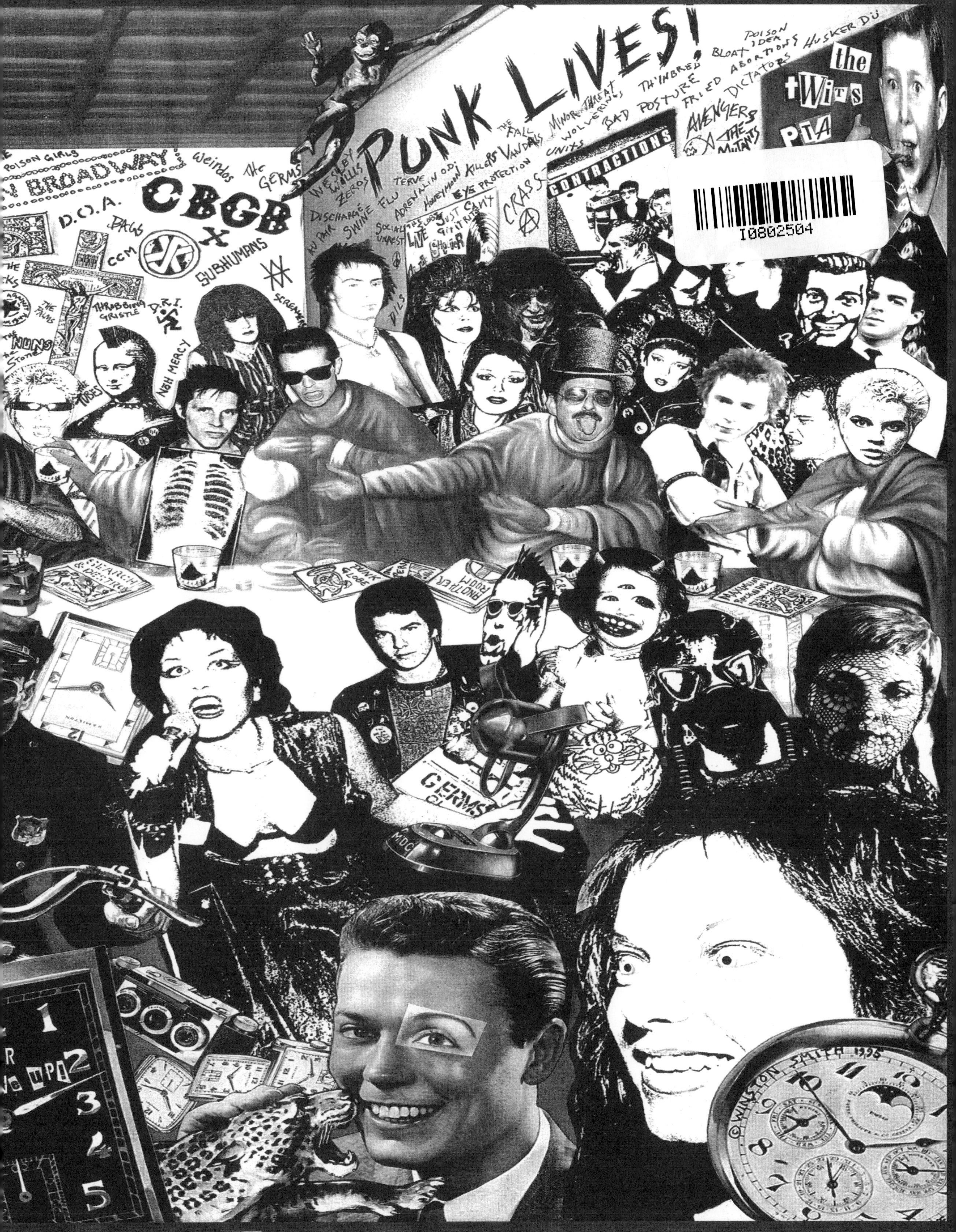
PUNK LIVES!
POISON GIRLS
BROADWAY
Weirdos
the GERMS
CBGB
D.O.A.
X
SUBHUMANS
THROBBING GRISTLE
D.R.I.
THE NUNS
NO MERCY
WESLEY WILLIS
ZEROS
DISCHARGE
AU PAIR
SWINE FLU
ADRENALIN O.D.
HONEYMOON KILLERS
EYE PROTECTION
THE FALL
VANDALS
MINOR THREAT
WOLVERINES
TH' INBRED
BAD POSTURE
UNITS
CRASS
CONTRACTIONS
BLOAT
POISON IDEA
FRIED ABORTIONS
DICTATORS
HUSKER DÜ
AVENGERS
THE MUTANTS
the TWITS
PTA
PUNK GLOBE
FRONTIER ROOM
GERMS
MDC
©WINSTON SMITH 1995

Fucked Up + Photocopied
Instant Art Of The Punk Rock Movement

Bryan Ray Turcotte & Christopher T. Miller

Art Direction by Bryan Ray Turcotte
Design by John Susoeff, Bryan Raymond Turcotte, Christopher T. Miller and Matt Neth
Raiders Edition Updated by Clint Woodside
Cover and Chapter Dividers By R.A. Fleming
Content Edited by Doug Woods, Bryan Raymond Turcotte and Christopher T. Miller
Stories Edited By John Susoeff
Project Coordinated by David Lopes

Published by Gingko Press
in association with
Kill Your Idols

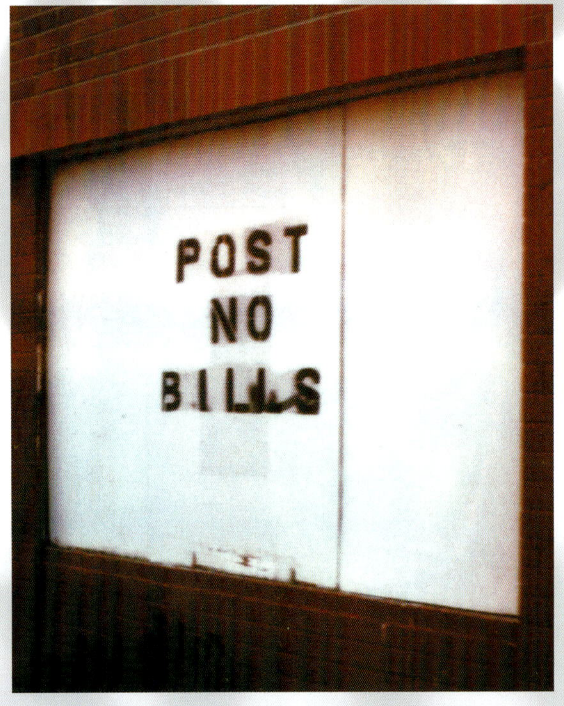

P.O. Box 48888
Los Angeles, CA 90048
killyouridols.com

The authors have endeavored to attribute and credit all work contained in this book. Any omissions brought to their attention shall be corrected in future editions.

Gingko Press Inc.
217 W. Richmond Ave
Richmond CA, 94801
gingkopress.com

"Raiders" edition, 2025

Printed in China

Bryan Ray Turcotte/Christopher T. Miller

Fucked Up + Photocopied: Instant Art Of The Punk Rock Movement

Bryan Ray Turcotte/Christopher T. Miller

ISBN: 978-1-58423-786-0

Contents

Inside Front and Back Cover:
"Never Give Up"
By WInston Smith

Contributing Writers

Charles Arjavac
KK Barrett
Jello Biafra
Bob Biggs
Brian Brannon
Dez Cadena
Joe Carducci
Robert Dapello
John Denney
Stephen Depace
Lorna Doom
Gary S. Floyd
Lars Fredrickson
Nathan Gates
Pearl E. Gates
Jill Heath
Scott Helland
Vis Helland
Doug Holland
Penelope Houston
Ken Inouye
Kim Kane
Joe Keithley
Scott Kempner
Tony Kinman
Evan Mack
Fat Mike
Keith Morris
Brendan Mullen
Corey O'Brien
Gavin O'Brien
Pushead
Hank Peirce
Al Quint
East Bay Ray
Jack Rivera
Craig Roose
Marc Rude
Corey Rusk
Jaime Sciarappa
Steve Schayer
Joe Sib
Winston Smith
Carol Ann Spalteholz
Shawn Stern
Ray Stevens II
John Susoeff
Carl Swanberg
Bryan Raymond Turcotte
Randall J. Biscuit Turner
Bill Vitale
Mike Watt
Danny Weizmann
Jimmy C. Wilsey
J. Yuenger

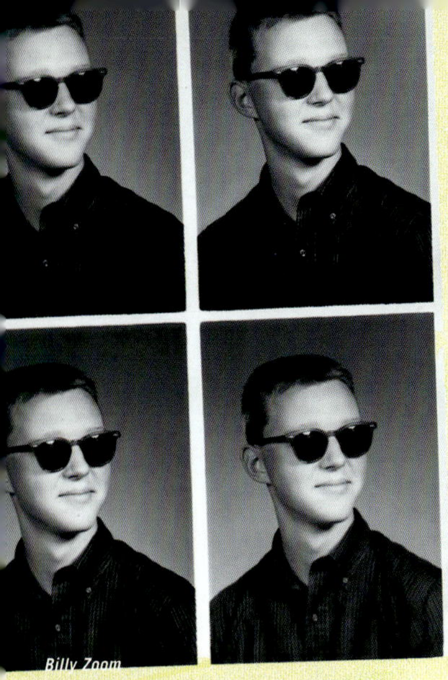
Billy Zoom

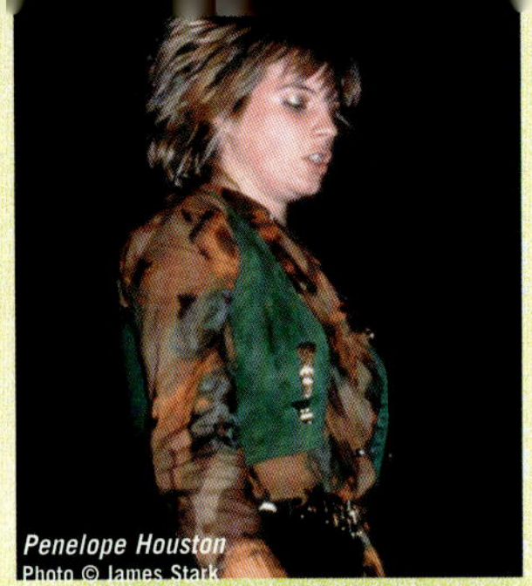
Penelope Houston
Photo © James Stark

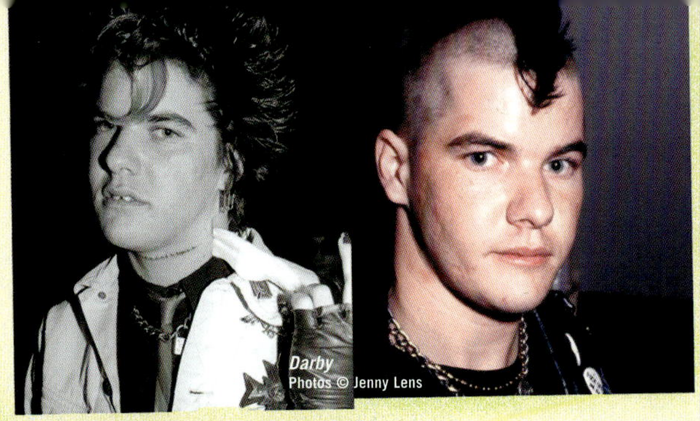
Darby
Photos © Jenny Lens

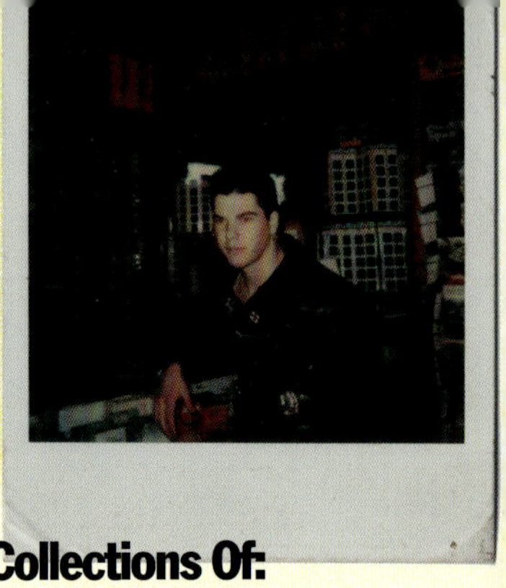

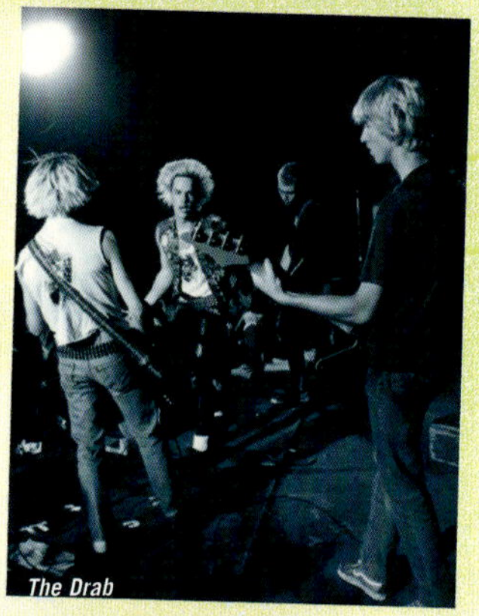
The Drab

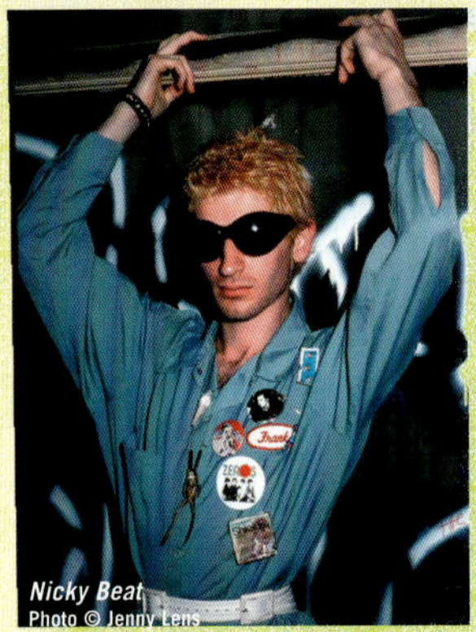
Nicky Beat
Photo © Jenny Lens

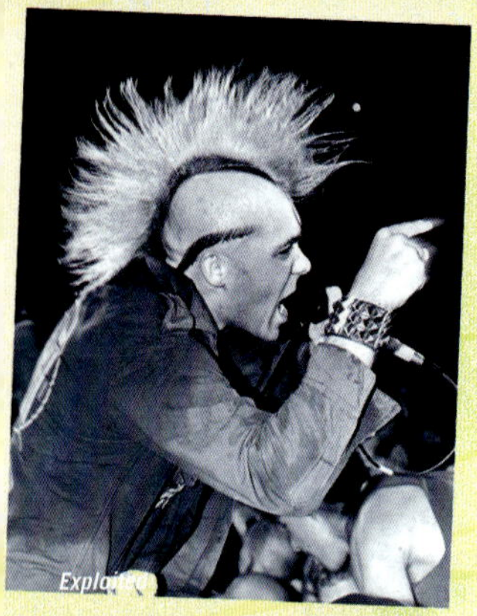
Explo

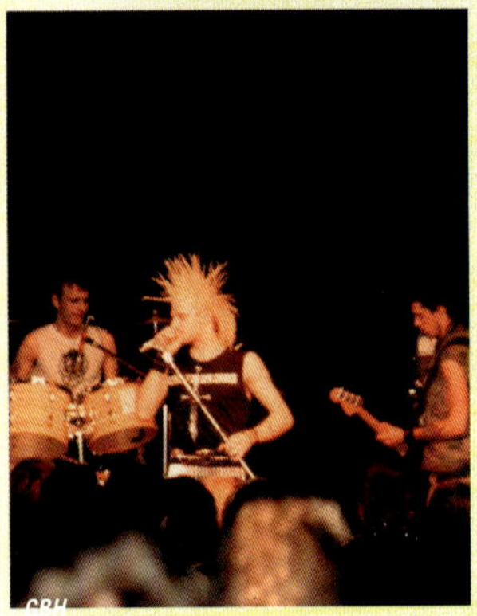
GBH

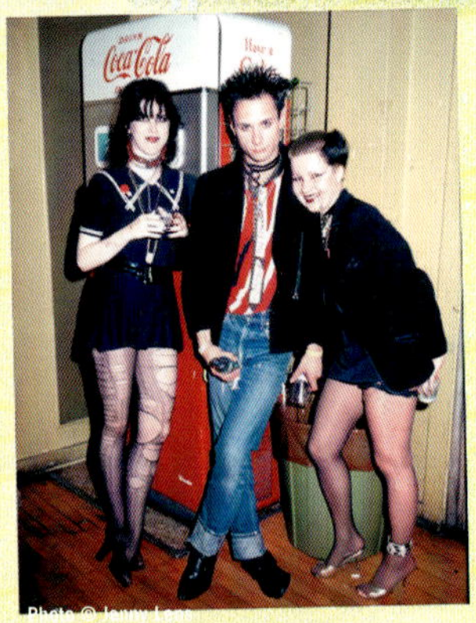

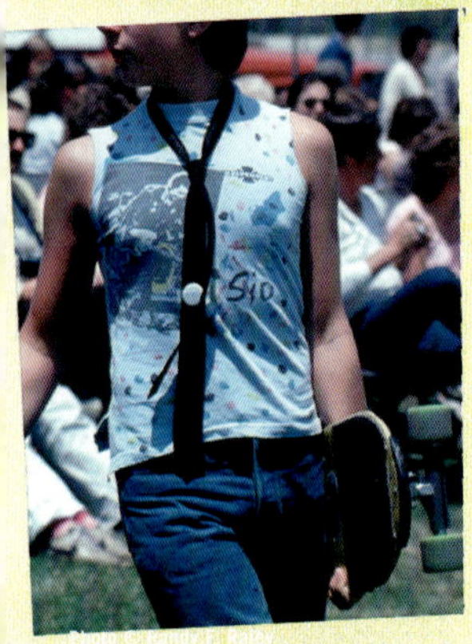

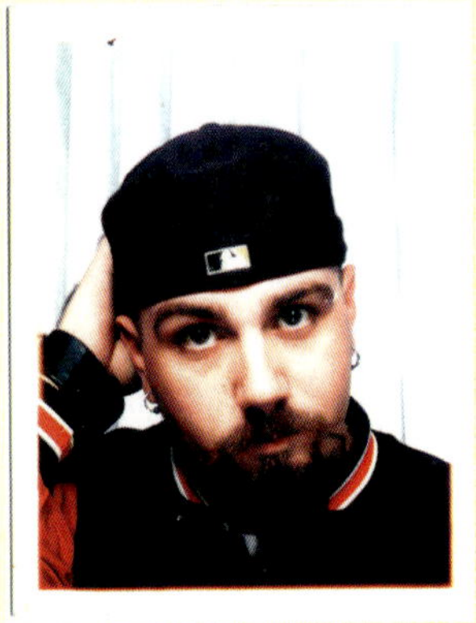
Bryan Ray Turcotte

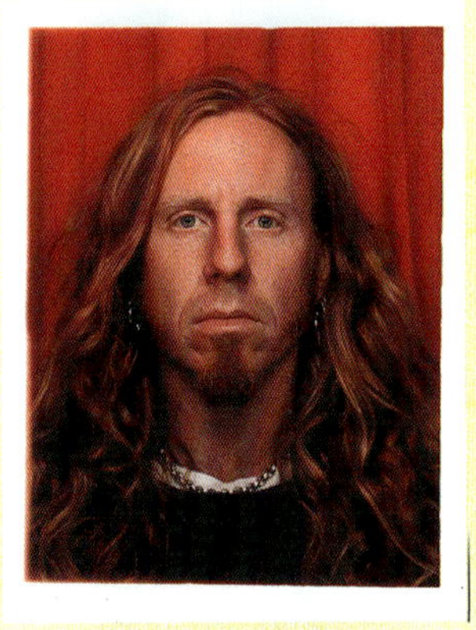
Christopher Tighe Miller

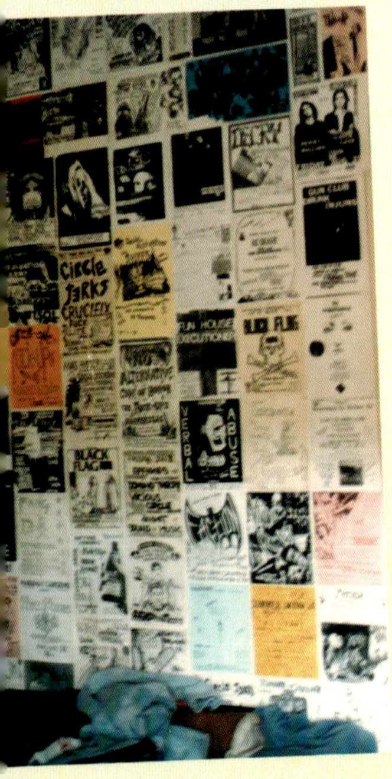

And on the eighth day
God created
PUNK ROCK

From The Collections Of:

Clay Allison
Robert Anderson
Charles Arjavac
Matt Arluck
Dave Arnson
Gary Benzel
Jello Biafra
Murray Bowles
Brian Brannon
Denny Burt
Joe Carducci
Larry Cartnell
Dean Chamberlain
Don Cowan
Shawn Cushman
Chris D.
Bev. Davies
John Denney
Stephen Depace
John Doe
Lorna Doom
Jeff Ellermeyer
Ronald Fleming
Gary S. Floyd
Glen E. Friedman
Victor Gastelum
Nathan Gates
Pearl E. Gates
Scott Garin
Gira/Jarboe
Juan Gomez
Steve Grimes
Danny Gromfin
Mike Guerena
Heather Harris
Jason Headley
Jill Heath
Scott Helland
Vis Helland
Gilbert Hernandez
Jaime Hernandez
Darren Hill
Paul Hischier
Doug Holland
John Holmstrom
Jason Honae
Penelope Houston
Craig Ibarra
Ken Inouye
Doug Kahl
Kim Kane
Joe Keithley
(Top Ten) Scott Kempner
Chip Kinman
Frank Kozik
Chris Leister
Jenny Lens
David Lopes
Robert Lopez
Margret Maat
Evan Mack
Ian Mackaye
Michelle Marini
Richard Hell Meyers
Fat Mike
Christopher T. Miller
Patrick Miller
Thurston Moore
Keith Morris
Mark Mothersbaugh
Brendan Mullen
Jeff Nelson
Corey O'Brien
Gavin O'Brien
Sis Onet
Melody Osorio
Gary Panter
John Paris
Mike Patton
Hank Peirce
Jeff Pezatti
Steve Pfauter
Michael Pilmer
Kevin Plamondon
Pushead
Al Quint
Randy F. Raley
East Bay Ray
Axxel G. Reese
Martin Rev
Eric Rife
Jack Rivera
Cliff Roman
Jeff Ross
Craig Roose
Marc Rude
Corey Rusk
Steve Schayer
Wendy Schecter
Jaime Sciarappa
Slash Magazine
Winston Smith
Smutty
Carol Ann Spalteholz
James Stark
Shawn Stern
Ray Stevens II
Carl Swanberg
John Tally-Jones
Tim Tanooka
Bridgitte Tirman
Bryan Raymond Turcotte
Randall J. Biscuit Turner
Bill Vitale
Marla Watson
Mike Watt
Danny Weizmann
Aaron White
Amy White
Darien Wilson
Jimmy C. Wilsey
Douglas Woods
J. Yuenger

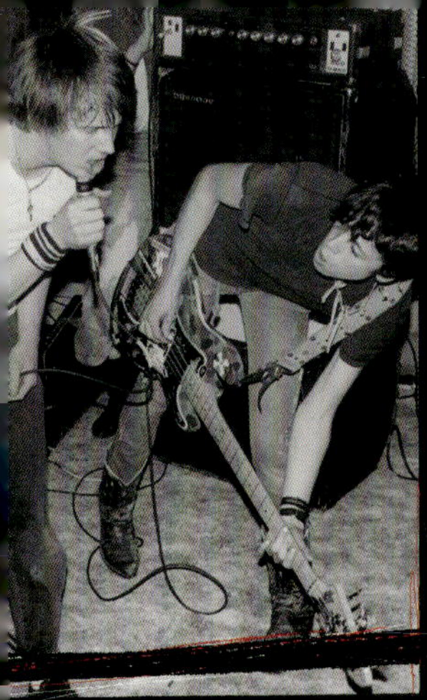

Tales Of Terror

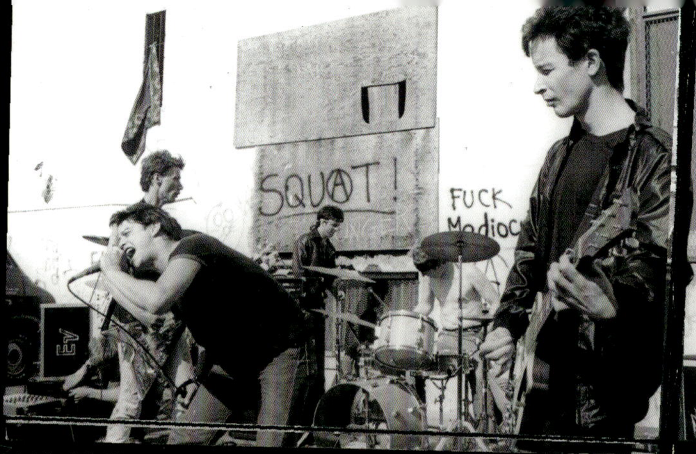

Fuck Ups At The Vats

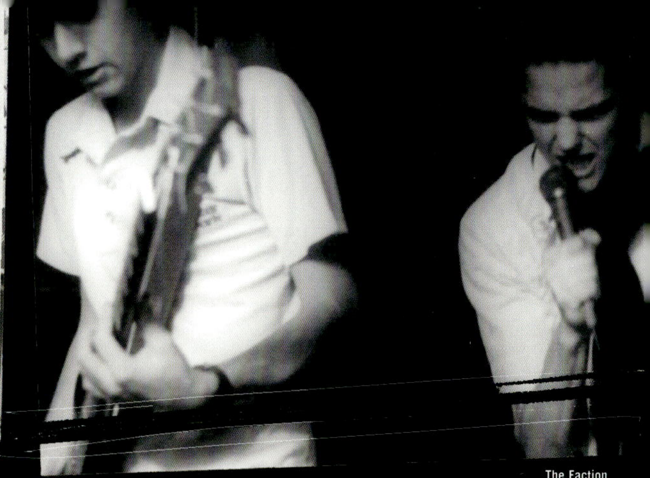

The Faction

The aggressive simplicity of these punk flyers have always felt like a graphic punch to the face. Like being tossed in the pit for the very first time.

They represent the spark that formed the scene, the beautiful raw energy and what it actually felt like. These flyers are as visceral as punk itself, raw, brazen, beautifully ugly and straight to the point.

All these years later they still threaten with the same venom as the day they were made, Fucked Up + Photocopied.

Bryan Raymond Turcotte
Kill Your Idols

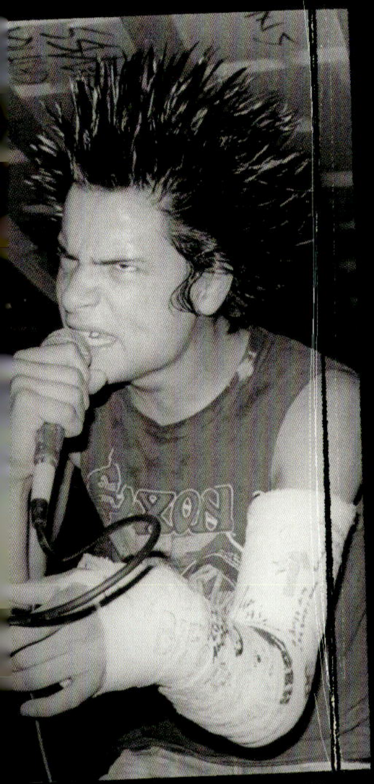

Ribsy

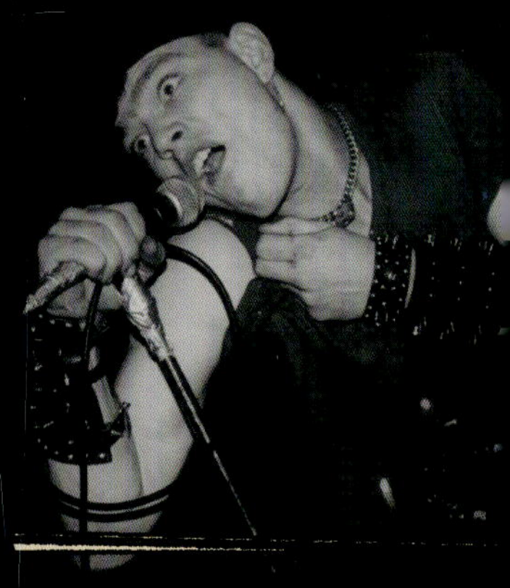

Urban Assault

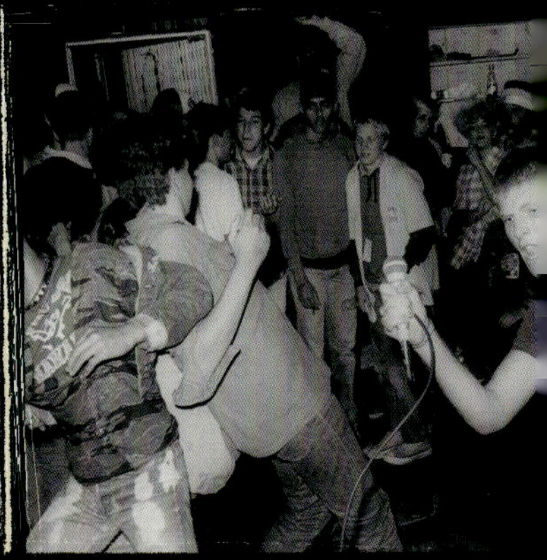

Grim Reality

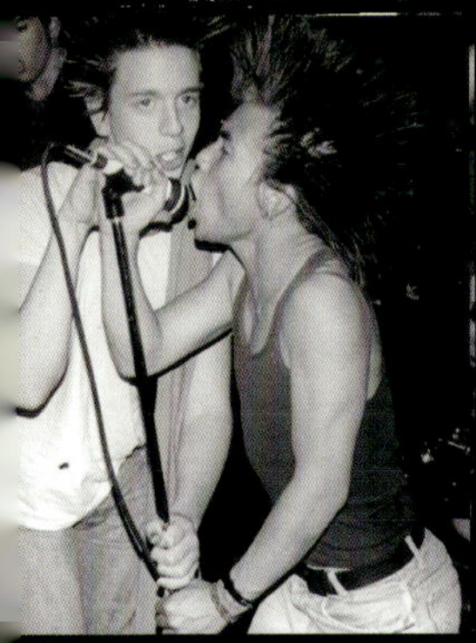

rucifix

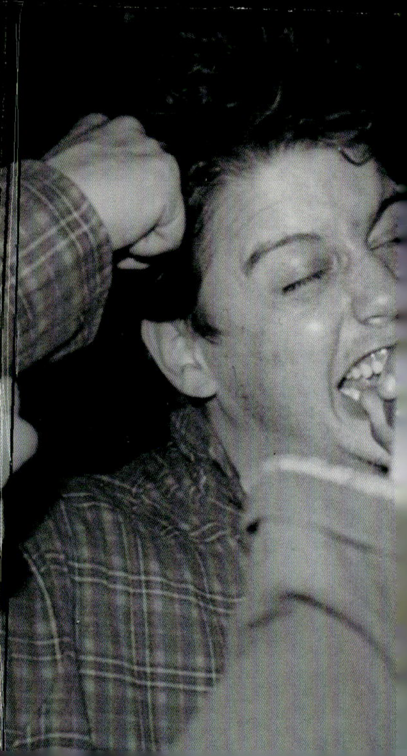

Fuck-Ups

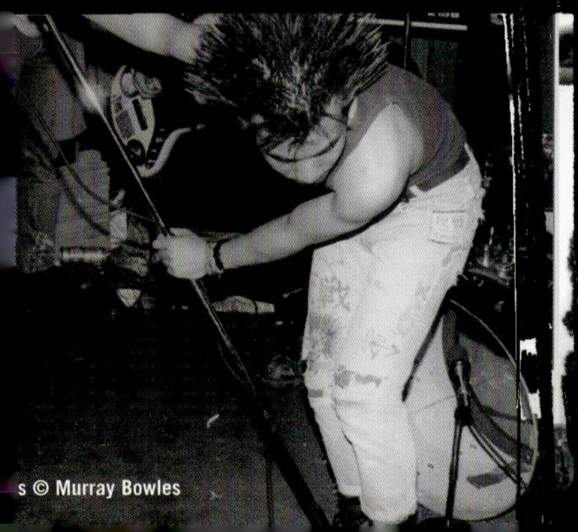

Crucifix

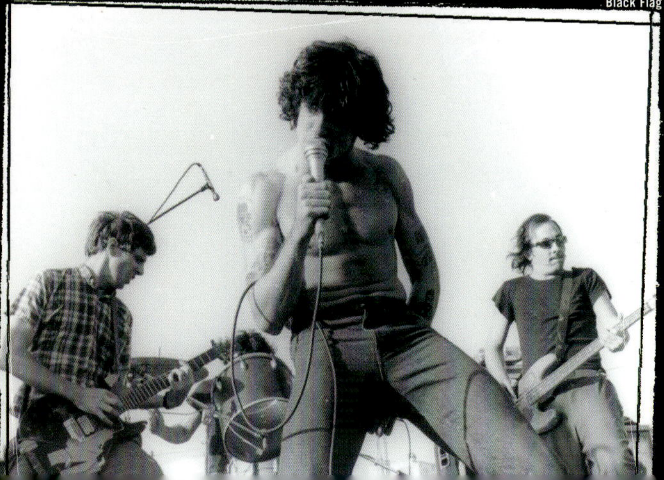

Black Flag

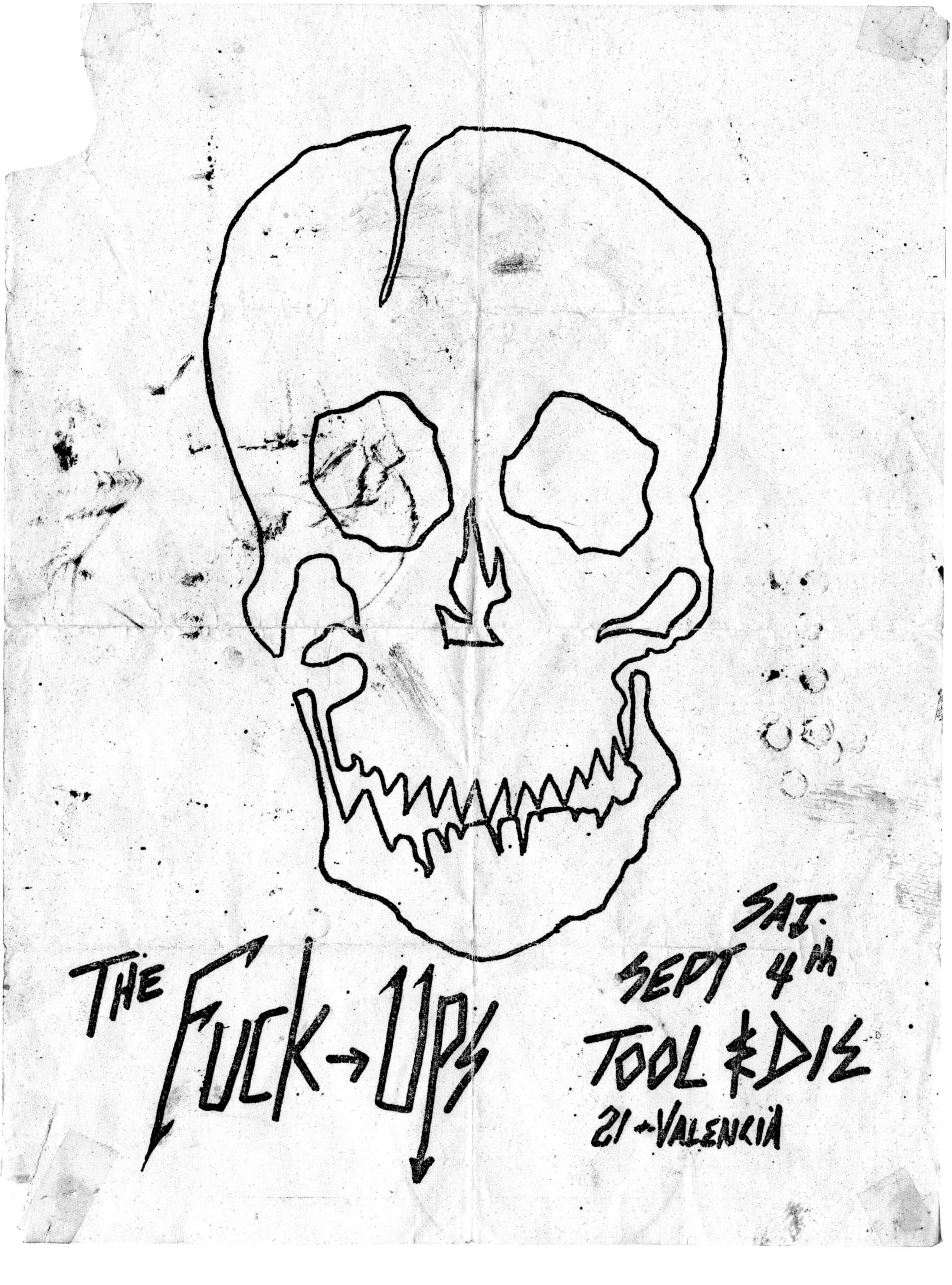
THE FUCK-UPS
SAT.
SEPT 4th
TOOL & DIE
21 + VALENCIA

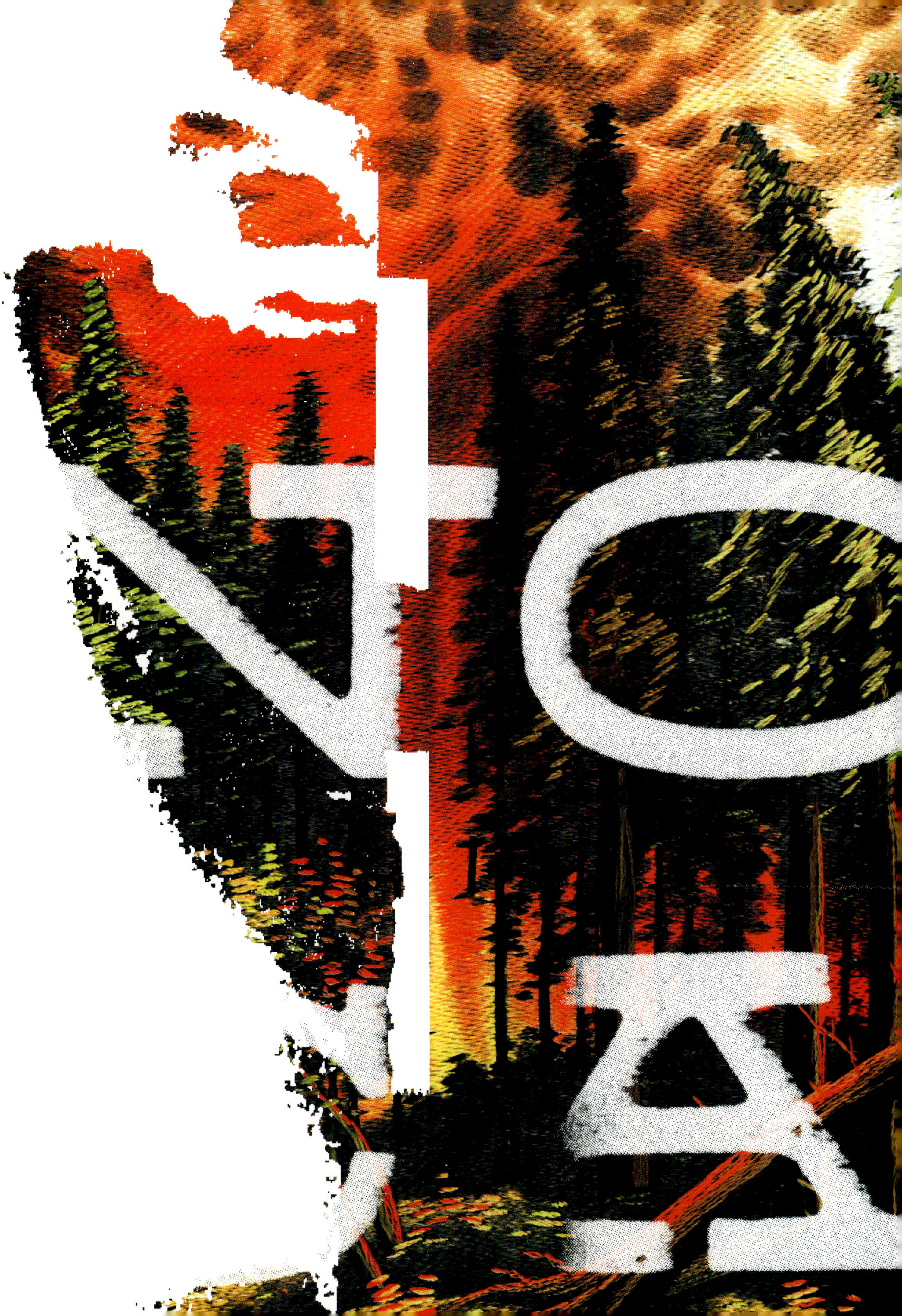

Make no mistake, the '70s sucked.

Only a bonehead would want to bring back any part of it in any form. When we were coming of age, we weren't dazed and confused, we were disgusted. **We missed the '60s!** All that fire, all that promise, all that fun-mellowed out, paved over, sold back to us as what we now call yuppie culture.

Rock and roll had been reduced to a spectator sport. The alternative scene many people take for granted today did not exist. there was no punk rock. Underground bands, independent records and 'zines were unheard of. In Colorado you either sounded as horrible as the Eagles or you didn't play. Live music was strictly for adults, with neatly trimmed Kenny Loggins beards, and corduroy jackets with patches on the elbows. Something drastic had to be done.

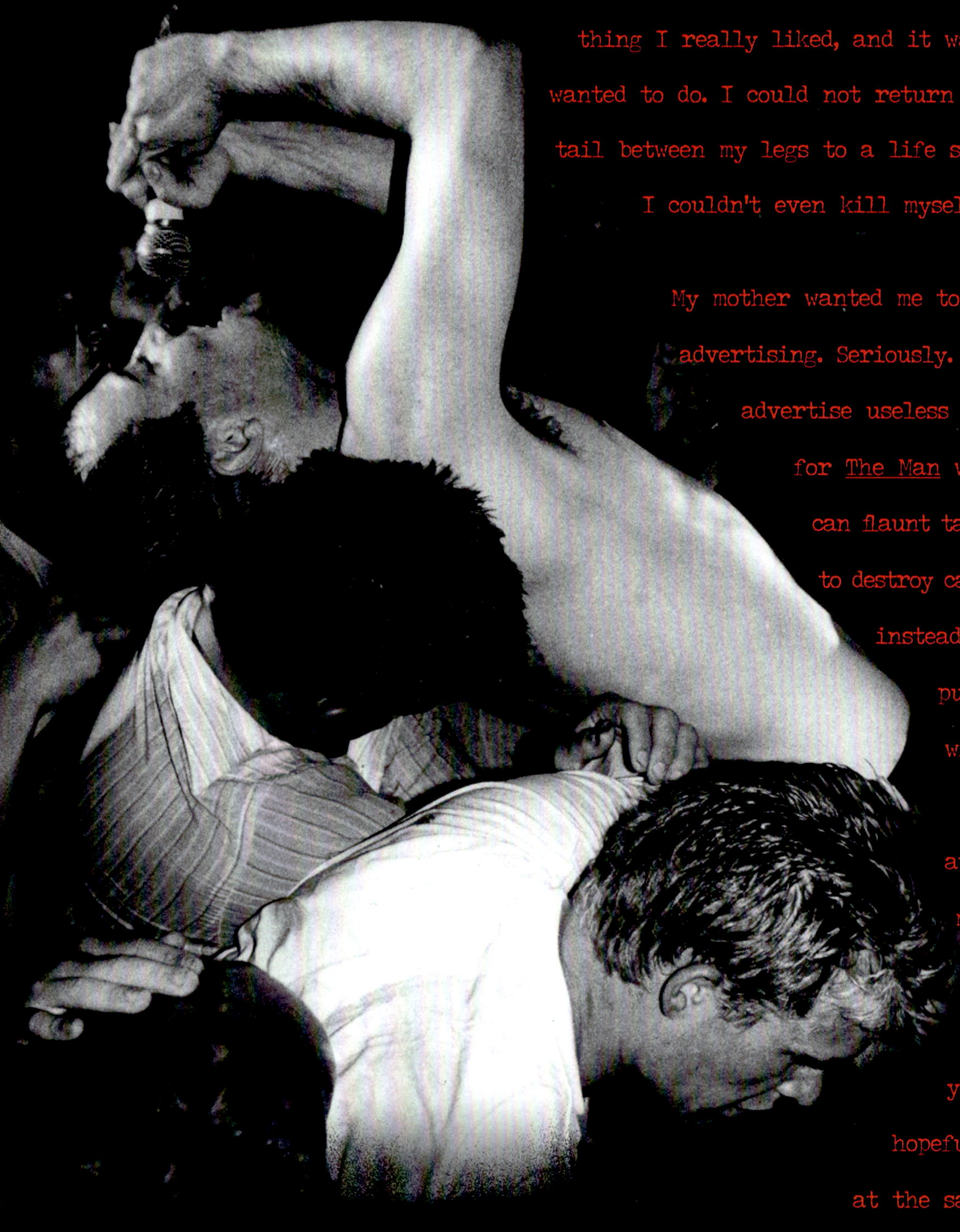

I headed west to San Francisco to dive face-first into punk rock. It was the only thing I really liked, and it was all I wanted to do. I could not return with my tail between my legs to a life so dismal I couldn't even kill myself right.

My mother wanted me to go into advertising. Seriously. But why advertise useless products for The Man when you can flaunt tasty ways to destroy capitalism instead? A good punk flyer will grab your attention, make you laugh, or piss you off - hopefully, all at the same time.

Jello Biafra
Photo © Marla Watson

Flyers had to be done quickly. Band names and the Mabuhay Gardens logo were cut out of old flyers and reused on the next. It was instant, it was cool. It was a hell of a lot of fun.

Computers were out of reach, rub-on letters were a luxury, so we improvised. Aping Jamie Reid's situationist-inspired cut-out art (Sex Pistols) was step one. Our own dark retakes on the plastic Amerika that spawned us came next. Without knowing it, we learned that putting any picture or collage on a punk flyer could make that image more ridiculous- or sinister- than ever.

Splicing the surreal gave me my name. I liked the way images of **Jello Biafra** (look it up, it's important) collide in the mind.

Punk was anything that pissed all over the 70s and stupidity in general. It was wide open. There was no "old school," we were blowing up the school. No one knew what was coming next- from England, New York, or the practice room down the hall.

The good natured peer pressure was not for everyone to sound the same, It was encouragement to every artist to be different.

Television, The Avengers, Devo and Survival Research Labs were all punk because no one had experienced anything like them. Plus, they scared the shit out of all the normaloids we hated.

own music, our own clothing, all out of nothing. It wasn't something we did on weekends, we had an agenda. Everyone's was different, and no one knew quite what it was. We were all trying to ride the same wild horse at once.

The scene was so small everyone went to every show. If a band stayed in one place too long we got bored. Playing the same set twice was unheard of. Groups like Negative Trend, SRL and- believe it or not- Dead Kennedys were more interested in offending the audience than being liked or being made pop stars. That punk attitude is what is missing from sterile retro punk today.

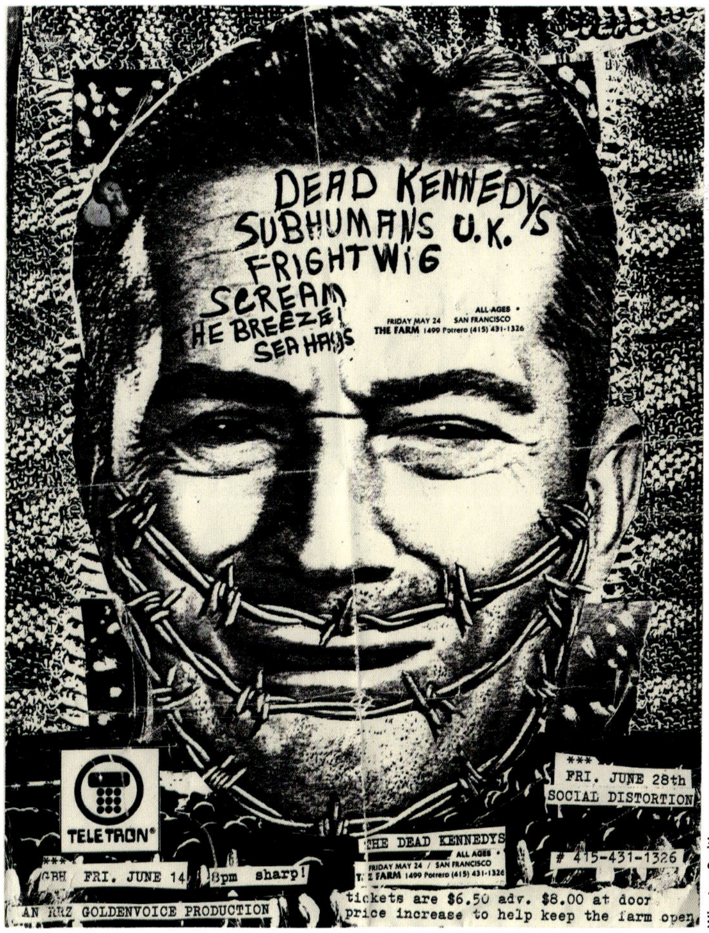

Winston Smith

What is now called punk may sound familiar, but too often the spirit has been replaced by rules - a kind of fundamentalism, even. The cartoony hardercore-than-thou crowd reminds me a little too much of Fonzie on Happy Days- they're as much fun to fuck with as Zeppelin and Skynyrd fans were way back when.

Good old daze? Poison. Magic and inspiration are where you find them. Stay curious and it's always there. Contradictory to what I just said or not, I've learned to respect that each generation has its own times, places, sounds and people, which mean as much to them as the best points in my life mean to me. Why take that feeling away by saying it was cooler way back when? Was it really?

The important stuff that lasts is from the people who go the extra mile to break the mold. Every time. That's what keeps me going. It's what I live for.

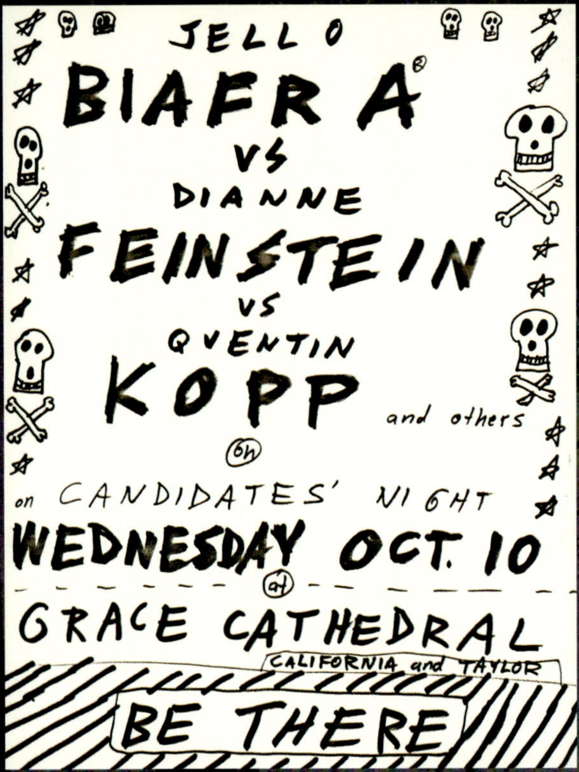

Jello Biafra

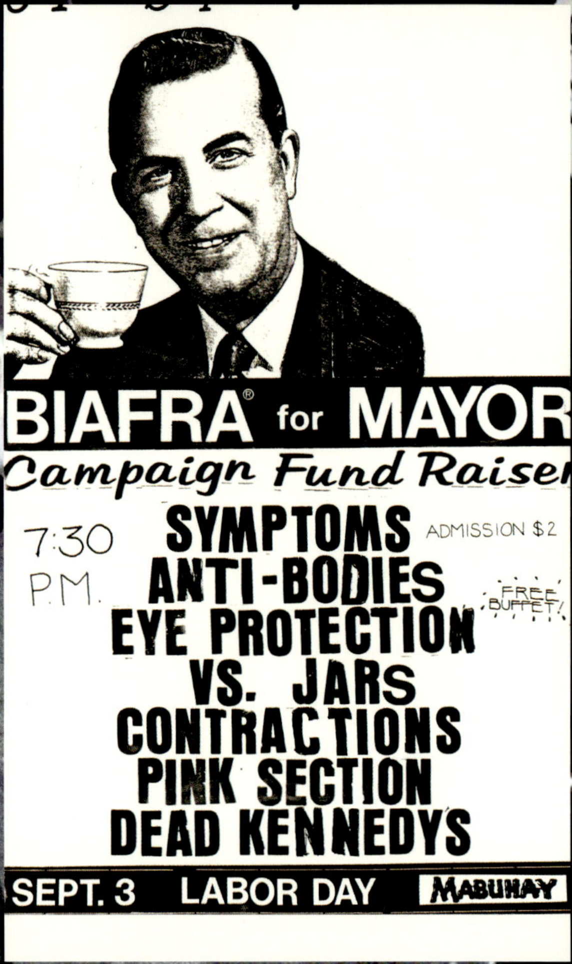

Bruce Slesinger

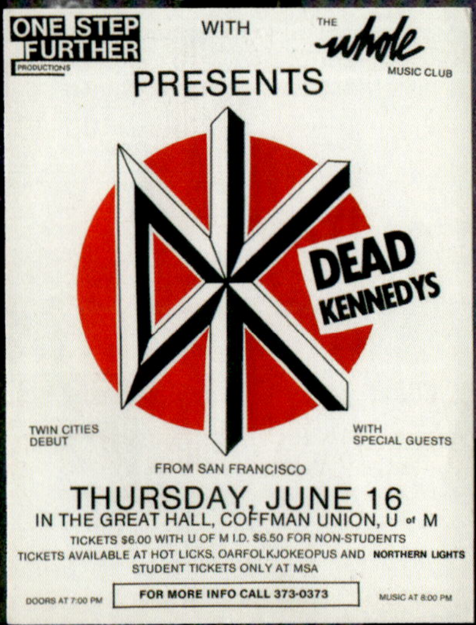

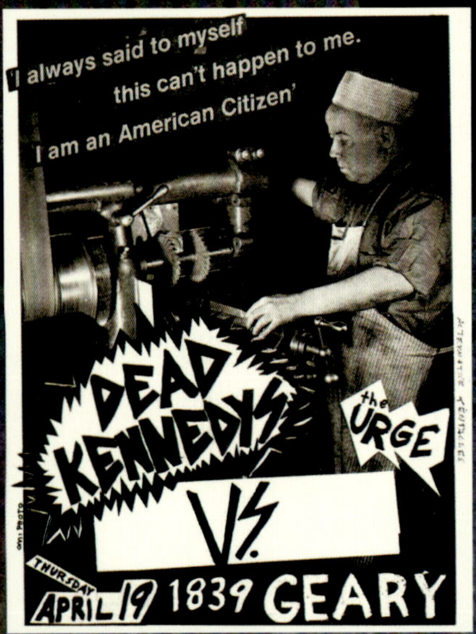

Jello Biafra

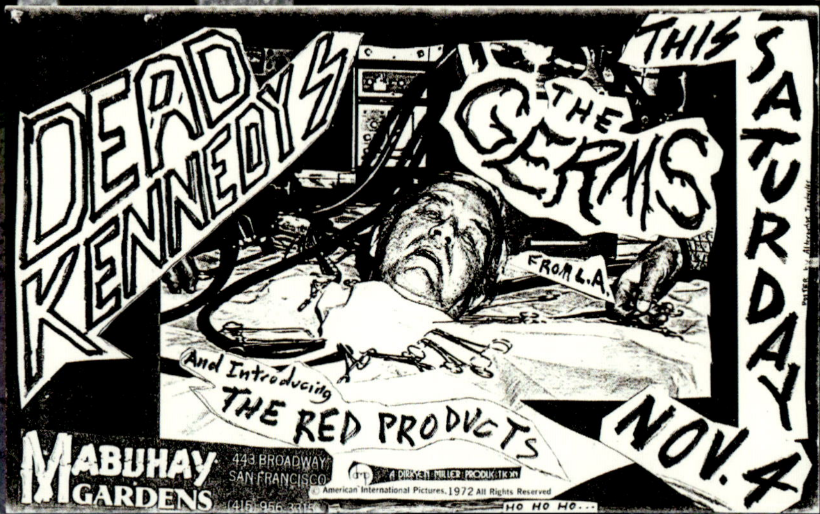

Jello Biafra

Jello's day in court
Photo © Heather Harris

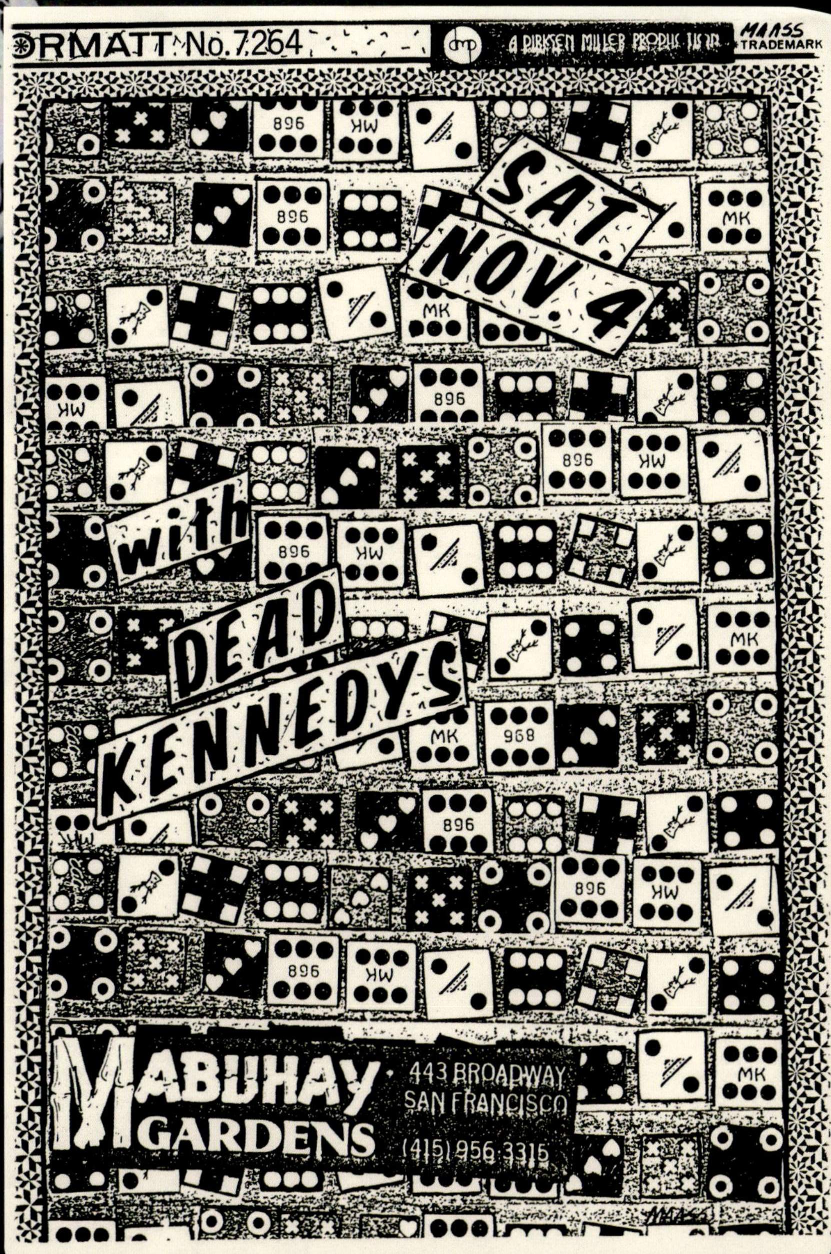

Bruce Slesinger

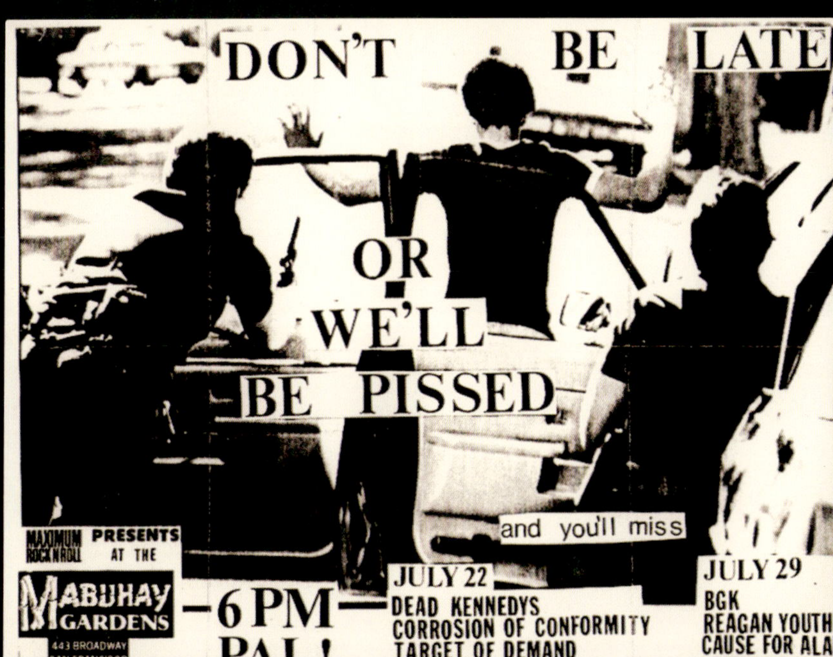

BACK IN THE LATE '70S AND EARLY '80S, A LOT OF BANDS CHANGED PUNK ROCK FOR THEMSELVES FROM THE MEDIA CIRCUS STARTED BY MALCOLM MCLAREN AND THE SEX PISTOLS TO SOMETHING MORE PERSONAL AND LOCAL, MORE ABOUT EXPERIMENTATION AND TOLERANCE. THERE WAS A FEELING THAT YOU DIDN'T NEED ANY SPECIAL TRAINING TO CREATE A PROJECT IF YOU HAD A GOOD IDEA TO EXPRESS. IN ADDITION TO THE BANDS AND MUSIC, ONE OF THE OUTLETS OF THIS EXPRESSION WAS FOR A BAND MEMBER OR A FRIEND TO CREATE A DIFFERENT POSTER FOR EACH PERFORMANCE. IT DIDN'T MATTER WHETHER A PUNKER HAD ART TRAINING OR NOT– **DIY,** DO IT YOURSELF, **WAS IN THE AIR.**

Continues...

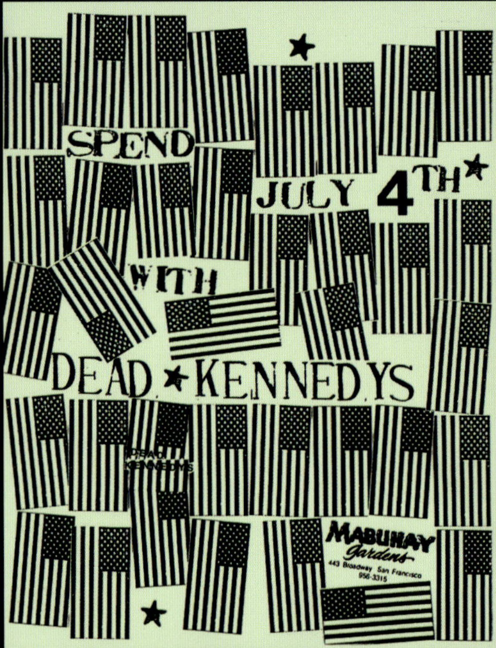

Bruce Slesinger

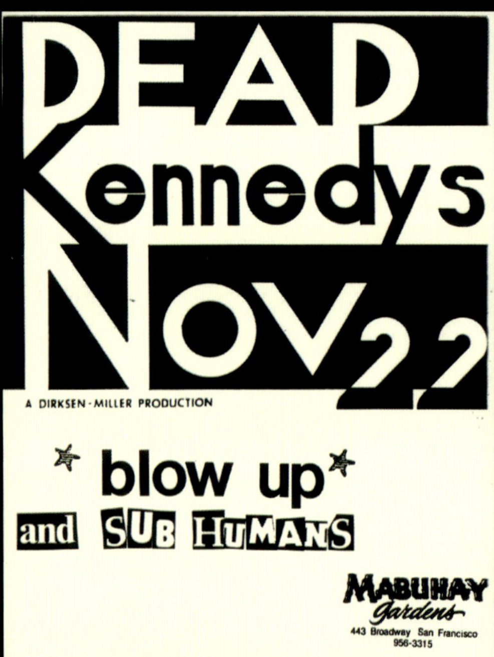

Bruce Slesinger

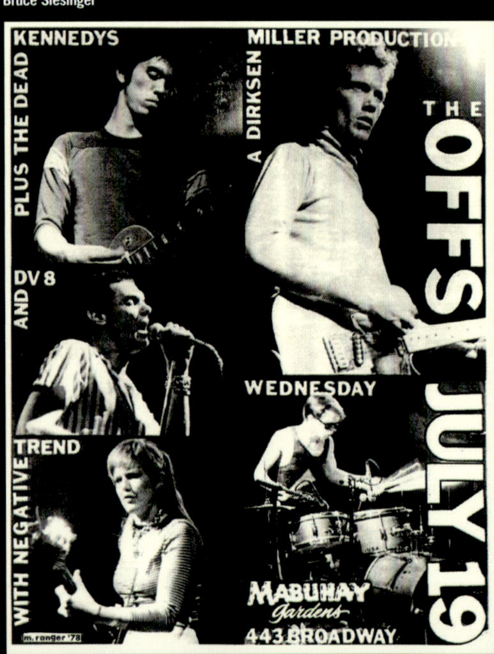

Flyer from first ever DKs show! — East Bay Ray

THERE WAS NO REASON TO WAIT FOR A BIG COMPANY TO COME ALONG AND FINANCE YOU, THE BIG COMPANIES WERE NOT INTERESTED IN PUNK ROCK. A LOT OF MUSICIANS LEARNED A LITTLE ABOUT MAKING ART BY ACTUALLY DOING IT AND A LOT OF VISUAL ARTISTS FOUND A NEW OUTLET FOR SOME INTERESTING EXPERIMENTS. THE XEROX COPY MACHINE MADE THESE POSTERS AND FLYERS EASY TO REPRODUCE–NOT MANY WERE ACTUALLY TAKEN TO A REAL PRINT SHOP*. MASS-PRODUCED OBJETS D'ART WERE BEING MADE BY PEOPLE WITH VERY LITTLE CAPITAL.

*I REMEMBER ONCE WE GOT A SUBSTANTIAL DISCOUNT FROM A DEAD KENNEDYS FAN WHO WORKED AT A PRINT SHOP - VERY SUBSTANTIAL.

EAST BAY RAY, OAKLAND CA 199

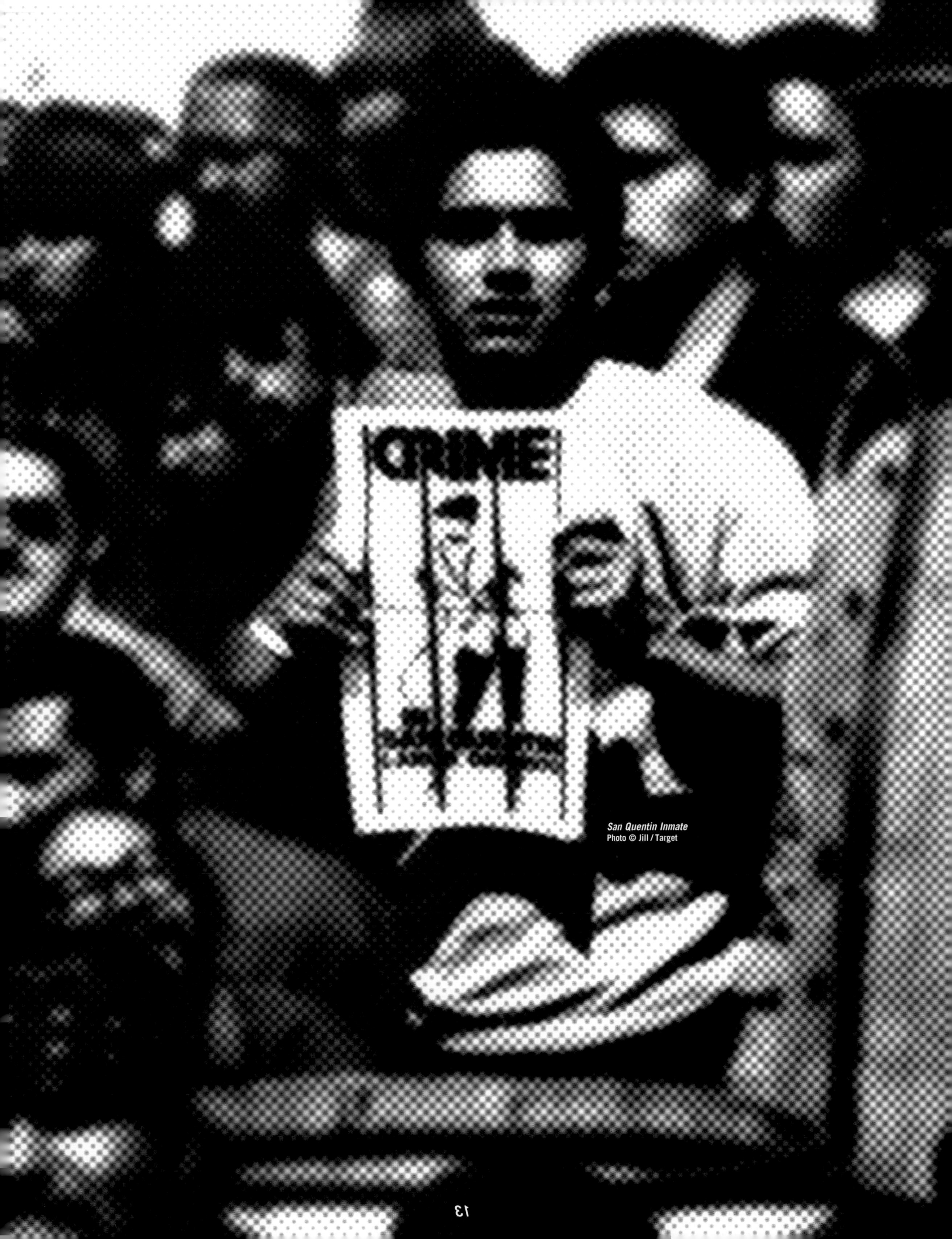

San Quentin Inmate
Photo © Jill / Target

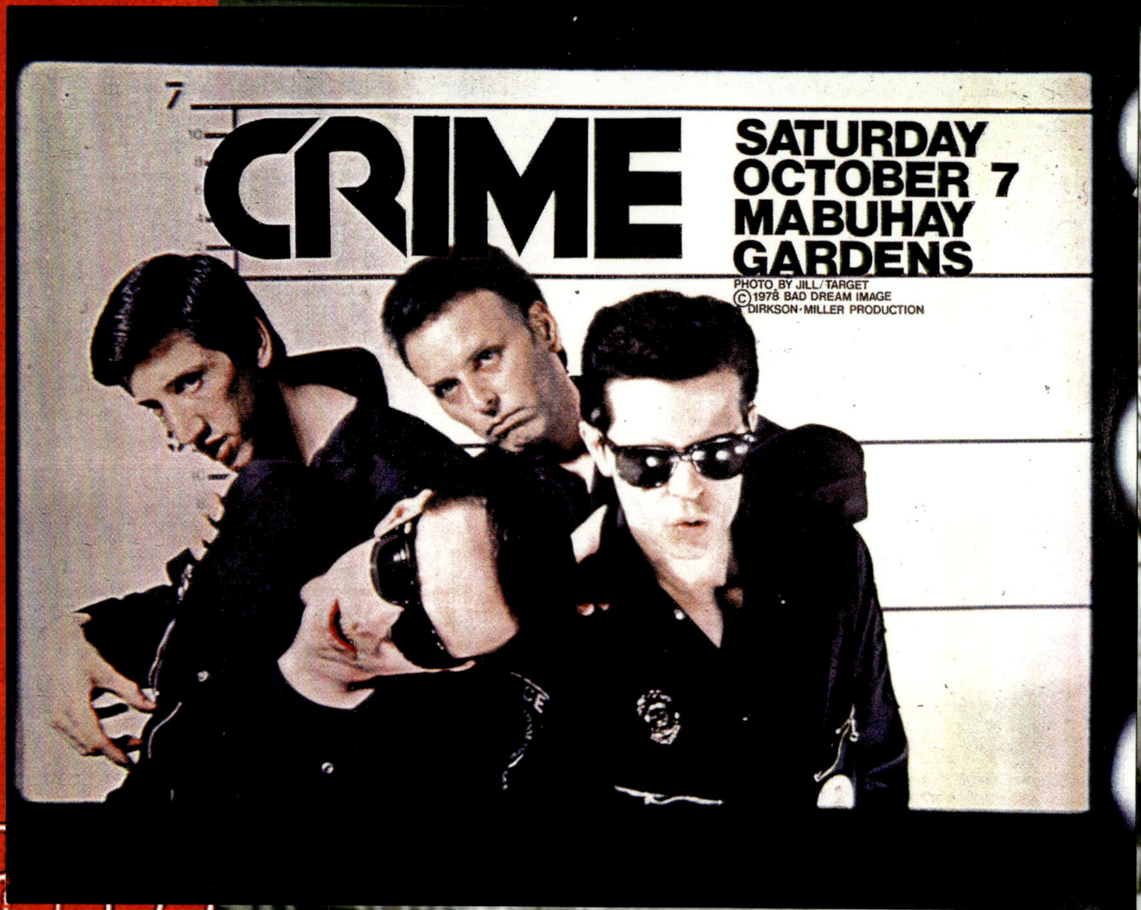

James Stark

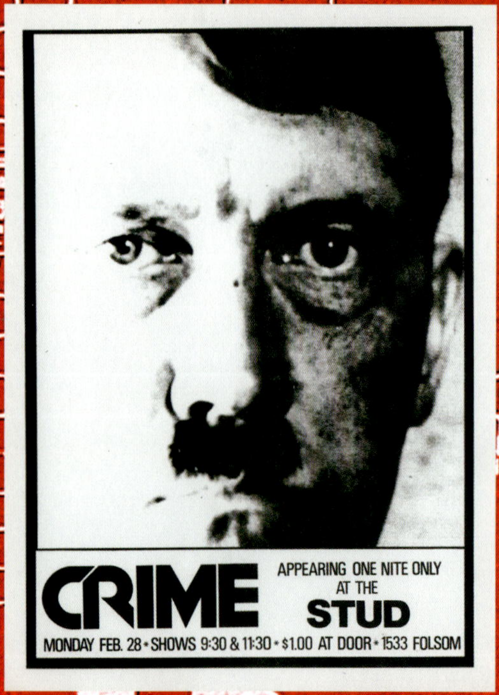

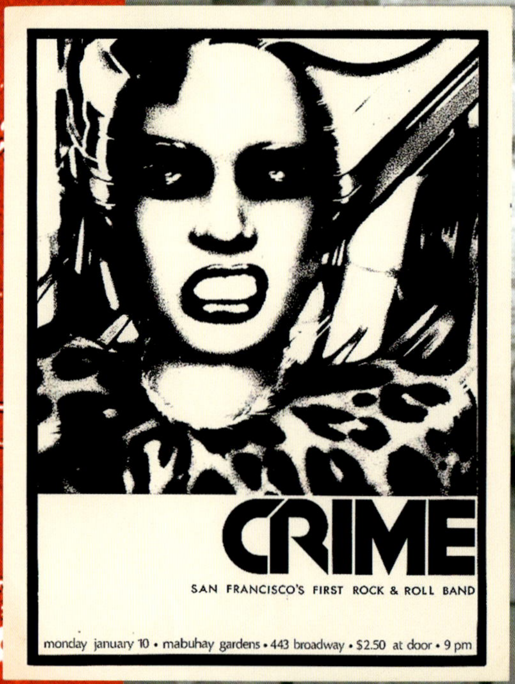

James Stark

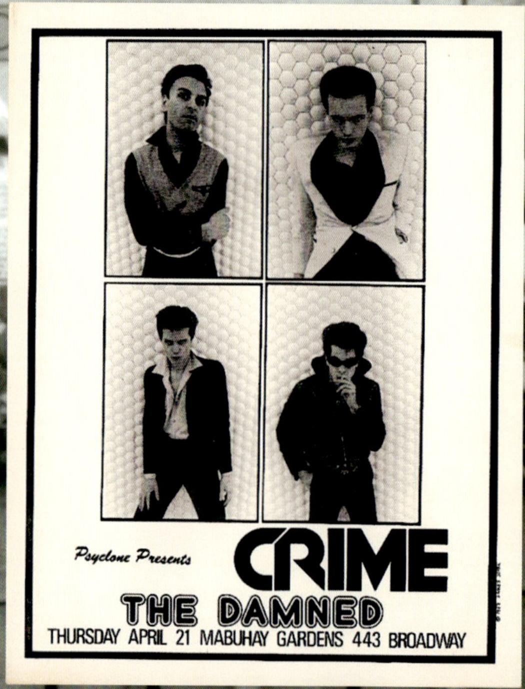

James Stark

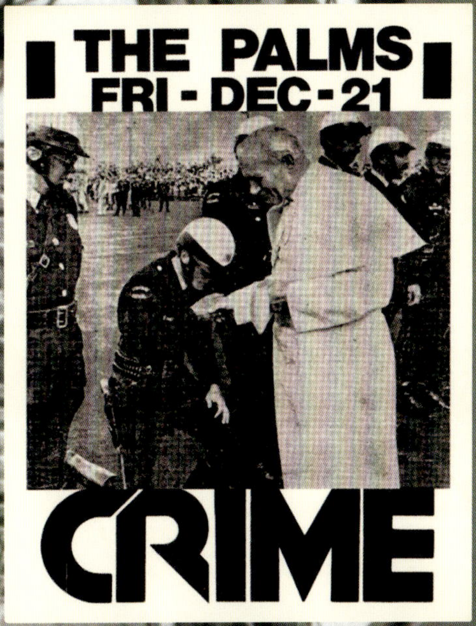

Joey D'Kaye

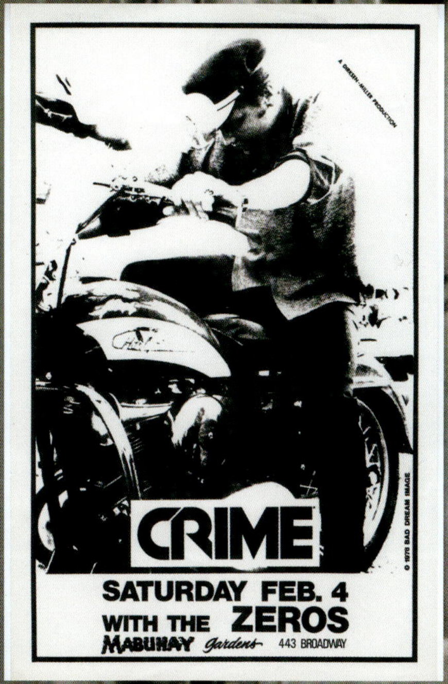

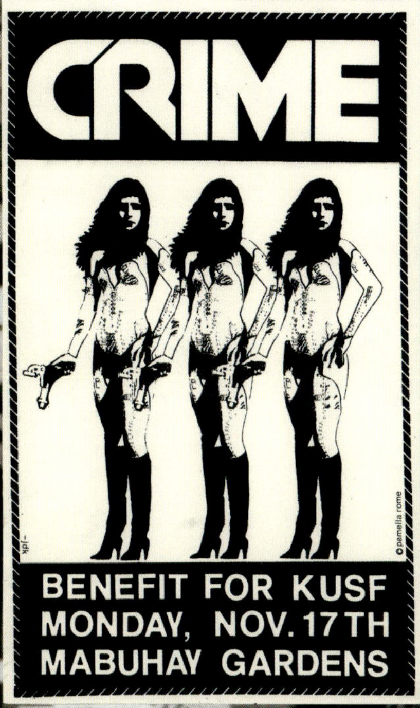

Design: Joey D'Kaye Im[illegible]ella Rome

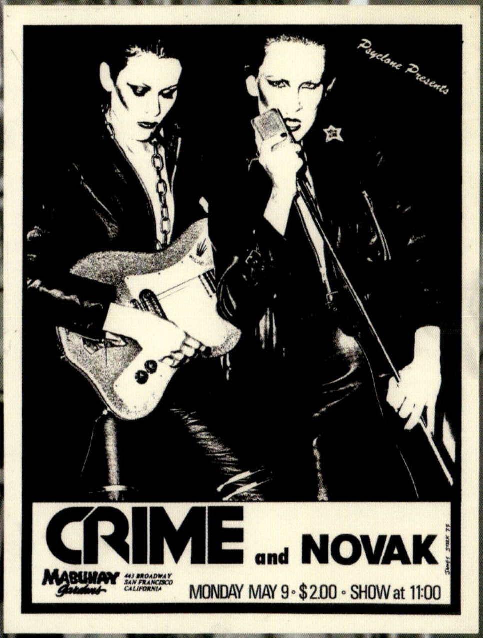

James Stark

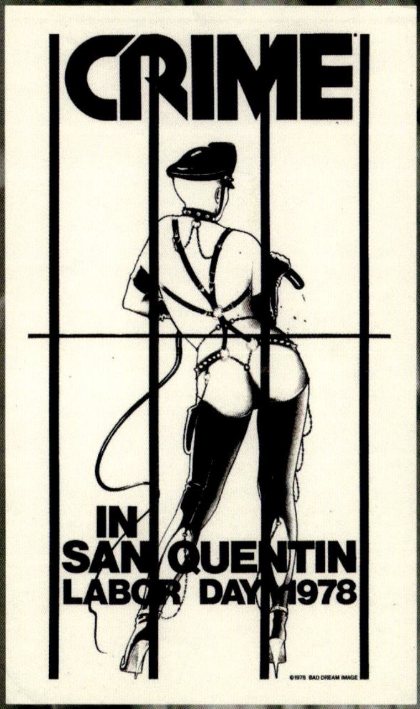

James Stark: Bad Dream Image

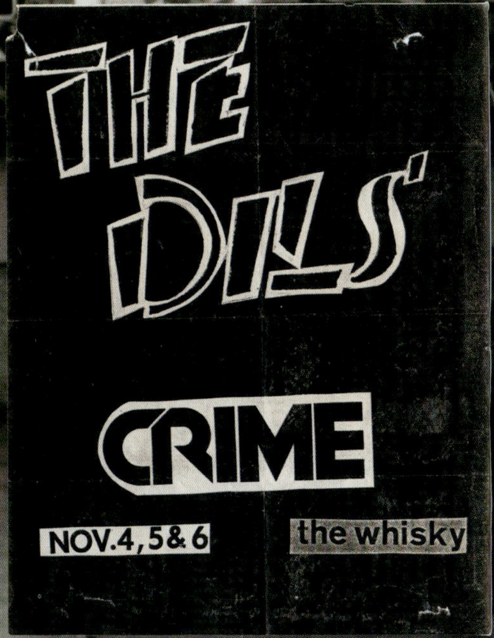

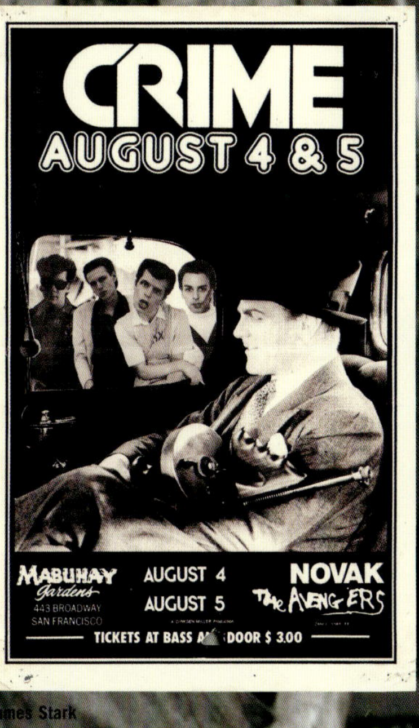

James Stark

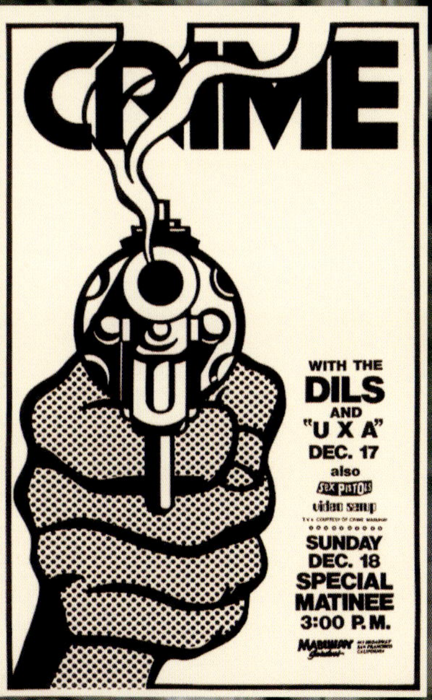

James St

Mab
© James Stark

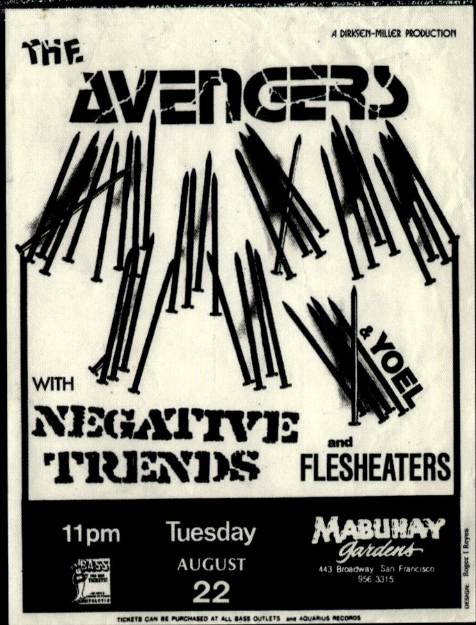

Roger I. Reyes

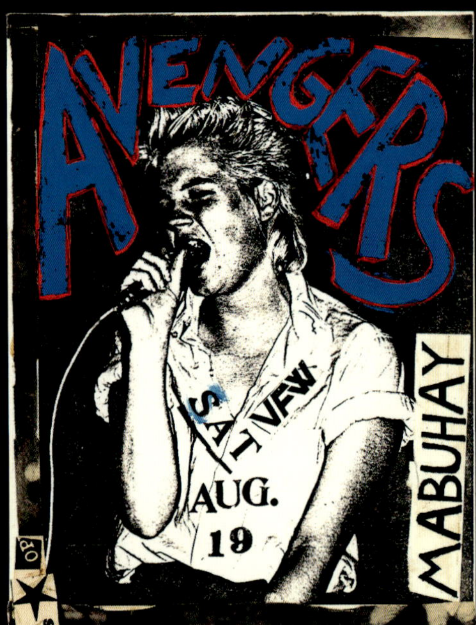

Penelope Houston

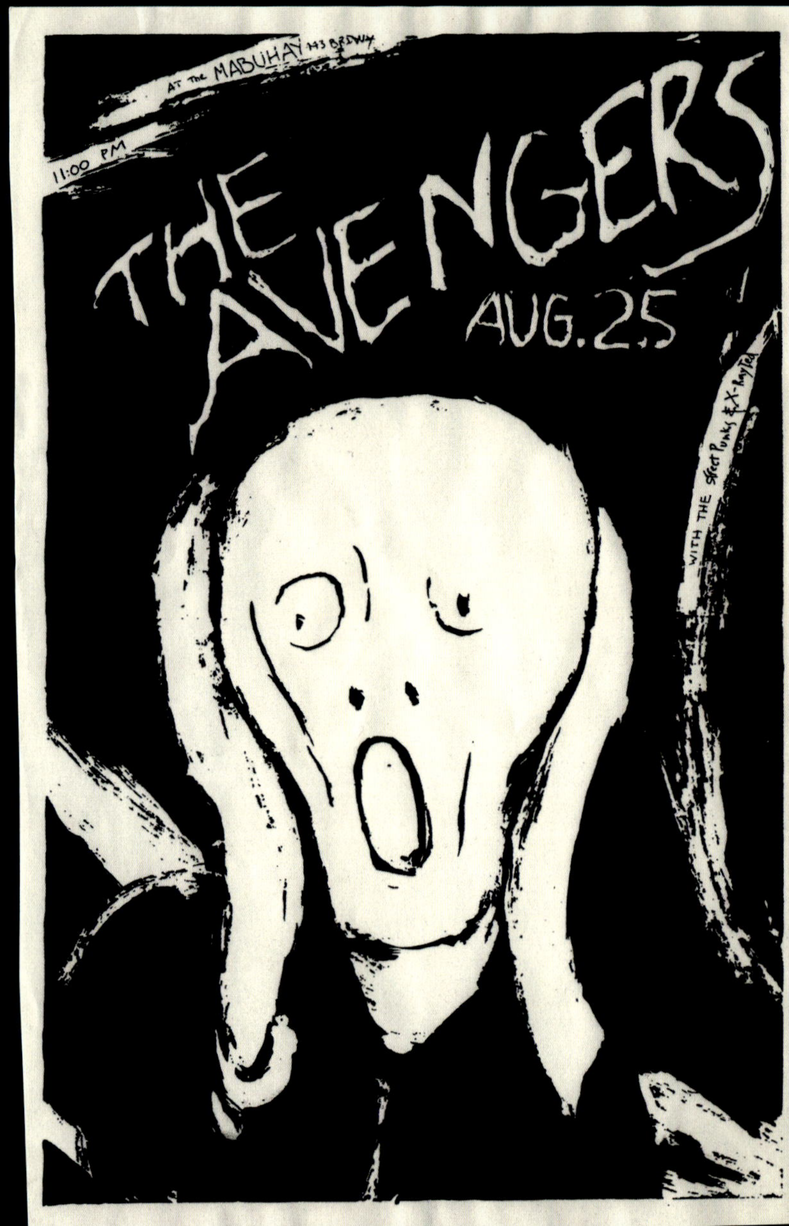

Penelope Houston

Saturday August 19, 1978
Mabuhay Gardens

Penelope: This is a recycled poster from a show 2 months earlier at the VFW hall in Santa Cruz, hence the VFW on my shirt. *UXA* and *The Lewd* opened. *The Lewd* was fronted by a screaming punk named Satz, whom I'd met years before in Seattle as *Satin Sheets,* a screaming drag queen in the infamous *Whiz Kids*. Other incarnations of Seattle's 'Kids' were the Screamers' Tommy Gear, who was *Melba Toast* when I met him, and *Tomata du Plenty*, who was, of course, *Tomata du Plenty.*

The Scream
Thursday August 25, 1977
Mabuhay Gardens

Penelope: This was our first headlining show. I can't remember a thing about it, but the black and white painting (stolen quite directly from Edvard Munch) got a lot of mileage in poster books, and even Life Magazine when they did their *Rock-n-Roll* issue. I had yet to drop out of the SF Art Institute, but it was imminent.

Penelope

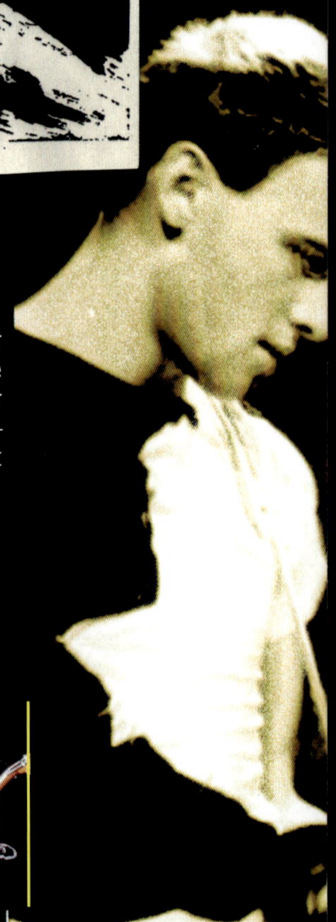

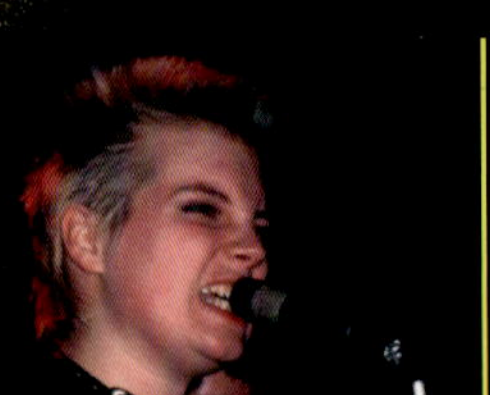

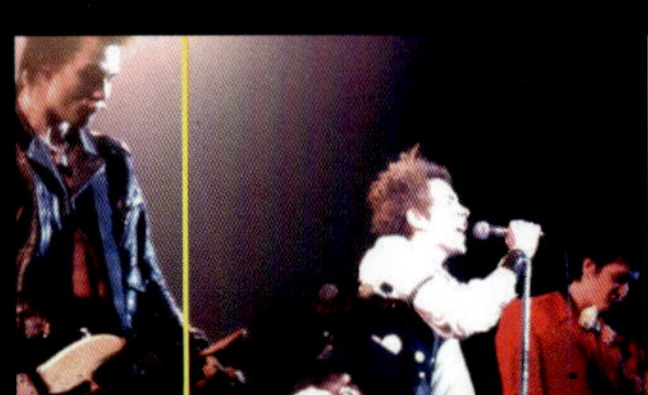

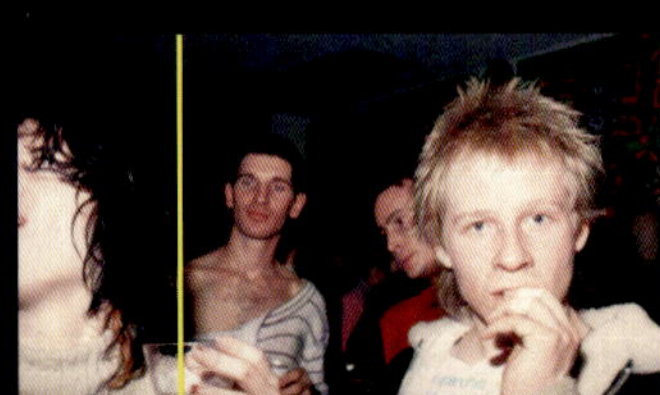

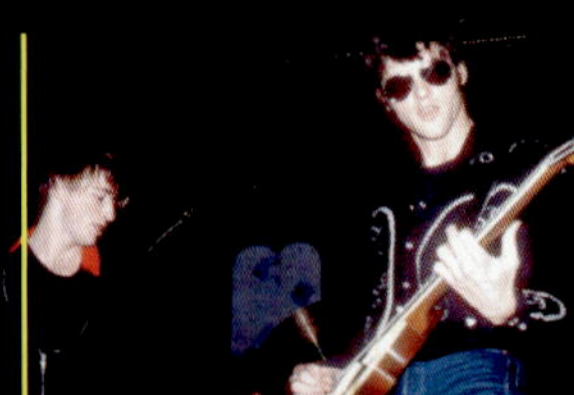

avengers and sex pistols at winterland

Photos © Jenny Lens

Photo © James Stark

guess endless enlarging on the Xerox machine just gets under your skin. The newest technology was a typewriter that

2

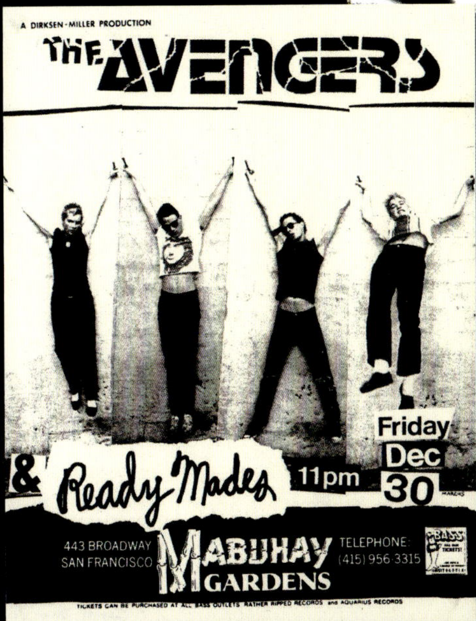

Photo: Marcus Leatherdale

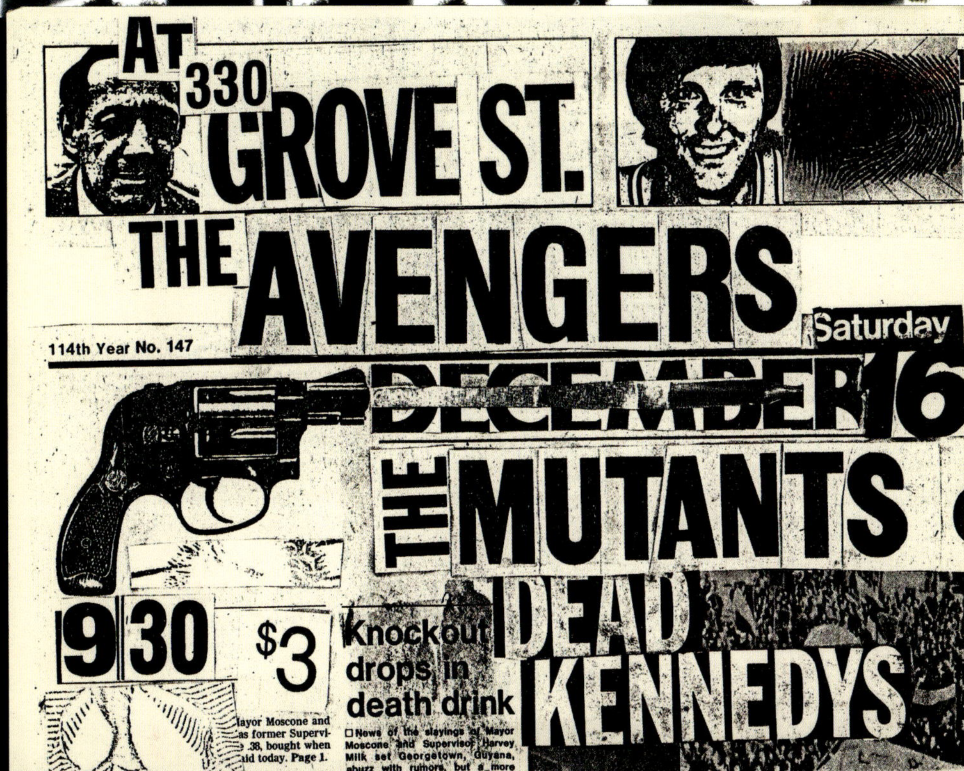

Penelope Houston

Penelope: I loved playing Grove Street because they had balconies that people would hang over, screaming.

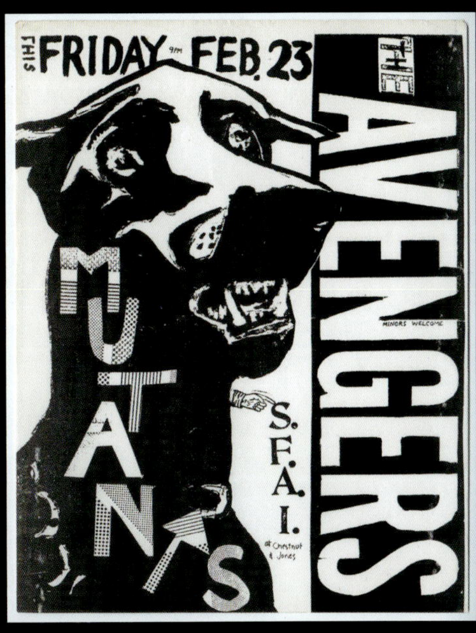

James Wilsey

Dog
Sept. 9th and 10th 1978
Mabuhay Gardens

I drew this poster in crayon in about five minutes. The image came from a pamphlet I found at the post office which told people to control their wild salivating animals when the mailman comes by. The image of a wild beast seemed to fit the way we played and acted. He's saying "Bop" because we'd recently discovered records by Gene Vincent and the Blue Capos (Be Bop A Lula, Bluejean Bop, Dance to the Bop, etc.)

The posters were so vital at the time - there was no outlet for legitimate advertising. It was fun because it was fast - you could draw something, get it copied, and have it pasted all over town in a matter of hours. I think it's also important to remember that it was an outlaw activity. I knew people who got busted postering, they got tickets and then were made to go and remove all the posters they had put up. We never got caught. We would cruise down the street in a pickup, keeping an eye out for the cops. Two people would jump out and work both sides of the street. (We thought we were pretty smart.) + **Jimmy Wilsey**

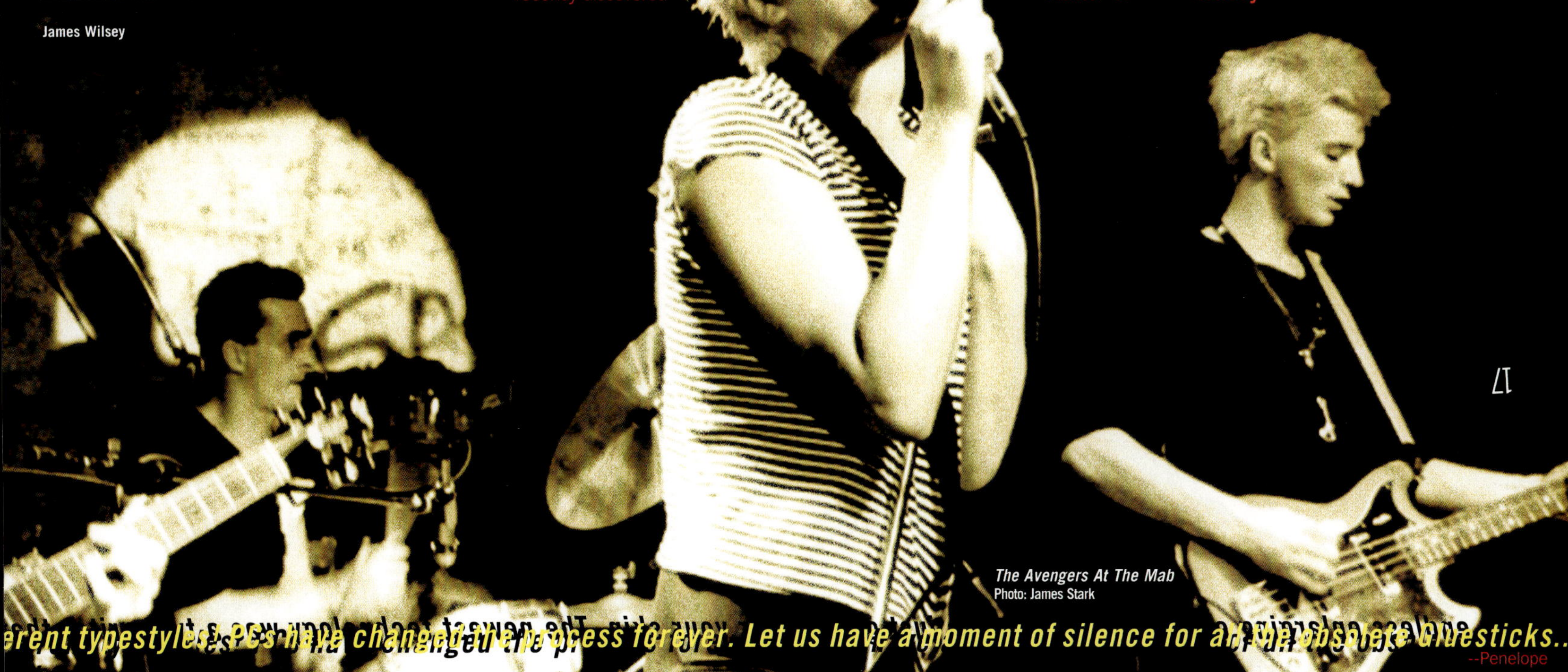

The Avengers At The Mab
Photo: James Stark

erent typestyles. PCs have changed the process forever. Let us have a moment of silence for all the obsolete gluesticks...
--Penelope

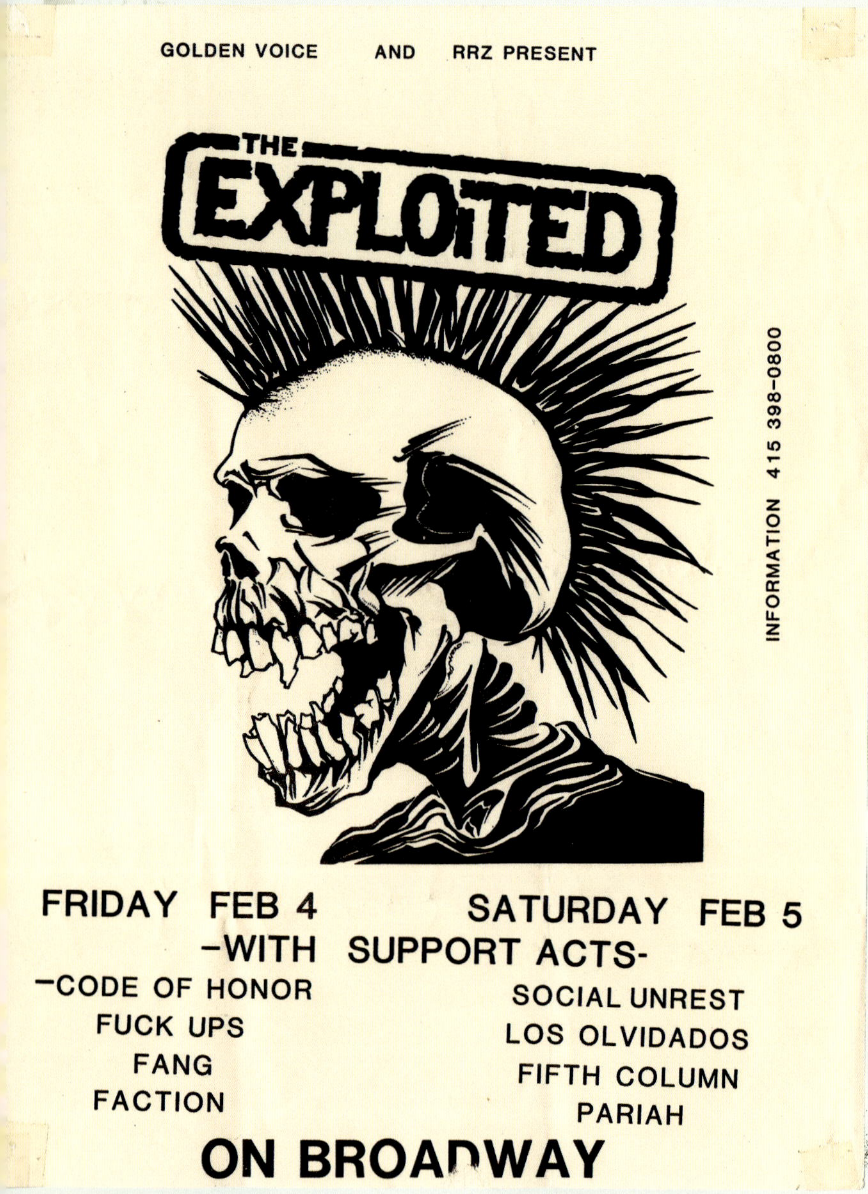

Pushead

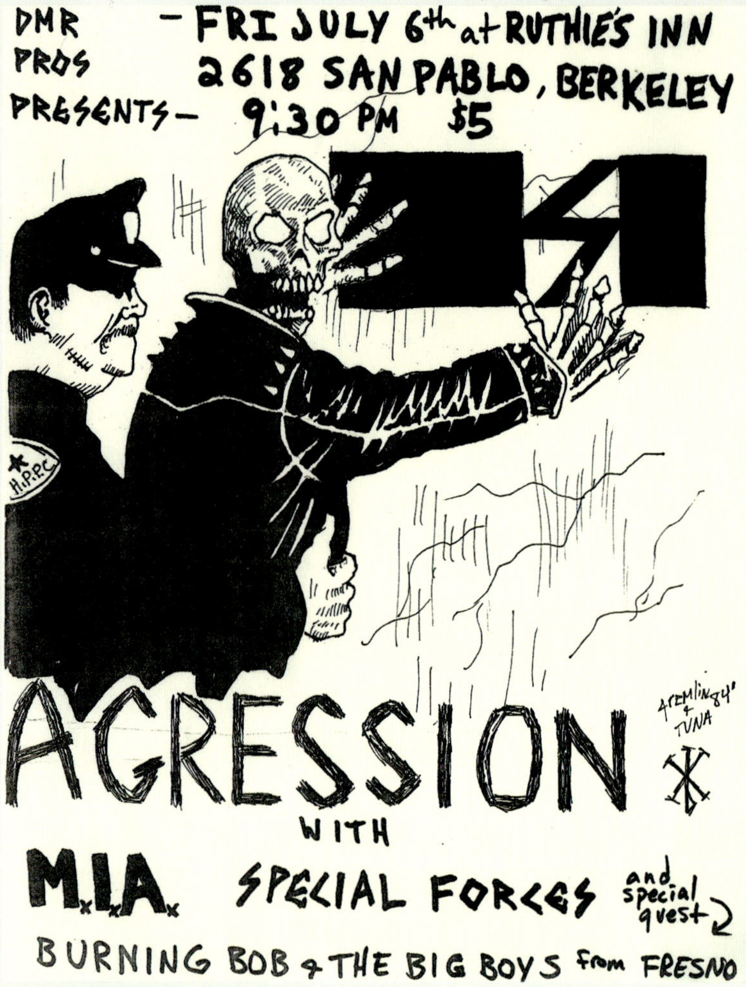

D.M.R.

Exploited Skull

This design was originally done for Shawn Stern/BYO when he was running Godzilla's. The actual Exploited show was canceled, but Stern did use it when it was rescheduled.

Like so many designs from this era, I received no money for my work. I just wanted to help out.

Pushead

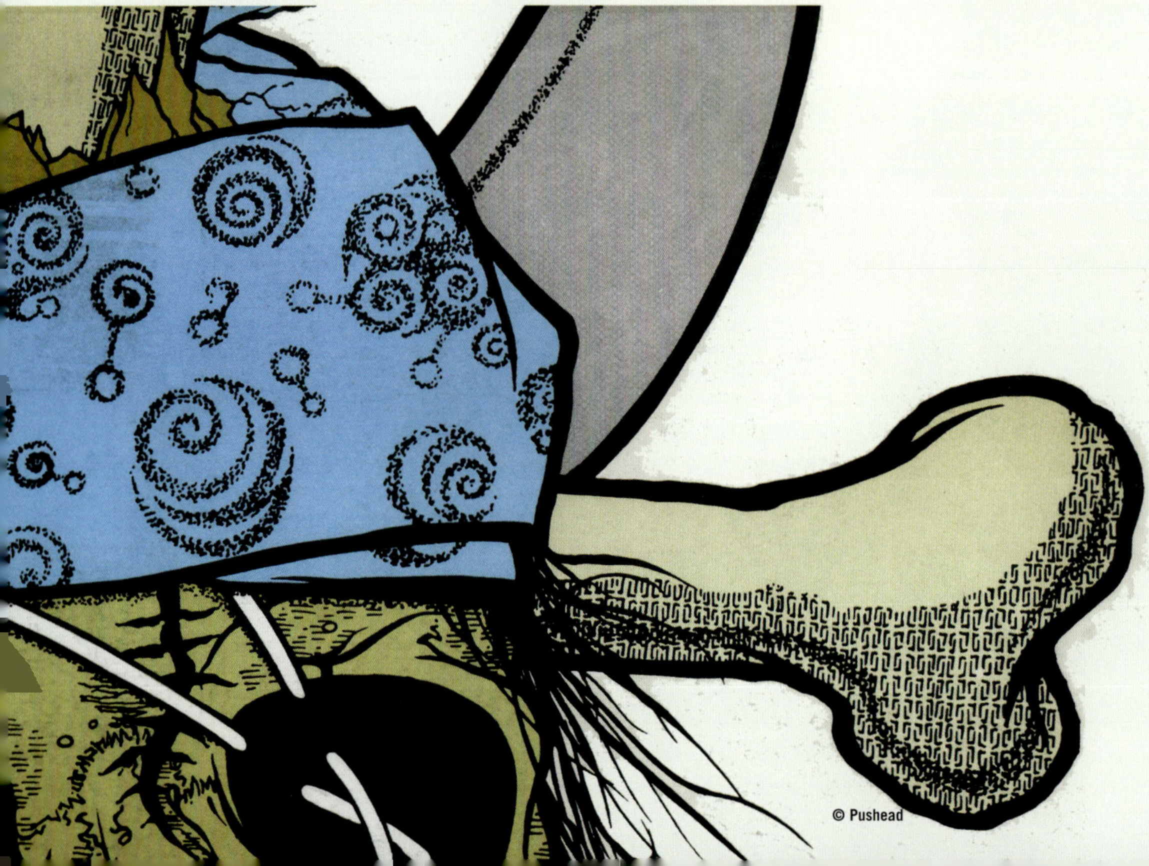

Skull Illustration: Asher

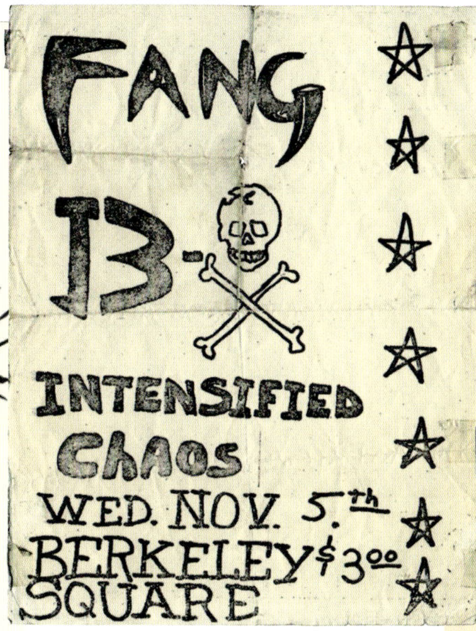

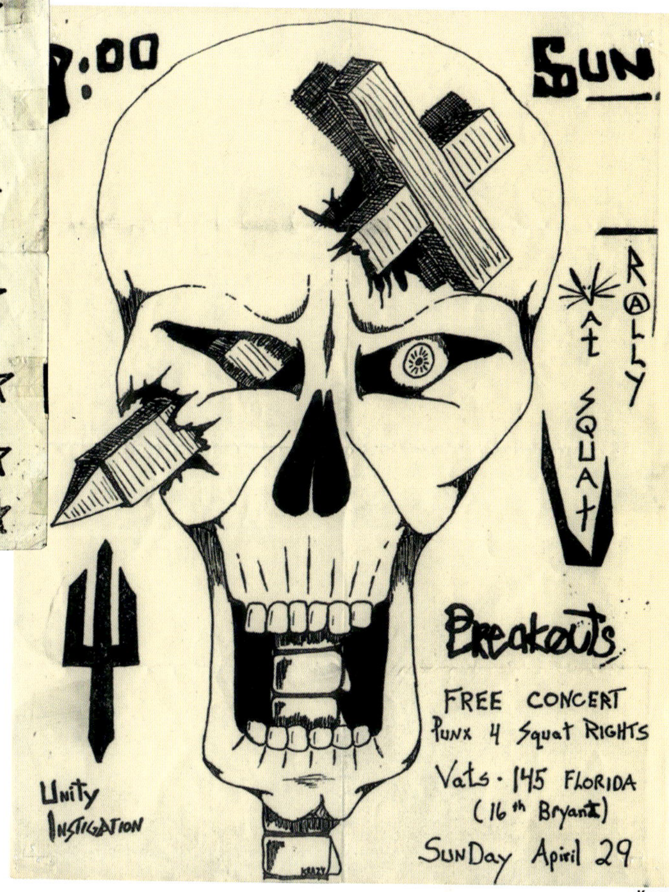

Krazy

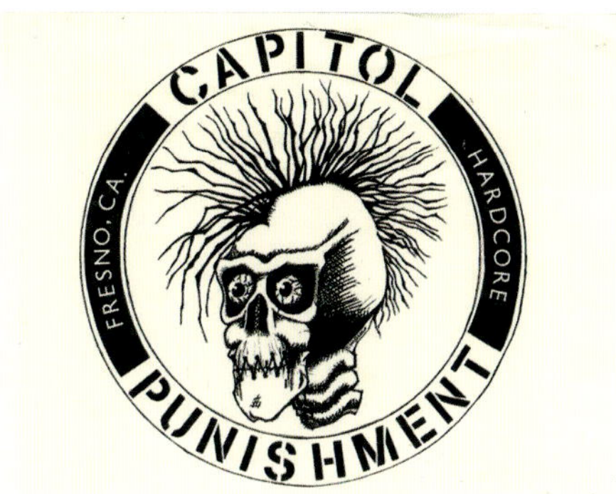

Tim Biskup

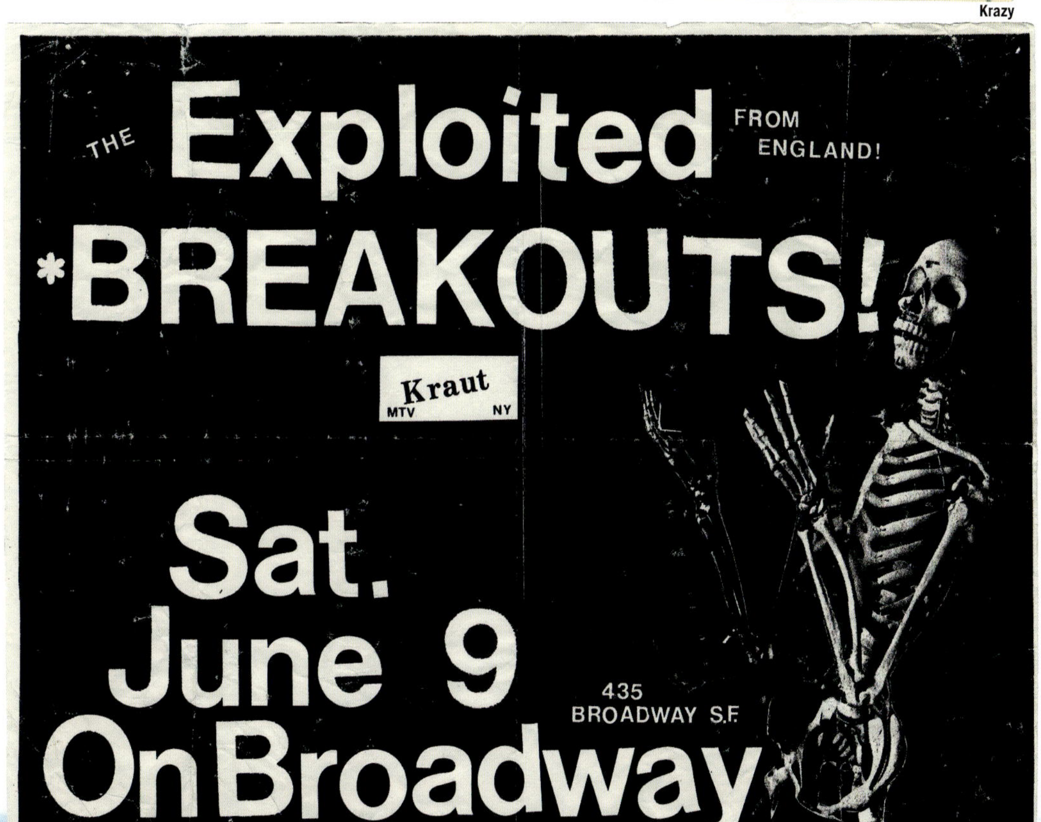

ʼresno Rocks! by Evan Mack

hen my family moved back to Fresno in 1980 I was 14 year d. (I had been born there, but we moved to Tempe, AZ for couple of years). I'd heard about Punk Rock. I'd read of Si cious' death in the newspaper, but hadn't actually heard the usic yet. Back in Fresno for the first time in a few years, a y old friends had turned into complete dorks, so I looked for w friends. I found them in the misfit skateboarders at schoo nese kids were all about getting into trouble, and listening to ... and The Sex Pistols. The music was the most revoltin uff I'd ever heard and I loved it. Hardcore had already begun ppening but it was slow to reach us. We heard some bands ere going to play on a weekday afternoon at some faux ... rk on the other side of town. I went with some schoolmates, d was blown away by the crazies there. The bands ... next to a picnic area and people were dancing violently the grass next to a man-made lake. Soon the pigs ... and pulled the plug. The show may have ended prematurely, t I was sold on punk. I didn't get to see many ... xt few years, and my only real connection to the music was weekly radio show, *Maximum Rock And Roll*, being broadcast t of Berkeley and picked up by a Fresno Public Radio station. ow this came to be is a mystery, due to the extremely small dience for it, but I listened every Tuesday night and recorded the show. I also managed to pick up a few records, but they were hard to come by.

en in 1983 my family moved to Modesto, CA. No one there seemed to have a clue about punk, and I was having a hard time with that. I read about San Francisco shows the paper, and within a few months convinced a couple of friends to go see a show with me. We drove to see GBH at *On Broadway*. The second we entered the place I as overcome by the smell (which took me a while to figure out- a combination of cloves and sweaty leather.) Six bands played and and we didn't get out of there until 3 . Every freak in the world seemed to be there and I knew instantly that this is what I had been looking for. The atmosphere of pure energy and reckless abandon was y dream come true. I went to as many shows as I could until On Broadway closed later that year. Then I started picking up flyers and began to explore shows all over the y Area. The flyers worked as advertising for the shows, a creative outlet for artists, and as wallpaper - everyone I knew covered their bedrooms from floor to ceiling with them. +

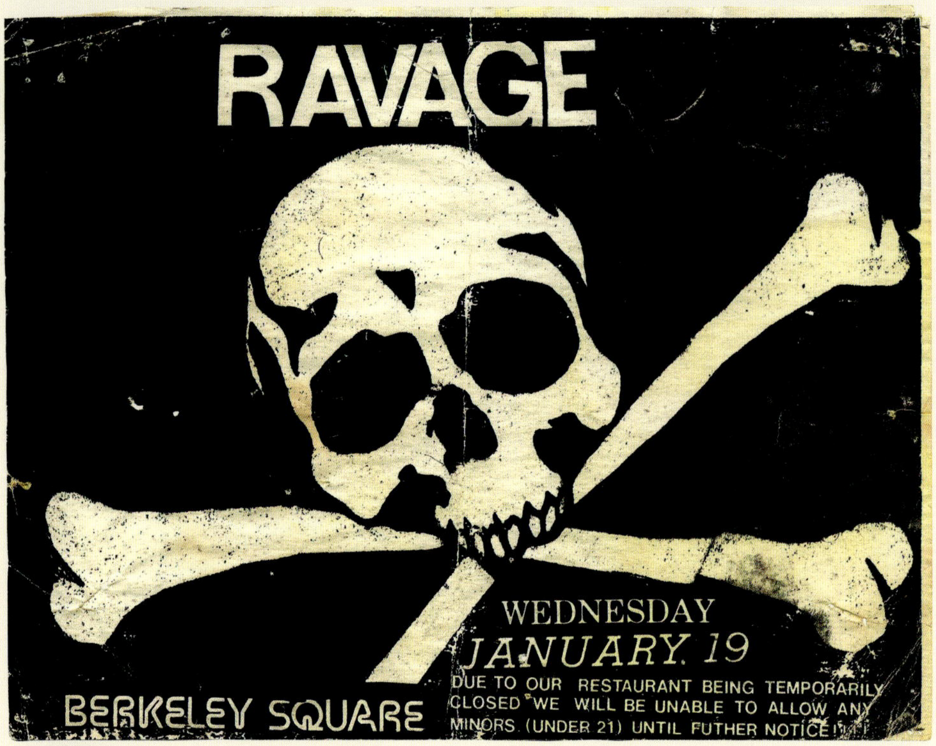

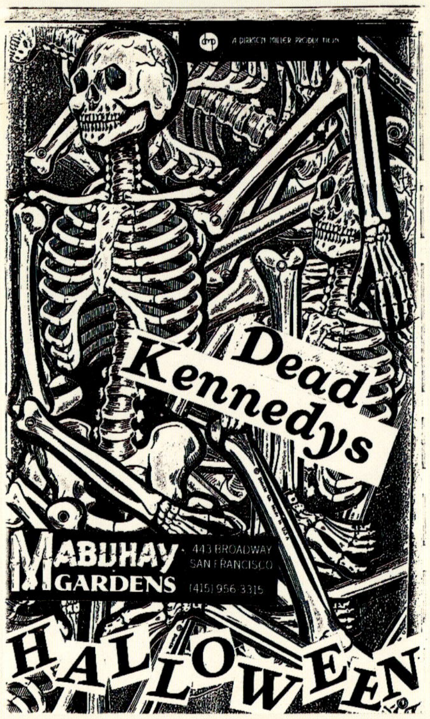

Bruce Slesinger

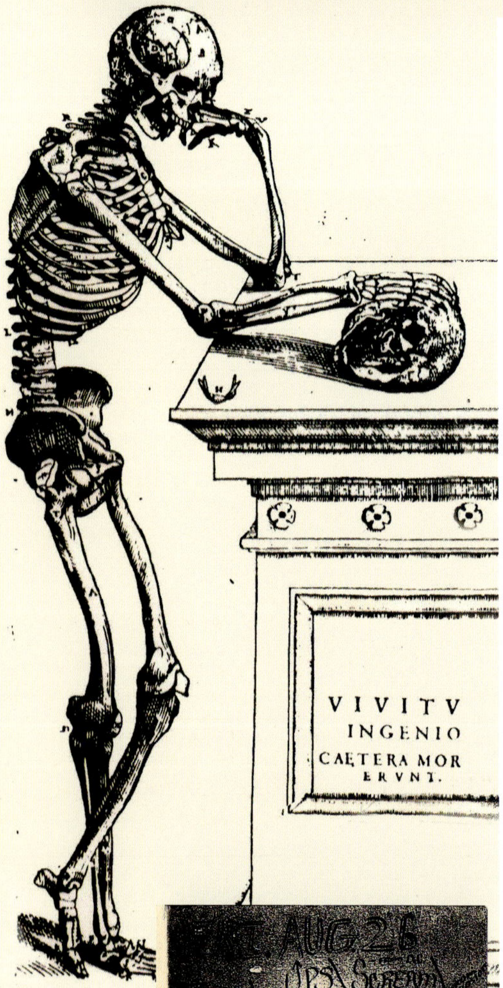

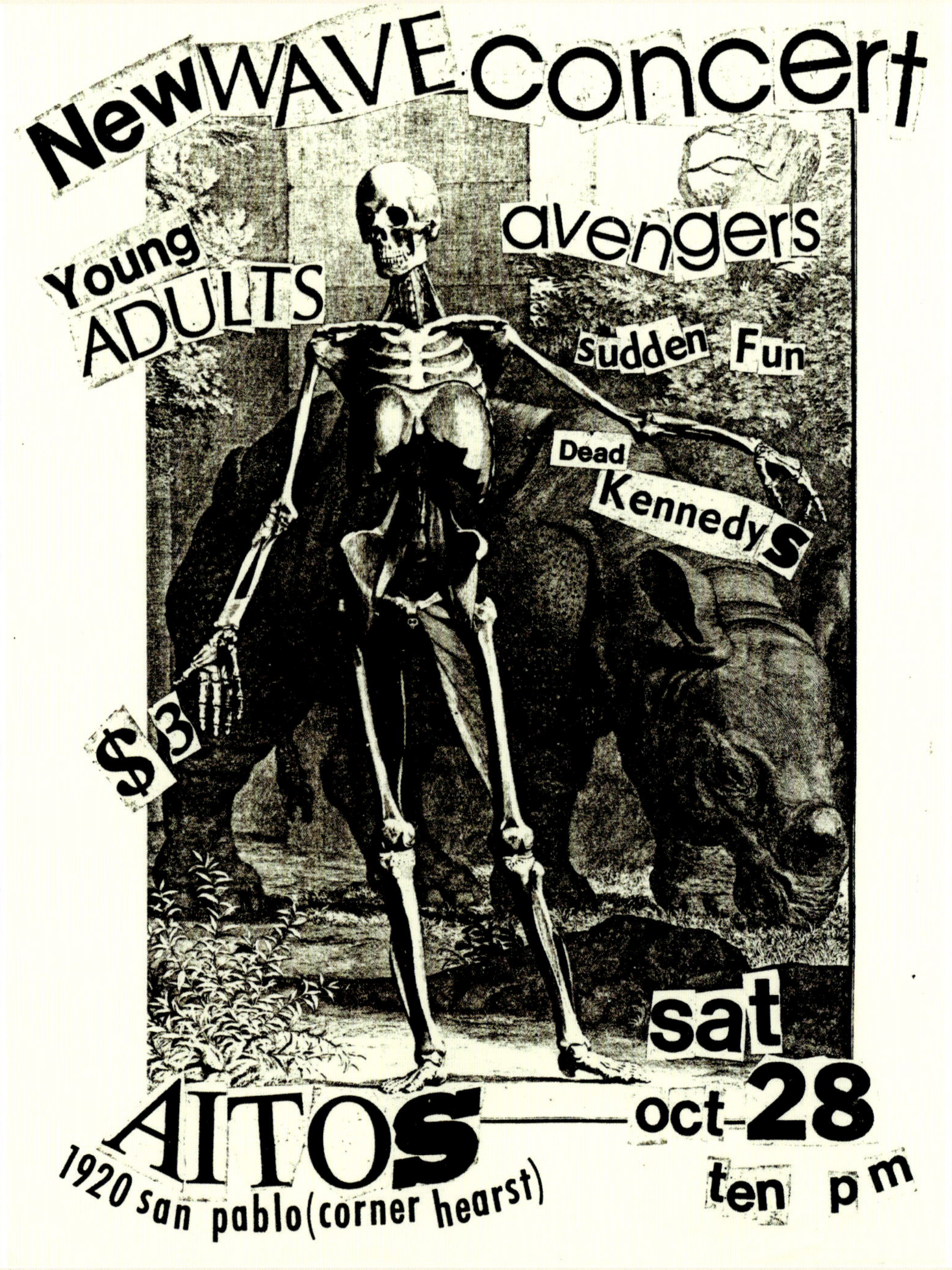

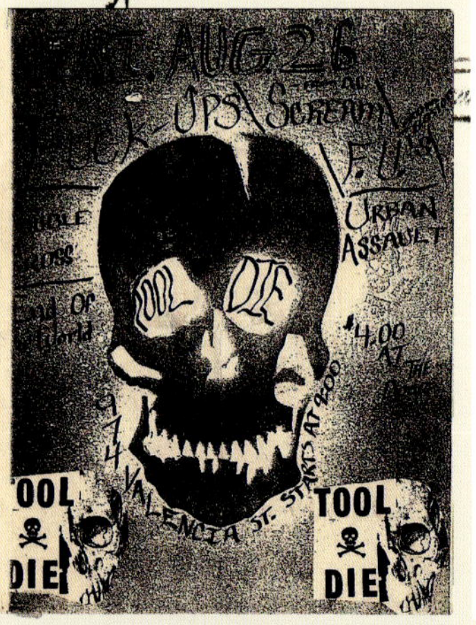

The Fuck-Ups

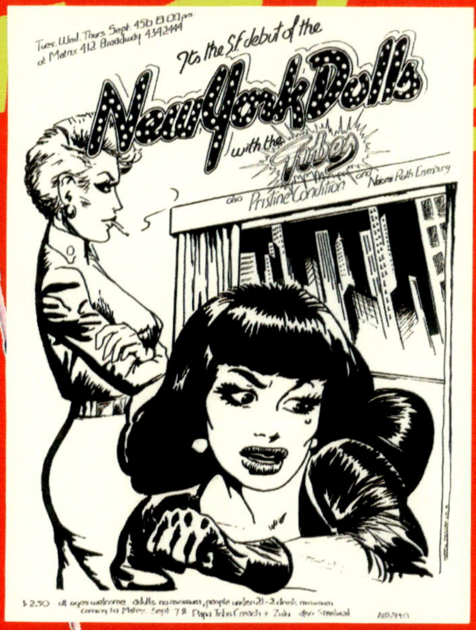

Aramid

Matrix Poster #3

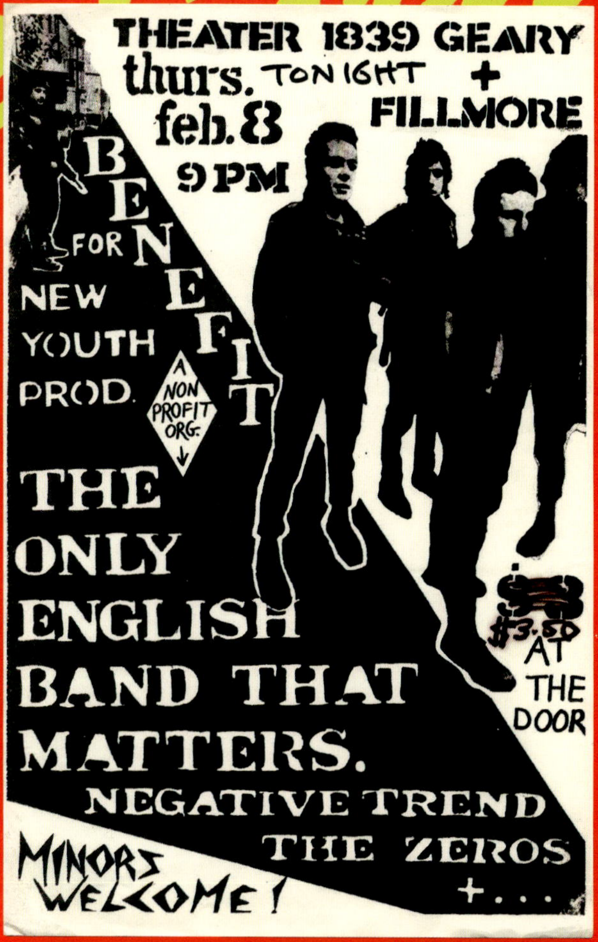

Alexis Scott / Sadie McFarlane

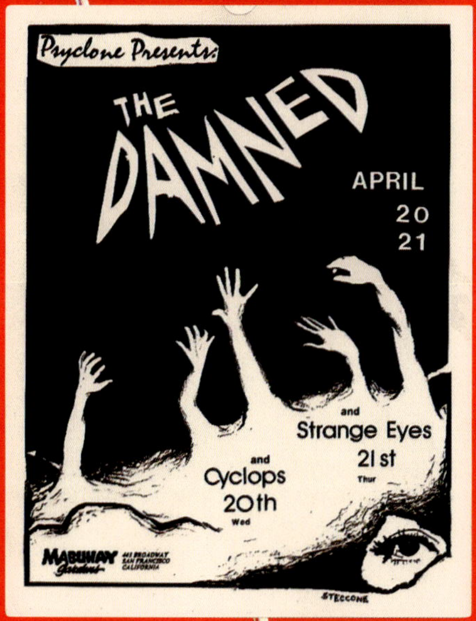

Judy Steccone

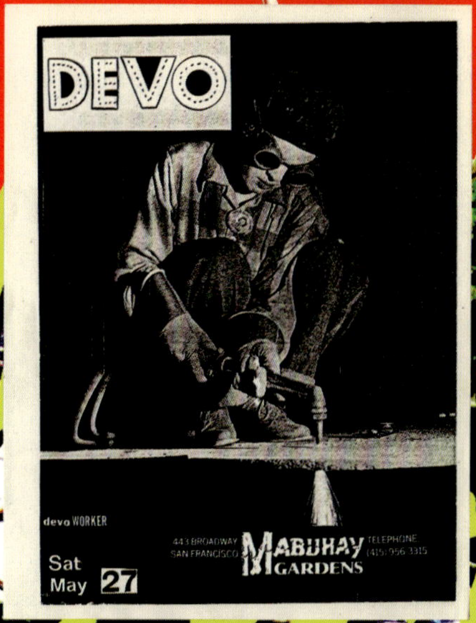

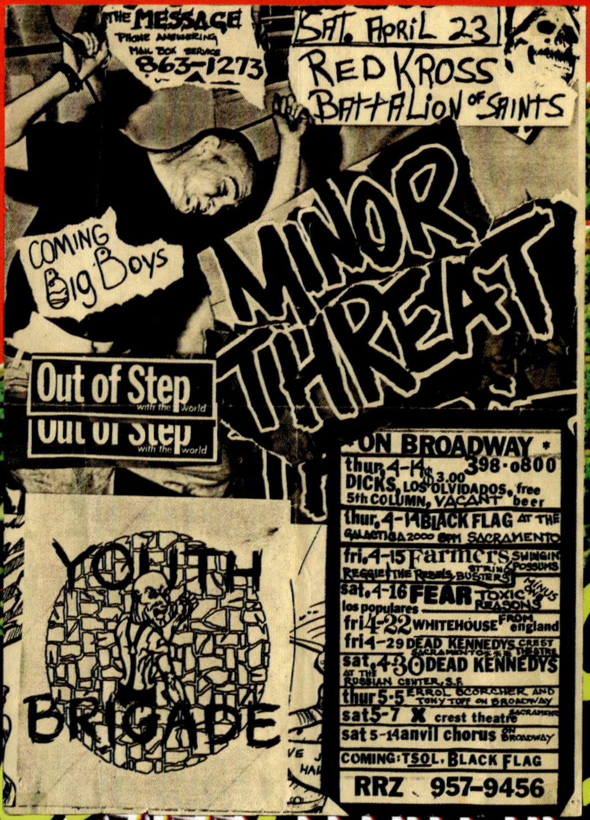

B A Y S M

New Varsity Theatre
Palo Alto CA 3 16 85

We are midway through our set when out of the corner of my eye I see something headed my way. I turn and step to the left and hear a crashing of cymbals and drums. I look at James, our drummer, and he is still playing, so on we go. When the song is over I see that someone threw a flag from a golf course at us. How the hell an eight foot pole with an orange flag got into the gig is beyond me. The most amazing thing is that not a drop of beer was spilled.

Thanks to everyone who ever came to see us play.
Bill V.
vocals, The Drab

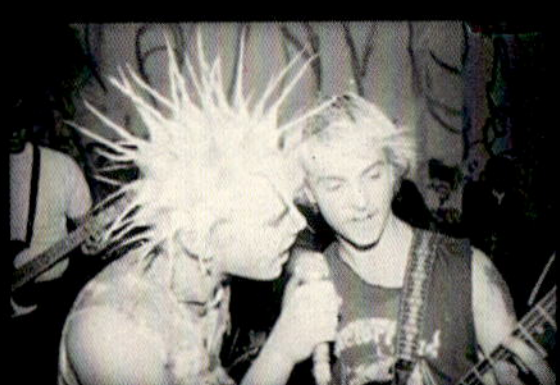

Drab Photo: Denise Vaughn

Flyers remind me of a time in my life when everything was new. Girls, drugs, alcohol, friends, but most importantly, the music.

Punk Rock...in 1998 the term sounds as old and tired as the reunited Sex Pistols. It's a shame because it wasn't that way when it started. And like everything else in this world that has any meaning, sooner or later it gets ruined.

Remember the Woodstock generation? Punkers hated those long haired artifacts with a passion, but now they strike up the same conversations of "back in my day, it was different. We had a reason...we were part of something."

Isn't it funny how everything comes full circle.

Joe Sib

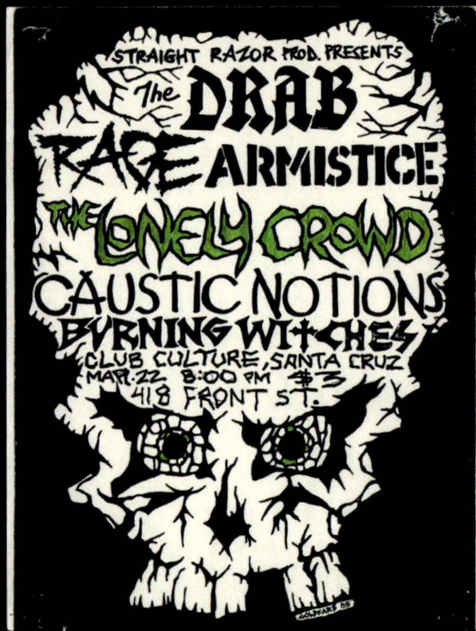

Andrew Goldfarb

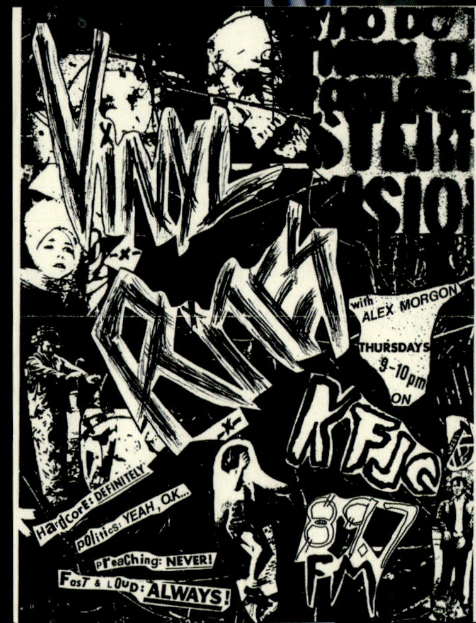

THE DRAB

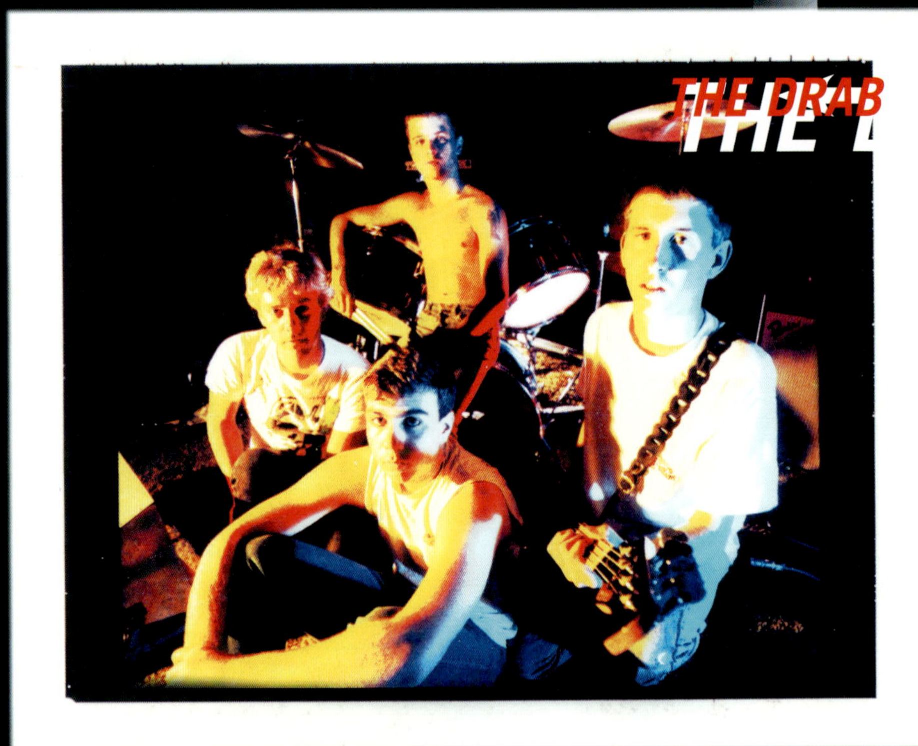

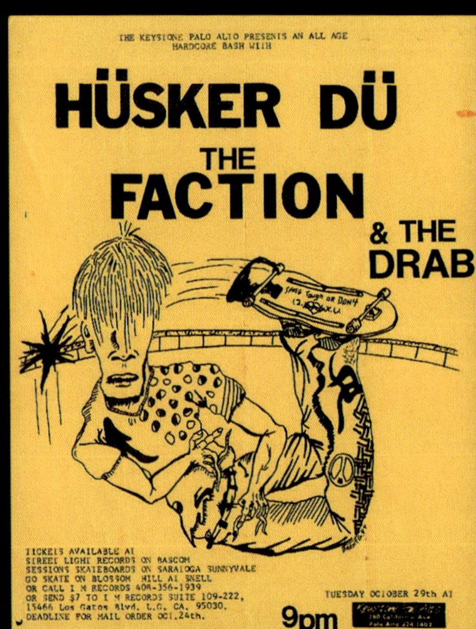

Brent G.

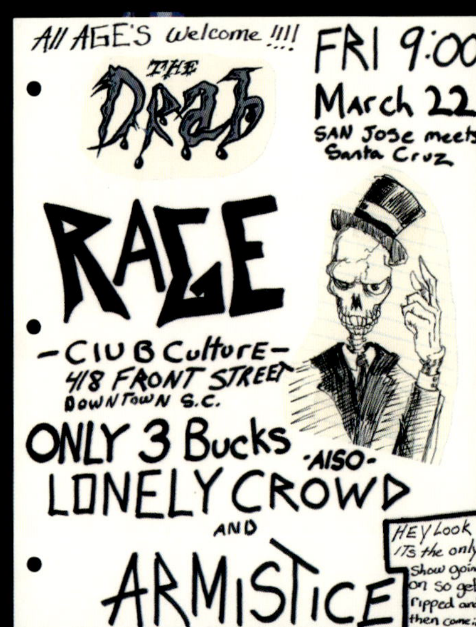

Bryan Turcotte & Joe Sib

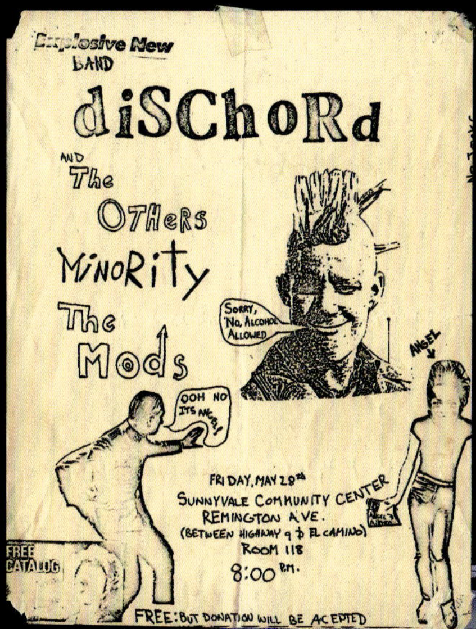

Now that I find myself old enough to consider my life and lifestyle from the late 70s to the mid 80s as part of my past, I find that aside from the obvious hair and fashion accoutrements, that I haven't really changed all that much. I always felt like an outsider in most social circles. With punk I had a chance not only to face those feelings of isolation, but via my mode of dress and judicious use of Knox gelatin, I let everyone around me know how I was feeling. I don't think that many of us have an incredible amount of photographic evidence of those days - documenting my life back then would have gotten in the way of swiveling in the pit, hanging around with Carol and the DMRs on Durant Street, or running from dirt-heads preparing to maul us with tennis rackets in their red oxide-primered Zeppelin-blasting '74 Camaros. Flyers to me are a more lucid memory of my experiences than any piece of original vinyl or reissue CD can ever come close to. And even more than the artistic and social statements they make, flyers have the power to invoke memories of some great days and nights in my life.

Carl Swanberg

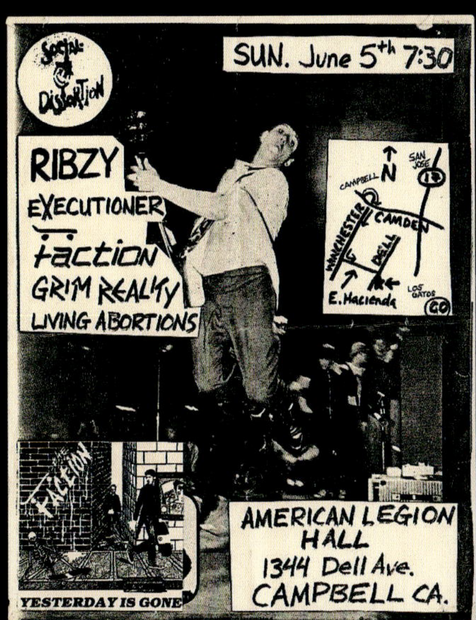

Mike Ness Photo: Glen E. Friedman

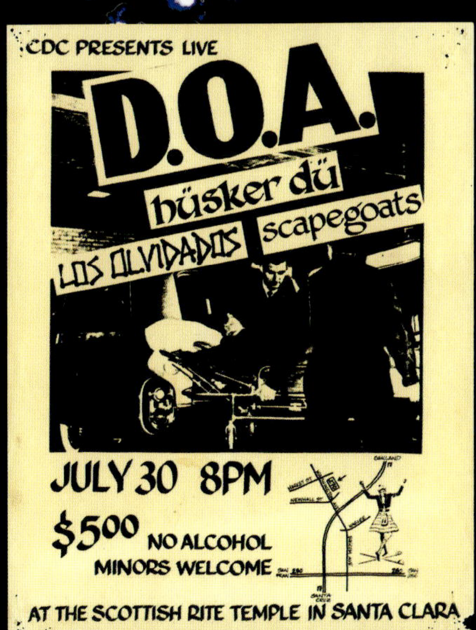

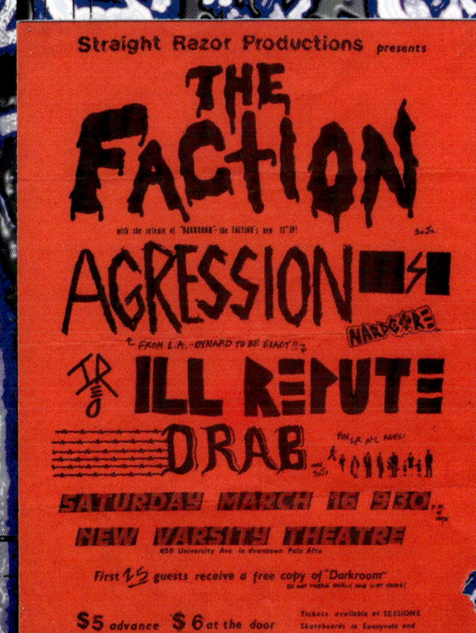

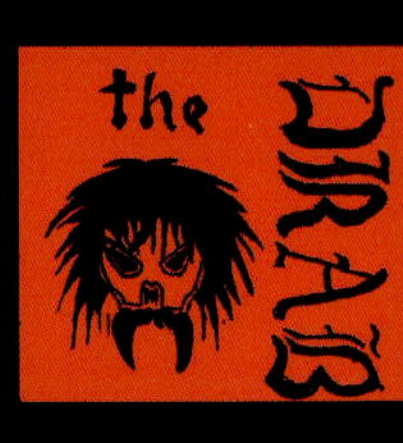

Bill Vitale of The Drab

Going down to the basement and swimming through the sealed boxes that contained our collection of flyers reminded us of how different the scene was back in the late '70s and early '80s, when being a punk was really dangerous.

The status quo were VERY concerned with how we wore our hair. Vans® shoes, straight-legged Levis® and short hair were all it took to get your ass kicked by complete strangers. Add a skateboard, and you were fair game to everyone: schoolmates, ex-friends, jocks, passers-by, teachers and especially cops. As we all now, these people eventually started wearing their hair short, with straight legs, and some even skated.

We'd to go to San Francisco three times a week to see great shows at places like *The Mab*, *On Broadway*, and the *Tool & Die*. It seemed that I was the only 16-year-old with a driver's license in San Jose's skate/punk scene, so I'd drive six other people into town several times a week.

San Jose had its fair share of truly great shows that we had the pleasure of surviving/attending. Dead Kennedys, Social Unrest and the Retorts was our first, and one of the only gigs in San Jose free of police rioting. In early 1980, The Angry Samoans, The VKTMS and local heroes Los Olvidados played at Studio 47, marking the last peaceful show in San Jose. After that, the cops went berserk. The Black Flag riot and Adolescents riots were particularly troubling.

By the time my band, The Faction, formed in 1982, the scene in San Jose was really good. Bands like The Retorts, Los Olvidados, Ribsy, The Unaware, Executioner and Grim Reality were all uniquely talented groups. Los Olvidados supported all the big touring bands in San Francisco because there wasn't a person in the Bay Area that didn't like them. Talk about talent!

The rest of America may have arrived 15 years late to what they think is punk, and maybe there were some who felt we were late back when we got started. The only thing that really matters is that twenty years ago, it was all new, it was all dangerous, and it was all ours.

Gavin O'Brien/Corey O'Brien
The Faction/Sonic Skates

Doyle smashes Timmy over the head w/Bass. Nor-Cal turns on the Misfits.

Tripple X Prod.

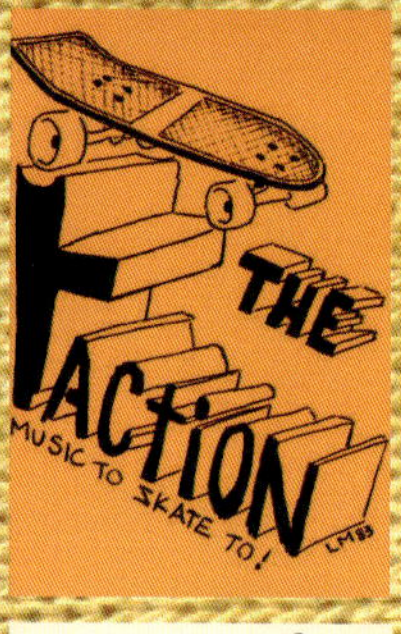

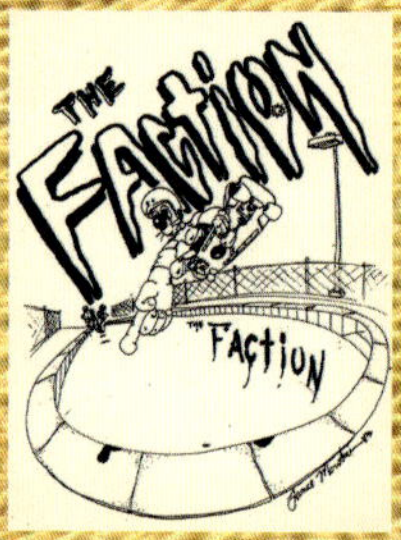

Lance Mountain

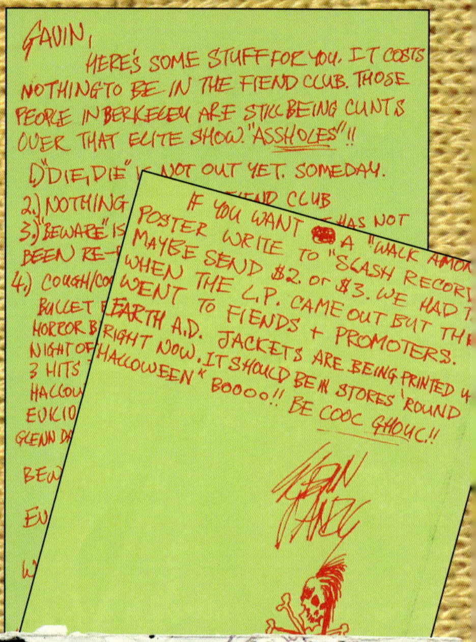

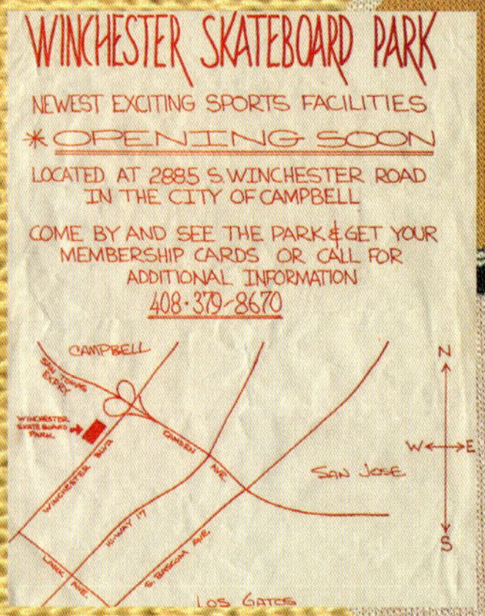

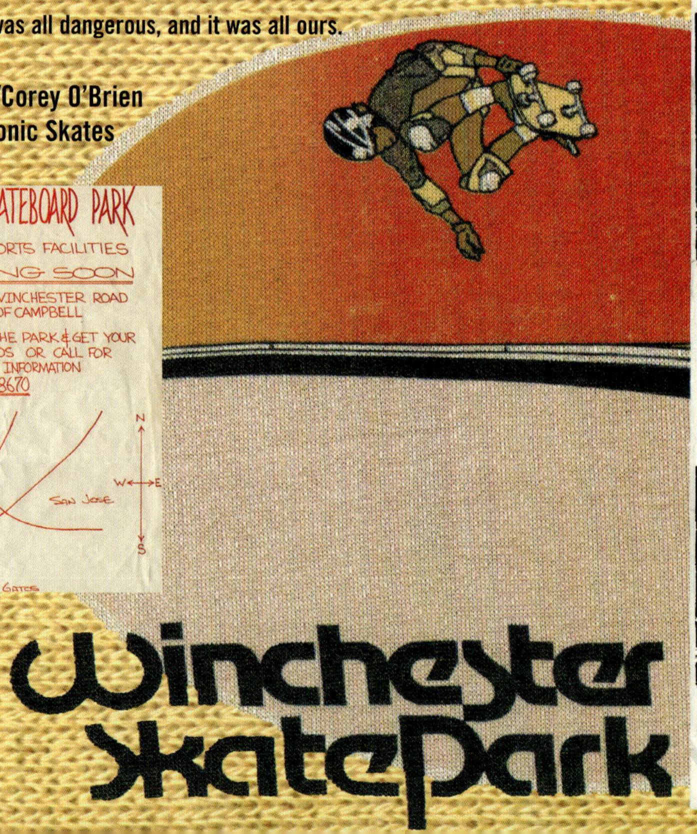

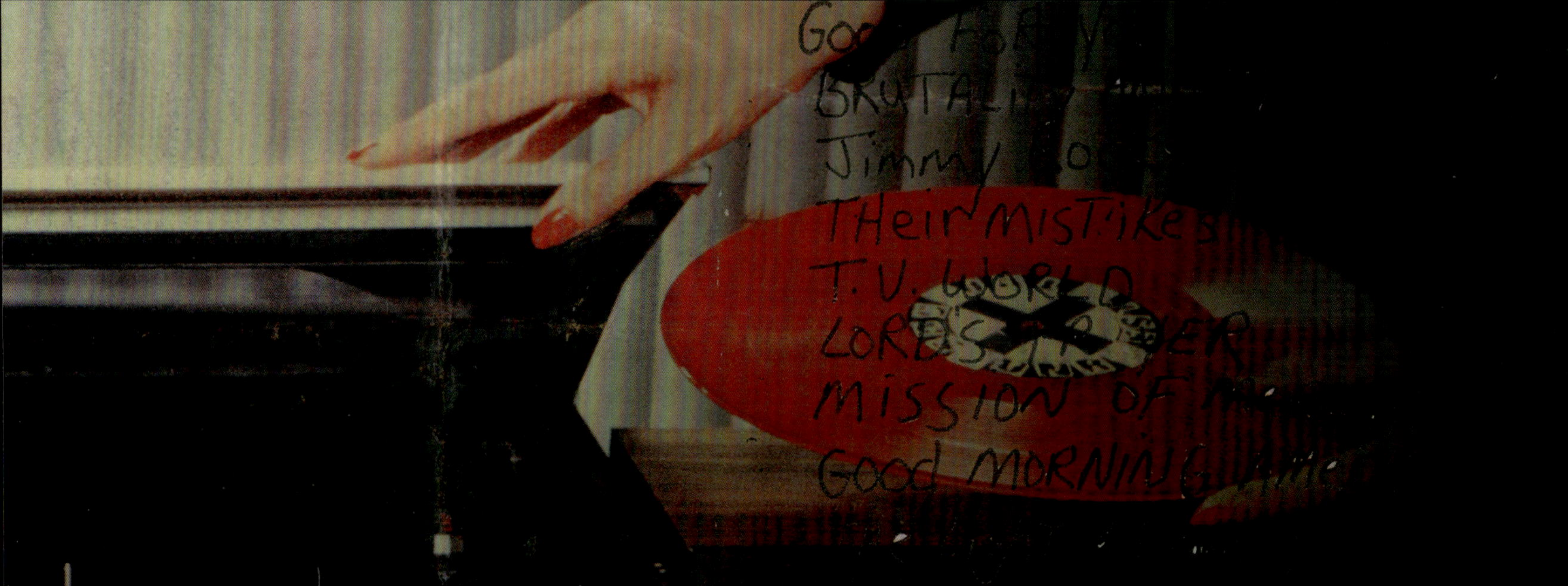

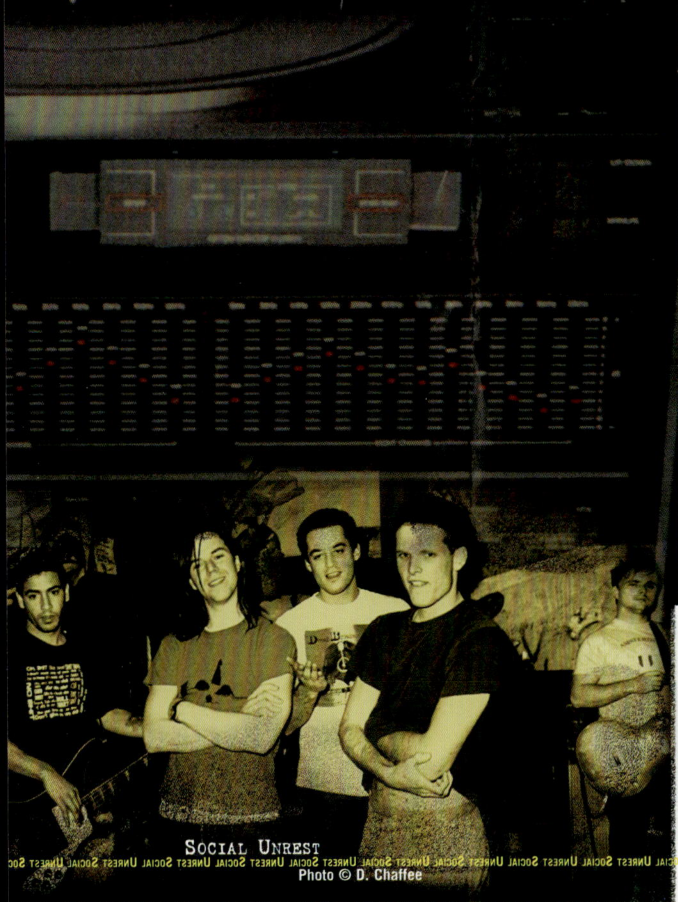

SOCIAL UNREST
Photo © D. Chaffee

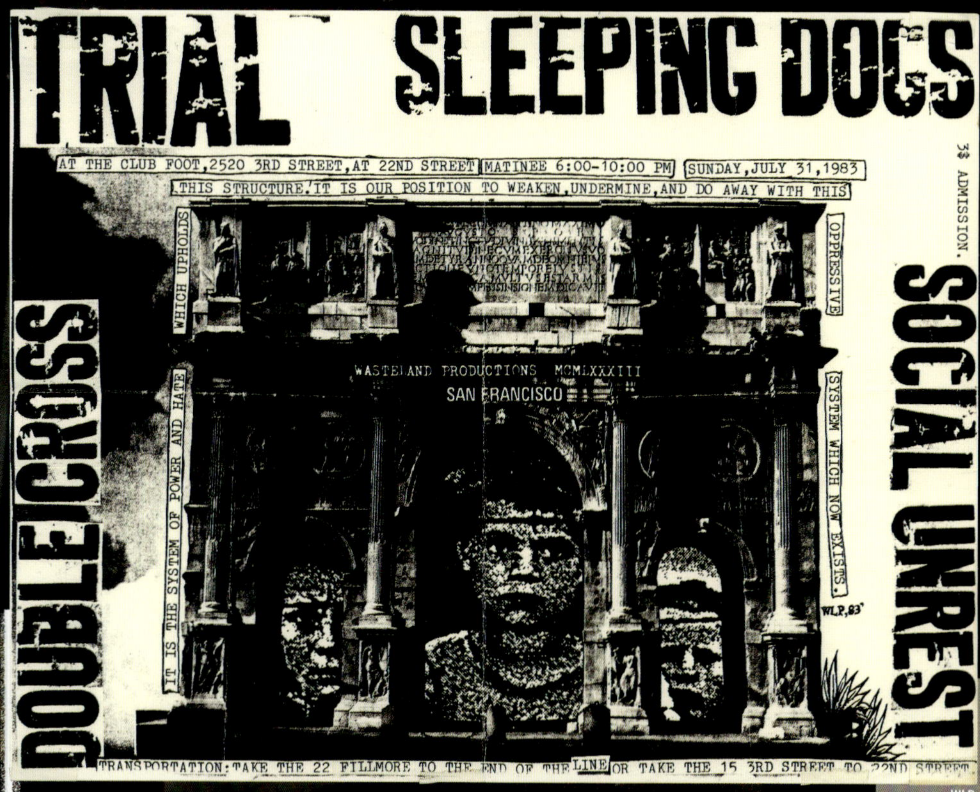

WLP

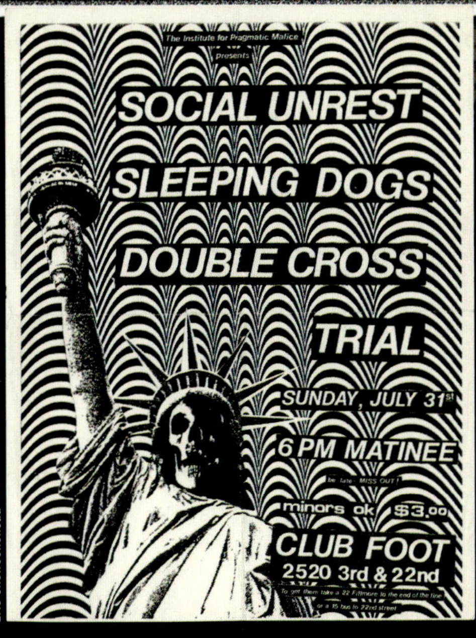

Eric Snowconehead

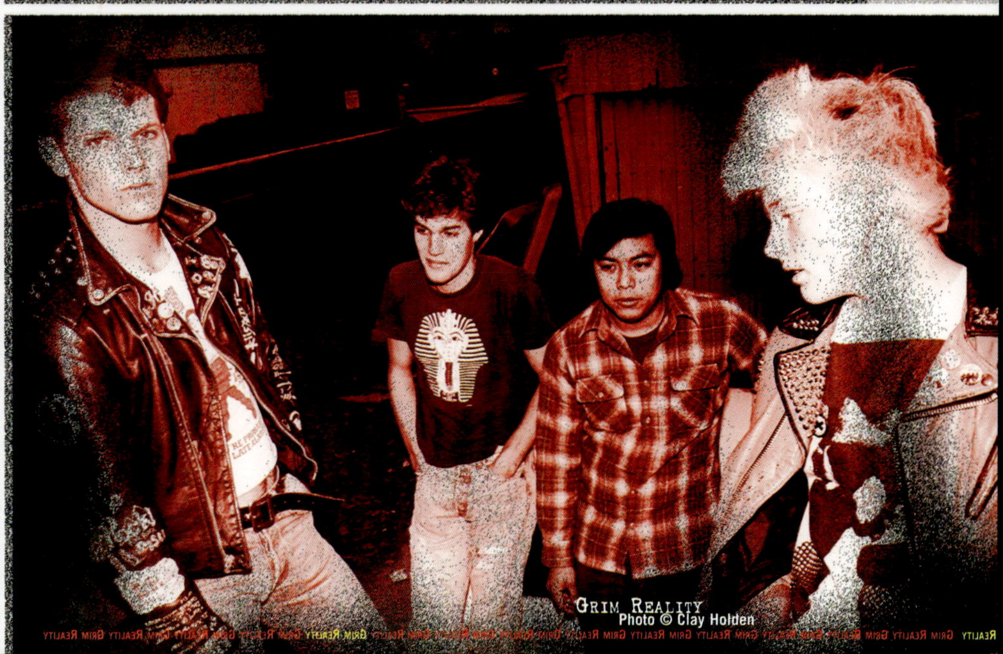

GRIM REALITY
Photo © Clay Holden

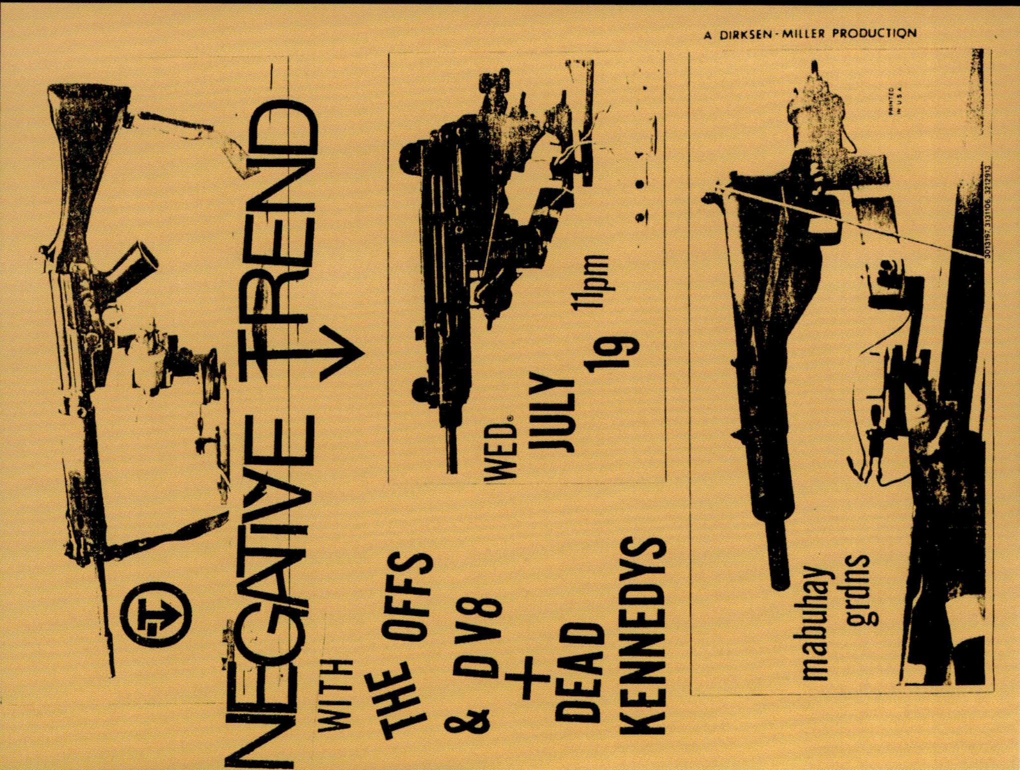

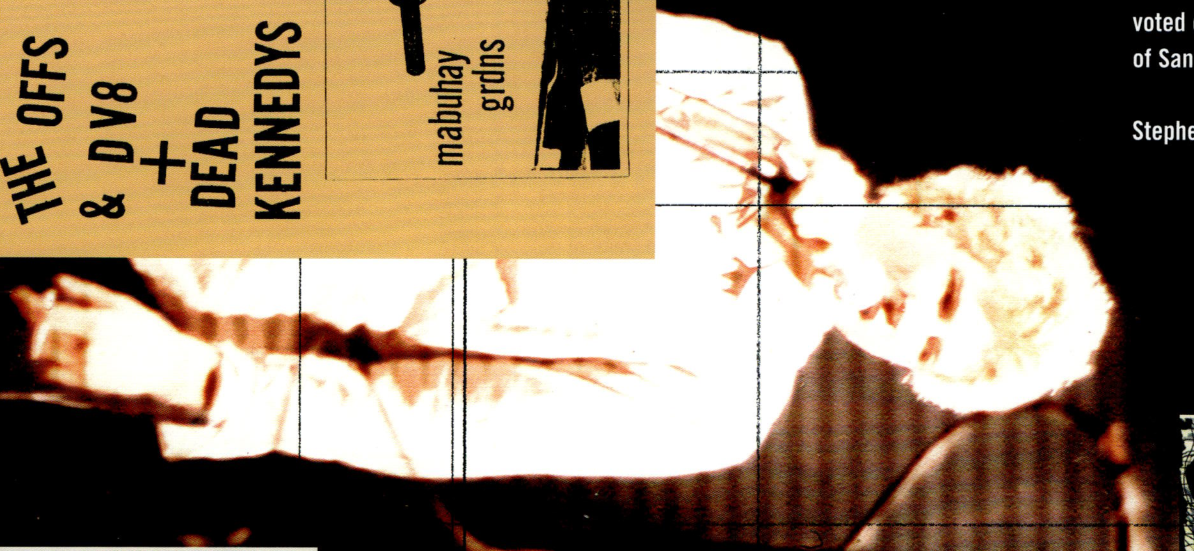

Will Shatter

In 1979 Flipper evolved out of three bands -
Will Shatter and myself from
Negative Trend,
Ted Falconi from SST,
and Ricky from The Sleepers.
Ricky was our original singer and came up with the
name of the band,
but he only lasted three months before being fired
because he was
unconscious
most of the time.
Flipper was both loved and hated, an,ɘmgiиɘ fun to
watch but tough to figure out. Generic Flipper was
voted one of the top ten albums ever to come out
of San Francisco.

Stephen DePace

Flipper
Photo © Wendy Schecter

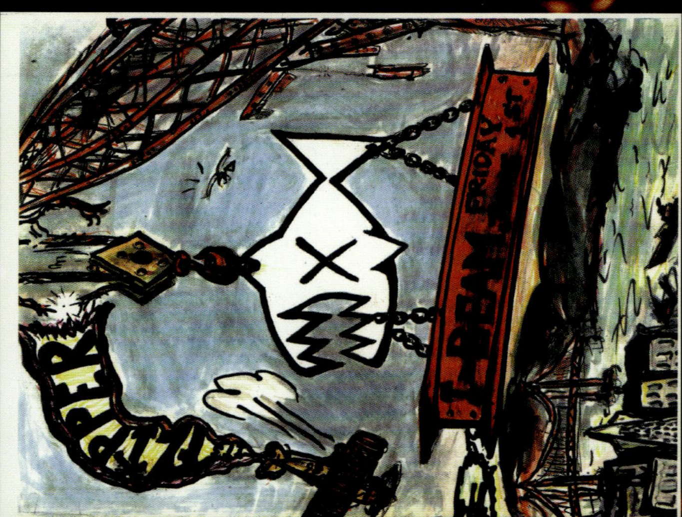

Ted Falconi

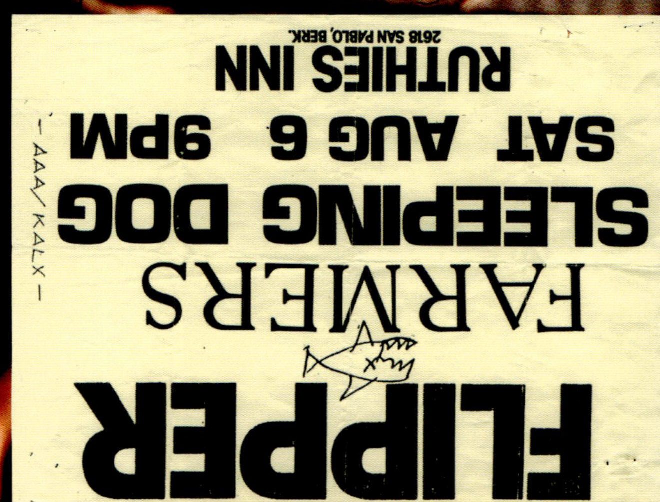

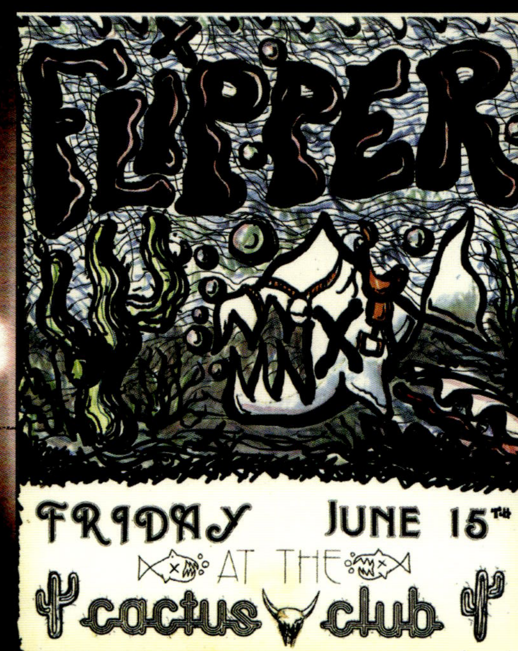

John Dougherty

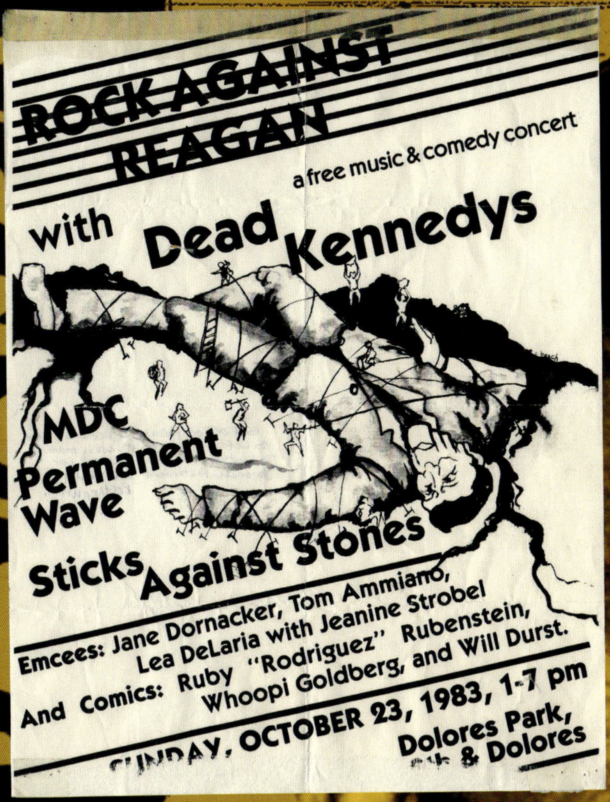

A. Beach

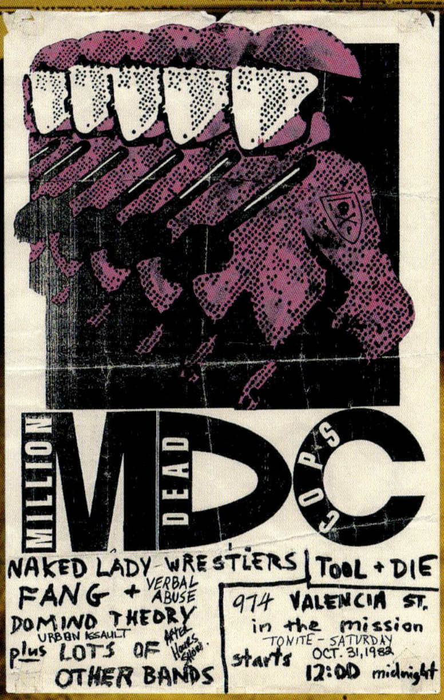

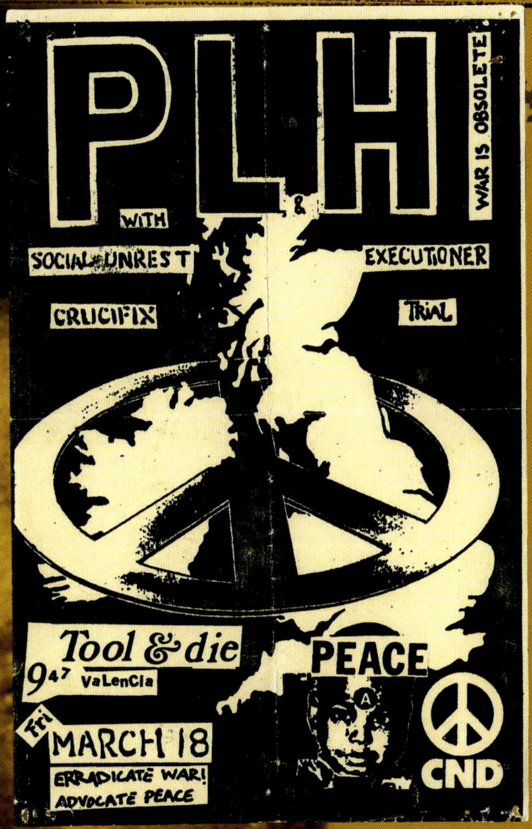

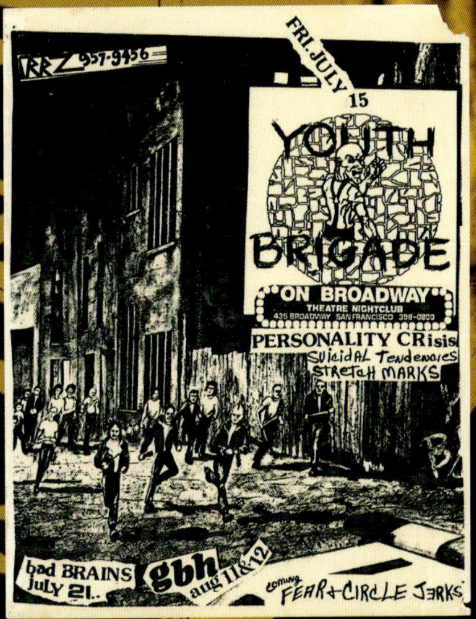

Kandy Stern

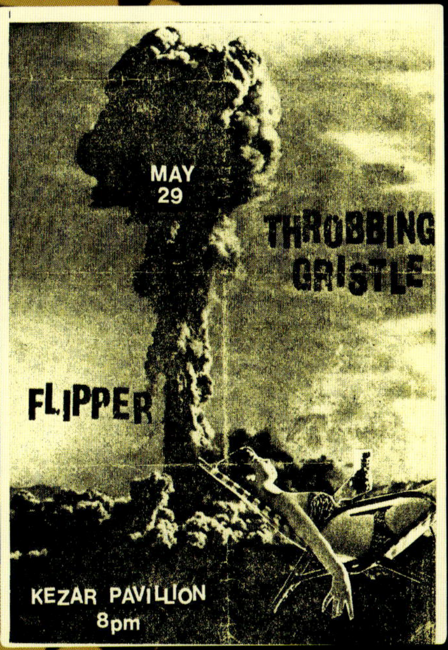

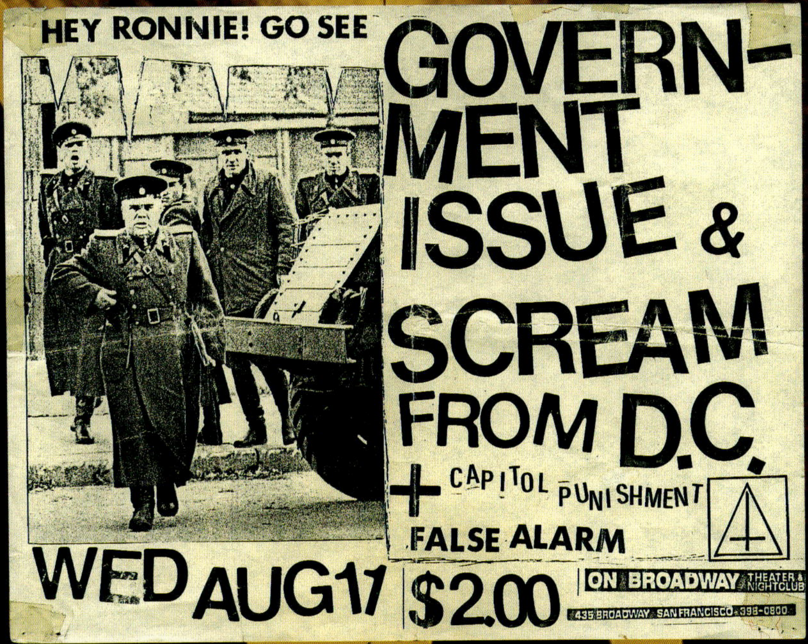

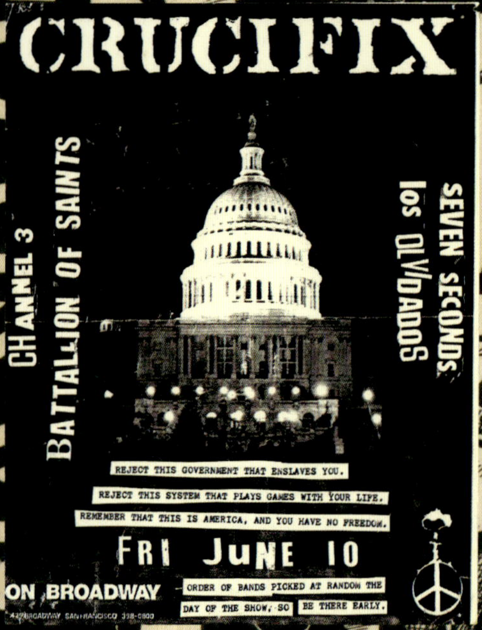
CRUCIFIX
CHANNEL 3
BATTALION OF SAINTS
SEVEN SECONDS
los OLVIDADOS
REJECT THIS GOVERNMENT THAT ENSLAVES YOU.
REJECT THIS SYSTEM THAT PLAYS GAMES WITH YOUR LIFE.
REMEMBER THAT THIS IS AMERICA, AND YOU HAVE NO FREEDOM.
FRI JUNE 10
ON BROADWAY
ORDER OF BANDS PICKED AT RANDOM THE DAY OF THE SHOW, SO BE THERE EARLY.

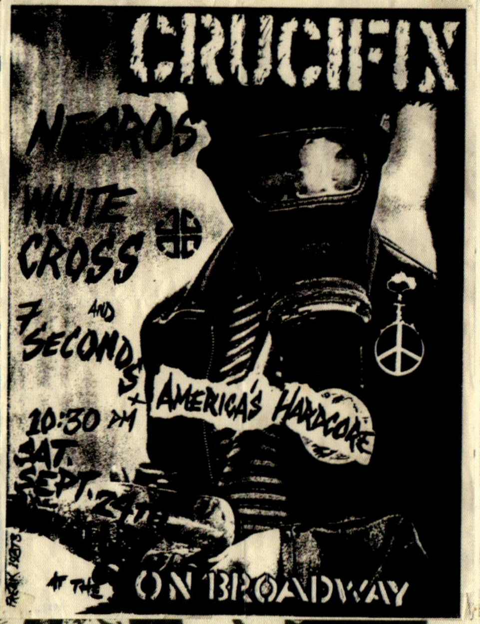
CRUCIFIX
NEGROS
WHITE CROSS
7 SECONDS
AMERICA'S HARDCORE
10:30 PM
SAT. SEPT. 24TH
AT THE ON BROADWAY

Fre

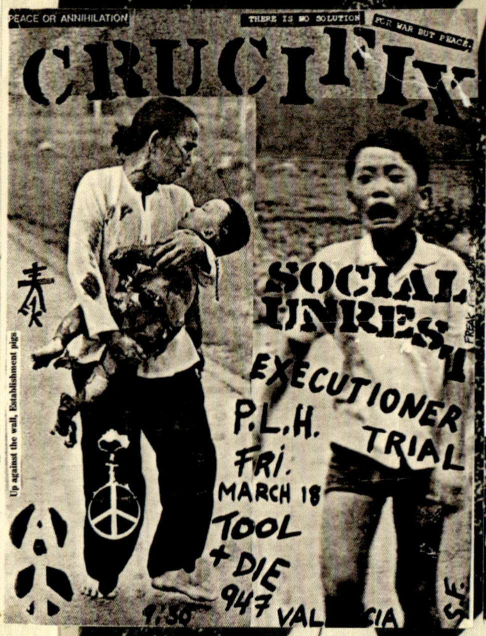
PEACE OR ANNIHILATION
THERE IS NO SOLUTION
FOR WAR BUT PEACE.
CRUCIFIX
SOCIAL UNREST
EXECUTIONER
P.L.H.
TRIAL
FRI. MARCH 18
TOOL + DIE
947 VALENCIA
Up against the wall, Establishment pigs

Freak

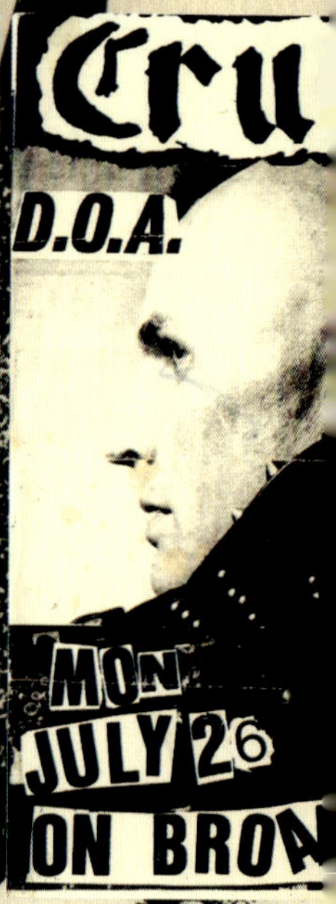
Cru
D.O.A.
MON JULY 26
ON BROA

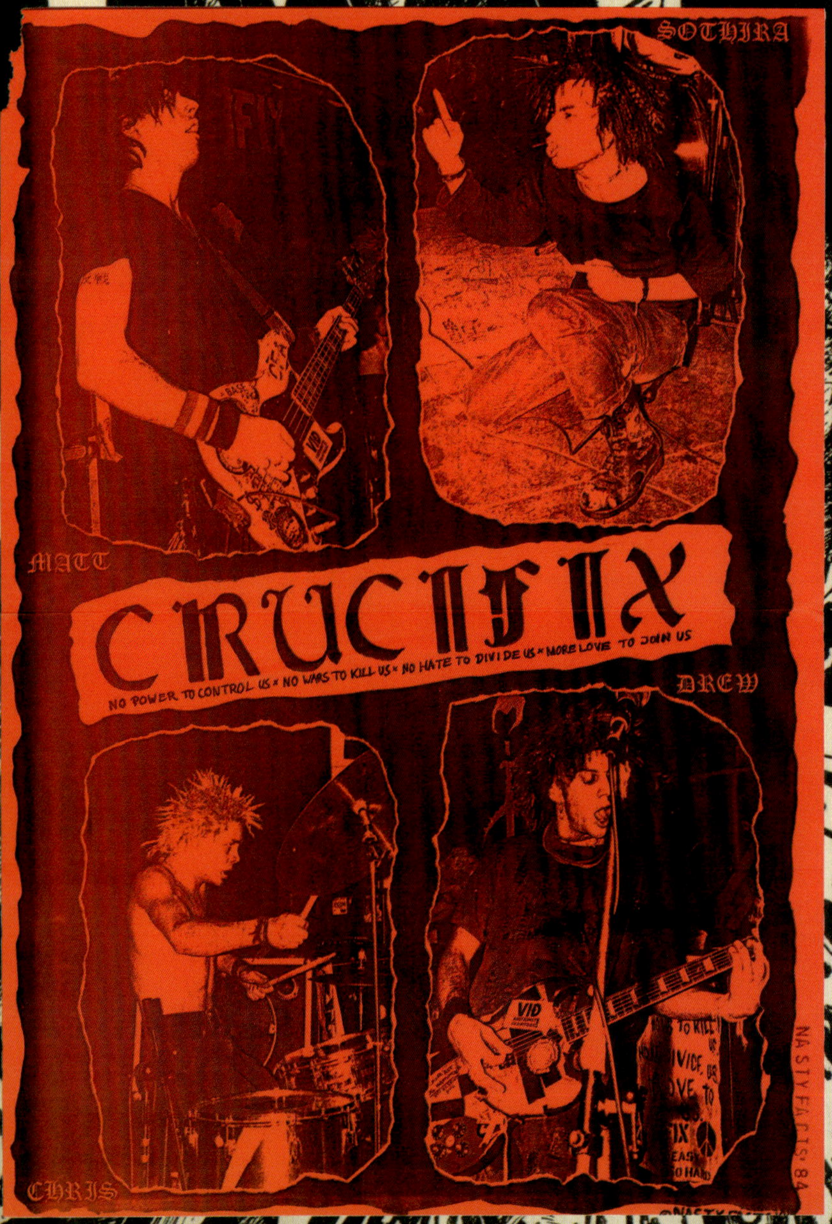
SOTHIRA
MATT
CRUCIFIX
NO POWER TO CONTROL US × NO WARS TO KILL US × NO HATE TO DIVIDE US × MORE LOVE TO JOIN US
DREW
CHRIS
NASTY FACTS 84

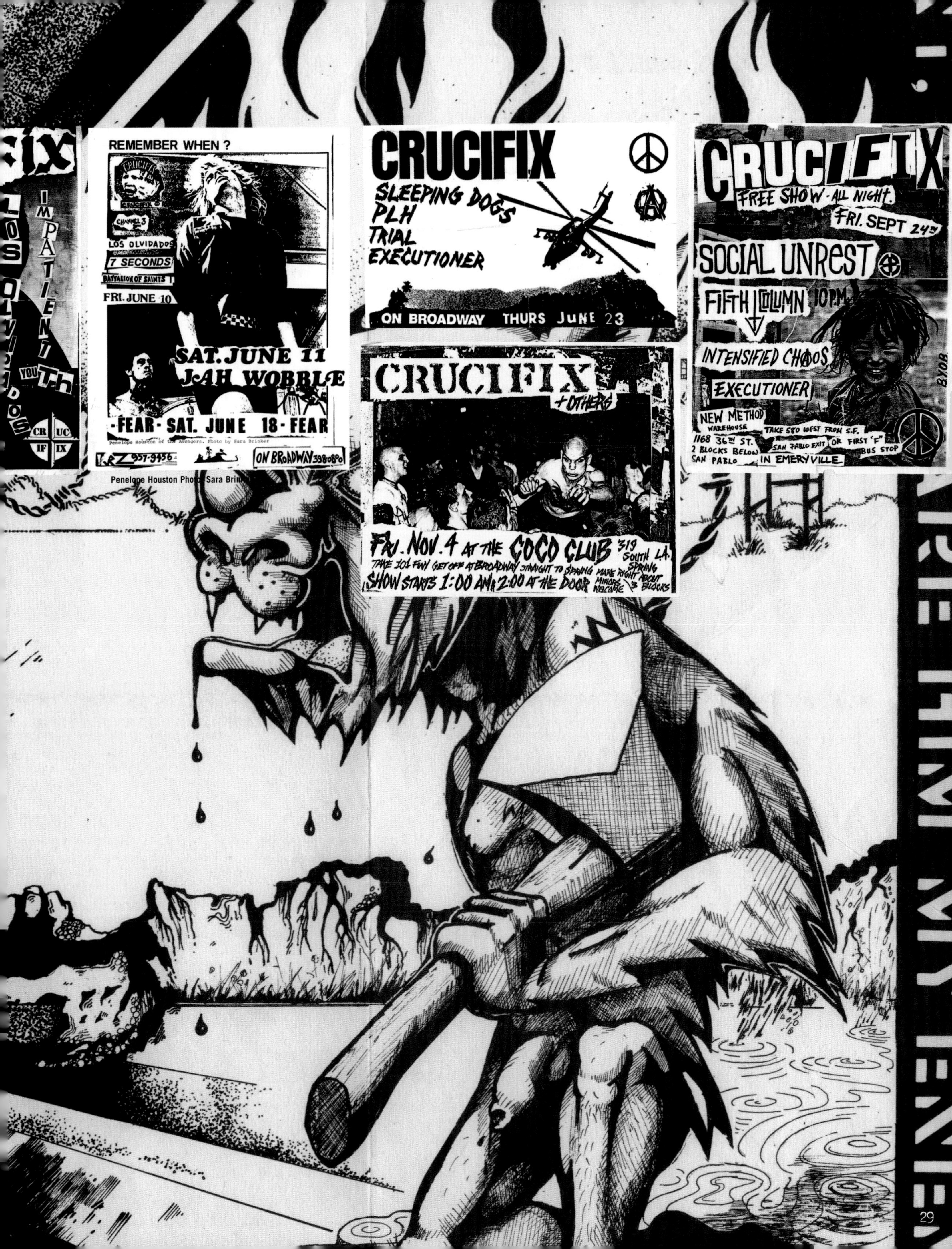

Penelope Houston Photo: Sara Brinker

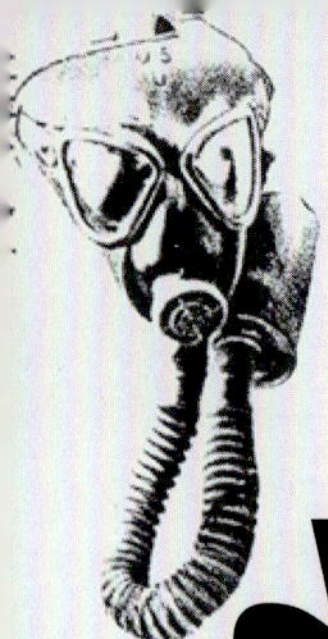

Winston Smith

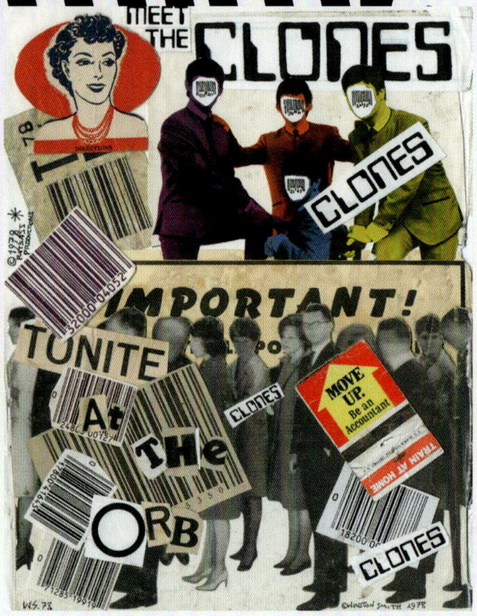

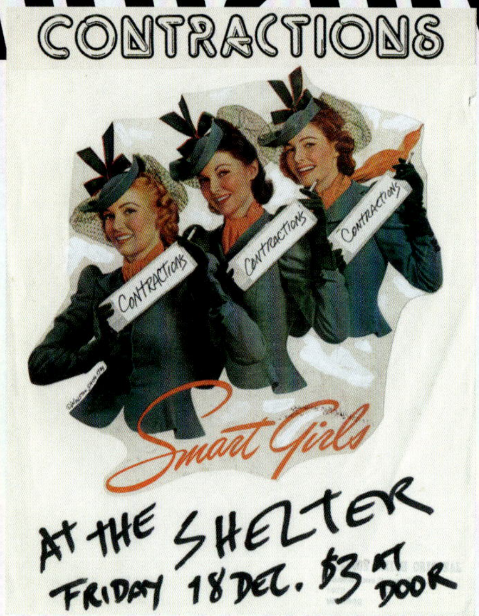

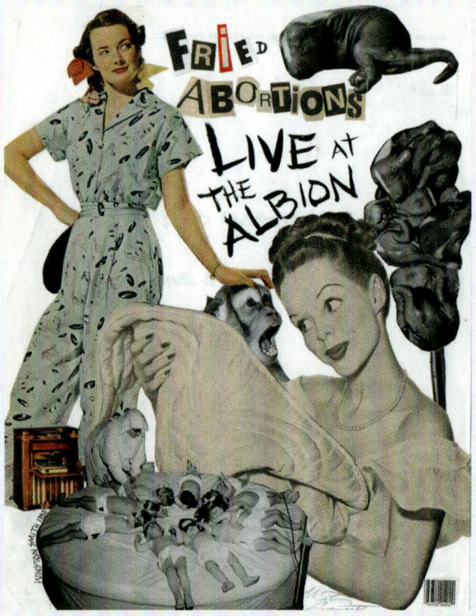

WHEN PUNK ROCK FIRST BEGAN TO REAR IT'S UGLY HEAD, THERE WAS AN EXPLOSION OF GIG FLYERS AND POSTERS FOR SHOWS THAT SUDDENLY SEEMED TO APPEAR ALL OVER SAN FRANCISCO.

SAN FRANCISCO IS A VERY SMALL CITY. IT'S ONLY 7-1/2 MILES ACROSS, VIRTUALLY AN ISLAND, SURROUNDED BY THE PACIFIC OCEAN AND THE BAY. BEING SO SMALL AND CONGESTED WITH AUTOMOBILES, IT'S A REAL WALKER'S TOWN. POSTERS, BOTH AS ART AND INFORMATION, HAVE ALWAYS BEEN A VALUABLE FORM OF COMMUNICATION HERE.

I'D STROLL ABOUT IN THOSE YEARS AND SEE THESE POSTERS ADVERTISING SHOWS AT THE MABUHAY GARDENS OR THE DEAF CLUB. SOME OF THEM WERE WILD, BUT MOST WERE LAME - EITHER INTENTIONALLY VAPID FROM AN ARTISTIC POINT OF VIEW OR JUST BECAUSE OF SHEER INEPT DESIGN. I REALIZE I'M NO MICHELANGELO, BUT I RECKONED I COULD DO AT LEAST AS WELL, IF NOT A TAD BETTER.

NOT REALLY KNOWING TOO MANY PEOPLE IN BANDS, I MADE UP SOME NAMES AND DESIGNED THEIR POSTERS. THEN, I'D WHEAT PASTE THESE POSTERS ALONG WITH MY ANTI-NUCLEAR AND ANTI-GOVERNMENT (AND ANTI-REAGAN, WHEN HE RAN FOR PRESIDENT IN 1980) ALL OVER THE WALLS AND SIGN POSTS OF SAN FRANCISCO. SOME OF THEM REMAINED IN PLACE FOR A VERY LONG TIME, AND SOME VANISHED OVERNIGHT. I DON'T KNOW IF THEY DISAPPEARED BECAUSE PEOPLE DIDN'T LIKE THEM OR BECAUSE THEY LIKED THEM SO MUCH THEY WANTED TO COLLECT THEM.

SOME OF THE BAND NAMES I'D INVENTED WERE:

THE RELEX
THE CLONES
ANONYMOUS TECHNICIANS
THE SIDE EFFEX
OUTSIDE AGITATORS
IDIOT CHILD
THE FUKKUPS
PEER PRESSURE
THE TWITS
PTA AND THE DIPSHITS
THE SLOBS
THE ROBOTS
PIPPIN YOUTH (PIPPIN WAS BIAFRA'S CAT)
LITTLE ROGER AND THE FLAVOR NUGGETS
JONNY TOXIC AND THE DOORSTOPS
THE SCABS
THE KOOTIES
CHAUVINISTS
LENNY AND THE SPITWADS
HALF-LIFE
THE CLIP-ONS
SPIN OFFS

DIRK DIRKSON ALWAYS WONDERED WHY THESE BANDS NEVER CAME INTO THE MAB OR ON BROADWAY TO GET BOOKINGS...

SINCE MOST OF THESE WERE KINDA OBVIOUS NAMES FOR BANDS, I'M SURPRISED THAT ONLY A FEW OF THEM GOT USED - THE FUCK UPS (DIFFERENT SPELLING) AND HALF-LIFE.

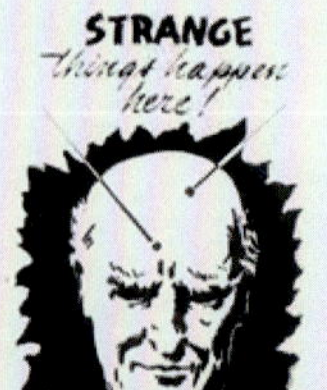

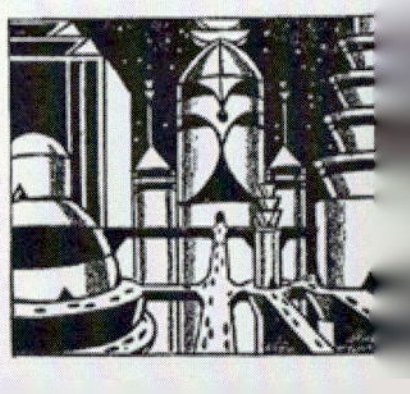

All of these flyers are FAKES!

(Contractions was a real band, but The Shelter wasn't a real club) All © Winston Smith

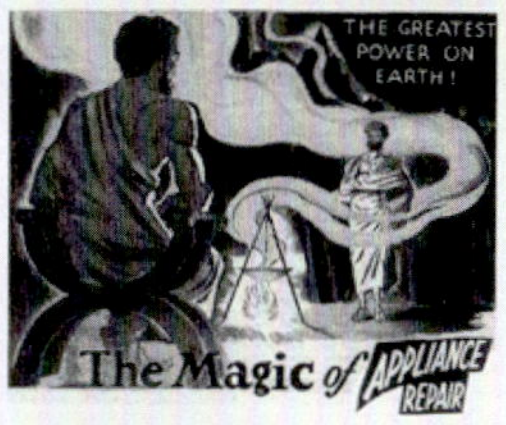

Winston Smith

VHEN PUNK ROCK FIRST 3EGAN TO REAR IT'S UGLY HEAD, THERE WAS AN EXPLOSION OF GIG FLYERS AND POSTERS FOR SHOWS THAT SUDDENLY SEEMED TO APPEAR ALL OVER SAN FRANCISCO.

SAN FRANCISCO IS A VERY SMALL CITY. IT'S ONLY 7-1/2 MILES ACROSS, VIRTUALLY AN ISLAND, SURROUNDED BY THE PACIFIC OCEAN AND THE BAY. BEING SO SMALL AND CONGESTED WITH AUTOMOBILES, T'S A REAL WALKER'S TOWN. POSTERS, BOTH AS ART AND NFORMATION, HAVE ALWAYS BEEN A VALUABLE FORM OF COMMUNICATION HERE.

'D STROLL ABOUT IN THOSE YEARS AND SEE THESE POSTERS ADVERTISING SHOWS AT THE MABUHAY GARDENS OR THE DEAF CLUB. SOME OF THEM WERE WILD, BUT MOST WERE LAME - EITHER NTENTIONALLY VAPID FROM AN ARTISTIC POINT OF VIEW OR JUST BECAUSE OF SHEER INEPT DESIGN. REALIZE I'M NO MICHELANGELO, BUT I RECKONED I COULD DO AT LEAST AS WELL, IF NOT A TAD BETTER.

NOT REALLY KNOWING TOO MANY PEOPLE IN BANDS, I MADE UP SOME NAMES AND DESIGNED THEIR POSTERS. THEN, I'D WHEAT PASTE THESE POSTERS ALONG WITH MY ANTI-NUCLEAR AND ANTI-GOVERNMENT (AND ANTI-REAGAN, WHEN HE RAN FOR PRESIDENT IN 1980) ALL OVER THE WALLS AND SIGN POSTS OF SAN FRANCISCO. SOME OF THEM REMAINED IN PLACE FOR A VERY LONG TIME, AND SOME VANISHED OVERNIGHT. I DON'T KNOW IF THEY DISAPPEARED BECAUSE PEOPLE DIDN'T LIKE THEM OR BECAUSE THEY LIKED THEM SO MUCH THEY WANTED TO COLLECT THEM.

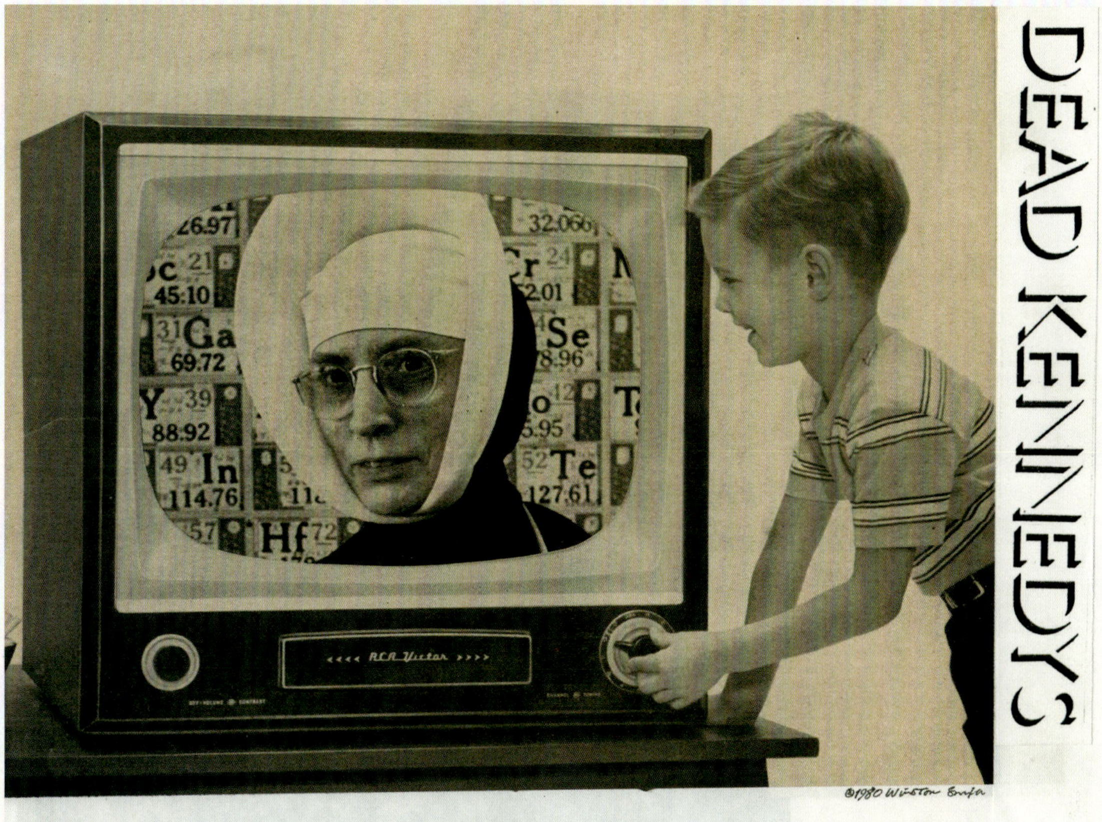

SOME OF THE BAND NAMES I'D INVENTED WERE:

THE REJEX
THE CLONES
ANONYMOUS TECHNICIANS
THE SIDE EFFEX
OUTSIDE AGITATORS
IDIOT CHILD
THE FUKKUPS
PEER PRESSURE
THE TWITS
PTA AND THE DIPSHITS
THE SLOBS
THE ROBOTS
PIPPIN YOUTH
(PIPPIN WAS BIAFRA'S CAT)
LITTLE ROGER AND THE FLAVOR NUGGETS
JONNY TOXIC AND THE DOORSTOPS
THE SCABS
THE KOOTIES
CHAUVINISTS
LENNY AND THE SPITWADS
HALF-LIFE
THE CLIP-ONS
SPIN OFFS

DIRK DIRKSON ALWAYS WONDERED WHY THESE BANDS NEVER CAME INTO THE MAB OR ON BROADWAY TO GET BOOKINGS...
SINCE MOST OF THESE WERE KINDA OBVIOUS NAMES FOR BANDS, I'M SURPRISED THAT ONLY A FEW OF THEM GOT USED - THE FUCK UPS (DIFFERENT SPELLING) AND HALF-LIFE.

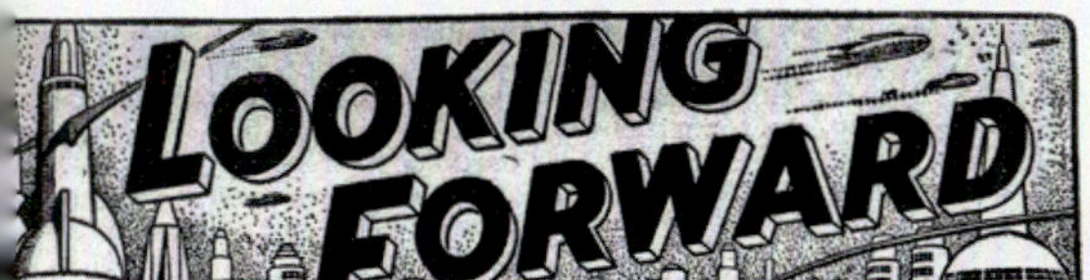

PEACE, LOVE, & BAN THE BOMB AND SMASH THE STATE!

W—

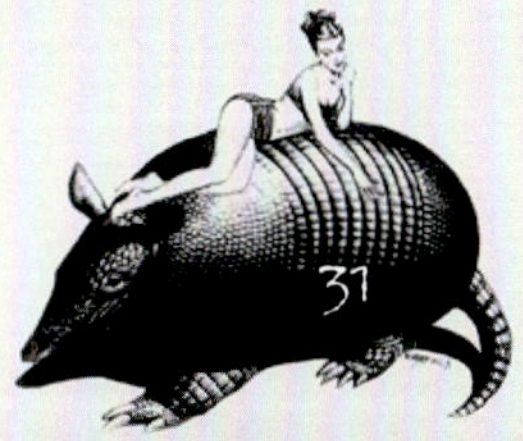

Winston Smith

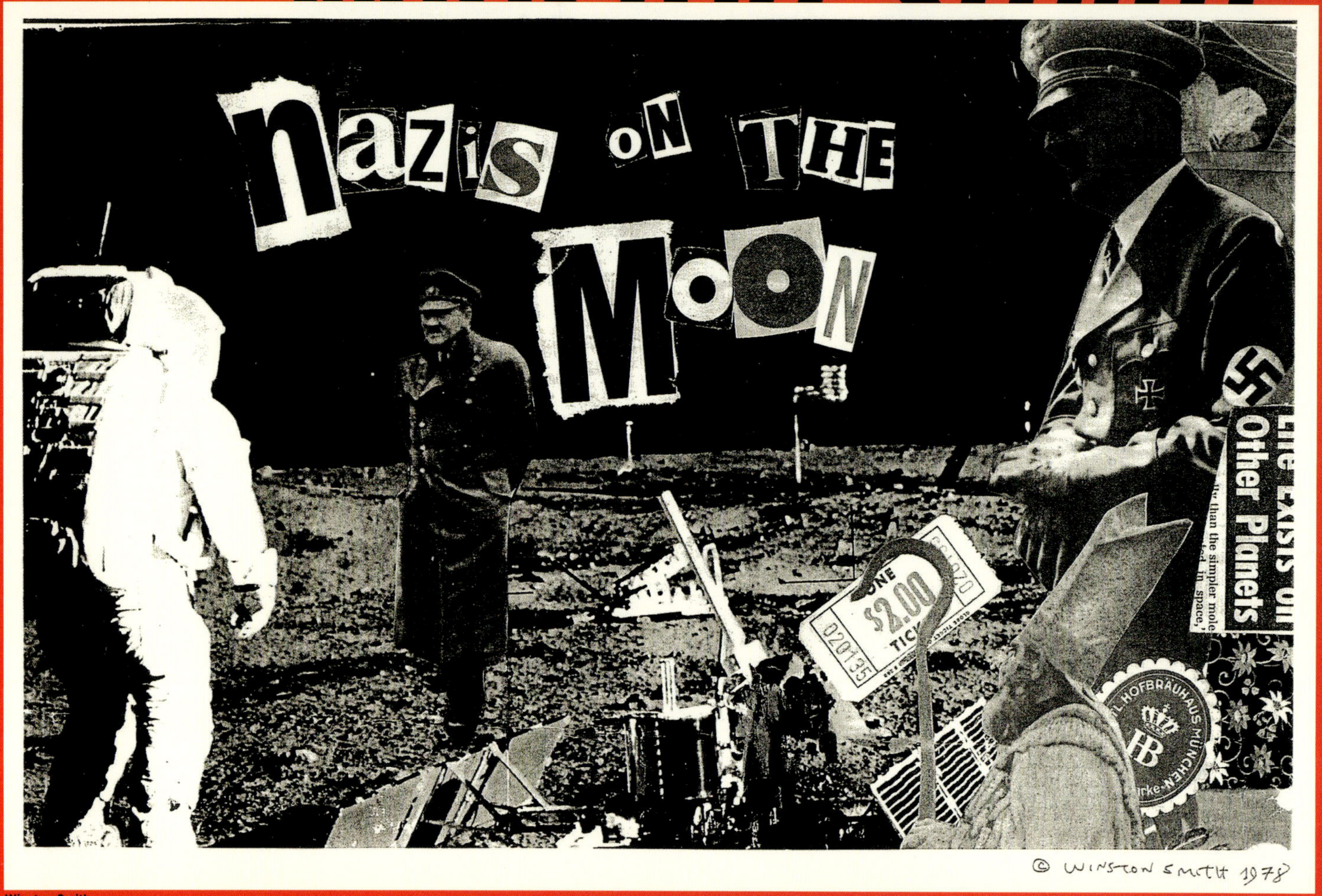

Winston Smith

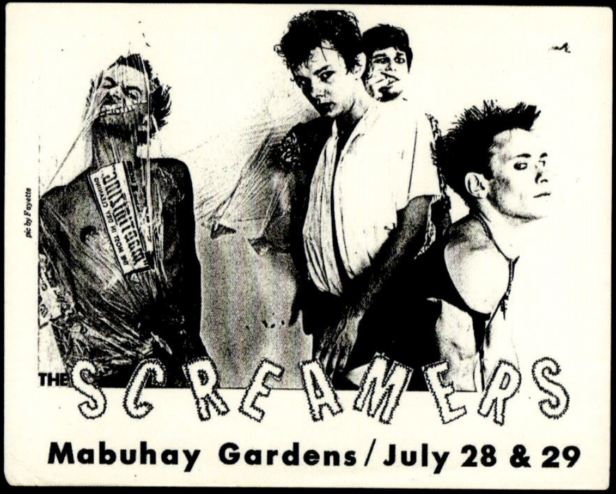

Screamers Photo: Fayette

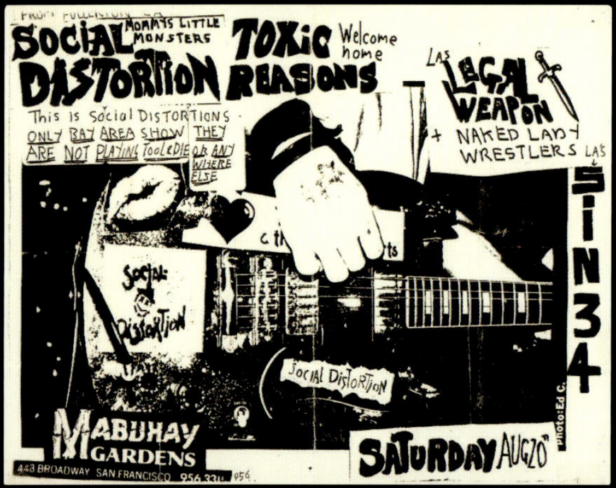

Photo : Ed Colver

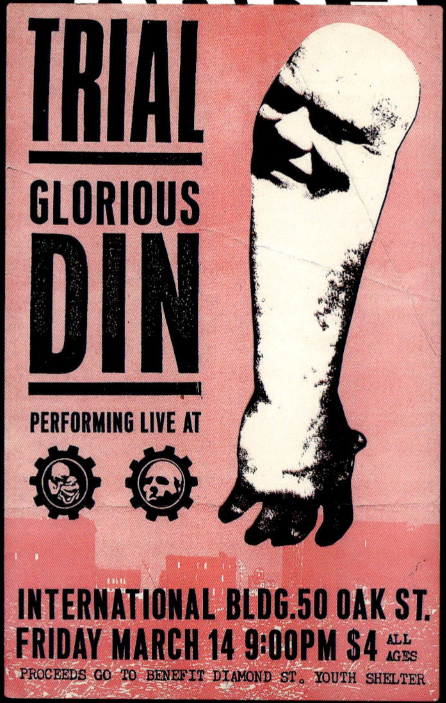

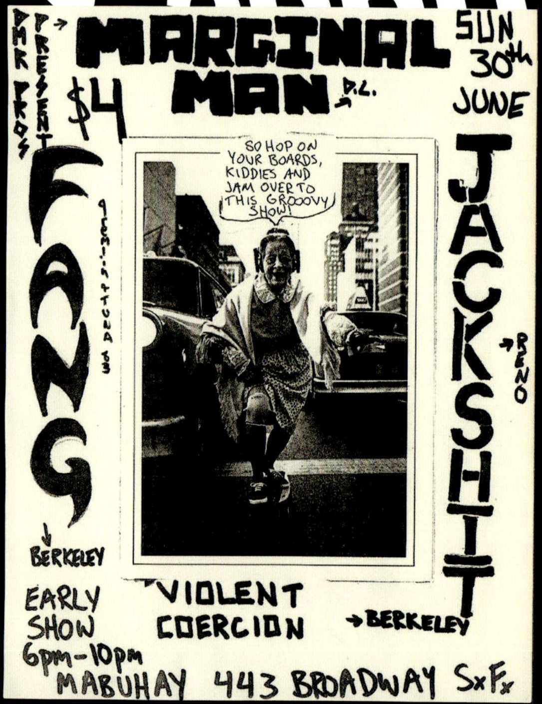

D.M.R.

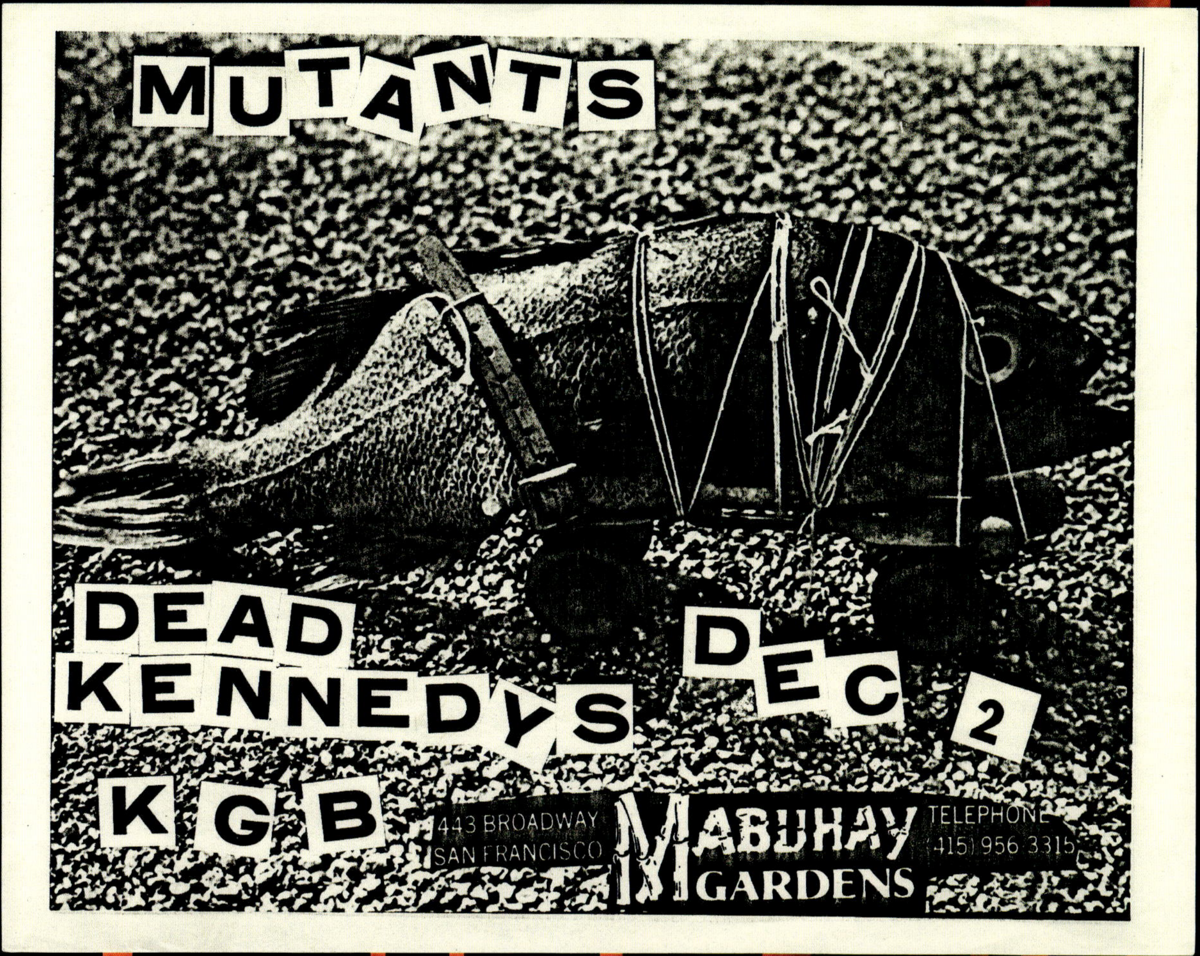

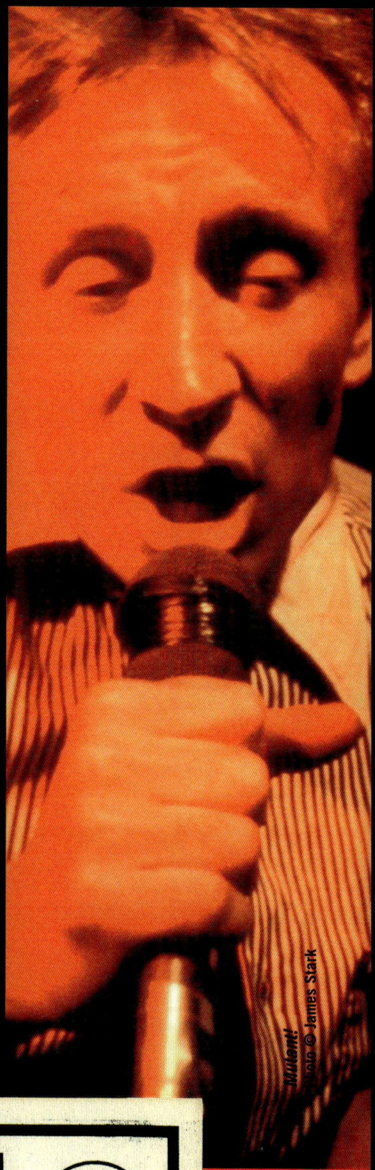

Mutant!
Photo © James Stark

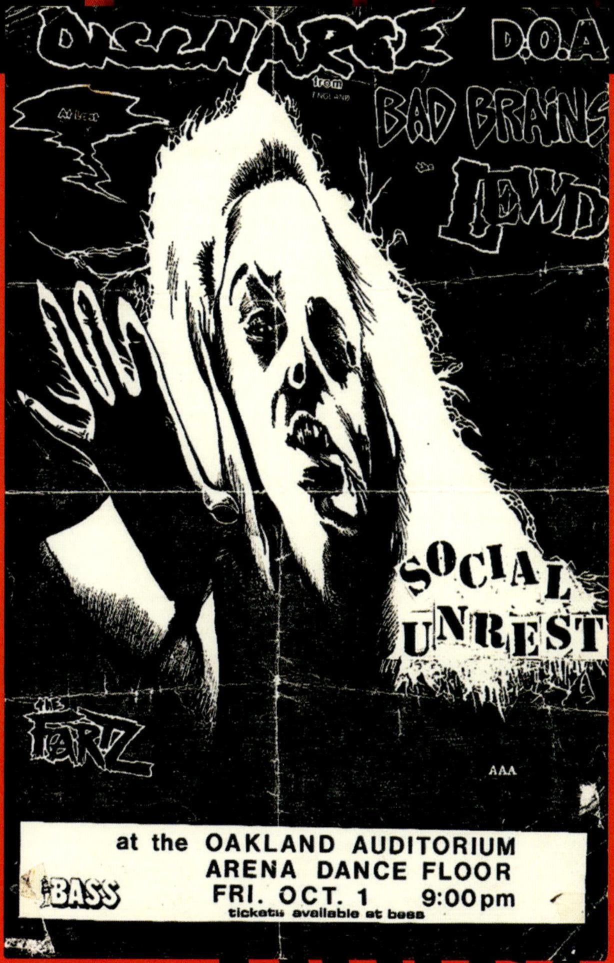

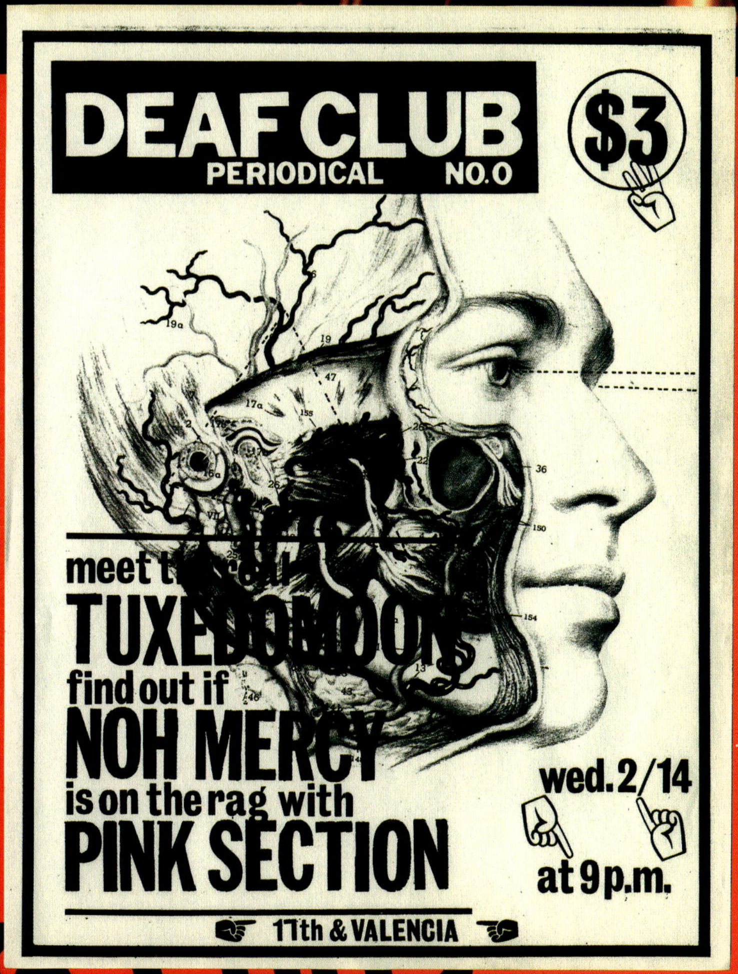

Odds & Ends

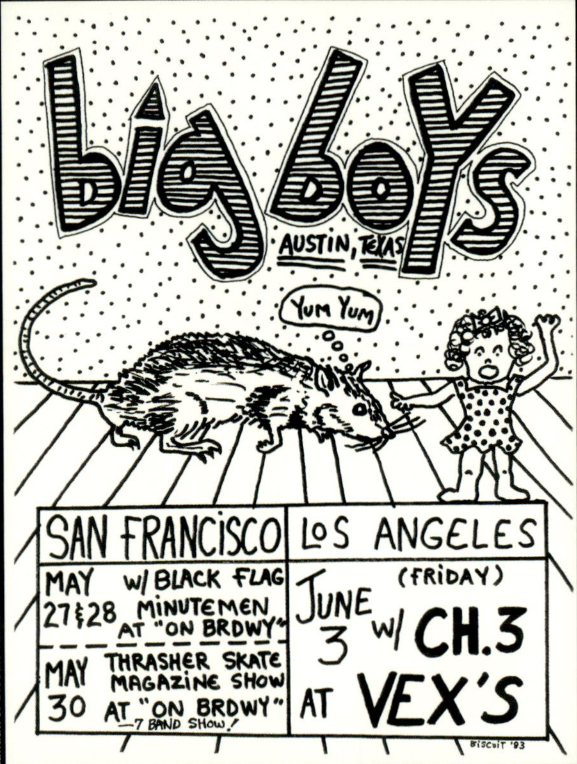

Randall J. Biscuit Turner

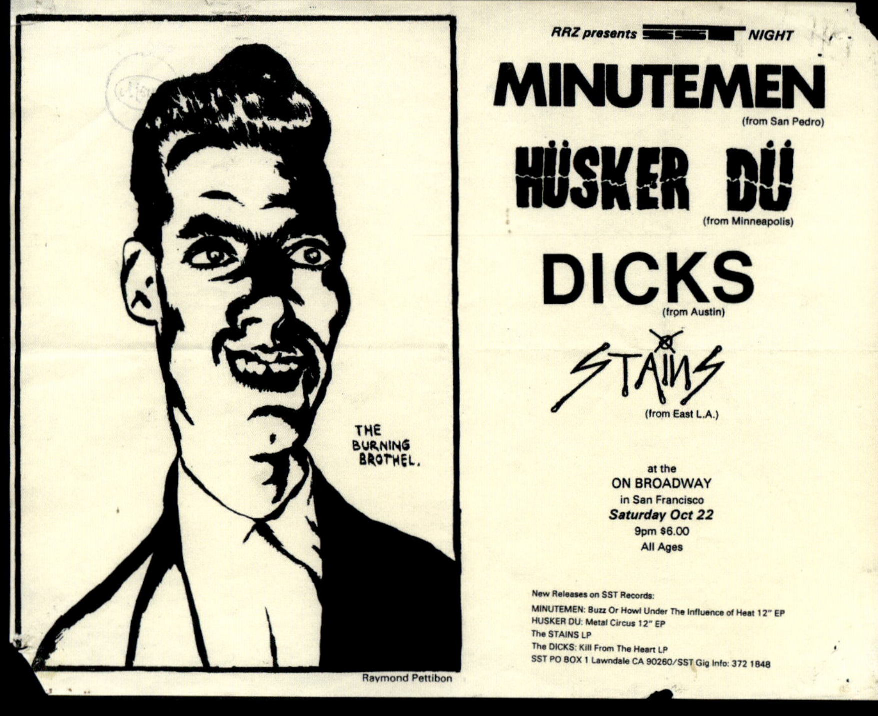

Raymond Pettibon

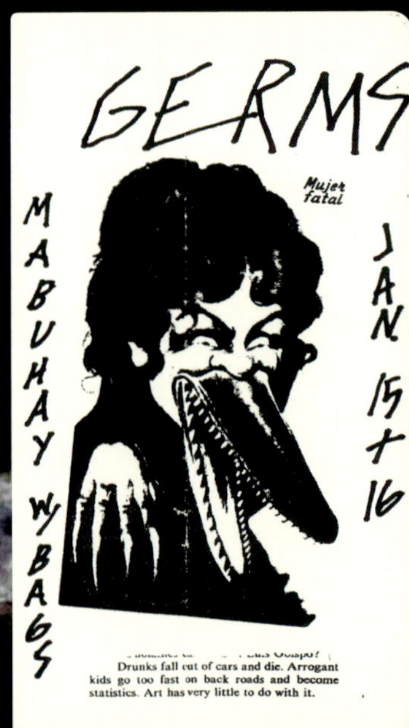

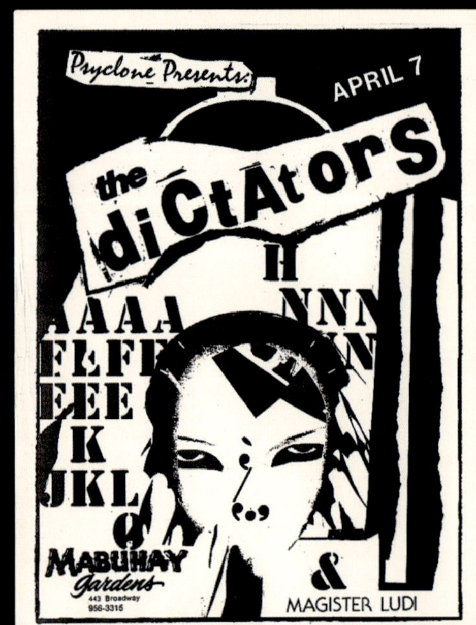

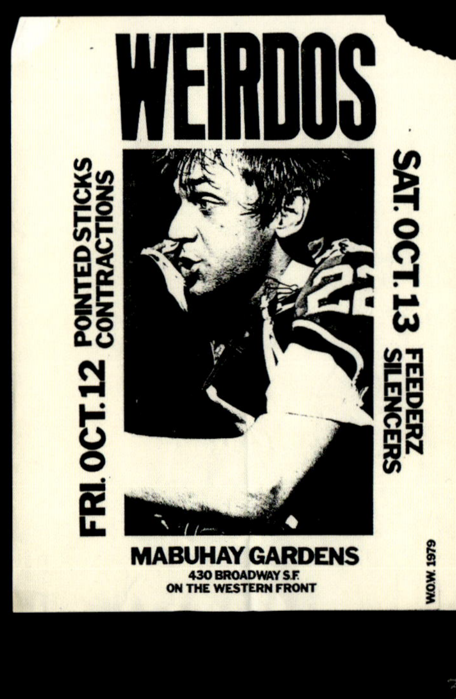

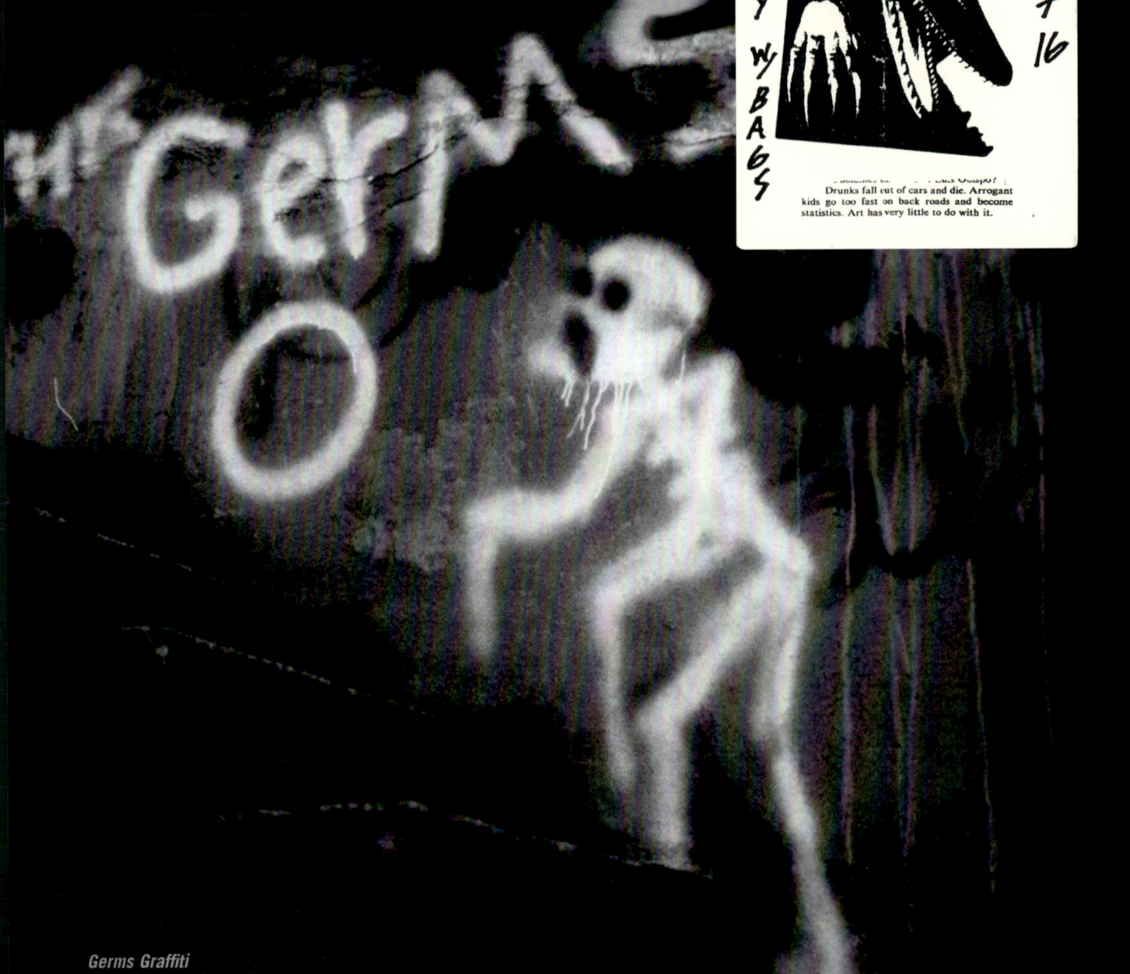

Germs Graffiti
Photo: © Doug Kahl

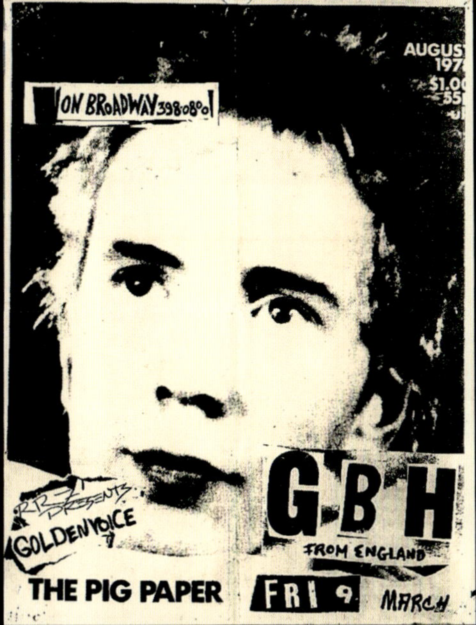

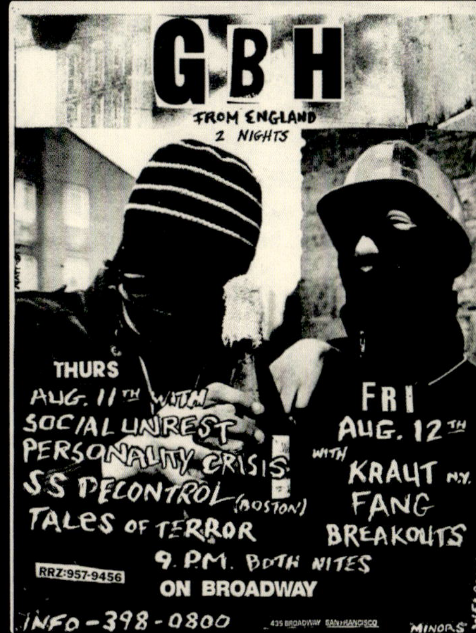

Matt

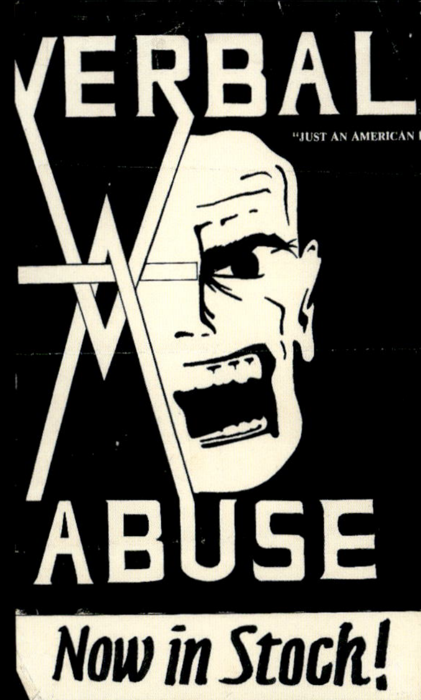

Lisa Deanne Smith

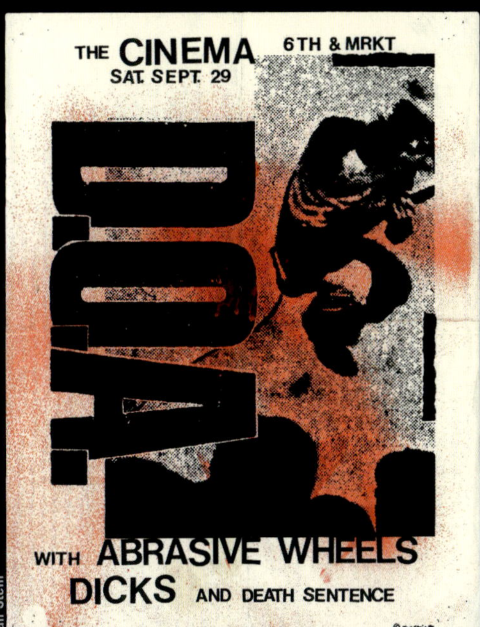

Ian Stein

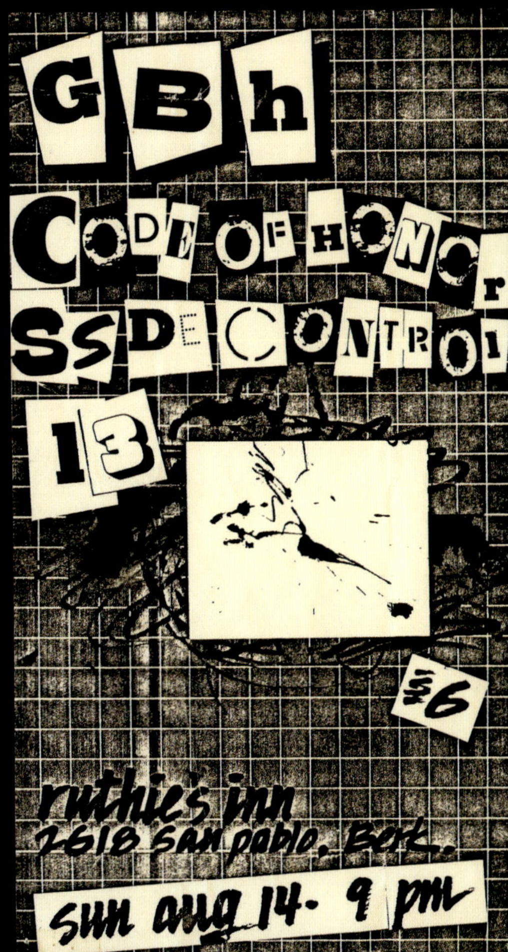

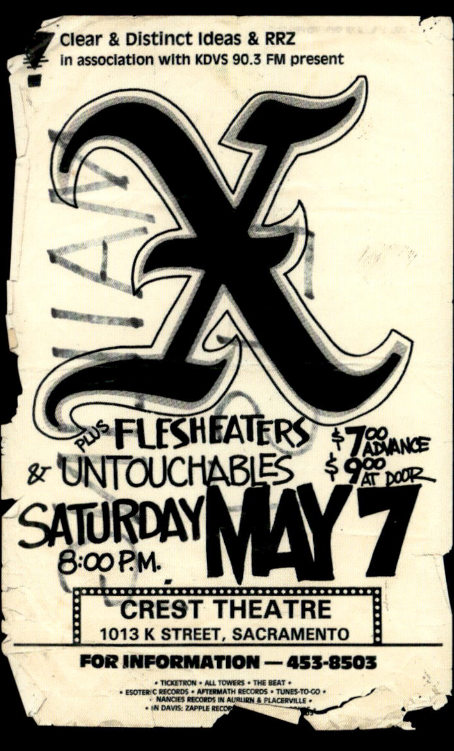

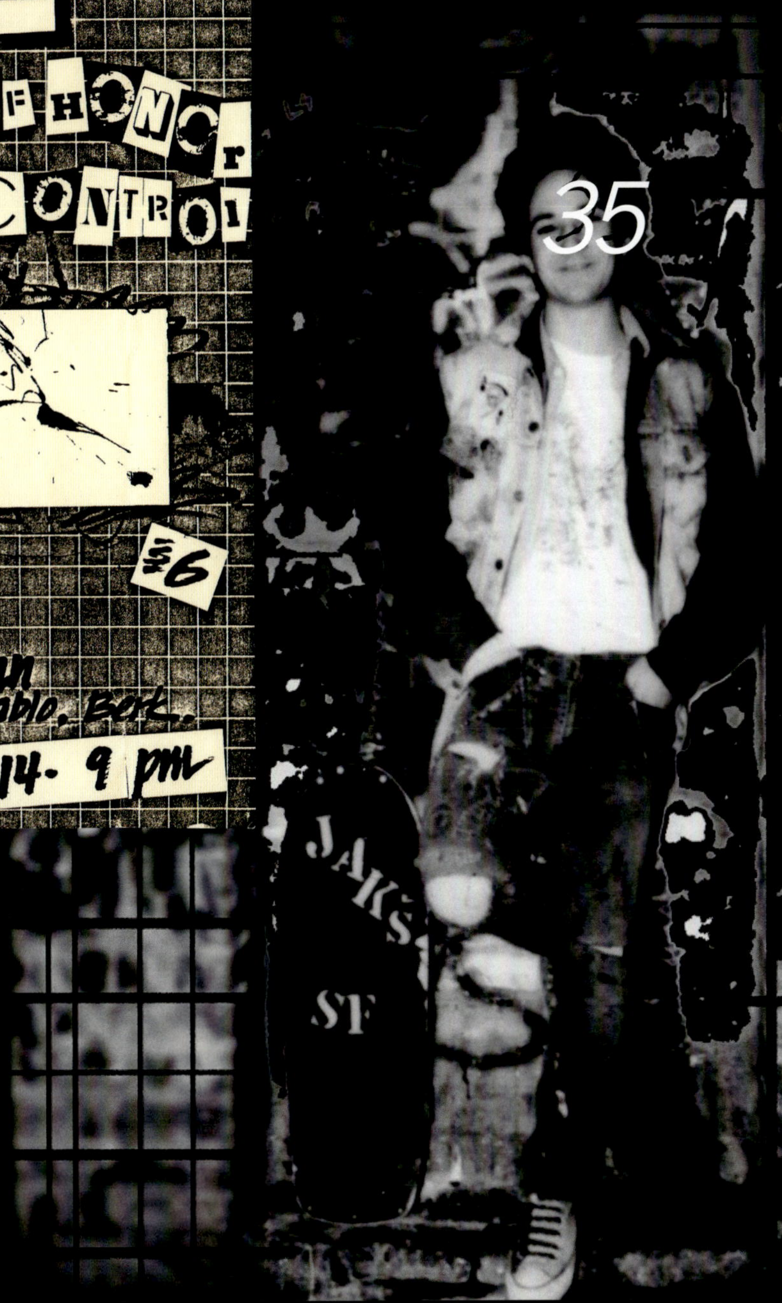

Jak's S.F.
Photo © Michelle Marini

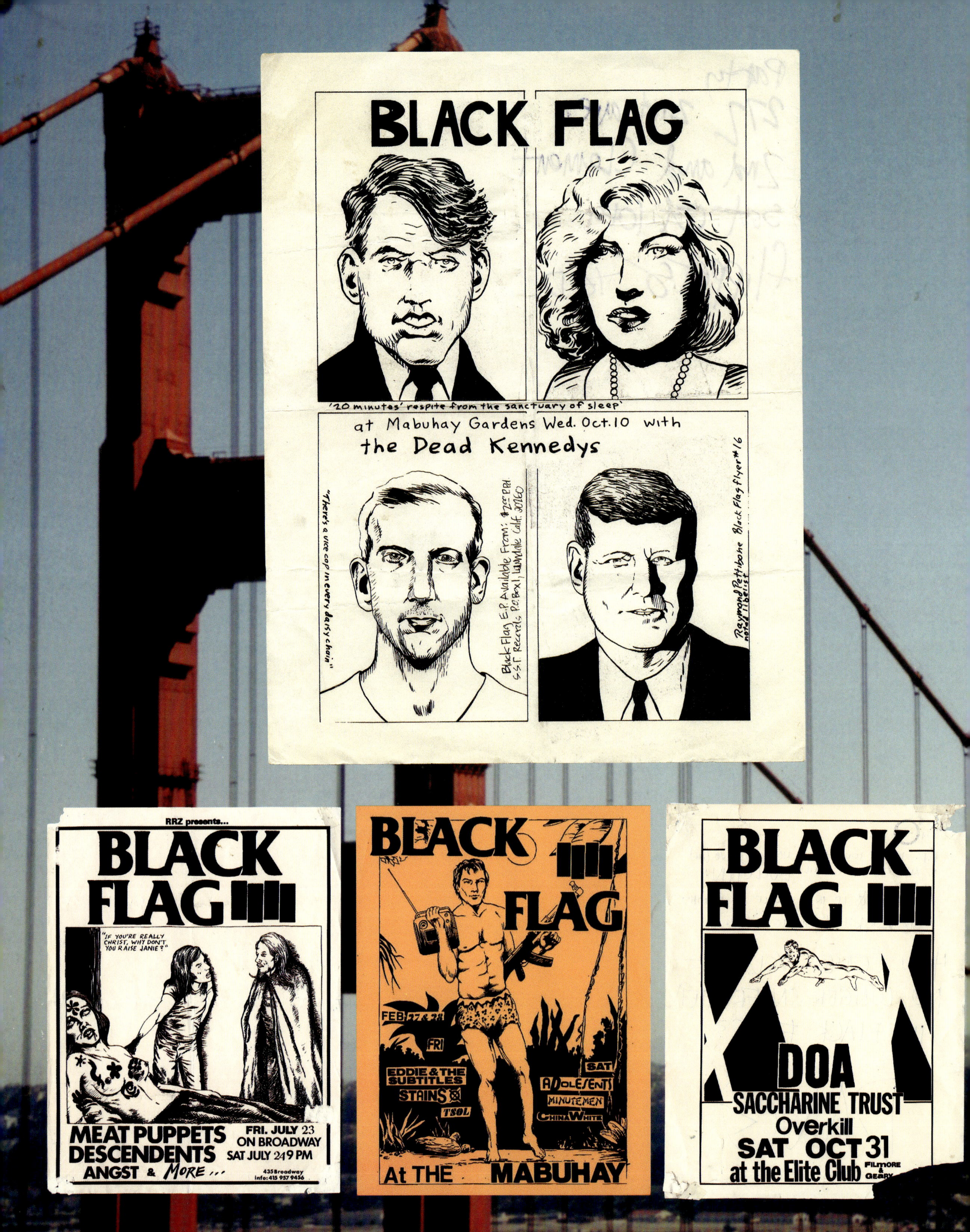

All On This Page: Raymond Petti

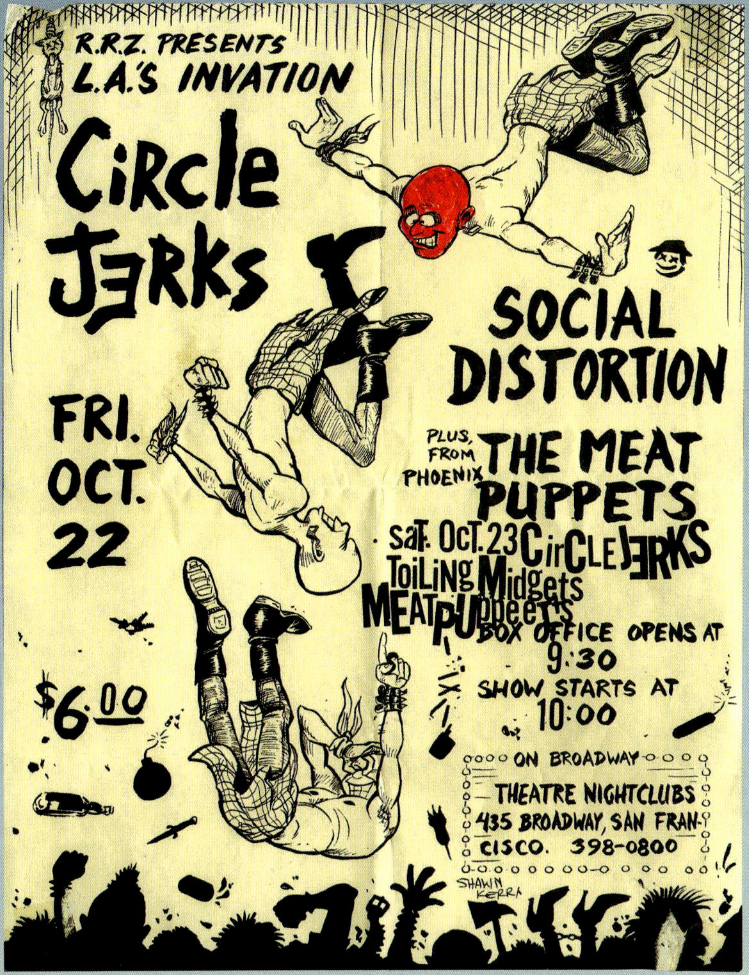

Shawn Kerri

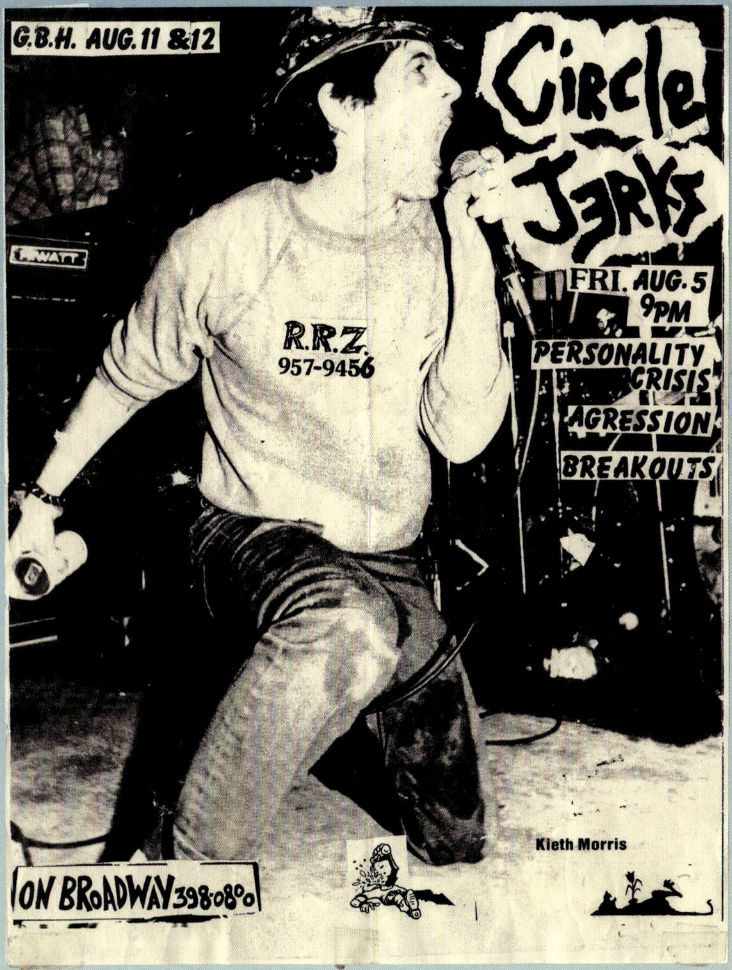

Photo: Glen E. Friedman

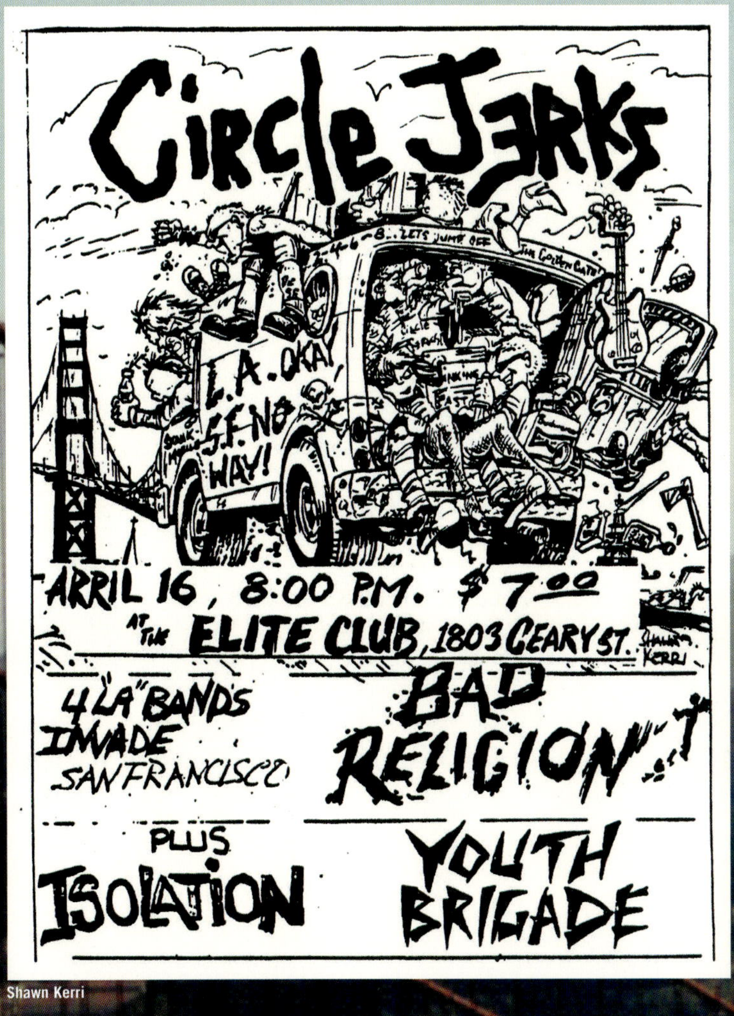

Shawn Kerri

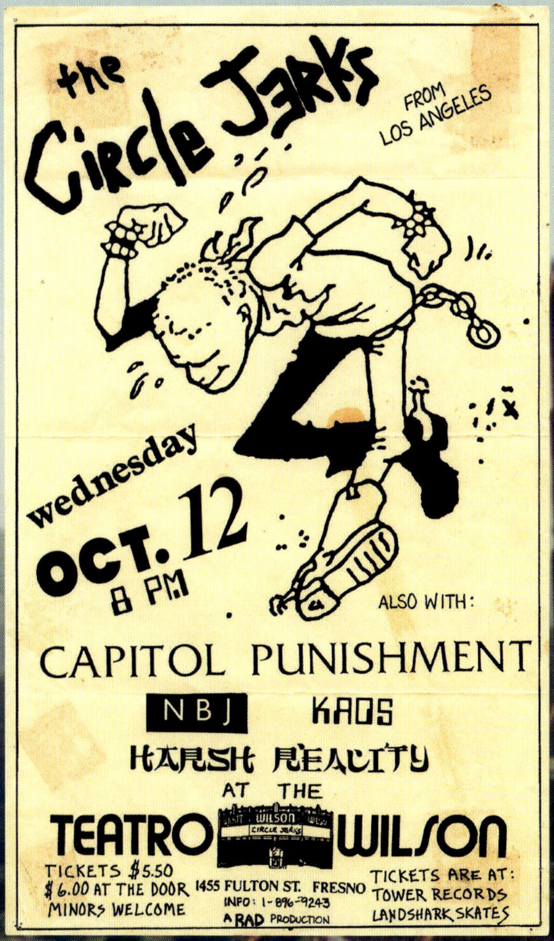

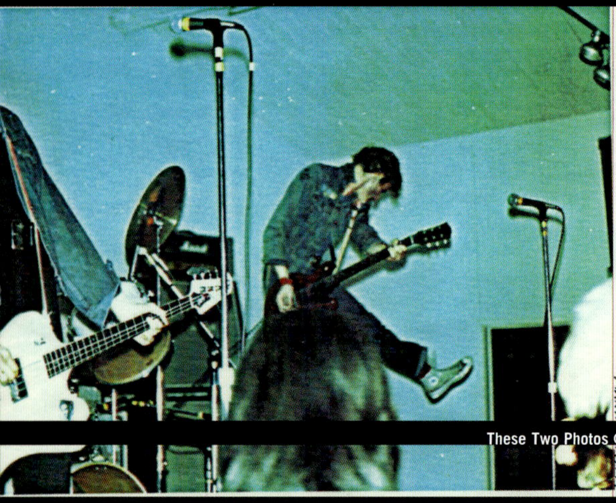
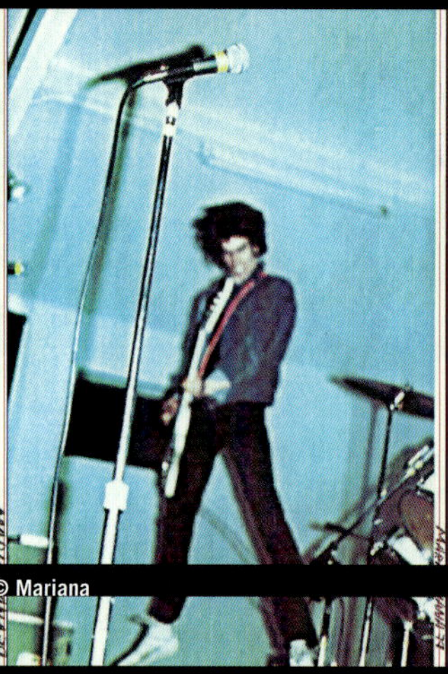

These Two Photos © Mariana

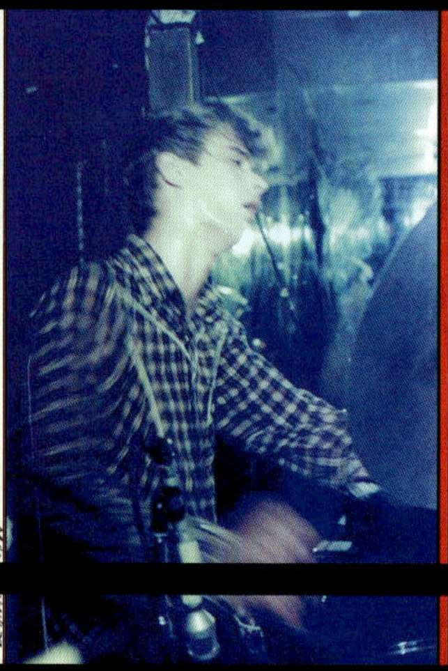
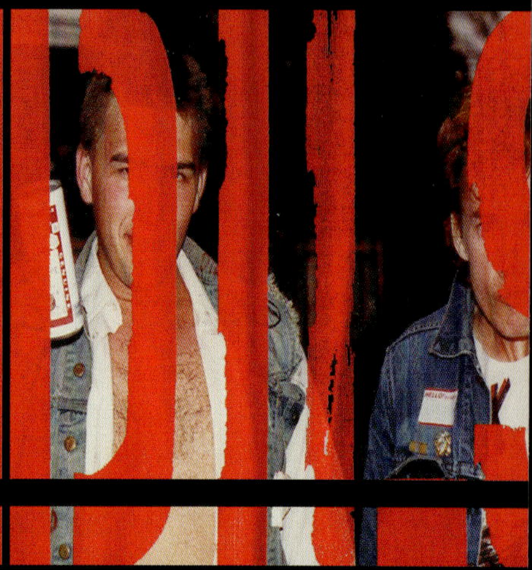

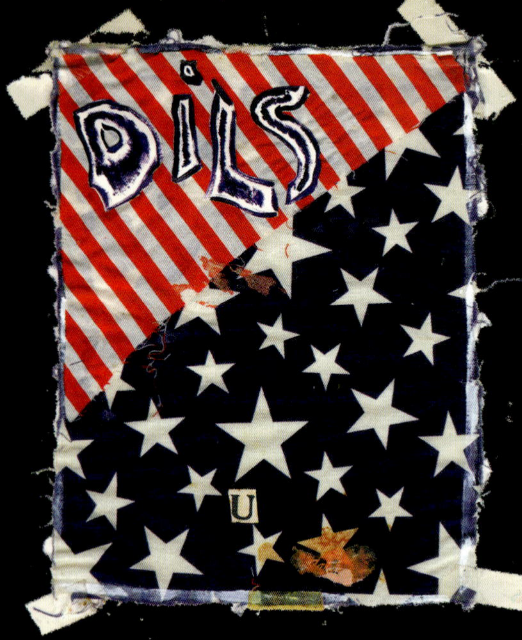

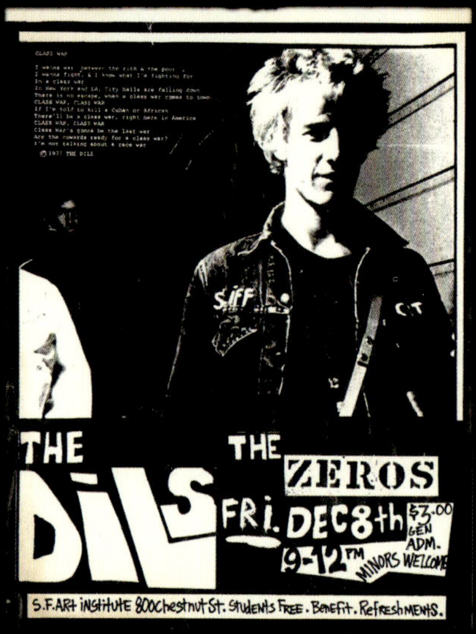

Tony Kinman

Photo: Kamera Zie

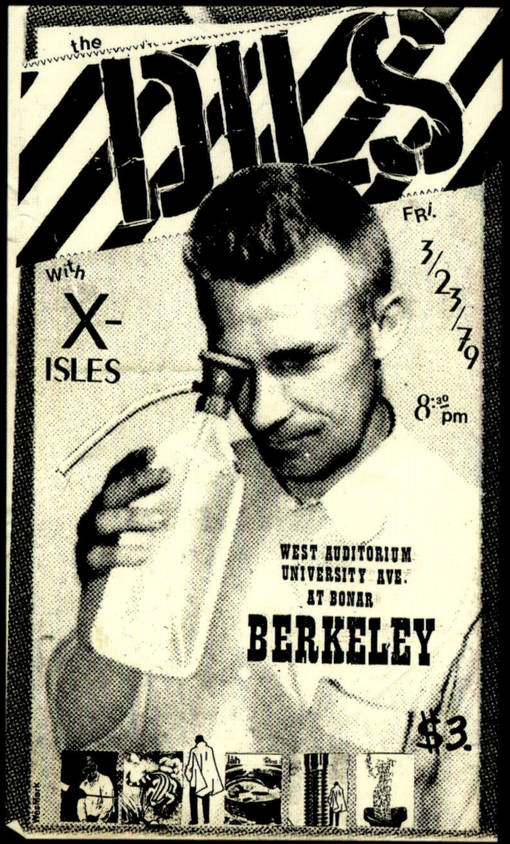

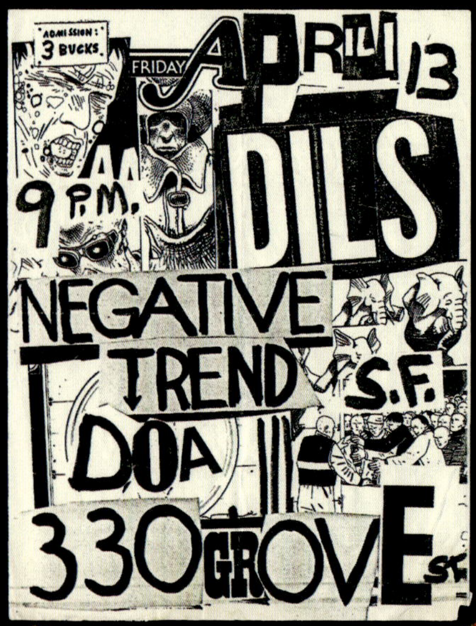

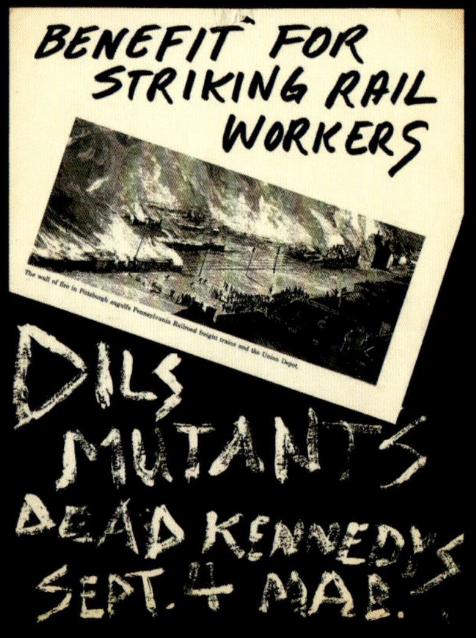

In the late seventies, a punk rocker was the only honorable thing to be.

Of course, it was pioneer days. No place to play, home-made clothing, Hostility on the part of the squares. We expected it. It was fun.

The sounds were cool. All the bands sounded different. It was absolutely underground. Record a single or two. Album? Who cares! Punk rock revolution!

It lasted a short time. In LA there were the mini-moguls. In SF, the junior commissars. It was inevitable that these rapacious dullards would eventually take over. When they did, there was no place for a man of honor.

It was time to move on, so I did.

Tony Kinman

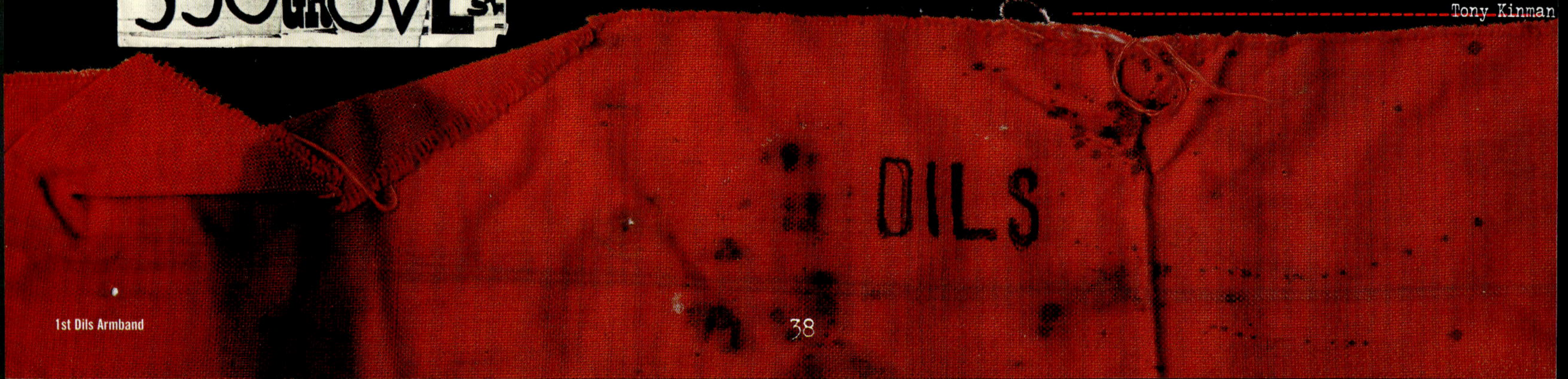

1st Dils Armband

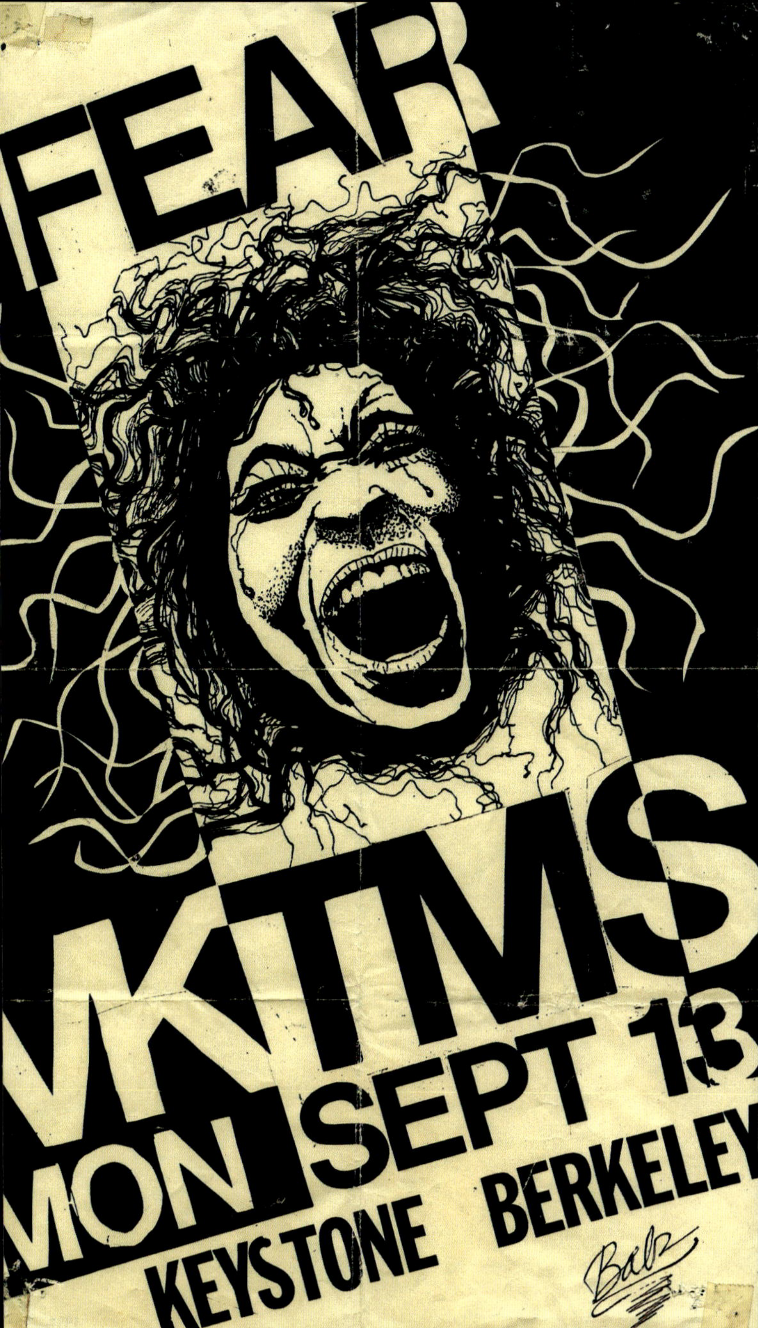

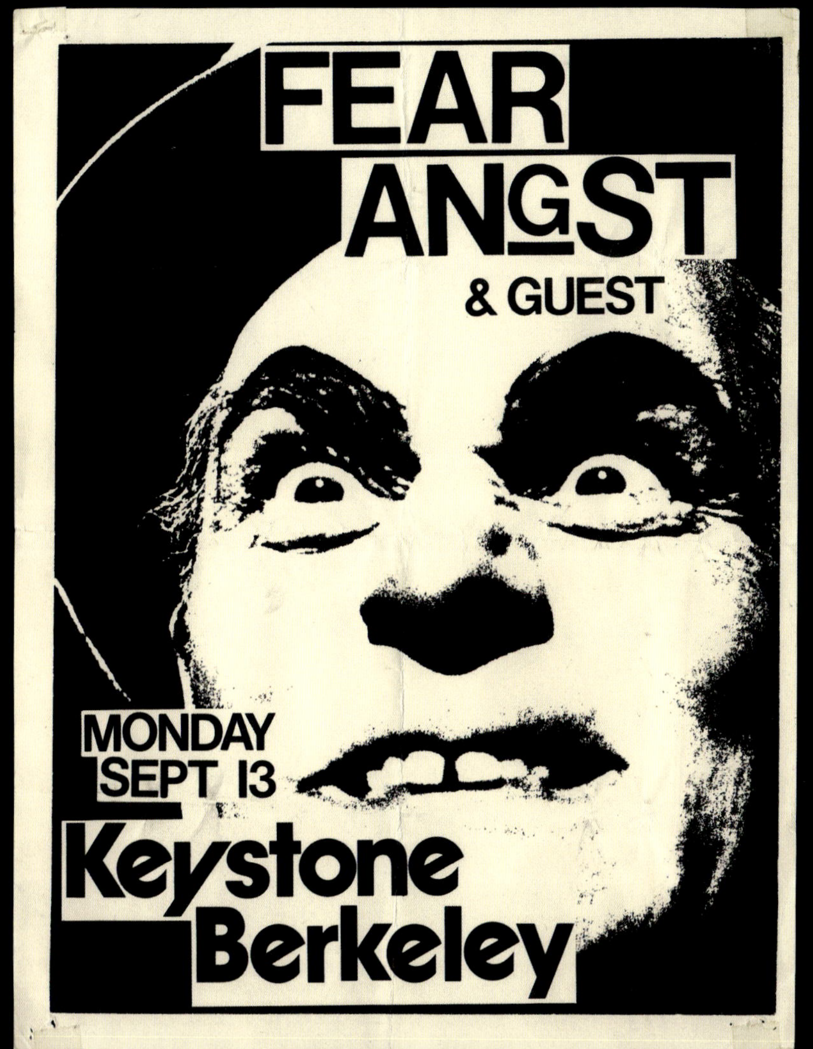

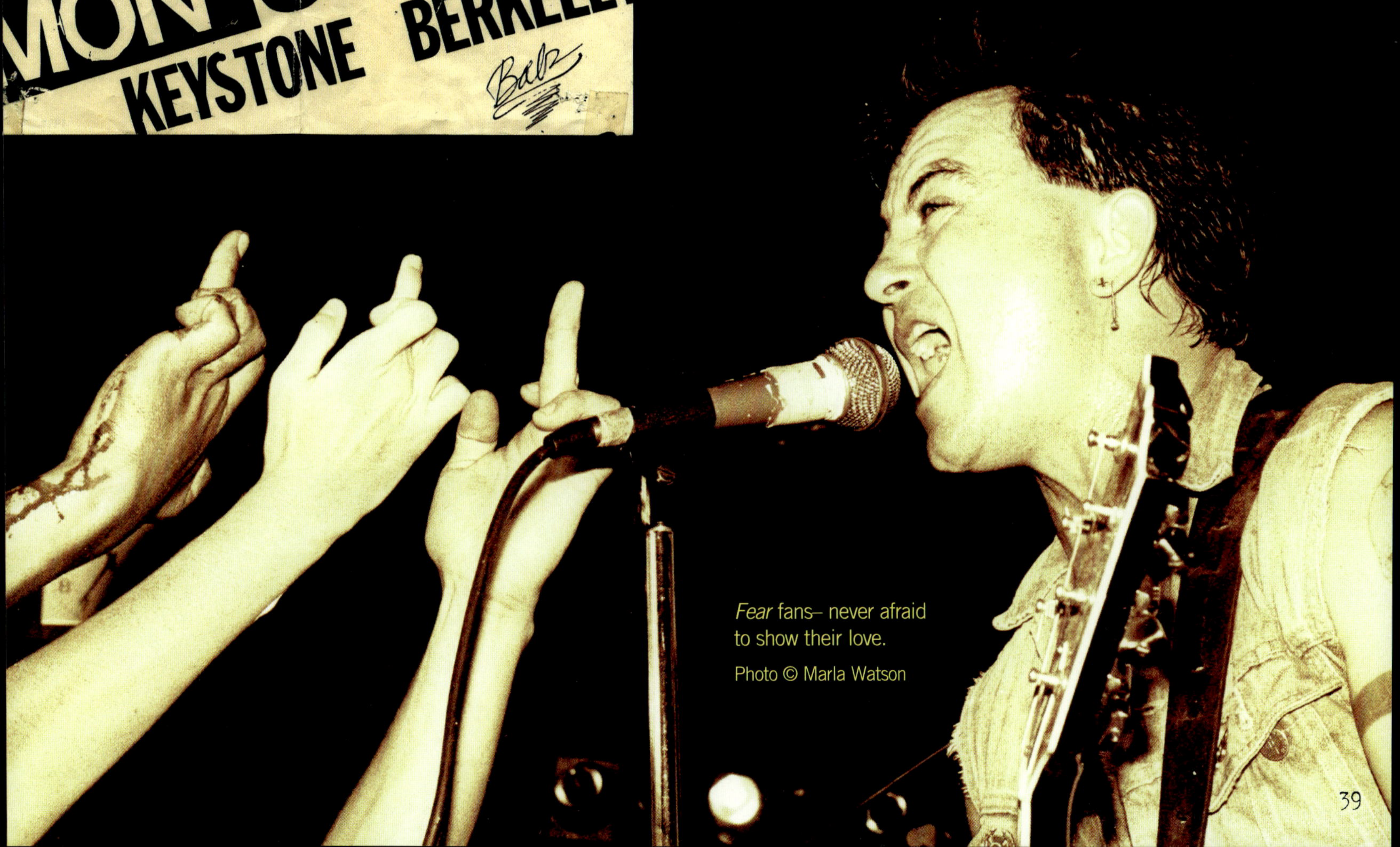

Fear fans– never afraid to show their love.

Photo © Marla Watson

Hand Scrawled Art

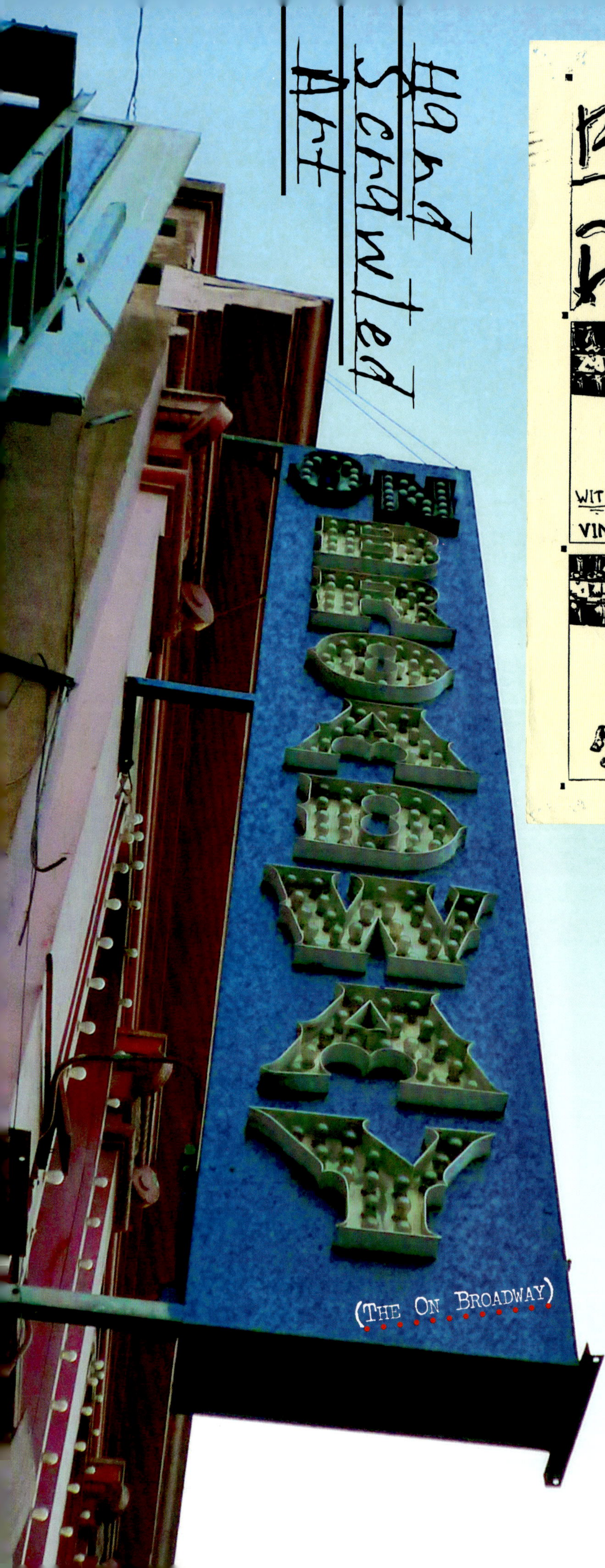

(The On Broadway)

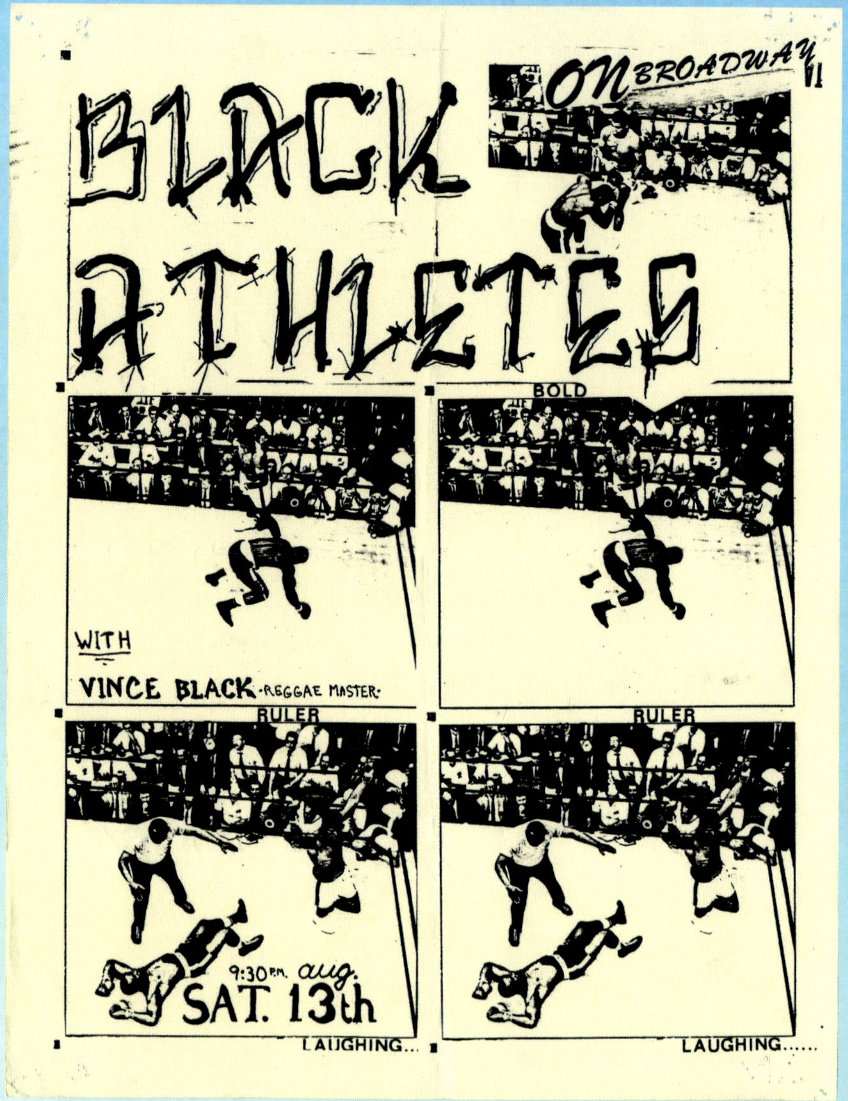

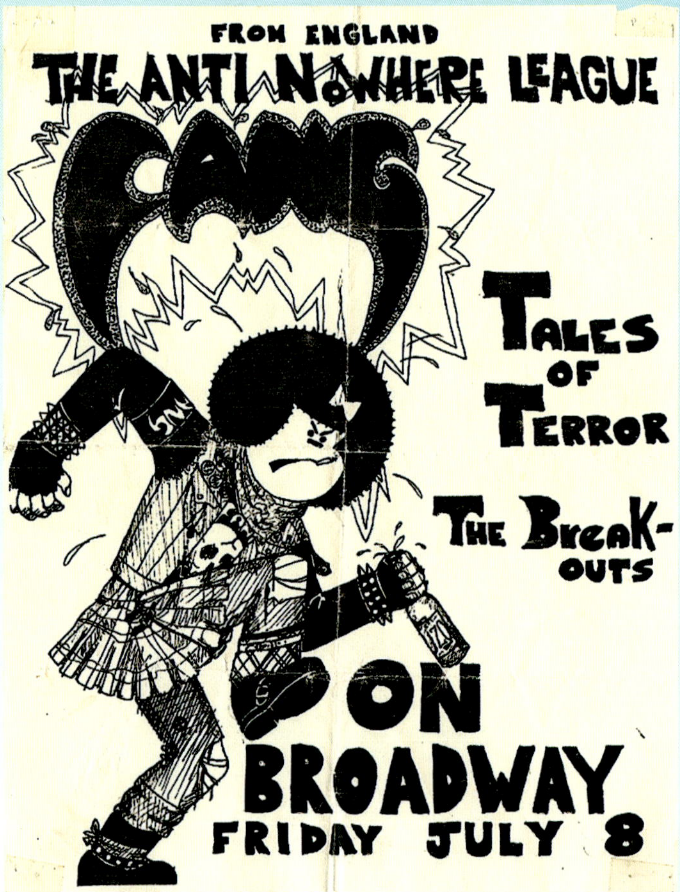

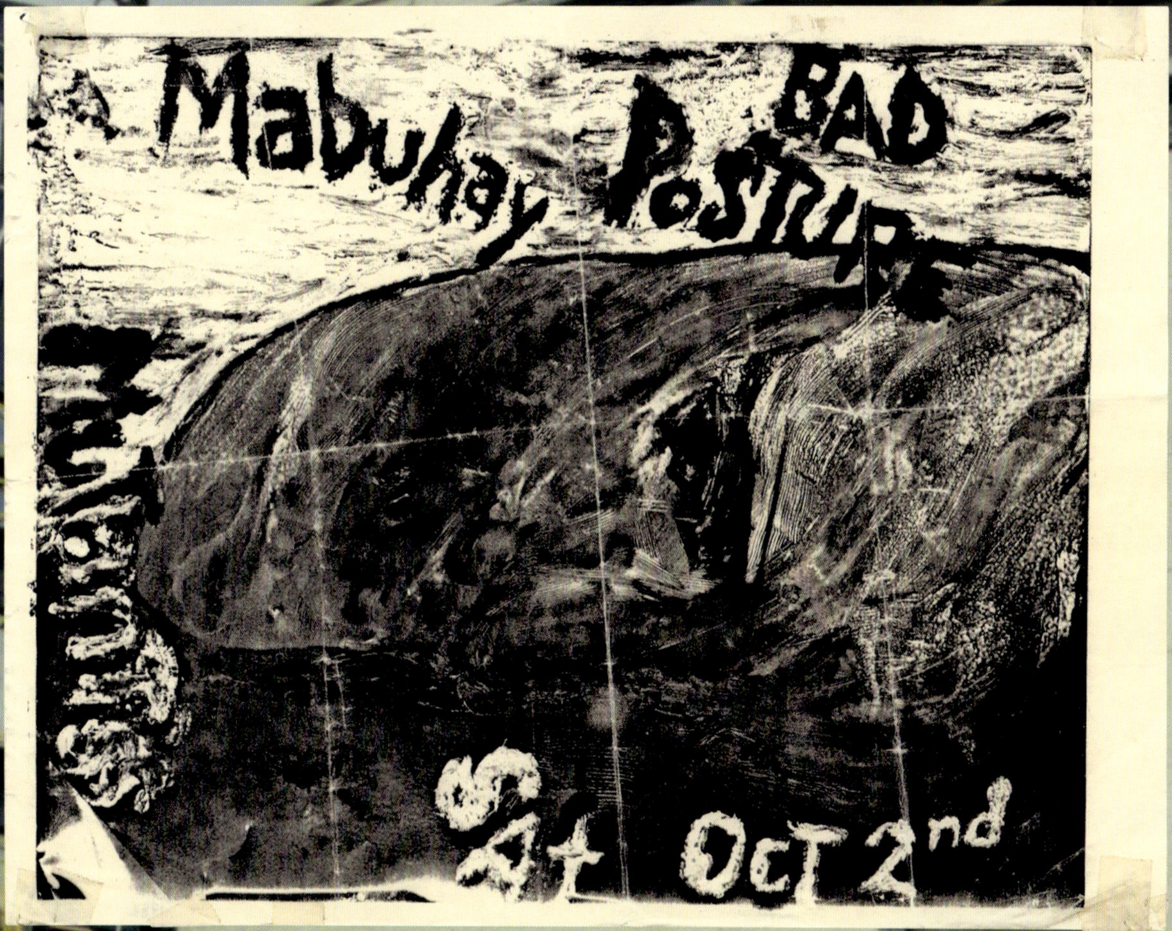

Two Flyers, same gig. Artist unknown

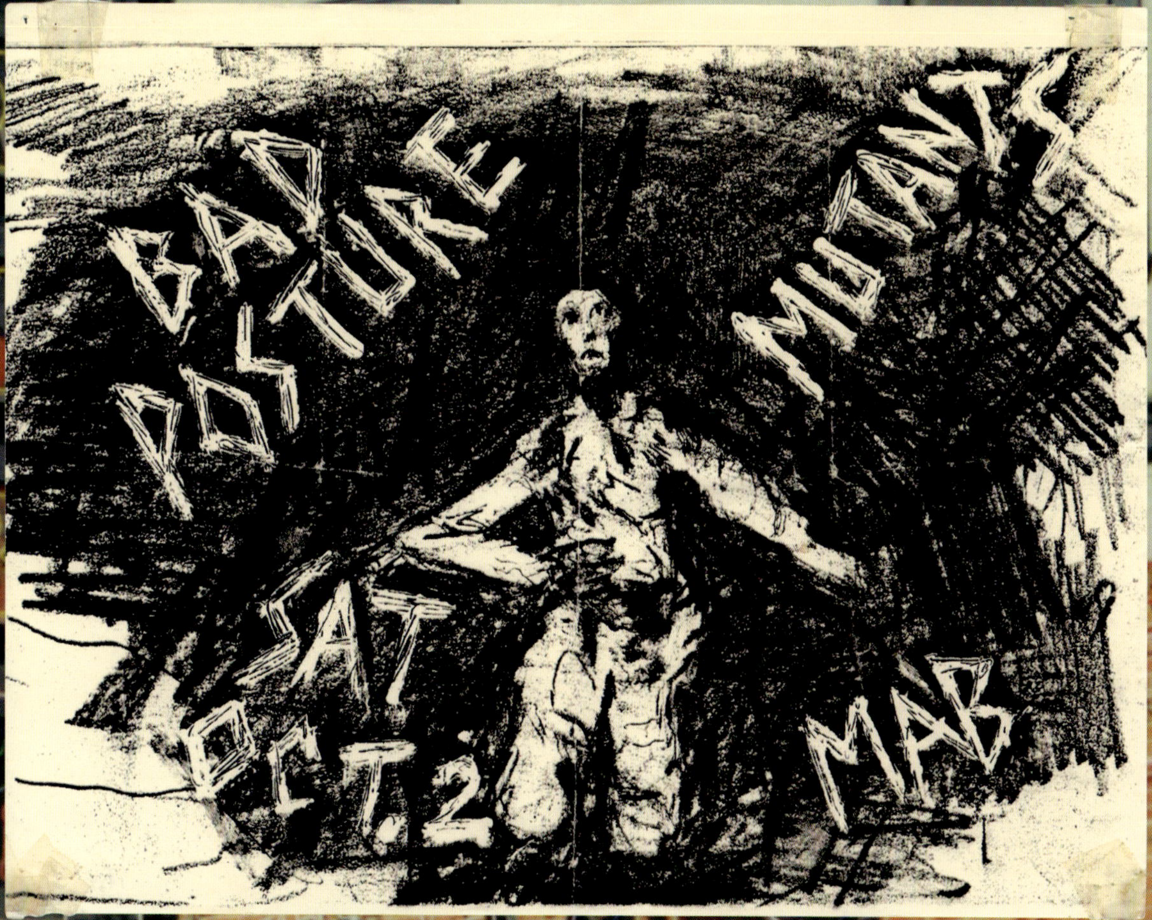

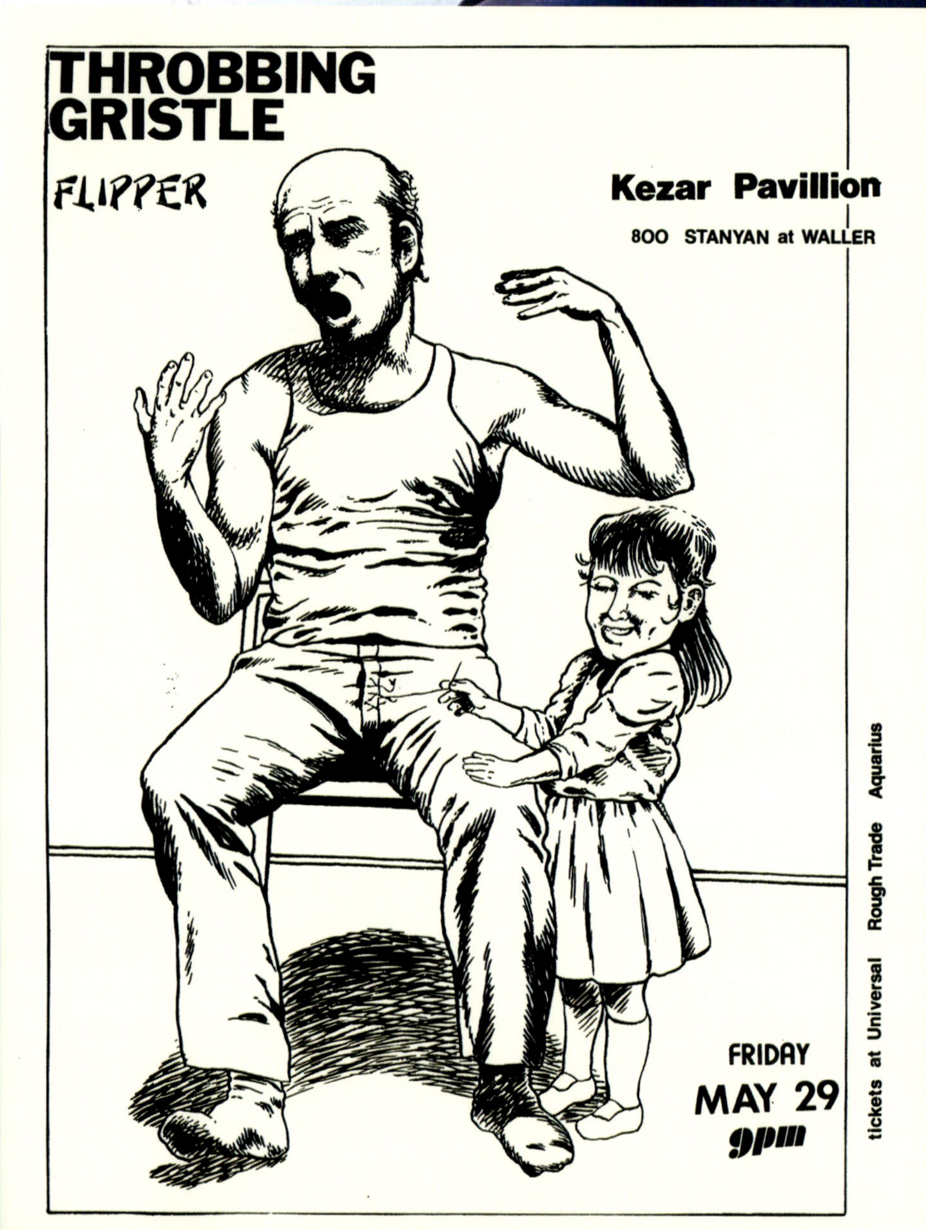

Raymond Pettibon

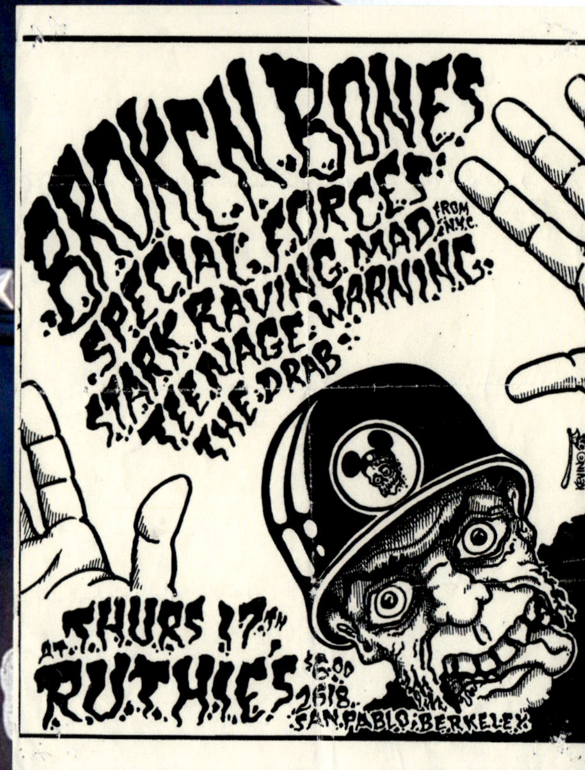

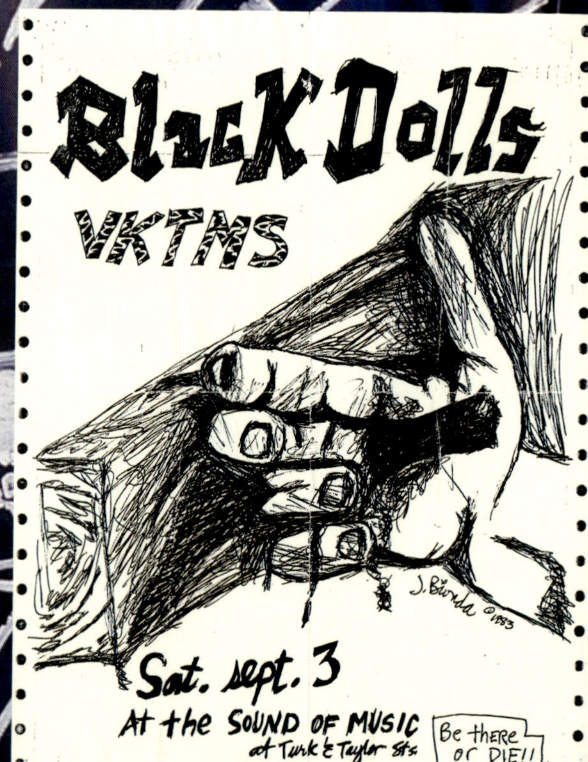

J Bianda

Alan Chilton

Hand Scrawled Art

Bryan's Jacket
Photo © Sheryl Nields

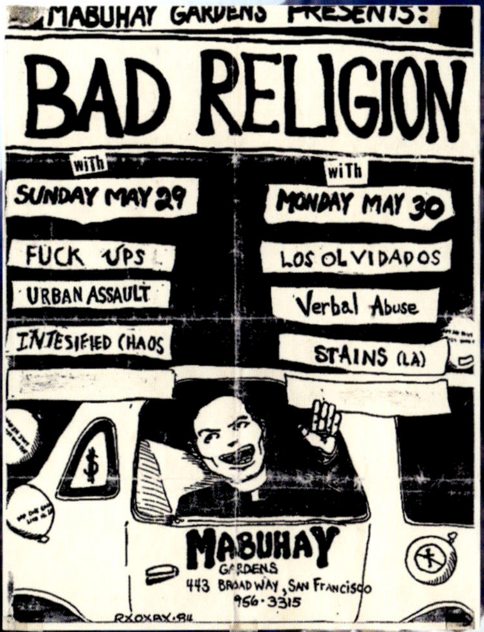

RxOxBx

Andrew Goldfarb AKA "13"

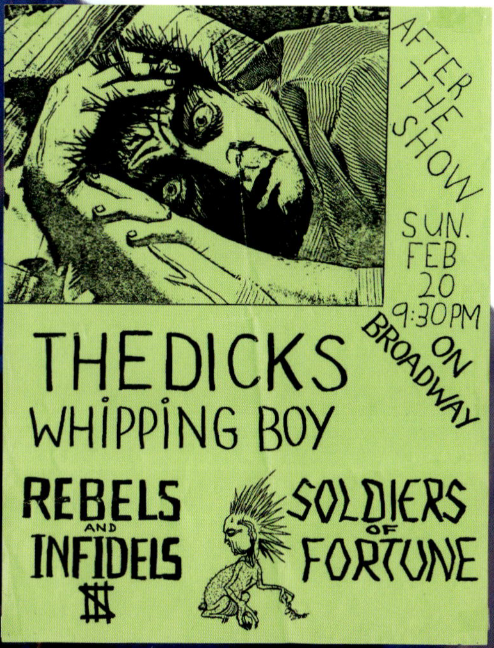

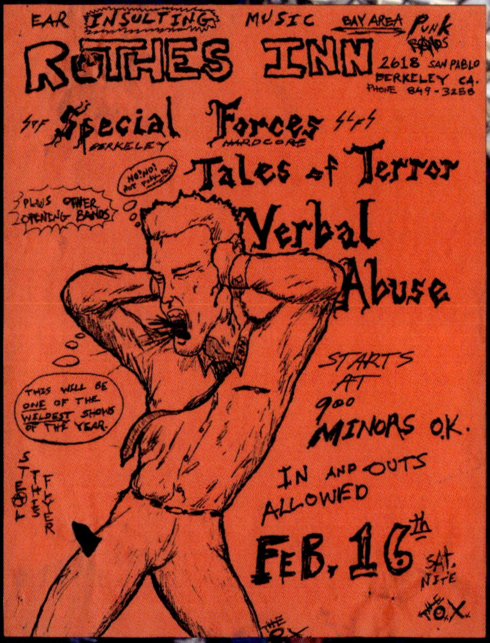

Orlando X

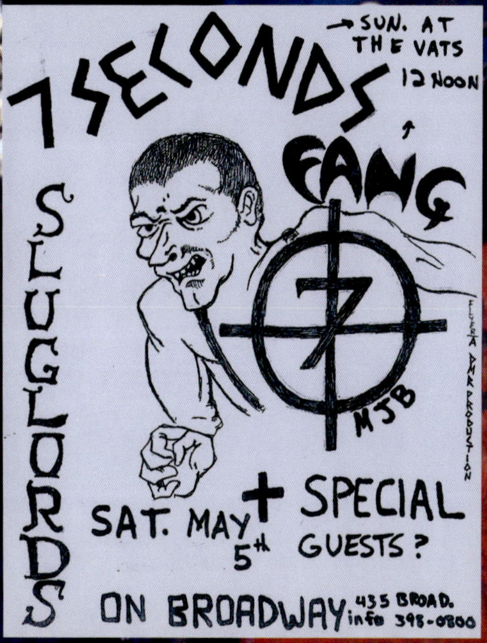

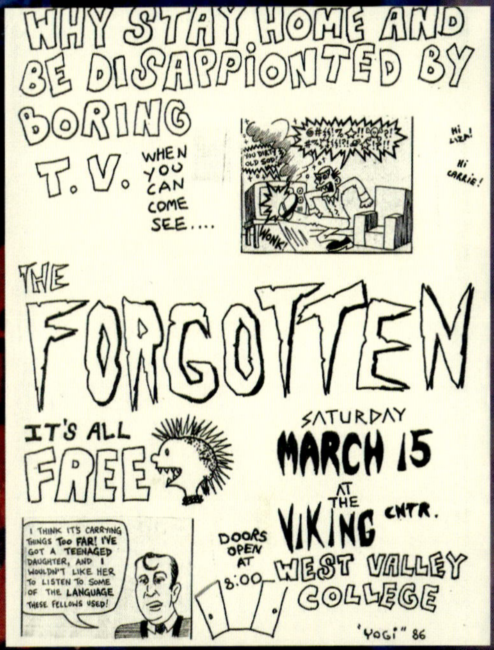

Yogi

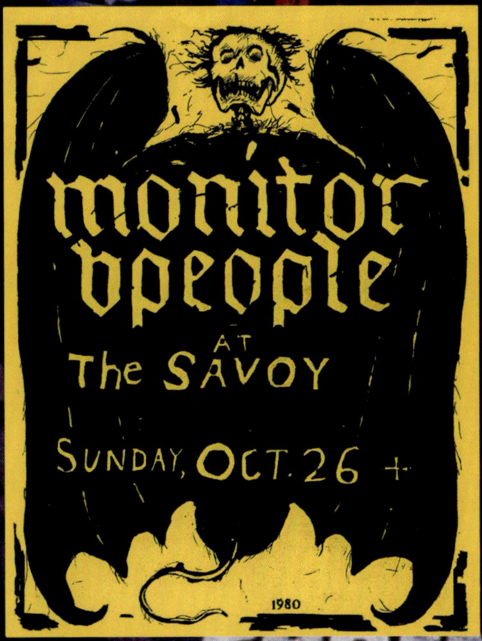

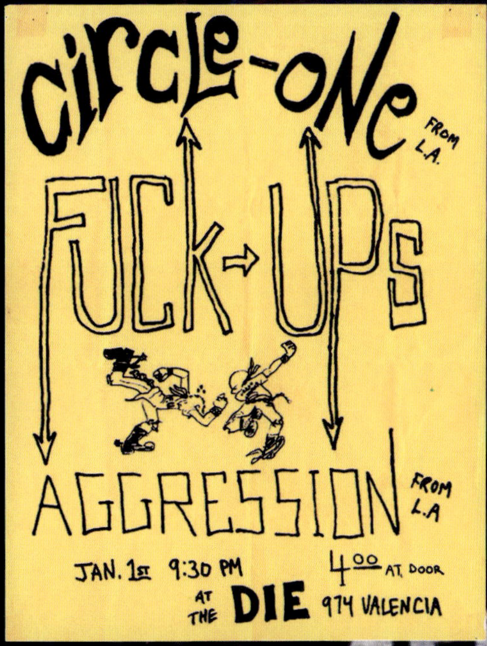

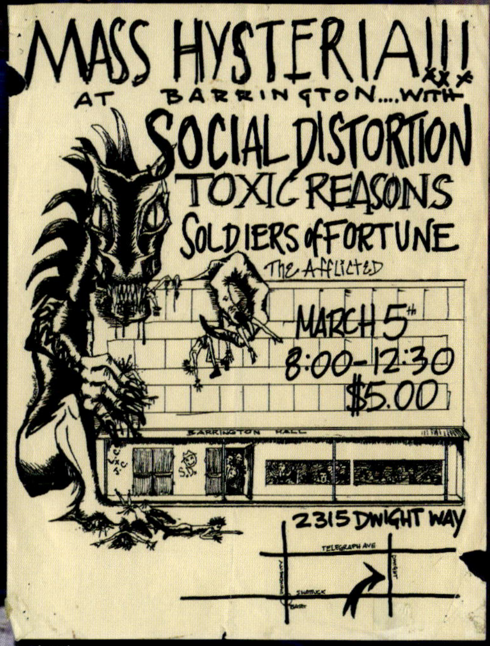

K. Bjornlie

Hand Scrawled Art

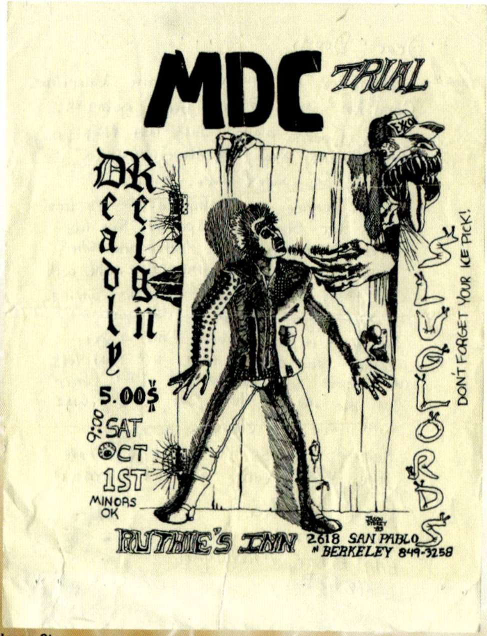

Jason Story

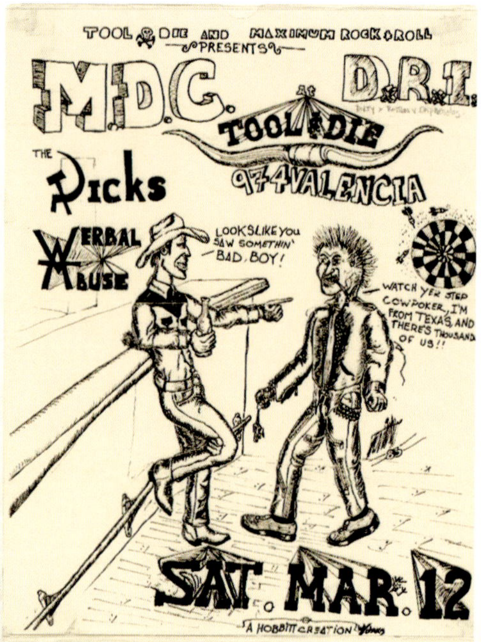

Hobbitt: Jak's Creation

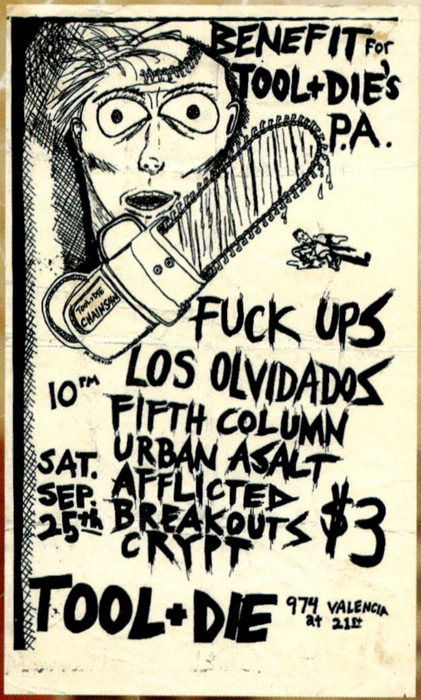

M. Girvin

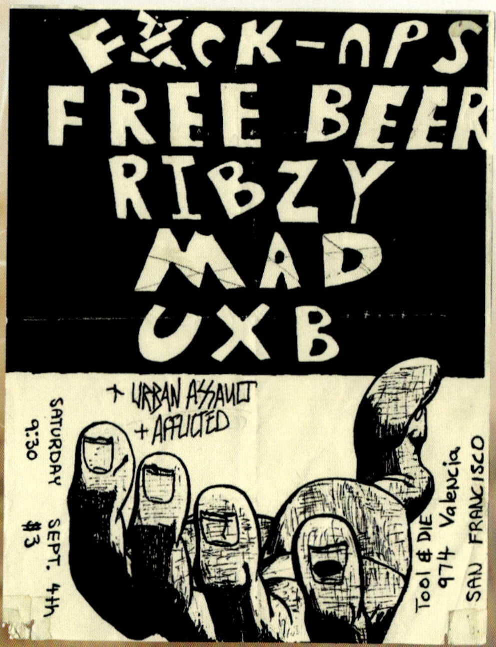

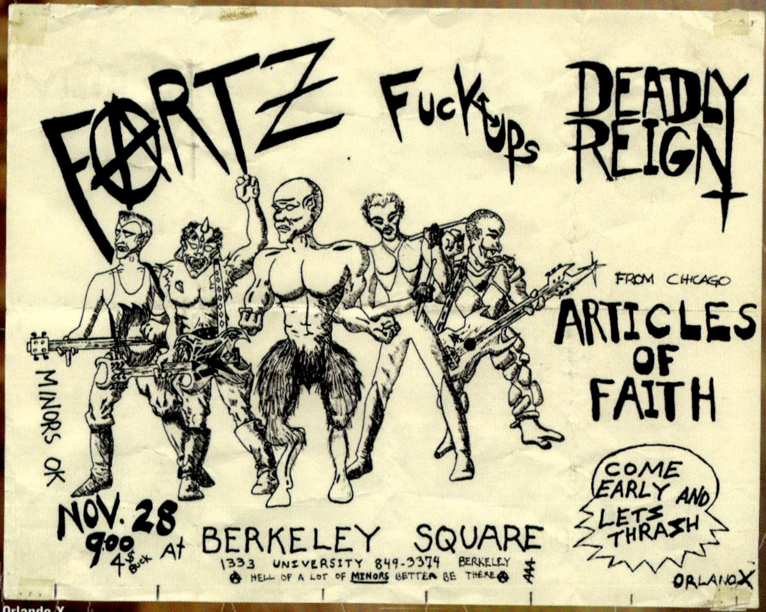

Orlando X

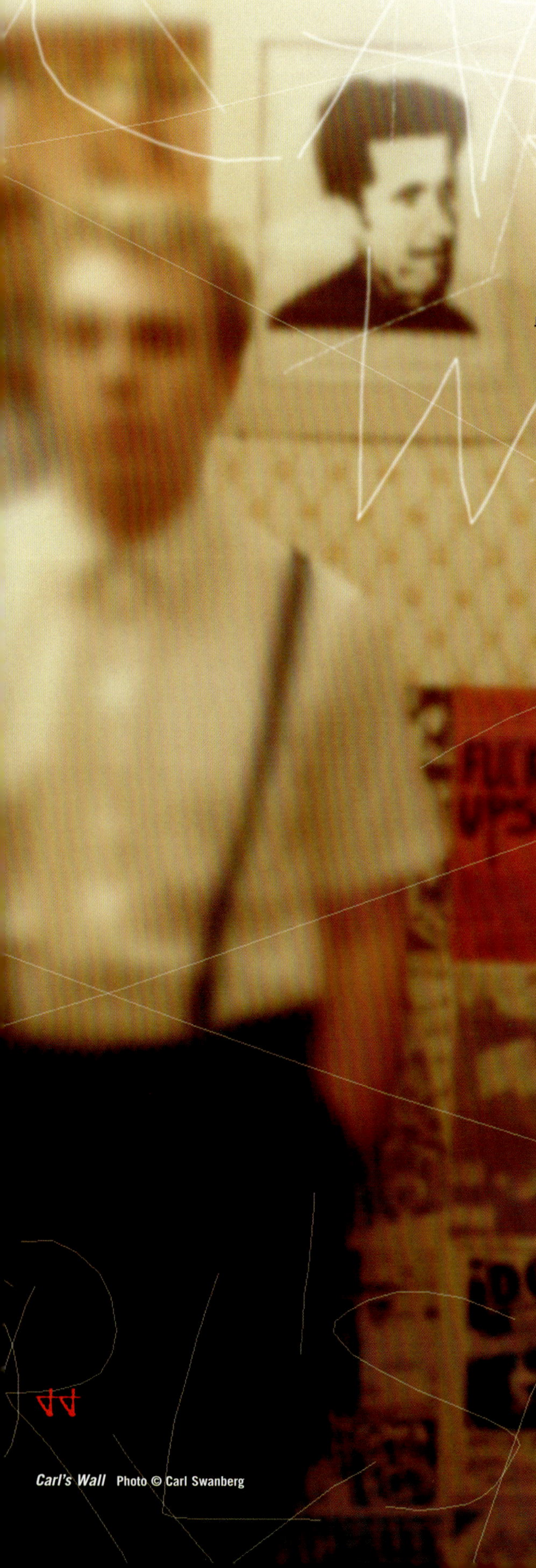
Carl's Wall Photo © Carl Swanberg

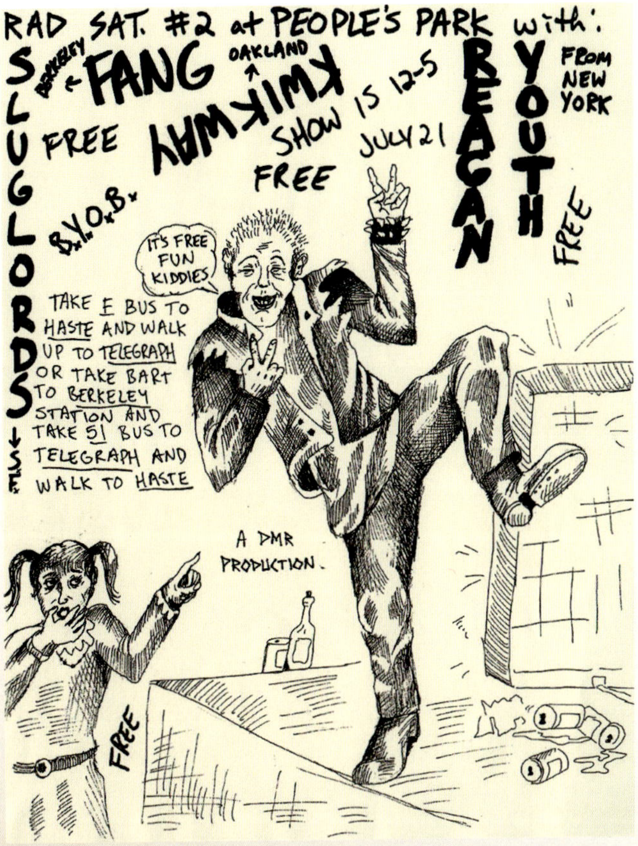

D.M.R.

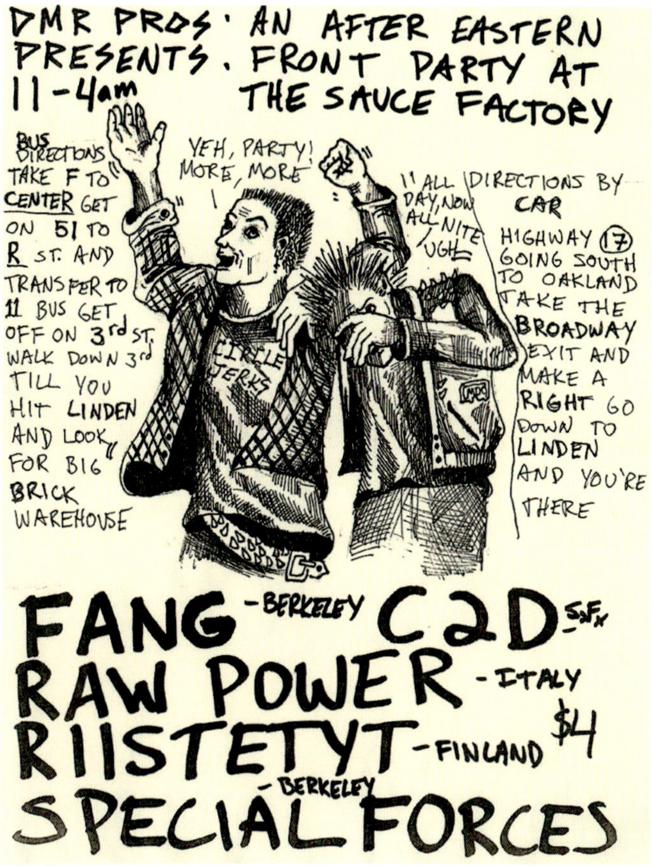

D.M.R.

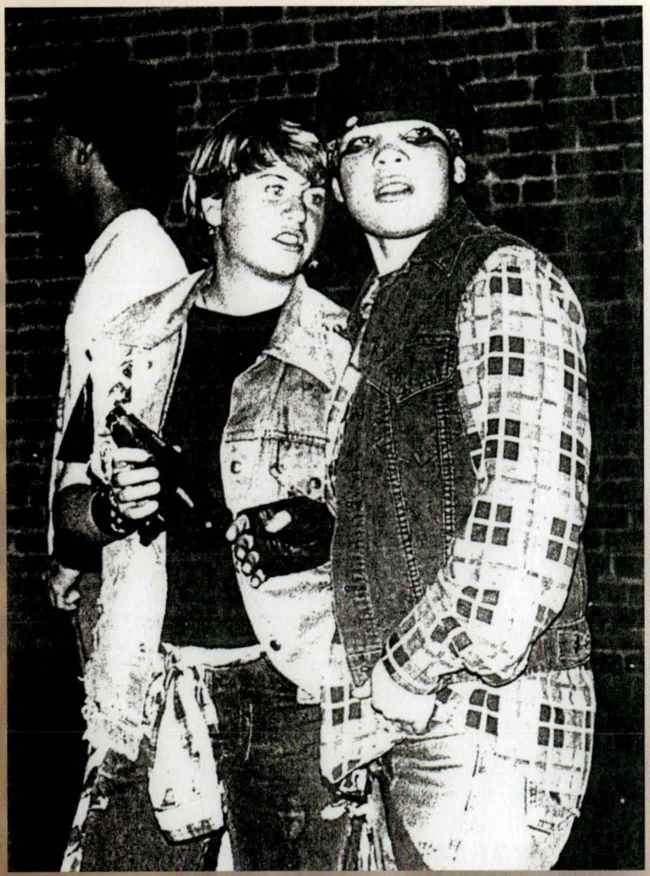

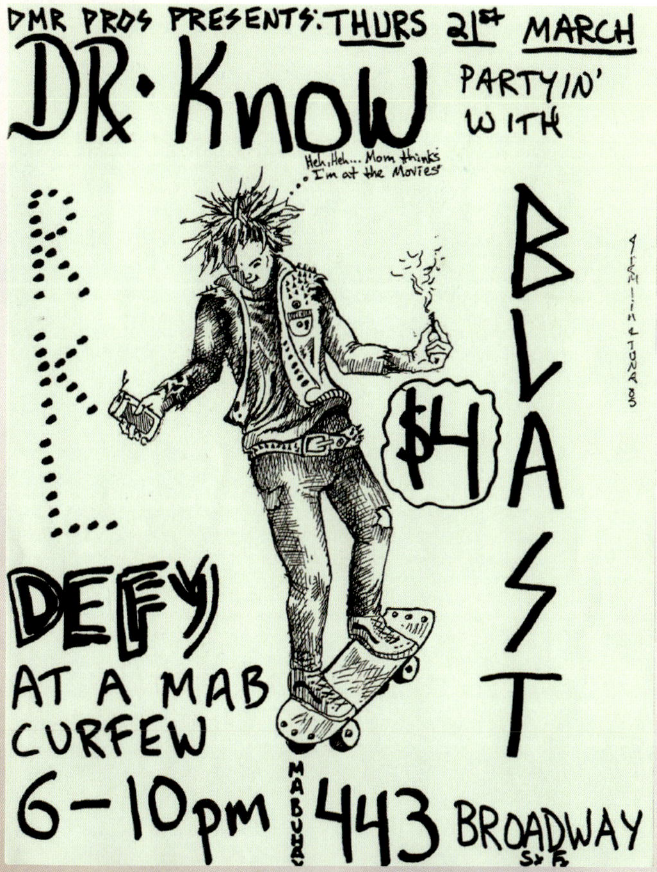

D.M.R.

D.M.R. Productions started doing shows in the Bay Area sometime in 1983 and continued until 1986. Our first production was a free show in Peoples Park near UC Berkeley. (I can't find this flyer, but I'm pretty sure that one of the bands was Special Forces.) After our second show in the park, the University banned us from using "their" property, because of the many complaints about the noise. We went on to do shows at various Bay Area clubs, including Ruthie's Inn in Berkeley, the Mab in the City, and a brief stint running our own club in Oakland. All our club shows were affordable and always between $1 and $6. All our shows were ALL AGES with the exception of one impromptu Raw Power gig at The Sound Of Music (which we only announced on the radio just the night before). D.M.R. Productions consisted of Carol Cross, Natasha Robinson, Aileen Sullivan, Rissa Schiff and Cliff Varnell. Some of the other gals who would help out included Courtenay, Dana, Sabrina and Danielle. Many thanks to Special Forces: they were always ready to do a show. Special thanks to the Sullivan family for housing and feeding many of the bands that played D.M.R. shows – you put up with a lot! D.M.R. Productions wasn't about money, It was all about our love for the music and the Bay Area scene.

Cheers, Carol

Skate Rock

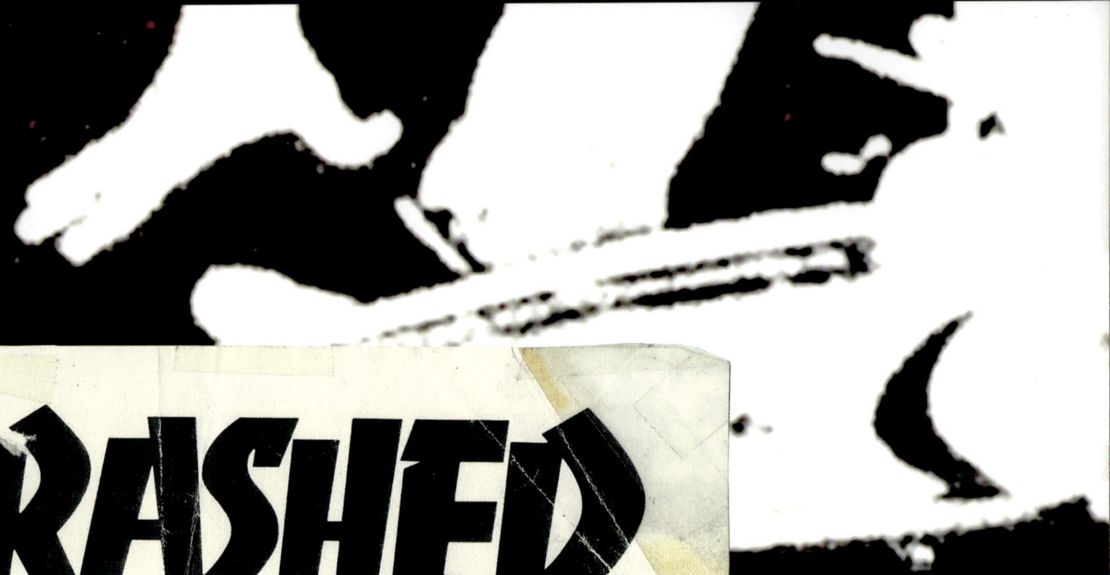

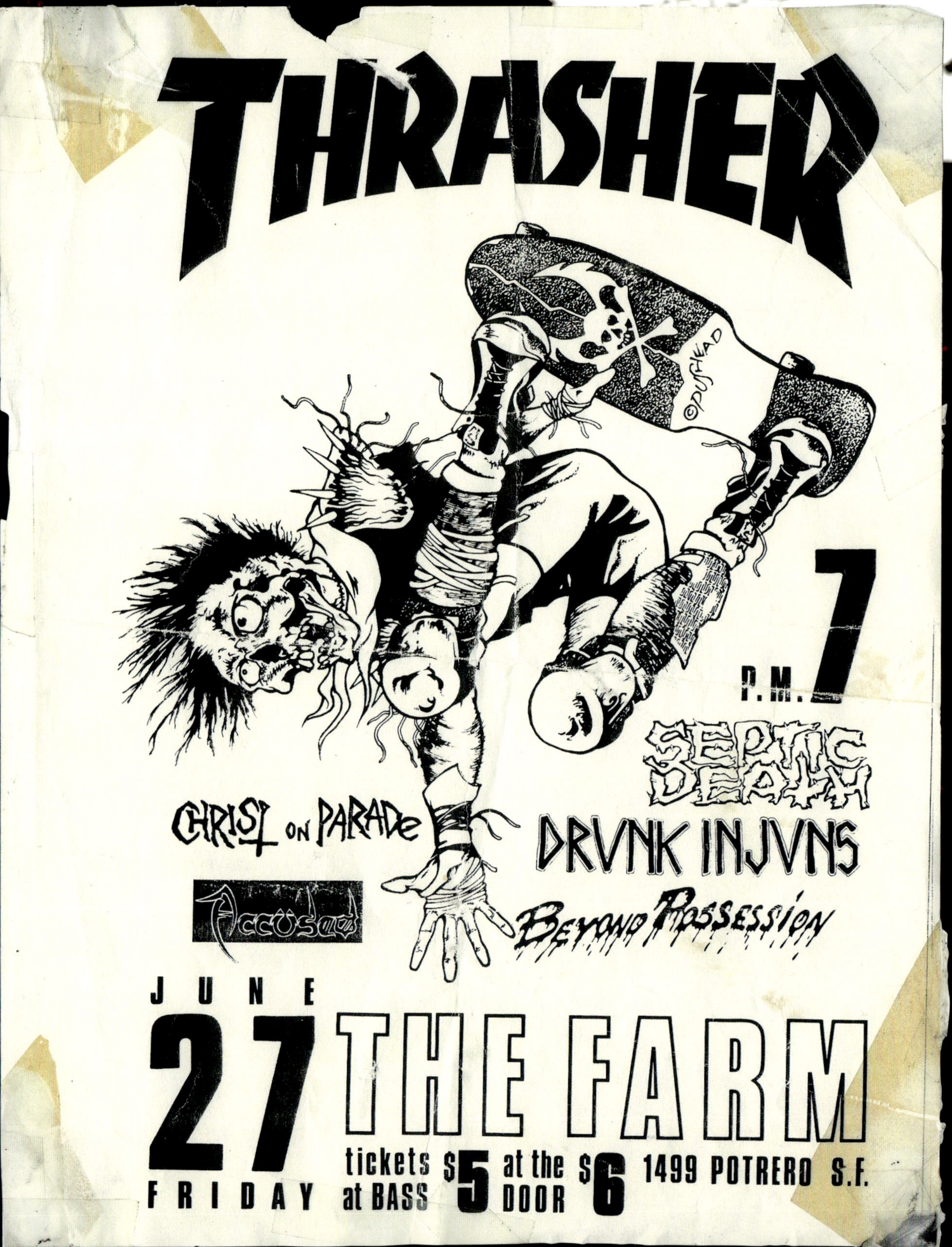

Pushead

I feel like I saw the birth of Skate Rock in 1983.

One Saturday night at the *Tool & Die* in SF's Mission District, *Thrasher Magazine* got together **The Scoundrelz** (with Tony Alva,) **The Faction**, **Los Olvidados** (my band) and **JFA**.

It was a warm evening in the Mission, which translates to an incredibly hot and humid night in the basement of the Tool & Die. There were probably 200 sweaty beer-soaked skaters standing in 120 degree heat, right in your face.

My memories of the night are a swirl of Jak's SF skate teams and the SSG (Scurbs Skate Gang) and possibly the CBS (City Boys Shred) all fucking with each other. It was like a scene out of a 60s surf film, except there was no beach party - it was all about hard-core skaters getting super fucked-up and swiveling (a dance that was part twisting and part skanking, less emphasis on slamming.) Mix in a bunch of suburban kids, add music, and everyone was raging.

When we finally made it up on stage, I saw the faces of skaters that I had admired now looking at me. The spirit and intensity of that night was just insane - the pushing, surging and screaming for music that belonged to us.
We were screwing around with the tempo of our songs, playing in country or reggae style, just to fuck with everyone. The sweat soaked through my pants, ran down my palms and onto the neck of my Fender, but I was so stoked.

Ray Stevens
Los Olvidados

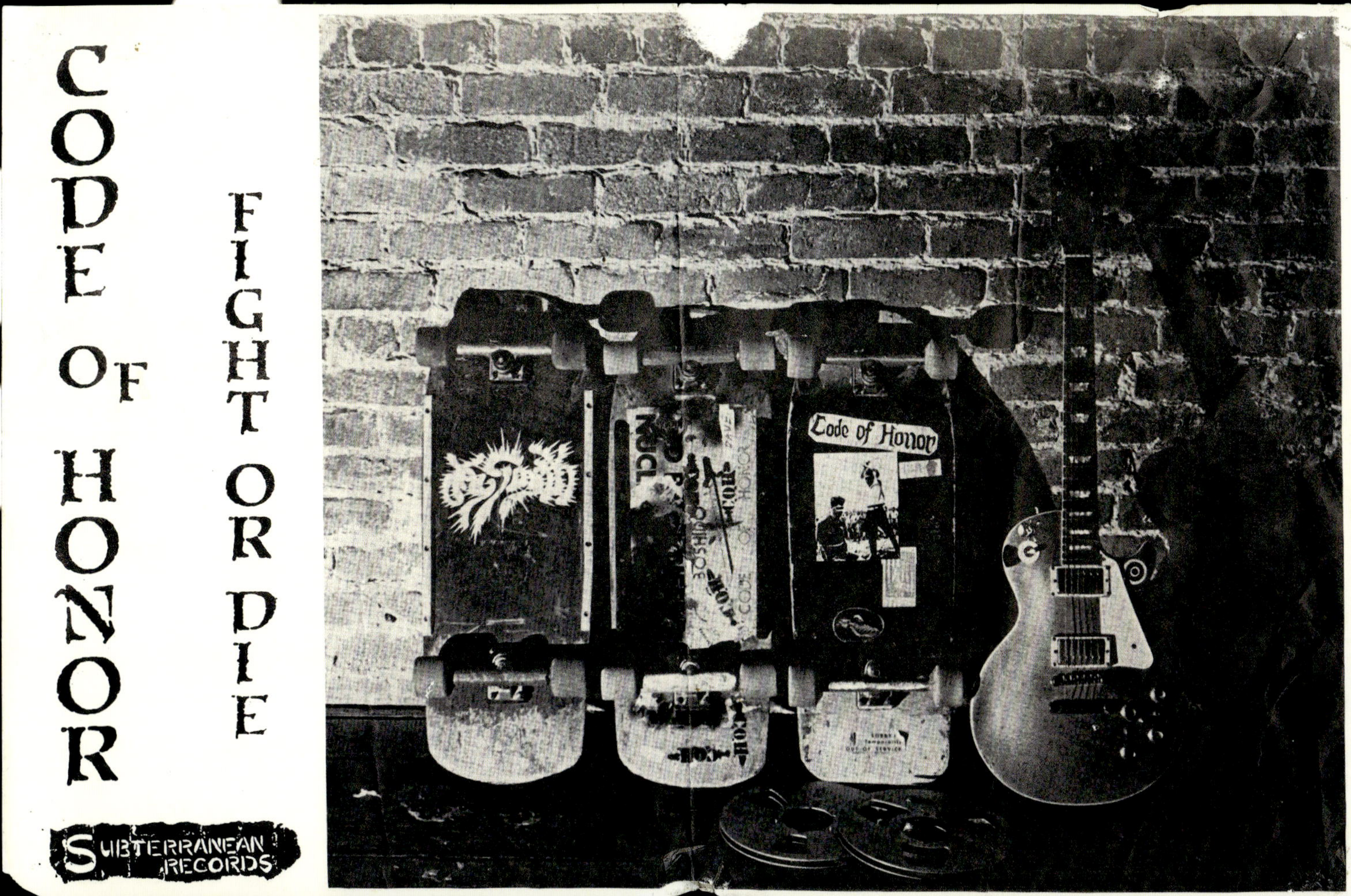

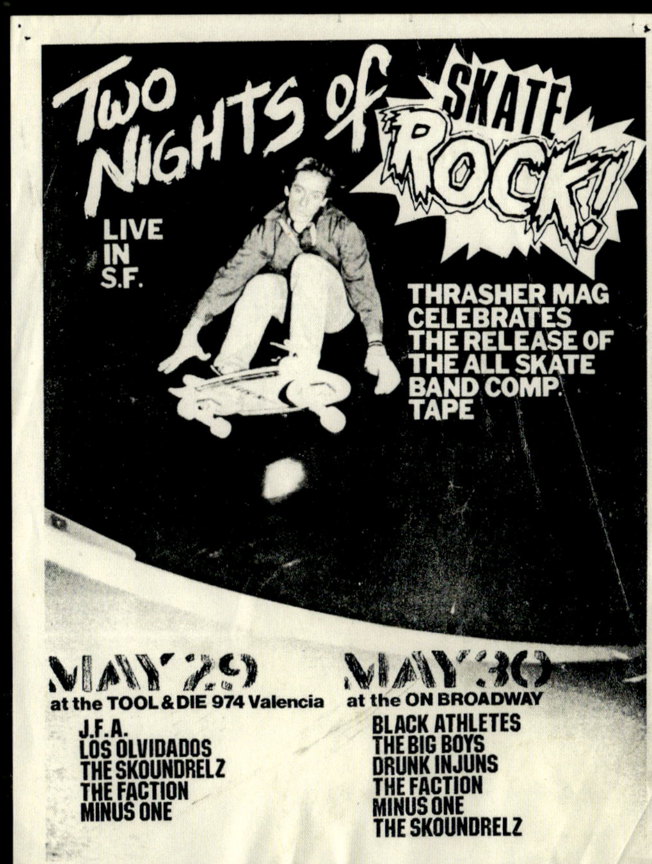

Back in the late '70s I can remember hearing a Joe Jackson song in which the lyrics mentioned "skateboards– I've almost made them respectable." I also remember wanting to kick that spindly little fucker's ass at that moment. It then occured to me that he had never taken his sorry life into his hands and entrusted it to a plexiglass board with urethane wheels, hurling that twig of a body down a hill at breakneck speed, only to catch a pebble and skim across asphalt at 30 mph. I knew he'd never know the feeling of picking himself up with four blood-streaked limbs, his left nipple torn partially from his chest.

Then I just felt really sorry for him.

If you don't know why punk and skateboarding go so well together, get back on your riding mower and finish the lawn Gomer, it's almost time for lunch.

J

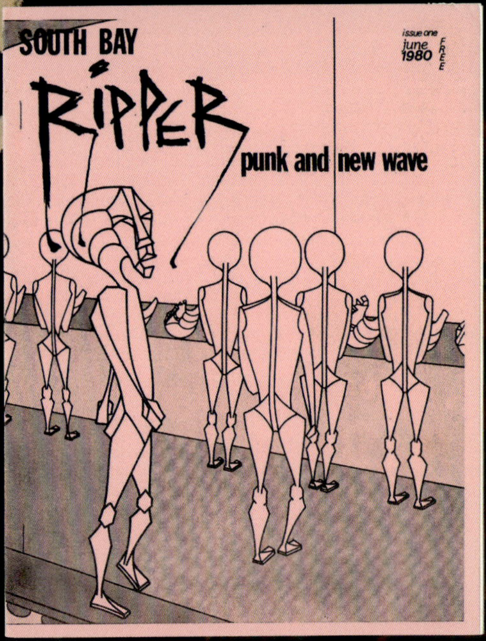

Tim Tanooka

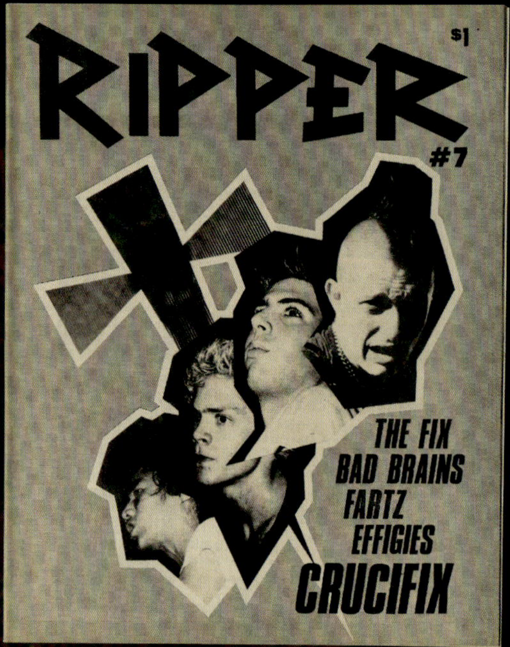

Tim Tanooka

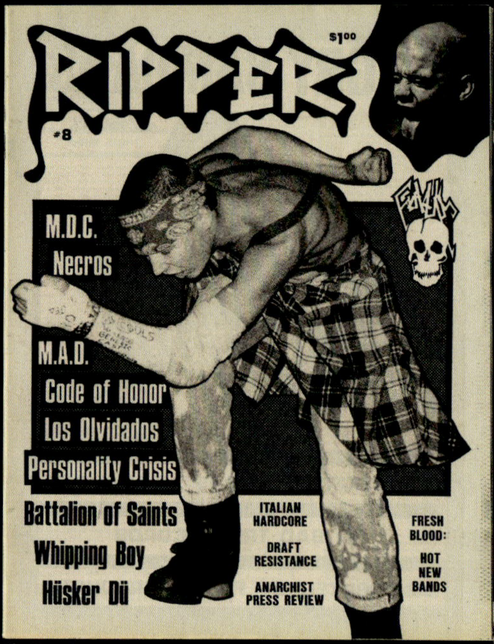

Tim Tanooka

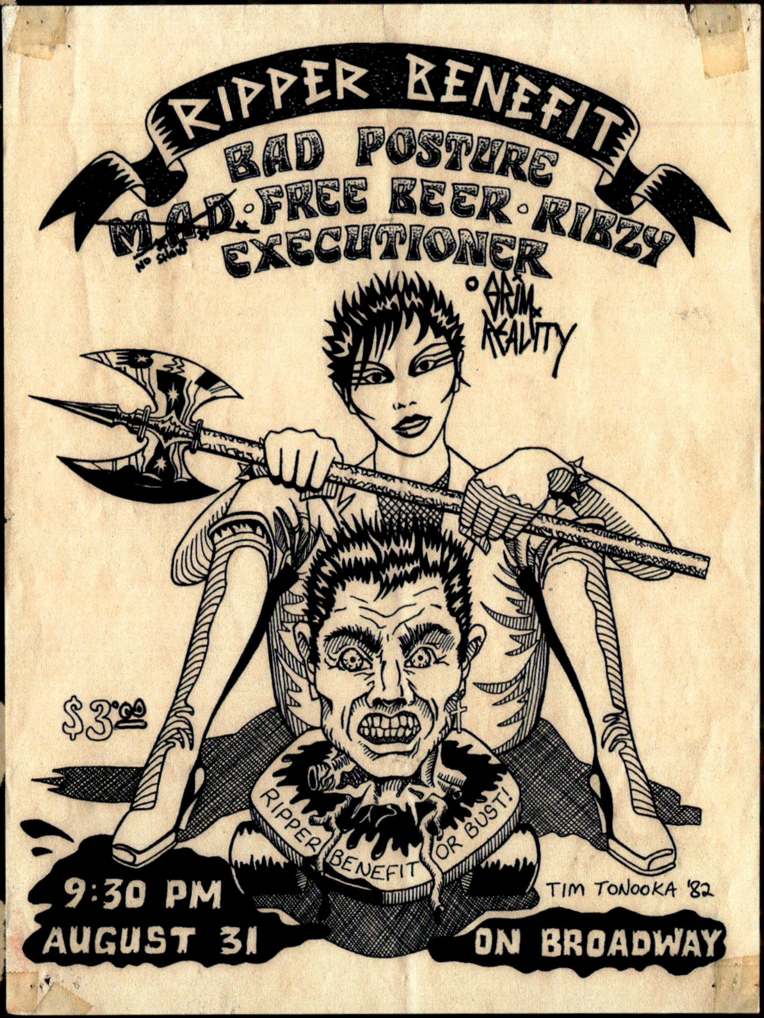

Tim Tanooka

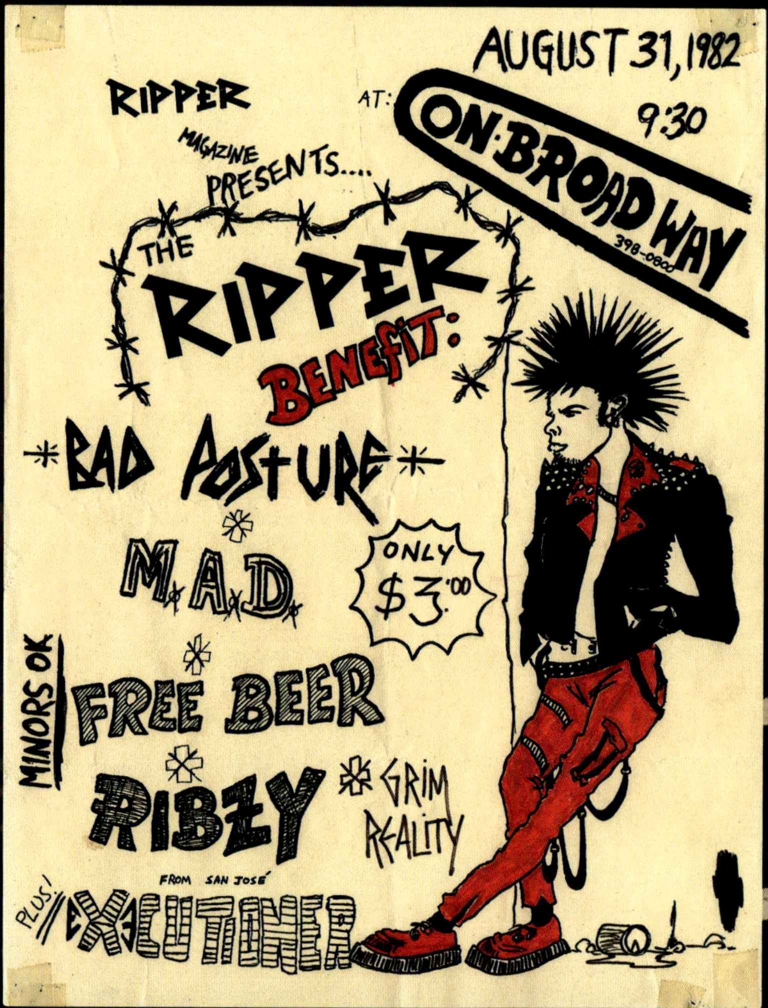

Jason Honae

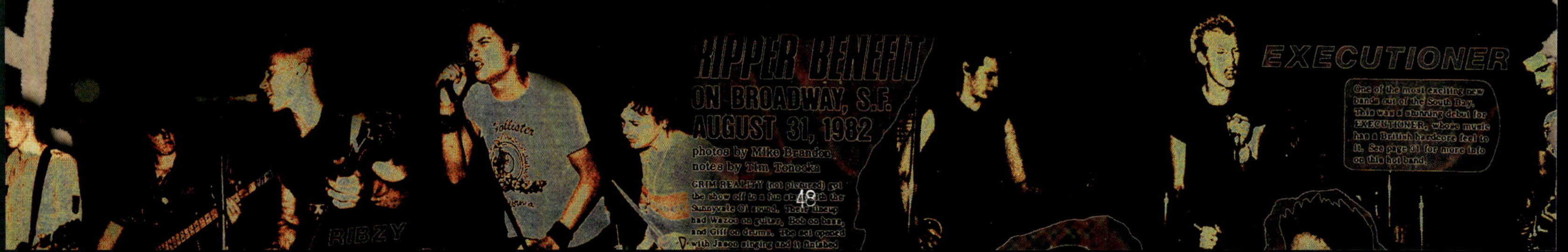

"Stolen" Art

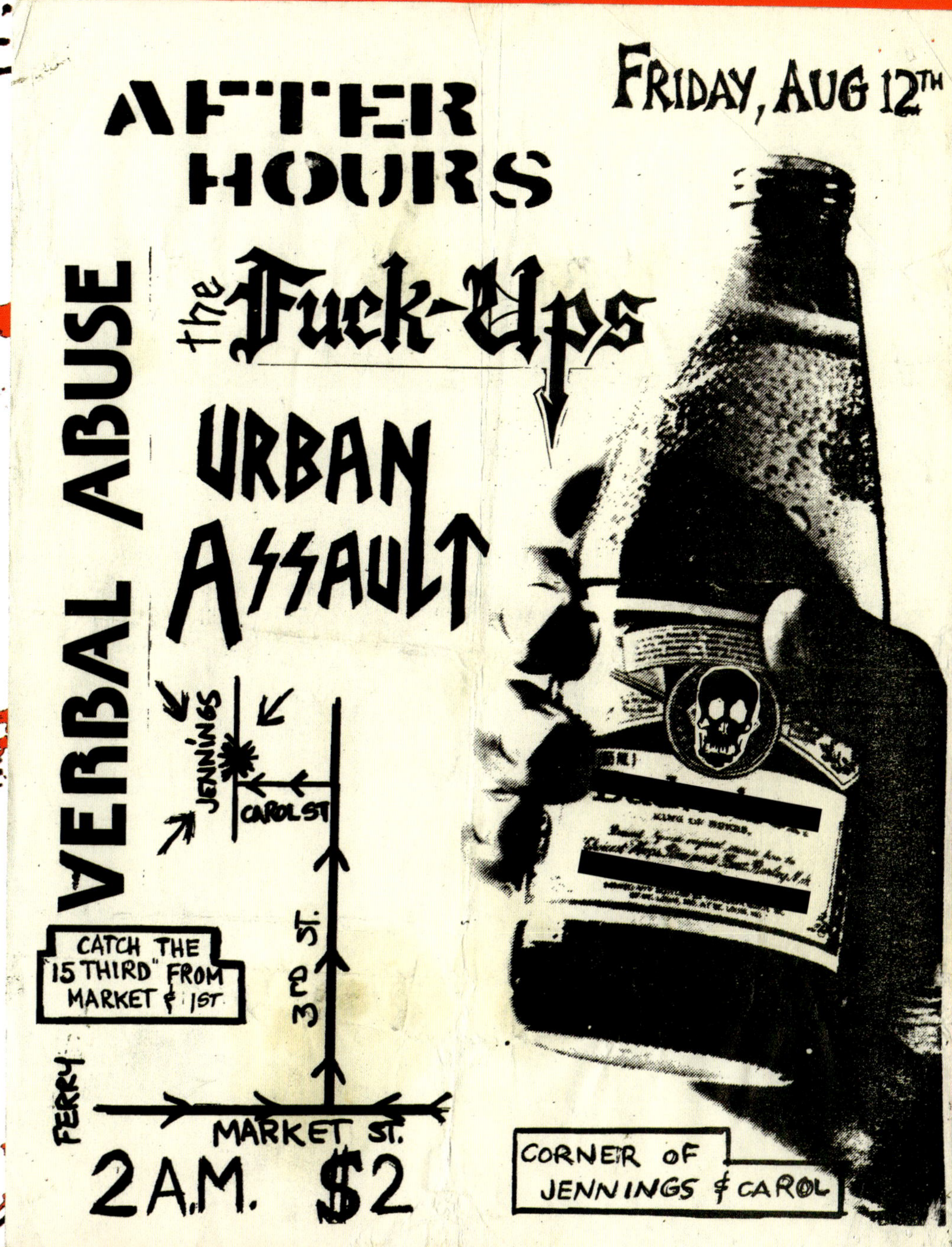

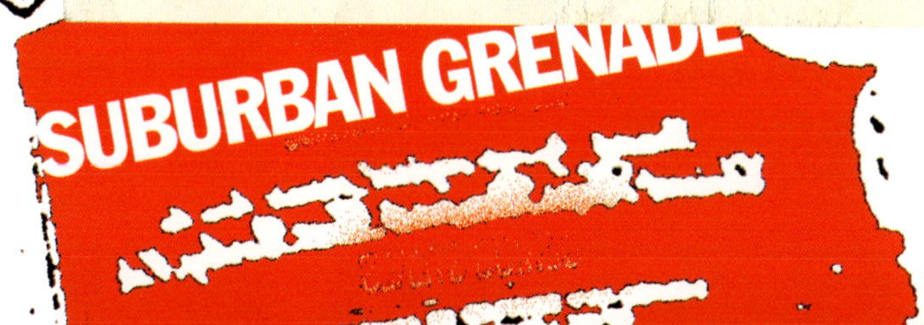

Punk music was fashioned out of pieces of vaudeville, blues, rock and reggae, so it made sense that the art that came with the scene was similar in nature. It was a perfect postmodern statement to put together a flyer out of newspaper clippings, retail catalogues, and pictures ripped out of magazines.

Clip out a celebrity photo, bore out the eyes, blacken a tooth, and you had instant contraband, pure blasphemy...a truly dangerous piece of art.

The best practitioners of this art form did with wit, smarts and without fear - the way all great art is created.

“Stolen” Art

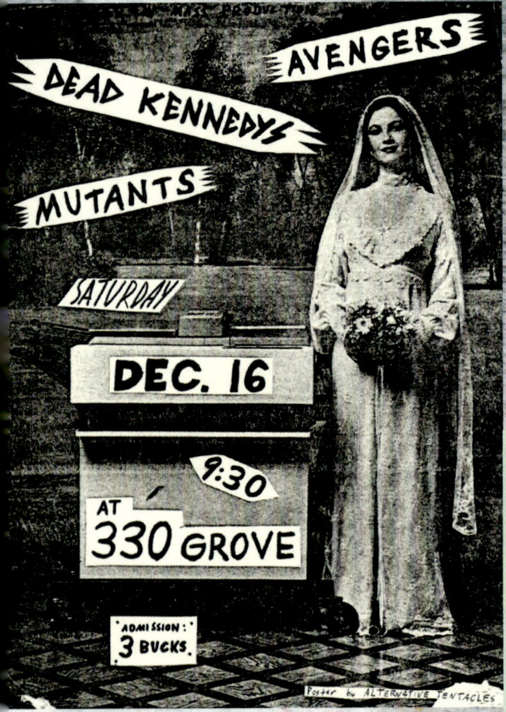

Jello Biafra

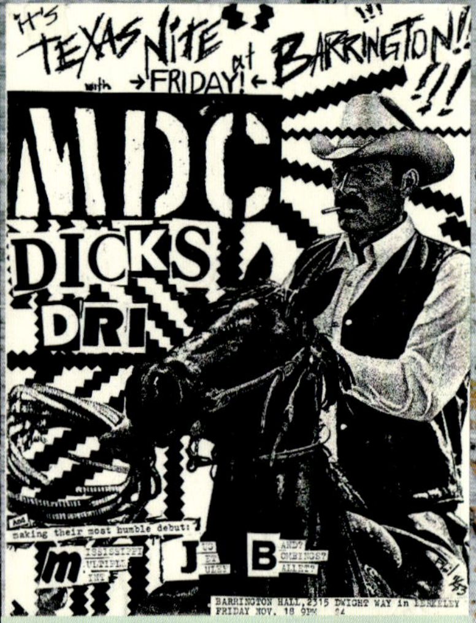

Phil

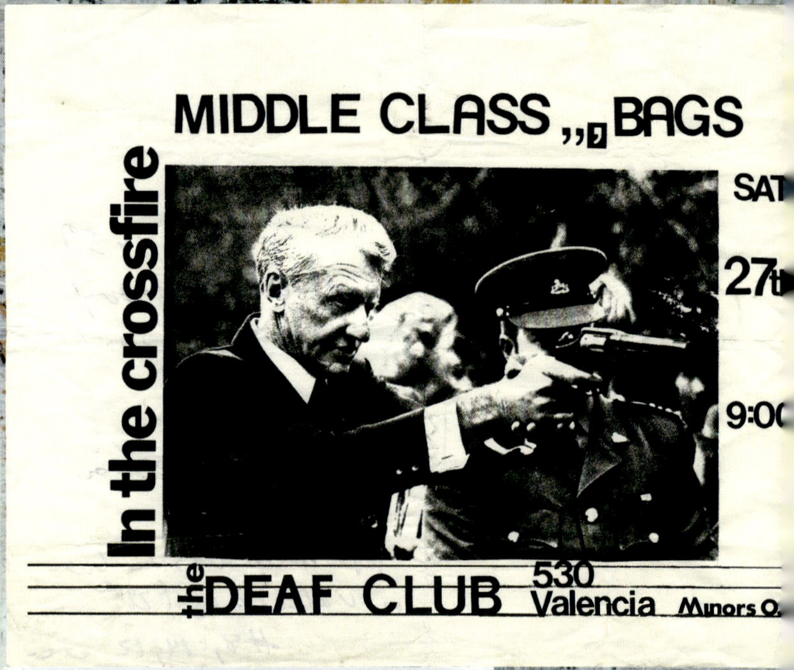

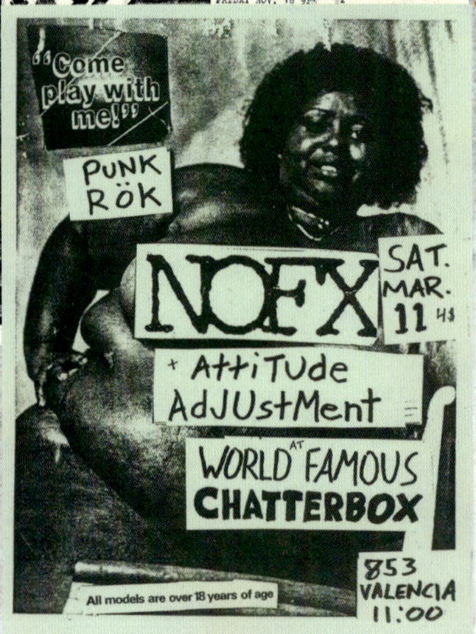

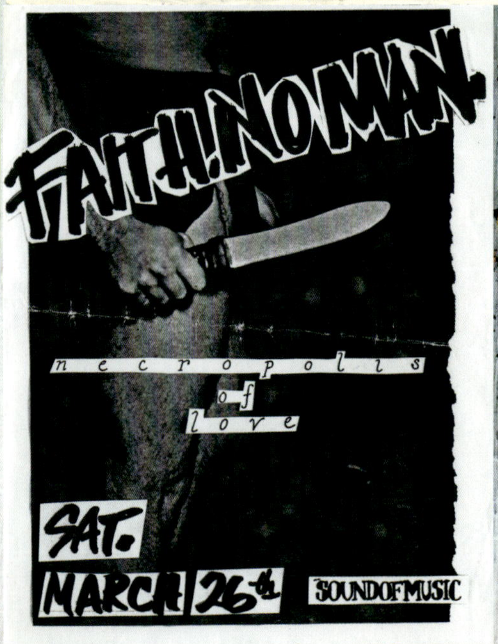

"Stolen" A

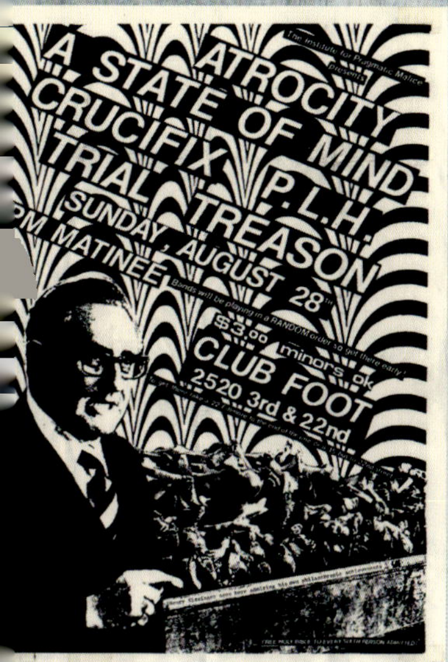

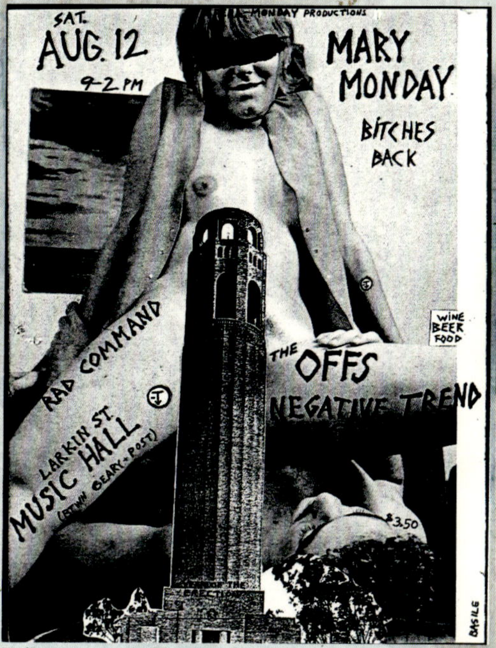

Basile

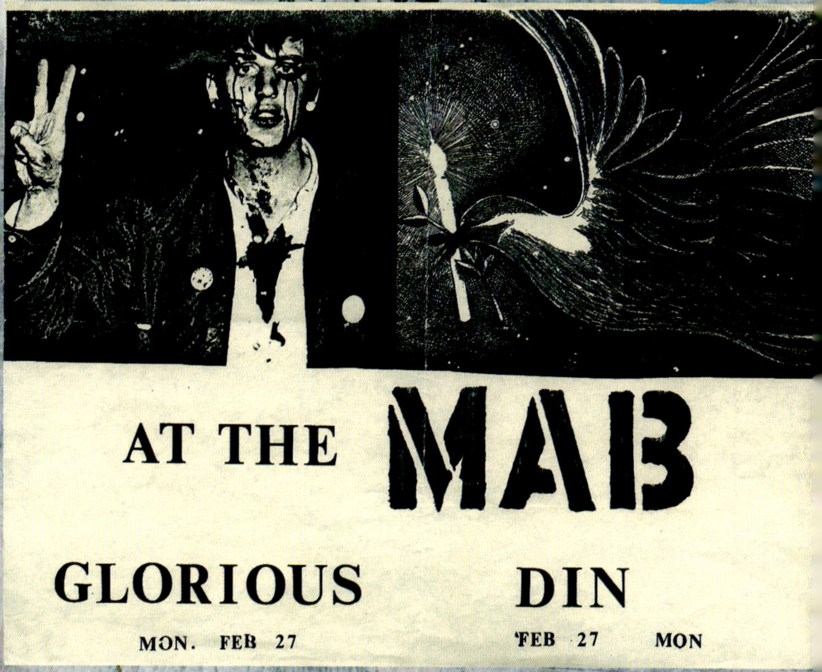

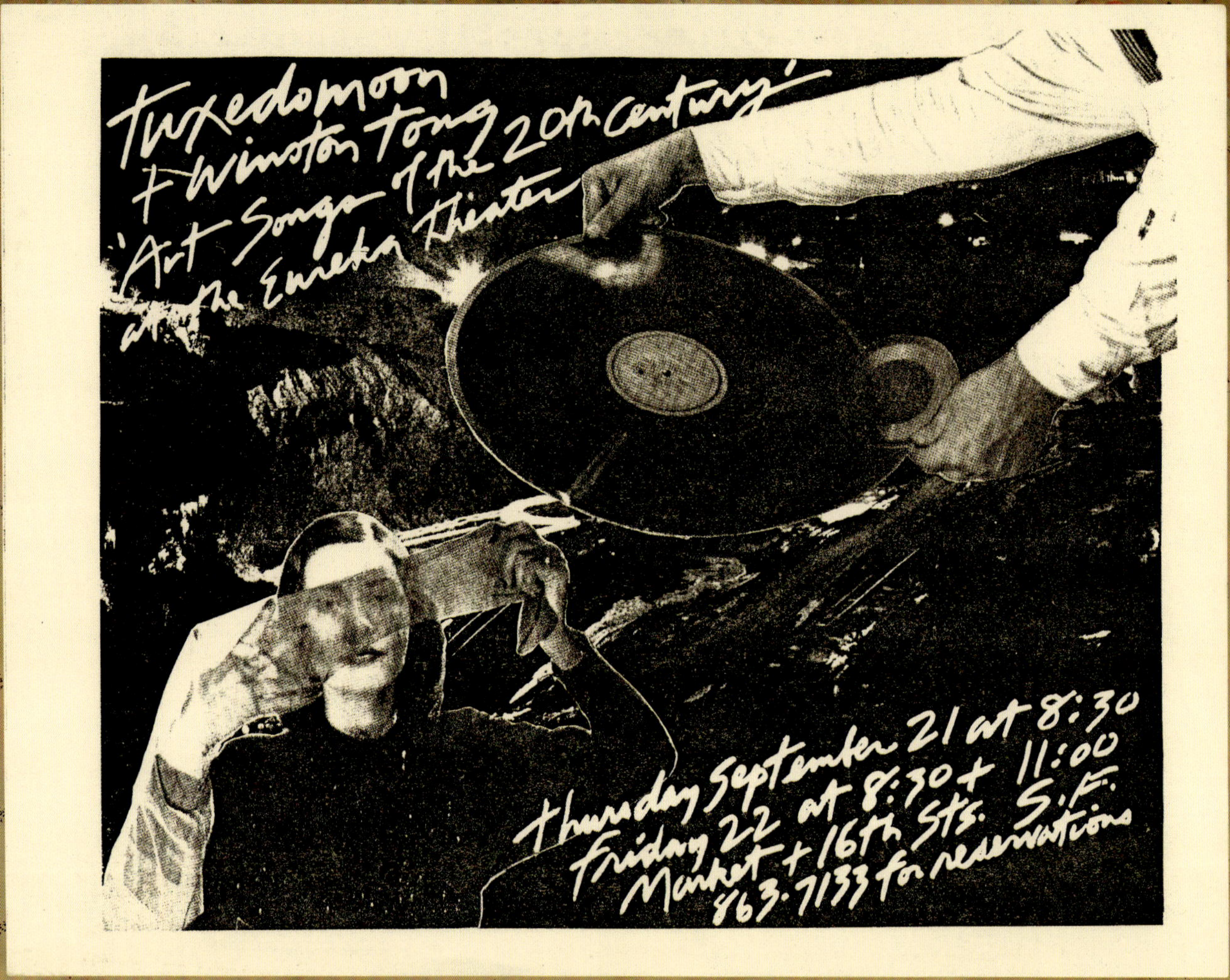

Winston Tong

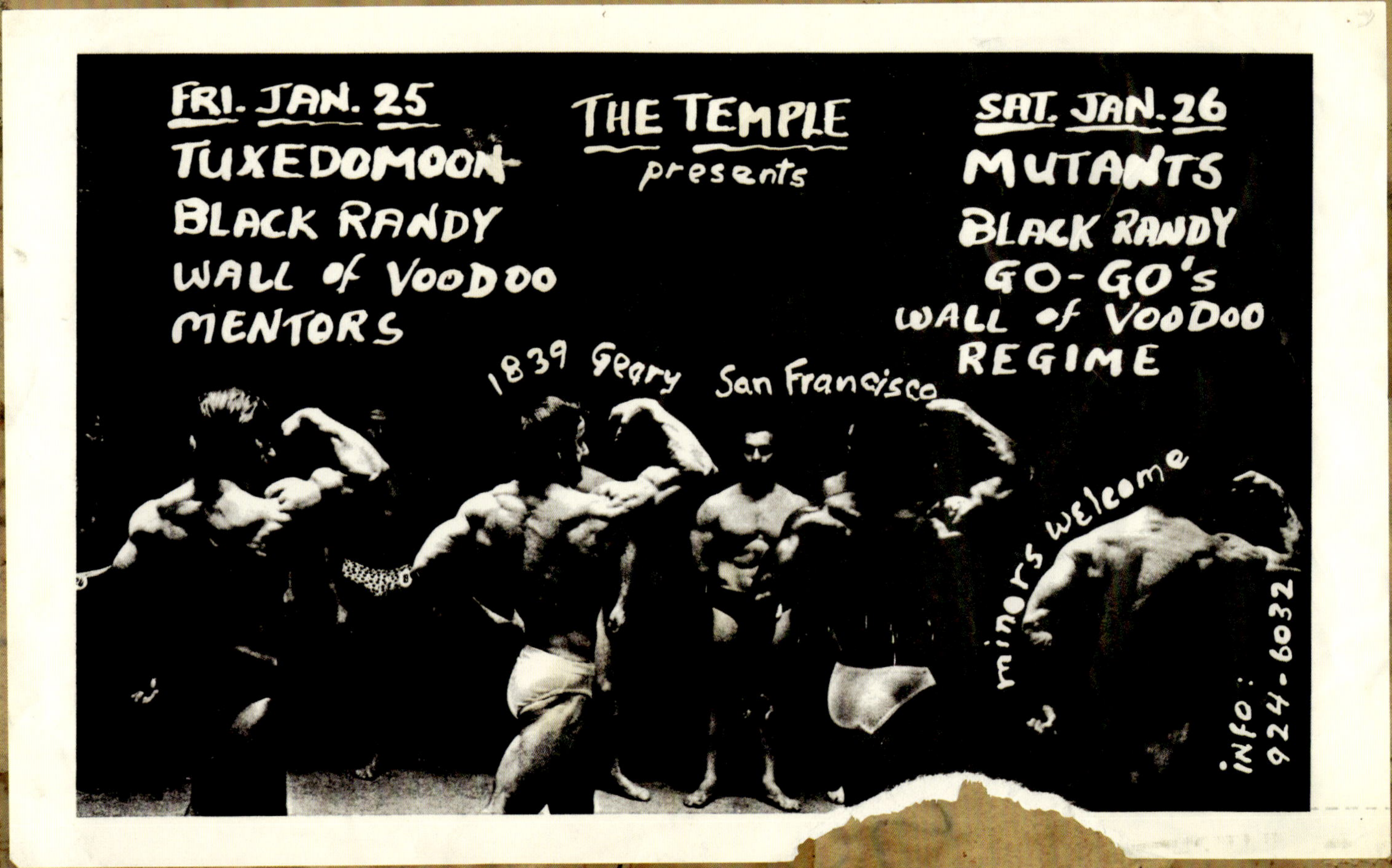

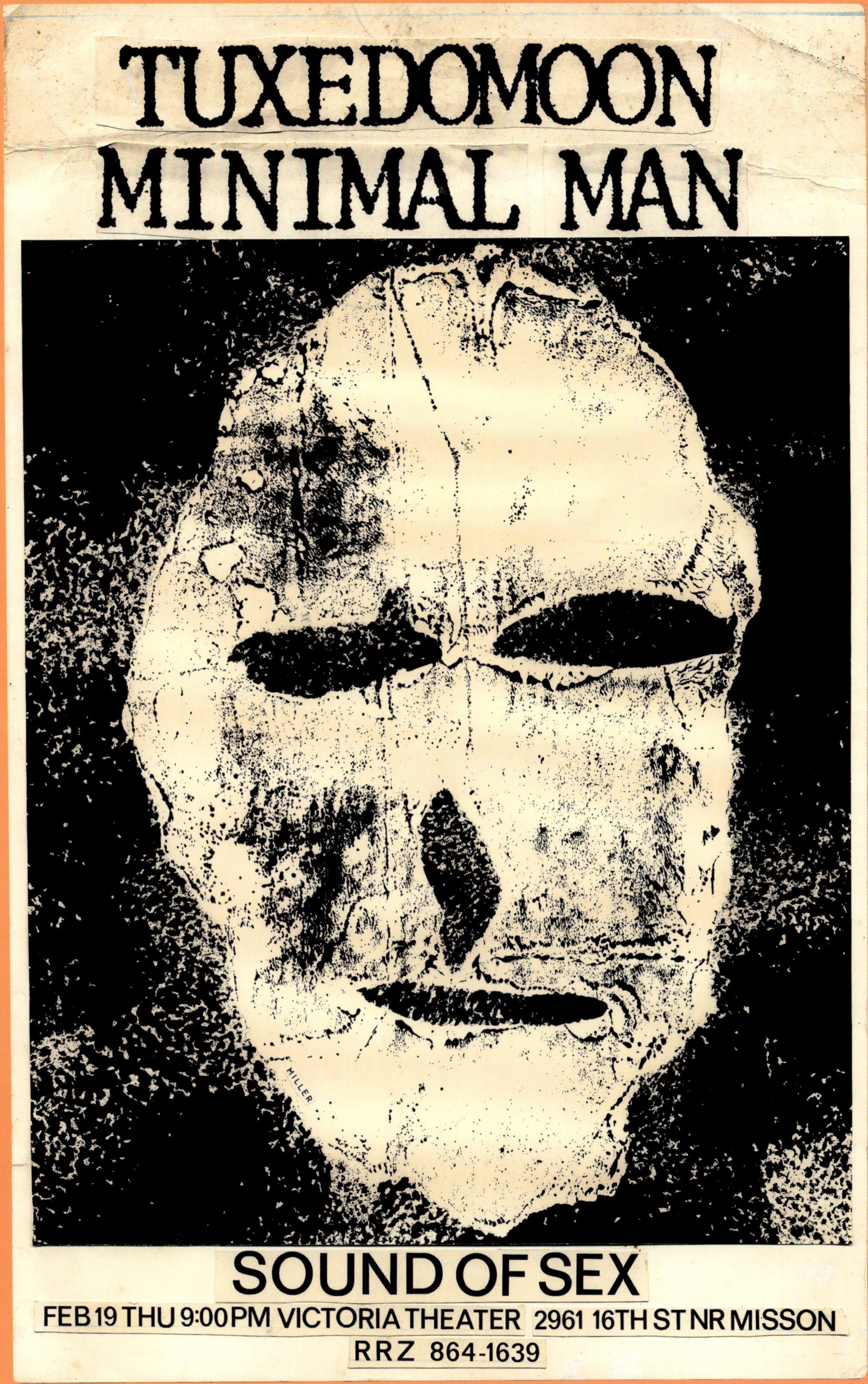

Patrick Miller

When punk rock first hit San Francisco in 1976, I was in a comedy group of a band called Leila & The Snakes. Jane Dornacker (aka Leila) had us doing a parody of punk as part of the show. It was my favorite bit, because I got to scream and shout in German while jumping on a pogo stick.

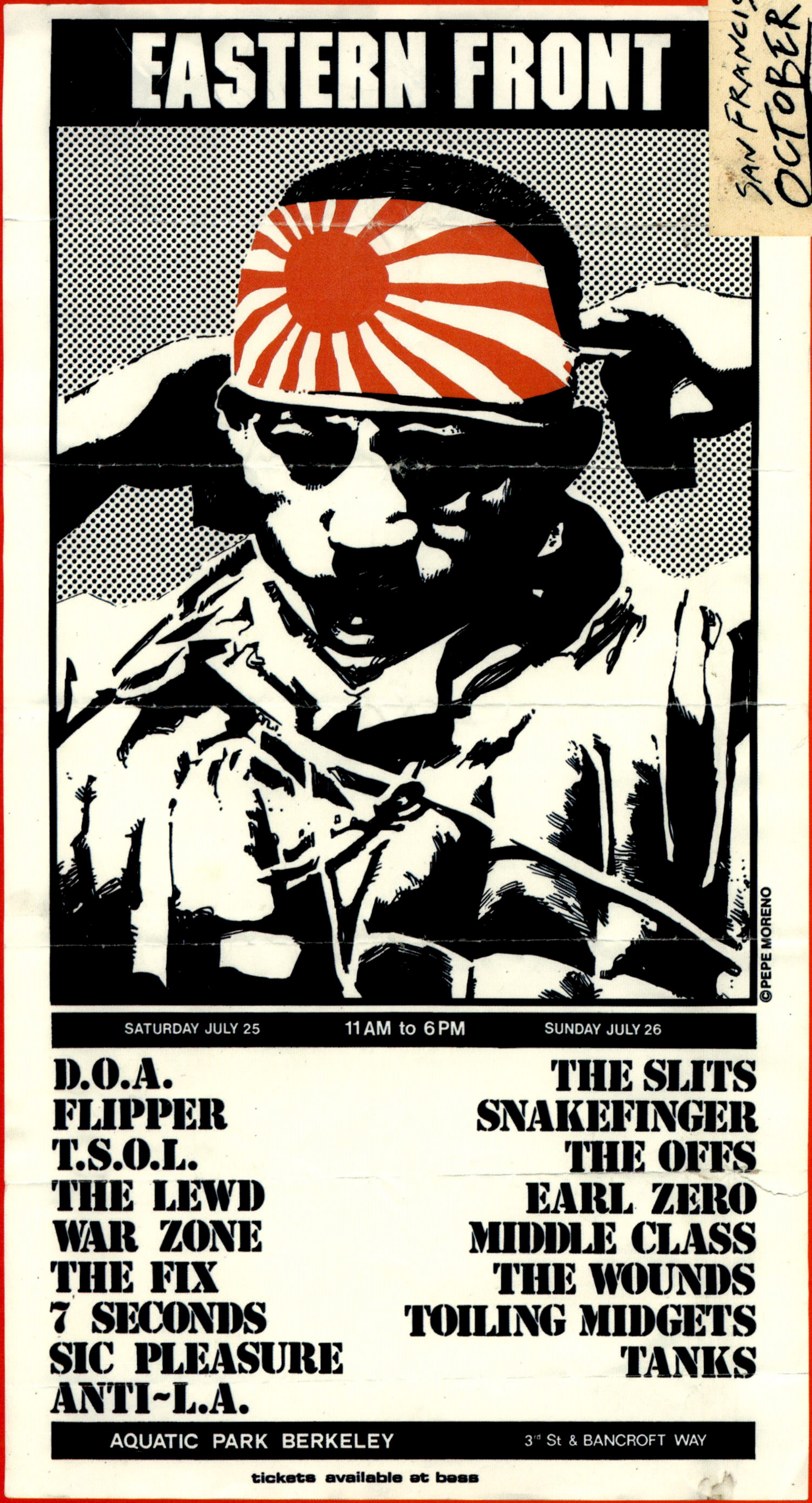

Pepe Moreno
Courtesy: Wes Robinson

I'd go check out new bands at the Mab every week. I really liked the groups that had a sense of humor about themselves - which was quite a number of them. Just get up there, bash it out and see what happens. The Mutants were good like that.

The violence was deliberate and mostly funny, too. Like everyone pretending to beat up Dirk Dirksen all the time. He was a great promoter for punk because he was so open-minded and seemed to see it just as it was - a bunch of kids just letting' off steam and having fun. He didn't even get mad when someone broke his nose one night.

I remember going to see the famous Sex Pistols show at Winterland, January 1978. I thought the music was great, but I was pissed off that the band, except for Sid, was wearing expensive designer clothes. That didn't seem too punk to me.

Dead Kennedys, The Avengers, Crime, The Nuns, The Dils and The Offs were in full swing and doing well when I left San Francisco in 1980. I think a good time was had by all. That's all I wanted out of it...make it loud, and make it fast!

Pearl E. Gates

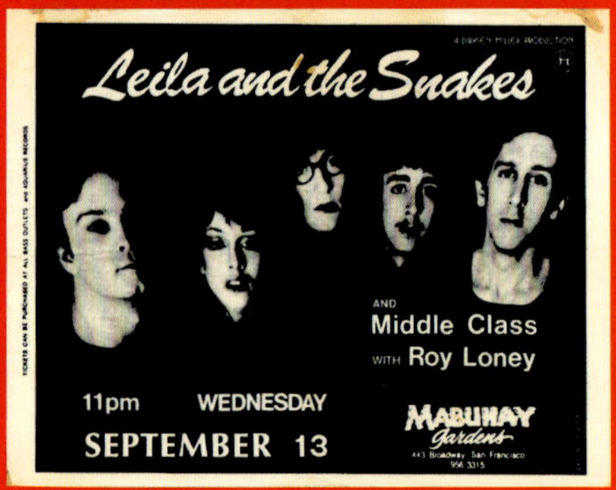

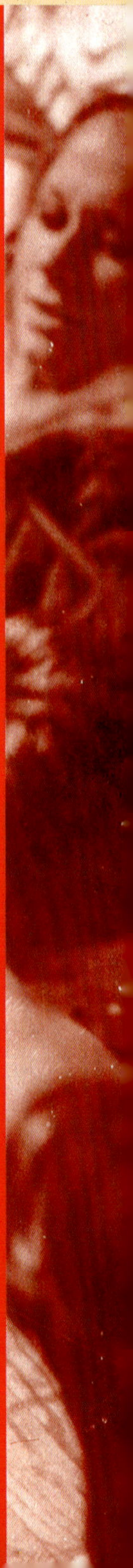

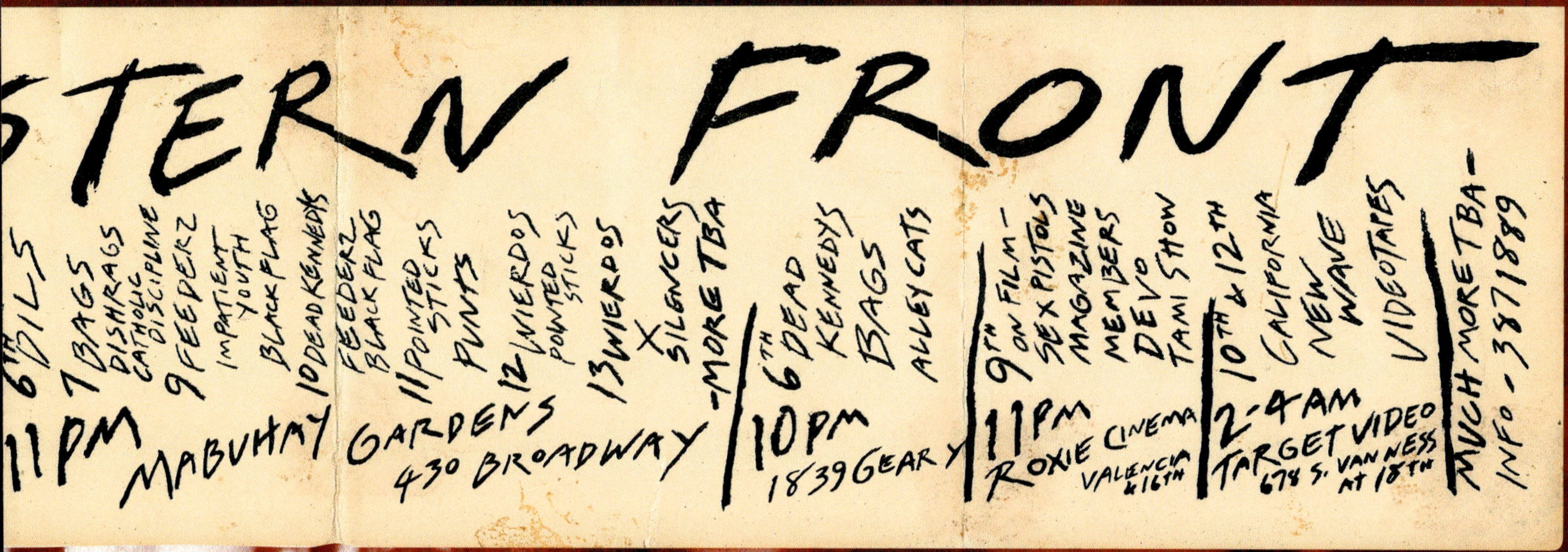

Winston Tong

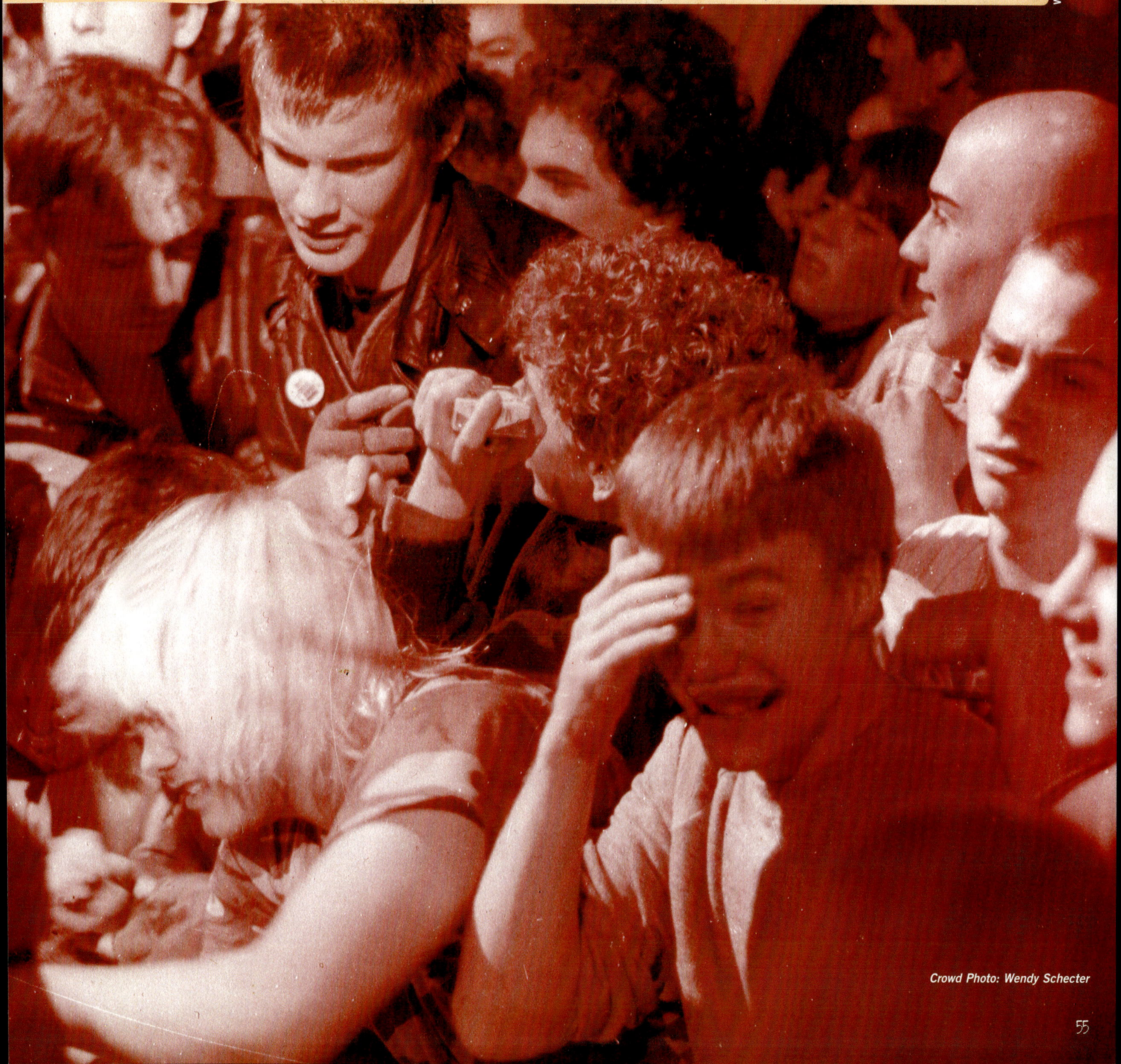

Crowd Photo: Wendy Schecter

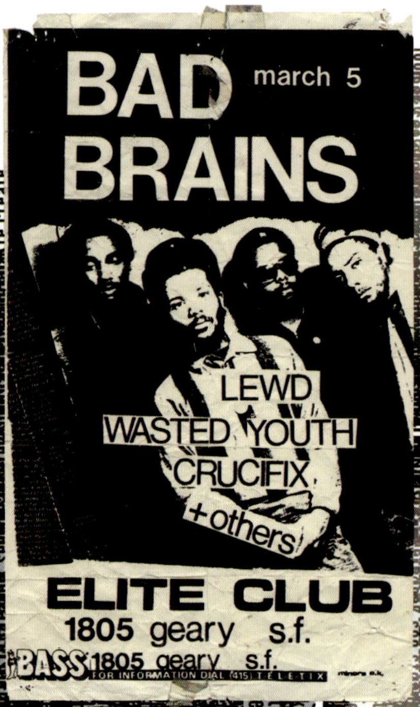

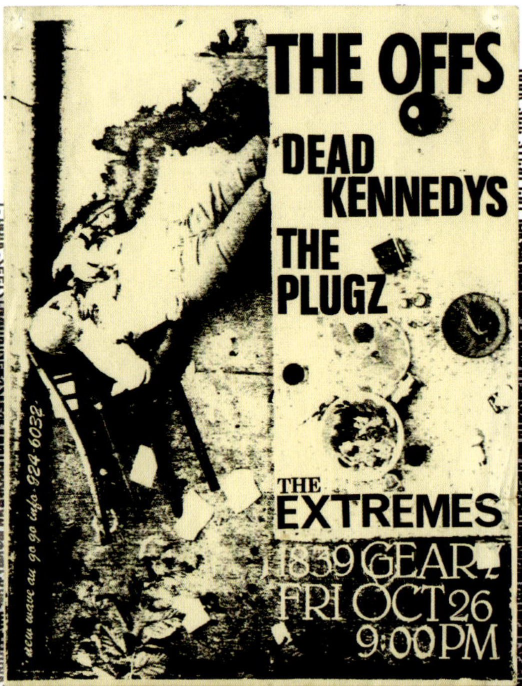

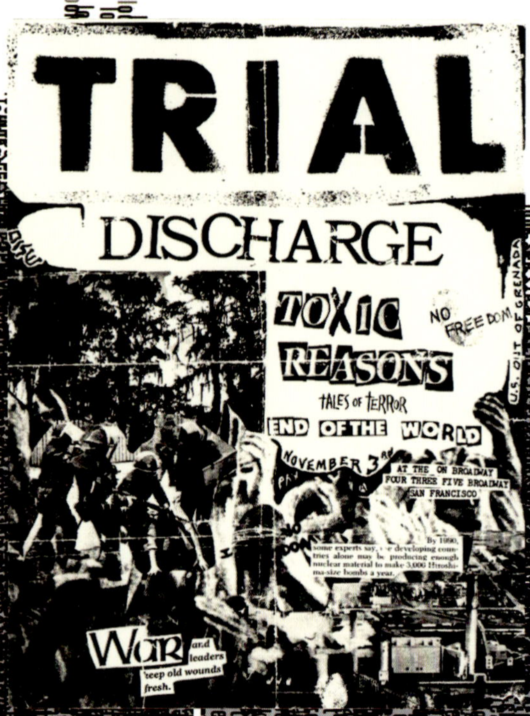

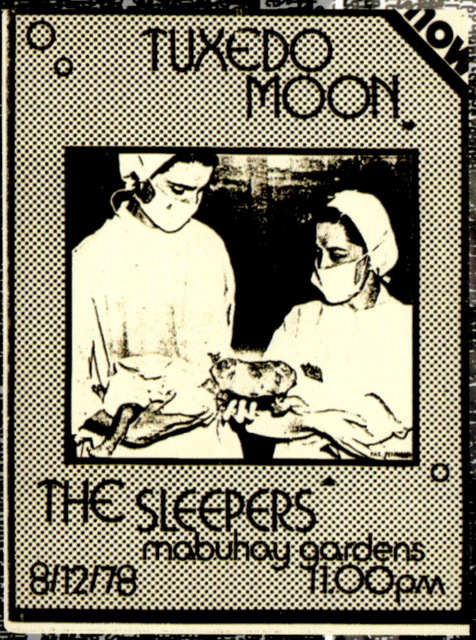

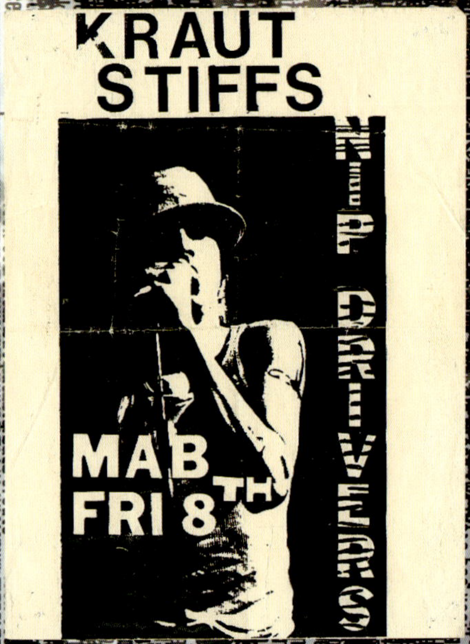

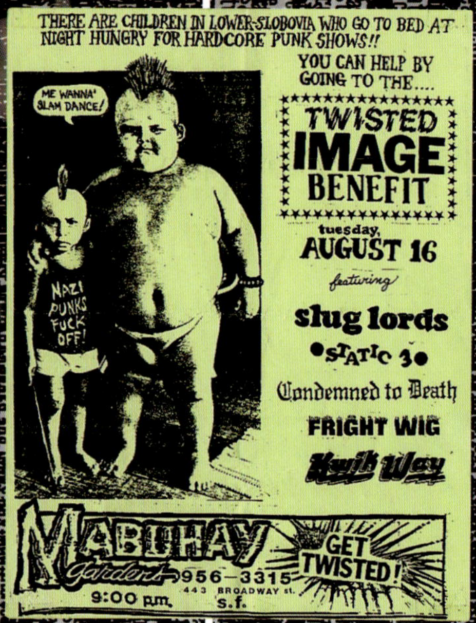

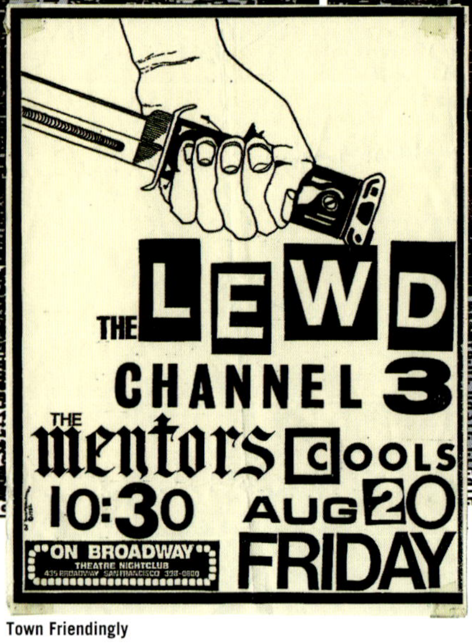

Town Friendingly

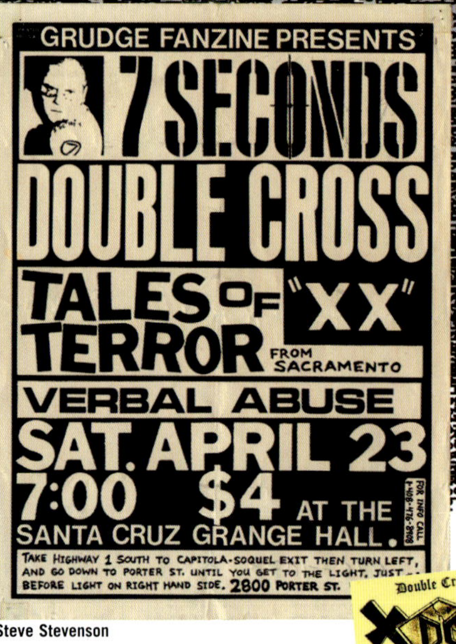

Steve Stevenson

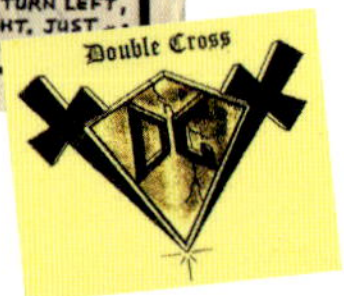

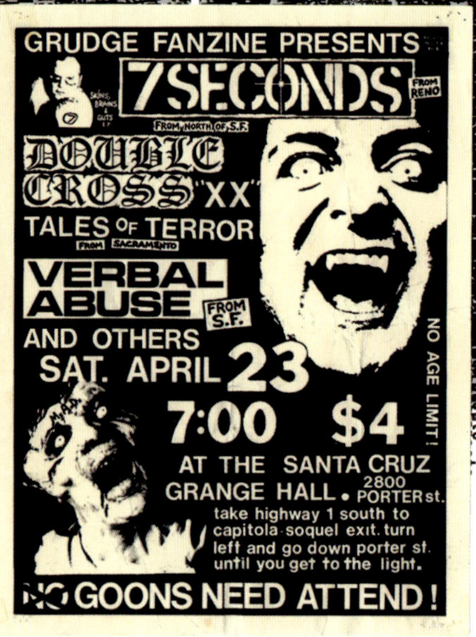

Steve Stevenson

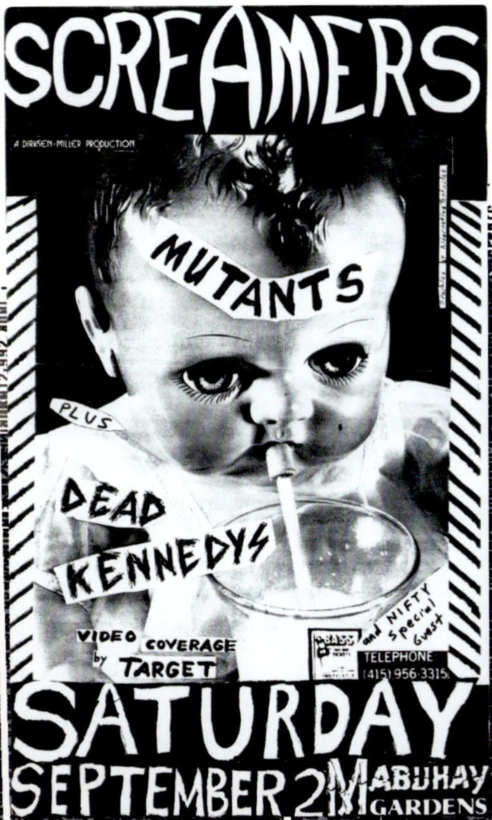

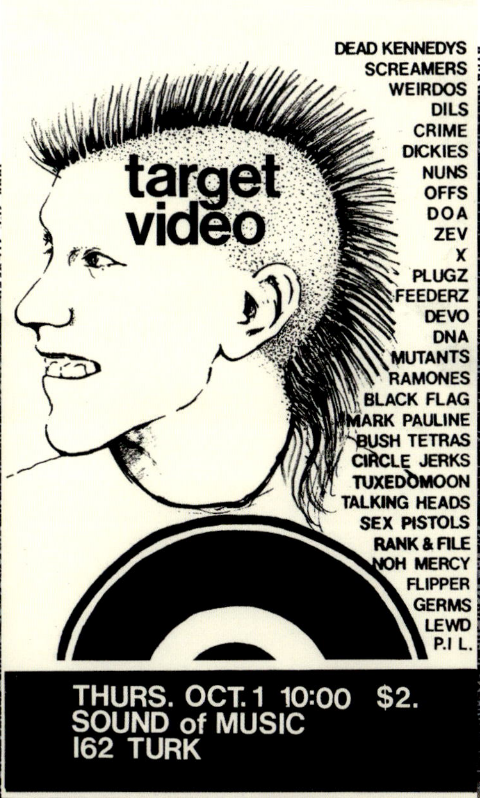

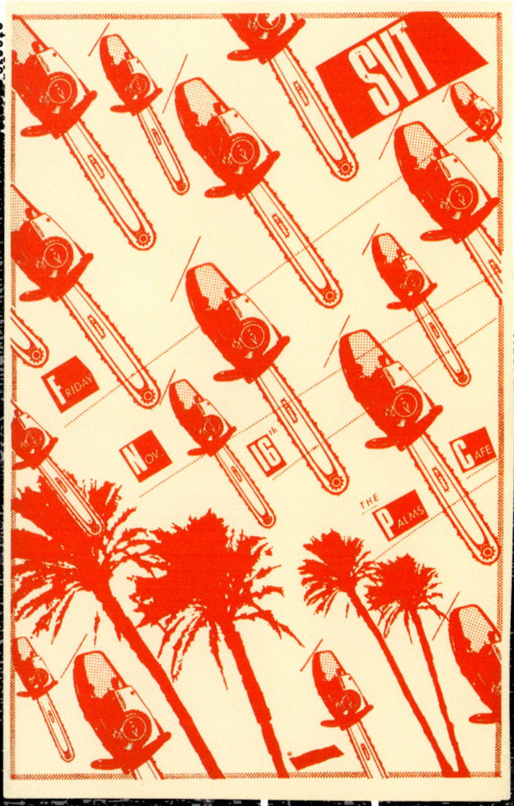

Richard Stutting

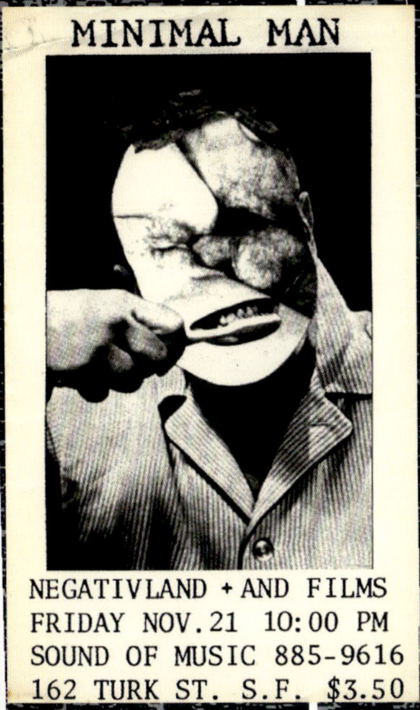

Patrick Miller

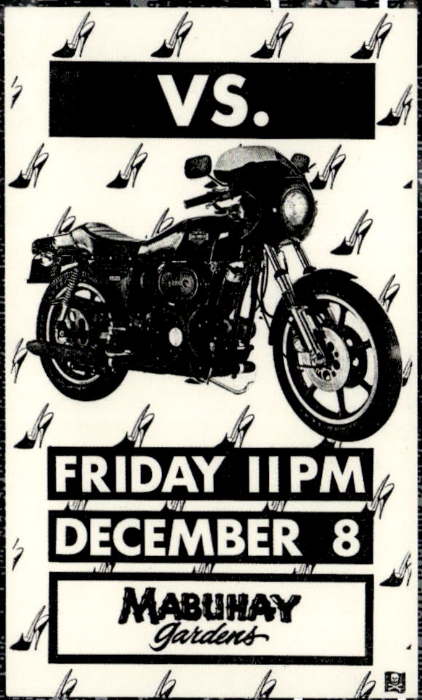

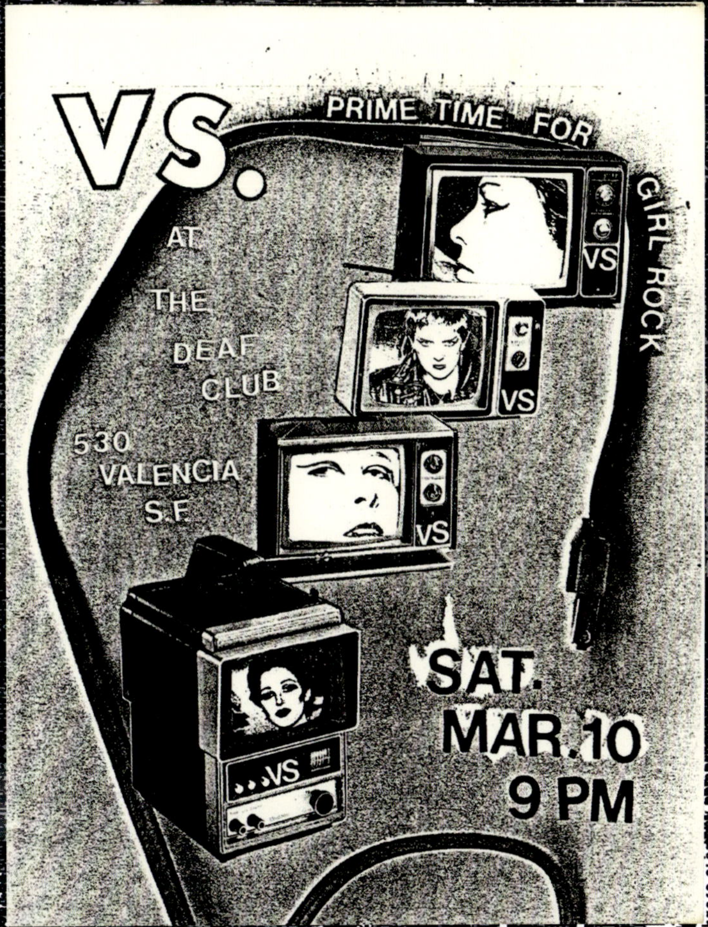

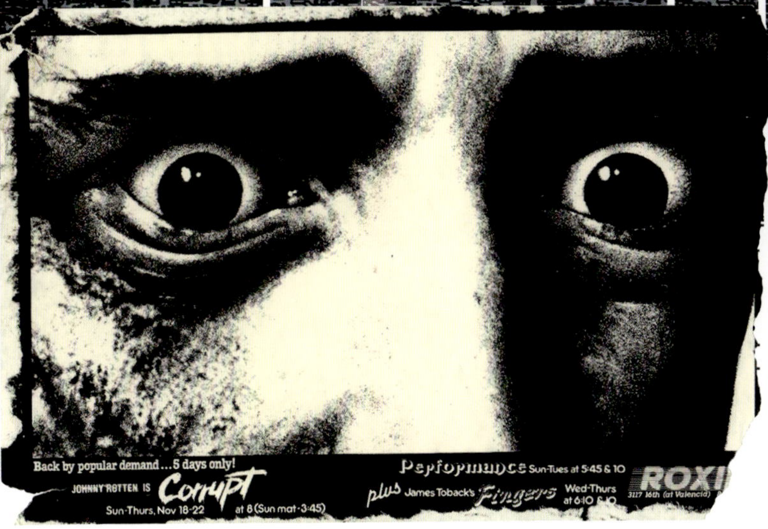

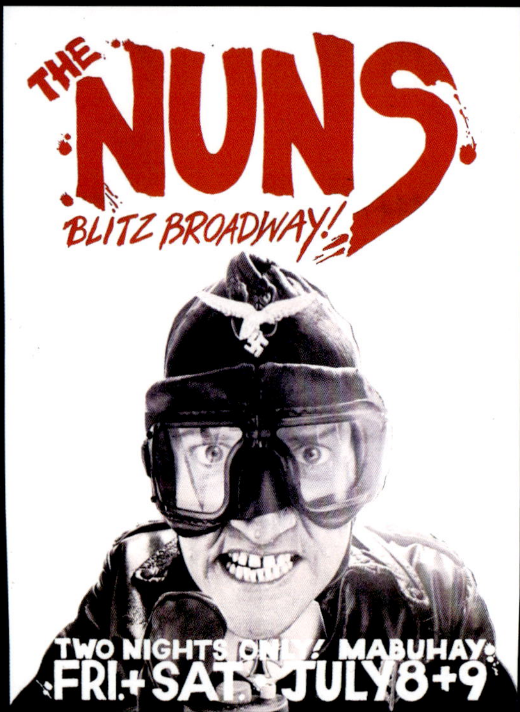

Edwin Heaven

Photo: Bartone

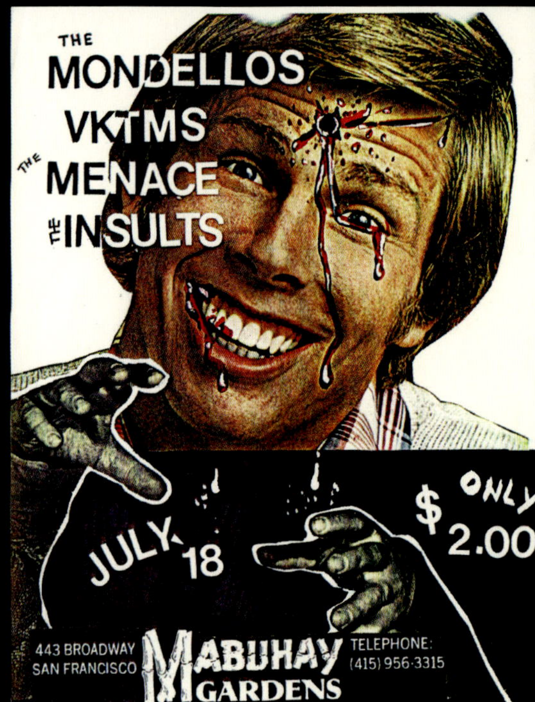

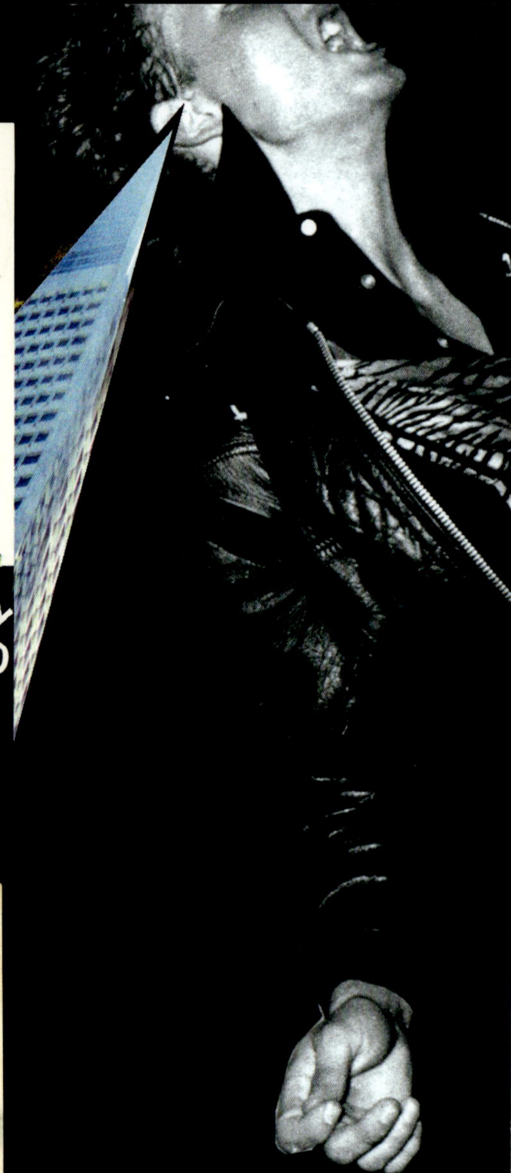

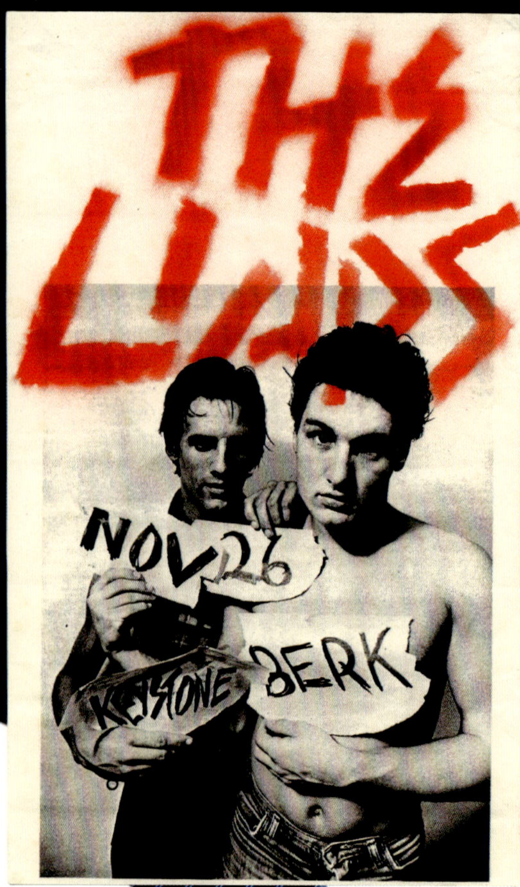

The Liars

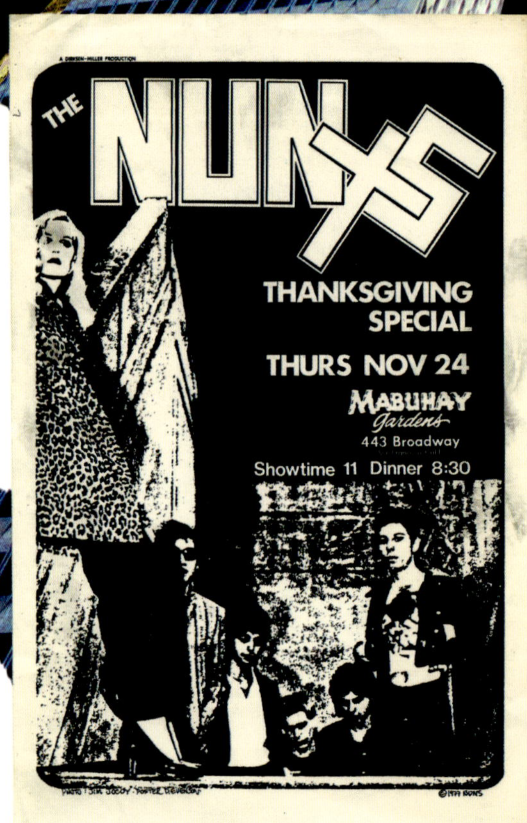

D. E[illegible]nson

Photo: Jim Jo[illegible]

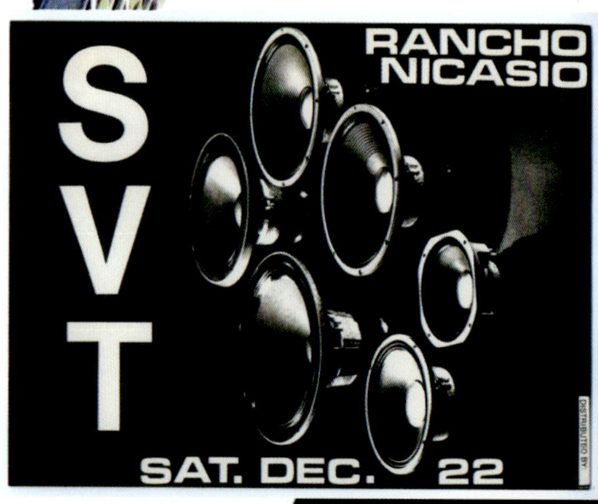

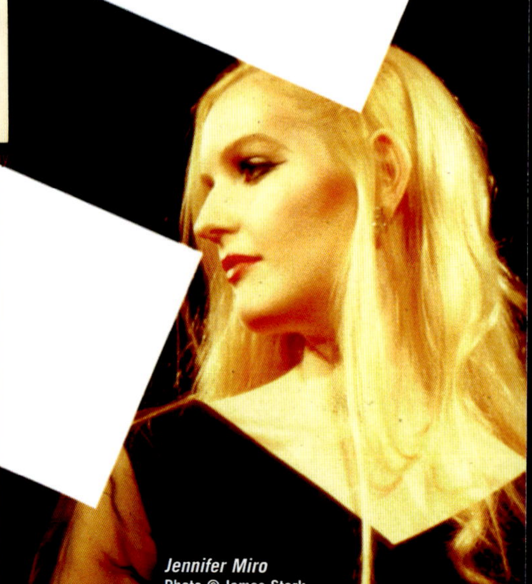

Jennifer Miro

Photo © James Stark

MY IDEA OF PUNK

PUNK HAS ALWAYS BEEN ABOUT ATTITUDE AND NOT FASHION. THATS WHAT I THINK ANYWAY. INDIPENDENT THOUGHT AND THE DESIRE TO MAKE YOUR LIFE WORK ON YOUR OWN TERMS ARE PUNK, NOT A PAIR OF DOC MARTENS AND A STUDDED LEATHER JACKET. I HAVE LONG HAIR, NOT SPIKY, AND I LISTEN TO BANDS LINKE KISS AND CHEAP TRICK BUT I ALSO LOVE G.B.H. AND THE RAMONES. MOST OF MY FREINDS FROM MY PUNK DAYS WERE SPIKY HAIRED OR SKINHEAD BUT I WAS JUST LIKE THEM IN MY THOUGHTS AND IDEALS. THATS WHY I WAS THE ONLY LONG HAIR METALHEAD IN A GANG OF PUNKS. AND IF WASN'T FOR THEM I WOULD PROBABALLY NEVER DISCOVERED MOTORHEAD UNTIL WAY LATER, I'M GRATEFUL FOR THAT. AS FAR AS MUSIC GOES PUNK ROCK HAS BEEN VERY THERAPUTIC ESPECIALLY BANDS LIKE SOCIAL DISTORTION, BAD RELIGION, CRUCIFIX, SOCIAL UNREST, DISCHARGE, EXPLOITED, ENGLISH DOGS, THE LIST IS ENDLESS. ALSO SHOWS WERE PROBALLY THE ONLY REAL THING ABOUT PUNK BEACAUSE THE PUNKS PUT THEM ON NOT SOME BIG TIME PROMOTER LIKE TODAY. 15 YEARS AGO IT WAS WAY FUCKING DIFFERENT AND NOT AS SAFE AS IT IS TODAY. I'VE SPENT 17 OF MY 30 YEARS THINKING THE PUNK IDEAL AND I WILL CONTINUE TO SEE THROUGH THE DAILY BULLSHIT THAT IS FED TO ME UNTIL THEY PLANT MY ASS IN THE FUCKING GROUND.

ROB DAPELLO
CAMPBELL, CA

It was the summer of 1983 and Social Distortion was playing my home town of Campbell, California. I had seen them the year before, around the same time of year. The Faction was playing, as well as Ribsy and Living Abortions. (I was fucked up at the time, so I don't remember much of the show.) In that calendar year I had my first Salty Dog, my first blowjob (man, I thought I was so cool), and fits of depression from thinking I had only one year left to see as many shows as possible (I had been listening to Crucifix and Discharge almost exclusively, and I was convinced that nuclear war was inevitable.)

A lot has changed since then, but I know at least one thing that hasn't: going to a show was always better than being bummed 'cuz no one likes you at school, or being upset that you don't fit in with the jocks who beat the shit out of you, or the world that your elders were in the process of shutting you out of. Better you get scabies from some punk chick you met in the city.

To this day, I think that's what attracts the most criminal-minded individuals I've ever met to Punk - It's an emotional outlet, one where you can leave your sweat out on the microphone, or your teeth on the dance floor. What a glorious place! NOW I fit in. Fuck all the cliques, and all the jaded old pricks who say "I remember when it was dangerous!" Who gives a fuck old man! Now, comb some royal crown into your hair, climb into your piece of shit car and get the fuck out! It's the new kids who get into Punk that makes it all worthwhile, that gives it a future. True inspiration comes from them collectively. It makes it Us! For the betterment of the scene, despite interference from THEM!

Who's THEM? It's different for everyone. Parents, cops, school, burnt out ex-punks, the government, whomever. THEM. That's what it's about to me. So fuck all of THEM if they don't like it...even you.

Lars Fredrickson

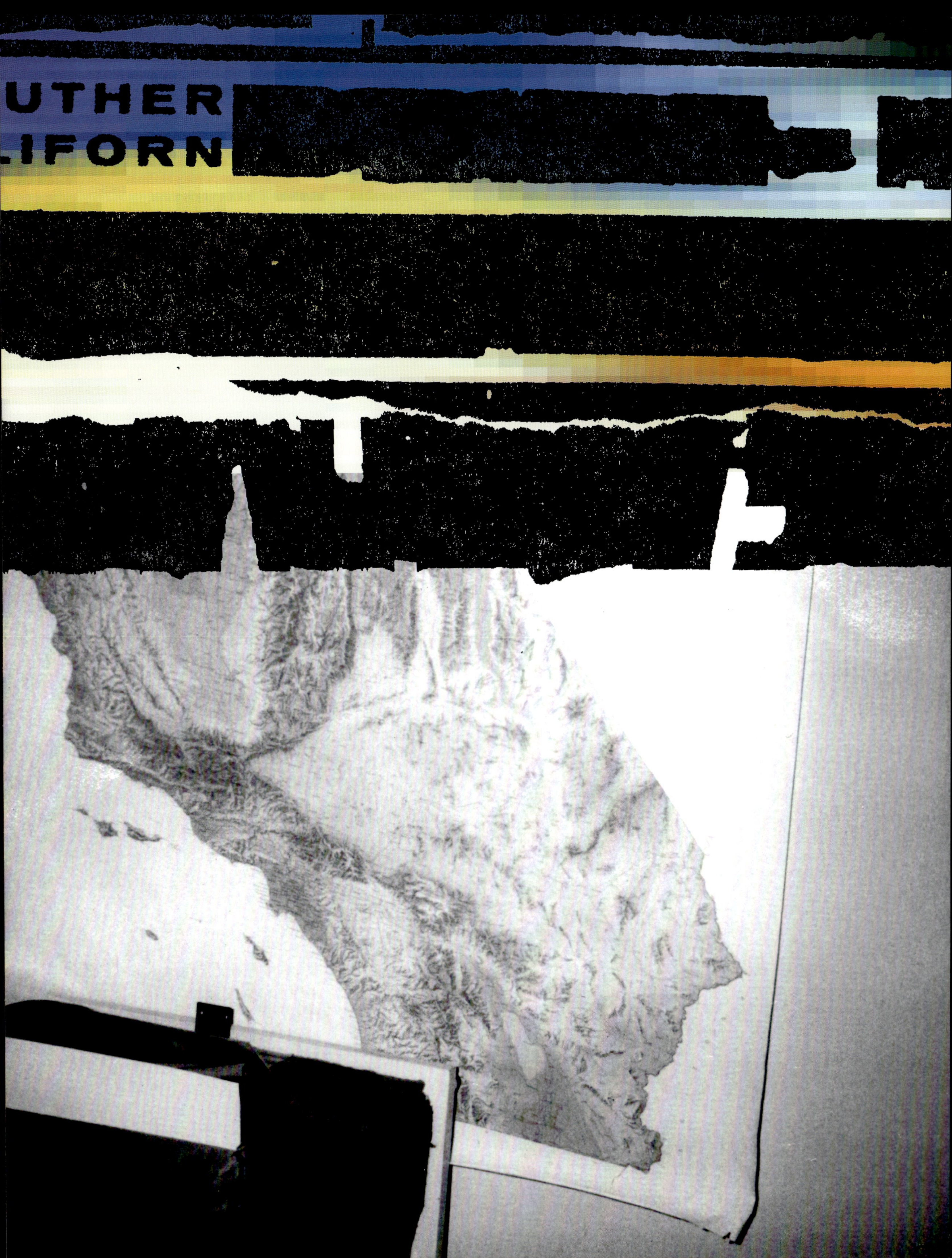
UTHER
LIFORN

Introductory Rant

By Brendan Mullen

By the time you read this, chances are it's close to the 21st century –or you're already in it – and you're an older nostalgia-seeking retro buff, a historian or a younger curio seeker wanting to examine some artifacts of dead culture from the 1900s, that classic century when young people and a variety of youth movements, one for each decade, made short-lived attempts to oppose the status quo.

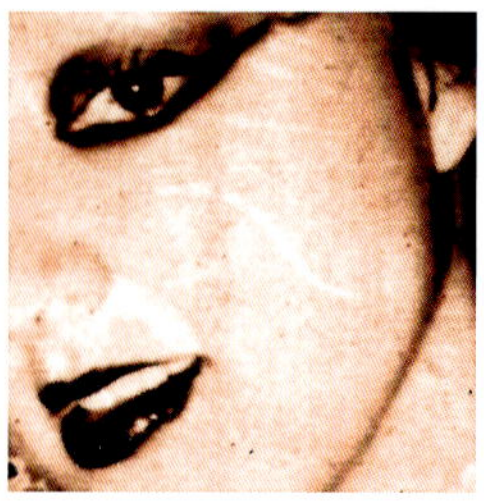

So who cares about a bunch of crummy old Punk Rock flyers from 20-plus years ago?

Fair question, and to that I respond: The invisible uncredited influence of Punk Rock is felt to the present day– whether the mainstream acknowledges it or not.

And so I maintain what you're really clutching in your paws is actual anthropological evidence that 20th century America's last pre-MTV, pre-cyber, last organically incubated and developed "oppositional youth" movement ever even existed.

You only have to look at creep-staffed ad agencies, representing international mega-conglomerate sneaker companies who appropriate and pervert punk rock slogans like *"just do it,"* not to promote self-empowerment like the original intent behind these flyers in this little book, but to sell shitloads of shabby shoes.

Back in ye olde merry 1900s, society had quaint names for youth and its culture. Cool terms like *juvenile delinquency*, *teen rebellion*, *post-adolescence* and *coming of age*.

Then there was, like, a short-lived era after World War II when young people could act and actually be, well, you know, like *young*, on their own terms, if only for a short while.

Coming-of-age was a permissible reflective time lapse and a general fuck-around period between adolescence and delving headlong into overt consumerism with higher education and naive idealism as a stop-gap.

Any such exuberant youthful dalliance during the '50s was largely demonized by our elders who originally identified it as delinquent, deviant or even *pathological*. The era which coined the term *teenager* gave a cultural collective identity to the previously invisible *us vs. them* dynamic of the '40s and even earlier: the young, the cool and the misunderstood vs the old, the stupid and the square.

By the mid-'60s, *youth culture* was eventually given a more high-falutin' moniker. The first wave of Psychedelic Flower Power was renamed *counterculture*, and, following hot on the heels of Beatlemania and Woodstock, *youth* began to be recognized on Madison Avenue as a massive mind-boggling marketing demograph in and of itself.

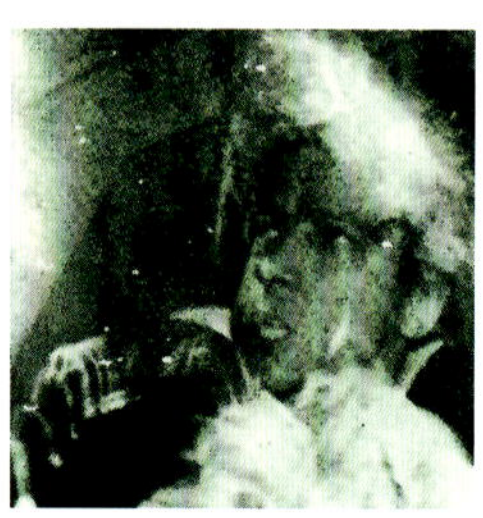

By the turn of the '60s, the original white middle class-and-up Woodstock hippies checked into psychiatric hospitals and drug rehab spas. Most of them, one way or another, straightened up and got jobs or went back to school for masters and doctorates. This was a class of kids whose parents were well-off enough to subsidize VW vans and slip junior the secret "credit cards" to finance the trips to the hash dens in Morocco and the ashrams of Tibet and India, with the intent of avoiding the Asian killing fields, where mostly blue collar and poor uneducated kids were picked off by infuriated local jungle snipers with no choice but to retaliate while their homes were being razed and their families disemboweled.

What Was Happening With Young People in the '70s And What The Hell Does That Have To Do With This Bunch Of Old Flyers?

As an especially alienated twenty-something during the '70s, it seemed to me that no one gave a toss what young people might have wanted, what we might have dreamt of, or any ideas we thought about as a collective. Our group fell between the cracks of social analysis, we were stereotyped as automatically being in cahoots with the *Me Decade* of mindless disco, cocaine, hard rock, Elton John, Fleetwood Mac, Peter Frampton, streaking and pornography-going-mainstream.

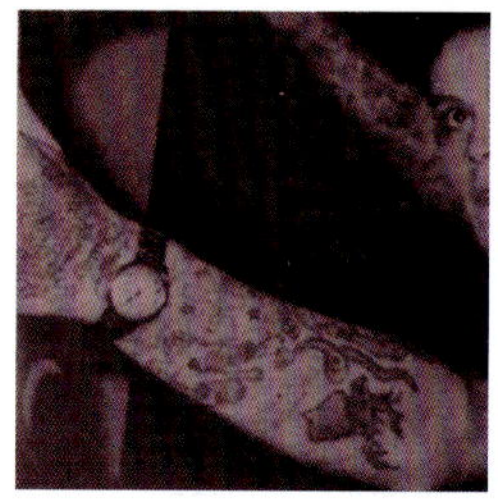

When I arrived in this country as an immigrant, the '70s media was flying sky-high from its biggest power-rush ever – Watergate – which proved QED that the newsmedia really was more powerful than the government since it had been able to take out a bent president that elected officials had refused to investigate. The down side of Watergate, of course, was that it fathered the culture of cynicism, distrust and furthered paranoia of elected officials that had begun with Vietnam. This social decline perception, especially among young people, was part of the *general malaise* theory Jimmy Carter ran down.

It also marked the dawn of the descent of mainstream news media as an independent watchdog doing its job in an allegedly free society, to a bullying scuzzy low-life hypocritical tabloid panderer by the late '90s.

Meanwhile, no one in the media or anywhere else appeared to give a rat's ass about we brats of the '70s, until social historian Dewar MacLeod, who is writing a book about Los Angeles Punk, noticed that social studies on youth seemed to jump from the '60s to the '90s.

Up to the late '90s media coverage and formal documentation was massive on the educated, more sophisticated beats, the blue-collar delinquents and the generally middle class *causeless rebel* of the '50s. The largely middle class-and-up Flower Power/Hippie era of the mid '60s had also been studied, researched and analyzed to death, with a gazillion coming-of-age big budget movies about that era.

Throughout the '70s the intellectual contingent of 'Nam-era boomers were now settling into careers in academic institutions whose entire focus was on debate and analysis of the '50s and especially the '60s, when youth culture - their culture - briefly became a movement to persuade Uncle Sam's army to refrain from the systematic mass murder of villagers and mostly unarmed peasants whose only crime was trying to survive through a different system of agriculture.

Prolonged Adolescence & Obsessive Credentialism

Meanwhile the new young people who missed the draft and came of age at the turn of the '70s remained invisible on the national cultural landscape. They were mostly stuck in schools because of the prevailing ideology among our elders about *obsessive credentialism*, so during the '70s young people were kept in school and out of the workplace.

Formal education had by now become a blind and meaningless exercise and not the all-access laminate pass to the Made-In-The-Shade good life that a college degree - any old college degree (it didn't matter,) was supposed grant you. College graduates were now accepting jobs previously held by less educated workers. As much as 10% of the young work force were overqualified for jobs in the '60s, and that figure rose to 25% in the '70s. High schools and colleges were fast becoming nothing more than places to harbor the surplus population in order to keep unemployment figures artificially low.

Too Young For Baby Boomerdom, Way Too Old For Gen X, And What About These Flyers?

So what about these handbills and posters... and what about those of us who fell between the cracks– slightly younger than the classic post-World War II boomers and born too early to be saddled with the dreaded **Gen X** tag?

I'll get back to the flyers in a minute, I promise, after I beg the question, *Where were we* **in-betweenies** *in the equation?* Those of us who were in our mid-to-late teens when the Flower Power era exploded, those of us who definitely took part in it – the loud music, travel, the rad politics, promiscuous sex and hallucinogenic drugs – but were too young to understand it properly. The real cool freaks always seemed to be older, and hey, they had longer hair and knew things our parents didn't. Some of our peers only saw it on TV or watched their older sibs, a few of us actually did drop out all the way.

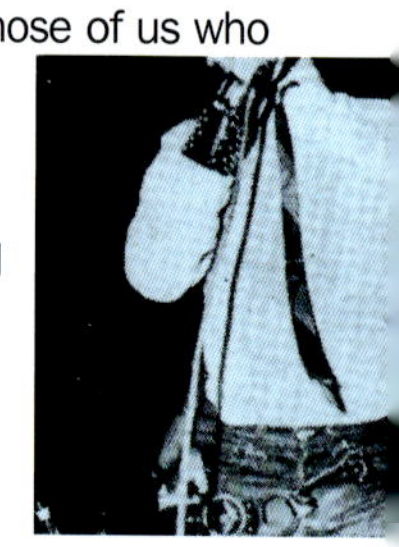

By the time mass media decided to focus on youth again in the late '80s, we were too old to be considered Gen X. One of its very own peers came up with that silly name tag for a generation that would consequently be ruthlessly dehumanized and robbed of its youth before most of them could even enjoy it.

Basically, all the Gen X ruckus was created by a few overeducated white kids with too much time who panicked and became hostile after some bright spark predicted the eventual bankruptcy of the Social Security System, thanks not to the socially retarded fiscal antics of the U.S. government, but– get this– to the children of the '60s! *Us! As if...Nevermind...Not Even...* to coin a few *au courant* catch-phrases. ...*Whatever.*

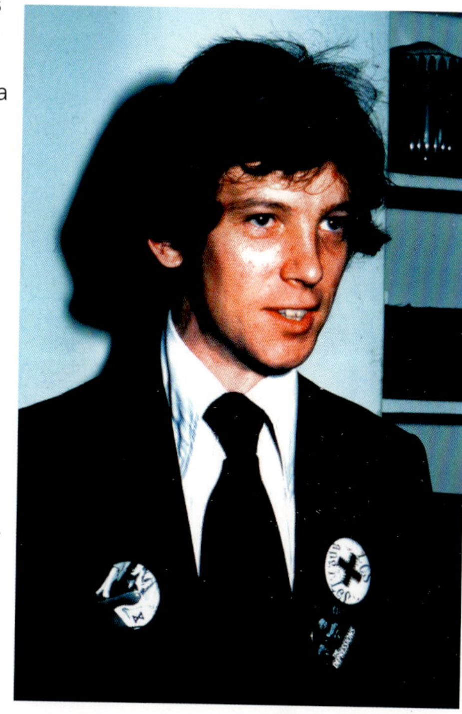

Brendan Mullen Photo © Jenny Lens

Other so-called Gen Xers simply pissed and moaned on the Internet about being left out. After spending a whole four to six years of their entire long lives in some stupid college, the degree meant jack-shit in the real world unless it was in computer science.

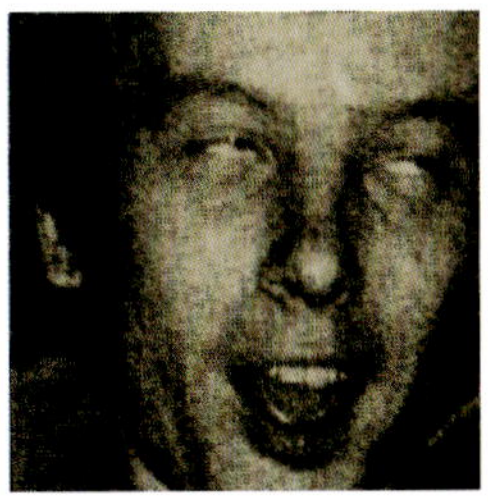

Of course, this upstart Gen X group hogged all the media space with their versions of the social malaises and complaints most of the '70s punkers originally bitched about, so our beloved little Punk Rock insurrection- represented by these crude, sometimes handwritten flyers, got pushed even deeper down into the cracks of obscurity, relegated to asterisk-footnote status by the new Gen X kids who eventually came to be immortalized as the generation of pouting crybabies.

The more self-aware Gen Xers snivelled, unknowingly, about a lot of the same political issues which these flyers were originally created to oppose or address while helplessly watching themselves reduced to a collective identity representing nothing more than the largest, most faceless LCD demograph since the onset of the Gutenberg Galaxy. It was all they could do, I suppose. By millenium's end, however, Gen X blubbering gradually subsided as this generation gave up the ghost, and, with no other choice aside from armed terrorism, cooperated all the way with the meltdown fusion of youth culture and mass media. Monopoly capitalism had won. Now there was nothing else. Besides, this generation had now become stuck with house and car payments, families and the same old bourgeoise shit they had originally accused the Boomers of copping out to.

So What Did Gen-X Actually Accomplish During Its "Golden Period?"

For a short while there during the early '90s a harmlessly fun '70s hard rock revival dressed up in LA punk fashions, modified for cold weather with an originally L.A hardcore punk attitude represented by– yup, you got it, ***these damned flyers,*** flared up in the city of Seattle. But the fun didn't last too long when the most prominent participants of the Seattle scene quickly opted to work in close collusion with MTV and the market share expansionist programs of David Geffen and a Euro-owned multinational megacorp, and so Seattle's garage/backyard barbeque/club scene became another major Madison Avenue and Wall Street coup, until it's two main icons woke up and committed suicide.

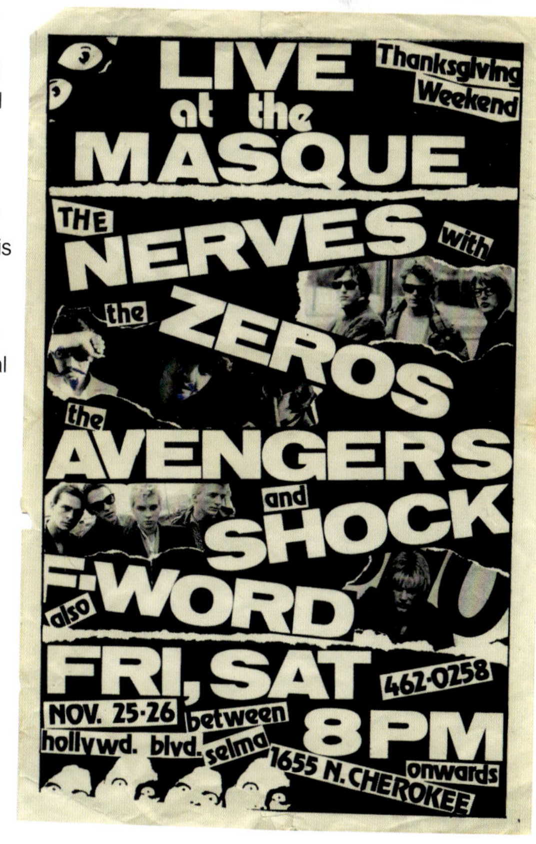

Paul Lesperance

One of these two icons shot its face off while the other shot its foot off by opting not to tour in huge venues controlled by corporate monopoly capitalist interests at a time when Seattle was at the peak of its commercial momentum. Not a single other major rock act who could have made a difference supported this stand, and the second icon, of course, lost.

Concurrently with the Seattle fiasco, other newly grooving young people went down the Euro path of tripping out on designer hallucinogenics, sucking on baby pacifiers and twirling luminous neon toys in open fields in the middle of the night to the special software sound of preprogrammed machines and digital tapes.

Another splinter group, the *Nouveau Bohemia,* quickly evolved from beaten-down cheap rent storefronts with espresso machines, open mikes and bad art, into franchise chains of smoke-free coffee shops with corporate poetry readings and "tie-in" promotional-spoken-word-readings-in-the-back-room with Hank "Ironman" Rollins, the latter day Kerouac of their dreams.

Probably the most vital and fabulous of all, the ascent of hip-hop to the mainstream, fully bankrolled and encouraged by major corporate interests, quickly neutered out. Stupidly, quickly and willingly, hip-hop morphed into narrow-minded narcissism, conspicuously excessive consumerism, female-bashing and gun-glamour, although the Native Tongues posse and other "non-playa" poor righteous b-boy affiliates created a kind of peacenik hip-hop movement which boldly maintained, if only barely. Meanwhile, "da playaz" skool of hip-hop lamely cussed over the top of electronically created drum loops bagged from their parents record collections and furiously waved their hands and fingers in excruciatingly embarrassing video clips. Nevertheless, they pulled off the ultimate scam: young black entrepreneurs fronting for the same white corporate creeps in joint venture pacts that sold untold millions of records to suburban white kids, who believed they were buying the ultimate incorrect get-back against their baby boomer parents.

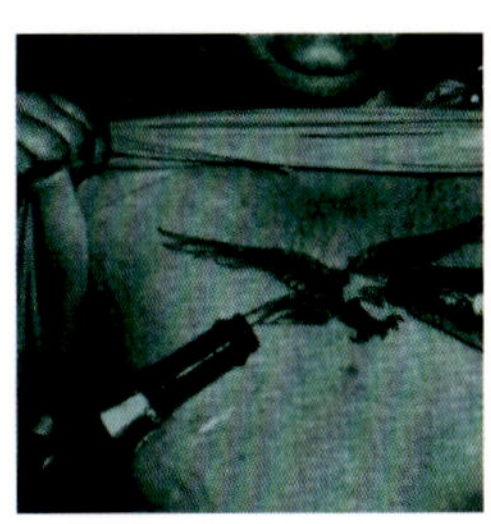

But it was an armed revolution of sorts anyway, in that it put guns in kids' hands, although there was no cohesive revolutionary ideology behind this call to arms. Barely knowing what to do with the weapons once they got their mitts on them, the kids, especially those living in blighted big city areas, turned inwards in frustration, and very conveniently for the status quo, they smoked each other. There was an alarmingly high statistical rate of kids from affluent ghettos who whacked their parents and a couple armed with serious automatic assault weapons even sprayed their campuses in rural high schools.

City of Los Angeles
FIRE DEPARTMENT

FIRE/LIFE SAFETY VIOLATION

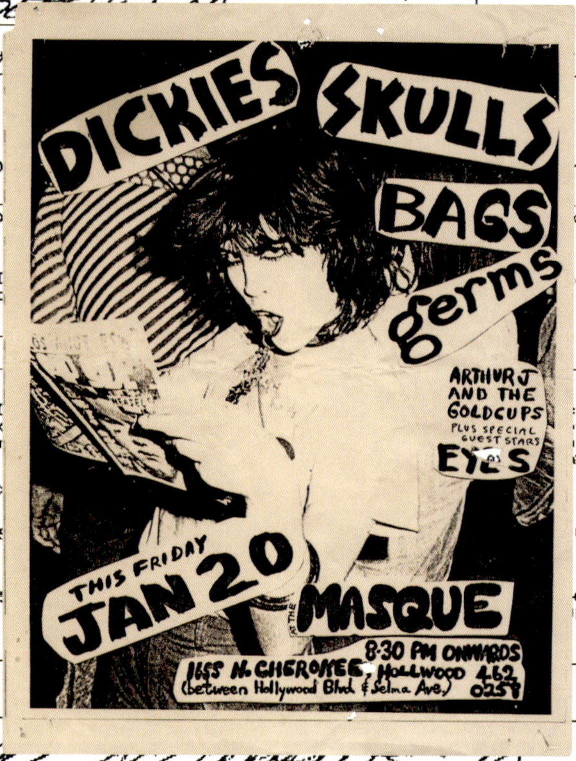

The Flipside benefit which never happened thanks to the Los Angeles Fire Dept.

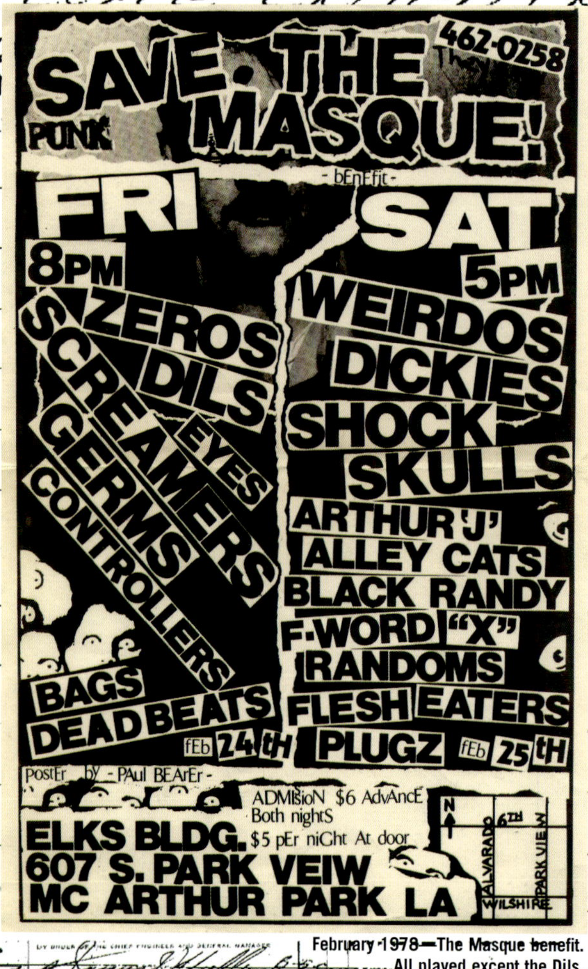

Paul Lesperance

February 1978—The Masque benefit. All played except the Dils.

Rage against the machine was limply diffused to *Rage Against Polygram,* a creepy patriarchal multinational mega conglomerate owned at the time (pre-Edgar Bronfman Jr.) by some old U-Boat commandants from World War II. These guys invested big-time in '90s American youth rage, with the given of allowing the kiddies a few bratty outbursts. It was now an era wherein hip, informed executives made budgetary allowances for "shocking" behavior and drug rehab time for artists...all in a day's work for maintenance of market share indexes and profit disbursements to their grubby little shareholders in the grand old global pyramid scheme of easy money for the planet's utterly useless.

Meanwhile, the current youth energy for self-definition appears largely dedicated, without irony, to absolute passive compliance with the dictates of mass media, especially advertising and marketing. Some of the hipper ones believed for a short while they were above it because they were adopting way-cool *post modern irony.*

This smirking ironic pose, which began in the late '80s, and (thank God,) appeared to reach its peak during the late '90s, was a stance of wholeheartedly embracing mass media and marketing while appearing to be distant and oppositional, 'cos you were *so coolly ironic.* Cool irony or whatever, was never anything less than total surrender, whichever way you looked at it or whatever semantics you used to disguise it. Generation X kow-towed and followed the same cop-out as the Baby Boomers they had originally ridiculed and decried.

Clutching for straws in a desperate search for some sort of self-definition, some late 90s kids embraced retro nostalgia and recycled the entire back catalog of Americana, from White Trash Tattoo Culture to Cheesy '70s Disco, Kitsch Exotica, '50s Cocktail Muzak, New Swing and early '80s pre-Techno Electro Pop, only to see everything morphed into Gap commercials overnight. The rest of the '90s kids were either asleep or couldn't figure it out and with no irony whatsoever simply bought everything outright as-is.

Sadly, by century's end the ultimate cool agenda was the hip-hop inspired *getting-paid-no-matter-what-it-takes* ideology, meaning the more quickly you sold out the cooler you became. Thus finalizing in one awesome swoop the Sweet Revenge Against The Boomers and their little youth ideology, and making the hedonistic '70s Me Decade look like a Good Samaritan movement.

Once again, the smarter kids gamely tried to convince themselves it was otherwise. They decided they were in the age of *cool collage* via their cool magazines with impossibly scrambled cool graphics and cool unreadable fonts. Buying into Beastie Boy fraudulence backed by amazing marketing savvy showed that you were down and understood irony and where it was at with *cut-and-paste collage* and the recycling of junk culture.

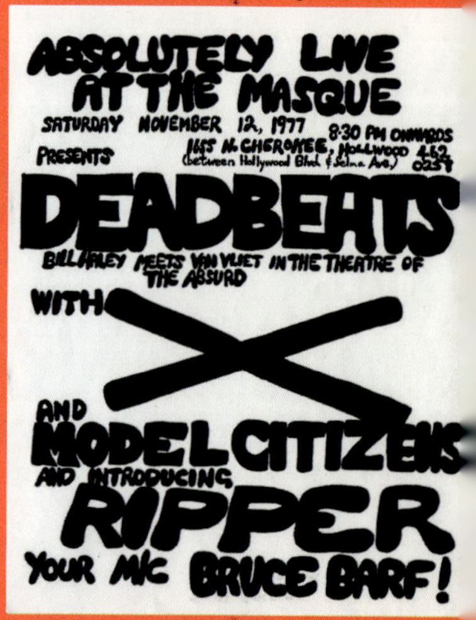

So Middle and Upper Class-Cool-AlternaSlacker-Whatever Irony really didn't count for jack in the real world, after all. (Any more than previous youthful dalliances had).

Even this wonderful tome you hold in your hands is available thanks to the ingenuity of Gingko and its distribution/marketing savvy in being able to get it into big corporate chains so that you can study its contents and proclaim yourself to have been there, done that, and now you're sending off the coupon inside for the t-shirt.

Masterpieces of primitive graphic design or scruffy naive folk art? Whatever. You decide, but whichever way you look at it, these flyers tell the story of the ascent of the Anybody-Just-Do-It culture of the late '70s. Groups of outlaw artists and other misfits fused their energy and muses with the original punk movement, and, in turn, created the impetus for the gradual penetration of the suburbs during the '80s, of American Hardcore, punk rock's truly ugly, angry little brother who grew up to be a real mother for ya. As Black Flag conceptualist and SST proprietor Greg Ginn might say, "You bet [the people who made these flyers] we've got something against you..."

So here it is folks, evidence that this last gasp, the Alamo of free-thinking, self-empowered American Youth actually ever existed. Here's sparse documentation that the invisible foot soldiers who fought *Cultural World War II* ever lived, the ones who went over the top first and fucking well *died hard.*

Now you have something to hold onto in the face of the terrifyingly hip wise-assed Bright Young Thing who might chirp up with something moronic like "Is there actually any need for anything other than mass culture? What did any alternative to it ever do? What would any alternative to it do now?" Or..."what's the point of wasting time with resistance when you're gonna lose anyway..."

And you respond, *Dickhead,* now you really have no name and no face. Ha-Ha. Enjoy it. And by the way, go fuck yourself and buy my book, *Nightmare In Punk Alley,* so I can get paid too, you punk rockin' muthafuckaz.

Brendan Mullen Los Angeles, 1999

Note: Some ideas in this piece were inspired by a thesis researched and written by punk social historian Dewar MacLeod

What exactly is THE WEIRDO'S SOUND?

Man with greater electronic reliability and now conveniently powered. . . . Superior noise . . . Incredible range . . . Flawless attack and sustain. tonal characteristics have enticed great-looking chassis as the devices, generates a sound to a pure deep organ fluttering performance and widely flexible delay, repeat, blending, alternately or simultaneously . . . Gleaming satin chrome razor sharp bite of screeching strings are whipped instead of plucked. The sweet violin-like gain-boost/overdrive up, as well as a hint of harmonic distortion. The cardioid pickup pattern feedback with rich sustaining sound power together in lightning fast runs . . . thereby enabling the playing of amazingly the full spectrum of sound in any proportion combined. The "ready-to-go" won't settle for less than the best! It is flat-top guitar rock feedback extremely unidirectional instantly — anywhere! . . . noise changes rate at which effect occurs. with superior wind, "pop," and built-in magnetic control allows breath noise suppression. Super wide range response, higher output level before feedback. True feature: a balanced tone quality and no losses while bending strings. Through manipulation of the controls, foot pedals of an electric round-hole "Hot" chord church pipe organ a complex matrix of fine comb filters that gently sweep the sound spectrum without loosening the rugged stage sound A high performance version of the variable depth chorus/vibrato, high volume and concert work. The unit has been completely redesigned Wired in parallel via an on/off magnetical flux over the entire field. Vacuum-injection sealing yields a higher lubricating precision with a switch which produces standard swoosh phase shifted mode The switch can be used for switching non-slip rubber lubrication ratio self-locking, slide signal-to-noise remarkably smooth screw adjustment into the soundhole with a heavy penetration of the hex wrench and many other humbuckers without modifications. And the result is rhythm AND tempo ranging from involuted overtones. terrific lines to slashing thin chops can be instantaneously and sensitively controlled through the player's use of attack and decay dynamics from the lightest touch to the heaviest clobber.

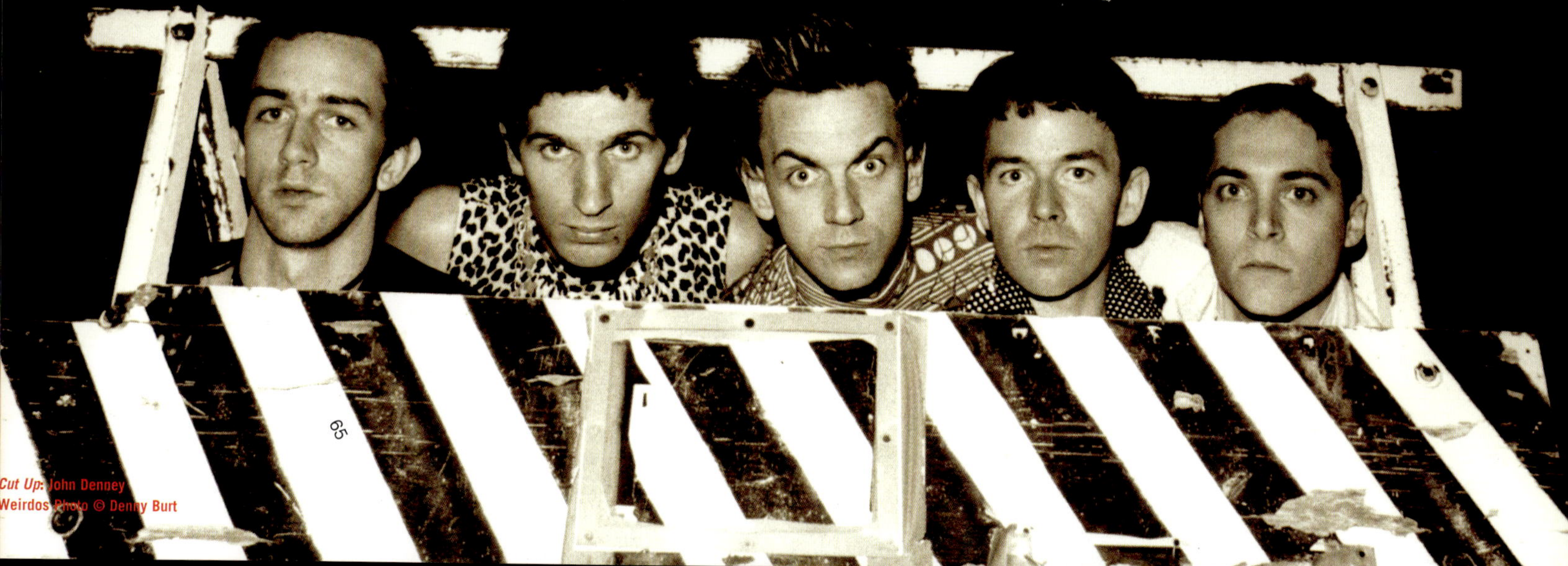

Cut Up: John Denney
Weirdos Photo © Denny Burt

Weirdoism by John Denney

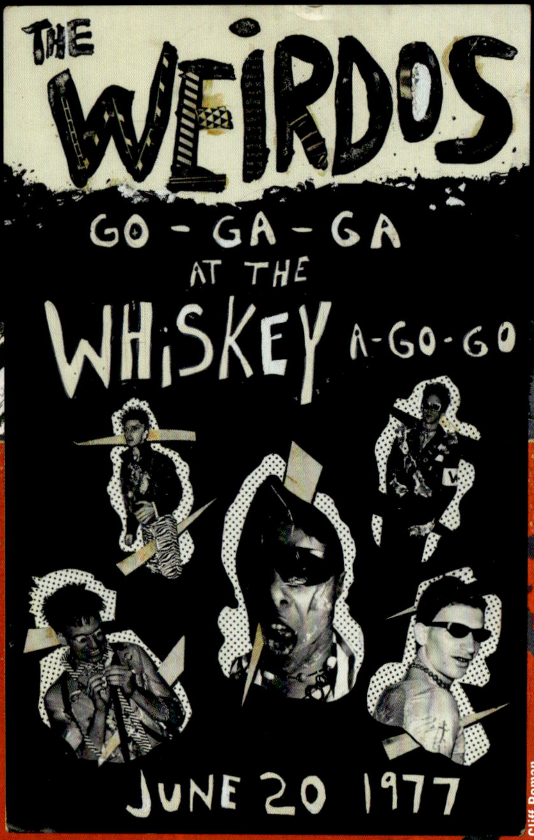

Cliff Roman

From 1977 until 1981, The Weirdos were a do-it-yourself operation from top to bottom. Not only did we write and arrange our music and lyrics, we ripped up and reassembled our clothing, cut our own hair, and designed all our logos, bumperstickers, t-shirts, record sleeves and flyers ourselves, not to mention forming the crew that flyered every telephone pole from here to Timbuktu, all done in the purest expression of Weirdoism.

We're all quite proud of being recognized as one of America's first Punk Rock bands: truth be told, we were a little apprehensive about that label at first. To us, Punk Rock was what was happening in London (Pistols, Clash, Damned, etc.) We distanced ourselves by proclaiming that we weren't punks, we were *weirdos from Hollywood!* We hoped our music reflected this - we thought the best way to be different was simply to be contrary. Irony was our form of rebellion– we adorned ourselves with happy faces, peace signs, plastic flowers and assorted doo-dads– accessories that were decidedly un-punk. But in July of 1977, Time Magazine printed a photo of the Weirdos as part of a Punk Rock feature story, so we relented and accepted the ***L.A. Punk Band*** classification. So much for artistic integrity.

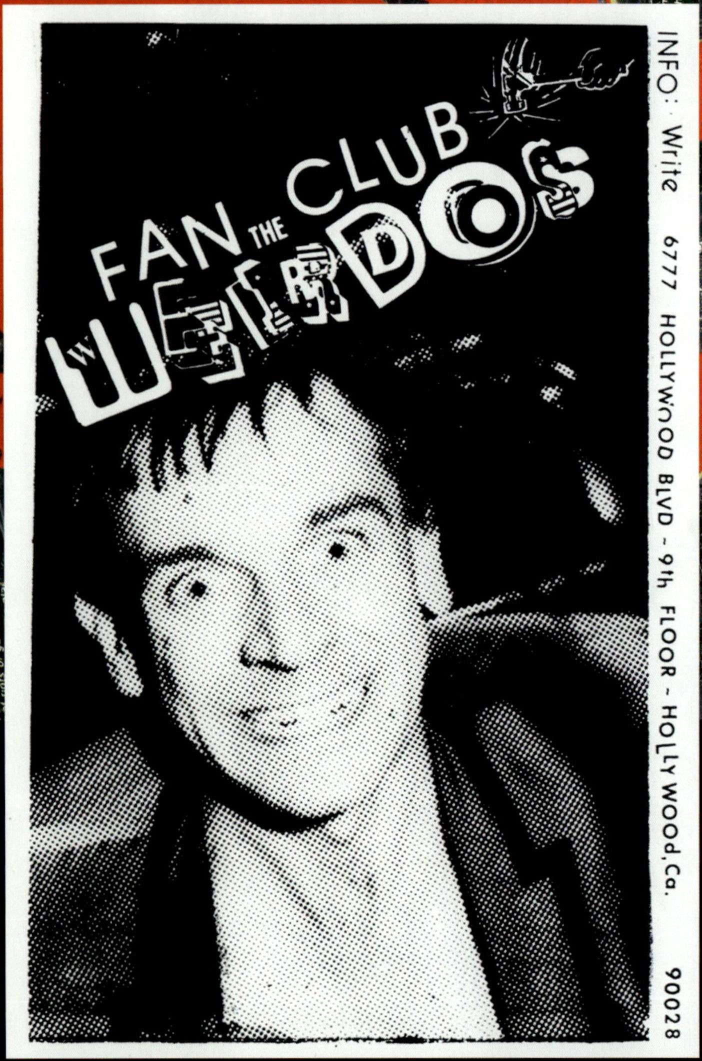

Cliff Roman

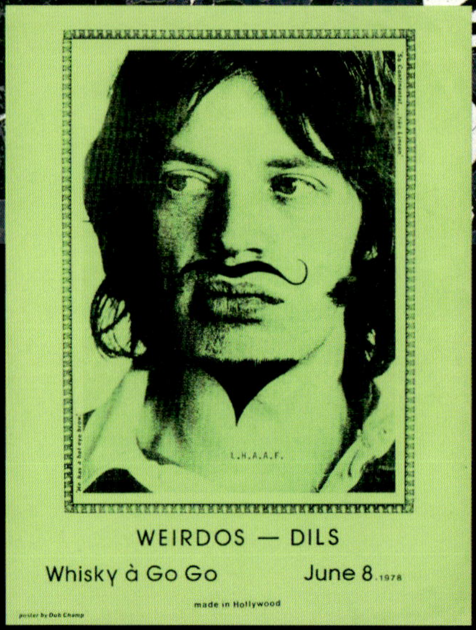

Cliff Roman

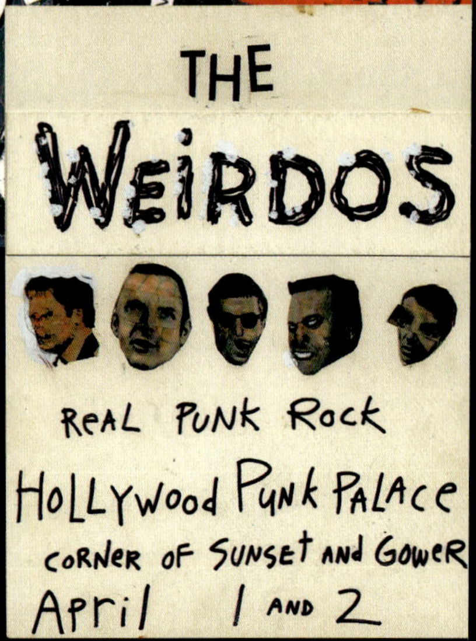

Cliff Roman

The Weirdos had their beginnings way back in 1971, when I met Cliff Roman in an art class at North Hollywood High School (art being one of the few classes I attended with any regularity.) Cliff and I became good friends, our comraderie centered on discussing art, music, girls, and all things weird. We experimented with music, even going so far as to call ourselves a band, which no one who knew us well took too seriously. Our imaginary band went by an assortment of names, including *Los Lords, The Razorblades,* and *Scab Country.* We adopted pseudonyms, Cliff calling himself *Young Metal*, I was *Revlon DiDi*, and our other cohort Steve Welborn went by the name *Bitch Cracker.*

We took trips, created artwork, engaged in sophomoric yet spirited conversations about art and the meaning of life. We fancied ourselves as some sort of new neo-Dada Beatniks, replete with short cropped Mod-like haircuts and kooky sunglasses. Besides our reverence for Duchamp and Man Ray, we explored music with equal vigor. We soaked up everything from Stockhausen, John Cage, Louis Armstrong and Miles Davis, to Rockabilly, Surf music and Captain Beefheart. We went to shows, including witnessing Iggy and The Stooges at the Whiskey A-Go-Go in 1973. At one point Iggy made his customary leap into the crowd, and we were face to face with him. Cliff seized the moment by pulling out a red marking pen and swiped a large red "X" on Iggy's bare chest. Iggy didn't even flinch, continuing the rest of the show with Cliff's "X" on his chest. A brilliant piece of art, I thought.

Soon, Cliff went to Cal Arts, and I went to the beach. Cliff met a fellow student by the name of Dave Trout, who shared many of Cliff's interests and opinions with respect to art and its presentation. This resulted in their collaboration on several art projects.

(Continues on Page 68)

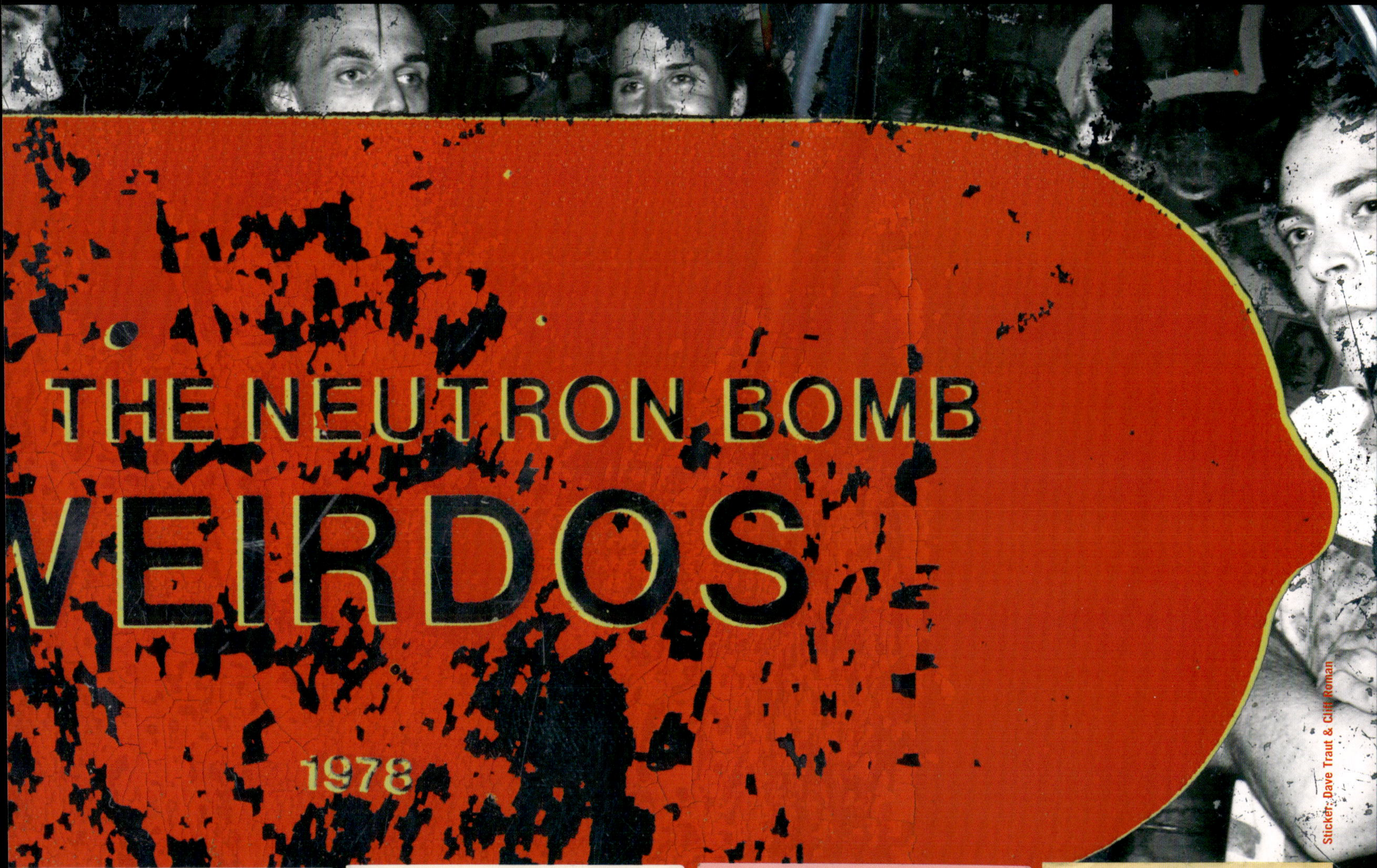

Sticker: Dave Traut & Cliff Roman

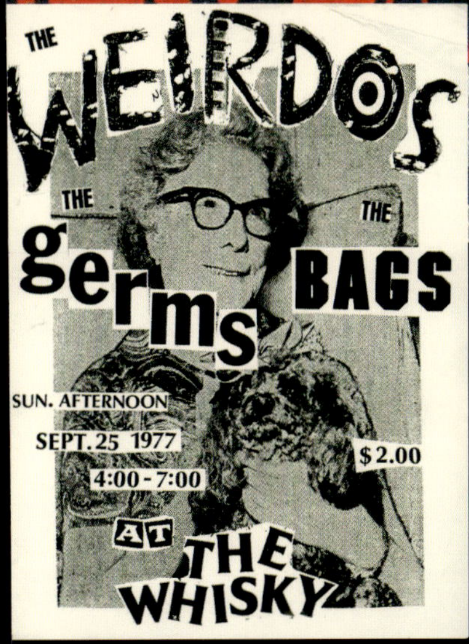

Denney

Darby cuts his foot wide open...

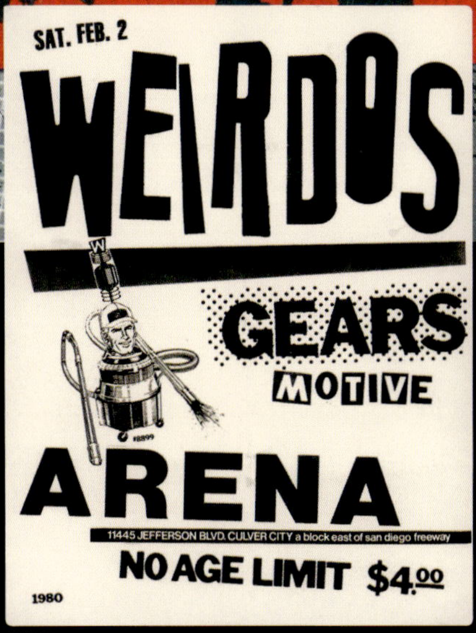

Cliff Roman

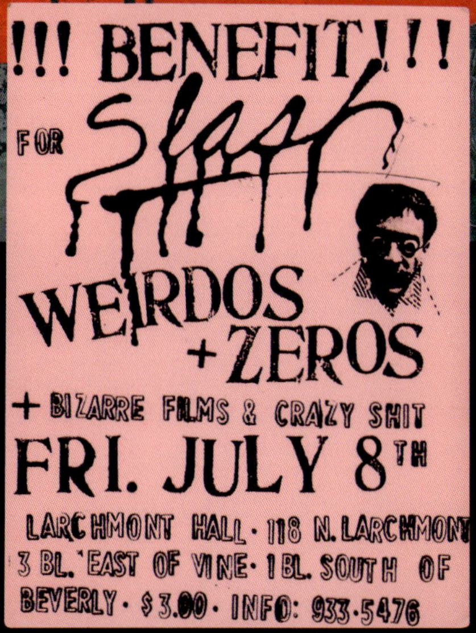

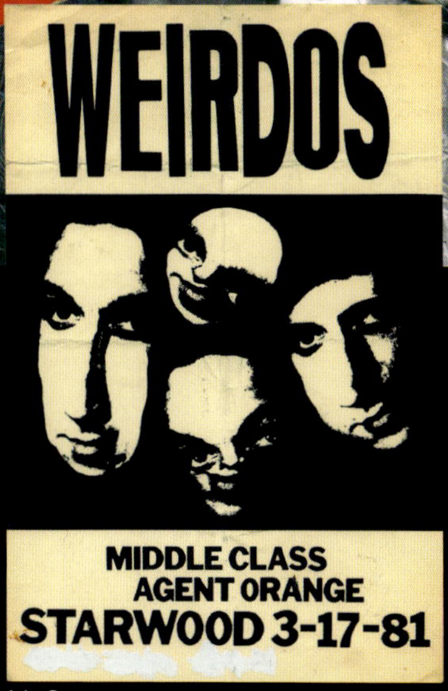

John Denney

At the time, Performance Art was emerging as a movement at Cal Arts, and the art world in general. In that atmosphere, they had the idea of starting a rock band as performance art– and the potential for fun seemed boundless.

At the same time, my younger brother Dix was taking a course in sound engineering, as well as surfing and playing guitar in a garage band. I was studying acting (or acting like I was studying acting). The timing was great. Cliff and Dave wanted my brother and I to form a band with them. A few jams later, the Weirdos were born, in December 1976.

In March of 1977, while rehearsing at a Hollywood studio, we were approached by Peter Case and his band at the time, *The Nerves*. They asked if we wanted to play a gig on April 2nd. Despite having no drummer, we couldn't refuse. We performed drummerless for three shows, until our MC, Phast Phreddie, hooked us up with a wild young guy named Nickey Beat. After one rehearsal we asked him to join the band, with the condition that he cut his long hair. Two minutes later he began burning it off, until we stopped him (due to the stench) and assured him that scissors would do the job just fine. As Nickey would tell you, the rest is history.

Later that month, *The Damned* came from London to LA (the first British punk band to do so) and when they came to check out our show at the Orpheum, Captain Sensible jammed with us on a bombastic version of *Pushin' Too Hard*. By summer we were headlining the fabled Whiskey and had generated a rabid following, which Kickboy Face of *Slash* magazine called "Weirdomania."

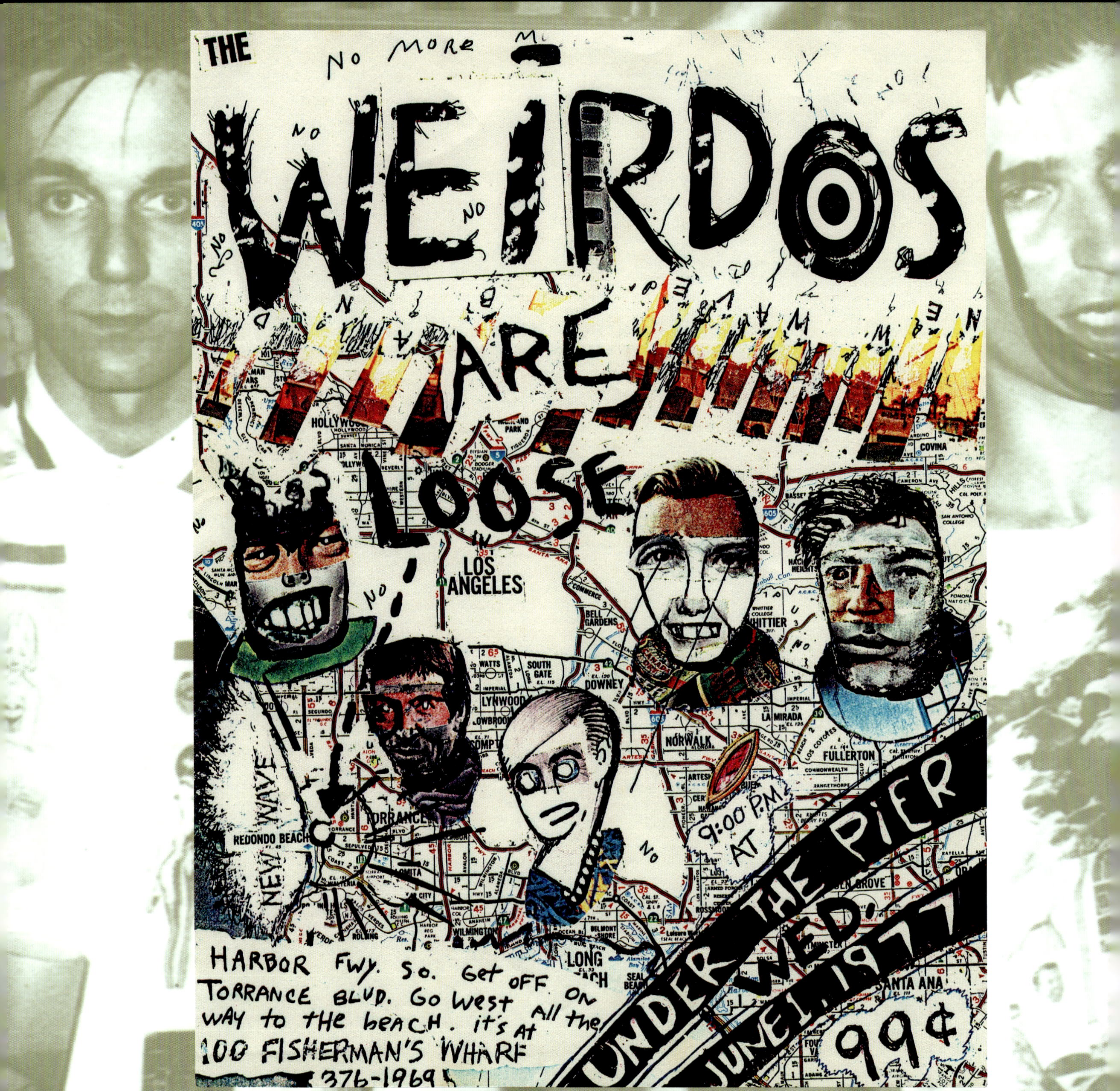

Cliff Roman

Other locals like *The Dils*, *The Screamers* and the *Germs* began making noise of their own. Shortly thereafter, Brendan Mullen opened the Masque, a basement club in an alley off Hollywood Boulevard. By that fall, Hollywood had an indigenous Punk scene, and a wild one at that. There was a slew of terrific bands, most notably *The Skulls, The Controllers, Arthur J and The Gold Cups, The Eyes, The Alleycats, The Deadbeats, Black Randy and The Metro Squad, The Zeros, The Dickies, the Go-Gos,* and *X.*

Around this time, a band from Ohio called *Devo* came to town and cleverly volunteered their services by opening up for the Weirdos on a number of occasions, which they parlayed into a record deal with Warner Brothers. *Bravo!*

My last acknowledgement: Musically speaking, the Weirdos were a speeded-up Rock and Roll hybrid, equal parts Stones, Faces, Who, Stooges and New York Dolls. But without a doubt, the main catalyst in the development of the Weirdos was the release of the Ramones' first album. That's what pushed us over the edge. See kids, we even respect our elders.

Over time, as our musicianship improved, the wacky trappings of our get-ups began to fall by the wayside, much to the chagrin of our early hardcore following. As we broadened our audience beyond the borders of Los Angeles county, we continued to refine and redefine the band. We embraced change as an essential aspect of The Weirdos ethos. Ultimately, this growth and change meant going our own ways, but those were great days!

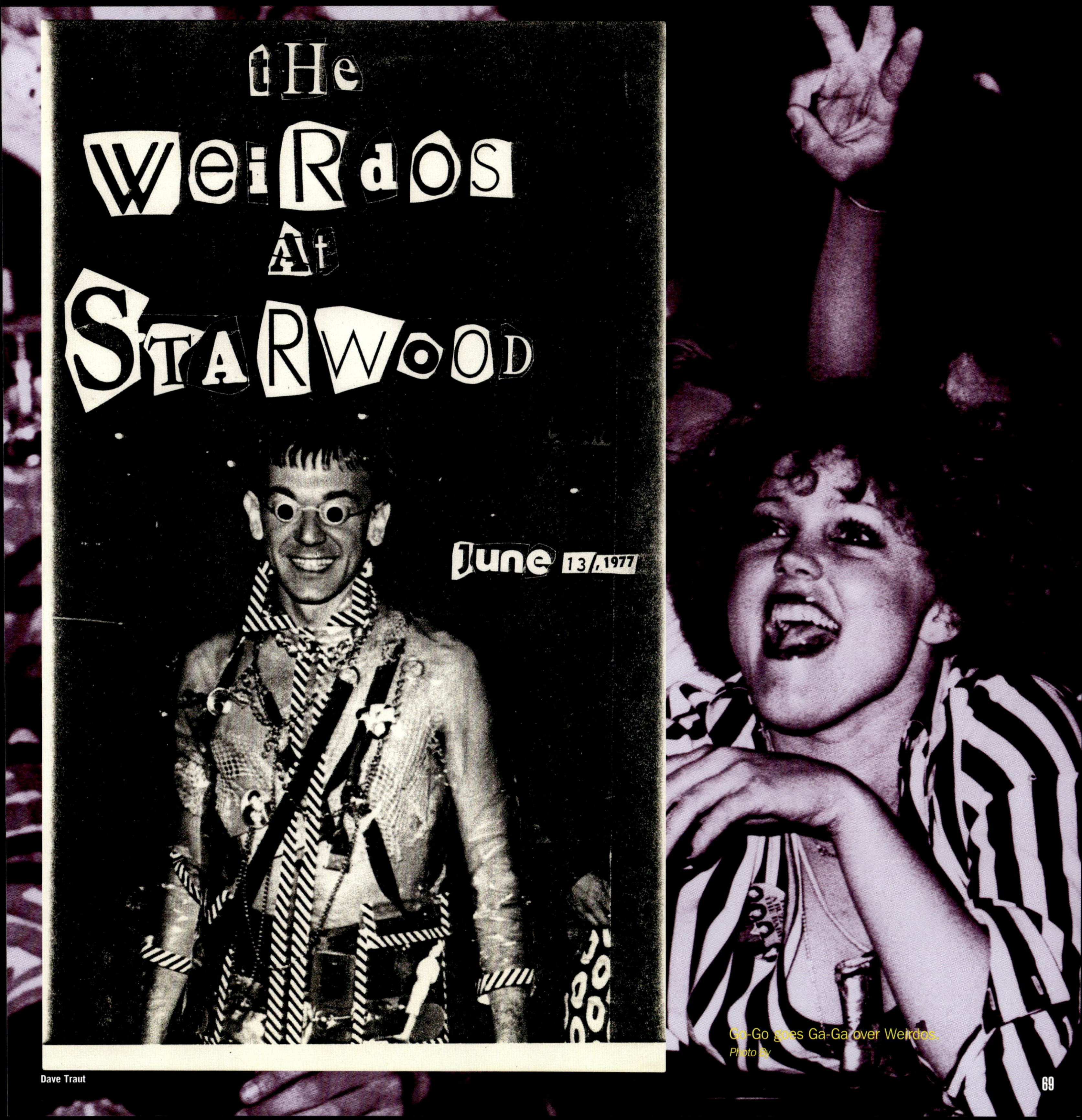

Dave Traut

Go-Go goes Ga-Ga over Weirdos.
Photo By

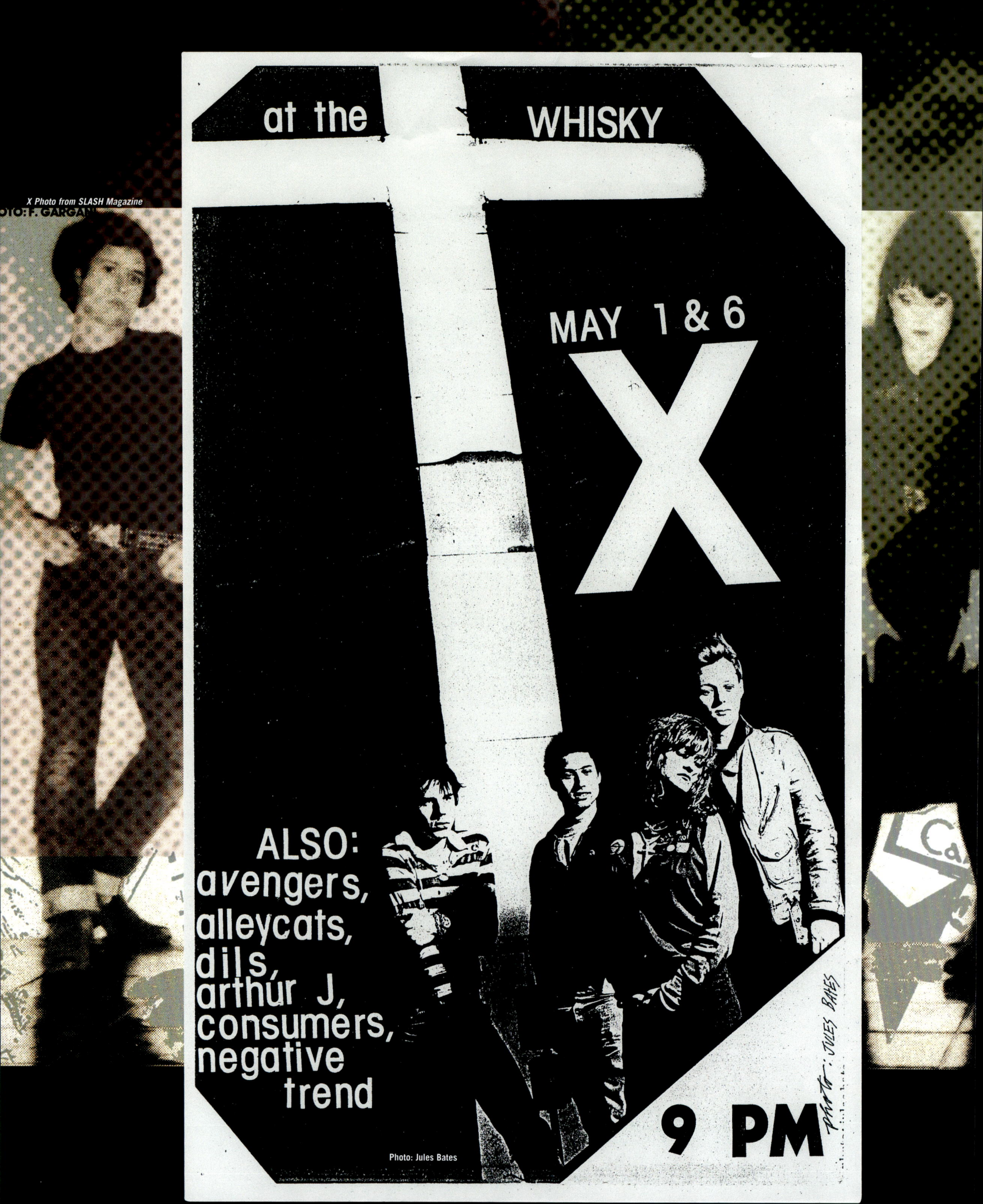

X Photo from SLASH Magazine
OTO: F. GARGAN

Photo: Jules Bates

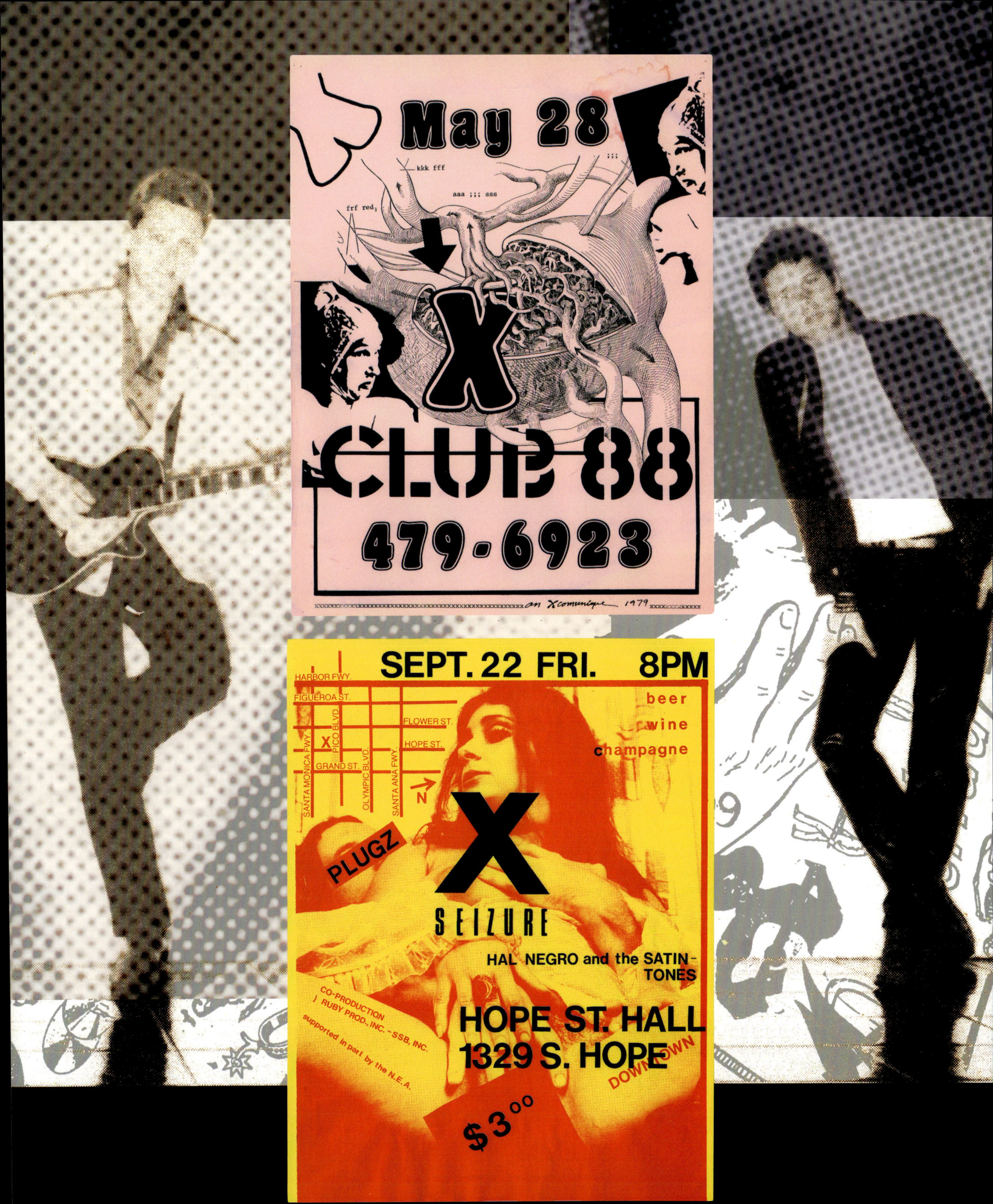
May 28
X
CLUB 88
479-6923
an Xcomunique 1979
SEPT. 22 FRI. 8PM
HARBOR FWY.
FIGUEROA ST.
FLOWER ST.
HOPE ST.
GRAND ST.
SANTA MONICA FWY.
PICO BLVD
OLYMPIC BLVD
SANTA ANA FWY.
N
beer
wine
champagne
PLUGZ
X
SEIZURE
HAL NEGRO and the SATIN-TONES
CO-PRODUCTION
J. RUBY PROD., INC. - SSB, INC.
supported in part by the N.E.A.
HOPE ST. HALL
1329 S. HOPE
DOWNTOWN
$3.00

Bob Biggs

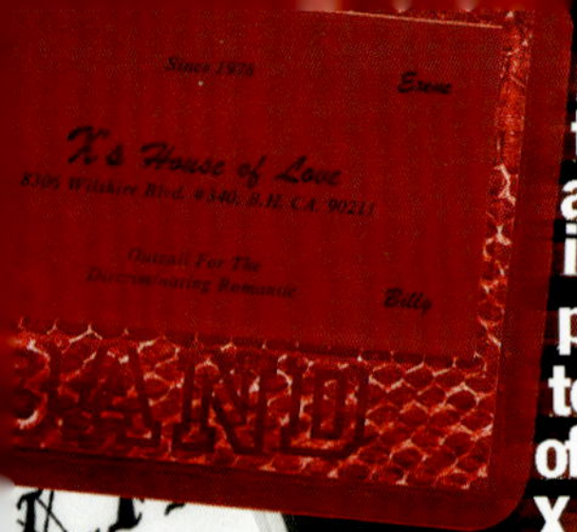

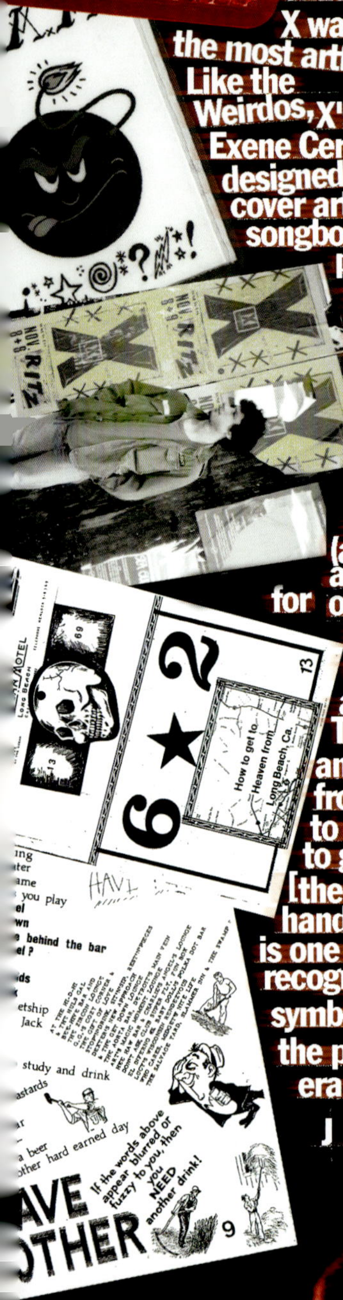

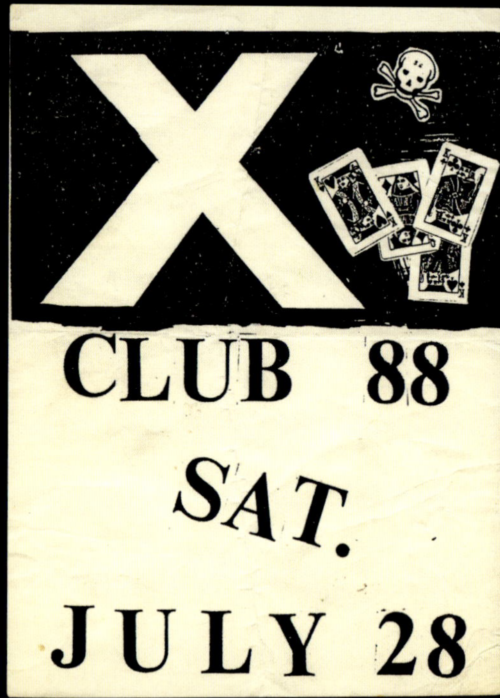

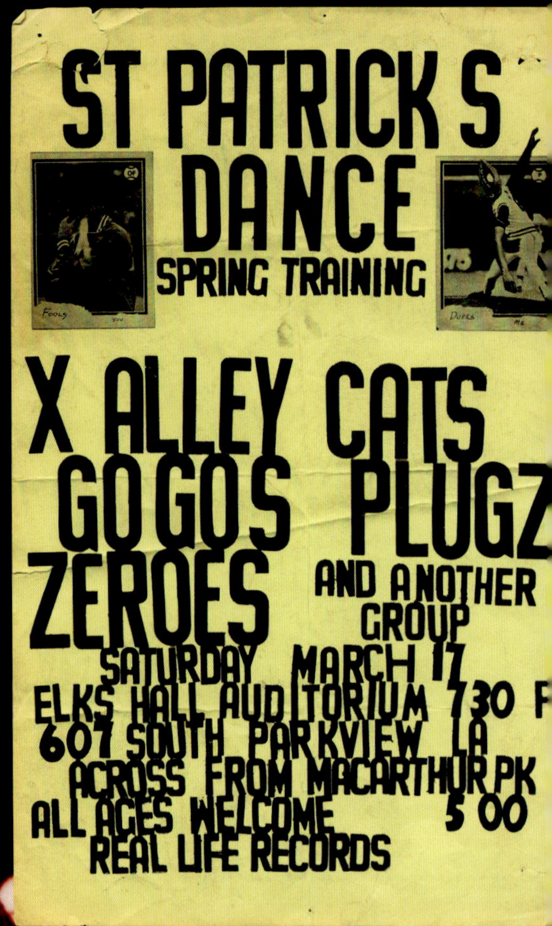

Aside from their stature as the most important punk band to come out of Los Angeles, X was also *the most artful.* Like the Weirdos, X's Exene Cervenkova designed the cover art, songbooks, posters, backstage passes and other paraphernalia, (comma) exhibiting, (among other things) a distaste for organized religion, and a love for 1950s kitsch and old clip art. Long before those avenues became clichés lifted by graphic designers everywhere. The band's logo, and it's metamorphosis from hand drawing to burning cross to germanic woodtype, [then back to it's hand-drawn roots,] is one of the most recognizable symbols of the punk era.+

J

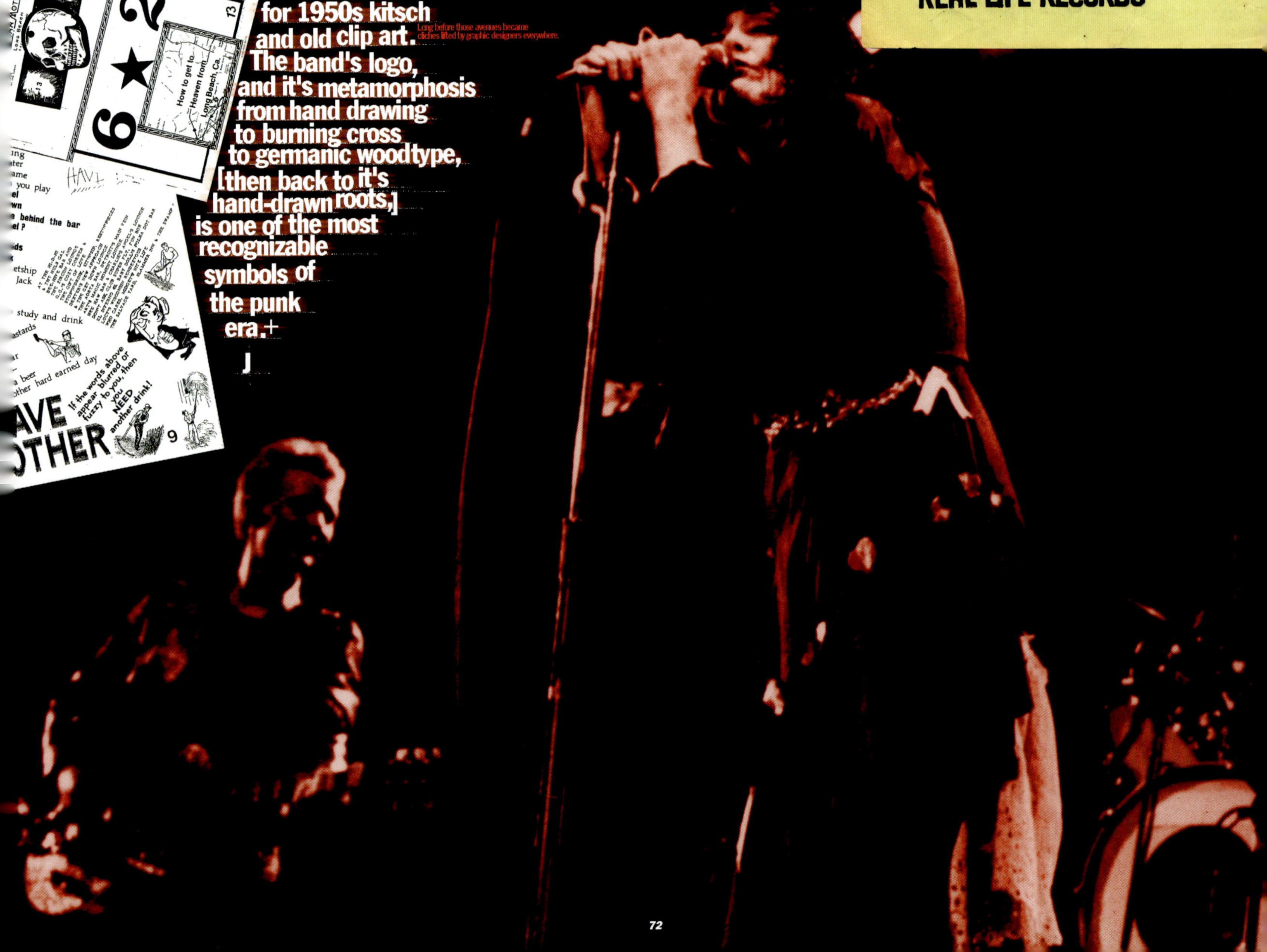

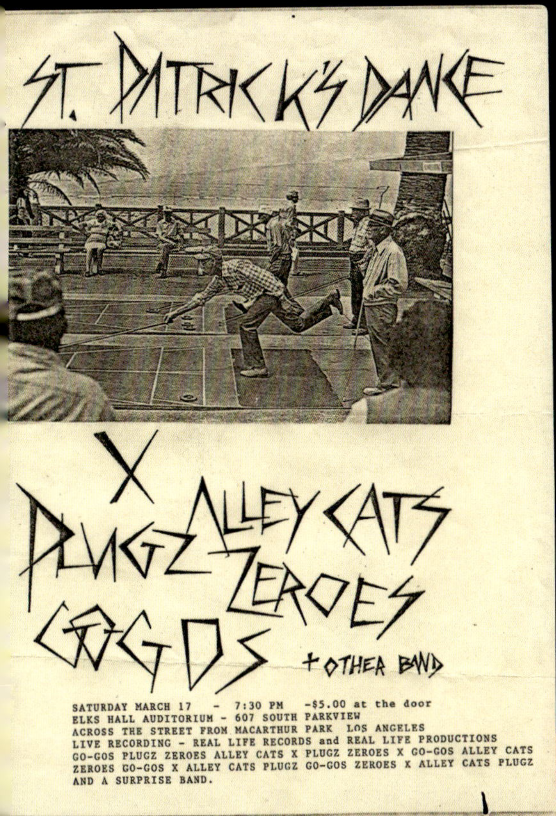

atrick's Day "Massacre": The First of many LAPD riots
n the media called "Punk Riots."

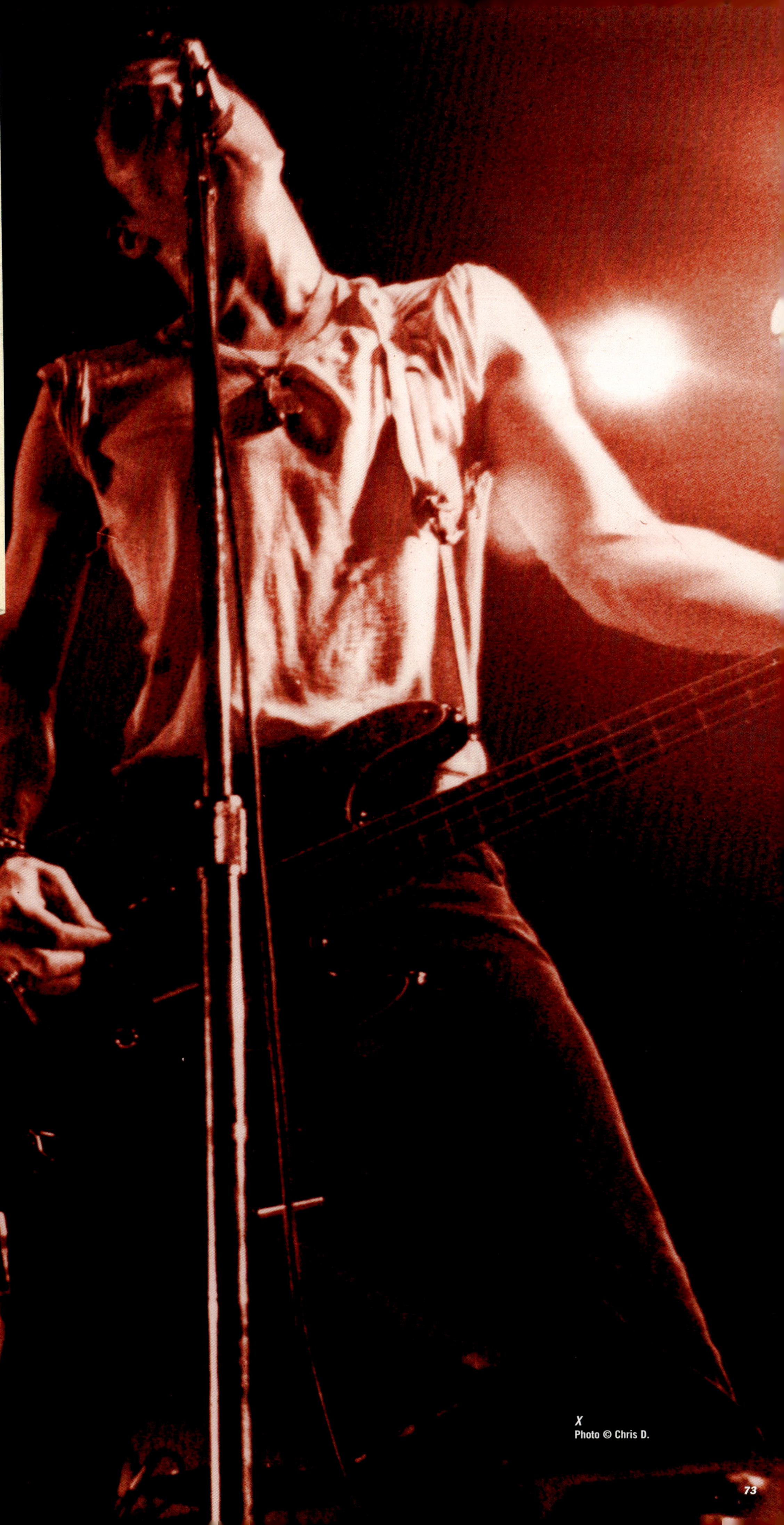

X
Photo © Chris D.

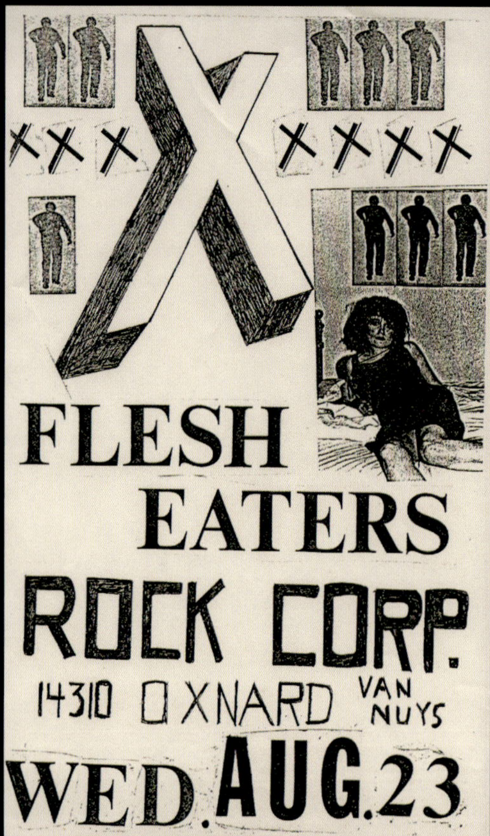

Chris D.

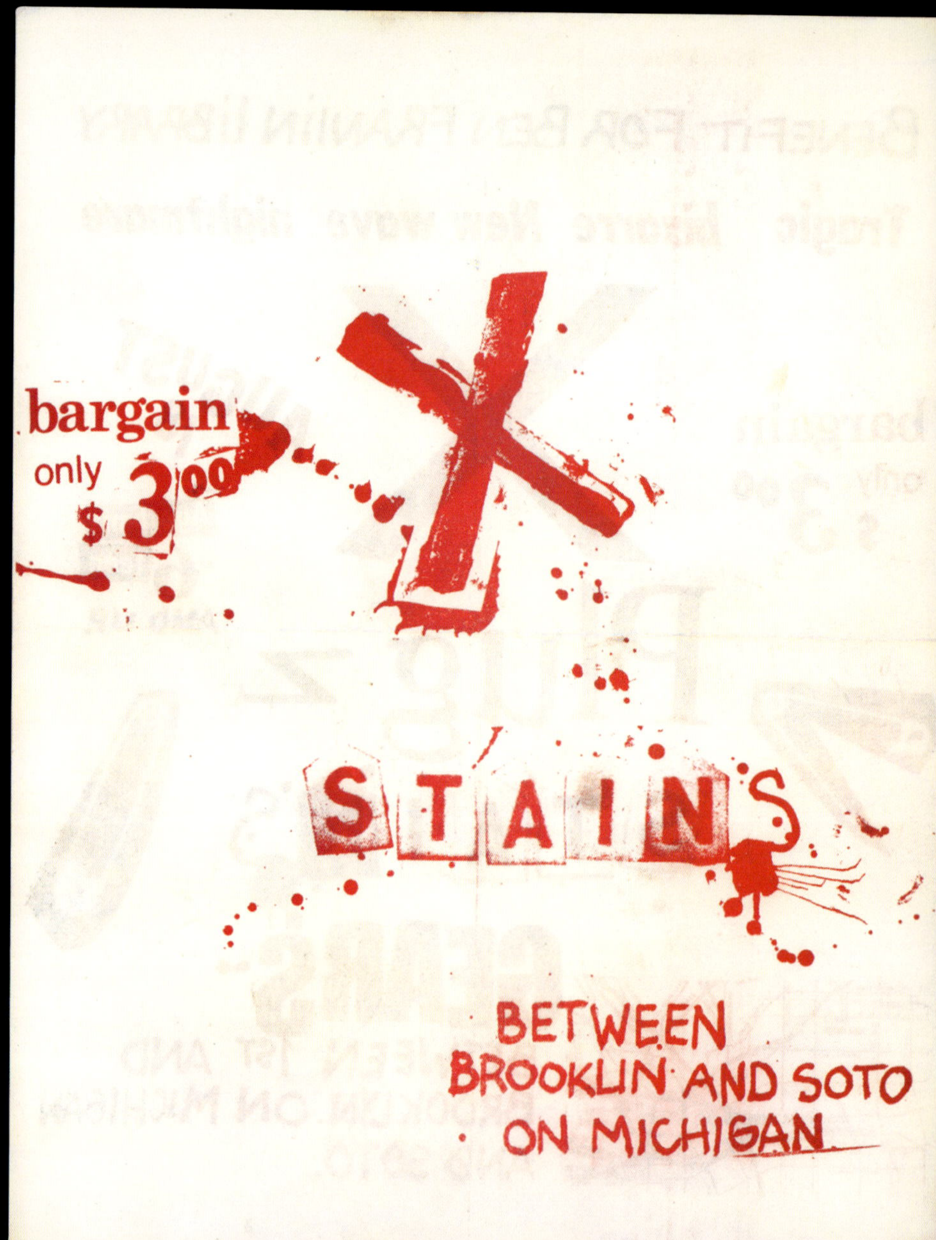

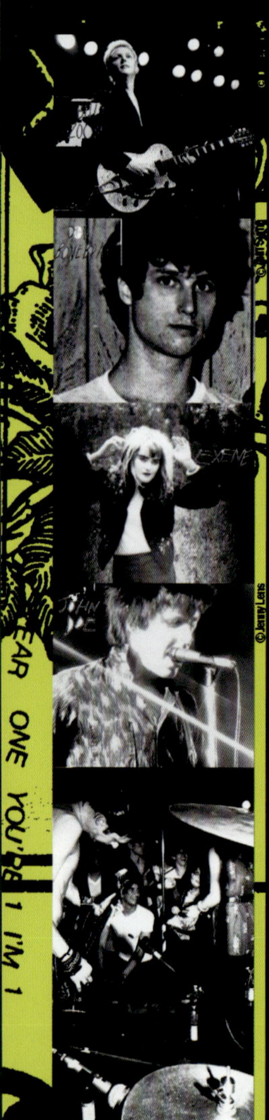

X

By Craig Roose

In the dull, dull, dull, literally nothing to do, (unless you were lucky enough to have the *"Z"* channel or *"Pong"*) late seventies, when punk was just emerging, the scene was the Hong Kong Cafe in Chinatown, Los Angeles. Or it was the Masque. Or it was the Starwood, The Whiskey, or some one-night-rented hall or dingy warehouse in the backstreets of nowhere, Los Angeles. It was too fuckin' fun and too bad you missed it, if you missed it...*and X was the best damn band that ever walked the land.*

It is hard to describe properly the feeling of the city at that time, but it was bland and lifeless and initially the world outside didn't know or give a damn about what these freaks (or weirdos, or queers) were doing in a basement or dive somewhere. Out there in the dark there was an incredibly exciting, energetic scene brewing. The time was ripe for a bunch of bored, frustrated and creative people to find their own individual expression and let go in a playground of spontaneous lunatics.

The doors were suddenly burst open for so many new ideas at once. People got very creative with personas and the image package of their bands. There were a lot of great bands that offered something you wanted to see again and again. Germs, Bags, Gun Club, Flesheaters, Alleycats, Fear, Suburban Lawns, etc. But X were the most powerful, dynamic, honest and deep-rooted of them all. They were the strongest voice in this scene and still carry the most lasting message.

To experience an X show was to be sucked into an emotional and powerful religious experience. There were real guts spilled here. Raw emotion, passion and pain. Their lyrics and music combined could practically knock the wind out of you. There was never a show where there wasn't a dedicated contingent fighting to get as close to Exene as possible to share the intensity of this experience. John Doe and Exene Cervenka were our own personal underground superheroes. A handsome biker-farm boy and his devil-doll bride. Backed, to boot, by a rockabilly icon and an all-American bulldozer on drums. They looked great. They sounded great. And every song was a rip-ass *keeper*. X were a combination of so many elements at once, it was mesmerizing. There were familiar elements of rockabilly, blues and jazz. Pieces of Americana, religion and social behavior thrown back at us for reconsideration and reevaluation.

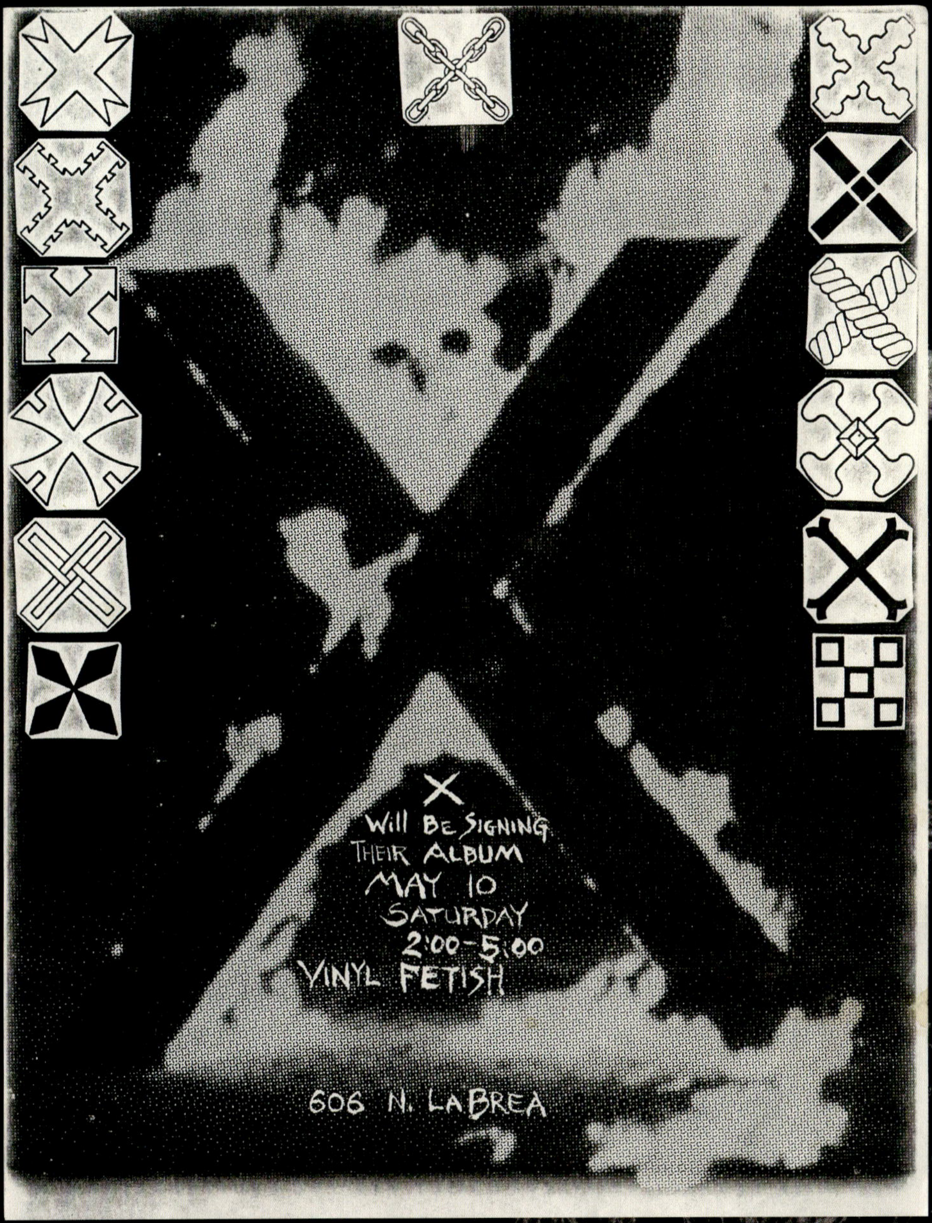

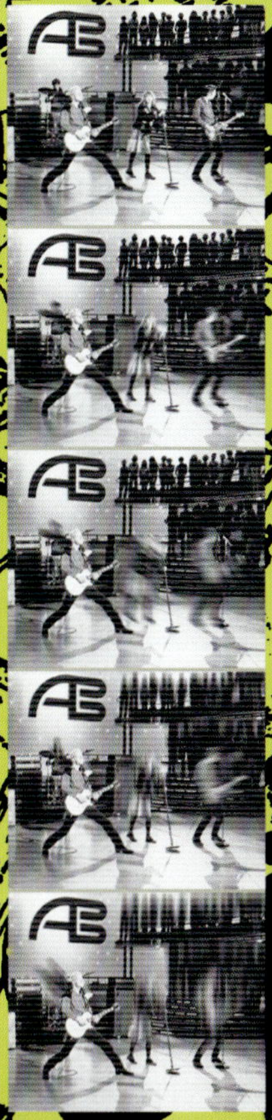

We even looked to them for fashion ideas (is there anything cooler than the band photo on the back of the *"Los Angeles"* album?) The crying, moaning harmonies or their sophisticated and humorous wordplay could strike a physical chord in you that made you feel and made you think– helped you heal. All the while they were giving 200% 40-mule-team velocity and a *"shut up and smoke"* attitude that kept you grounded and not feeling too sorry for yourself.

The punk rock approach allowed a lot of room for experimentation. You didn't have to be a singer to sing, you could channel emotion, mostly. That was Exene. Like Patsy Cline, Billie Holliday and an evangelist all rolled into one, then set on fire. The combination of John's already powerful vocals and Exene's emotion created something so unique and gut-wrenching, there was no other way to play it. It was what it was. It was original. It was real. It was alive. And blended with the break-neck musicianship of Billy Zoom, John Doe and D.J. Bonebrake, you got X. Something that doesn't come along every day, but something that I know will last forever. And they're a lot better than *"Pong."* +

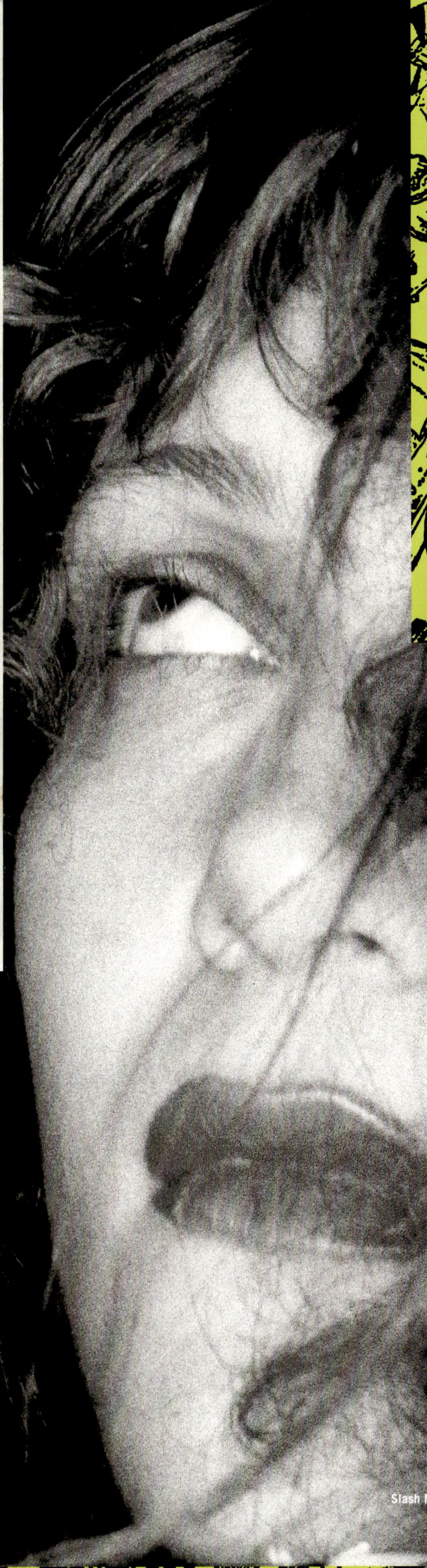

Exene
Slash Magazine Cover Vol. 1 #6

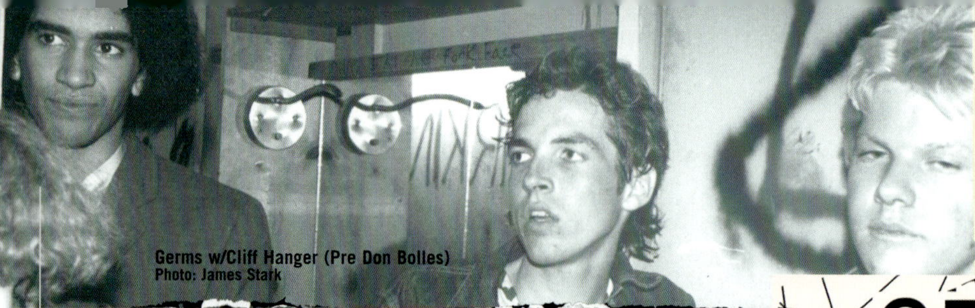

Germs w/Cliff Hanger (Pre Don Bolles)
Photo: James Stark

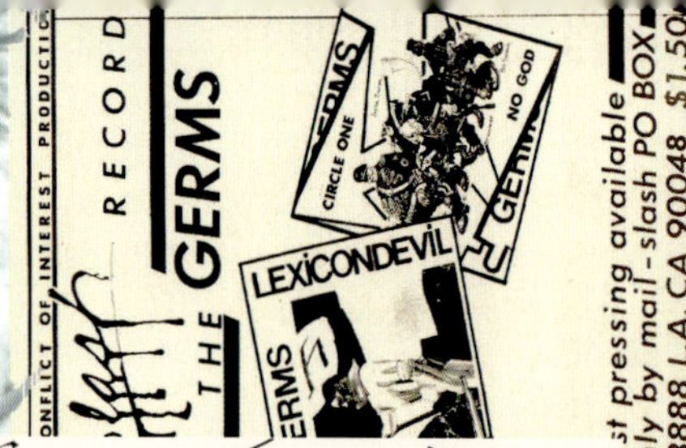

"...at Okie Dogs"

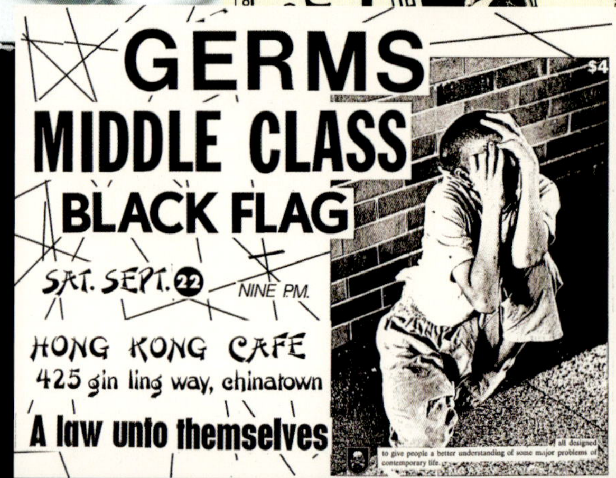

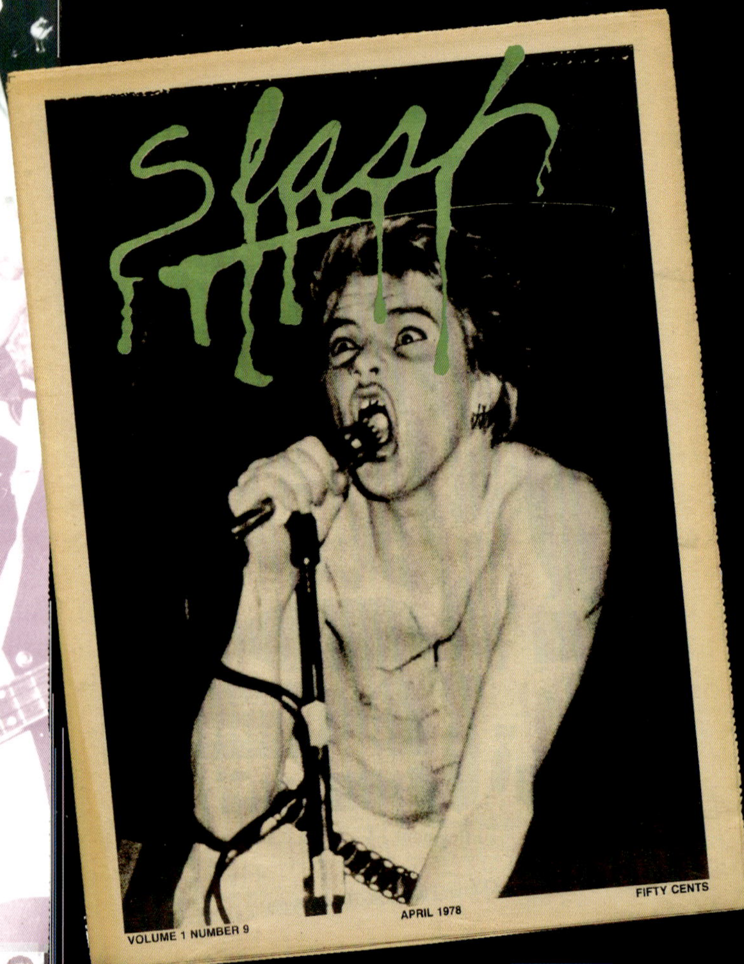

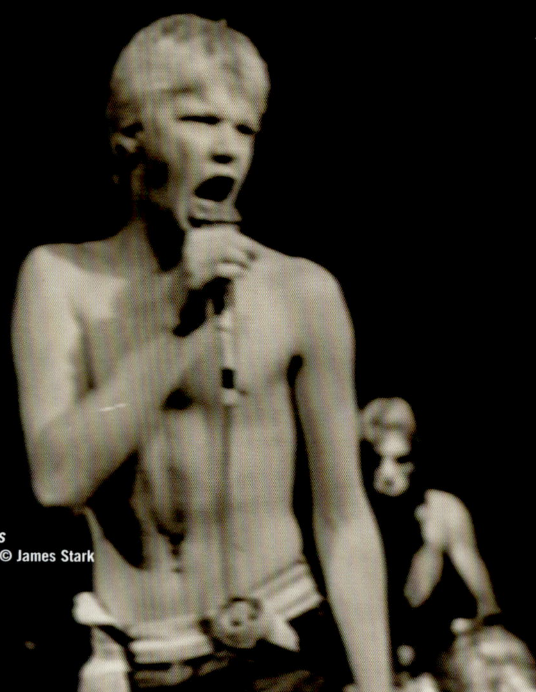

Germs
Photo © James Stark

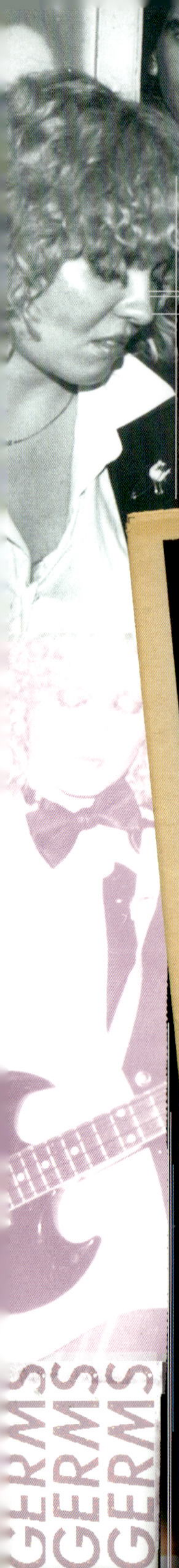

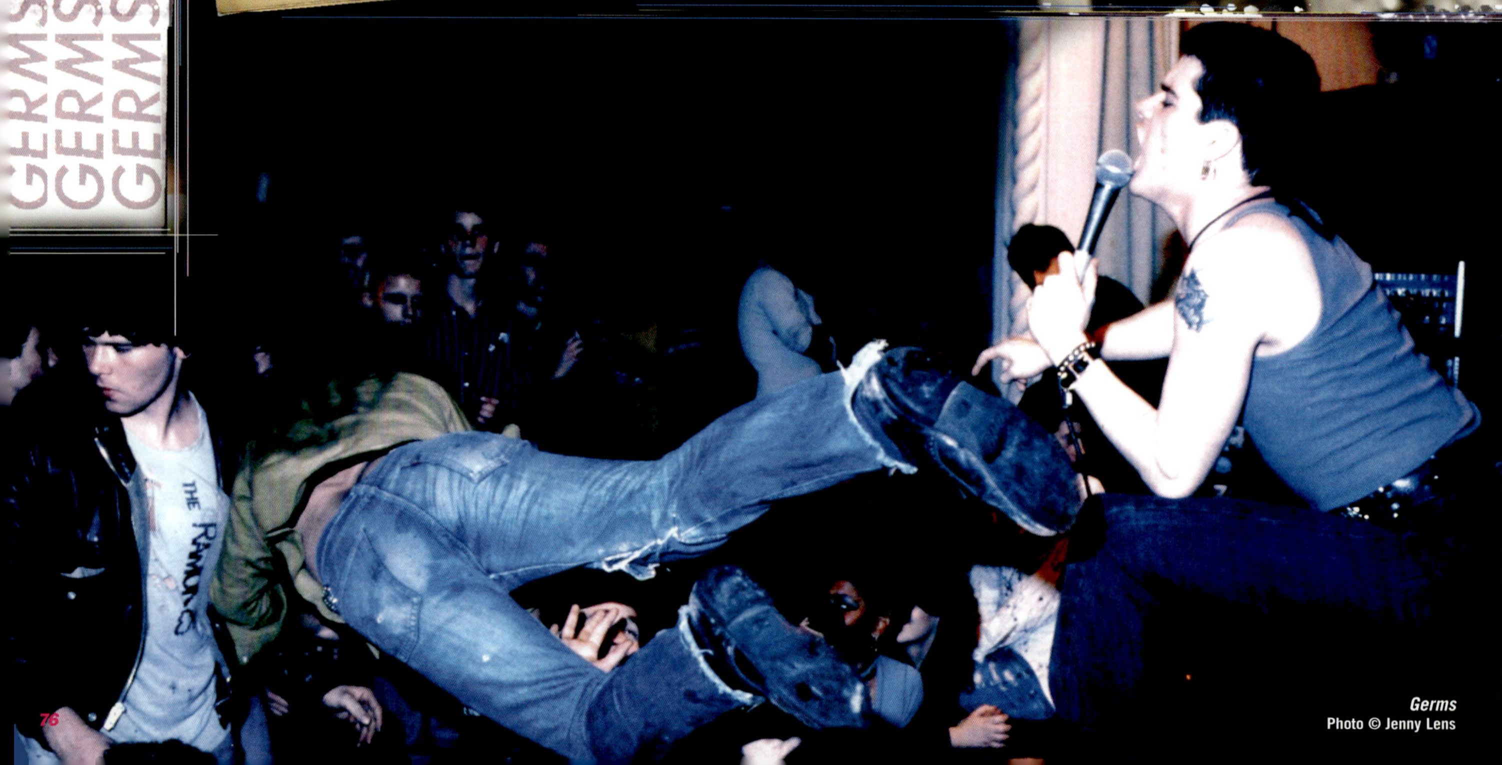

Germs
Photo © Jenny Lens

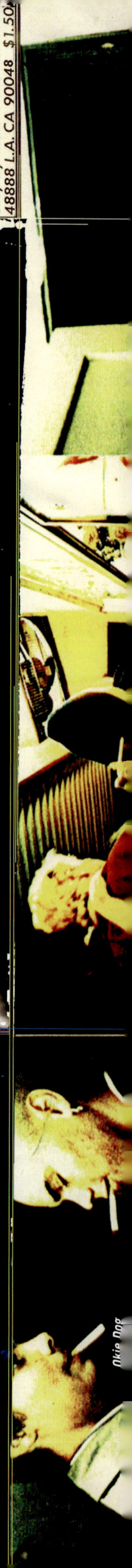

Okie Dog

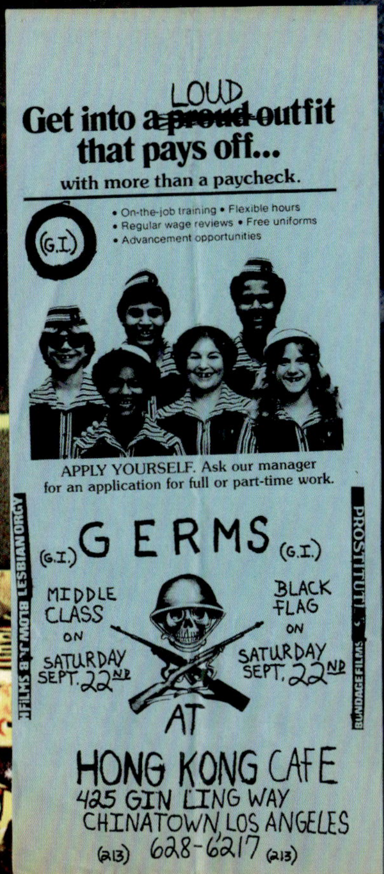

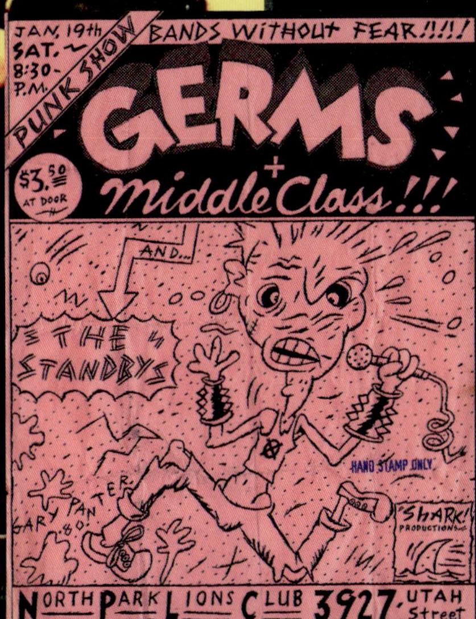

© Gary Panter

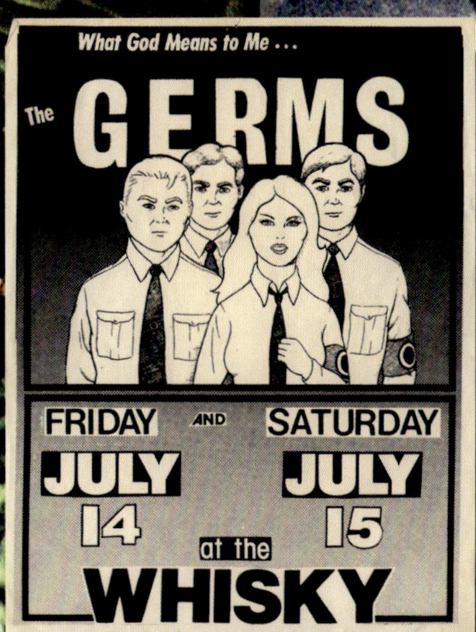

Don Bolles

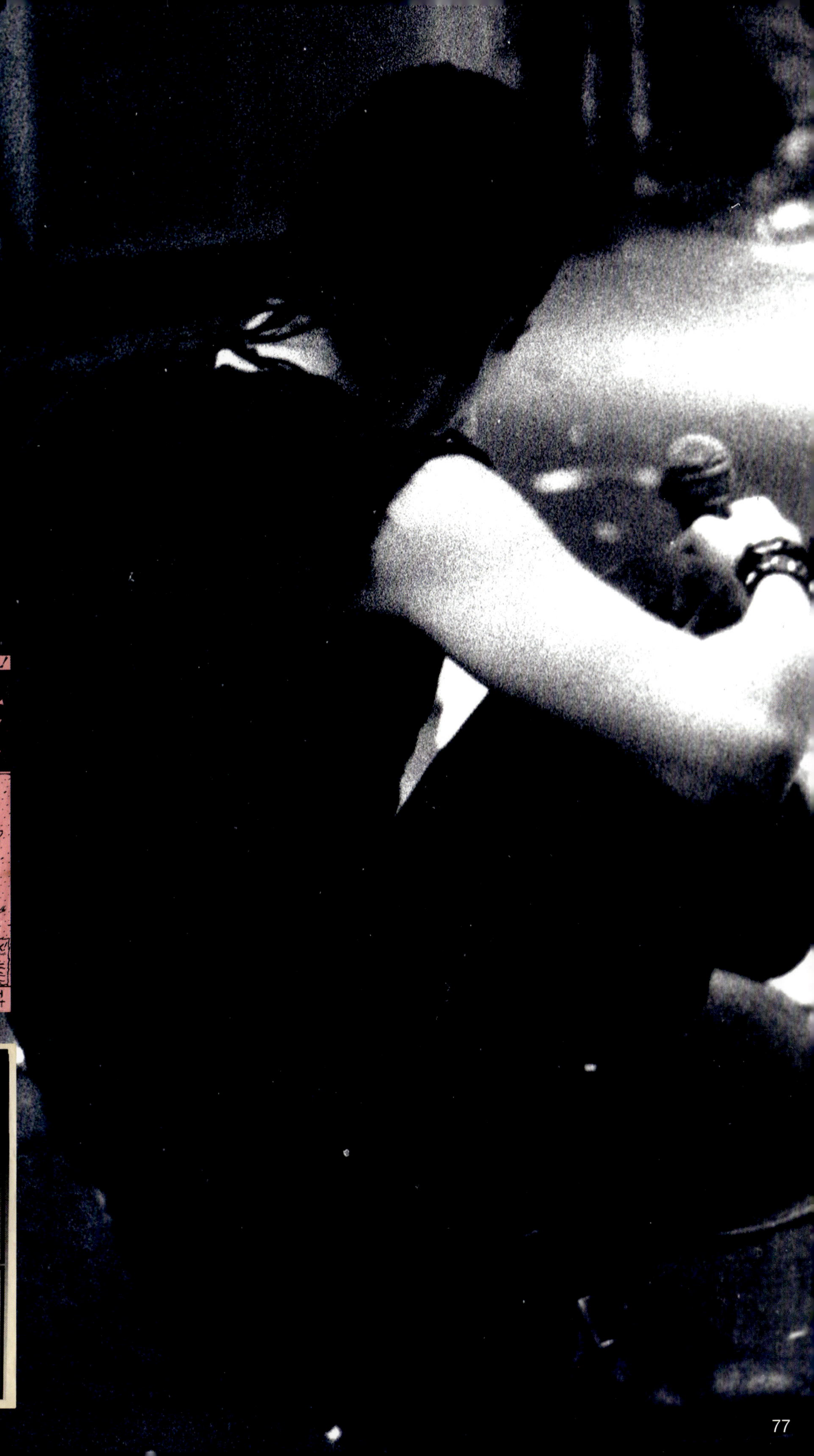

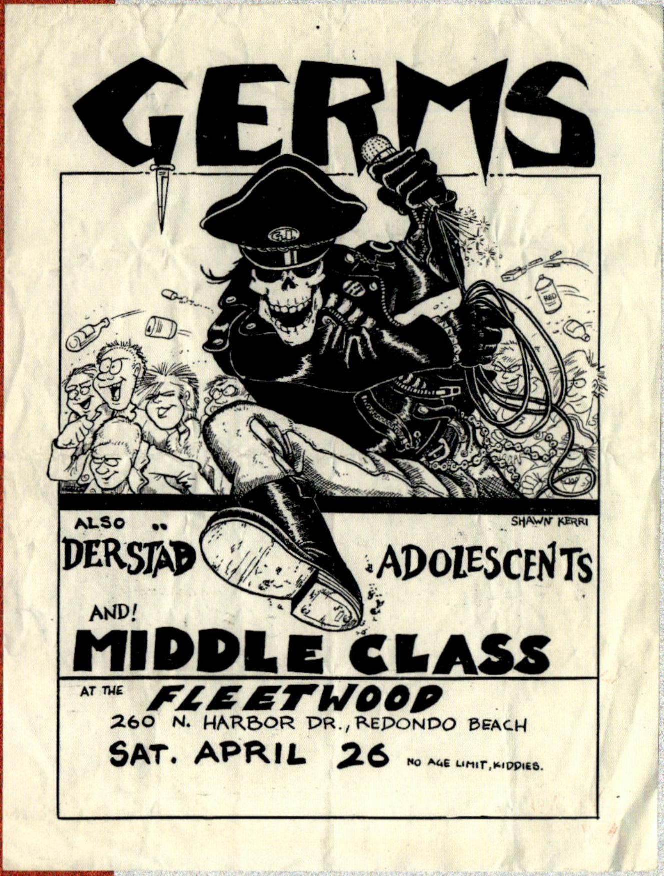

Shawn Kerri

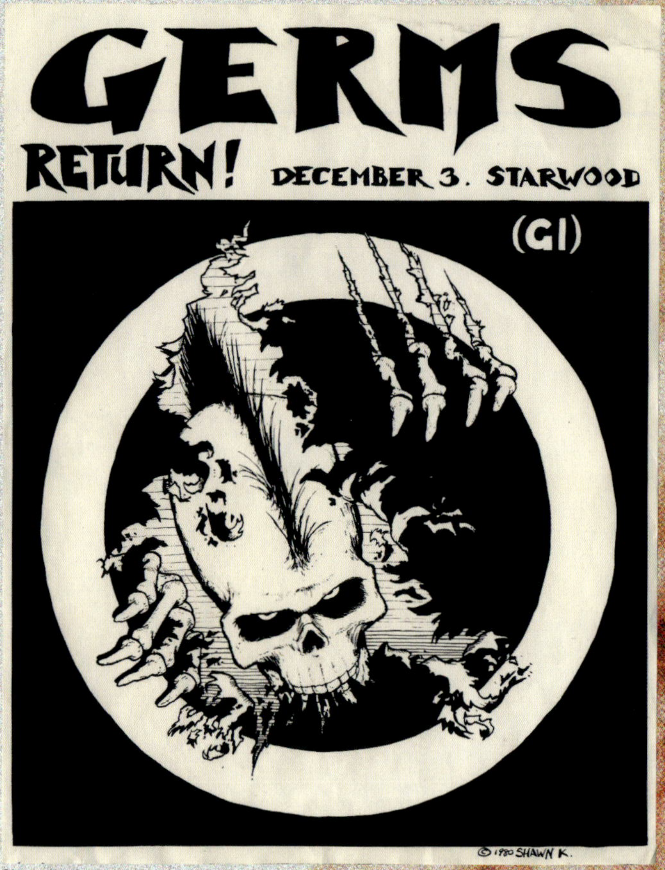

Shawn Kerri

The final appearance.

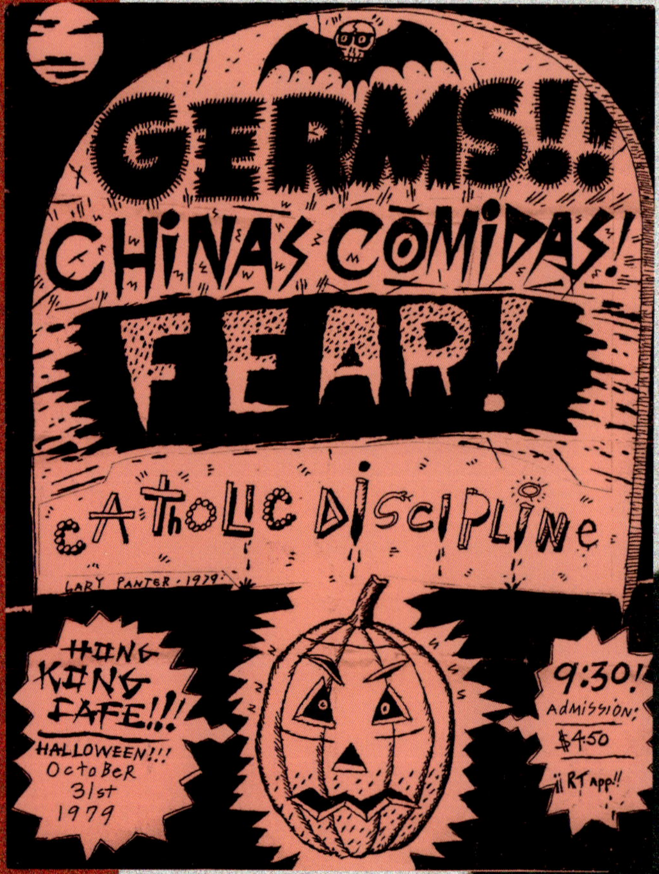

© Garry Panter

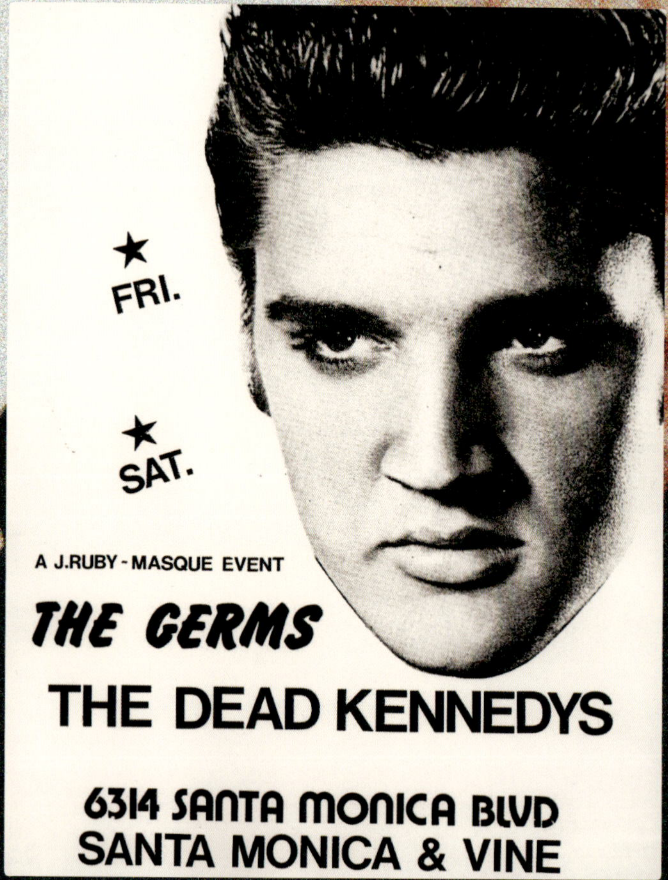

Bob Biggs

Lorna Doom
Photo: © Denny Burt

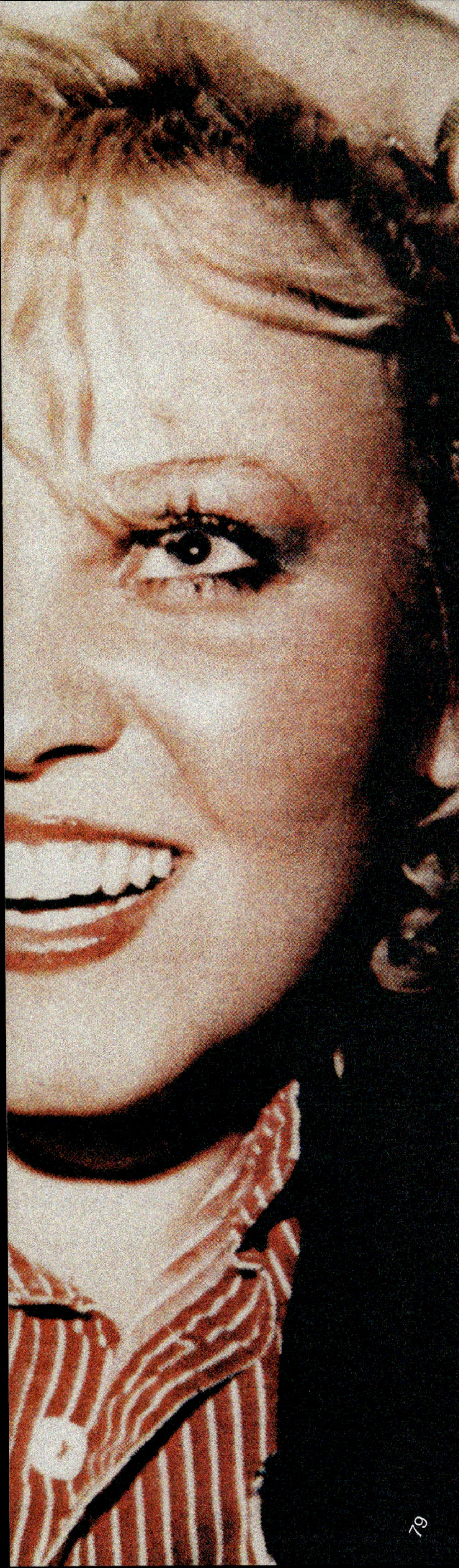

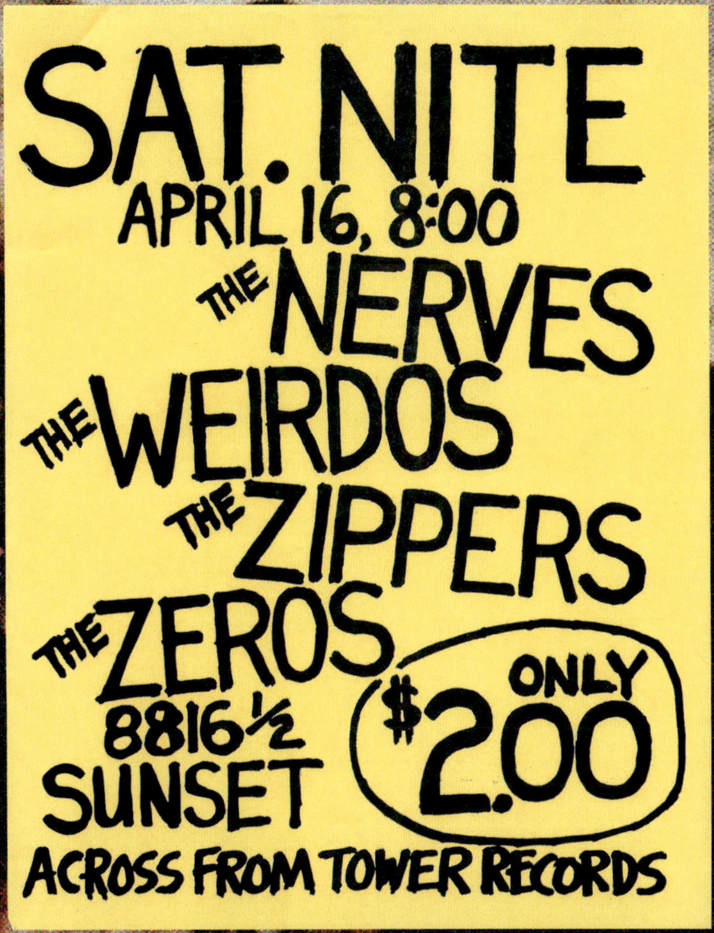

Germs (Unbilled) First Show

Dave Traut

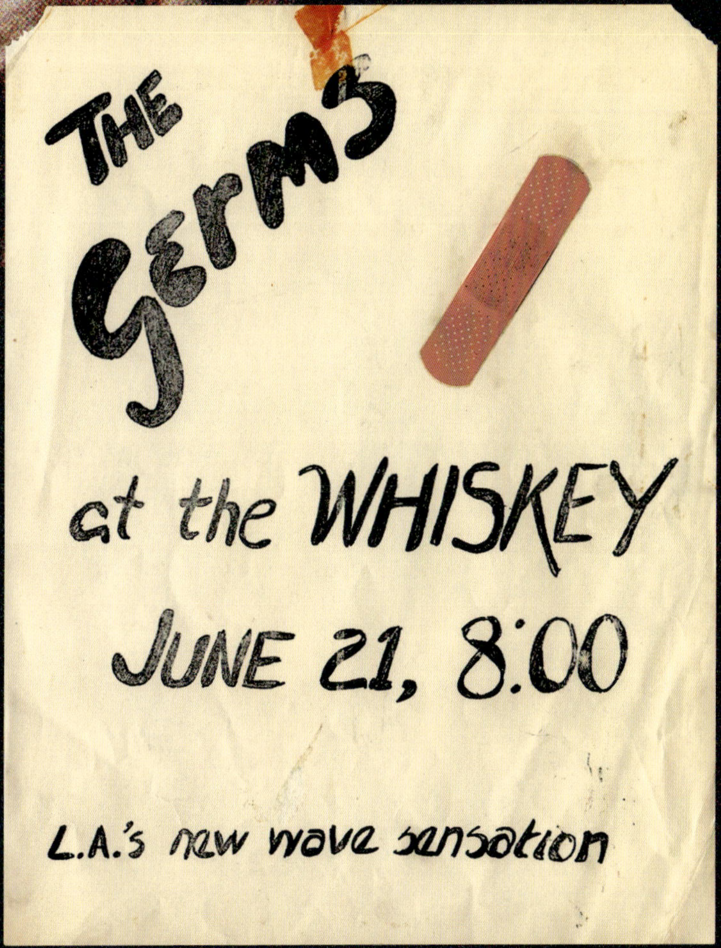

1159 North Genesee Avenue (1979)

Melissa Hutton's West Hollywood apartment off Santa Monica Blvd. became the new official Germs home/hangout for both band members and friends who had previously clustered at the Canterbury Apartments near the Masque.

Most afternoons were complemented by a shifting constellation of a half-dozen people coming and going to receive a new haircut or color by Melissa, or just to hang around.

Between 4:00 and 5:00 Darby and entourage would arrive. We'd pool our money to have a "chi chi" party, named after a drink which consisted of pineapple and coconut juices, and vodka. Darby would then proceed to share his secret recipe for a perfect Top Ramen, explain his theory for the Germs burn, and generally entertain everyone thoroughly.

From there it was into someone's car–off to some other band's show, followed by a party somewhere. We would always end up at Oki Dogs, and then later at Melissa's.

I will always remember those times as very warm... very friendly... very wild.

Lorna Doom

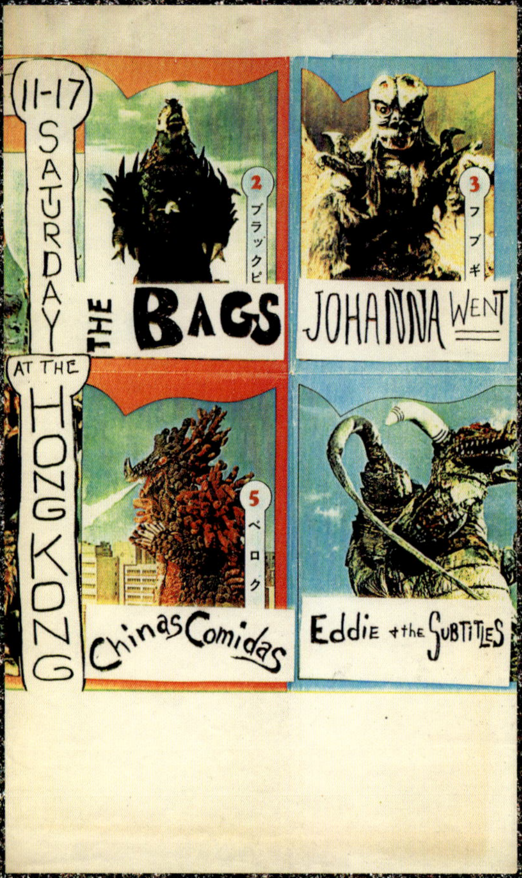

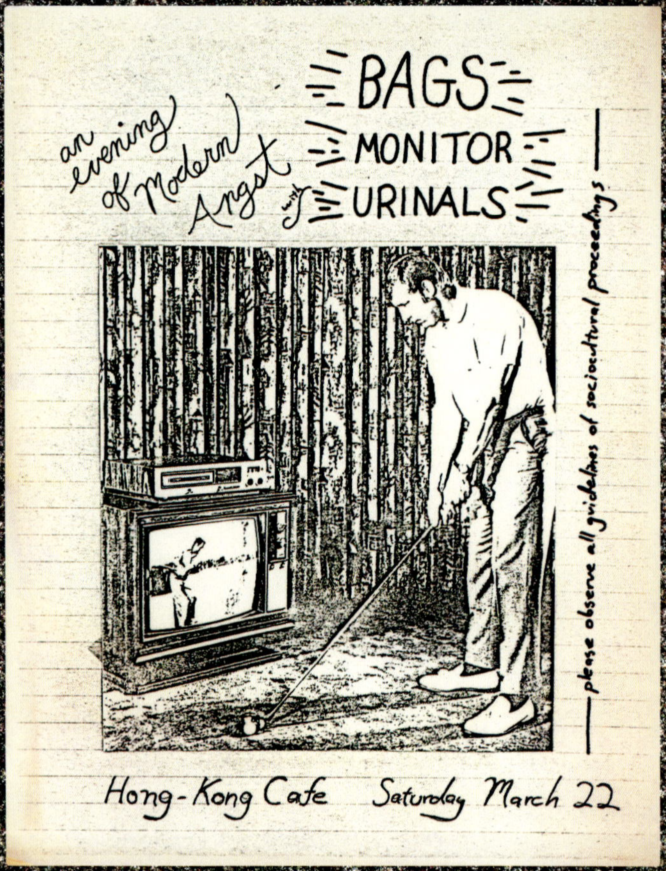

John Tally-Jones

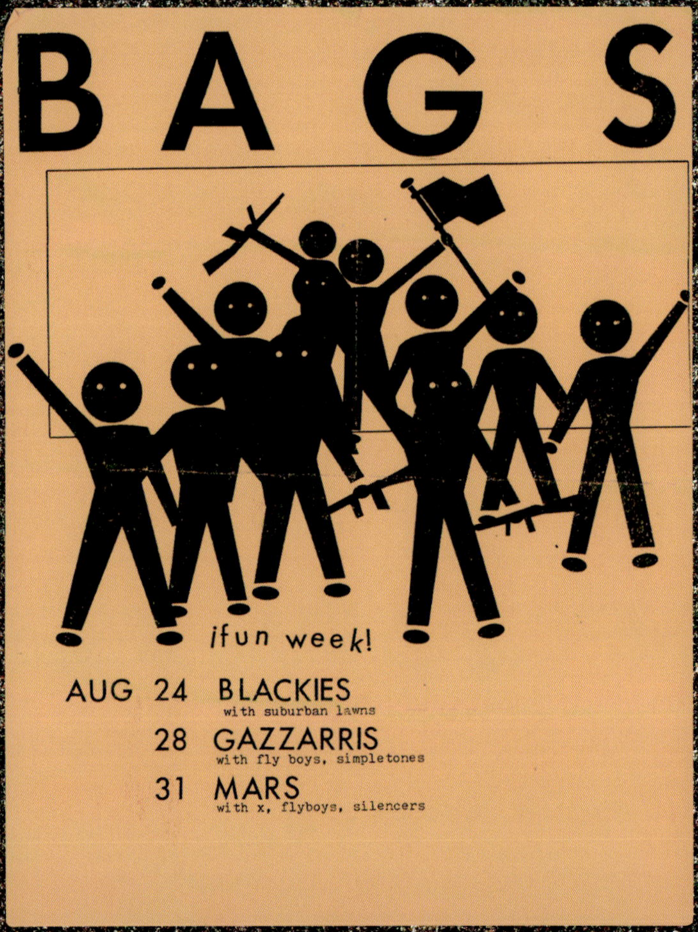

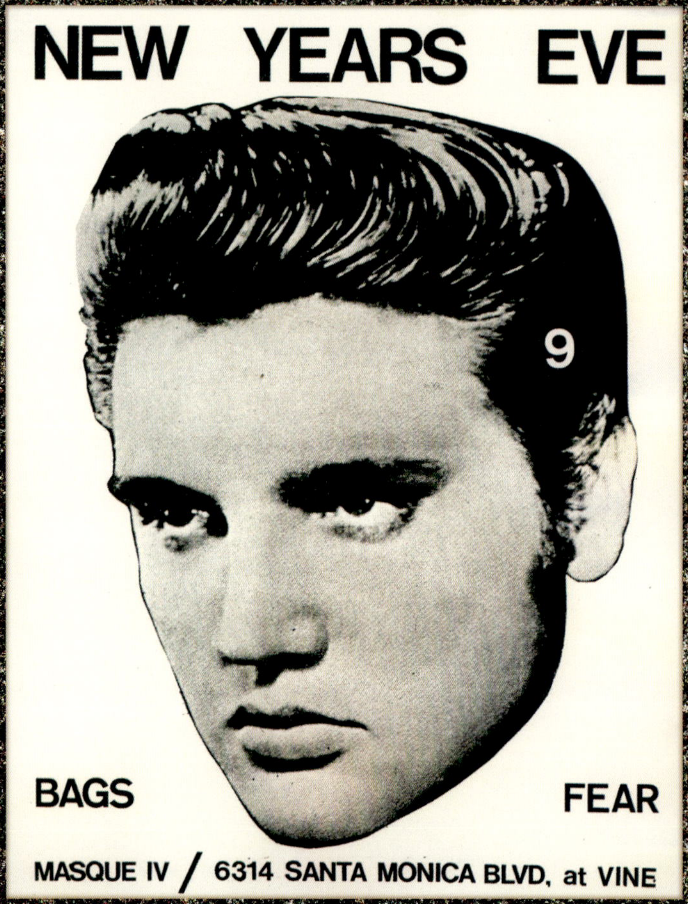

Bob Biggs

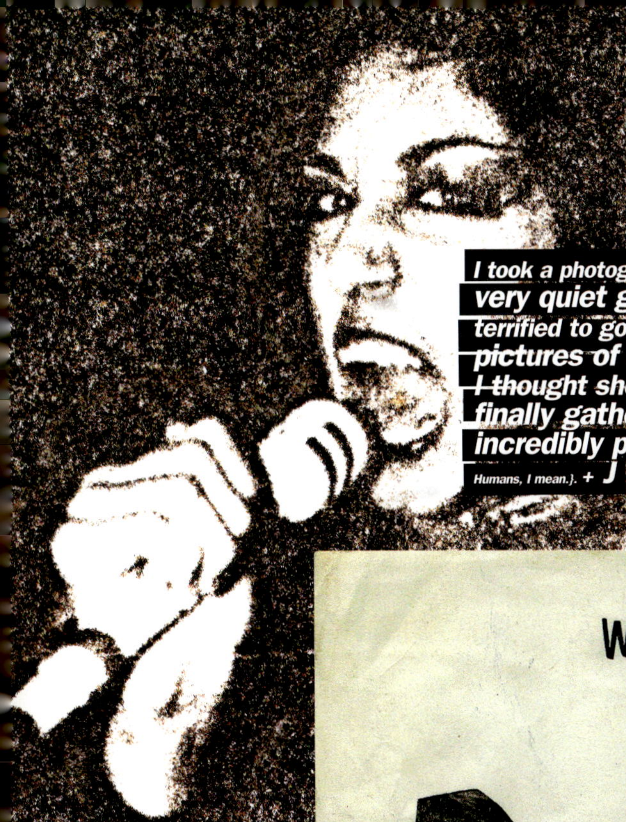

I took a photography course in 1980. One of my classmates pointed to a very quiet girl in the corner and told me it was Alice Bag. I was terrified to go near her, because I'd heard her music and seen scary pictures of her in Creem magazine slow-dancing with Lydia Lunch. I thought she'd tear me apart if I even looked at her wrong. When I finally gathered the courage to say hello to her, of course she was incredibly polite and one of the nicest people in the class. {See what miserable fucks we can be? Humans, I mean.}. + J

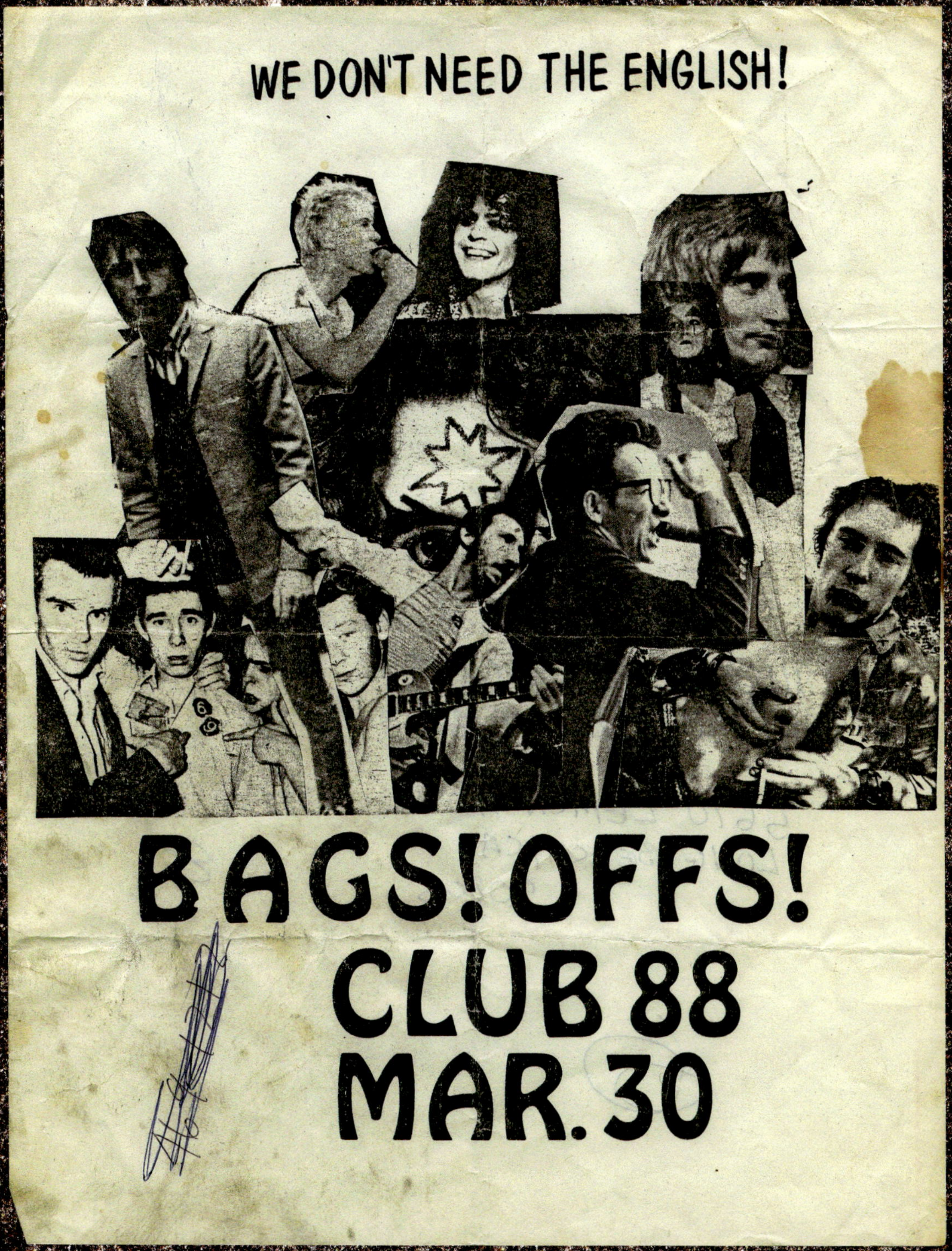

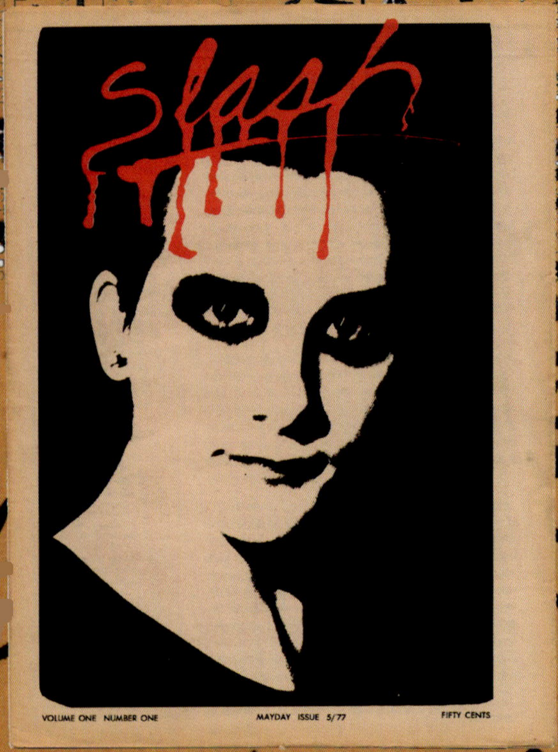

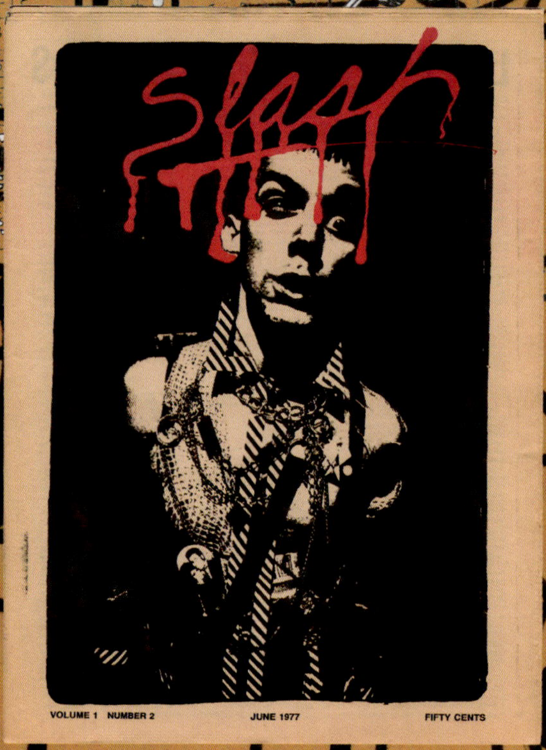

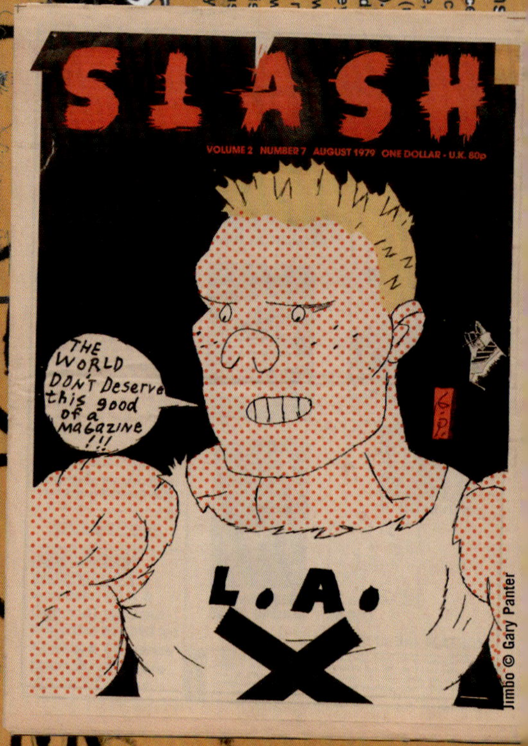

Jimbo © Gary Panter

SLASH MAGAZINE

I had the advantage, or disadvantage, depending on your perspective, of being older than most people in the punk scene (except maybe for *"Kickboy Face"* Claude Bessy.) I had lived through the '60s, and thus learned that youth movements occurred in cycles, they changed constantly, and they had short lifespans.

'77: The Look and The Sound

[by Bob Biggs]

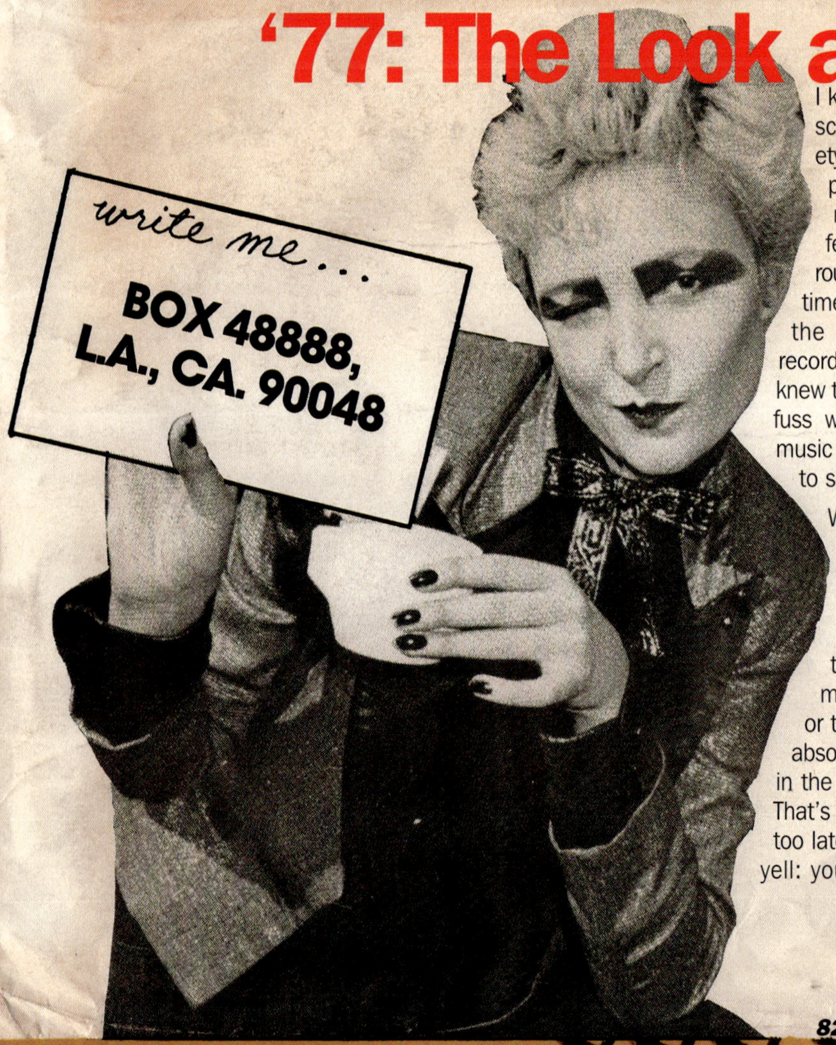

I knew what would happen to the LA punk scene: it would be assimilated into society after making its contribution to cultural progress. This knowledge certainly did not dull the excitement of the day, those few years before 1980. They were raw, rough, aggressive, bombastic and exciting times. Nobody was making any money off the scene, not the bands, magazines, record labels or clubs, but I think many of us knew that if we could make enough of a public fuss with blue hair, sharp objects, concrete music and obnoxious flyers, we could give birth to something substantial - and we did.

We learned and executed the number one rule of manipulating pop culture: to shock. We accomplished that, but we were so busy fighting for visibility that we really didn't achieve much of anything else. The shock effect of the punk movement was fine, but with no agenda or tangible set of values, only the style was absorbed into popular culture. You can see it in the flyers: they're sexy, violent and absurd. That's what makes them great. But we learned too late that it's probably not enough just to yell: you've got to have something to say. +

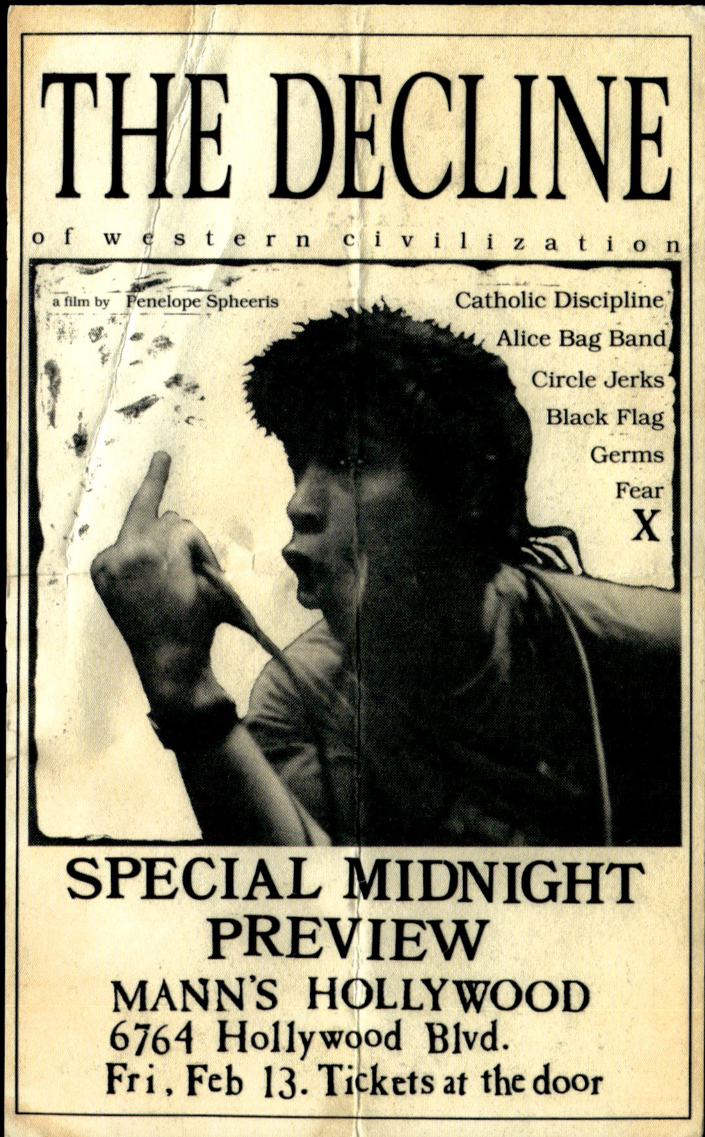

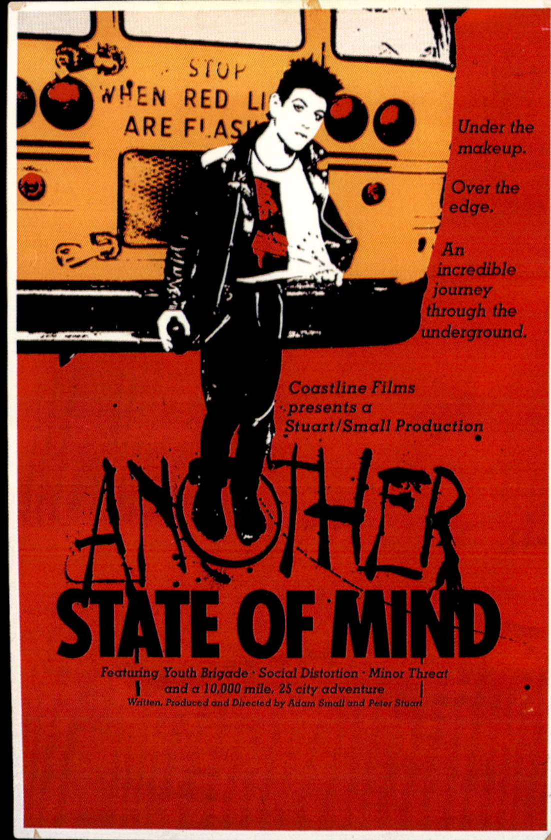

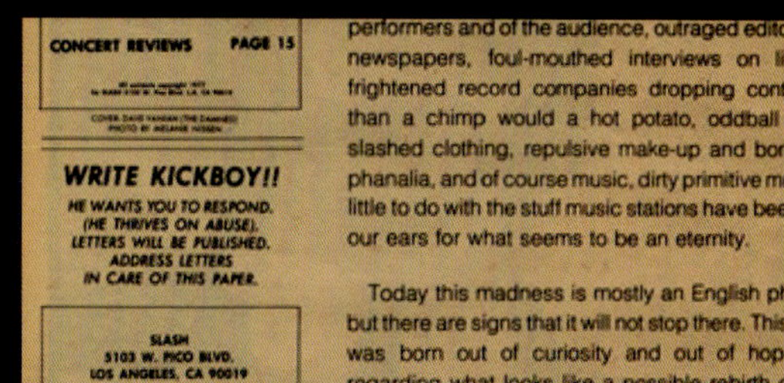

CONCERT REVIEWS PAGE 15

WRITE KICKBOY!!
HE WANTS YOU TO RESPOND.
(HE THRIVES ON ABUSE).
LETTERS WILL BE PUBLISHED.
ADDRESS LETTERS
IN CARE OF THIS PAPER.

SLASH
5103 W. PICO BLVD.
LOS ANGELES, CA 90019

performers and of the audience, outraged edito newspapers, foul-mouthed interviews on liv frightened record companies dropping contr than a chimp would a hot potato, oddball slashed clothing, repulsive make-up and bon phanalia, and of course music, dirty primitive mu little to do with the stuff music stations have bee our ears for what seems to be an eternity.

Today this madness is mostly an English ph but there are signs that it will not stop there. This was born out of curiosity and out of hope regarding what looks like a possible rebirth o

[Claude Bessy]

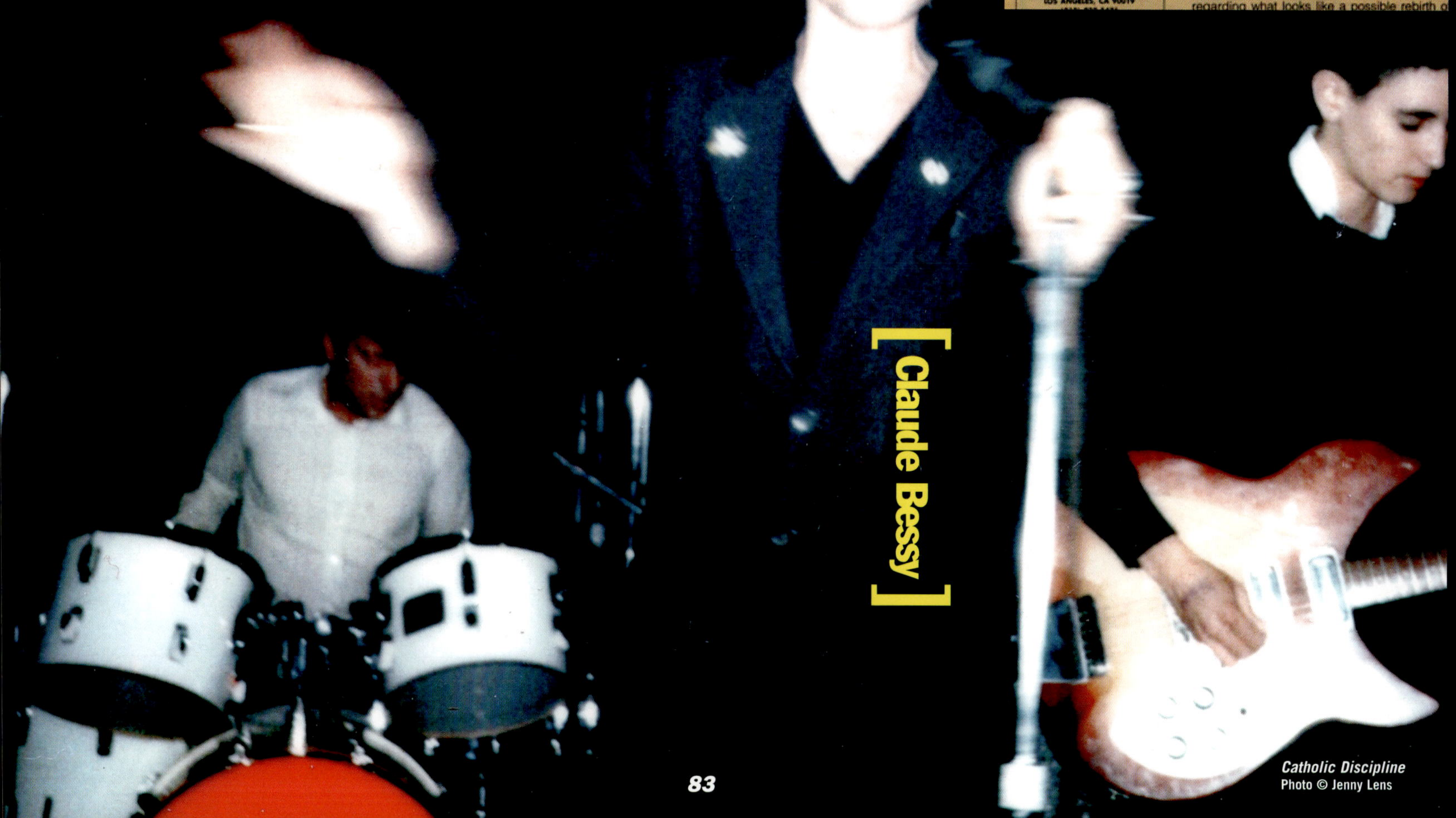

Catholic Discipline
Photo © Jenny Lens

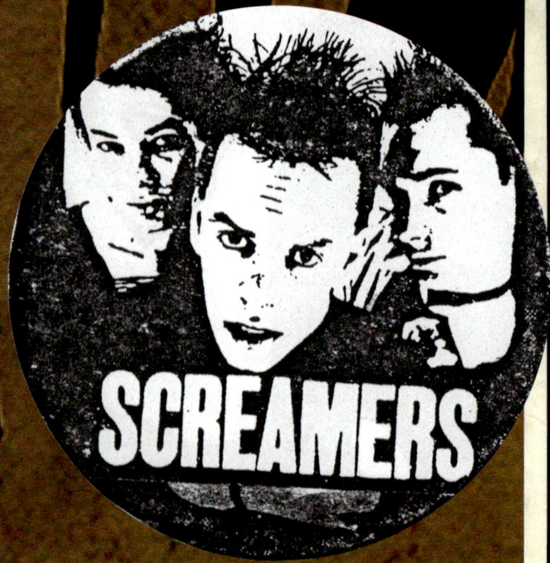

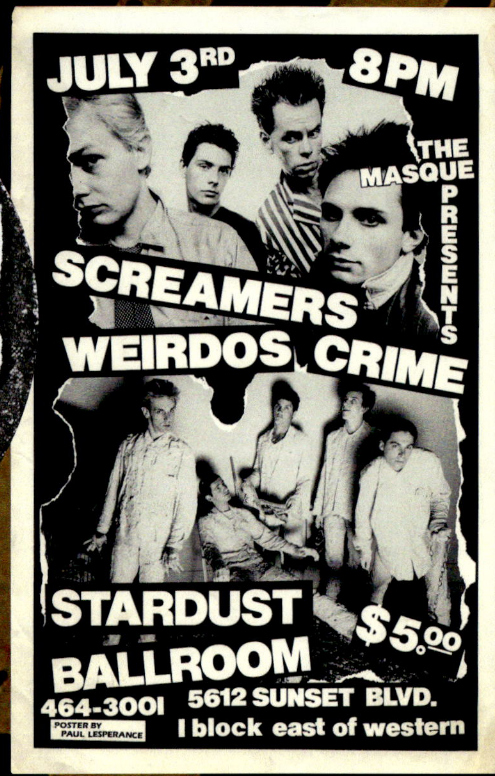

Screamers Photo: Erik Blum
Weirdos Photo: Jules Bates
Paul Lesperance

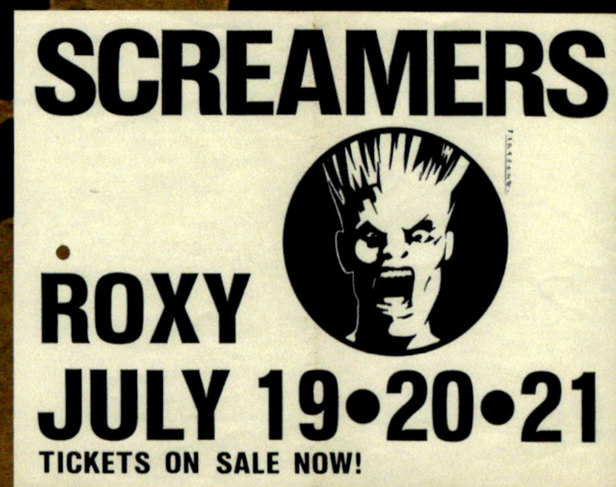

© Gary Panter

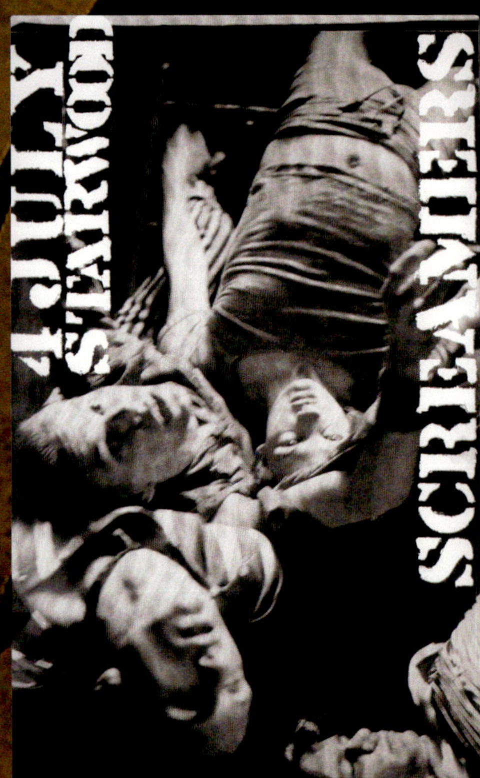

THE THING IS;
WE WERE OF PURE SONIC DESIRE.
ABANDON THE INSTRUMENT
INSTRUMENT THE ABANDON
HAMMER OVERDRIVEN ART DAMAGE INTO DISTORTED MINDFUCK PAST SUSTAINED ECHO TO MAKE MASS MASS CONGEALS OVERHEAD SQUEEZING FLESH PAST BONE TO BRAIN FODDER. CONSTANT FOOT-SNARE-TOM BLUNDER KICKING SAND INTO THE TRAN-SISTERS OF THREE BANAL CRIMINALS OF THE 70's. AN ARP ODYSSEY SYNTHESIZER, THE POLITE FENDER RHODES ELECTRIC PIANO, AND THE RHYTHM ACE BEAT BOX. THESE THREE VICTIMS OF THE LIGHT TOUCH LOVED TO BE JAIL-RAPED INTO SOLDIERS OF DISCIPLINE BY CHOKING THEM THROUGH A DAISY CHAIN OF BIG MUFFY'S FUZZY TWEAKERS AND OPEN-NECK FED THE INTIMATE DANCING STEROID GARGLE OF ONE WE CALLED THE SINGER...WAS IT TENDER?
THE THING IS;
WE WANTED TO BE OF OUR TIME,
ELIMINATE NOSTALGIA: A MISGUIDED ADRIFTNESS TOWARDS SUNSHINE WHEN CONCRETE BECKONED.

KK BARRETT

Screaming Punk
© Gary Panter

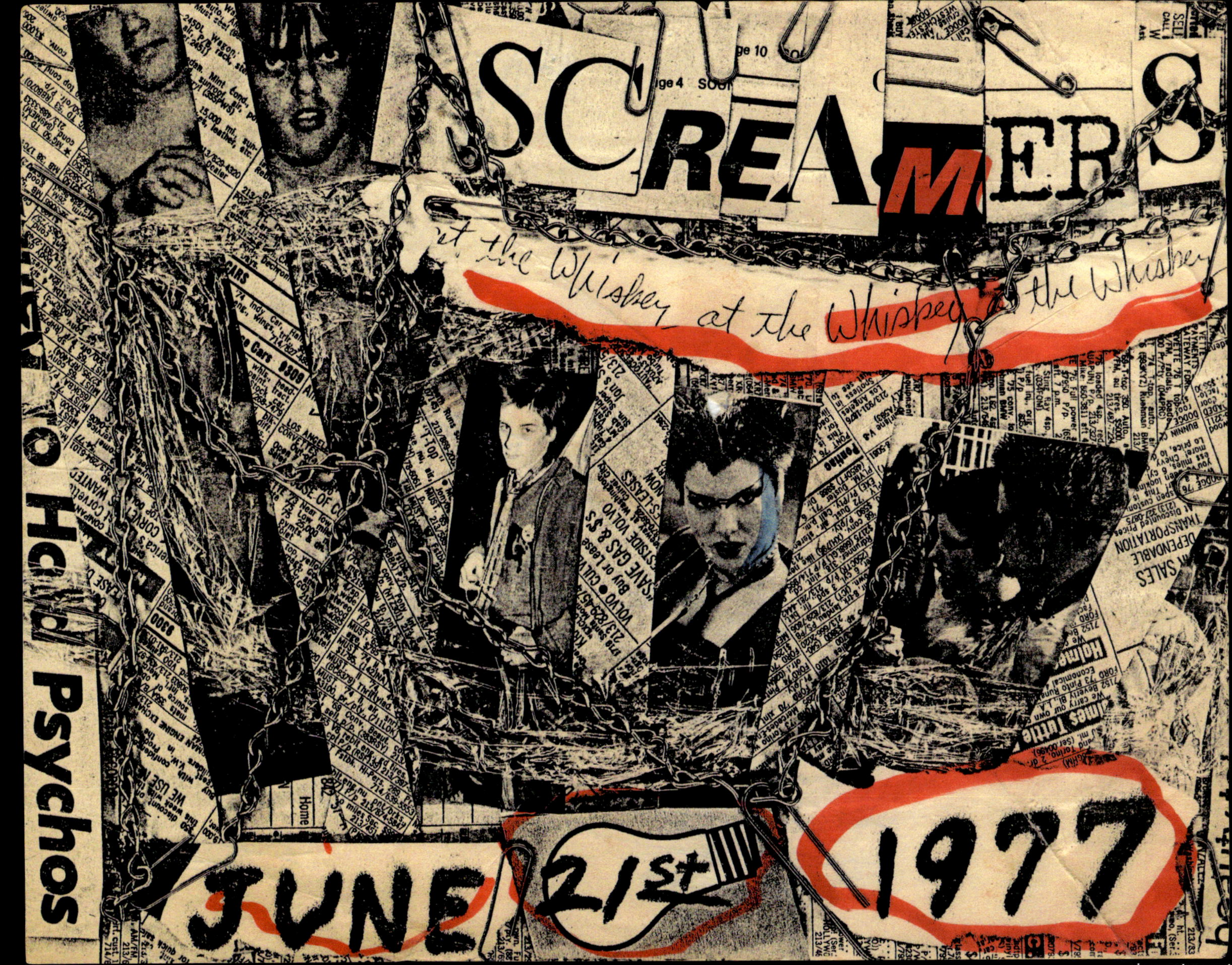

gig never happened

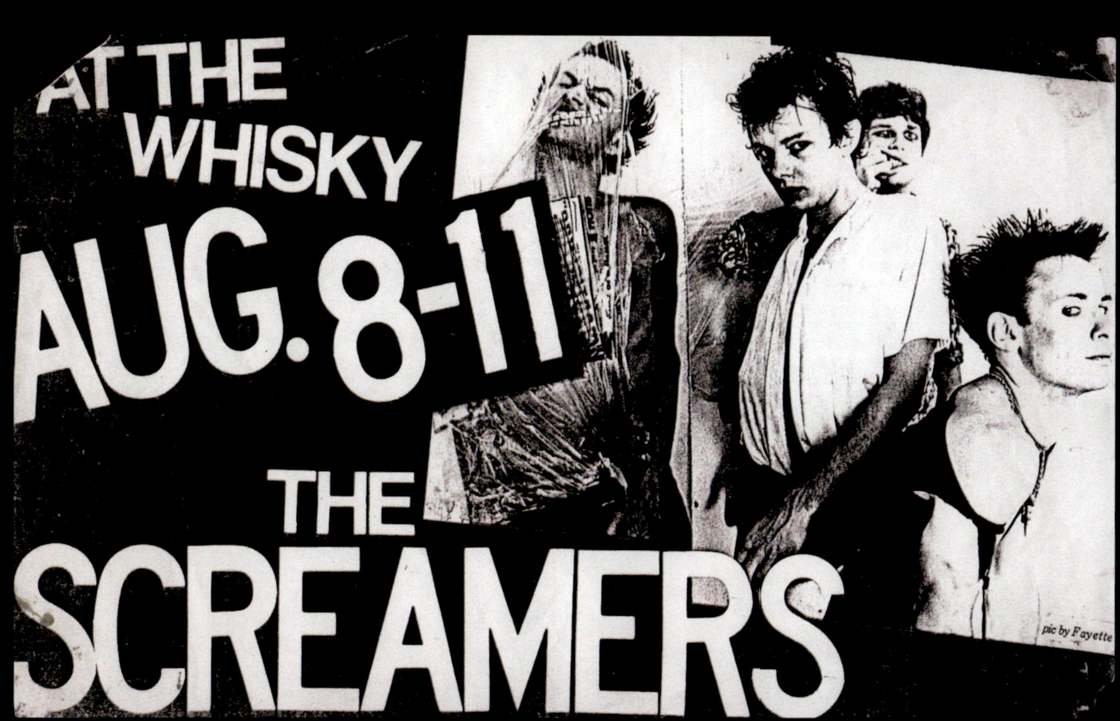

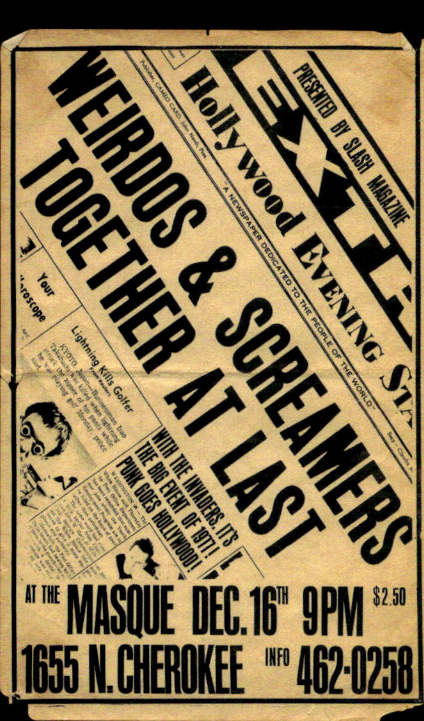

MINUTEMEN

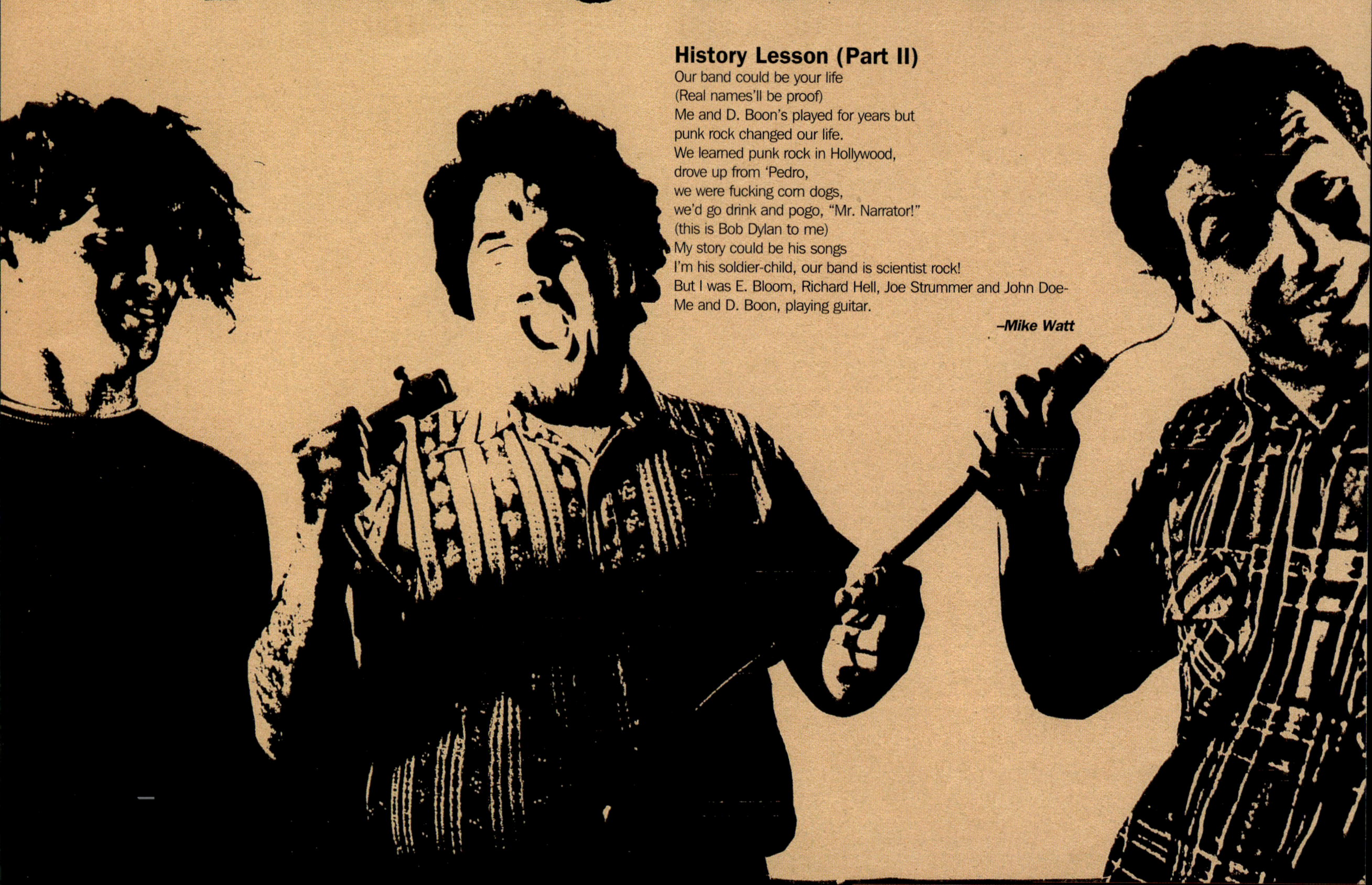

History Lesson (Part II)

Our band could be your life
(Real names'll be proof)
Me and D. Boon's played for years but
punk rock changed our life.
We learned punk rock in Hollywood,
drove up from 'Pedro,
we were fucking corn dogs,
we'd go drink and pogo, "Mr. Narrator!"
(this is Bob Dylan to me)
My story could be his songs
I'm his soldier-child, our band is scientist rock!
But I was E. Bloom, Richard Hell, Joe Strummer and John Doe-
Me and D. Boon, playing guitar.

–Mike Watt

The Joy of Touring by Mike Watt ***January 1983*** I was with the Minutemen touring Europe with Black Flag. In Geneva we stayed at a squatter's place. After drinking their homemade shine, they told us it was mad from rotten fruit and shit they found in dumpsters and garbage cans. I tried to use the bathroom but because this was a squat, there was no plumbing. I opened a door and found turds piled three feet off th toilet. The stench overpowered me, throwing me to the floor. I pissed my pants, but somehow managed to close that door. I cannot accurately relate the reek of that stink. ***Fall 1985*** I go to pick up a friend at Newar Airport after a soundcheck in Manhattan. That whole tour I was wearing army clothes with a beard - kind of a Castro parody. At the airport I ran into some automatic doors that would *not* open. When I opene them myself, two plainclothes policemen grabbed me and threw me against a counter and completely *(COMPLETELY)* searched me, saying "What's up with you, Mr Iranian!" ***Food Poisoning*** I have a gut like a turke vulture after 20 tours, but when I first hit the road food poisoning was a constant hazard. In winter of 1985 we were touring with REM and I got the bug in Land o' Lakes, Florida. It soon became useless to kee changing my pants, so I tied a shirt around my waist and rags around the bottoms of my pant legs. Three days later my pants were full to the knees.

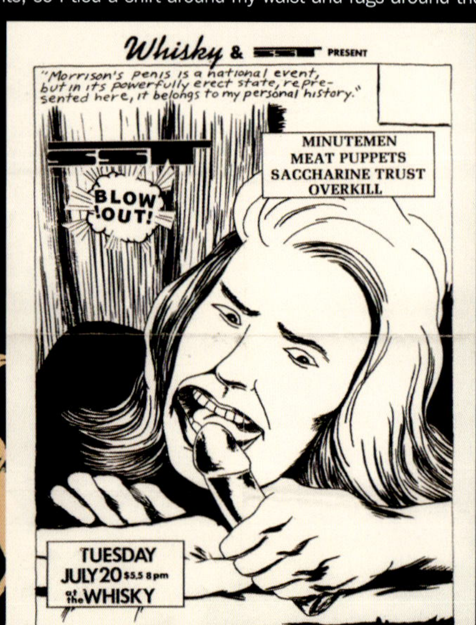

Raymond Pettibon

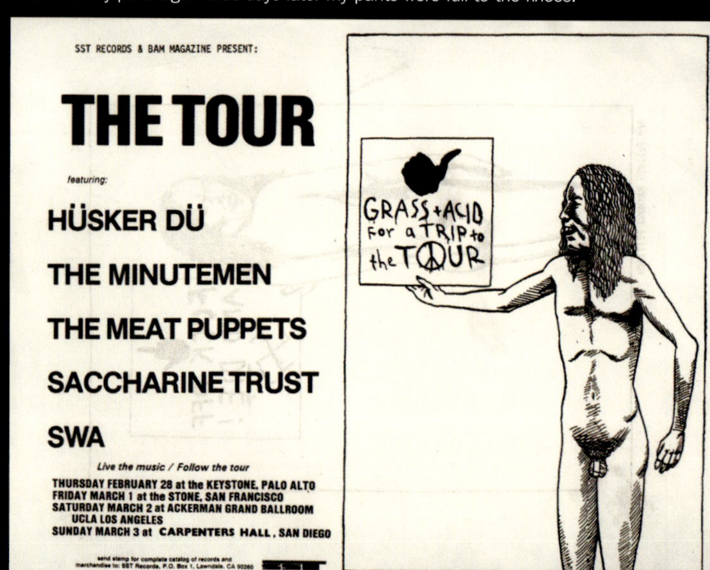

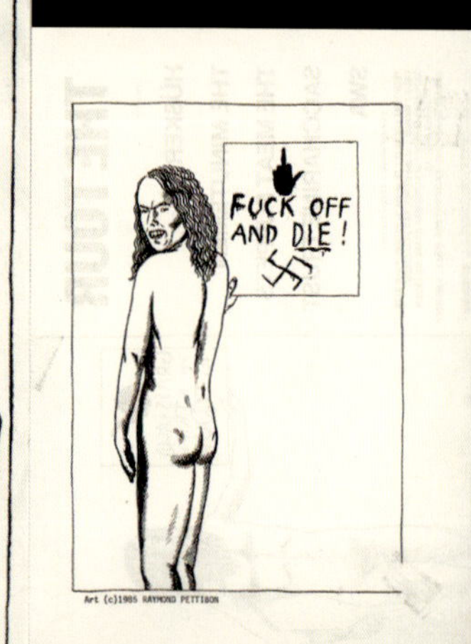

Raymond Pettibon

Page 86: ***R.I.P.*** • D Boon • Robert Dapello • Scotty Volmer • Darby Crash • Will Shatter • Sid Vicious • Billy Rath • Jerry Nolan • Johnny Thunders • Arthur Killer Kane • Nilly Murcia • Jay Adams • Bob Casale • Alan Myers • Derf Scratch • Dee Dee Ramone • Joey Ramone • Johnny Ramone • Tommy Ramone • Artura Vega • Shawn Kerri • Mad Marc Rude • Ian Dury • Jay Reatard • Joe Strummer • Lux Interior • Malcolm McLaren • Nikki Sudden • Randall J. Biscuit Turner • Rik L Rik • Rozz Williams • Ron Asheton • Sc Asheton • Stevo Jensen • Tim Yohannan • Pig Champion • Tomata du Plenty • Leee Black Childers • Poly Styrene • John Peel • Dennis Danell • Dimwit • Tim Rawbiz Williams • Se Dunnigan • Mike Dunnigan • J. P. Toulon • Jennifer MIro • Raybeez • Ben Zanotto • Randy Kaye • Dirk Dirksen • Lance Loud • Patrick Miller • Bryan Gregory • Bruce Kalberg • Dave Insurgent • Robert Quine • Chuck Wagon • Annie Larue • Yvonne Pinto • Lester Bangs • John Dougherty • Wendy O. Williams • Stiv Bator • Claude Bessy • Jeffrey Lee Pierce • Rob Rit Craig Lee • David Wiley • El Duce • Brendan Mullen • Black Randy • Hillel Slovak • G.G. Allin • Brad Barnett • Ian Curtis • Rob Graves • Bill Bartell • Drew Bernstein

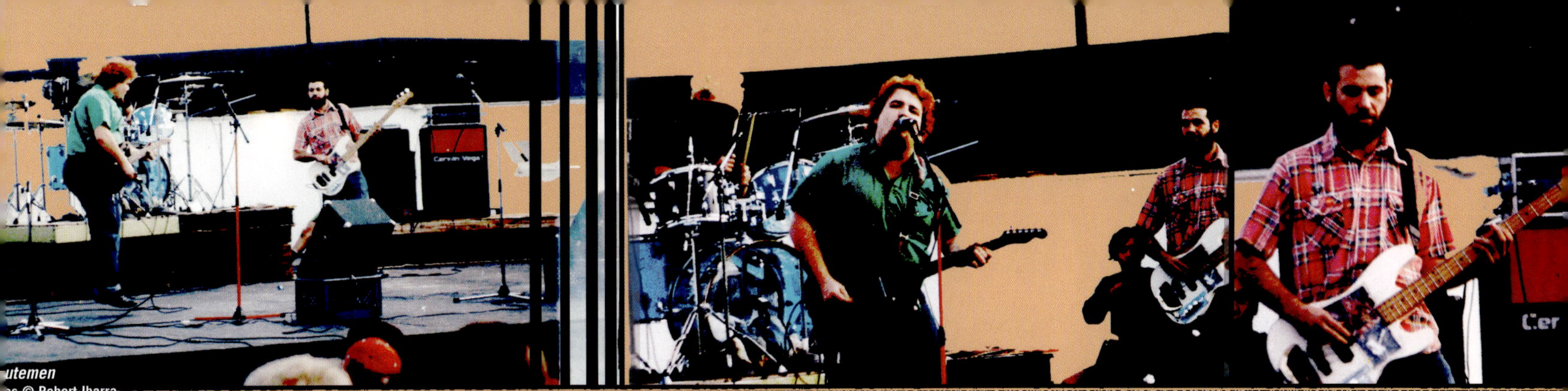

utemen
os © Robert Ibarra

N D. BOON GETS AIRBORNE AT LAST SHOW FOR MINUTEMEN

Photographs, Set List and flyer from Last 'Pedro Gig, November 16, 1985 at Angels Gate Cultural Center Amphitheater

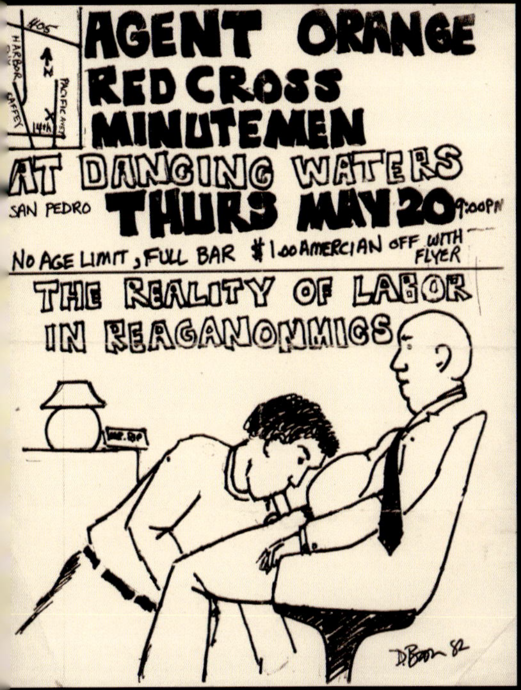

. Boon

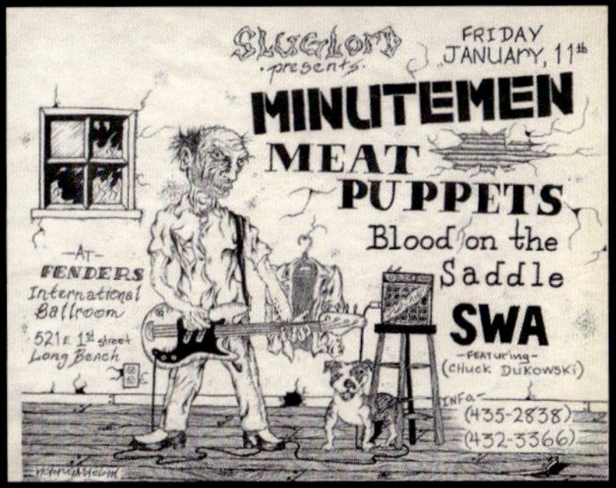

Victor Gastelum

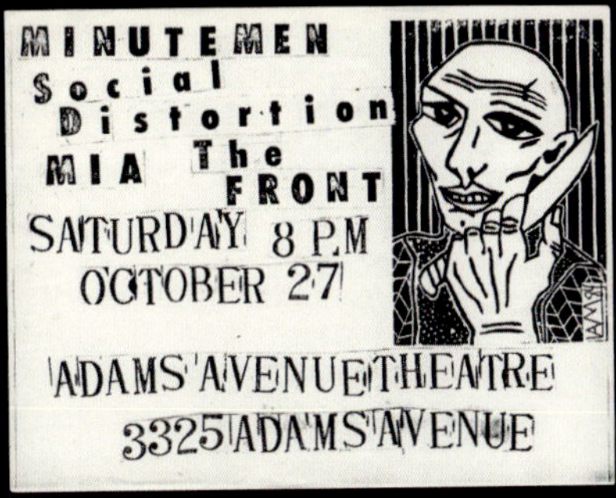

A.M.

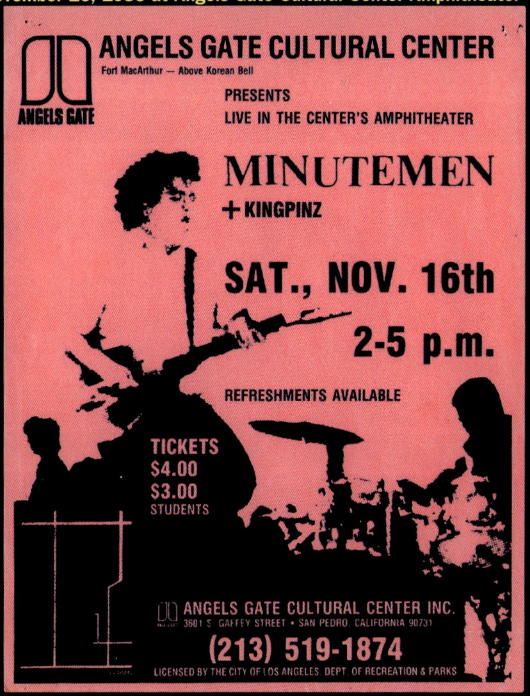

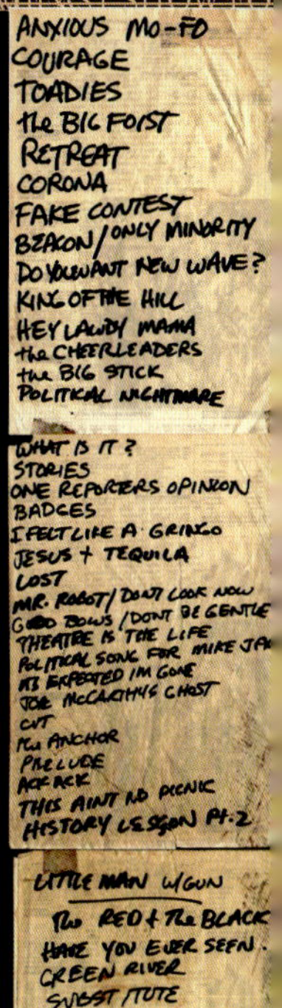

Joe Carducci

Gig flyers work. That's why they're all over the place. You can't depend on the putative music media to do their job. They're all media professionals looking for professional musicians. They don't want to know about your cruddy garage band. You are well beneath them. It's not in their purview to help anyone out. They program music and spread gig info about bands that THEY need, not bands that need THEM.

Your cruddy band is left to depend on the few record stores, book stores, newsstands, etc. responsible enough to leave space for flyer stacks near the door, municipal lamp posts and the Xerox Corporation of America.

Print shops themselves are frequently cultural information centers themselves. Before Punk there was so little musical activity that lamp posts and record stores were bare. The mid-seventies music industry was primed for platinum via radio and *Rolling Stone*– simple, no need to get offset ink on your fingers or wheat paste all over your pants. The only bands that got signed were those first signed to management contracts by established/known/connected individuals or companies. you know, kinda like today. (Only way worse, kids. that may have been our advantage. Good luck to you– you'll need it.)

My brother had a band from 1969 to 1976. No flyers. No flyers in college in 1974. No flyers in Chicago in 1975. Saw my first relevant non-frat party flyer in Hollywood for the *Ramones*. (Didn't go.) Saw a *Dogs* flyer too. (Didn't go.) I'd never been to a gig except for my brother's band, and *Tangerine Dream*. Portland in 1978-79 and Berkeley in '80-81– I saw lots of flyers and started going to the gigs: *Zeros, DOA, Dils, Dead Kennedys, Wipers, Neo Boys, Screamers, Crime, Weirdos, Flipper, Black Flag, Monitor, Sleepers, Avengers, Pink Section, Alley Cats,* ooowee, you name it. I thought I knew flyers, then I moved back to Los Angeles. There had never been flyers-as-medium like the flyers for a Los Angeles *Black Flag* gig in the years 1979-1983. Black Flag produced radio spots for these gigs and flew planes with banners over outdoor rock festivals, but mostly they did flyers. Pettibon, Pettibon everywhere. Los Angeles County. Orange County. Mugger and Robo on foot, walking from Hermosa to Hollywood, gluing Pettibon on every light post on Crenshaw: Dukowski and Dez driving the van, high school to high school to Anaheim. They'd all come back splattered survivors of the paste orgy of all time. Then they'd all go out to the *Iron Maiden* gig and put a flyer on every car's windshield in the parking lot of the Long Beach arena. Thousands of flyers for a gig at Devonshire Downs, or the Stardust Ballroom. Some of them are still up. Archaeologists of the 30th century will think *Black Flag* was the name of the municipal electrical utility.

I'm not into handbills myself. I kept a few for gigs at my place in Laramie, but they are merely utilitarian. I went to Tower in New York last month to place 8-1/2" x 14" flyers for my film and found that their counter was full of tiny handbills and full color rave cards. I kicked their ass with my flyers. Right on.

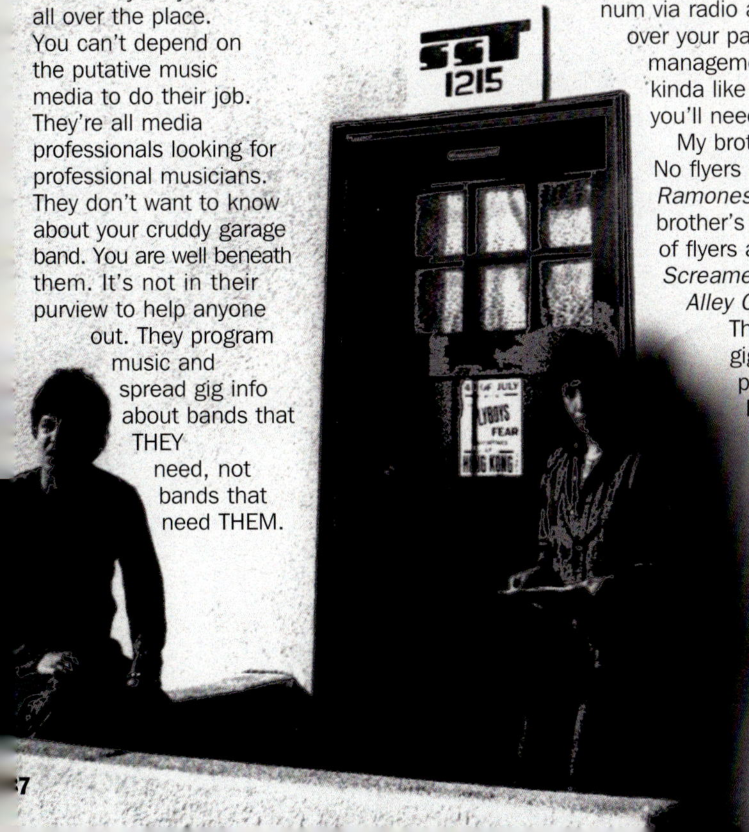

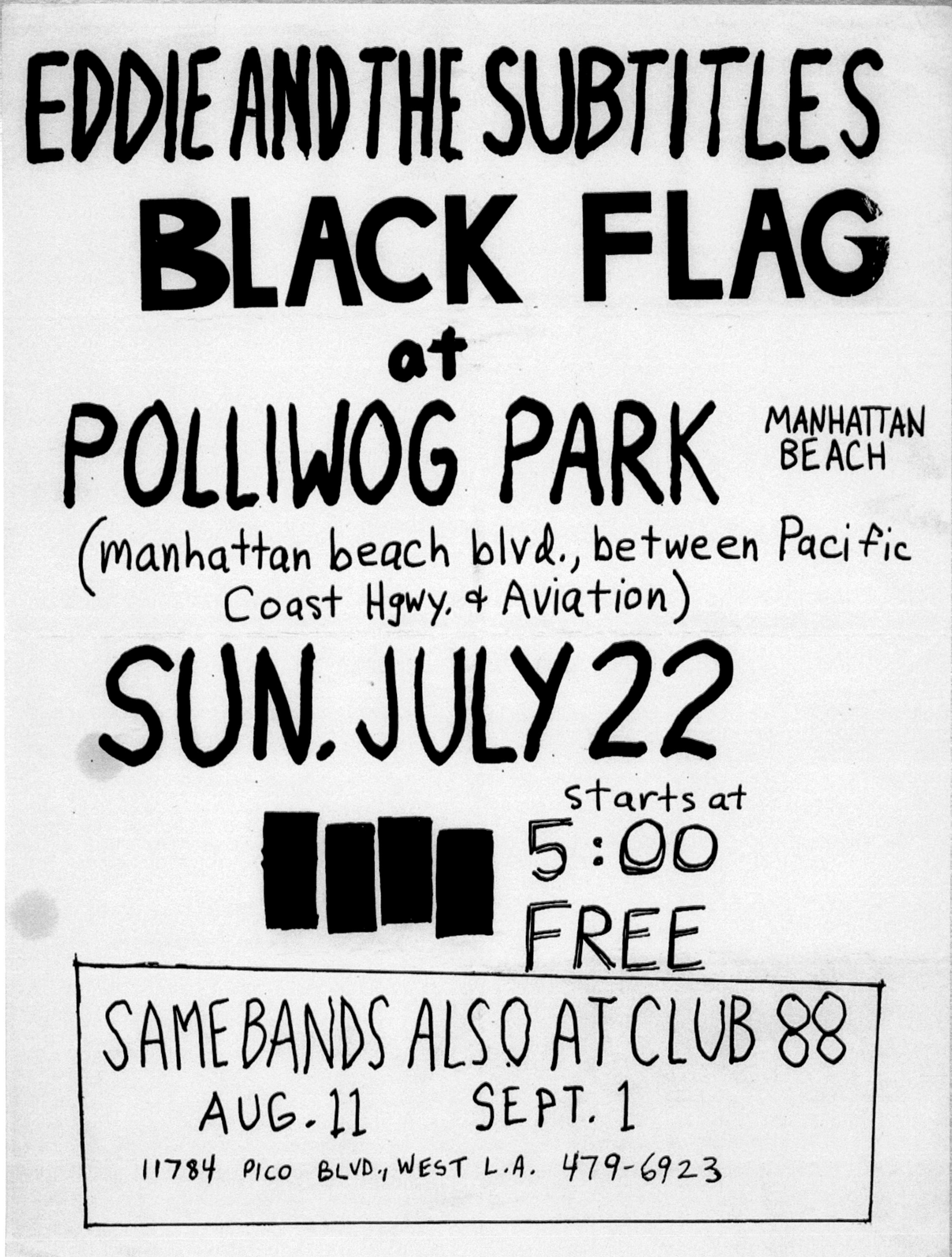

Black Flag claimed to be a Fleetwood Mac cover band so that park officials would let them play. Over 1,000 people showed up—all hell broke loose.

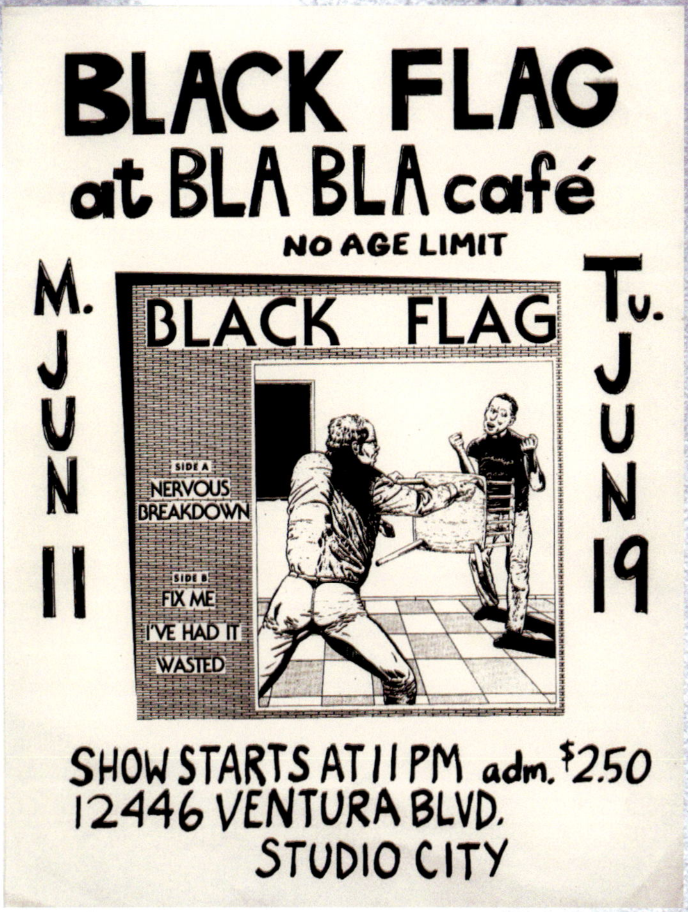

Raymond Pettibon

1st night: all hell broke loose.
2nd night: cancelled.

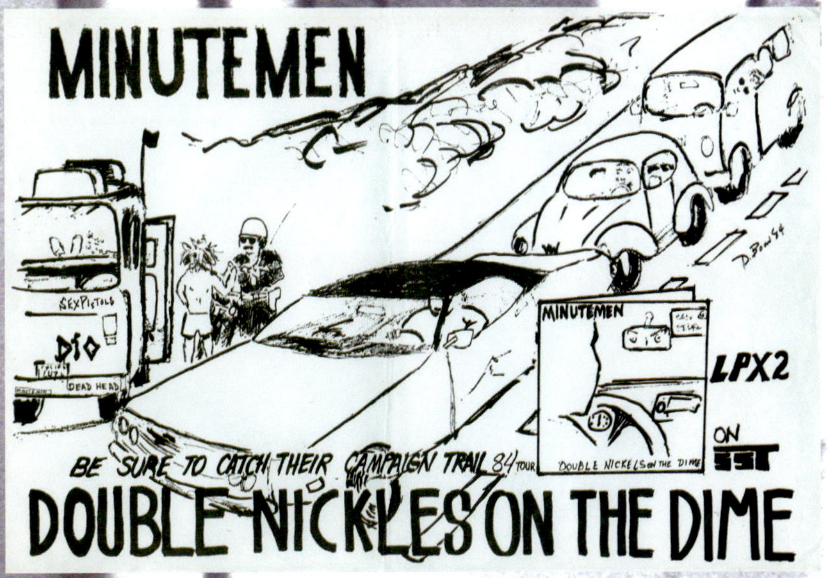

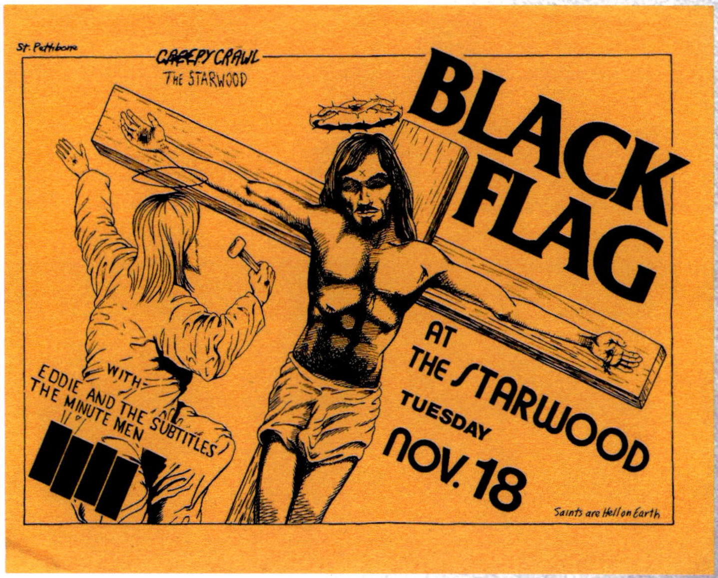

Raymond Pettibon

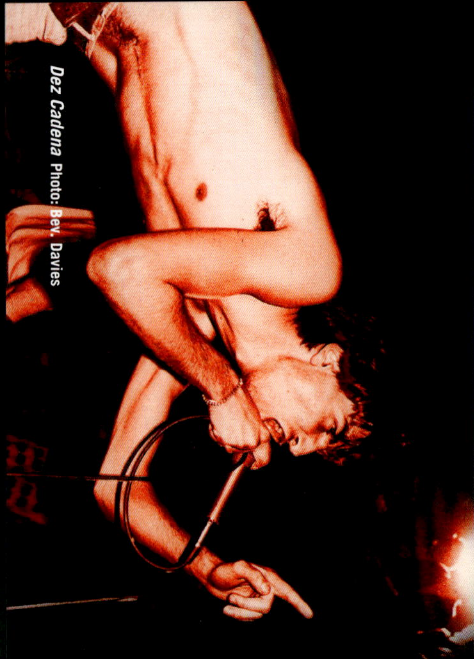

Dez Cadena Photo: Bev. Davies

Ever since I can remember, the fight to maintain individuality has been the driving force of my existence.

I owe this to my father and his commitment to free thinking. Like him, my struggle manifests itself in the creation of music.

High School was a major lesson in social retardation. The only escape from that banality was music and art.

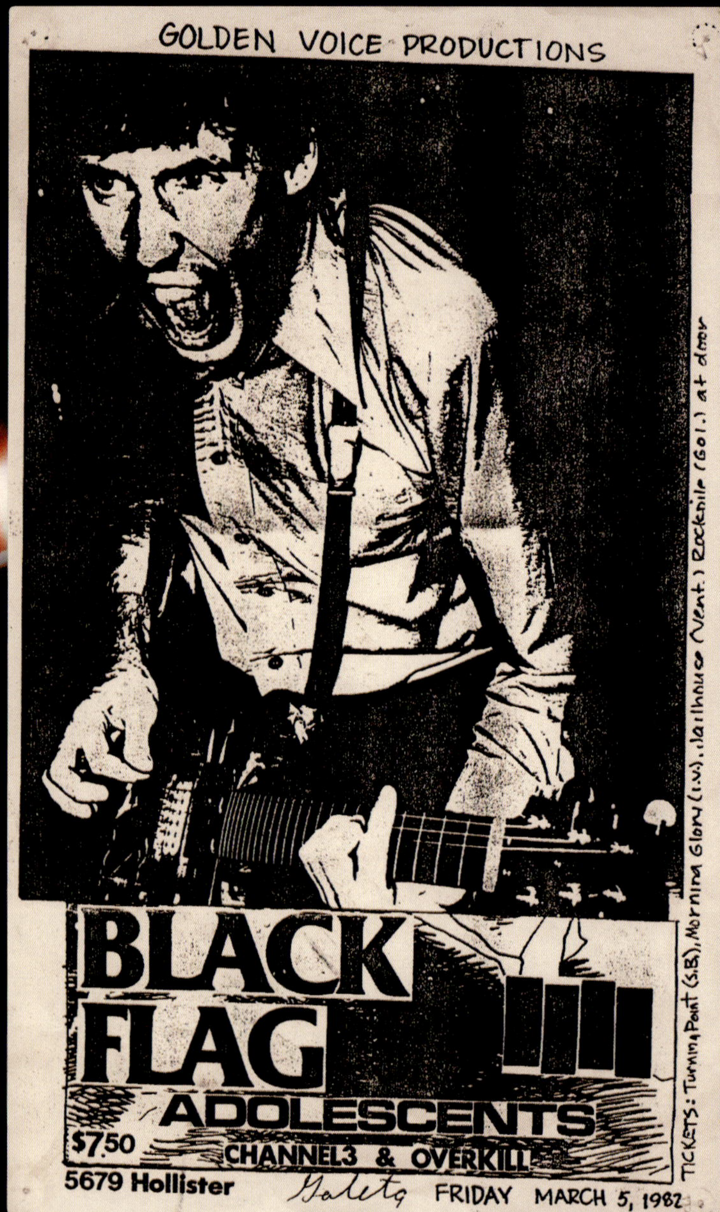

I stumbled onto this form of expression via Rodney Bingenheimer's radio show in '78 and '79. I'd gather with friends and tune in on Sunday nights, taping the show to acquire the music of Angeleno bands like Germs, Controllers, Screamers, Bags, Eyes, etc. It was the best place to find out about new bands and venues, not to mention the only way to hear music from England and New York. I knew Rodney was a scenester from the '60s from listening to the first Larry "Wildman" Fisher album and GTOs lps, but it wasn't until 1974 when my family moved to Hermosa Beach from Newark NJ, that I finally realized who Rodney was. He basically formed the scene here

Other than Rodney's show, the only other forms of communication for bands and gigs was word of mouth, or flyers. To me, each individual flyer represented a very separate and individual experience. I used to collect them, until I started playing in "serious" bands, then I lost interest (I was too busy handing our own flyers out.)

Black Flag's philosophy on advertising was, "Let everyone know the name of your band whether they like it or not!" You'd grab a bucket of paste and flyer every locker at some high school. (Preferably not your own, it was too easy to get busted. Call the dean at Huntington Beach High School for more information on this subject.)

A book like this is great for an old fart like myself to remember the good ol' days, but it's hard for me to romanticize about Punk rock. And if you're younger than I am, don't romanticize it - get twisted and make your own scene.

Dez Cadena

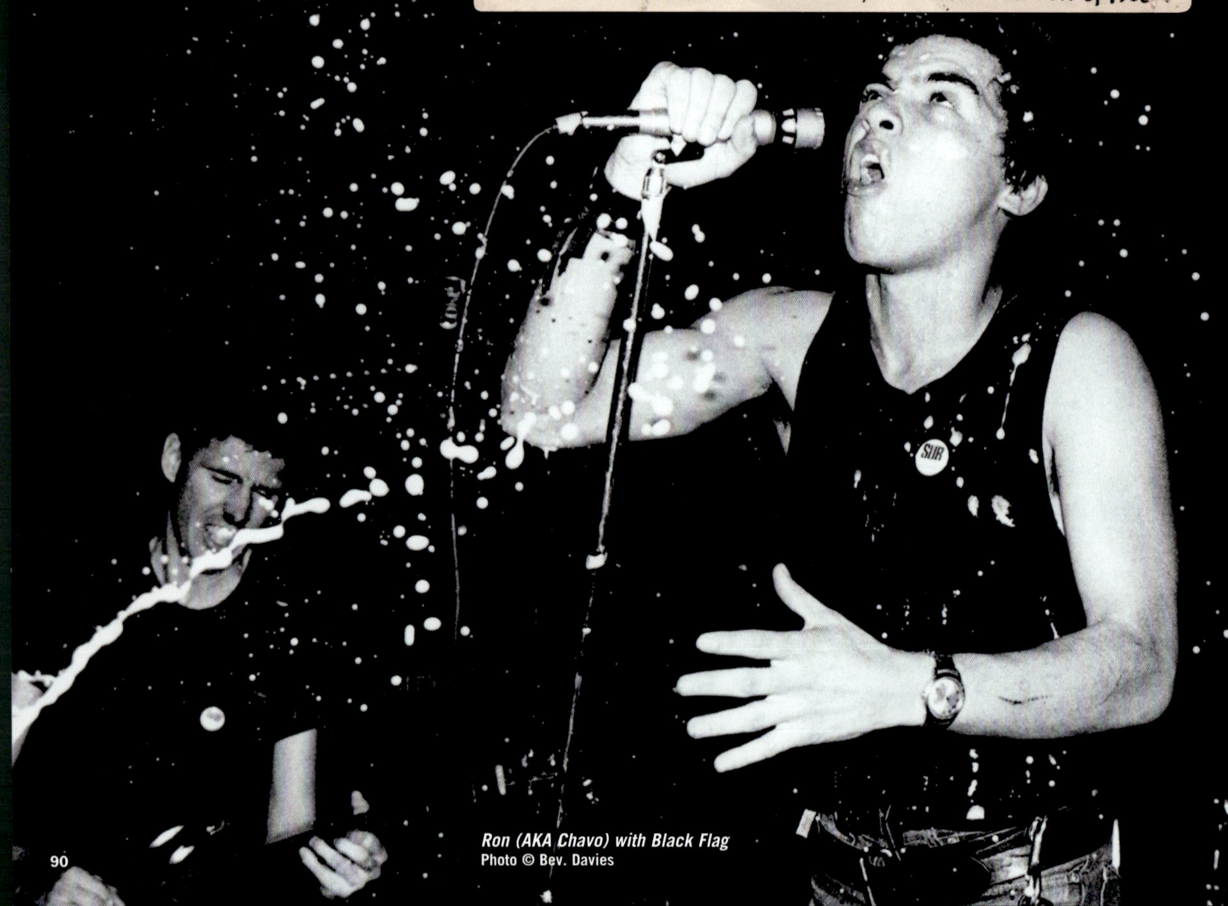

Ron (AKA Chavo) with Black Flag
Photo © Bev. Davies

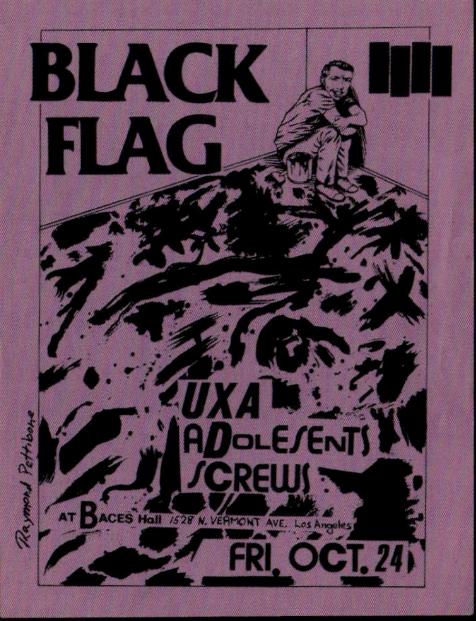
BLACK FLAG
UXA
ADOLESENTS
SCREWS
AT BACES Hall 1528 N. VERMONT AVE. Los Angeles
FRI. OCT. 24
Raymond Pettibone

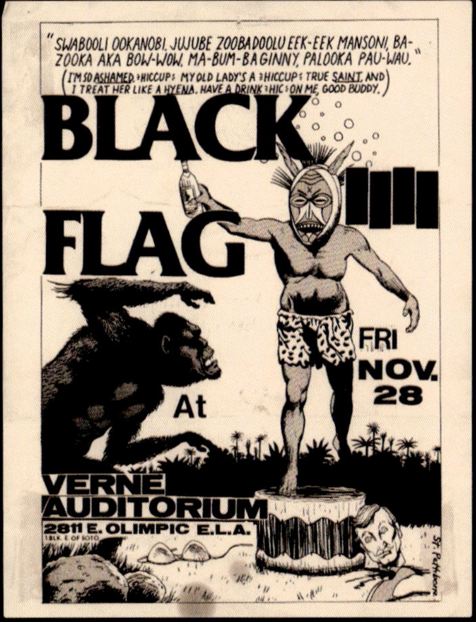
"SWABOOLI OOKANOBI, JUJUBE ZOOBADOOLU EEK-EEK MANSONI, BAZOOKA AKA BOW-WOW, MA-BUM-BAGINNY, PALOOKA PAU-WAU."
I'M SO ASHAMED (HICCUP) MY OLD LADY'S A (HICCUP) TRUE SAINT, AND I TREAT HER LIKE A HYENA. HAVE A DRINK (HIC) ON ME GOOD BUDDY.
BLACK
FLAG
FRI
NOV.
28
At
VERNE AUDITORIUM
2811 E. OLYMPIC E.L.A.

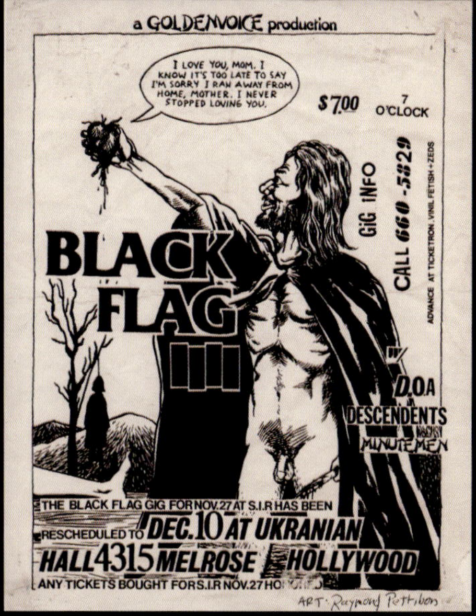
a GOLDENVOICE production
I LOVE YOU, MOM. I KNOW IT'S TOO LATE TO SAY I'M SORRY I RAN AWAY FROM HOME, MOTHER. I NEVER STOPPED LOVING YOU.
$7.00
7 O'CLOCK
GIG INFO
CALL 660-5829
BLACK FLAG
W/
D.O.A
DESCENDENTS
MINUTEMEN
THE BLACK FLAG GIG FOR NOV.27 AT S.I.R HAS BEEN
RESCHEDULED TO DEC.10 AT UKRANIAN
HALL 4315 MELROSE HOLLYWOOD
ANY TICKETS BOUGHT FOR S.I.R NOV.27 HO...
ART: Raymond Pettibon

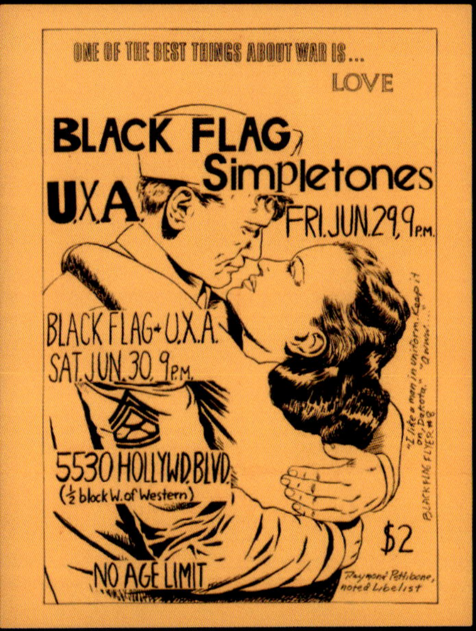
ONE OF THE BEST THINGS ABOUT WAR IS...
LOVE
BLACK FLAG
Simpletones
U.X.A
FRI. JUN. 29, 9 P.M.
BLACK FLAG + U.X.A.
SAT. JUN. 30. 9 P.M.
5530 HOLLYWD. BLVD.
(½ block W. of Western)
$2
NO AGE LIMIT
Raymond Pettibone, noted Libelist

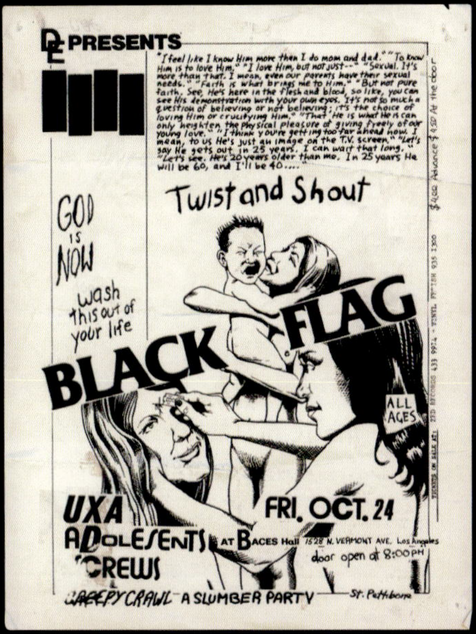
PRESENTS
GOD is NOW
wash this out of your life
Twist and Shout
BLACK FLAG
ALL AGES
FRI. OCT. 24
UXA
ADOLESENTS
SCREWS
AT BACES Hall 1528 N. VERMONT AVE. Los Angeles
door open at 8:00 PM
CREEPY CRAWL A SLUMBER PARTY

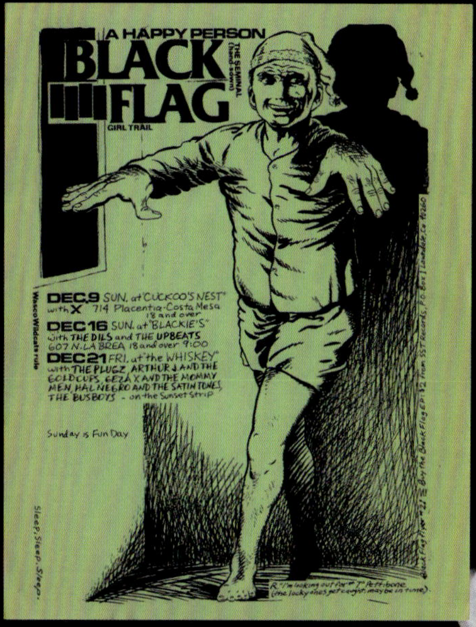
A HAPPY PERSON
BLACK FLAG
DEC 9 SUN. at "CUCKOO'S NEST" with X 714 Placentia - Costa Mesa
DEC 16 SUN. at "BLACKIE'S" with THE DILS and THE UPBEATS 607 N. LA BREA
DEC 21 FRI. at the "WHISKEY" with THE PLUGZ, ARTHUR J. AND THE GOLD CUPS, GEZA X AND THE MOMMY MEN, HAL NEGRO AND THE SATIN TONES, THE BUSBOYS - on the Sunset Strip
Sunday is Fun Day

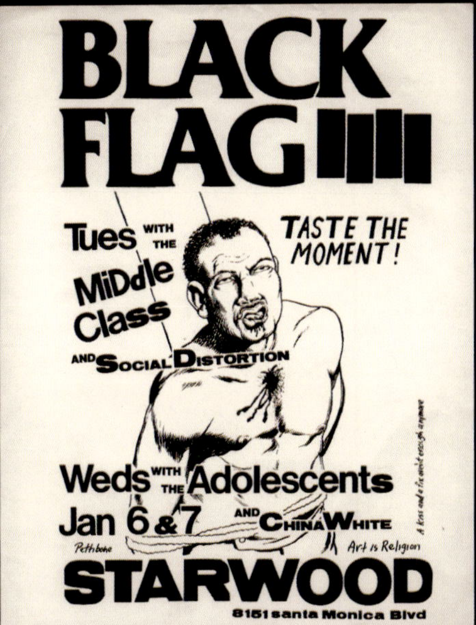
BLACK FLAG
Tues WITH THE Middle Class
AND Social Distortion
TASTE THE MOMENT!
Weds WITH THE Adolescents
AND China White
Jan 6 & 7
Pettibone
Art is Religion
STARWOOD
8151 santa Monica Blvd

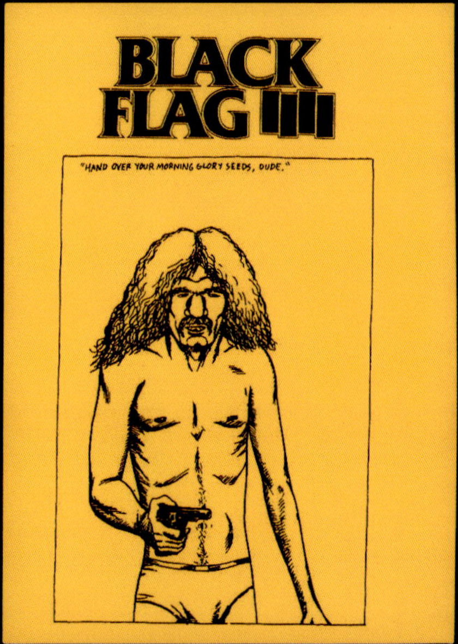
BLACK FLAG
"HAND OVER YOUR MORNING GLORY SEEDS, DUDE."

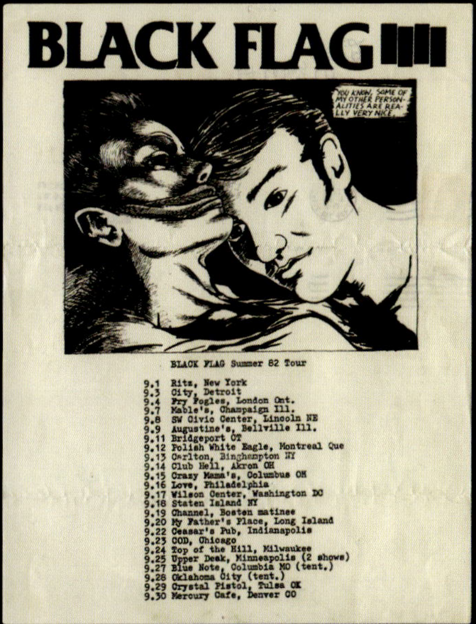
BLACK FLAG
YOU KNOW, SOME OF MY OTHER PERSONALITIES ARE REALLY VERY NICE.
BLACK FLAG Summer 82 Tour
9.1 Ritz, New York
9.3 City, Detroit
9.4 Fry Fogles, London Ont.
9.7 Mable's, Champaign Ill.
9.8 SW Civic Center, Lincoln NE
9.9 Augustine's, Bellville Ill.
9.11 Bridgeport CT
9.12 Polish White Eagle, Montreal Que
9.13 Carlton, Binghampton NY
9.14 Club Hell, Akron OH
9.15 Crazy Mama's, Columbus OH
9.16 Love, Philadelphia
9.17 Wilson Center, Washington DC
9.18 Staten Island NY
9.19 Channel, Boston matinee
9.20 My Father's Place, Long Island
9.22 Ceasar's Pub, Indianapolis
9.23 COD, Chicago
9.24 Top of the Hill, Milwaukee
9.25 Upper Deck, Minneapolis (2 shows)
9.27 Blue Note, Columbia MO (tent.)
9.28 Oklahoma City (tent.)
9.29 Crystal Pistol, Tulsa OK
9.30 Mercury Cafe, Denver CO

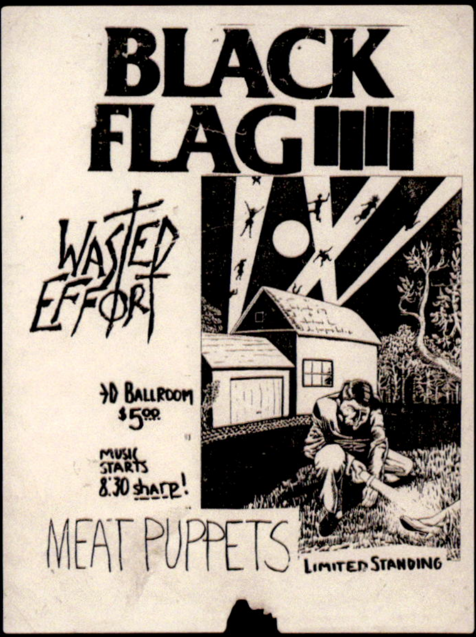

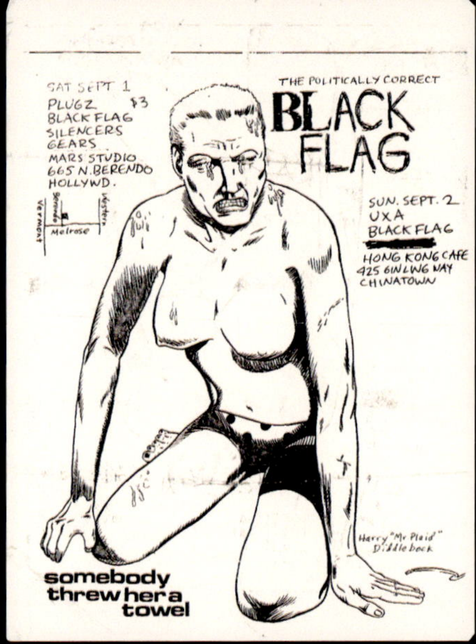

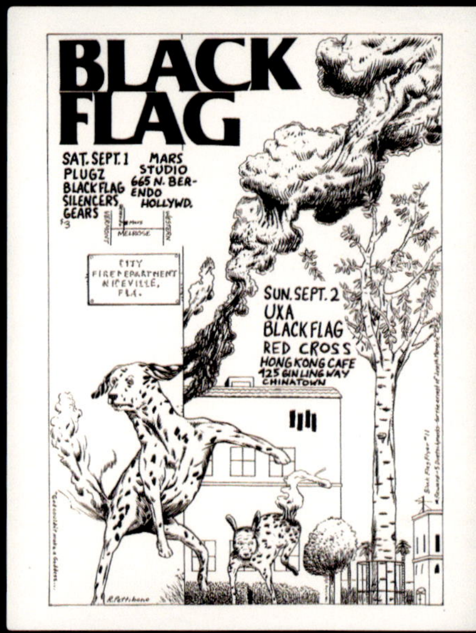

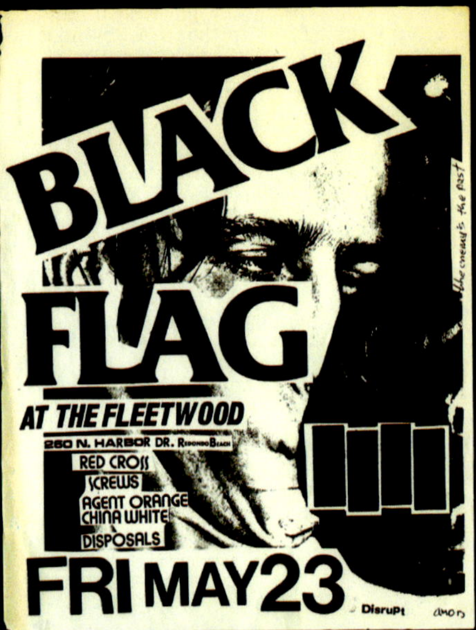

Except this one. We don't know who designed it...

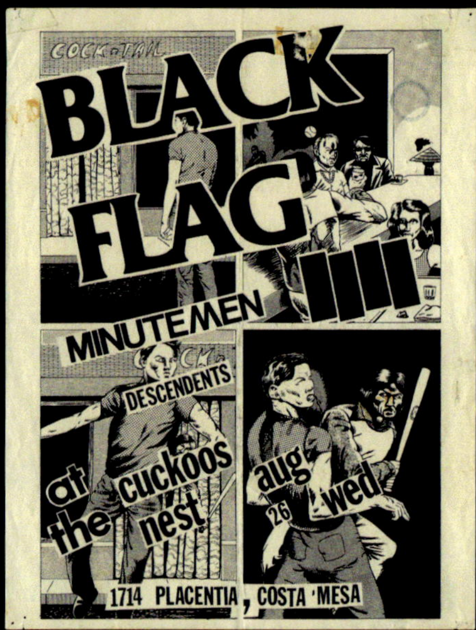

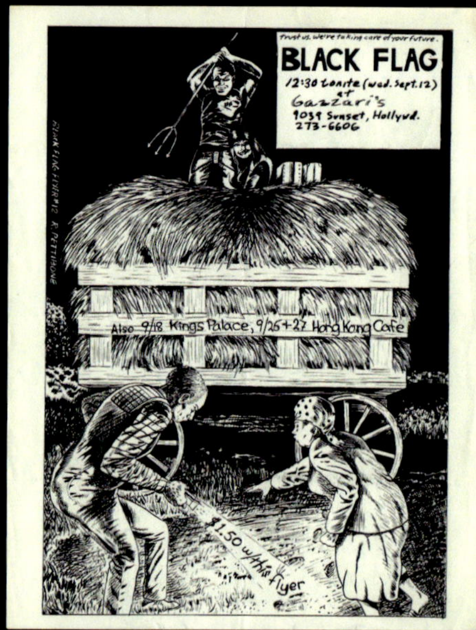

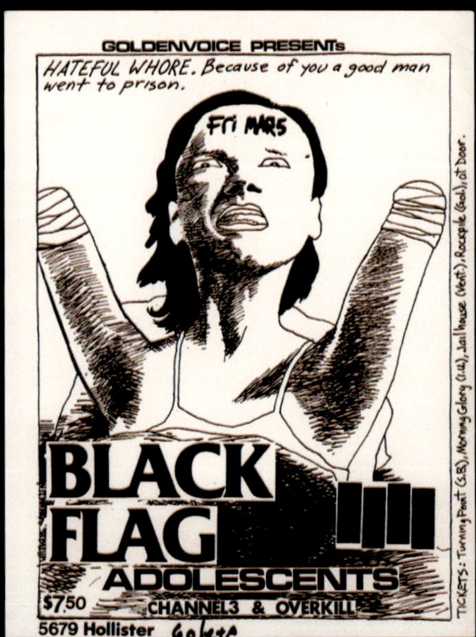

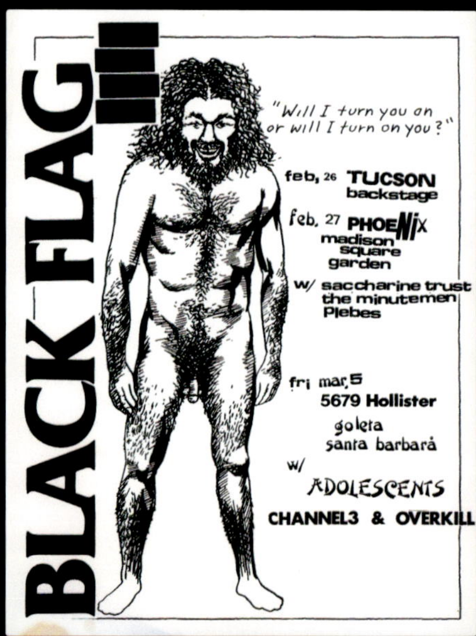

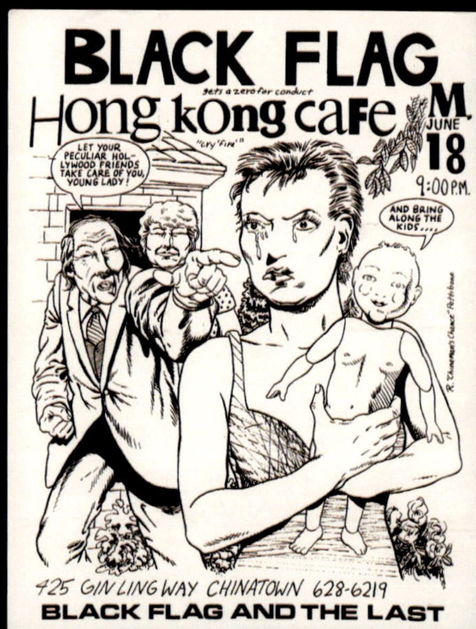

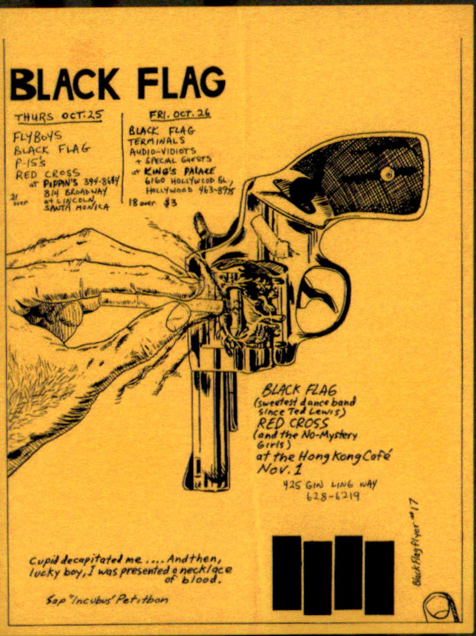
BLACK FLAG
THURS OCT. 25
FLYBOYS
BLACK FLAG
P-15's
RED CROSS
at PIPPIN'S 394-8689
814 BROADWAY
at LINCOLN, SANTA MONICA
FRI. OCT. 26
BLACK FLAG
TERMINALS
AUDIO-VIDIOTS
+ SPECIAL GUESTS
at KING'S PALACE
6160 HOLLYWOOD BL.
HOLLYWOOD 463-8915
18 over $3
BLACK FLAG
(sweetest dance band since Ted Lewis)
RED CROSS
(and the No-Mystery Girls)
at the Hong Kong Café
Nov. 1
425 GIN LING WAY
628-6219
Cupid decapitated me.... And then, lucky boy, I was presented a necklace of blood.
Sap "Incubus" Petitbon
Black Flag Flyer #17

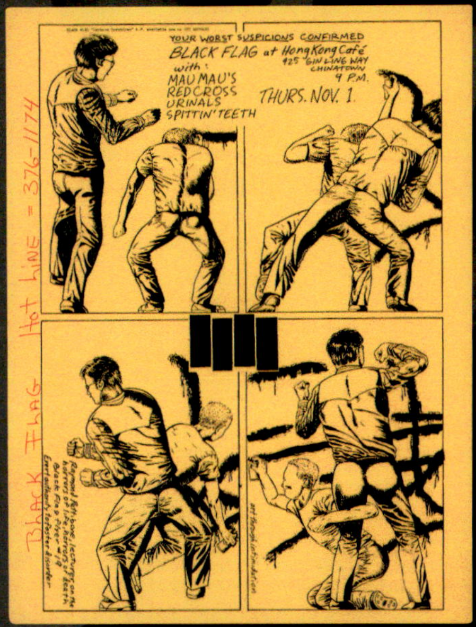
YOUR WORST SUSPICIONS CONFIRMED
BLACK FLAG at Hong Kong Café
425 GIN LING WAY
CHINATOWN
9 P.M.
with:
MAU MAU'S
RED CROSS
URINALS
SPITTIN' TEETH
THURS. NOV. 1.
BLACK FLAG Hot Line = 376-1174

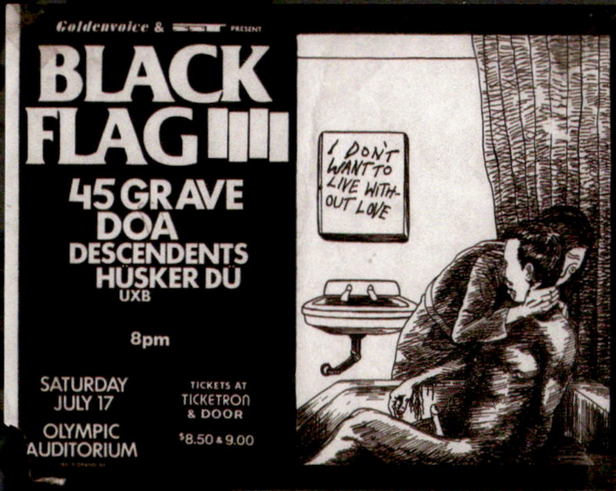
Goldenvoice & PRESENT
BLACK FLAG
45 GRAVE
DOA
DESCENDENTS
HÜSKER DÜ
UXB
8pm
SATURDAY JULY 17
OLYMPIC AUDITORIUM
TICKETS AT TICKETRON & DOOR
$8.50 & 9.00
I DON'T WANT TO LIVE WITHOUT LOVE

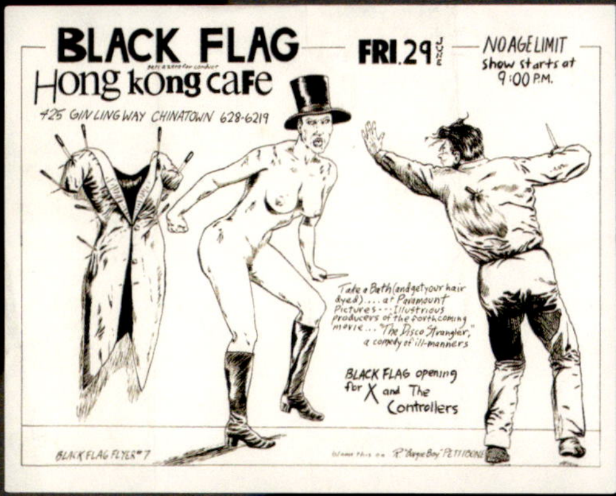
BLACK FLAG
FRI. 29
NO AGE LIMIT
Show starts at 9:00 P.M.
Hong kong cafe
425 GIN LING WAY CHINATOWN 628-6219
Take a Bath (and get your hair dyed)... at Paramount Pictures -- illustrious producers of the forthcoming movie... "The Disco Strangler," a comedy of ill-manners
BLACK FLAG opening for X and The Controllers
BLACK FLAG FLYER #7

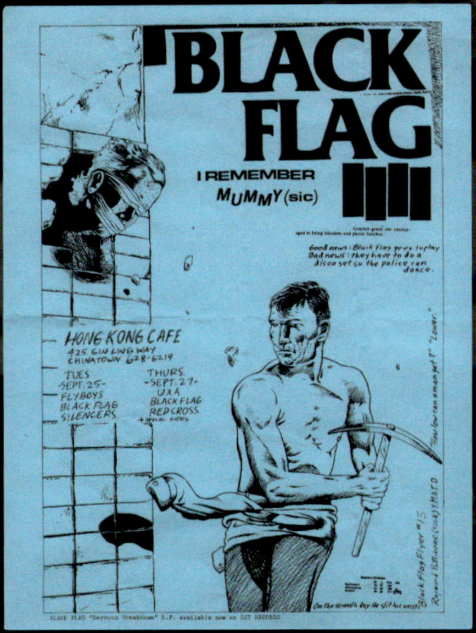
BLACK FLAG
I REMEMBER
MUMMY (sic)
Good news: Black Flag goes to play
Bad news: they have to do a disco set so the police can dance.
HONG KONG CAFE
425 GIN LING WAY
CHINATOWN 628-6219
TUES
-SEPT. 25-
FLYBOYS
BLACK FLAG
SILENCERS
THURS
-SEPT. 27-
UXA
BLACK FLAG
RED CROSS
Black Flag Flyer #15

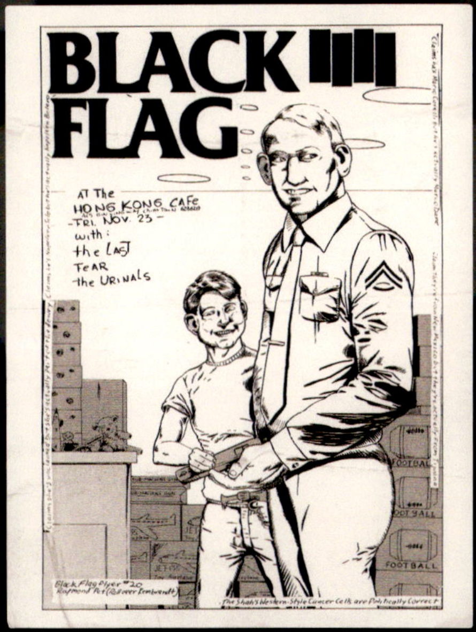
BLACK FLAG
AT The
HONG KONG CAFE
-FRI. NOV. 23-
with:
the LAST
TEAR
the URINALS
FOOTBALL
Black Flag Flyer #20

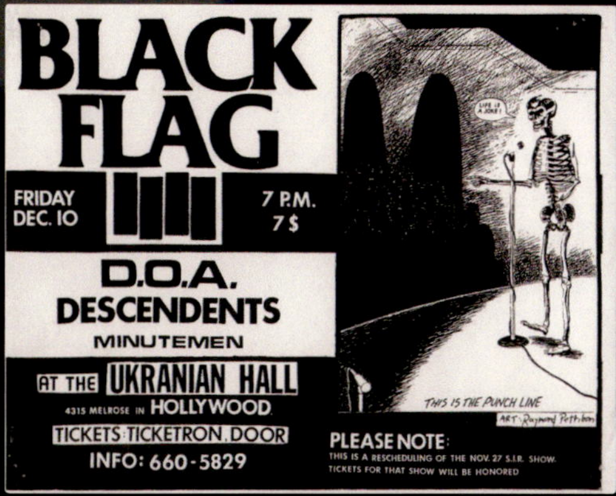
BLACK FLAG
FRIDAY DEC. 10
7 P.M.
7$
D.O.A.
DESCENDENTS
MINUTEMEN
AT THE UKRANIAN HALL
4315 MELROSE IN HOLLYWOOD
TICKETS: TICKETRON. DOOR
INFO: 660-5829
THIS IS THE PUNCH LINE
PLEASE NOTE:
THIS IS A RESCHEDULING OF THE NOV. 27 S.I.R. SHOW.
TICKETS FOR THAT SHOW WILL BE HONORED

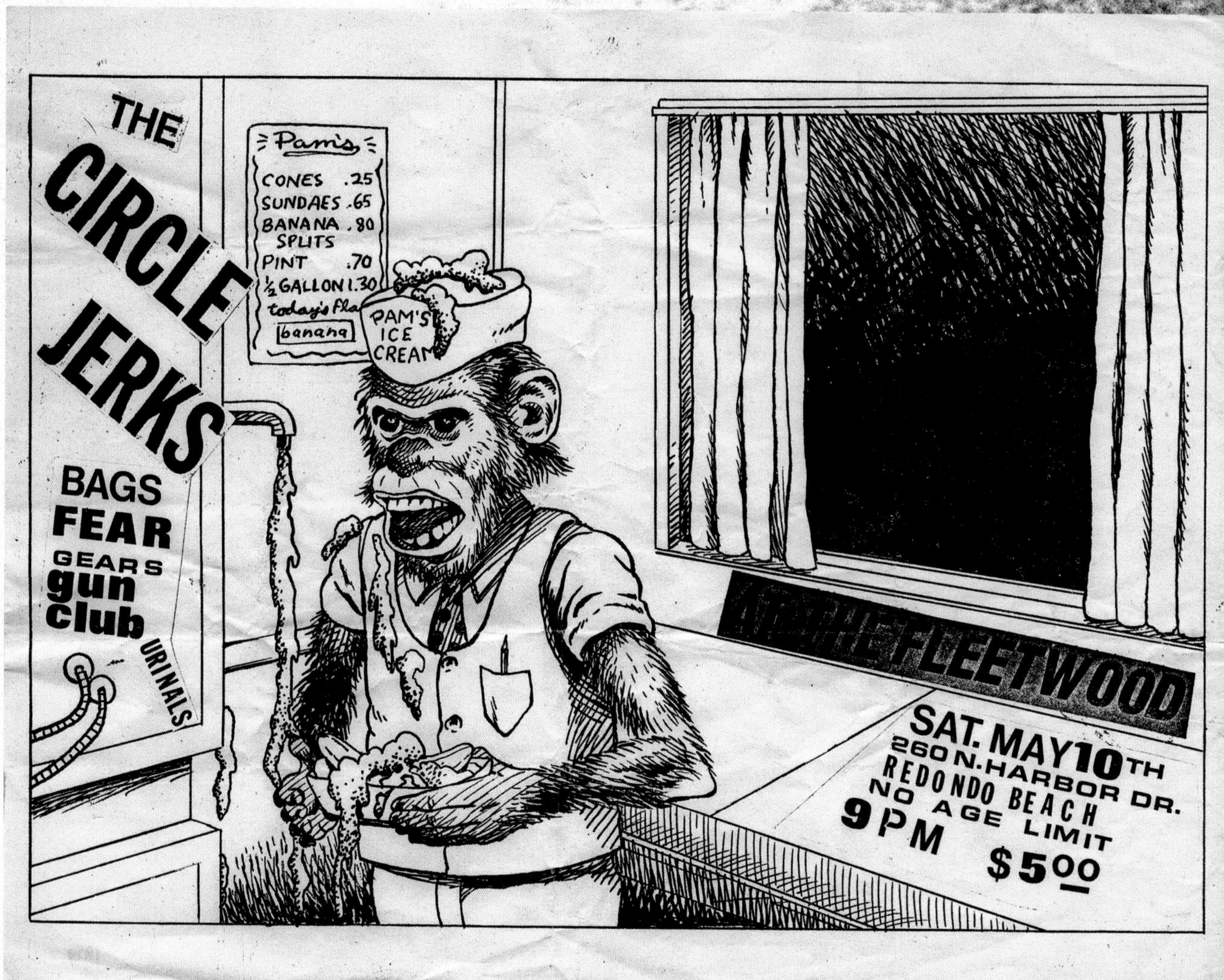

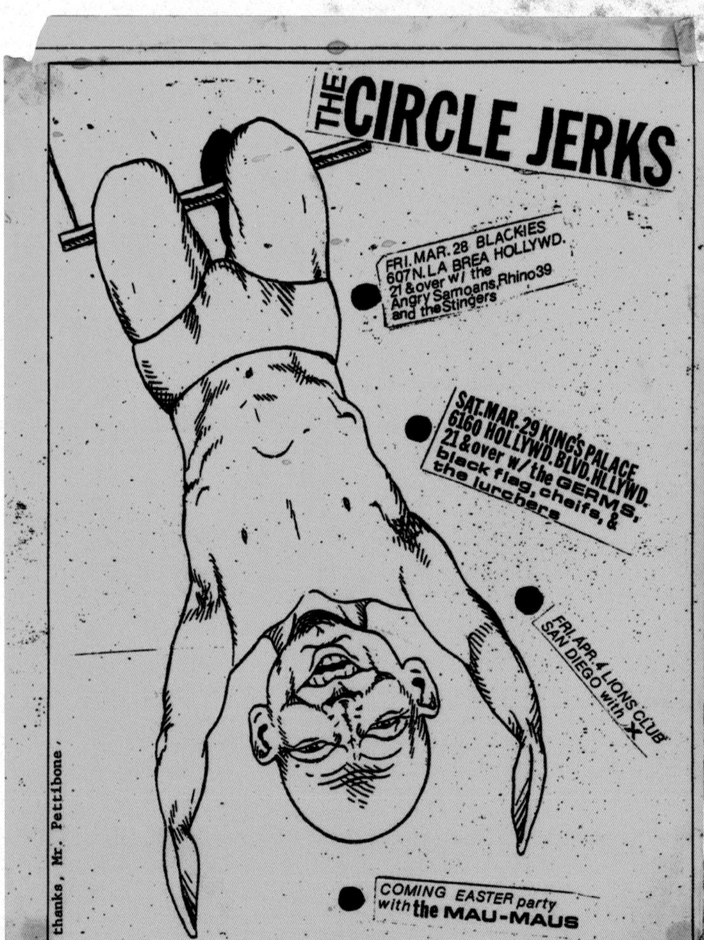

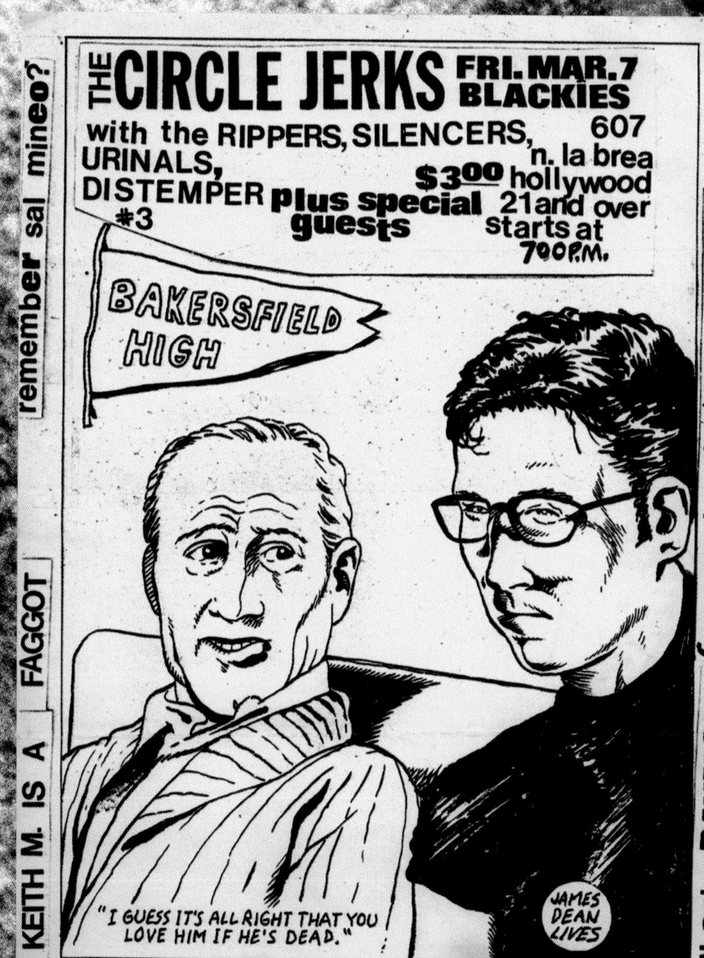

All of these flyers by Raymond Pettibon too

Keith Morris
Photo © Maria Watson

It's two o'clock in the morning along a pitch-black stretch of Pacific Coast Highway.

By Keith Morris

(Bare and desolate, a thick salty mist starting to settle.)

Chuck and I are looking out for cops as Robo pastes Black Flag flyers on walls, traffic light control boxes, lamp posts and anything else paper can stick to.

(Pile into a tiny Ford and it's off to the next intersection for a repeat performance.)

We stop for beer and cigarettes, clothes and fingers sticky from glue.

(Then we continue our work, pasting flyers for another few miles.)

20 dozen posters later we are pretty damned pleased with ourselves.

No confrontation with local authority figures

until later when a local city official presents Greg Ginn with a court order and a fine for defacing public property.

They wanted us to go away, but we had advertising to do.

Midnight to 3 am: it was time to do some damage!

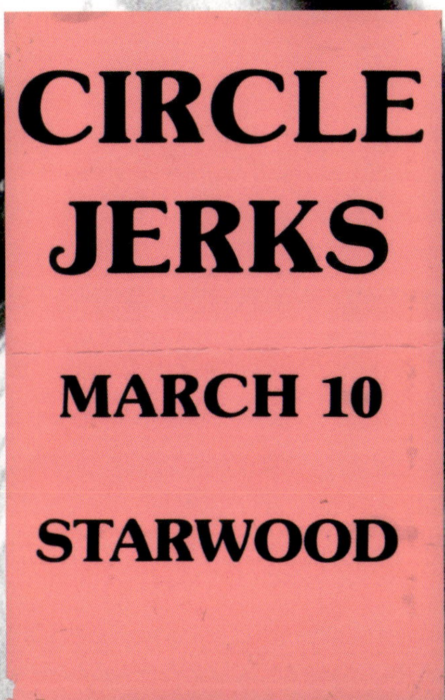

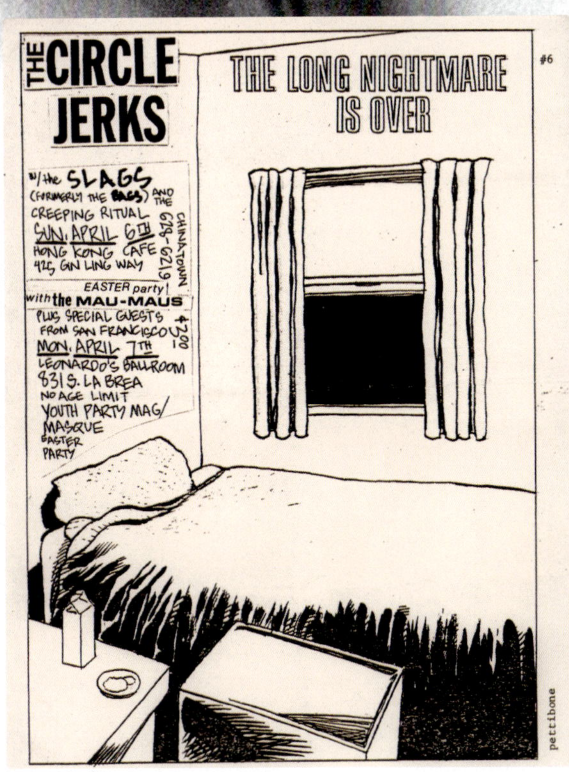

Raymond Pettibon

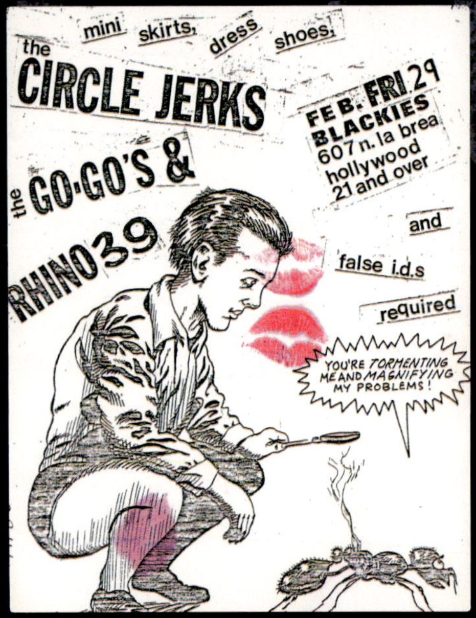

Raymond Pettibon

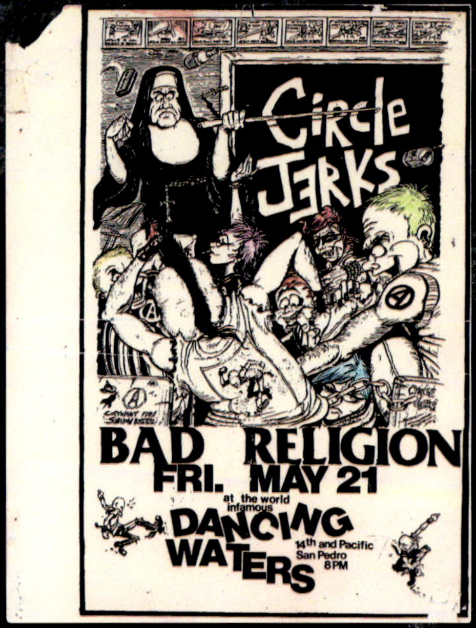

Shawn Kerri

Skank Kid: Shawn Kerri

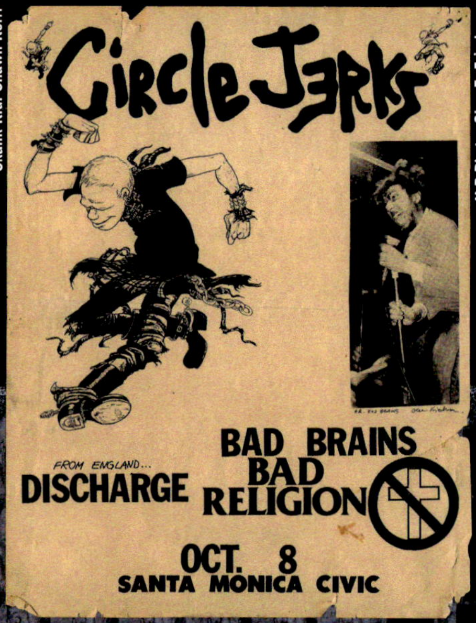

H.R.Photo: Glen E. Friedman

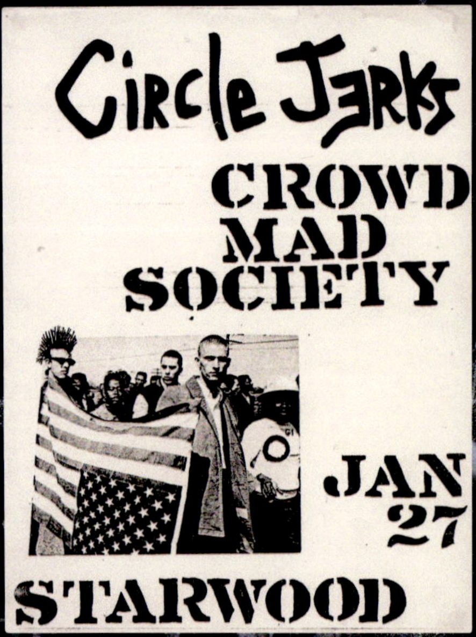

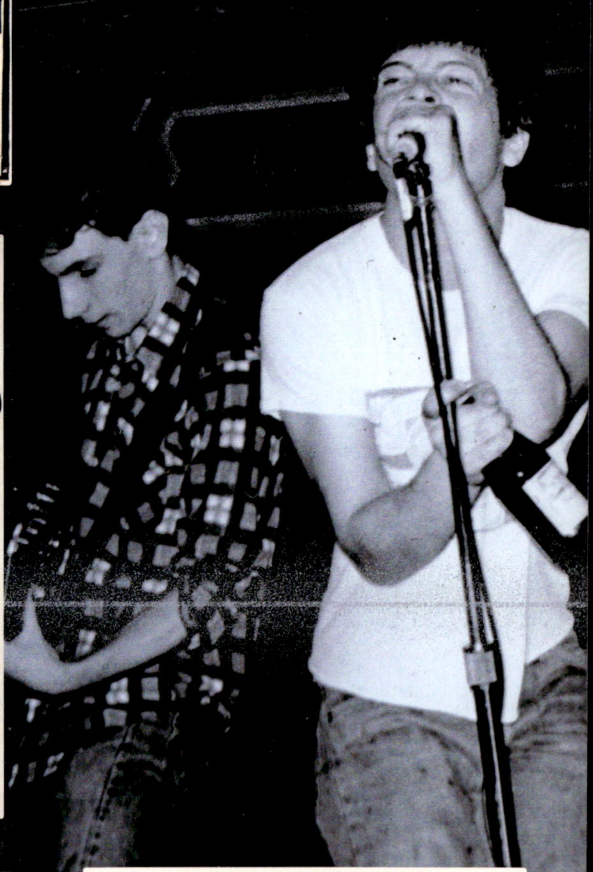

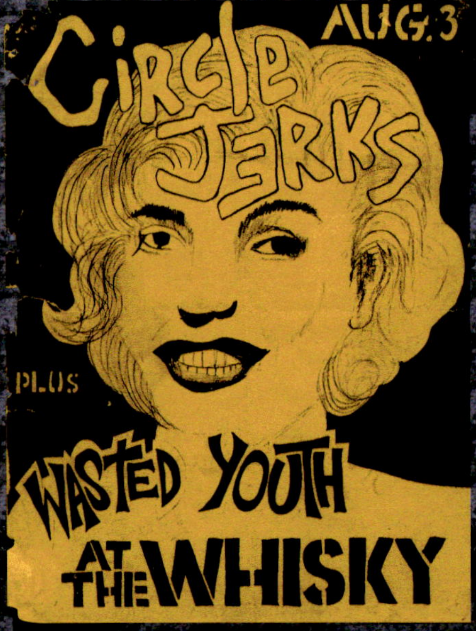

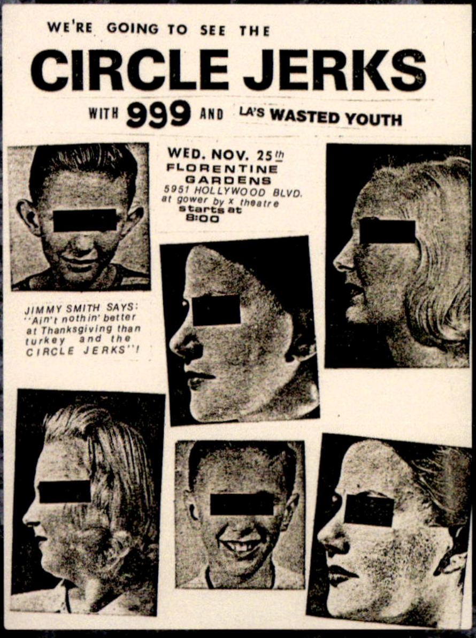

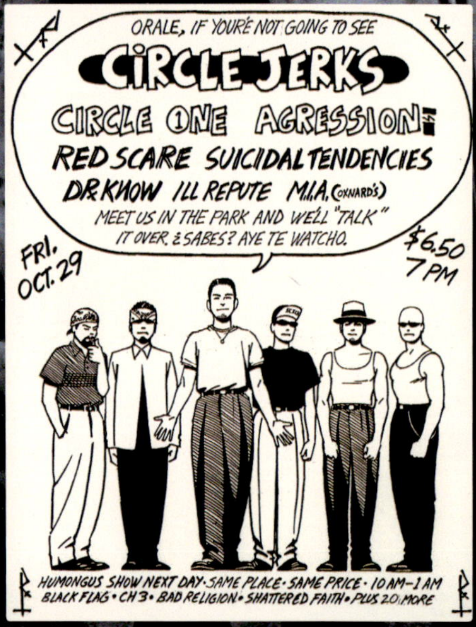

Jaime Hernandez

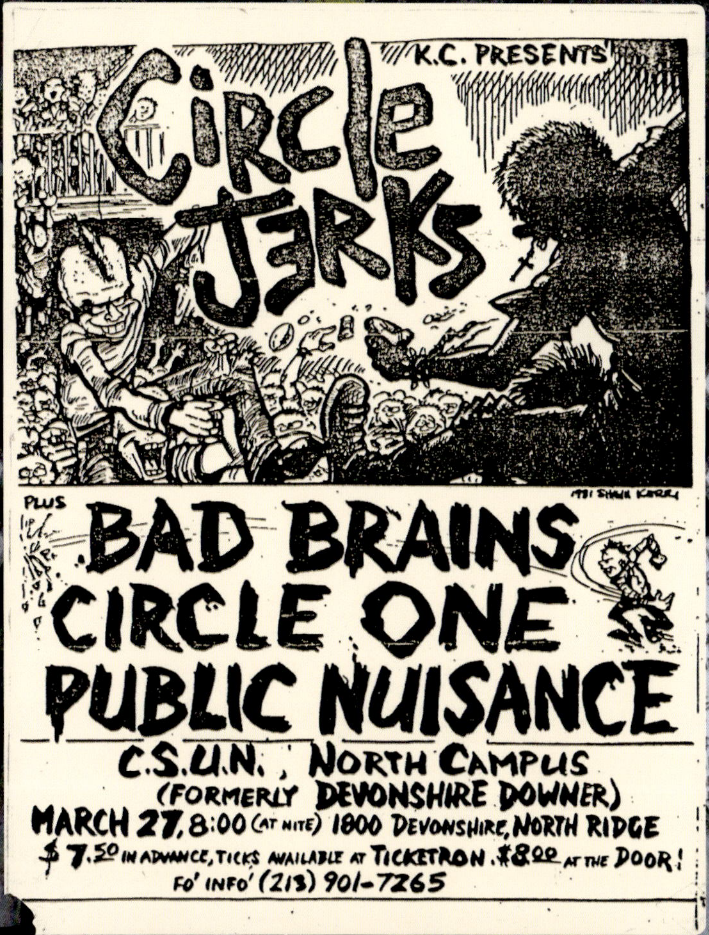

Shawn Kerri

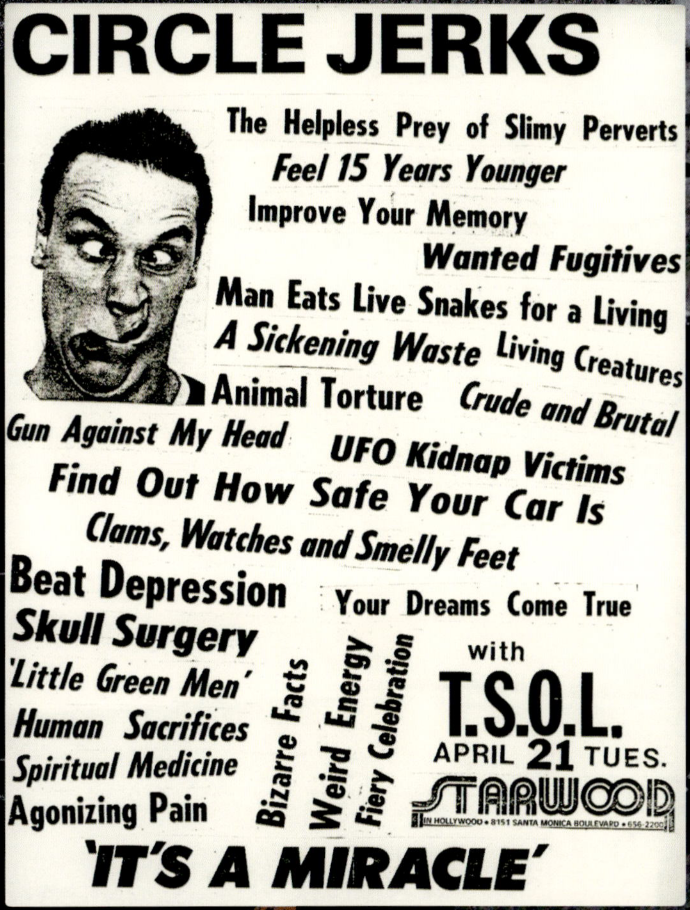

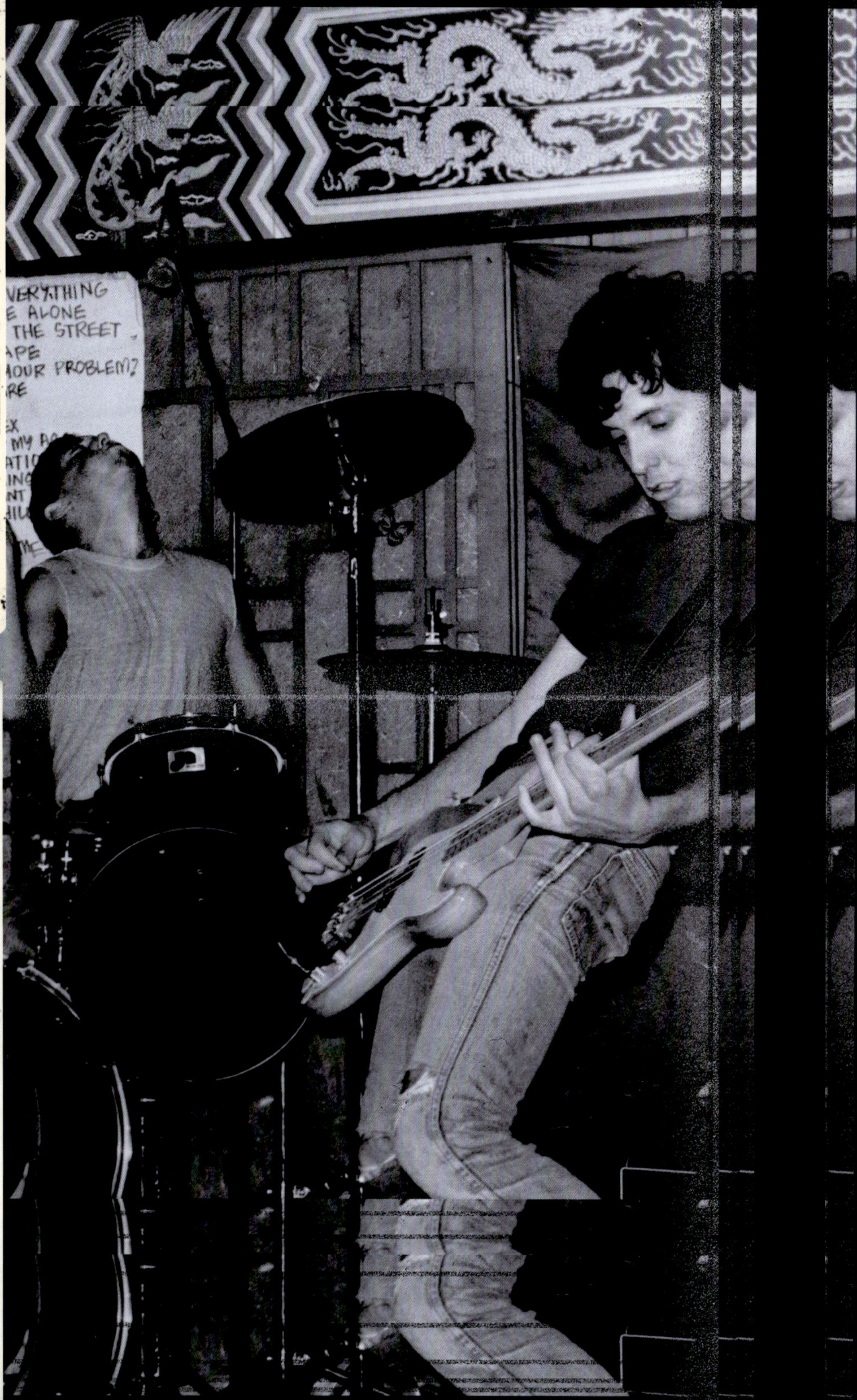

Circle Jerks At The Hong Kong Cafe
Photo © Mark Seldis
Courtesy: Slash Magazine

PUBLIC SERVICE ANNOUNCEMENTS

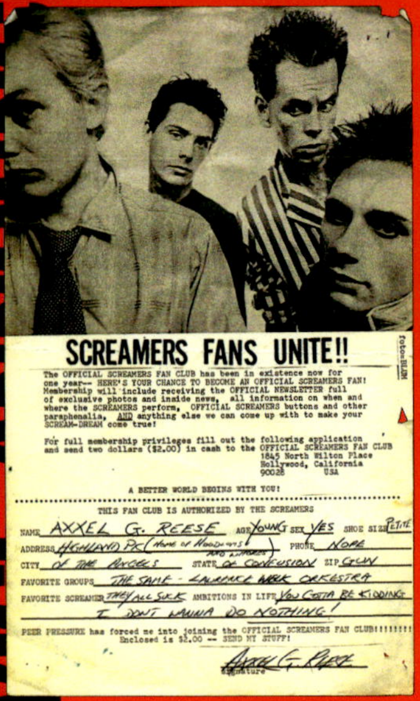
SCREAMERS FANS UNITE!!

foto=BLUM

The OFFICIAL SCREAMERS FAN CLUB has been in existence now for one year-- HERE'S YOUR CHANCE TO BECOME AN OFFICIAL SCREAMERS FAN! Membership will include receiving the OFFICIAL NEWSLETTER full of exclusive photos and inside news, all information on when and where the SCREAMERS perform, OFFICIAL SCREAMERS buttons and other paraphenalia, AND anything else we can come up with to make your SCREAM-DREAM come true!

For full membership privileges fill out the following application and send two dollars ($2.00) in cash to the OFFICIAL SCREAMERS FAN CLUB
1845 North Wilton Place
Hollywood, California
90028 USA

A BETTER WORLD BEGINS WITH YOU!

THIS FAN CLUB IS AUTHORIZED BY THE SCREAMERS

NAME AXXEL G. REESE AGE YOUNG SEX YES SHOE SIZE PETITE
ADDRESS HIGHLAND PK (Home of Hoodlums and Winners) PHONE NOPE
CITY OF THE ANGELS STATE OF CONFUSION ZIP GUN
FAVORITE GROUPS THE SAME - LAWRENCE WELK ORKESTRA
FAVORITE SCREAMER THEY ALL SUCK AMBITIONS IN LIFE YOU GOTTA BE KIDDING! I DONT WANNA DO NOTHING!

PEER PRESSURE has forced me into joining the OFFICIAL SCREAMERS FAN CLUB!!!!!!!!
Enclosed is $2.00 -- SEND MY STUFF!

Axxel G. Reese
signature

Dave Traut & Cliff Roman

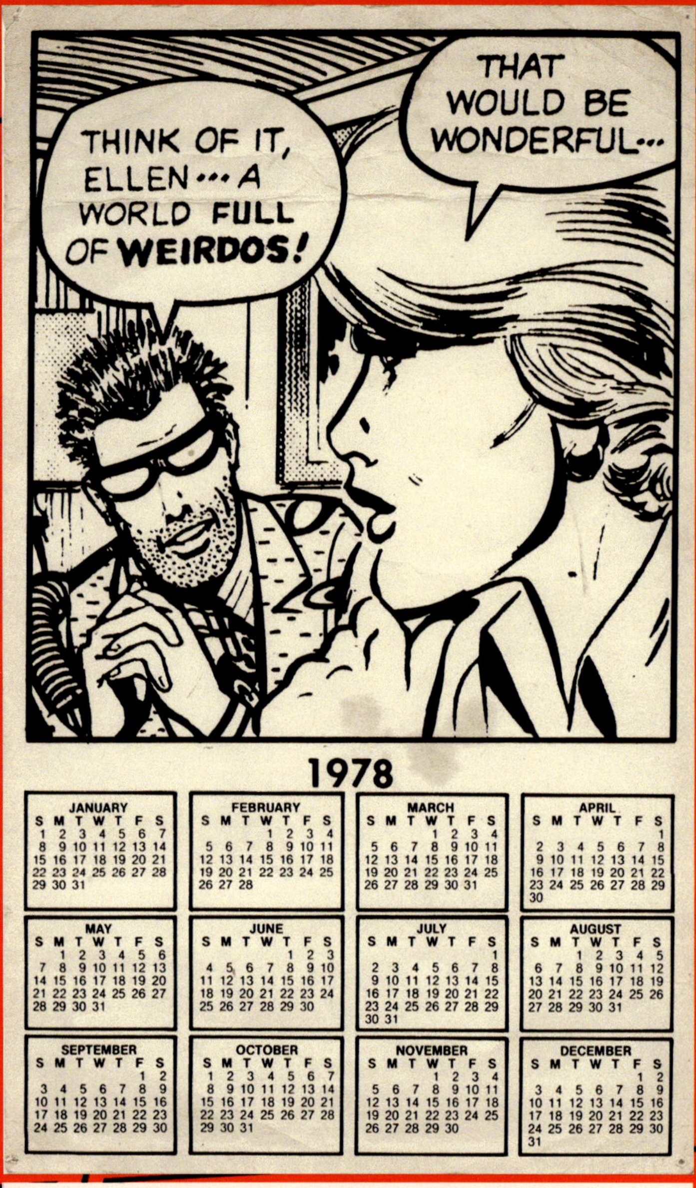

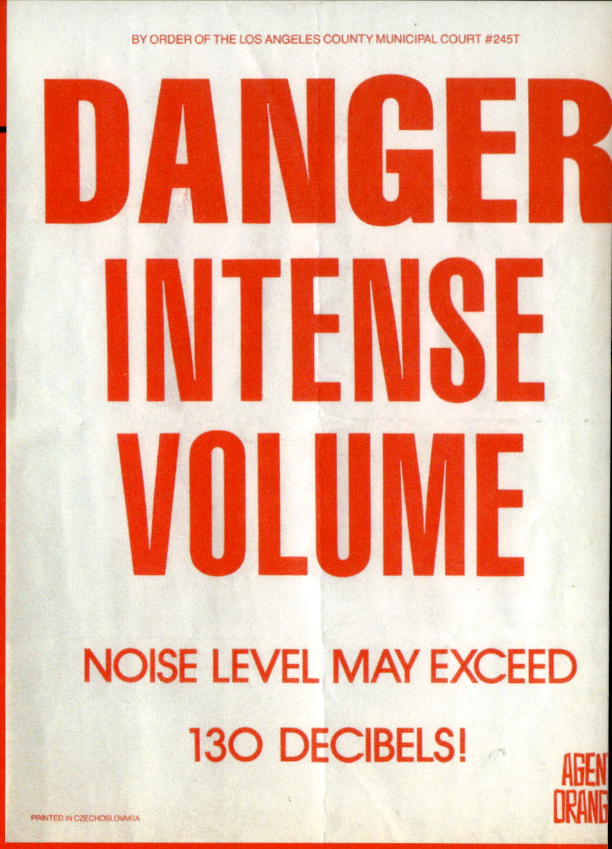

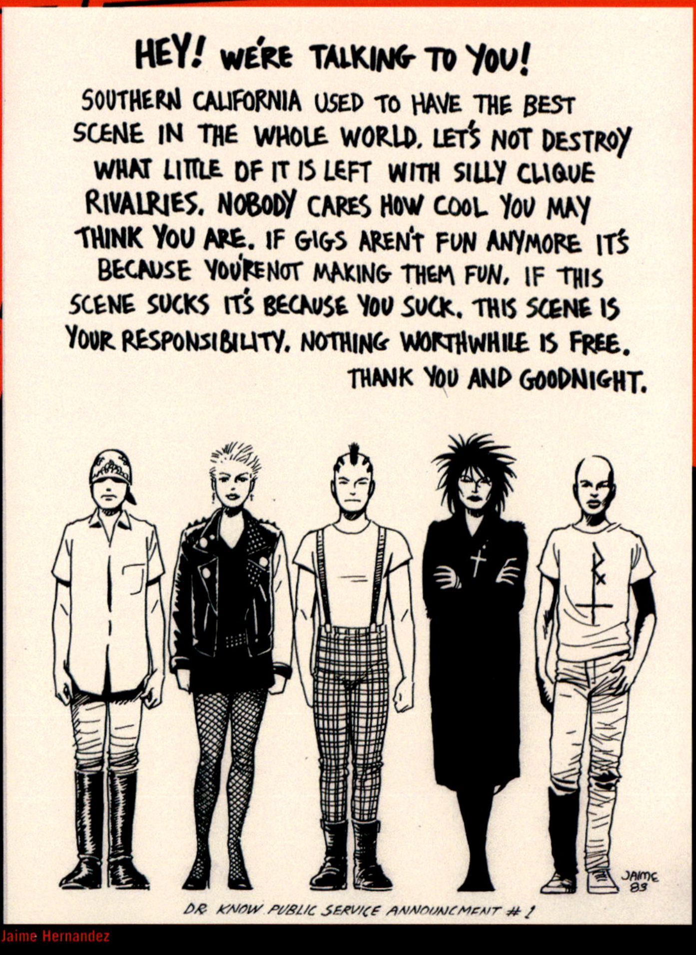

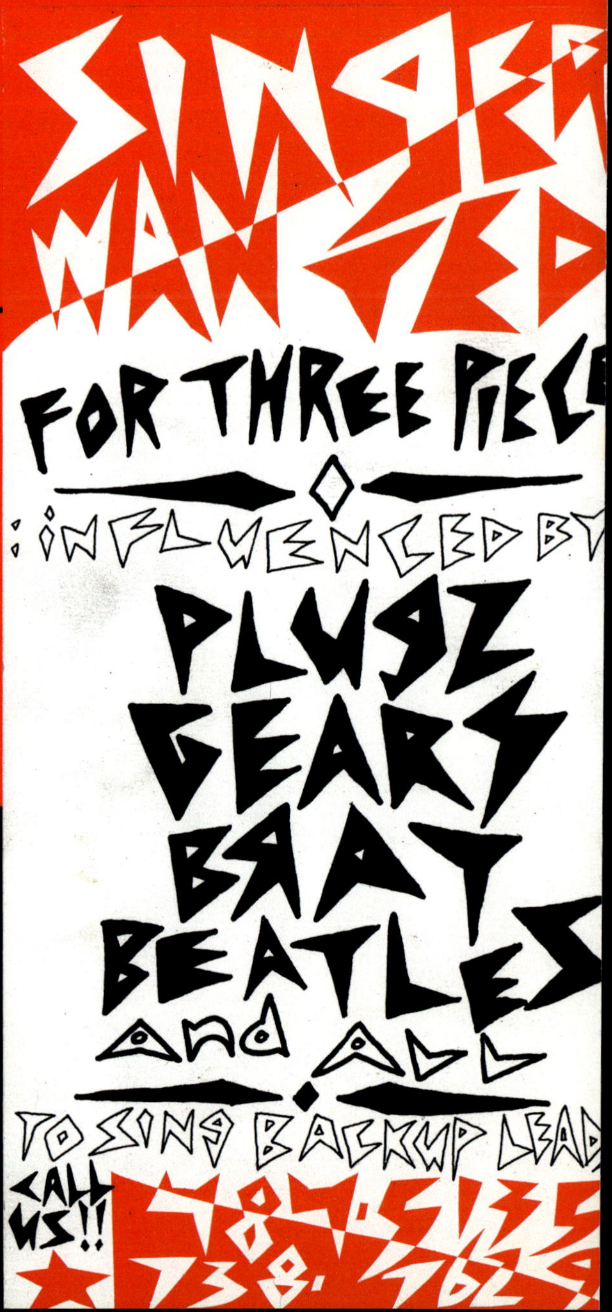

Jaime Hernandez

Dave Traut

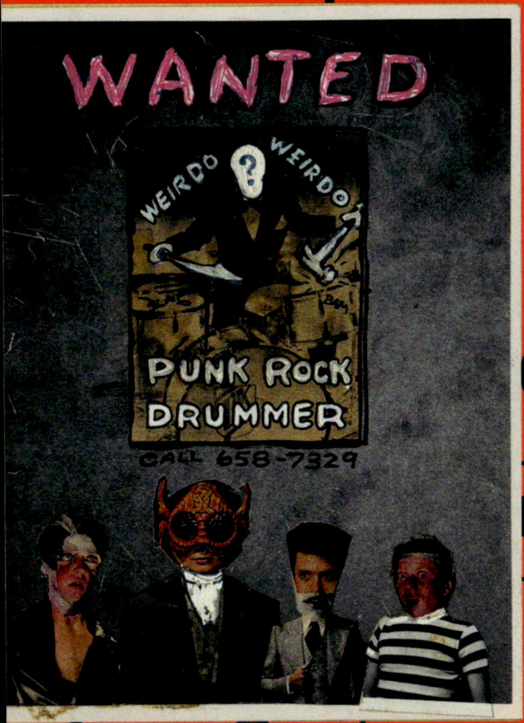

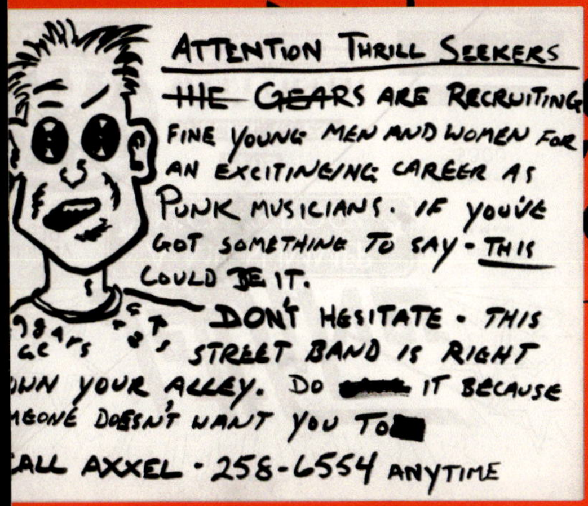

G. Reese

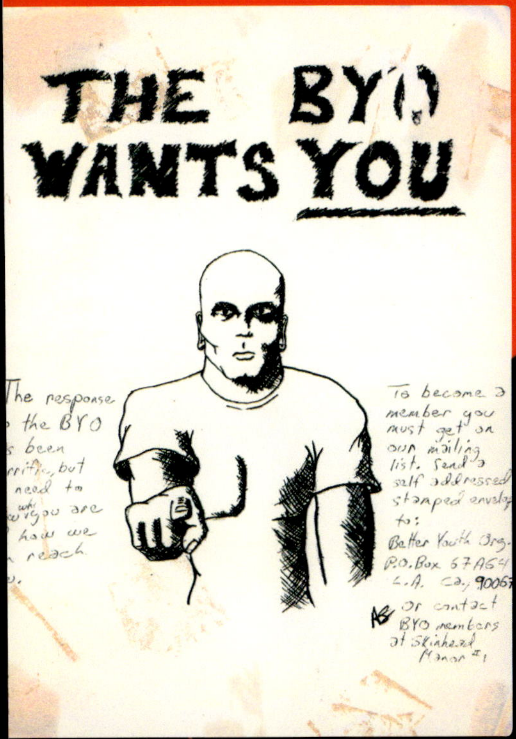

Stern

Better Youth Organization

presents

Youth Movement '82

THURSDAY, FEBRUARY 11, 1982 — 7:00 P.M.

HOLLYWOOD PALLADIUM

6215 Sunset Blvd., Hollywood

ANOTHER B.Y.O. PRODUCTION

No 1290

People ask me what it was like back in the old daze, as if it was some golden age. I don't believe any of us thought we were doing anything special, but I know now that there was something amazing going on in Los Angeles in the late '70s and early '80s.

There weren't a lot of bands but there was a real community supporting the music, art and ideas. LA had the biggest punk shows in the world for a few years there, with regular crowds at the Olympic Auditorium of 3,000 - 5,000 totally fucked up and crazy kids. Most of the time we were ignored by a music business that swallows the new flavor of the week, and with it any integrity and creativity the bands might have. The business of capitalism has obviously been the driving force in punk lately, but we tried hard to put on shows with great lineups and kept the door price low so anyone could afford to come and have a great time. There were no worries about guarantees or who played in what order, or selling t-shirts. So few of us had records out, we were just doing it to have some fun.

Sure, the shows soon got so big and out of control that other forces stepped in, like record companies, security guards and cops. But for awhile, it was just a movement, where anyone who cared could be a part of something that really mattered. What's stopping people from creating another one?

Peace, Love and Support Independent Rock
Shawn Stern

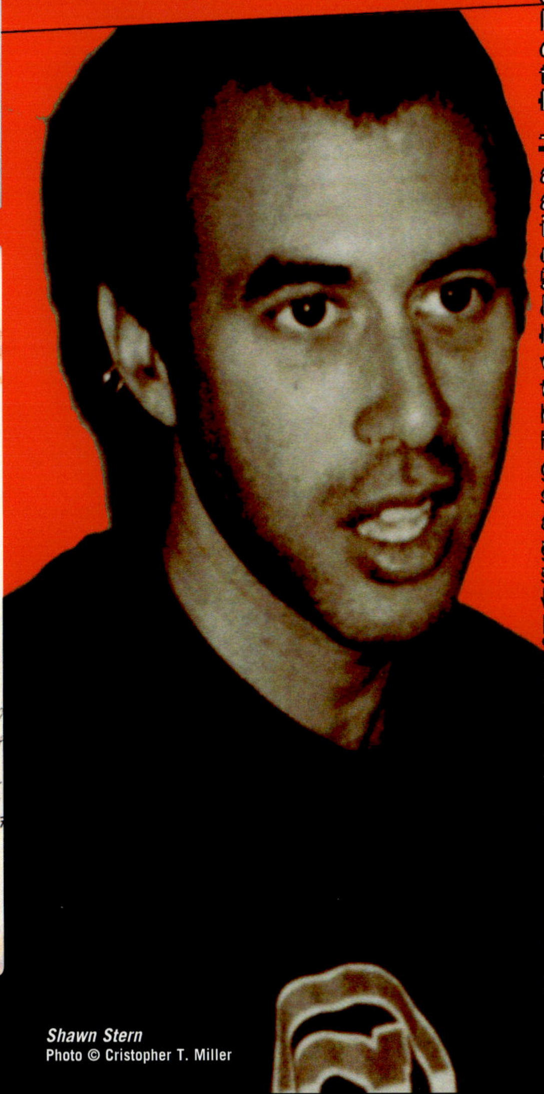

Shawn Stern
Photo © Cristopher T. Miller

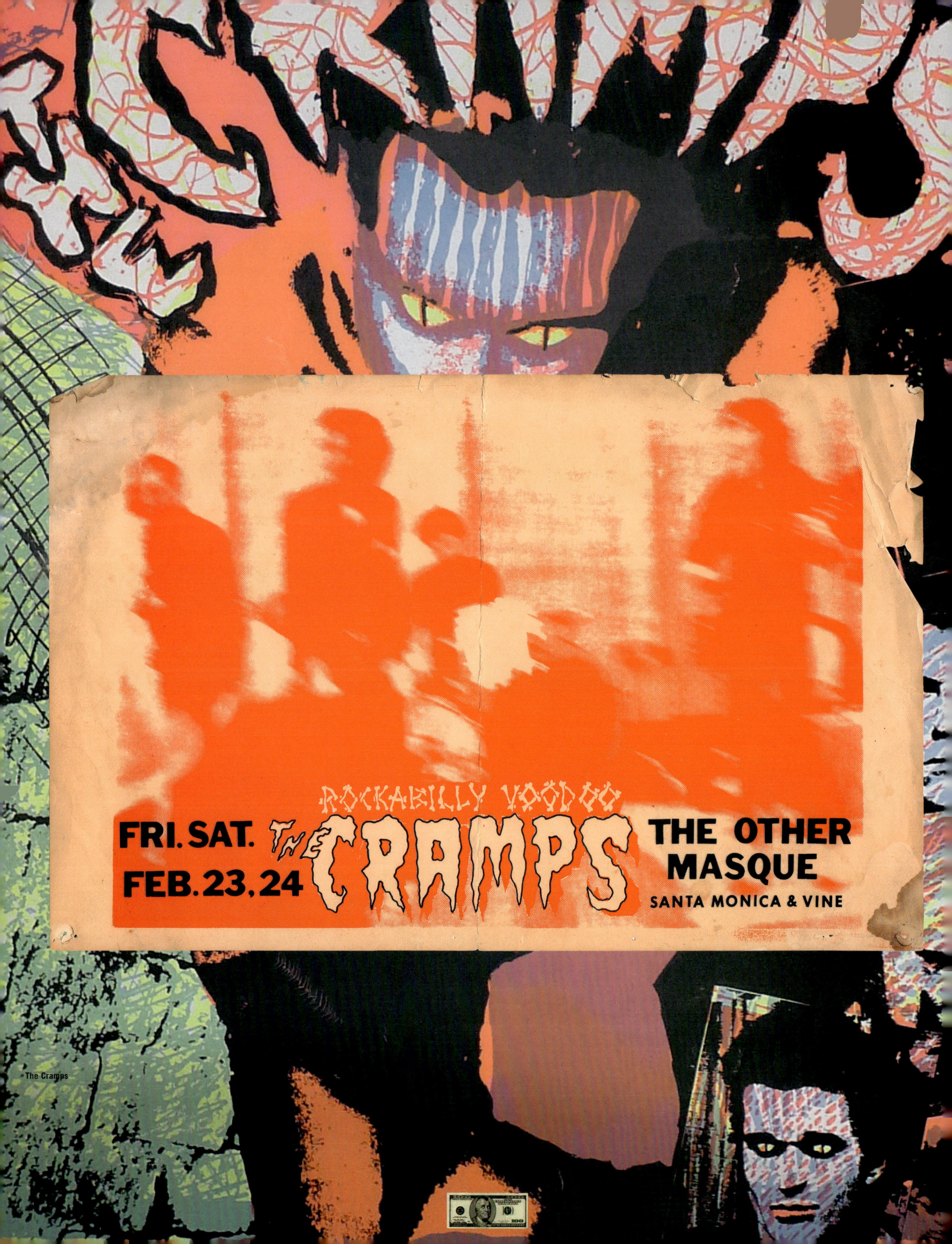
ROCKABILLY VOODOO
FRI. SAT.
FEB. 23, 24
THE CRAMPS
THE OTHER MASQUE
SANTA MONICA & VINE

The Cramps

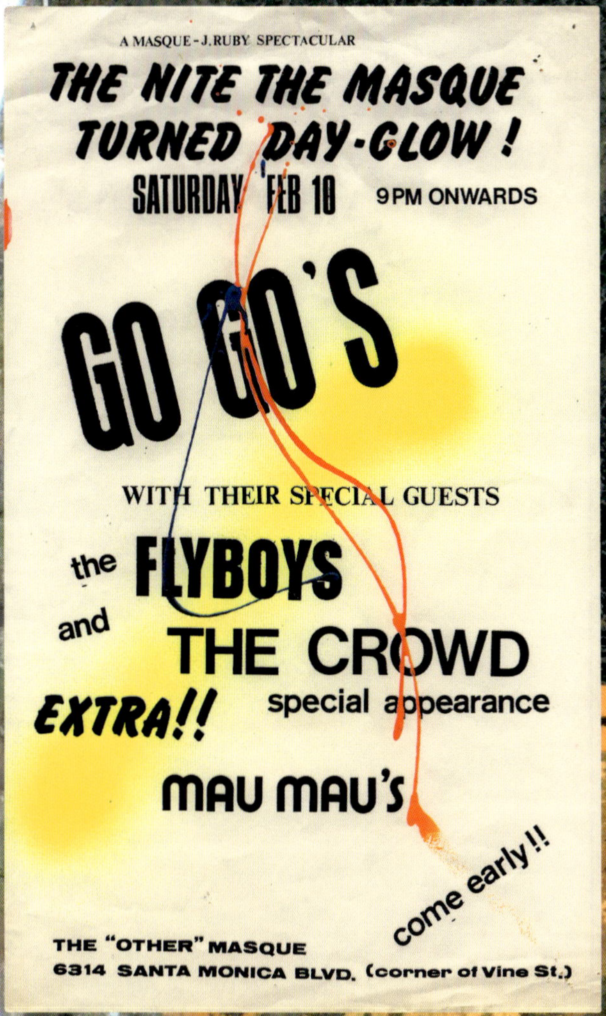

Brendan Mullen

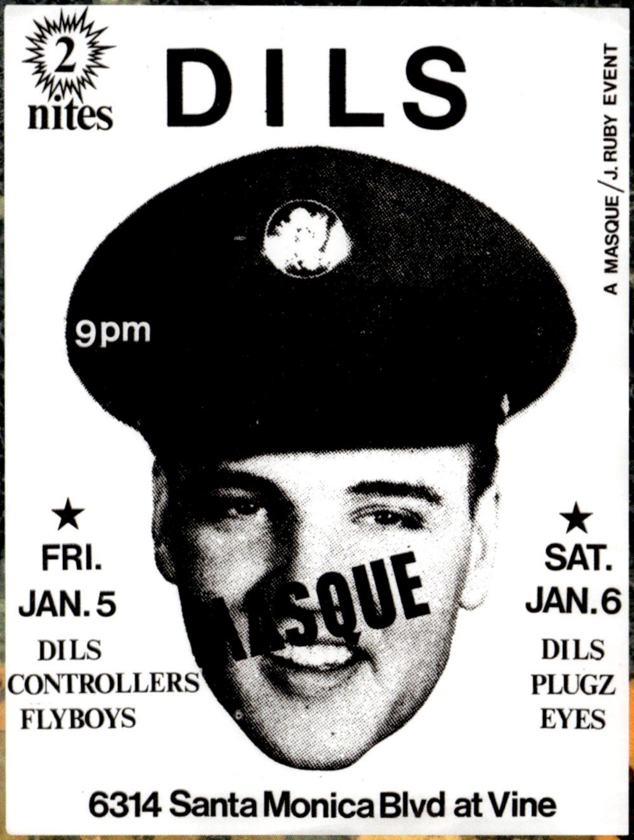

Bob Biggs

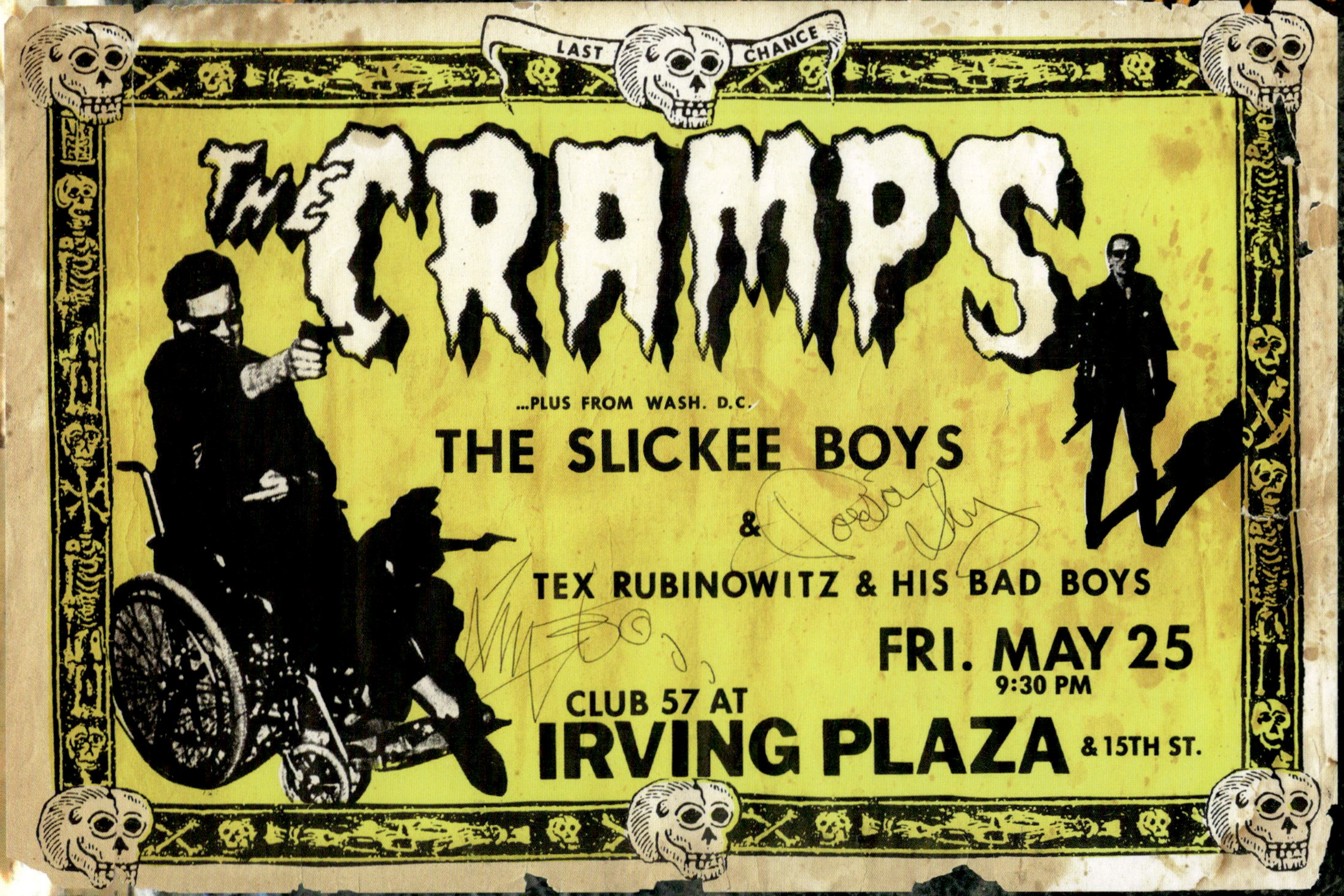

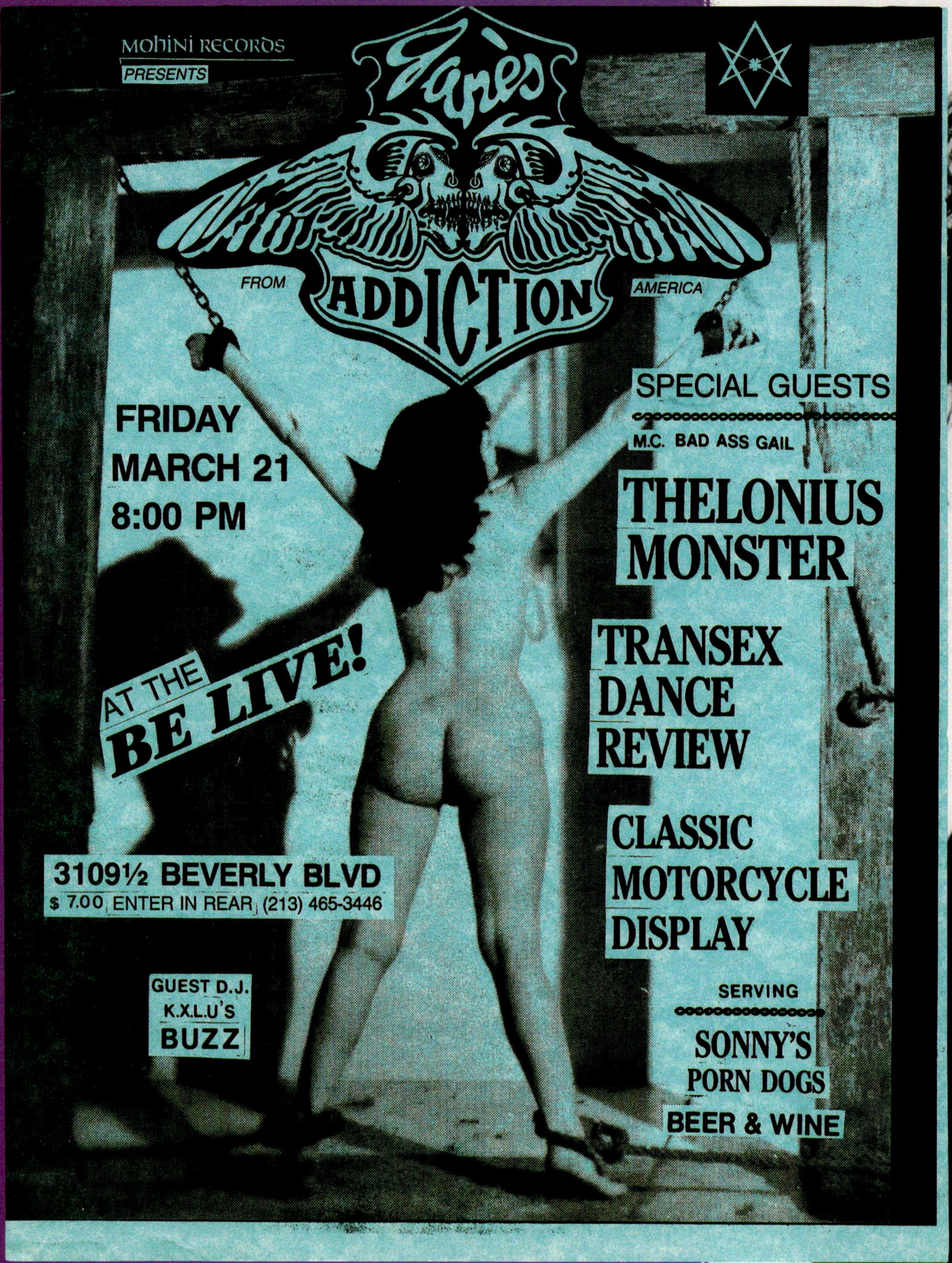

Perry Farrell

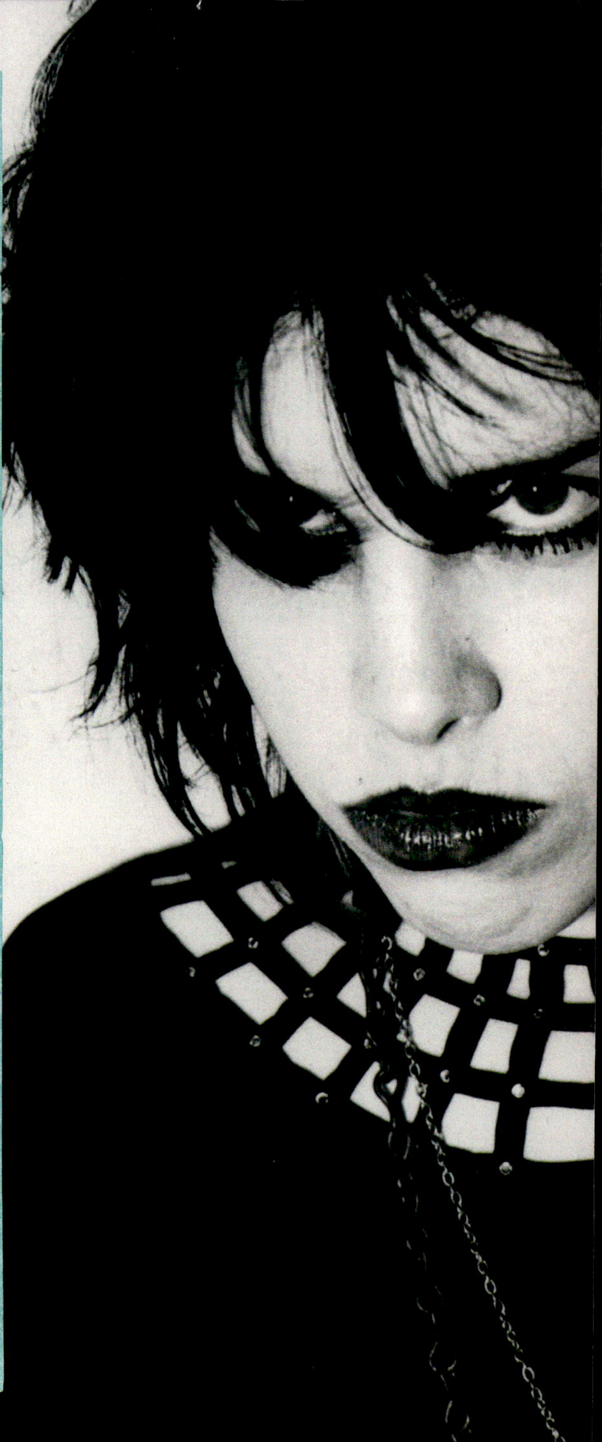

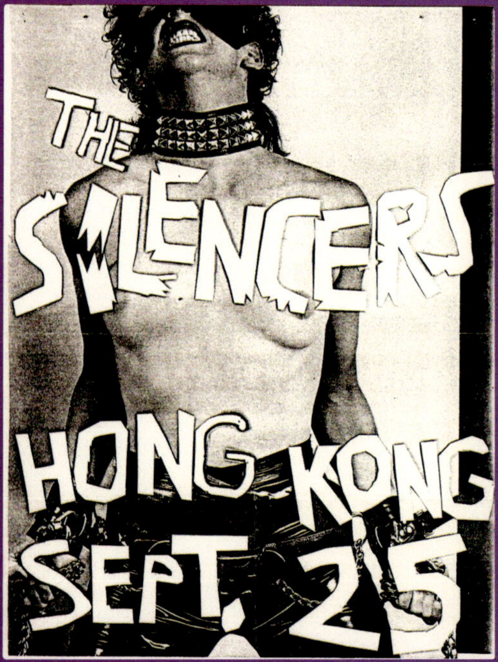

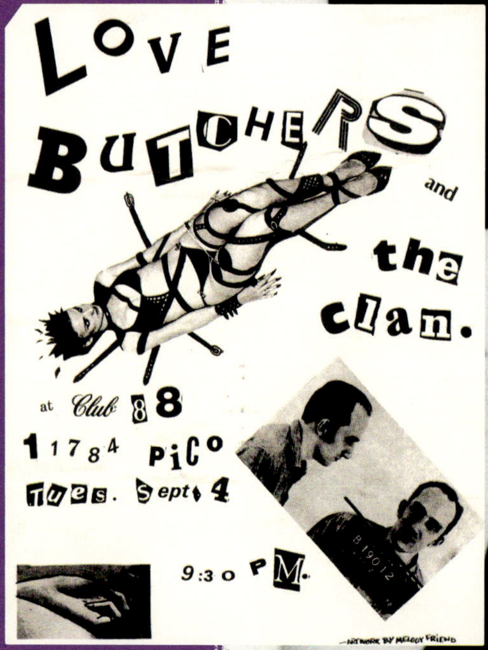

Melody Friend

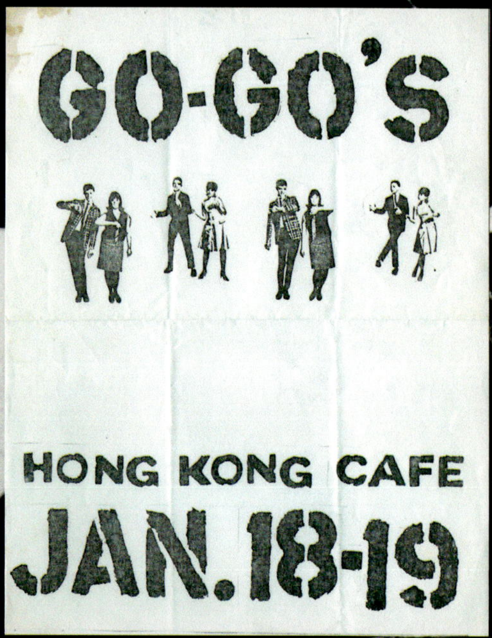

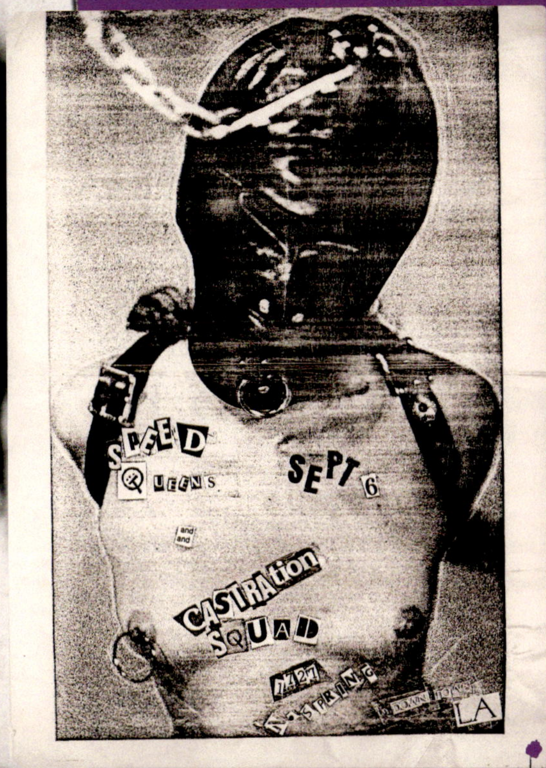

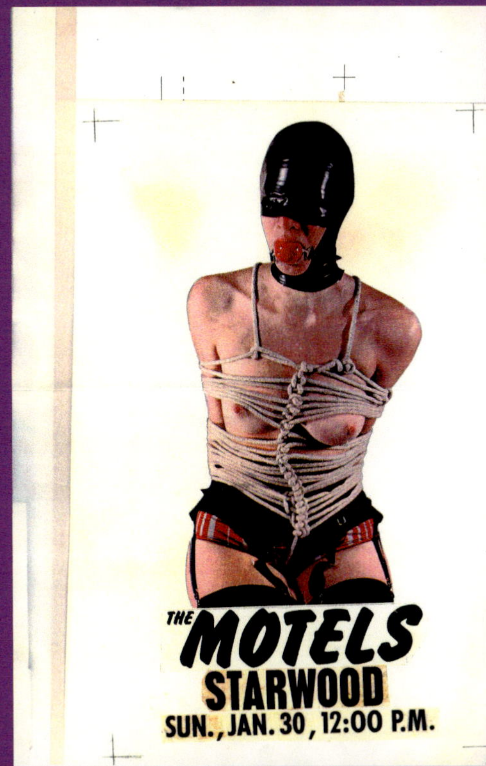

Dean Chamberlain

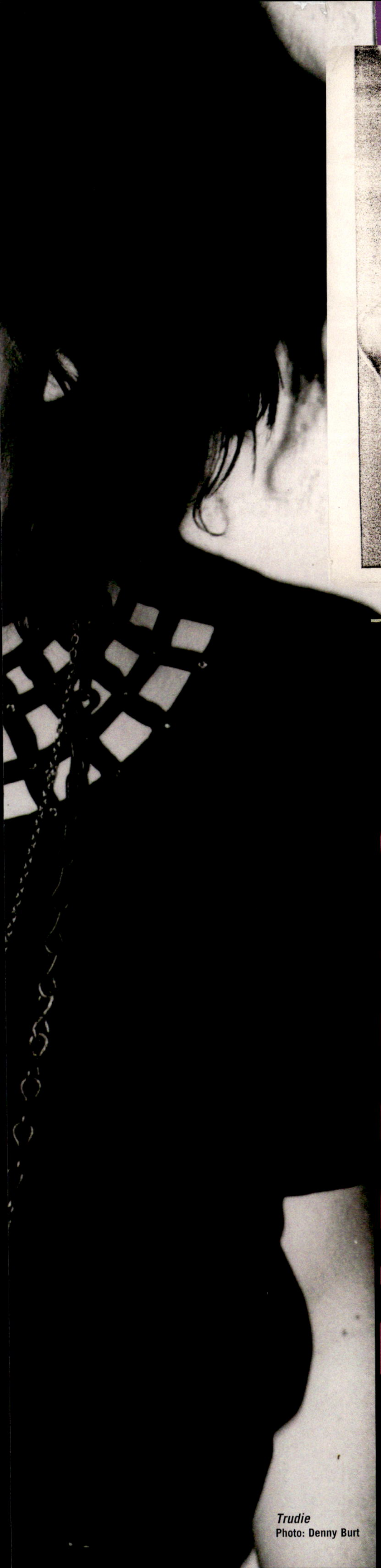

Trudie
Photo: Denny Burt

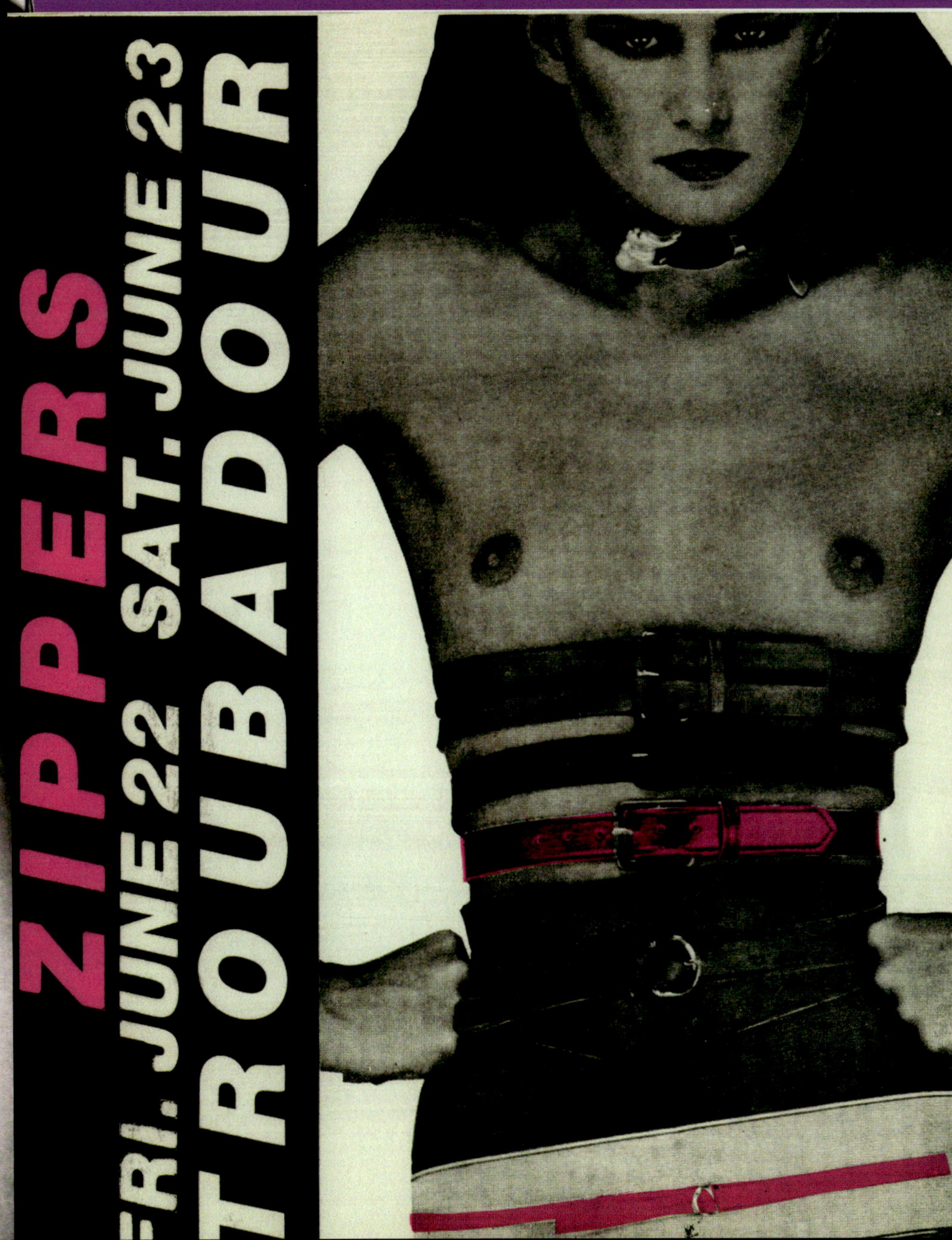

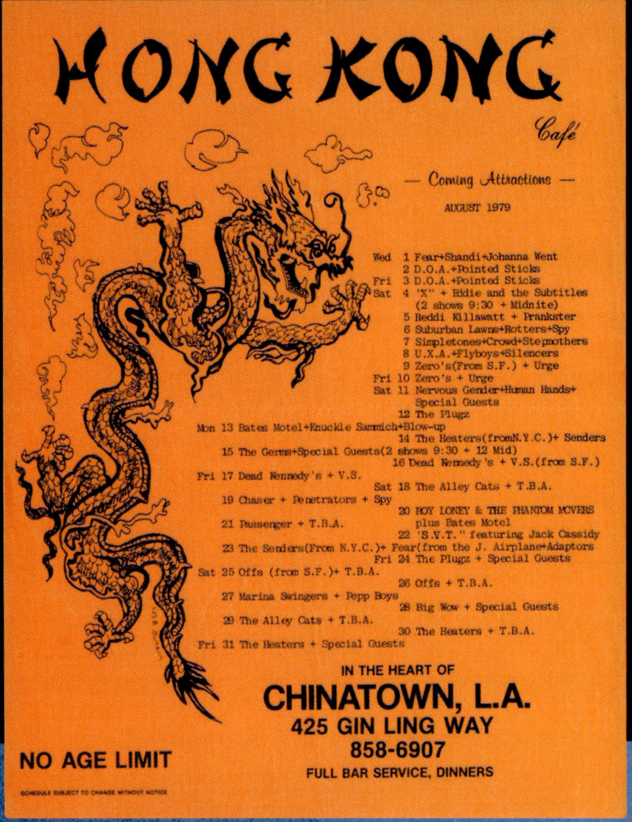
HONG KONG
Café
— Coming Attractions —
AUGUST 1979
Wed 1 Fear+Shandi+Johanna Went
2 D.O.A.+Pointed Sticks
Fri 3 D.O.A.+Pointed Sticks
Sat 4 "X" + Eddie and the Subtitles
(2 shows 9:30 + Midnite)
5 Reddi Killawatt + Prankster
6 Suburban Lawns+Rotters+Spy
7 Simpletones+Crowd+Stepmothers
8 U.X.A.+Flyboys+Silencers
9 Zero's(From S.F.) + Urge
Fri 10 Zero's + Urge
Sat 11 Nervous Gender+Human Hands+
Special Guests
12 The Plugz
Mon 13 Bates Motel+Knuckle Sammich+Blow-up
14 The Heaters(fromN.Y.C.)+ Senders
15 The Germs+Special Guests(2 shows 9:30 + 12 Mid)
16 Dead Kennedy's + V.S.(from S.F.)
Fri 17 Dead Kennedy's + V.S.
Sat 18 The Alley Cats + T.B.A.
19 Chaser + Penetrators + Spy
20 ROY LONEY & THE PHANTOM MOVERS
plus Bates Motel
21 Passenger + T.B.A.
22 'S.V.T." featuring Jack Cassidy
23 The Senders(From N.Y.C.)+ Fear(from the J. Airplane+Adaptors
Fri 24 The Plugz + Special Guests
Sat 25 Offs (from S.F.)+ T.B.A.
26 Offs + T.B.A.
27 Marina Swingers + Pepp Boys
28 Big Wow + Special Guests
29 The Alley Cats + T.B.A.
30 The Heaters + T.B.A.
Fri 31 The Heaters + Special Guests
NO AGE LIMIT
IN THE HEART OF
CHINATOWN, L.A.
425 GIN LING WAY
858-6907
FULL BAR SERVICE, DINNERS

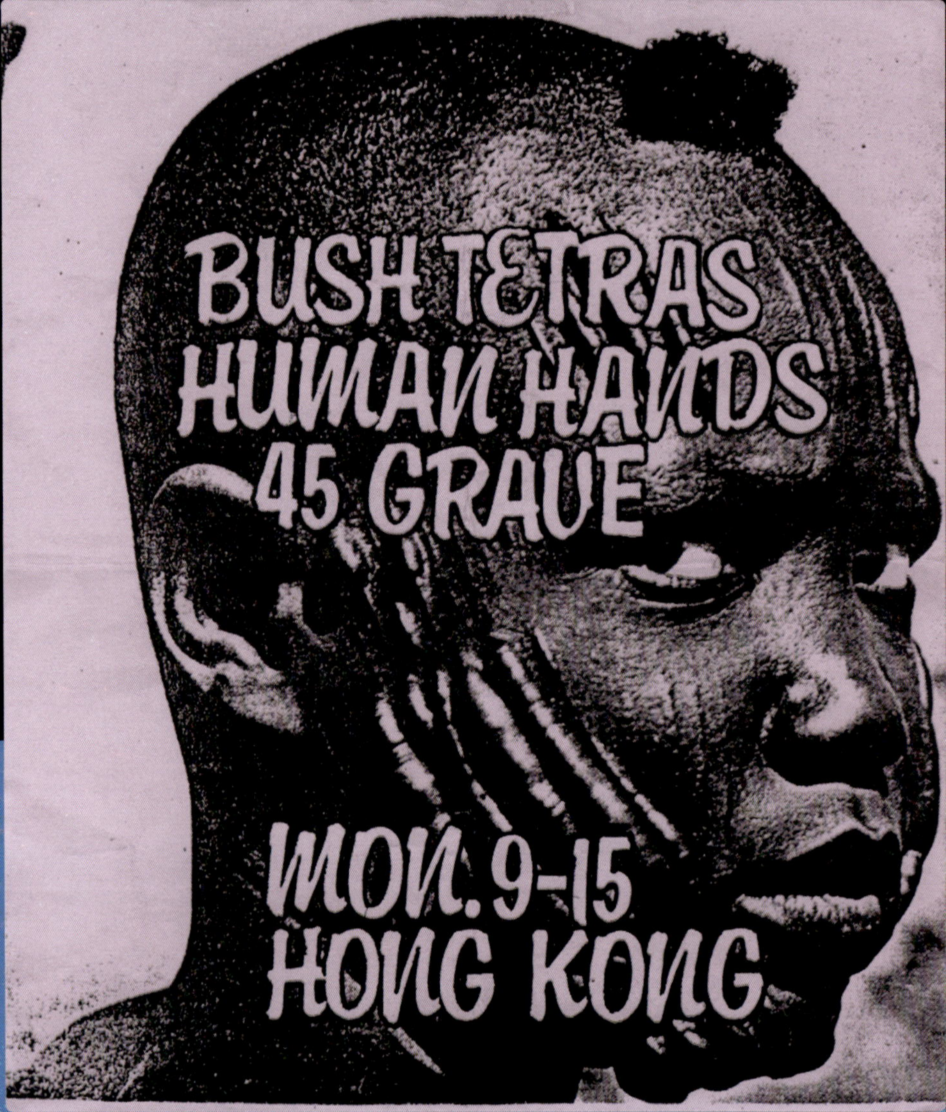
BUSH TETRAS
HUMAN HANDS
45 GRAVE
MON. 9-15
HONG KONG

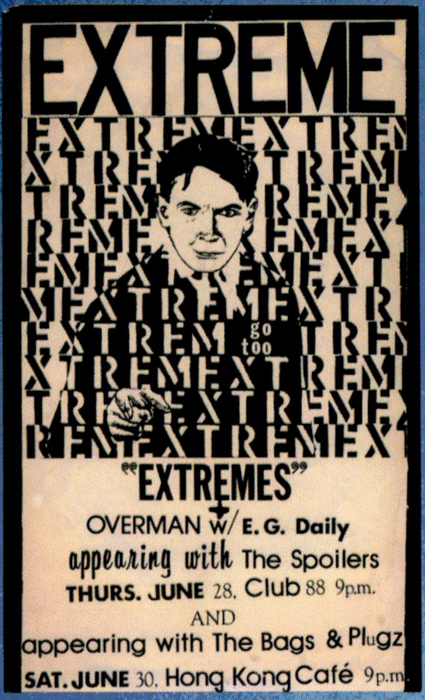
EXTREME
go too
"EXTREMES"
OVERMAN w/ E.G. Daily
appearing with The Spoilers
THURS. JUNE 28. Club 88 9p.m.
AND
appearing with The Bags & Plugz
SAT. JUNE 30. Hong Kong Café 9p.m.

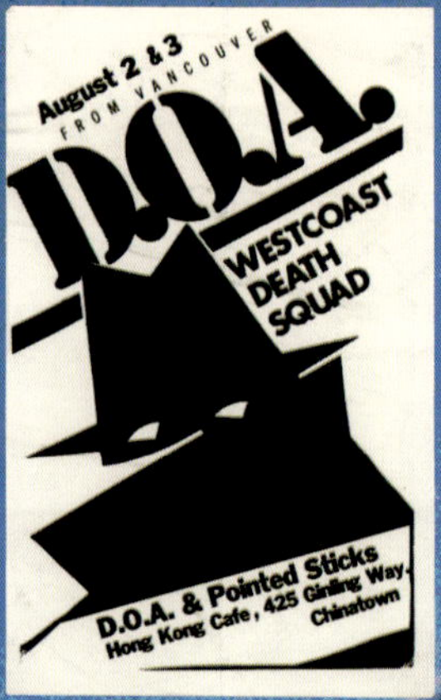
August 2 & 3
FROM VANCOUVER
D.O.A.
WESTCOAST
DEATH
SQUAD
D.O.A. & Pointed Sticks
Hong Kong Cafe, 425 Ginling Way,
Chinatown

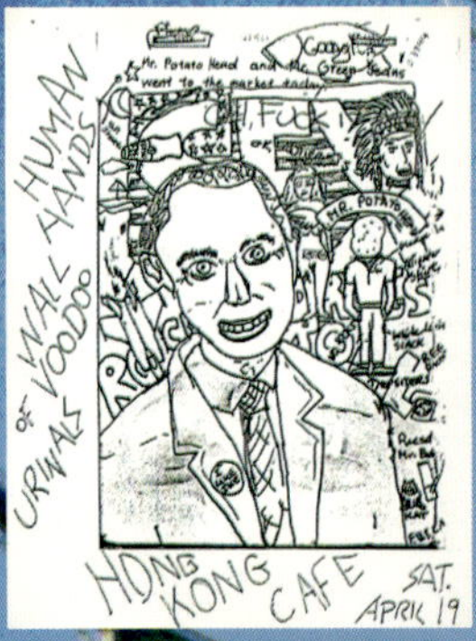
HUMAN HANDS
URINALS
of WALL VOODOO
HONG KONG CAFE
SAT. APRIL 19

Stan Tom

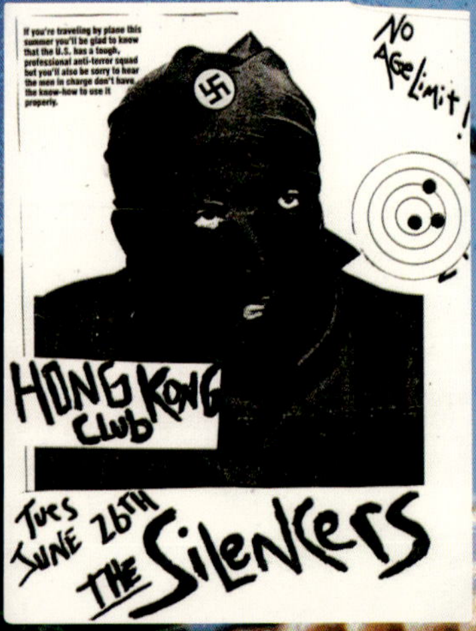
If you're traveling by plane this summer you'll be glad to know that the U.S. has a tough, professional anti-terror squad but you'll also be sorry to hear the men in charge don't have the know-how to use it properly.
No Age Limit!
HONG KONG club
Tues June 26th
THE Silencers

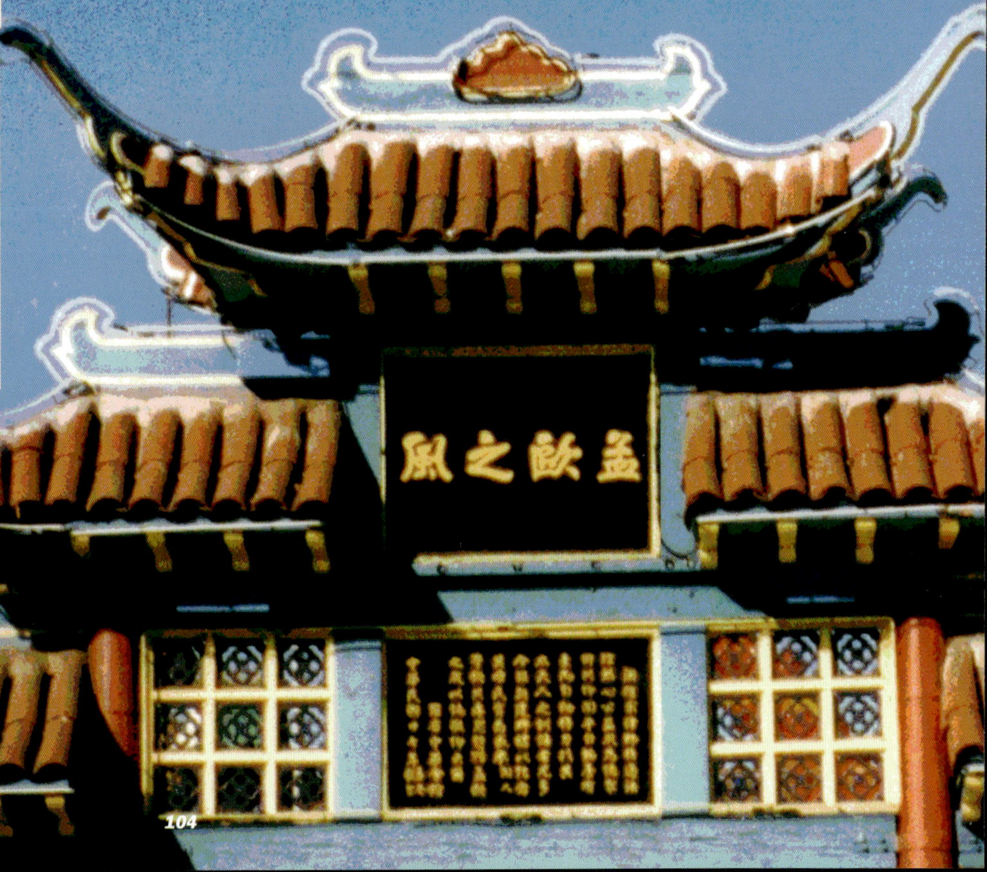

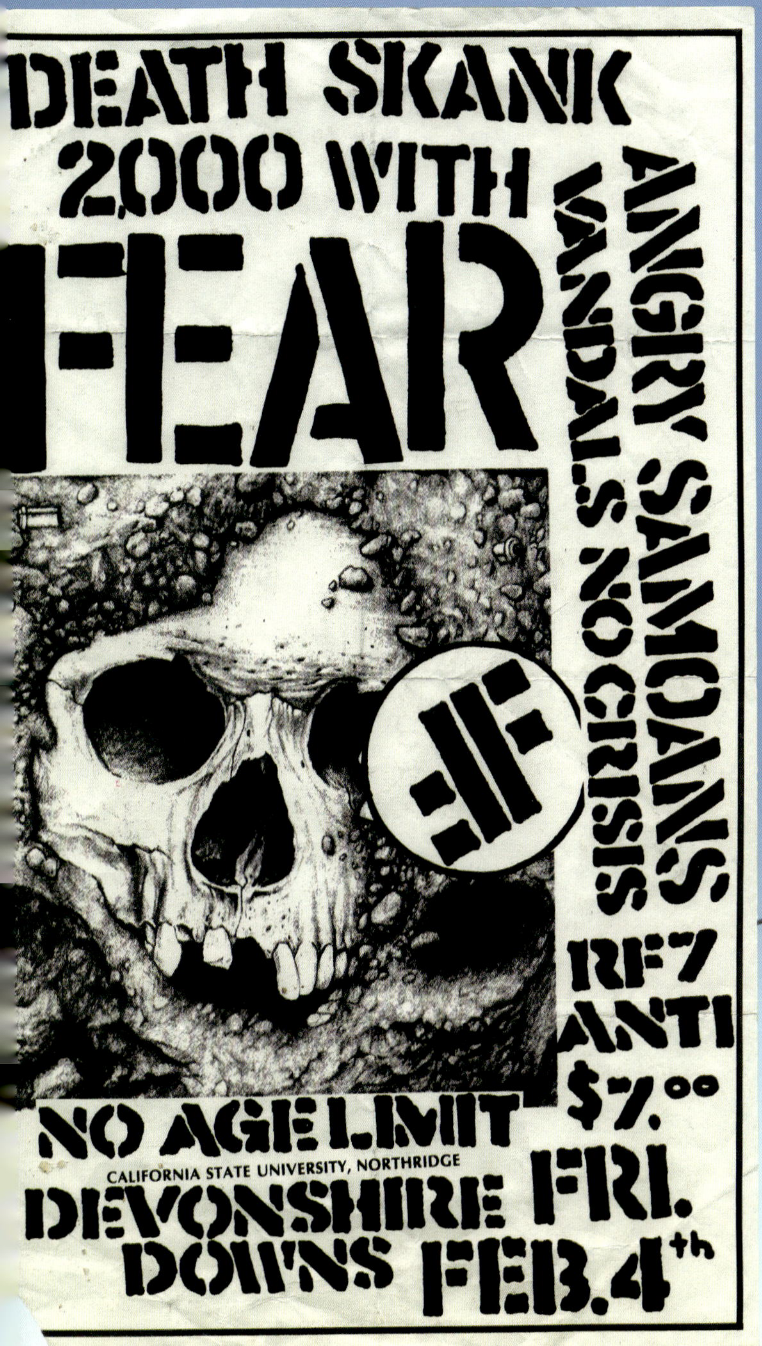

Mad Marc Rude

The Valley

Shawn Kerri

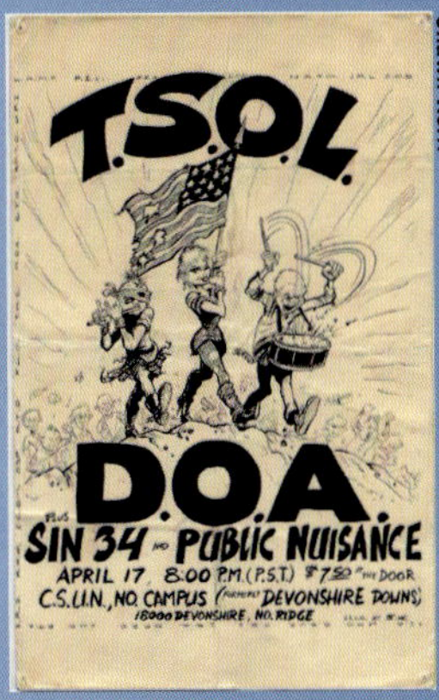

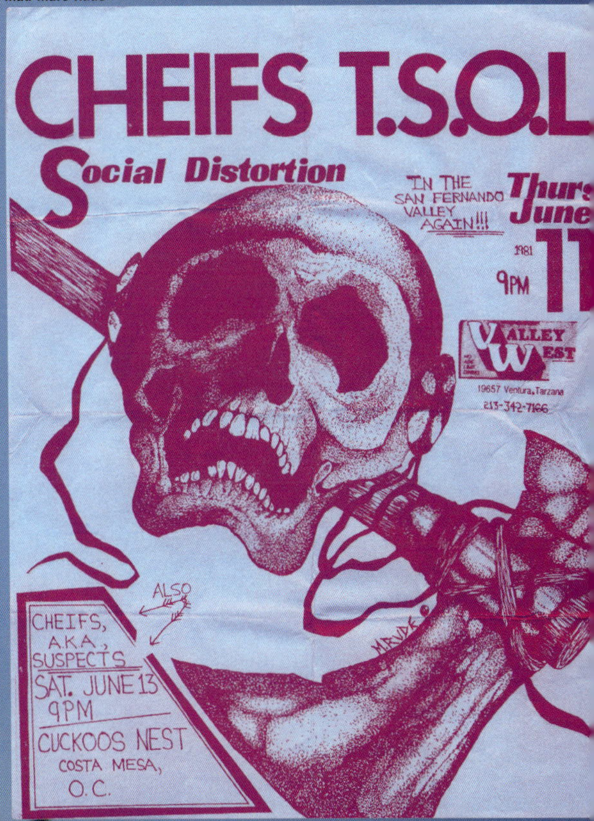

In the San Fernando Valley you were either a West End Punk or an East End Punk, depending on which side of the freeway at Sepulveda you lived on. This territorial pissing really didn't mean much, just a longer drive to Godzillas or the Whiskey, or the swap meet at the Country Club. Wherever you lived, being a punk in the Valley was a dangerous choice. There was always some **Trans-Am-driving-longhaired-cowboy hat-with-roach-clip-attached** around to give you shit. You couldn't take the bus without getting pelted with comments and sundry bullshit someone threw at you. School was worse, especially if you went to an all-boys Catholic high school. Anyone brave enough not to ditch was surrounded at lunch by a heaving mass of burly fuckheads pissed off that you didn't have the decency to listen to Genesis or REO Speedwagon, and ready to kick your ass. Even the teachers made fun of us.

But when we got together at a show, we were no longer the minority. Bad Religion, Red Cross, China White, UXA, Circle Jerks, Wasted Youth - they, and many more, all belonged to us.

Some of my friends express a sadness that the Green Day kids walking down the street don't know that we were creating the scene they mosh around in...leaving a trail of flyers and endless stories behind us... we talk about Oki Dog before it became a Fatburger, how outrageous it was to pay $7 to see the Damned at *Godzillas*. Then someone pipes in with a bad impression of Claude Bessy– *"There's no such thing as punk rock - it's just a figment of some lame cunt's imagination!"*

The flyers collected here are more than pieces of wallpaper that made it into a book. they represent actual events, shows we attended and remember fondly. +

Steve Schayer

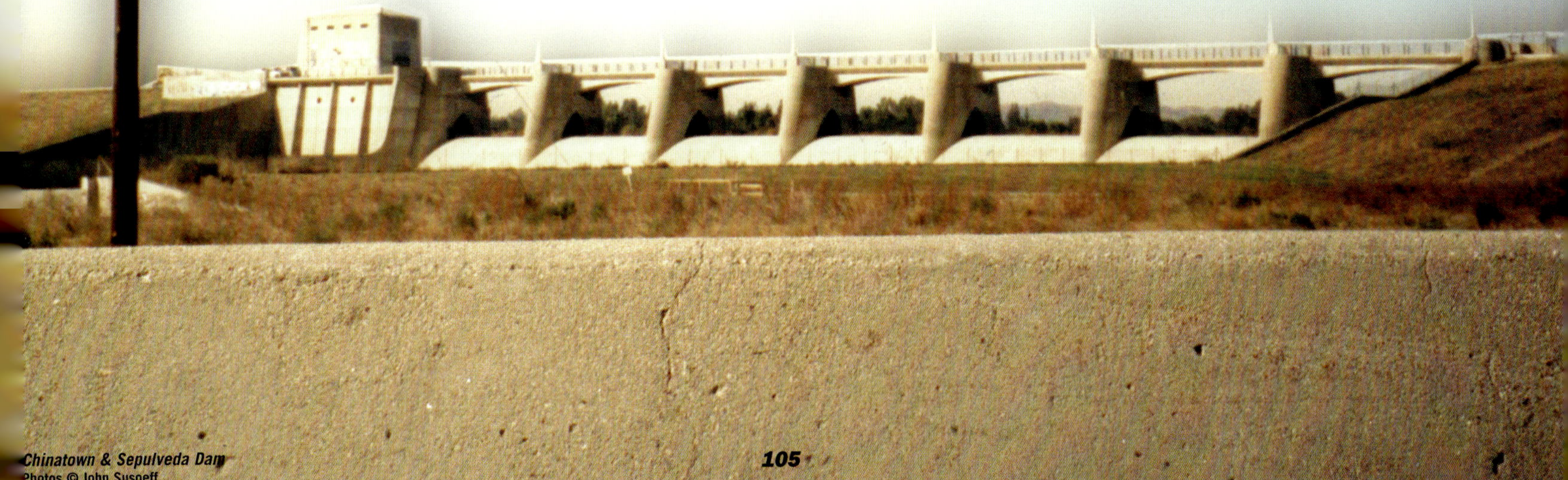

Chinatown & Sepulveda Dam
Photos © John Susoeff

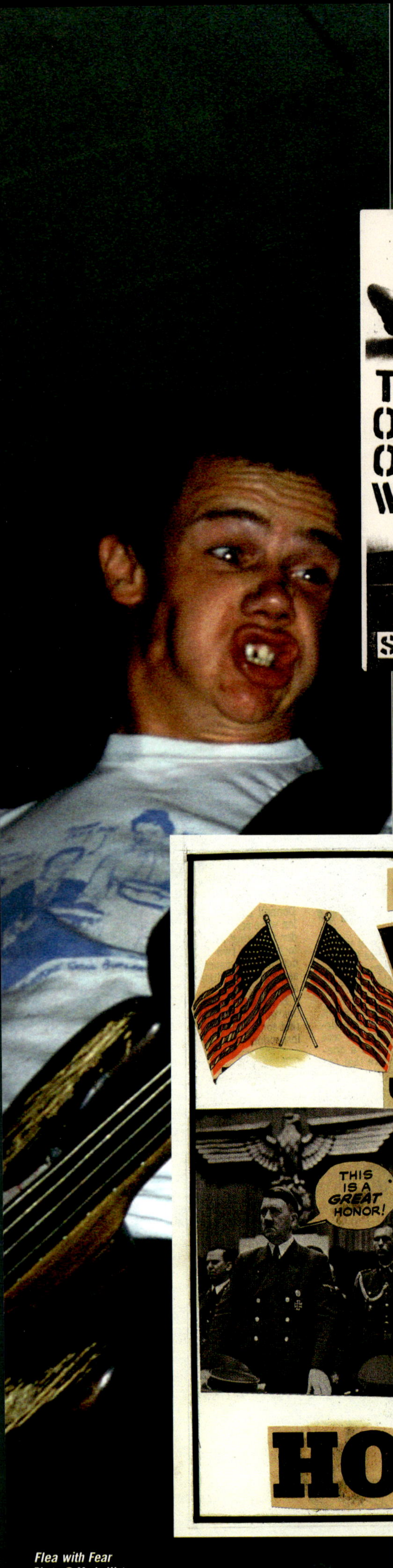

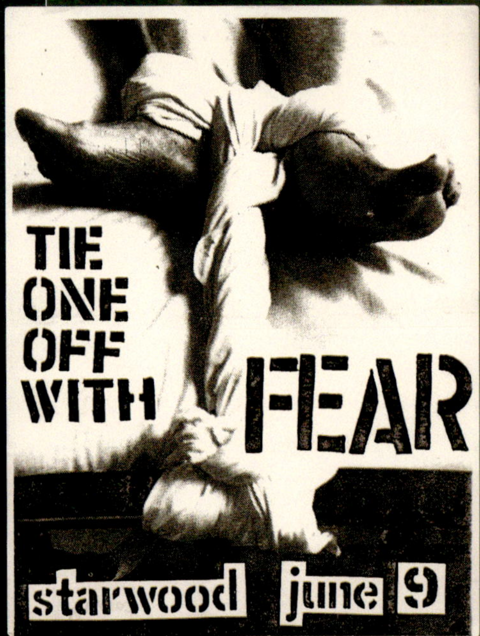

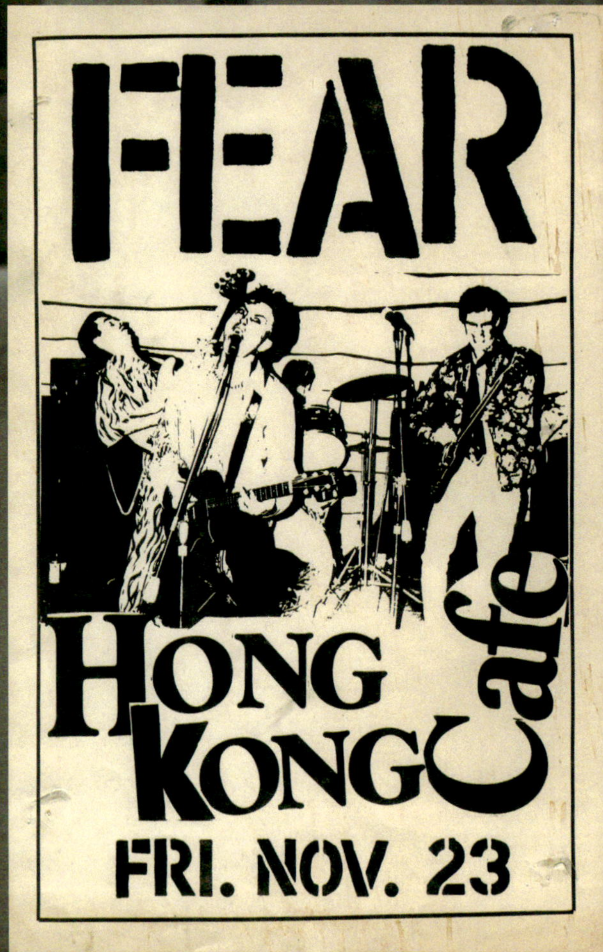

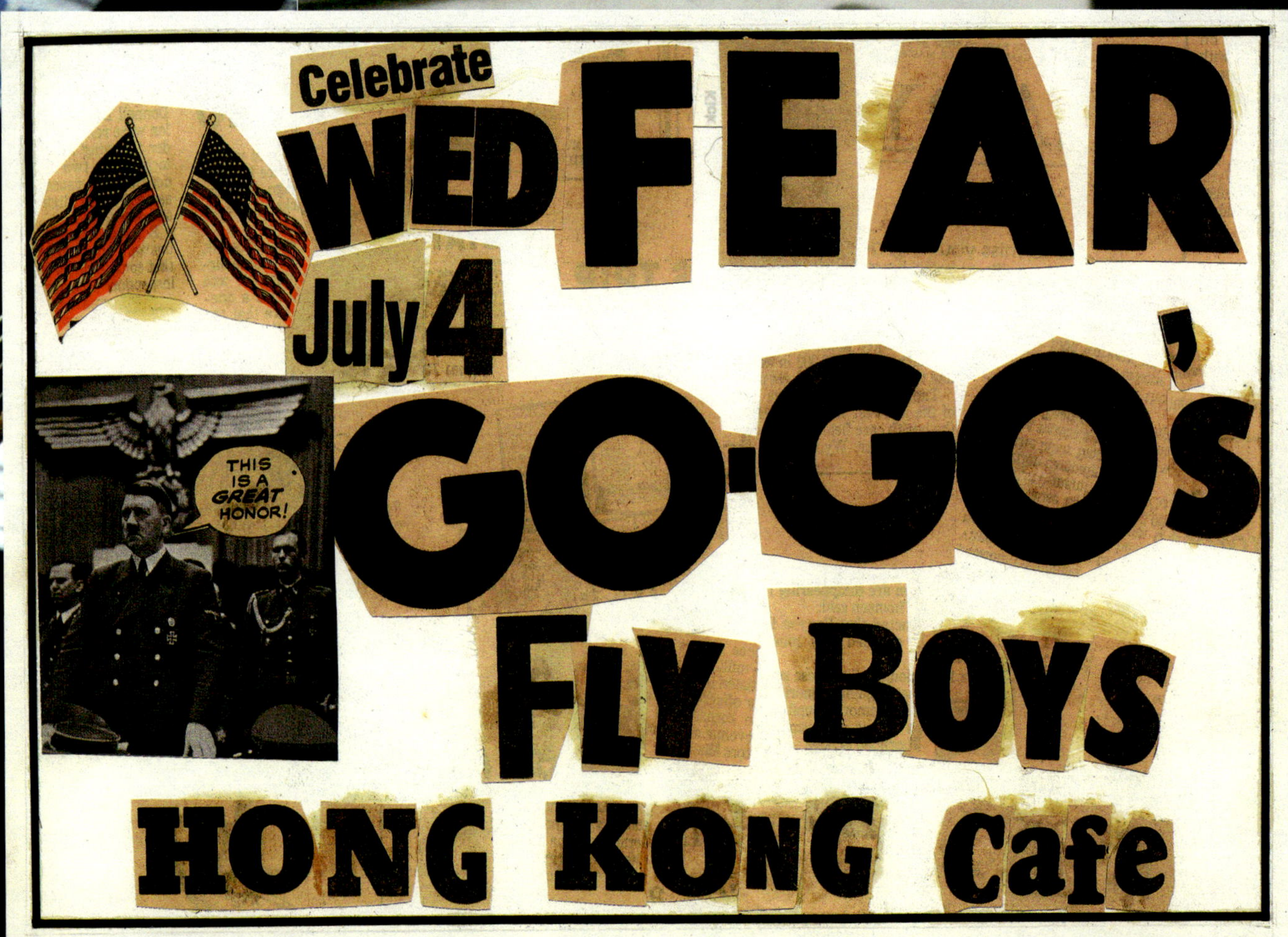

Flea with Fear
Photo © Marla Watson

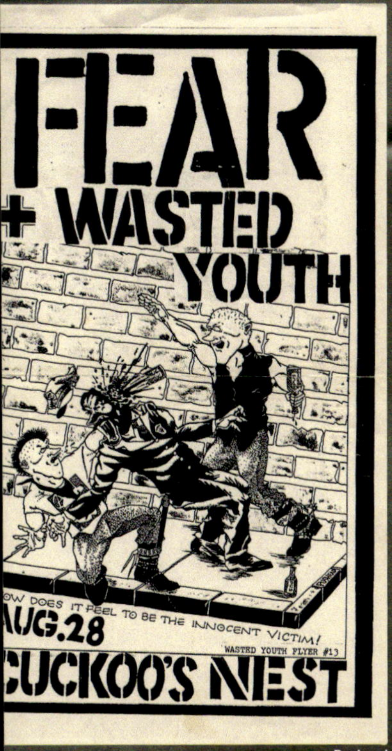

Pushead

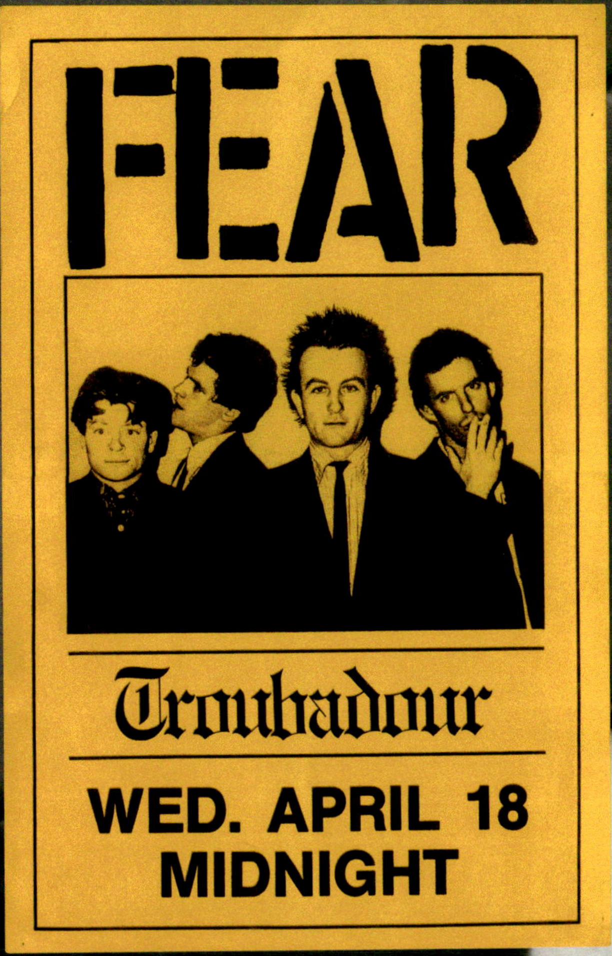

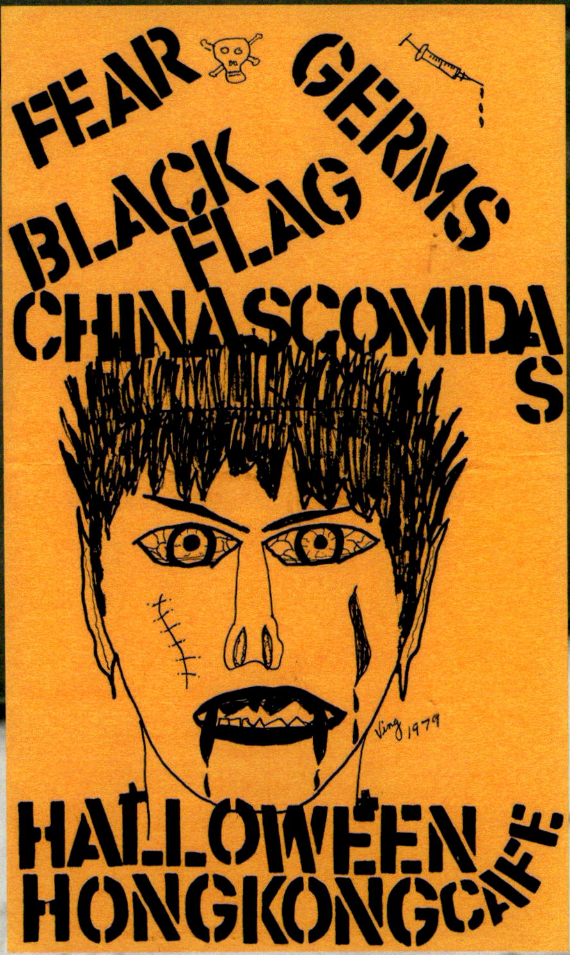

Lee Ving

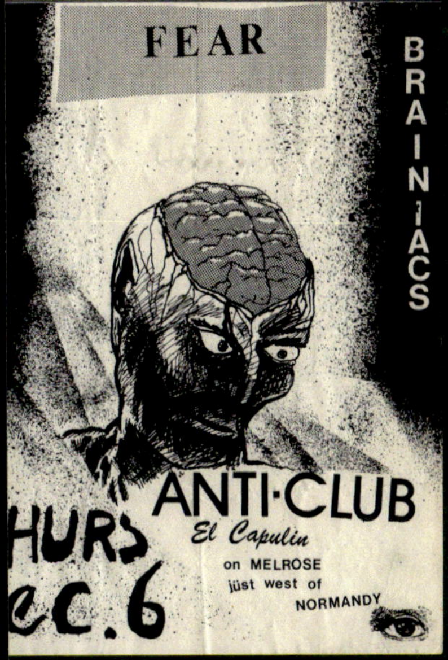

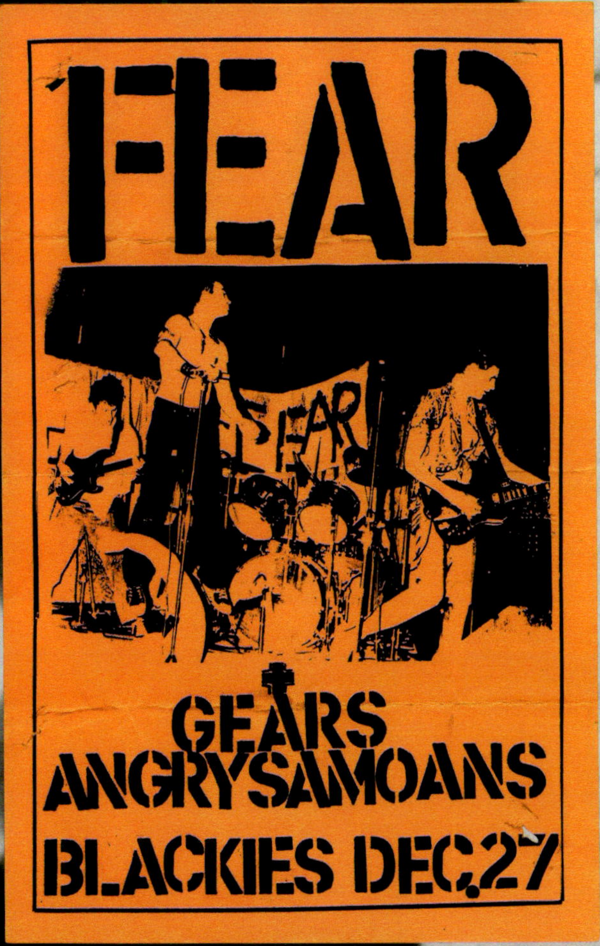

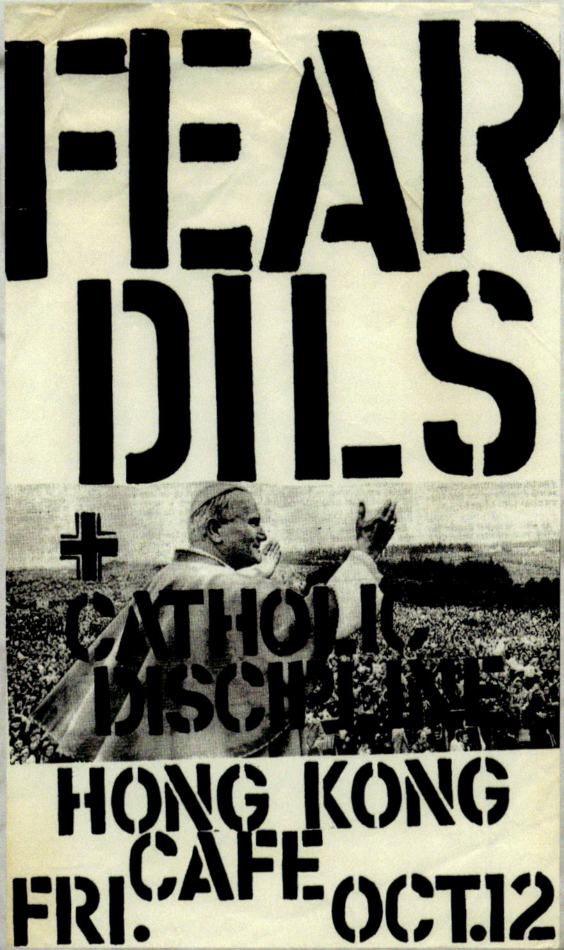

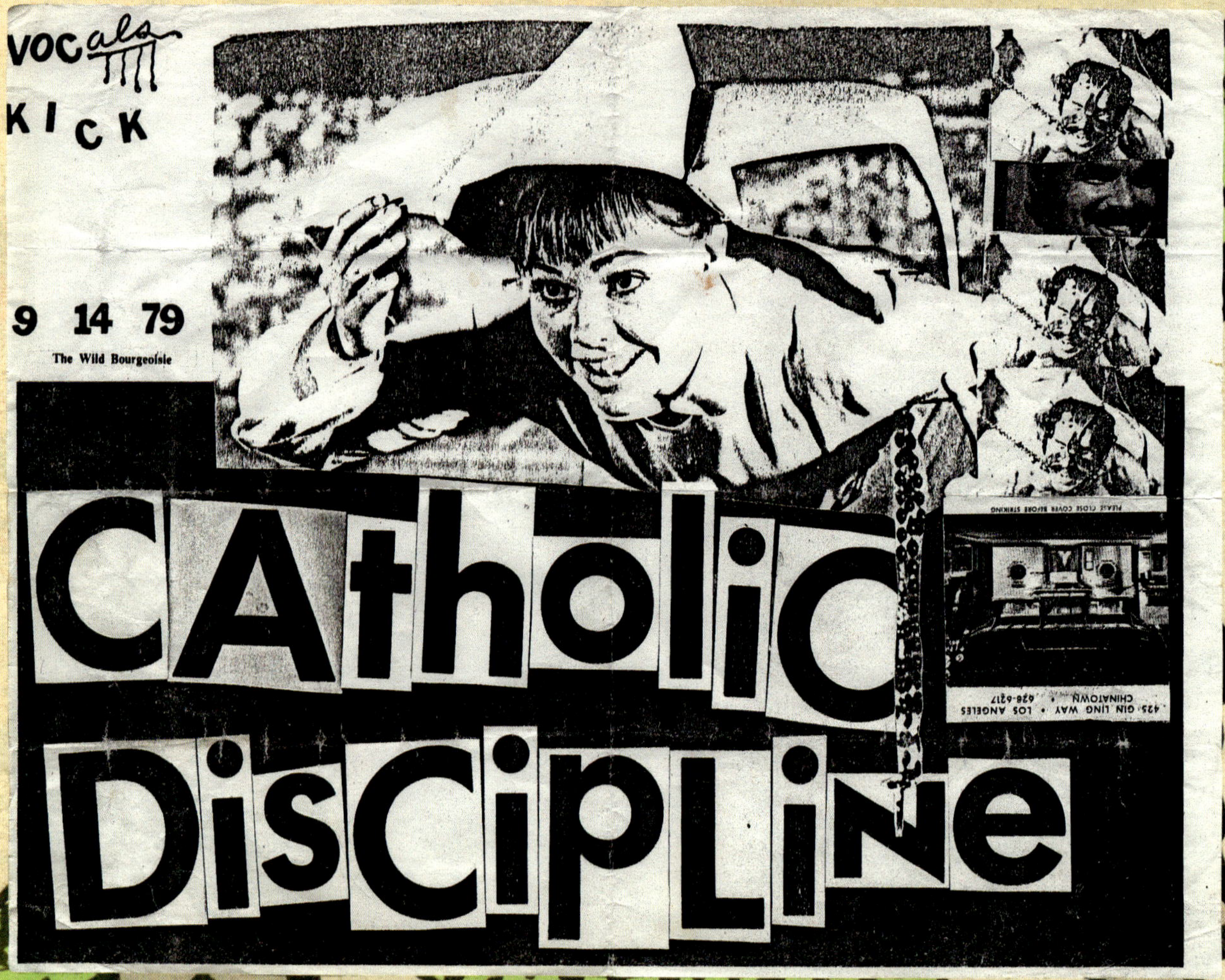
vocals
KICK
9 14 79
The Wild Bourgeoisie
Catholic Discipline

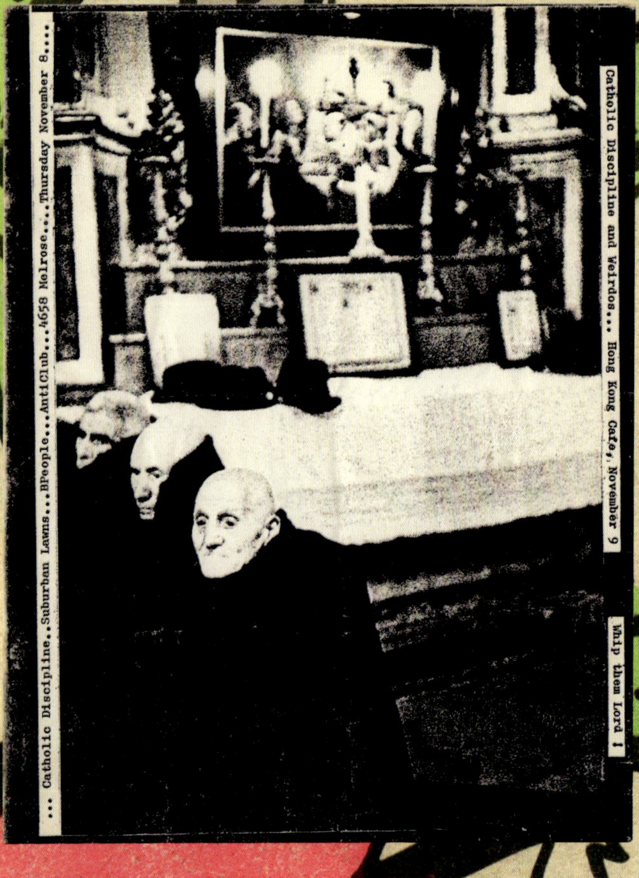
... Catholic Discipline...Suburban Lawns...BPeople...AntiClub...4658 Melrose....Thursday November 8....
Catholic Discipline and Weirdos... Hong Kong Cafe, November 9
Whip them Lord !

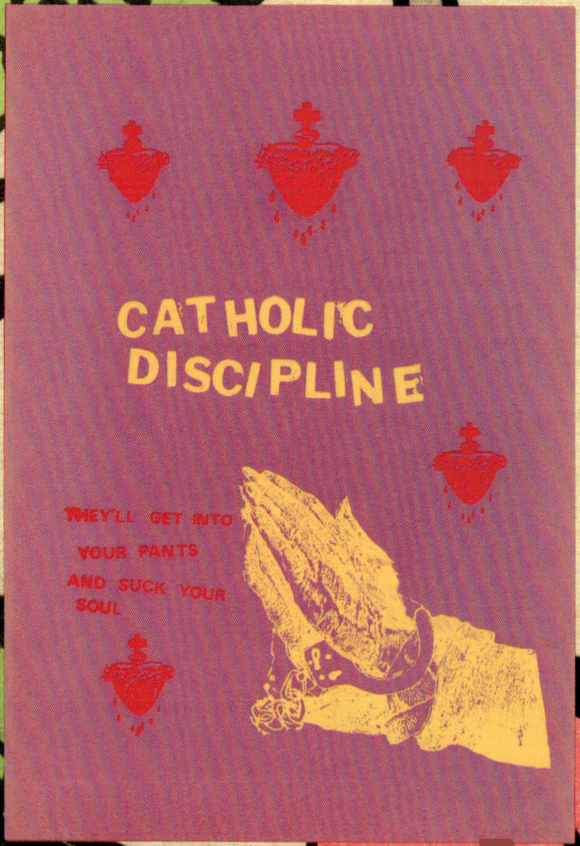
CATHOLIC DISCIPLINE
THEY'LL GET INTO YOUR PANTS AND SUCK YOUR SOUL

Chris D.

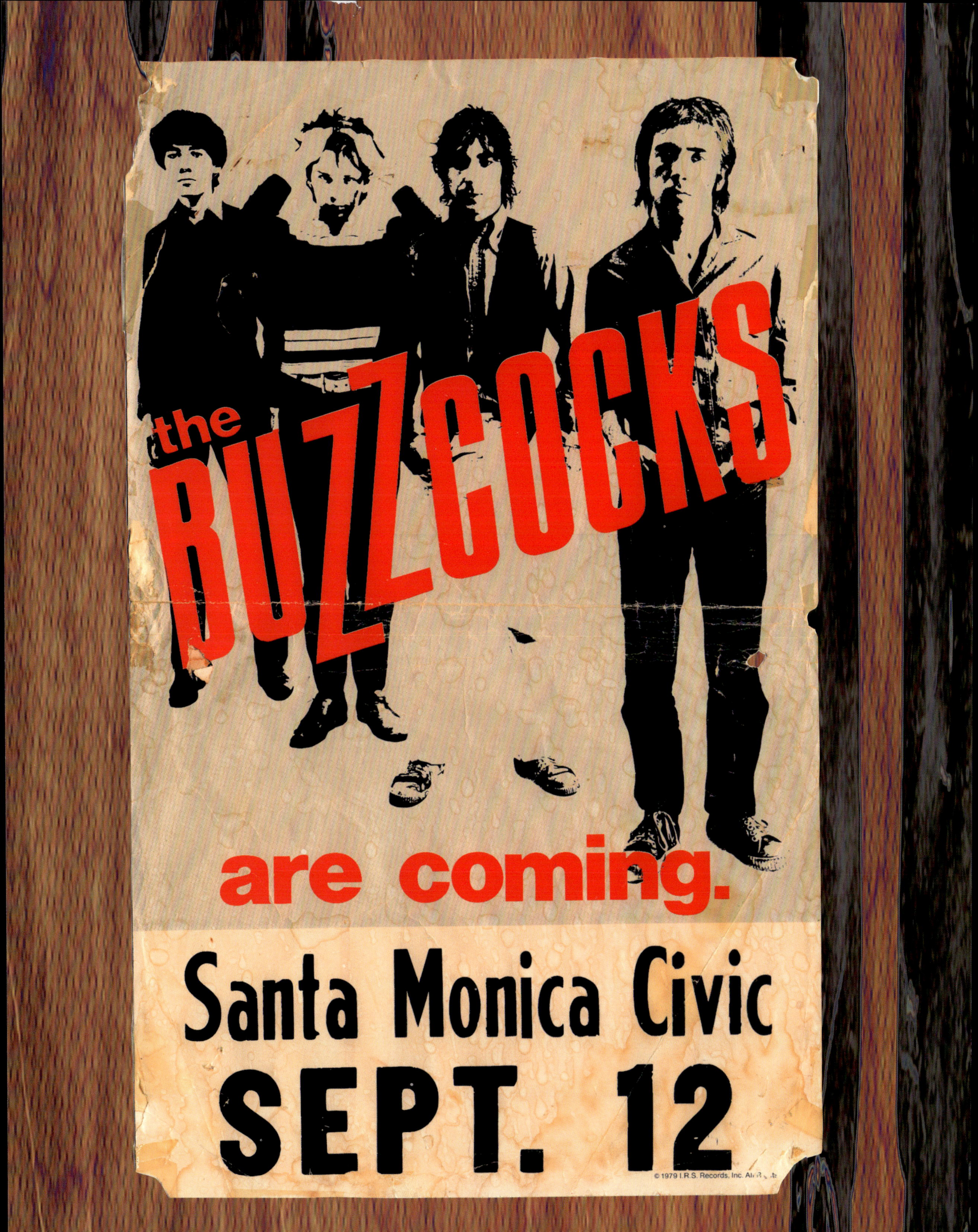

the
BUZZCOCKS
are coming.
Santa Monica Civic
SEPT. 12
© 1979 I.R.S. Records, Inc.

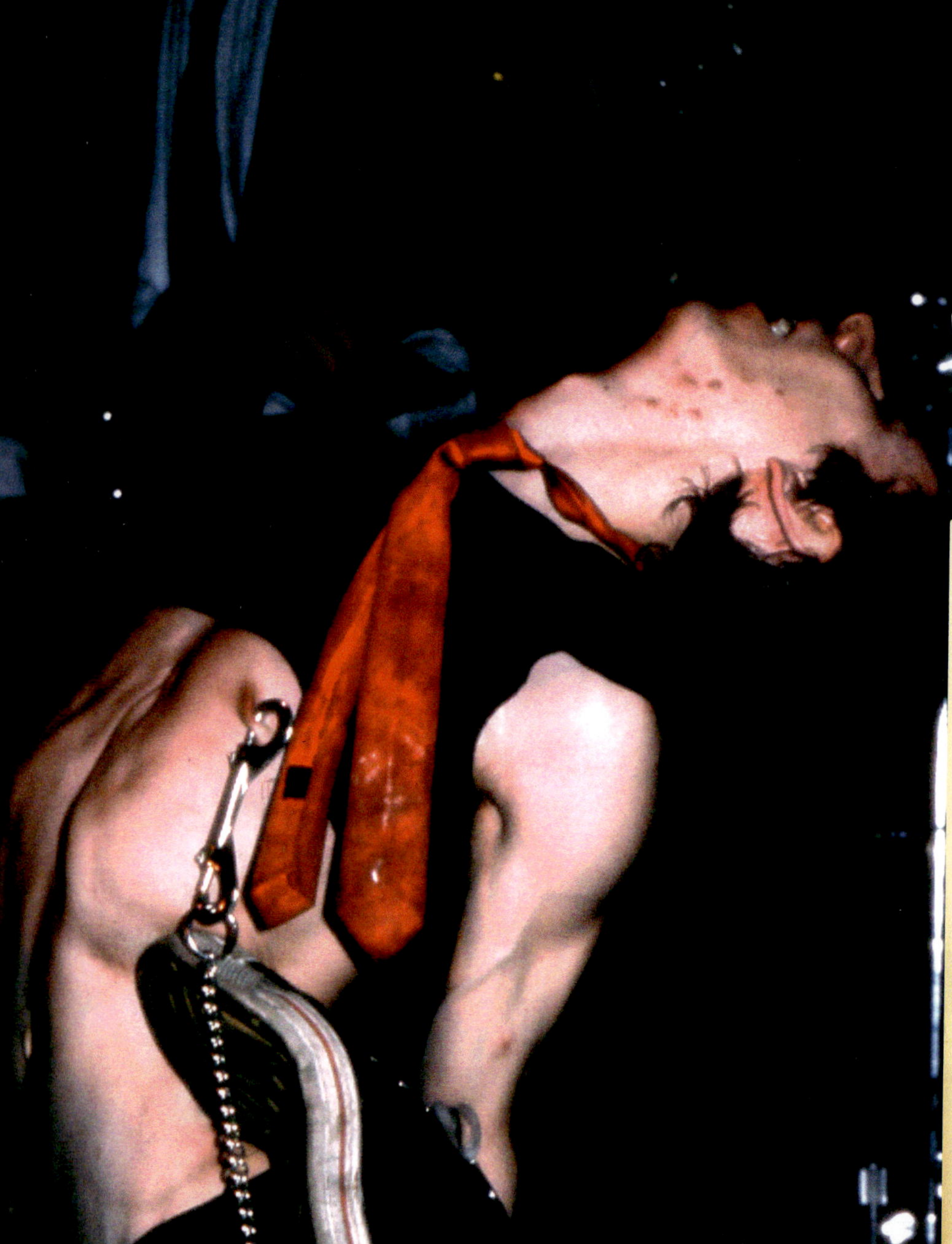

Stiv Bators
Photo © Jenny Lens

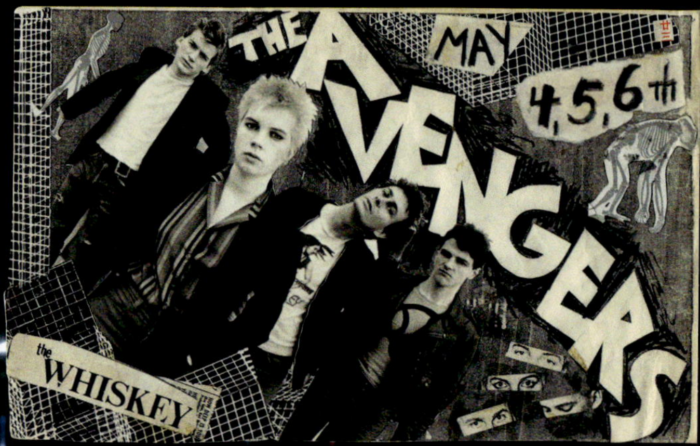

Penelope Housto

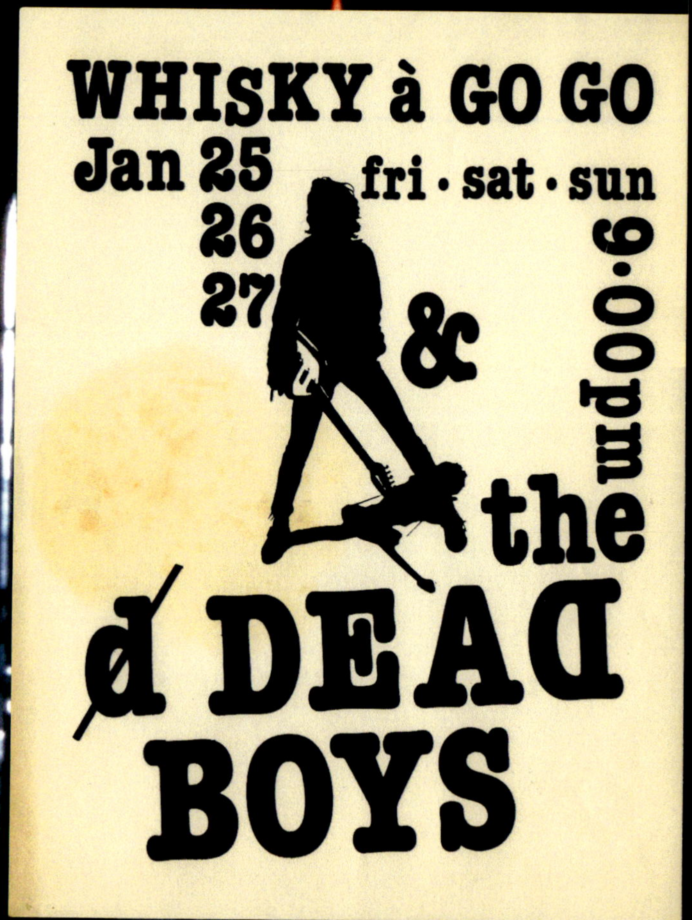

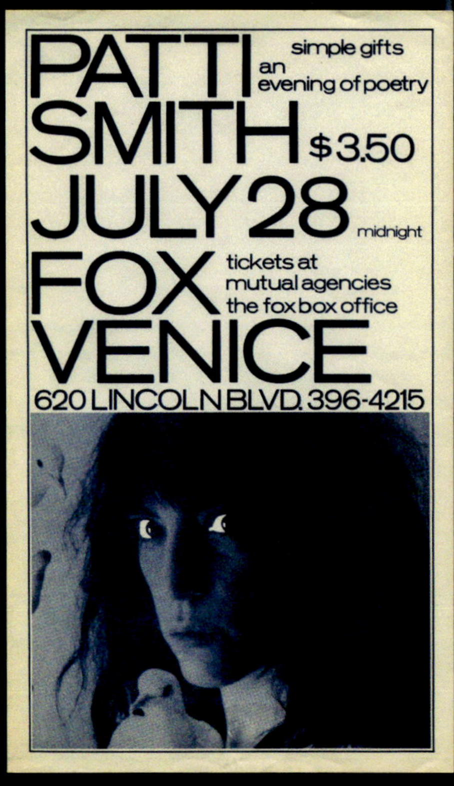

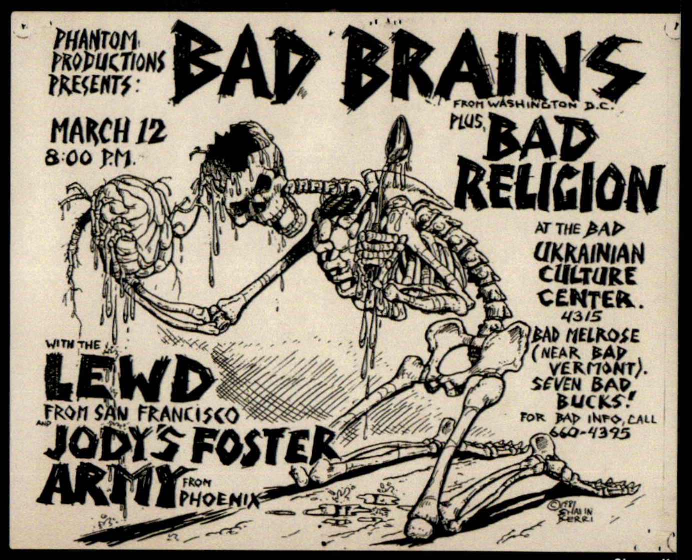

.Shawn Ke

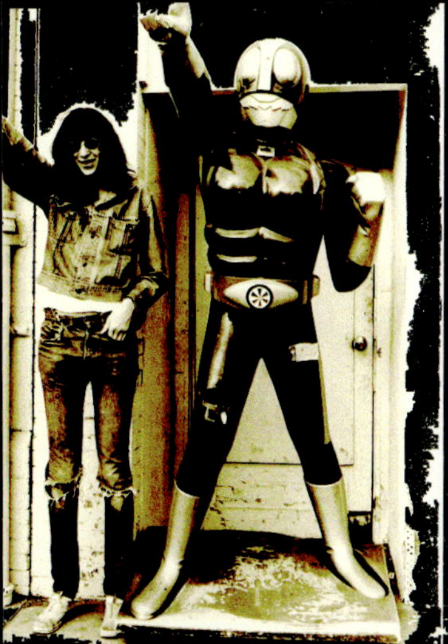

ey Ramone
oto © Jenny Lens

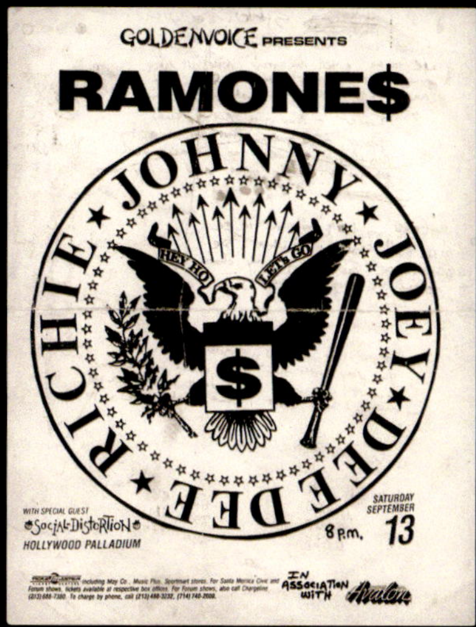

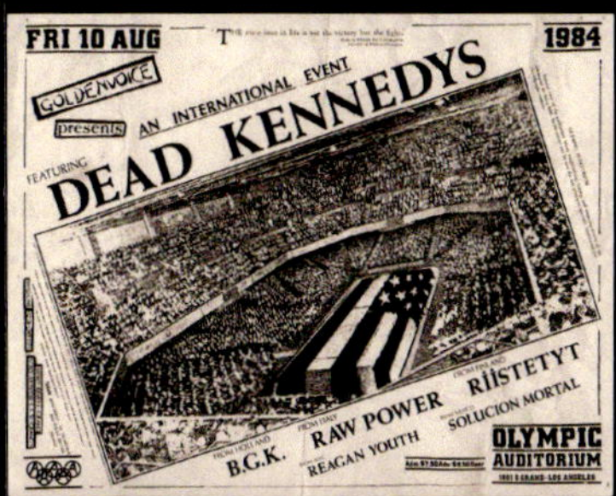

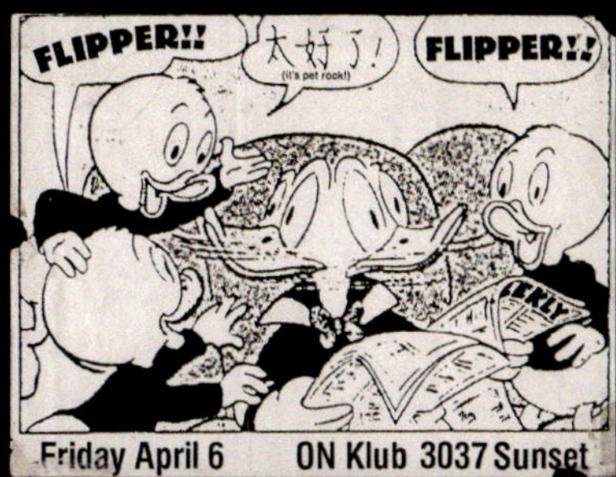

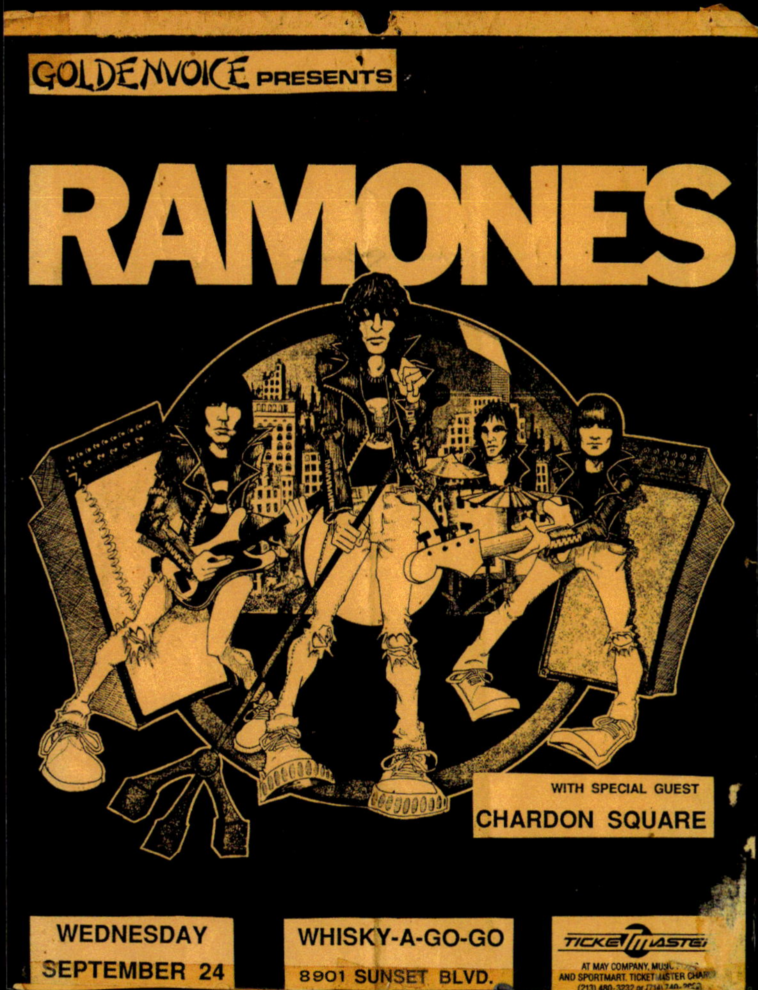

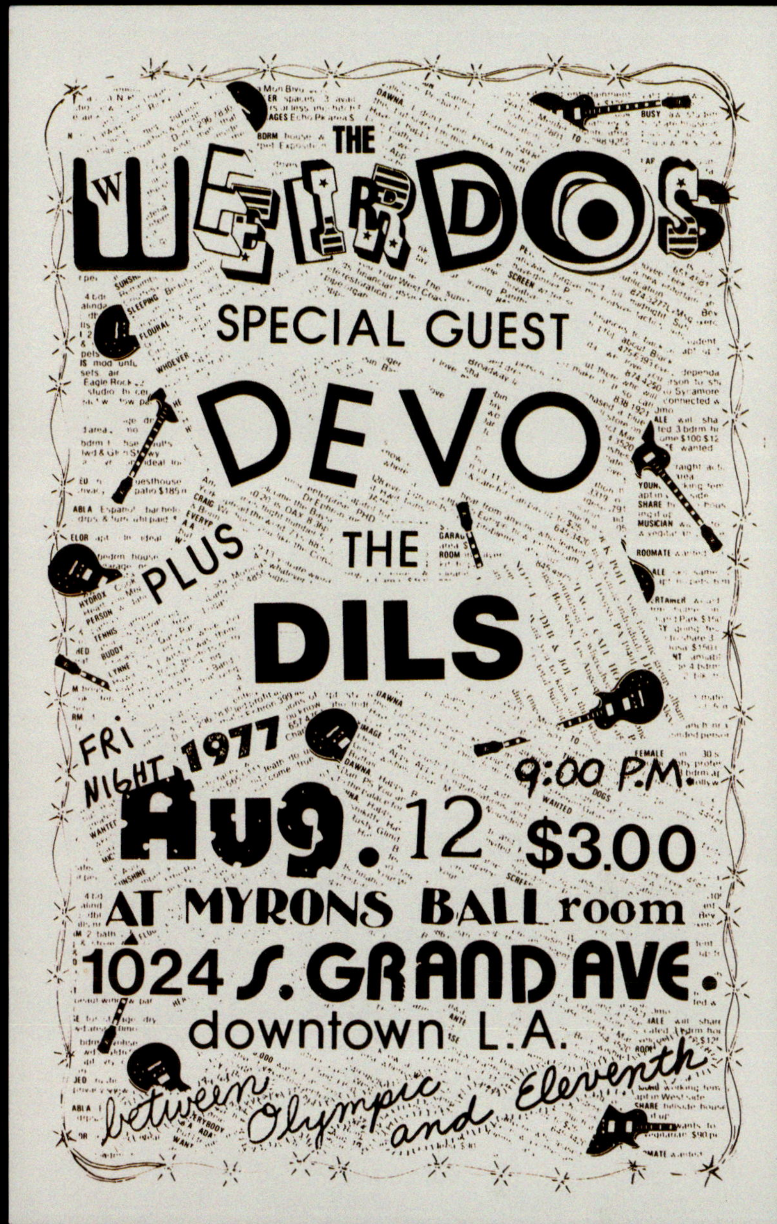

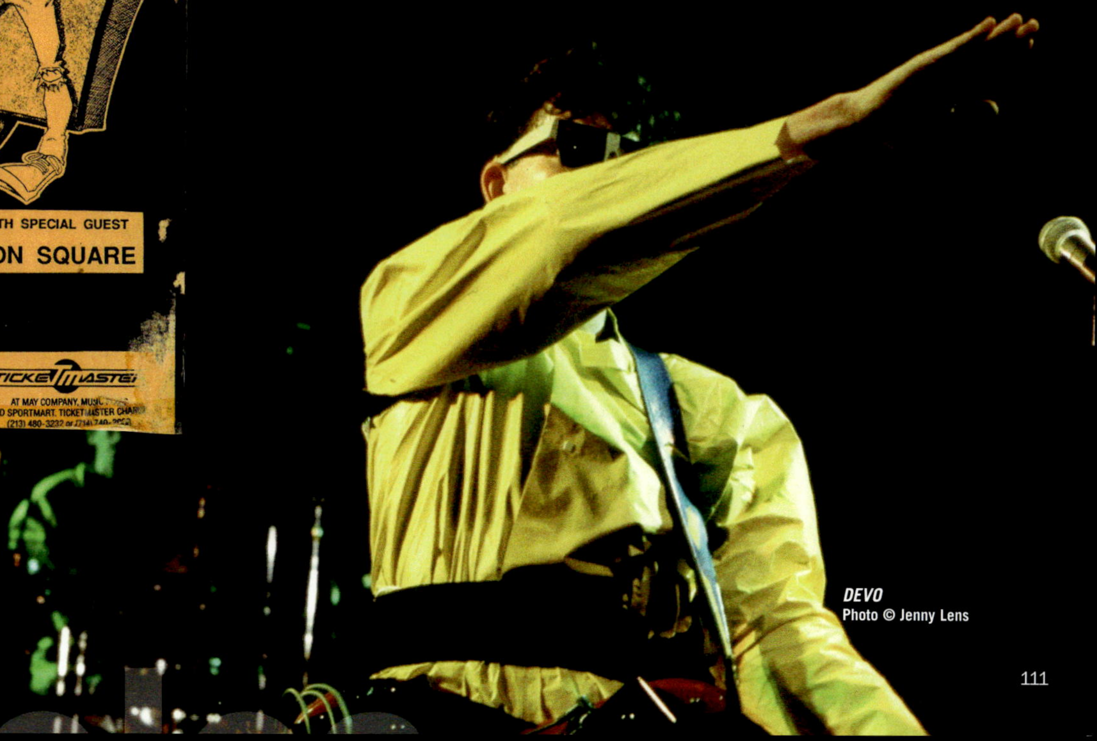

DEVO
Photo © Jenny Lens

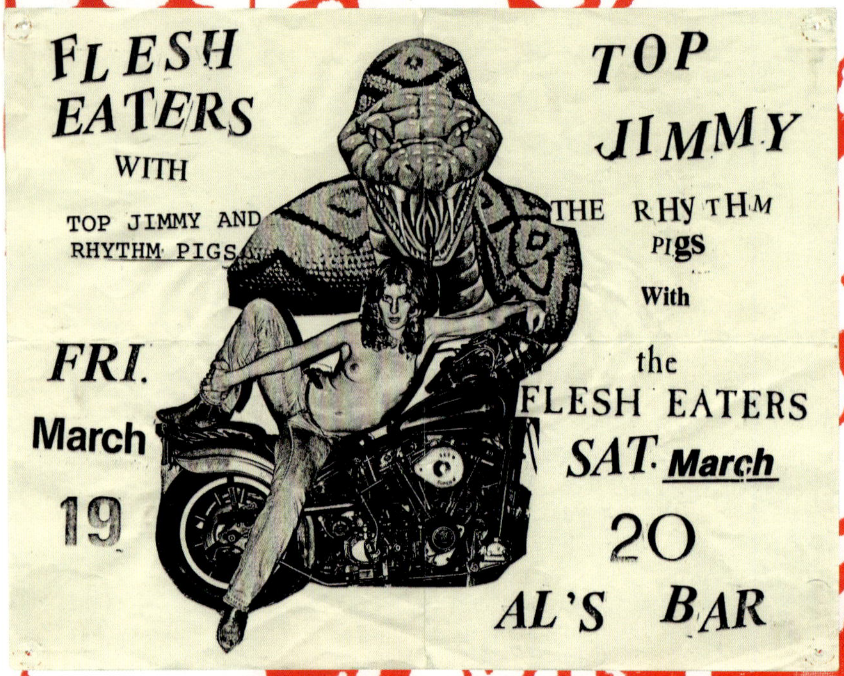
FLESH EATERS
WITH
TOP JIMMY AND RHYTHM PIGS
FRI. March 19
TOP JIMMY
THE RHYTHM PIGS
With
the FLESH EATERS
SAT. March 20
AL'S BAR

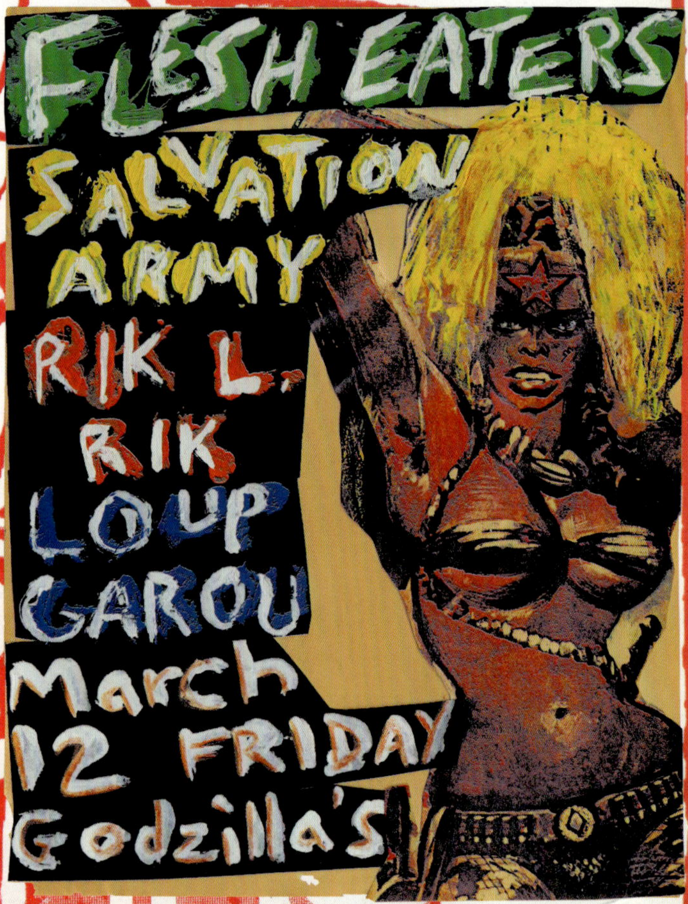
FLESH EATERS
SALVATION ARMY
RIK L. RIK
LOUP GAROU
March 12 FRIDAY
Godzilla's

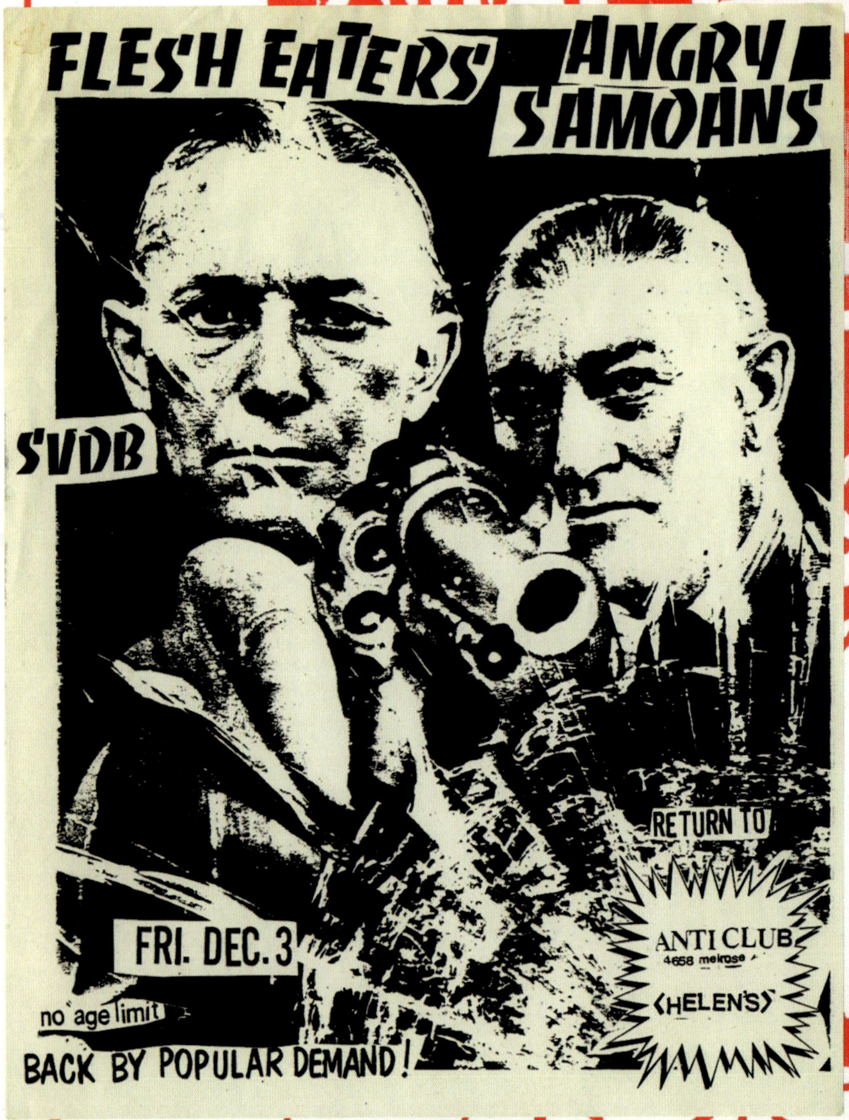
FLESH EATERS
ANGRY SAMOANS
SVDB
RETURN TO
ANTI CLUB
4658 melrose
<HELEN'S>
FRI. DEC. 3
no age limit
BACK BY POPULAR DEMAND!

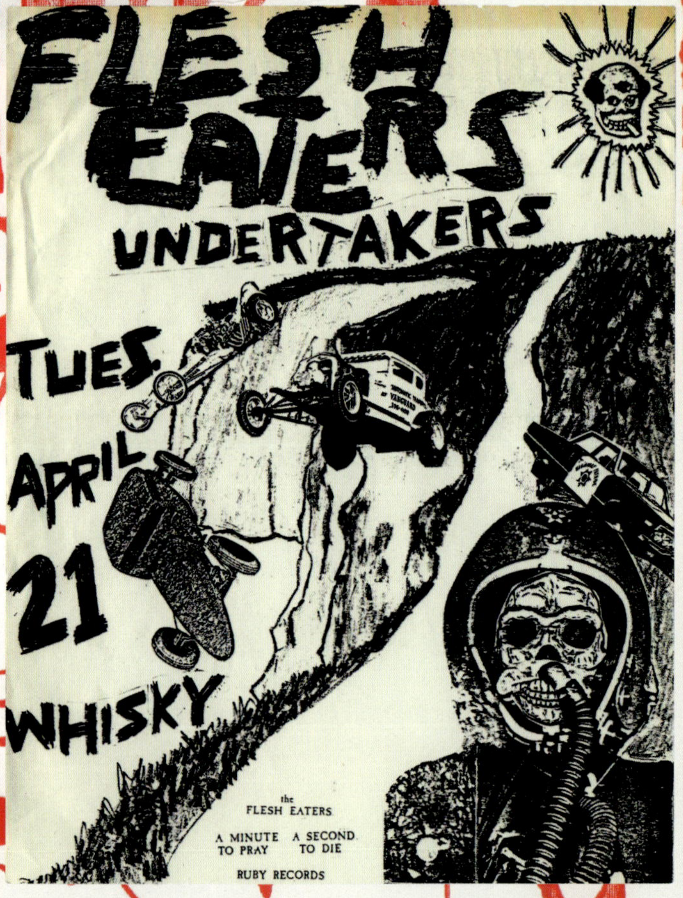
FLESH EATERS
UNDERTAKERS
TUES APRIL 21
WHISKY
the FLESH EATERS
A MINUTE TO PRAY A SECOND TO DIE
RUBY RECORDS

All: Chris D.

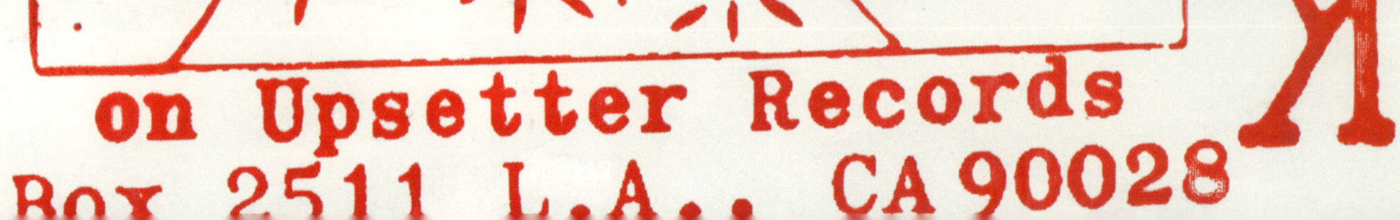
on Upsetter Records
Box 2511 L.A., CA 90028

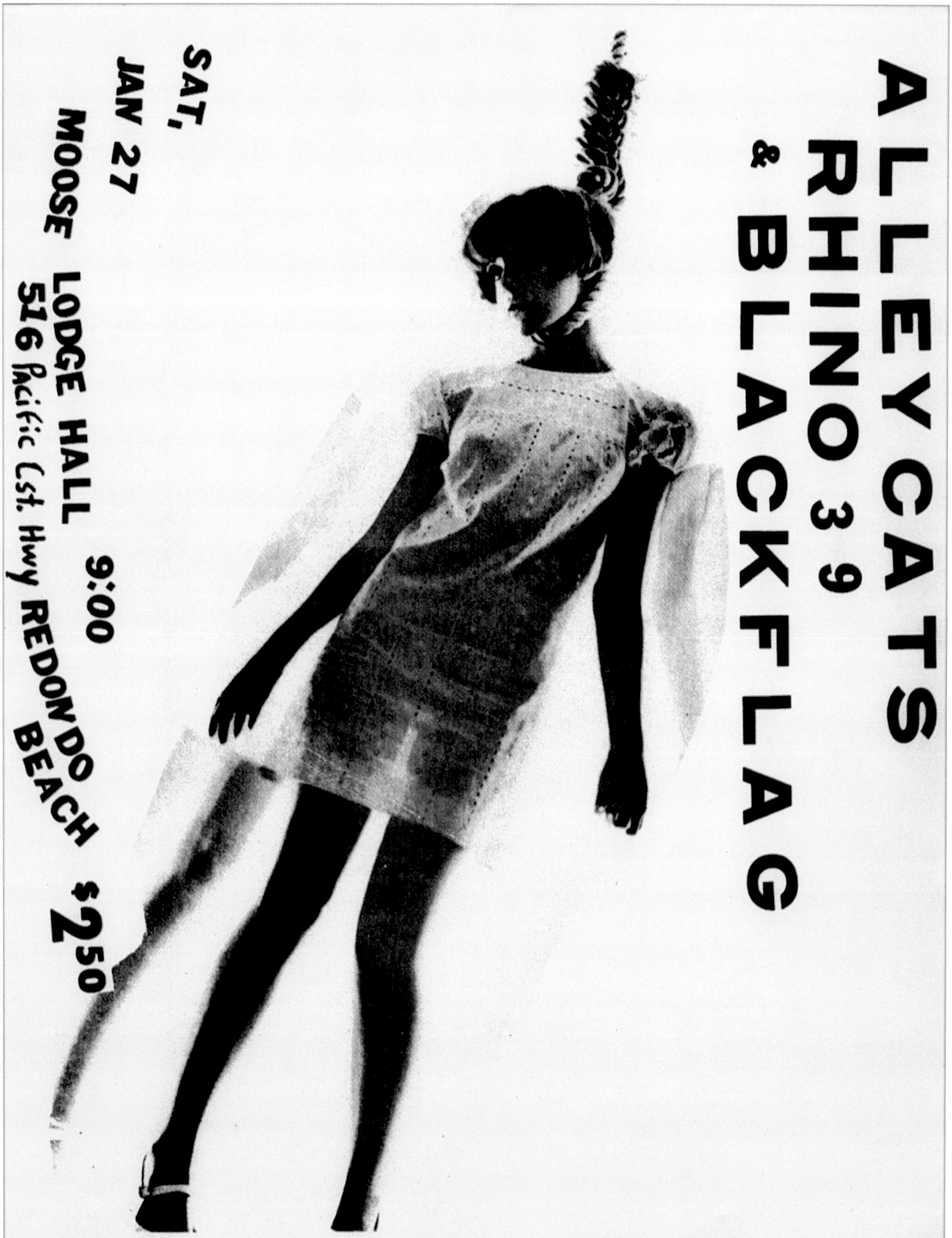

Black Flag's first club show...1979.

MOWING

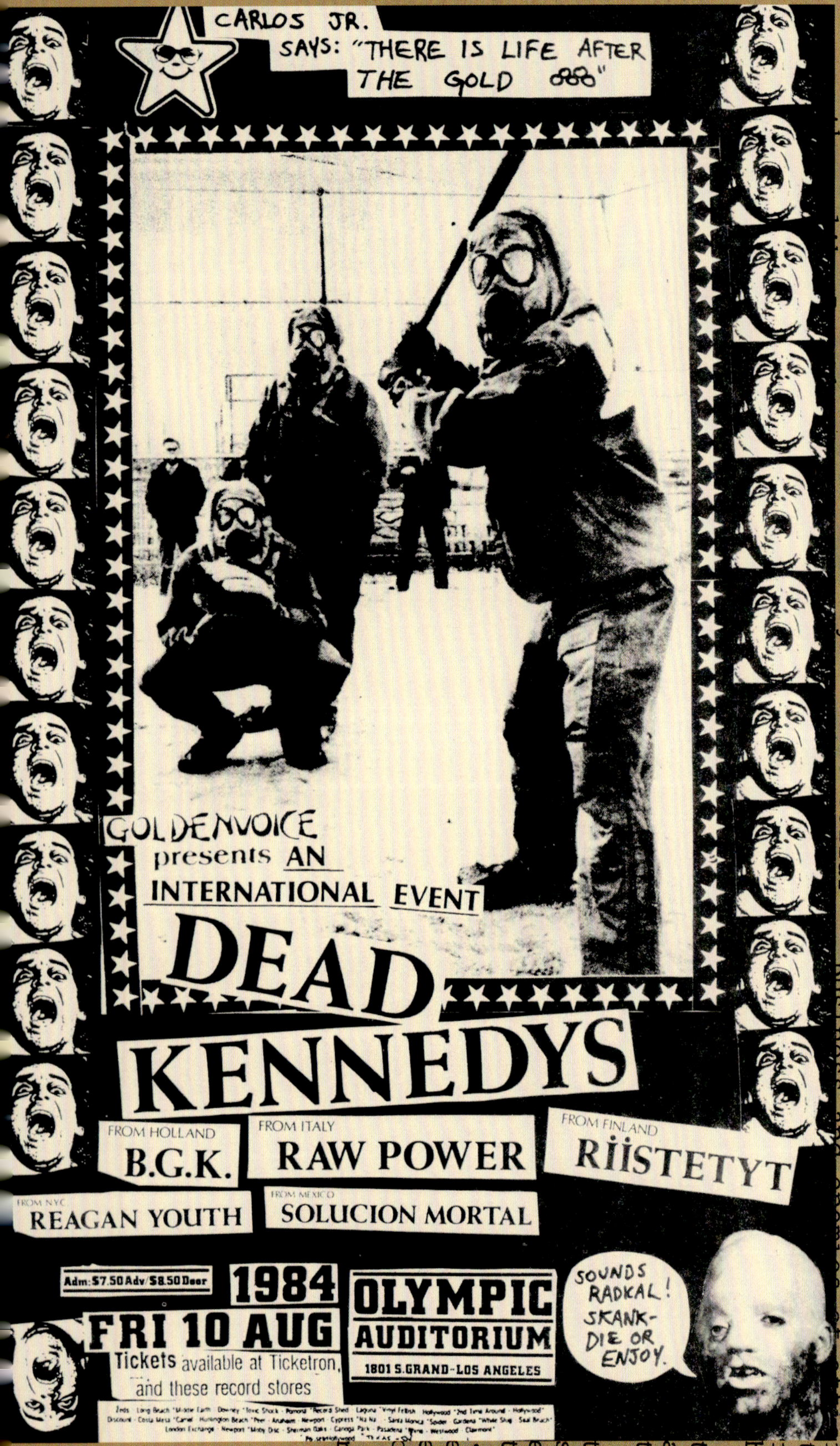

Jello Biafra

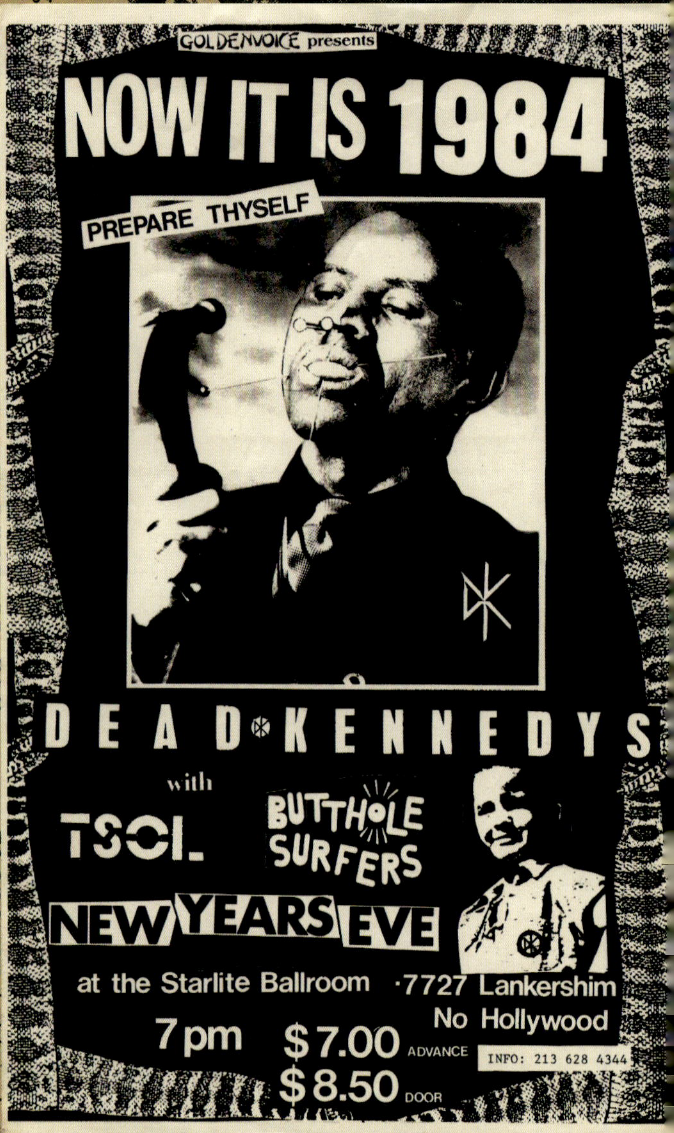

Jello Biafra

MOWING DOWN THE PEOPLE

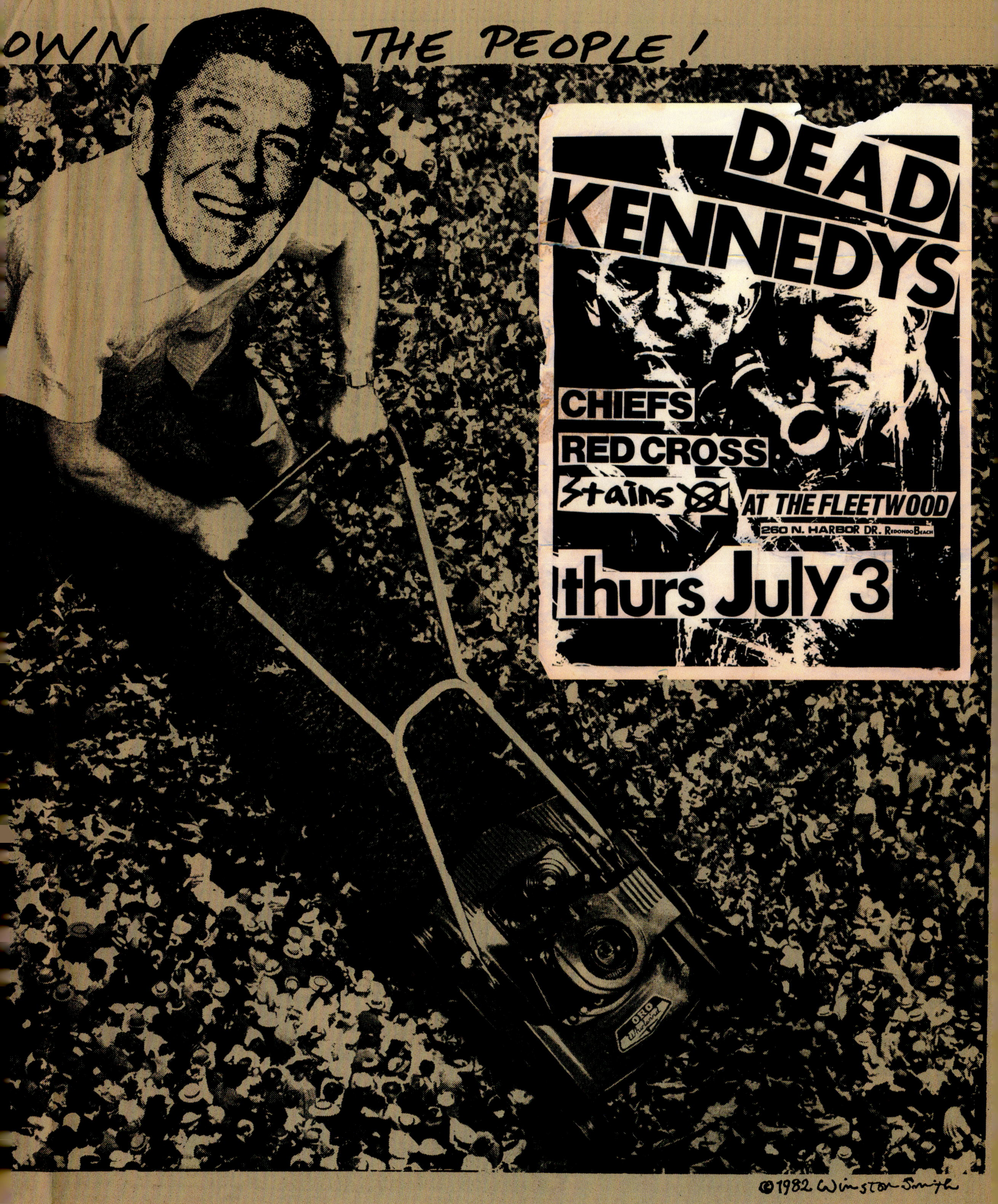
OWN THE PEOPLE!
DEAD KENNEDYS
CHIEFS
RED CROSS
Stains
AT THE FLEETWOOD
260 N. HARBOR DR. REDONDO BEACH
thurs July 3
©1982 Winston Smith

Crossing The Bridge: East Los Angeles

It's kinda scary when I think about it, but its been 20 years since I first tuned into "Rodney on the Roq," dyed my hair and bought my first Punk/New Wave records (the usual stuff: Ramones, Devo, Blondie, Clash.) It was a little later that I got into the juicy hard stuff, Black Flag, Germs, MC-5, Dolls, Stooges and Hawkwind. It was like being pummeled by a Panzer tank, and I loved it.

Soon I needed someplace to hang out and be "Punk." I joined the Stains and started going to shows in Chinatown, Al's Bar, and various lofts around town. With no MTV to show us how to be angry or depressed, we went to clubs, bought the records and read the fanzines. (Maybe it was a reaction to too many Brady Bunch episodes and Kimba reruns, who knows?) The best thing about the scene was that it managed to infiltrate the Barrio, deep into the heart of Boyle Heights–that's East L.A. for all you non-Californios! We even had our own club, The Vex, on Brooklyn Avenue, caddy-corner to the house I grew up in. The East LA scene was just a few bands that hated each other, with scary names like The Stains, Violent Children, The Brat, Los Illegals, The Undertakers, and later on, Los Lobos. We weren't exactly Ronnie & The Pomona Casuals or Rosie and Thee Originals, but we had our moments.

After 1981 the scene lost its urgency and newness. OC bands came to town and the scene was polarized, not much fun. Darby wasn't around to bum a quarter, Chuck D was giving interviews to Rhona Barrett, and I became obsessed with the blues and playing guitar, so much so that I turned down playing drums with Black Flag on its Canadian tour in '82. I was only 17, but I'd already lost interest - though, deep down, I'll be a punk forever.

Gilbert Berumen
AKA Jack Rivera

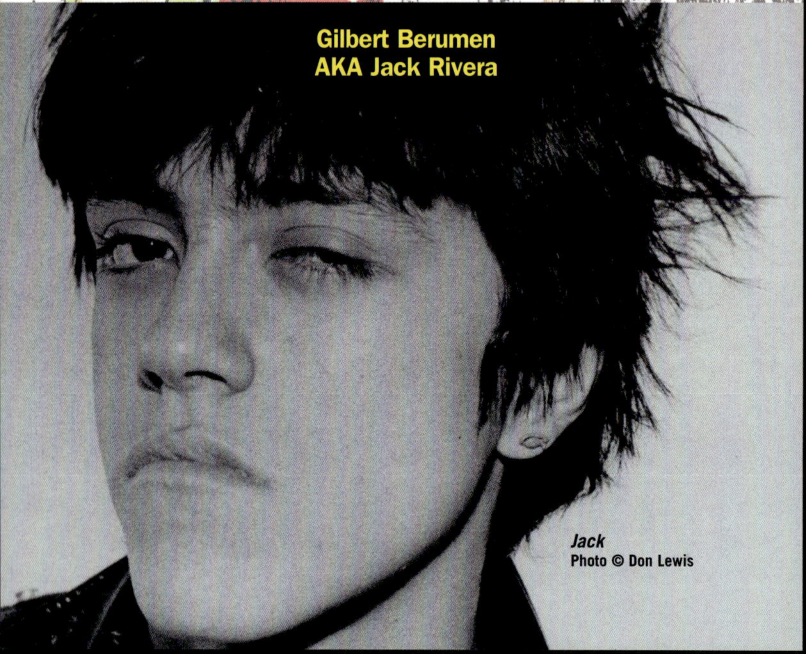

Jack
Photo © Don Lewis

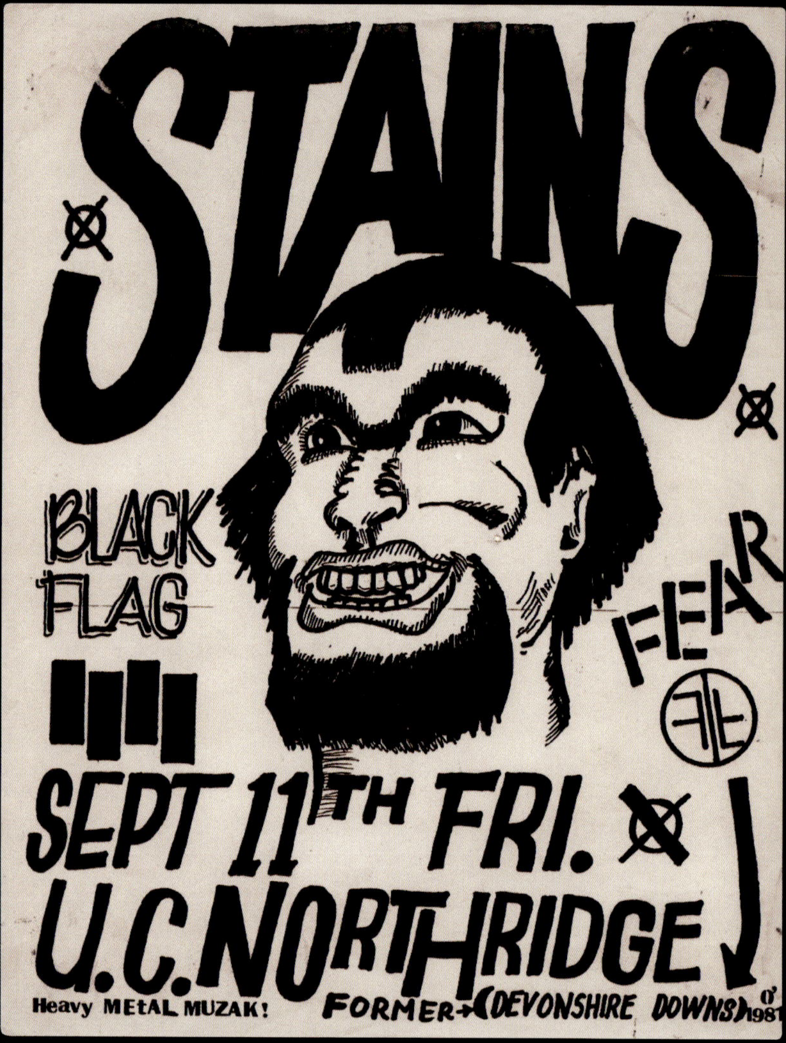

0

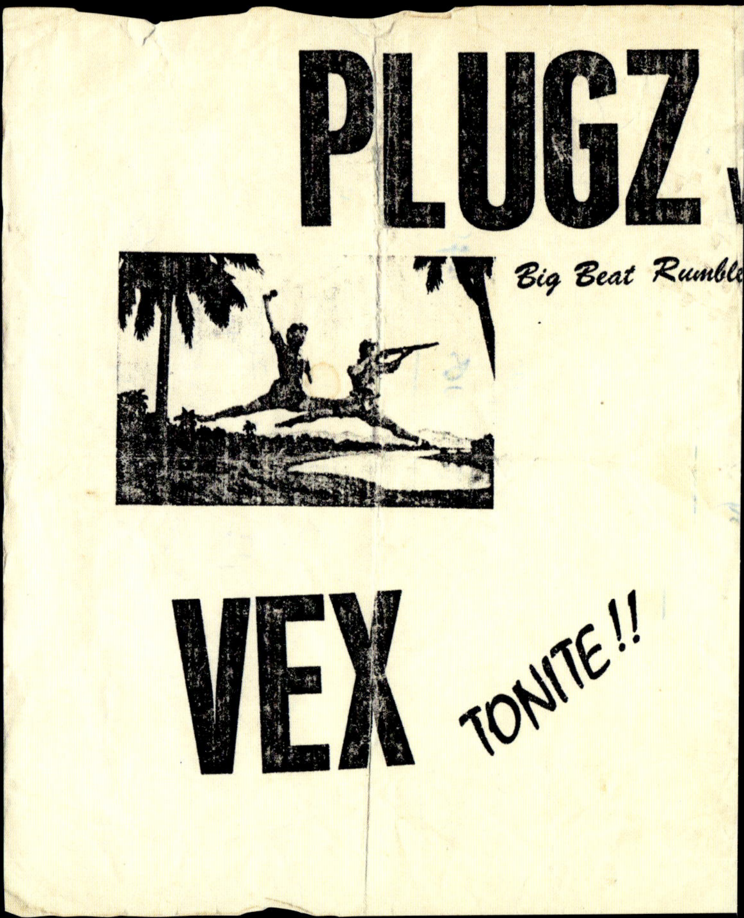

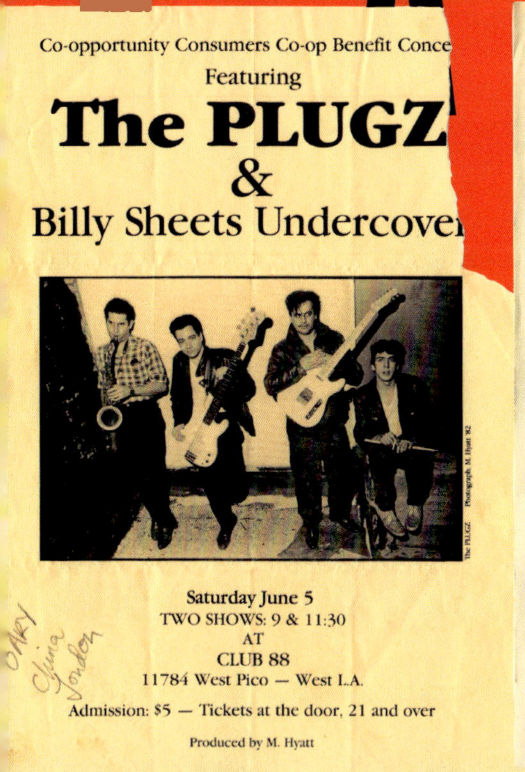

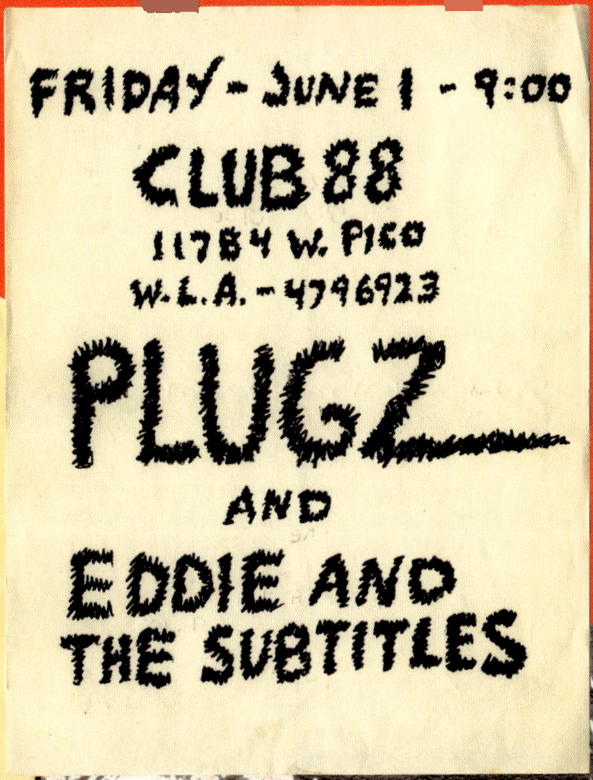

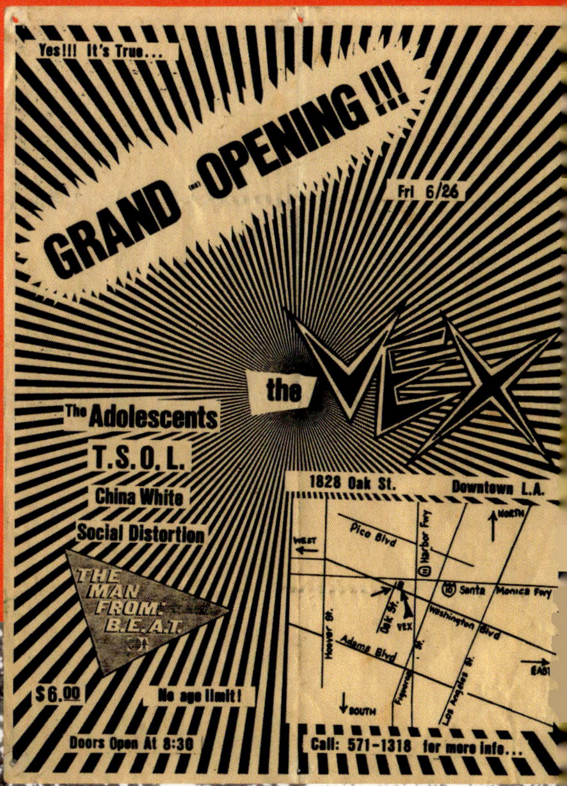

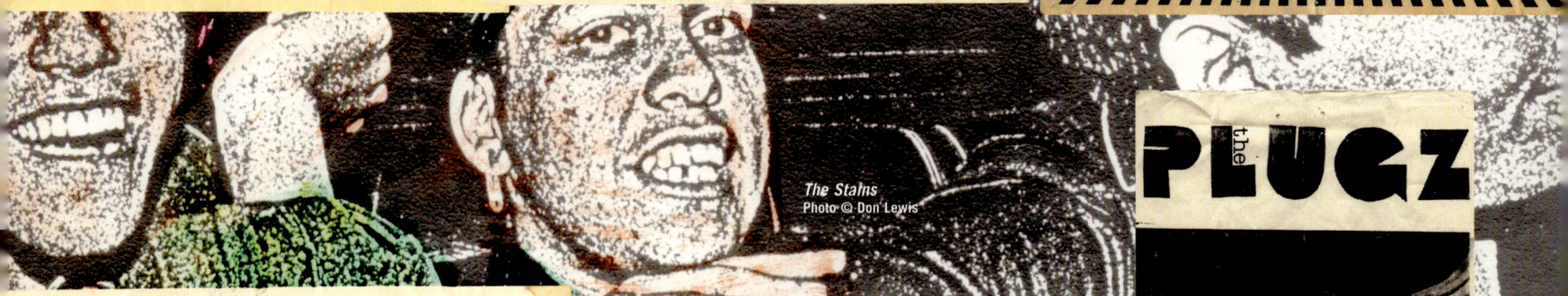
The Stains
Photo © Don Lewis

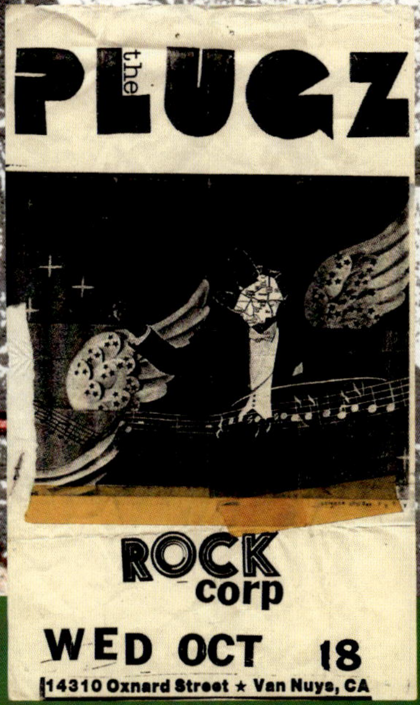

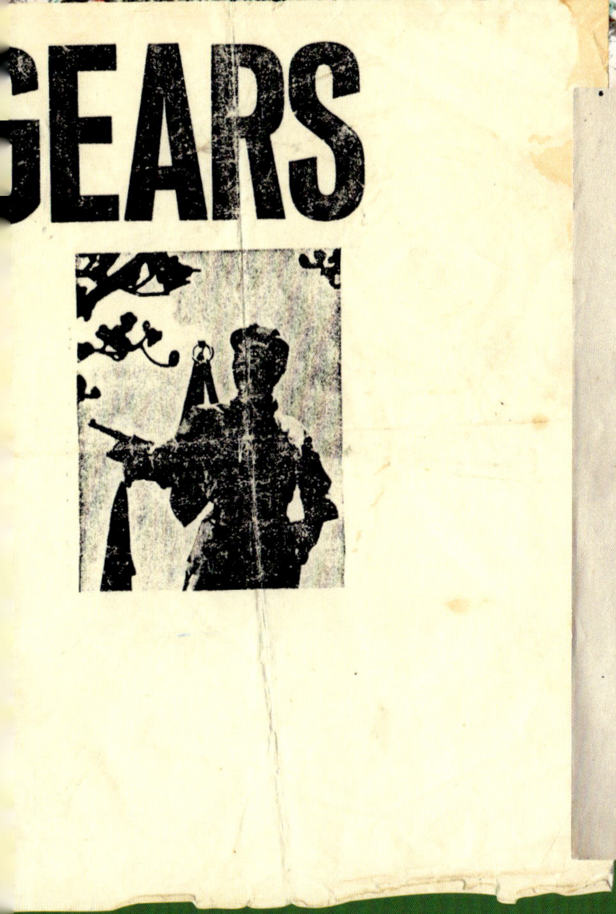

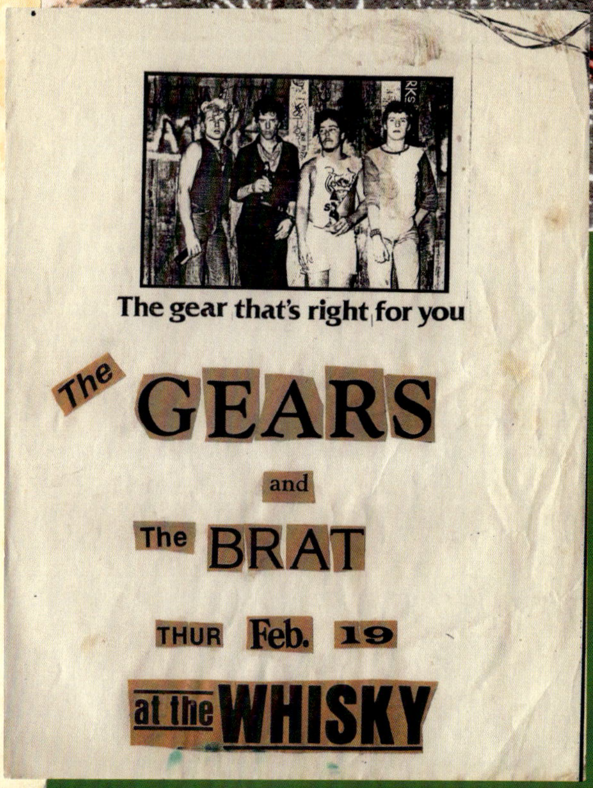

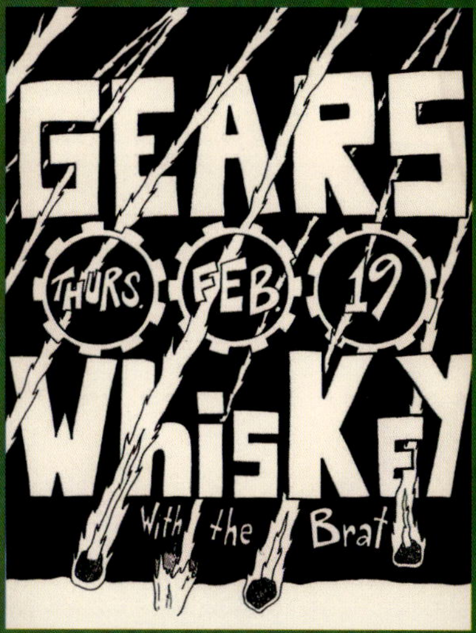

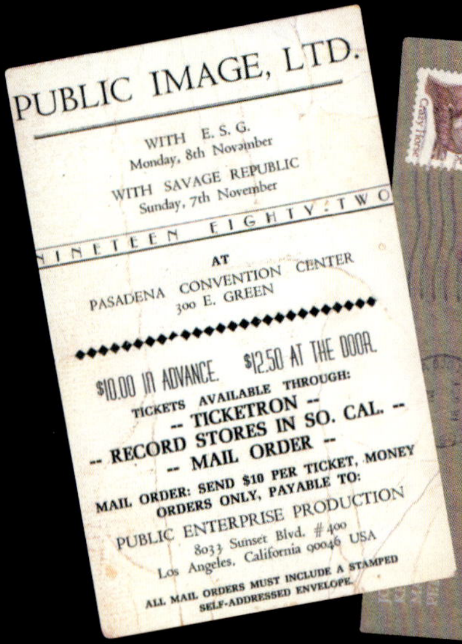

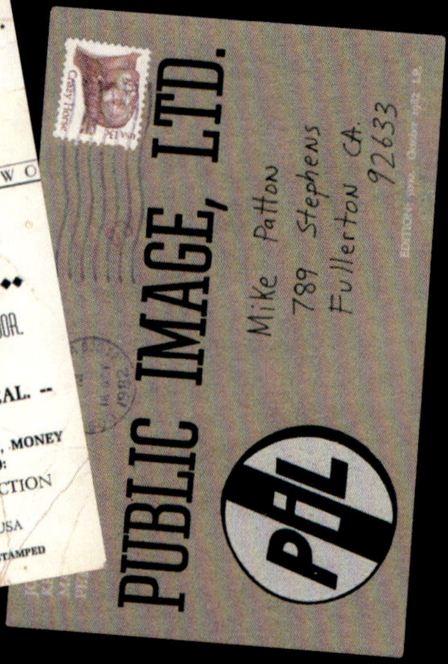

PASADENA

PerkinsPalace

Human Hands

Ice House

B People

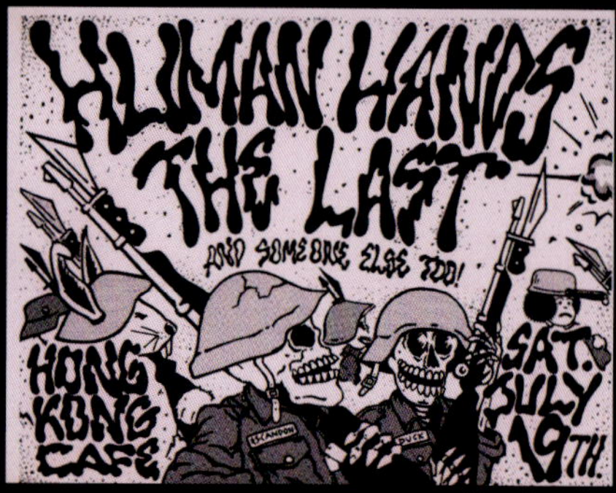

Steve Escandon

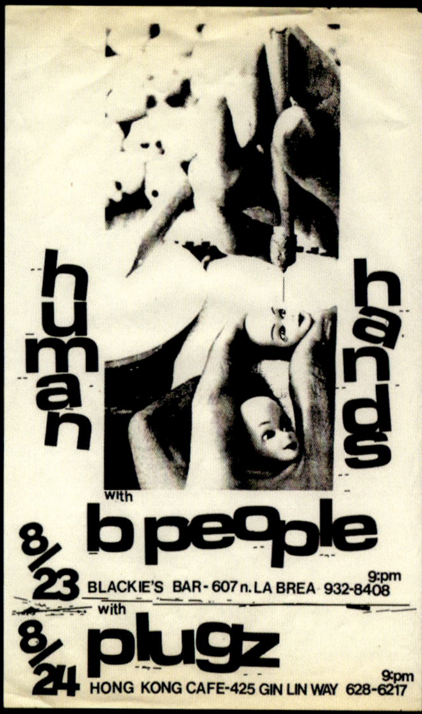

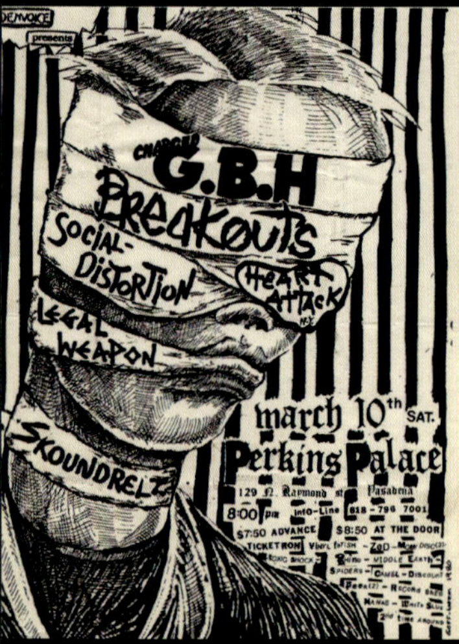

Goef Worm

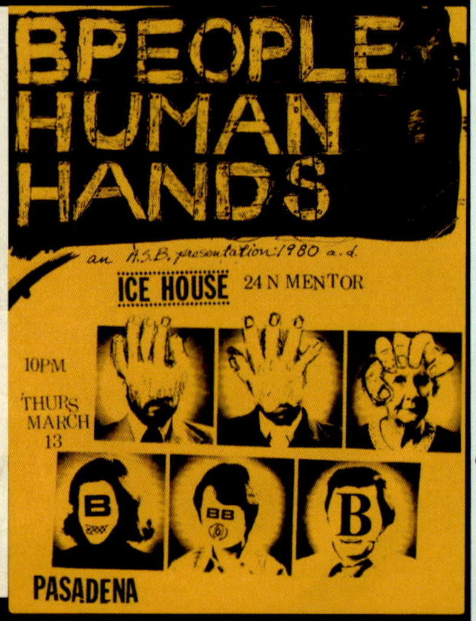

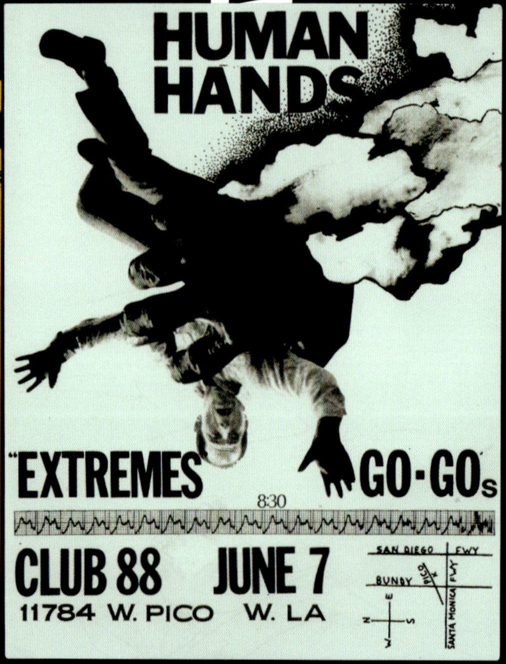

Juan Gomez

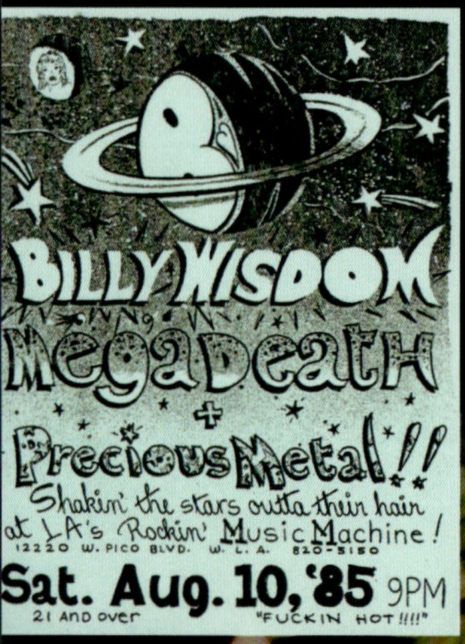

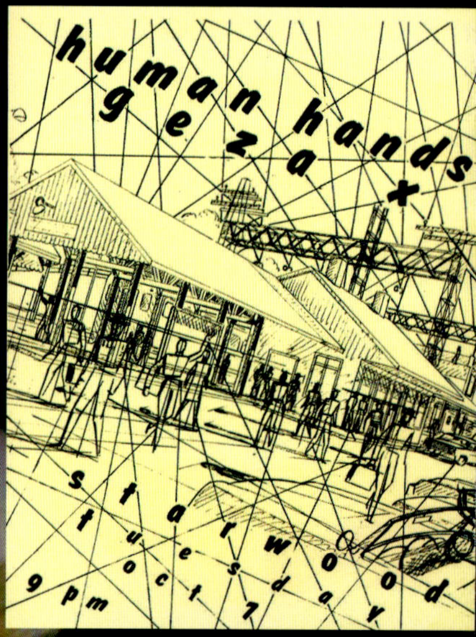

David Wiley

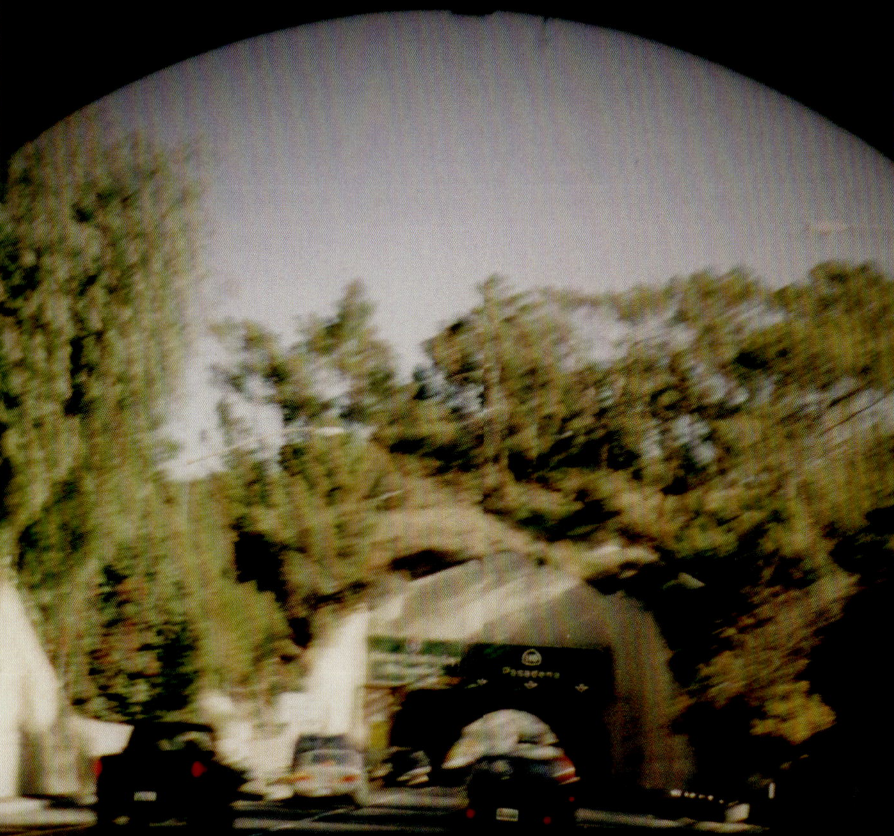

110 Tunnels to Pasa

Photo © John S

Victor Gastelum

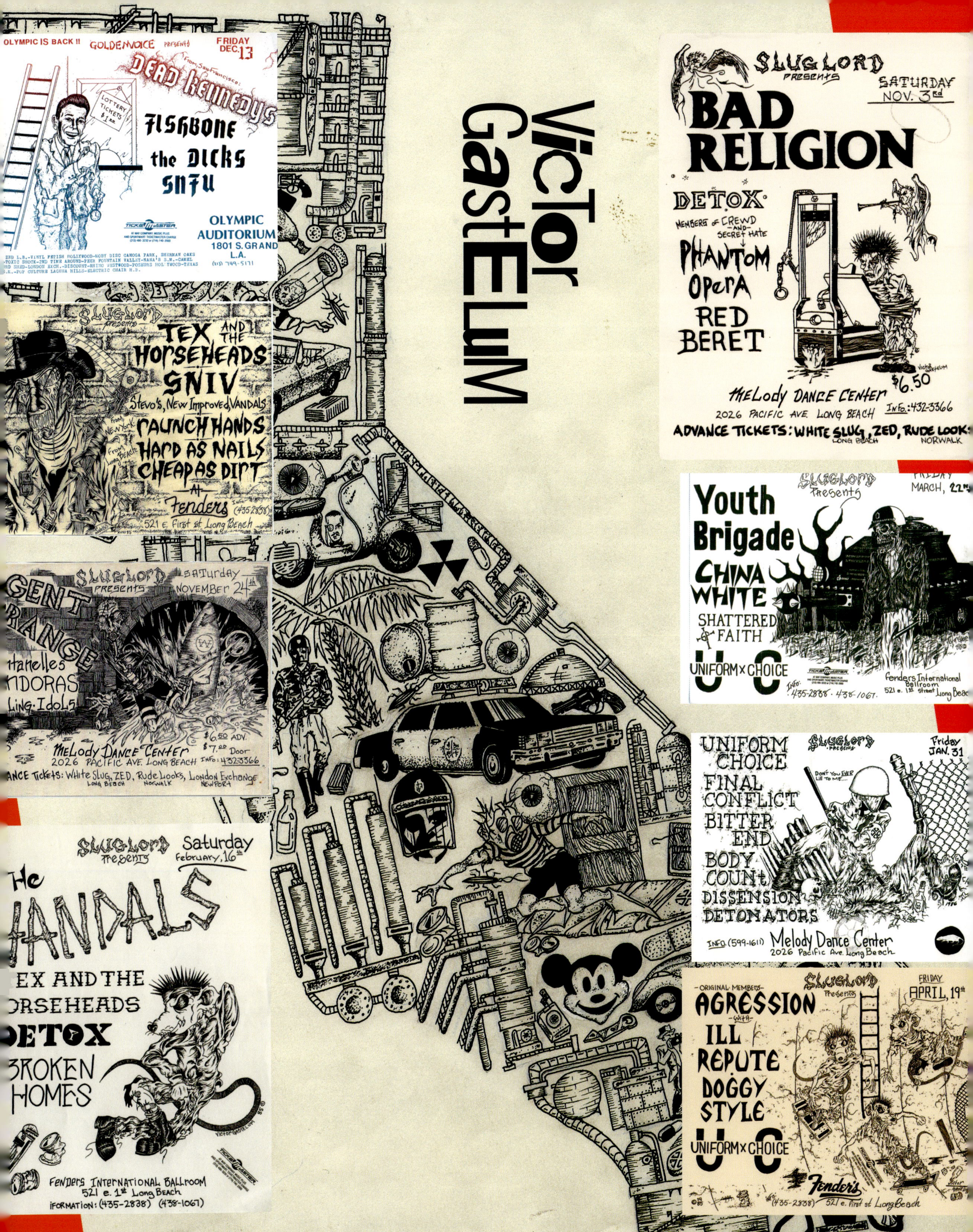

 All on this page Victor Gastelum

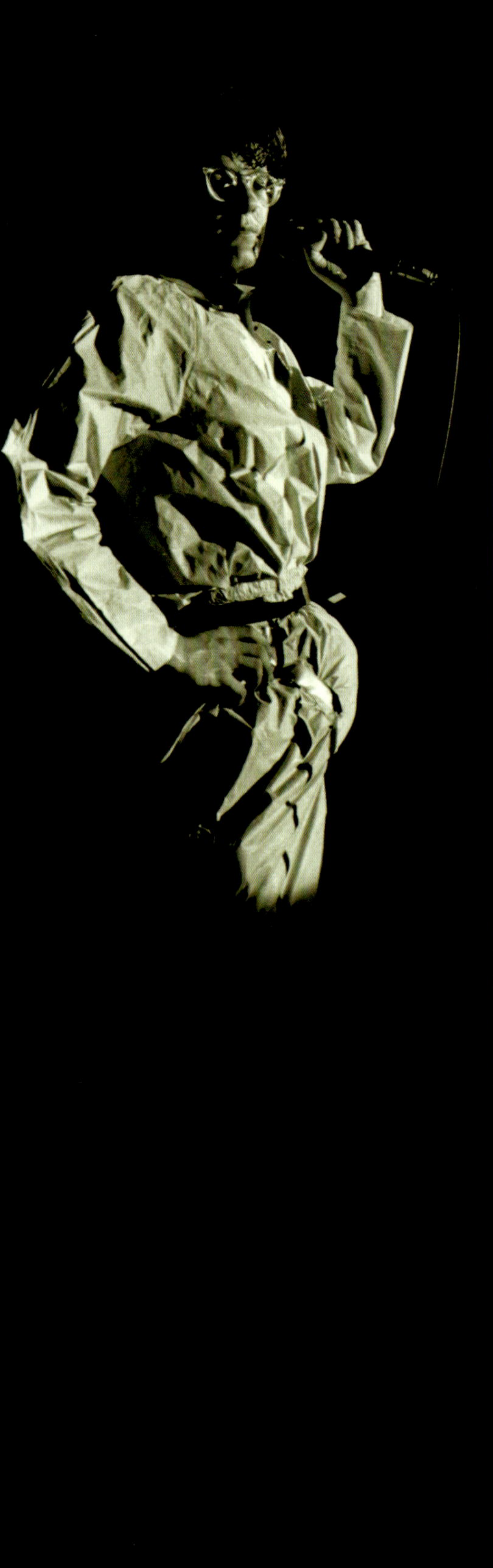

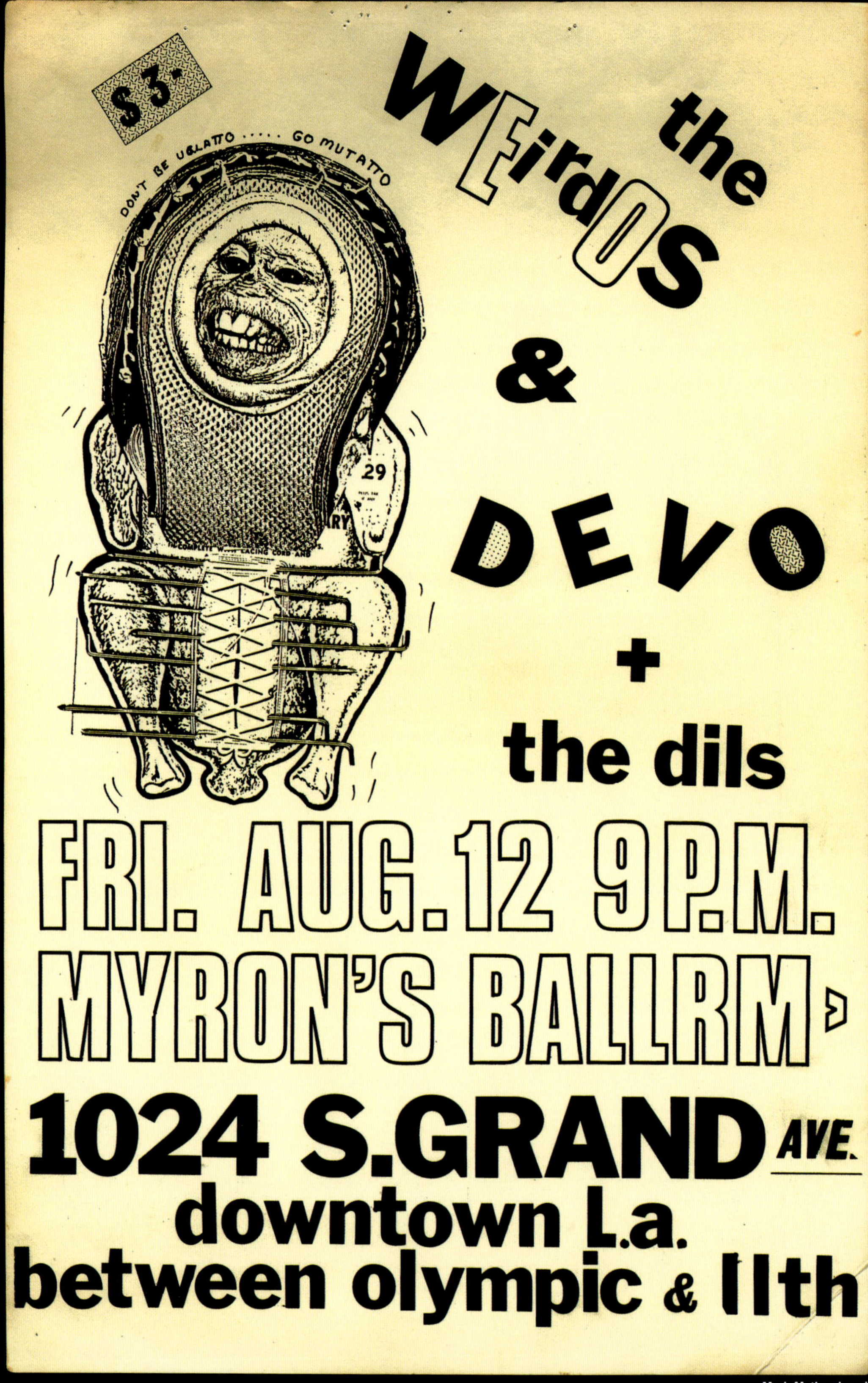

Mark Mothersbaugh

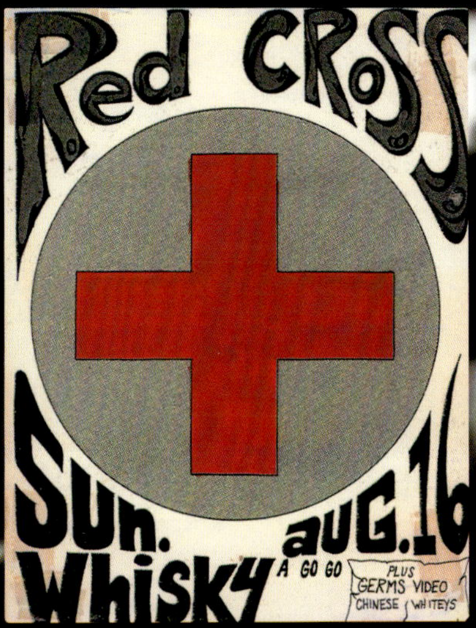

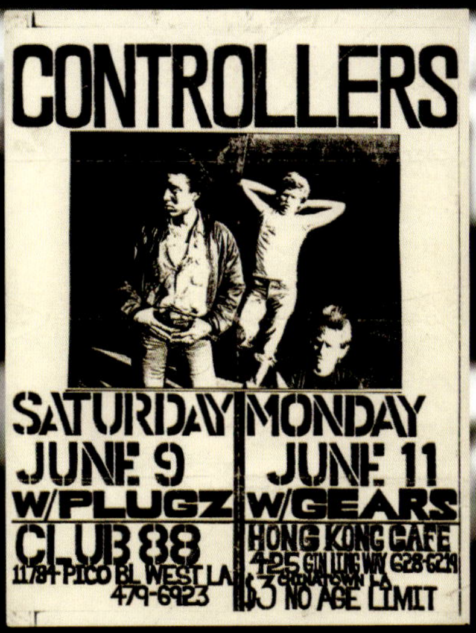

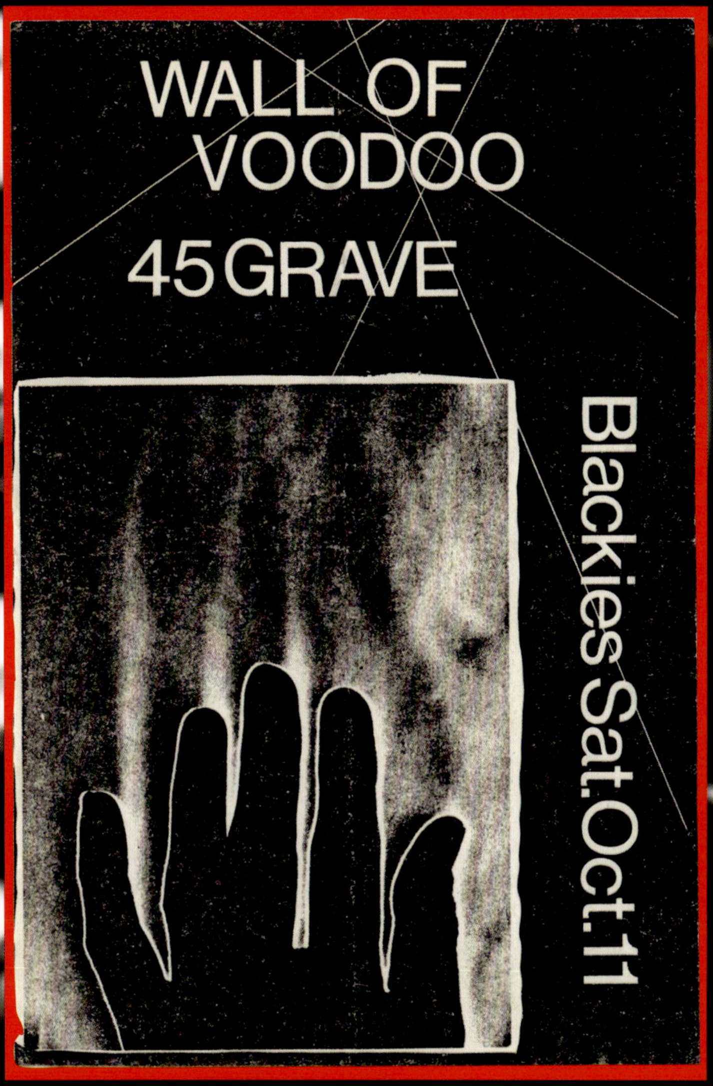

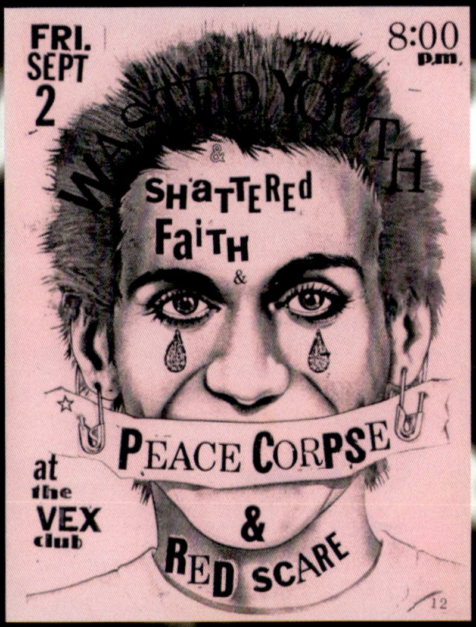

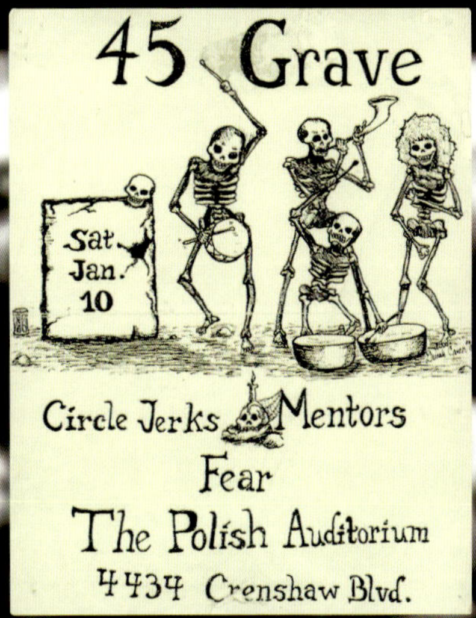

Dinah Cancer

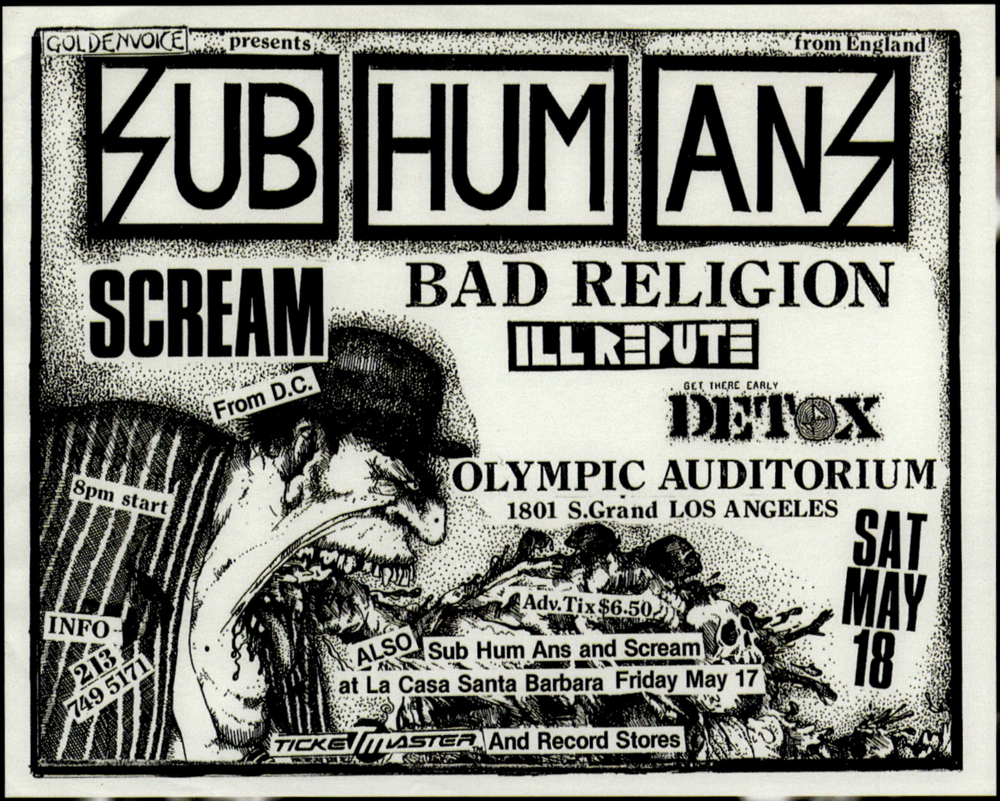

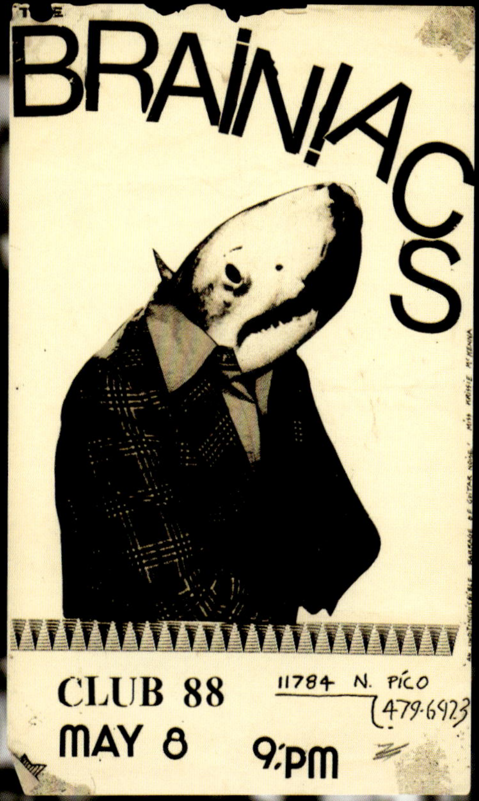

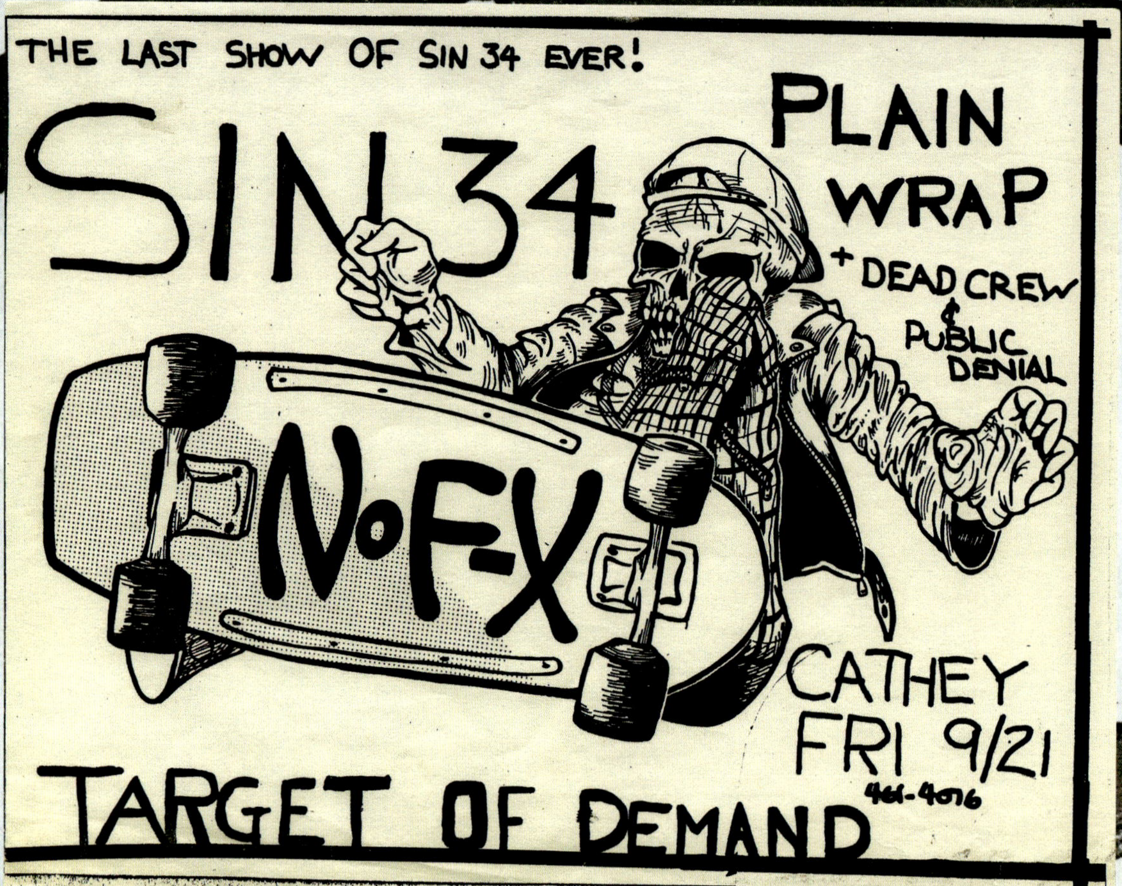

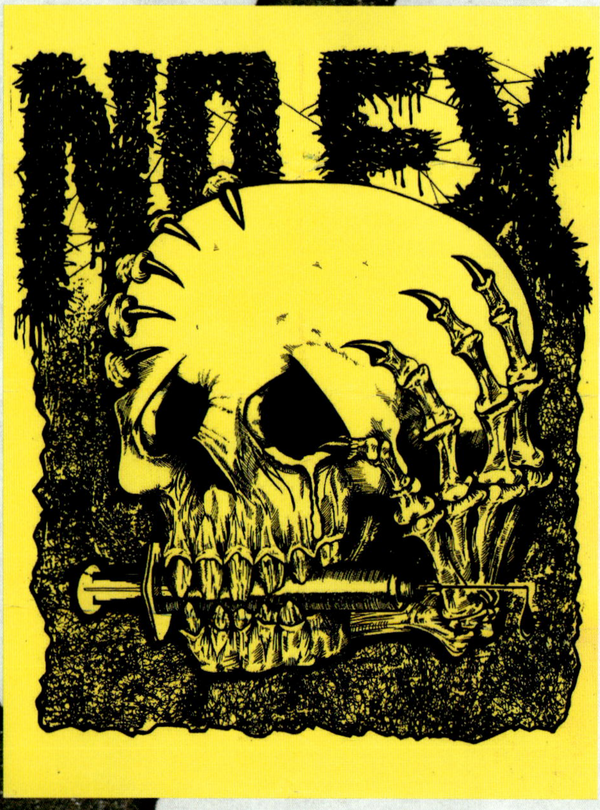

Stoked: Fat Mike and The Cathay De Grande

The first time we played the Cathay we weren't on the bill. It was a straight edge show with Unity and Justice League. I was in the parking lot beer-bonging my second quart of Olde English when Erik came up to me and said that we could use Justice League's equipment and play four songs. That was great, since we only knew five songs at the time. It was our first show, we played badly and nobody liked us, but we were stoked.[1]

The fourth time we played the Cathay, was with Circle One, Dont Know, Ill Repute and two or three other bands. the promoter Mike told us that too many bands showed up and that he would give us 13 bucks if we didn't play. That was the most money we had ever made. We were stoked.[2]

The last time we played the Cathay was the night before it closed. We played badly, nobody liked us. We were bummed because we knew there would never be another club like the Cathay, but I had oral sex with an ex-girlfriend in a booth downstairs while Beyond Possession was playing.

I was stoked.[3]

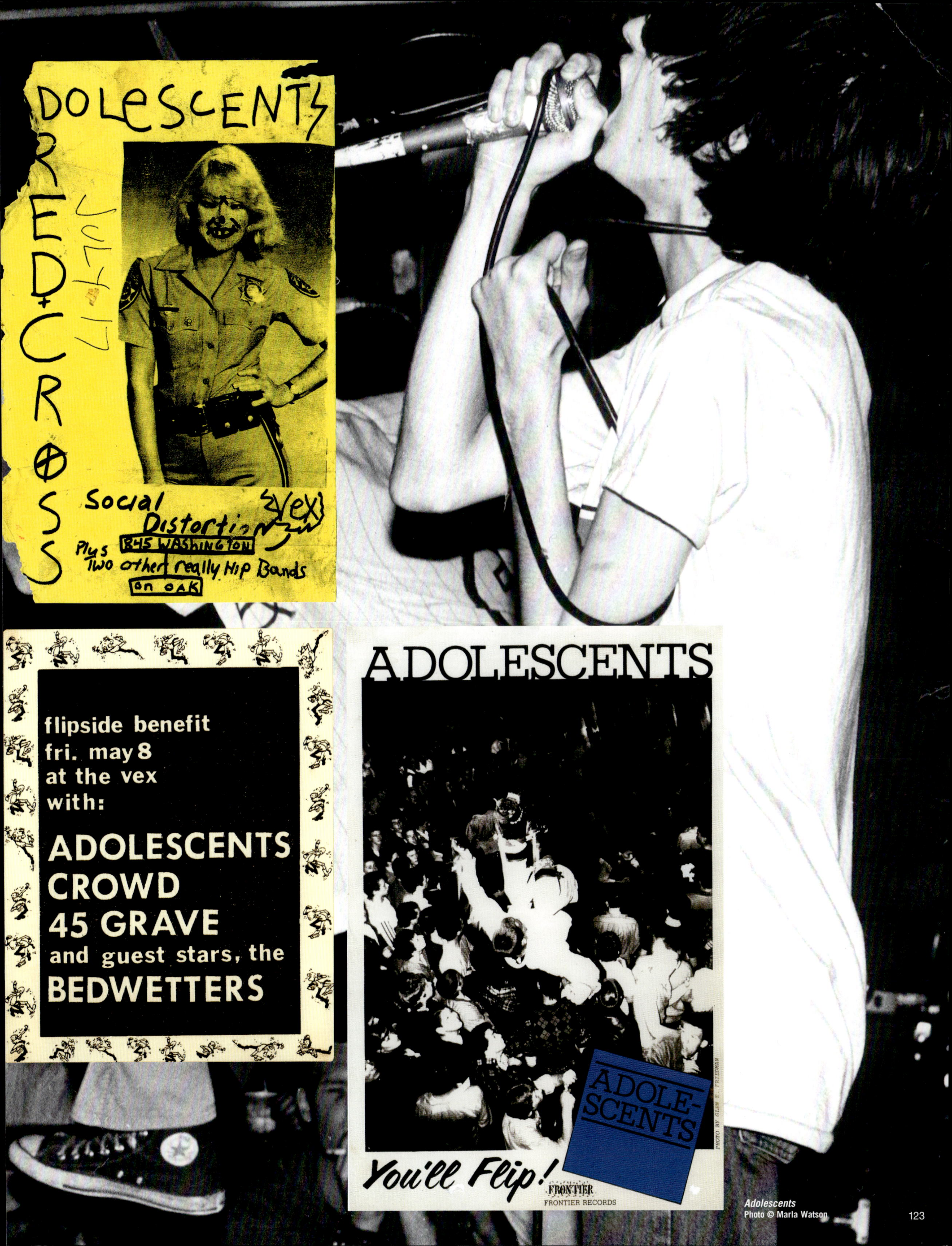

Adolescents
Photo © Marla Watson

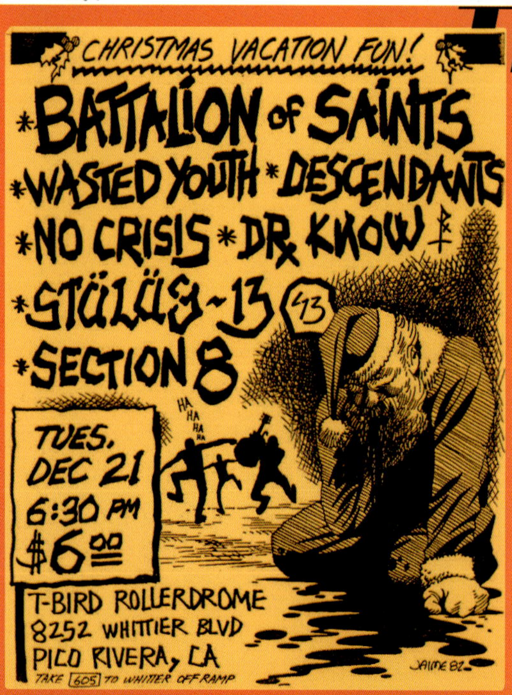

THEHer

XAIME H.

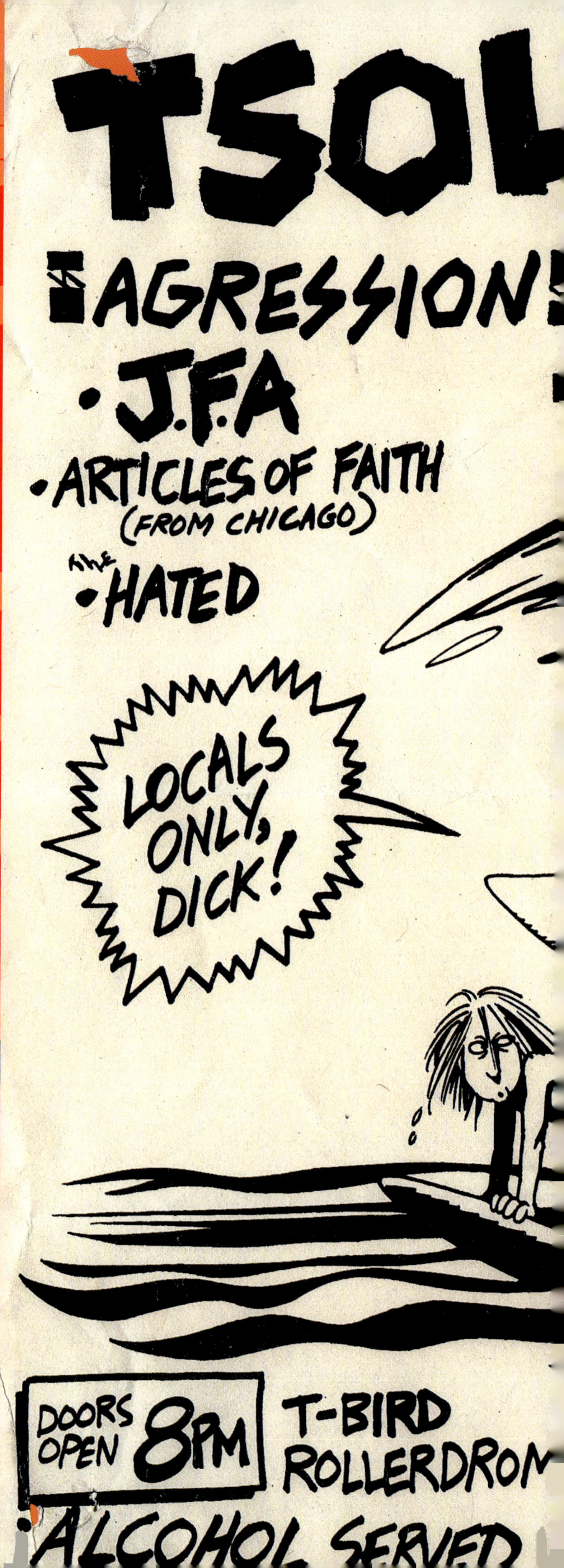

All: Jaime Hernandez

Jaime Hernandez

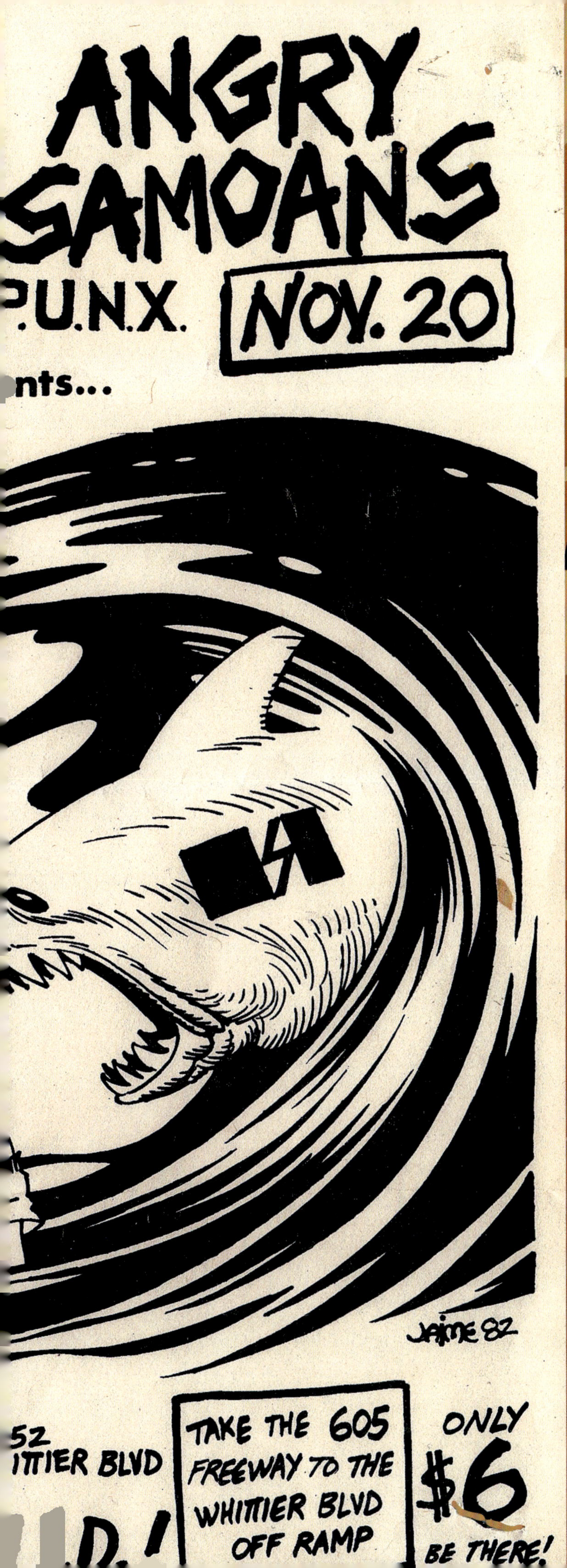

rnandezBROS

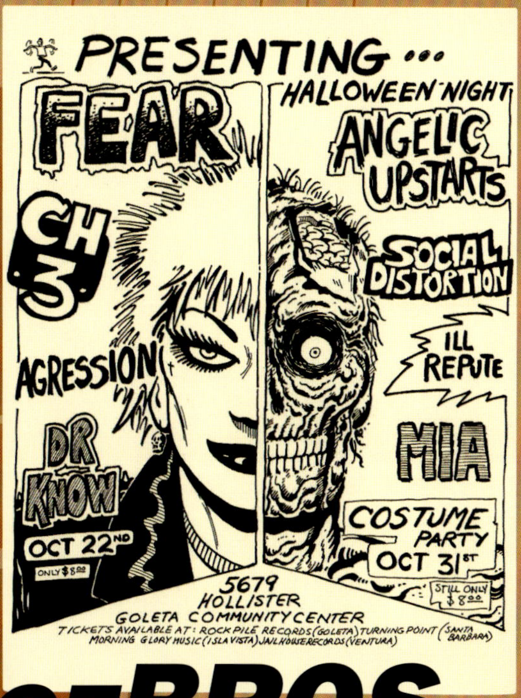

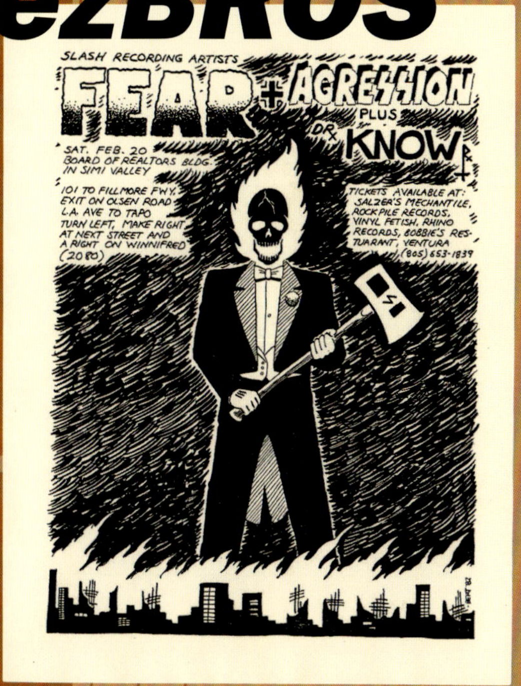

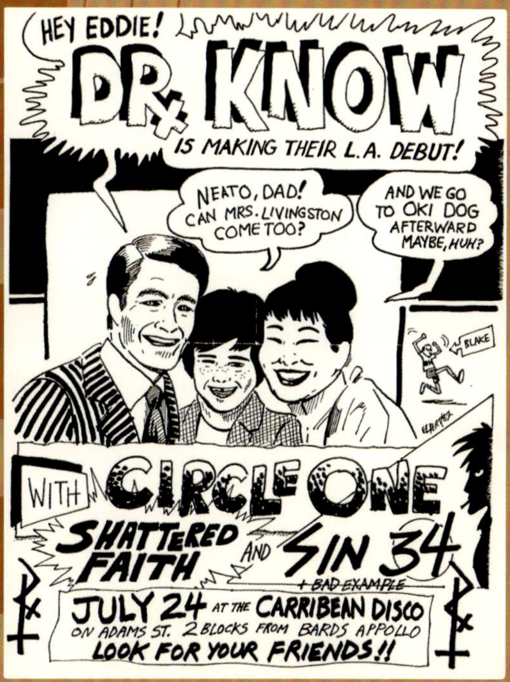

All: Gilbert Hernandez

START

Fear is playing a show at the Hong Kong Cafe, downtown LA (not so uncommon, it's the early 80s, so Fear, Middle Class, UXA Circle Jerks were always playing somewhere in the LA Basin.) Lee Ving is doing the usual shit, playing hard and insulting even harder. The Hong Kong was a decent sized place but they had tables everywhere, so the pit was limited in size. Shawn Kerri, the girl who drew the Circle Jerks skanking kid, and I drove up to LA from San Diego, in a '57 Chevy, like the road warriors that we were. High on speed and wine, we went to LA for Vinyl Fetish, Oki Dogs, Germs and Slash...a city we didn't particularly like became our second home and our first love. Back to the Hong Kong Cafe: I'm bouncing around the dance floor, singing along..."I don't care about you, FUCK YOU!" There's a

gives me a few good shots, no big deal, until the last one gets me in the taint (you know, taint the balls, taint the ass.) So I punch her in the face really fucking hard. In the next moment a number of no-neck Neandrethals want to kill me. One spits beer down the back of my shirt, and I hear the sound of chain unraveling, chain with my name on it. I grab Shawn and we head to the car. In the trunk we just happen to have a sword - yes, a fucking SWORD - and a steel axe I made at the shipyards where I worked. We went back to the club, sword down Shawn's pant leg, axe in my jacket. There was a fountain near the Hong Kong where punks assembled after shows. We saw Darby and the Blue Circle Gang. Finally the no-necks show up and we stepped up to the plate. Shawn pulls out the sword and says "which of you motherfuckers is first?!" No-necks backed down, saying no problem, it's cool!" Shawn doesn't think everything is so cool and waves the sword and goes after them - they lost their shit and ran fast, and we laughed very hard. Darby came over, swore that was the best thing he'd ever seen, gave me an AXE pin off his jacket, and slapped a big kiss on me.

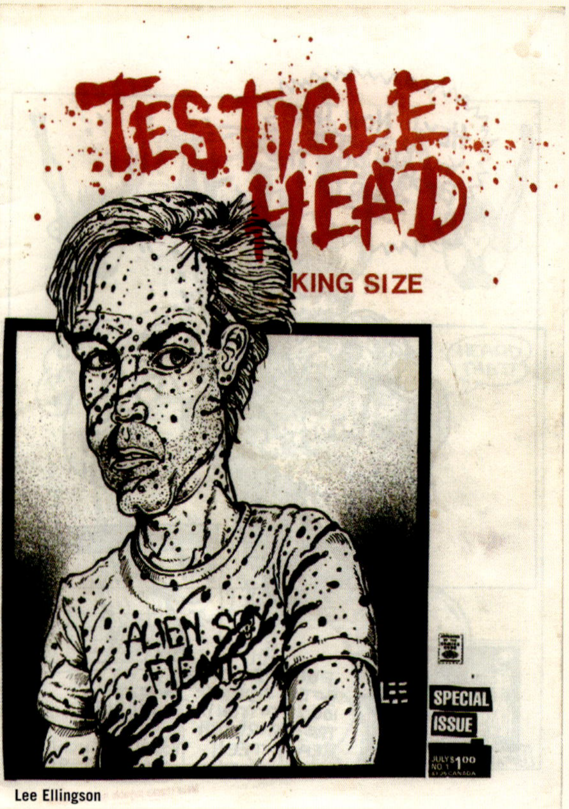

Lee Ellingson

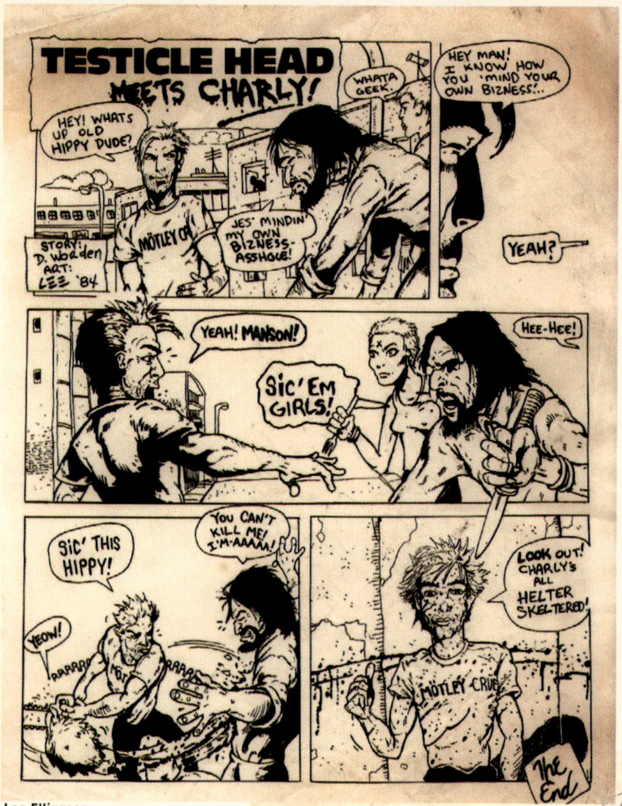

Lee Ellingson

Lee Ellingson

DEPARTMENT OF THE ARMY • HEADQUARTERS • U.S. ARMY RECRUITING COMMAND • FORT SHERIDAN, ILLINOIS 60037

9 November 1981

Jello Biafra
5645 Guincho Ct.
San Diego, CA 92124

Dear Jello Biafra:

Thank you for your interest in the Army Reserve. I think you'll be even more interested when you learn more about it -- new horizons, career training, extra money in your pocket!

The enclosed booklet will give you some interesting information about the Army Reserve and the opportunities and challenges a career in the Reserve can offer you.

Joining the Army Reserve can be a rewarding step forward. Your part-time service in a local Army Reserve unit can open up many new opportunities: to learn a skill that can be useful for a lifetime; to grow and progress; to meet many new and interesting people: and, perhaps of most importance, to do something different, challenging, and vital. An Army Reservist is part of an essential organization that serves our country well. That's why we say that "Part Of What You Earn Is Pride".

Look over all of the facts. It's your future, and it deserve your careful thought. Then talk the whole thing over with y Army Reserve Representative.

3877a Clairemont Dr
San Diego, CA 92117
Phone (714) 270-2501

You owe it to yourself to find out all you can. There's no

Encl.

That kind of thing would never happen now: punk is a serious business, full of corporate tools getting rich talking about old school and keeping it real. I did the very first Offspring album cover, before they were on Epitaph Records, for $125. Now that they're *big bank* they reissued the record with new artwork. That's not very **old school** or **keeping it** very **real**, and hey, I could've used the exposure, *you pussies.* If you really care about punk you might try having some fucking respect for the art.

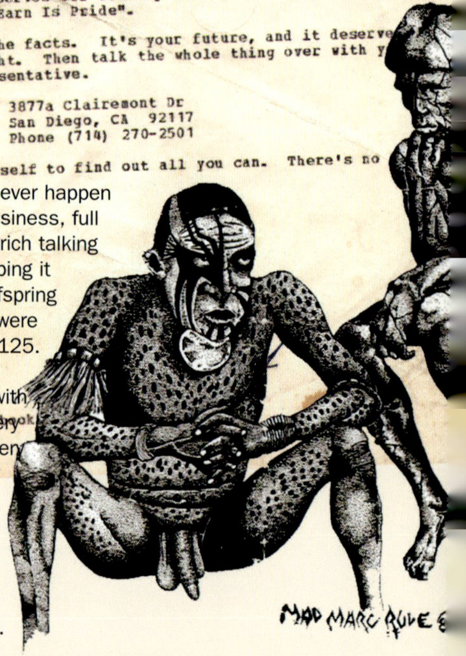

FINISH

Mad Marc Rude

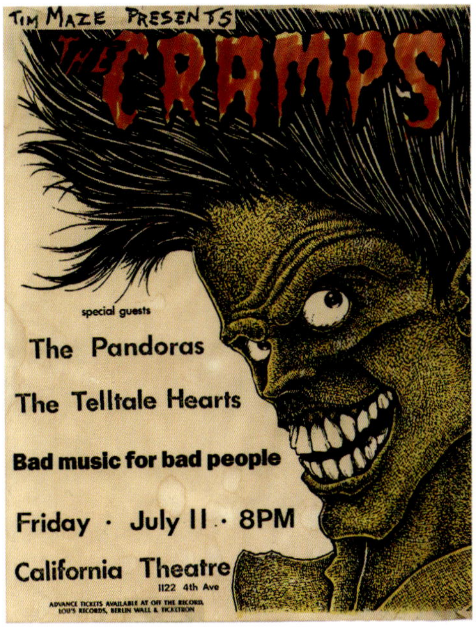

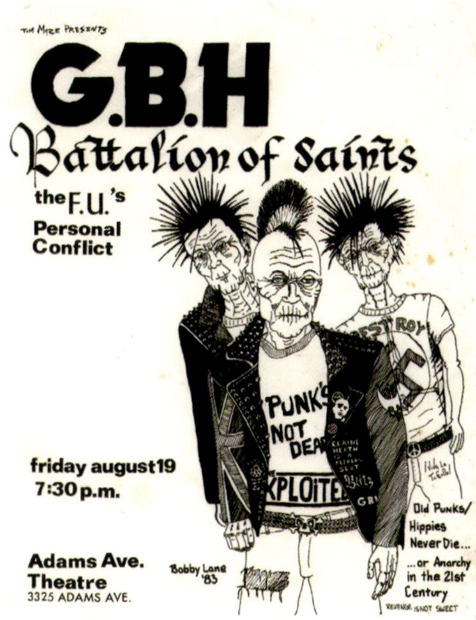

Bobby Lane

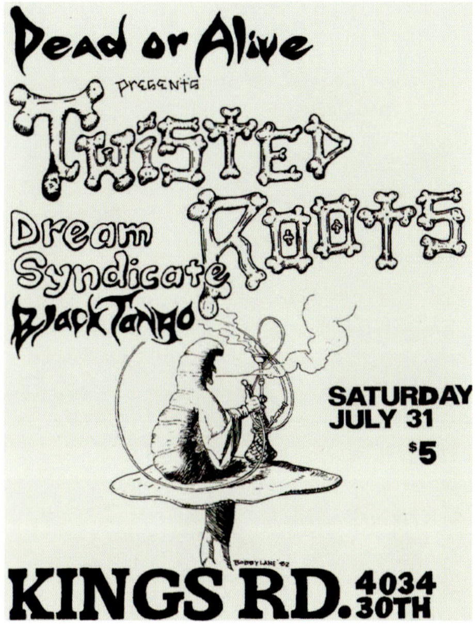

Bobby Lane

sd

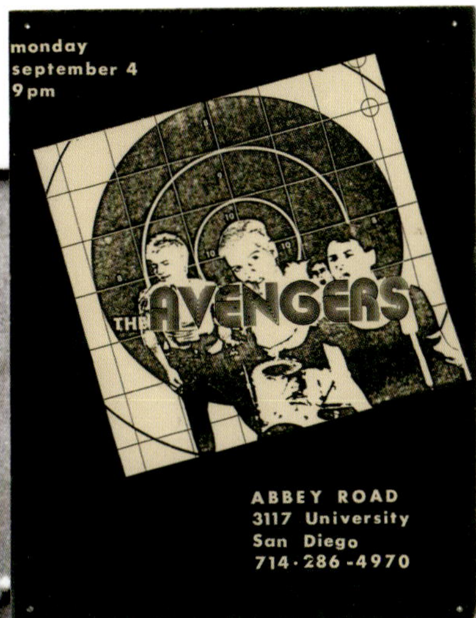

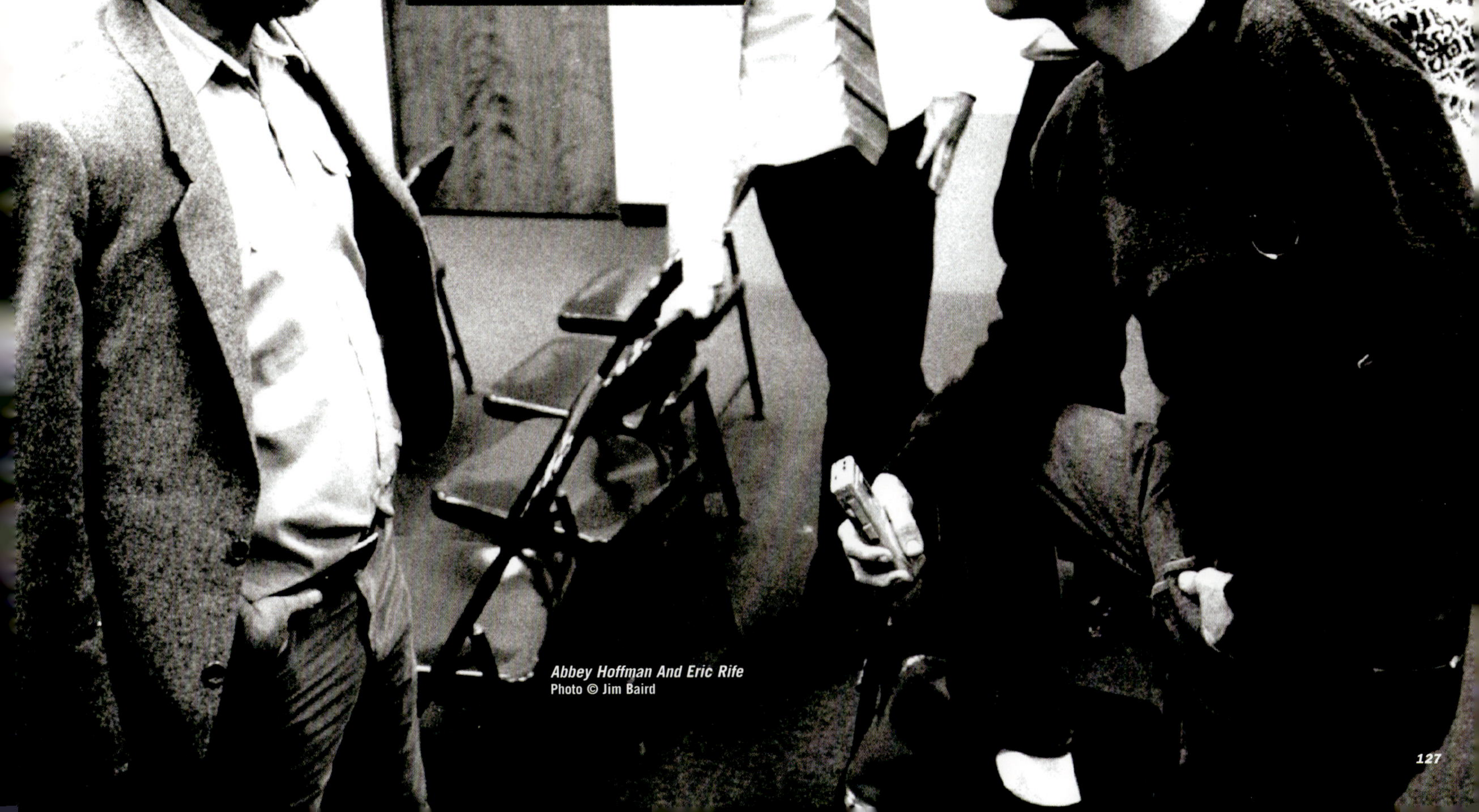

Abbey Hoffman And Eric Rife
Photo © Jim Baird

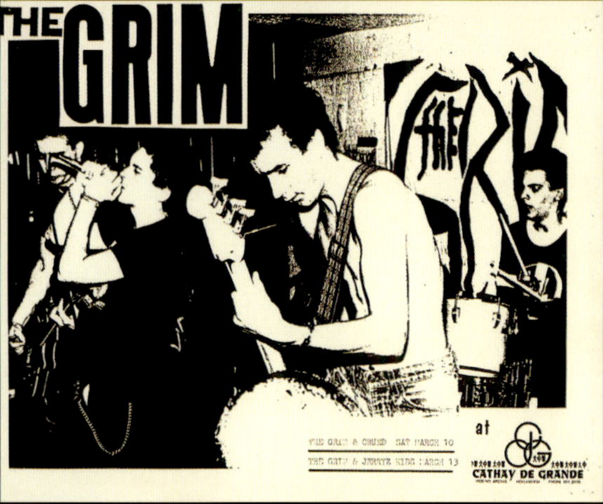

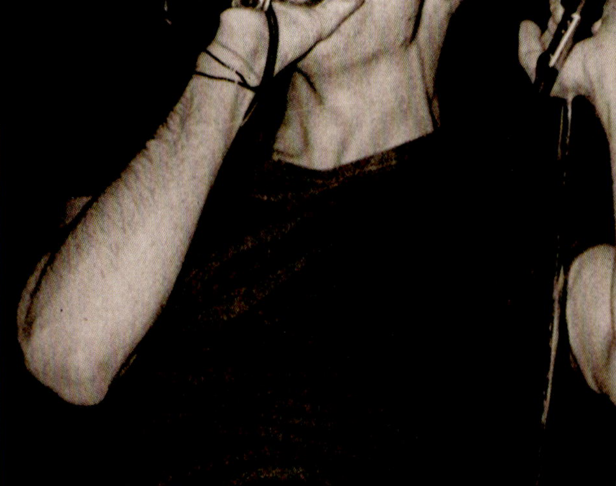

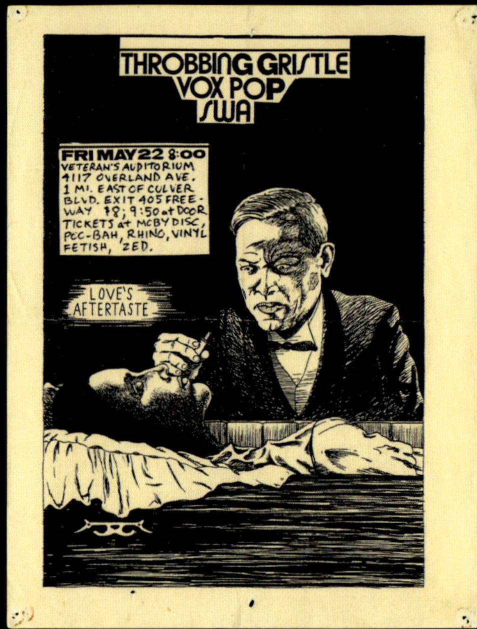

Raymond Pettibon

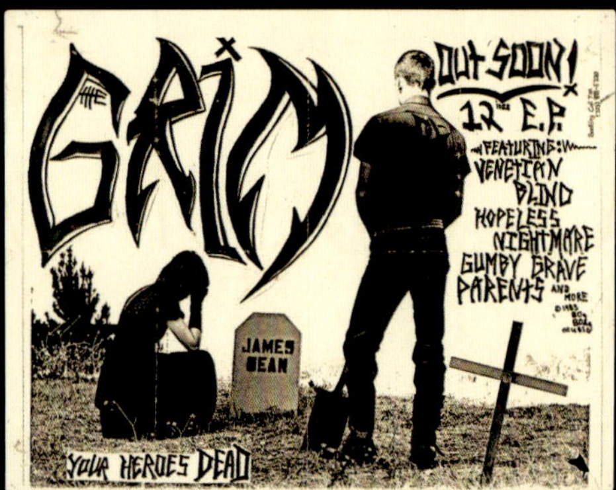

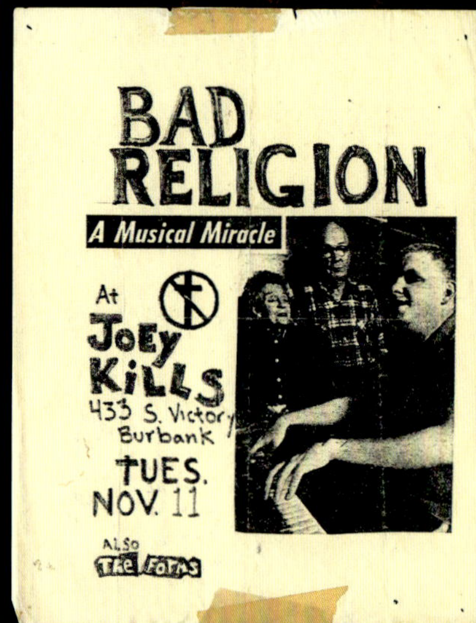

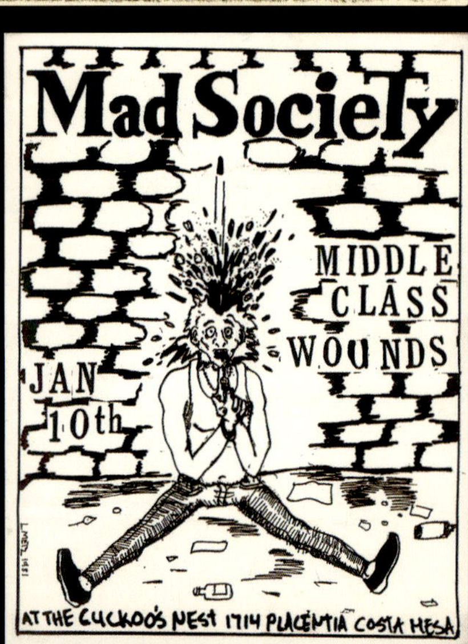

L. Metz

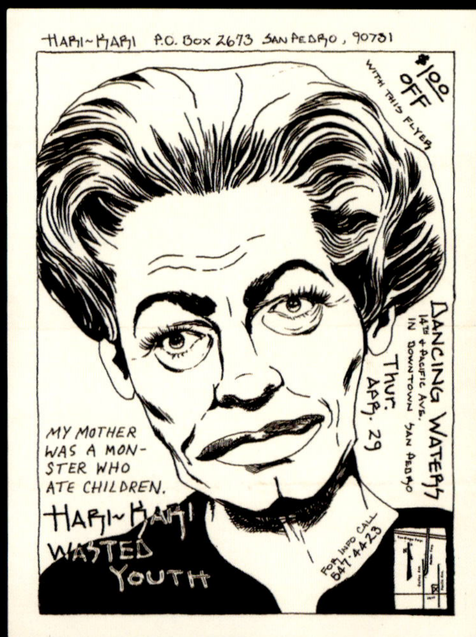

Raymond Pettibon

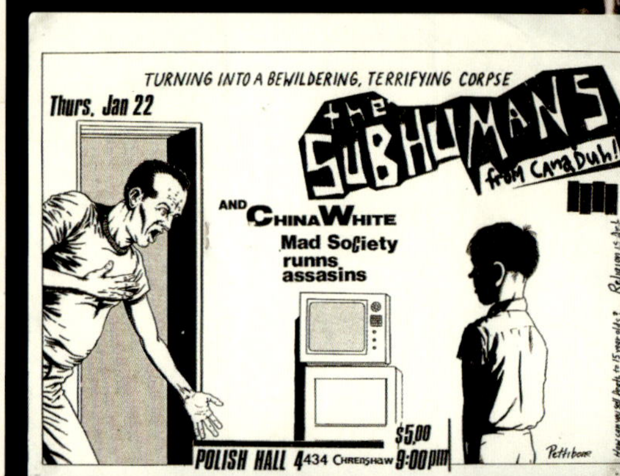

Raymond Pettibon

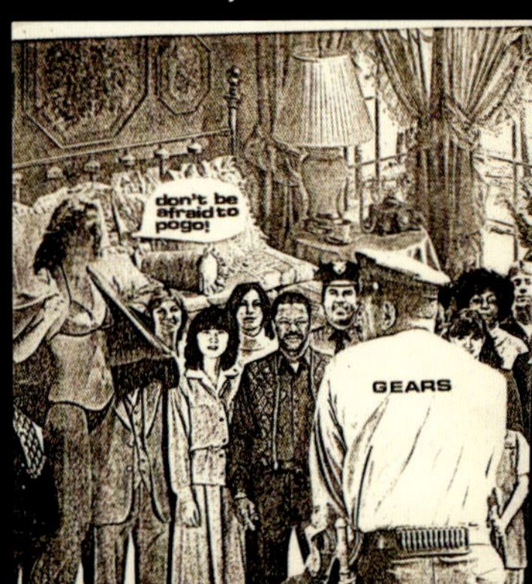

Axxel G. Reese

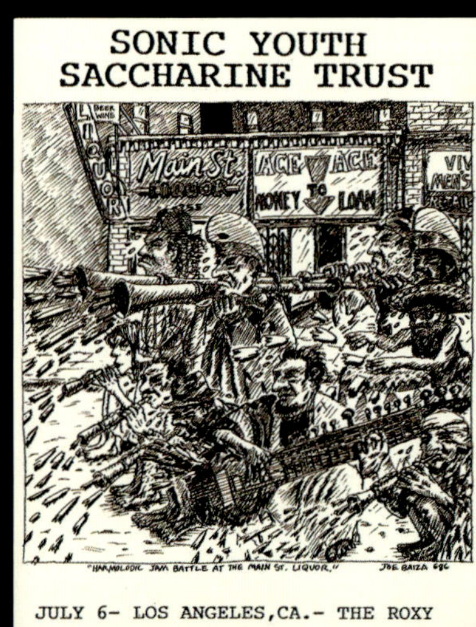

Joe Baiza

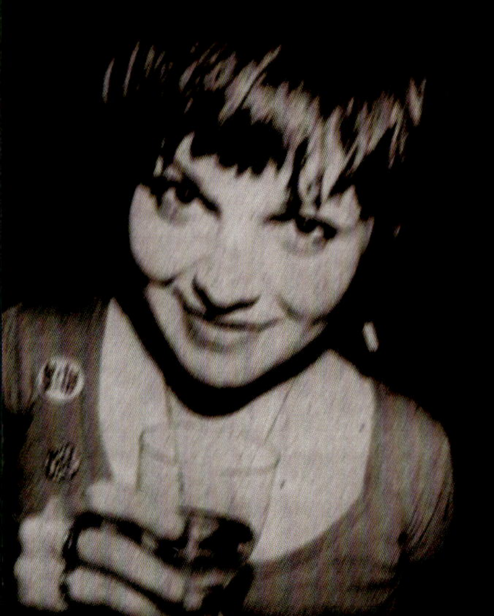

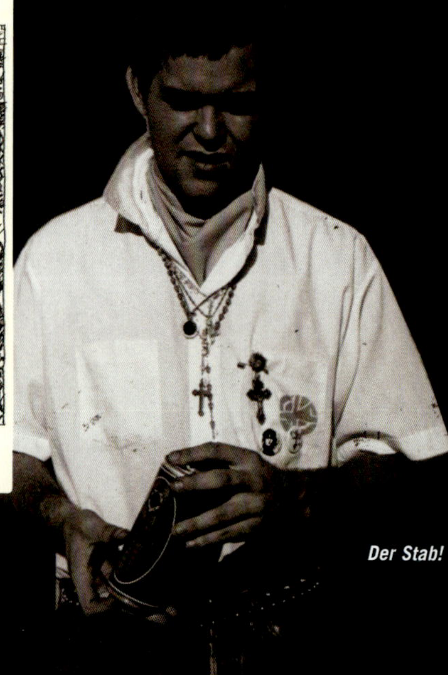

Der Stab!

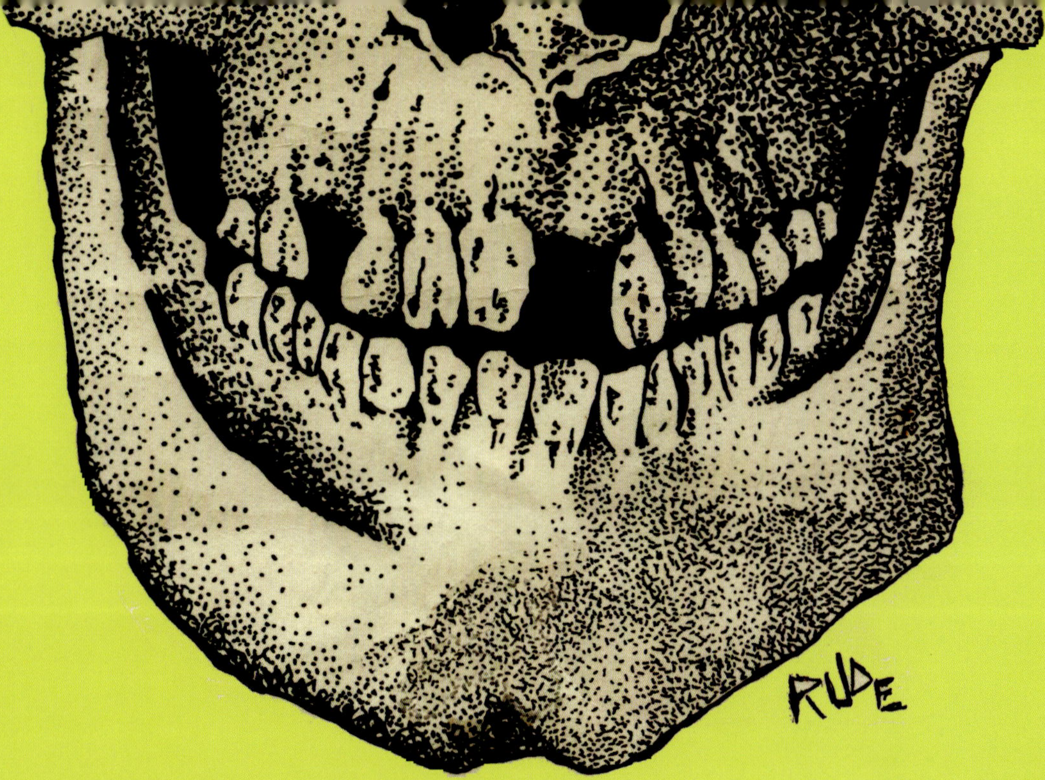

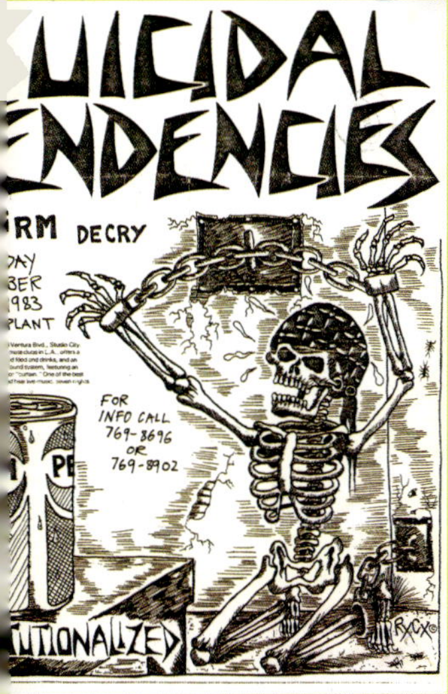

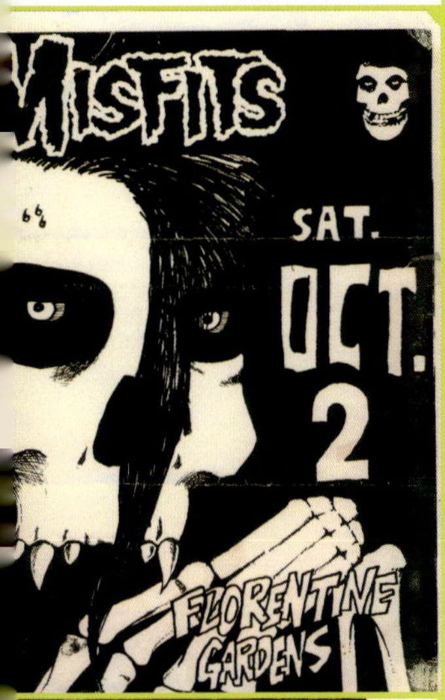

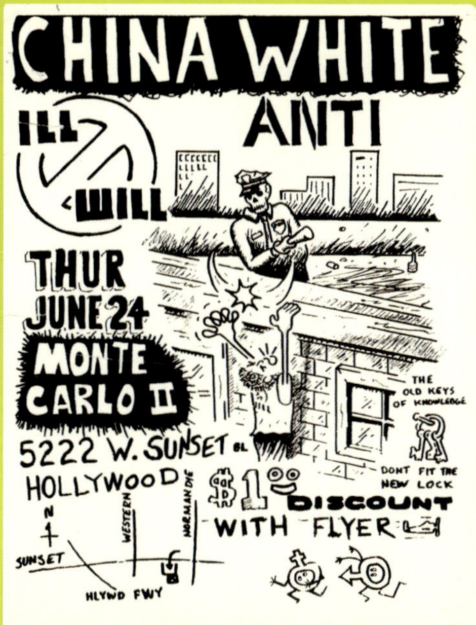

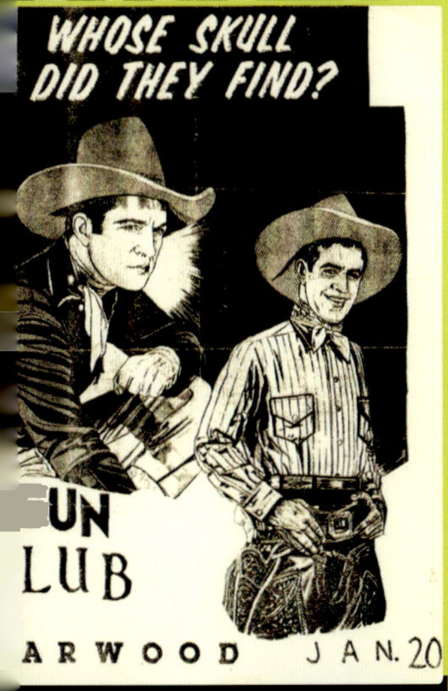

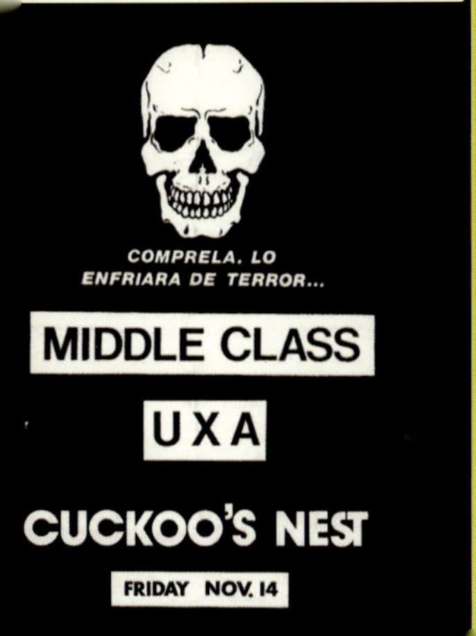

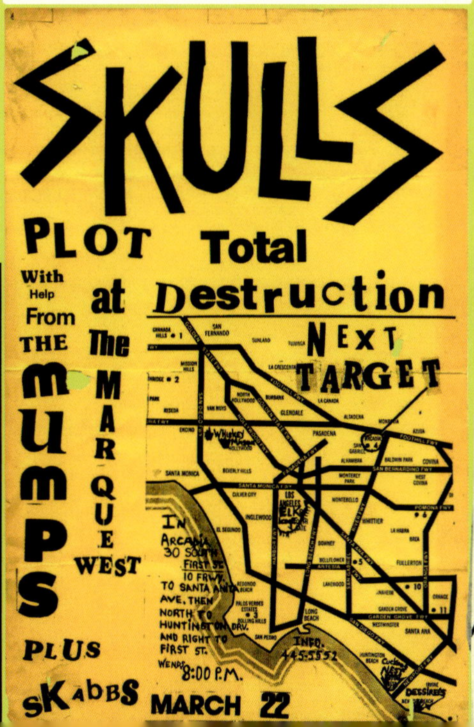

Mad Marc Rude

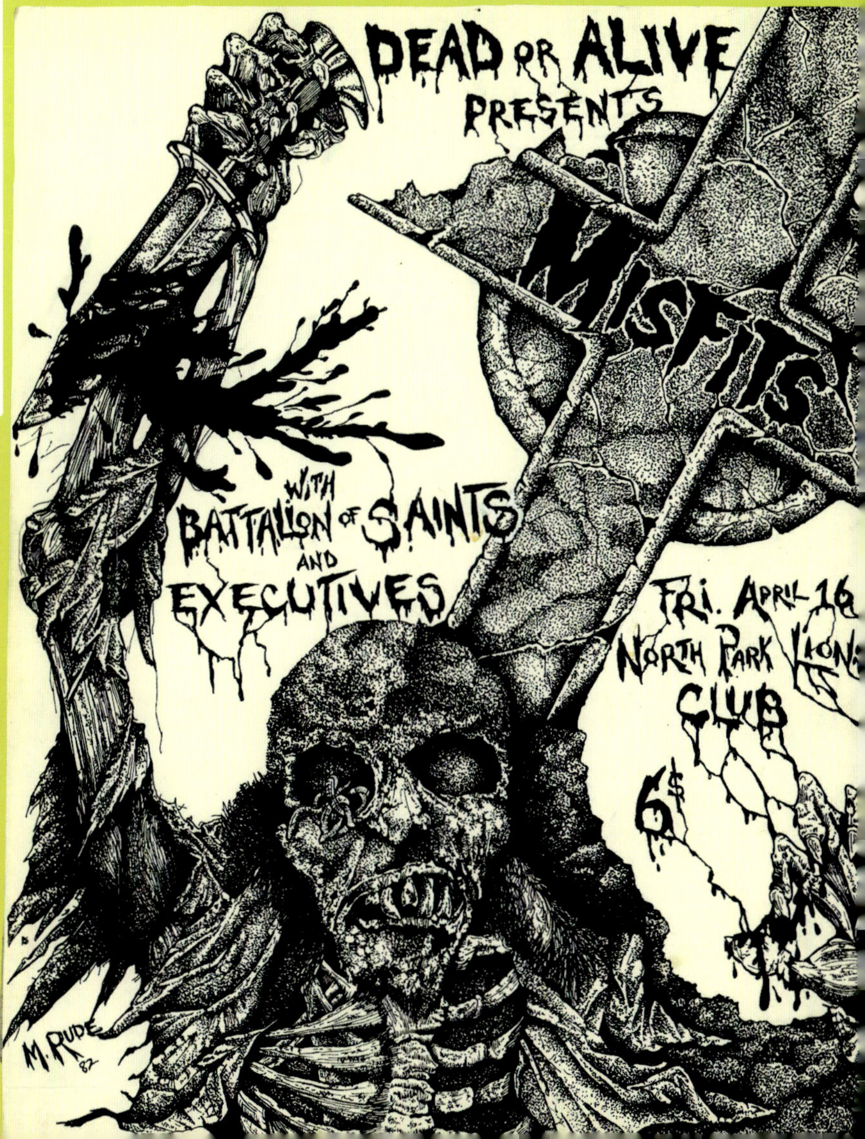

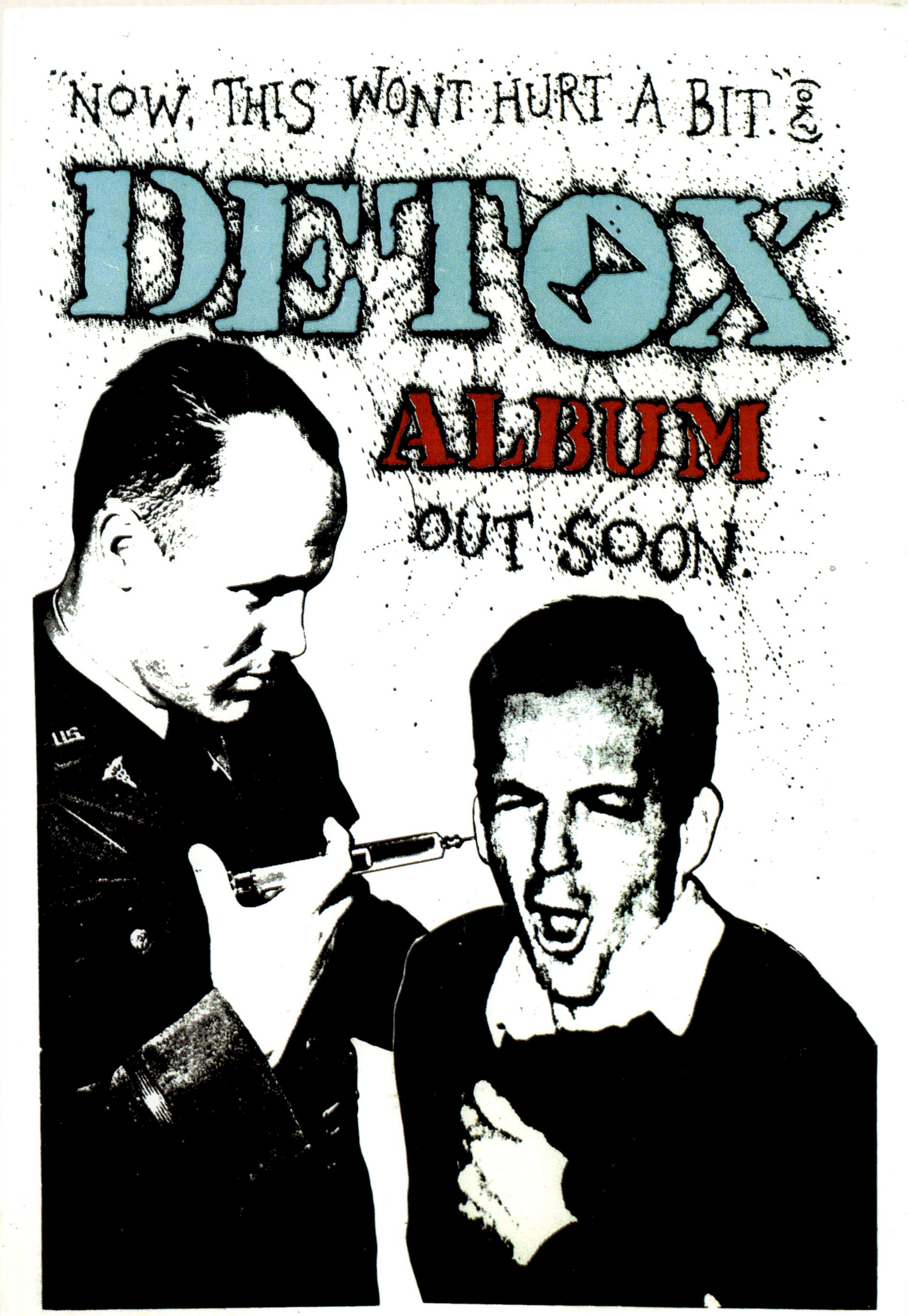

Steve Human

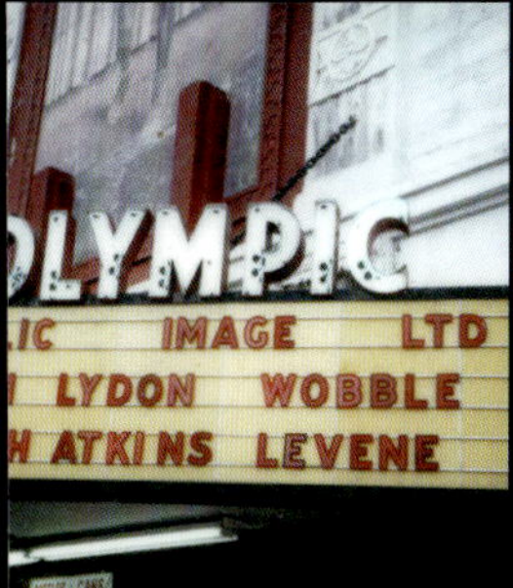

The front lines of the punk battleground: the murals with boxer's portraits couldn't have been more appropriate

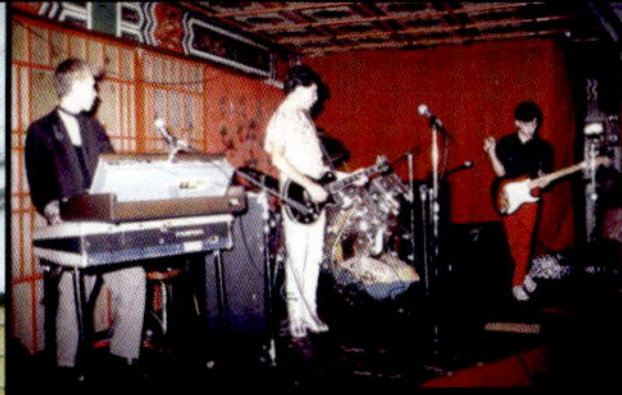
Extremes at The Hong Kong Cafe

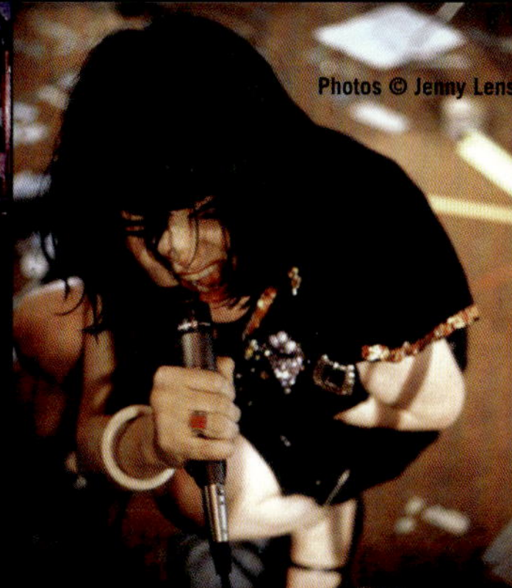
Photos © Jenny Lens

Exene belts it out at Club 88

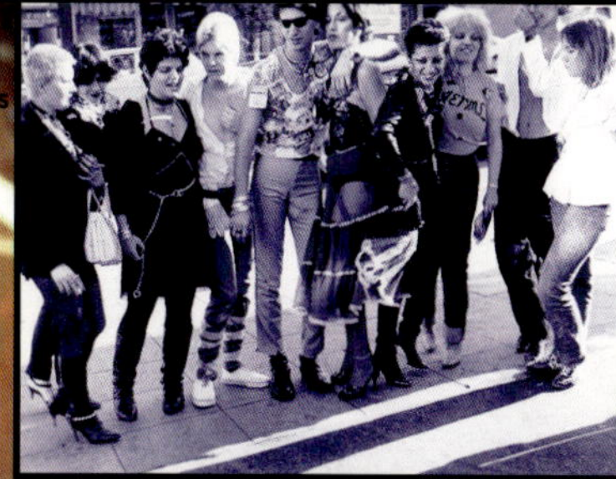
LA Punks

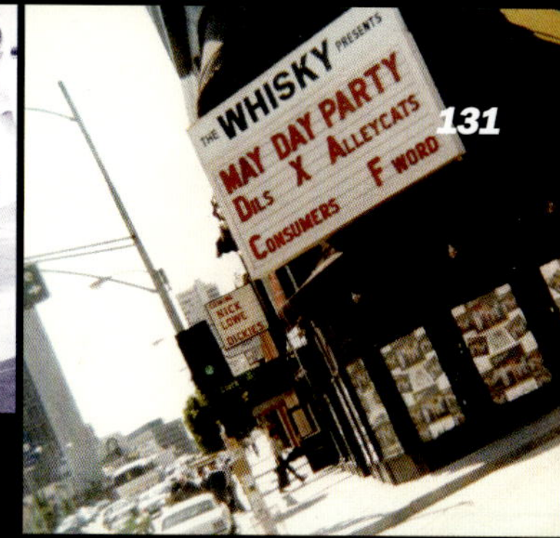

What the Whisky useta look like...

R.I.P. : Club 88, Arons, The Cuckoo's Nest, The Vex, The Capitol Records Swap Meet, The Masque, The Other Masque, Perkins Palace, etc. etc.

Cliff Roman

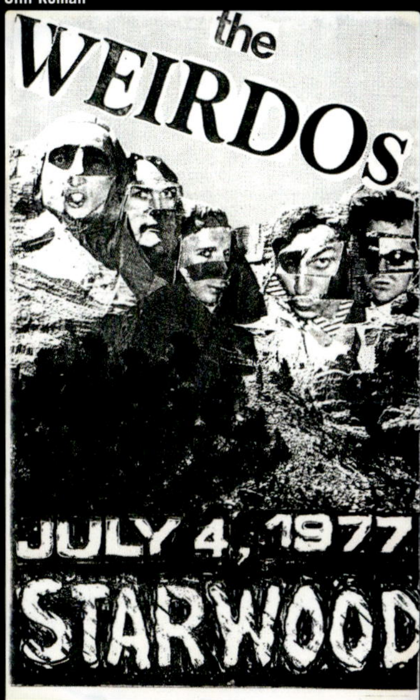

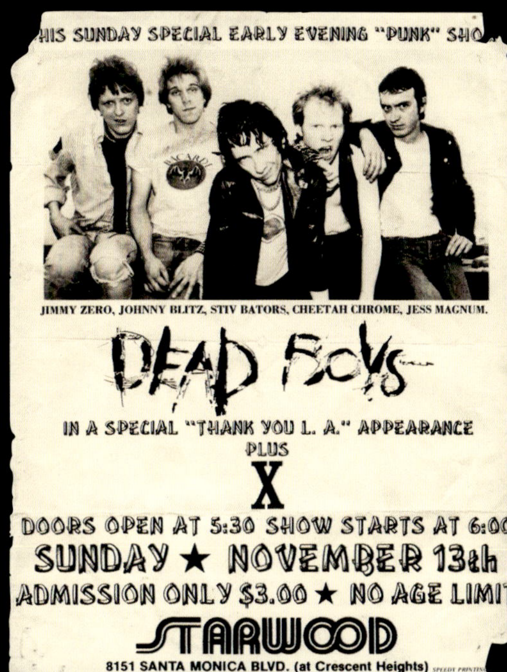

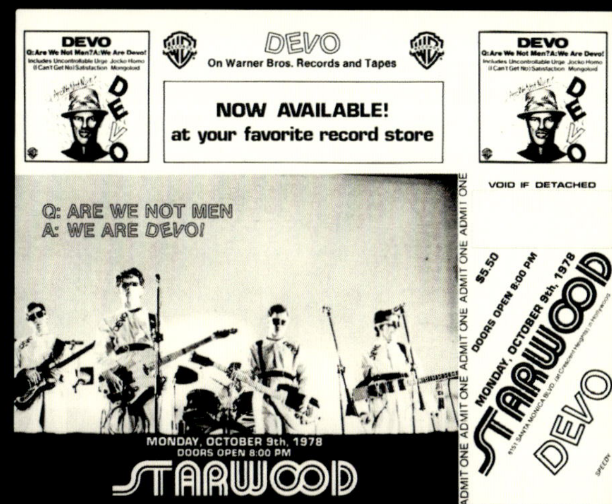

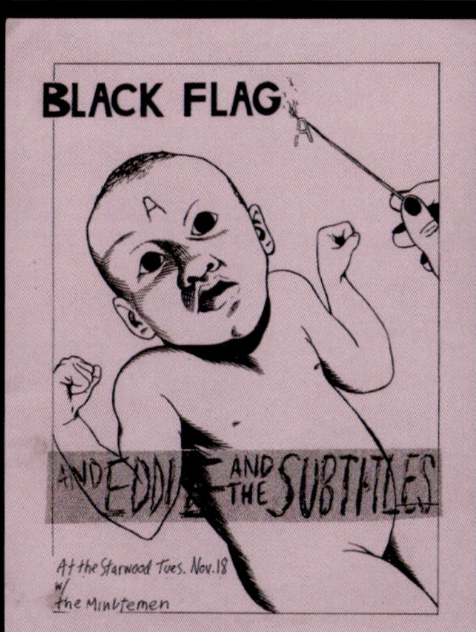

Raymond Pettibon

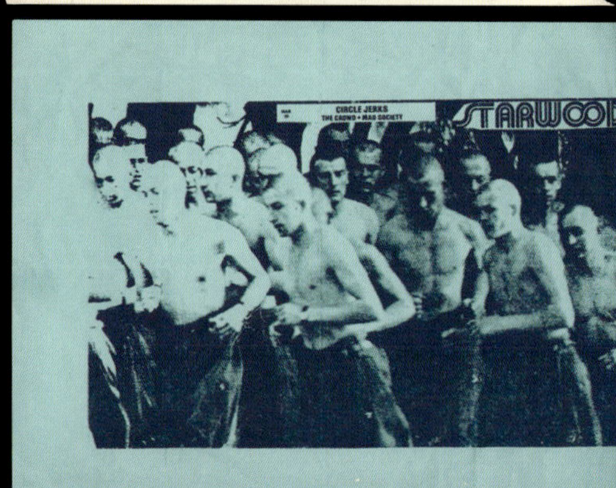

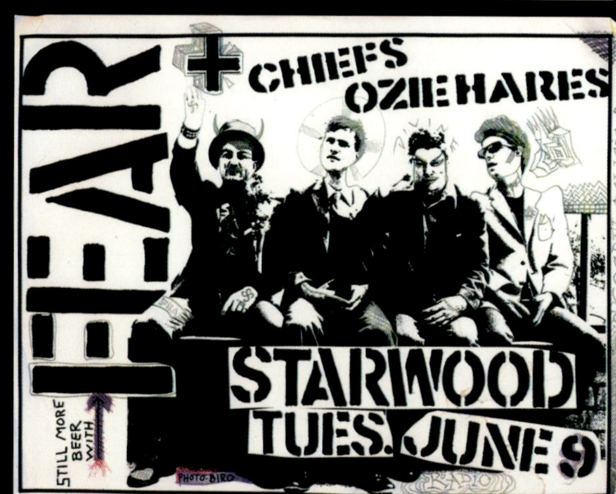

Fear Photo: Biro

The Starwood

It's amazing what rummaging through a closet or driving down the street can do to trigger your memory. I look to the corner of Santa Monica and Crescent Heights Boulevards expecting to see the Starwood, and I'm still disappointed at the sight of a strip mall. A drive down Sunset by the Whisky yields not a venerable old rock institution, but a purple and yellow eyesore. But punk was supposed to be about knocking down institutions, and finding an old X ticket stub at the bottom of a drawer, I realize that it wasn't the temples we worshipped in that makes me wax nostalgic. I miss the people I was with, the fury of the performances, and the urgency of the moment. + J

Road to the promised land

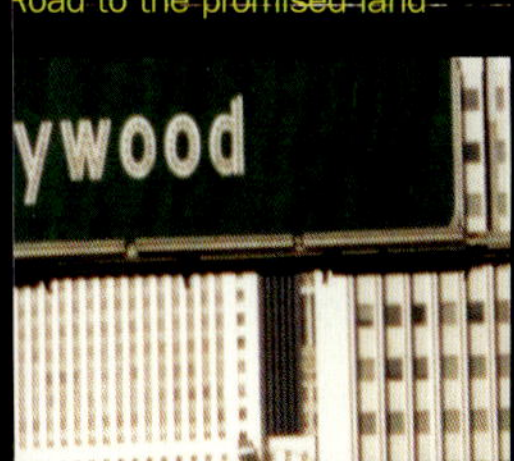

Part of the strip mall

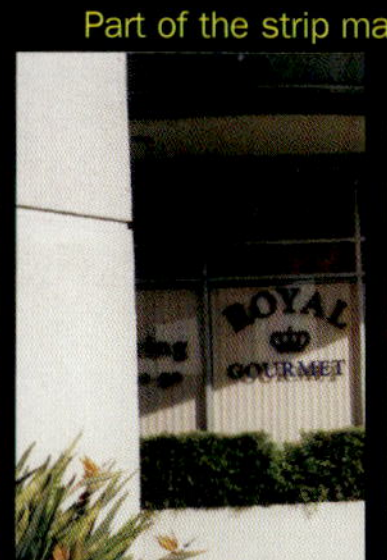

where The Starwood useta be

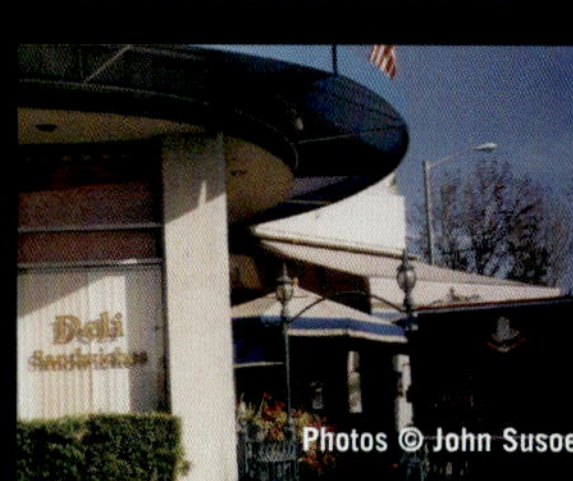

Photos © John Susoeff

I miss Aron's and the Capitol Records Swap Meet more than ever

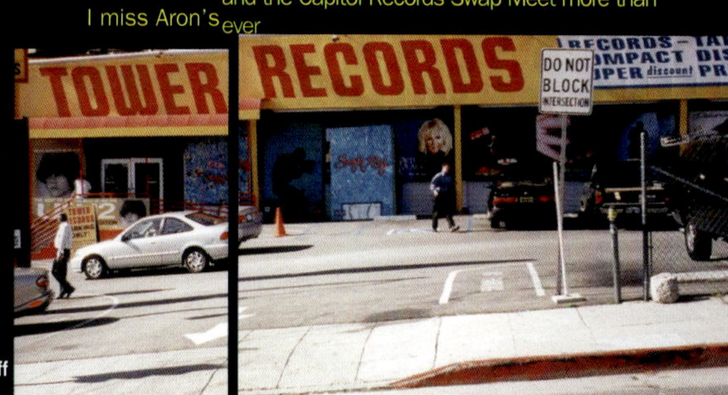

...what the Whisky looks like today

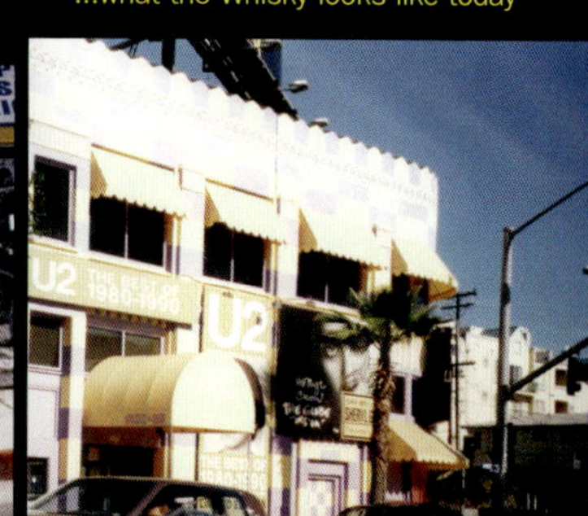

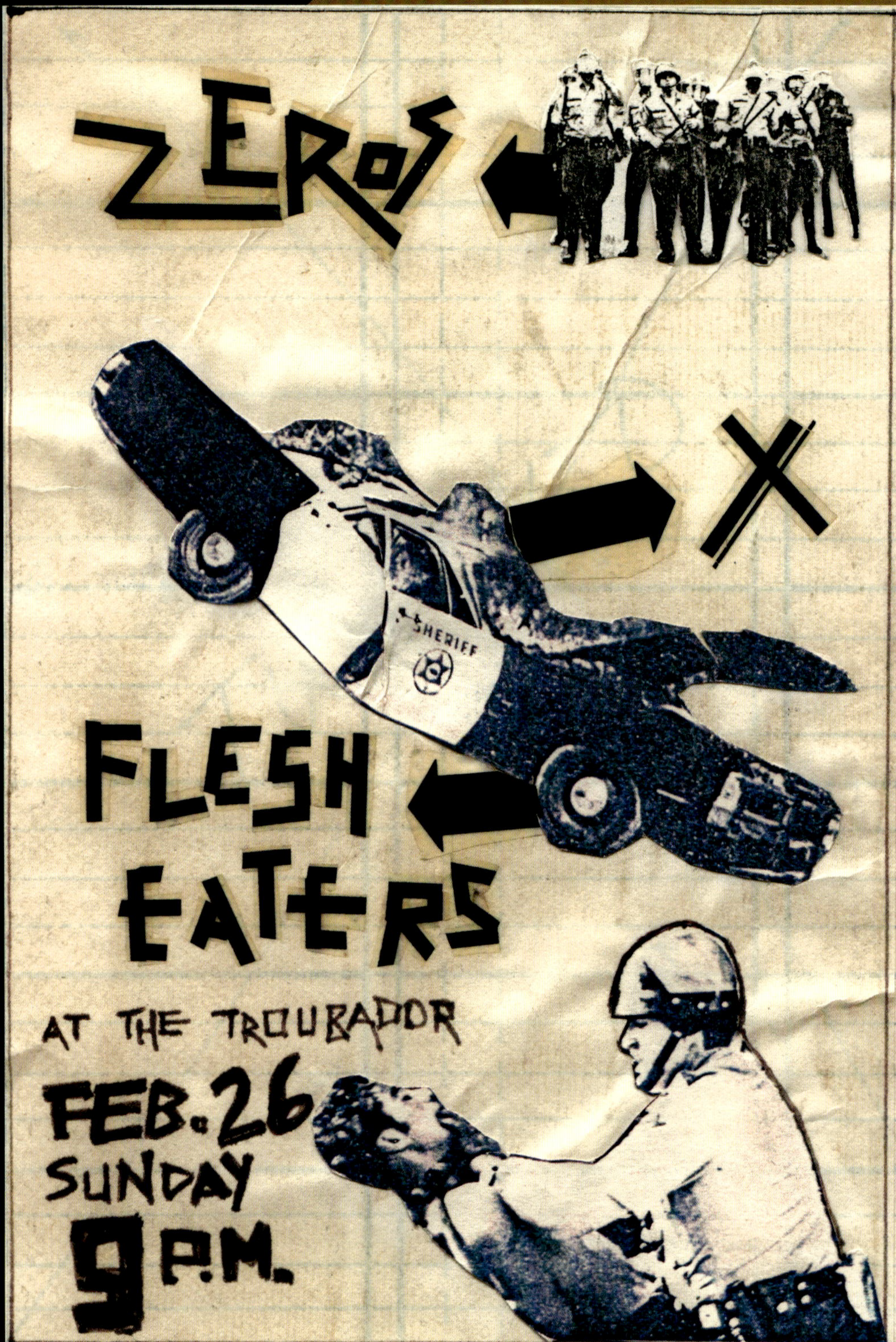
ZEROS
X
SHERIFF
FLESH EATERS
AT THE TROUBADOR
FEB. 26
SUNDAY
9 P.M.

Chris D.

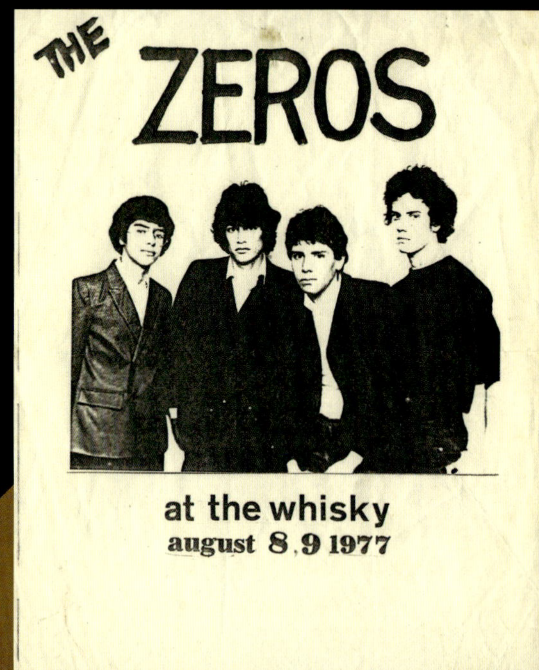
THE ZEROS
at the whisky
august 8,9 1977

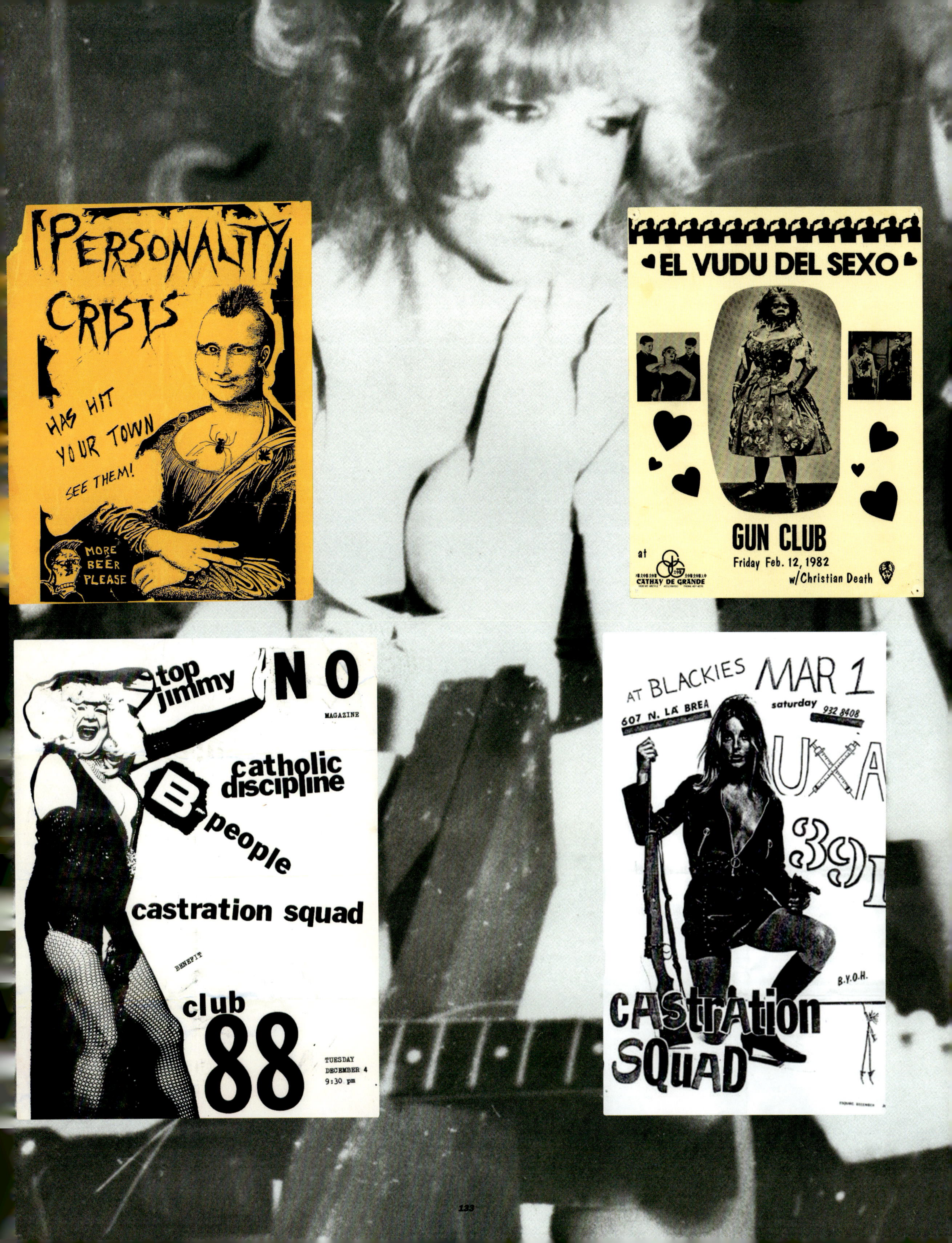
PERSONALITY CRISIS
HAS HIT YOUR TOWN
SEE THEM!
MORE BEER PLEASE
EL VUDU DEL SEXO
GUN CLUB
at
CATHAY DE GRANDE
Friday Feb. 12, 1982
w/Christian Death
top jimmy
NO
MAGAZINE
catholic discipline
B people
castration squad
BENEFIT
club 88
TUESDAY
DECEMBER 4
9:30 pm
AT BLACKIES
MAR 1
607 N. LA BREA
saturday
932 8408
UXA
B.Y.O.H.
CASTRATION SQUAD

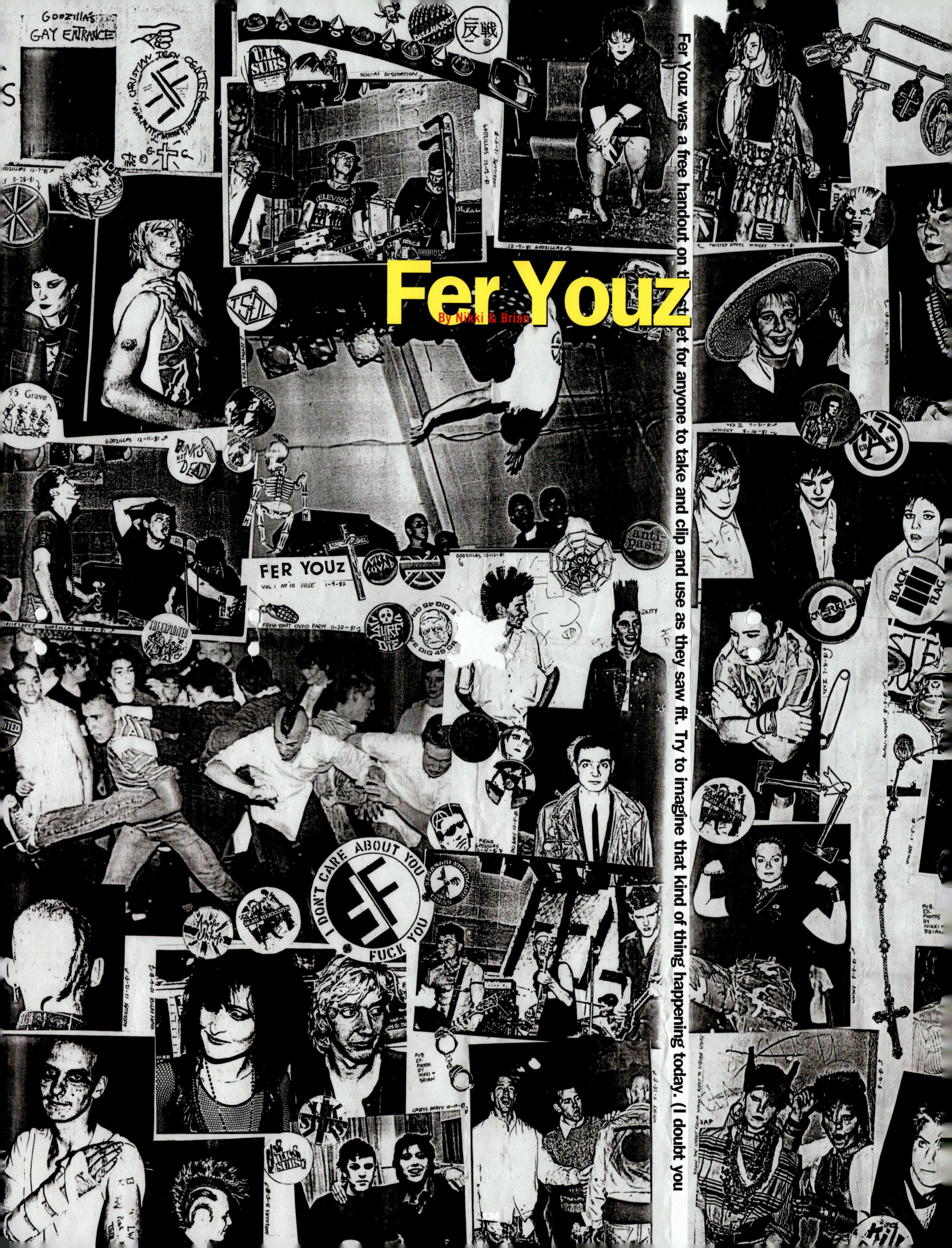

Fer Youz

By Nikki & Brian

Fer Youz was a free handout on the street for anyone to take and clip and use as they saw fit. Try to imagine that kind of thing happening today. (I doubt you can.)

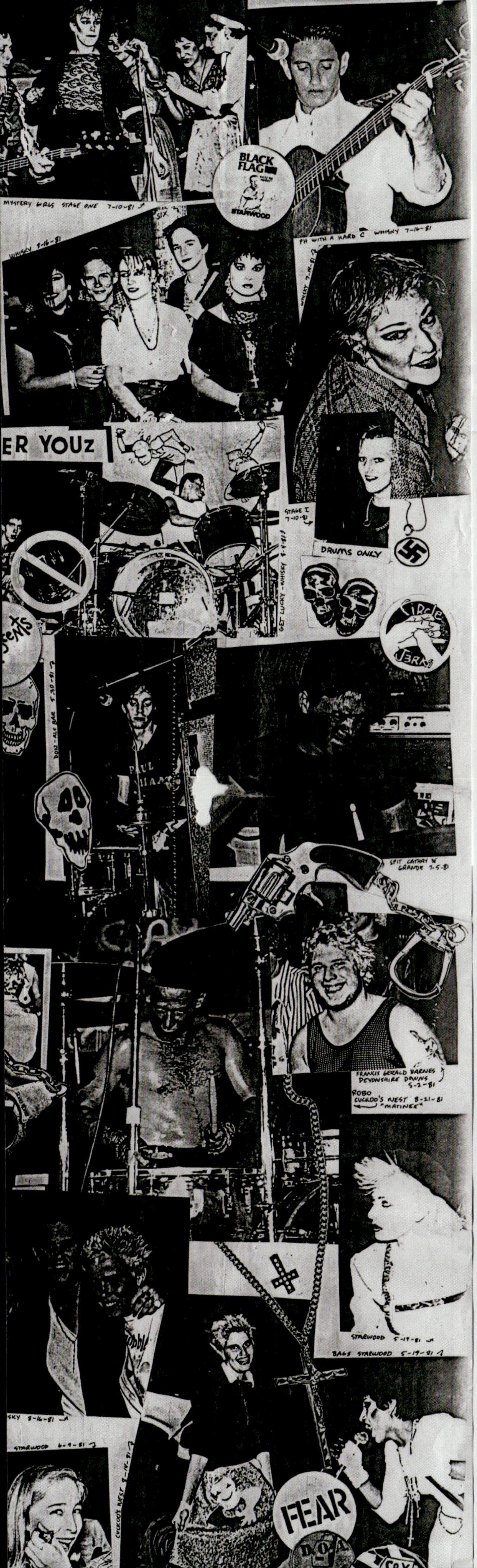

Rag In Chains - Danny Weizmann

My Take On Punk

by Danny Weizmann

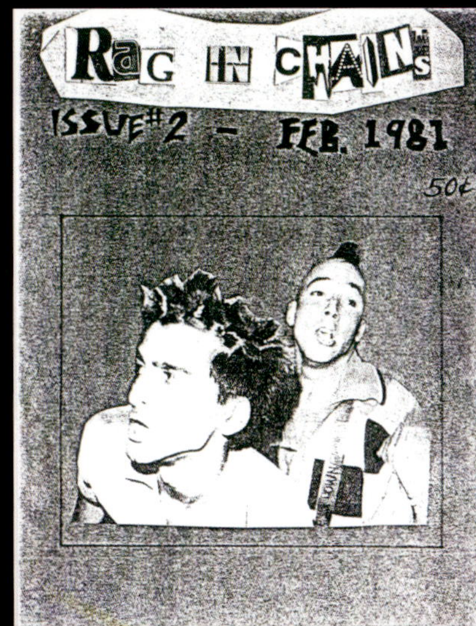

Punk was fun and freeing. Los Angeles in the late '70s and early '80s was sunny and spacious, lawless and sybaritic.

At 13 I used my bar mitzah money to start the fanzine ***Rag In Chains,*** under the nom de plume *Shredder.*

My Thomas Starr King Junior High pals and I would steal photos, conduct interviews on Hollywood Boulevard, stick it all together with rubber cement, take it down to a copy house in Gower Gulch on Sunset, and run them off by the hundreds. Then on Saturdays we'd place them in stores up and down Melrose - a quiet, desolate stretch at the time - on consignment at Tiger Rose, Cowboys and Poodles, Vinyl Fetish...

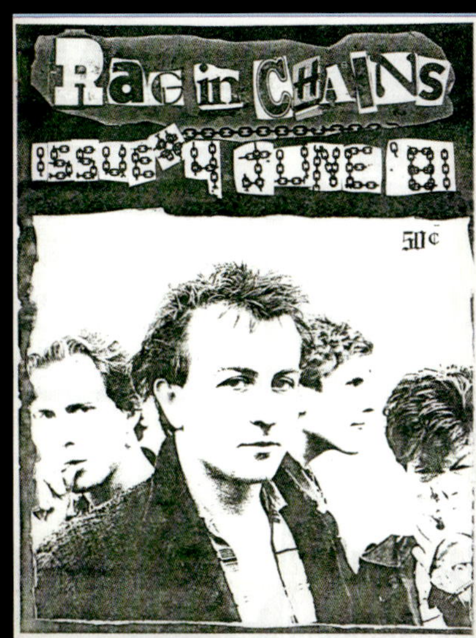

We were completely winging it. We'd hang out at Oki Dog, The Starwood, Marina Skate Park, Foster's Freeze, Hong Kong Cafe, Poseur on the Strip... cracking jokes and causing trouble. In punk there was no future, no money, no other place to go. It was all for the moment, and it was rad.

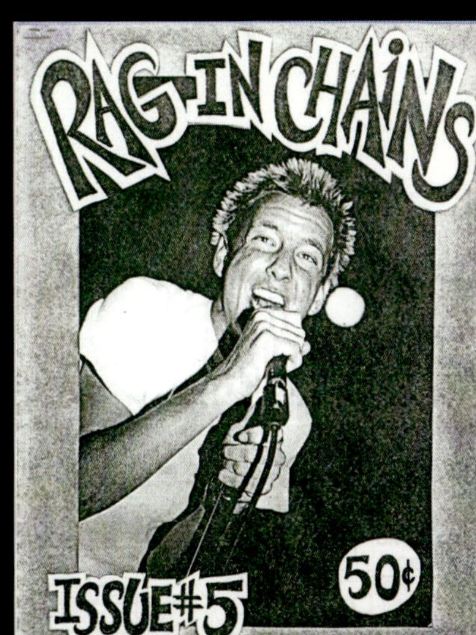

It was a revolution, but in an innocent and funny way. It was so cool to jump on the bus down Hollywood or Beverly or Fairfax and see another punk - from Redondo or Highland Park, Echo Park... making an instant connection in a big lonely city. I love those memories.

The 1984 Olympic Games, MTV, Reagan, Bush and natural entropy reversed the energy. Natch.

But it was fun while it lasted. +

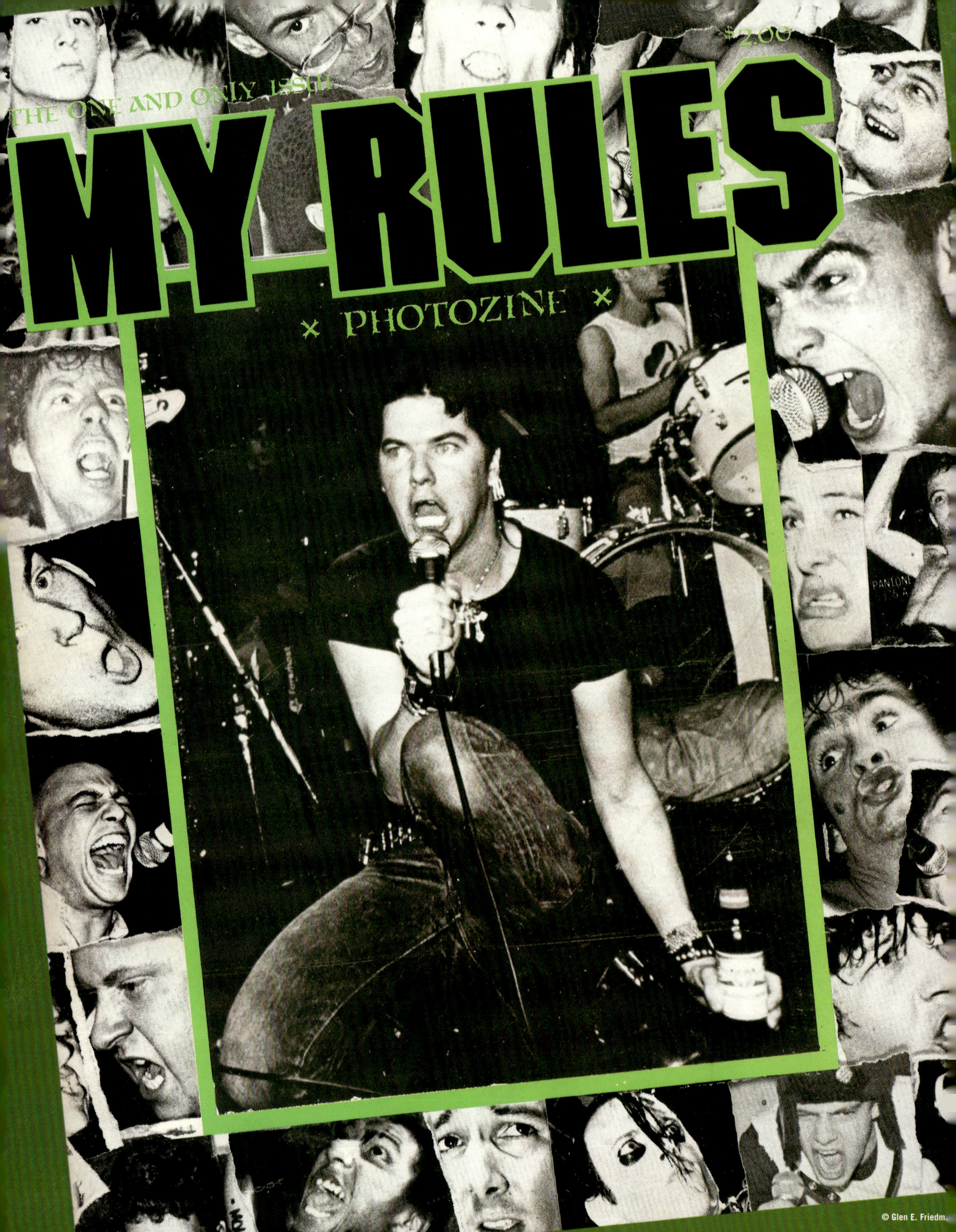
$2.00
THE ONE AND ONLY ISSUE
MY RULES
× PHOTOZINE ×

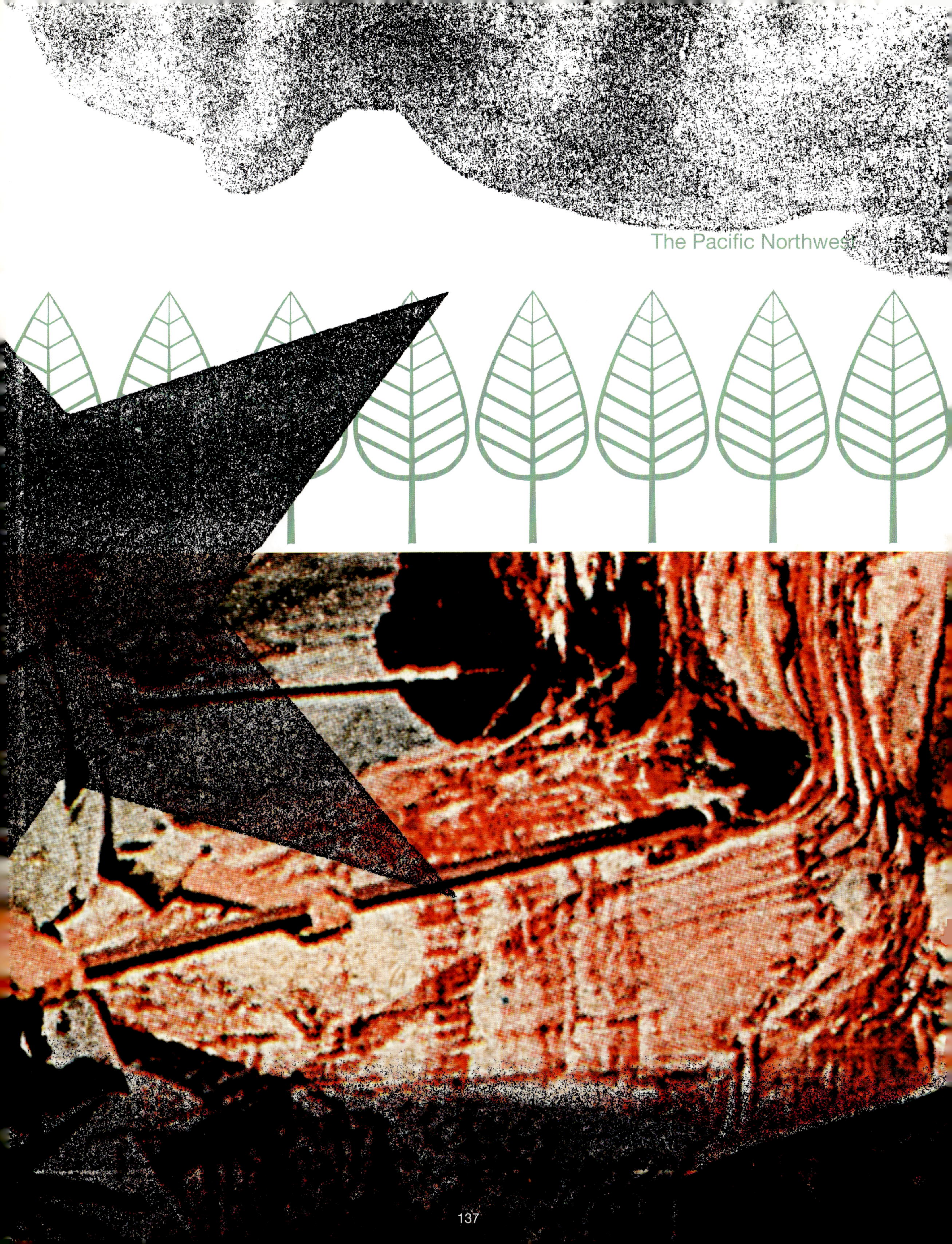
The Pacific Northwest

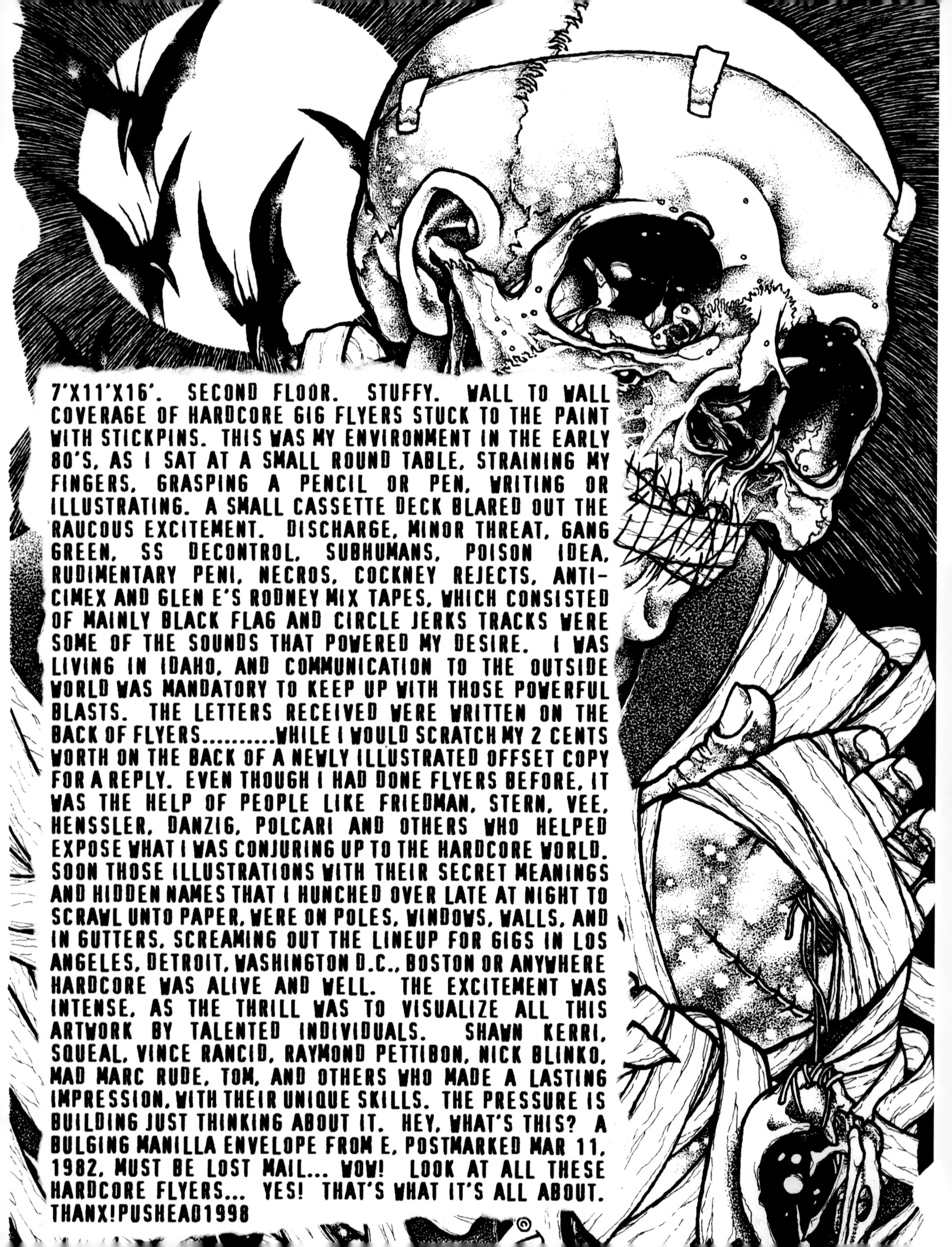

7'X11'X16'. SECOND FLOOR. STUFFY. WALL TO WALL COVERAGE OF HARDCORE GIG FLYERS STUCK TO THE PAINT WITH STICKPINS. THIS WAS MY ENVIRONMENT IN THE EARLY 80'S, AS I SAT AT A SMALL ROUND TABLE, STRAINING MY FINGERS, GRASPING A PENCIL OR PEN, WRITING OR ILLUSTRATING. A SMALL CASSETTE DECK BLARED OUT THE RAUCOUS EXCITEMENT. DISCHARGE, MINOR THREAT, GANG GREEN, SS DECONTROL, SUBHUMANS, POISON IDEA, RUDIMENTARY PENI, NECROS, COCKNEY REJECTS, ANTI-CIMEX AND GLEN E'S RODNEY MIX TAPES, WHICH CONSISTED OF MAINLY BLACK FLAG AND CIRCLE JERKS TRACKS WERE SOME OF THE SOUNDS THAT POWERED MY DESIRE. I WAS LIVING IN IDAHO, AND COMMUNICATION TO THE OUTSIDE WORLD WAS MANDATORY TO KEEP UP WITH THOSE POWERFUL BLASTS. THE LETTERS RECEIVED WERE WRITTEN ON THE BACK OF FLYERS..........WHILE I WOULD SCRATCH MY 2 CENTS WORTH ON THE BACK OF A NEWLY ILLUSTRATED OFFSET COPY FOR A REPLY. EVEN THOUGH I HAD DONE FLYERS BEFORE, IT WAS THE HELP OF PEOPLE LIKE FRIEDMAN, STERN, VEE, HENSSLER, DANZIG, POLCARI AND OTHERS WHO HELPED EXPOSE WHAT I WAS CONJURING UP TO THE HARDCORE WORLD. SOON THOSE ILLUSTRATIONS WITH THEIR SECRET MEANINGS AND HIDDEN NAMES THAT I HUNCHED OVER LATE AT NIGHT TO SCRAWL UNTO PAPER, WERE ON POLES, WINDOWS, WALLS, AND IN GUTTERS, SCREAMING OUT THE LINEUP FOR GIGS IN LOS ANGELES, DETROIT, WASHINGTON D.C., BOSTON OR ANYWHERE HARDCORE WAS ALIVE AND WELL. THE EXCITEMENT WAS INTENSE, AS THE THRILL WAS TO VISUALIZE ALL THIS ARTWORK BY TALENTED INDIVIDUALS. SHAWN KERRI, SQUEAL, VINCE RANCID, RAYMOND PETTIBON, NICK BLINKO, MAD MARC RUDE, TOM, AND OTHERS WHO MADE A LASTING IMPRESSION, WITH THEIR UNIQUE SKILLS. THE PRESSURE IS BUILDING JUST THINKING ABOUT IT. HEY, WHAT'S THIS? A BULGING MANILLA ENVELOPE FROM E, POSTMARKED MAR 11, 1982, MUST BE LOST MAIL... WOW! LOOK AT ALL THESE HARDCORE FLYERS... YES! THAT'S WHAT IT'S ALL ABOUT. THANX!PUSHEAD1998

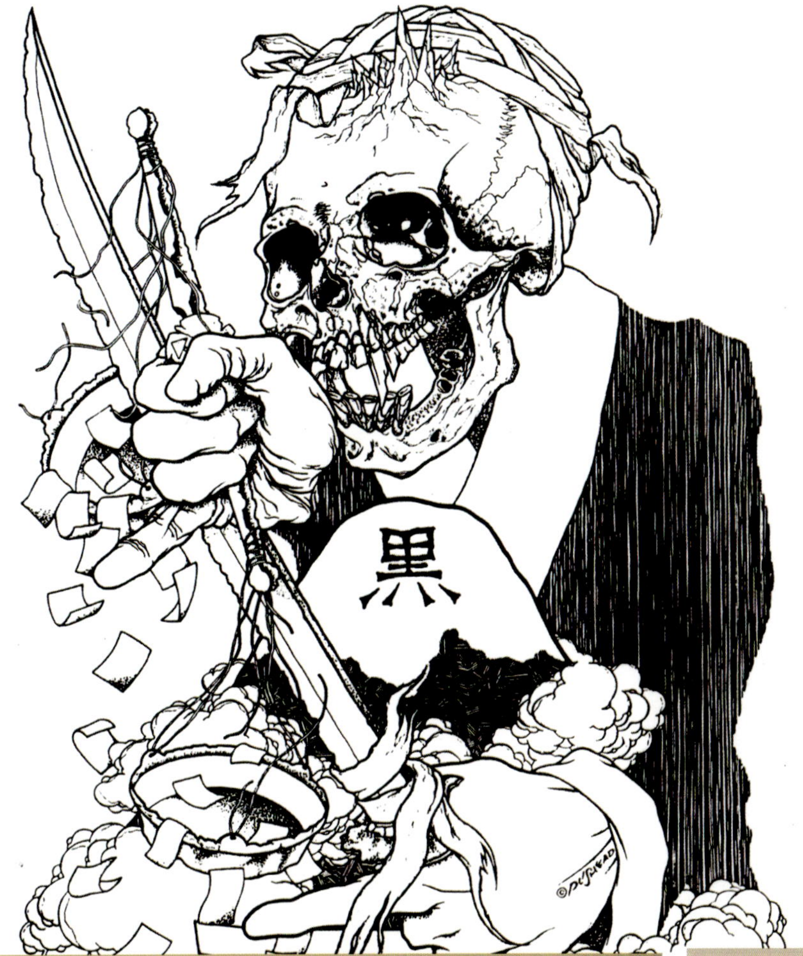

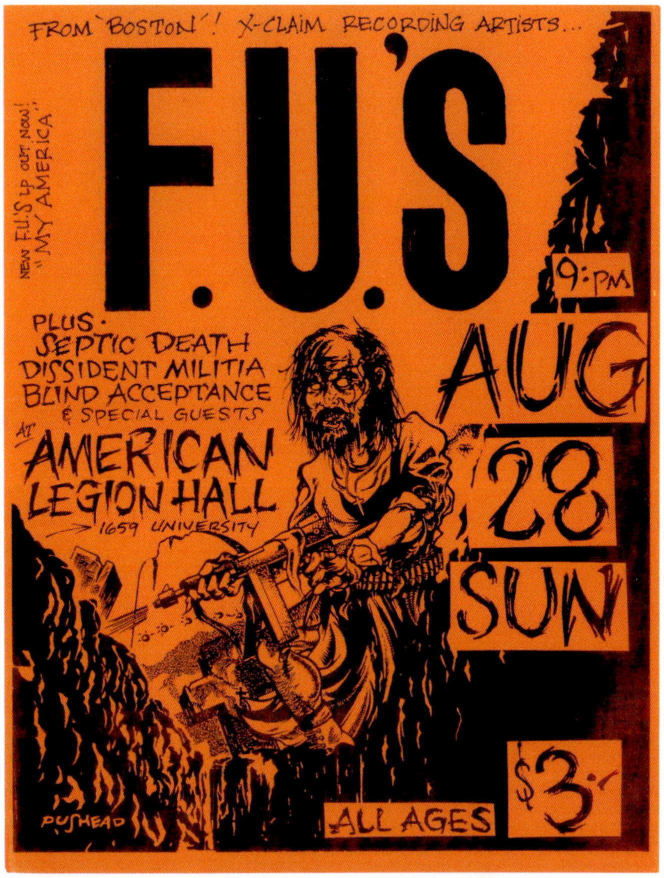

FROM 'BOSTON'! X-CLAIM RECORDING ARTISTS...
NEW F.U.'S LP OUT NOW! "MY AMERICA"
F.U.'S
9:PM
PLUS-
SEPTIC DEATH
DISSIDENT MILITIA
BLIND ACCEPTANCE
& SPECIAL GUESTS
AT AMERICAN LEGION HALL
1659 UNIVERSITY
AUG
28
SUN
$3.-
ALL AGES
PUSHEAD

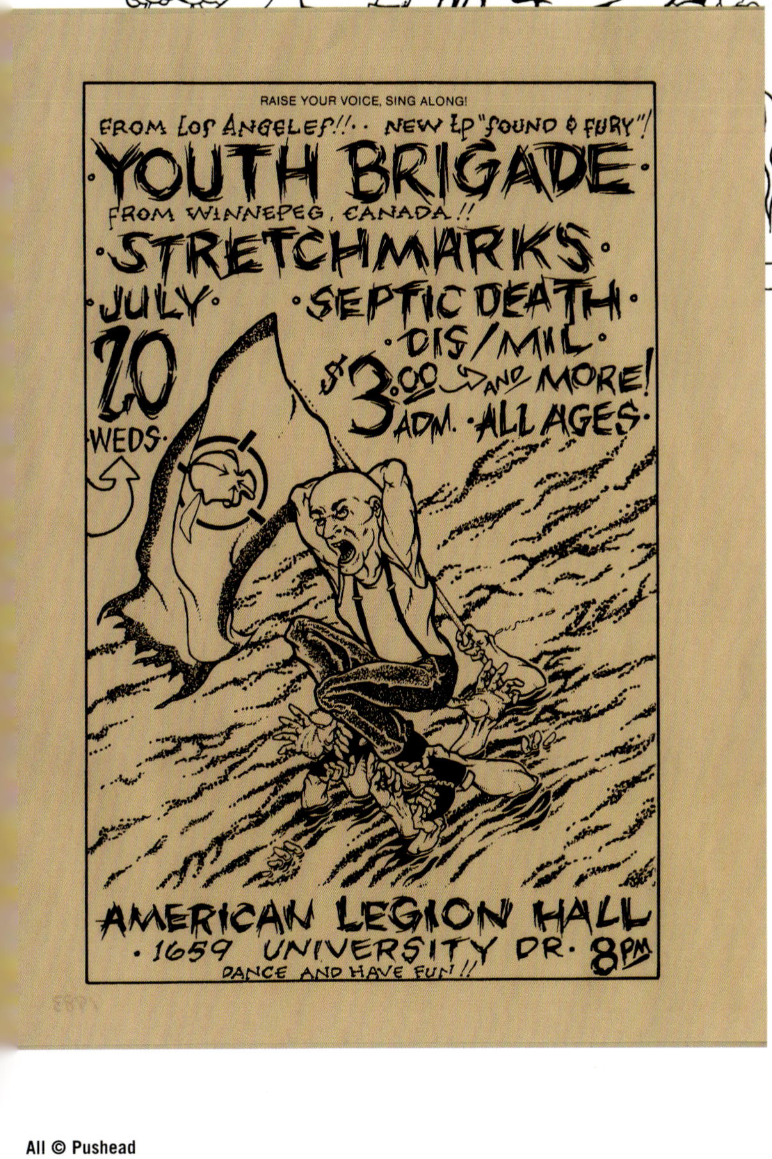

RAISE YOUR VOICE, SING ALONG!
FROM LOS ANGELES!!.. NEW LP "SOUND & FURY"!
YOUTH BRIGADE
FROM WINNEPEG, CANADA!!
STRETCHMARKS
JULY
20
WEDS
SEPTIC DEATH
DIS/MIL
$3.00 ADM.
AND MORE!
ALL AGES
AMERICAN LEGION HALL
1659 UNIVERSITY DR. 8PM
DANCE AND HAVE FUN!!

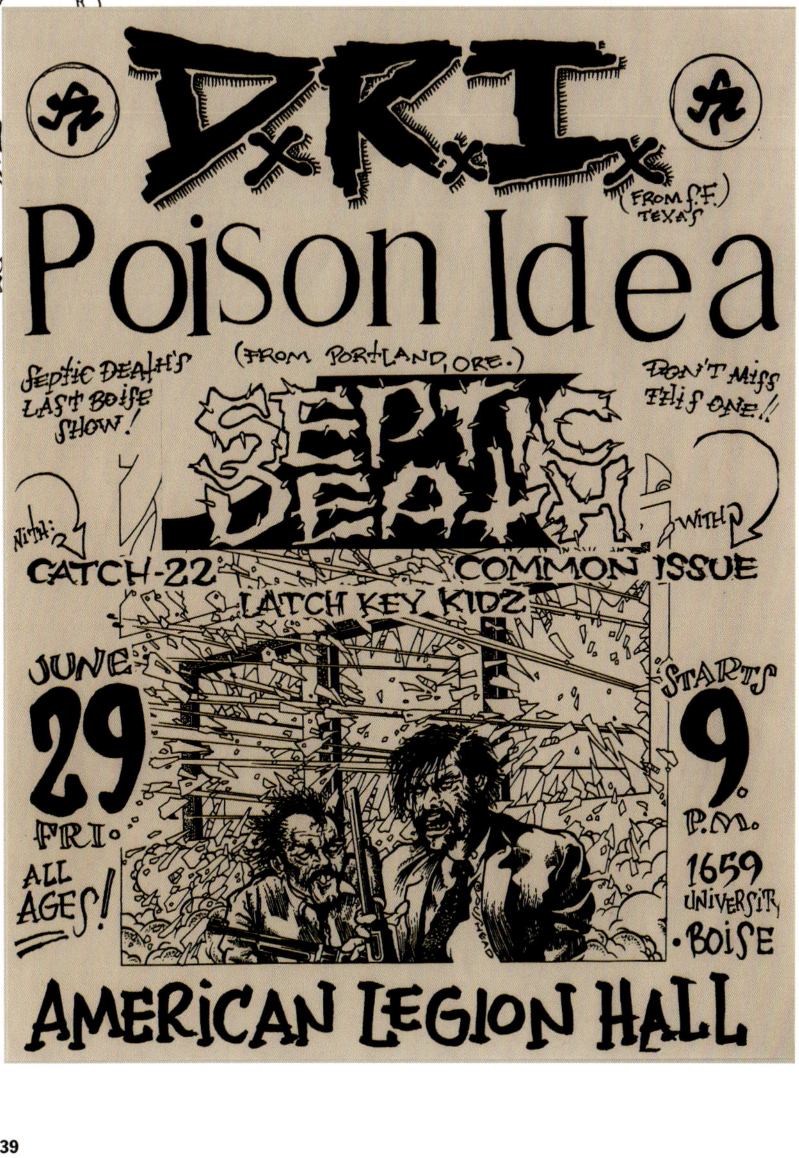

D.R.I.
(FROM S.F. TEXAS)
Poison Idea
(FROM PORTLAND, ORE.)
SEPTIC DEATH'S LAST BOISE SHOW!
DON'T MISS THIS ONE!!
SEPTIC DEATH
WITH
CATCH-22
COMMON ISSUE
LATCH KEY KIDZ
JUNE
29
FRI.
ALL AGES!
STARTS
9.
P.M.
1659 UNIVERSITY
BOISE
AMERICAN LEGION HALL

PUSHEAD

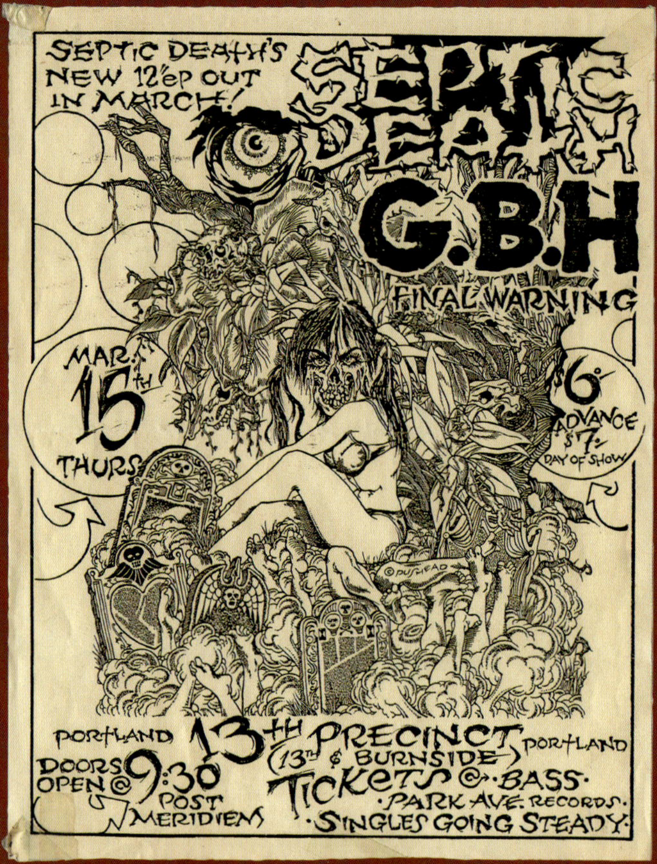
SEPTIC DEATH'S NEW 12"EP OUT IN MARCH
SEPTIC DEATH
G.B.H
FINAL WARNING
MAR. 15th THURS
$6 ADVANCE $7 DAY OF SHOW
PORTLAND 13th PRECINCT 13th & BURNSIDE PORTLAND
DOORS OPEN @ 9:30 POST MERIDIEN
TICKETS @: BASS
PARK AVE. RECORDS
SINGLES GOING STEADY

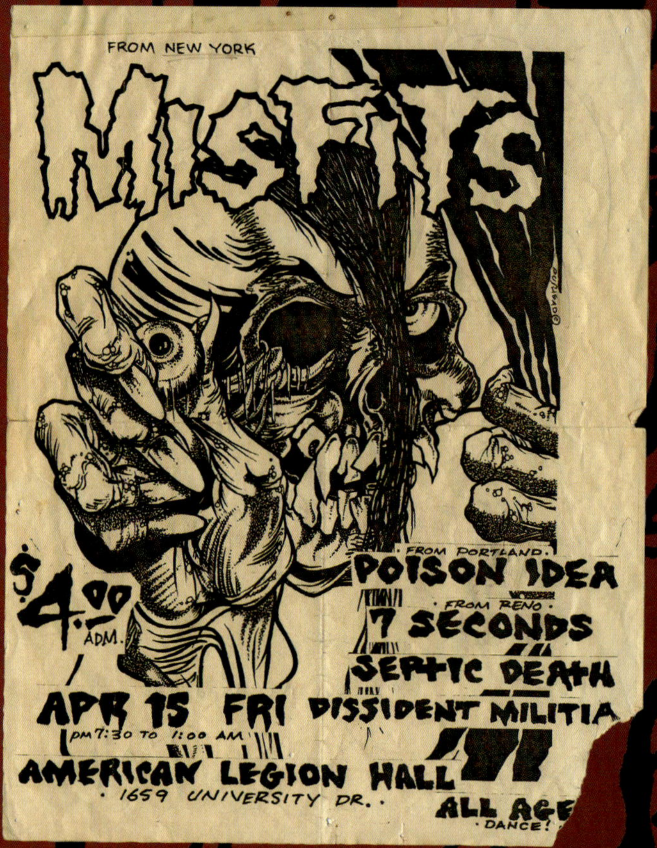
FROM NEW YORK
MISFITS
$4.00 ADM.
FROM PORTLAND POISON IDEA
FROM RENO 7 SECONDS
SEPTIC DEATH
APR 15 FRI DISSIDENT MILITIA
pm 7:30 to 11:00 AM
AMERICAN LEGION HALL
1659 UNIVERSITY DR.
ALL AGE DANCE!

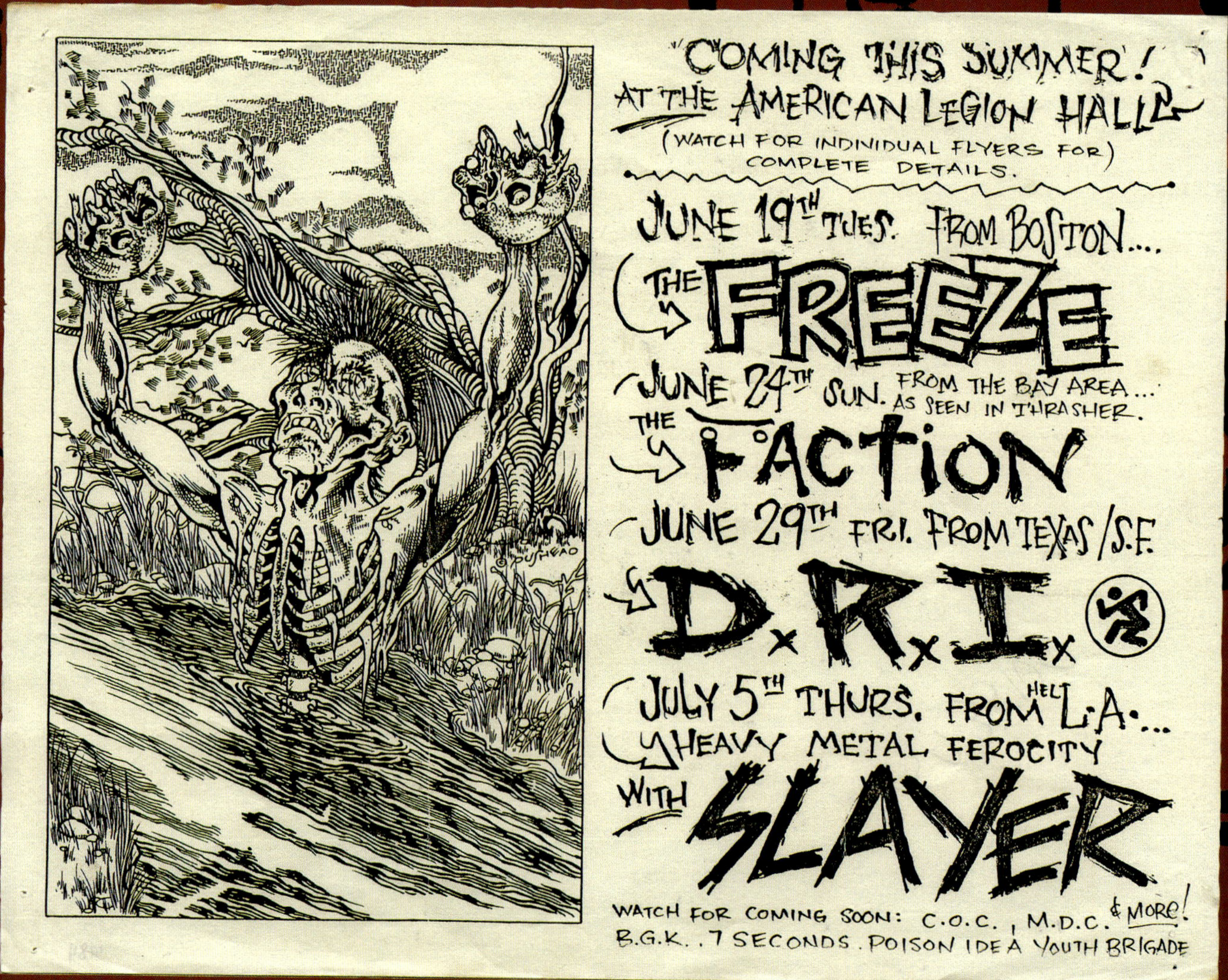
COMING THIS SUMMER! AT THE AMERICAN LEGION HALL
(WATCH FOR INDIVIDUAL FLYERS FOR) COMPLETE DETAILS.
JUNE 19th TUES. FROM BOSTON....
THE FREEZE
JUNE 24th SUN. FROM THE BAY AREA... AS SEEN IN THRASHER.
THE FACTION
JUNE 29th FRI. FROM TEXAS / S.F.
D.R.I.
JULY 5th THURS. FROM HELL L.A....
HEAVY METAL FEROCITY
WITH SLAYER
WATCH FOR COMING SOON: C.O.C., M.D.C. & MORE!
B.G.K., 7 SECONDS, POISON IDEA, YOUTH BRIGADE

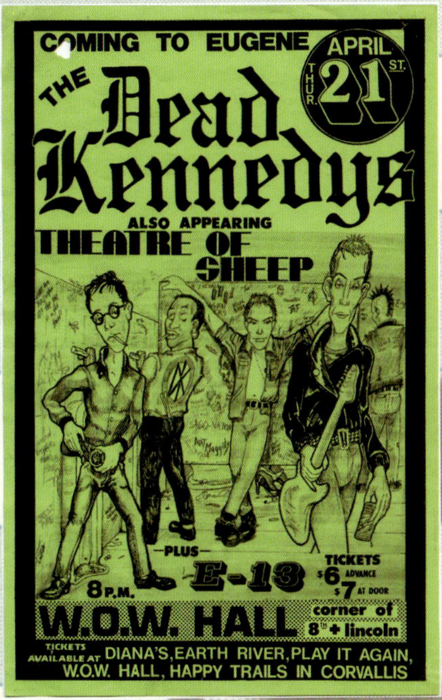
COMING TO EUGENE
APRIL
THUR 21 ST.
THE Dead Kennedys
ALSO APPEARING
THEATRE OF SHEEP
—PLUS—
E-13
8 P.M.
TICKETS $6 ADVANCE $7 AT DOOR
W.O.W. HALL corner of 8th + lincoln
TICKETS AVAILABLE AT DIANA'S, EARTH RIVER, PLAY IT AGAIN, W.O.W. HALL, HAPPY TRAILS IN CORVALLIS

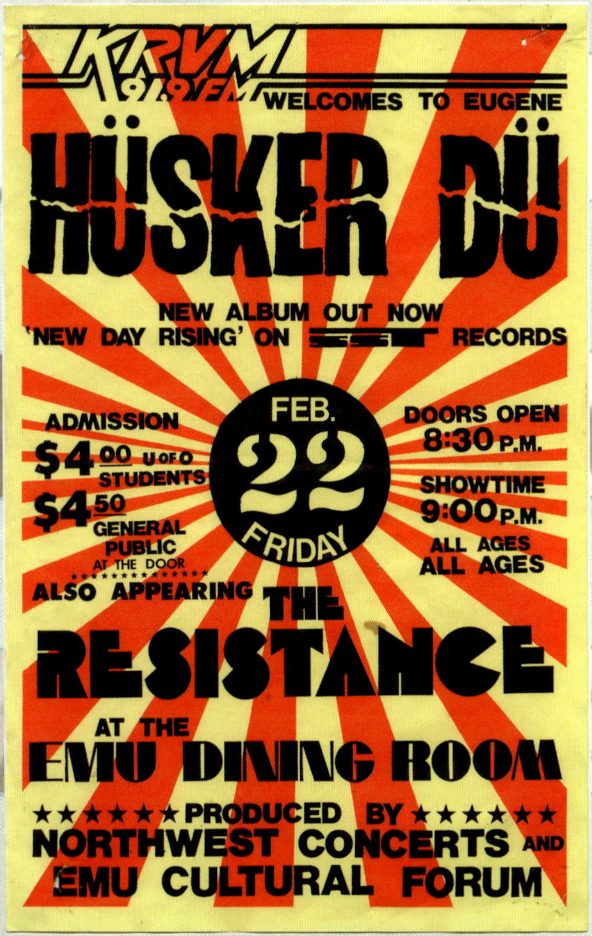
KRVM 91.9 FM WELCOMES TO EUGENE
HÜSKER DÜ
NEW ALBUM OUT NOW
'NEW DAY RISING' ON SST RECORDS
ADMISSION
$4.00 U of O STUDENTS
$4.50 GENERAL PUBLIC AT THE DOOR
FEB. 22 FRIDAY
DOORS OPEN 8:30 P.M.
SHOWTIME 9:00 P.M.
ALL AGES
ALL AGES
ALSO APPEARING THE RESISTANCE
AT THE EMU DINING ROOM
★★★★★ PRODUCED BY ★★★★★
NORTHWEST CONCERTS AND
EMU CULTURAL FORUM

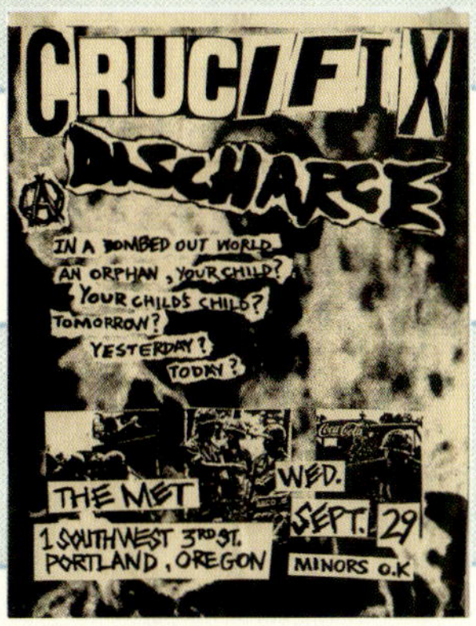
CRUCIFIX
DISCHARGE
IN A BOMBED OUT WORLD
AN ORPHAN, YOUR CHILD?
YOUR CHILDS CHILD?
TOMORROW?
YESTERDAY?
TODAY?
THE MET
1 SOUTHWEST 3RD ST. PORTLAND, OREGON
WED. SEPT. 29
MINORS O.K.

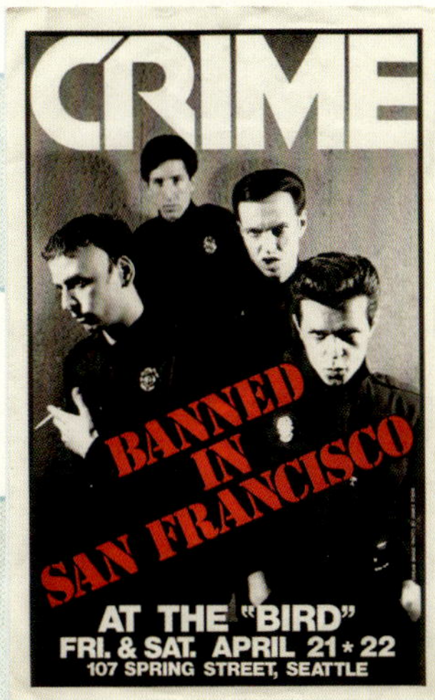
CRIME
BANNED IN SAN FRANCISCO
AT THE "BIRD"
FRI. & SAT. APRIL 21 ★ 22
107 SPRING STREET, SEATTLE

James Stark

PSUEDOE productions
welcomes
D.O.A.*
and
COFFIN BREAK
and
NIRVANA
18 and over
THURS 1 DEC
at THE UNDERGROUND
4518 University Way NE • 548-9362
$8.00 at the door
doors open at 7:30pm

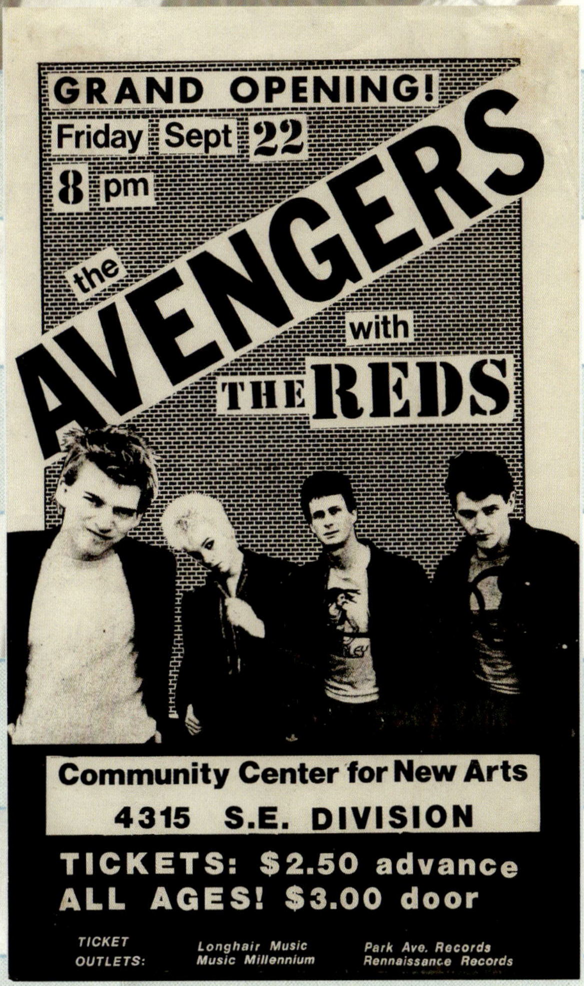
GRAND OPENING!
Friday Sept 22
8 pm
the AVENGERS
with
THE REDS
Community Center for New Arts
4315 S.E. DIVISION
TICKETS: $2.50 advance
ALL AGES! $3.00 door
TICKET OUTLETS:
Longhair Music
Music Millennium
Park Ave. Records
Rennaissance Records

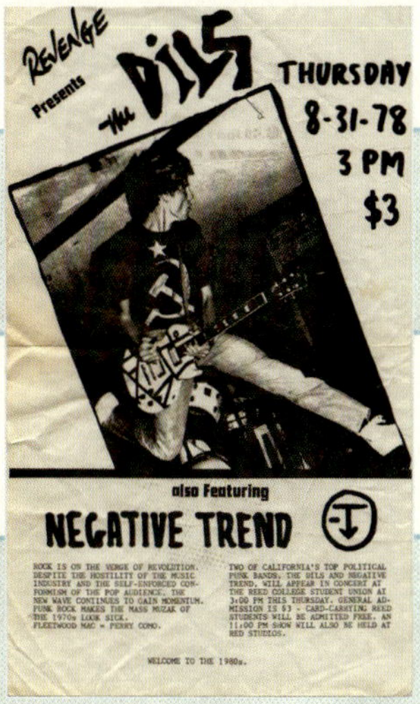
REVENGE Presents
the DILS
THURSDAY
8-31-78
3 PM
$3
also Featuring
NEGATIVE TREND

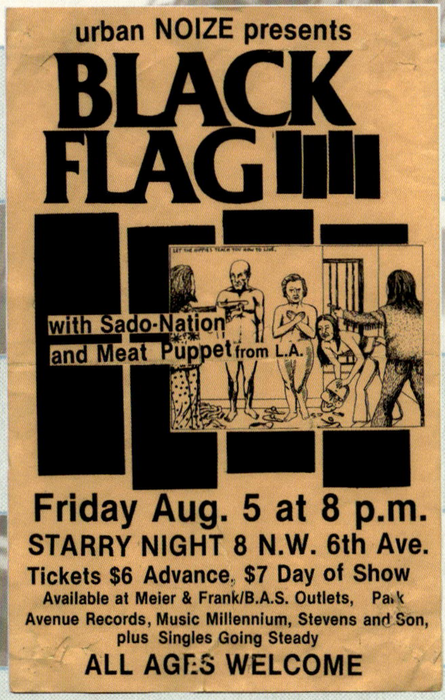
urban NOIZE presents
BLACK FLAG
with Sado-Nation
and Meat Puppet from L.A.
Friday Aug. 5 at 8 p.m.
STARRY NIGHT 8 N.W. 6th Ave.
Tickets $6 Advance, $7 Day of Show
Available at Meier & Frank/B.A.S. Outlets, Park Avenue Records, Music Millennium, Stevens and Son, plus Singles Going Steady
ALL AGES WELCOME

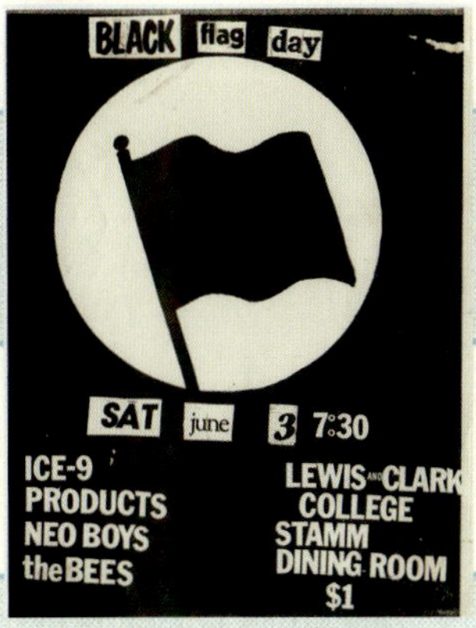
BLACK flag day
SAT june 3 7:30
ICE-9
PRODUCTS
NEO BOYS
the BEES
LEWIS and CLARK COLLEGE
STAMM DINING ROOM
$1

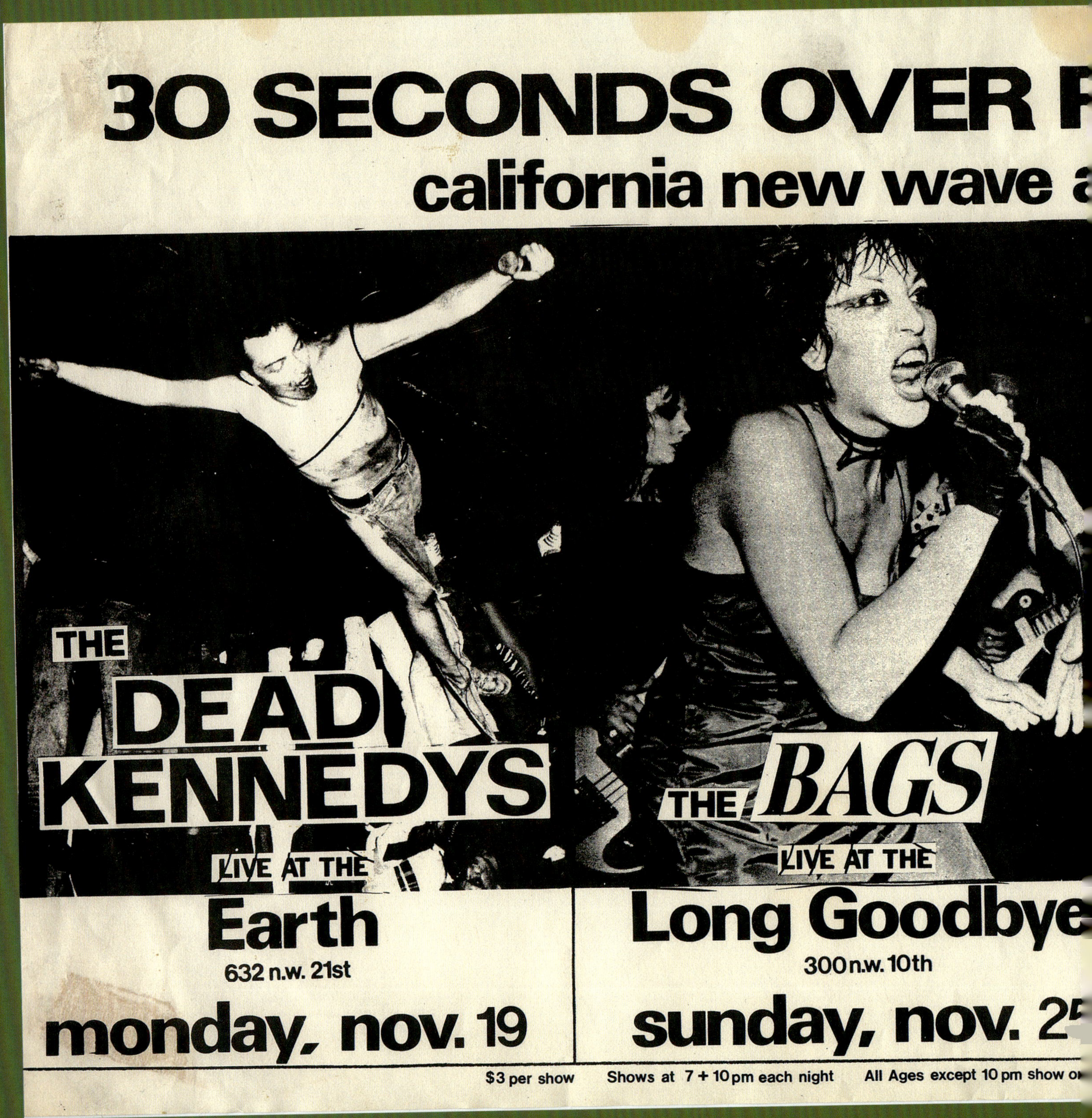

New Wave?

Great Punk Rock Moments In Oregon History, Part One
DKs (Long Goodbye)
This average Oregonian guy and his girlfriend were sitting at a table close to the stage. Jello Biafra runs up to the table and dumped the guy's ashtray into his pitcher of beer. I thought, "Hmmmmm, he's not from around here."
(Charles Arjavac, Sado Nation)

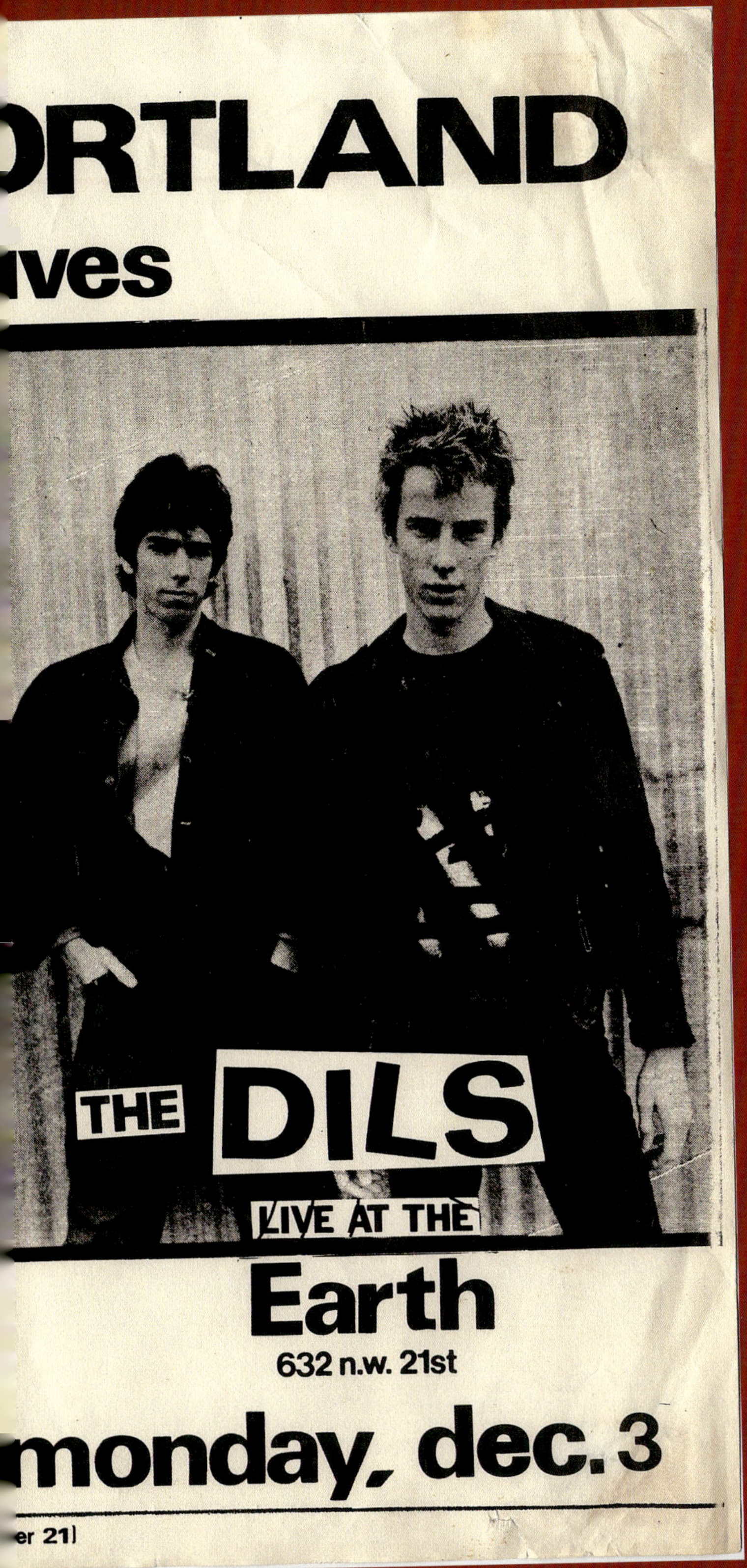

Great Punk Rock Moments In Oregon History, Part Two
10/29/79 (Earth Tavern)
Nine bands, including the Wipers, Neo Boys, Cleavers and The Rubbers played a show recorded live for release as the "10/29/79" Portland compilation album. The show was heavily supported and a large crowd showed up. This night marked the recording debut of the Rubbers featuring Bob and Bruce Loose, future members of the Cheifs, and Flipper.
(Charles Arjavac, Sado Nation)

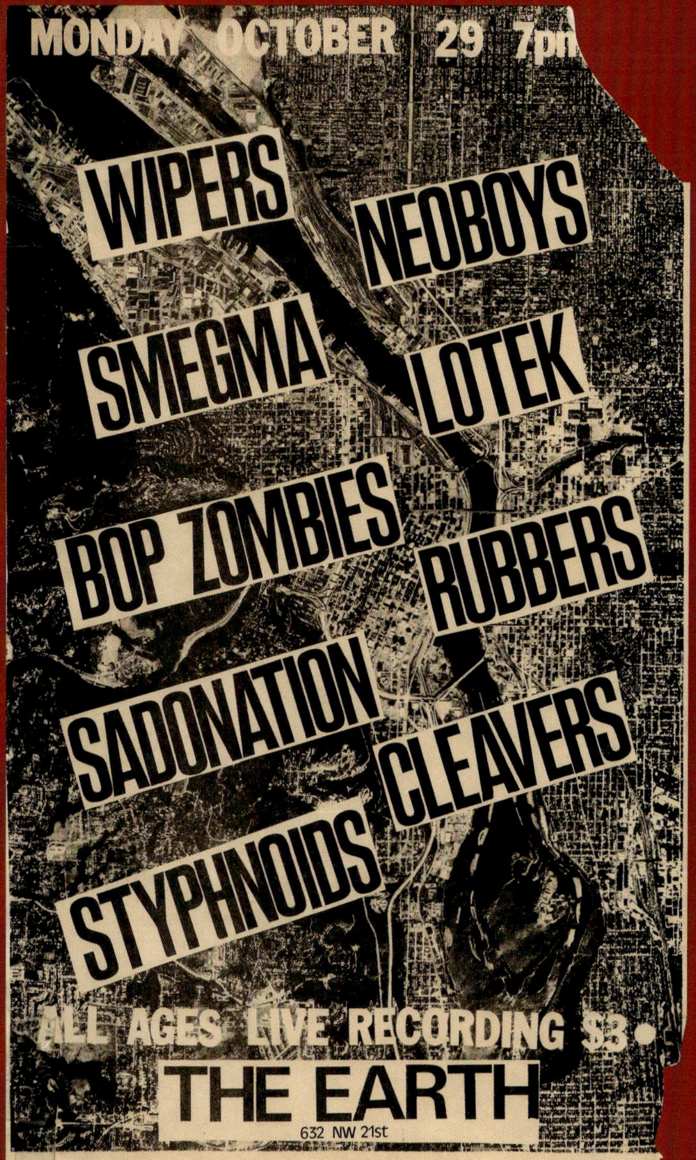

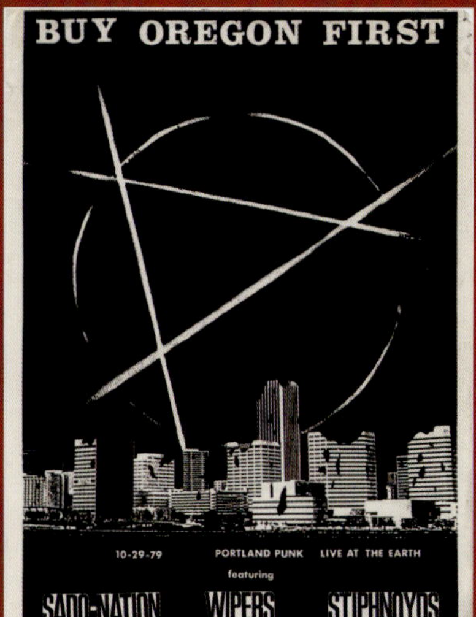

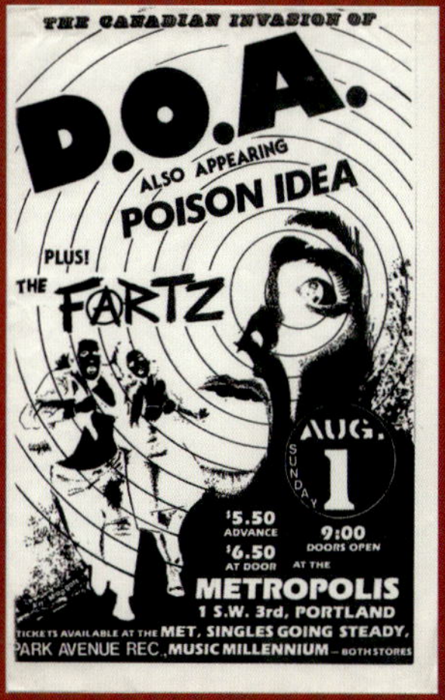

Janice Moreland

Great Punk Rock Moments In Oregon History, Part Three
Fear (The Met)
After the gig, Derf Scratch told us there was a party at their motel room. We followed him backstage to get directions, where we found singer Lee Ving bent over a table counting money. He looked up at us and said, "We didn't come here to make friends." Needless to say, there was no party that night. (Charles Arjavac, Sado Nation)

Great Punk Rock Moments In Oregon History, Part Four
The Portland Evening News
A news crew came down to film a show for a feature on punk rock. They filmed me playing drums and overdubbed someone commenting on how punks traded food stamps for beer. My family was never so proud. (Charles Arjavac, Sado Nation)

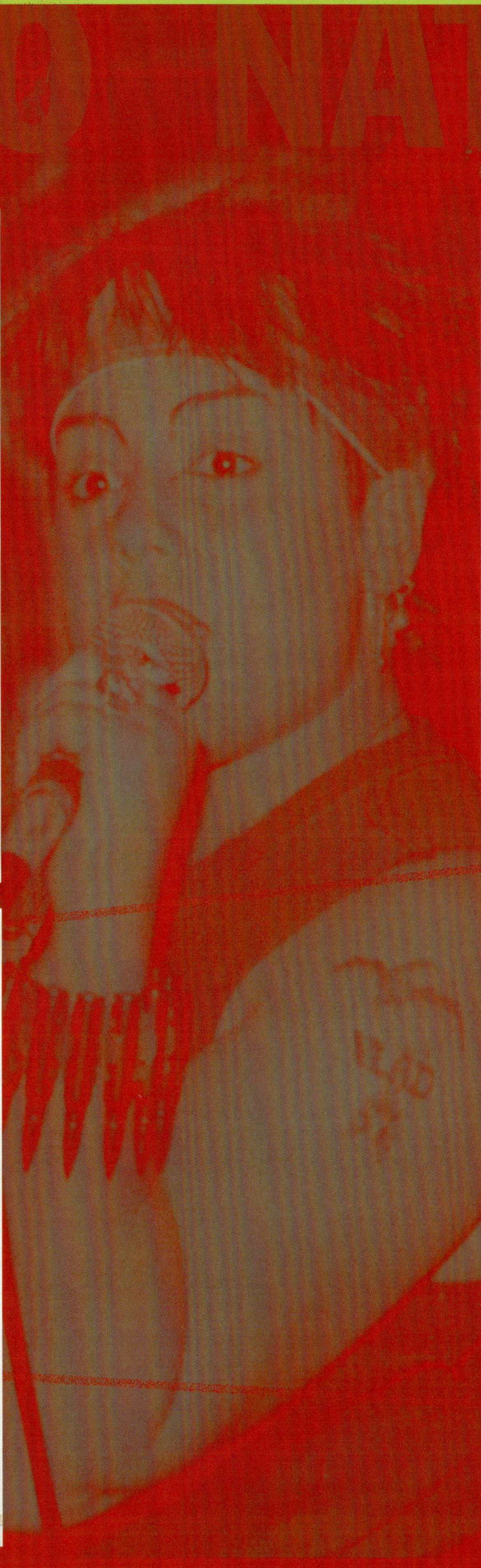

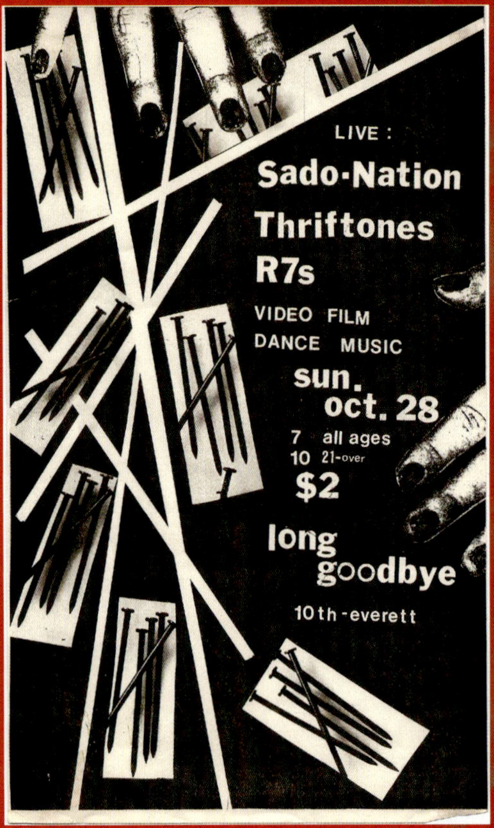

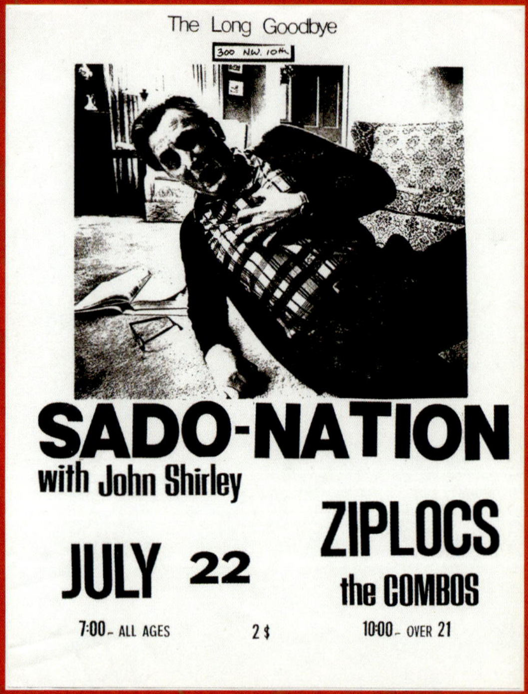

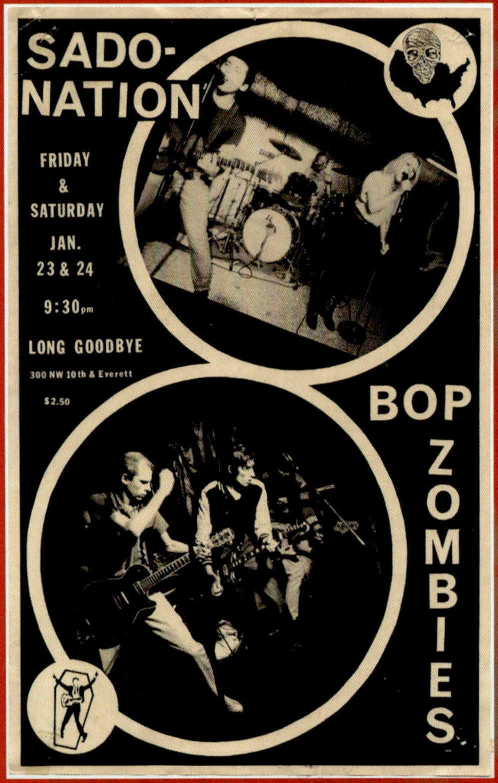

Janice Moreland

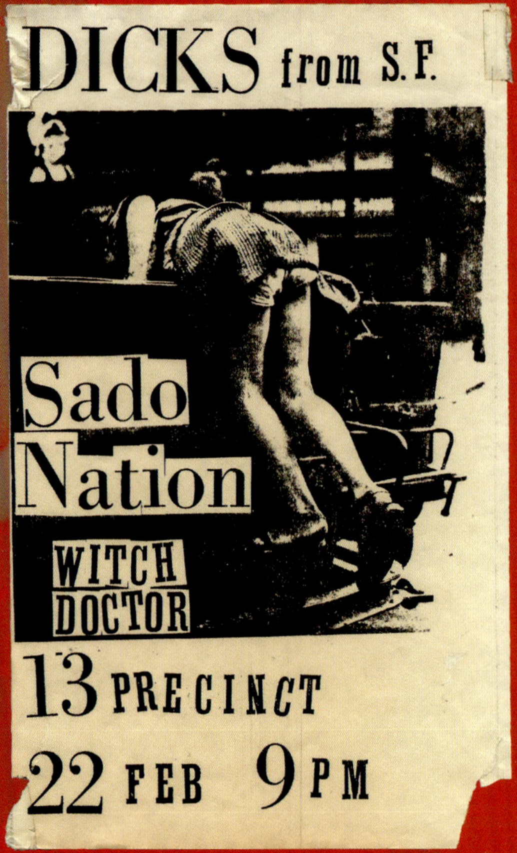

Mish Bondage

Mish Bondage — Sado Nation
Photo © Murray Bowles

THE WIPERS

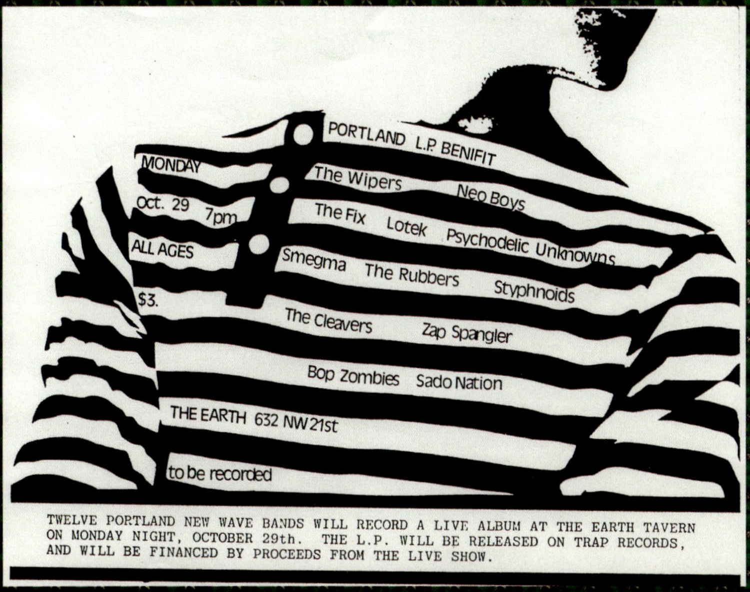

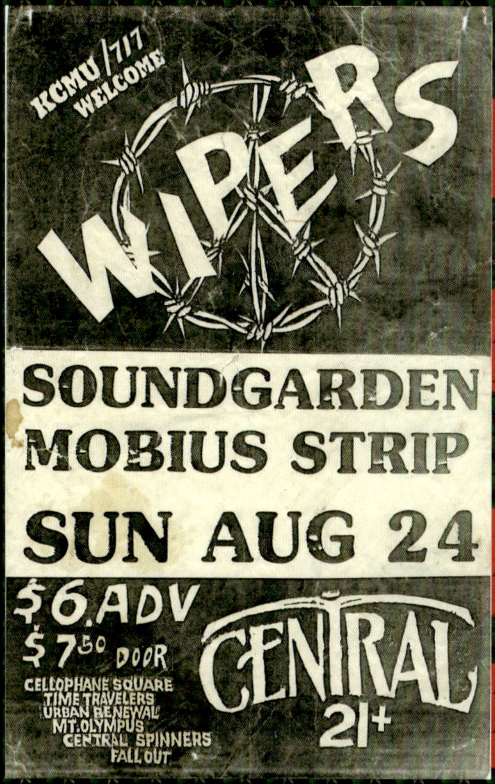

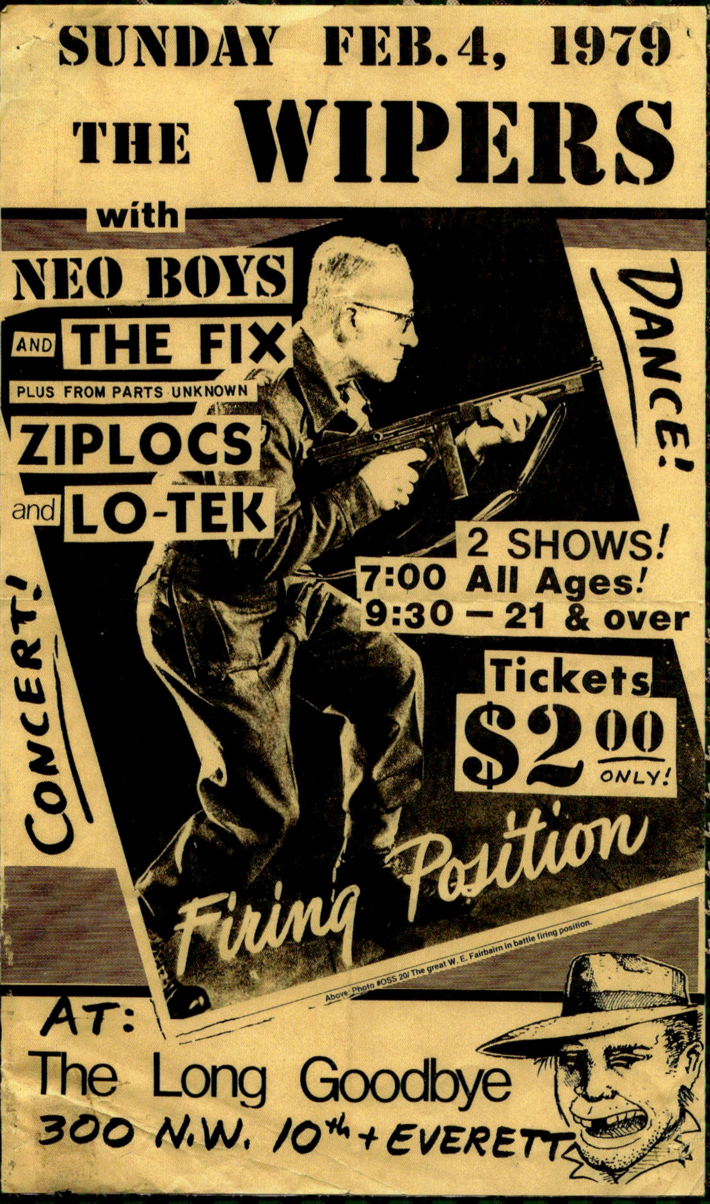

Great Punk Rock Moments In Oregon History, Part Five

The Wipers (Long Goodbye/Earth Tavern

By 1980, it became apparent the Wipers would be the band that put our town on the map. With the lineup consisting of Greg Sage, Sam Henry and Dave Koppel, the Wipers would perform some of the greatest live shows in the history of Portland, Oregon.

(Charles Arjavac, Sado Nation)

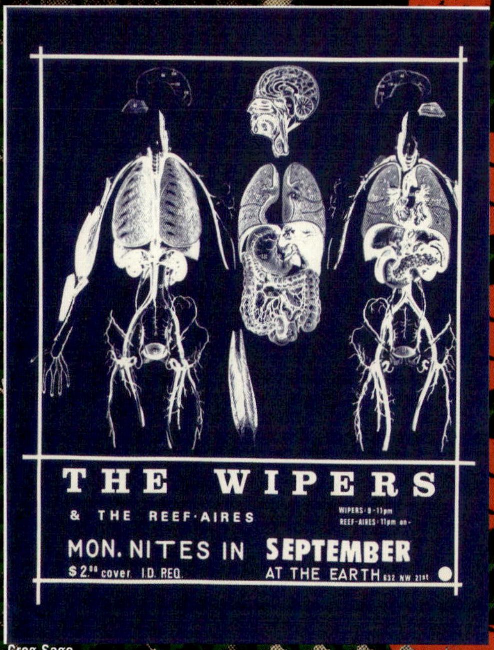

Greg Sage

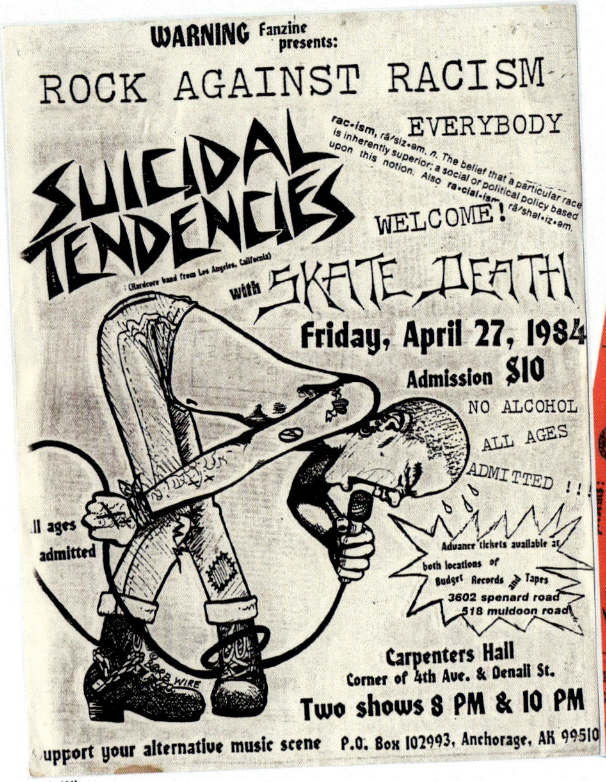

Barb Wire

Punk rock reaches Alaska...

(yes, Alaska.)

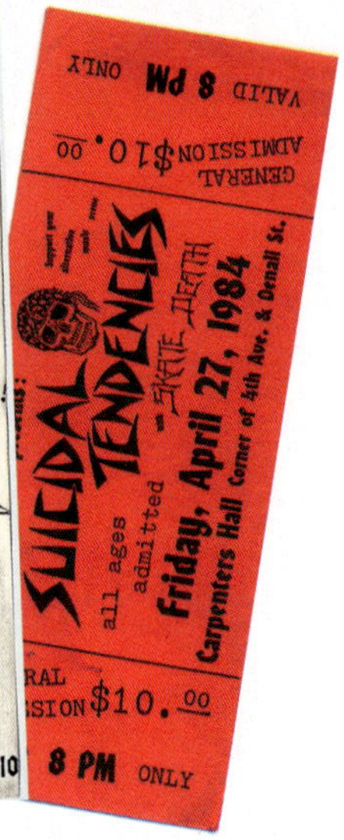

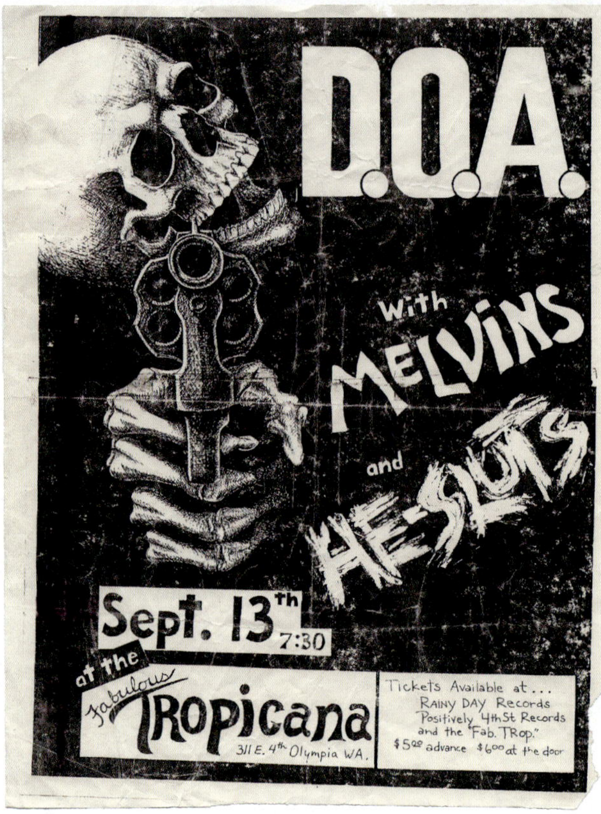

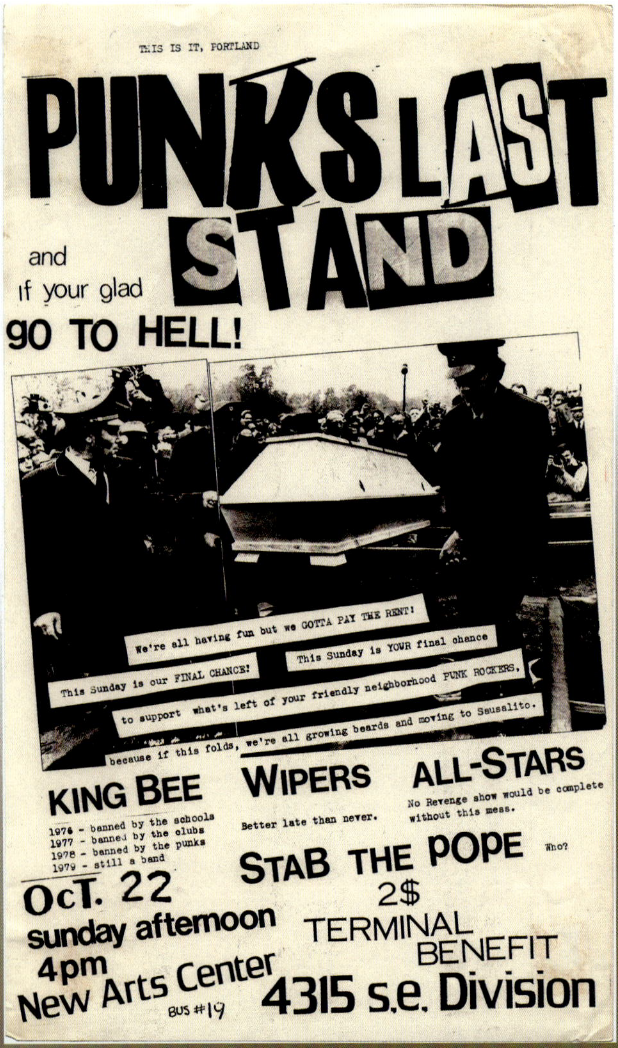

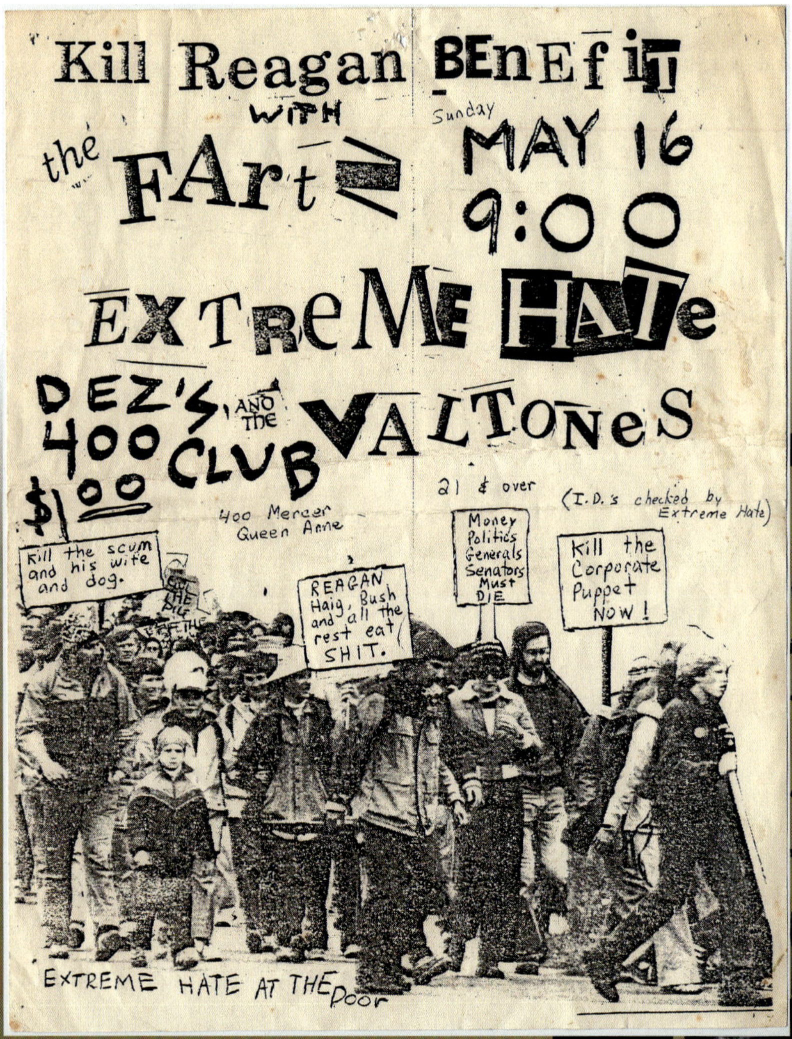

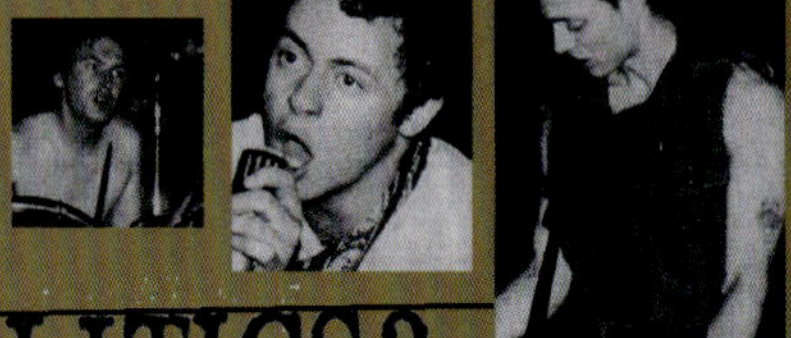

...DID YOU FIRST GET INTO ANARCHIST POLITICS?

THE WEST

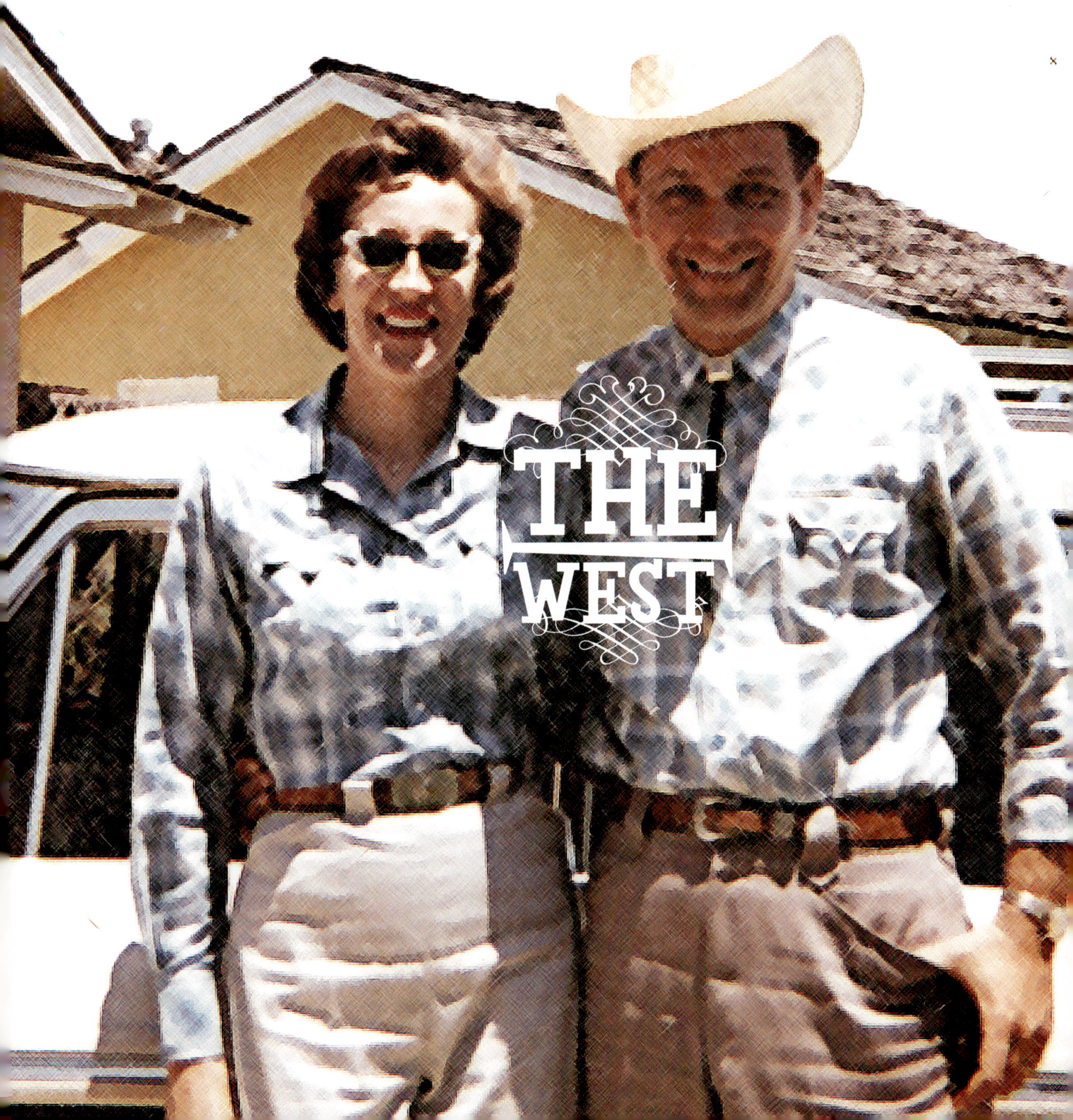

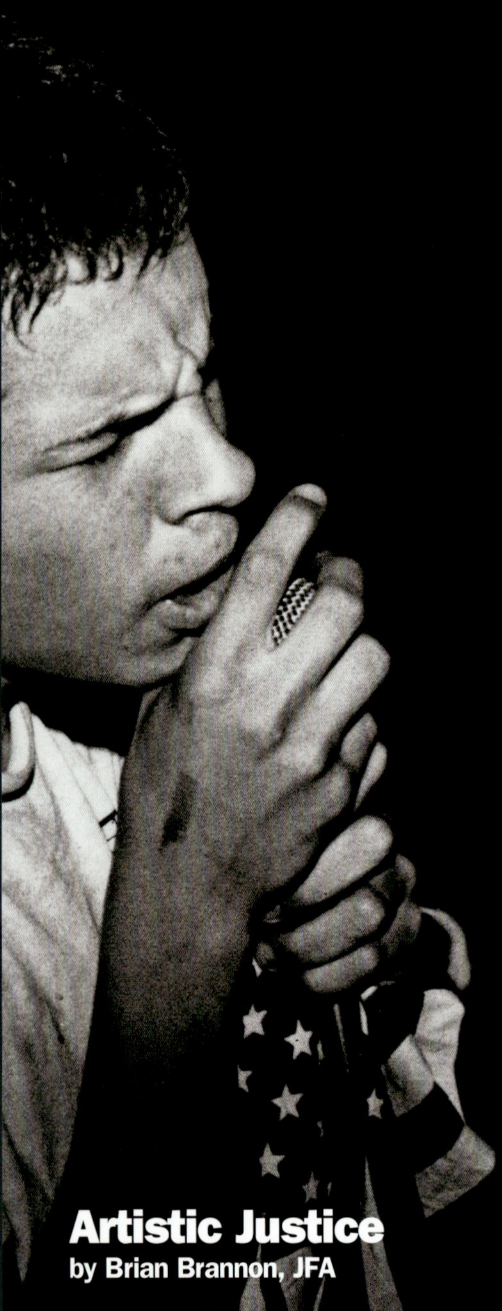

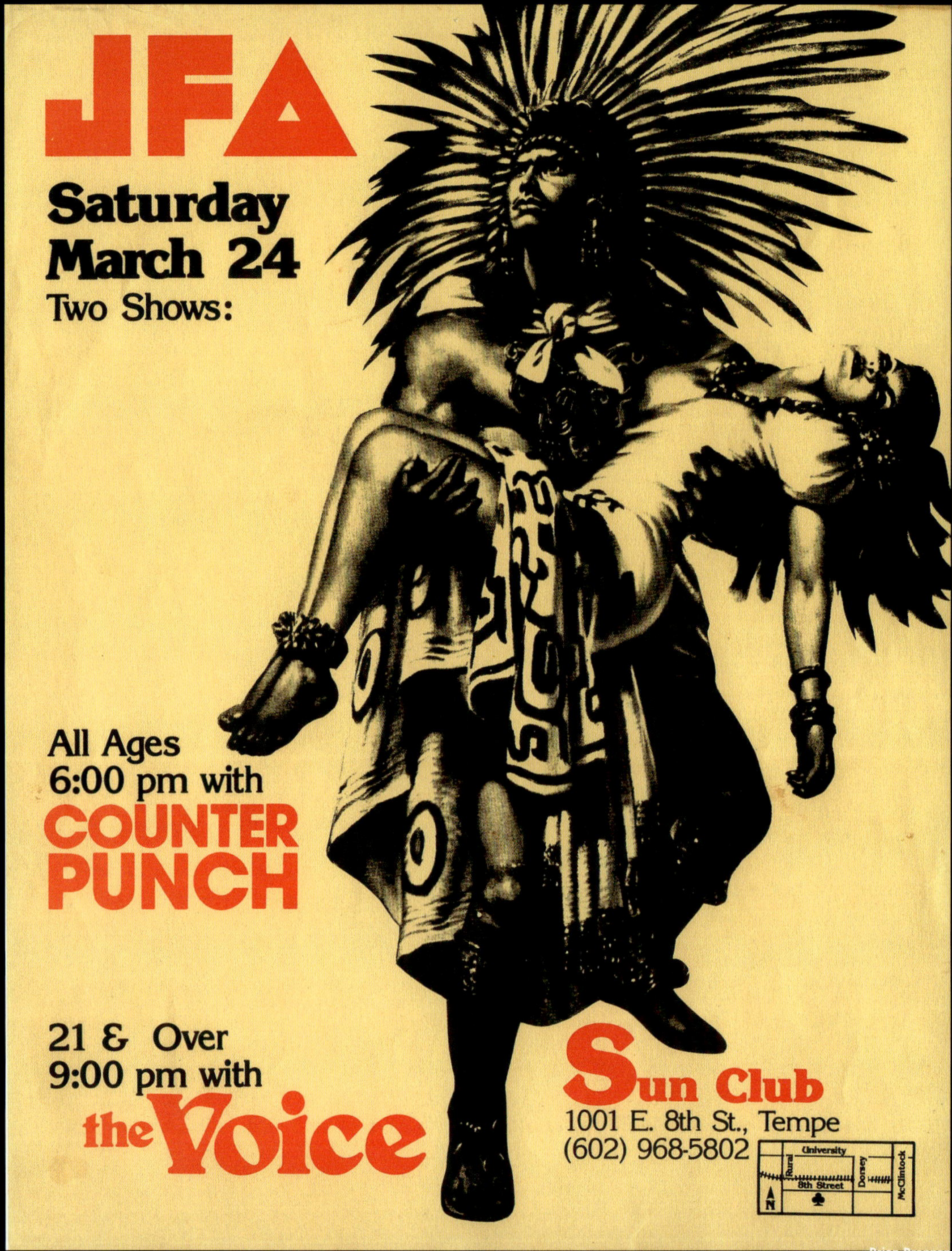

Brian Brannon

Artistic Justice

by Brian Brannon, JFA

Flyers were a key ingredient in my adolescent aesthetic. While some people might have walked into my room and saw cheap xeroxed paper wallpaper, what I saw was fine art– memories of a hundred bands, gigs, bouncers, emotions, friends, clubs, riots, girls.

Somehow the key moments of every show I had seen or wanted to see were all captured in the names, dates, drawings and photos plastered on my walls. Some of the early JFA flyers were even more special because they were drawn by my best buddy, crazy Sean Merli.

Me, Sean and his older brother Eric went way back. We all got into punk together despite their Mormon parents, who strictly forbade any such behavior.

One day I got the call to skate over to the Merli residence and dig through their garbage. Their mom had just thrown out all their good records– Clash, Pistols, Flyboys, Devo, B-52s.

It only took me a few minutes to get over there and rescue the booty, but sitting in that dumpster in the Arizona sun caused some serious vinyl warpage. I took the records home, set my needle on extra heavy, and the records played just fine.

Except for the Flyboys - it took us the longest time to figure out that their record played at 45 rpm and not 33-1/3. There we sat, thinking the guy had the coolest deep voice, but that the music was slow and plodding. When we turned it to the correct speed, we couldn't believe they played that fast.

Back to the flyers: Being some of the first punkers at Saguaro High School in Scottsdale Arizona, and FRESHMEN to boot, got me and Sean hassled more than a little by the jockier guys, not to mention the rockers, preppies, shit-kickers and pretty boys. It was the jocks we hated most. Me, Sean and Eric had a dream band going, which we called *The Deceased.*

One day I decided to get some spray paint and stencils and wrote on the back of a t-shirt in 4-inch-high letters, *"JOCKS SUCK."* On the front I scribbled our band's motto: *"The Deceased Don't Care."*

My fashion choice for school the next day was complete.

Brian Brannon
Photo © Sue Moped

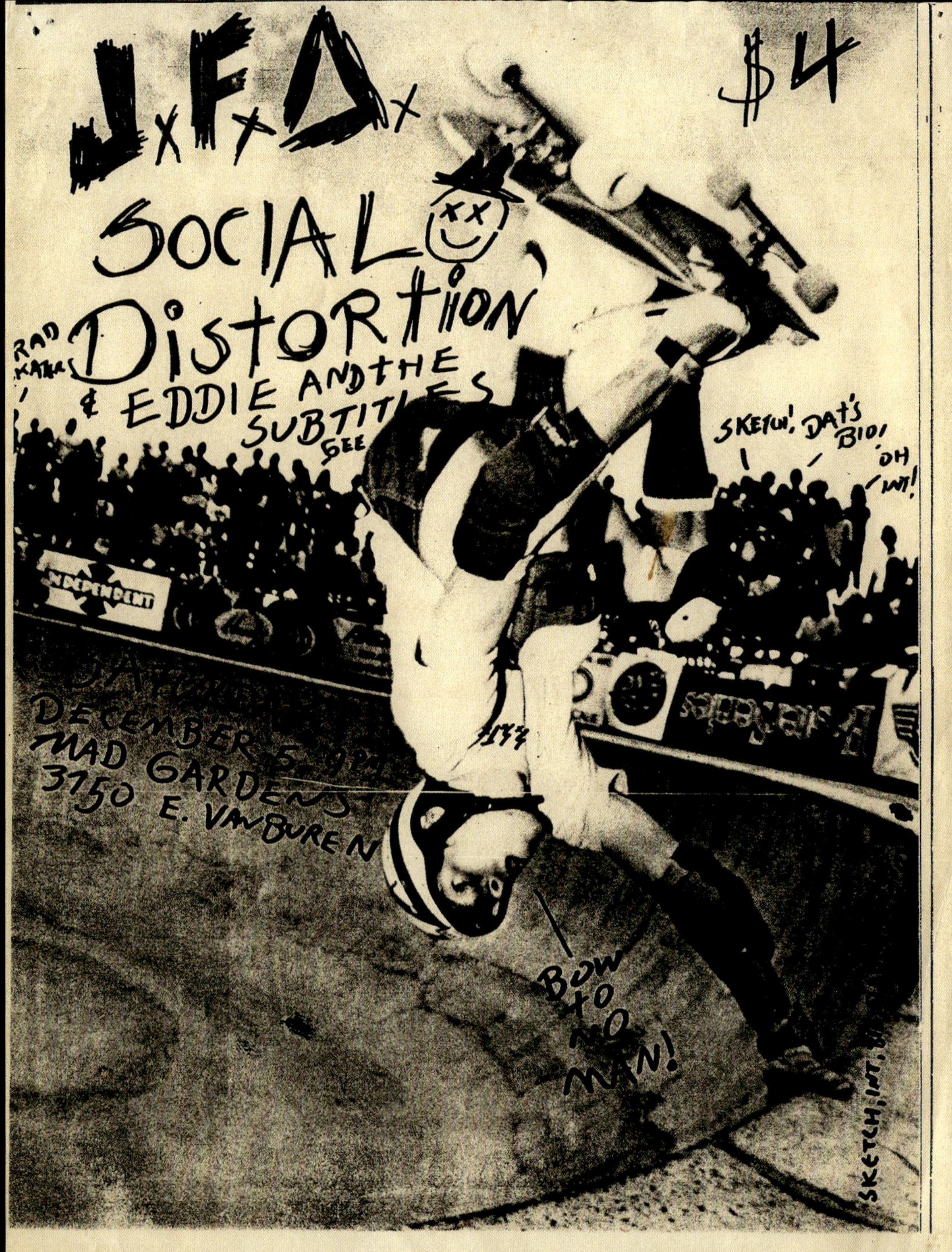

Brian Brannon

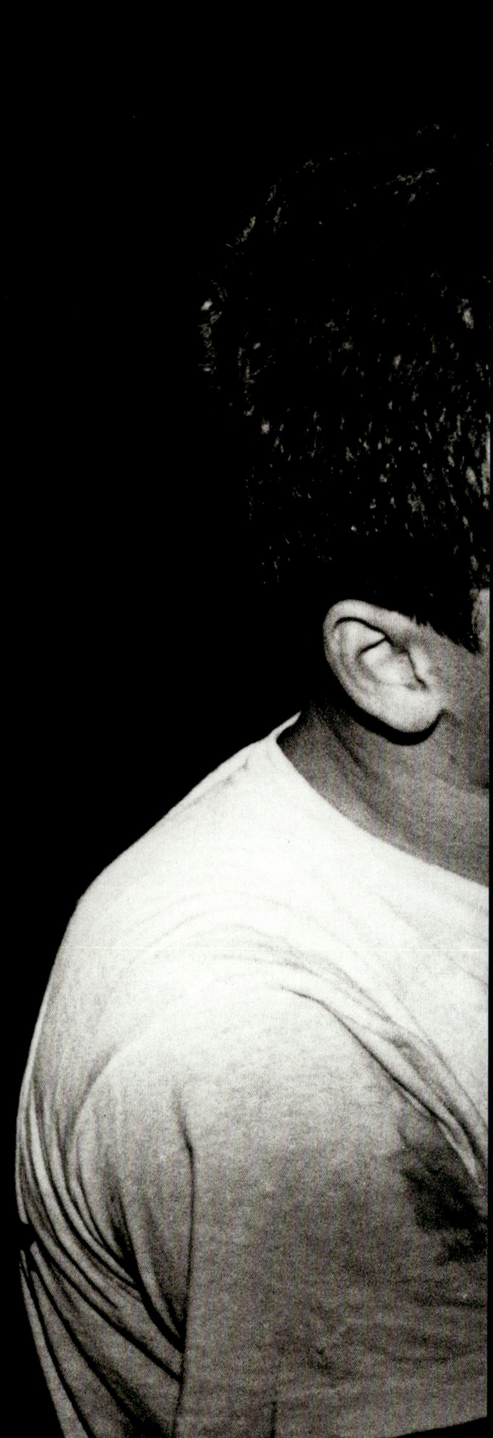

It was chilly the next morning so I wore a jacket to school, which covered the message I had for my schoolmates when I first showed up. *Then I thought, What kind of man am I? What was the point if I'm not going to follow through?* Before first period, off came the jacket.

I drew immediate stares. Everywhere I walked people stopped and pointed. The shit was beginning to hit the fan.

It didn't take long for the jocks to organize (for jocks, anyway.) By third period they had gathered in roving packs which I casually avoided contact with. Fifth period was lunch, and by then everyone knew of the punky little freshman's assertion.

When I walked down the courtyard towards the lunch area, groups of jocks and prepsters closed in behind me with more joining in as I walked past. The snack bar was packed, and I took my place at the back of the line.

I was immediately surrounded by vicious athletic types ready to pound my brains in. I don't remember what happened next, but I think someone said something, then I replied. Someone grabbed me from behind, yanking on my collar. I got pushed, someone grabbed the bottom of my shirt, then someone else, then someone else– my shirt became the rope in a game of tug-of-war while random blows were being delivered to my head and midsection.

That ruckus finally subsided when the shirt was ripped completely off my back. All that remained was an oversized collar hanging around my neck.

They proceeded to march me over to the benches where one of them grabbed and held my arms behind my back. The whole football team was lining up to take turns smashing my face in. It was time for some fast thinking.

One of the biggest and ugliest dudes was at the front of the line. He stepped up and delivered a jab to my stomach. I was ready for it and it didn't hurt, but I sure acted like it did. I fell to the ground coughing and gasping in spasm. I hammed it up so good they actually split, thinking they had killed me.

Continues next page

Sure, it was a wussy move, but what choice did I have?

I wore my jacket shirtless to my next class, then ditched the rest of the day, knowing the bloodthirsty jocks would kill me after school if they saw that I was alive and well.

Things were tense for days after, but it eventually died down. Nowadays if you look around, most of the jocks are punkers, or at least think they are.

Being a punk meant everyone from cops to parents, to schoolmates and teachers were united in hating you. That whole stage of my life is best represented by a flyer for an early JFA-TSOL gig at Madison Square Gardens in Phoenix. It has an illustration my buddy Sean drew of a punker puppeteer about to kick ass on a couple of jock puppeteers. That's what I call artistic justice.

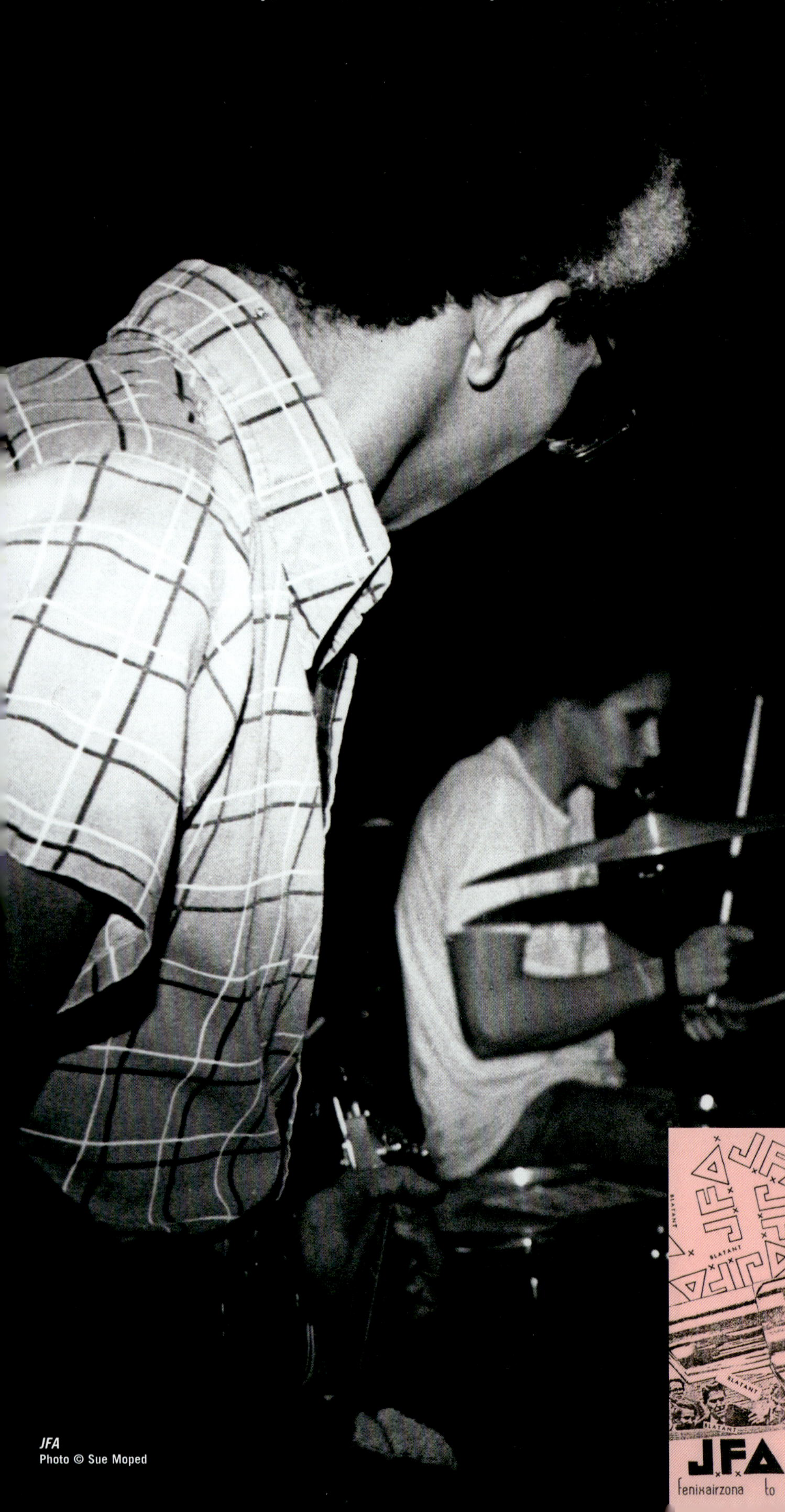

JFA
Photo © Sue Moped

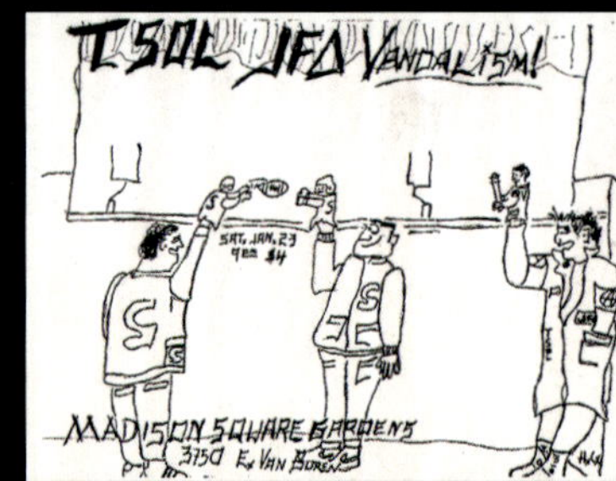

Sean

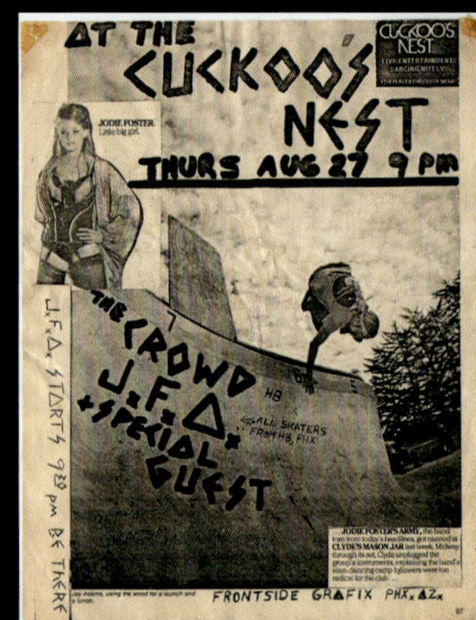

Don Redondo - Orange County venue - oops!

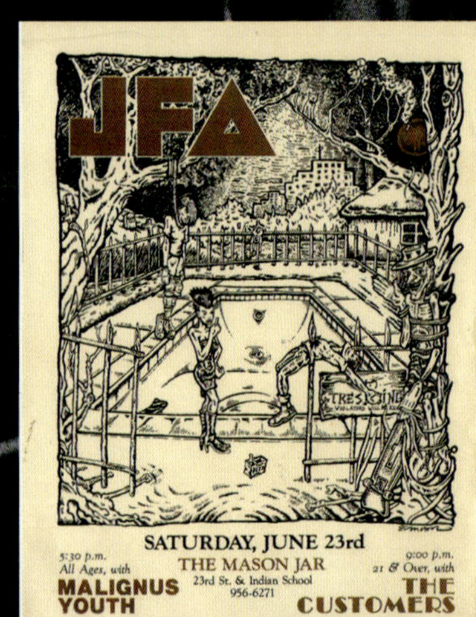

Sam Esmoer

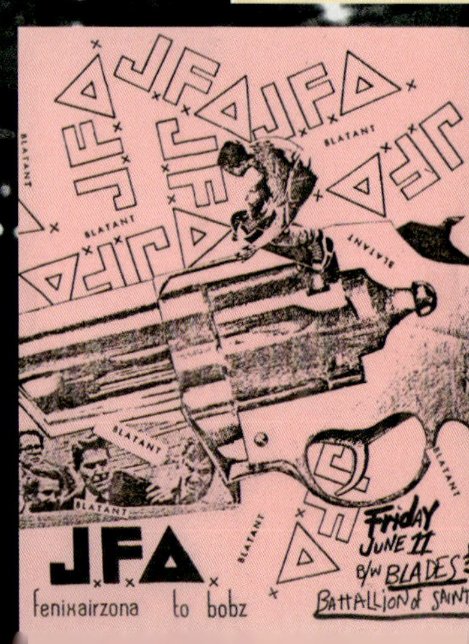

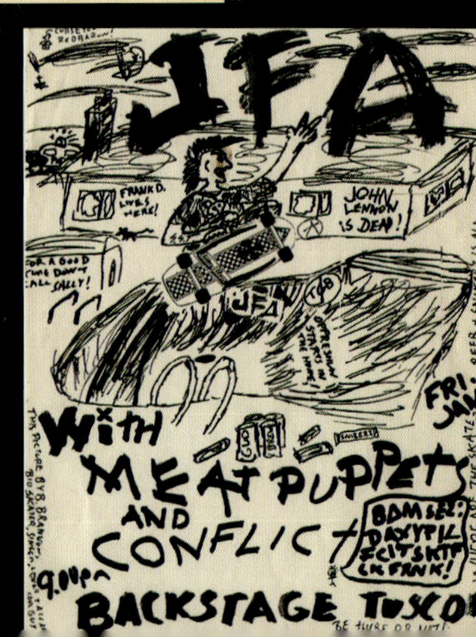

Brian Brannon

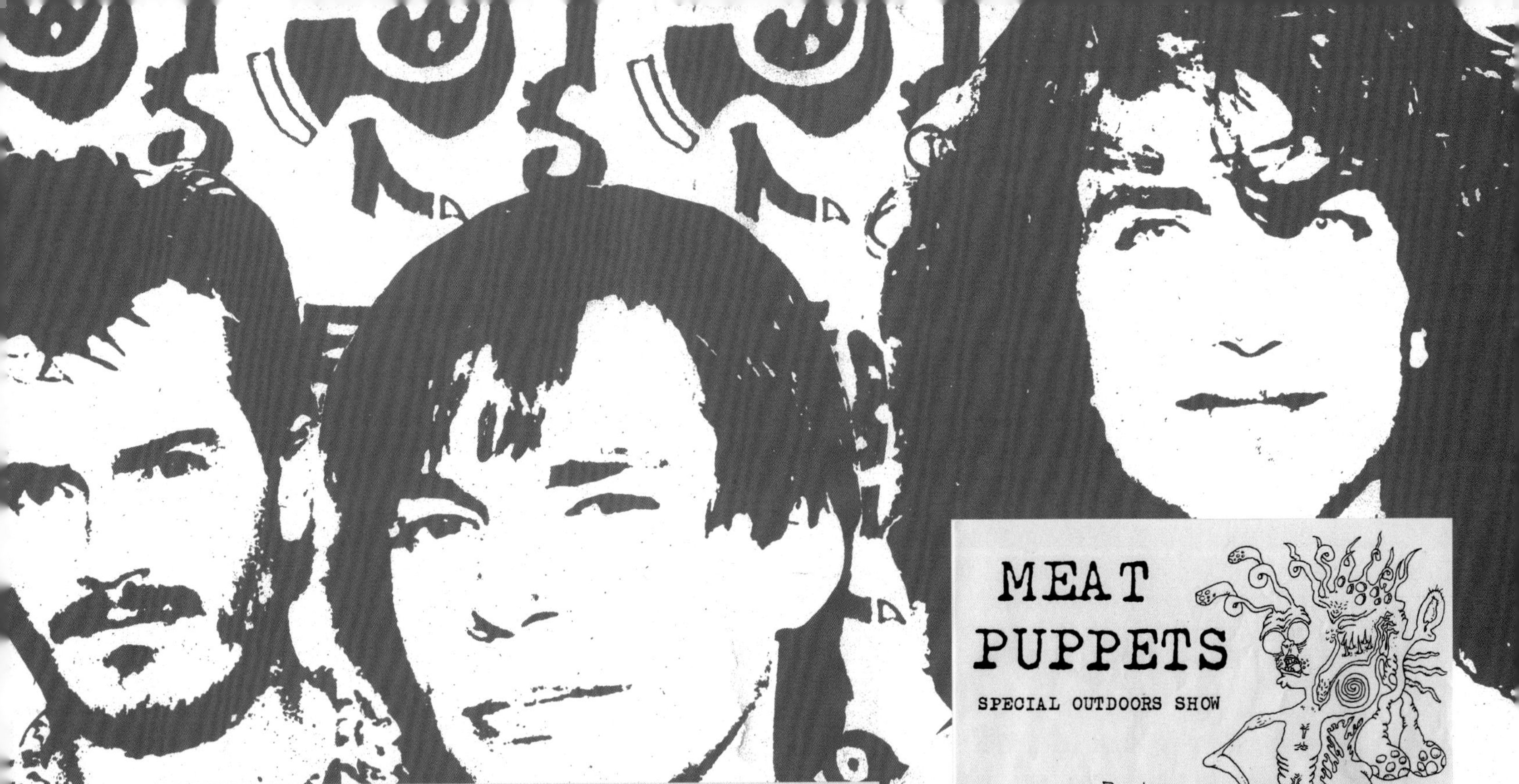

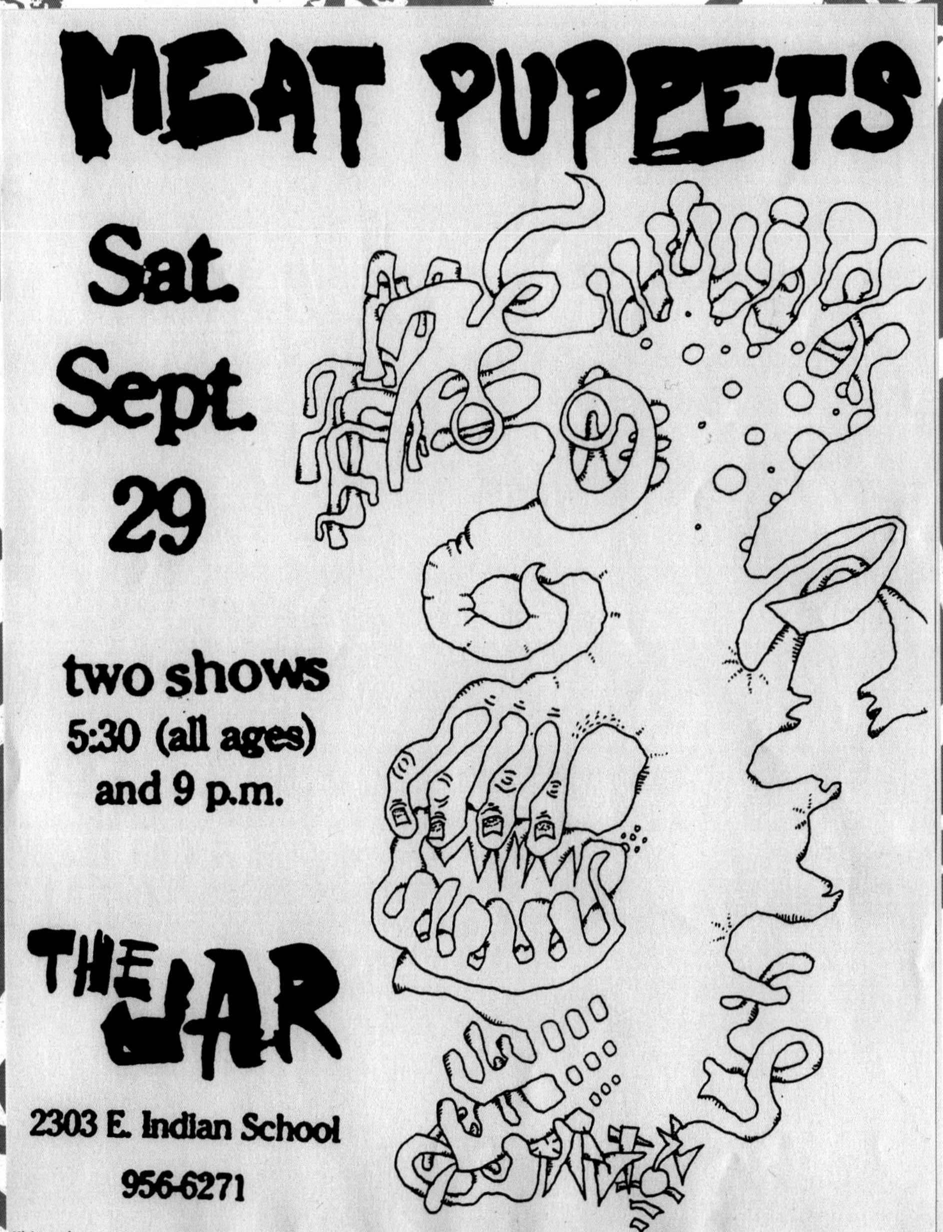

Kirkwood

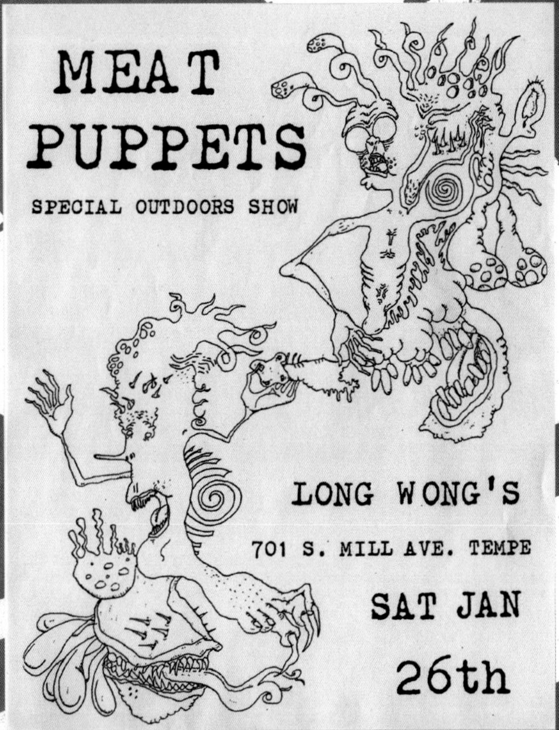

Kirkwood

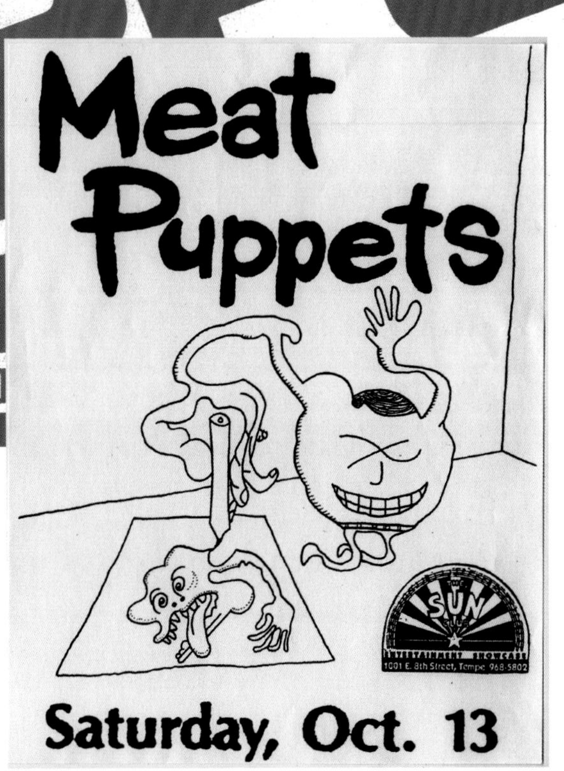

Kirkwood

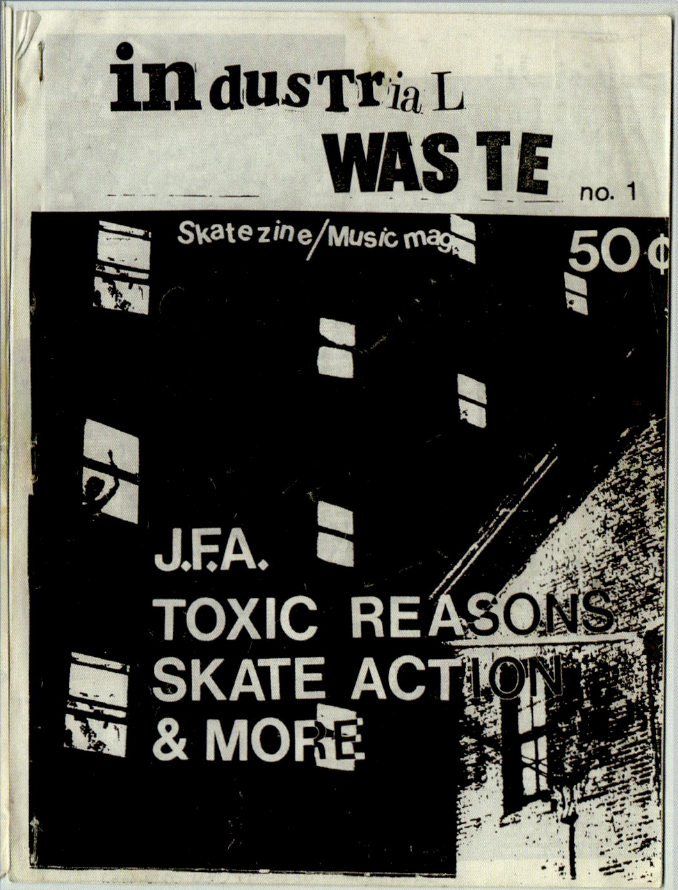
industriaL
WASTE
no. 1
Skatezine/Music mag.
50¢
J.F.A.
TOXIC REASONS
SKATE ACTION
& MORE

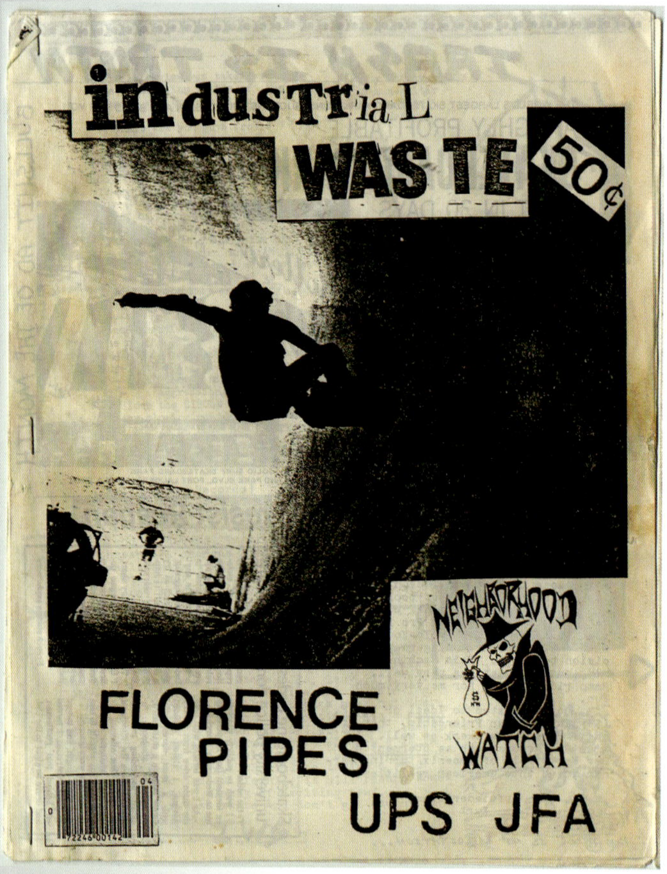
industriaL
WASTE
50¢
NEIGHBORHOOD
WATCH
FLORENCE
PIPES
UPS JFA

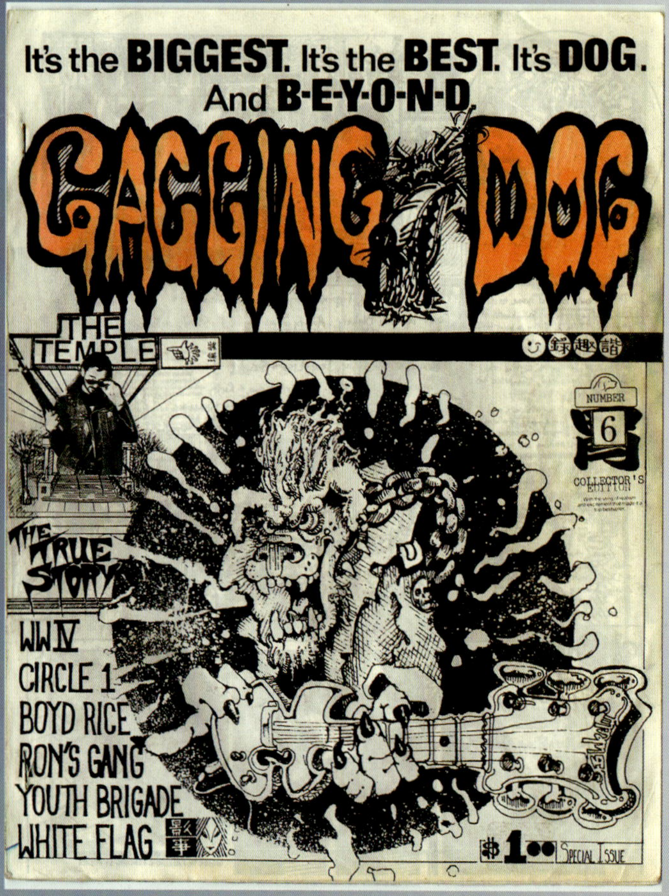
It's the BIGGEST. It's the BEST. It's DOG.
And B-E-Y-O-N-D
GAGGING DOG
THE TEMPLE
NUMBER
6
COLLECTOR'S EDITION
THE TRUE STORY
WW IV
CIRCLE 1
BOYD RICE
RON'S GANG
YOUTH BRIGADE
WHITE FLAG
$1.00
SPECIAL ISSUE

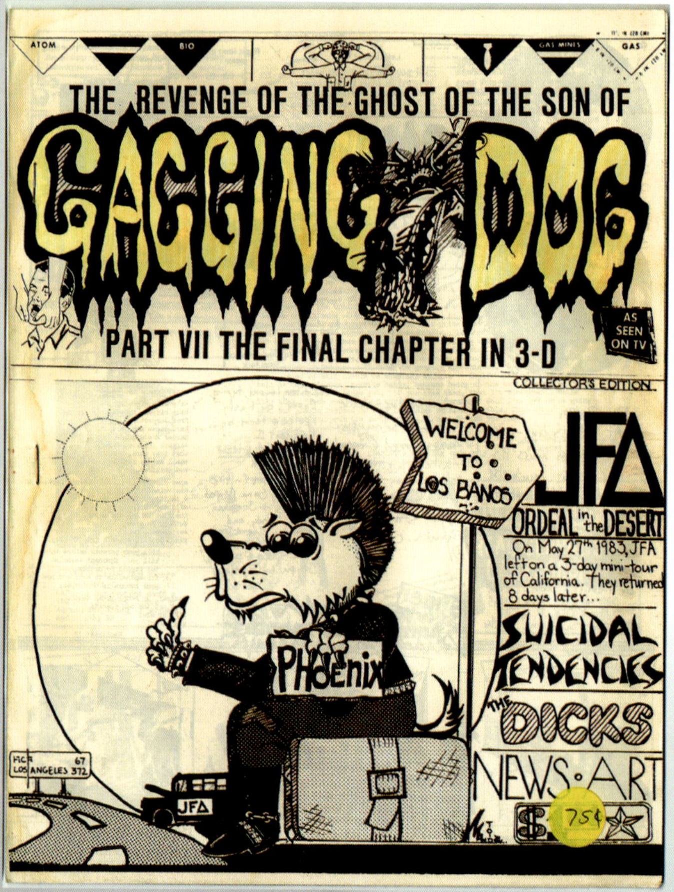
ATOM
BIO
GAS
THE REVENGE OF THE GHOST OF THE SON OF
GAGGING DOG
AS SEEN ON TV
PART VII THE FINAL CHAPTER IN 3-D
COLLECTORS EDITION
WELCOME TO LOS BANOS
JFA
ORDEAL in the DESERT
On May 27th 1983, JFA left on a 3-day mini-tour of California. They returned 8 days later...
SUICIDAL TENDENCIES
THE DICKS
NEWS·ART
Phoenix
JFA
LOS ANGELES
75¢

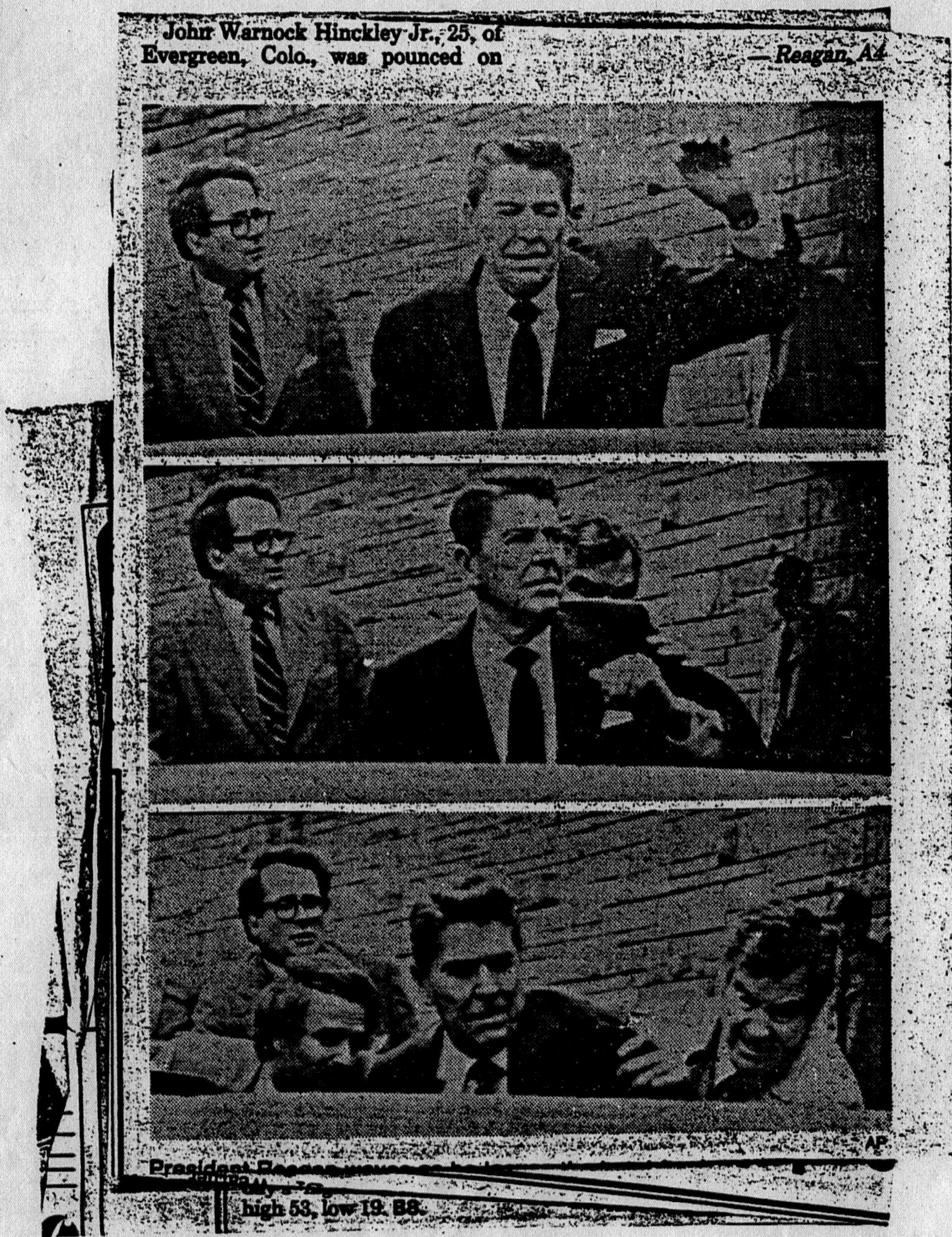

ADOLESCENTS LA
MEAT PUPPETS
JODIE FOSTER'S ARMY
THE FARM LA

SATURDAY FEB 20 9pm
MAD GARDENS 3750 e VAN BUREN

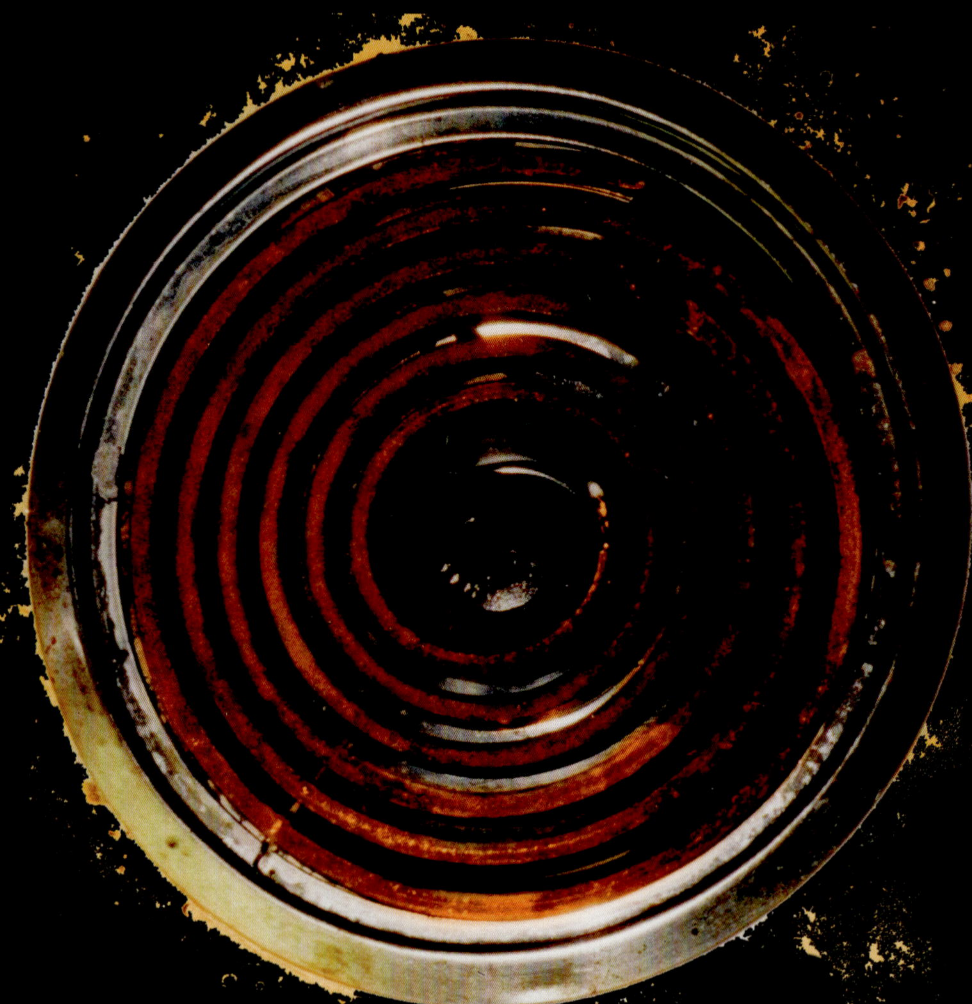

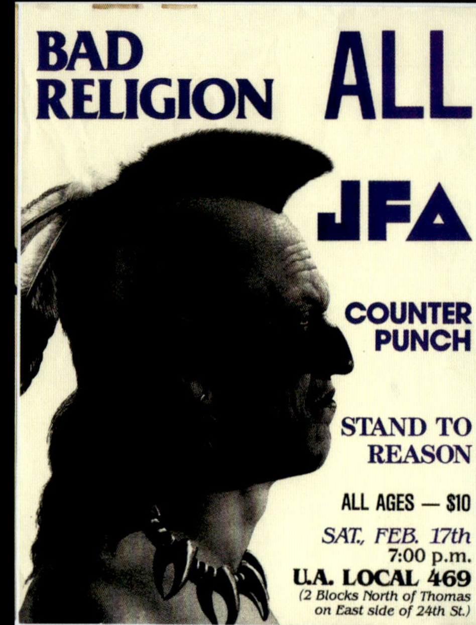

Brian Brannon

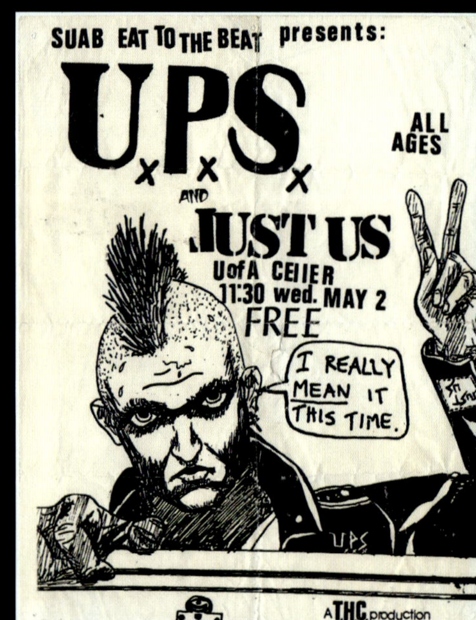

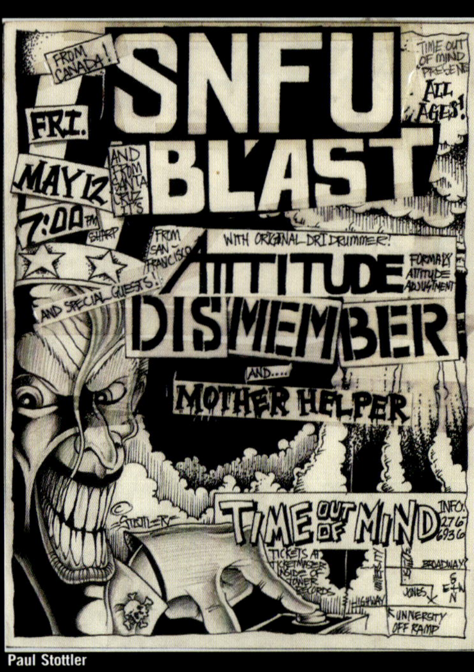

Paul Stottler

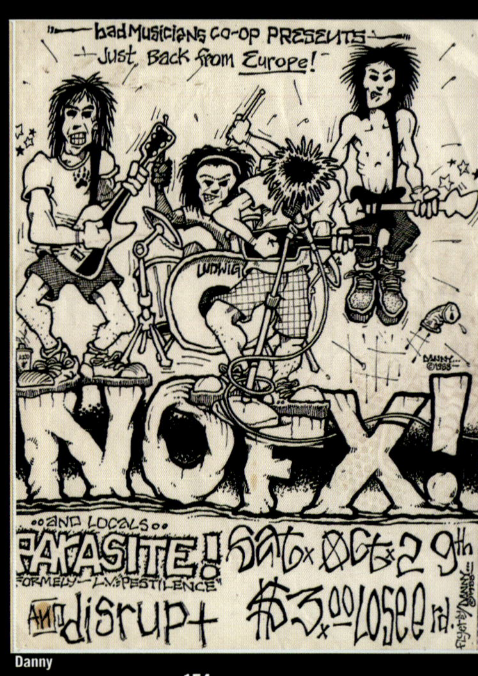

Danny

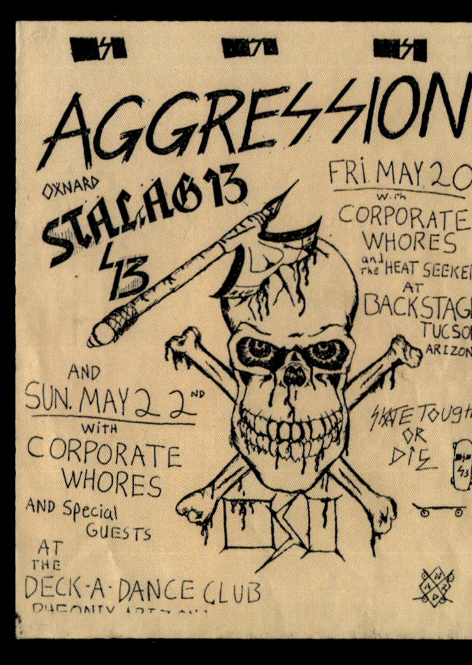

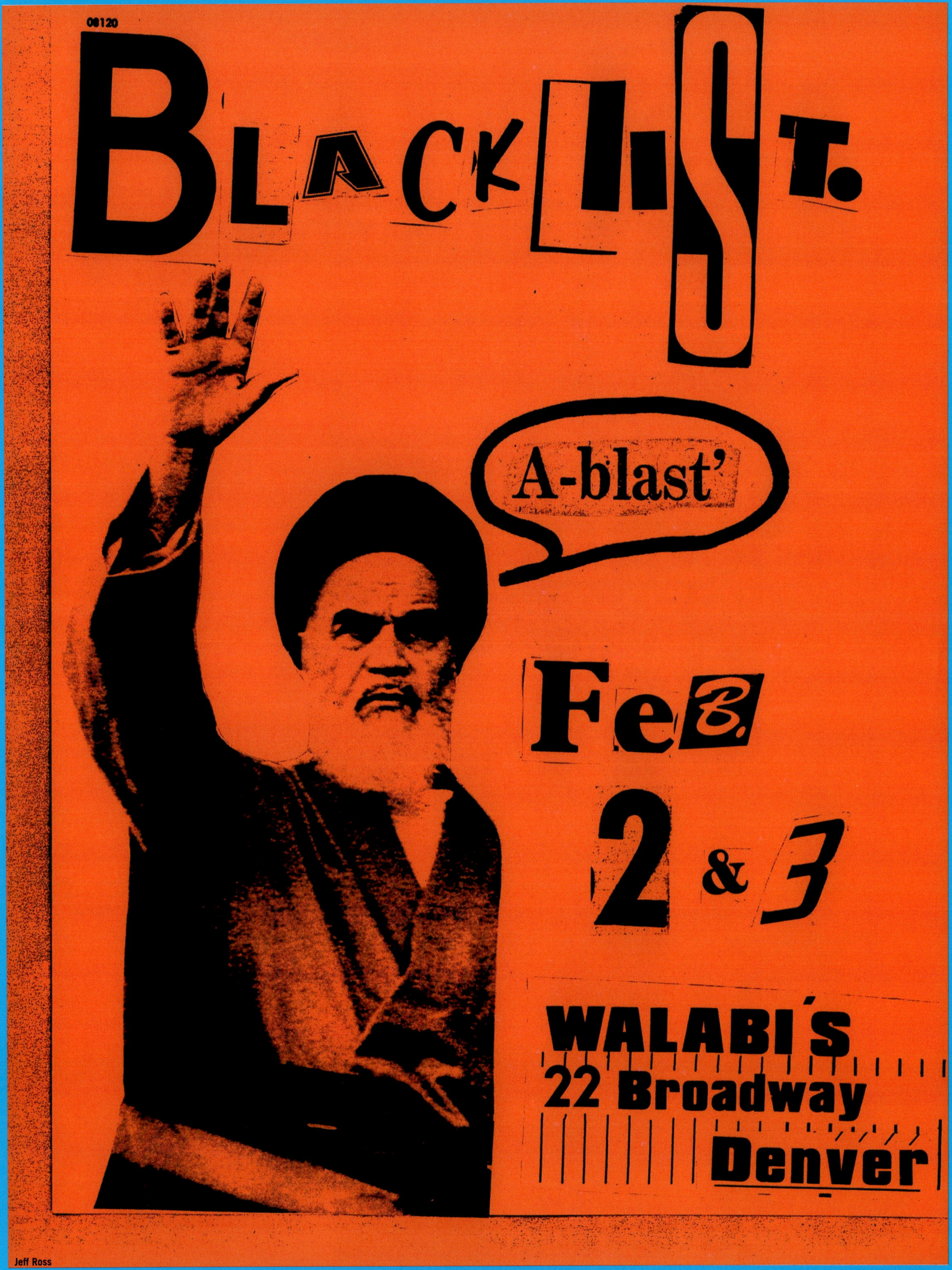

Jeff Ross

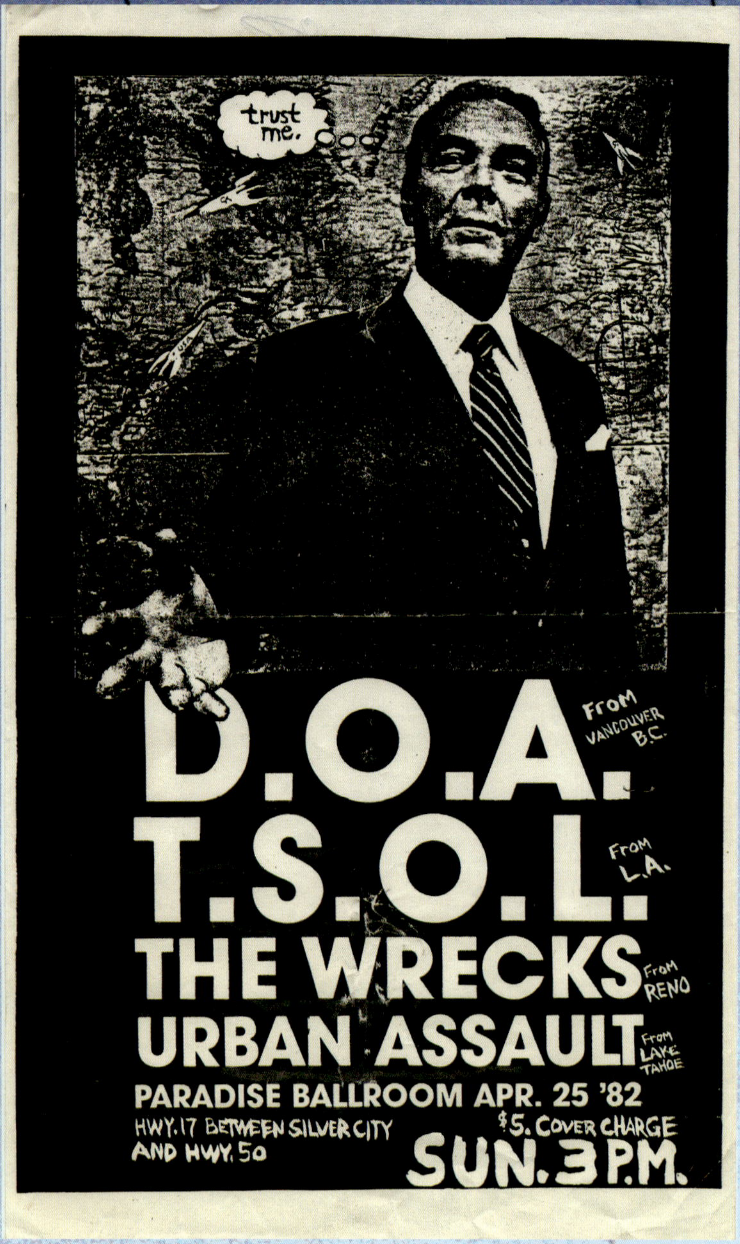
trust me.
D.O.A.
FROM VANCOUVER B.C.
T.S.O.L.
FROM L.A.
THE WRECKS
FROM RENO
URBAN ASSAULT
FROM LAKE TAHOE
PARADISE BALLROOM APR. 25 '82
HWY. 17 BETWEEN SILVER CITY AND HWY. 50
$5. COVER CHARGE
SUN. 3 P.M.

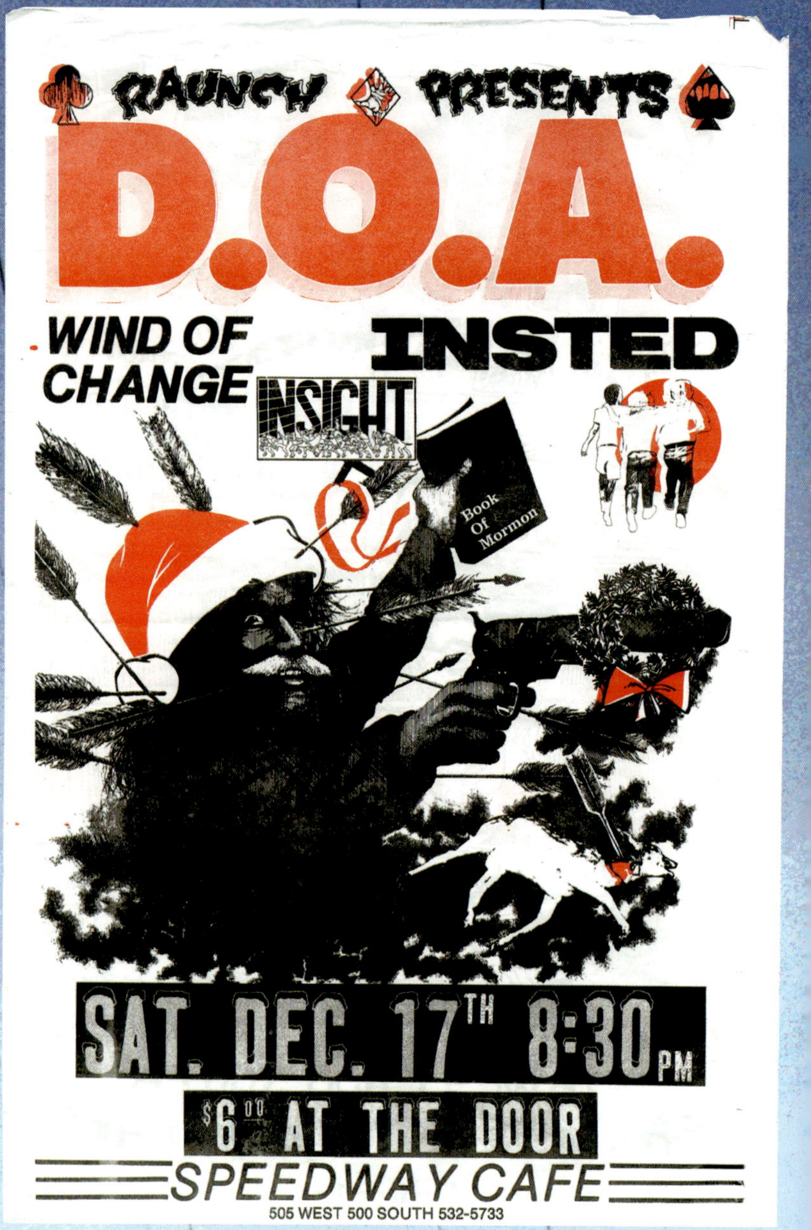
RAUNCH PRESENTS
D.O.A.
WIND OF CHANGE
INSTED
INSIGHT
Book Of Mormon
SAT. DEC. 17TH 8:30 PM
$6.00 AT THE DOOR
SPEEDWAY CAFE
505 WEST 500 SOUTH 532-5733

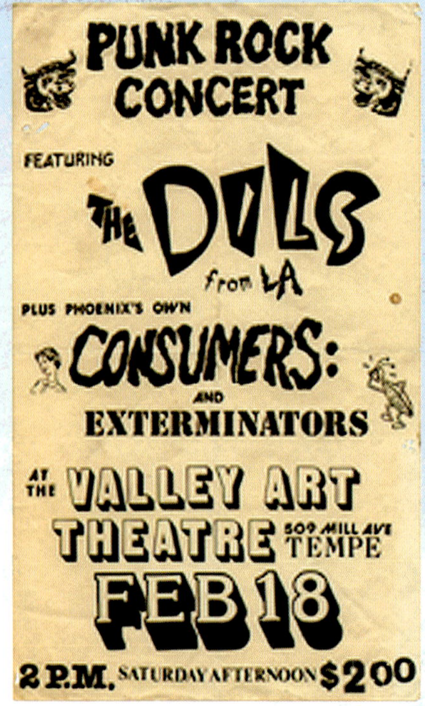
PUNK ROCK CONCERT
FEATURING
THE DILS
from LA
PLUS PHOENIX'S OWN
CONSUMERS:
AND
EXTERMINATORS
AT THE VALLEY ART THEATRE
509 MILL AVE TEMPE
FEB 18
2 P.M. SATURDAY AFTERNOON $2.00

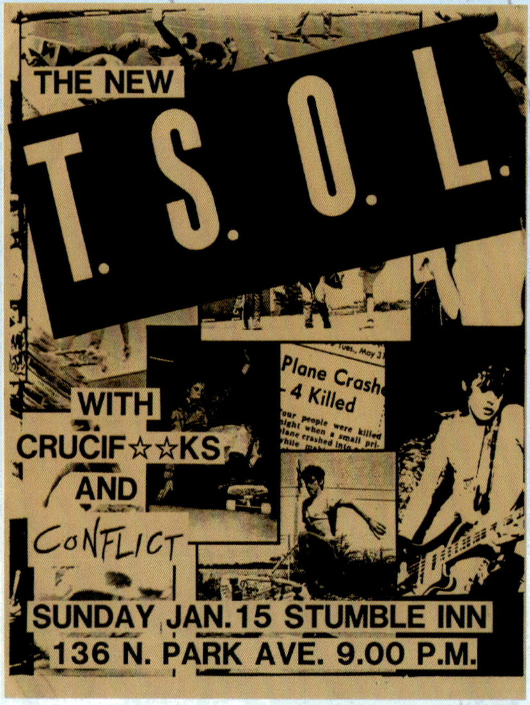
THE NEW
T.S.O.L.
Plane Crash 4 Killed
WITH
CRUCIF☆☆KS
AND
CONFLICT
SUNDAY JAN. 15 STUMBLE INN
136 N. PARK AVE. 9.00 P.M.

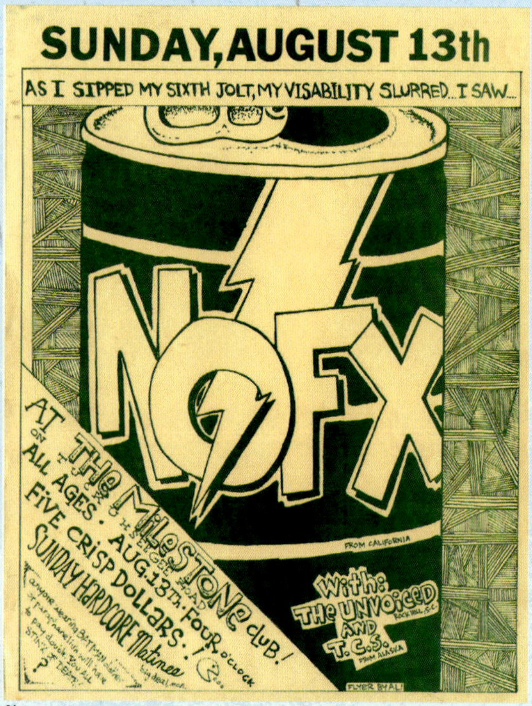
SUNDAY, AUGUST 13th
AS I SIPPED MY SIXTH JOLT, MY VISABILITY SLURRED... I SAW...
NOFX
FROM CALIFORNIA
AT The MILESTONE CLUB!
ON ALL AGES · AUG. 13TH · FOUR O'CLOCK
FIVE CRISP DOLLARS!
SUNDAY HARDCORE Matinee
With: THE UNVOICED
AND
T.C.S.
FROM ALASKA
FLYER BY AL!

AI

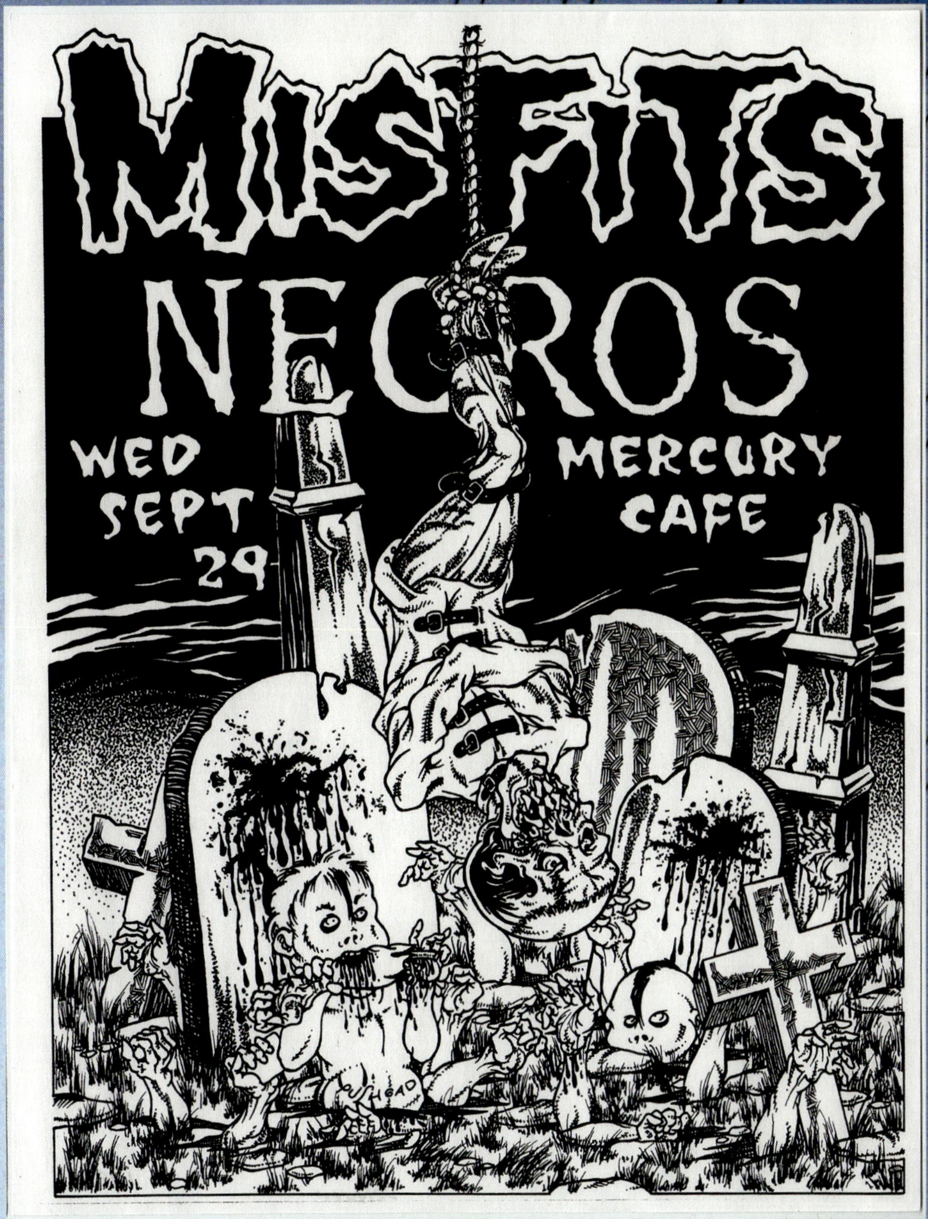

Pushead

Denver

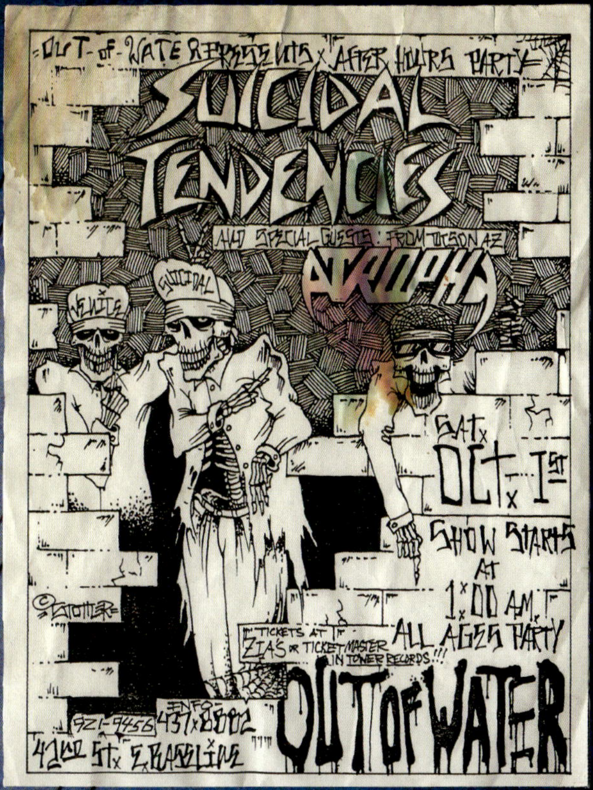

Paul Stottler

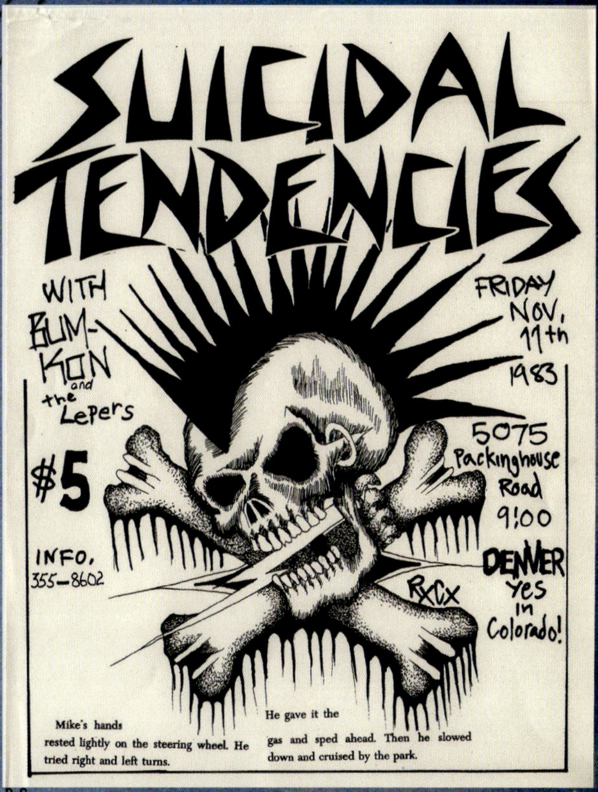

RxCx

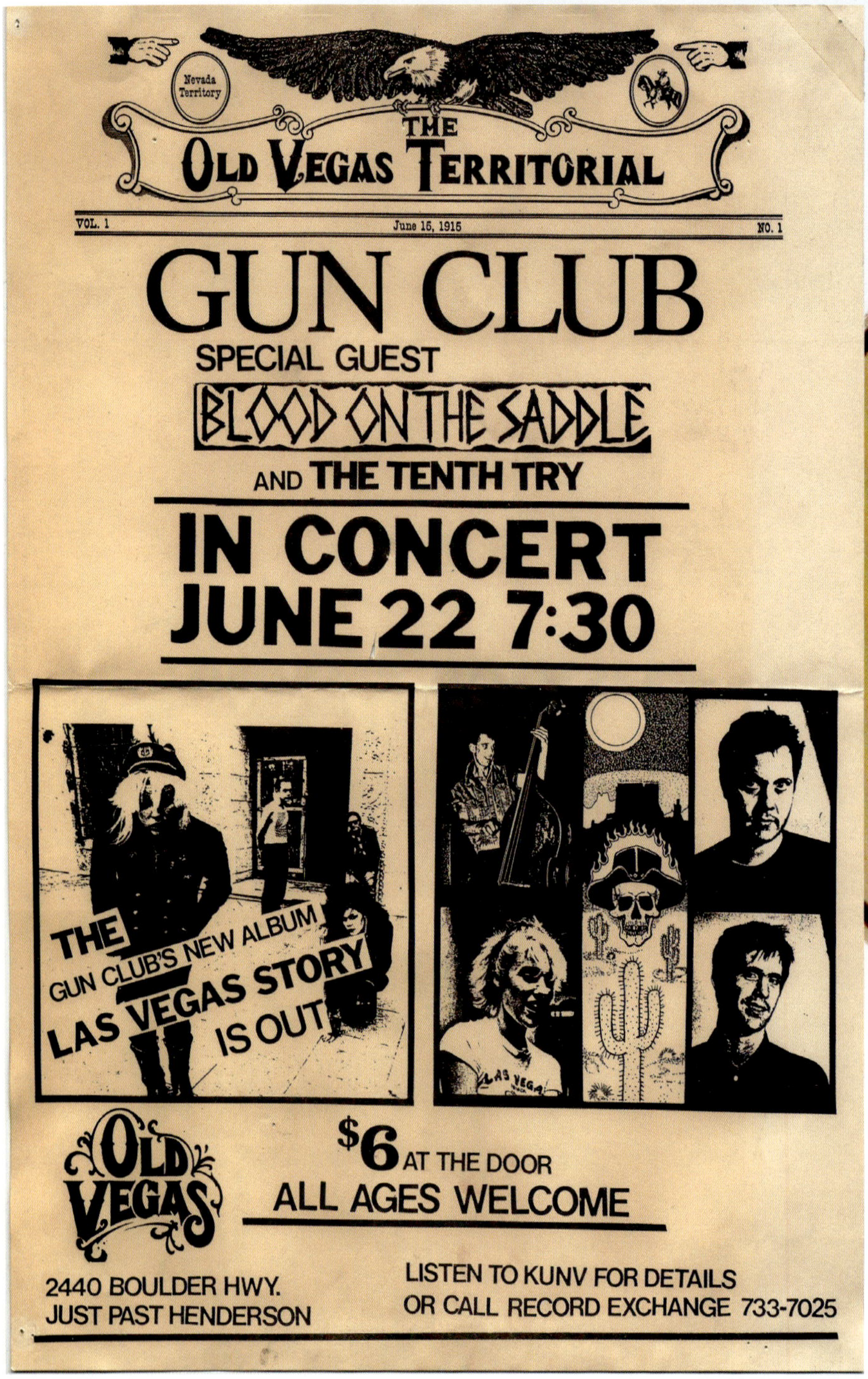
Nevada Territory
THE
OLD VEGAS TERRITORIAL
VOL. 1
June 15, 1915
NO. 1
GUN CLUB
SPECIAL GUEST
BLOOD ON THE SADDLE
AND THE TENTH TRY
IN CONCERT
JUNE 22 7:30
THE GUN CLUB'S NEW ALBUM LAS VEGAS STORY IS OUT
LAS VEGAS
OLD VEGAS
$6 AT THE DOOR
ALL AGES WELCOME
2440 BOULDER HWY.
JUST PAST HENDERSON
LISTEN TO KUNV FOR DETAILS
OR CALL RECORD EXCHANGE 733-7025

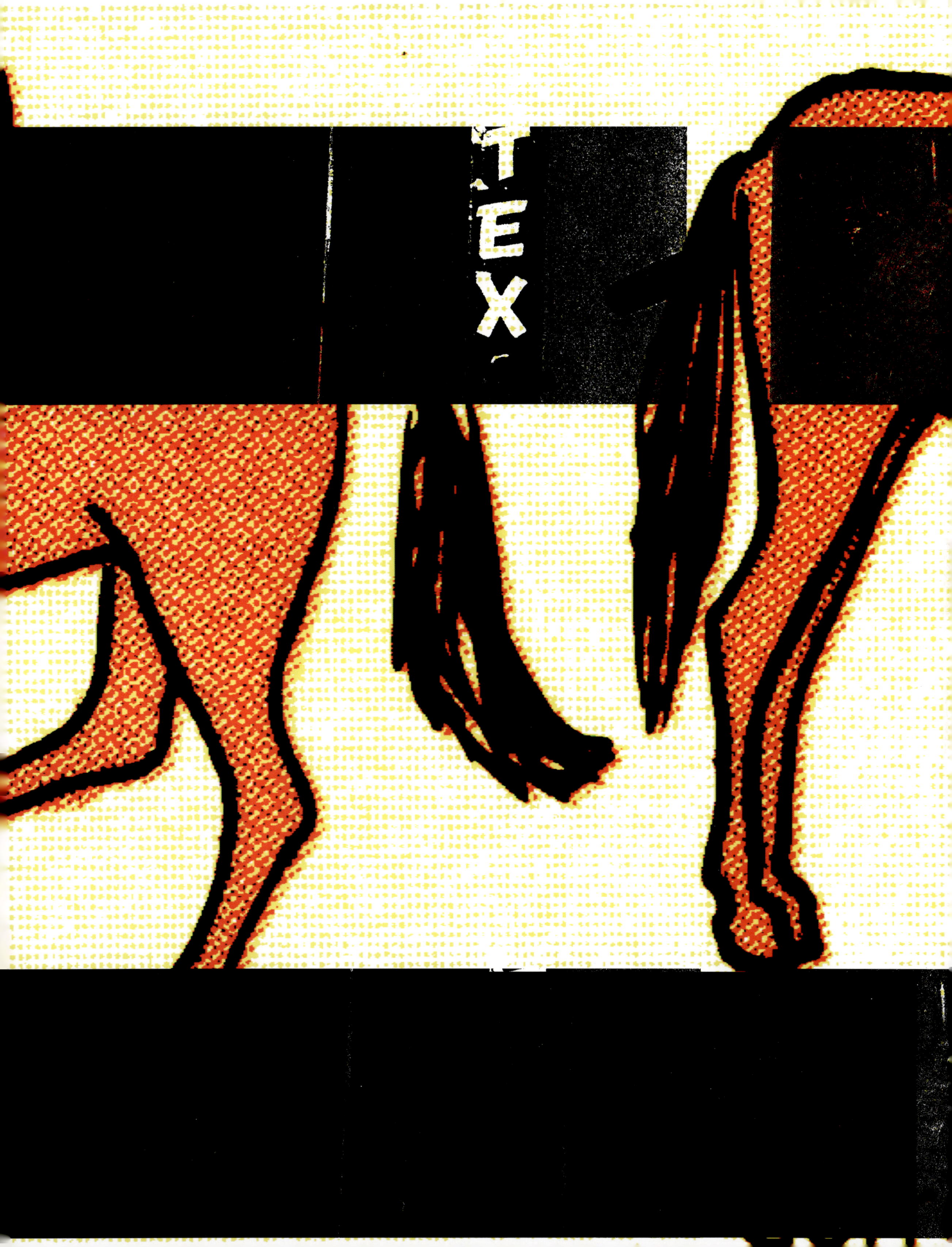
TEX

In 1980 I cut my hair. This was no small act, hair (long hair) being the primary indicator of your disaffection at the point, and I dug the rebellious rush of shifting from 70s hippie skate kid (or freak) to the 17-year-old nihilist outsider skate kid (or freak.) Punk's anti-hair possibilities were not widely accepted in Texas at that time, which is very odd considering that my flat-top buzz-cut was about as redneck as you could get.

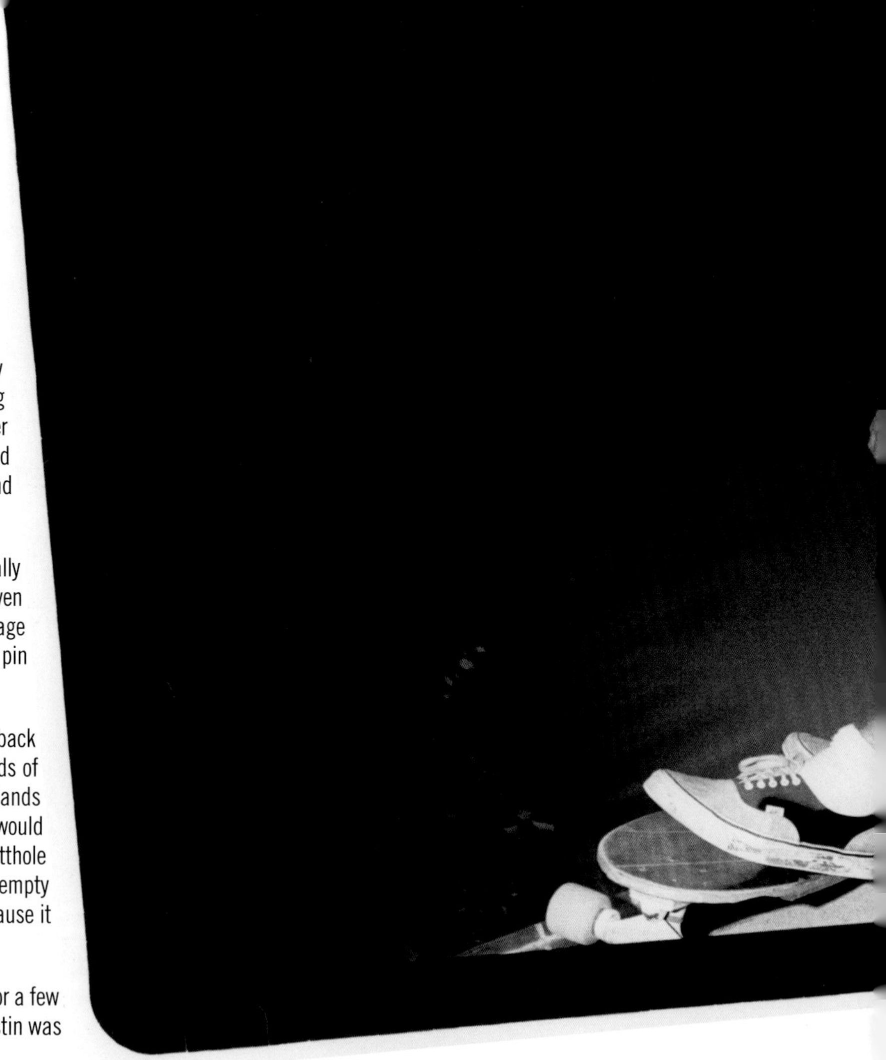

My brother's band, the Big Boys, had just celebrated their first record release party at Inner Sanctum, and I took off for the Speedway Barber Shop, famous for plumping up Freddie Fender's pompadour. A couple of friends tagged along, and I'll never forget the looks on their faces as the huge clumps of hair hit the ground. $2.75 and ten minutes later I had committed, joined the un-group, became an individual, and admitted the obvious: I'm a punk.

MTV was a ways away from dictating cool yet, and Punk Rock had not been officially appropriated by major labels yet. Radio wouldn't touch it. the only time Punk was even mentioned in the media was Mike Wallace commenting sardonically on some footage of pasty, nail-headed British punks sneering, dripping blood from the huge safety pin through their cheek and spitting out teeth.

This pre- internet, pre-MTV lack of information created an insular scene - an outback oasis in the wastelands of Texas that never failed to surprise the van-touring bands of skaters and other disenfranchised youth from similar scenes across the country. Bands like Husker Du, Minutemen, J.F.A., Fear, Minor Threat, X, these bands from far away would prove to be powerful, if distant, cousins to The Big Boys, The Dicks, Scratch Acid, Butthole Surfers, all doing the musical equivalent of climbing a fence and skateboarding an empty pool. No one told you to do it, a lot of people advised against it - but you did it because it felt right to you.

Underage drinking, drugs, 5 bands, $3 to get in, then skate home plowed to sleep for a few hours before school. The thing I loved most about the burgeoning punk scene in Austin was that it was truly scary - Anything could happen...

Anything except a record deal, that is. The concept was so preposterous as to never even occur to anyone, and that made the music (and the screaming, feedback, noise and bodily function) simply about right...now. Do it yourself - anyone can do this. YOU can do this. Do SOMETHING. Not one Big Boys gig went by without one of the guys admonishing the crowd to "start your own band!"

Start your own band. Make a fanzine. Cut your hair. Make up some T-shirts. Create a poster.

A lot of bands saved up money from odd jobs and put out a record, which had to be "self-promoted," a grand term for all the schlepping around involved...then slamming out 100 free copies on some unsuspecting copier at work, or imposing on your pal's night shift at Kinko's to get it printed on color paper.

Frequently there were 5 or 6 different posters for the same show, one or more from each band on the bill. In a time before Photoshop®, Illustrator® and QuarkXpress®, punk rock was handmade. Anything that could be put in the 1/8" focus of a Xerox® machine while the light was travelling back and forth under the glass could be your art. Hand lettering and the drummer's face plastered against the copier window touted your 11:00 slot Thursday at Raul's.

The ultimate poster campaign was from madman David Yow, and his "poster band" Toxic Shock. David (Yow is his real name, how punk is that?) sang in such illustrious bands as G.O.D. (God On Drugs,) Toxic Shock (named after the gruesome-newscast-soundbyte diagnosis-of-death fashionable in 1981), Scratch Acid and currently Jesus Lizard. He can "draw real purty," and has a sick mind to boot.

Toxic Shock was a non-existent band, but David advertised it on telephone poles around town, an artistic expression that was reported (well, commented on,) in the local media. Andy Warhol would have loved it. It was punk that was more Lenny Bruce than Sid Vicious, but it was definitely punk.

There was a Punk Poster Art show at UT once, but no one was thinking historical relevance at the time, when there were details like guest lists, eviction notices and term papers to contend with.

As producer and imminent space clarinetist Spot said on the liner notes of a Big Boys record, "If you were there, no explanation is necessary; if you weren't, no explanation will ever be satisfactory..."

Nathan Gates

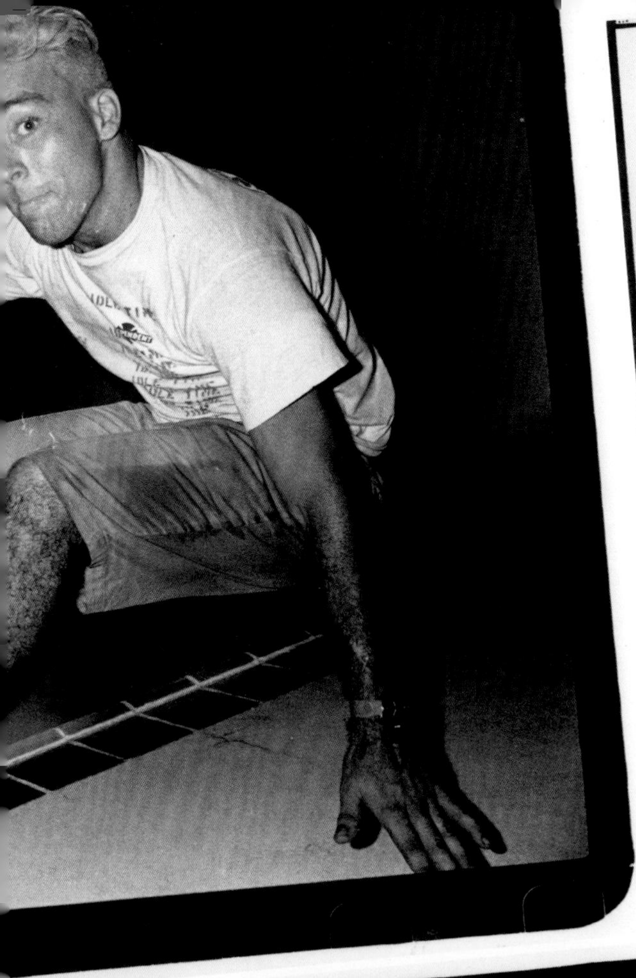

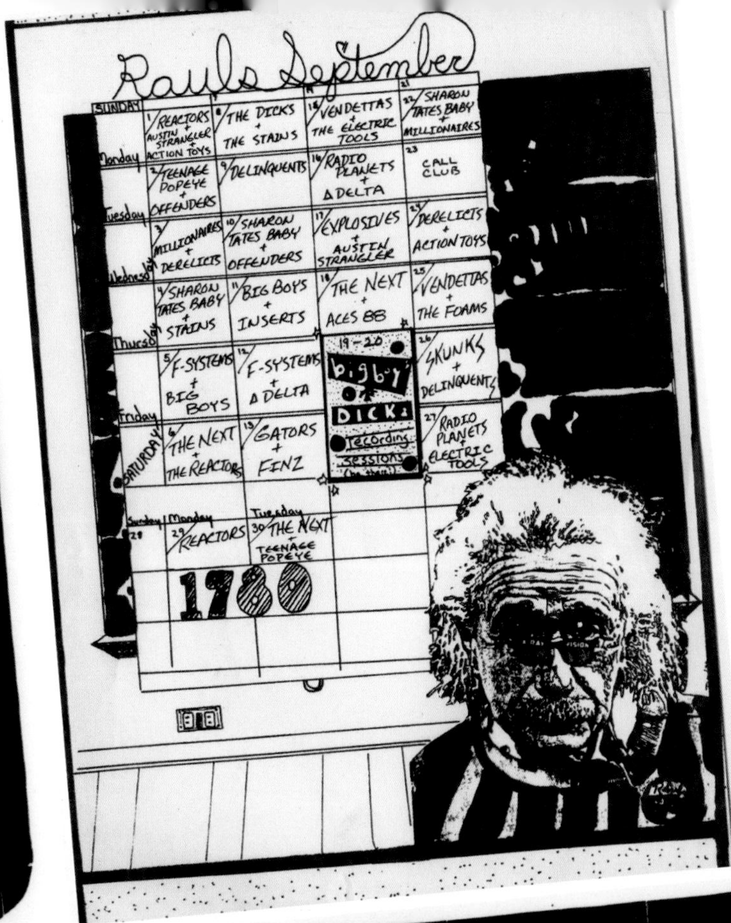
Rauls September
SUNDAY
Monday
Tuesday
Wednesday
Thursday
Friday
SATURDAY
1 REACTORS + AUSTIN STRANGLER + ACTION TOYS
8 THE DICKS + THE STAINS
15 VENDETTAS + THE ELECTRIC TOOLS
22 SHARON TATES BABY + MILLIONAIRES
2 TEENAGE POPEYE + OFFENDERS
9 DELINQUENTS
16 RADIO PLANETS + Δ DELTA
23 CALL CLUB
3 MILLIONAIRES + DERELICTS
10 SHARON TATES BABY + OFFENDERS
17 EXPLOSIVES + AUSTIN STRANGLER
24 DERELICTS + ACTION TOYS
4 SHARON TATES BABY + STAINS
11 BIG BOYS + INSERTS
18 THE NEXT + ACES 88
25 VENDETTAS + THE FOAMS
5 F-SYSTEMS + BIG BOYS
12 F-SYSTEMS + Δ DELTA
19–20 big boy DICKS recording sessions
26 SKUNKS + DELINQUENTS
6 THE NEXT + THE REACTORS
13 GATORS + FINZ
27 RADIO PLANETS + ELECTRIC TOOLS
Sunday 28
Monday 29 REACTORS
Tuesday 30 THE NEXT + TEENAGE POPEYE
1780

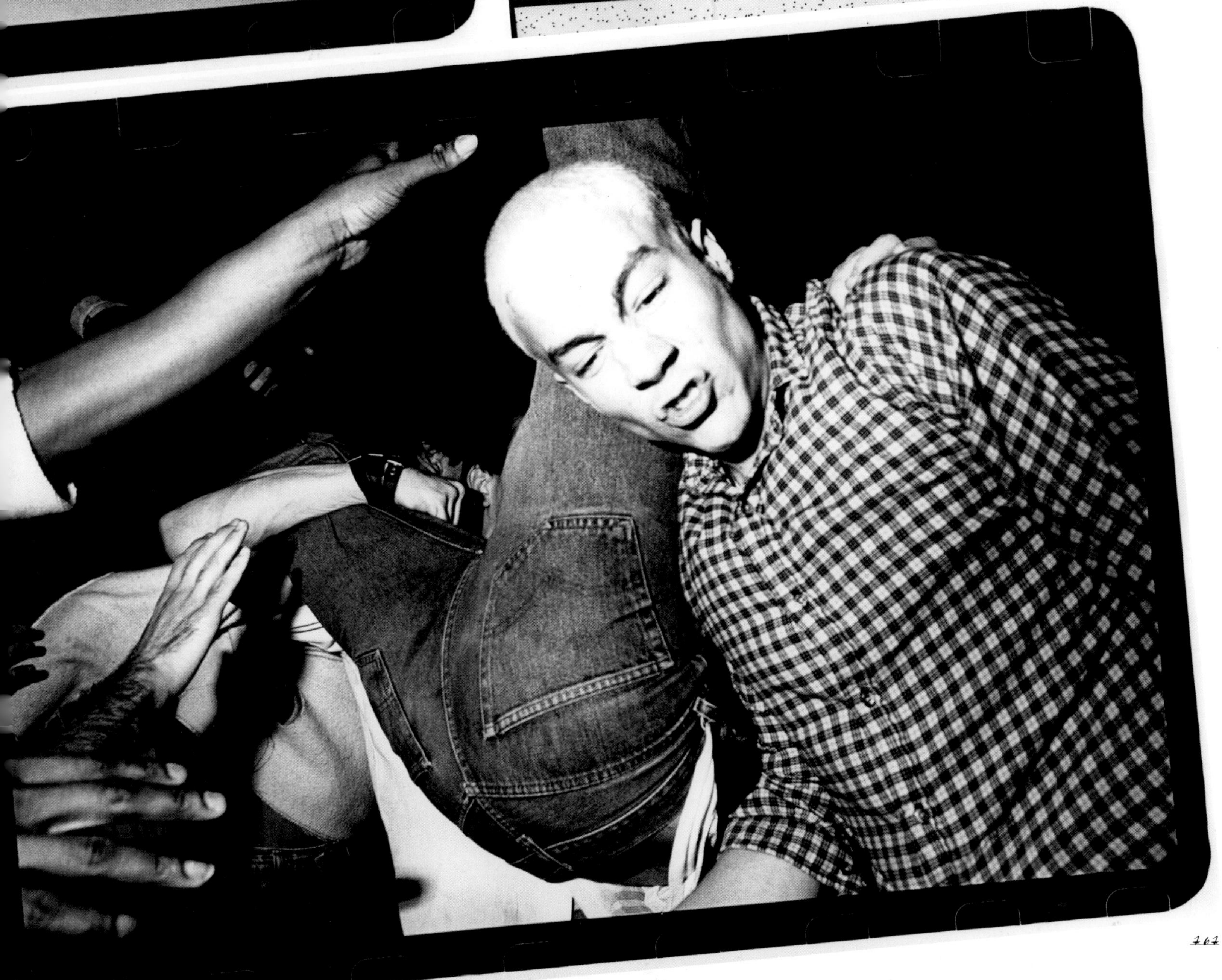

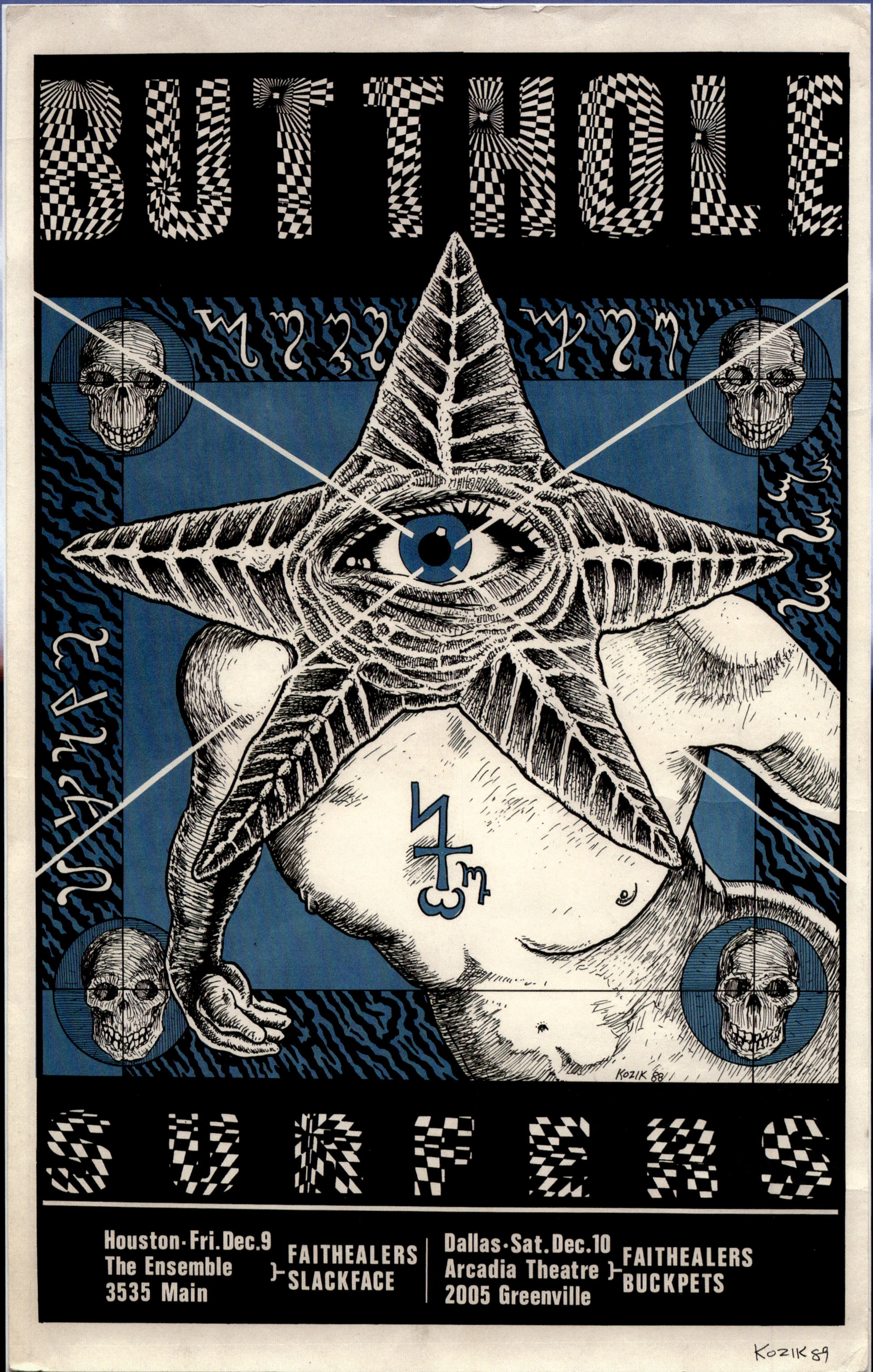
BUTTHOLE
SURFERS
KOZIK '88
Houston · Fri. Dec. 9
The Ensemble
3535 Main
FAITHEALERS
SLACKFACE
Dallas · Sat. Dec. 10
Arcadia Theatre
2005 Greenville
FAITHEALERS
BUCKPETS
KOZIK 89

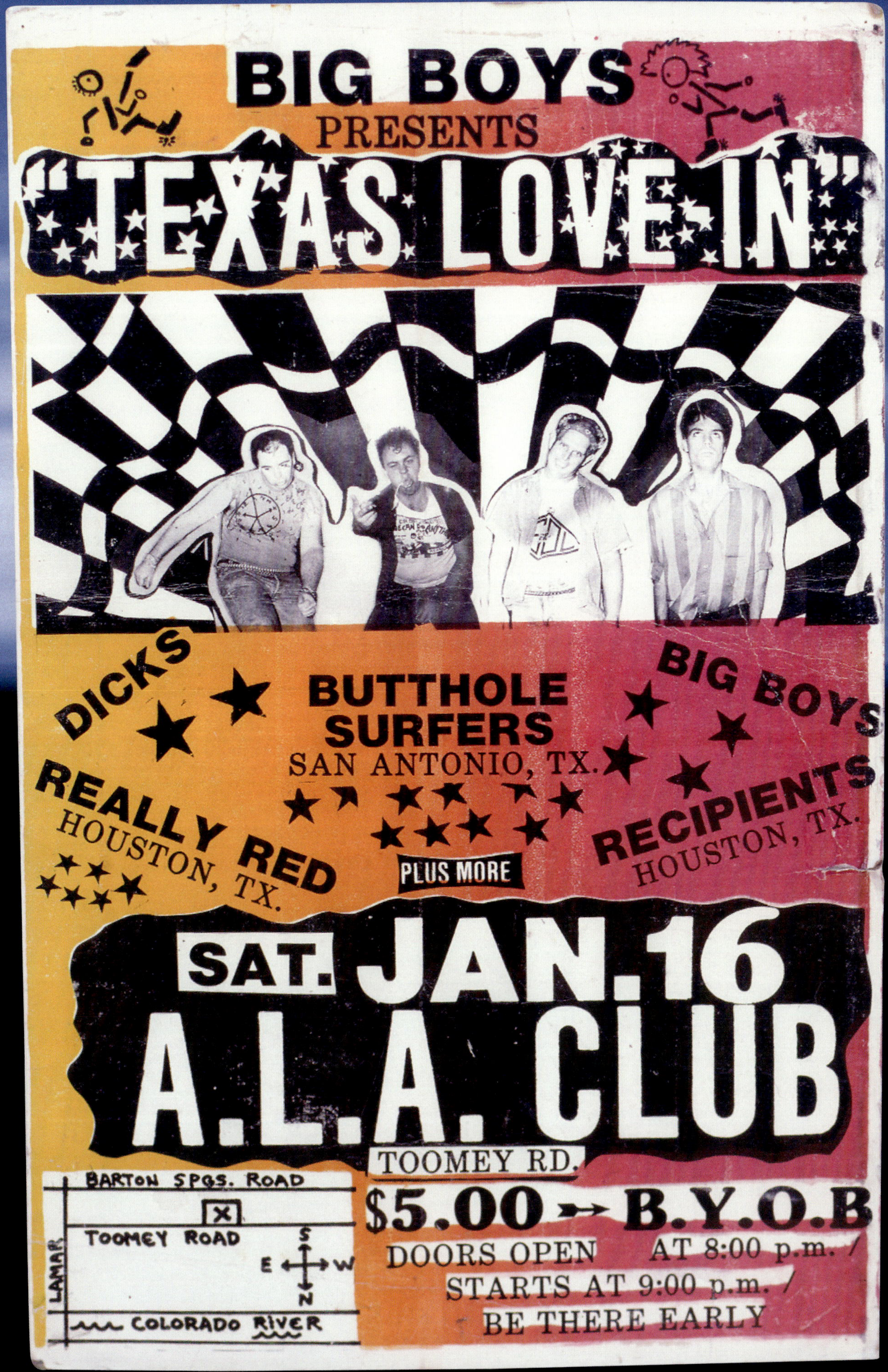

Randall L. Biscuit Turner

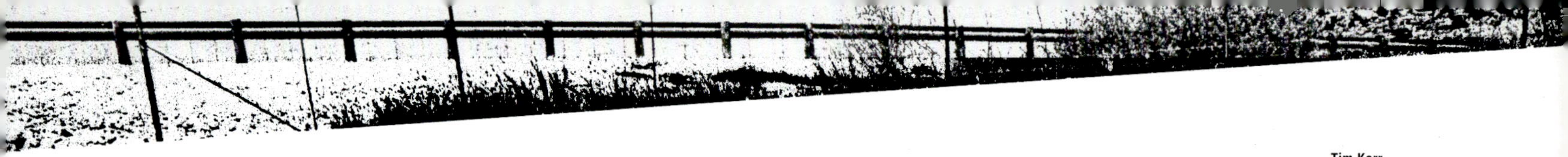

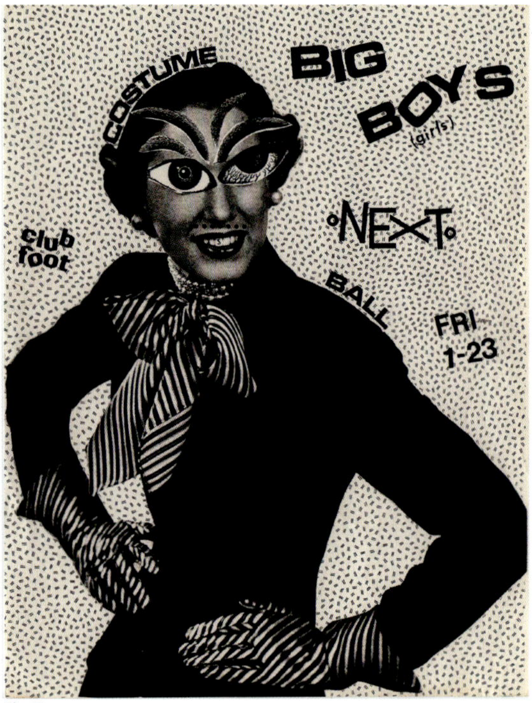

Tim Kerr

Tim Kerr

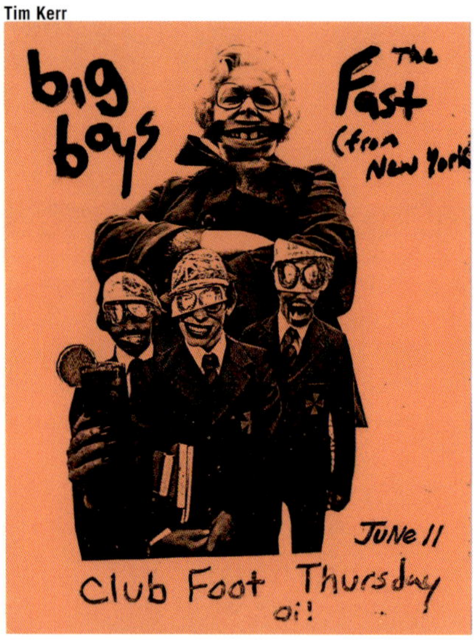

Tim Kerr

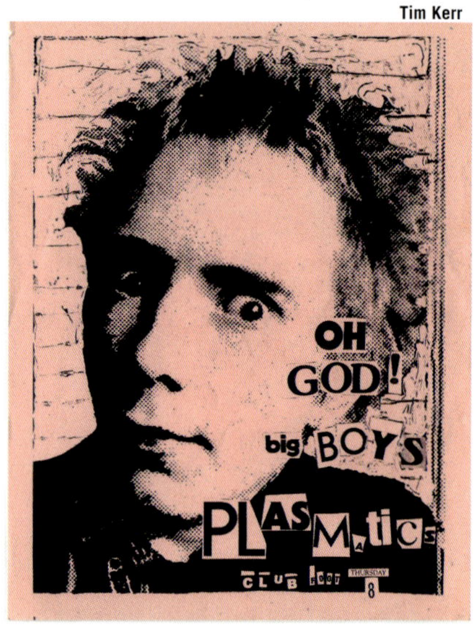

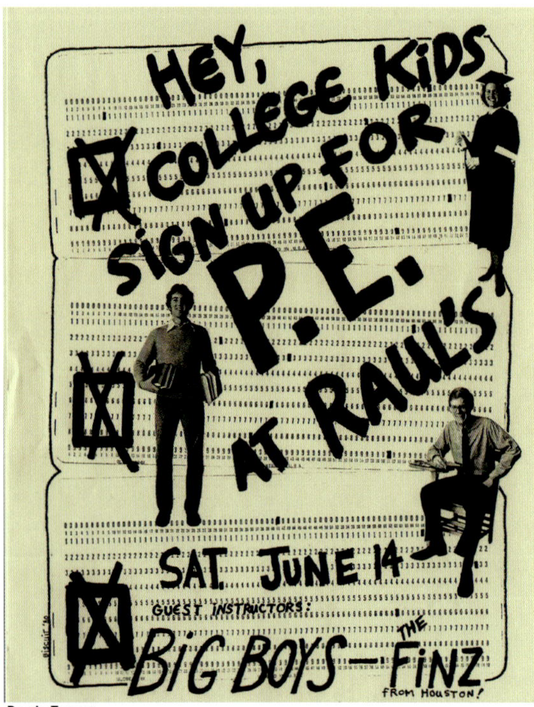

Randy Turner

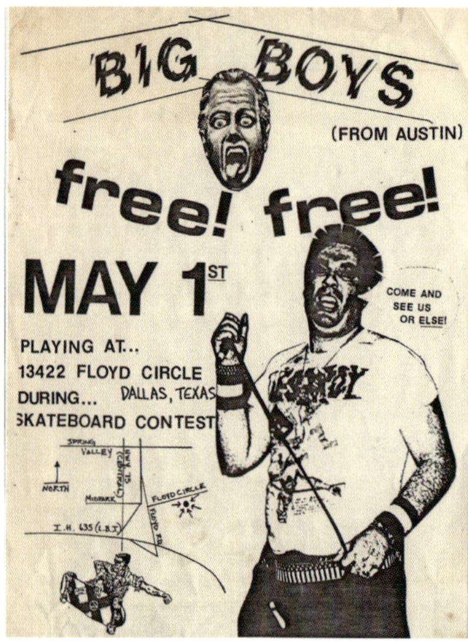

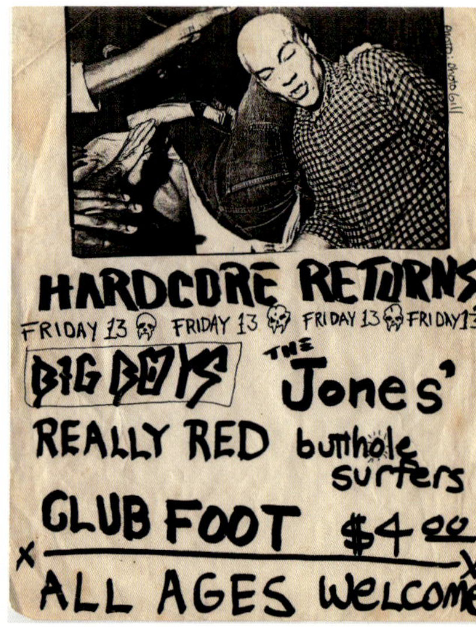

Photo of Andrew Gates: Photo Bill

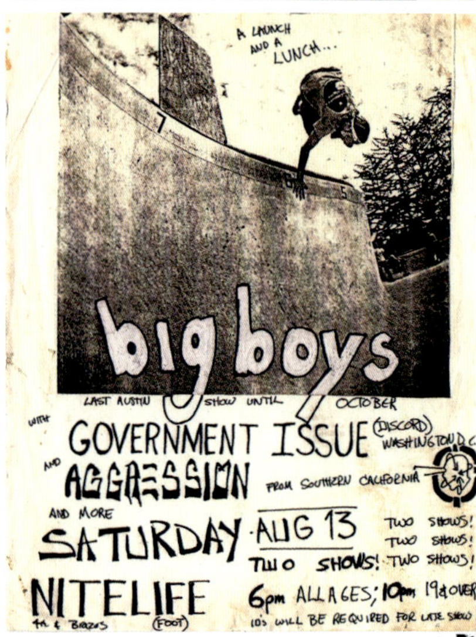

Tim Kerr

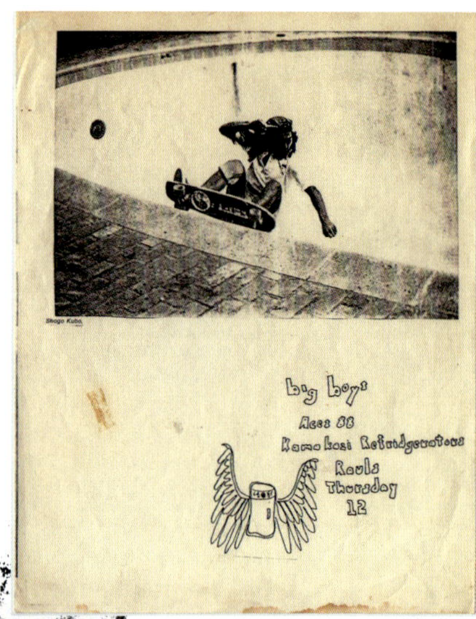

Tim Kerr

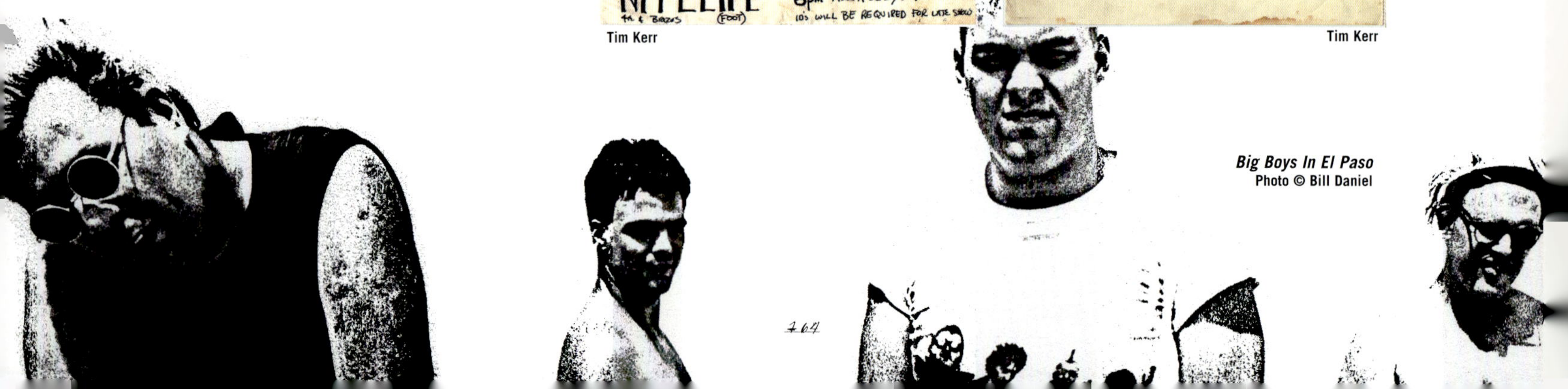

Big Boys In El Paso
Photo © Bill Daniel

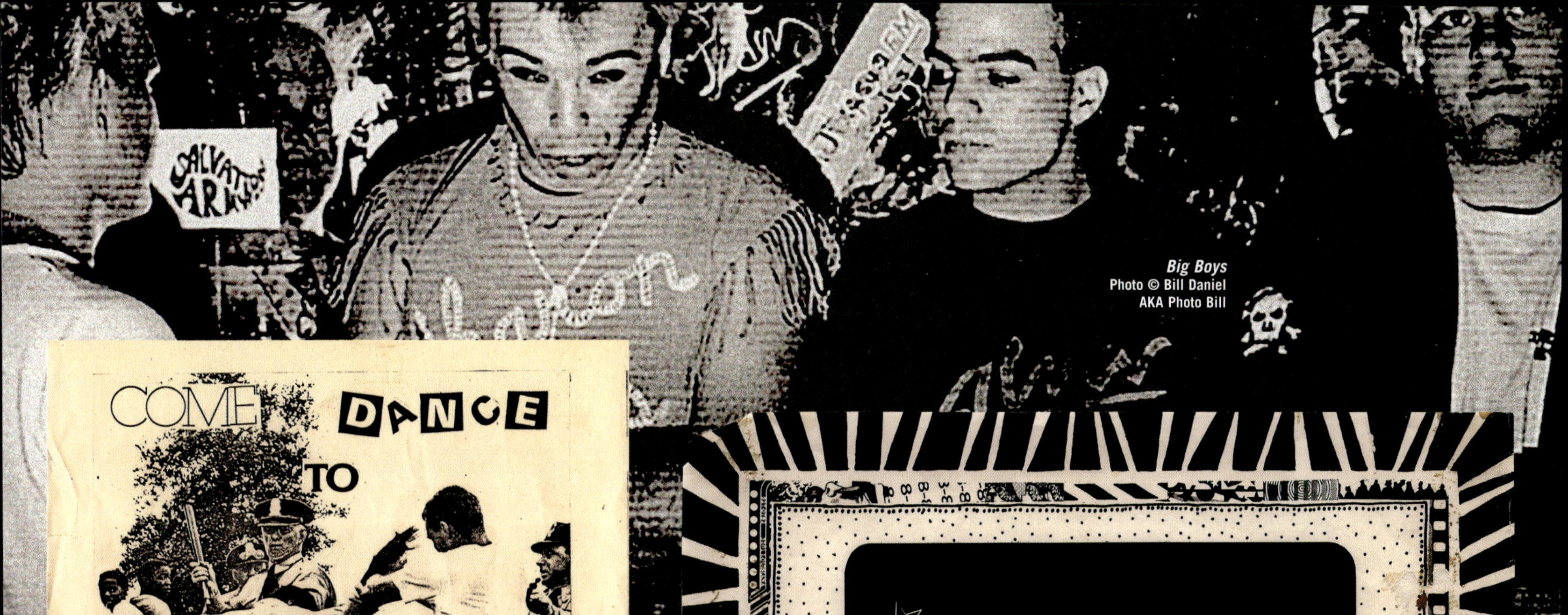

Big Boys
Photo © Bill Daniel
AKA Photo Bill

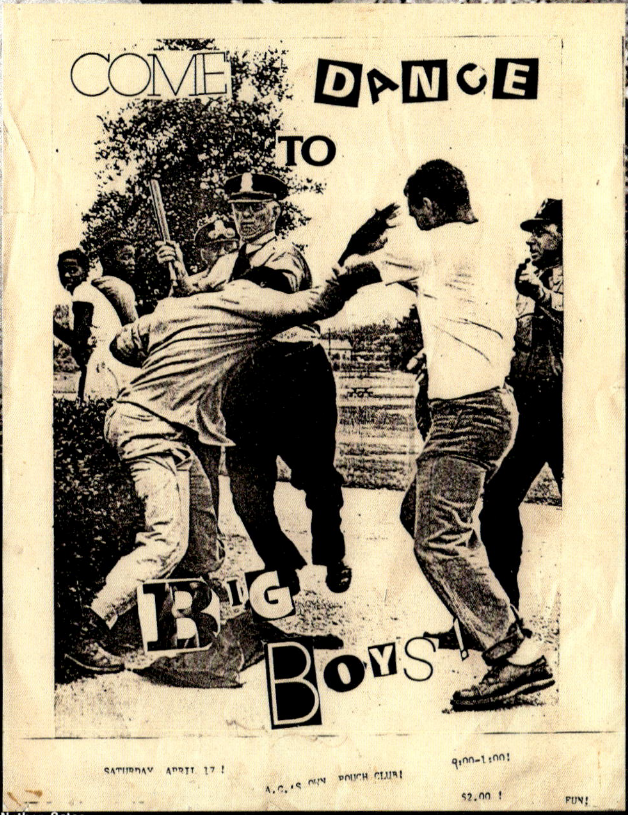

Nathan Gates

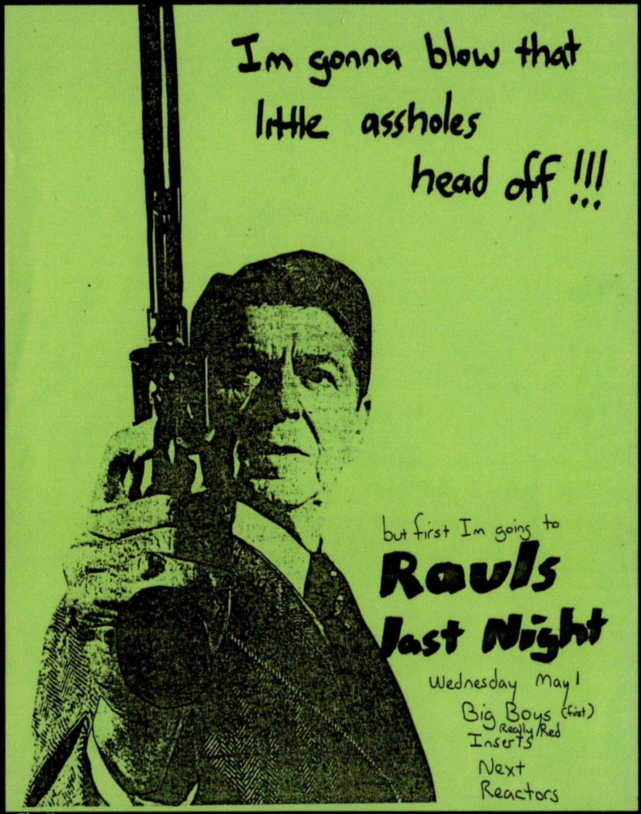

Tim Kerr

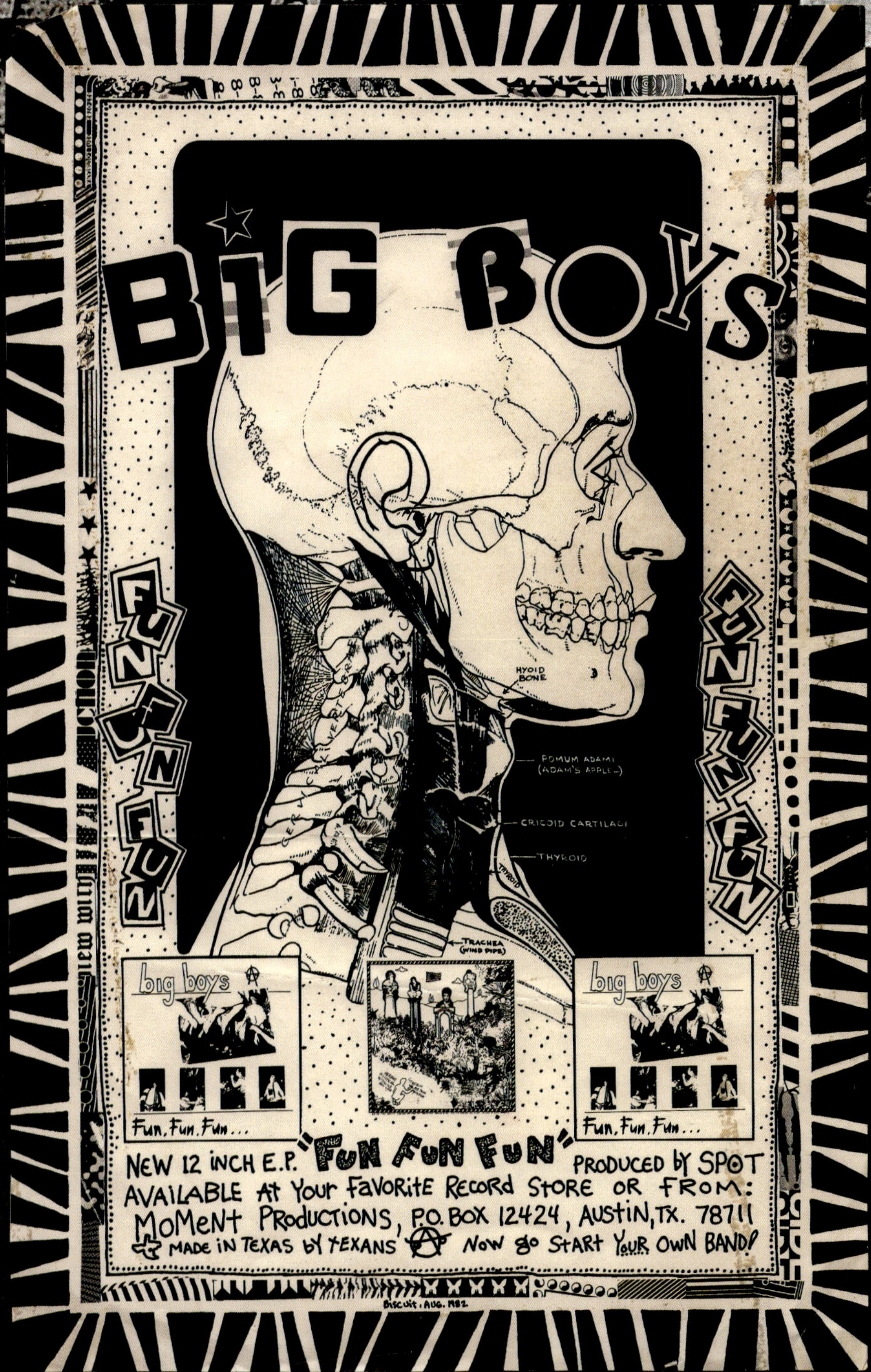

Randy Turner

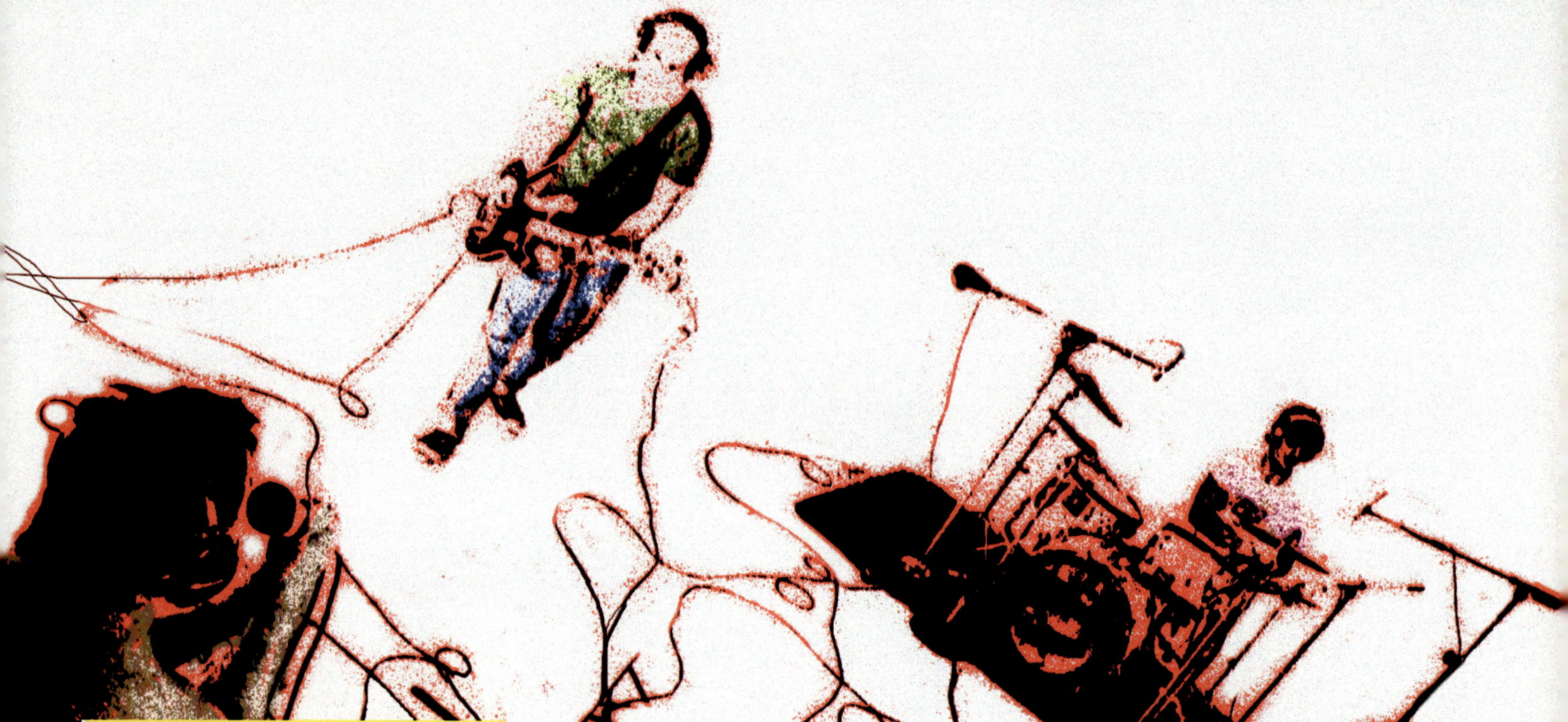

Tim Kerr

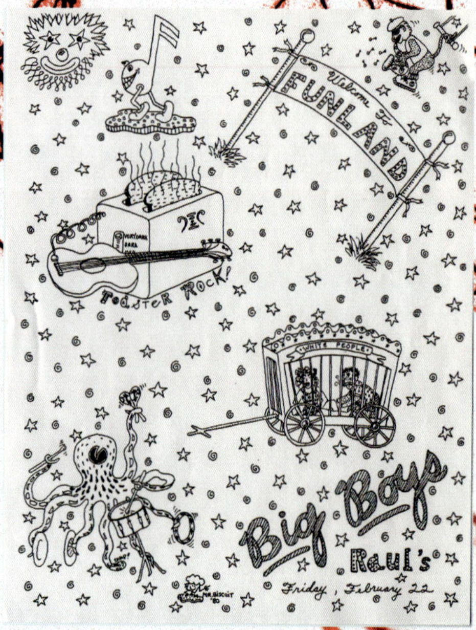

Randy "Biscuit" Turner

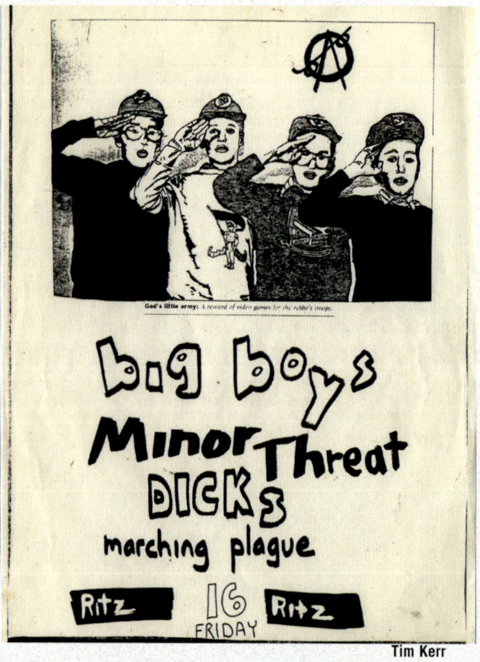

Tim Kerr

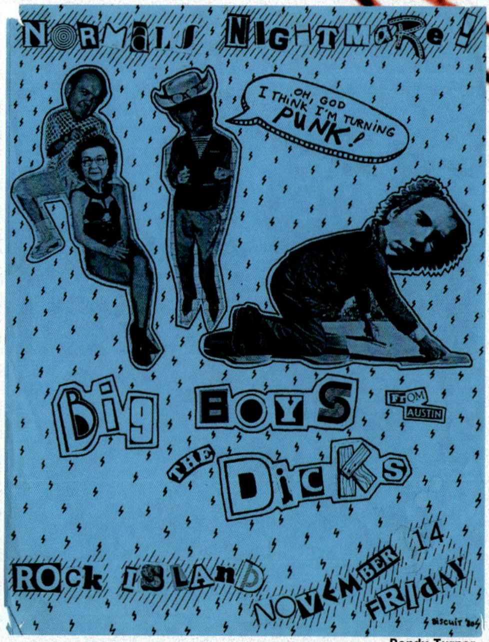

Randy Turner

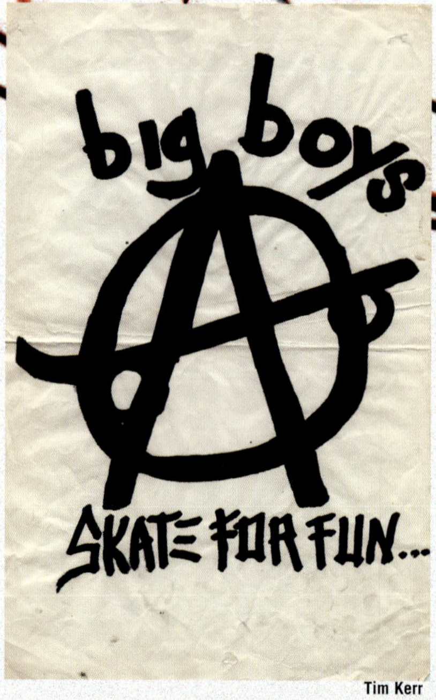

Tim Kerr

Big Boys In The S
Photo © Bill

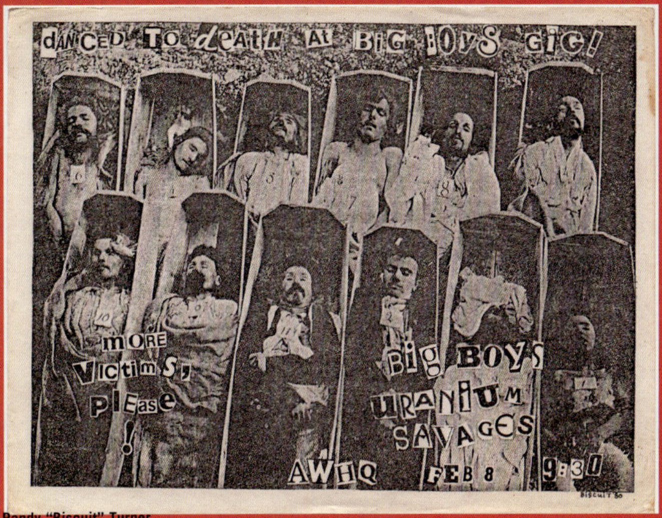

Randy "Biscuit" Turner

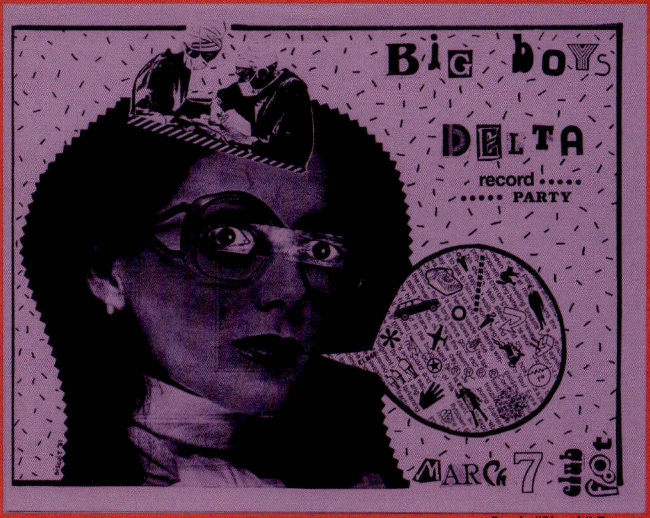

Randy "Biscuit" Turner

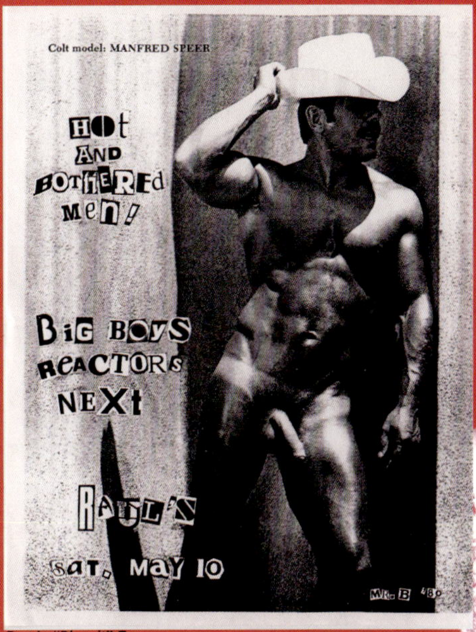

Randy "Biscuit" Turner

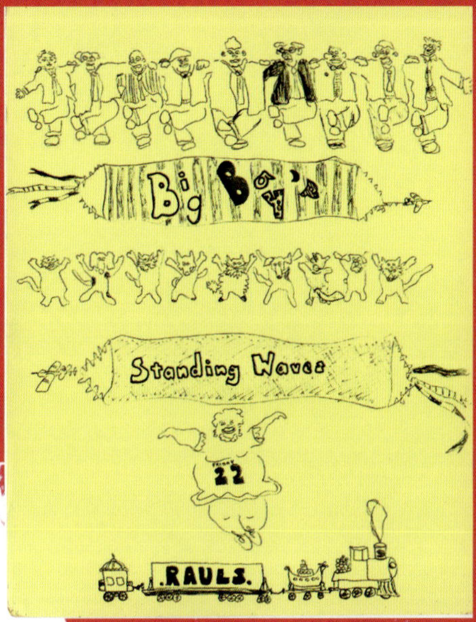

Tim Kerr

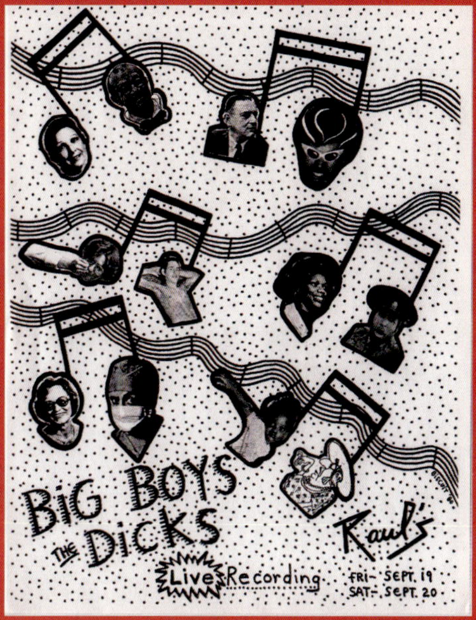

Randy Turner

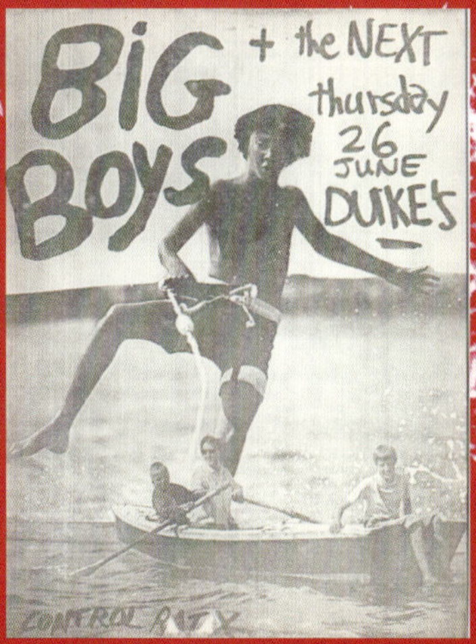

The Pecker Rears Its Ugly Head

by Randall J. "Biscuit" Turner

My bandmate Gary turned to me and said, "This flyer is controversy bound," and "dumb-ass/sexy/cool times 9." The night before we had showered the inner city with hundreds of posters of nekkid men promising wild punk rock perversity. Before noon the next day a 400 lb. African-American Alcoholic Beverage Commission Officer showed up at Raul's, the venue, completely pissed. He proceeded to hassle the owner, Steve, who already knew of "the flyer." Steve was arrested, laughing all the way to the hoosegow. He knew this was meaningless bullshit, that would only further the fine name of his club, the finest punk rock club in the Southern United States. He was sprung in two hours, thanks to my bail money, but was charged with a class C misdemeanor for advertising "butts with beer". We had a wailin' six band benefit to help pay the fine, and made more than the fines, money which went to buy kegs and food. The poster became a huge collector's item, and I was begged by millions for copies, to which I bowed and artfully complied. +

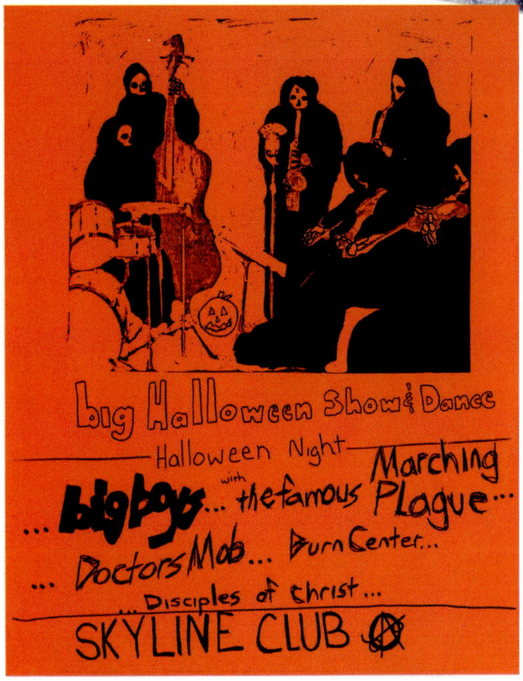

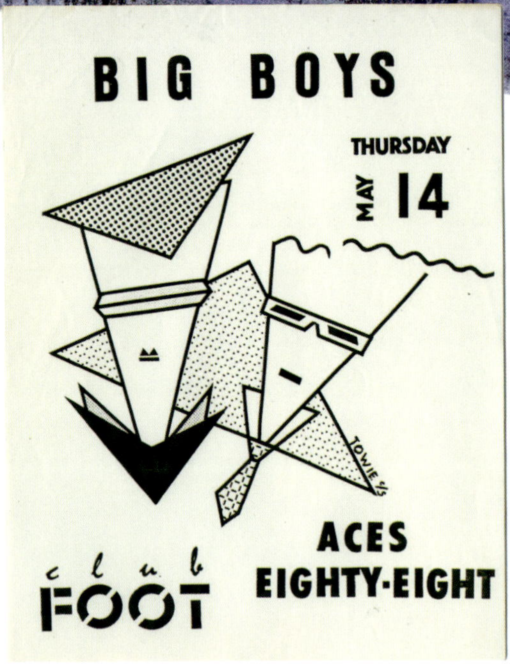

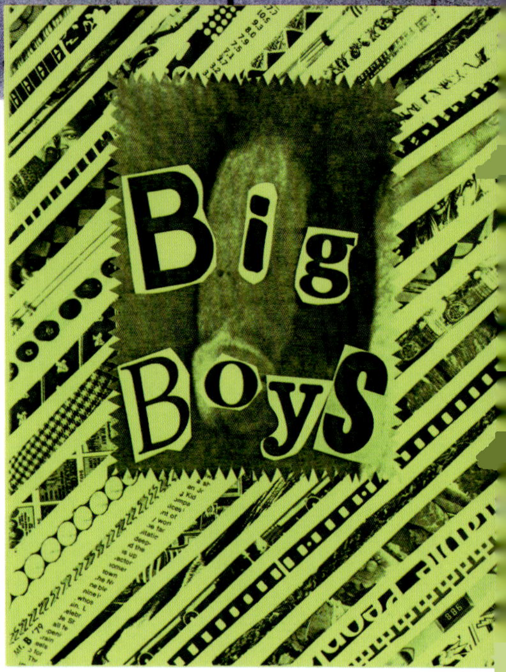

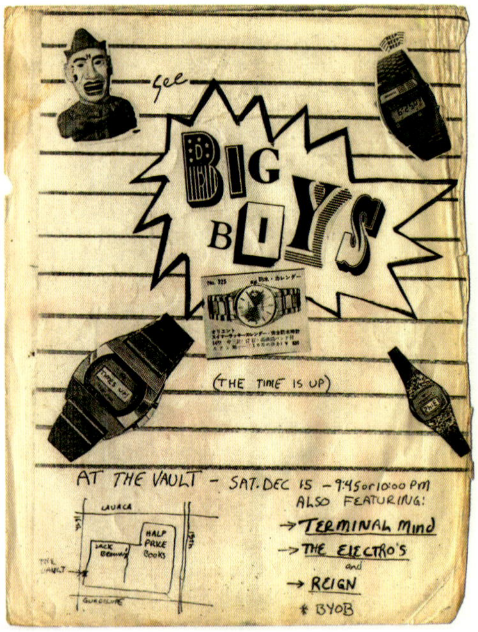

Big Boys' third show...

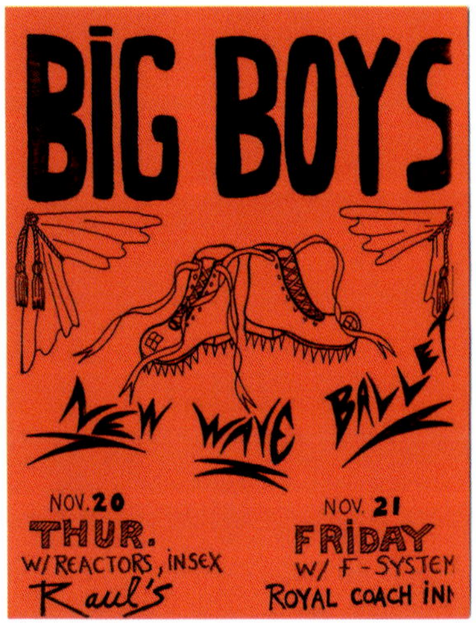

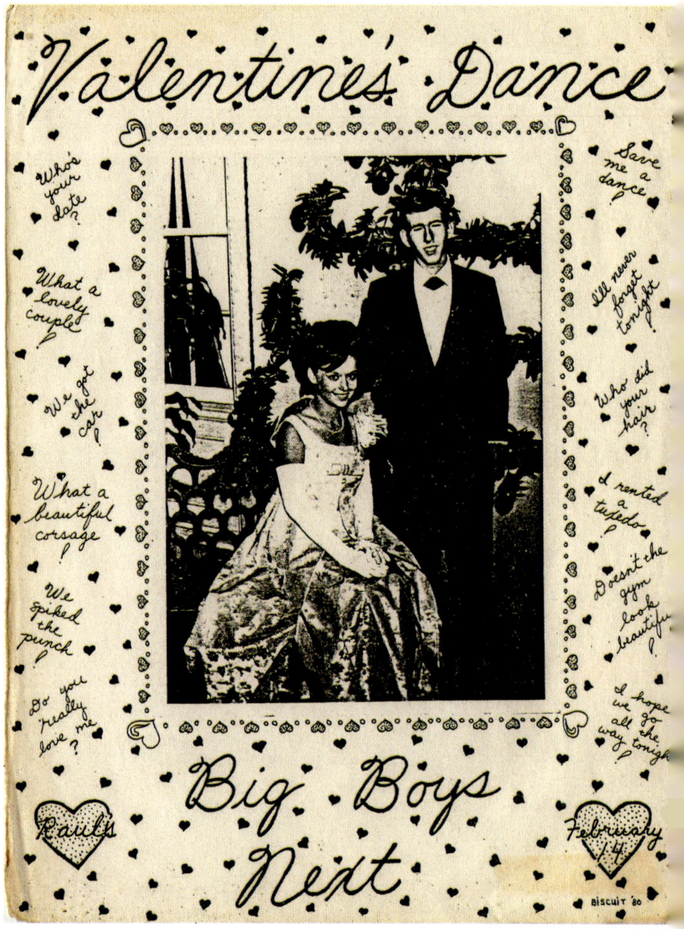

Randy "Biscuit" T

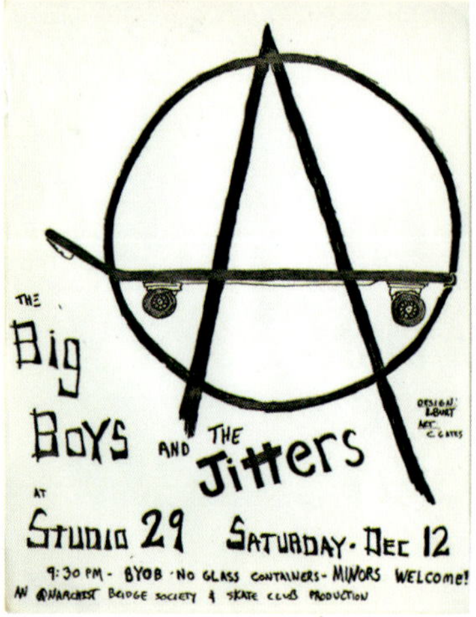

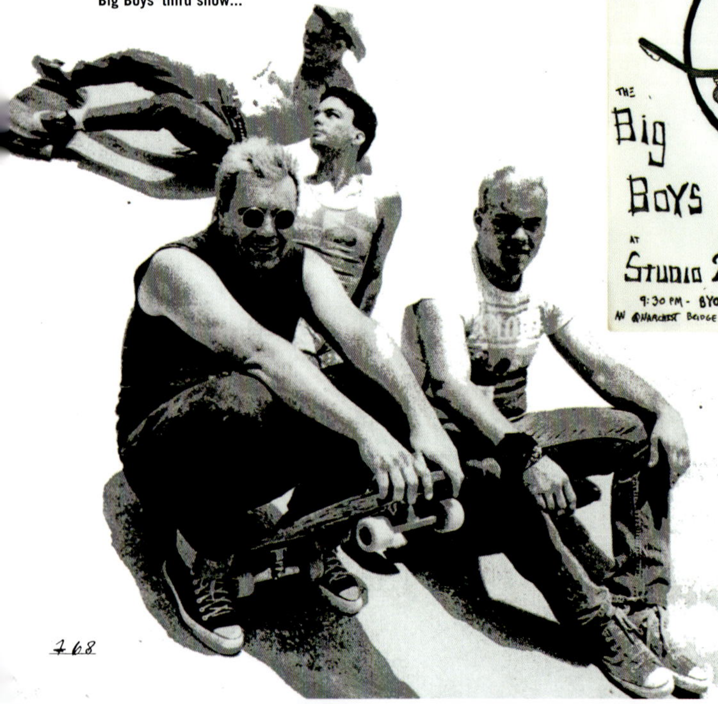

Big Boys
Photo © Bill Daniel

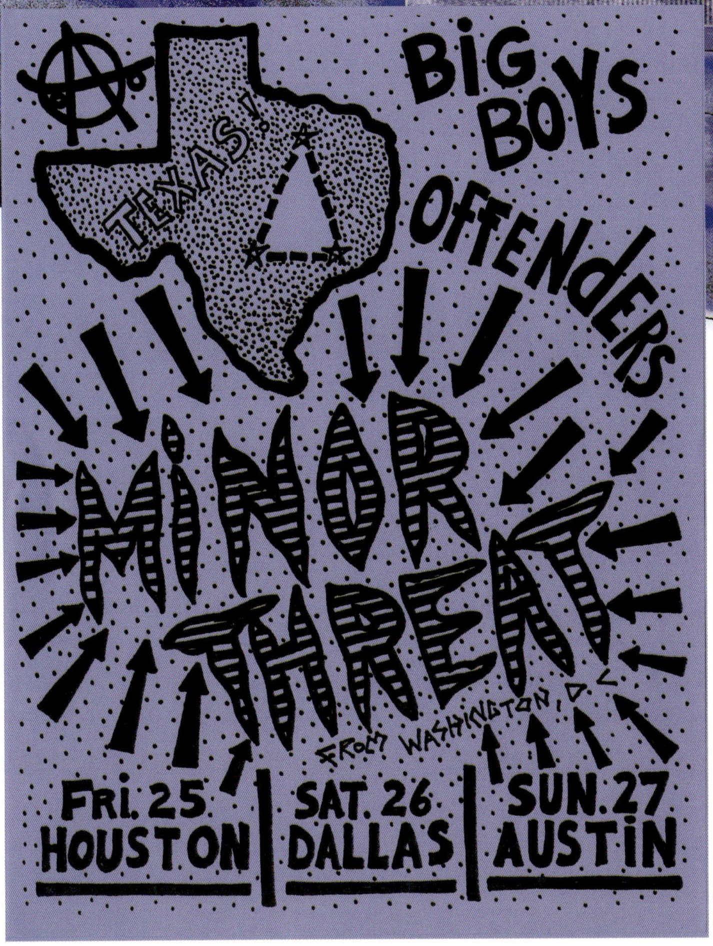

Randy "Biscuit" Turner

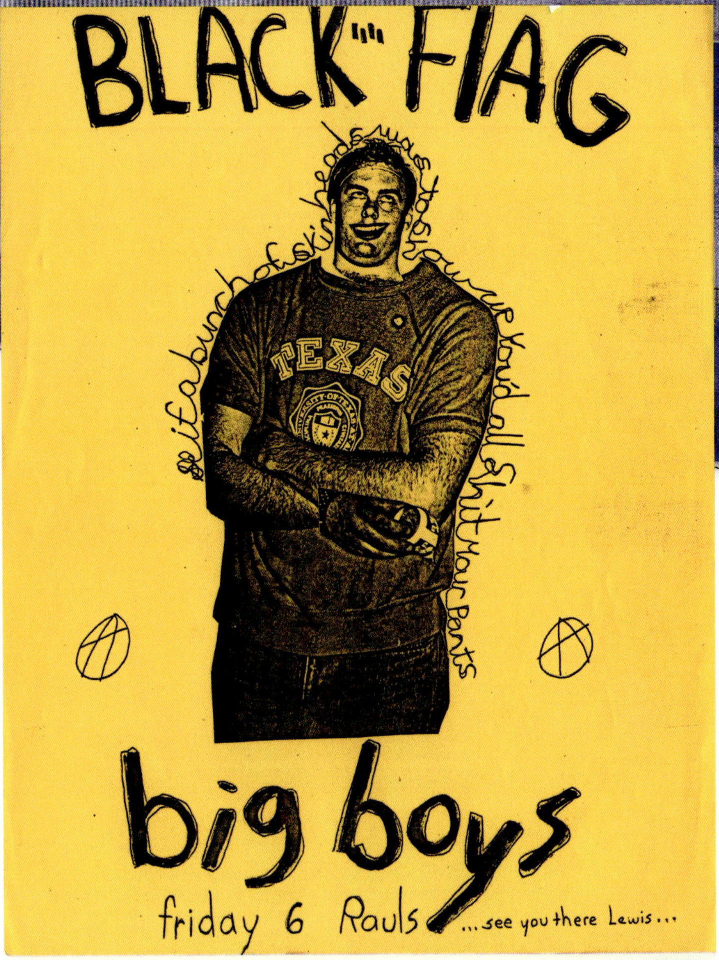

Tim Kerr

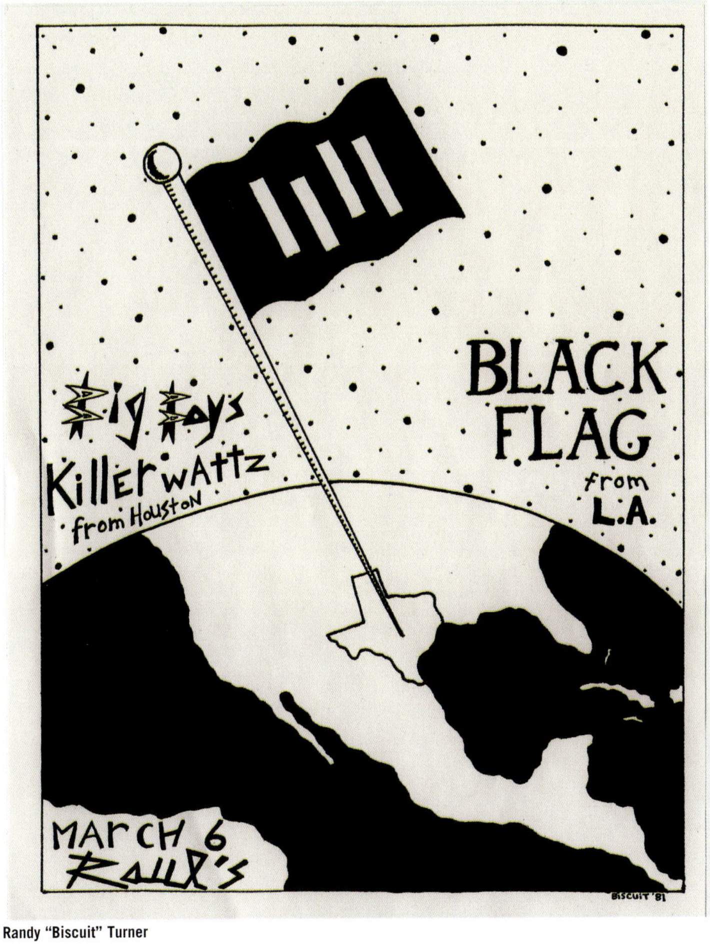

Randy "Biscuit" Turner

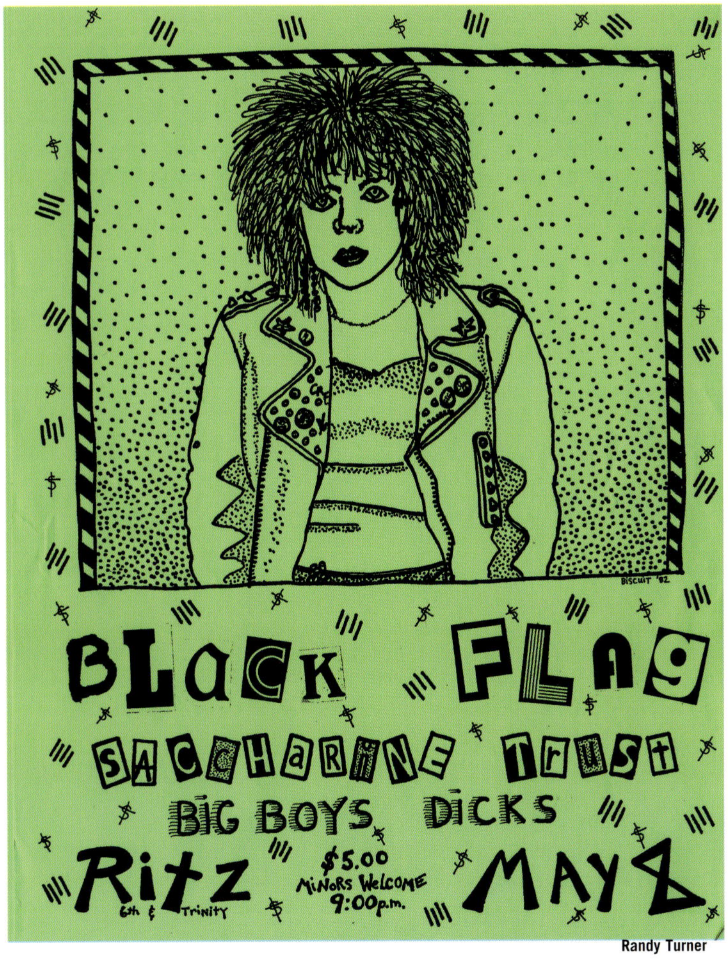

Randy Turner

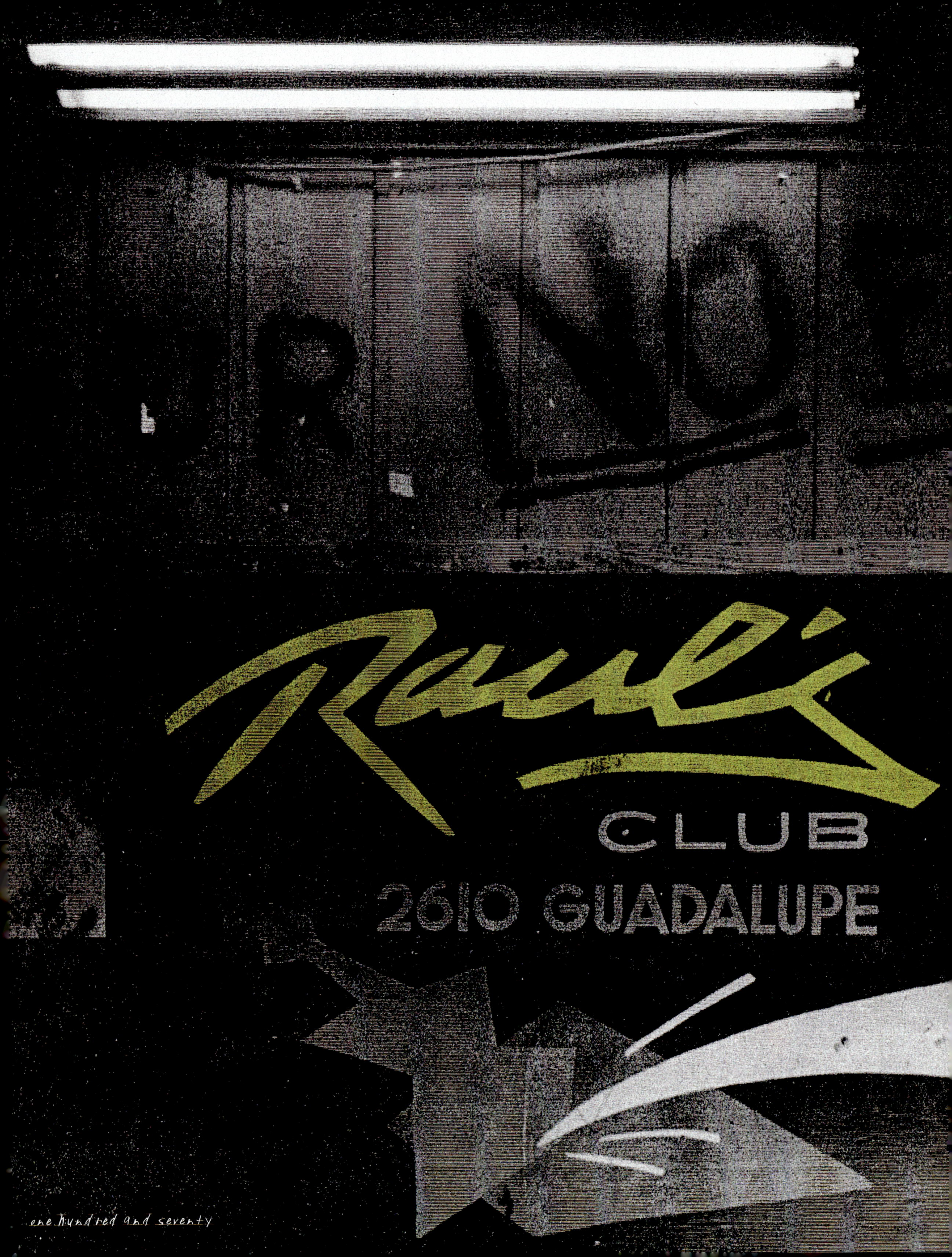
Raul's
CLUB
2610 GUADALUPE

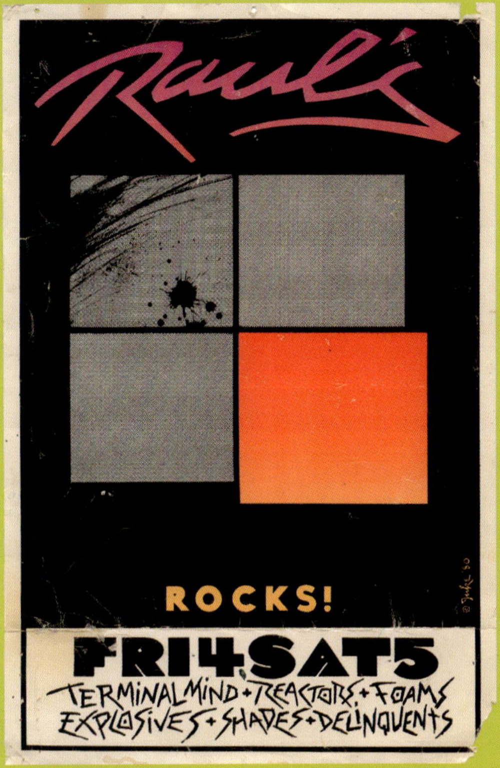

Guy Juke

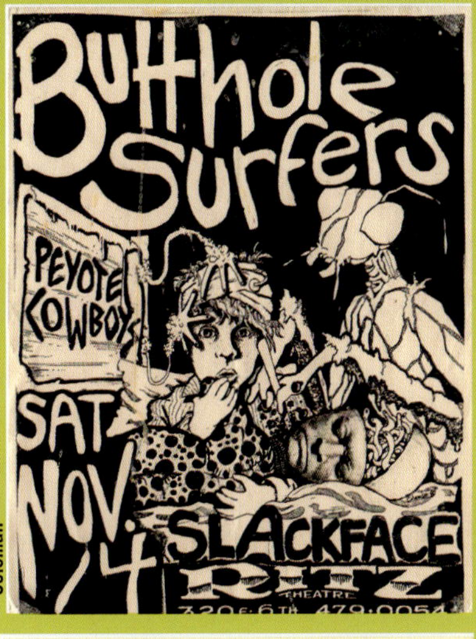

Coleman

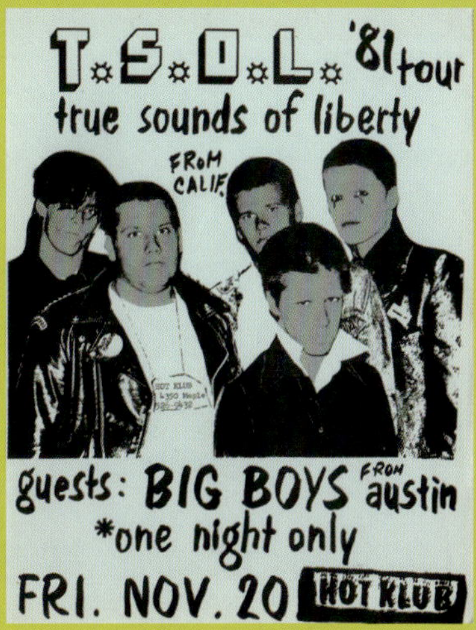

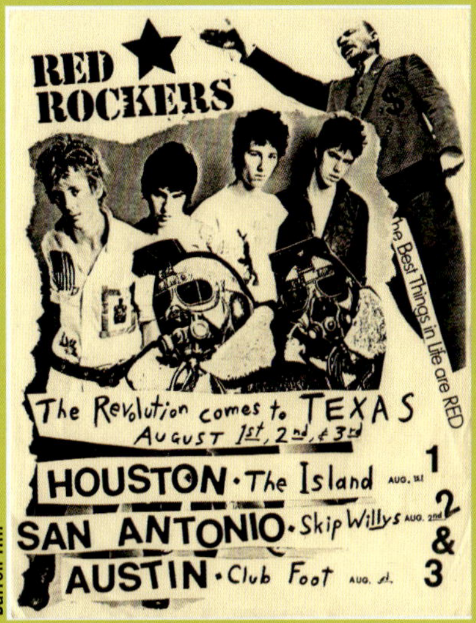

Darren Hill

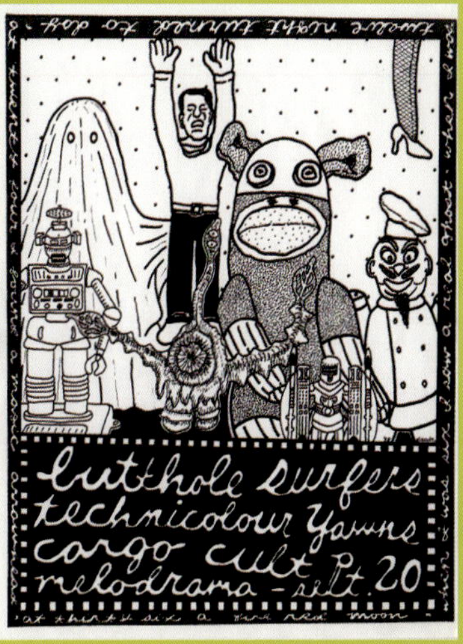

Randy Turner

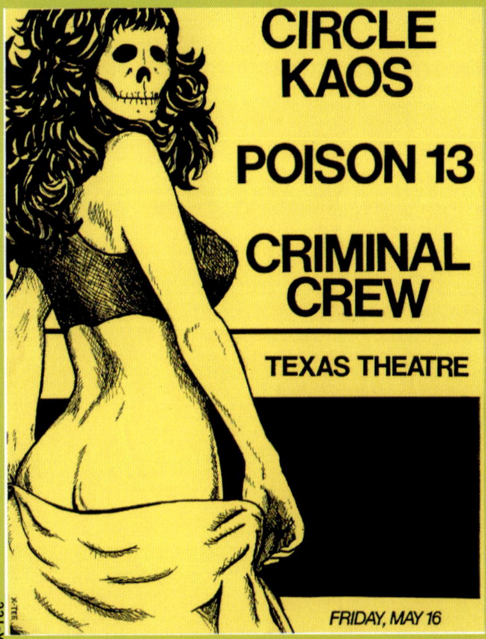

X-Tee

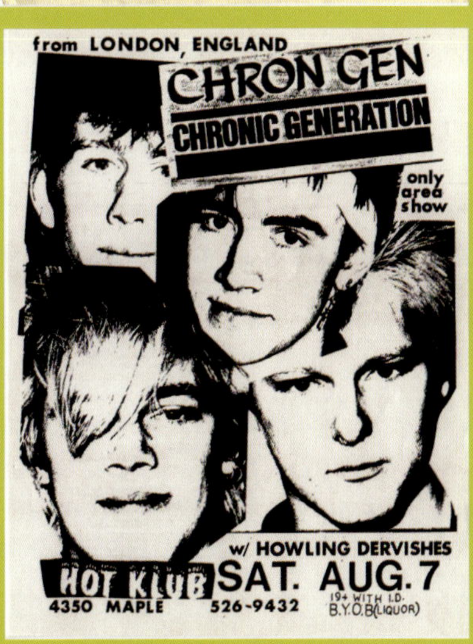

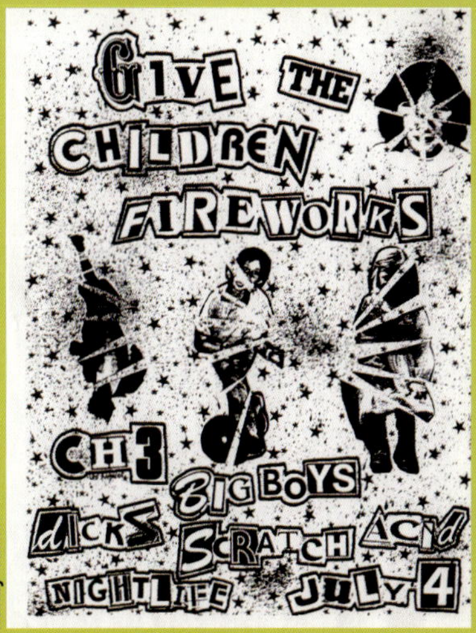

Randy Turner

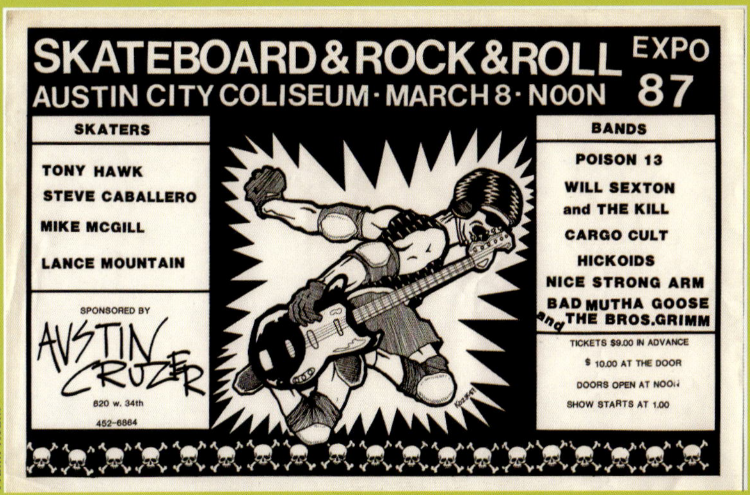

Frank Kozik

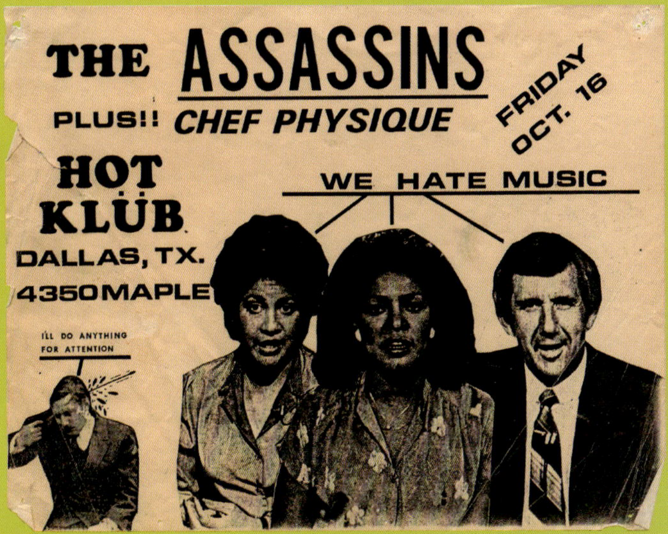

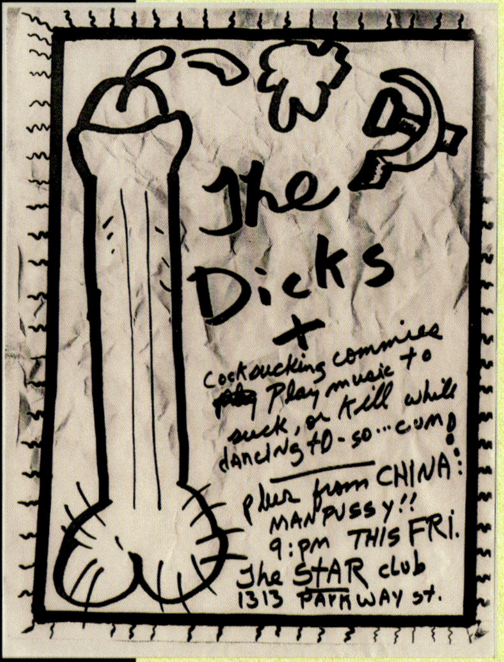

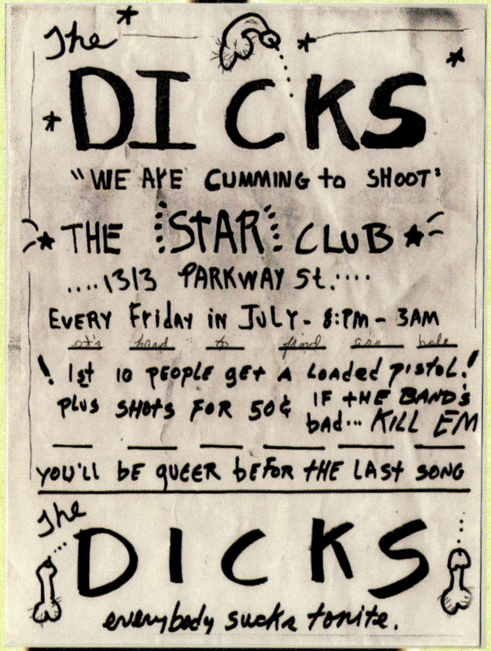

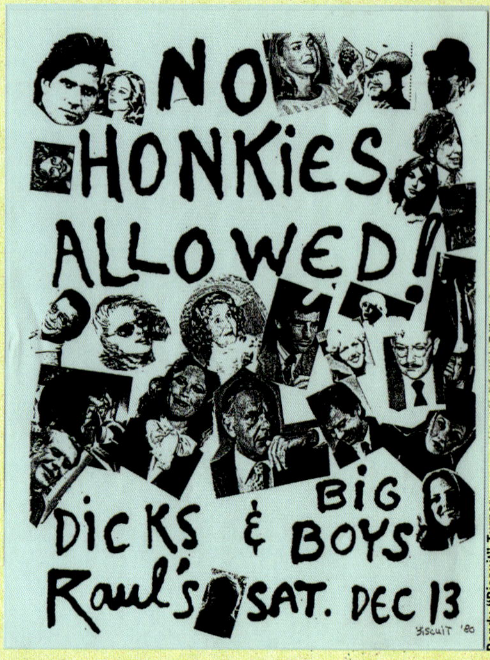

Randy "Biscuit" Turner

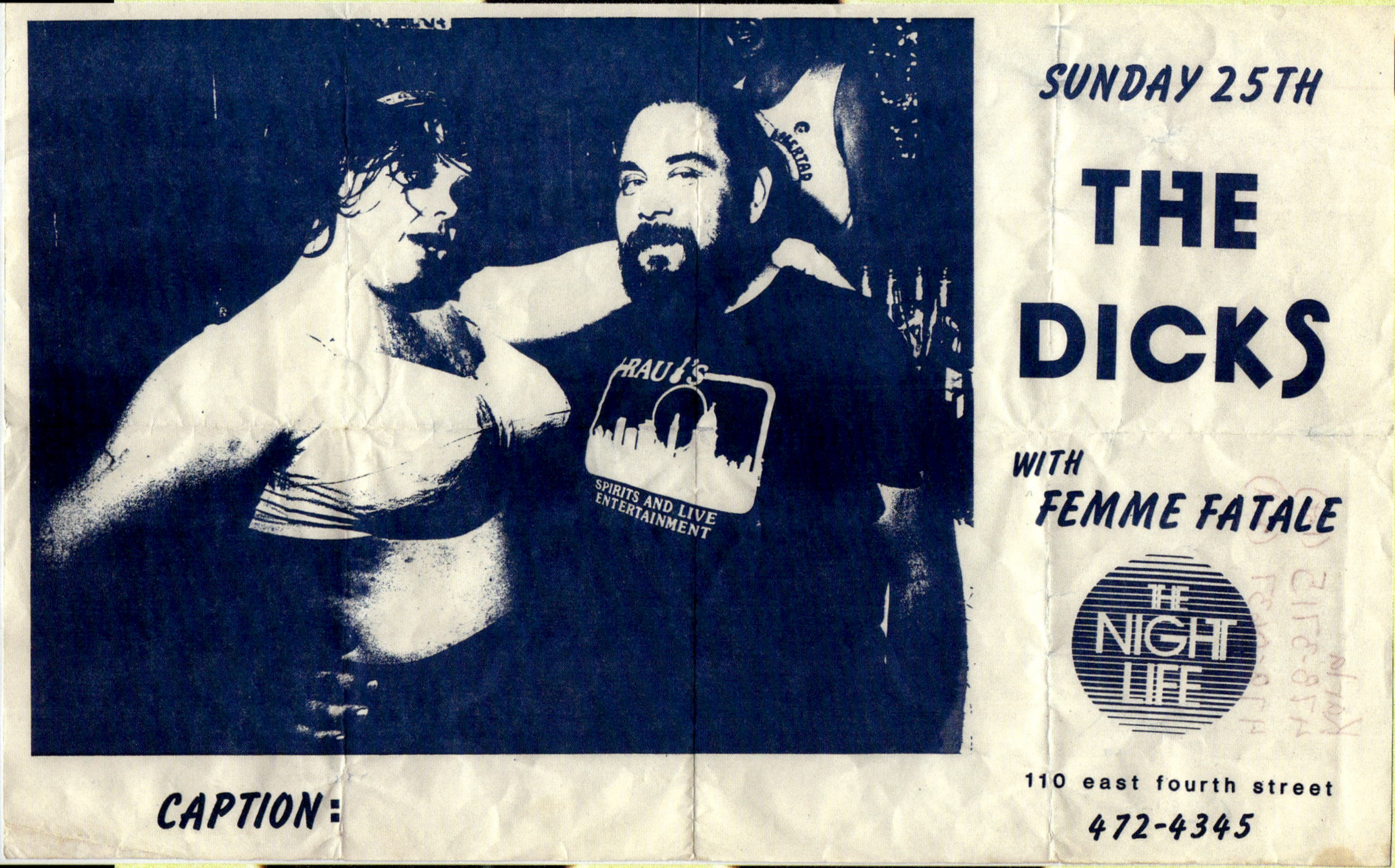

The Lies Become Truth

by Gary S. Floyd

I'd seen the Ramones in Austin and San Francisco. Later I saw the Sex Pistols. Then I knew I wanted to be in a punk rock band. Everything was ripe for change. Flip-flopping from Austin to San Francisco in 1978 and '79, I decided Texas was too hot. People were burning up mad, drunk, and a little club named Raul's, right on the main Drag, was the spot they burned the hottest. My obvious choice was Austin.

I wanted a band so badly—I had been in some weird little hippie things in high school, but I wanted a sound to match my attitude—bad, bad music, lousy singing and lots of lukewarm beer from anyone who set down a can and walked away. Being a queer who just happened to enjoy the sound of my own desire, I decided to lie and say, "Yeah, I'm in a band—the Dicks." People believed me. I'd hear them say, "There's that queer that sings for The Dicks." I loved it. I had to say we'd played, so I made up a club, the Star Club on Parkway, with fake or very unclear dates. People even started to say they'd seen us. It was easy. CONTINUED NEXT PAGE

Then I met Glen, Pat and Buff, and we really did start to play, in the heat of Raul's during a summer that seemed to last forever.

Of course, it didn't. I moved back to San Francisco. The Dicks ended. Other bands came and went. People have died that everyone thought would live forever.

Now I follow the Hindu path to spiritual liberation. Who would've ever guessed that? But the Star club hasn't changed. It's still right there, waiting for someone to make it happen. +

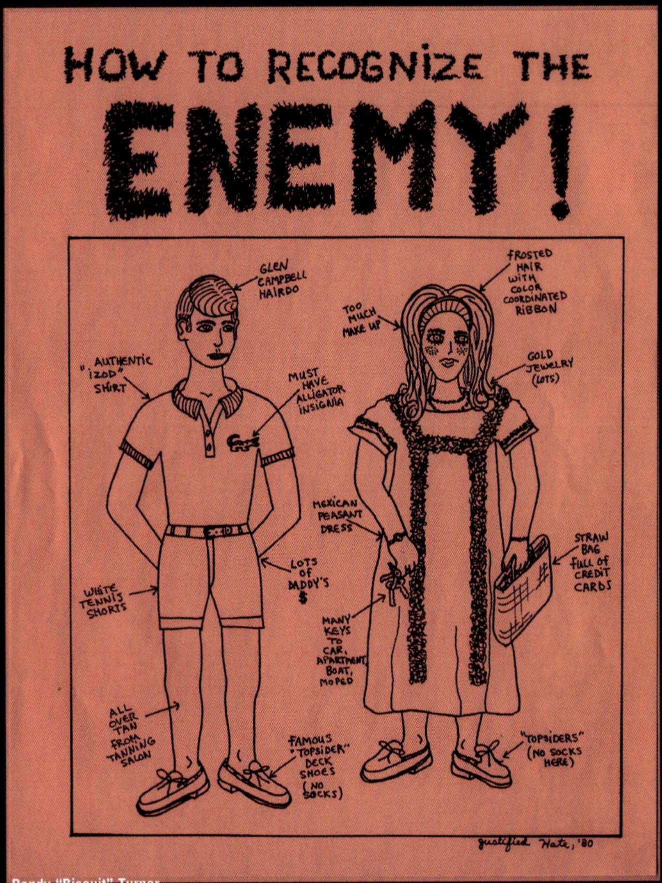

Randy "Biscuit" Turner

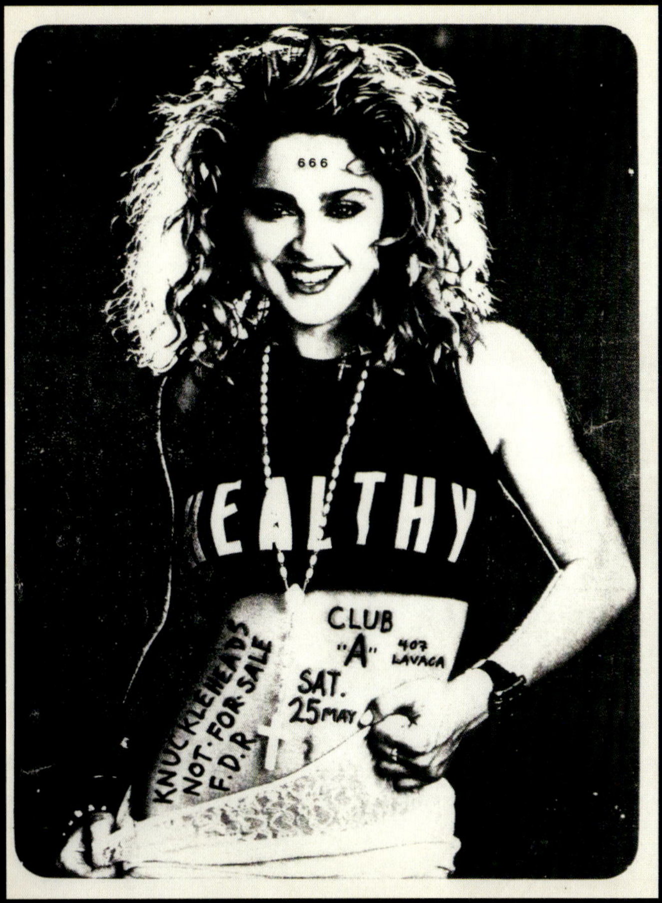

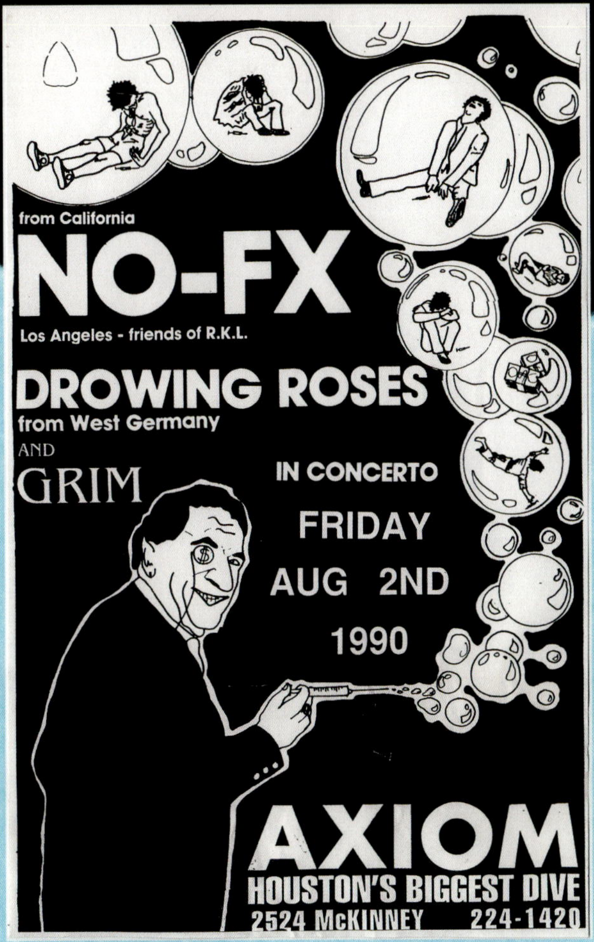

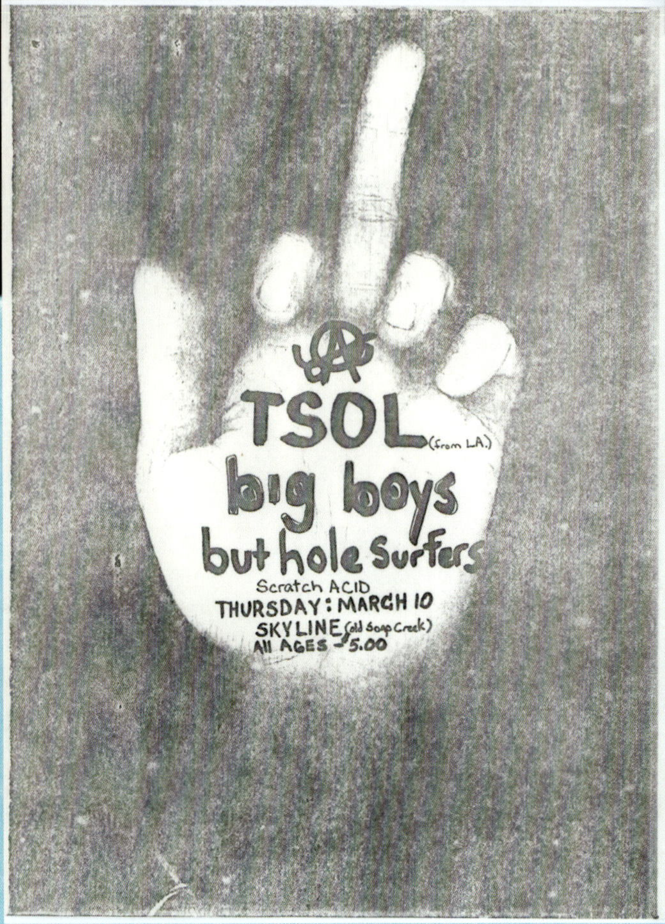

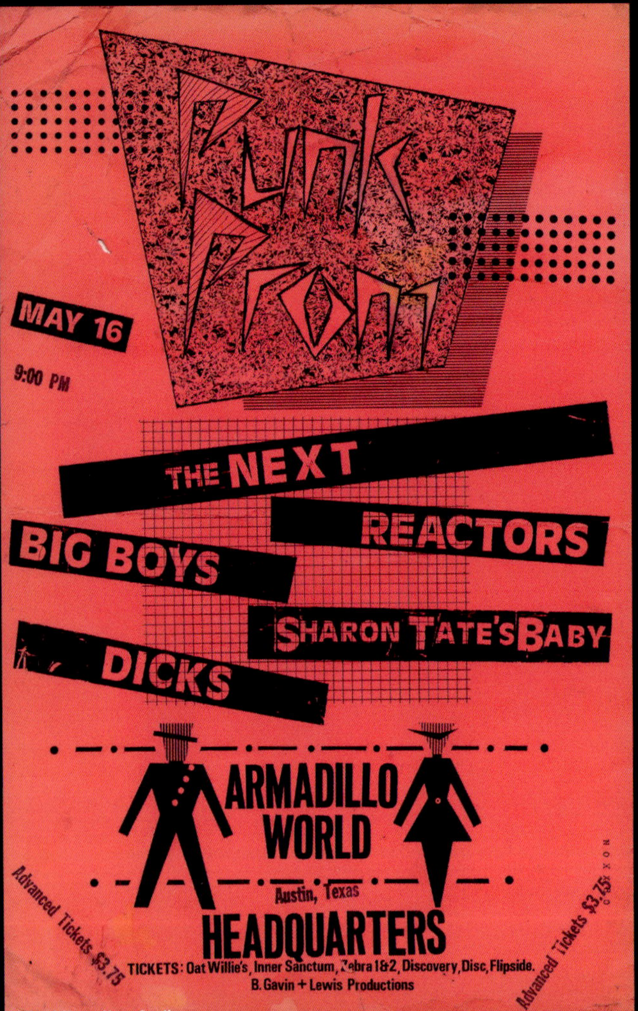

Michael Nott - Noxx Studios

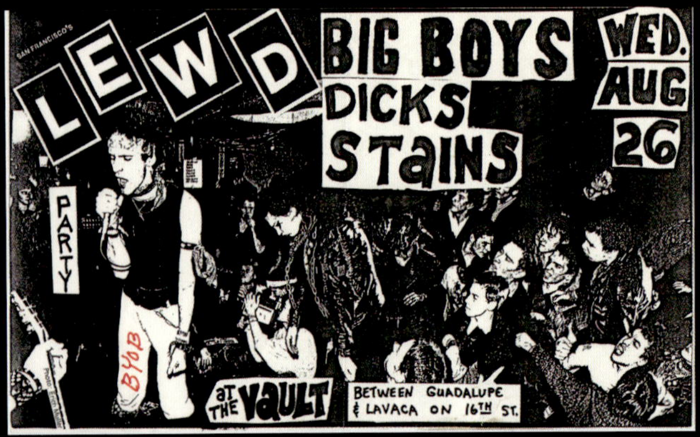

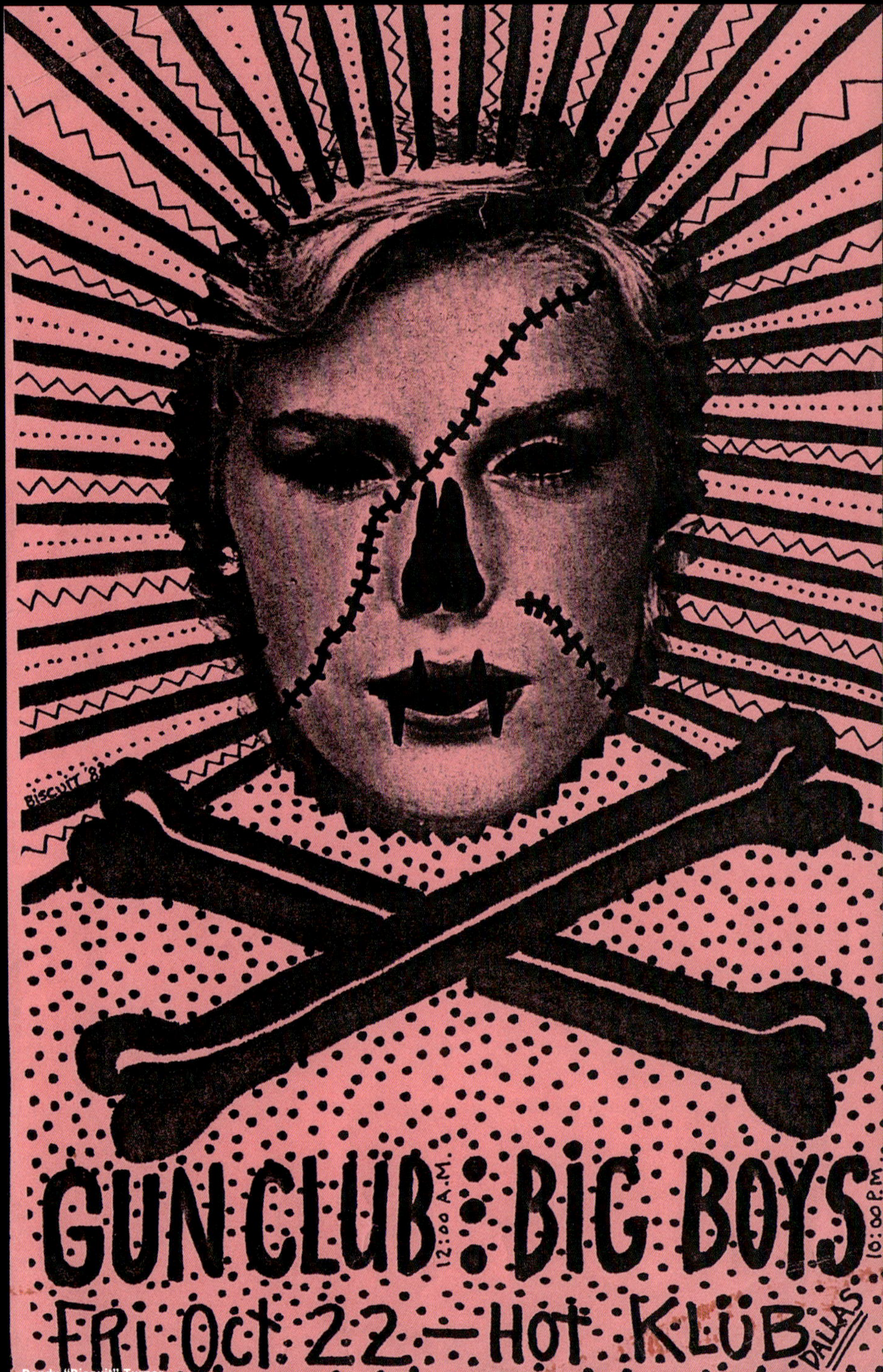

Randy "Biscuit" Turner

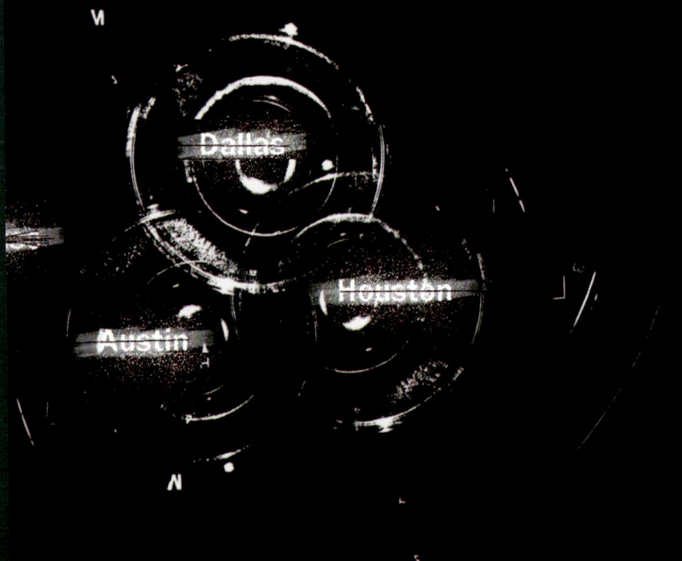

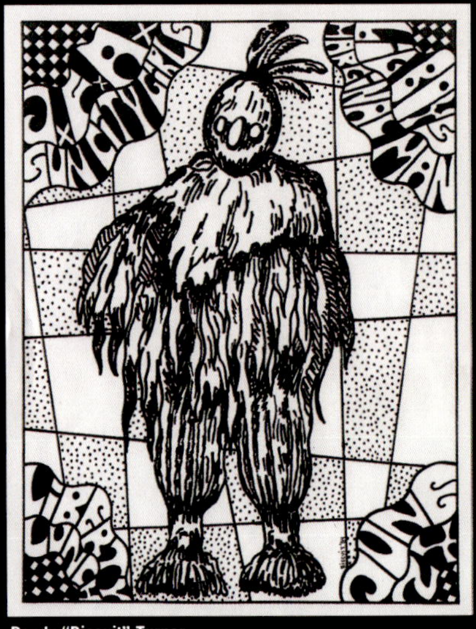

Randy "Biscuit" Turner

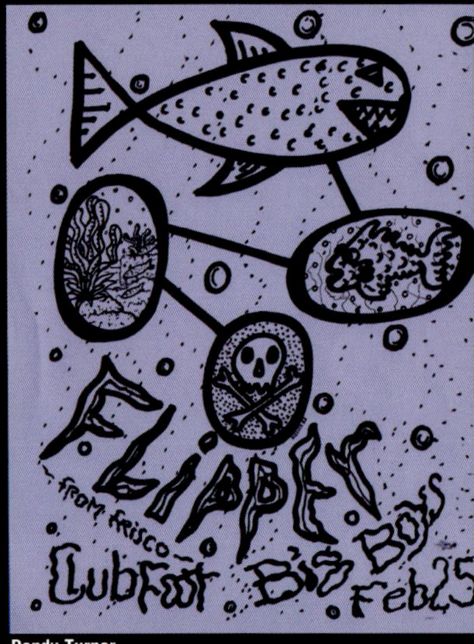

Randy Turner

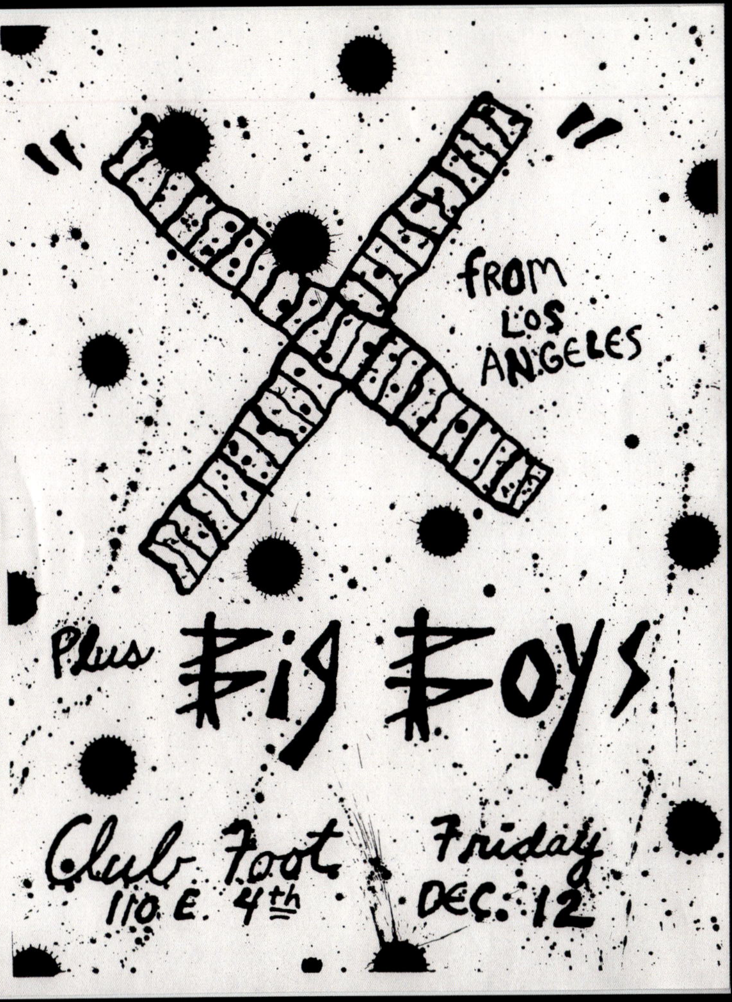

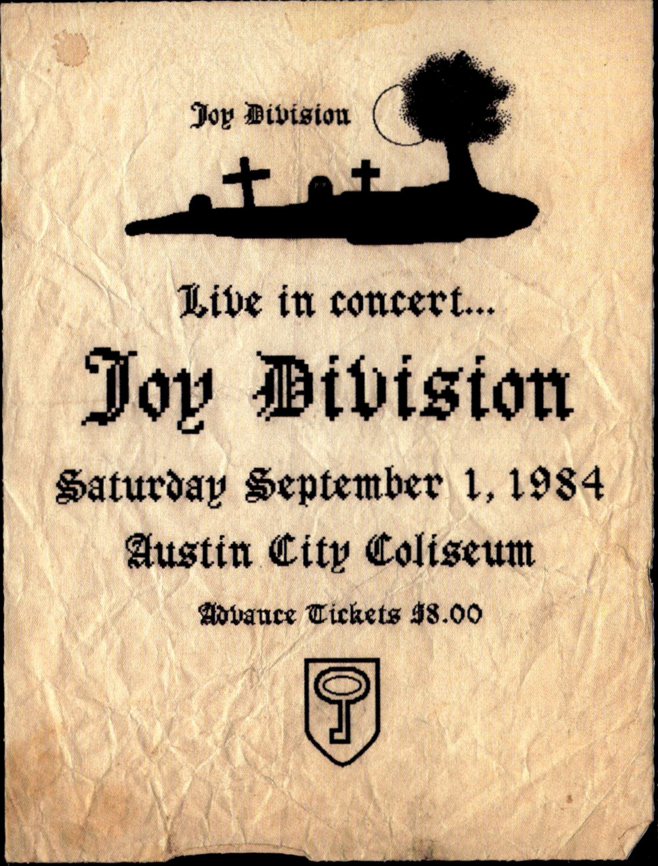

Mike Laird

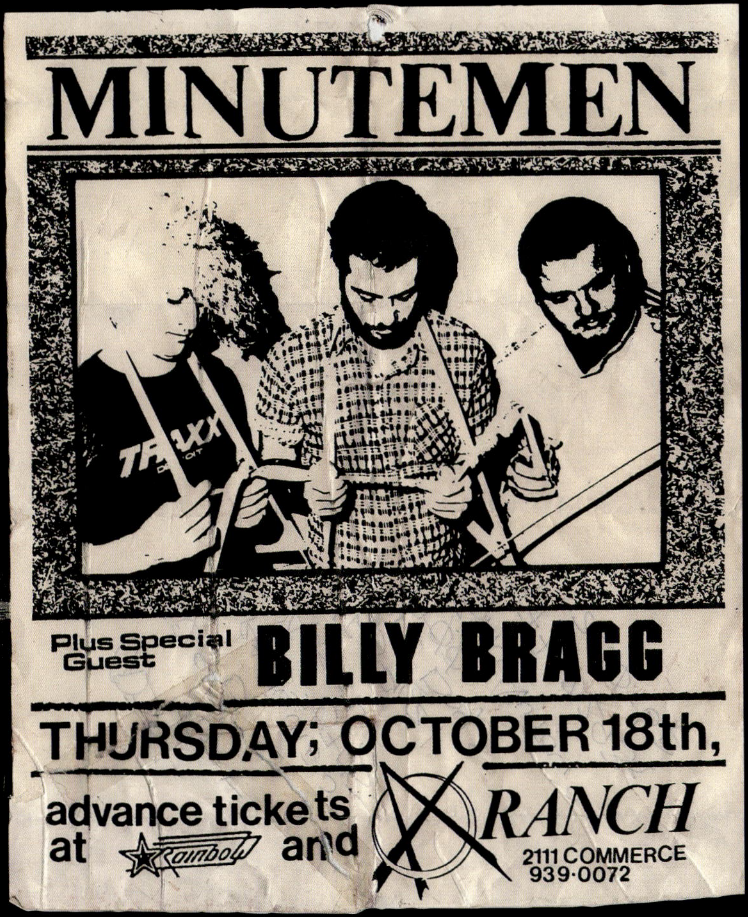

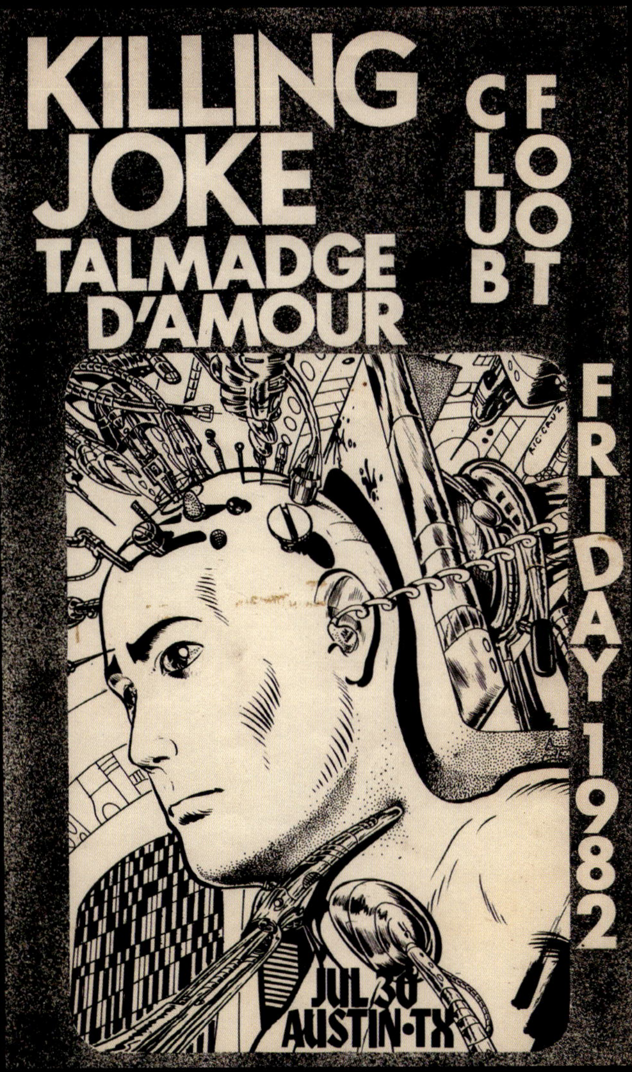

Ric Cruz

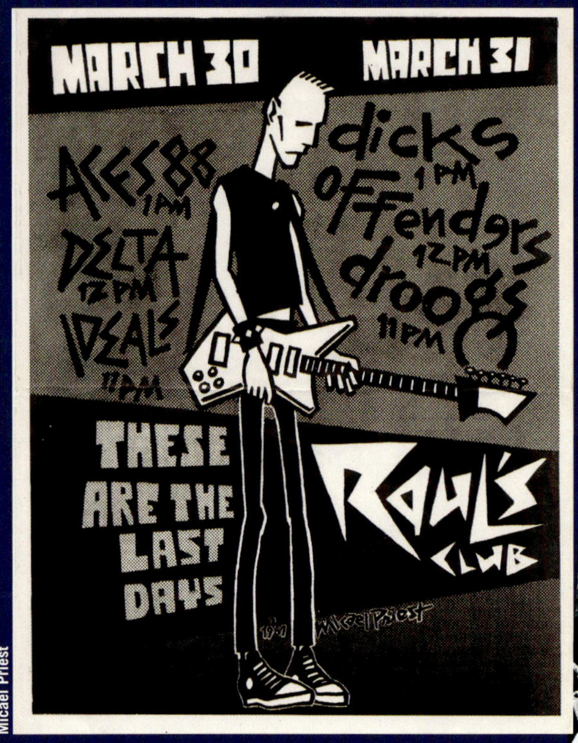

Micael Priest

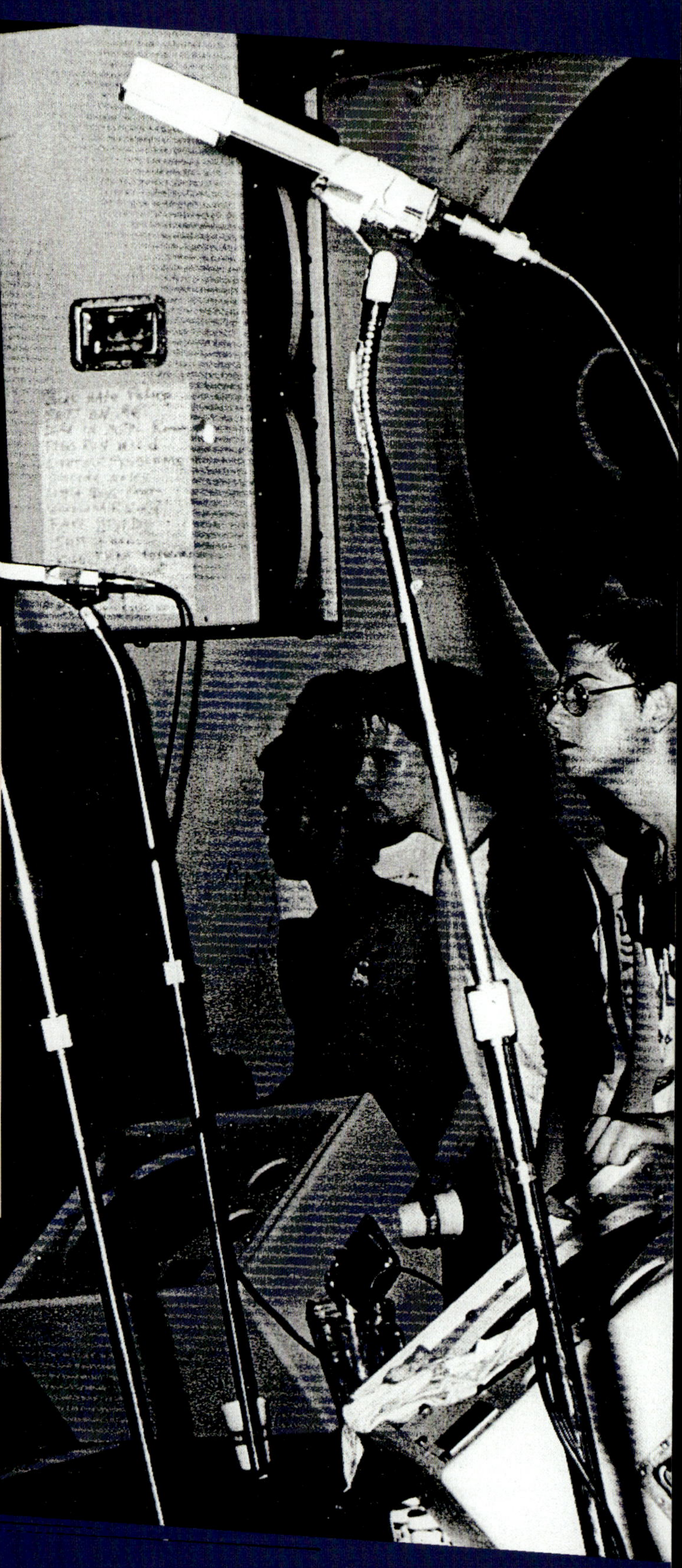

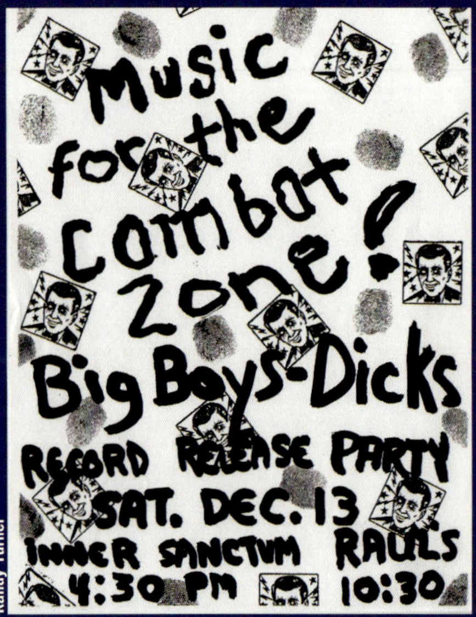

Randy Turner

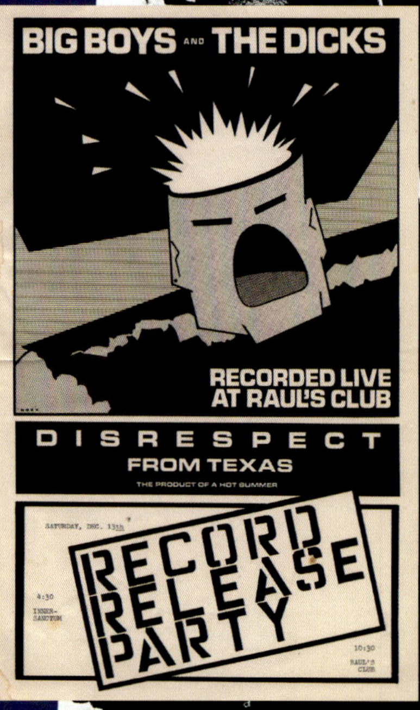

Michael Nott - Noxx Studios

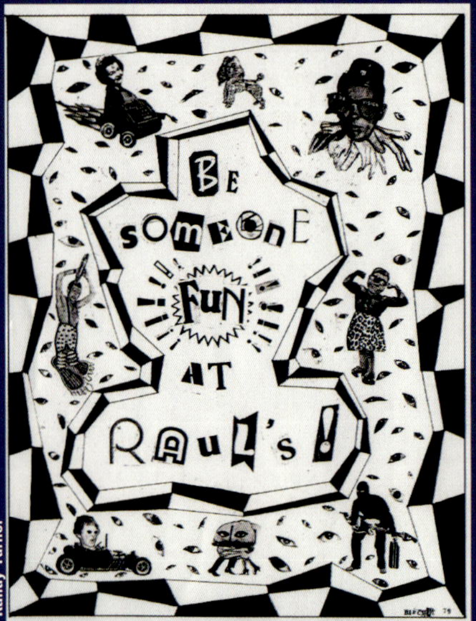

Randy Turner

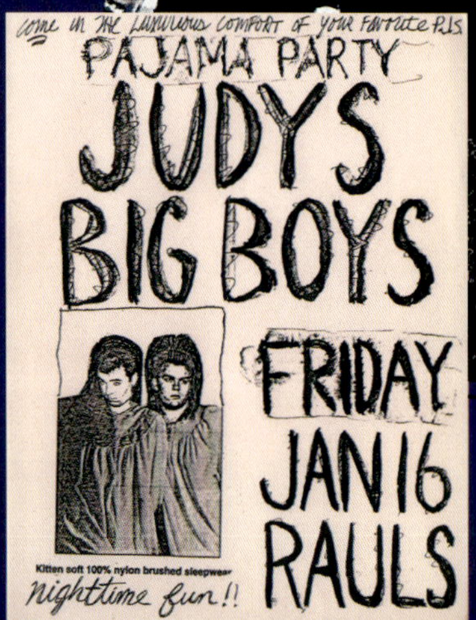

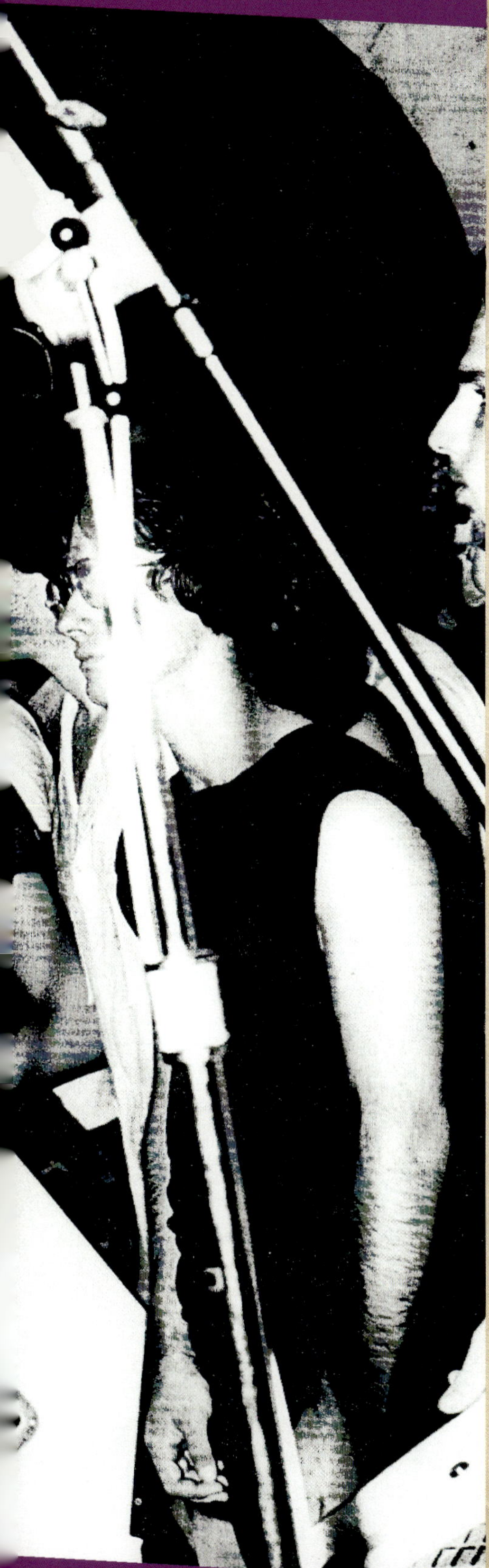

Big Boys Live - Recording At Raul's

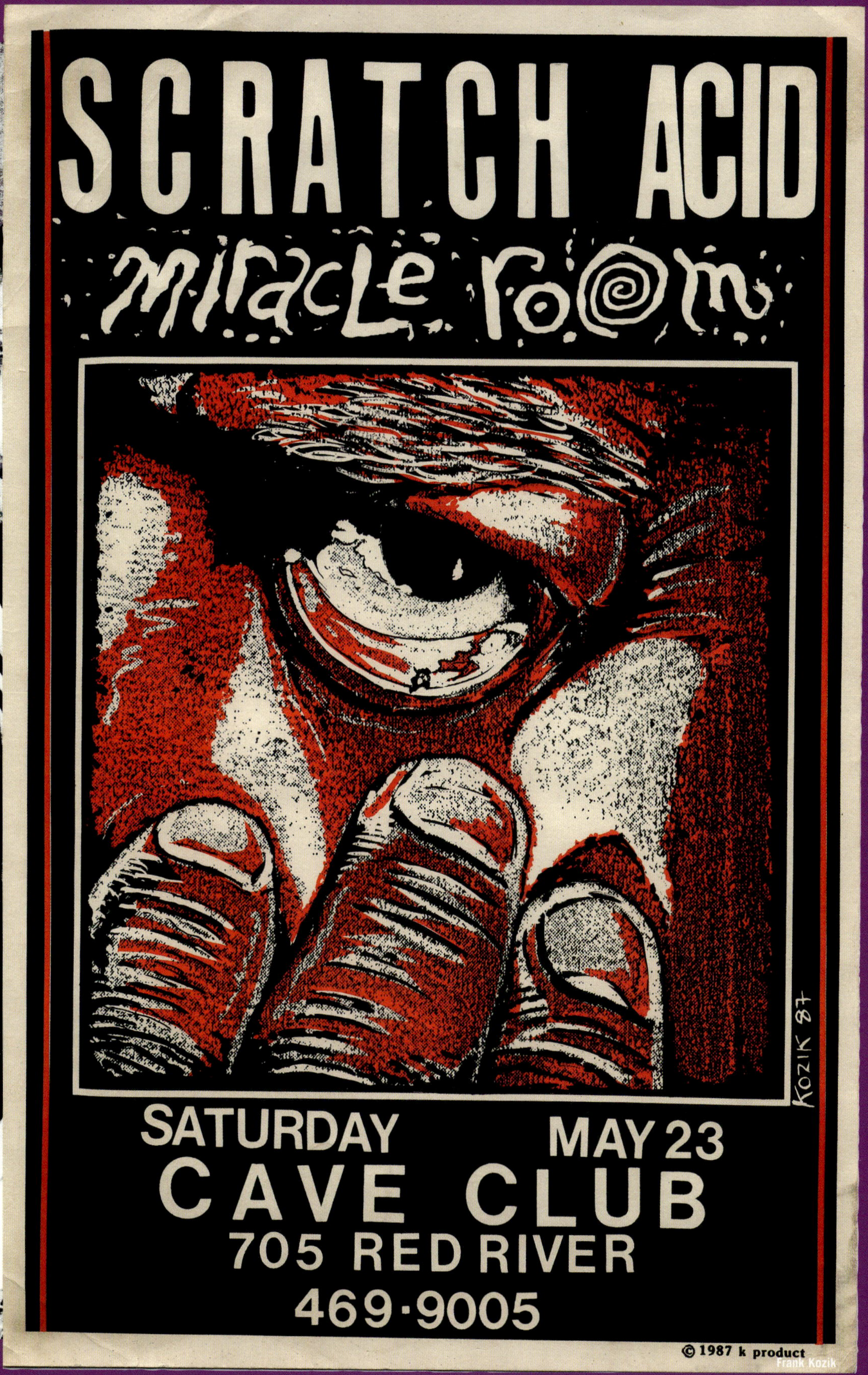

Frank Kozik

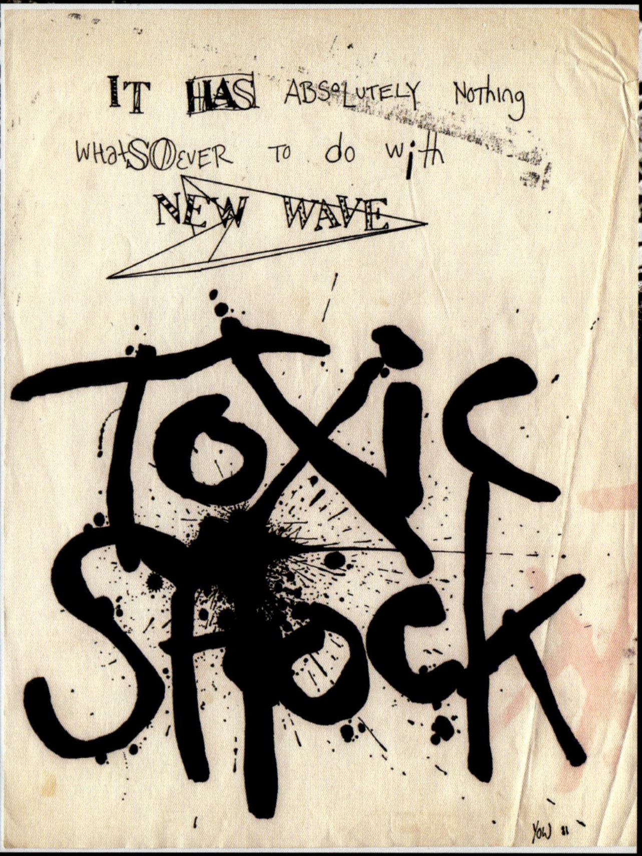

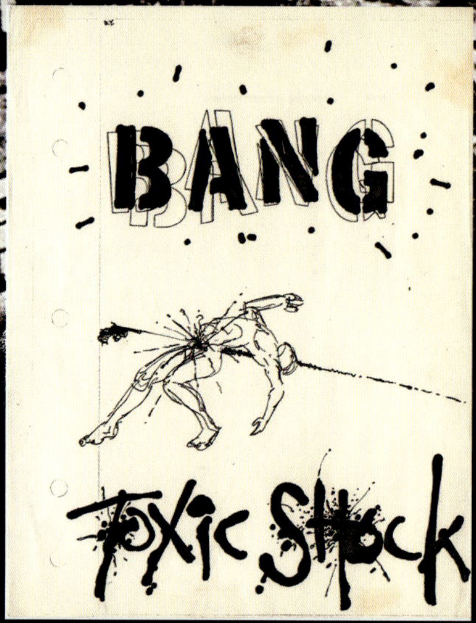

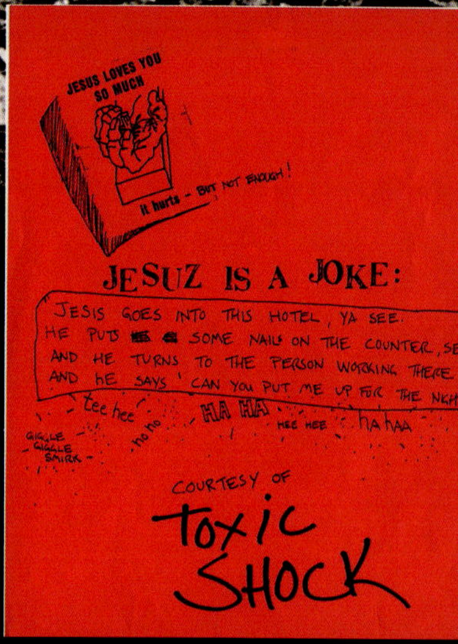

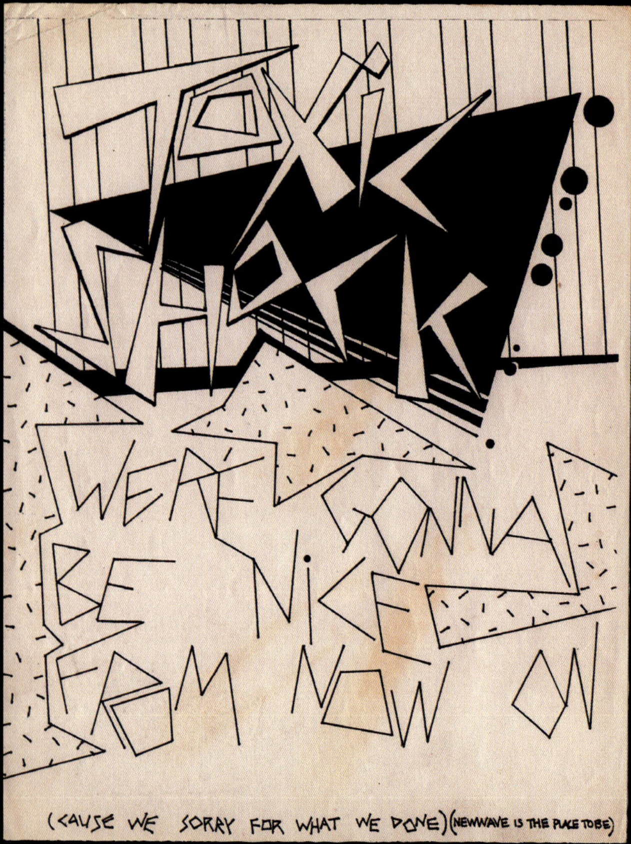

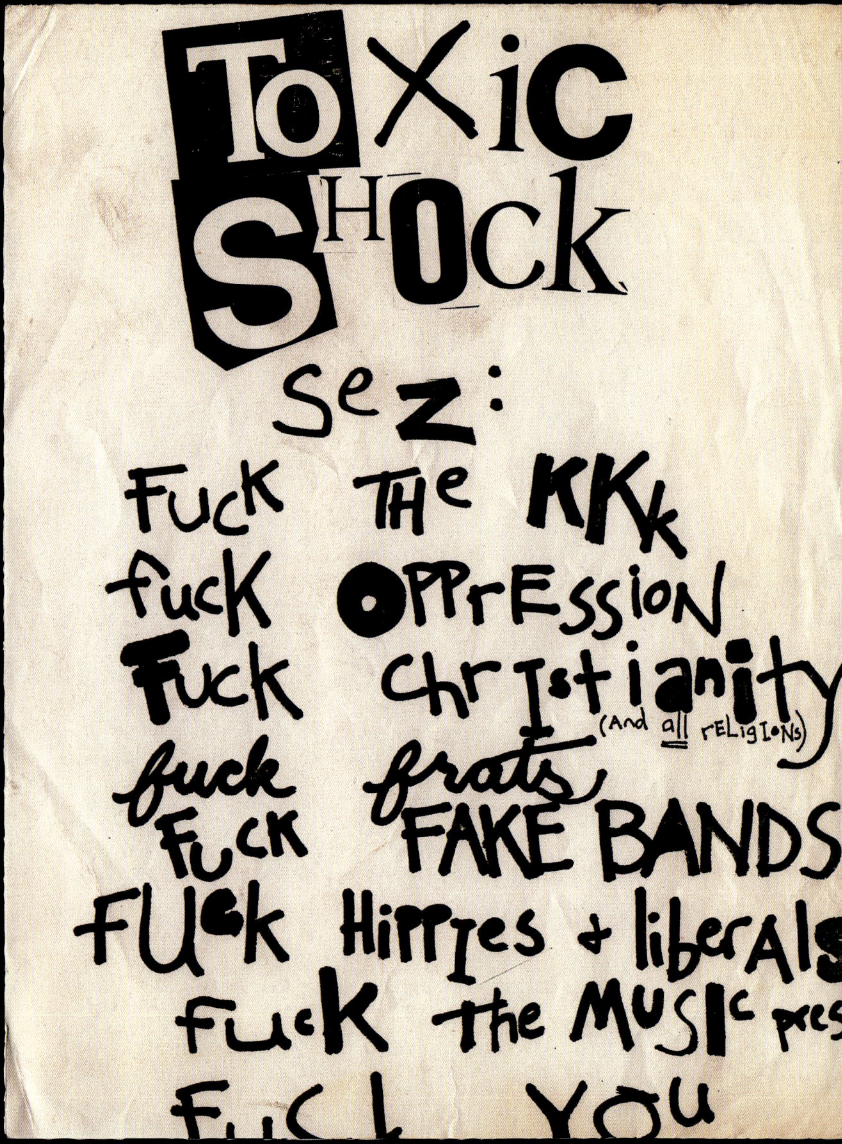

All of these flyers by David Y

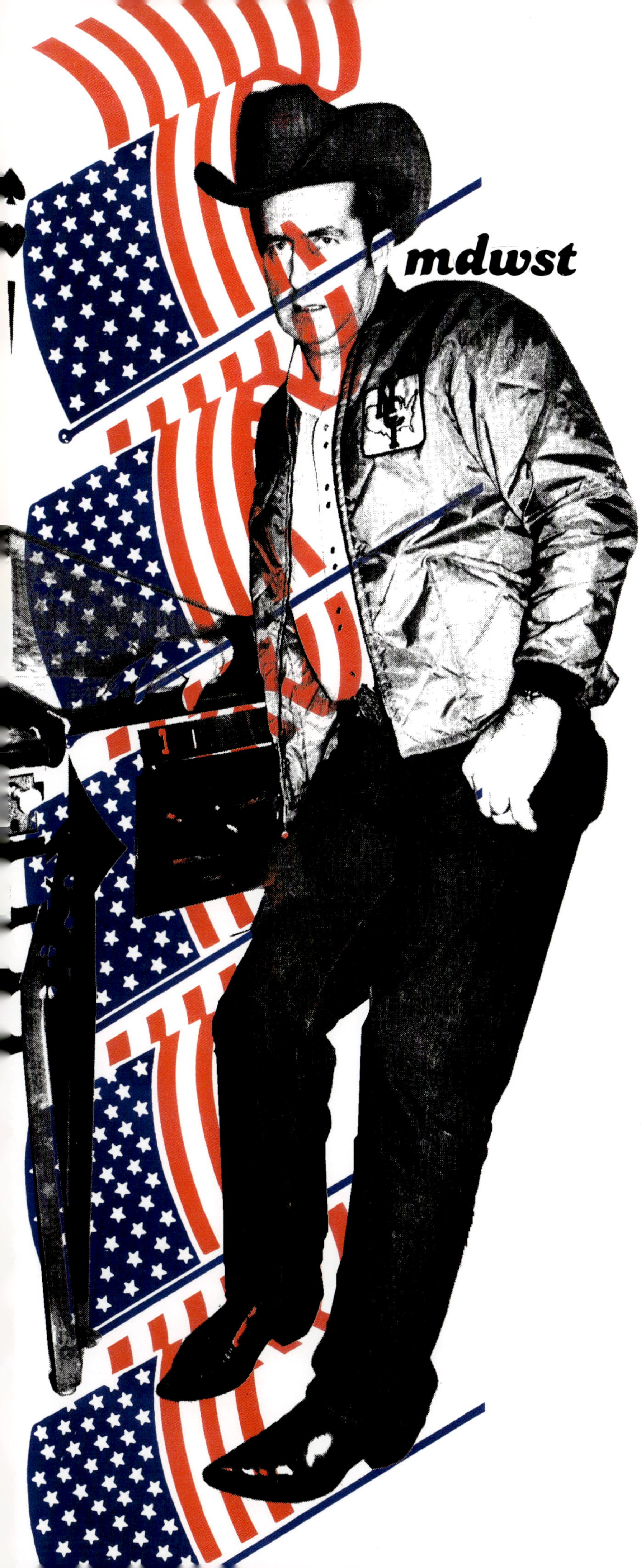
mdwst

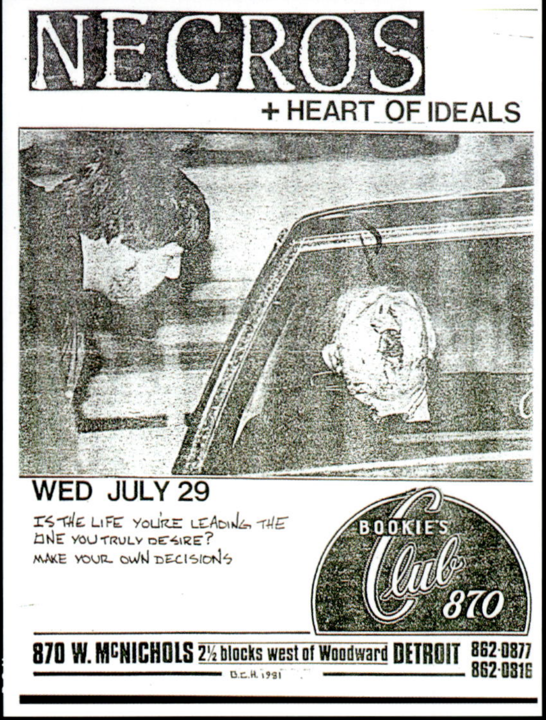

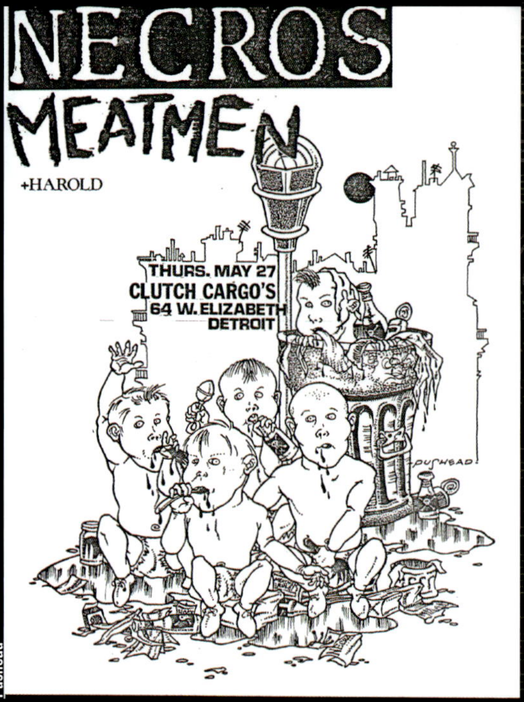

Pushead

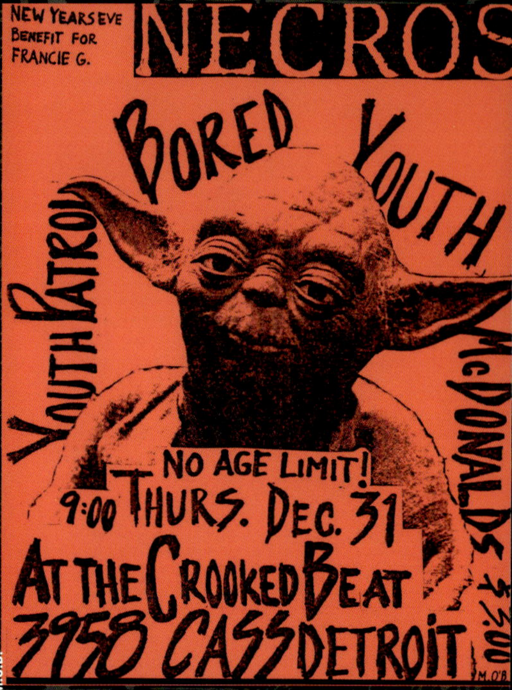

M.O.B.

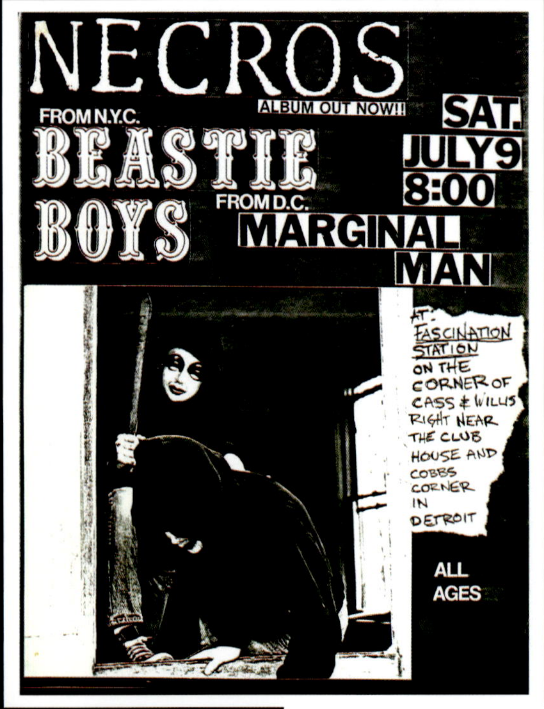

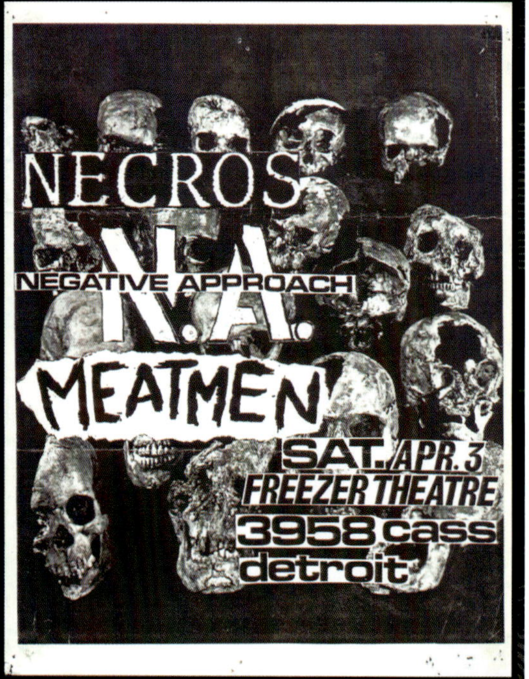

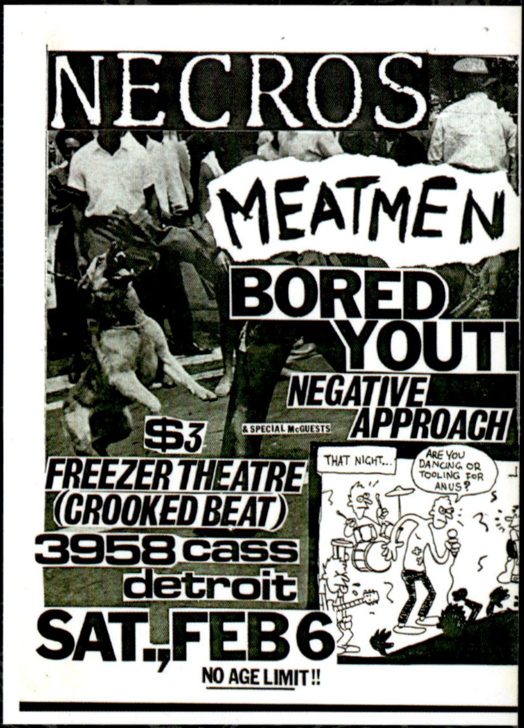

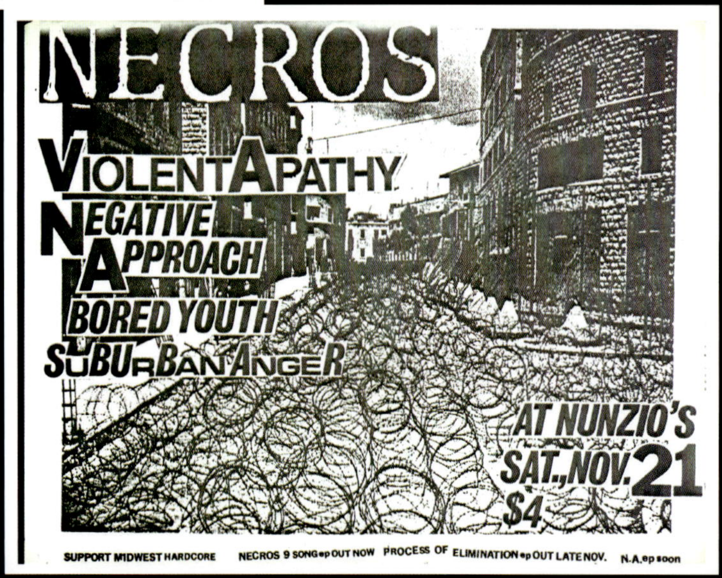

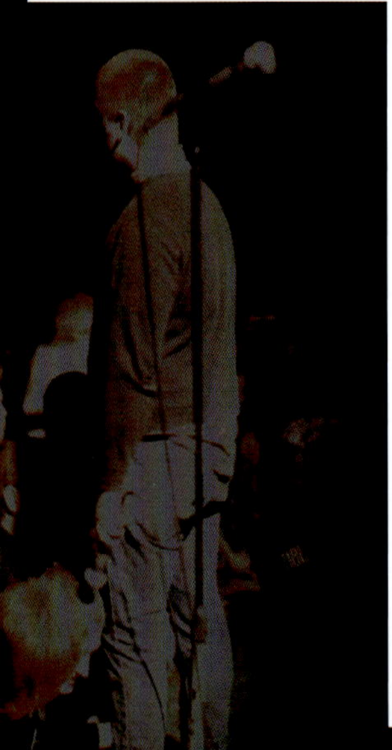

Barry of Necros
Photo © Wendy Schecter

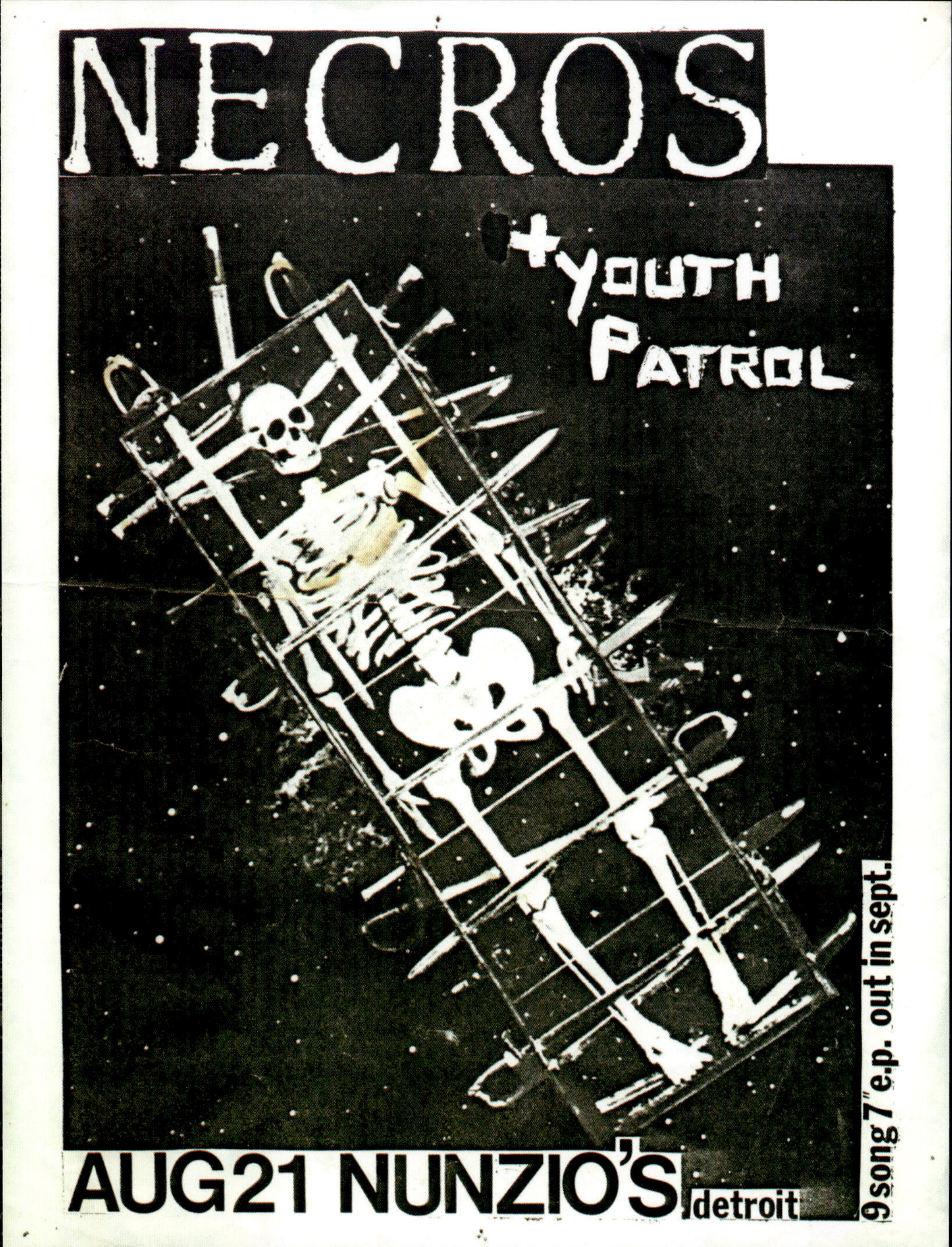

"I am not going to be of any help regarding who designed what. I might have done some, and I'm sure that some of the band members did some, but it was too long ago for me to remember."

Corey Rusk

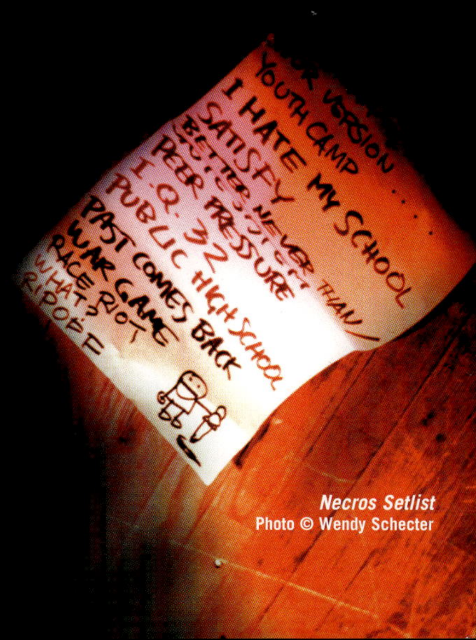

Necros Setlist
Photo © Wendy Schecter

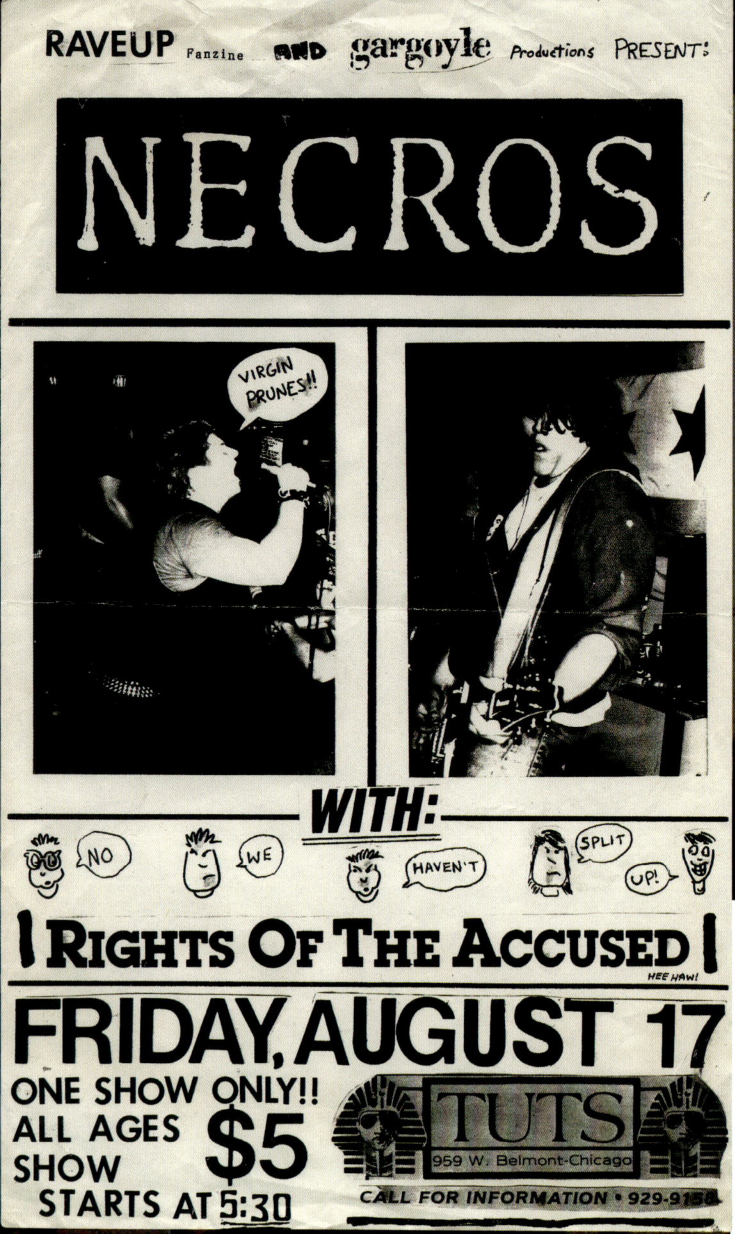
RAVEUP Fanzine AND gargoyle Productions PRESENT:
NECROS
VIRGIN PRUNES!!
WITH:
NO
WE
HAVEN'T
SPLIT
UP!
RIGHTS OF THE ACCUSED
HEE HAW!
FRIDAY, AUGUST 17
ONE SHOW ONLY!!
ALL AGES SHOW
$5
STARTS AT 5:30
TUTS
959 W. Belmont-Chicago
CALL FOR INFORMATION • 929-9158

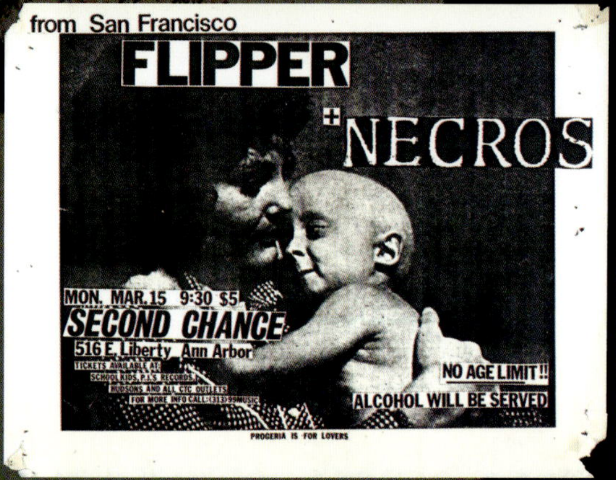
from San Francisco
FLIPPER
+ NECROS
MON. MAR.15 9:30 $5
SECOND CHANCE
516 E. Liberty Ann Arbor
NO AGE LIMIT!!
ALCOHOL WILL BE SERVED
PROGERIA IS FOR LOVERS

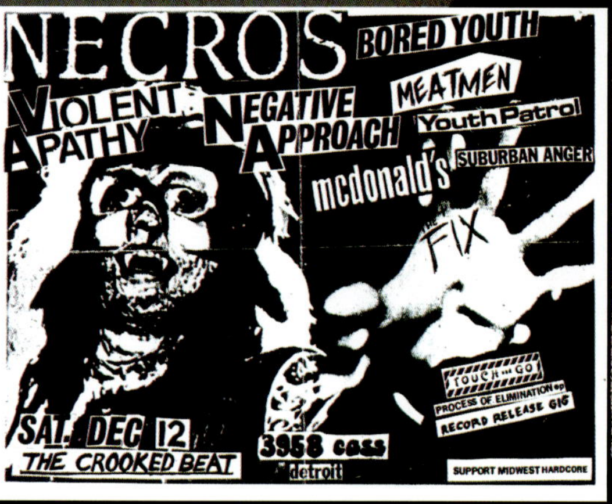
NECROS
BORED YOUTH
VIOLENT APATHY
NEGATIVE APPROACH
MEATMEN
Youth Patrol
SUBURBAN ANGER
mcdonald's
FIX
TOUCH AND GO
PROCESS OF ELIMINATION EP
RECORD RELEASE GIG
SAT. DEC 12
THE CROOKED BEAT
3958 cass
detroit
SUPPORT MIDWEST HARDCORE

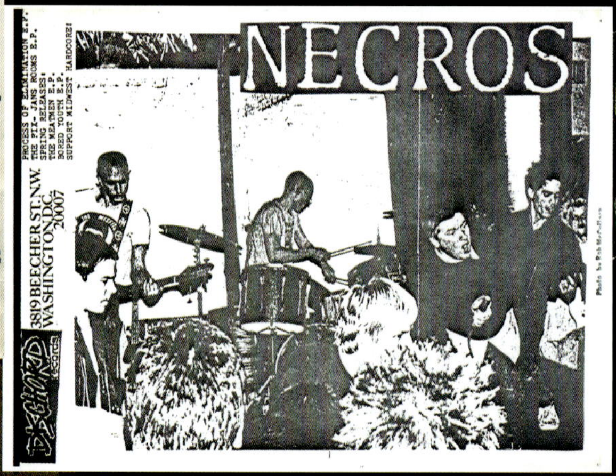
NECROS
3819 BEECHER ST. N.W.
WASHINGTON, D.C.
20007
SUPPORT MIDWEST HARDCORE!
DISCHORD records

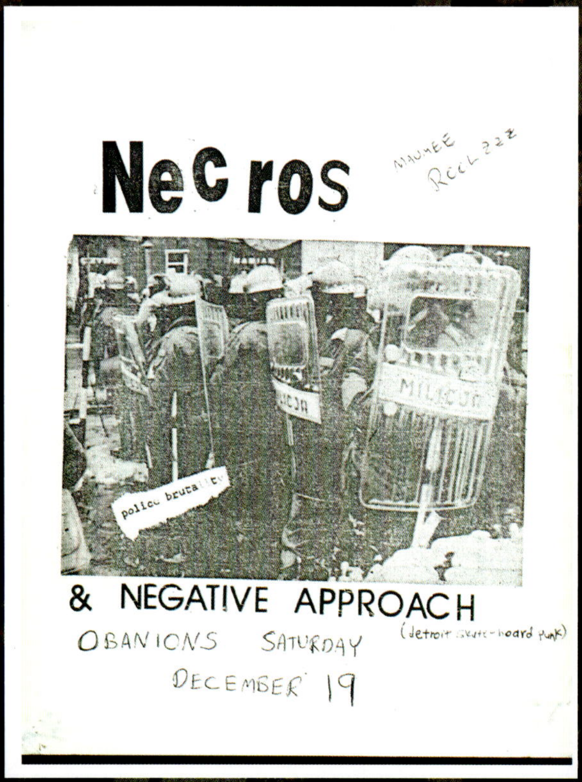
NeCros
MAUMEE ROCK ???
police brutality
MILICJA
& NEGATIVE APPROACH
(detroit skate-board punk)
OBANIONS SATURDAY
DECEMBER 19

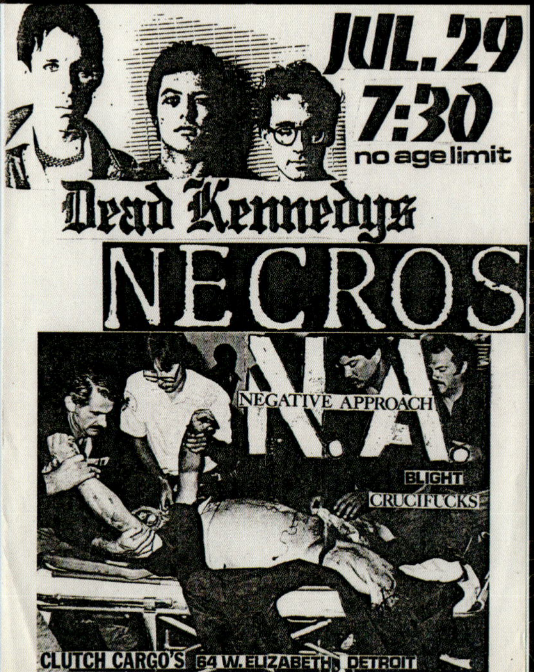
JUL. 29
7:30
no age limit
Dead Kennedys
NECROS
N.A.
NEGATIVE APPROACH
BLIGHT
CRUCIFUCKS
CLUTCH CARGO'S 64 W. ELIZABETH DETROIT

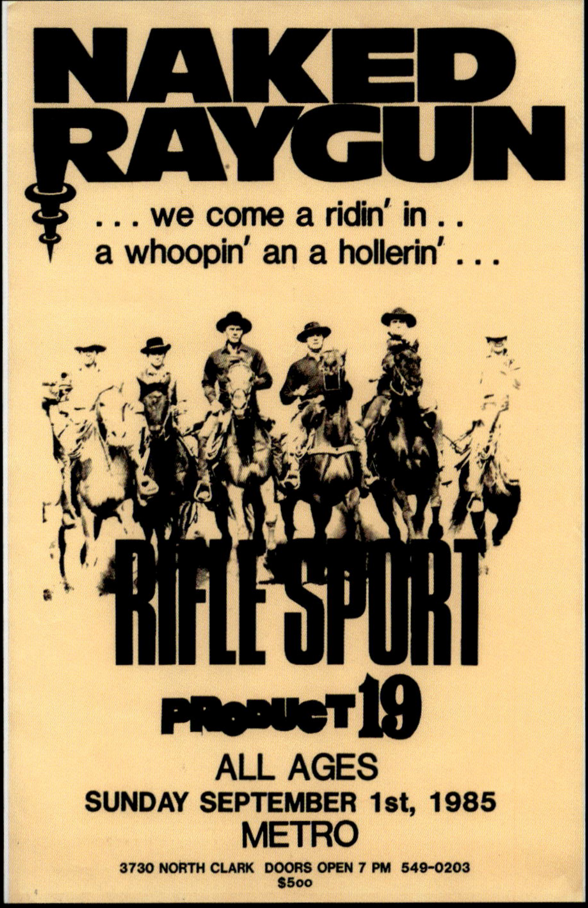
NAKED RAYGUN
. . . we come a ridin' in . .
a whoopin' an a hollerin' . . .
RIFLE SPORT
PRODUCT 19
ALL AGES
SUNDAY SEPTEMBER 1st, 1985
METRO
3730 NORTH CLARK DOORS OPEN 7 PM 549-0203
$5oo

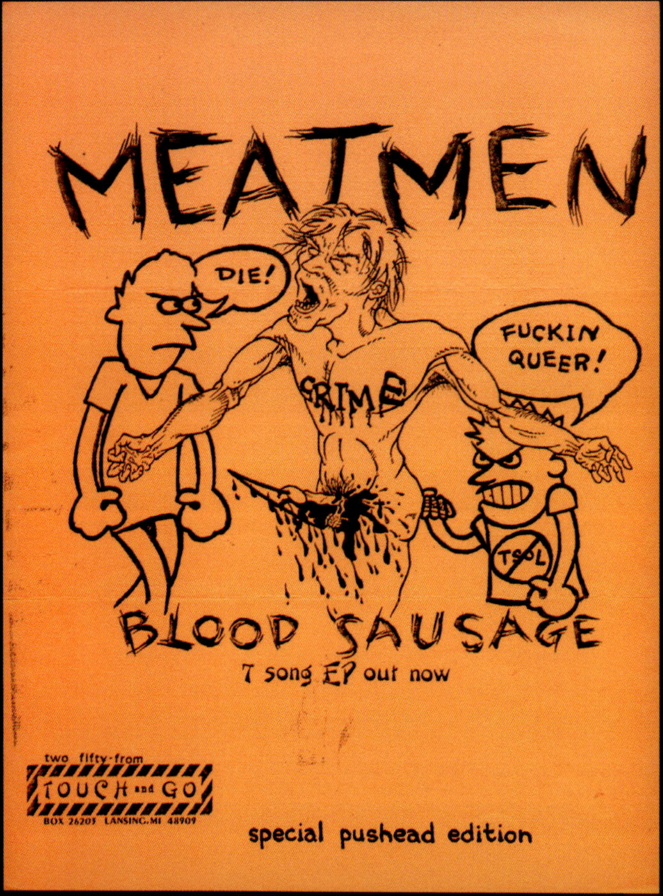
MEATMEN
DIE!
FUCKIN QUEER!
CRIME
TSOL
BLOOD SAUSAGE
7 song EP out now
two fifty from
TOUCH and GO
BOX 26203 LANSING, MI 48909
special pushead edition

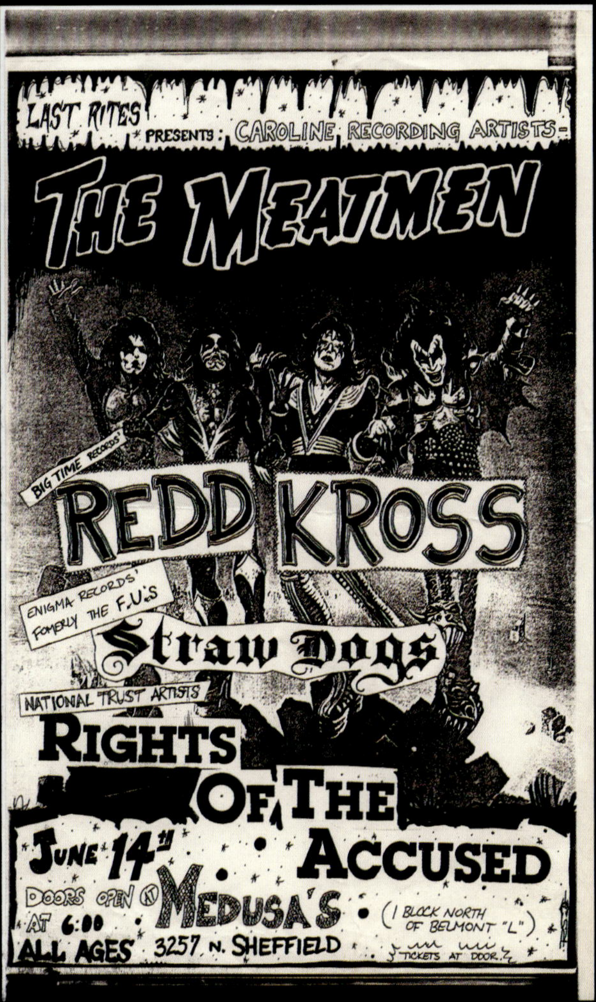
LAST RITES PRESENTS: CAROLINE RECORDING ARTISTS-
THE MEATMEN
BIG TIME RECORDS
REDD KROSS
ENIGMA RECORDS' FORMERLY THE F.U.'S
Straw Dogs
NATIONAL TRUST ARTISTS
RIGHTS OF THE ACCUSED
JUNE 14th
DOORS OPEN AT 6:00
ALL AGES
MEDUSA'S
3257 N. SHEFFIELD
(1 BLOCK NORTH OF BELMONT "L")
TICKETS AT DOOR

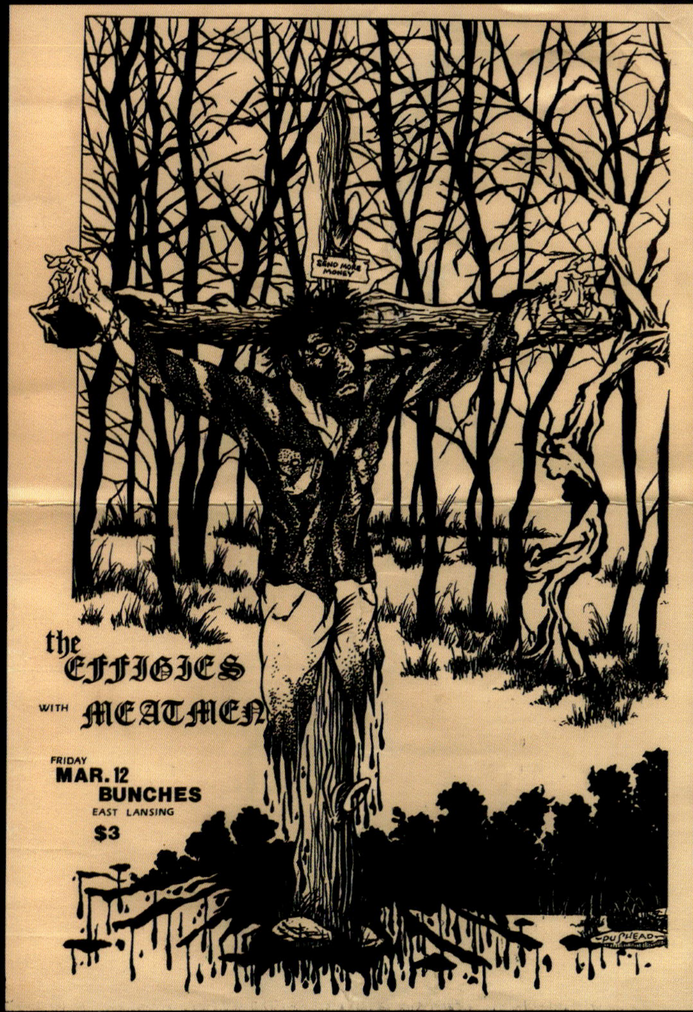
SEND MORE MONEY
the EFFIGIES
WITH MEATMEN
FRIDAY
MAR. 12
BUNCHES
EAST LANSING
$3
PUSHEAD

Pushead

About Punk Rock J Yuenger

About the worst trade I ever made: a handwritten Minor Threat setlist I found onstage, swapped for a chrome bullet belt. The show was at a rundown disco in Chicago called the Central American Social Club (or "The Hall" in common parlance,) and it was amazing. It was one of those nights when there's a bunch of sweaty kids onstage singing along the whole time, knowing every word, who buy t-shirts or stickers from the band out by their van after the gig and everyone's really cool and your crappy teenage life seems to be okay for a week. (The belt got stolen out of a car three months later.)

About the Necros logo painted on the back of my leather jacket, along with that image of a skeleton in a box with a bunch of swords sticking through it. I'd be riding the bus or walking down the street and an African-American person would see it and yell, *"Negroes?* What do you mean, *Negroes!?"*

About the stage dive I was about to make at a Die Kreuzen show when their singer Danny got me in a headlock. His homemade punk bracelet studded with nails left a huge gash half an inch above my right eye.

About an hour by bus and subway to get to Wax Trax! Records, the only place in Chicago to buy imports and indie records. I remember kids who would drive two hours up from southern Illinois to see little local hardcore bands play. There were no real channels of communication about the music or what was going on in the scene, other than word of mouth, fanzines and flyers. Everyone I met had a real mania to KNOW. Early on it seemed all you could do to get information was to run up to every person you saw wearing a punk shirt or button, and hit them up for details.

About Naked Raygun, a goofy art-damaged noise band that gradually turned into a supercool, supertight melodic punk machine. They kept one goofy thing about them, their guitarist played sax as well. One day someone stole the saxophone, and instead of replacing it they just stopped playing the songs that featured sax.

About Bad Brains: I heard a couple of the band members talking backstage once at a club called COD's in 1982 and wondered how guys from Maryland might have picked up Jamaican accents. I also remember the show they played that night, and sixteen years later bands are still trying and failing to capture that sound and spirit.

About Husker Du: I loved that they could play a whole set of songs without stopping once.

About cops: most of them fat and mean, with leather jackets and their haircut: sideburns, long in back (think Jim Belushi) which is still the height of Chicago law enforcement fashion. I can remember walking to school and being stopped and searched by the same two plainclothesmen every other day for a year. It was some kind of game: they never stopped expecting to find some kind of contraband on me even though I'd never have anything in my pockets besides guitar picks, and a cassette (Misfits *Walk Among Us* on one side, Void/Faith on the other). I never alternated my route or tried to sneak past them because I felt I was striking some kind of blow for punk rock.

About the best show I can remember was the Big Boys. It was a consensus among everyone I knew - I don't remember everything about the show, just that it was incredibly hot in "The Hall" that night, but the good time punk rock lunacy of the gig carried out to the street, where there was a big group of kids running around singing the *"whoa whoa"* chorus of the song "We Got Your Money" at the top of their lungs.

About the reasons we did it: For some, it was purely social. Others had an interest in politics and bucking the system. (My friend John was always one of those guys with a CRASS logo on his jacket. He went on to open a political bookstore. My friend Scott ended up in a free speech battle with the city of Chicago after the mayor shut down his installation in the Art institute, which required the viewer to stand on the American flag.)

Still others were about the music. By 1985-86, when most of my peers in the scene were going to college, work, or finding another way to drift apart, I realized that I'd been ignoring other kinds of music: metal, Stooges, '60s garage bands, hip-hop. For me, it's always been music.

A few years ago I started playing my scratchy old hardcore records again–first as a kind of anthropological study (the one-time only sound of bored kids with pawn shop equipment in anonymous recording studios that no one could recreate if they tried) and then as a warning from the past (music made by people who do it purely for the love of it doesn't go stale). Later, as I started to buy the recordings on CD, because a lot of those songs are really good. That's what it's about.

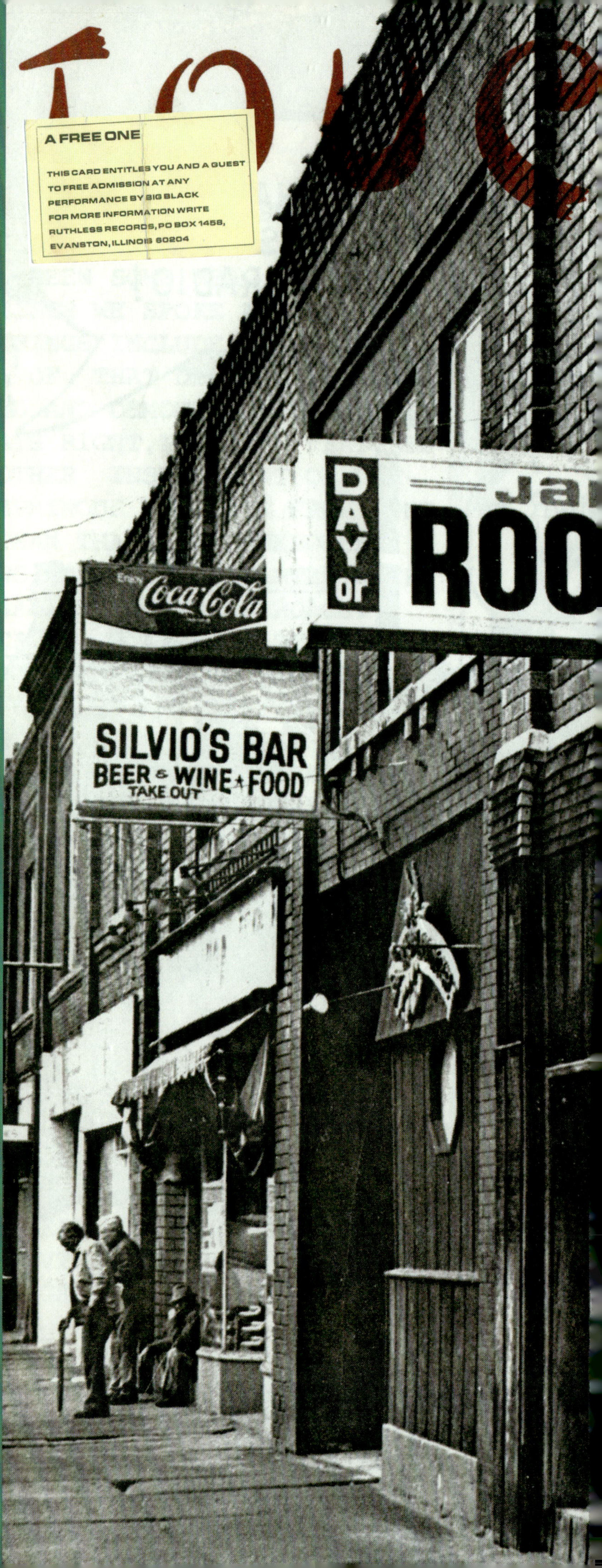

big boys
FROM AUSTIN TEXAS
WITH
die kreuzen
FROM MILWAUKEE
AND
THE LATIN DOGS
GRAYSTONE HALL 7816 MICH. AVE!
no age limit!
WEST OF LIVERNOIS AVE. & EAST OF WYOMING AVE
IN detroit
NEAR DEARBORN
FRIDAY SEPT. 2

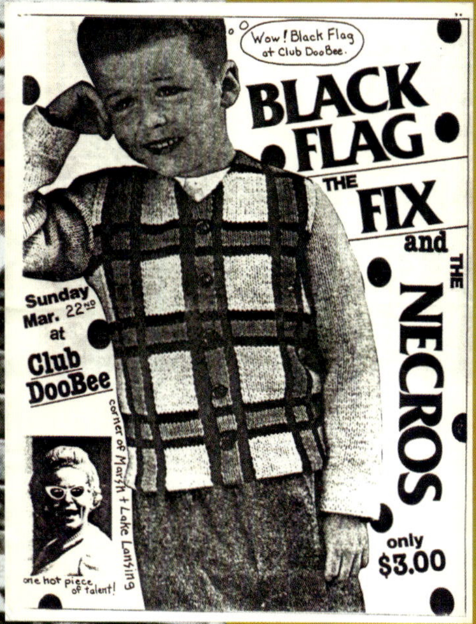
Wow! Black Flag at Club DooBee.
BLACK FLAG
THE FIX
and
THE NECROS
Sunday Mar. 22nd at Club DooBee
only $3.00

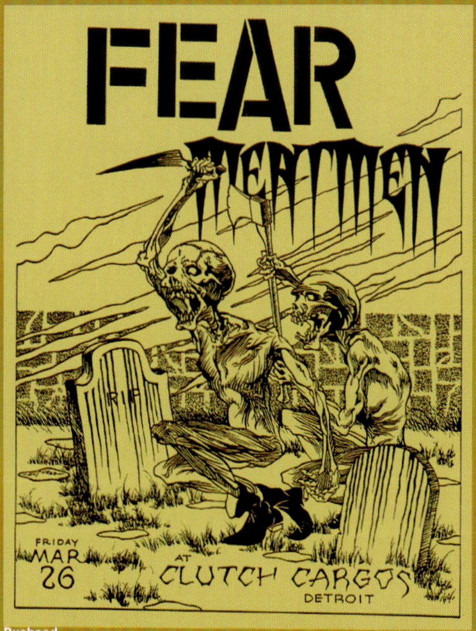
FEAR
DEATHMEN
FRIDAY MAR 26
AT CLUTCH CARGOS
DETROIT

Pushead

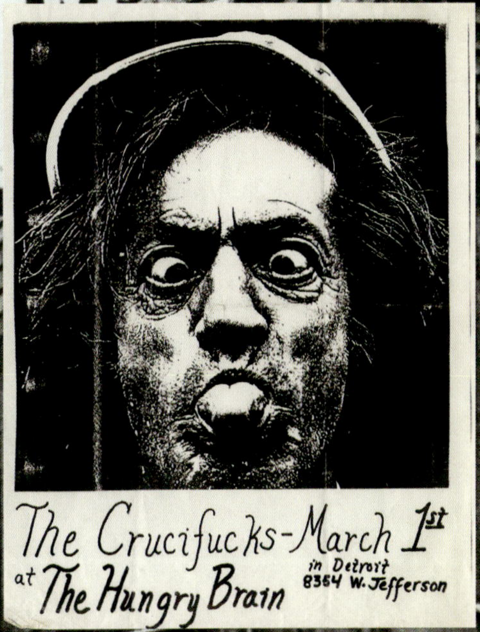
The Crucifucks - March 1st
at The Hungry Brain
in Detroit
8364 W. Jefferson

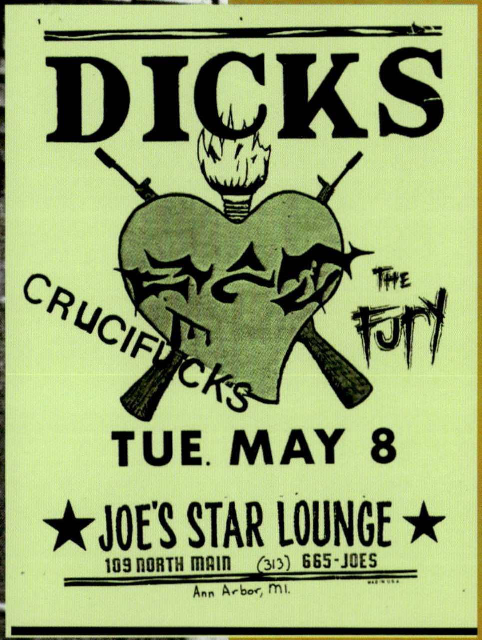
DICKS
CRUCIFUCKS
THE FURY
TUE. MAY 8
★ JOE'S STAR LOUNGE ★
109 NORTH MAIN (313) 665-JOES
Ann Arbor, MI.

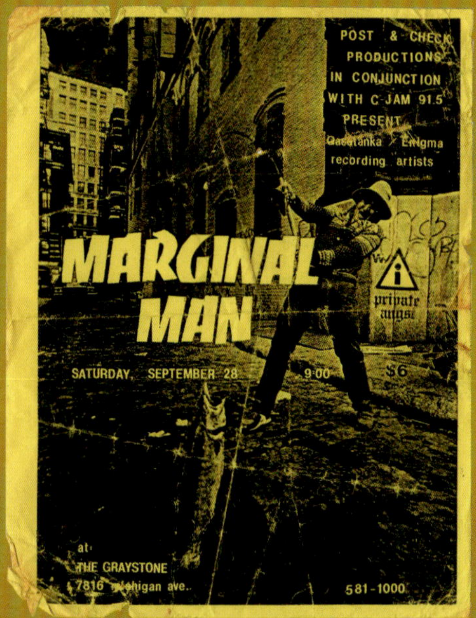
POST & CHECK PRODUCTIONS
IN CONJUNCTION WITH C-JAM 91.5
PRESENT
MARGINAL MAN
SATURDAY, SEPTEMBER 28
9:00
$6
at THE GRAYSTONE
581-1000

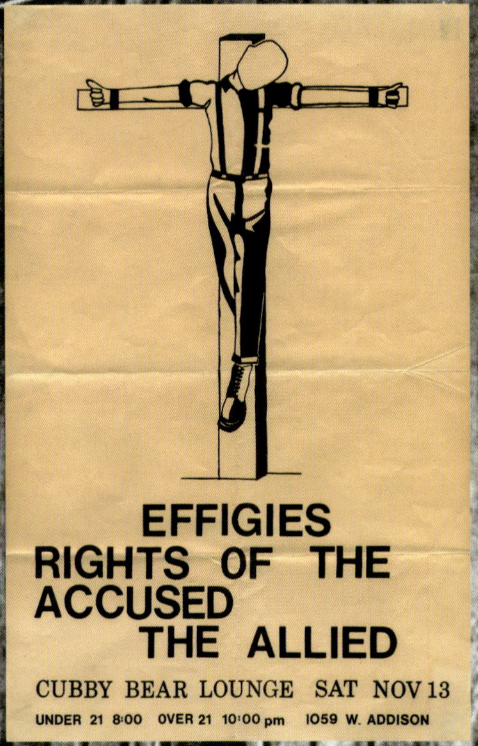
EFFIGIES
RIGHTS OF THE ACCUSED
THE ALLIED
CUBBY BEAR LOUNGE SAT NOV 13
UNDER 21 8:00 OVER 21 10:00 pm 1059 W. ADDISON

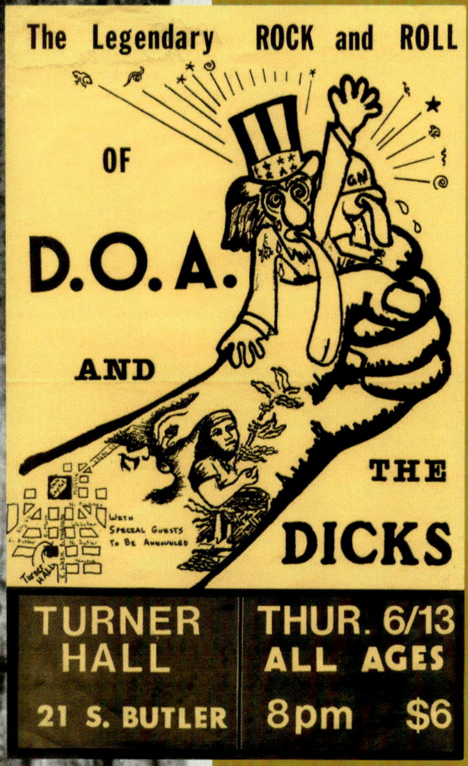
The Legendary ROCK and ROLL
OF
D.O.A.
AND
THE
DICKS
TURNER HALL
THUR. 6/13
ALL AGES
21 S. BUTLER
8pm $6

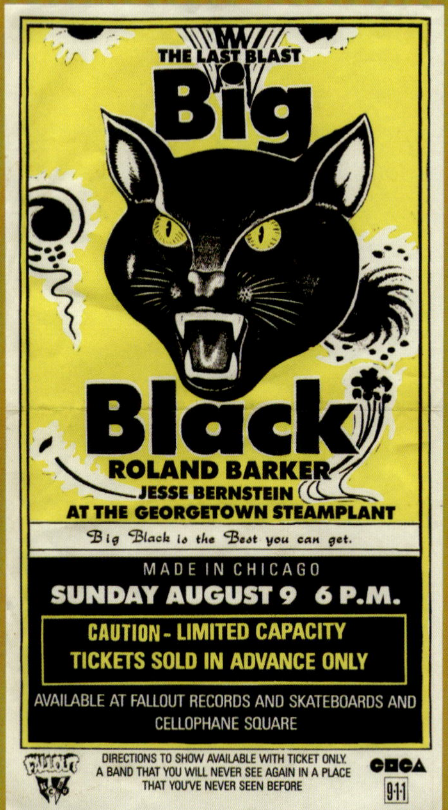
THE LAST BLAST
Big Black
ROLAND BARKER
JESSE BERNSTEIN
AT THE GEORGETOWN STEAMPLANT
Big Black is the Best you can get.
MADE IN CHICAGO
SUNDAY AUGUST 9 6 P.M.
CAUTION - LIMITED CAPACITY
TICKETS SOLD IN ADVANCE ONLY
AVAILABLE AT FALLOUT RECORDS AND SKATEBOARDS AND CELLOPHANE SQUARE
DIRECTIONS TO SHOW AVAILABLE WITH TICKET ONLY.
A BAND THAT YOU WILL NEVER SEE AGAIN IN A PLACE THAT YOU'VE NEVER SEEN BEFORE

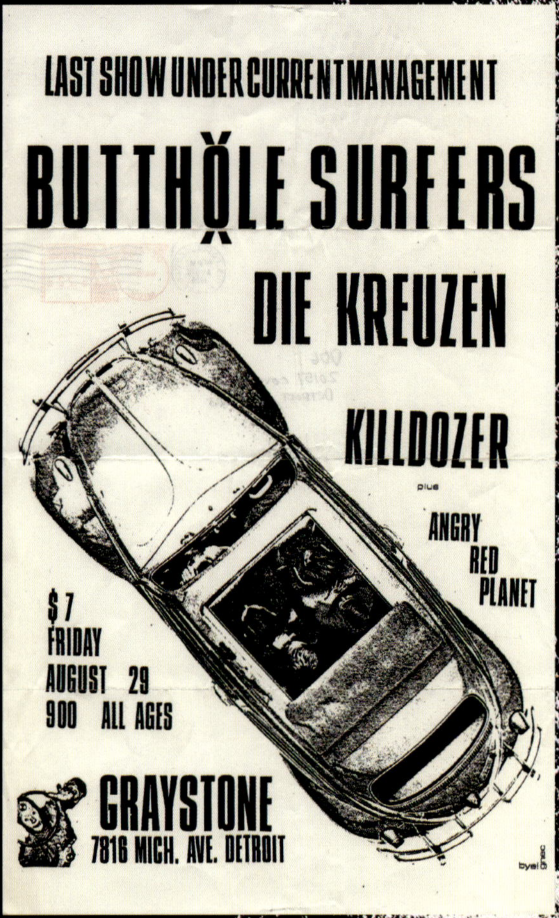
LAST SHOW UNDER CURRENT MANAGEMENT
BUTTHOLE SURFERS
DIE KREUZEN
KILLDOZER
plus
ANGRY RED PLANET
$7
FRIDAY
AUGUST 29
900 ALL AGES
GRAYSTONE
7816 MICH. AVE. DETROIT

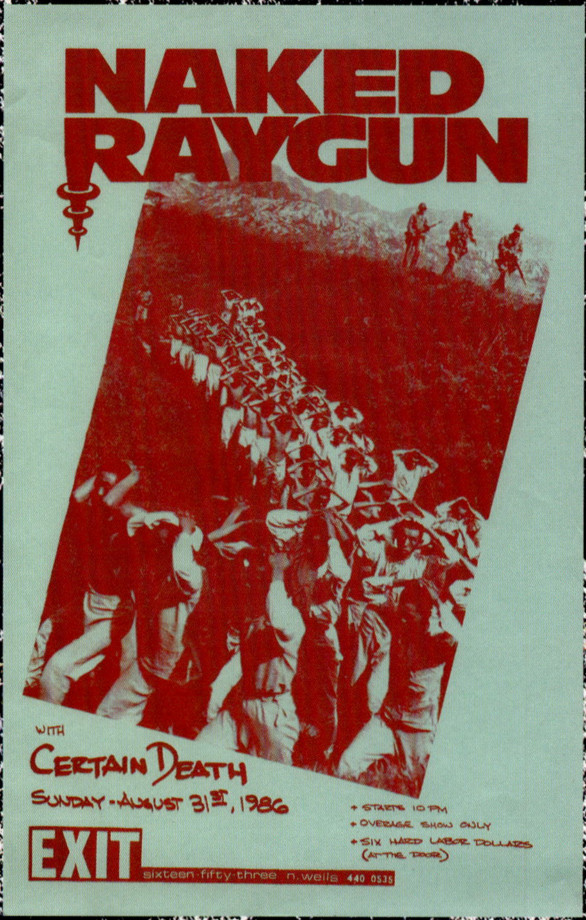
NAKED RAYGUN
WITH
CERTAIN DEATH
SUNDAY - AUGUST 31ST, 1986
STARTS 10 PM
OVERAGE SHOW ONLY
SIX HARD LABOR DOLLARS (AT THE DOOR)
EXIT
sixteen-fifty-three n. wells 440 0535

GNEC

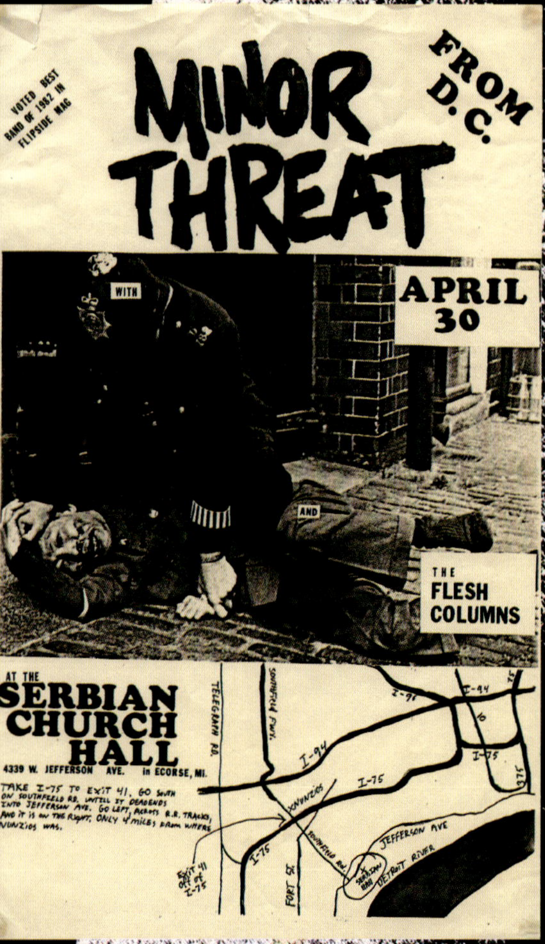
VOTED BEST BAND OF 1982 IN FLIPSIDE MAG
MINOR THREAT
FROM D.C.
WITH
APRIL 30
AND
THE FLESH COLUMNS
AT THE
SERBIAN CHURCH HALL
4339 W. JEFFERSON AVE. in ECORSE, MI.

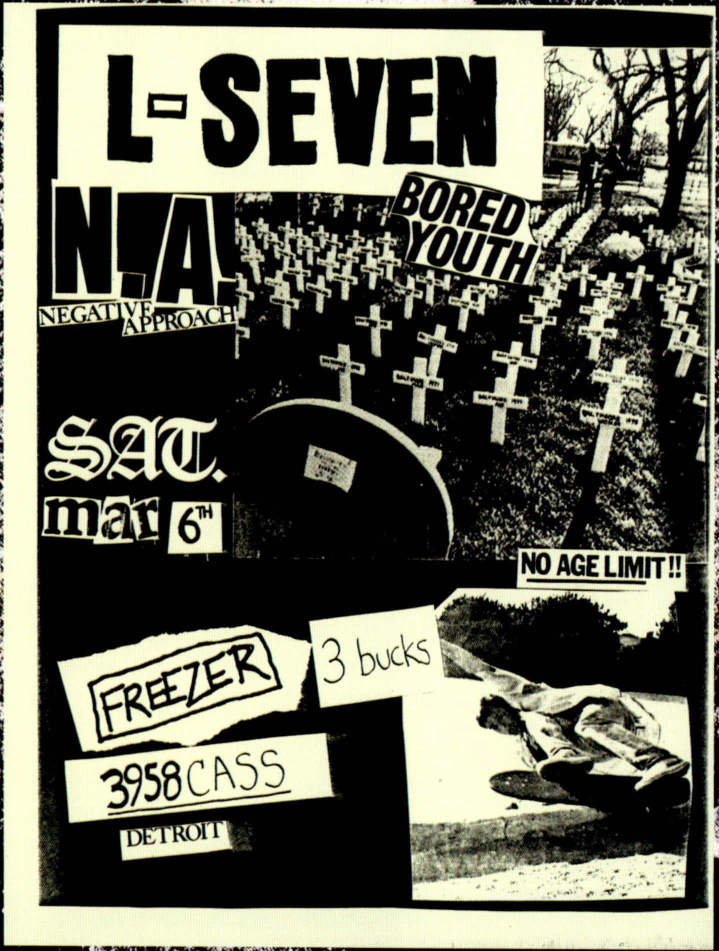
L-SEVEN
N.A.
NEGATIVE APPROACH
BORED YOUTH
SAT.
mar 6TH
NO AGE LIMIT!!
FREEZER
3 bucks
3958 CASS
DETROIT

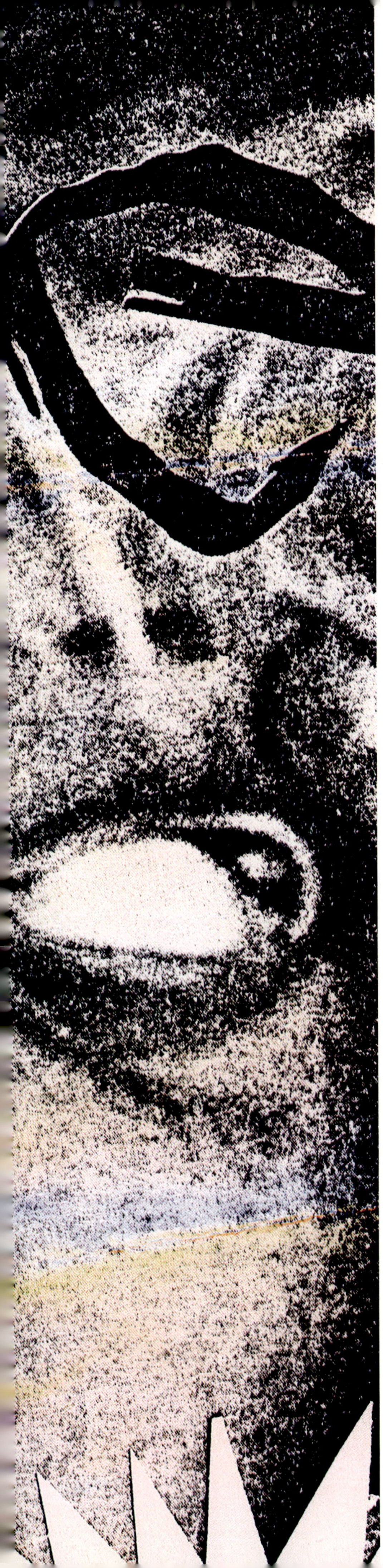

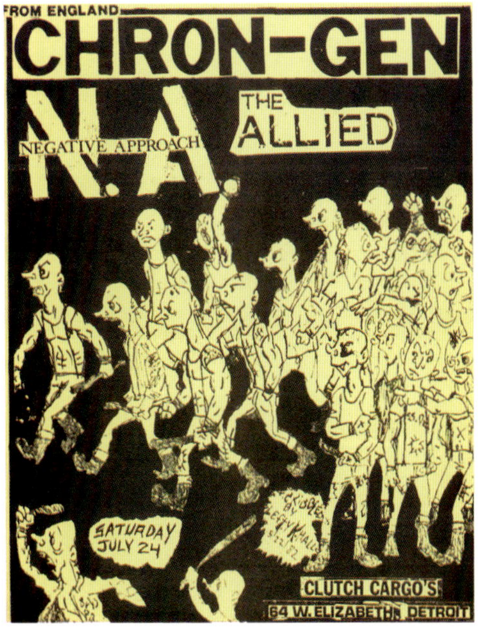
FROM ENGLAND
CHRON-GEN
N.A
NEGATIVE APPROACH
THE ALLIED
SATURDAY JULY 24
CLUTCH CARGO'S
64 W. ELIZABETH DETROIT

Lefty K. Hall

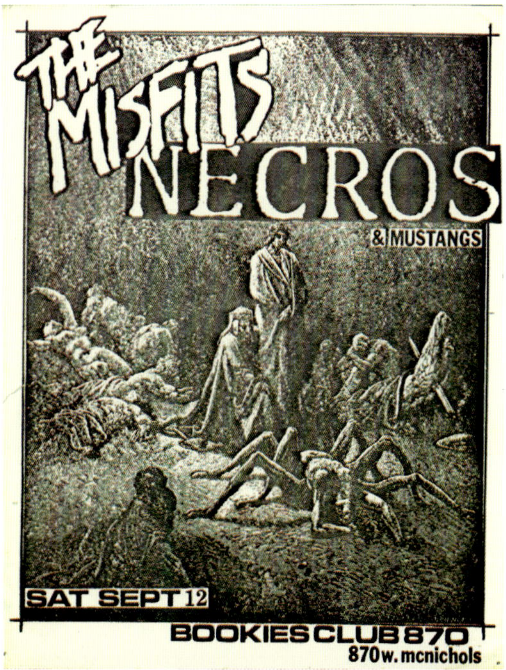
THE MISFITS
NECROS
& MUSTANGS
SAT SEPT 12
BOOKIES CLUB 870
870 w. mcnichols

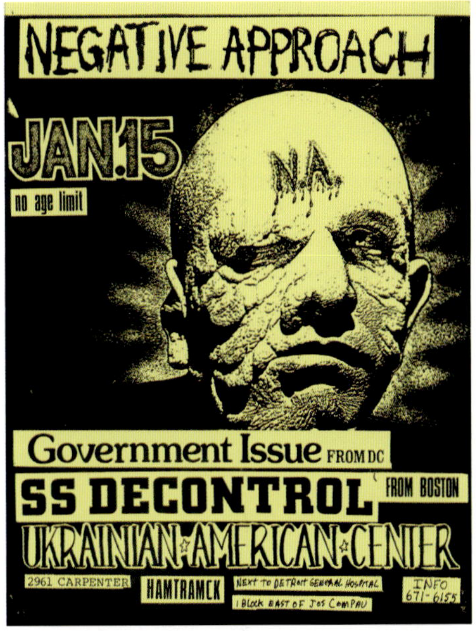
NEGATIVE APPROACH
JAN.15
no age limit
N.A.
Government Issue FROM DC
SS DECONTROL
FROM BOSTON
UKRAINIAN AMERICAN CENTER
2961 CARPENTER
HAMTRAMCK
INFO

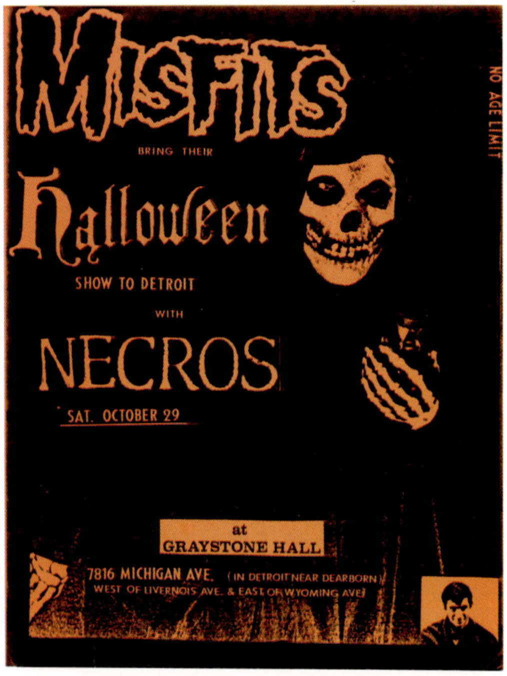
MISFITS
BRING THEIR
Halloween
SHOW TO DETROIT
WITH
NECROS
SAT. OCTOBER 29
NO AGE LIMIT
at
GRAYSTONE HALL
7816 MICHIGAN AVE. (IN DETROIT NEAR DEARBORN)
WEST OF LIVERNOIS AVE. & EAST OF WYOMING AVE.

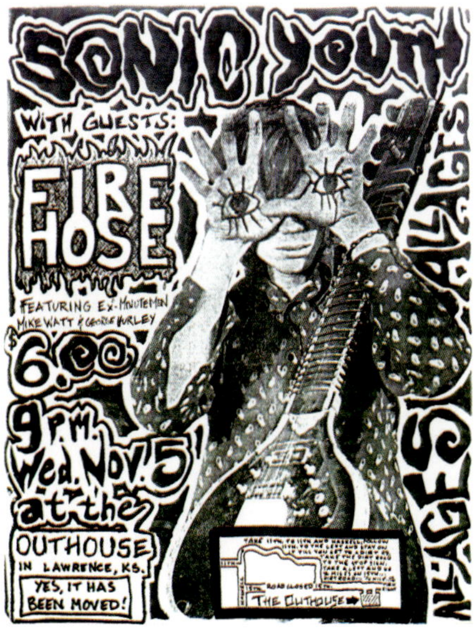
SONIC YOUTH
WITH GUESTS:
FIREHOSE
ALL AGES
6.00
9 pm.
Wed. Nov. 5
at the
OUTHOUSE
IN LAWRENCE, KS.
YES, IT HAS BEEN MOVED!
THE OUTHOUSE

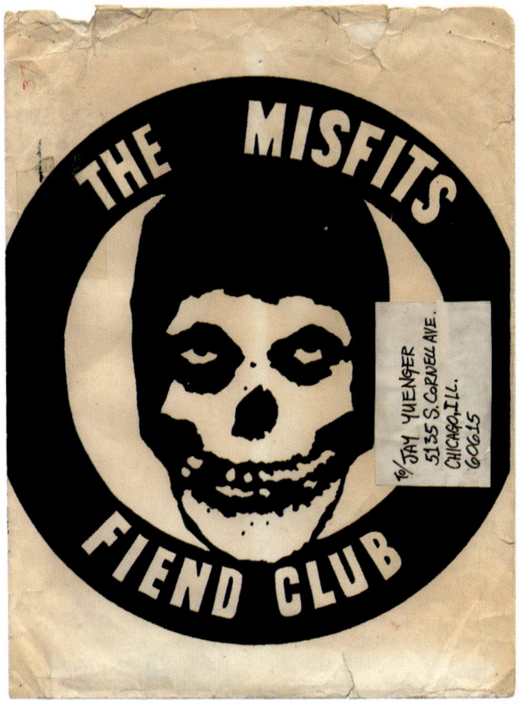
THE MISFITS
FIEND CLUB
JAY YUENGER
5135 S. CORNELL AVE.
CHICAGO, ILL.
60615

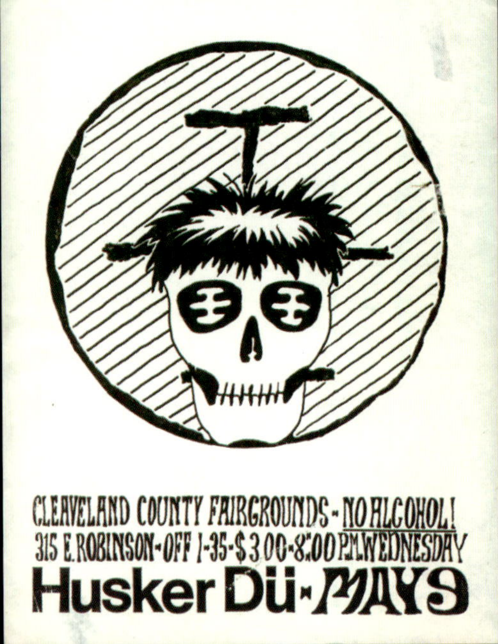

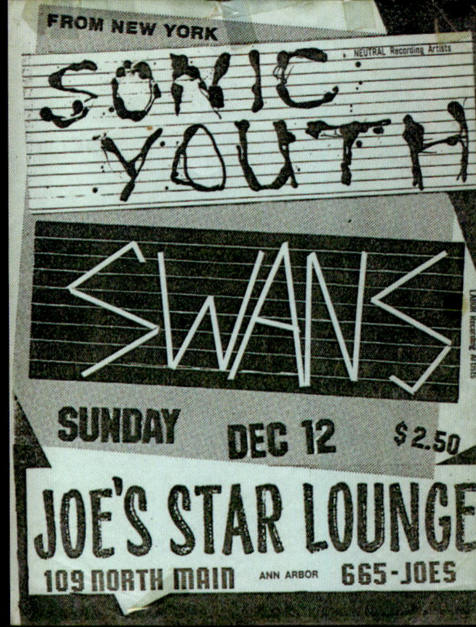

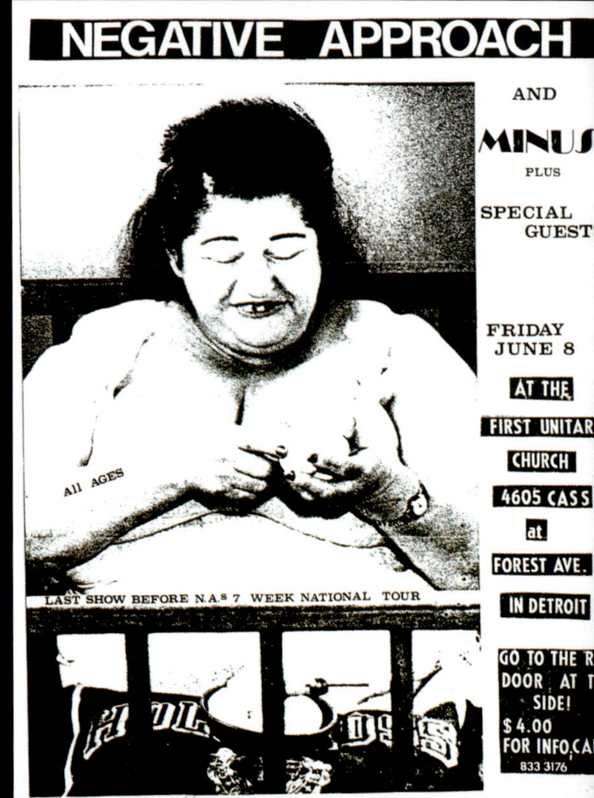

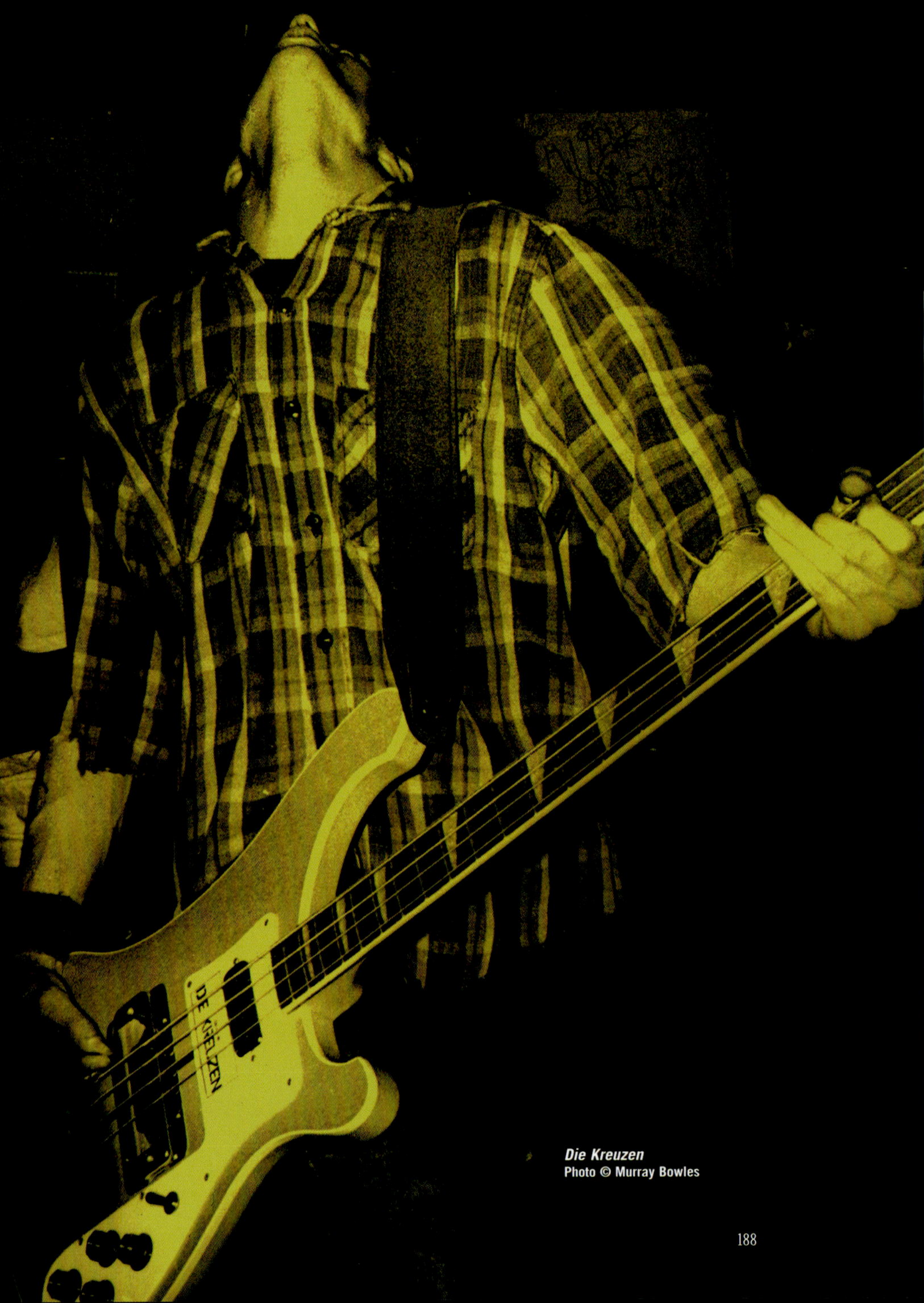

Die Kreuzen
Photo © Murray Bowles

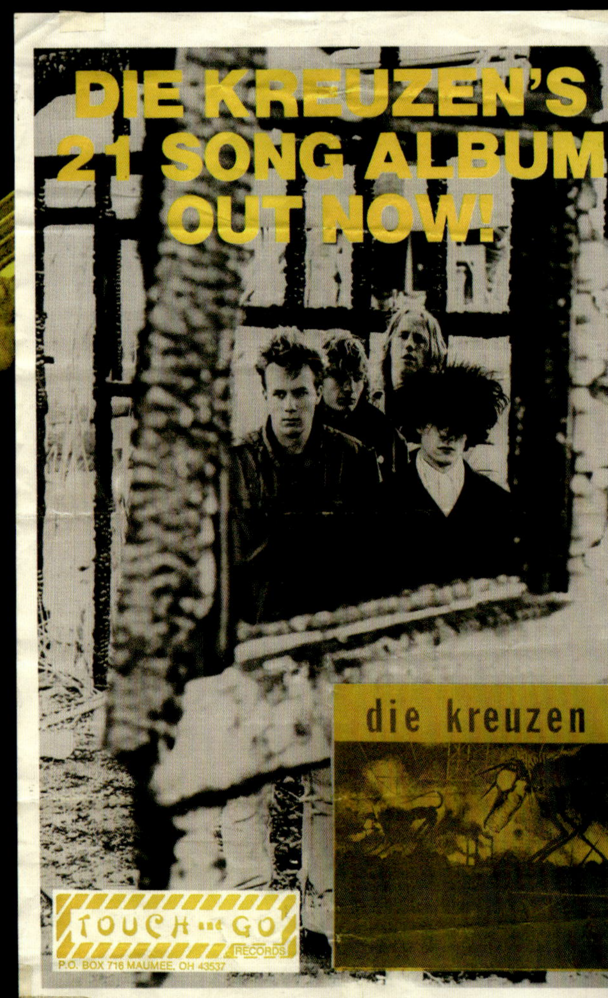

BOSTON

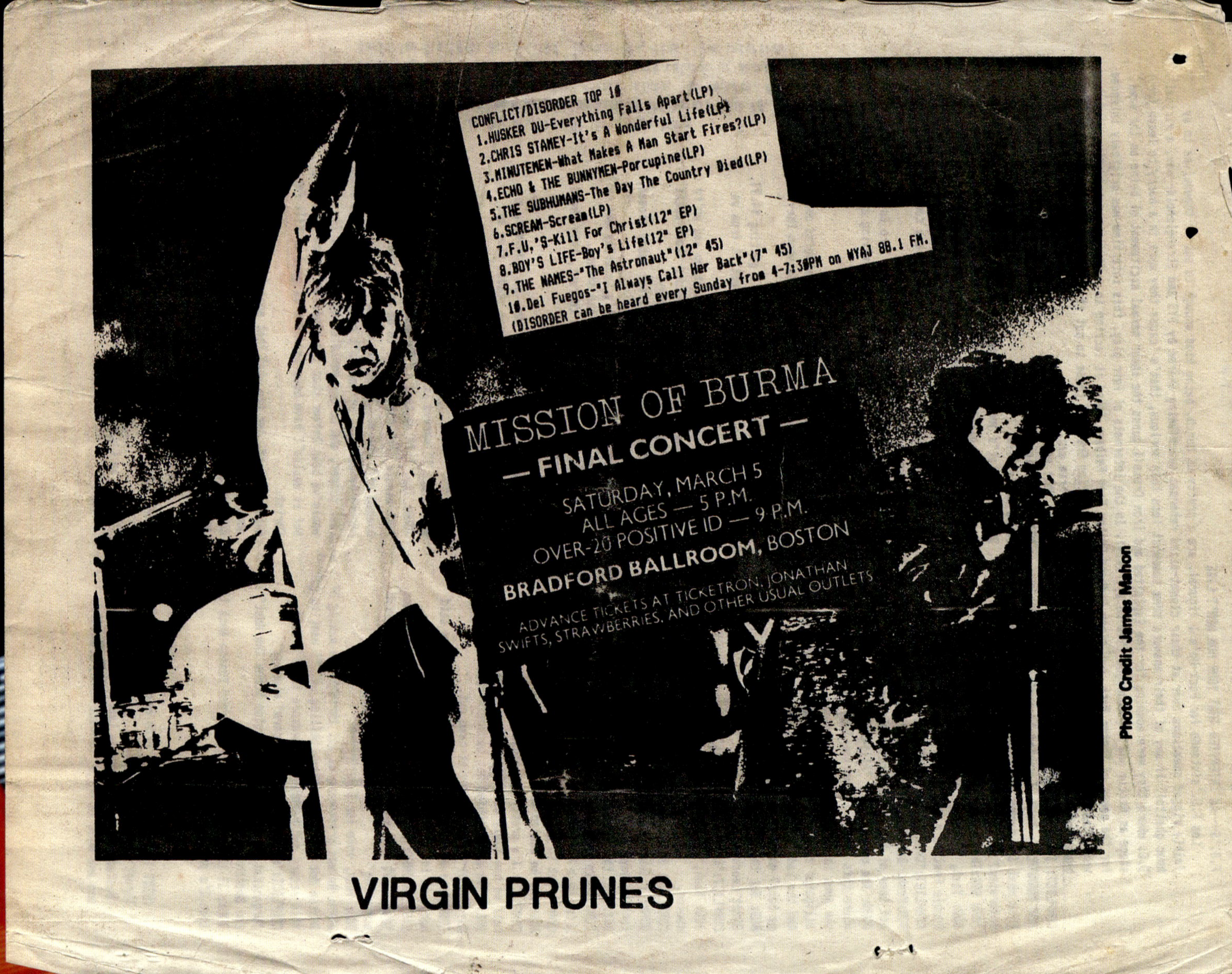

Photo: James Mahon

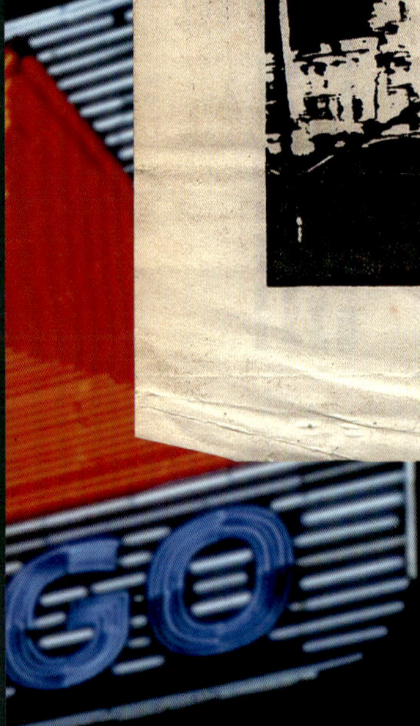

Punk Is Dead

by Hank Peirce

"We are a generation of obscenities. The most oppressed people in this country are...the middle class. They don't have anything to rise up against and fight against. We will have to invent new laws to break...the first part of the yippy program is to kill your parents...until you're prepared to kill your parents you're not ready to change this country. Our parents are our first oppressors." –Jerry Rubin

Punk is dead. There, I've said it, let's now get on with creating a new world. Yes, just like hippies, just like Jerry Rubin, punk is dead. Once books are published discussing the importance of any movement, it signifies the death of that movement. I'm not saying that punk was useless, it was a life preserver for many of us. It was the *Island of Misfit Toys* that those of us drowning in a sea of conformity swam to. Today, sadly, that island is prime real estate, overbuilt by consumerism and eroded by waves of conformity. Worst of all, WE let it happen. It must be destroyed before the nostalgia cruises begin.

Punk is dead. I say this because until the youth of the world recognizes that the life force of punk has dissipated, no one will create anything better. If you're a teenager and read this, listen carefully. Don't follow us, don't do what we did, just learn from our mistakes. Beware the traps of consumerism that we stepped into. Don't let yourself be marketed as a rehash of something that has gone before, or as the *rebellion du jour.* Beware the hatred and ignorance fed to you by those who came earlier. Don't believe that your distrust of authority is just a phase that you're going through. It wasn't necessarily better *in the day,* and not everything has been achieved. Look to the future, not the past, and build a better world on our corpses.

Punk is dead, long live punk, kill your parents.

CITGO Sign
Photo © Beth Schneckenburger

GOD, GUNS, & GUTS:

THE

F.U.'S

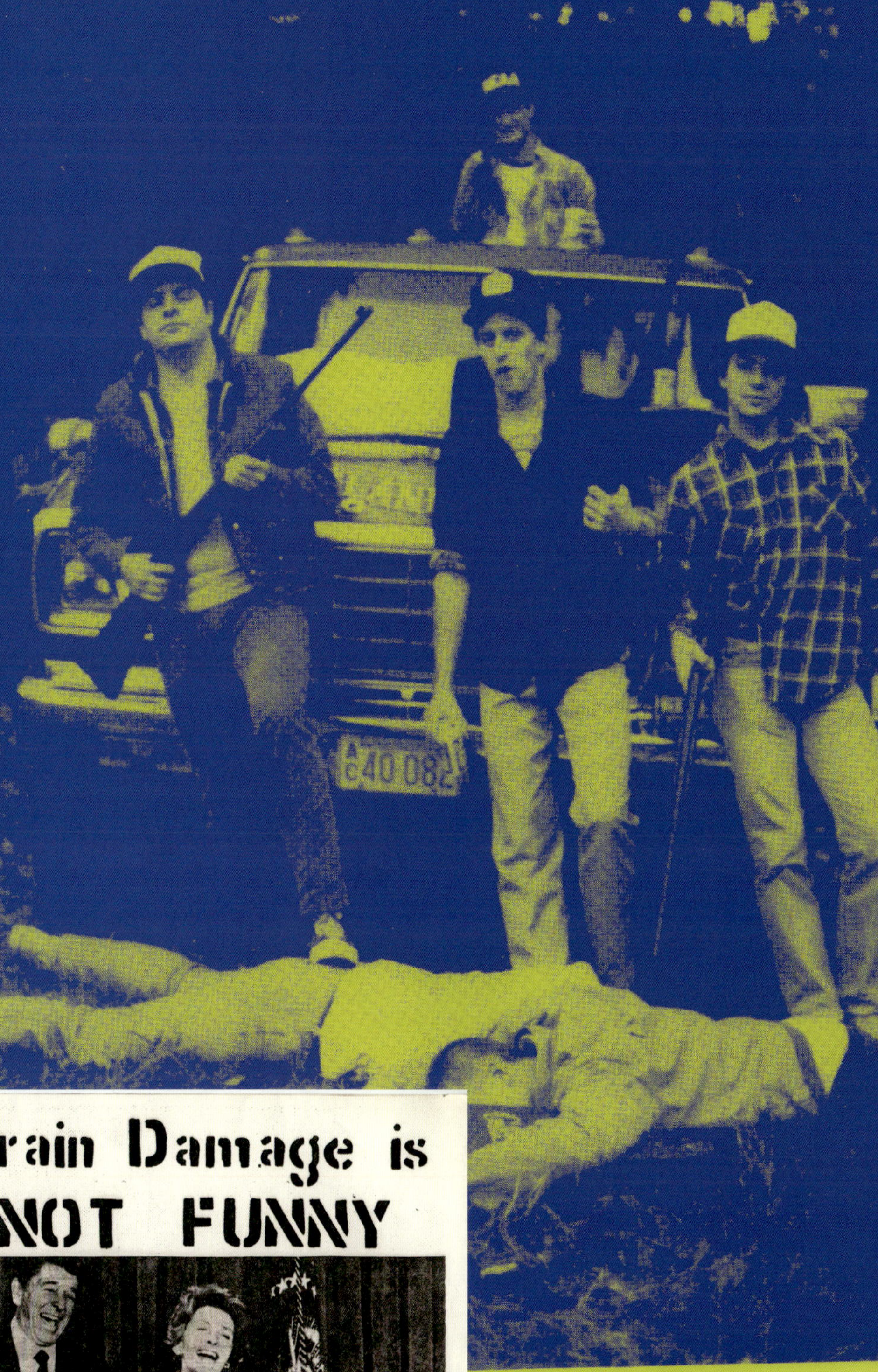

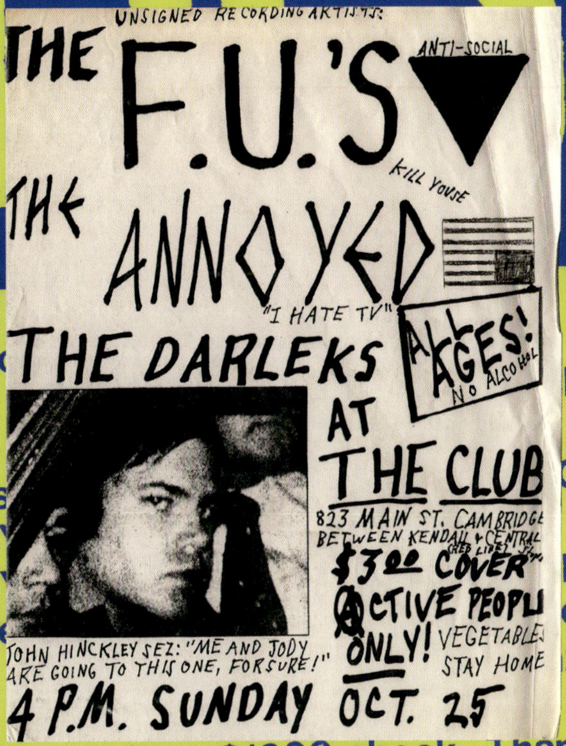

ere's another $1000 check. Thanks a

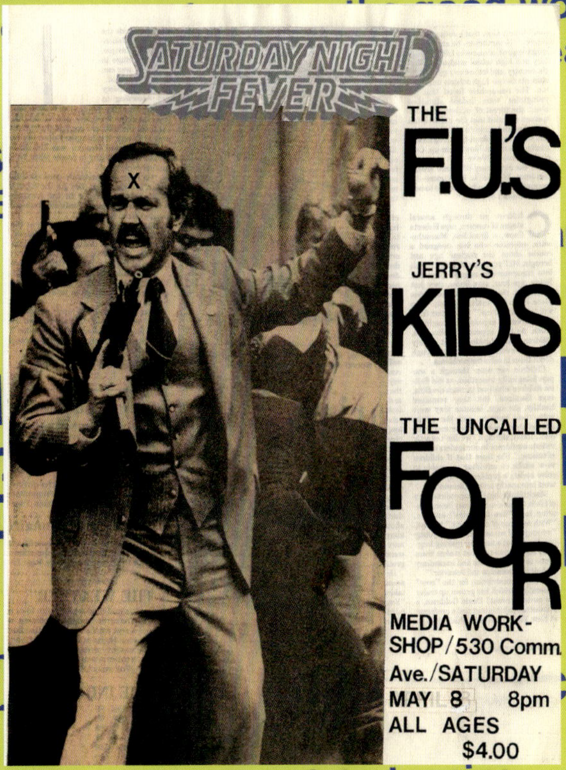

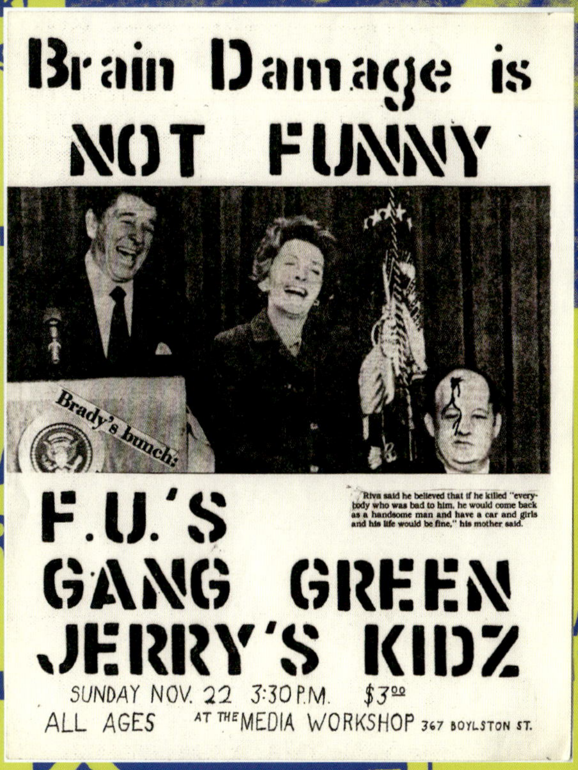

TO SPREAD
AT THE SAME

AVAILABLE FOR $4 ea. pp
) FROM:
F.U.'s c/o Bob Furapple
45 Lydon Way
Dorchester, MA 02124

And that neo-fascist classic:

CLAIM!

All on this page: Steve Grimes

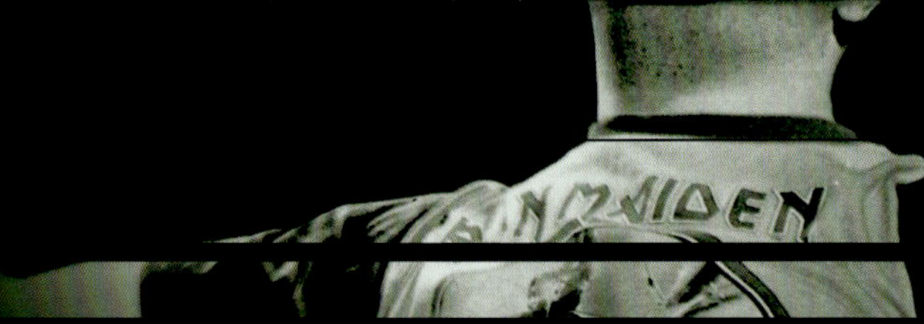

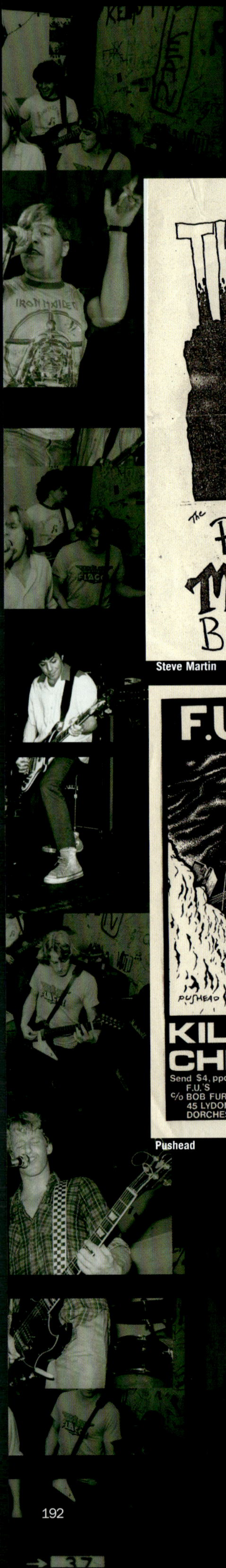

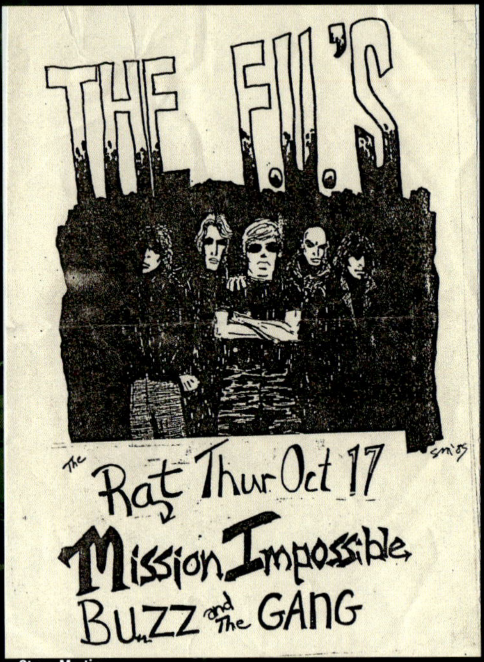

Steve Martin

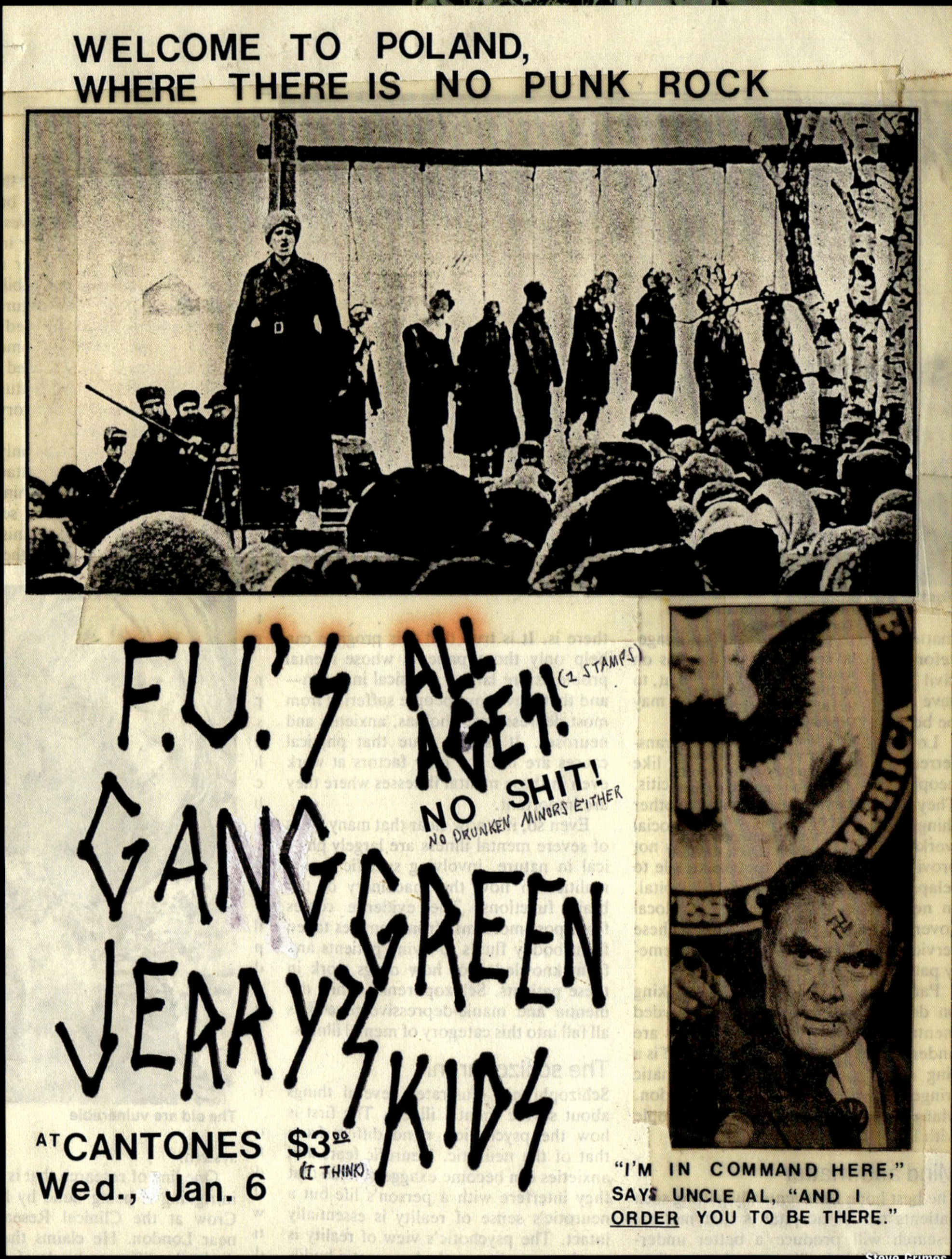

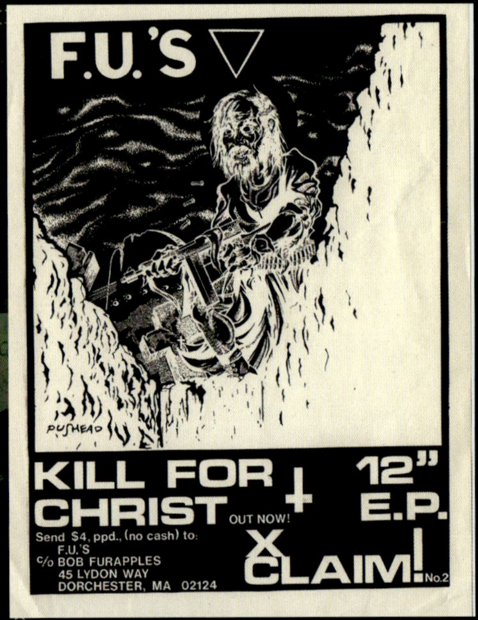

Pushead

Steve Grimes

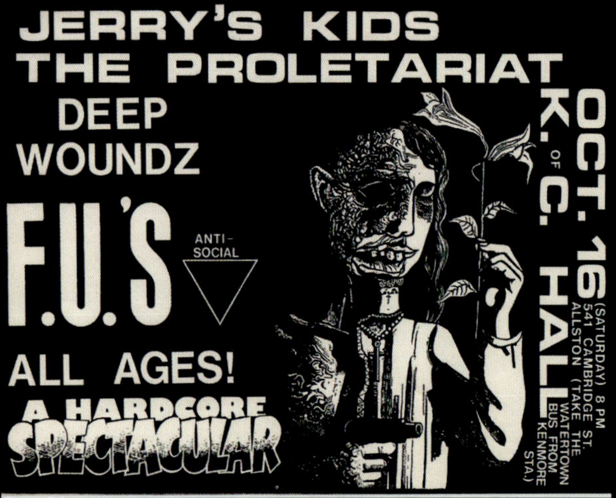

Steve Grimes

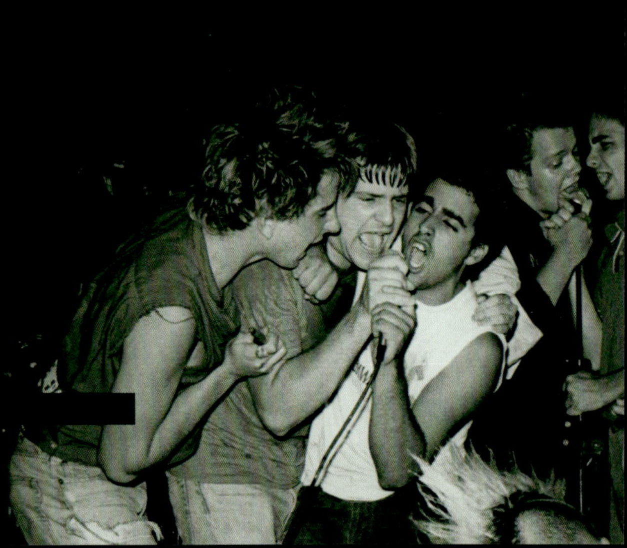

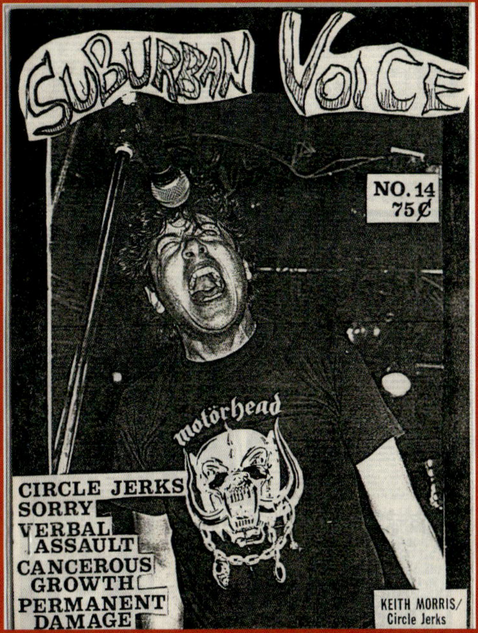

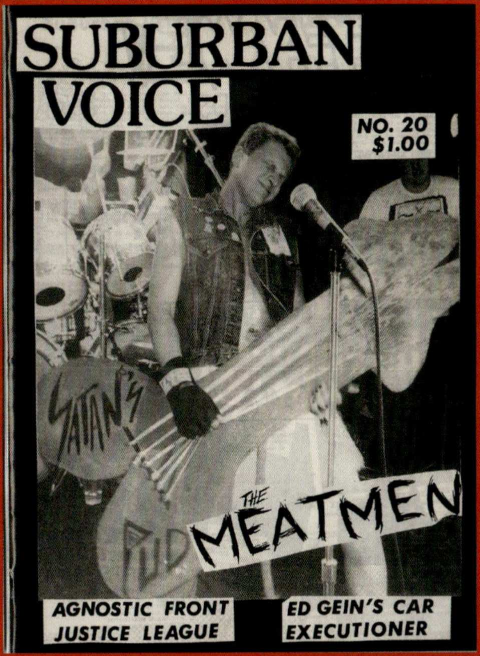

This music means everything to me...

By Al Quint

This music means everything to me...

It's getting out of work at 6 pm, throwing off my corporate monkey suit, rolling down the window and blasting Discharge's *Hear Nothing, See Nothing, Say Nothing* at 60 mph on Rt. 128.

This music means everything to me...

It's waiting for Bad Brains to show up for a gig, which they do at 1:45 am (and the show has to be over by 2:00 am). Then they play the most ravaging 15 minutes of music you've ever seen to a mass of thrashing, gyrating arms, legs and bodies, perfectly synchronized to the music.

This music means everything to me...

It's coming home with arms black and blue after a Misfits show at a church in Cambridge. It's John Sox of the FU's yelling "hit the beach!" during their rendition of *The Ballad of the Green Berets* and a sea of humanity flying in every direction, belly-first, from the stage. Robo of the Misfits came up to me after the show and gave me a handful of change to purchase the 2nd issue of my 'zine, mimeographed at a grade school at which my mom was a substitute teacher.

This music means everything to me...

It's piling friends and acquaintances into the car and driving two-and-a-half hours to the Guiding Star Grange In Greenfield to see Crucifix for the first time. It's the discovery of a scene seemingly out in the middle of nowhere, with bands like All White Jury, Outpatients, Deep Wound and BIU.

This music means everything to me...

It's seeing Husker Du three nights in a row and still managing to drag my ass into work each day after...spending two weeks of vacation listening to *Zen Arcade*, a brilliant record – punk in spirit, but moving into unexpected directions at a time when there weren't so many divisions and subcategories, and music didn't have to fit into a neat little marketable package.

This music means everything to me...

It's the idealism of youth, an oasis of understanding and a musical and ideological escape valve from the real world, a world where you spend your waking hours working at something you despise, and allowing music's ideals and idealism to keep you reasonably sane through it all.

This music means everything to me...

It's being amazed (shocked?) by the fact that I still feel as strongly about this stuff after 16 years of doing a 'zine. It's all the bands I've seen, the people I've met, and the friendships made. Punk rock is often just entertainment or an adolescent rite of passage, but for the true believer, it's an inseparable part of your being.

Al Quint is the publisher of Suburban Voice Fanzine

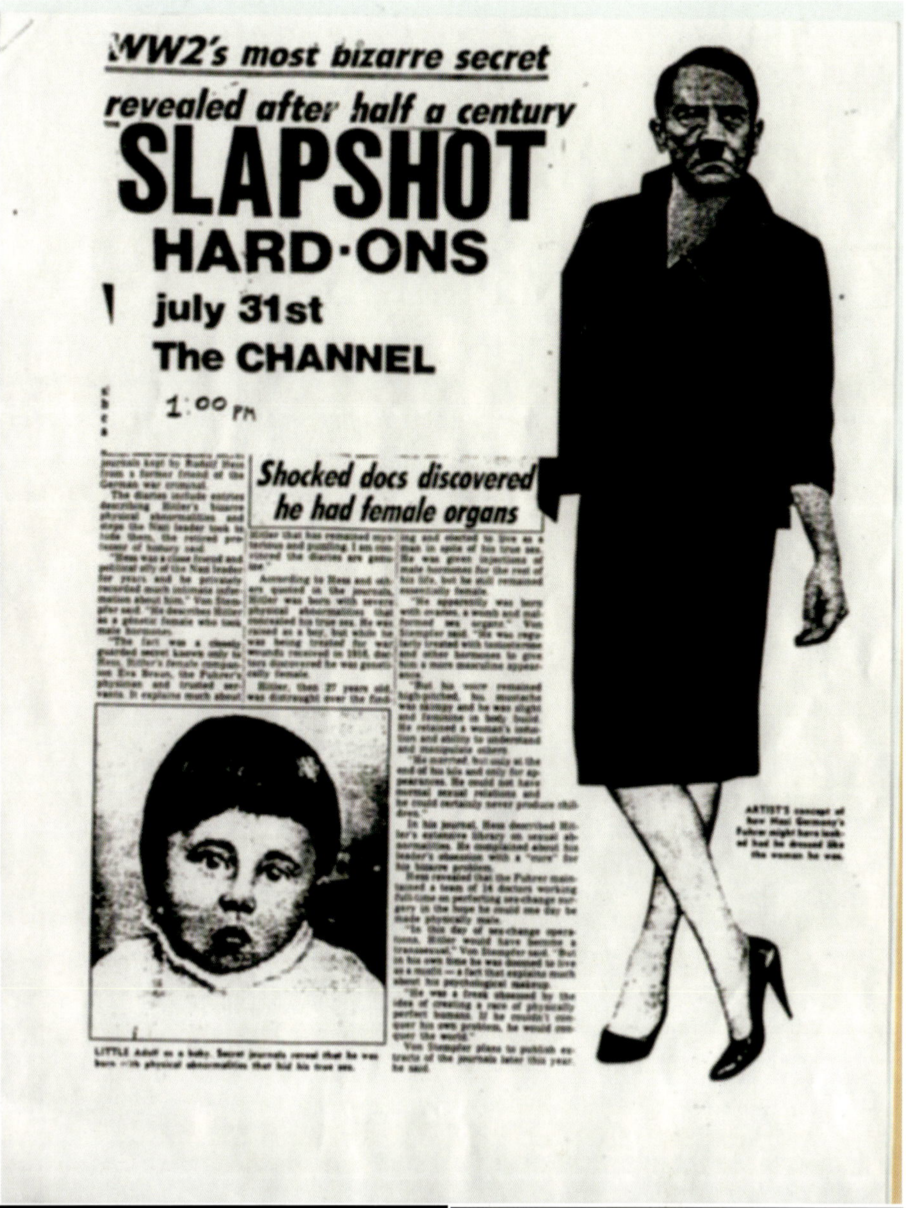

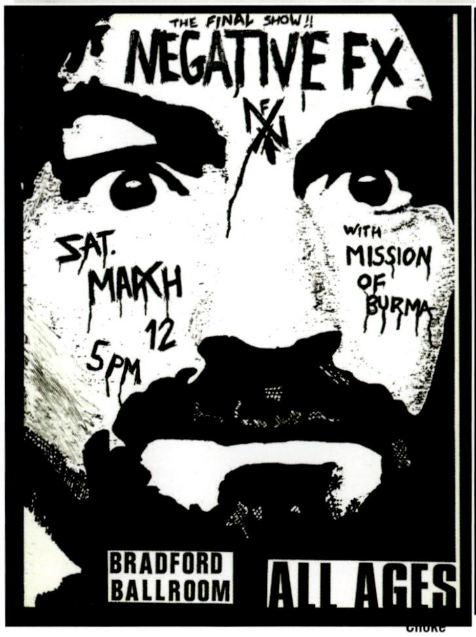

Choke

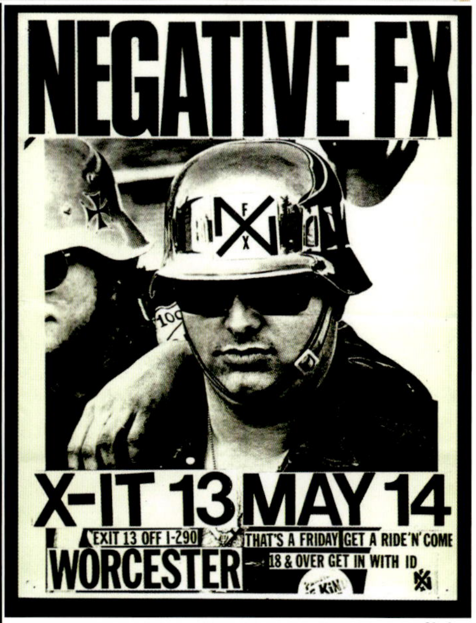

Choke

We flyered the shit out of our city before every show, hating every minute of it- especially in the winter. Anyone in a band from the Northeast who had wheat paste frozen on their hands in 20 degree weather will tell you why. But it got people to the shows." - Jaime Sciarappa - SSD

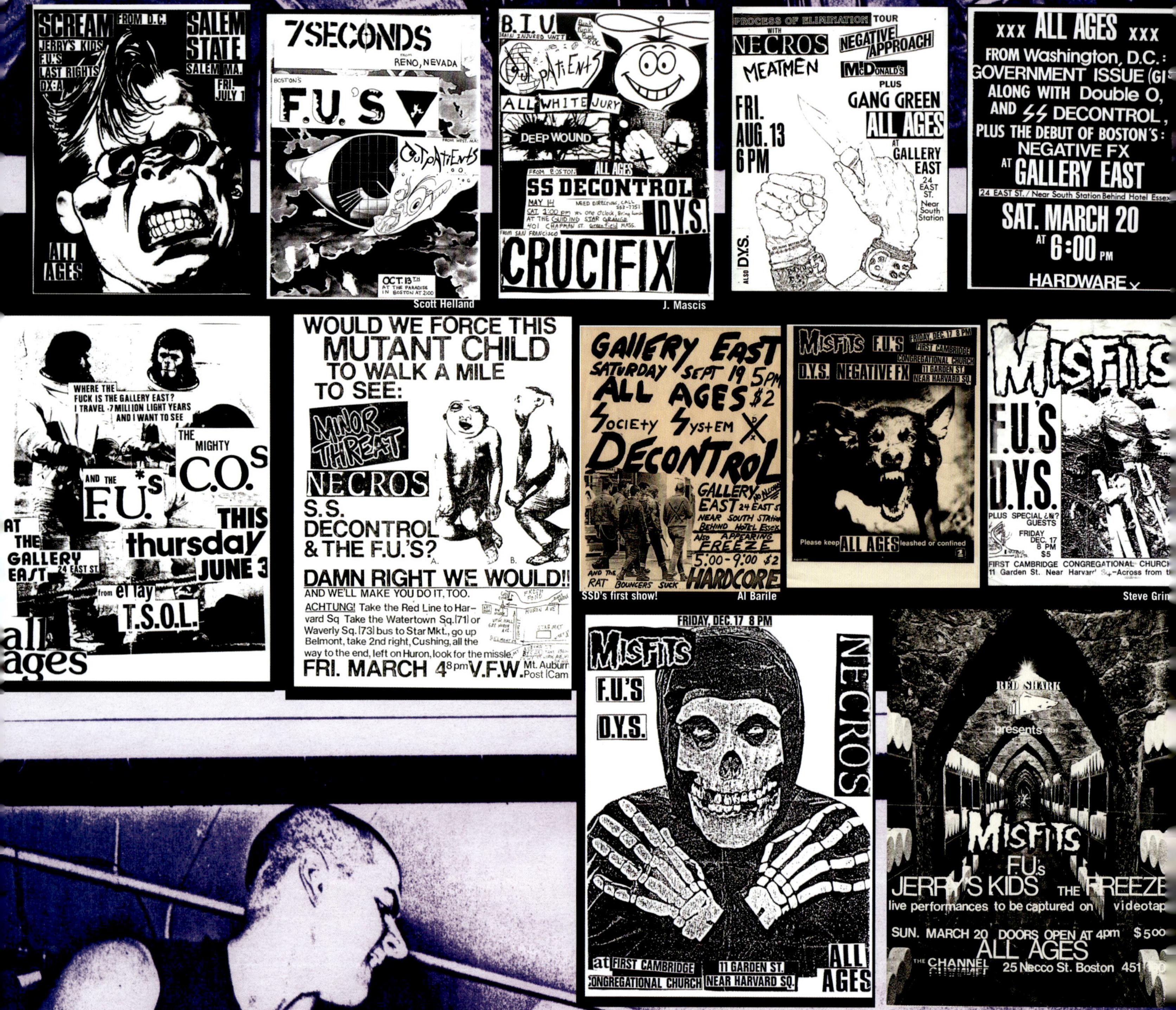

Scott Helland

J. Mascis

SSD's first show!

Al Barile

Steve Grin

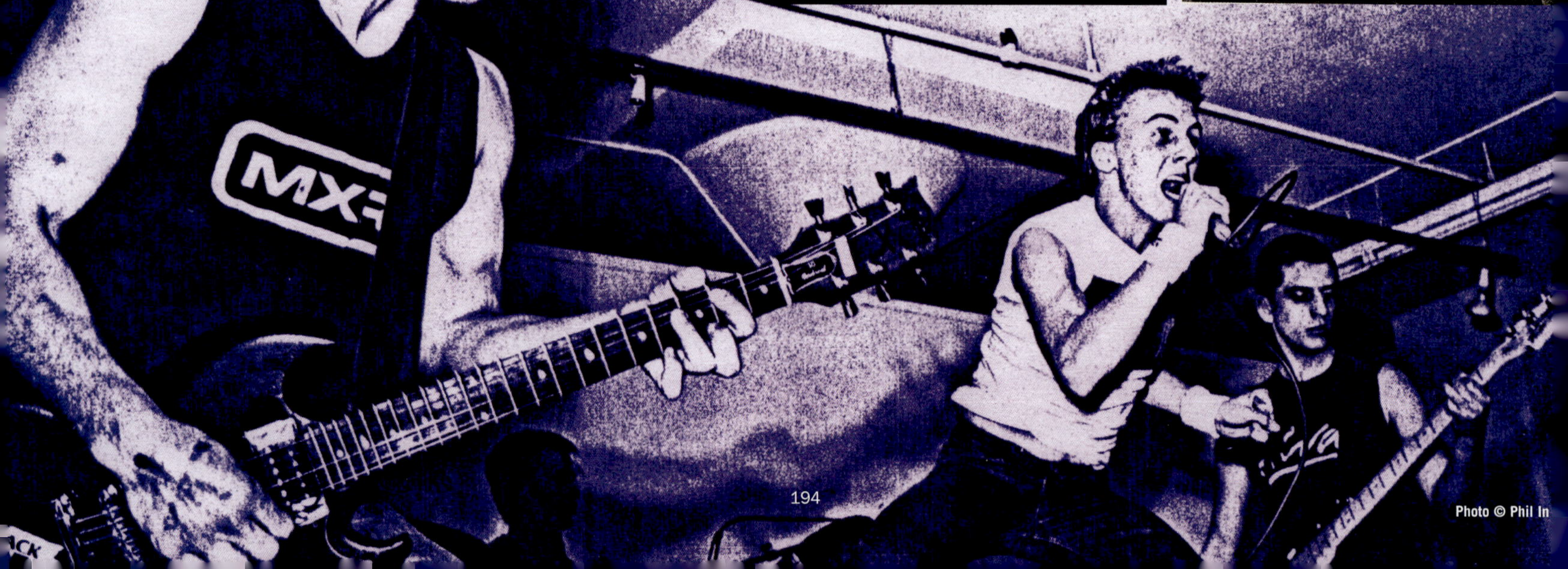

Photo © Phil In

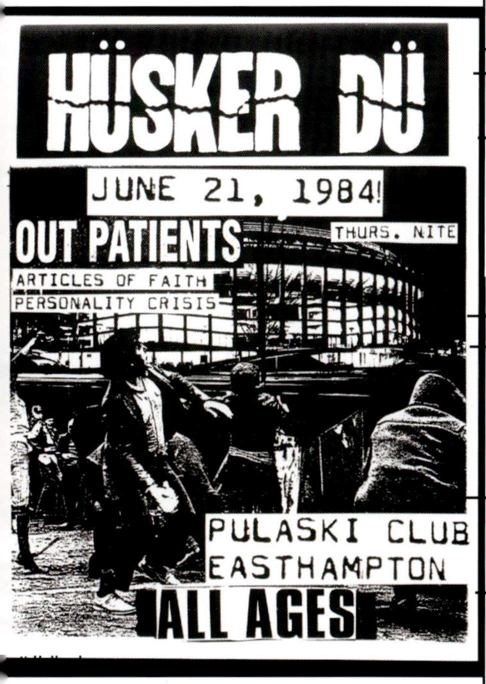

Going Mental
Vis Helland Outpatients

Hardcore was an explosion. Our fuse was lit when my band Mace needed a bass player. My brother Scott (14 years old) was already playing with Lou Barlow and J Macsis in Deep Wound. He joined us and we took on the name/concept "Outpatients."

We were tired of our school system, our lame town conscience and local rock scene. We'd just walk onstage and go mental, to the point of hyperventilation. I never collapsed, but I vomited my adrenaline a few times.

We played with hundreds of bands, from Canada to Argentina, including a lot of local shows. The scene was vibrant with shows, rumors, fanzines, pirate radio stations, and relatively little violence. Wow! Twenty years have passed and I still want to go mental!

WesternMass
Scott Helland Outpatients

A veteran of all-night flyer-pasting runs, I've got a good collection of flyers from 1982-1986. Stacks of yellowing paper, glue and tape residue, and tack and nail holes.

February 5, 1982, the Guiding Star Grange Hall in Greenfield, MA. was the site of the first hardcore show I can remember. A bunch of bands from the area played - Deep Wound, All White Jury, Brain Injured Unit, PSD, and our band Outpatients. It was a great show, it was a good turnout, and BANG!, just like that there was a Western Mass scene.

I had just turned 15, the Outpatients had just recorded our first album, and we started putting on shows with a few friends, most of time playing and running the PA ourselves. Bands came and went over the next few years (No Preservatives, Black Christmas, Catharsis) and great bands like Black Flag, Husker Du, IFA and Crucifix came through, as well as Bostonians like SSD, FUs, Cancerous Growth and Siege.

It was a small scene - the only places to play were the Greenfield Grange Hall and Easthampton Pulaski Club, since the local clubs didn't open their doors to hardcore bands until way later. eventually Westfield State, UMass and Smith College started to book shows.

Western Mass' scene was an interesting alternative to Boston's great scene– our bands had a hard time fitting into Beantown's clique.

And the scene still exists, with bands like Bloodbath, Push-Button Warfare and Doom Nation still playing shows.

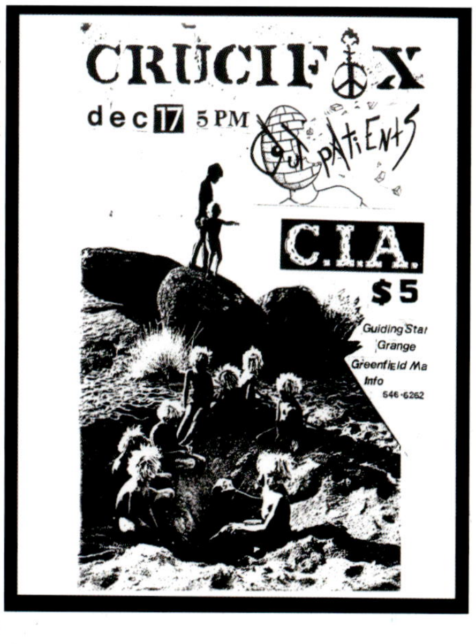

Vis Helland/Cathy E. Trix

Al Barile

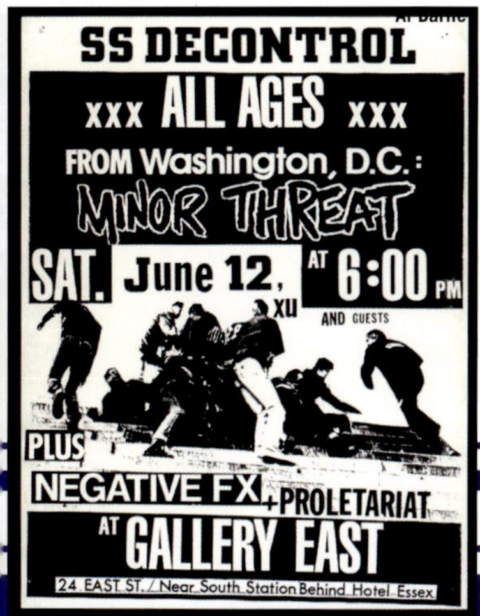

Al Barile

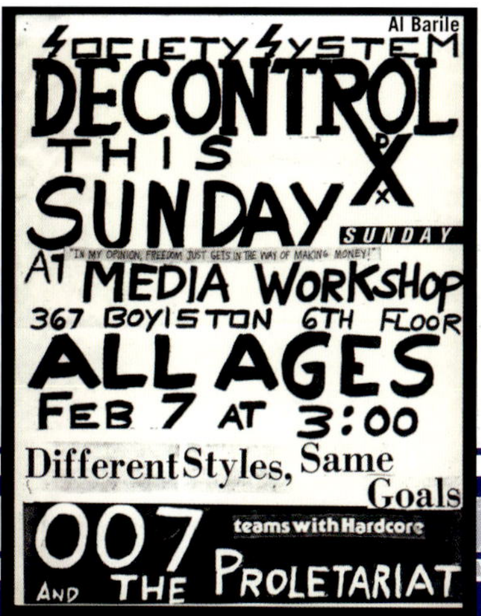

Al Barile

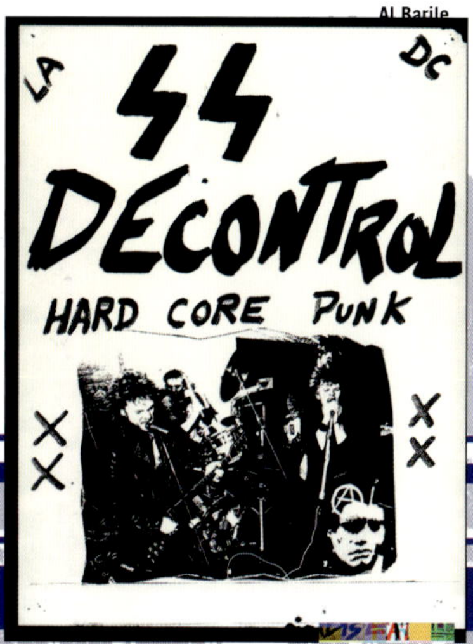

Al Barile

aime Sciarappa - SSD

Hardcore for me was all about seeing the bands live. The thing I remember most was that feeling that anything co[...] on in the air. Anyone who's seen Black Flag (in any of its many forms) knows what I'm talking about. It was this cra[...] Boston had so many great bands - I'll spare you the list. In addition it was a regular stop for every band on tour. [...] cause we wanted every show to be an event. We flyered the shit out of our city before every show, hating every min[...] ıyone in a band from the Northeast who had wheat paste frozen on their hands in 20 degree weather will tell you w[...] Here's a list of my favorite shows, in no particular order, between 1981-1984. The SSD gigs on this list aren't esent because we were playing, but because everyone else was so awesome that night. Hope you were there!

Misfits, DYS and FUs, Cambr[...] M[...] The Misfits playing in a church hall- how cool is that? I think th[...]

inor Threat, SSD Agnostic Front-Camde[...] Ian MacKaye of Minor Threat got hit by a car before the sho[...] sti[...] de it back in time to play. They were amazing that night. I think this show is still around on video.

ead Kennedys, DOA and SSD- Paramount Thea[...] DOA rocked. There was a riot outside after the sh[...] punkers just liked a little extra mayhem at their shows.

[...] Brains-Any Show When they weren't playing reggae, they were the most powerful band of all time, without a[...]

rocess Of Elimination Tour, NY and Boston The Meatmen and Negative Approach in one night - give me a f[...]

[...]igies-[...] Monica Civic The biggest show SSD ever played. Our first taste of the hugen[...] LA [...]

ission of Burma, Negative FX- Bradford Ballroom, Boston MA By the 2nd or 3rd song of Negative FX's [...] were ating the shit out of a bouncer, while continuing to play. This was Mission of Burma's last gig.

ack Flag and Bad Brains- Irving Plaza, NYC The roughest pit I've ever been in. The DC guys showed up for this show, meaning NY, Boston d Washington DC punks all in the same pit- way too much testosterone for one room. Black Flag played again that night at the A7 Club (a 20'x20' hole the wall by Needle Park.) Some guy named Henry from DC sold me a 7-inch earlier that evening of his band SOA. I remember him jumping up to sing one ng with Black Flag that night. The rest, of course, is history.

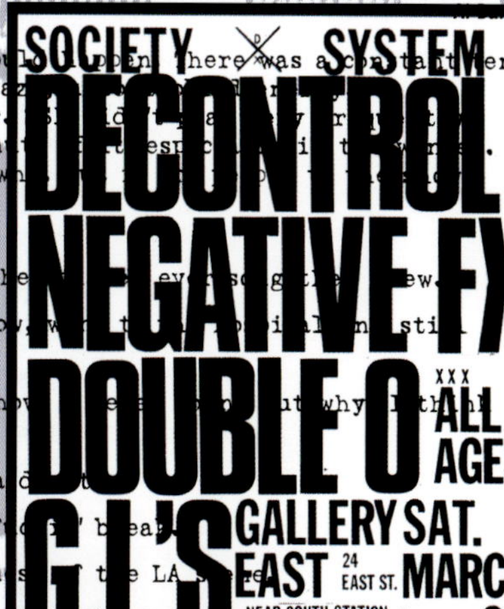

ing The White House
© Phil In Phlash

BOSTON

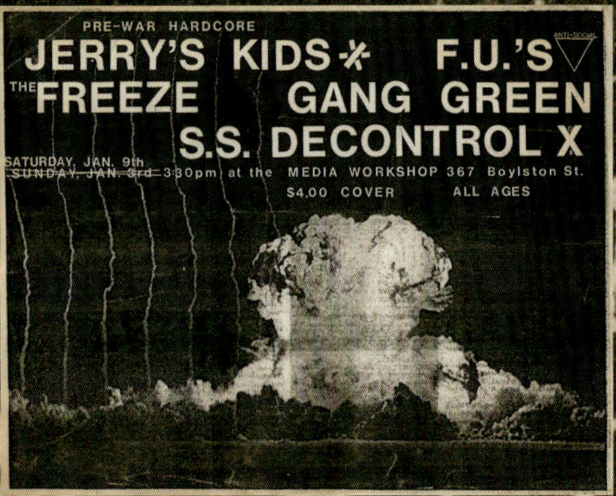
PRE-WAR HARDCORE
JERRY'S KIDS F.U.'S
THE FREEZE GANG GREEN
S.S. DECONTROL X
SATURDAY, JAN. 9th SUNDAY, JAN. 3rd 3:30pm at the MEDIA WORKSHOP 367 Boylston St.
$4.00 COVER ALL AGES

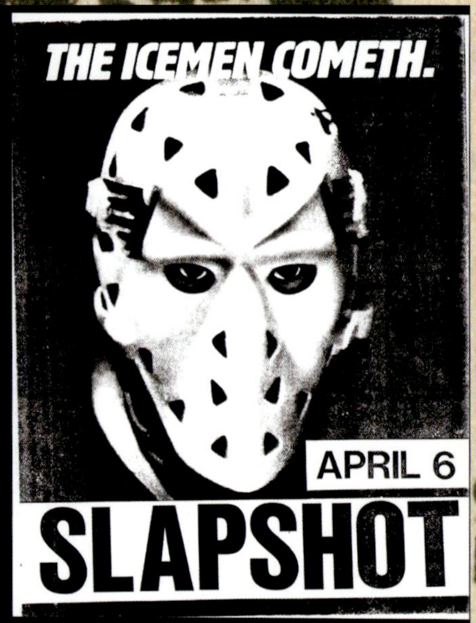
THE ICEMEN COMETH.
APRIL 6
SLAPSHOT

Mark McKay

PARADISE CLUB
AUGUST 18
SATURDAY
1984
MATINEE
BATTALION OF SAINTS
CORROSION OF CONFORMITY

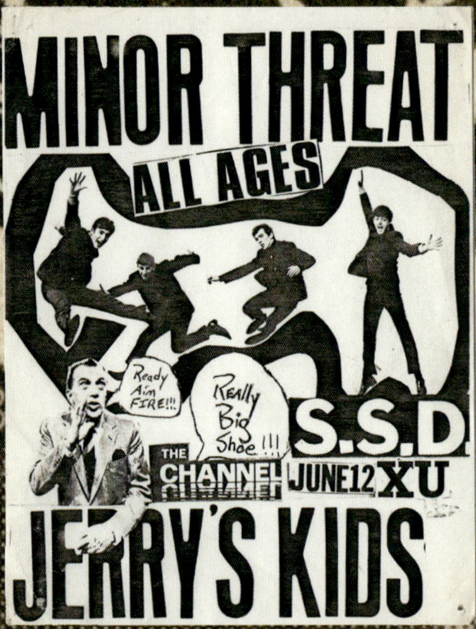
MINOR THREAT
ALL AGES
Ready Aim FIRE!!!
Really Big Shoe!!!
S.S.D
THE CHANNEL
JUNE 12
XU
JERRY'S KIDS

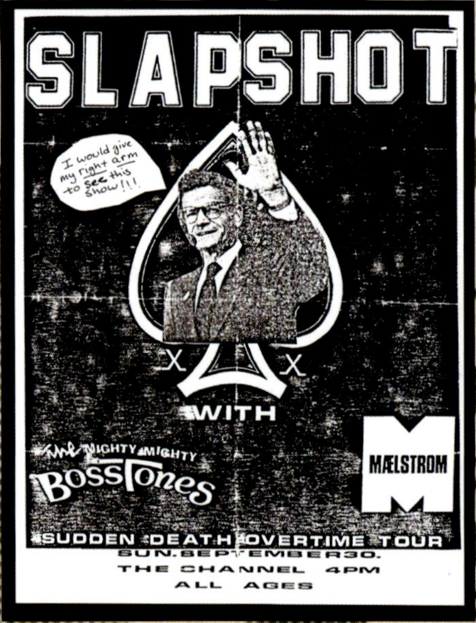
SLAPSHOT
I would give my right arm to see this show!!!
WITH
THE MIGHTY MIGHTY BOSSTONES
MÆLSTROM
SUDDEN DEATH OVERTIME TOUR
SUN.SEPTEMBER30.
THE CHANNEL 4PM
ALL AGES

BOSTON'S HARDEST
MAIN EVENT
THANKSGIVING DAY WEEKEND
STRAW DOGS
VS.
Gang green
King of Bands
FORMERLY THE F.U.'S
T.T. THE BEARS
NOV 30th

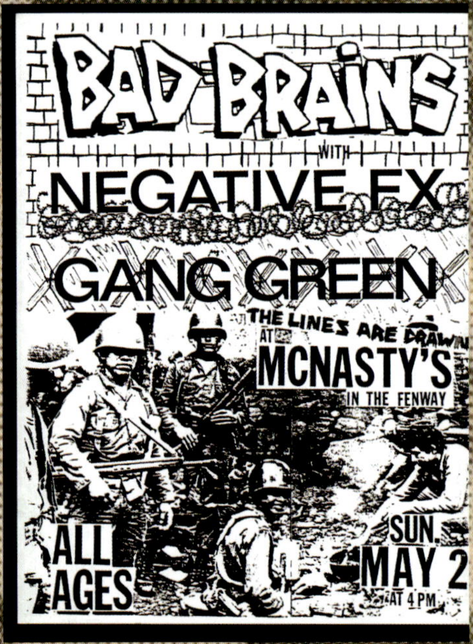
BAD BRAINS
WITH
NEGATIVE FX
GANG GREEN
THE LINES ARE DRAWN
AT MCNASTY'S
IN THE FENWAY
ALL AGES
SUN. MAY 2
AT 4 PM

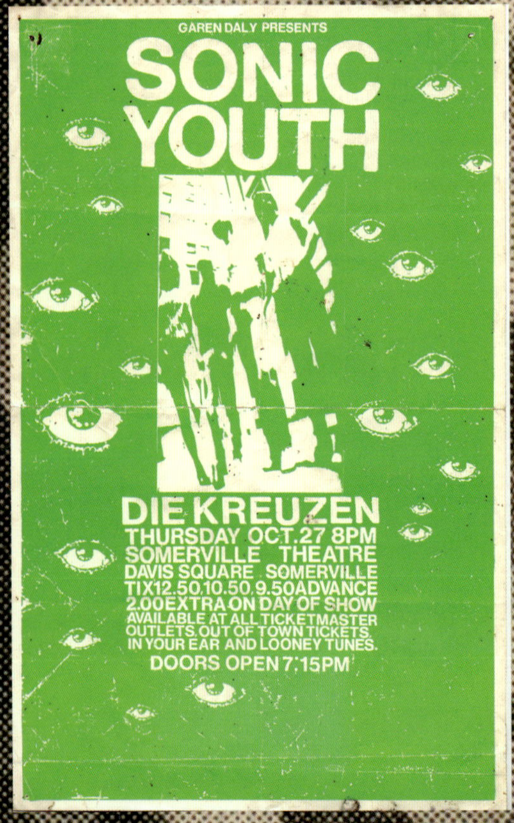
GAREN DALY PRESENTS
SONIC YOUTH
DIE KREUZEN
THURSDAY OCT.27 8PM
SOMERVILLE THEATRE
DAVIS SQUARE SOMERVILLE
TIX 12.50 10.50 9.50 ADVANCE
2.00 EXTRA ON DAY OF SHOW
AVAILABLE AT ALL TICKETMASTER OUTLETS, OUT OF TOWN TICKETS, IN YOUR EAR AND LOONEY TUNES.
DOORS OPEN 7:15PM

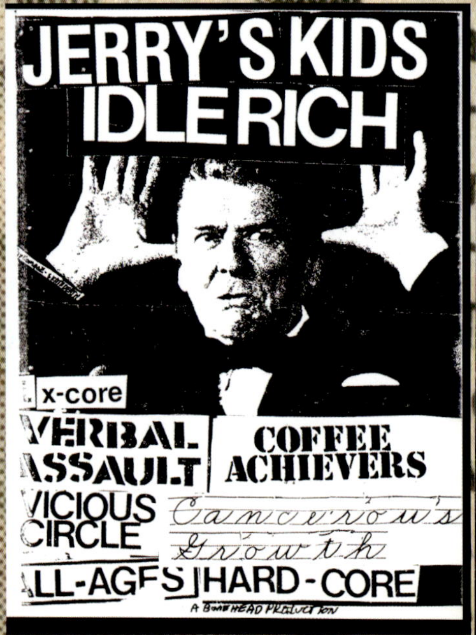
JERRY'S KIDS
IDLE RICH
x-core
VERBAL ASSAULT
COFFEE ACHIEVERS
VICIOUS CIRCLE
Cancerous Growth
ALL-AGES HARD-CORE

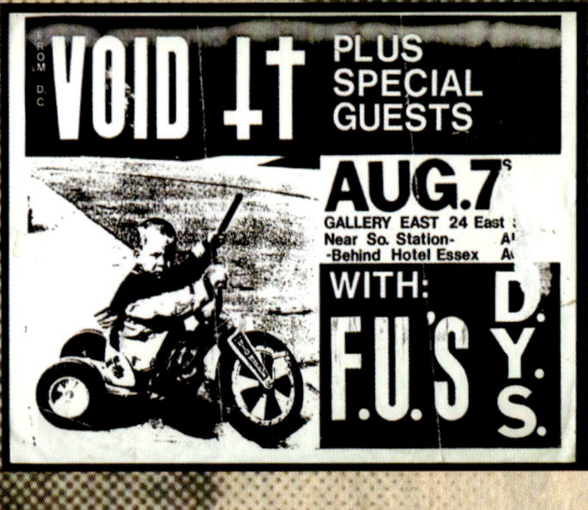
VOID
PLUS SPECIAL GUESTS
AUG.7
GALLERY EAST 24 East
Near So. Station
Behind Hotel Essex
WITH:
F.U.'S
D.Y.S.

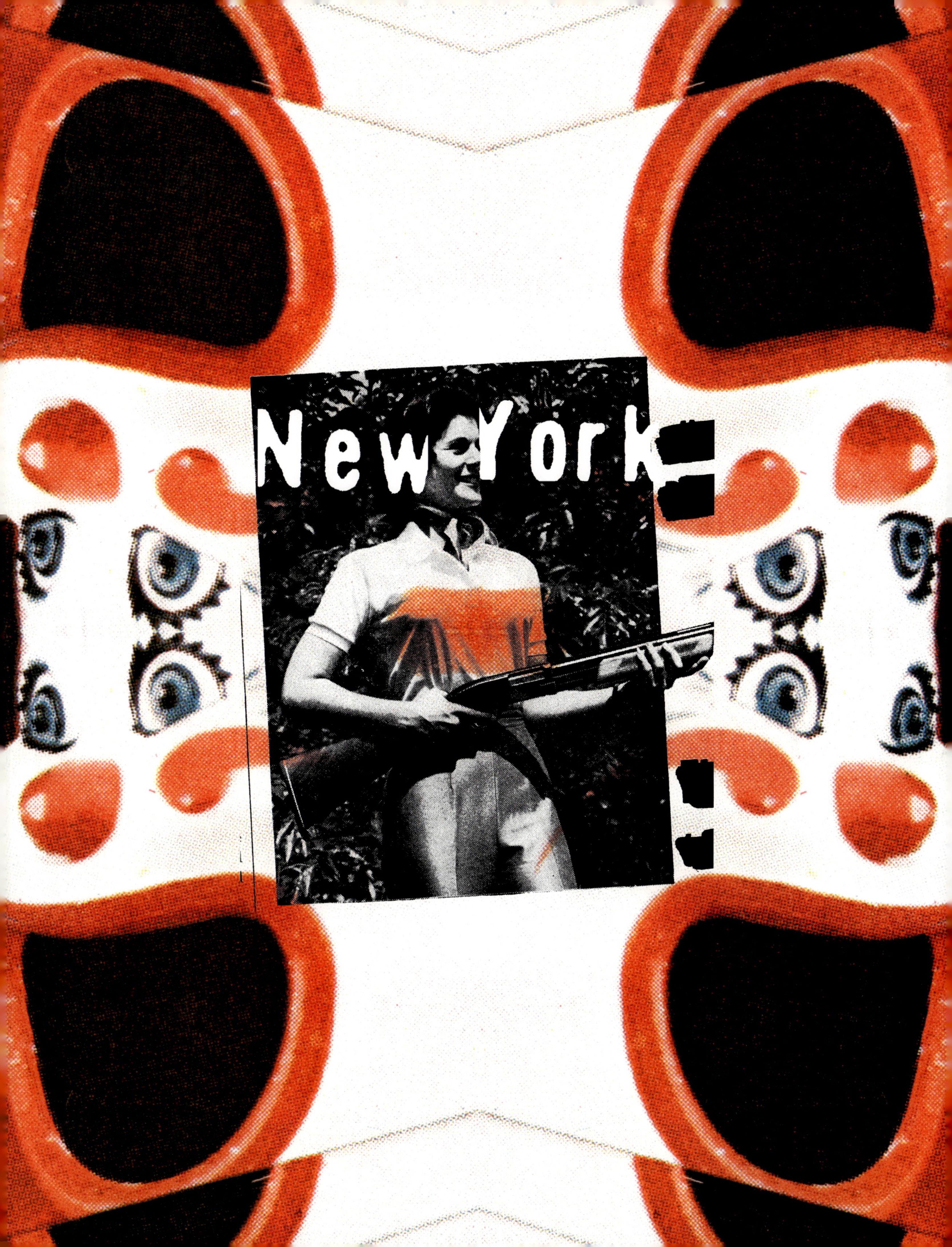
New York

John Holmstrom

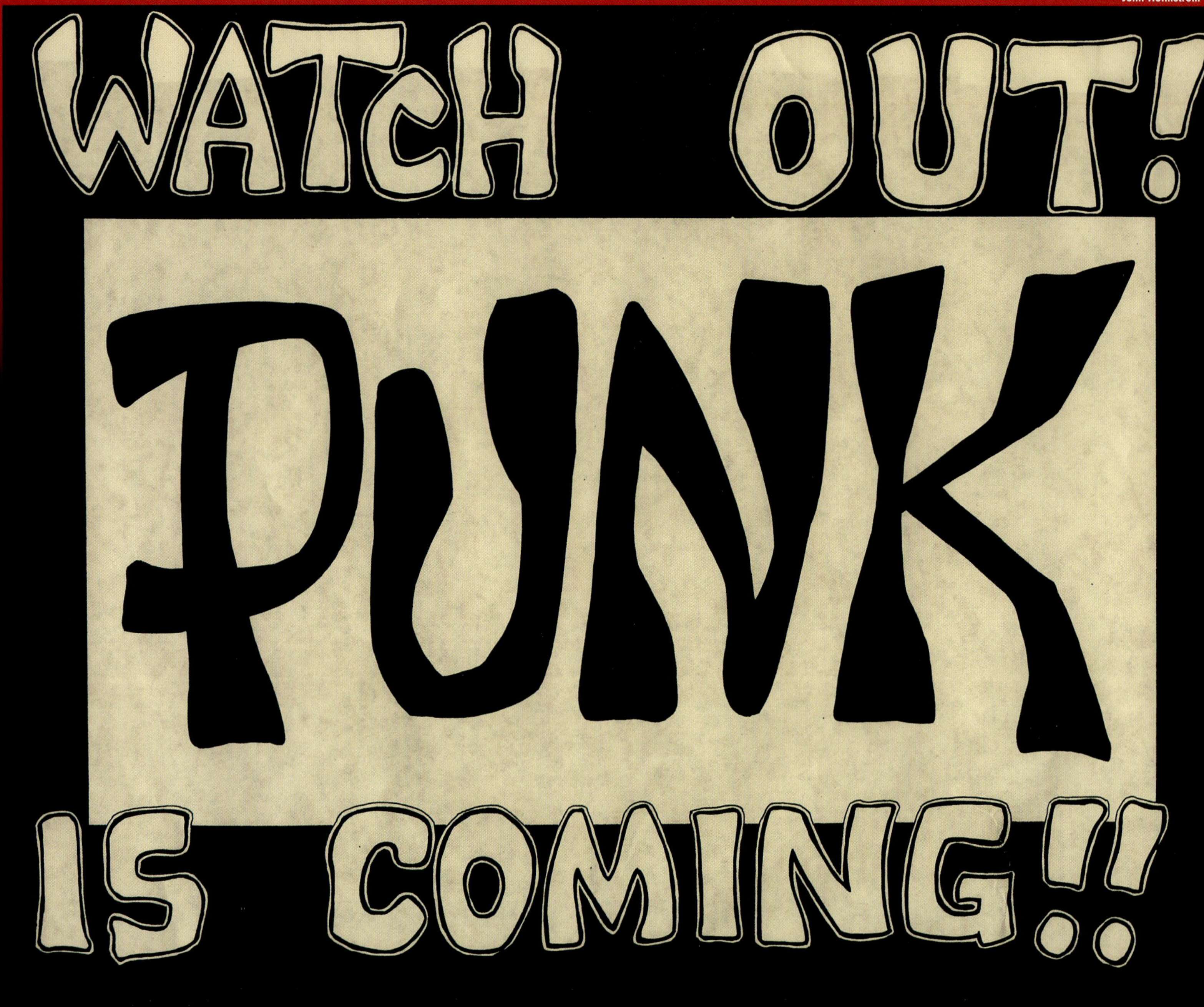

Ged Dunn Jr., Eddie McNeil and I postered these all over NYC in November and December, 1975.
John Holmstrom

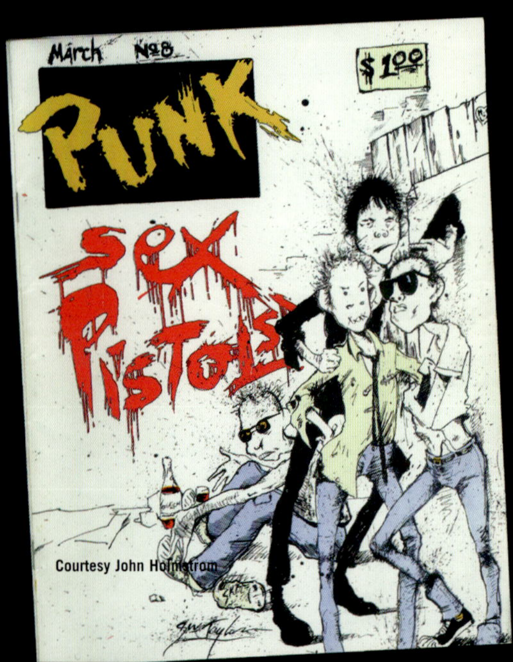

Courtesy John Holmstrom

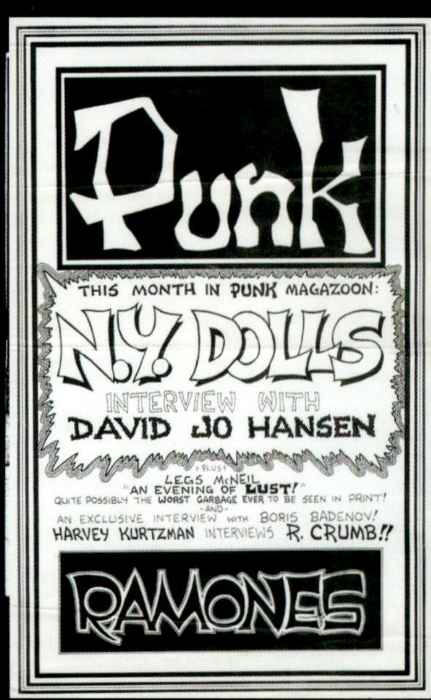

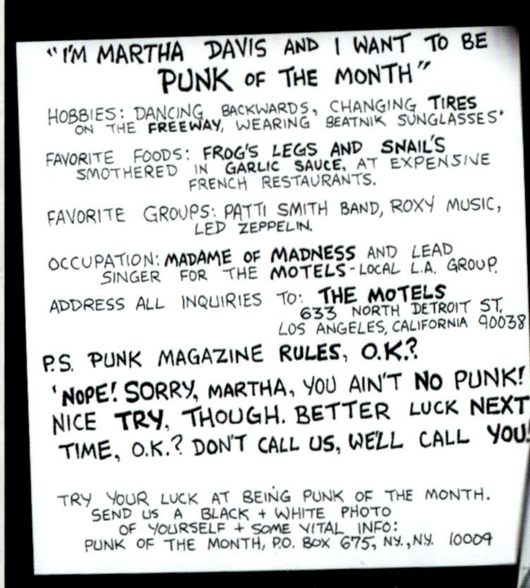
"I'M MARTHA DAVIS AND I WANT TO BE PUNK OF THE MONTH"

HOBBIES: DANCING BACKWARDS, CHANGING TIRES ON THE FREEWAY, WEARING BEATNIK SUNGLASSES'

FAVORITE FOODS: FROG'S LEGS AND SNAIL'S SMOTHERED IN GARLIC SAUCE, AT EXPENSIVE FRENCH RESTAURANTS.

FAVORITE GROUPS: PATTI SMITH BAND, ROXY MUSIC, LED ZEPPELIN.

OCCUPATION: MADAME OF MADNESS AND LEAD SINGER FOR THE MOTELS - LOCAL L.A. GROUP.

ADDRESS ALL INQUIRIES TO: THE MOTELS
633 NORTH DETROIT ST.
LOS ANGELES, CALIFORNIA 90038

P.S. PUNK MAGAZINE RULES, O.K.?

'NOPE! SORRY, MARTHA, YOU AIN'T NO PUNK! NICE TRY, THOUGH. BETTER LUCK NEXT TIME, O.K.? DON'T CALL US, WE'LL CALL YOU!

TRY YOUR LUCK AT BEING PUNK OF THE MONTH. SEND US A BLACK + WHITE PHOTO OF YOURSELF + SOME VITAL INFO:
PUNK OF THE MONTH, P.O. BOX 675, N.Y., N.Y. 10009

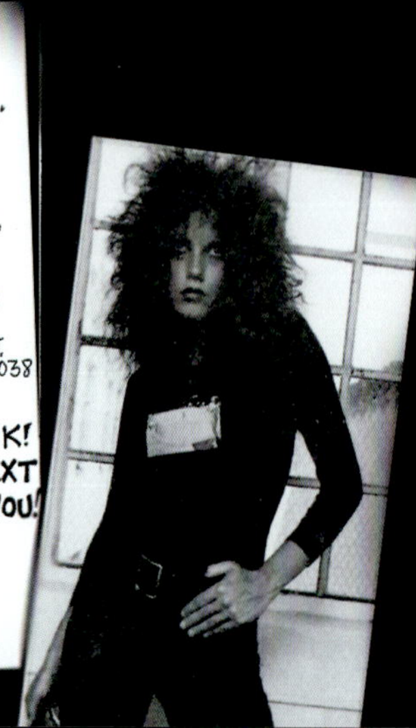

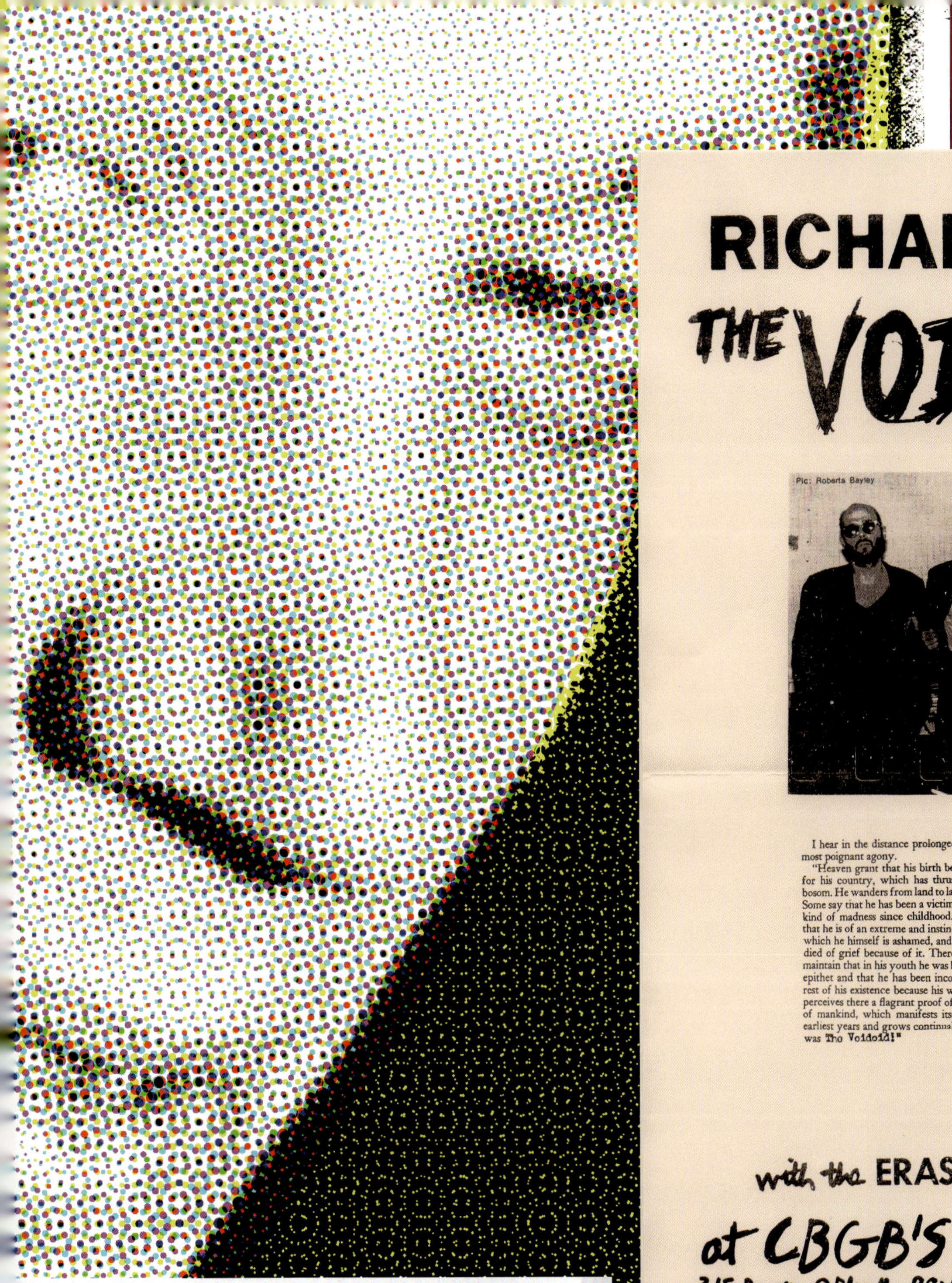

RICHARD HELL &

THE VOIDOIDS

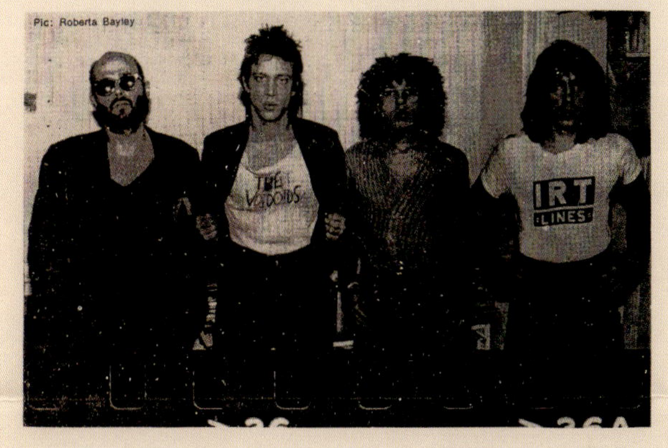

I hear in the distance prolonged shrieks of the most poignant agony.

"Heaven grant that his birth be not a calamity for his country, which has thrust him from its bosom. He wanders from land to land, hated by all. Some say that he has been a victim of some special kind of madness since childhood. Others believe that he is of an extreme and instinctive cruelty, of which he himself is ashamed, and that his parents died of grief because of it. There are those who maintain that in his youth he was branded with an epithet and that he has been inconsolable for the rest of his existence because his wounded dignity perceives there a flagrant proof of the wickedness of mankind, which manifests itself during their earliest years and grows continually. This epithet was Tho Voidoid!"

I hear in the distance prolonged shrieks of the most poignant agony.

"They add that night and day without rest nor respite horrible nightmares cause him to bleed through the ears and mouth; and that ghosts sit at the head of his bed and, driven despite themselves by an unknown force, fling in his face, now softly, now in tones like the roar of battle, and with implacable persistence, that loathsome and persistent epithet, which will perish only when the universe perishes. Some say that love brought him to this state; or that his cries are the expression of remorse for some crime, shrouded in the night of his mysterious past. But most think that he is tortured by incommensurable pride, as Satan was, and that he would like to be God's equal."

I hear in the distance prolonged shrieks of the most poignant agony.

Lautréamont

with the ERASERS and the GHOSTS

at CBGB'S April 20, 21, 22

315 Bowery @ Bleecker 982 4052 Thursday, Friday, Saturday

Richard Hell

TOM VERLAINE--guitar, vocals, music, lyrics: Facts unknown.

RICHARD HELL--bass, vocals, lyrics: Chip on his shoulder. Mama's boy. No personality. Highschool dropout. Mean.

RICHARD LLOYD--guitar, vocals: bleach-blond - mental insitutions - male prostitue - suicide attempts

BILLY FICCA--drums: Blues bands is Philadelphia. Doesn't talk much. Friendly.

TELEVISION'S music fulfills the adolescent desire to fuck the girl you never met because you've just been run over by a car. Three minute songs of passion performed by four boys who make James Dean look like Little Nemo. Their sound is made distinctive by Hell's rare Dan Electro bass, one that pops and grunts like no model presently available, and his unique spare patterns. Add to this Richard Lloyd's blitzcrieg chop on his vintage Telecaster and Verlaine's leads alternately psychotic Duane Eddy and Segovia on a ukelele with two strings gone. Verlaine, who uses an old Fender Jazzmaster, when asked about the music said, "I don't know. It tells the story. Like "The Hunch" by the Robert Charles Quintet or "Tornado" by Dale Hawkins. Those cats could track it down. I'll tell you the secret."

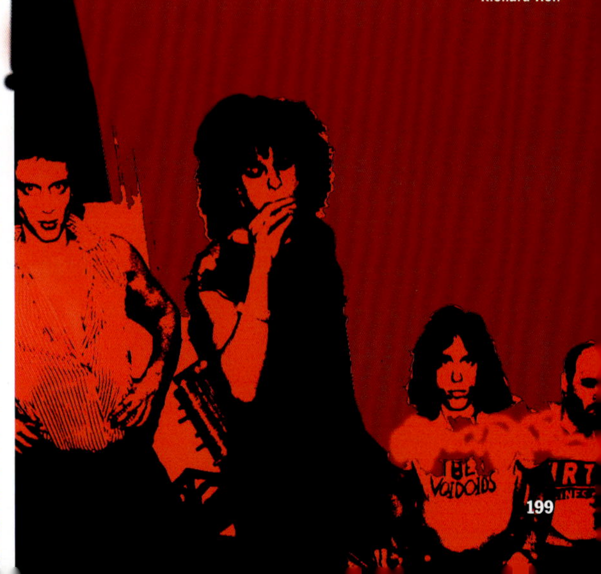

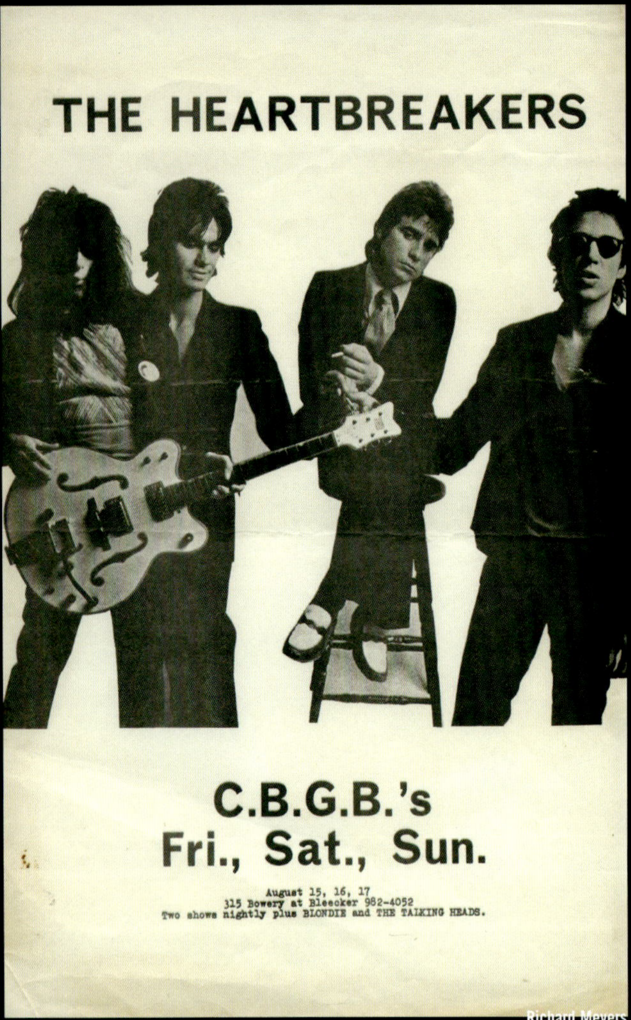

Richard Meyers

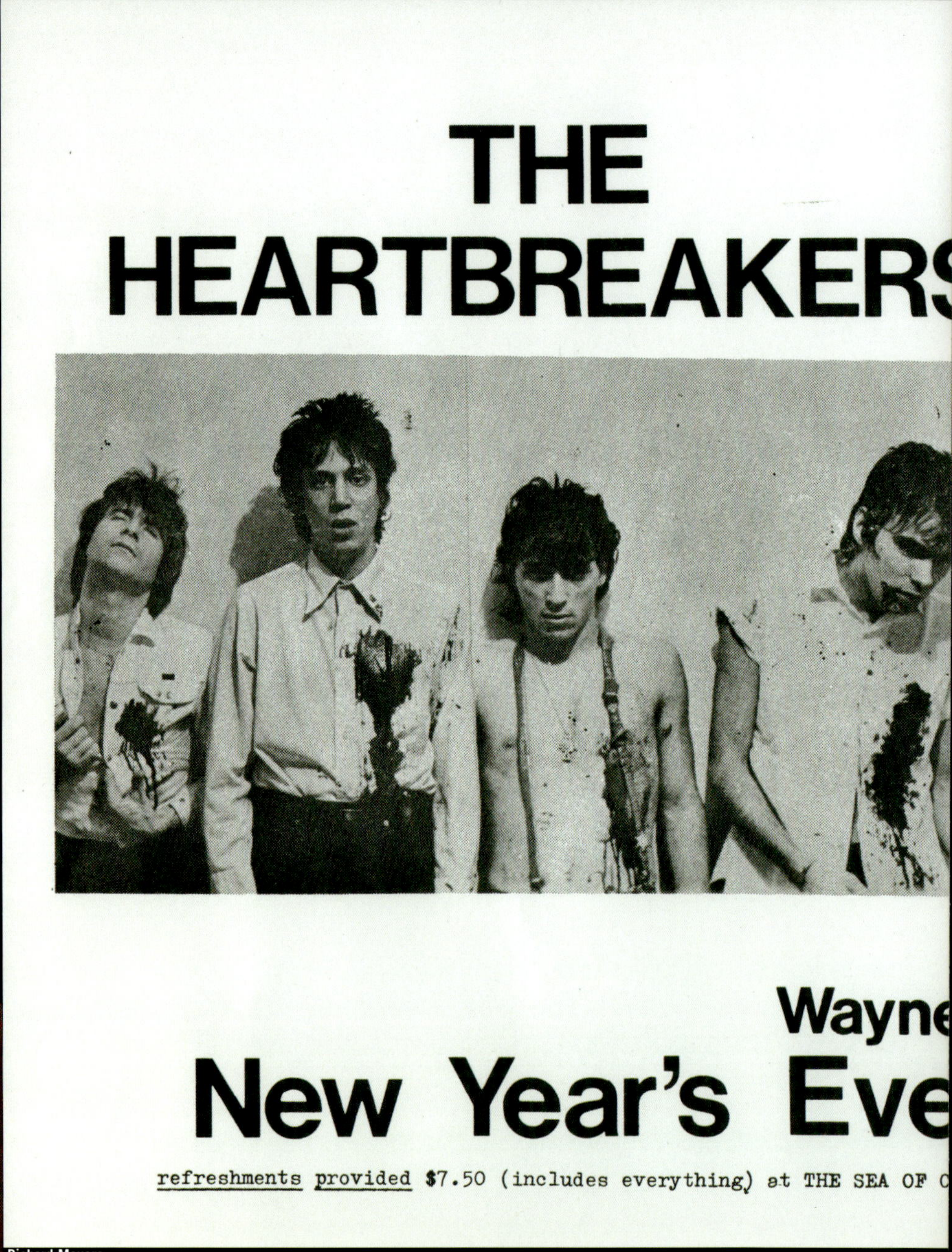

Richard Meyers

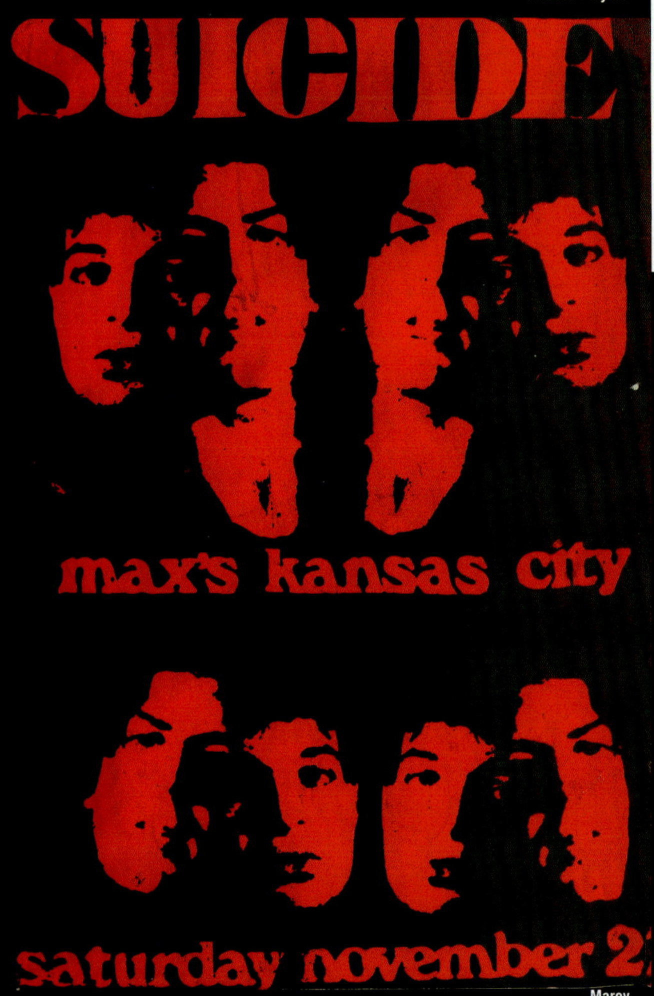

Marev

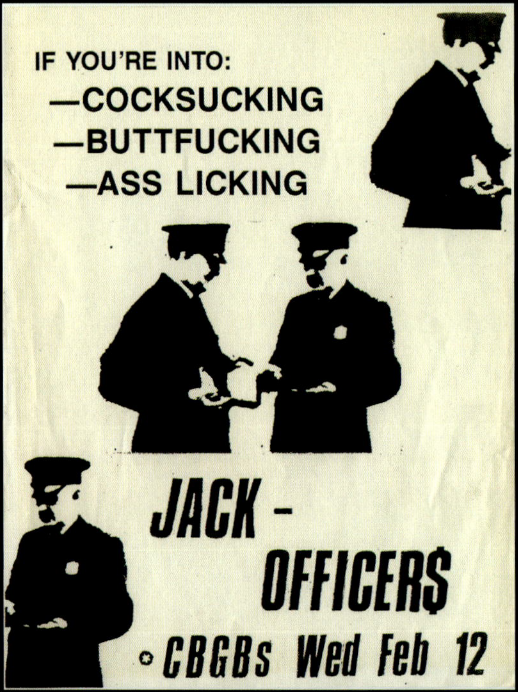

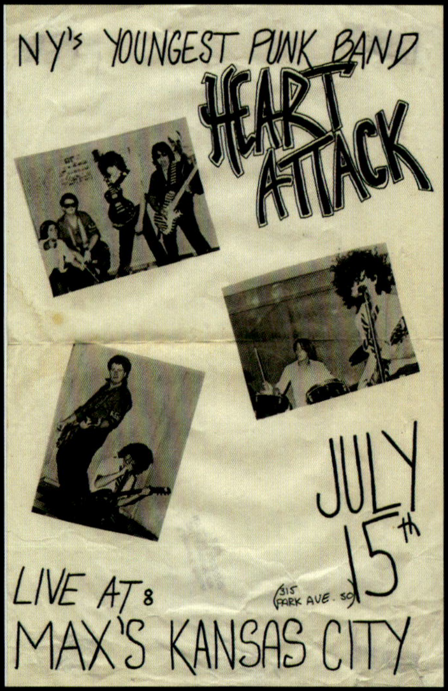

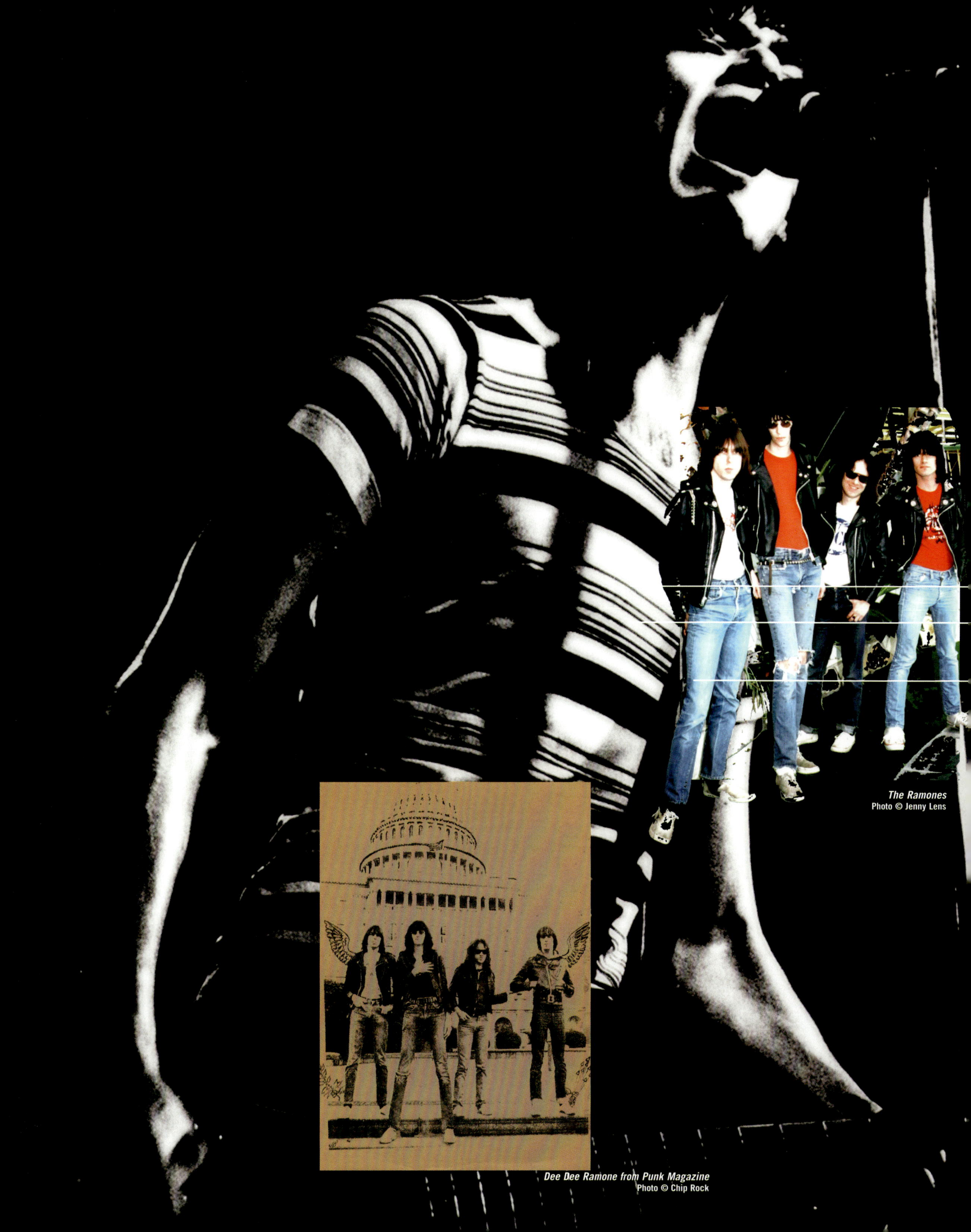

The Ramones
Photo © Jenny Lens

Dee Dee Ramone from Punk Magazine
Photo © Chip Rock

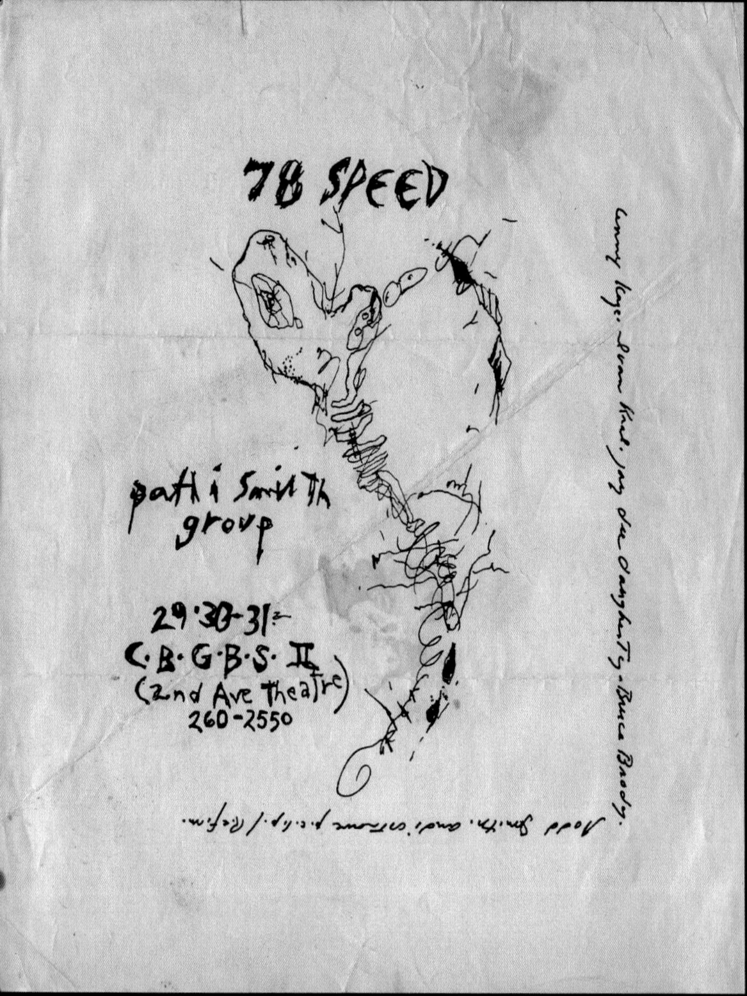

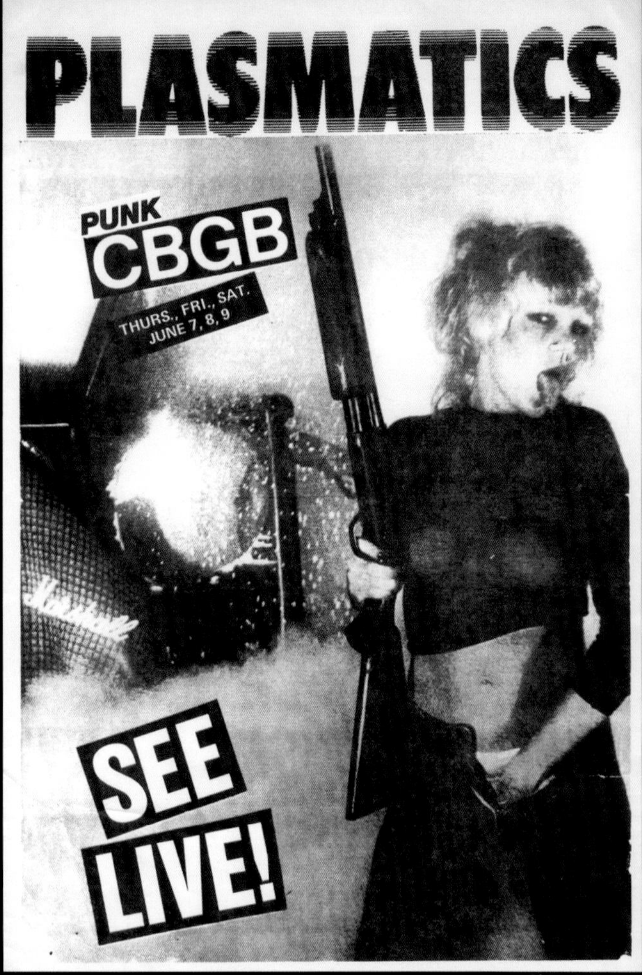

Richard Meyers

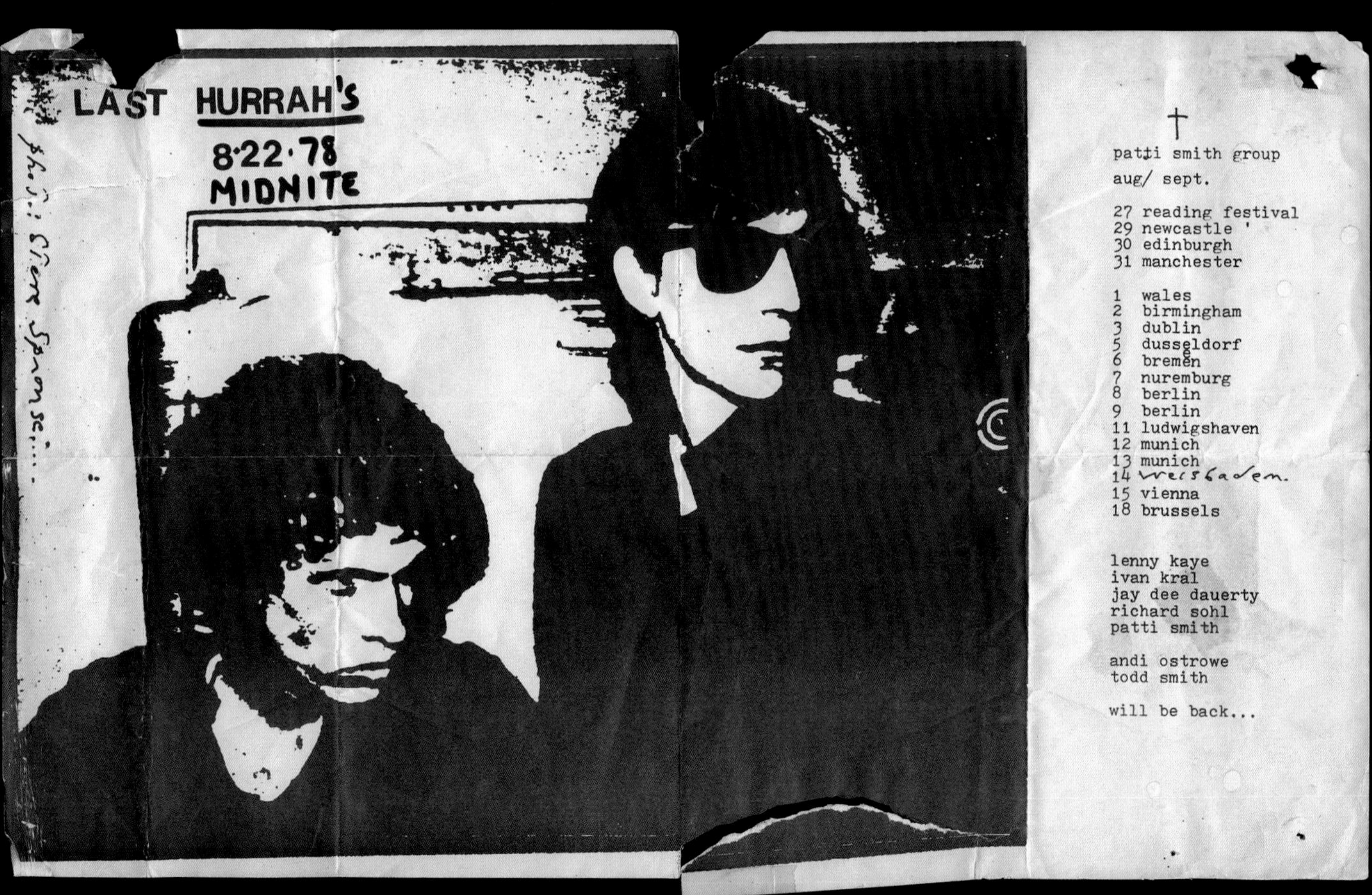

Photo: Steve Sprouse

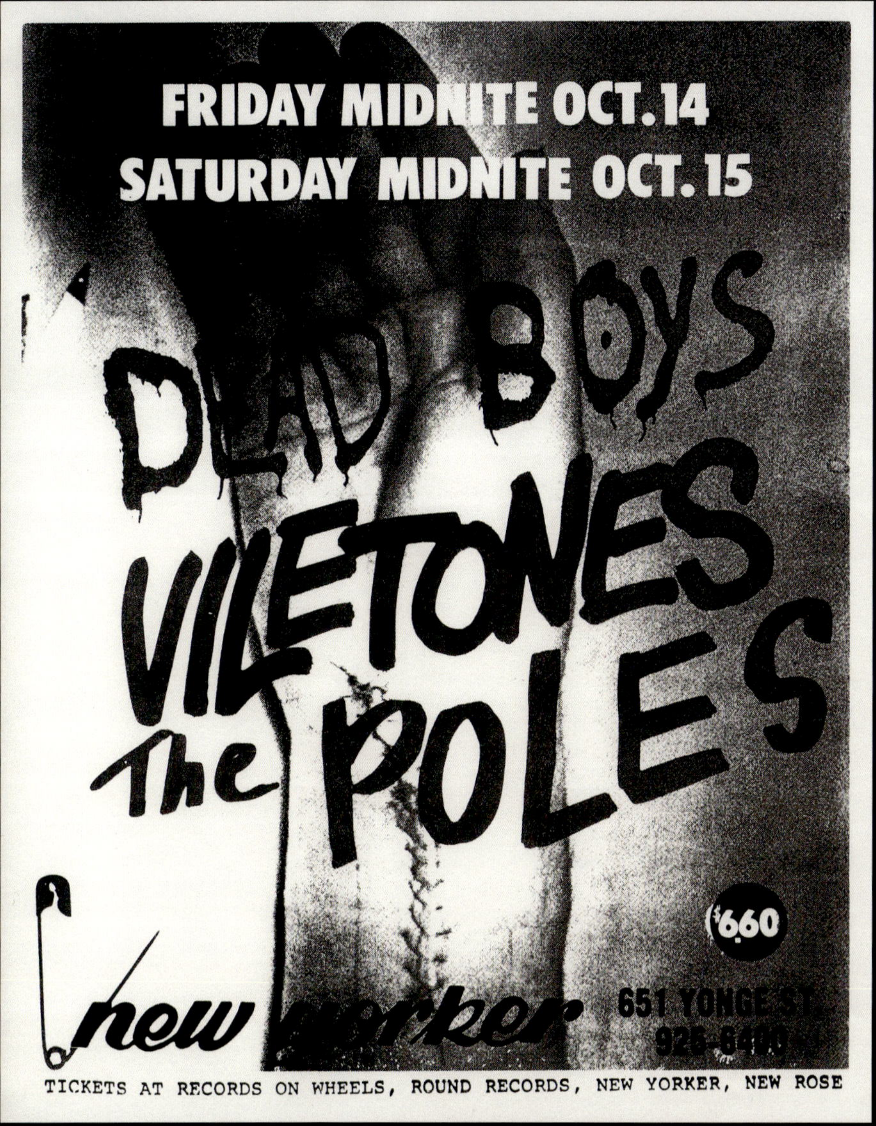

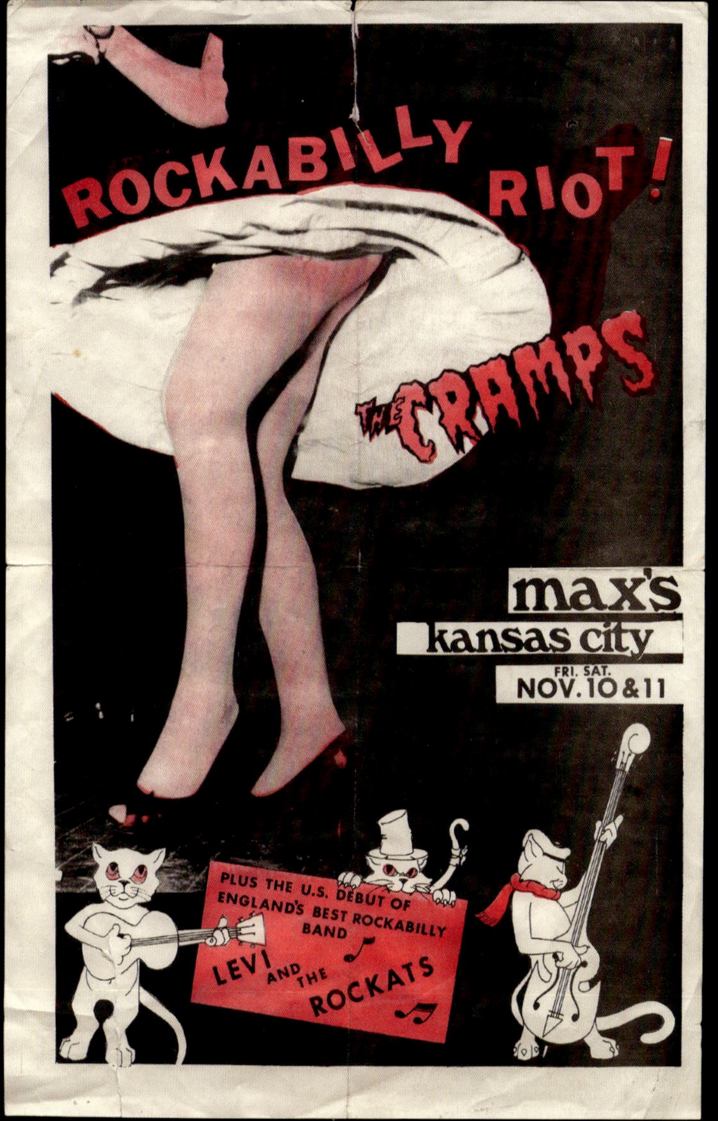

The Cramps

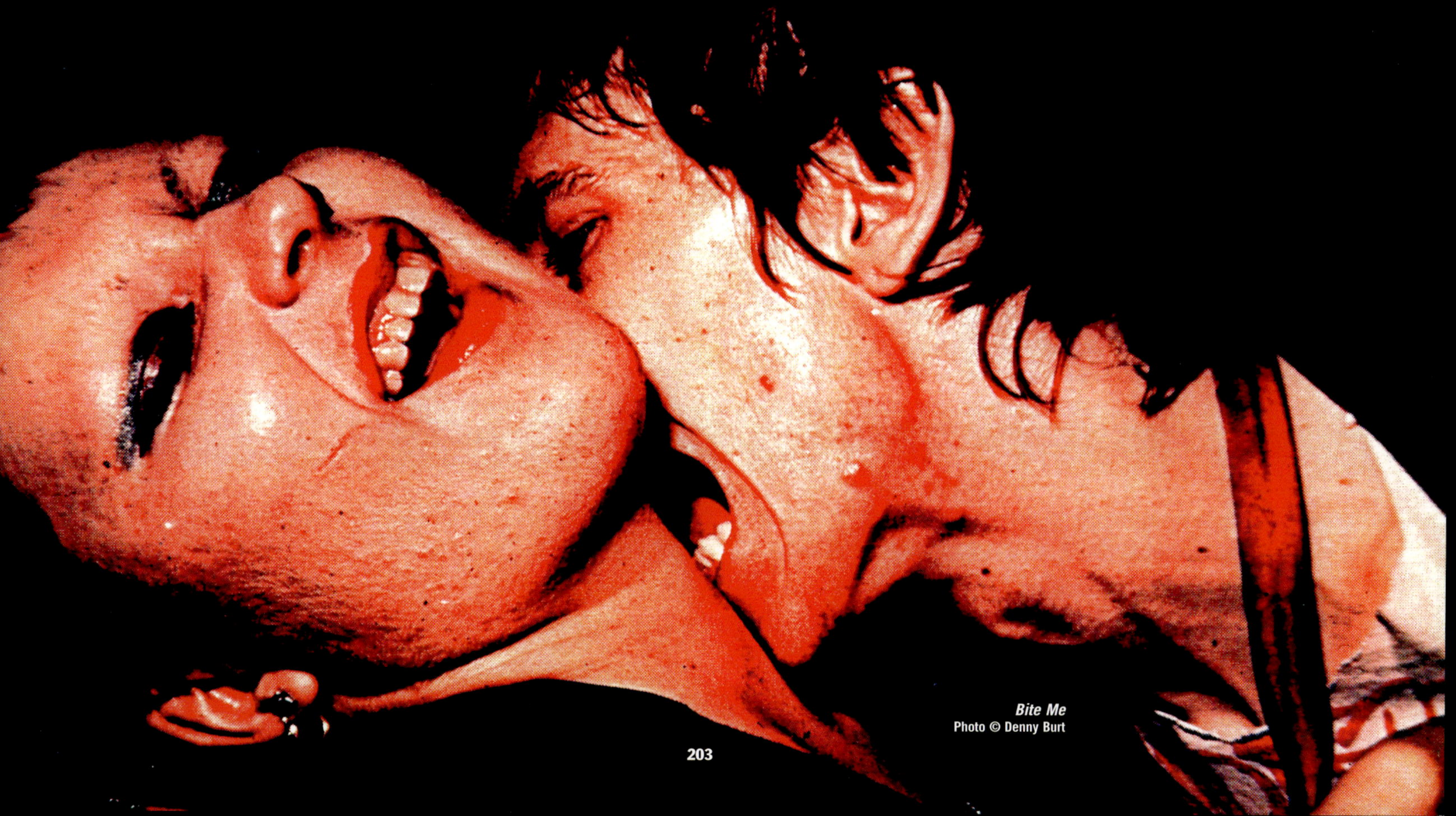

Bite Me
Photo © Denny Burt

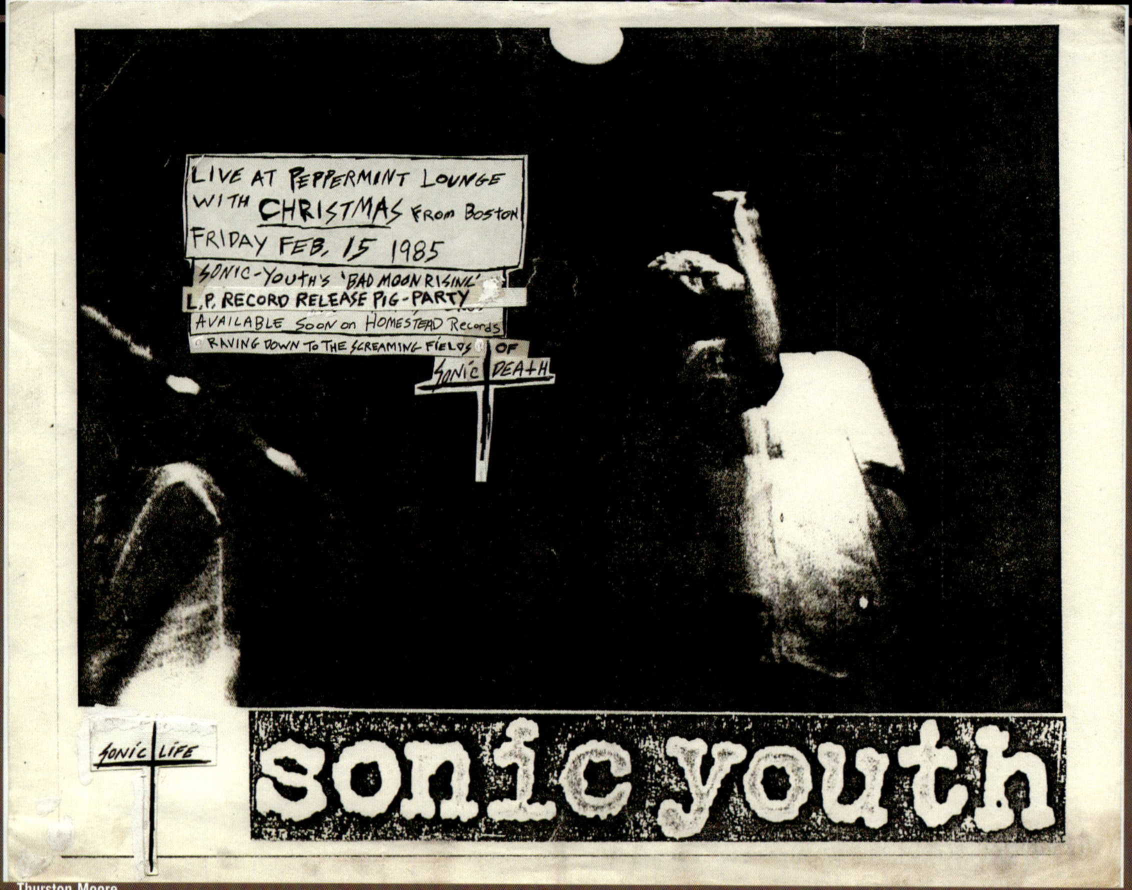

Thurston Moore

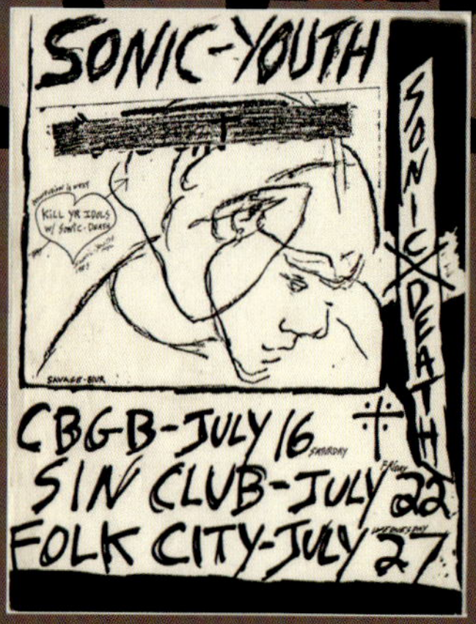

Thurston Moore

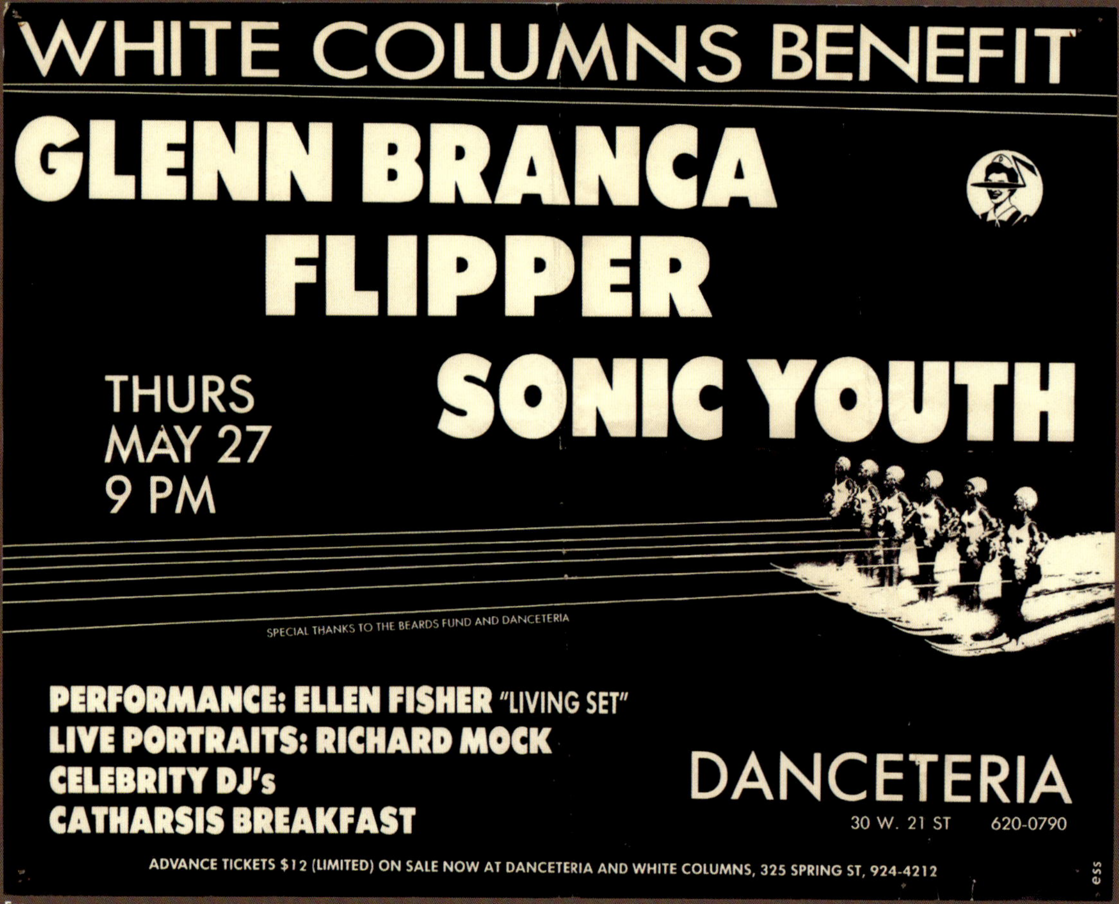

Ess

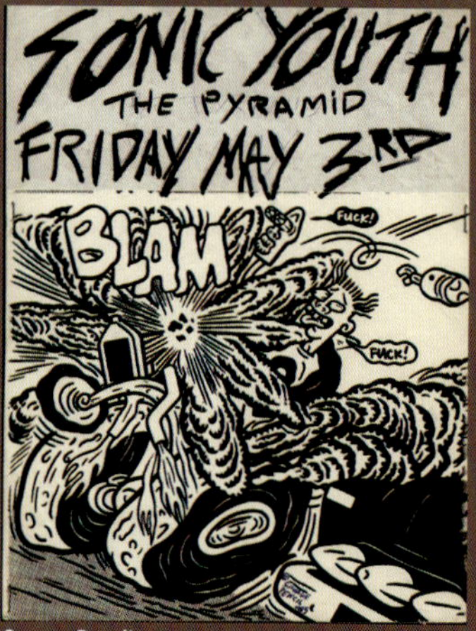

Savage Pencil

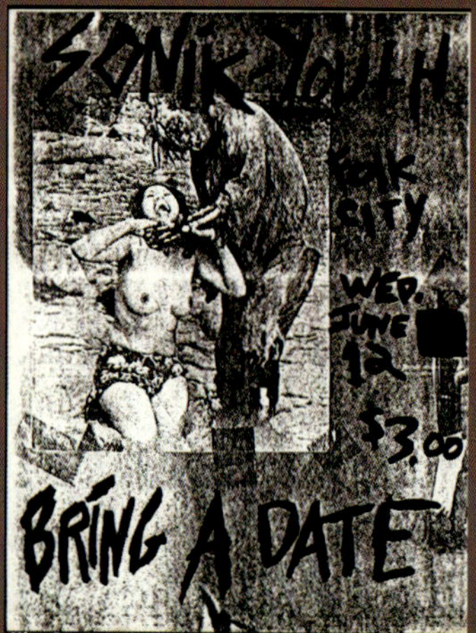

Kim Gordon

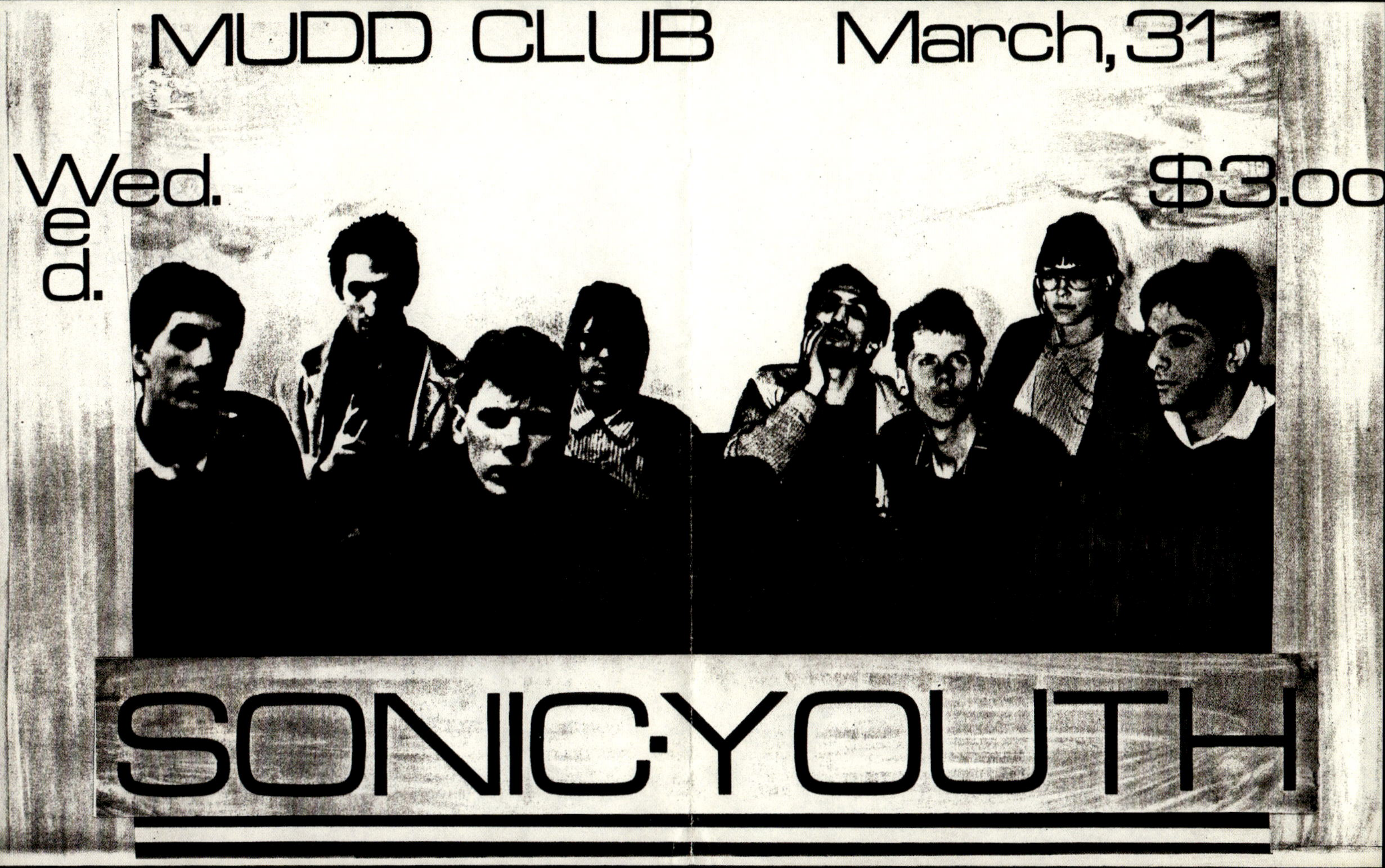

Kim Gordon & Thurston Moore

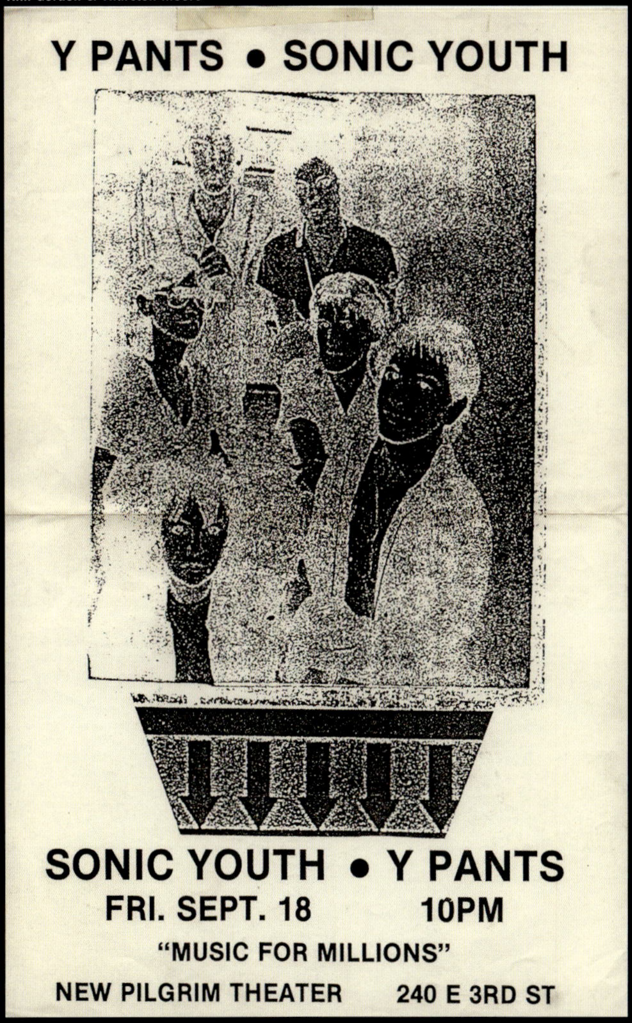

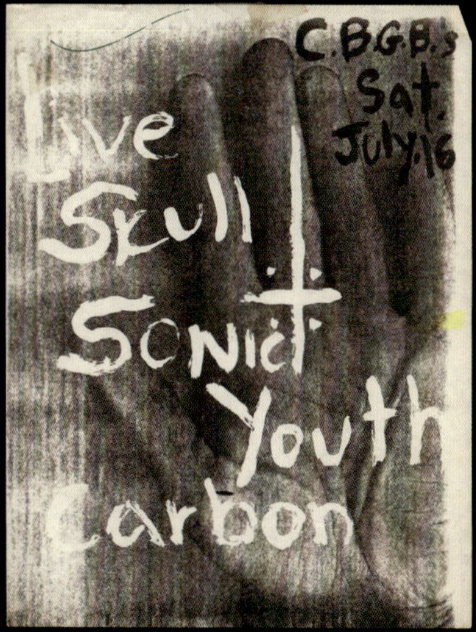

Kim Gordon & Thurston Moore

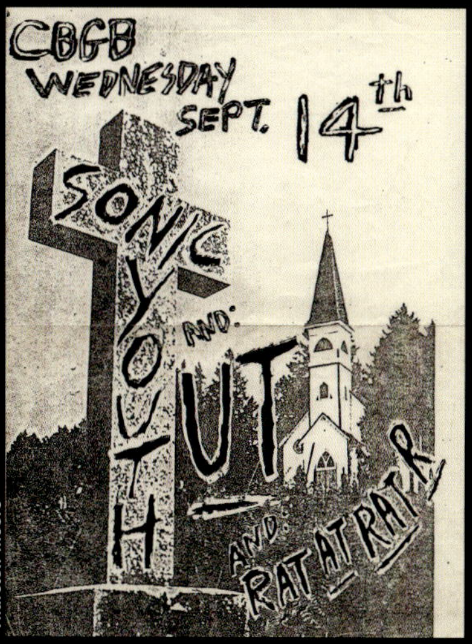

Thurston Moore

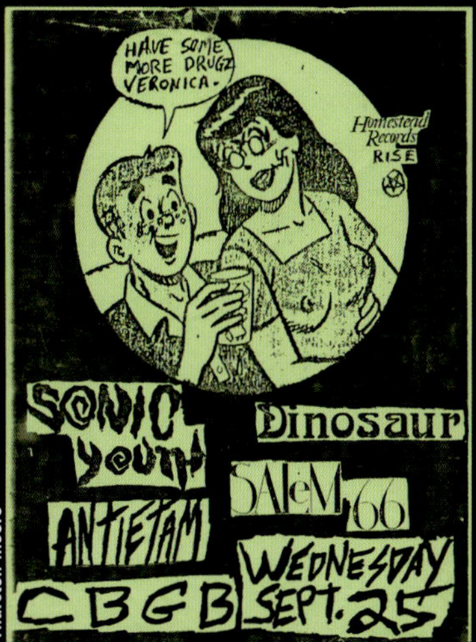

Thurston Moore

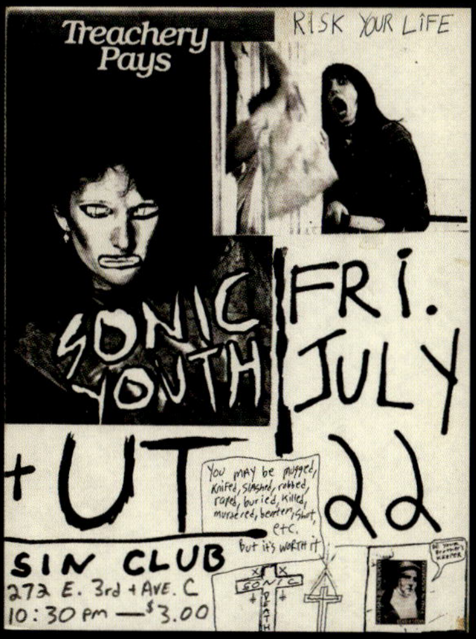

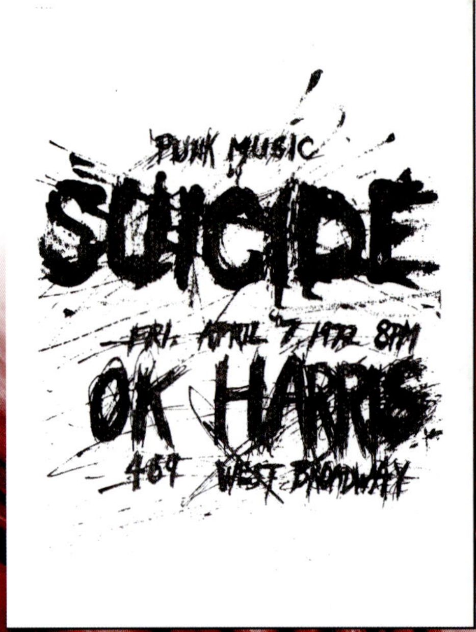
PUNK MUSIC
SUICIDE
FRI. APRIL 7 1972 8PM
OK HARRIS
469 WEST BROADWAY

PUNK MUSIC
by
SUICIDE
at
MUSEUM
729 BROADWAY
EVERY FRIDAY NIGHT
10 PM
no admission

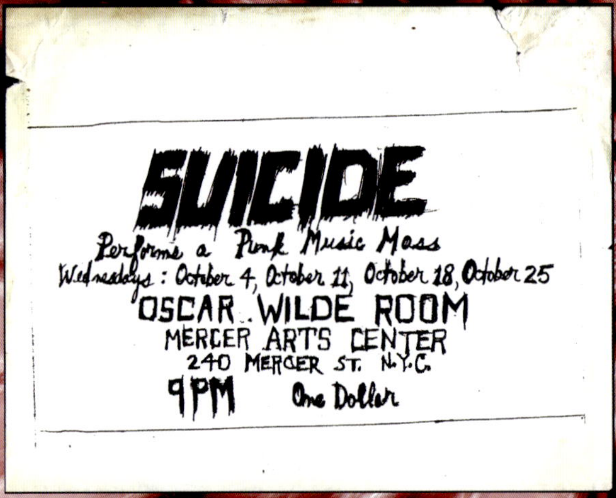
SUICIDE
Performs a Punk Music Mass
Wednesdays: October 4, October 11, October 18, October 25
OSCAR WILDE ROOM
MERCER ARTS CENTER
240 MERCER ST. N.Y.C.
9PM One Dollar

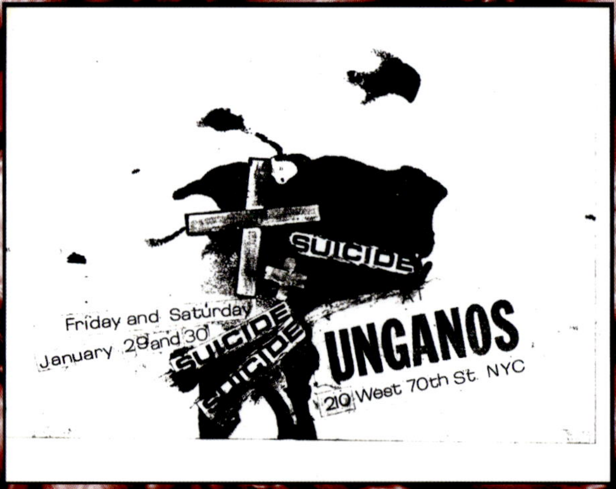
SUICIDE
Friday and Saturday
January 29 and 30
SUICIDE
SUICIDE
SUICIDE
UNGANOS
210 West 70th St. NYC

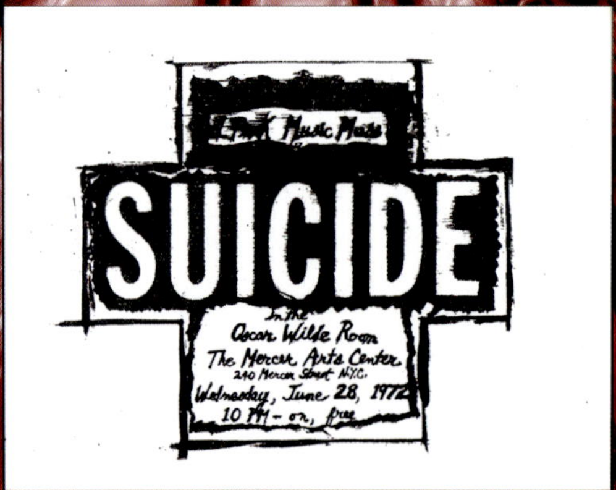
Punk Music Mass
SUICIDE
In the
Oscar Wilde Room
The Mercer Arts Center
240 Mercer Street N.Y.C.
Wednesday, June 28, 1972
10 PM - on, free

All: Suicide

Belmar

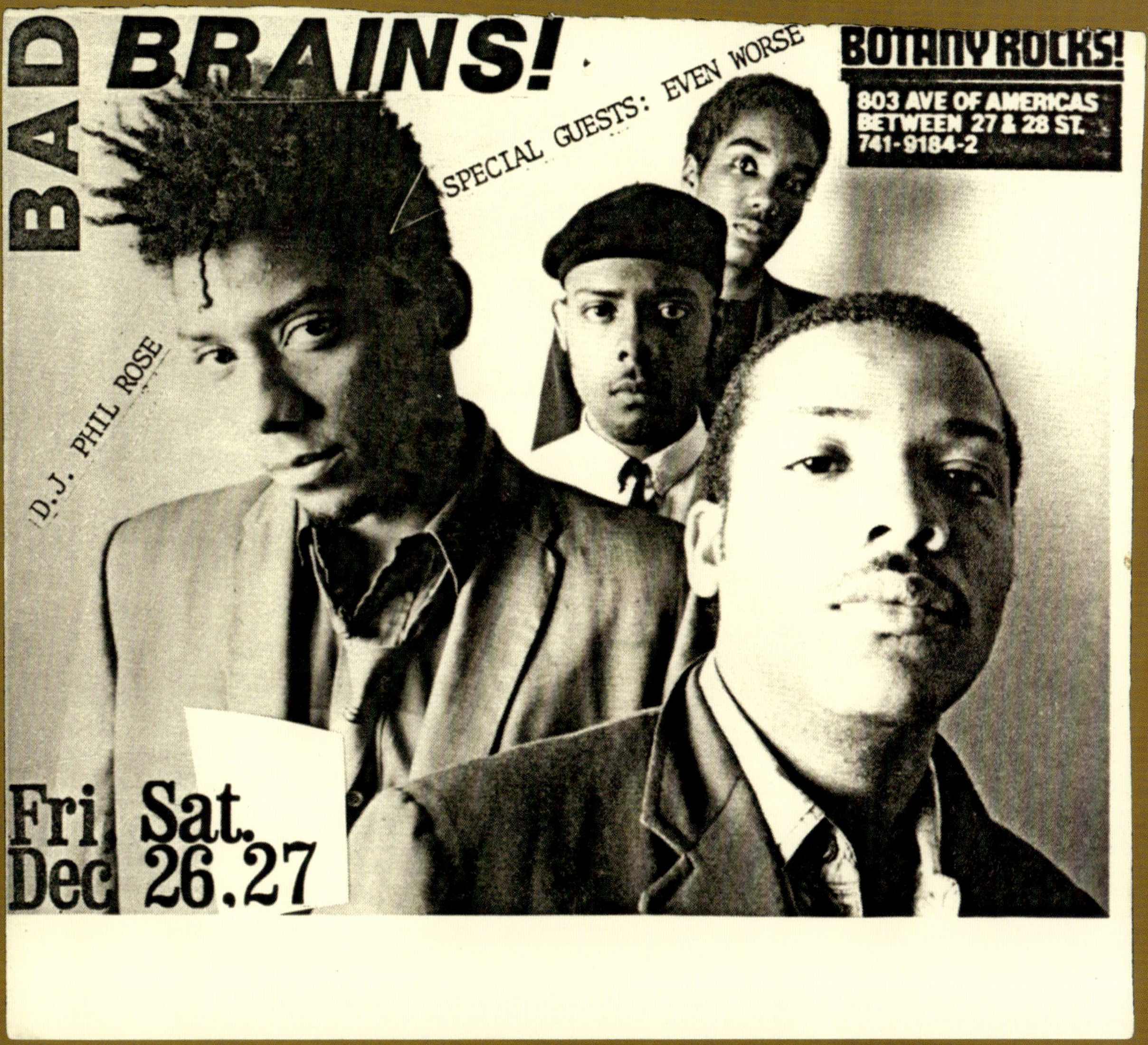

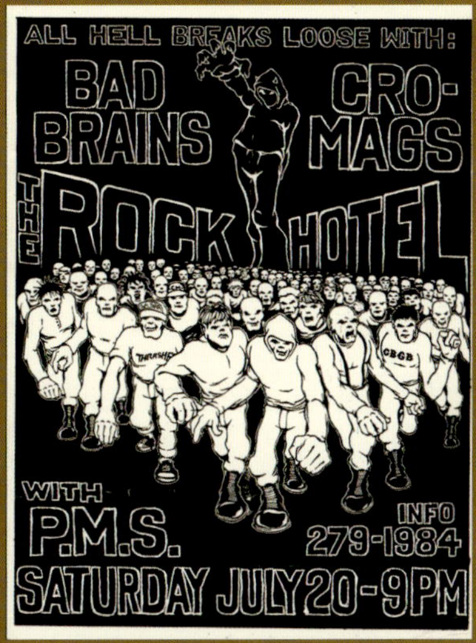

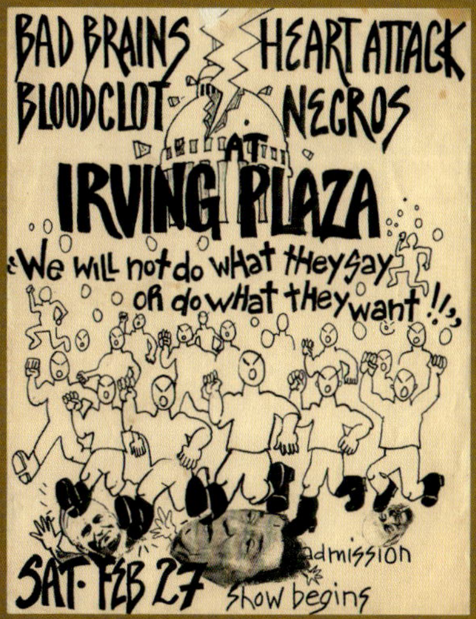

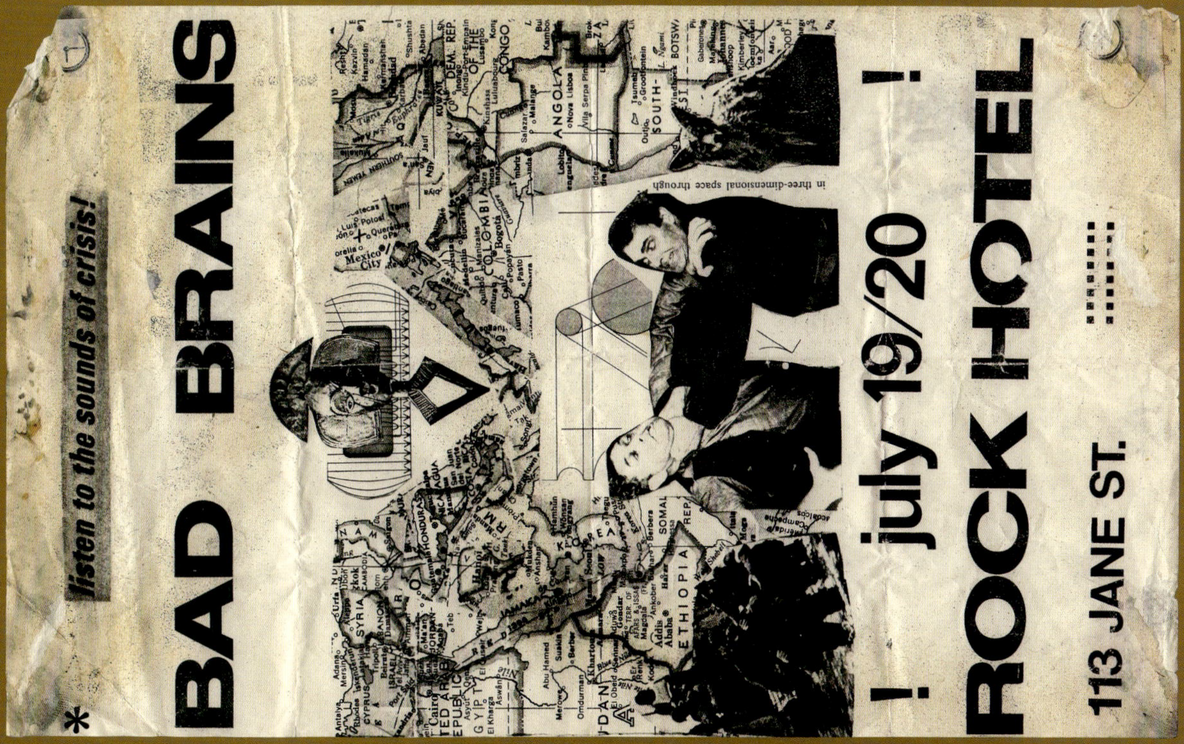

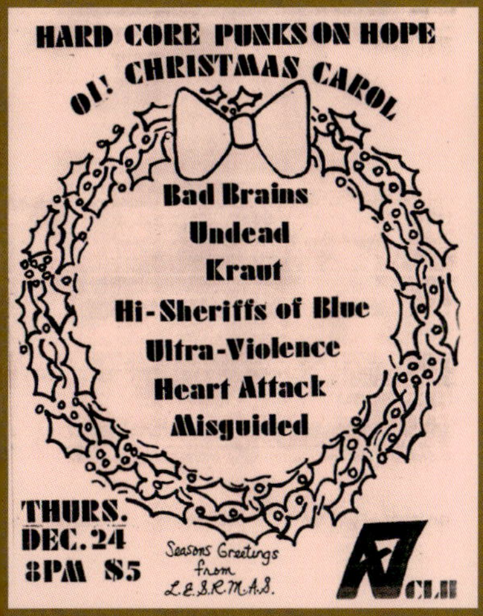

Dave Gibson

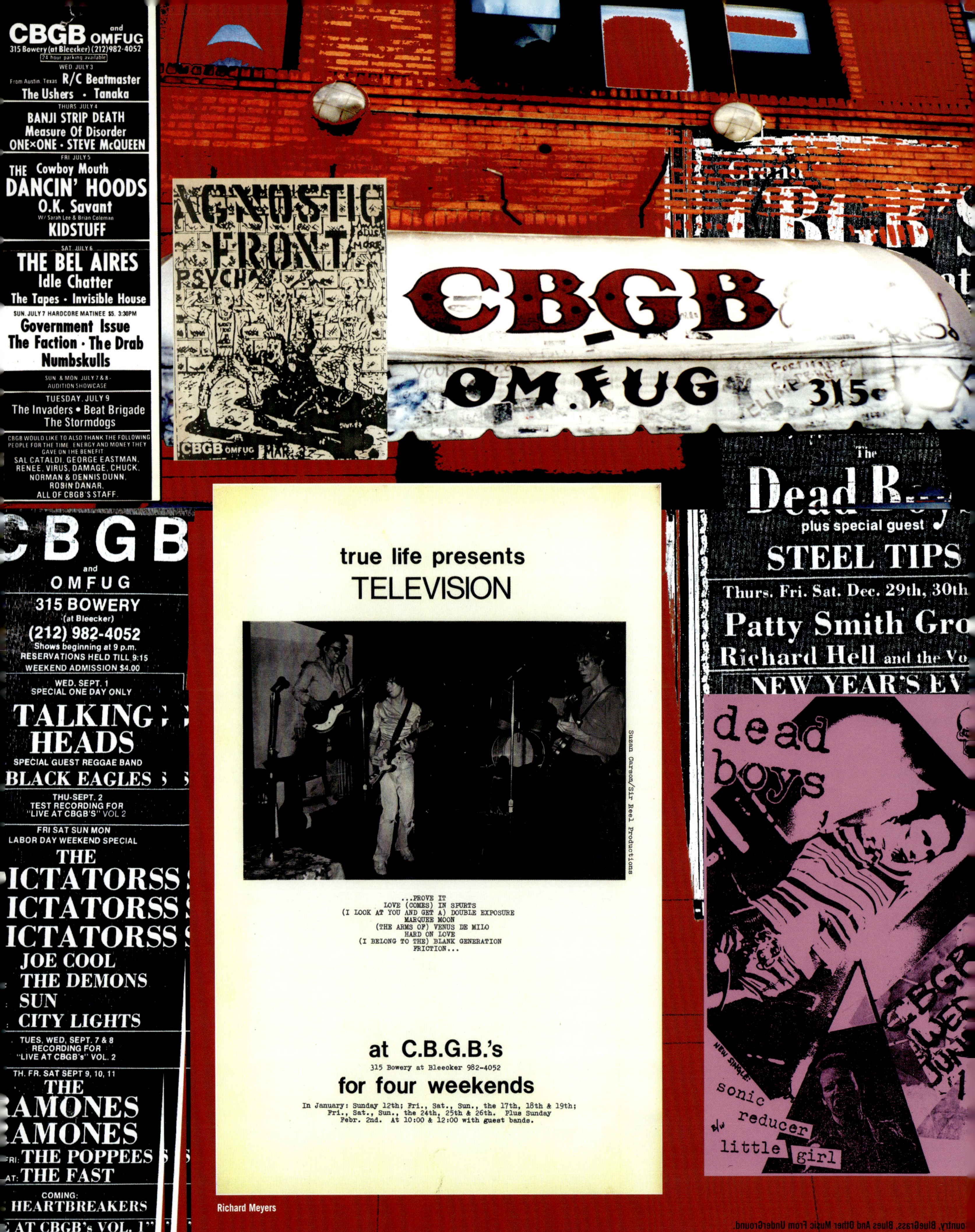

Richard Meyers

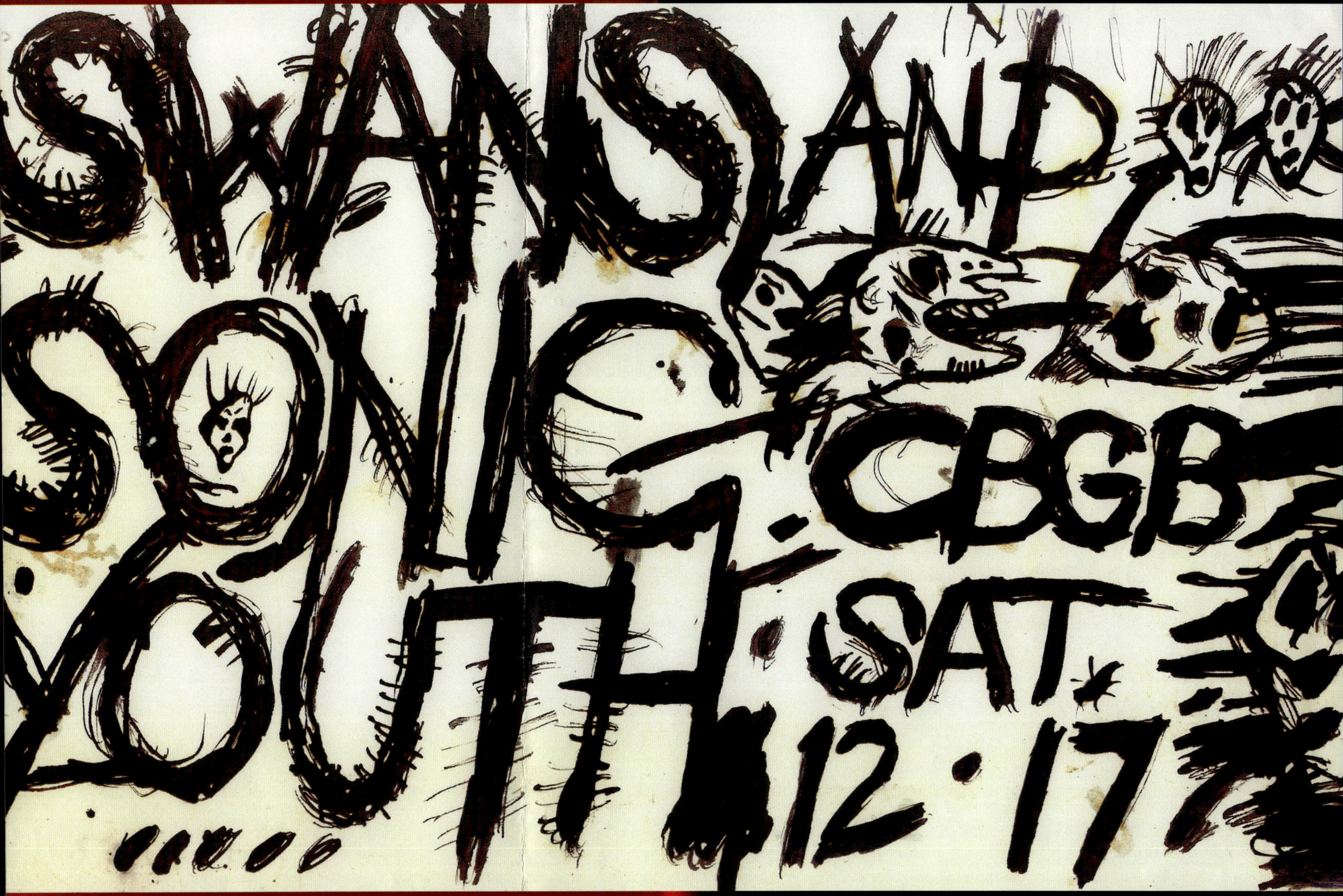
SWANS AND SONIC YOUTH
CBGB
SAT
12·17

Gira/Jarboe

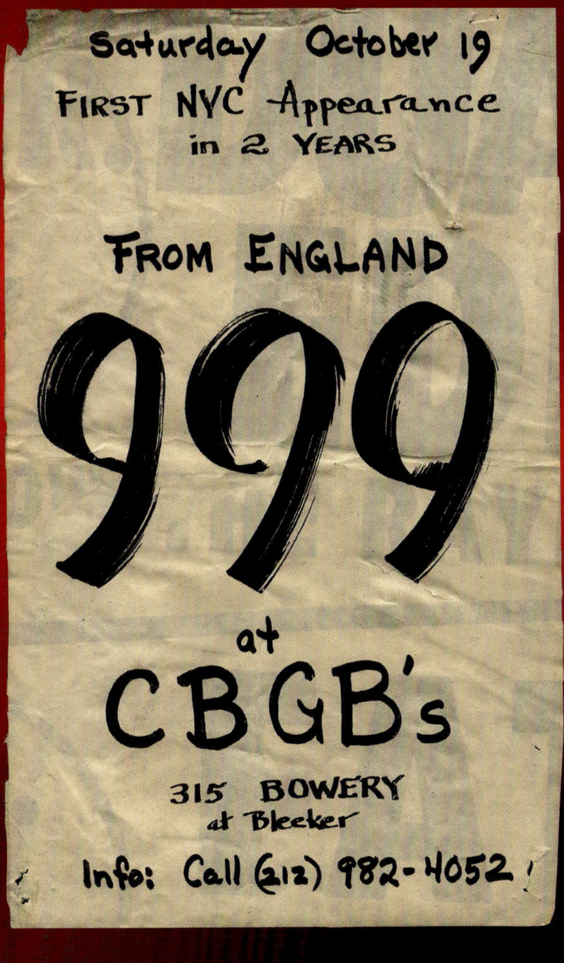
Saturday October 19
FIRST NYC Appearance in 2 YEARS
FROM ENGLAND
999
at
CBGB's
315 BOWERY
at Bleeker
Info: Call (212) 982-4052

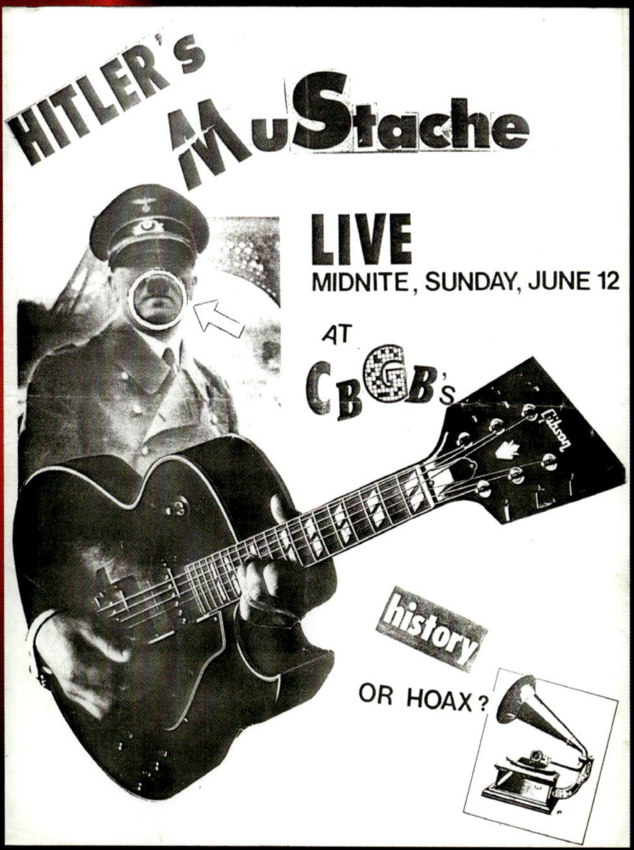
HITLER'S MuStache
LIVE
MIDNITE, SUNDAY, JUNE 12
AT
CBGB's
history
OR HOAX?

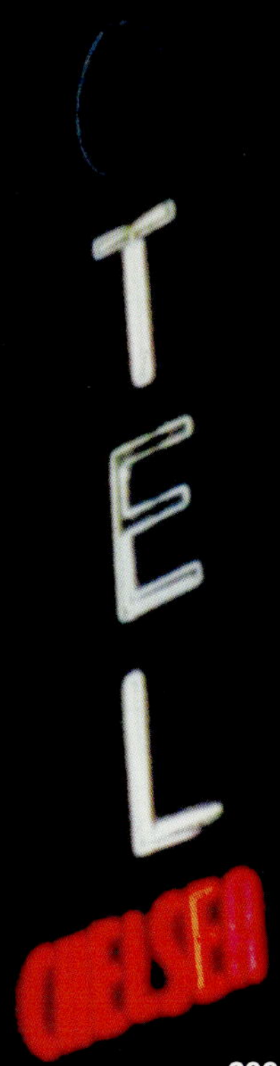
TEL
CHELSEA

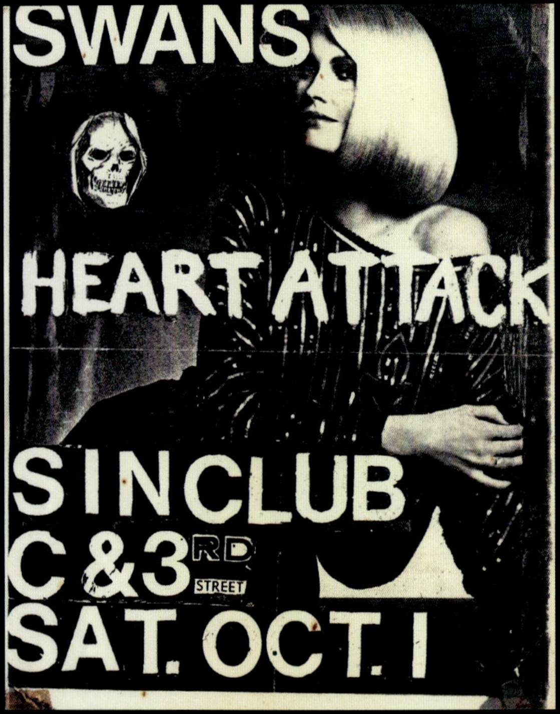

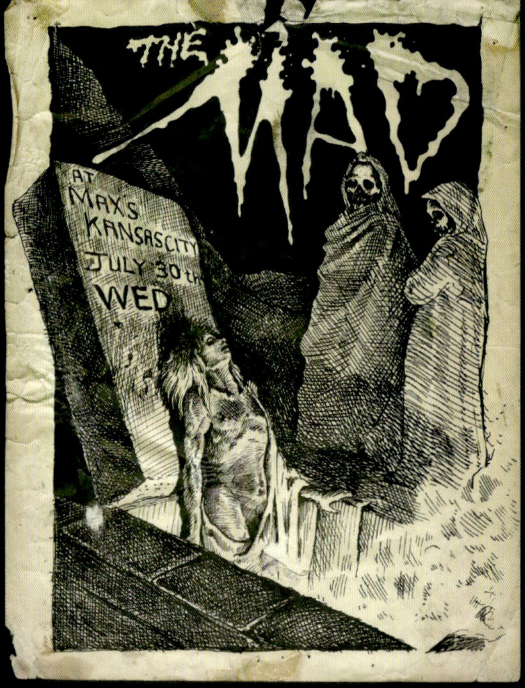

Mad George

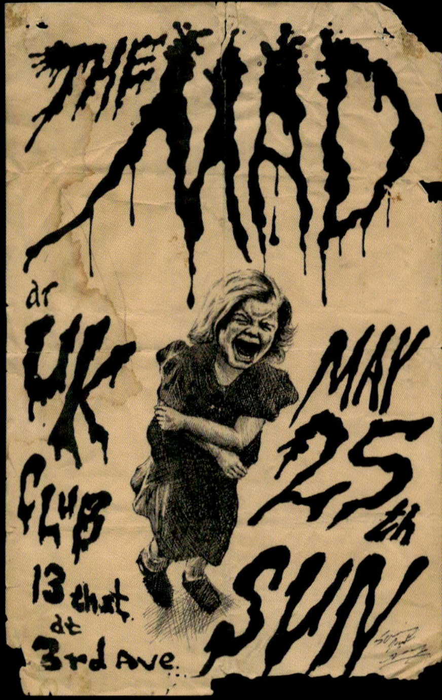

Mad George

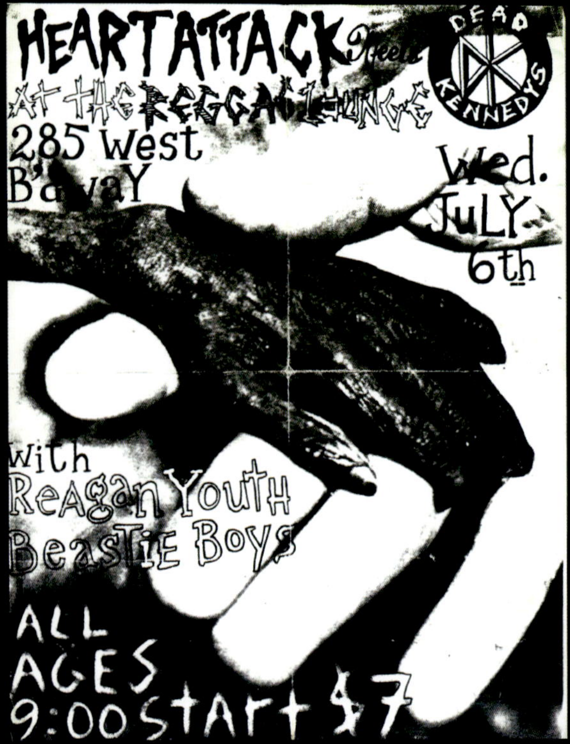

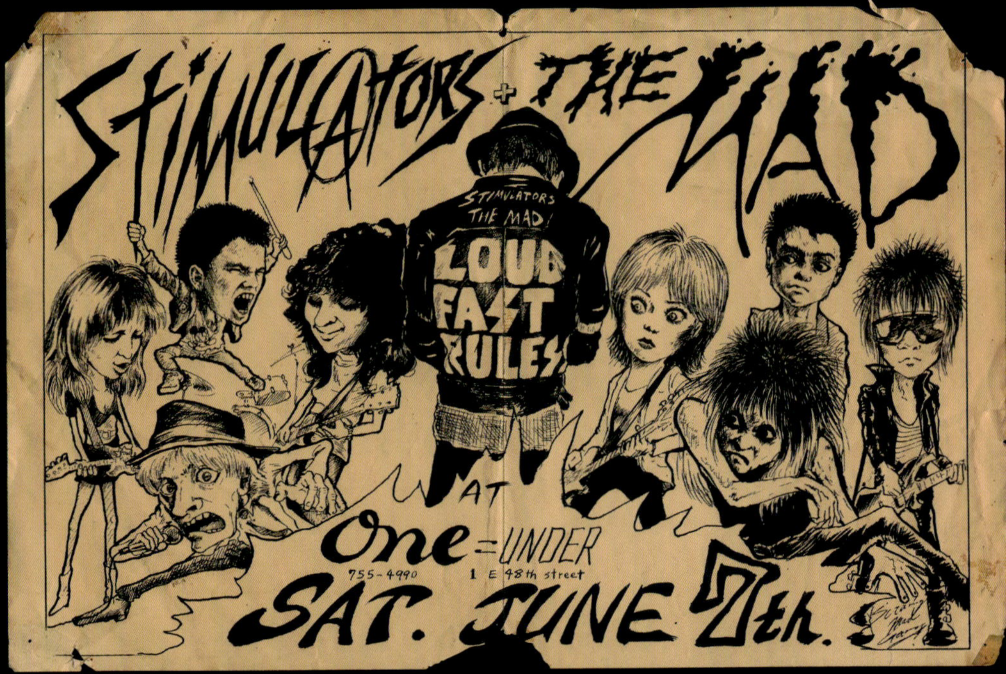

Mad George

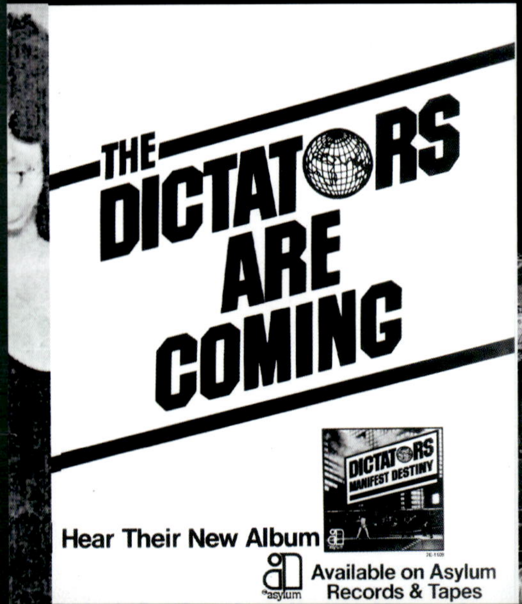

"NYC is not only the area between 14th St. and Chinatown.
We hailed proudly from the Bronx -
Middle-class wiseguys
with a fire for rock and roll
that burned brighter and longer than any of us would have guessed back then."
Top Ten, The Dictators

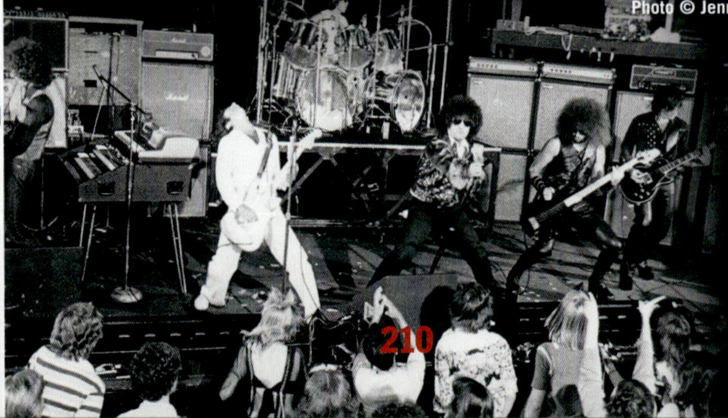

Dictators
Photo © Jenny Lens

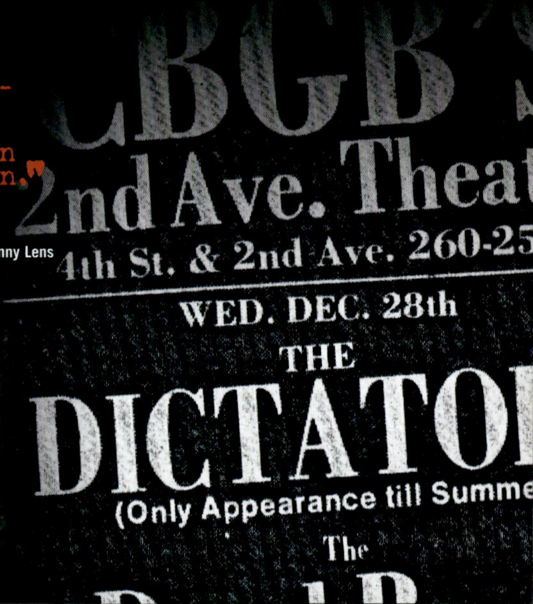

Don Cowan

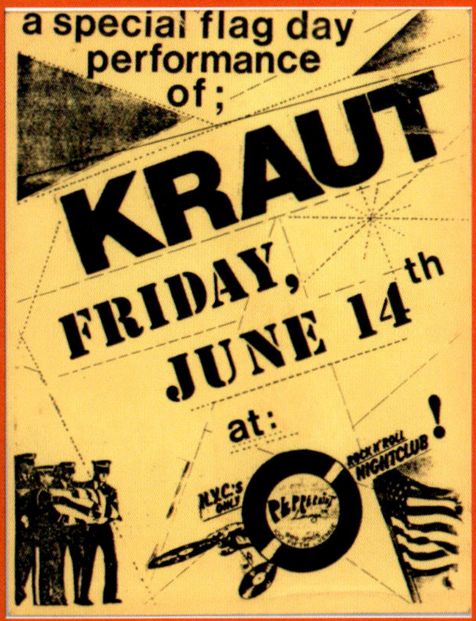

Don Cowan

First Rock Hotel Flyer!

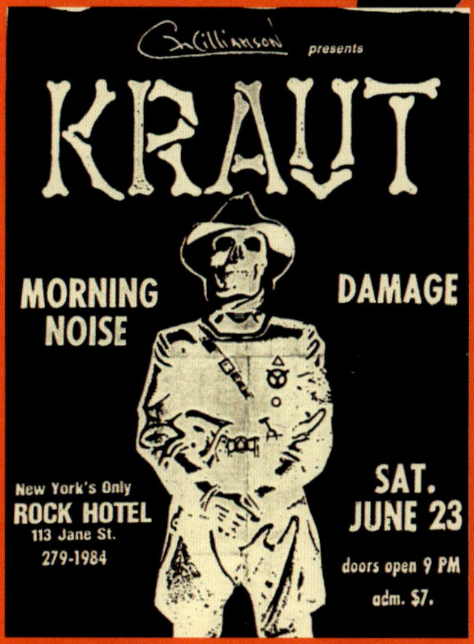

Doug Holland

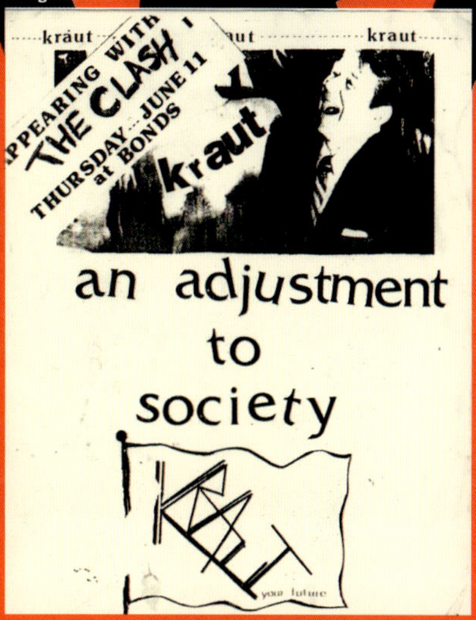

Doug Holland

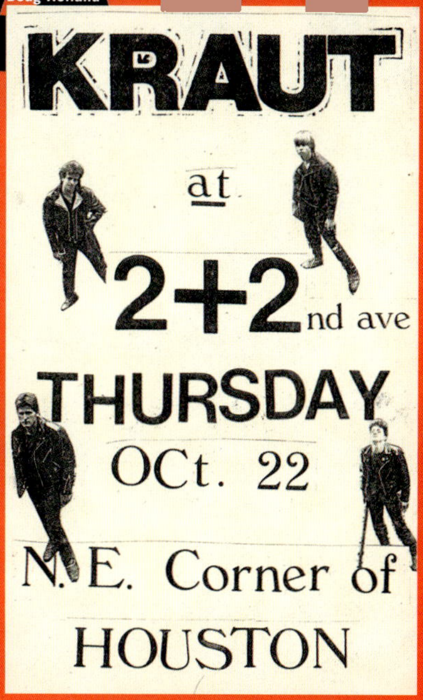

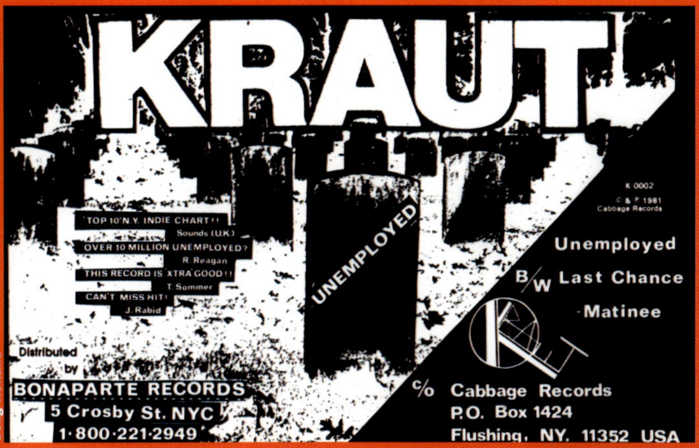

Don Cowan

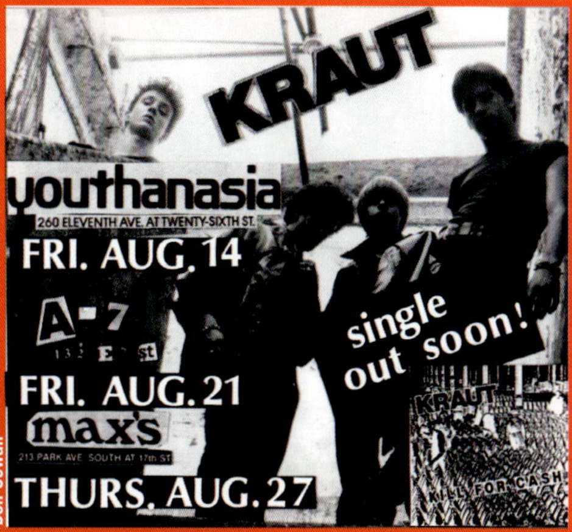

Doug Holland

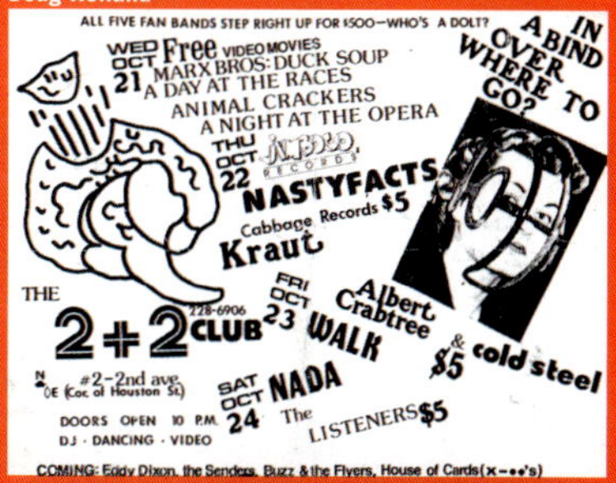

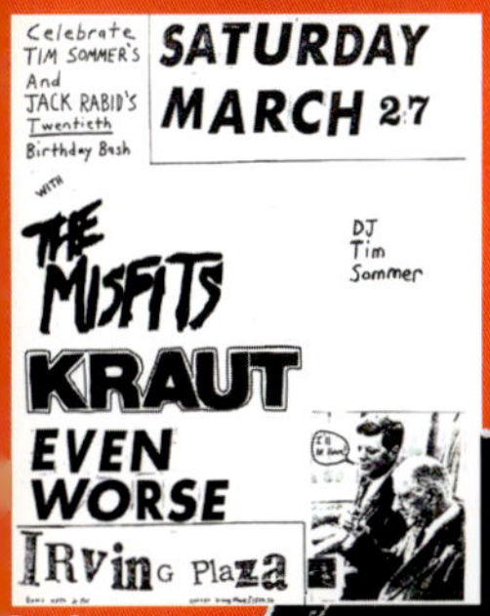

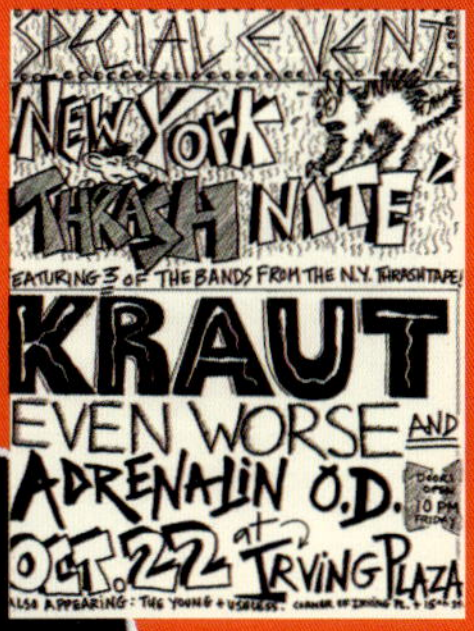

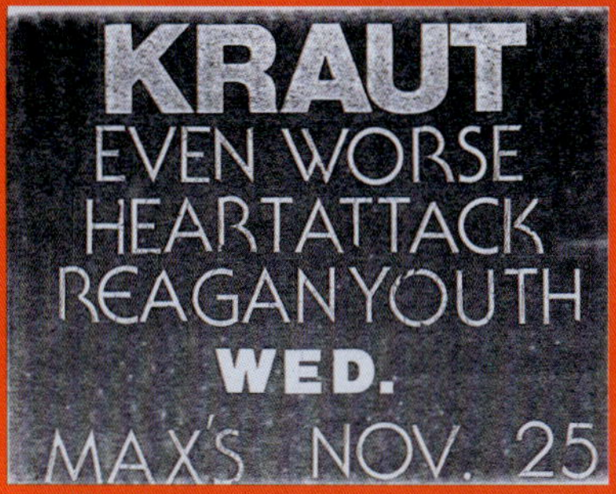

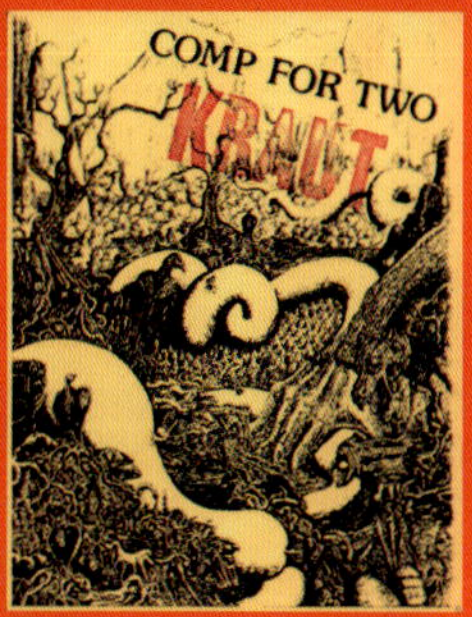

Don Cowan

Doug Holland

Don Cowan

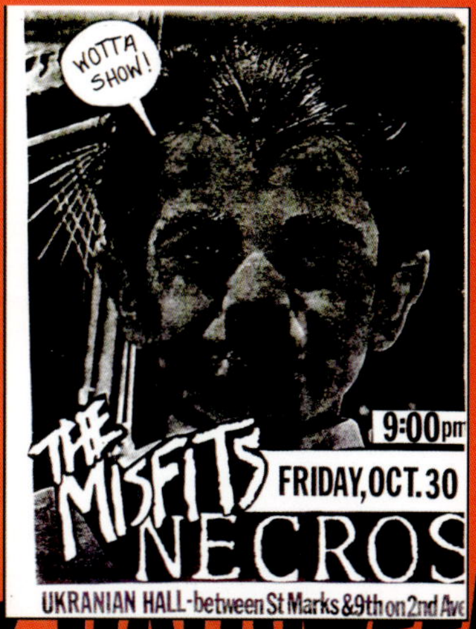

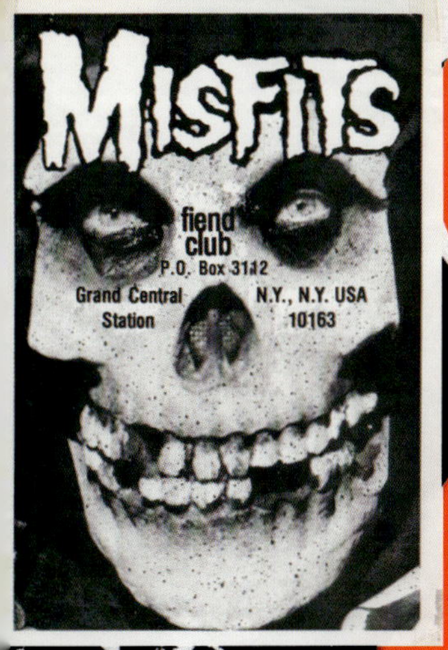

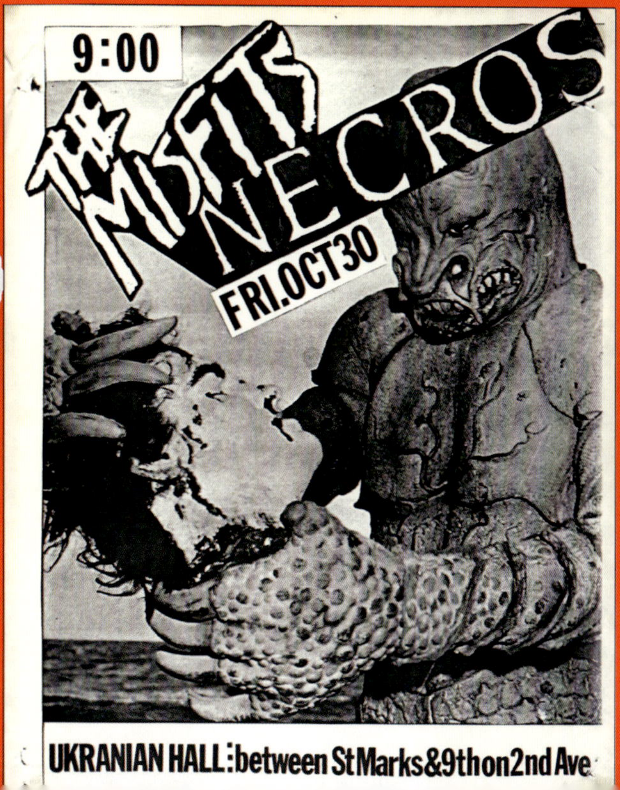

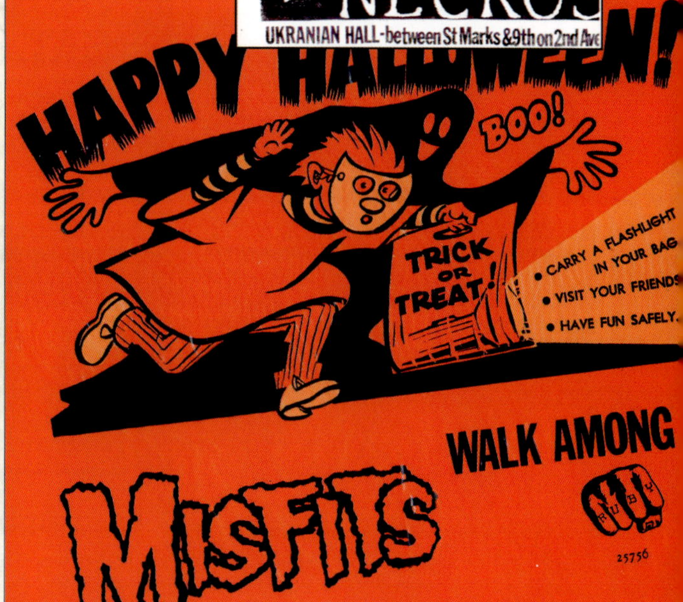

Misfits Trick Or Treat Bag

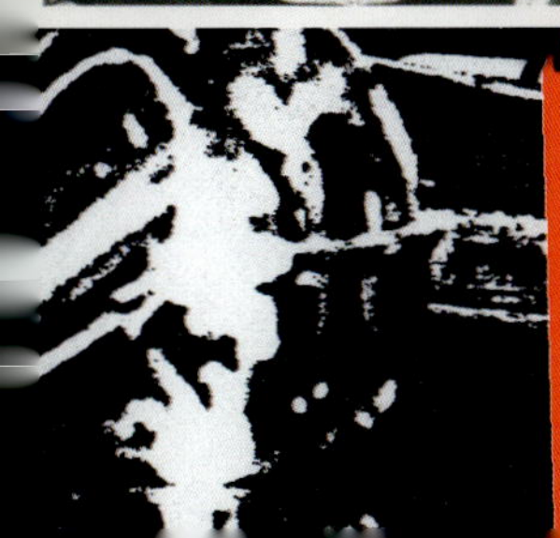

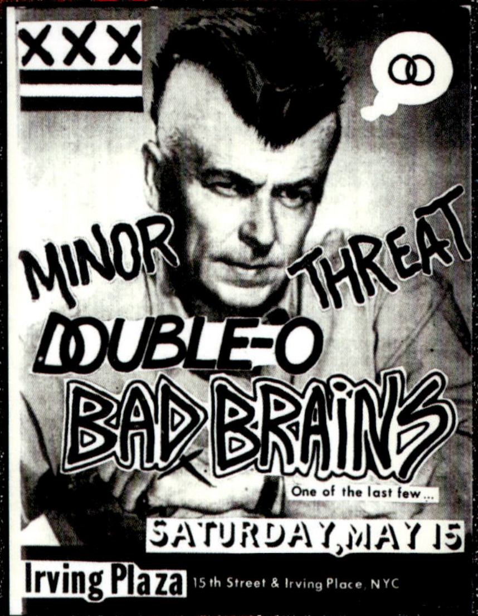
MINOR THREAT
DOUBLE-O
BAD BRAINS
One of the last few...
SATURDAY, MAY 15
Irving Plaza 15th Street & Irving Place, NYC

PARTY TIME!
SFA NEW YORK
+
GO!
LAURA'S HOUSE
july 8th · 2pm

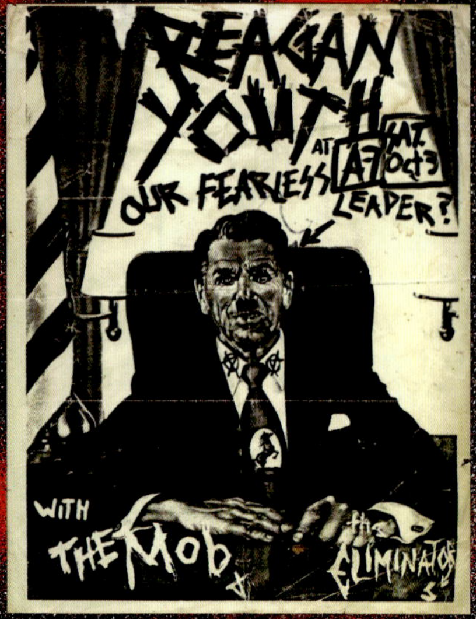
REAGAN YOUTH
AT A7
SAT. Oct 3
OUR FEARLESS LEADER?
WITH
THE MOB
the ELIMINATORS

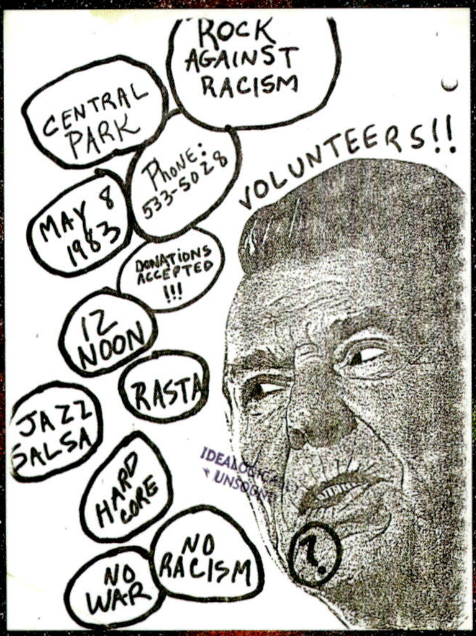
ROCK AGAINST RACISM
CENTRAL PARK
MAY 8 1983
Phone: 533-5028
VOLUNTEERS!!
DONATIONS ACCEPTED !!!
12 NOON
RASTA
JAZZ SALSA
HARD CORE
NO WAR
NO RACISM

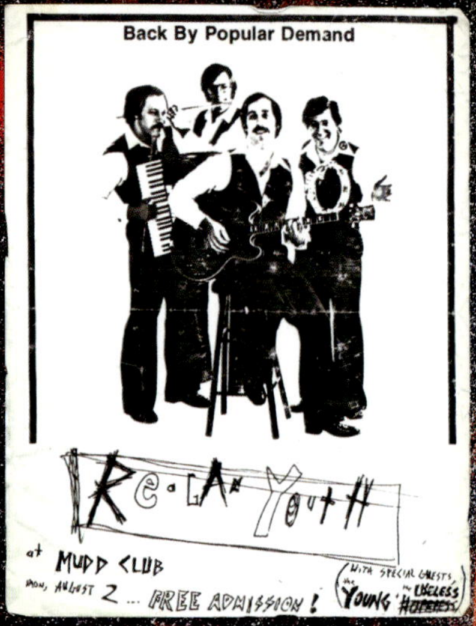
Back By Popular Demand
REAGAN YOUTH
at MUDD CLUB
MON, AUGUST 2 ... FREE ADMISSION!
WITH SPECIAL GUESTS
YOUNG USELESS HOTHEADS

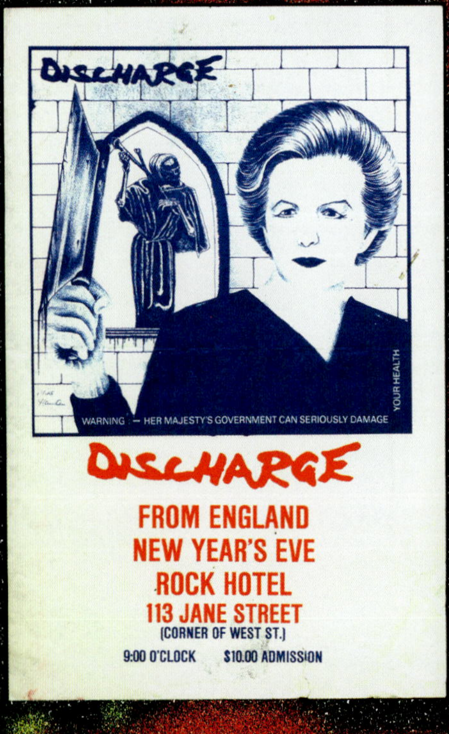
DISCHARGE
WARNING — HER MAJESTY'S GOVERNMENT CAN SERIOUSLY DAMAGE YOUR HEALTH
DISCHARGE
FROM ENGLAND
NEW YEAR'S EVE
ROCK HOTEL
113 JANE STREET
(CORNER OF WEST ST.)
9:00 O'CLOCK $10.00 ADMISSION

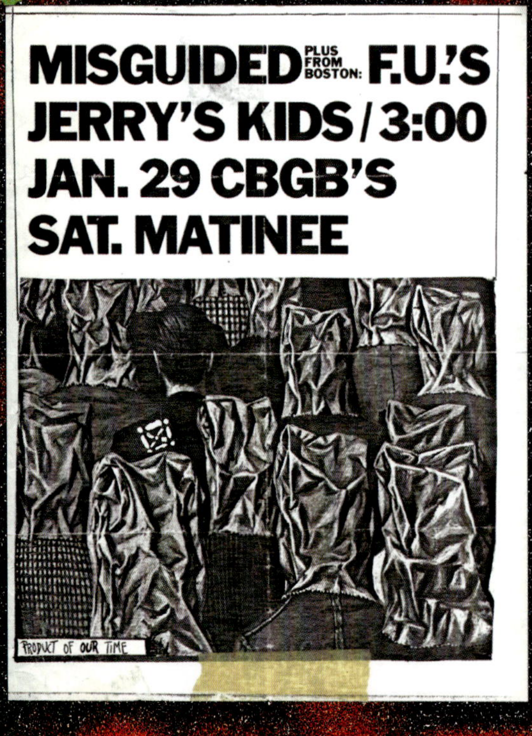
MISGUIDED PLUS FROM BOSTON: F.U.'S
JERRY'S KIDS / 3:00
JAN. 29 CBGB'S
SAT. MATINEE
PRODUCT OF OUR TIME

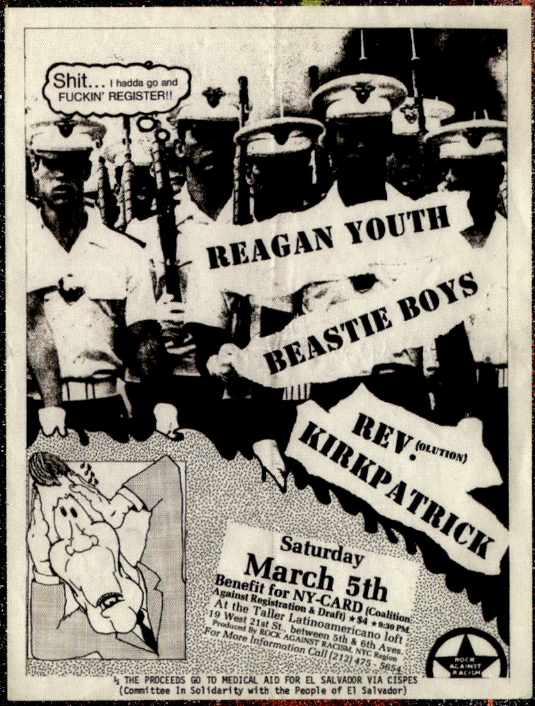
Shit... I hadda go and FUCKIN' REGISTER!!
REAGAN YOUTH
BEASTIE BOYS
REV. (OLUTION) KIRKPATRICK
Saturday
March 5th
Benefit for NY-CARD (Coalition Against Registration & Draft) • $4 • 9:30 PM
At the Taller Latinoamericano loft
19 West 21st St. between 5th & 6th Aves.
For More Information Call (212) 475-9654
½ THE PROCEEDS GO TO MEDICAL AID FOR EL SALVADOR VIA CISPES
(Committee In Solidarity with the People of El Salvador)
ROCK AGAINST RACISM

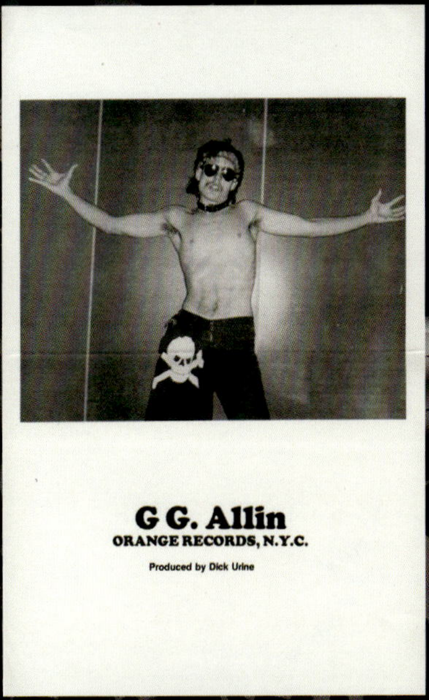

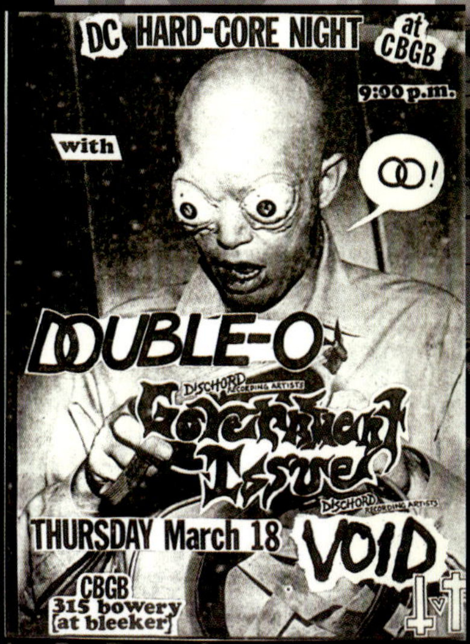

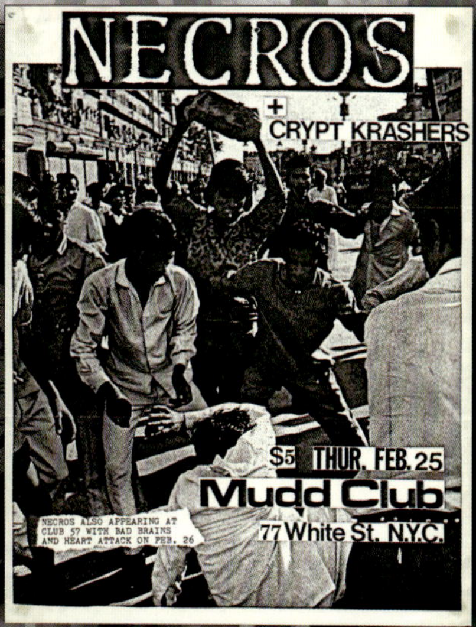

K. Crowley

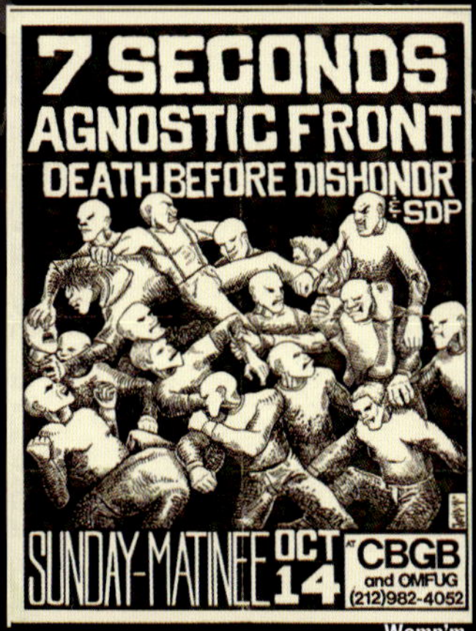

Womp'm

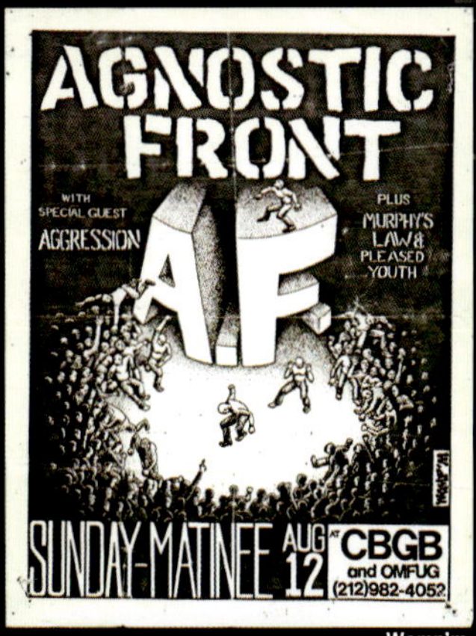

Womp'm

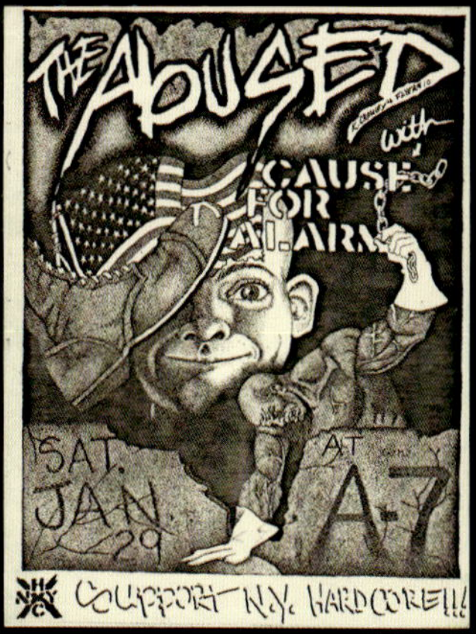

K. Crowley

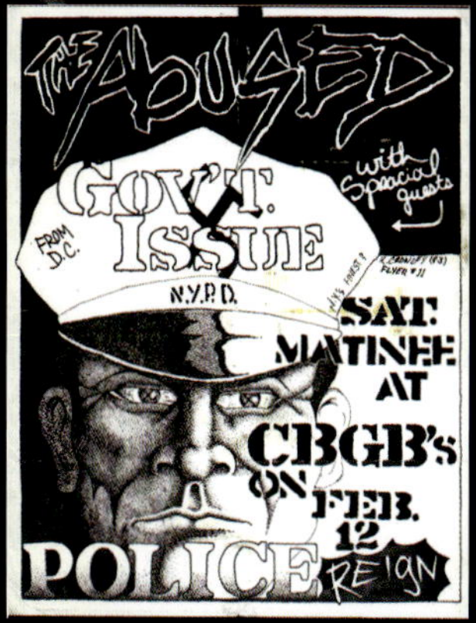

K. Crowley

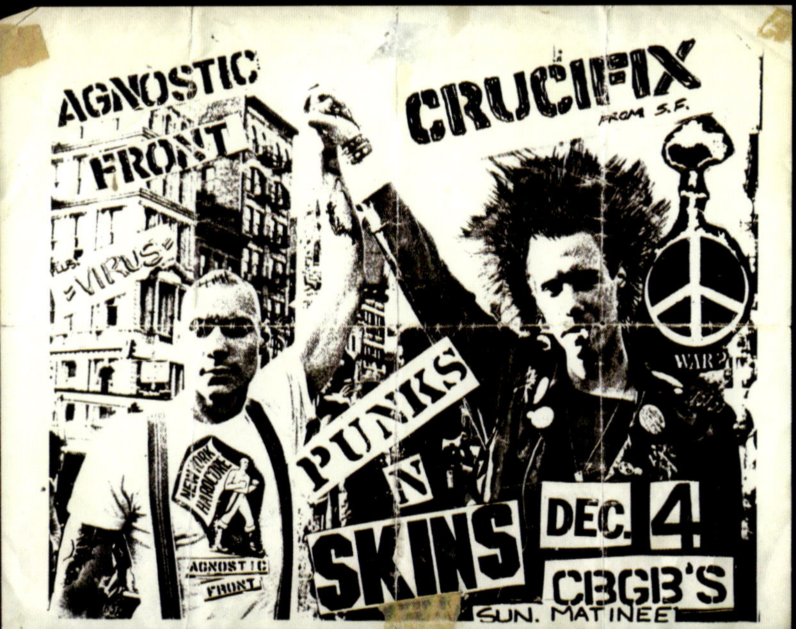

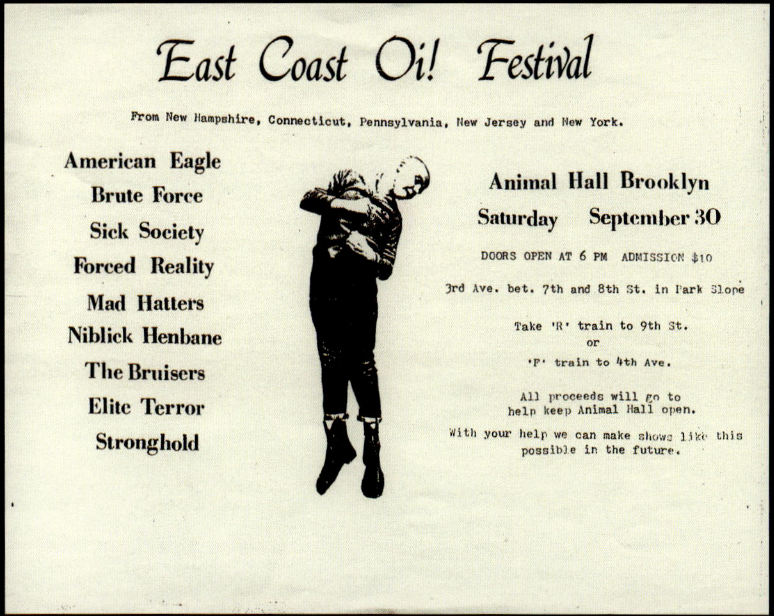

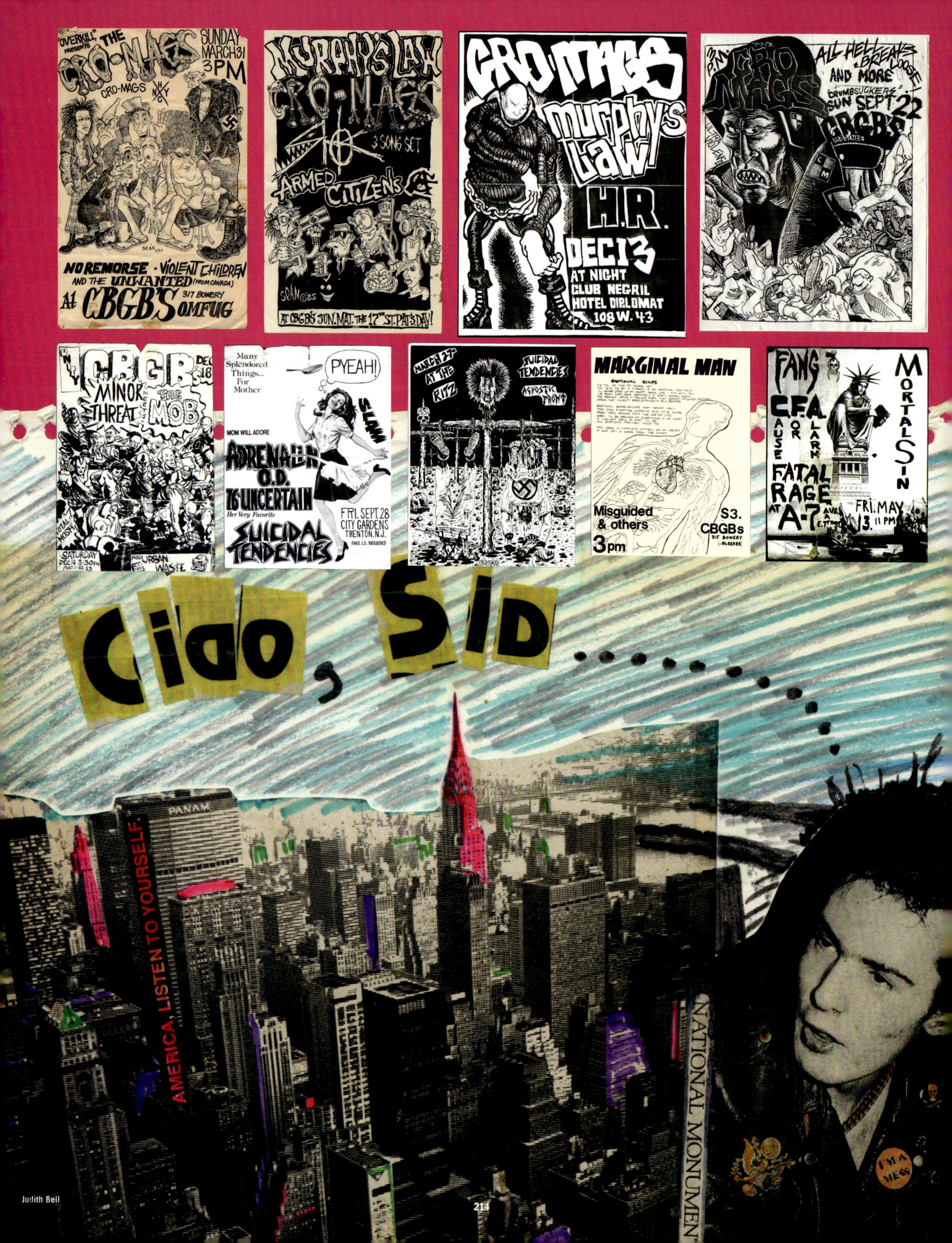
"OVERKILL" PRESENTS THE CRO-MAGS
SUNDAY MARCH 31 3PM
NO REMORSE · VIOLENT CHILDREN
AND THE UNWANTED (FROM CANADA)
At CBGB'S OMFUG 317 BOWERY
MURPHY'S LAW
CRO-MAGS
3 SONG SET
ARMED CITIZENS
AT CBGB'S SUN. MAT. THE 17TH ST. PAT'S DAY!
CRO-MAGS
murphy's law
H.R.
DEC 13
AT NIGHT
CLUB NEGRIL
HOTEL DIPLOMAT
108 W. 43
CRO MAGS
ALL HELL BREAKS LOOSE
AND MORE
"CRUMBSUCKERS"
SUN SEPT 22
CBGB'S
CBGB
DEC 18
MINOR THREAT
THE MOB
SATURDAY
URBAN WASTE
Many Splendored Things... For Mother
PYEAH!
SLAM
MOM WILL ADORE
ADRENALIN O.D.
76 UNCERTAIN
Her Very Favorite
SUICIDAL TENDENCIES
FRI. SEPT 28
CITY GARDENS
TRENTON, N.J.
FAKE I.D. REQUIRED
MARCH 29TH AT THE RITZ
SUICIDAL TENDENCIES
AGNOSTIC FRONT
MARGINAL MAN
Misguided & others
3pm
$3.
CBGBs
315 BOWERY
FANG
C.F.A.
CAUSE FOR ALARM
FATAL RAGE
AT A-7
FRI. MAY 13.
MORTAL SIN
Ciao, Sid
PANAM
AMERICA, LISTEN TO YOURSELF.
NATIONAL MONUMEN
I'M A MESS

Judith Bell

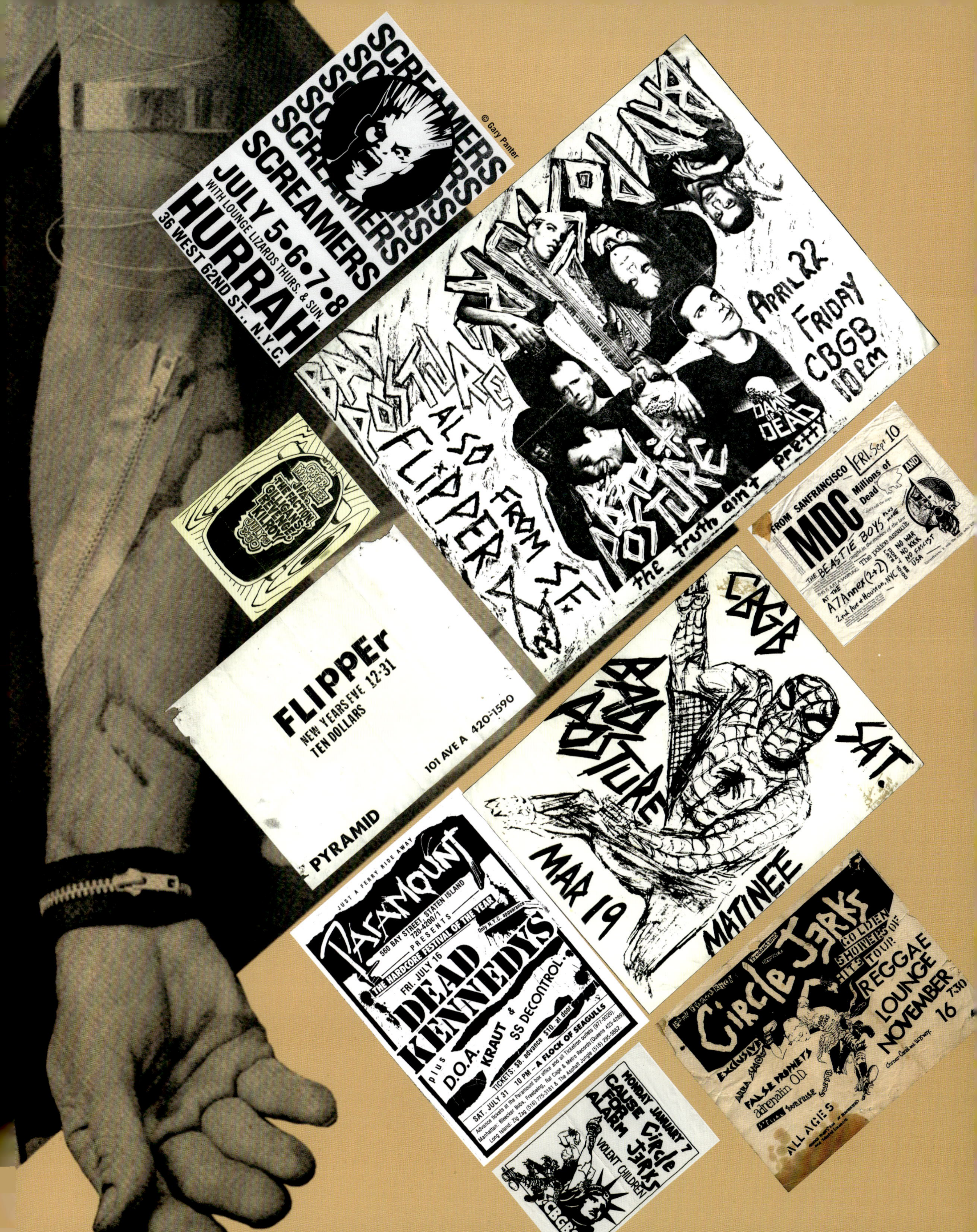
SCREAMERS
JULY 5•6•7•8
WITH LOUNGE LIZARDS THURS. & SUN.
HURRAH
36 WEST 62ND ST., N.Y.C.
© Gary Panter
BAD POSTURE
ALSO FLIPPER FROM S.F.
APRIL 22 FRIDAY CBGB 10 P.M.
the truth ain't pretty
FROM SAN FRANCISCO
MDC
Millions of Dead
FRI. SEP 10
THE BEASTIE BOYS
A7 Annex
FLIPPEr
NEW YEARS EVE 12-31
TEN DOLLARS
101 AVE A 420-1590
PYRAMID
CBGB
BAD POSTURE
SAT.
MAR 19
MATINEE
JUST A FERRY RIDE AWAY
PARAMOUNT
560 BAY STREET, STATEN ISLAND
720-4200/1
PRESENTS
THE HARDCORE FESTIVAL OF THE YEAR
FRI. JULY 16
DEAD KENNEDYS
plus D.O.A. KRAUT & SS DECONTROL
Only N.Y.C. appearance
TICKETS: $8. advance $10. at door
SAT. JULY 31 10 PM – A FLOCK OF SEAGULLS
Circle Jerks
GOLDEN SHOWER OF HITS TOUR
REGGAE LOUNGE
NOVEMBER 16
7:30
FALSE PROPHETS
adrenalin O.D.
ALL AGES
MONDAY JANUARY 7
CAUSE FOR ALARM
Circle Jerks
VIOLENT CHILDREN
CBGBS

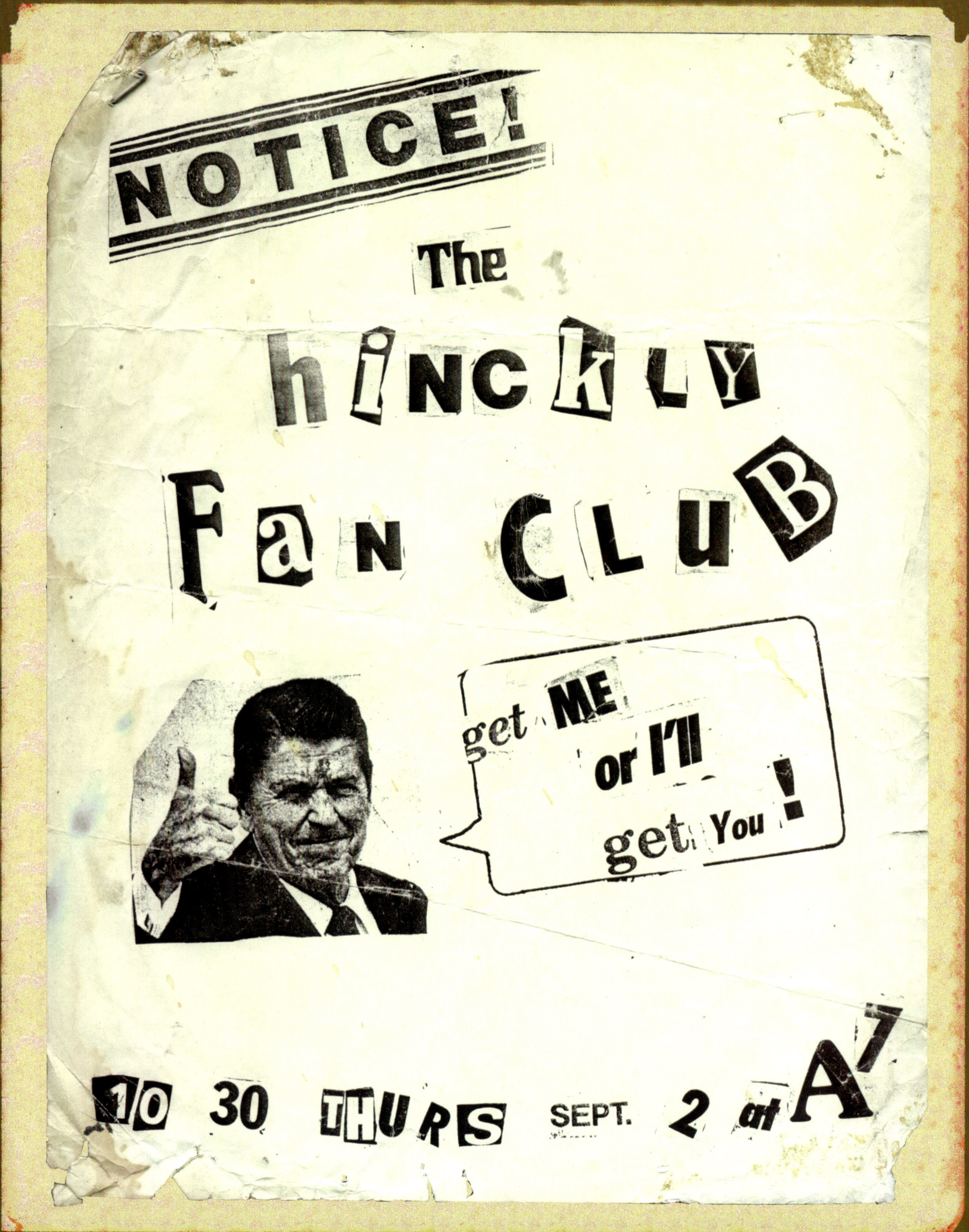
NOTICE!
The
hinckly
Fan Club
get ME
or I'll
get You !
10 30 THURS SEPT. 2 at A7

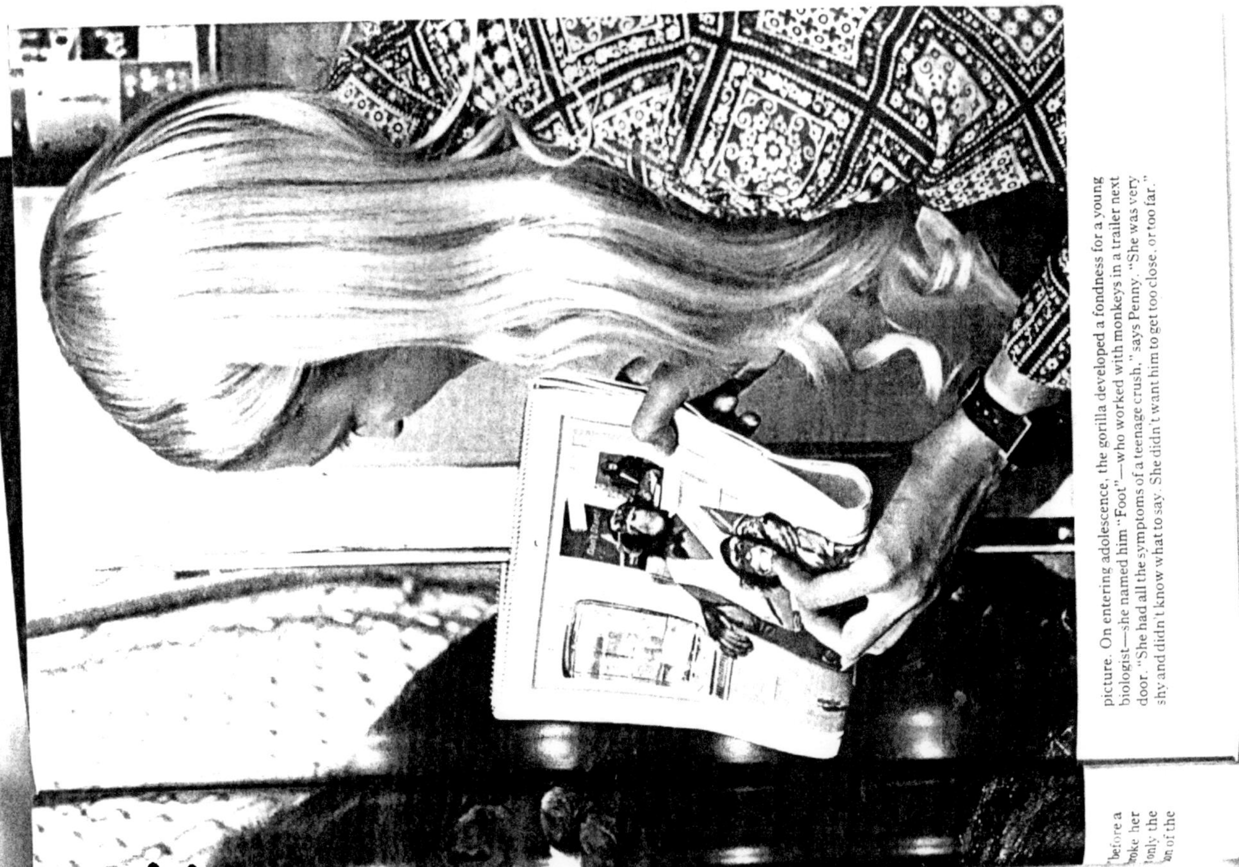

Washington 25, D.C.

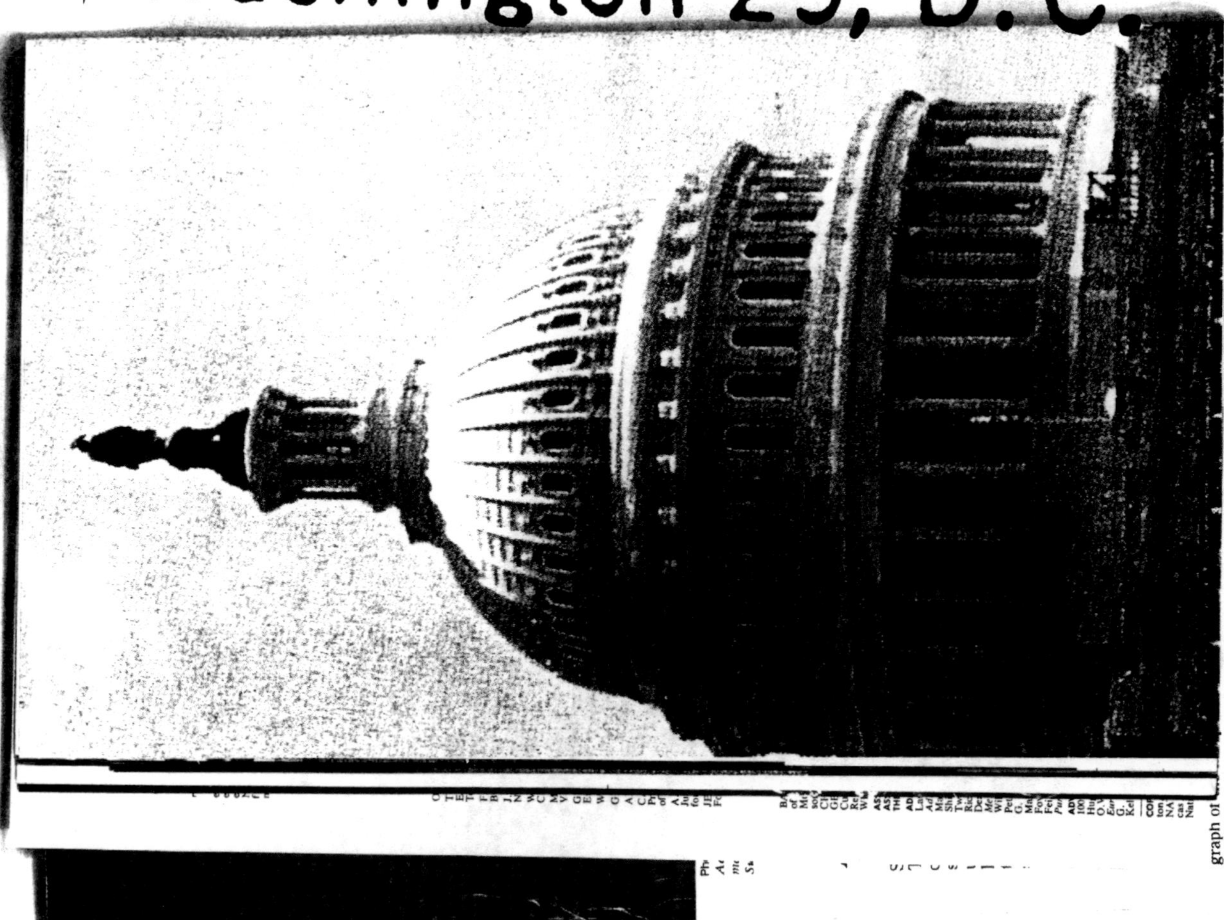

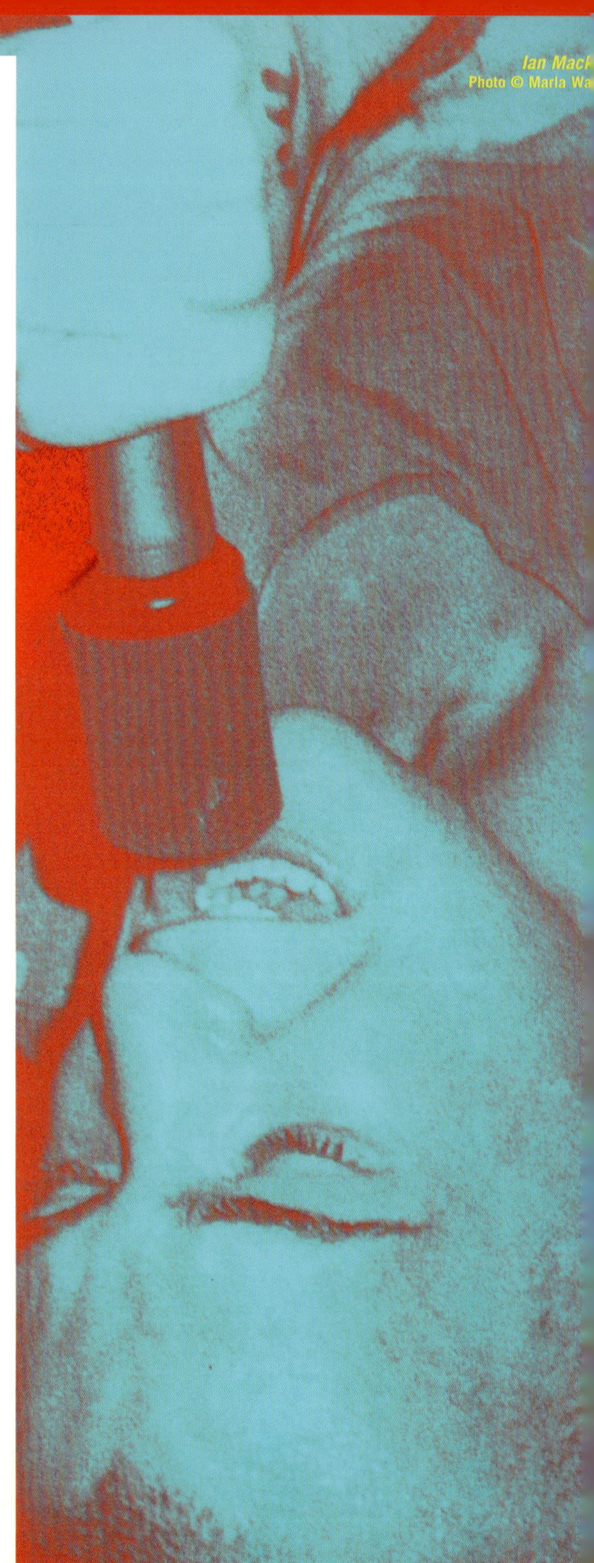

Ian Mack
Photo © Marla Wa

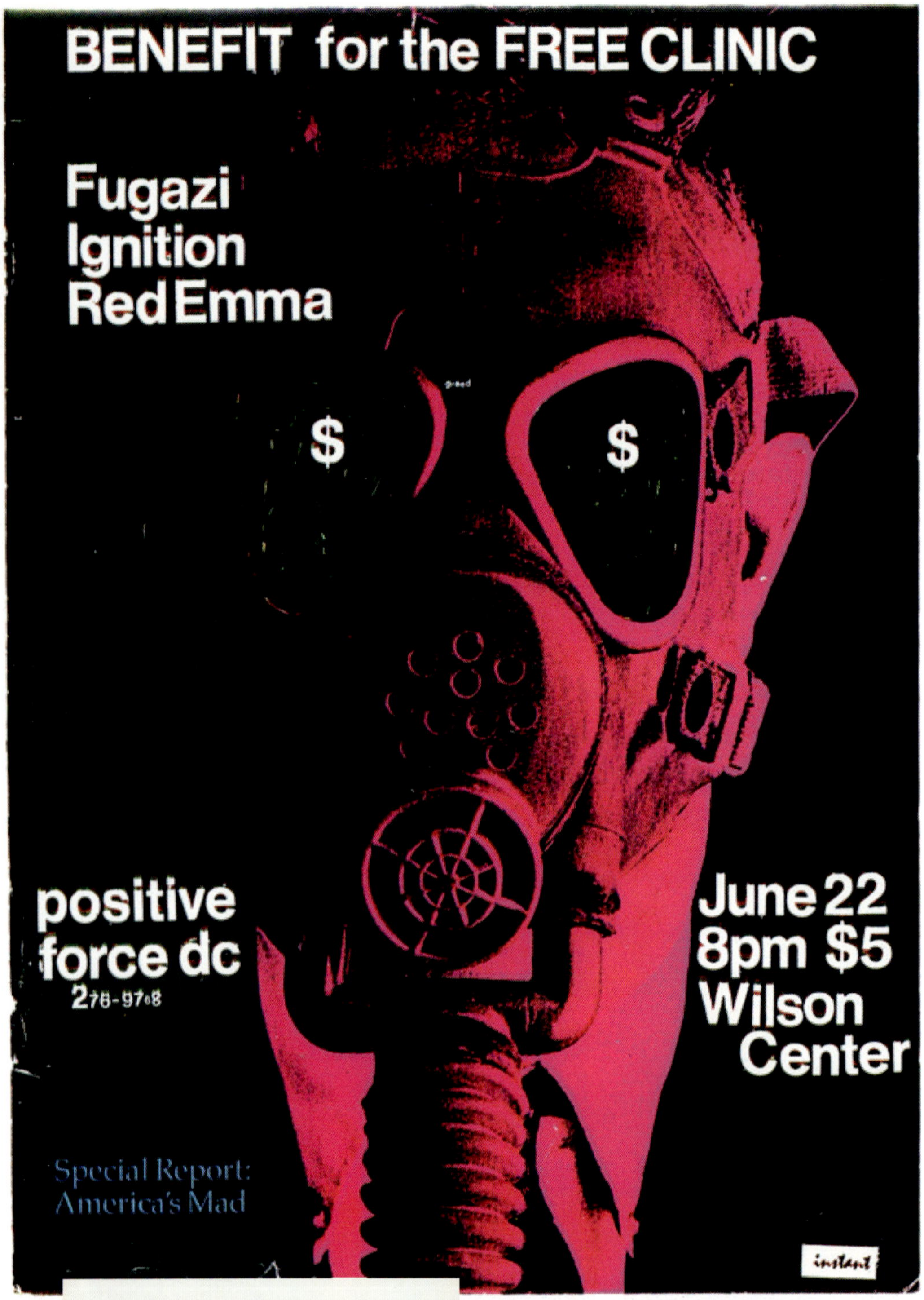

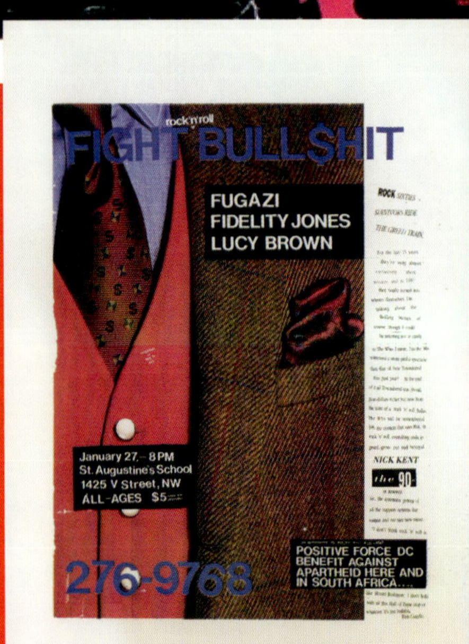

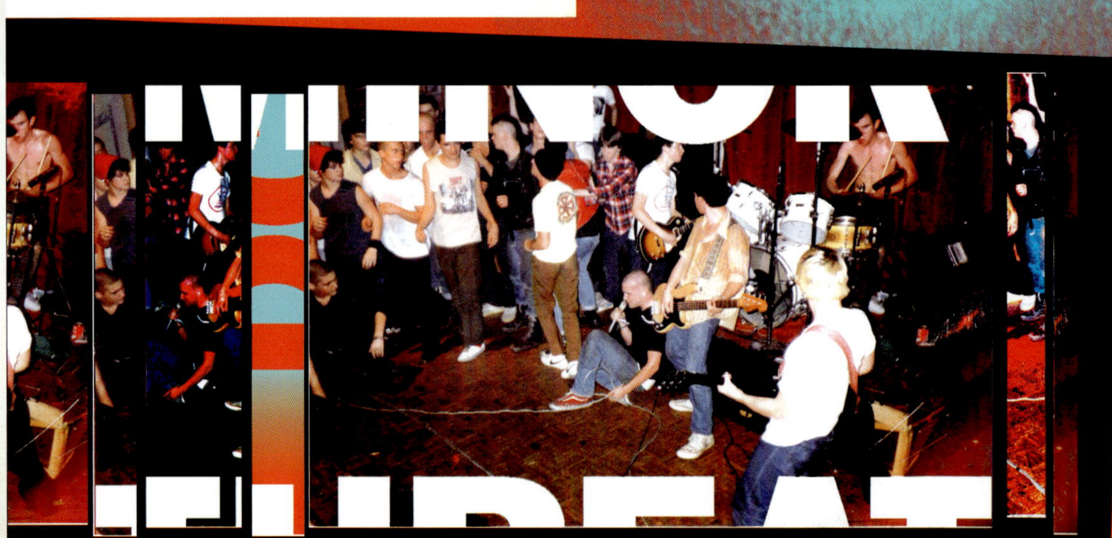

Minor Threat at The Wilson C
Photo © Angie Scia

Both Posters: Mark Anderson

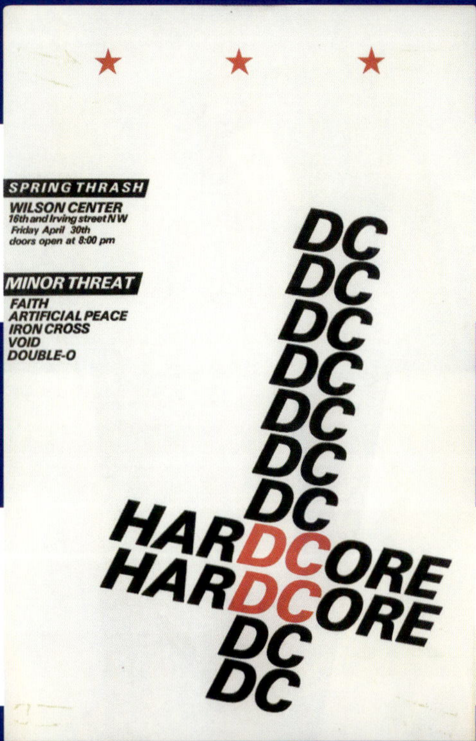
SPRING THRASH
WILSON CENTER
16th and Irving street N W
Friday April 30th
doors open at 8:00 pm
MINOR THREAT
FAITH
ARTIFICIAL PEACE
IRON CROSS
VOID
DOUBLE-O
DC
HARDCORE
HARDCORE
DC

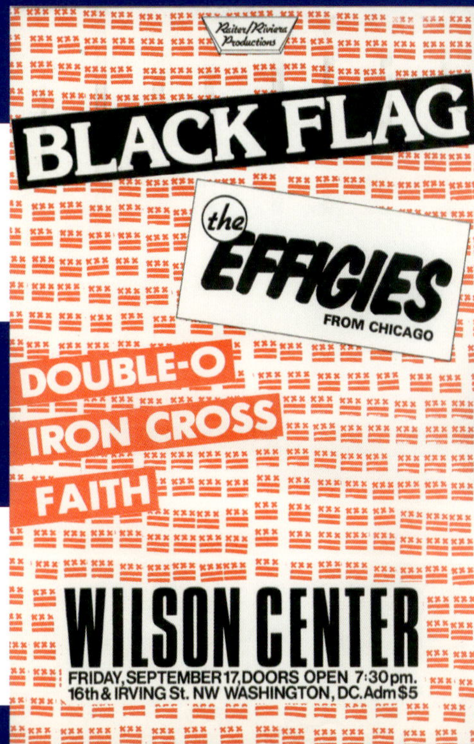
BLACK FLAG
the EFFIGIES
FROM CHICAGO
DOUBLE-O
IRON CROSS
FAITH
WILSON CENTER
FRIDAY, SEPTEMBER 17, DOORS OPEN 7:30pm.
16th & IRVING St. NW WASHINGTON, DC. Adm $5

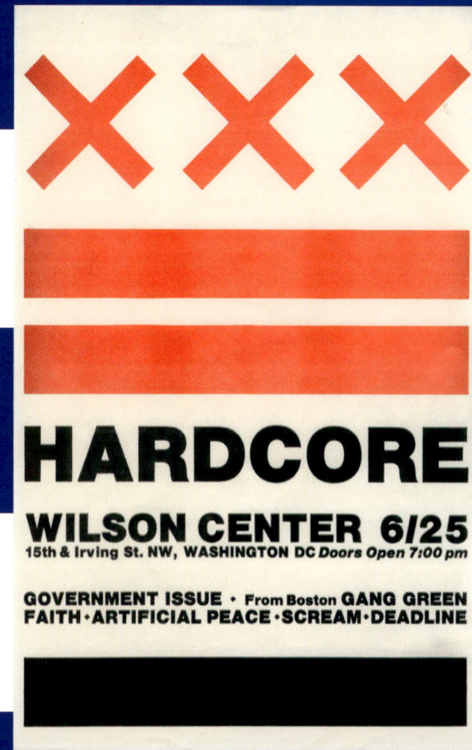
HARDCORE
WILSON CENTER 6/25
15th & Irving St. NW, WASHINGTON DC Doors Open 7:00 pm
GOVERNMENT ISSUE • From Boston GANG GREEN
FAITH • ARTIFICIAL PEACE • SCREAM • DEADLINE

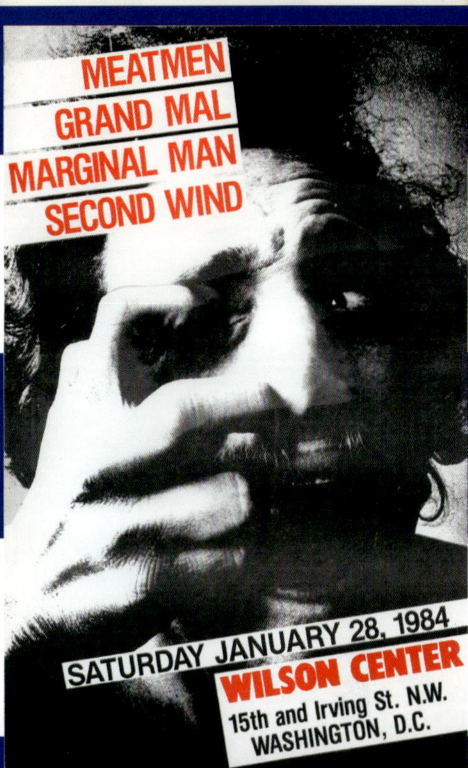
MEATMEN
GRAND MAL
MARGINAL MAN
SECOND WIND
SATURDAY JANUARY 28, 1984
WILSON CENTER
15th and Irving St. N.W.
WASHINGTON, D.C.

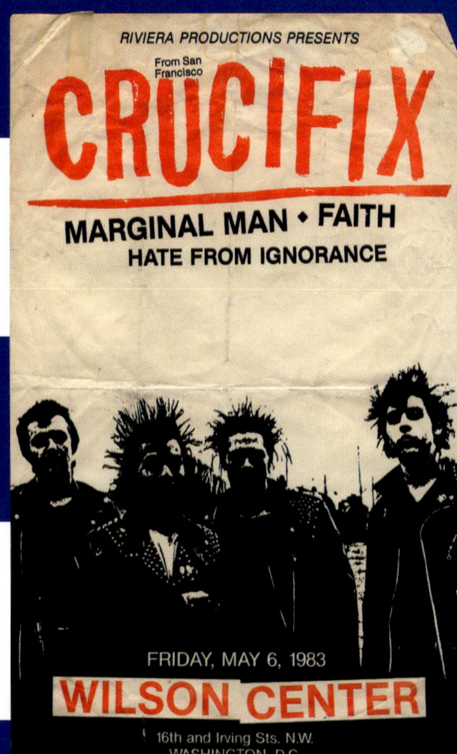
RIVIERA PRODUCTIONS PRESENTS
From San Francisco
CRUCIFIX
MARGINAL MAN • FAITH
HATE FROM IGNORANCE
FRIDAY, MAY 6, 1983
WILSON CENTER
16th and Irving Sts. N.W.
WASHINGTON, D.C.

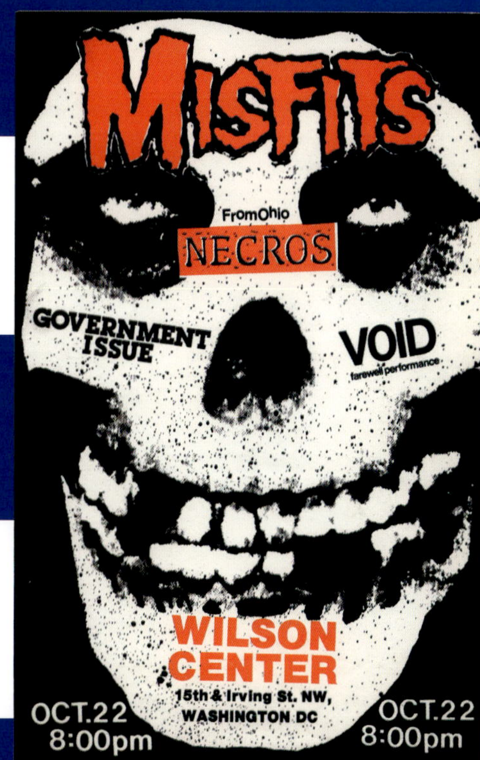
MISFITS
From Ohio
NECROS
GOVERNMENT ISSUE
VOID
farewell performance
WILSON CENTER
15th & Irving St. NW,
WASHINGTON DC
OCT.22
8:00pm
OCT.22
8:00pm

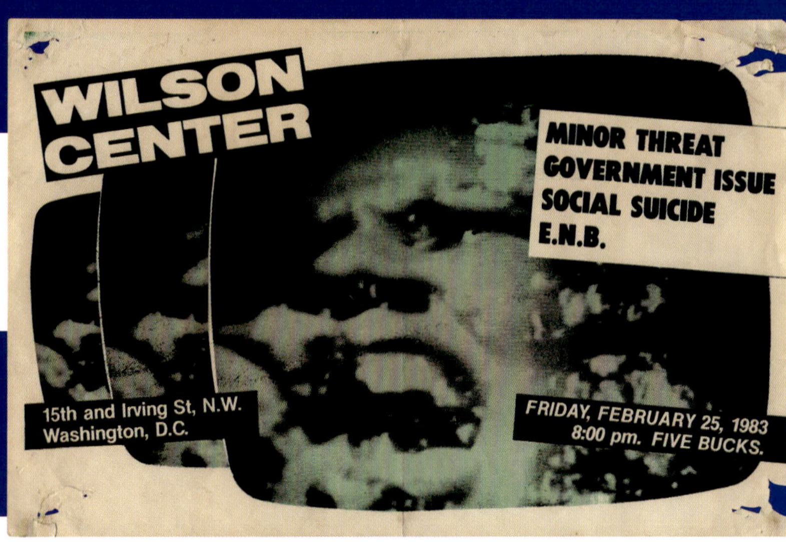
WILSON CENTER
MINOR THREAT
GOVERNMENT ISSUE
SOCIAL SUICIDE
E.N.B.
15th and Irving St, N.W.
Washington, D.C.
FRIDAY, FEBRUARY 25, 1983
8:00 pm. FIVE BUCKS.

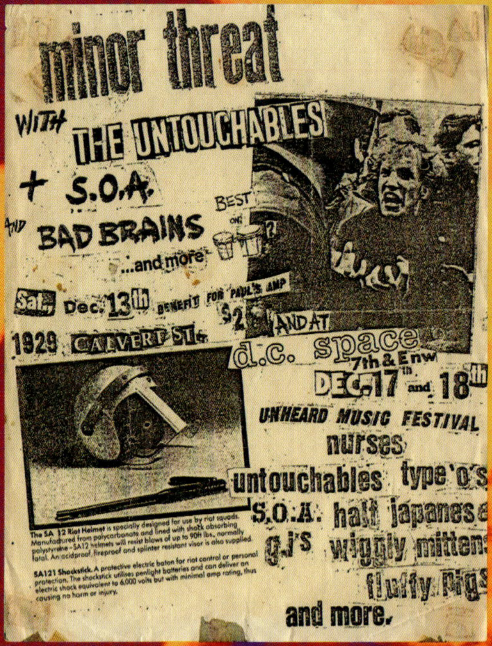

Ian Mackaye

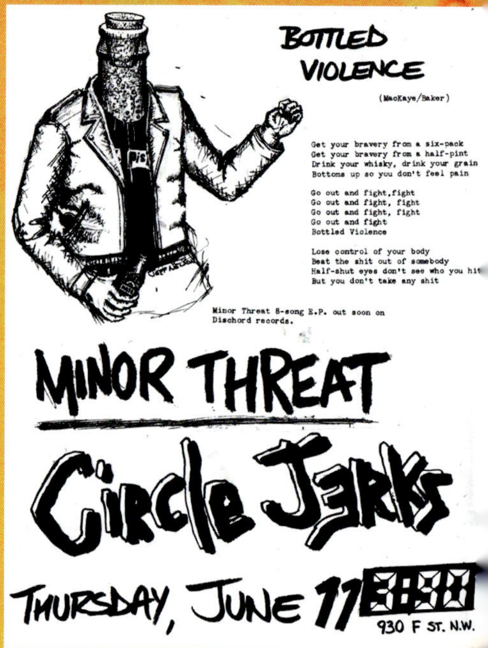

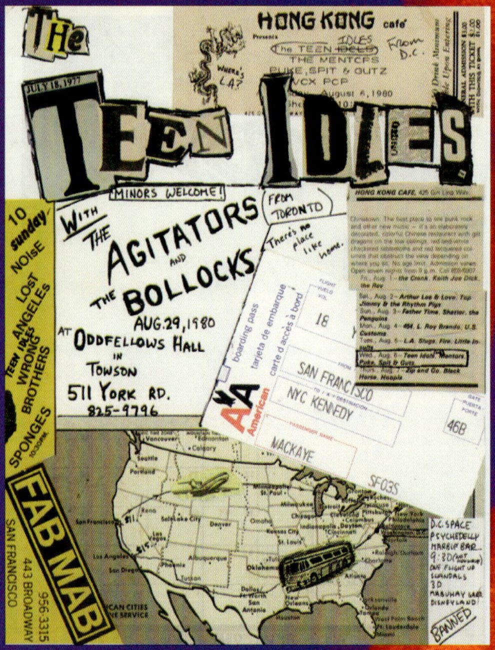

Jeff Nelson

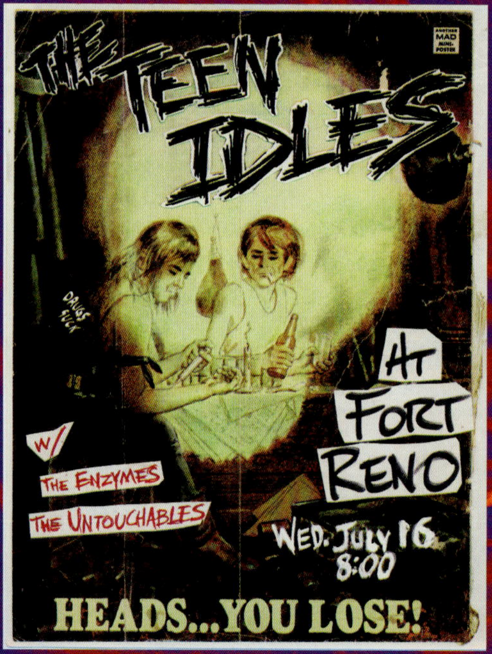

Nathan Strejcek

Jeff Ne

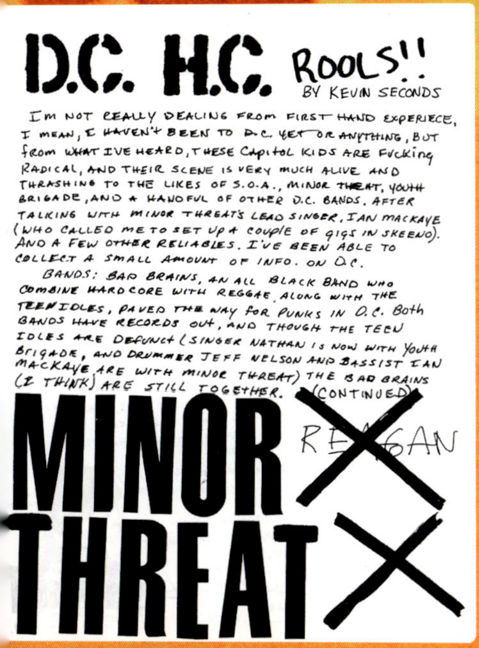

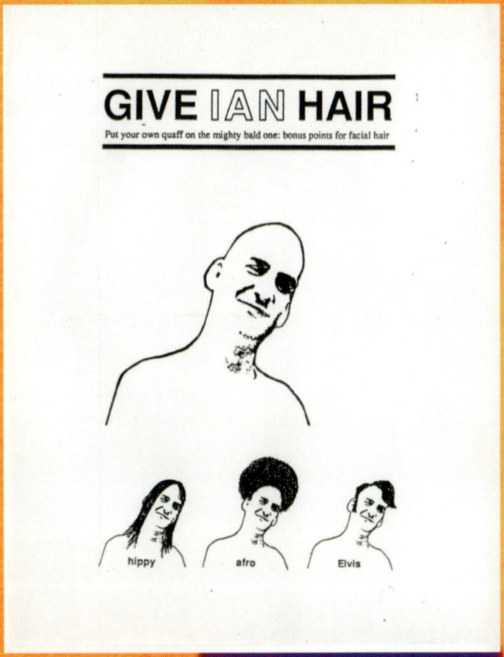

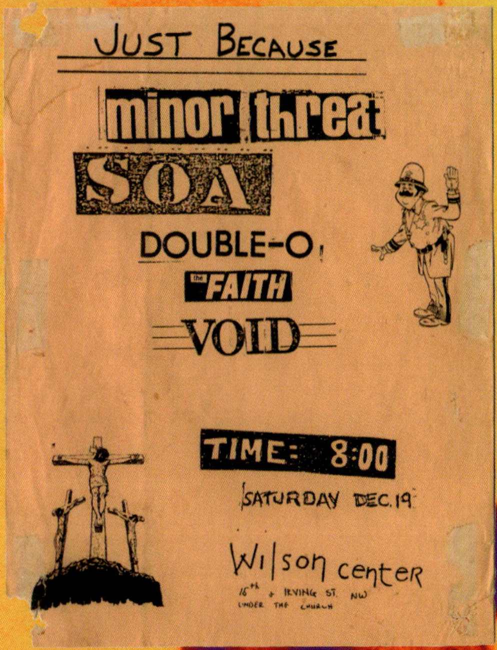

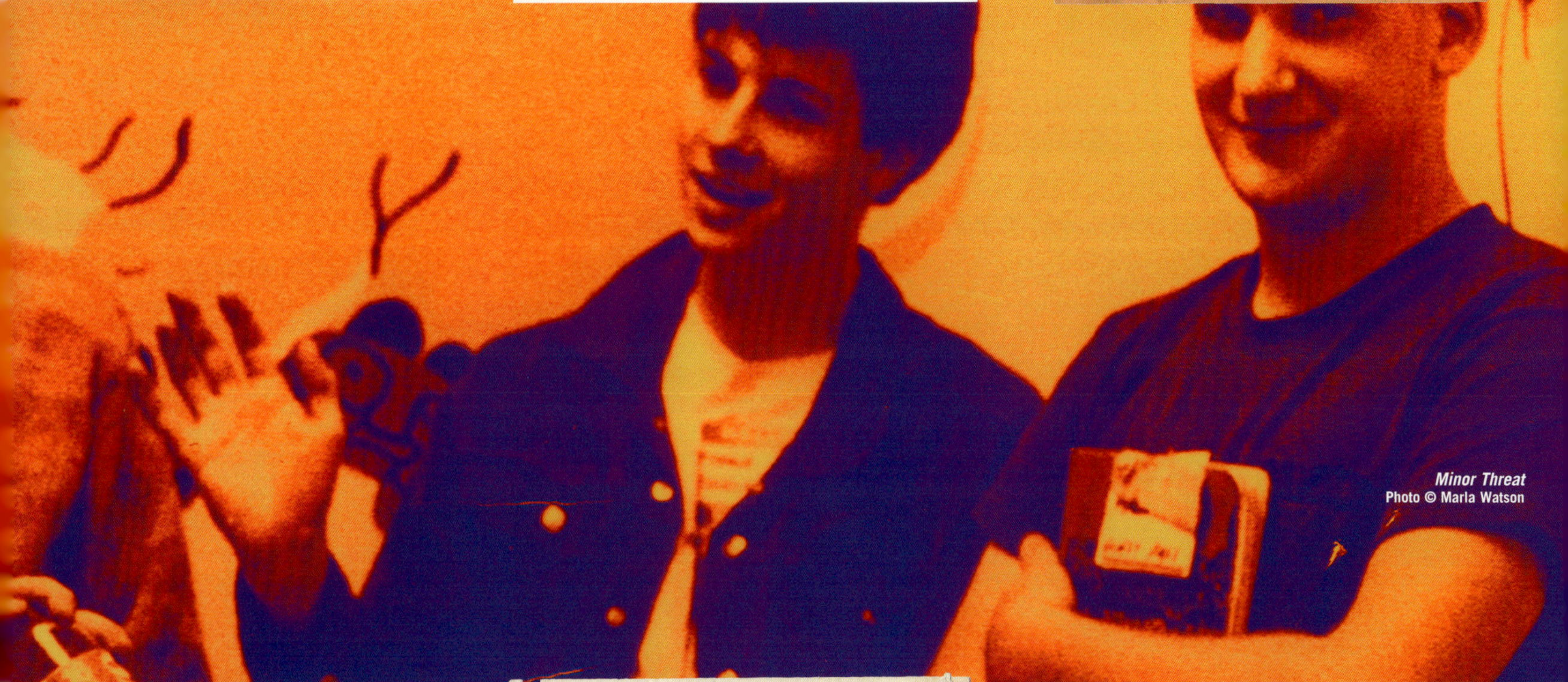

Minor Threat
Photo © Marla Watson

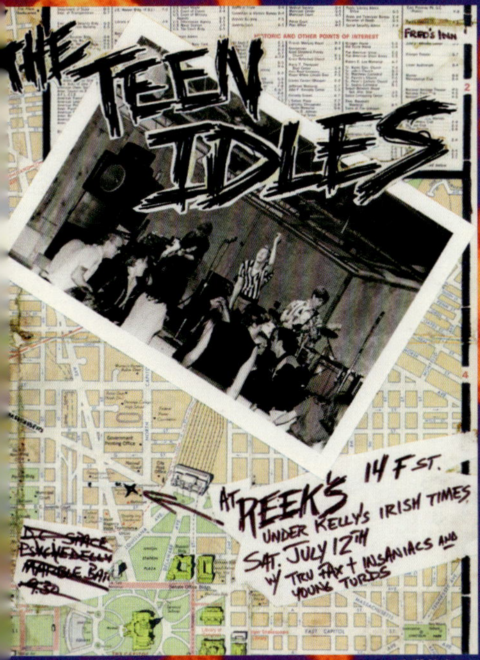

Jeff Nelson

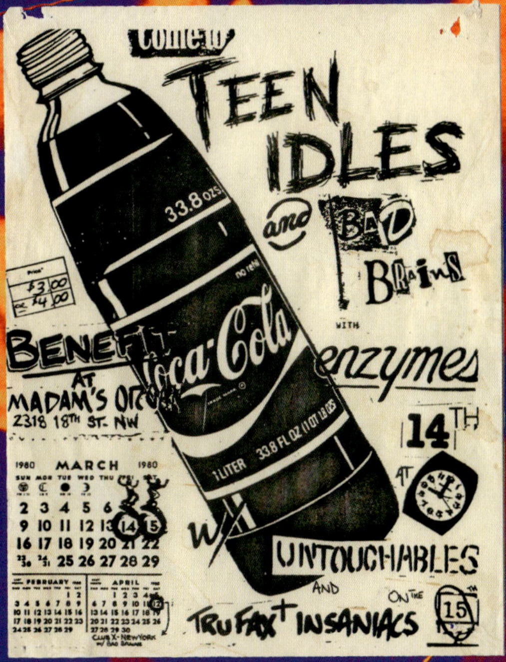

Jeff Nelson

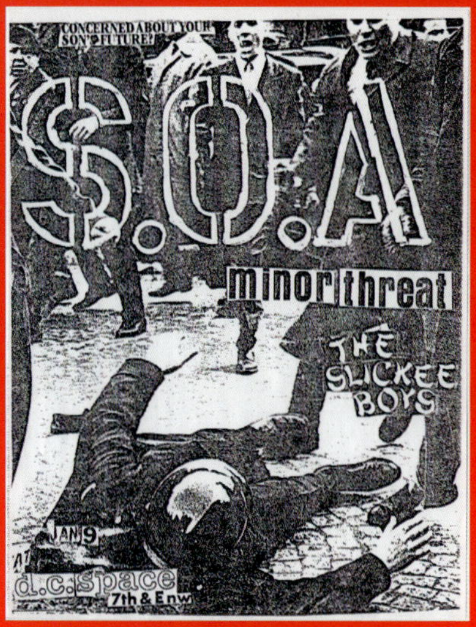

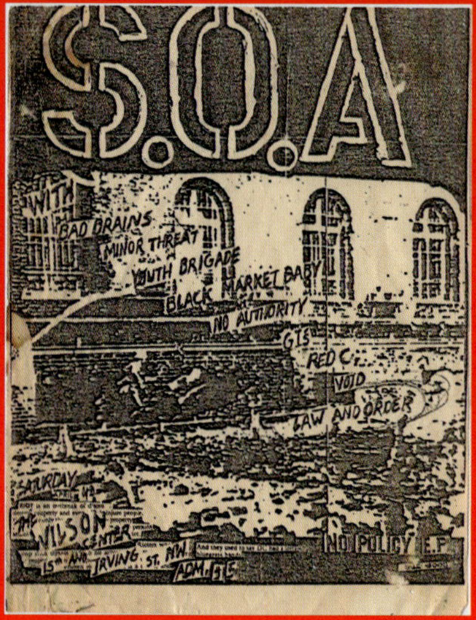

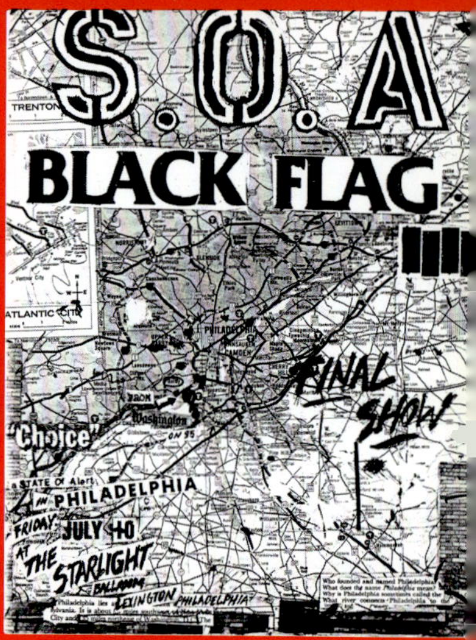

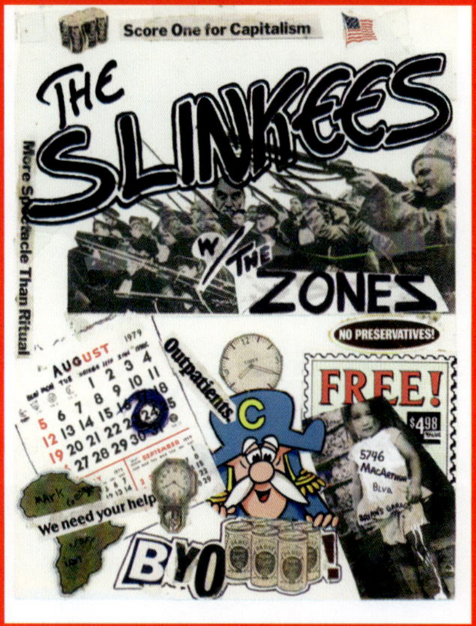

Jeff Nelson

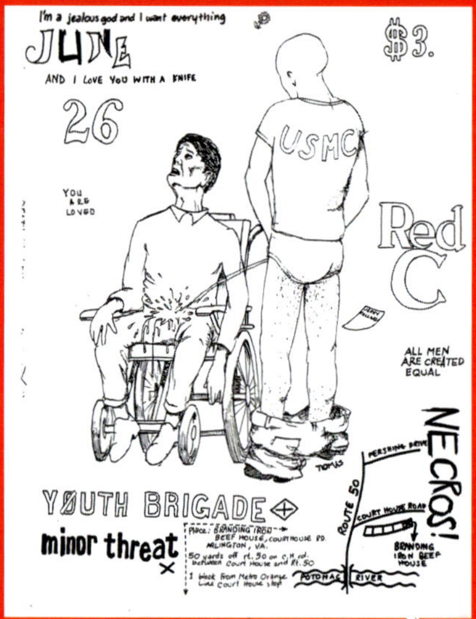

Thomas

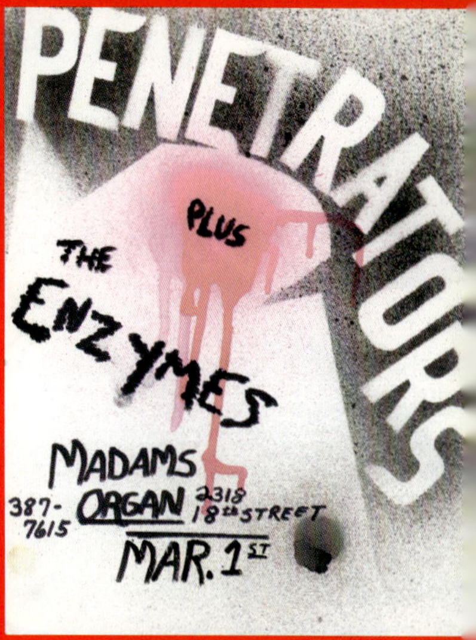

Andre & James Lee

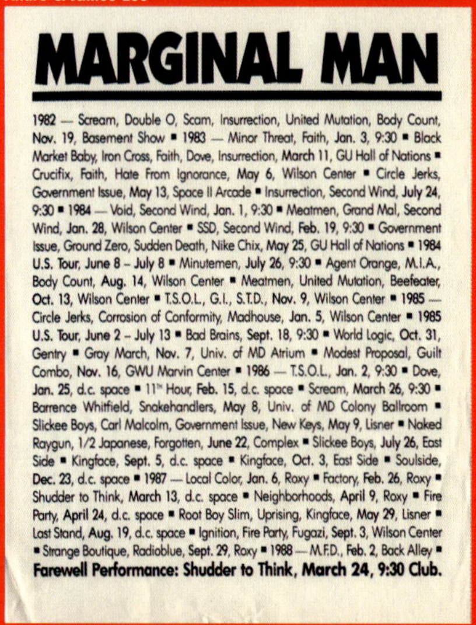
MARGINAL MAN

1982 — Scream, Double O, Scam, Insurrection, United Mutation, Body Count, Nov. 19, Basement Show ▪ 1983 — Minor Threat, Faith, Jan. 3, 9:30 ▪ Black Market Baby, Iron Cross, Faith, Dove, Insurrection, March 11, GU Hall of Nations ▪ Crucifix, Faith, Hate From Ignorance, May 6, Wilson Center ▪ Circle Jerks, Government Issue, May 13, Space II Arcade ▪ Insurrection, Second Wind, July 24, 9:30 ▪ 1984 — Void, Second Wind, Jan. 1, 9:30 ▪ Meatmen, Grand Mal, Second Wind, Jan. 28, Wilson Center ▪ SSD, Second Wind, Feb. 19, 9:30 ▪ Government Issue, Ground Zero, Sudden Death, Nike Chix, May 25, GU Hall of Nations ▪ 1984 U.S. Tour, June 8 – July 8 ▪ Minutemen, July 26, 9:30 ▪ Agent Orange, M.I.A., Body Count, Aug. 14, Wilson Center ▪ Meatmen, United Mutation, Beefeater, Oct. 13, Wilson Center ▪ T.S.O.L., G.I., S.T.D., Nov. 9, Wilson Center ▪ 1985 — Circle Jerks, Corrosion of Conformity, Madhouse, Jan. 5, Wilson Center ▪ 1985 U.S. Tour, June 2 – July 13 ▪ Bad Brains, Sept. 18, 9:30 ▪ World Logic, Oct. 31, Gentry ▪ Gray March, Nov. 7, Univ. of MD Atrium ▪ Modest Proposal, Guilt Combo, Nov. 16, GWU Marvin Center ▪ 1986 — T.S.O.L., Jan. 2, 9:30 ▪ Dove, Jan. 25, d.c. space ▪ 11th Hour, Feb. 15, d.c. space ▪ Scream, March 26, 9:30 ▪ Barrence Whitfield, Snakehandlers, May 8, Univ. of MD Colony Ballroom ▪ Slickee Boys, Carl Malcolm, Government Issue, New Keys, May 9, Lisner ▪ Naked Raygun, 1/2 Japanese, Forgotten, June 22, Complex ▪ Slickee Boys, July 26, East Side ▪ Kingface, Sept. 5, d.c. space ▪ Kingface, Oct. 3, East Side ▪ Soulside, Dec. 23, d.c. space ▪ 1987 — Local Color, Jan. 6, Roxy ▪ Factory, Feb. 26, Roxy ▪ Shudder to Think, March 13, d.c. space ▪ Neighborhoods, April 9, Roxy ▪ Fire Party, April 24, d.c. space ▪ Root Boy Slim, Uprising, Kingface, May 29, Lisner ▪ Last Stand, Aug. 19, d.c. space ▪ Ignition, Fire Party, Fugazi, Sept. 3, Wilson Center ▪ Strange Boutique, Radioblue, Sept. 29, Roxy ▪ 1988 — M.F.D., Feb. 2, Back Alley ▪ **Farewell Performance: Shudder to Think, March 24, 9:30 Club.**

Mad George

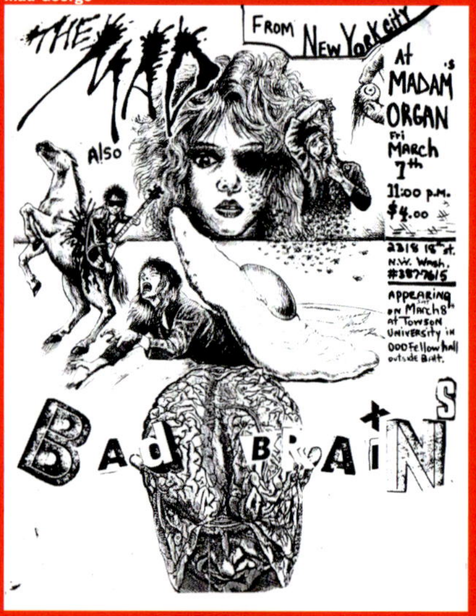

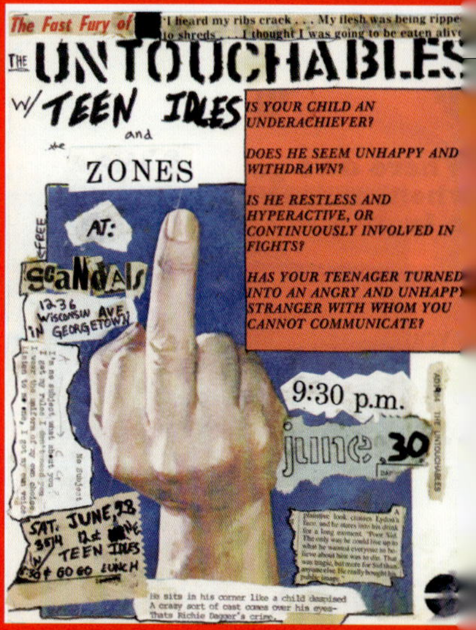

21

by Ken Inouye
(Marginal Man)

We left DC in June and headed south to North Carolina to headline a bill w/Corrosion of Conformity. Continued south to Florida, formed a clockwise loop of the US through Texas, up through California, then east through the heartland. 30 shows in 35 days, slept on a lot of floors, (that's not sleeping.)

On the way to Atlantic City, our van died. We needed a new engine, so we rented a U-Haul truck, and decided to go home to DC for a day or so. We'd pick up our van on our way back to Boston. In a U-Haul only 2 or 3 people can fit up front. We were a 5 piece band, so, two of us had to stay "in the box", (back with the equipment.) Our bass player Andre and I were the lucky souls stuck back with the gear-four to five hours of total darkness. (See the movie Papillon and check out the scene on solitary confinement for an idea of how our trip went.) The truck was by no means waterproof. During a thunderstorm the truck leaked like a sieve and we scrambled around in the dark with flashlights, trying to keep the gear dry, while bouncing around at 60 mph. It was a riot.

When we got home the next day, I slept all day. When I woke up we loaded up Steve's mom's station wagon to make the trip back up to Boston to headline a matinee at The Channel w/Raw Power (from Italy) and Psycho. As you can imagine, (maybe you can't,) we had no room in the stationwagon with the gear of five band members. I slept for the first shift of the drive, on top of the guitar cases in back, four inches from the roof.

We were on time, everything was cool. I ran into Ray Cappo of *Youth of Today* outside the club. (We'd been trying to work out a deal to play in Providence.) I proceeded to help him and his friends sneak in with my backstage pass. I'd sneak them in, have a band member bring the pass back out to me, and tell them to inform anyone who asked that they were roadies. Between Ray and his friends and a few other folks I knew, I snuck 20 people into the club. I'm sure the bouncers were suspicious of the size of our road crew that day.

The Channel was a big rock club type of place, thankfully unobsessed with haircut metal that was so prevalent at the time.The only punk bands that got to play were more well-known, like Black Flag or Dead Kennedys. There was a good sized stage, good sound and PA, and clean bathrooms. That was all fine and dandy, but the fact that we got fed was huge. (I'd already lost 15 pounds on this tour.) Getting this treatment from kids putting on shows was one thing, but clubs never did stuff like this. I was told the club thought the show was going to sell real well.

I had been looking forward to this show.Boston crowds were always, let's say, "exuberant."But it looked like today was not going to be one of those days. The club had gotten moody about slamdancing and stage diving, so they weren't going to allow any of that kind of crowd activity. (It was well-known that the Channel was owned by the Mob,so we wanted to avoid any trouble if we could.) There wasn't any trouble with the two opening bands. Almost immediately after starting our set, we noticed the bouncers strong-arming the kids, telling them not to MOVE, let alone *dance.*

Six songs in, the club told us that unless we stopped "causing a riot," they would stop the show. I couldn't believe the club was freaking out about this crowd-they were far from causing a riot. Even looking back twelve years later, that audience was pretty tame.

About halfway through our next song, "Missing Rungs," the club pulled the plug and called the police. They couldn't have picked a better song to pull the plug on–by the time the power had died in the amps and the PA, we were in a sing-along part of the song where the phrase *"rat race"* is chanted through to the end.

Club management was visibly nervous, and my emotions were a mix of being pissed about the show being shut down and amusement that the club owners and bouncers were beginning to sweat.

Everyone in the band realized that while the crowd originally was far from causing trouble, now that the plug was pulled there was a very real possibility that there'd be a riot. All it would have taken from us was one wrong word and things would have gotten very ugly. The cops had shown up, primed and ready for the shit to hit the fan, and that only made matters worse.

Using well chosen words and an assurance that we'd come back soon and play got the kids to leave without tearing the place apart. The bouncers gave us attitude the whole time. It was almost as if these assholes wanted us to start something so they could pound our faces in, with the help of the cops. These bouncers were the epitome of the big chicken-shit jock who can't feel safe taunting someone half his size unless his friends and the police are there to back them up.

As I loaded some guitars into the station wagon, one of the bouncers jeered, "you'll never work in this town again." At that point I had to stop and laugh uncontrollably. I felt like we were living out some bad late night movie.

As we pulled out of town, Andre turned to me and said, "Hey Kenny. Happy birthday." In all the insanity, it had completely slipped my mind. I turned 21 that day. +

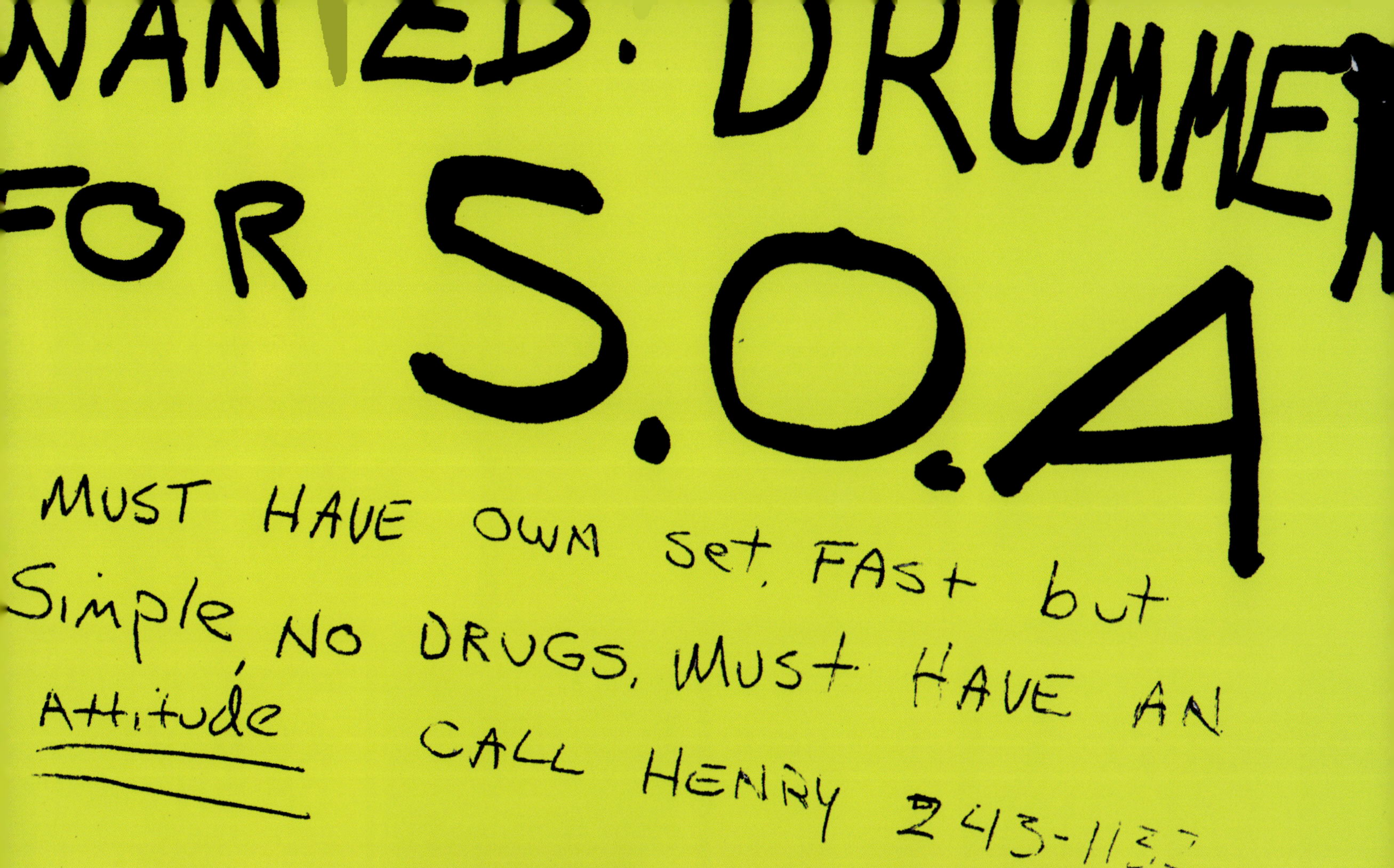
WANTED: DRUMMER
FOR S.O.A
MUST HAVE OWN set, FAST but
Simple, NO DRUGS, Must HAVE AN
Attitude CALL HENRY 243-1132

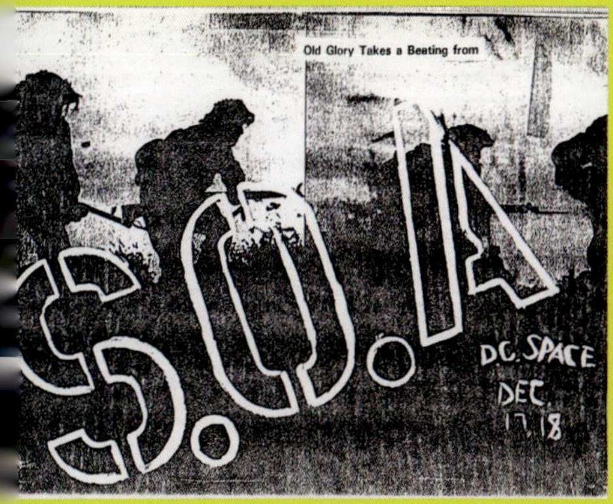
Old Glory Takes a Beating from
S.O.A
D.C. SPACE
DEC.
17, 18

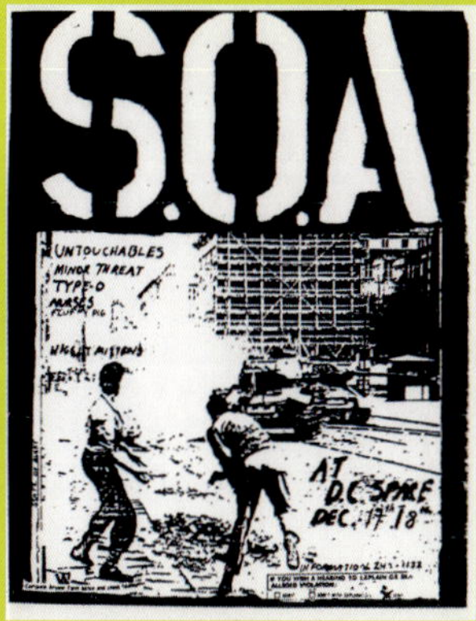
S.O.A
UNTOUCHABLES
MINOR THREAT
AT D.C. SPACE
DEC. 17th 18th

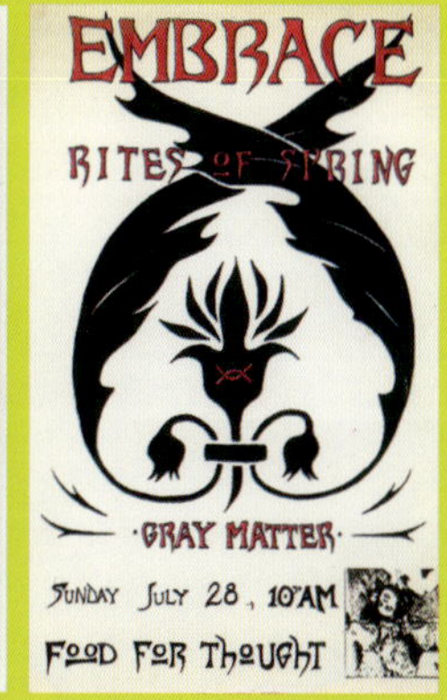
EMBRACE
RITES OF SPRING
GRAY MATTER
SUNDAY JULY 28, 10AM
FOOD FOR THOUGHT

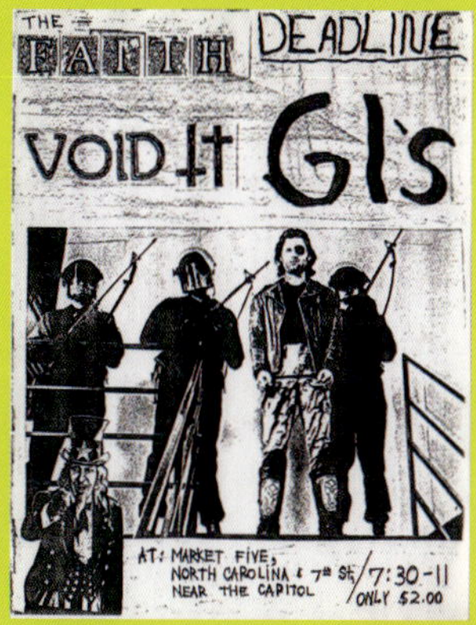
THE FAITH
DEADLINE
VOID
GI's
AT: MARKET FIVE,
NORTH CAROLINA & 7th ST.
NEAR THE CAPITOL
7:30-11
ONLY $2.00

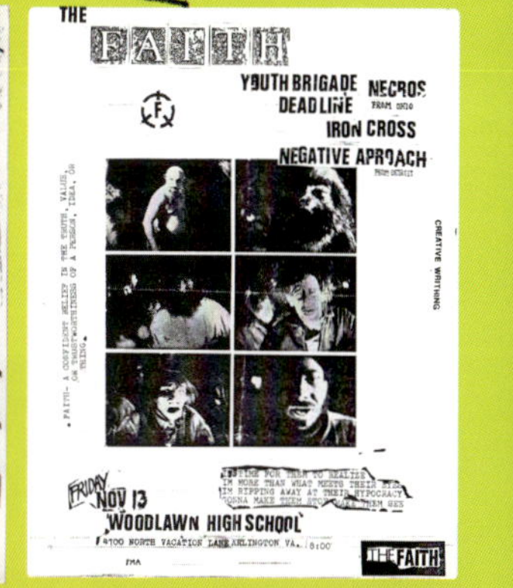
THE FAITH
YOUTH BRIGADE
NECROS
DEADLINE
IRON CROSS
NEGATIVE APROACH
FRIDAY NOV 13
WOODLAWN HIGH SCHOOL
THE FAITH

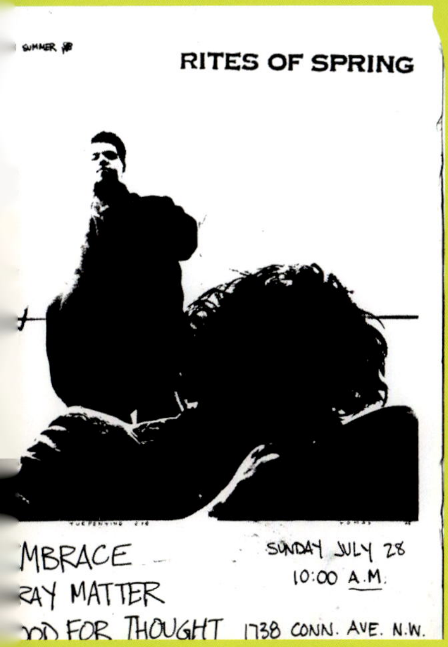
RITES OF SPRING
EMBRACE
GRAY MATTER
FOOD FOR THOUGHT
SUNDAY JULY 28
10:00 A.M.
1738 CONN. AVE. N.W.

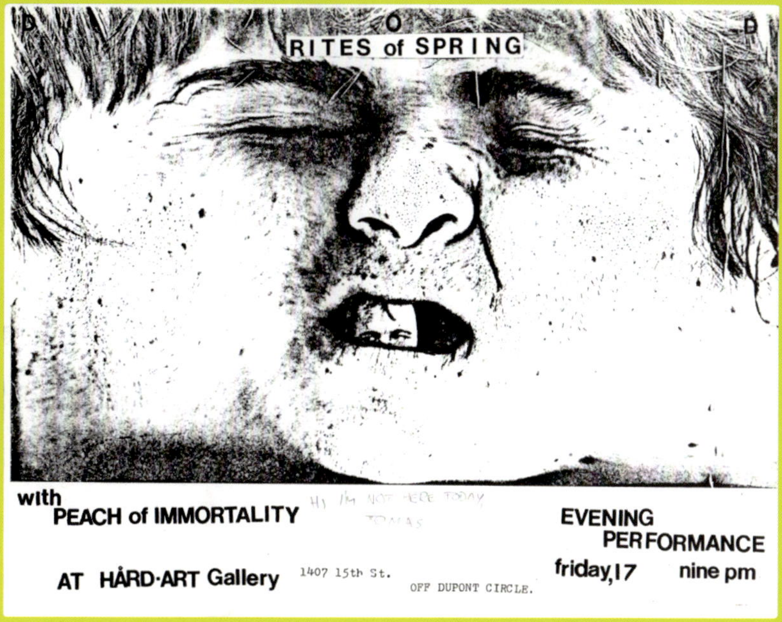
RITES of SPRING
with
PEACH of IMMORTALITY
AT HARD-ART Gallery
1407 15th St.
OFF DUPONT CIRCLE
EVENING
PERFORMANCE
friday,17
nine pm

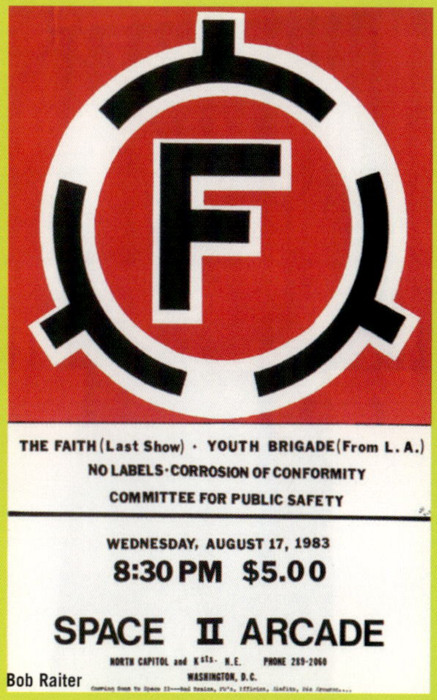
F
THE FAITH (Last Show) · YOUTH BRIGADE (From L. A.)
NO LABELS · CORROSION OF CONFORMITY
COMMITTEE FOR PUBLIC SAFETY
WEDNESDAY, AUGUST 17, 1983
8:30 PM $5.00
SPACE II ARCADE
WASHINGTON, D.C.
Bob Raiter

All 9353 flyers by Bruce Merkle

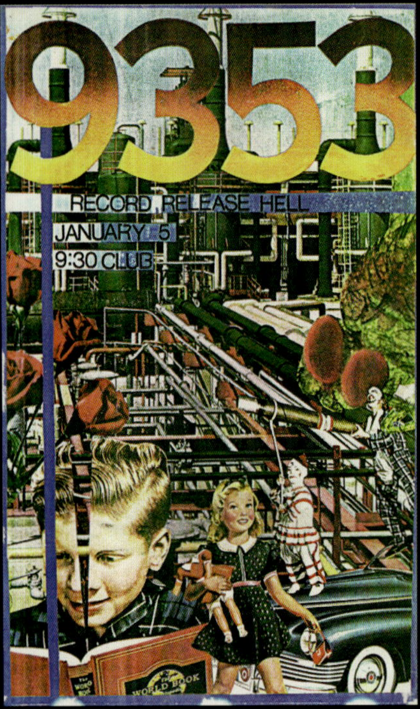

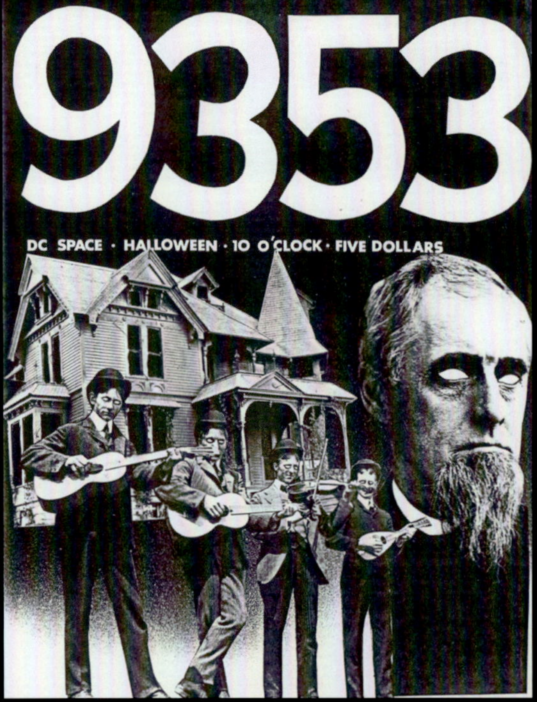

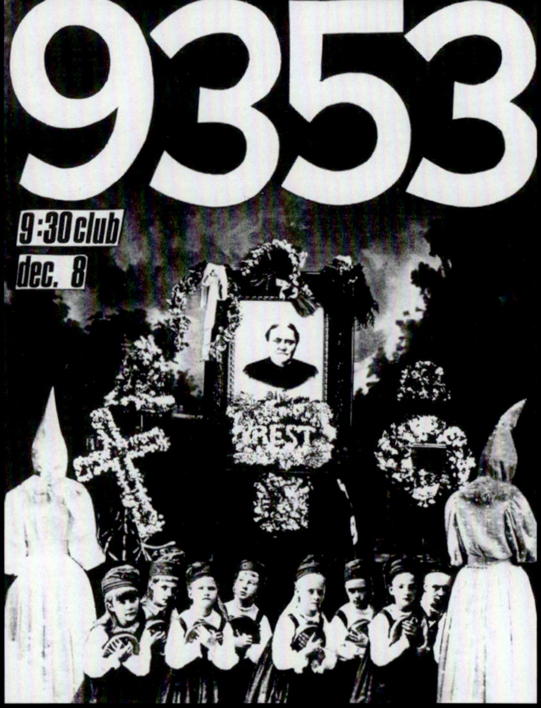

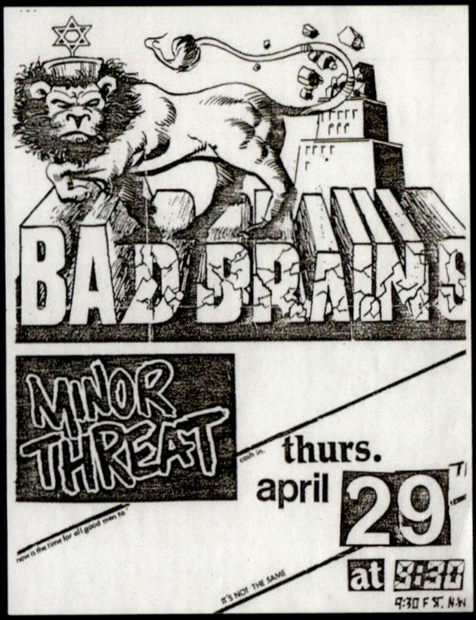

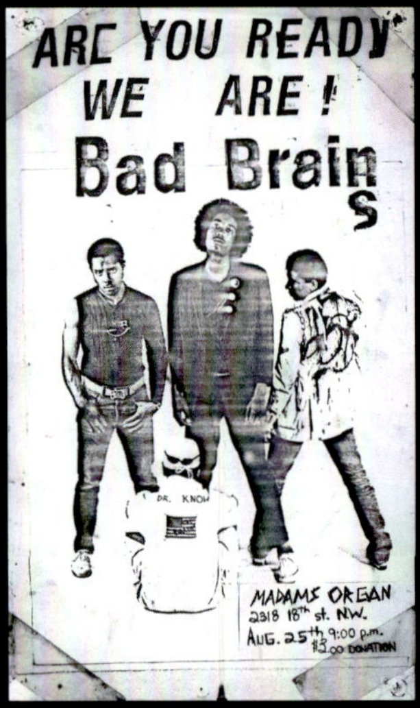

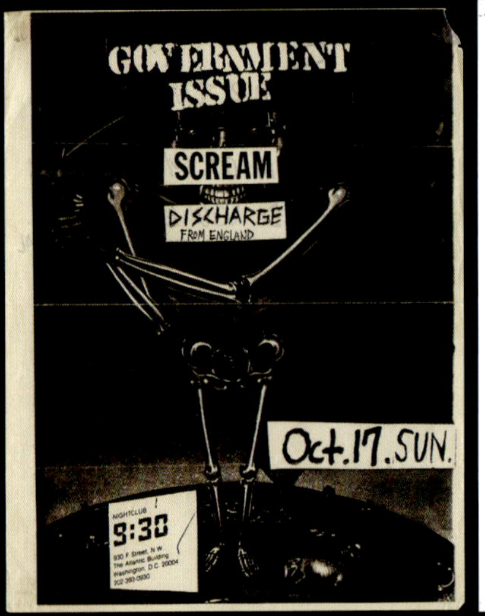

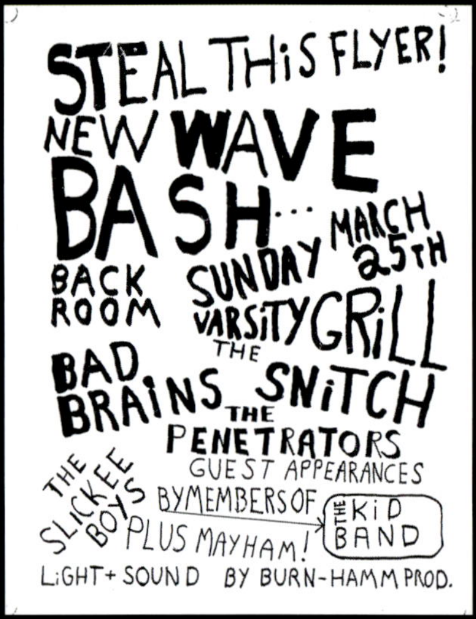

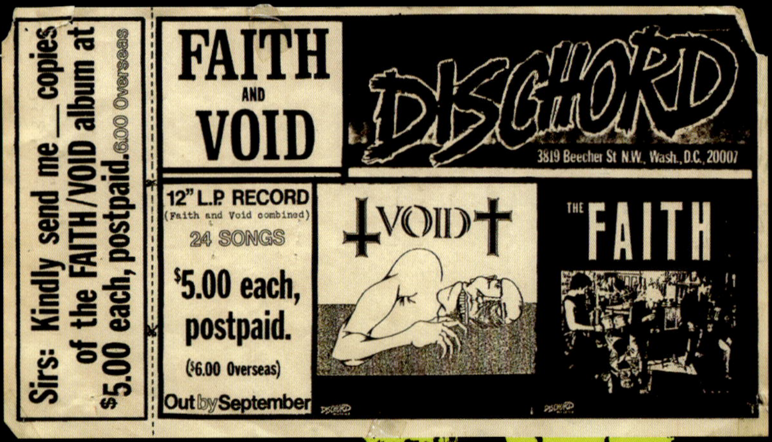

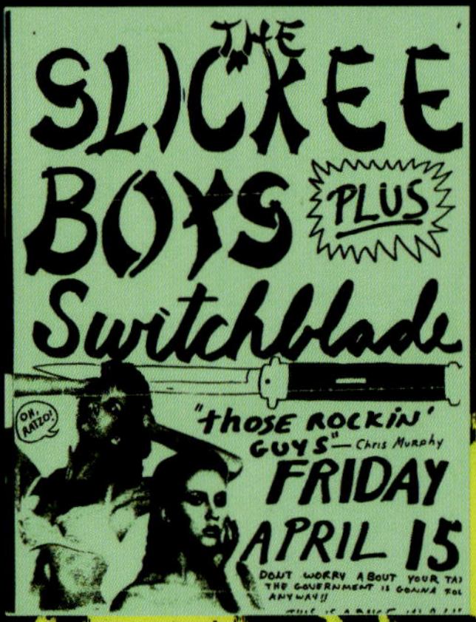

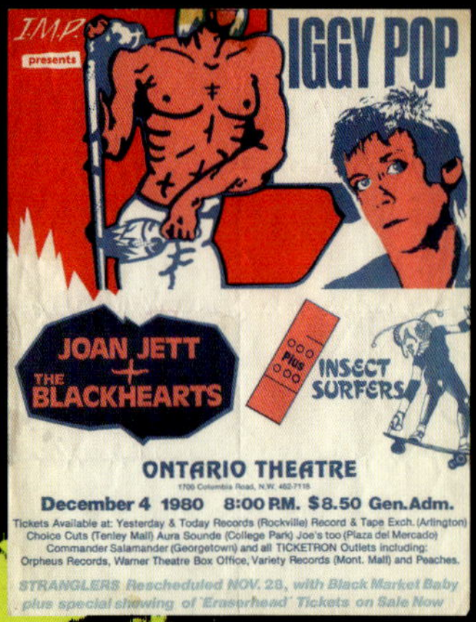

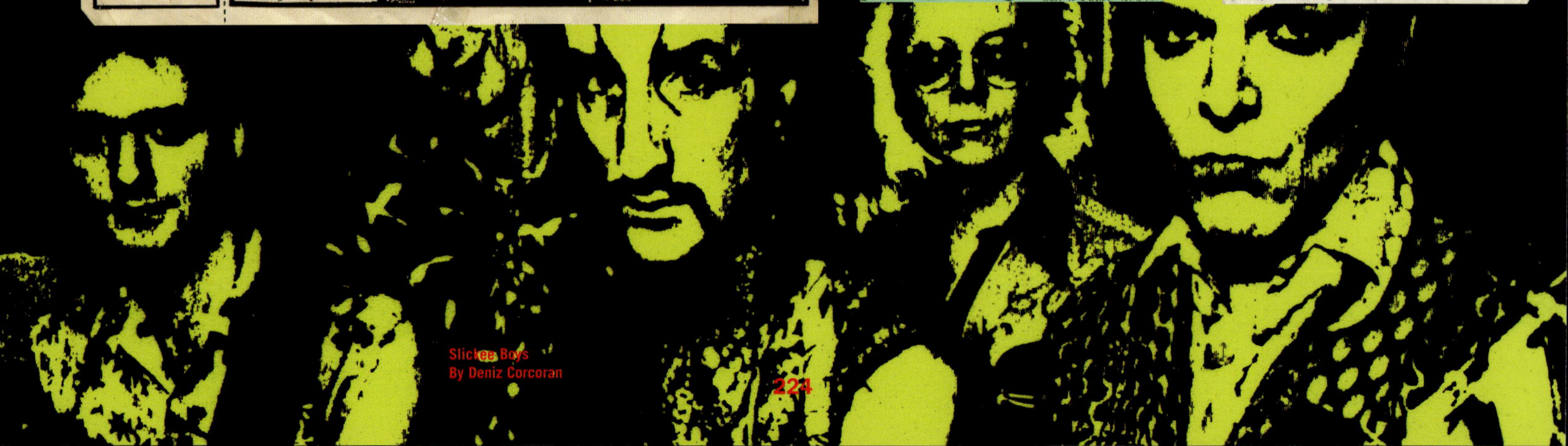

Slickee Boys
By Deniz Corcoran

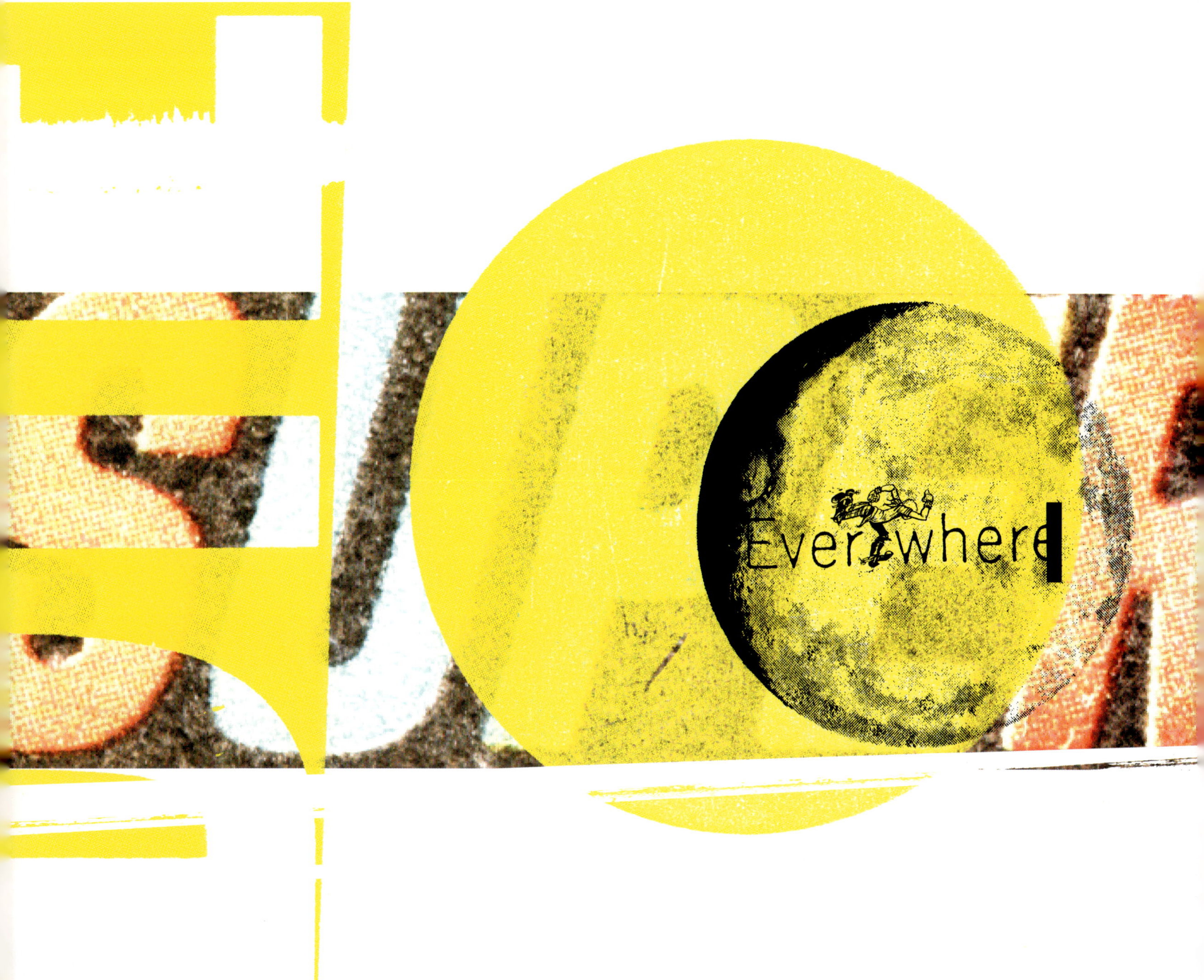
Everywhere

HÜSKER DÜ
NONE OF THE ABOVE
NO DIRECTION
I'M SORRY
NORTH BASE NATIONAL GUARD ARMORY 7:30 PM
SATURDAY, JAN. 22
ALL AGES
4 BANDS / $3.50

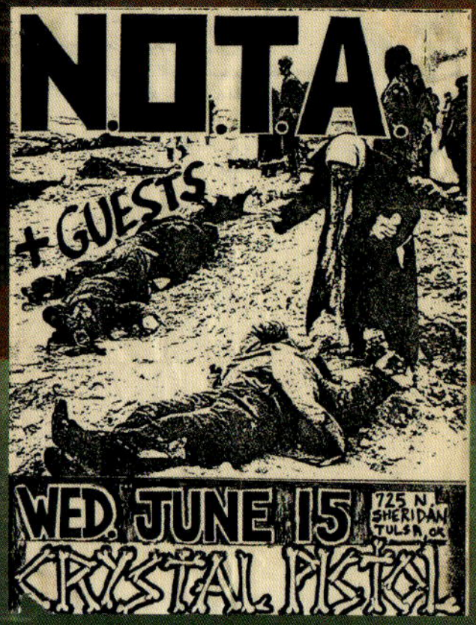
N.O.T.A.
+ GUESTS
WED. JUNE 15
CRYSTAL PISTOL

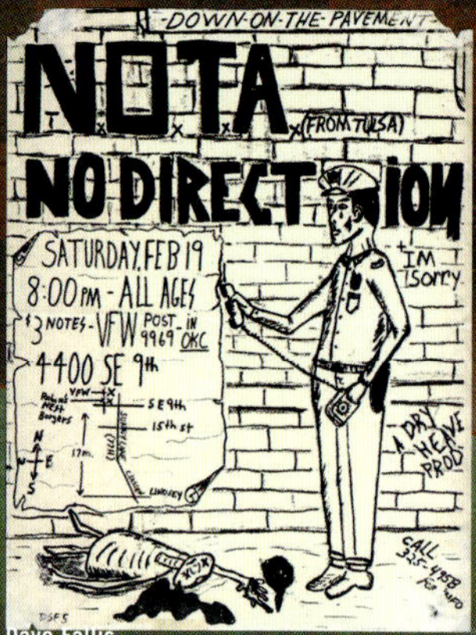
DOWN ON THE PAVEMENT
N.O.T.A.
NO DIRECTION
SATURDAY, FEB 19
8:00 PM - ALL AGES
VFW POST
I'M SORRY

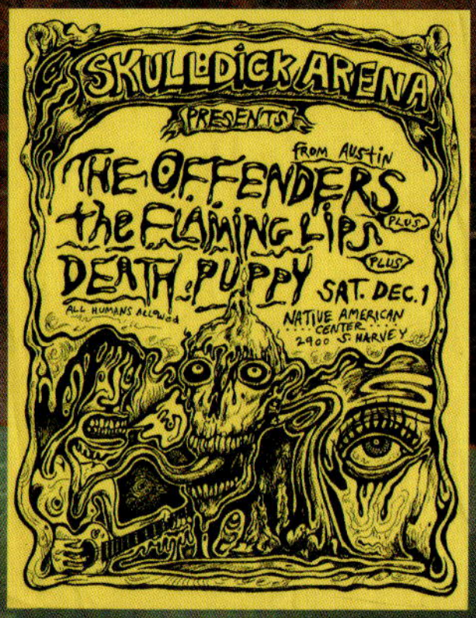
SKULLDICK ARENA
PRESENTS
THE OFFENDERS
THE FLAMING LIPS
DEATH PUPPY
SAT. DEC. 1

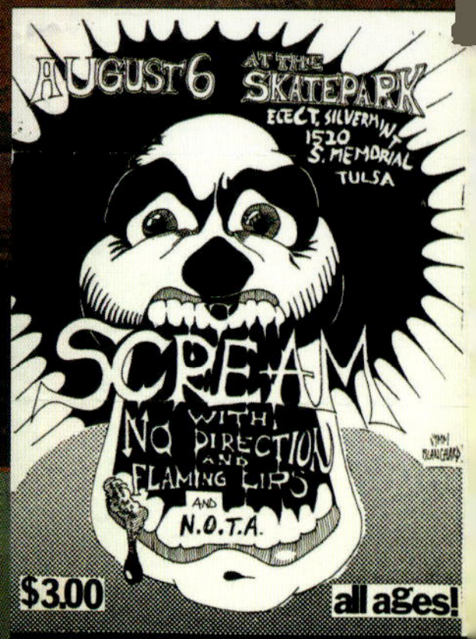
AUGUST 6
SKATEPARK
SCREAM
WITH
NO DIRECTION
FLAMING LIPS
N.O.T.A.
$3.00
all ages!

Dave Fallis

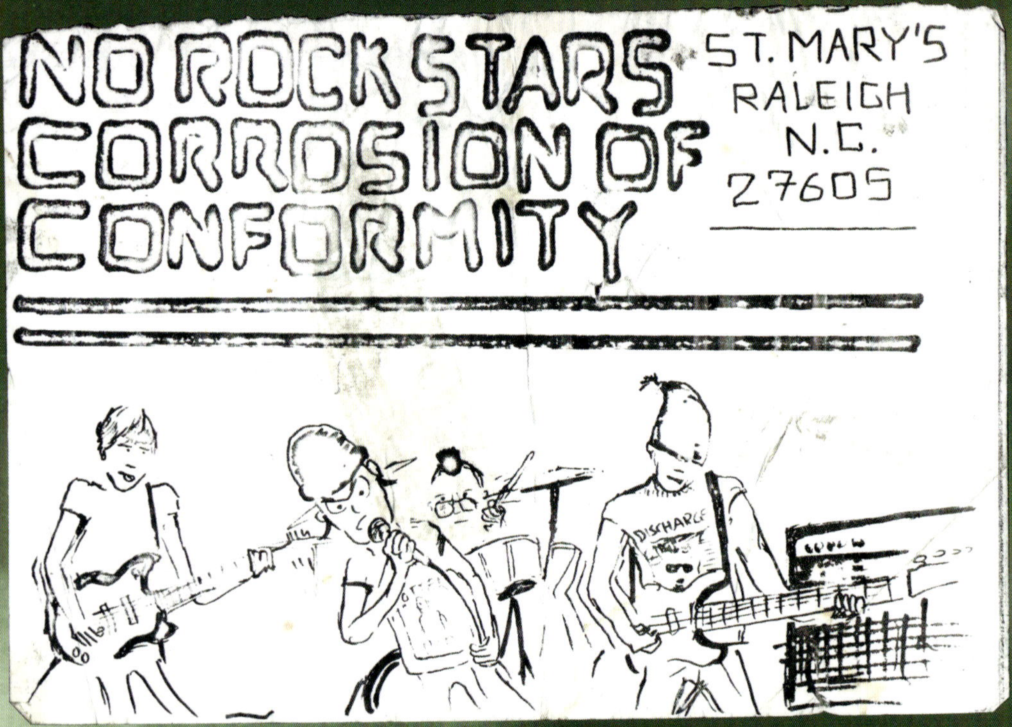
NO ROCK STARS
CORROSION OF CONFORMITY
ST. MARY'S
RALEIGH
N.C.
27605
DISCHARGE

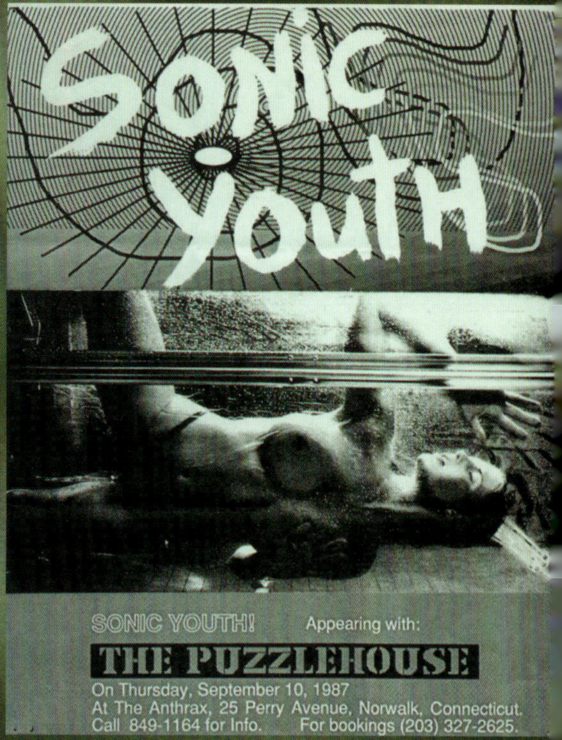
SONIC YOUTH
SONIC YOUTH! Appearing with:
THE PUZZLEHOUSE
On Thursday, September 10, 1987
At The Anthrax, 25 Perry Avenue, Norwalk, Connecticut.
Call 849-1164 for Info. For bookings (203) 327-2625.

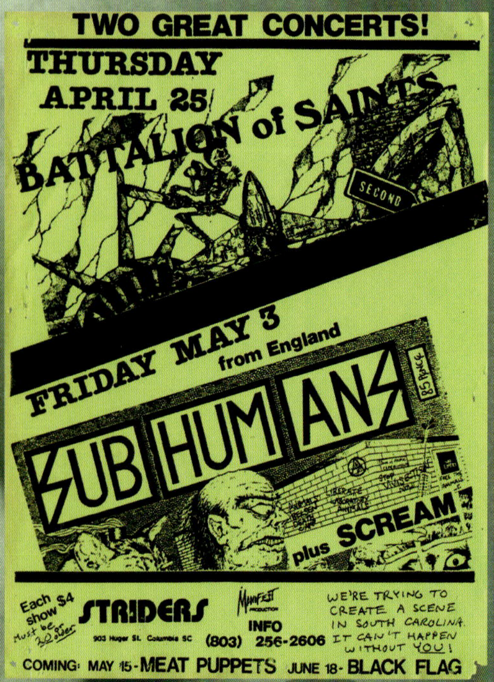
TWO GREAT CONCERTS!
THURSDAY
APRIL 25
BATTALION of SAINTS
FRIDAY MAY 3
from England
SUBHUMANS
plus SCREAM
Each show $4
STRIDERS
INFO
(803) 256-2606
WE'RE TRYING TO CREATE A SCENE IN SOUTH CAROLINA. IT CAN'T HAPPEN WITHOUT YOU!
COMING: MAY 15 - MEAT PUPPETS JUNE 18 - BLACK FLAG

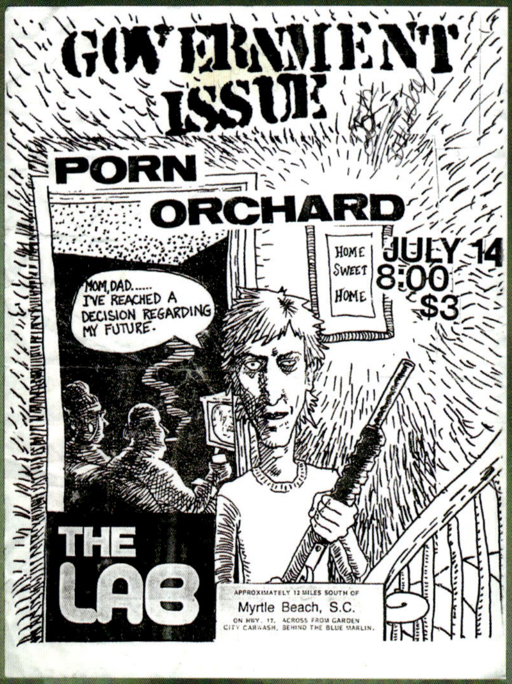
GOVERNMENT ISSUE
PORN ORCHARD
JULY 14
8:00
$3
HOME SWEET HOME
MOM, DAD...... I'VE REACHED A DECISION REGARDING MY FUTURE.
THE LAB
Myrtle Beach, S.C.

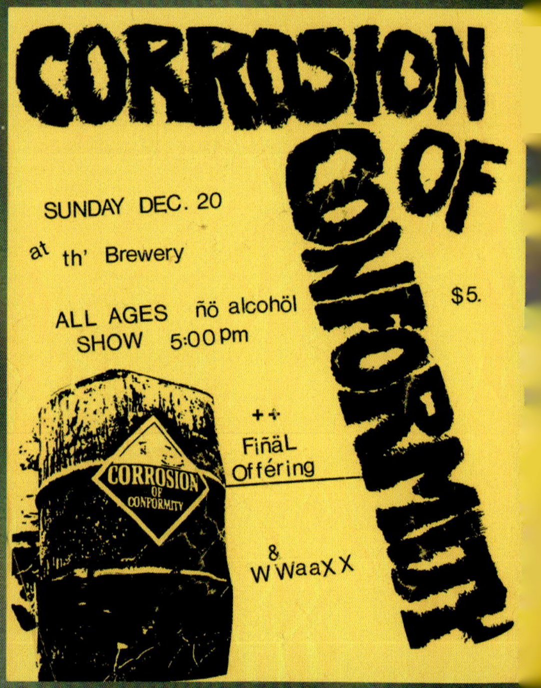
CORROSION OF CONFORMITY
SUNDAY DEC. 20
at th' Brewery
ALL AGES SHOW
ñö alcohöl
5:00 pm
$5.
+ Fiñal Offéring
& W WaaXX

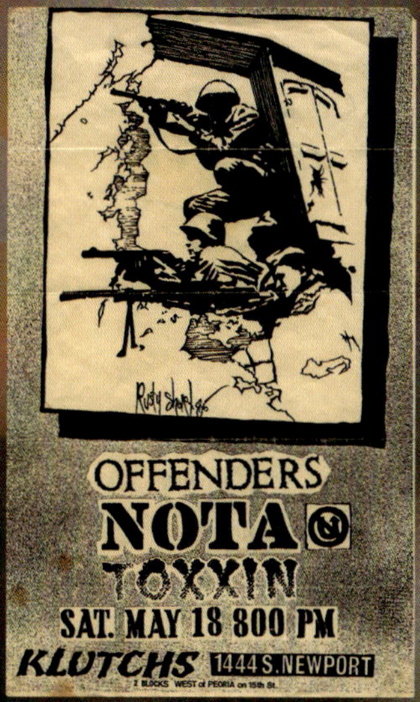

Rusty Short

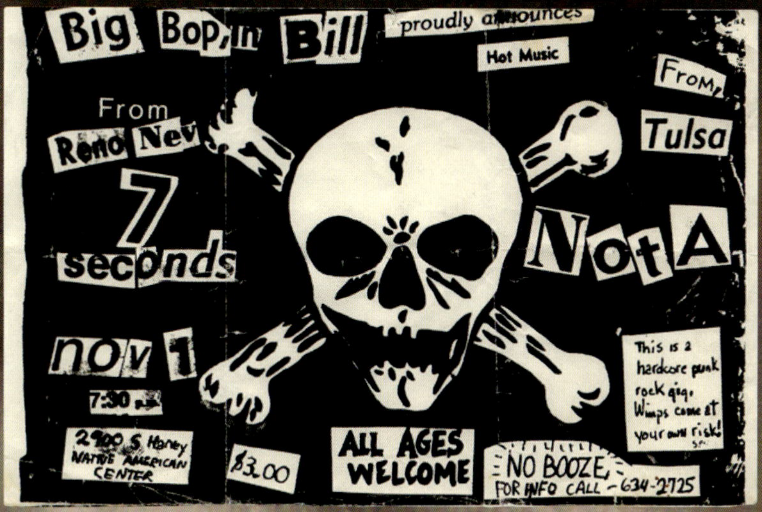

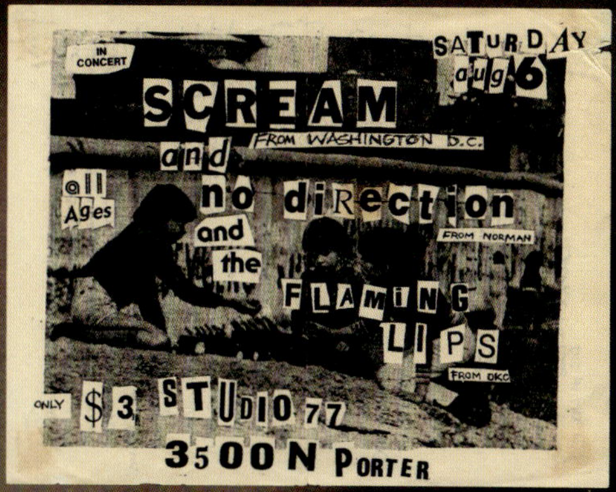

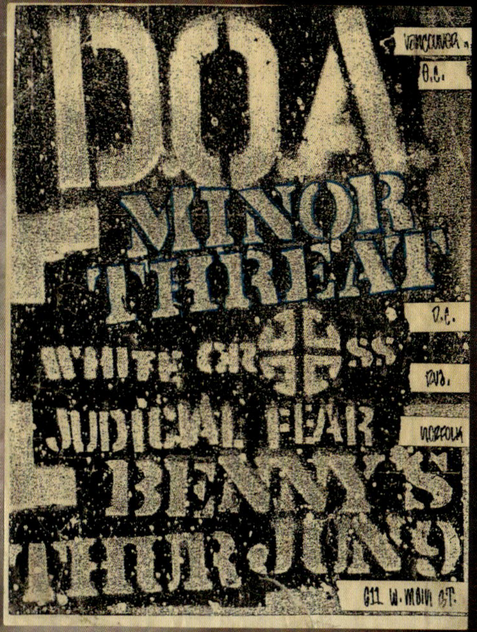

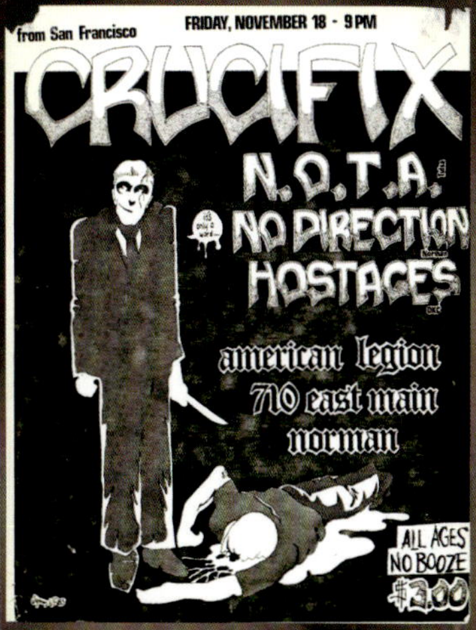

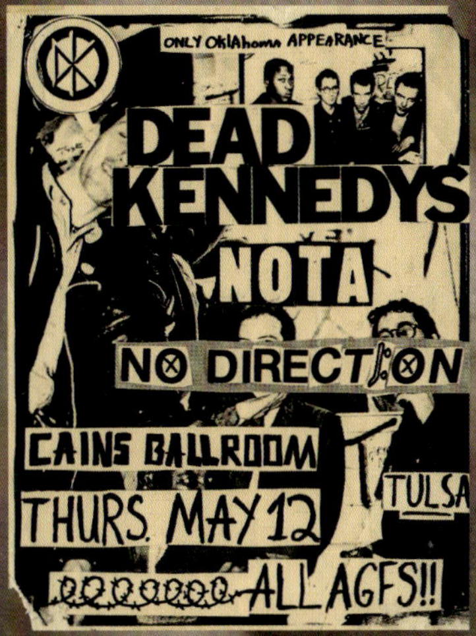

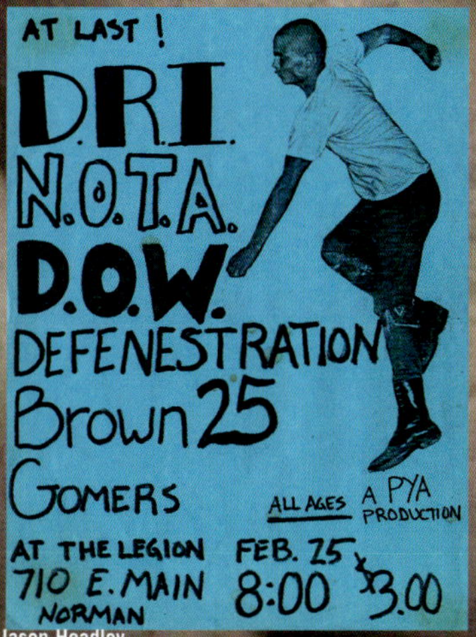

Jason Headley

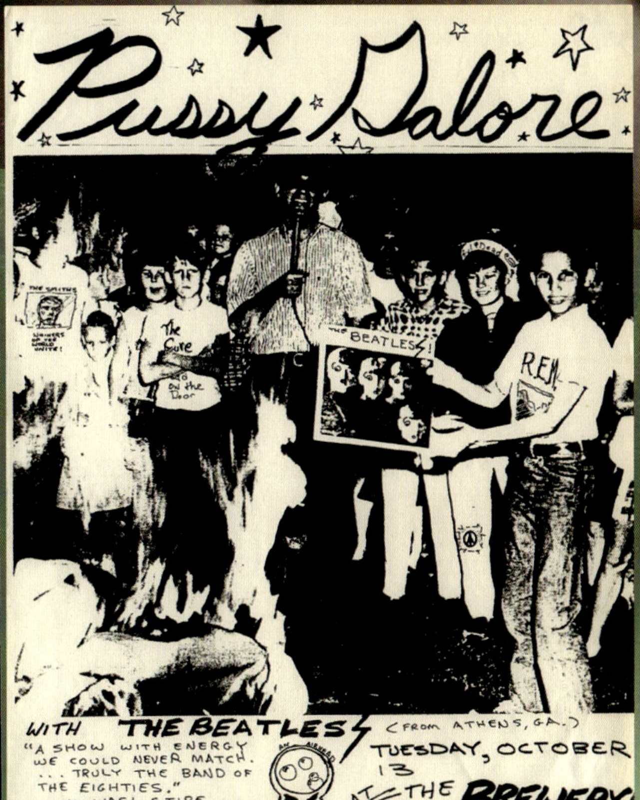

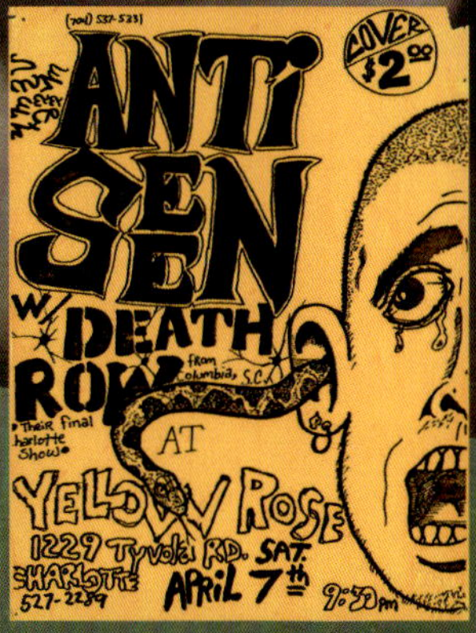

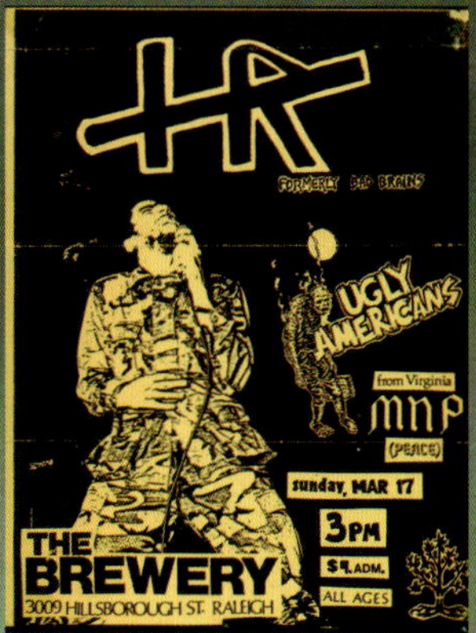

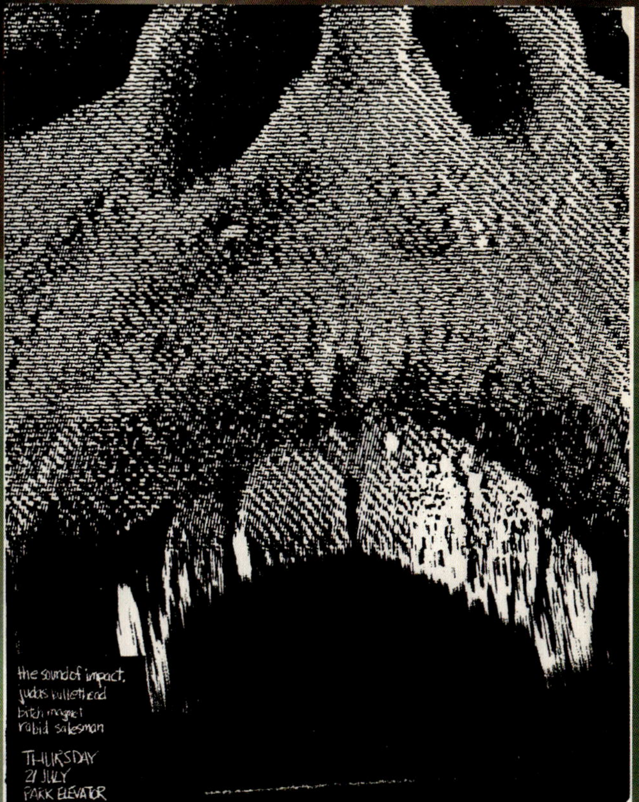

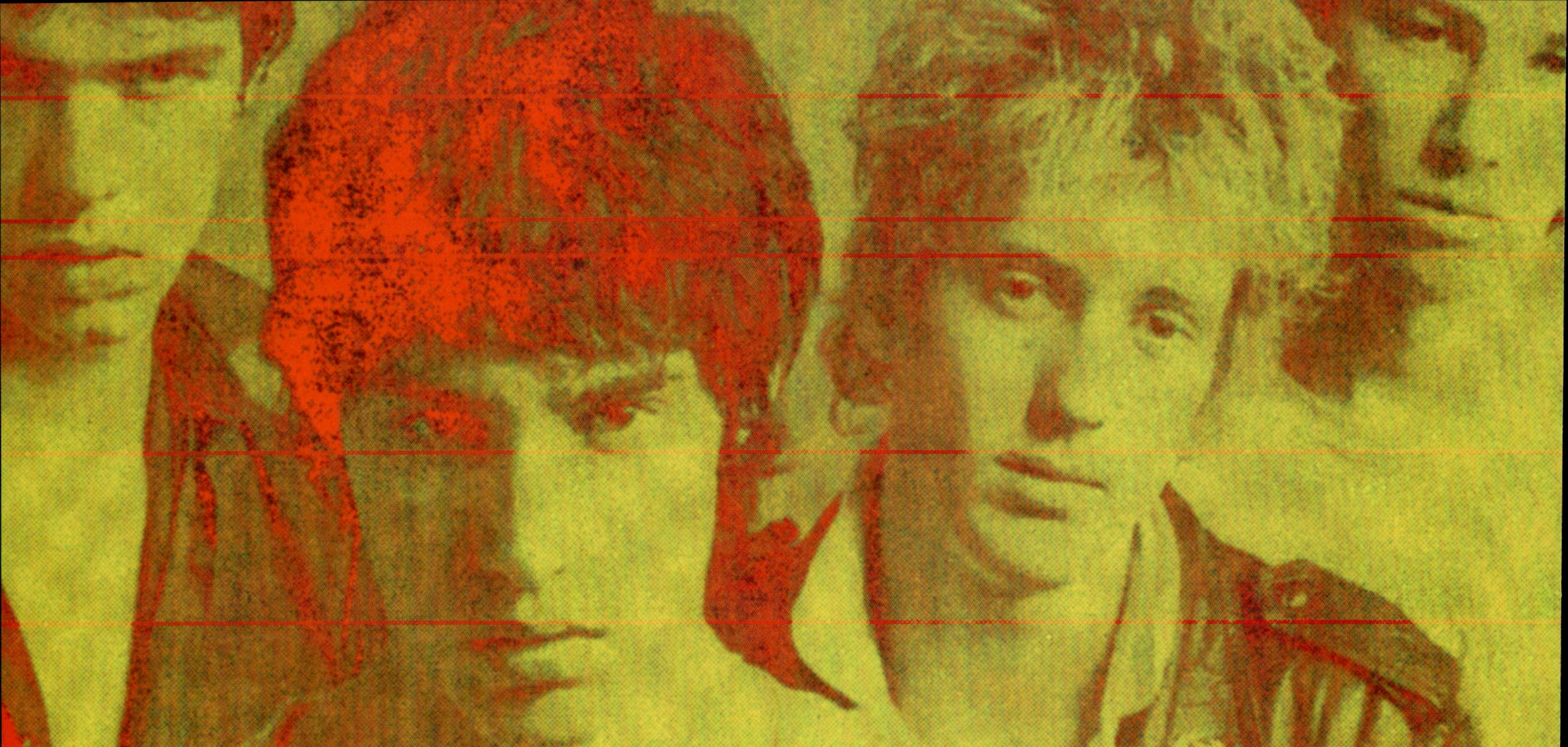

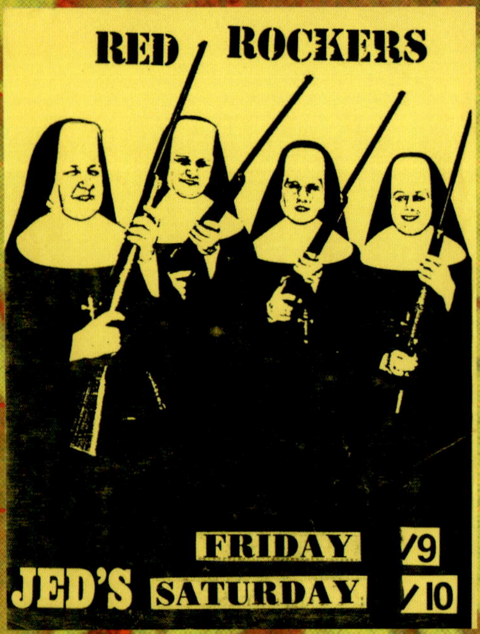

Darren Hill

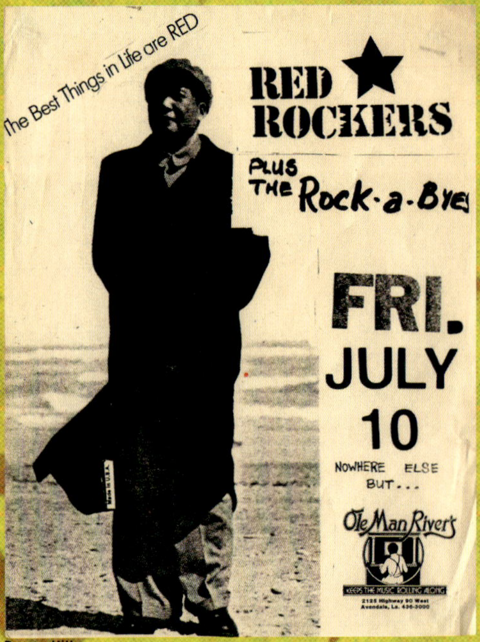

Darren Hill

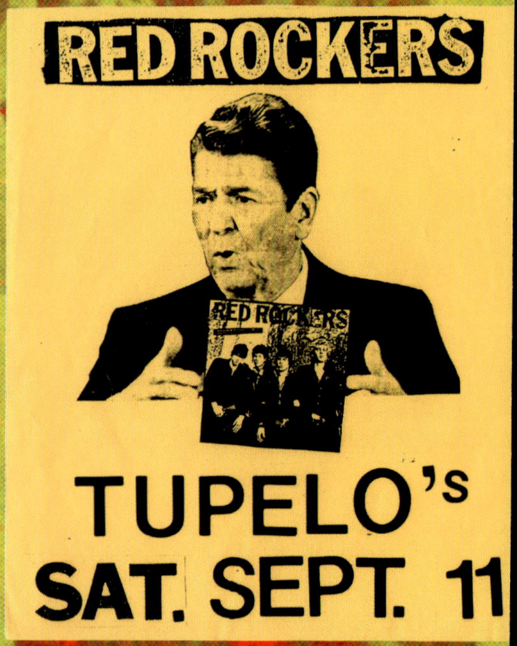

Darren Hill

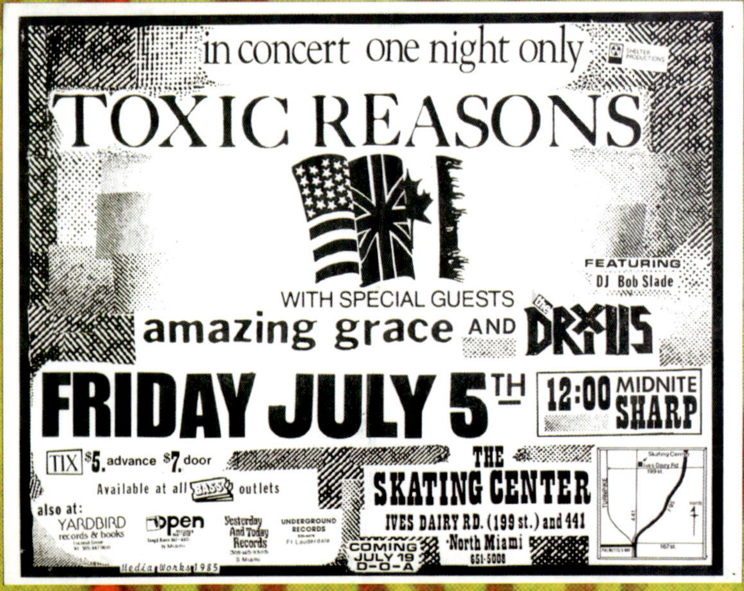

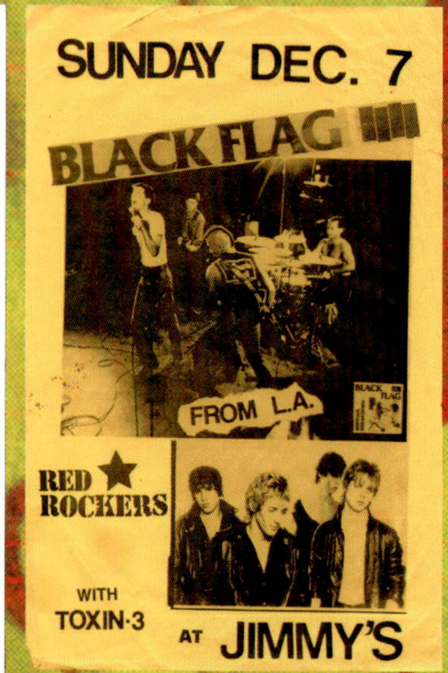

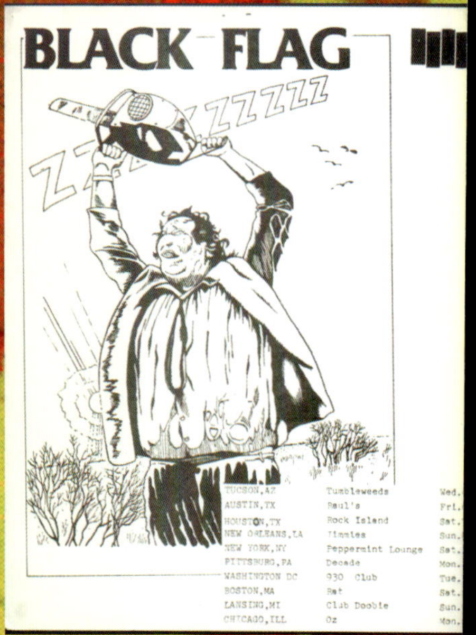

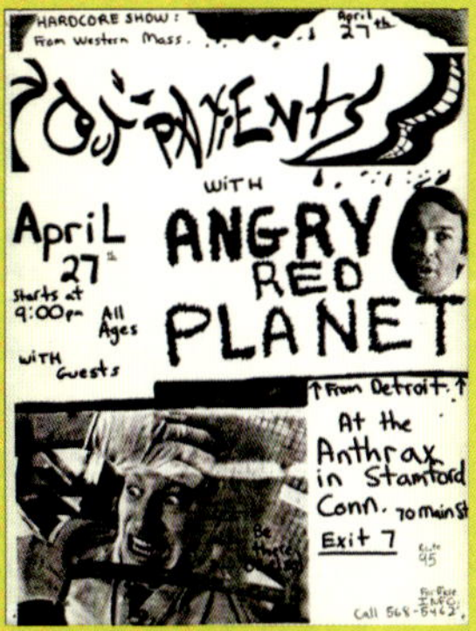

Scott Helland

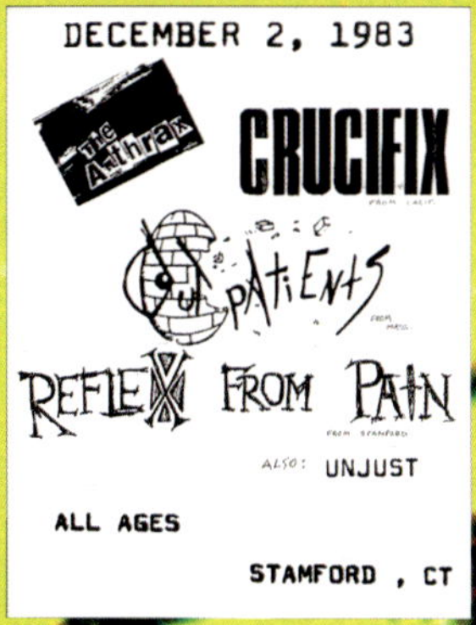

Scott Helland

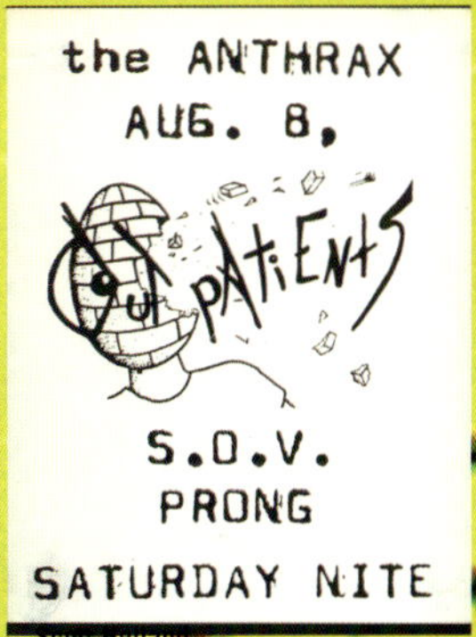

Scott Helland

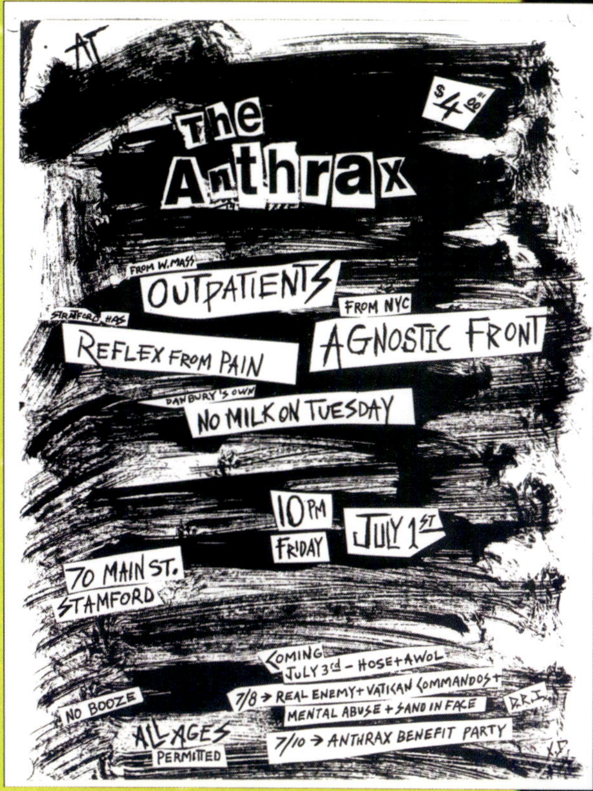

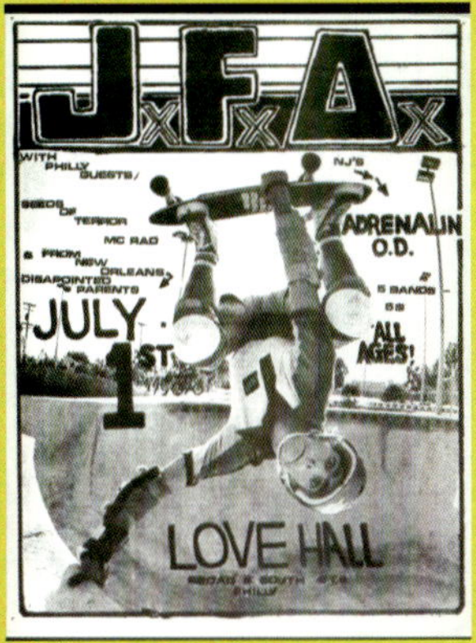

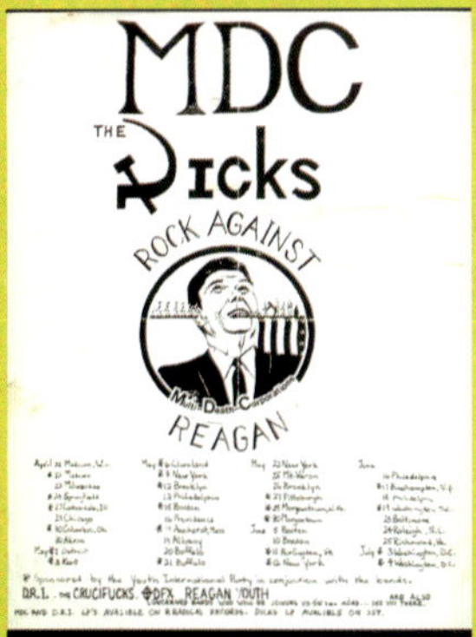

Lisa Deanne Smith

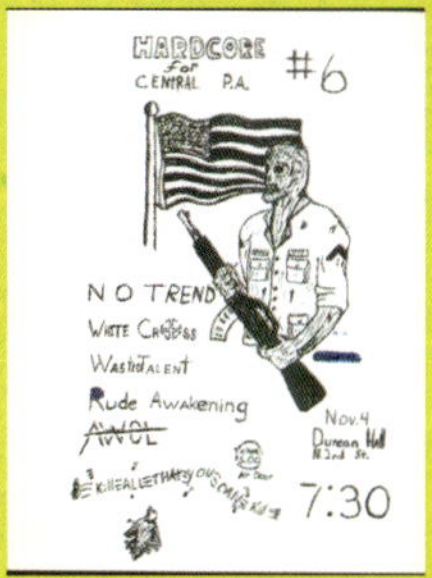

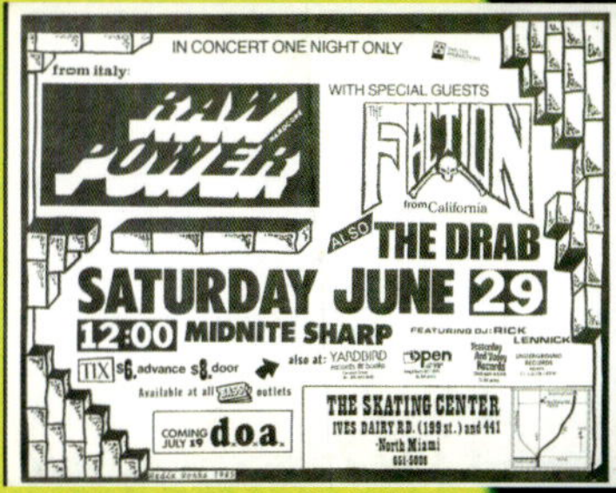

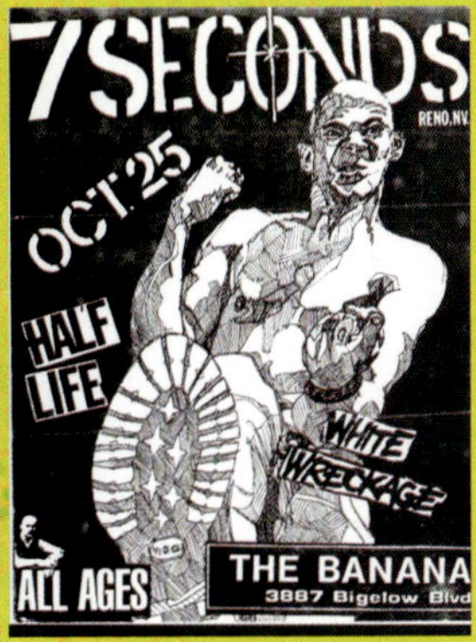

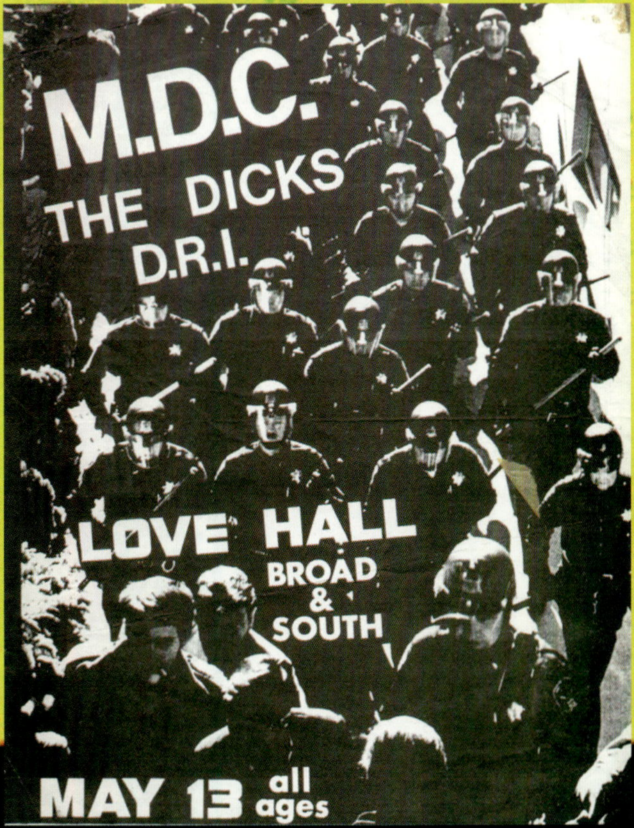

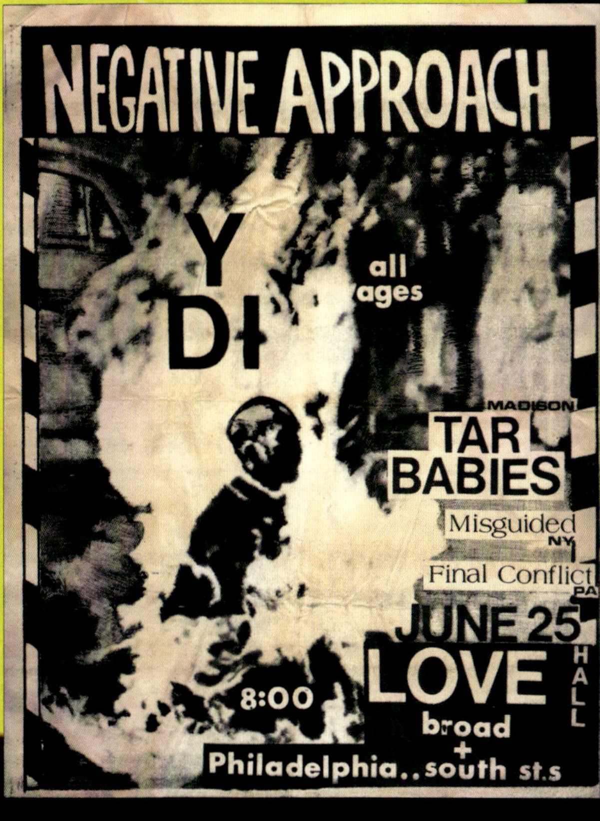

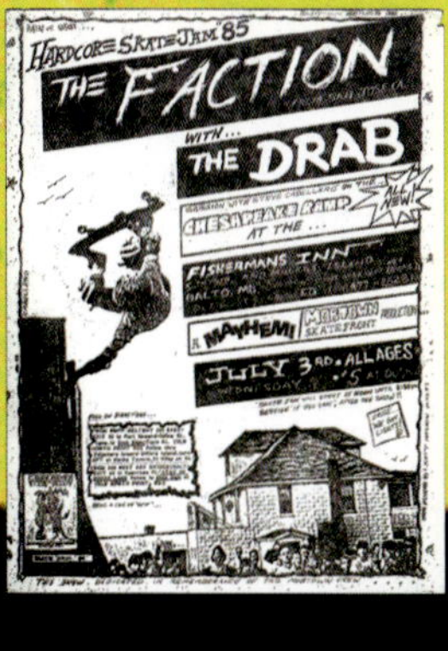

Addicted
Blood River
Garlands Pit
Time Is Running Out
Pay back
Afraid to Die
Anti-War
Dreams
Aggressive Systems
Pain of Mind
D-Day
Look What We've Done Now
Dismember Me
Ocean
Wired
Beach Creep
(Condemned to Death)

RE-IGNITION
ROCK FOR LIGHT
LET ME HELP
DAY TRIPPER
HOUSE (BANNED VOYAGE)
COPTIC
I AGAINST I
DUB
I+I SURVIVE
FOOLS GOLD
SACRED LOVE
SOUL CRAFT
SECRET 77
MOVIES
I LOVE I JAH
QUICKNESS
PAY TO CUM

SOUL KITCHEN
RIDING W/ MARY
HOW I...
L.D.
HAVE NOTS
REAL CHILD O'HELL
SEX & DYING
DESPERATE
SOME OTHER TIME
UNHEARD MUSIC
HUNGRY WOLF
PHONE'S OFF
MOTEL ROOM
WHITE GIRL
ONCE OVER TWICE
BECAUSE I DO
SUGARLIGHT
BEYOND & BACK
JOHNY HIT & RUN
U.T. B.B.S.
YEAR 1

Mr. Big
Give me a break
Not worth it
Blow up
National Guard
Hate the Rich
Class war
Lone house
Tell me what I want to hear
Sound of the rain
New kicks
Same things never change
Red Rockers rule
Golden gate
Love done gone
Tell her I love her
Poor woman
C-A-R
Can't shake it
Spliff City

THE MEMBRANES
MUSIC TO ...

All Hell
Samhain
All Murder
The Shift
The Howl
Die, Die
Unholy Passion
Black Dream
Halloween II
Hungry End
Misery
Horror Biz
He-Who-Cannot-Be-Named

Revenge
American Waste
We Heard It Before
Depression
Beat My Head Against the Wall
Nervous Breakdown
Jealous Again
We Got to Run
My Rules
Spray Paint
Damaged I
Life of Pain
No Values
Six Pack
... Man

UNITY
NOT NORMAL I
Typical America
Leach
WASTED Youth
That fun to you
Do you even care
Drug Fools
How much Art
Arms Race
SPY
Police
WAR Threat
Jack Itch
Screw
violent Attack
Not Normal II
Fight them
The End
DECONTROL

Teen Idle
Milk
Trans Am
Stepping Stone
Sneakers
At the Hop
Adventure
Do you Love Me
Commie Song
Pipe bomb
Fiorucci Nitemare
Dead Head → No Fun

LETTER BOMB
BACK AGAINST THE WALL
PATRICK GOLDSTEIN
WILD IN THE STREETS
RED TAPE
PAID VACATION
TRAPPED
DENY EVERYTHING
WHAT'S YOUR PROBLEM
BEHIND THE DOOR
SKANK
BEVERLY HILLS, CENTURY CITY
OPERATION
LIVE FAST, DIE YOUNG
GROUP SEX
WORLD UP MY ASS
JUST LIKE ME

L-Times
Black Spiders
Bad Brains
Modern Love
Hell Hole
Krista's Gotta Run
Time Bomb
Play Full
Senseless
Money

1. Good For You
2. Brutality and the Truth
3. Jimmy Rocks
4. Their Mistakes
5. T.V. World
6. Lord's Prayer
7. Mission of Mercy
8. Good Morning America
9. The Light
10. Bed of Nails
11. Talk's Cheap
12. Berlin, Berlin
13. Making Room for Youth
14. Got No Time
15. Rat in a Maze
16. Rock-N-Roll Babylon
17. Ignorance and Arrogance
18. Public Enemy #1

Security
Nervous
Funk Affectionate
Fight back
Brick wall
Damage 43
Prison
Baby lets play god
We got your money
Im sorry
History
Whats the word
Red green
Lesson
Jump the fence
We're not in it to lose
Fun Fun Fun

REVENGE
I DON'T CARE
WHITE MINORITY
GIVE US A BREAK
MACHINE
I'VE HAD IT
NERVOUS BREAKDOWN
PARENTS AND RELATIVES
DEPRESSION
JEALOUS AGAIN
FIX ME
WASTED
RED TAPE
POLICE STORY
GIMME, GIMME, GIMME
NO VALUES
CLOCKED IN
LEAVE ME ALONE
NEW CODE

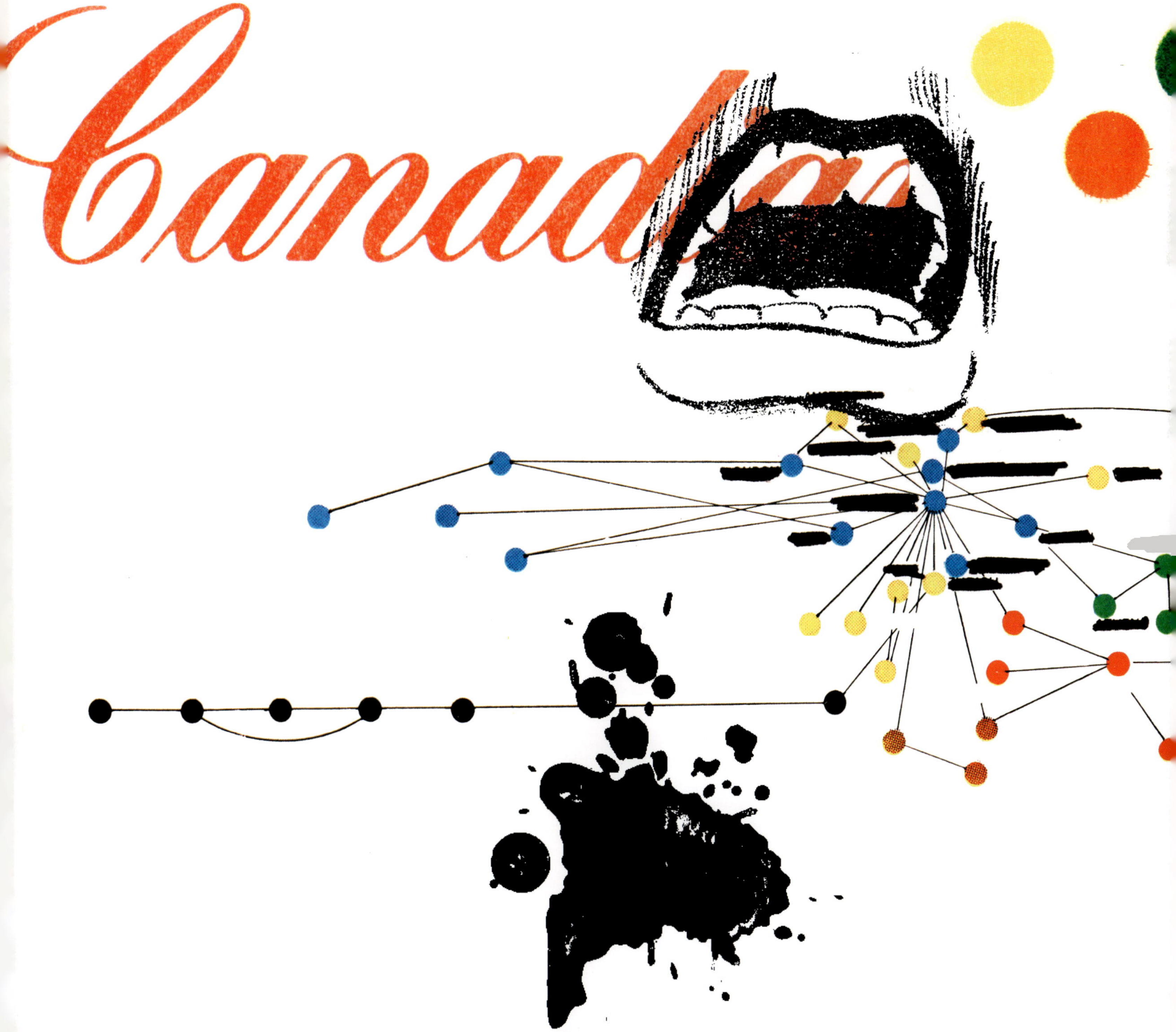
Canad

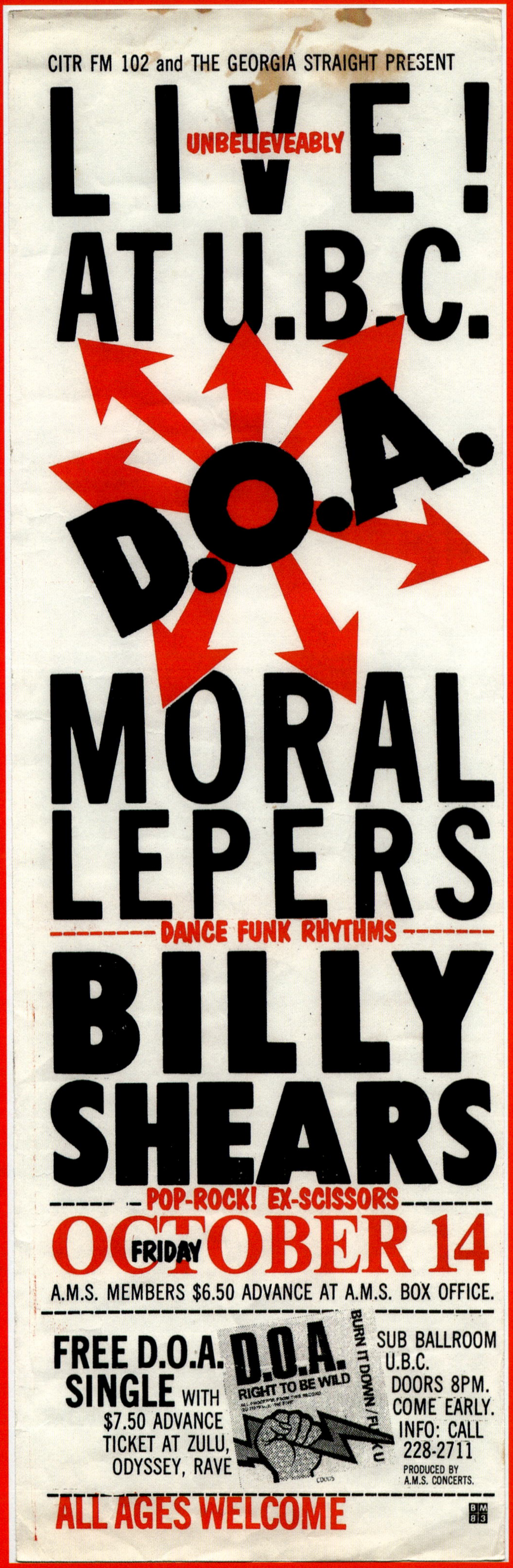

The Road To Milan: DOA Euro Tour 1984

David Lester

March 29 It's 7 am. Checkpoint Charlie, our Germa
driver, is yelling, *"Come on babies! You must wa
up! Come on babies! We must go!"* My girlfrien
Laura and I roll out of our makeshift bed on the flo
of some squat. Lester (anarchist/manager/writer Ke
Lester) is also yelling by this time, telling us tha
there's only one train to Yugoslavia, and it leaves
45 minutes. We pile into the worst looking van in th
country of Germany (we'd been pulled over by cop
once or twice a day for 10 days in this piece of shi
and hit the road. We make it to the Ljubljana Expres
with 30 seconds to spare.

Inside Tito's Socialist Experiment

**I wake up enroute to Ljubljana. Its our first visi
to a communist country. The train is full of soldier
the locals are laughing at us and calling us capitalists..
It's all slightly surreal.**

**When we get there, we meet Marion and Igor, who race us to the National Radio station, past cyrillic signs, porn, tiny Eastern cars, and pseudo-Western shops. At the radio station we are interviewed but don't get to say much, because o
the time involved using interpreters.**

**The gig starts and 800 people go out of their minds. Mostly punk rock virgins, the audience does well, rushing the stage, knocking over mike
and monitors and smashing into us. Two girls interview our heartthrob Ian for a Yugo "Sixteen"
type magazine.**

March 30

***On the train to Zagreb, the capital of Croatia, Ig
tells us of spending 2 months in jail for wearing
"Nazi Punks Fuck Off" button, interpreted by loc
authorities as being a pro-fascist statement. We c
it to our show from the train station and the cab
demands American dollars. We grab our stuff and t
him to fuck off. We play a great show to 1000 peop
with state-owned gear.***

The Night Train to Milan

**Popping the tops off several
bottles of wine, we then bid farewell to
Igor and Marion and continue west to
Italy.
We're having trouble finding a place
to stash our gear. We come across an
empty
compartment, locked with a sign in
Slovenian that we're sure says "Fuck o
Private!" Ian, in a drunken stupor rips
open the door and 6 of us pile into com
fortable chairs. Some of the band ende
up sleeping in the aisle, not everyone
in our entourage fit in the cabin.
A conductor comes by, asks us for our
tickets,
and we produce our 2nd class ducats.
He starts yelling, someone tells him to
fuck himself, and he leaves in a huff.
15 minutes later
he returns with border cops wearing
big blue overcoats and white helmets
screaming
at us for our passports. They slap our
drummer Greg across the face, Ian tak
a shot at one of them and the cop bac
hands him. They grab our passports an
throw us off the train. These guys mea
business- we were fucked.
Ian starts walking around
in a stupor muttering, "Let's
nuke this place," I grab
him and shake him by his
collar, "Shut up, shut Up,
shut up!" Lester pays the
conductor the difference
between 2nd and 1st class
and they let us back on the
train, only to find 6 Italians
had taken our seats, and
we ended up sleeping in
the aisle anyway.**

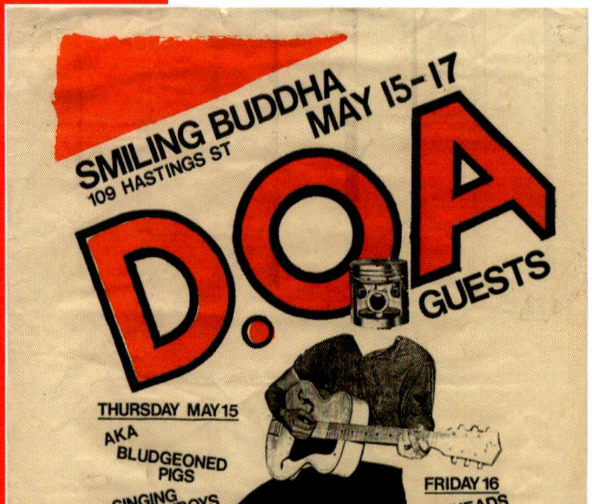

No Budget Studios

Milan

When we finally arrive in Milan everyone has to tak
a giant crap, There are no toilets to be found in ou
squat and the toilet backstage at the show doesn't
flush. Nine of us go in there and lay cable, and poo
Dave was the last to go, so he had to use the stand
up method.

We play to 2000 people - the p.a. is shit, it's utter
chaos, but its the first North American Punk band
these people have seen, and they even know some
the songs. Our payoff for the show is Airline tickets
London, this is the end of our first European tour. C
driver arrives in the a.m. to take us to the airport i
beat-to-shit VW van that won't go more than 10 mp
Ian is screaming at the driver, who speaks no Engli
and is too busy burning out what's left of the clutch
to pay any attention to him, and the fucking van die
on the side of the road. Greg commandeers 2 taxis
take us to the airport and they ream us for $100 ea
for a 10 minute ride. +

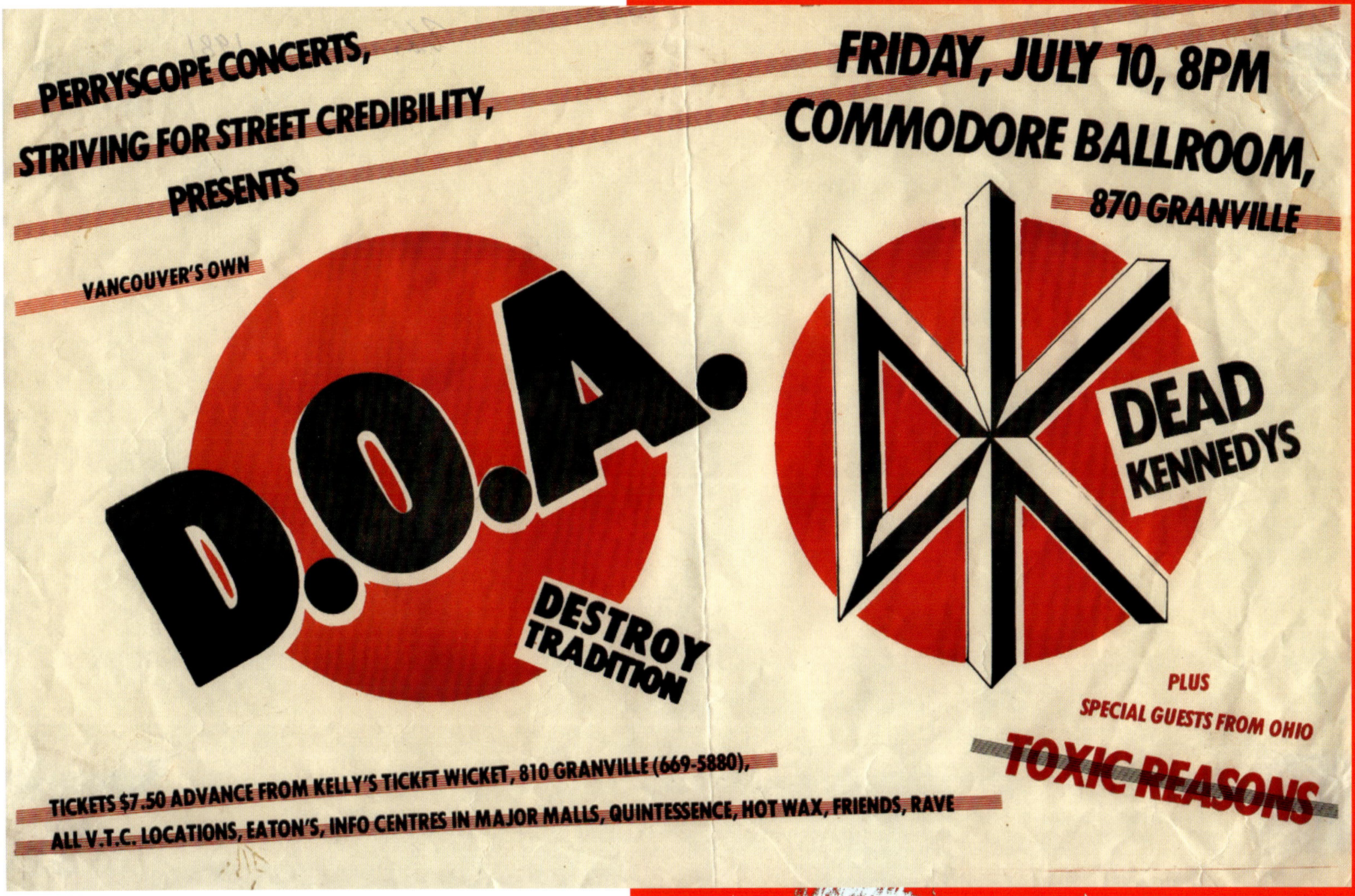

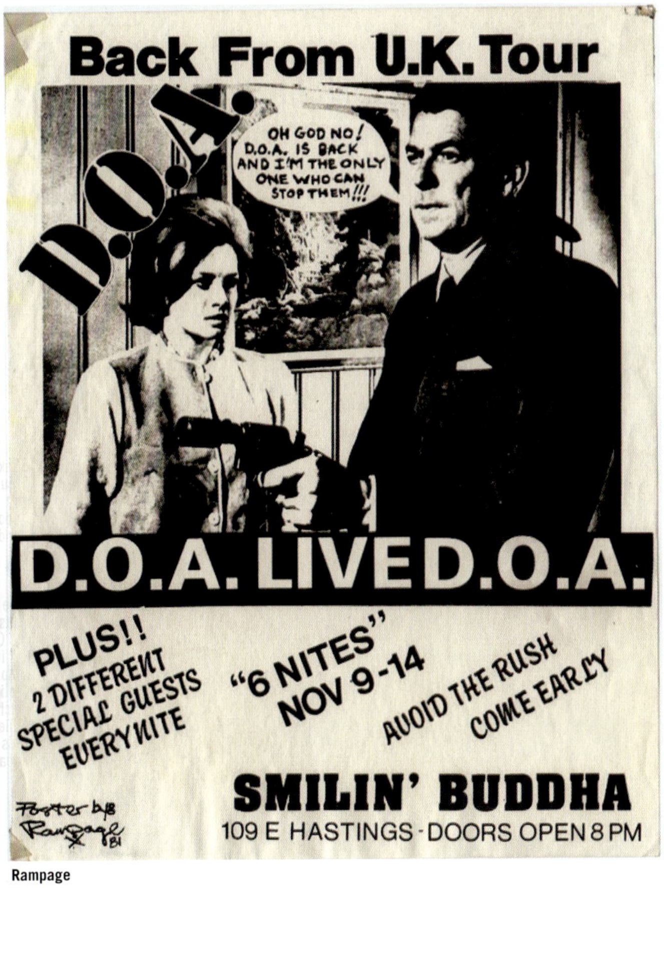

Rampage

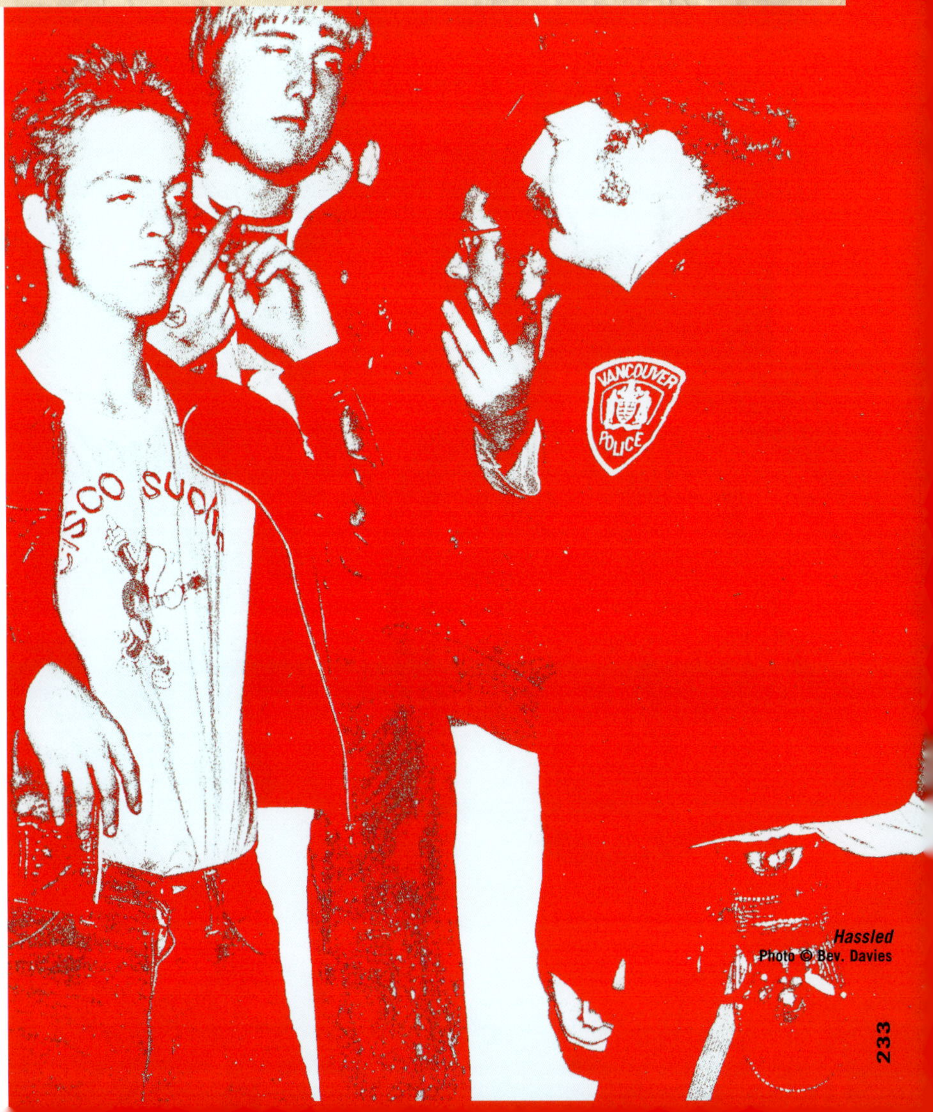

Hassled
Photo © Bev. Davies

Top Three D.O.A. Photos © Bev. Davies

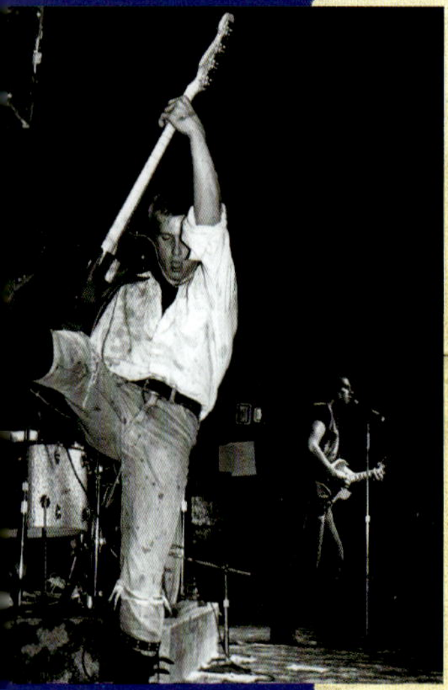

PARTICIPATION NOT DECIMATION!!!

TO WHOM IT MAY CONCERN:

IN FRONT OF THE STAGE IS A FREE FRAME OF REFERENCE. IT'S PHYSICAL, FUN, IT'S FOR EVERYONE WHO WANTS TO TAKE A RISK.

IT IS NOT FOR THE STRONG TO SMASH THE WEAK, THE BIG TO MUSCLE THE LITTLE, OR MEN TO MASH WOMEN. IT IS NOT A COMBAT ZONE FOR ANY ONE PERSON OR GROUP OF PEOPLE TO CONTROL.

EVERYONE, SHOULD BE ABLE TO PARTICIPATE. TOGETHER WE CAN CREATE AND EXPAND THE BOUNDS OF FREEDOM

FOR THE BEST: D.O.A.

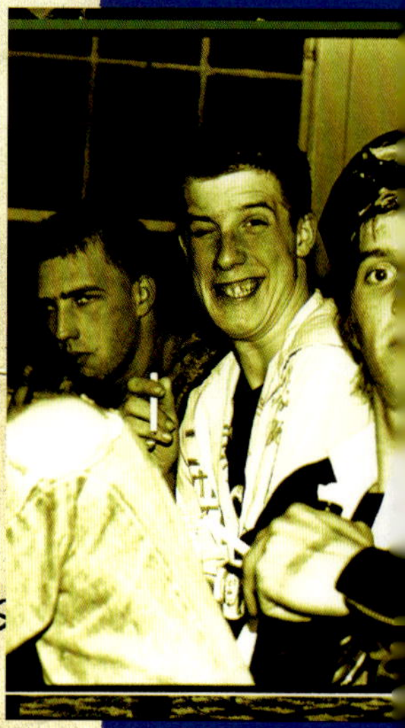

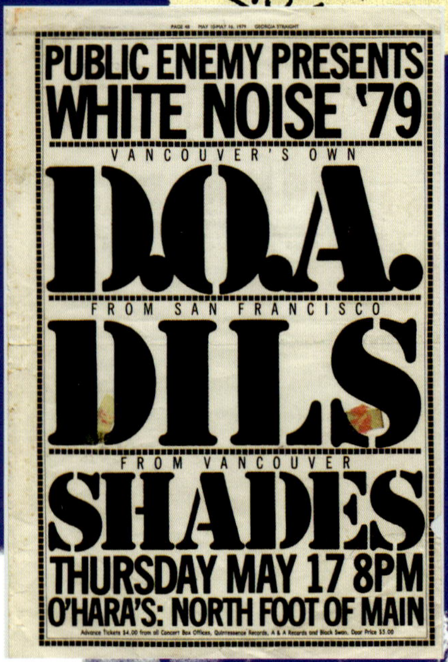

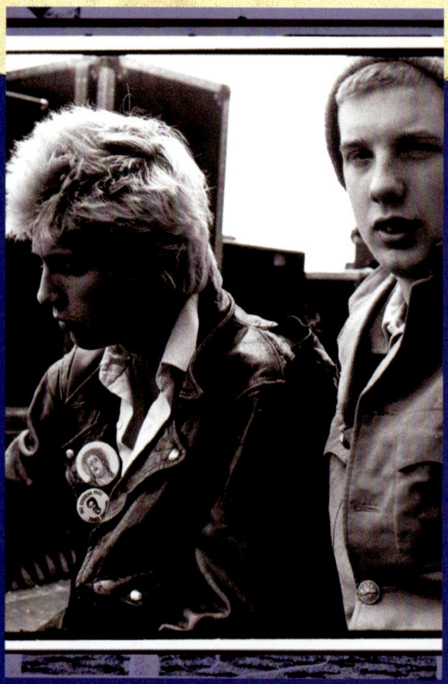

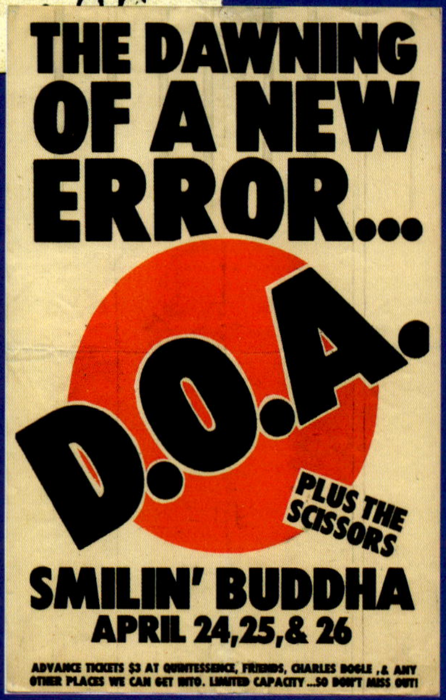

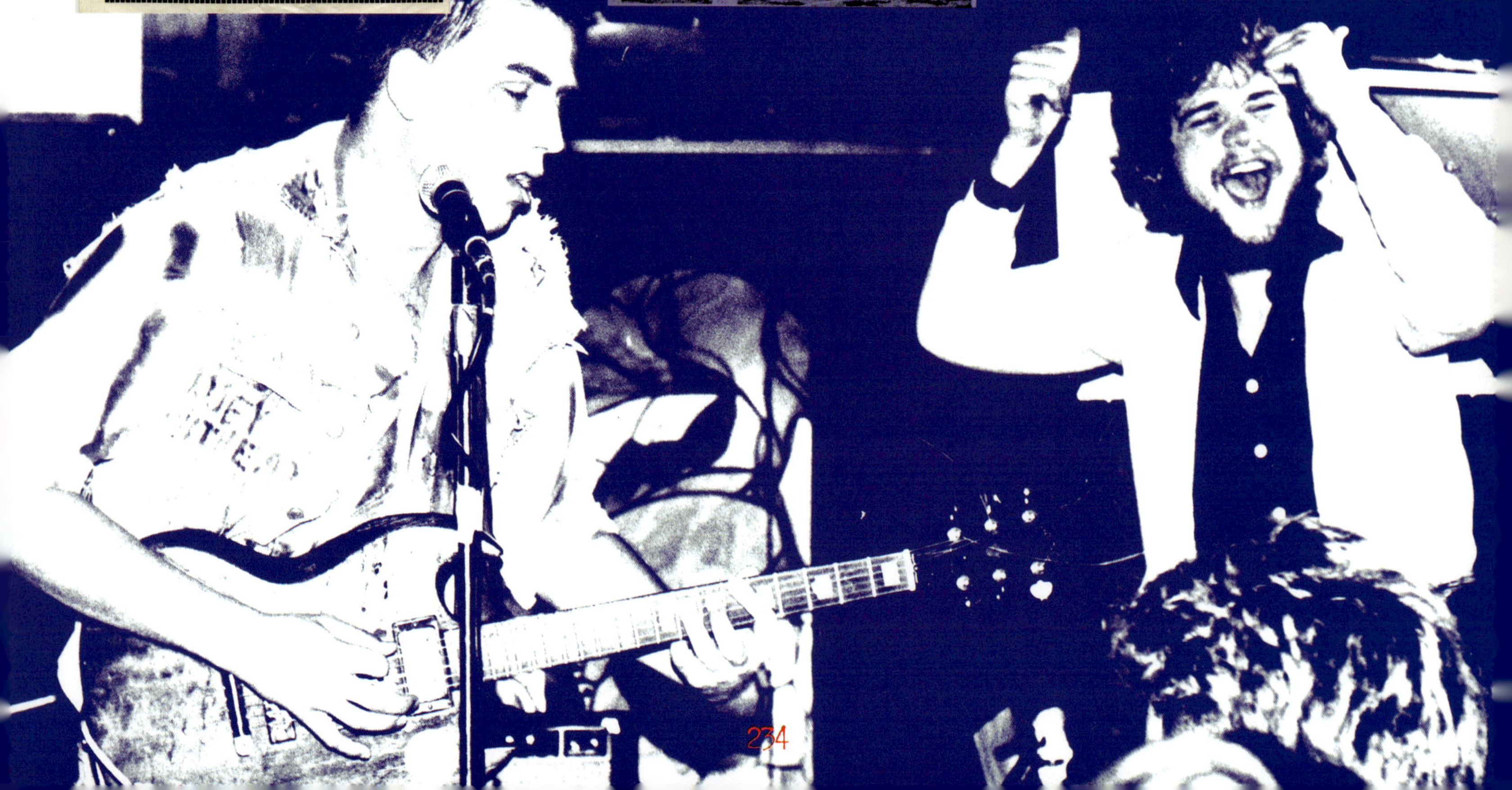

Psalm 23, Spunk 24 By Jill Heath

Punk rock is my goddess; I do not want.
She maketh me to revel in diversity,
And leadeth me not to believe that the grass is always greener,
On the other side of that white picket fence;
And encourageth me not to lay me down
In that grass-is-always greener pasture.
But lo, helpeth me to recognize manufactured homogeneous culture
For the suffocating slow death that it is.

She lifteth me up,
And giveth my soul room to breathe, grow and thrive,
Guiding me on a path of outward calm and inner peace,
With which to face a world,
That inclineth me to contempt and loathing, as much as not,
Shielding me from the crushing weight
Of its (not-so-) subtle oppression.
She drieth my tears of frustration and rage,
Oft times before they are shed.

Yea, I do walk through a valley of the shadow of death–
I call it white-bread culture;
And I fear no evil, for punk rock art with me.
Comfortable with that darkness,
(in a way deemed fatuous and obsessive
by the shallow yardstick of callow media culture),
Needing no rod, no staff nor shepherd's crook
For I am not a sheep,
And desire not to be herded,
To my appointed preyed-upon place in the newest target market.
My awareness of, and freedom from,
These tools of manipulation and coercion
IS my comfort,
Not thy rod, thy staff nor thy crook.

Punk rock, my goddess, prepareth not,
Nor spreadeth a table for me
In the sight of mine enemies,
But rather encourageth me to set mine own table,
With food I have cooked myself.
I prepare a feast (organic, vegetarian),
That does not come out of a box
And was not bought at a chain store that has a head office.
But instead I put my money where I later place my food
And hand it our in a store with an on-site owner/operator
That I know by name and face,
Developing a taste for the work of cooking–
My sustenance;
In turned giving me sustenance sufficient,
To be a 'difficult' guest at dinner,
But more importantly, feeding the interest in being a host.
My cup runneth over and so I feed those around me,
Offering up food as but one proof of my happy existence.

Punk rock raiseth me up,
And hath given me a conscience, political and otherwise,
Without which I may have believed
The fiction of my high school history text books;
She showeth me the examples of Helen and Scott Nearing,
Dalton Trumbo, and a host of others,
Who hath also influenced and encouraged me to bear
With good grace, the potential wight of living as an outsider;
Rather than castigate the arrogance and conceit of the world,
"Let these self-same twin evils follow you, like a curse,
All the days of your lives."

She giveth me ears to hear Gil Scott-Heron and Fugazi,
John Trudell and Tom Waits, the Goats and Diamanda Galas,
Nomeansno and Los Lobos, Consolidated and X,
Finding them riotously complementary.

She leadeth me to the march on Washington
(Sunday, the 25th of April, 1993),
To revel in the chorus of voices–of strangers and mine own,
Rising, swelling, spilling out of the subway at Dupont Circle,
To the rewritten tune of the Amen chorus,
the new words ecstatically booming out of that cavernous space:
"Ga-aa-ay men, Ga-aa-ay men, Ga-aa-ay men and les-bi-ans (bisexuals!!!)"
Complete with soloists of astounding beauty,
One woman's voice spiralling out of the Metro,
As the escalator raises her skywards;
She turns and sings to those behind her,
the song simultaneously carried back into the earth,
By other vibrating vocal chords
Making a gliding, graceful descent.

Punk rock granteth goodness and mercy unfailing
seemingly in such short supply elsewhere,
But found easily in the generosity of my far-flung-but-close-knit-tribe.
She restoreth my faith and revitalizeth me,
She replenisheth my soul and reneweth life within me,
On an ongoing daily basis
And through continued contact with my extended tribe.

Surely these things shall follow me all the days of my life:
And I shall dwell in the house of punk rock my whole life long,
Forever, Amen.

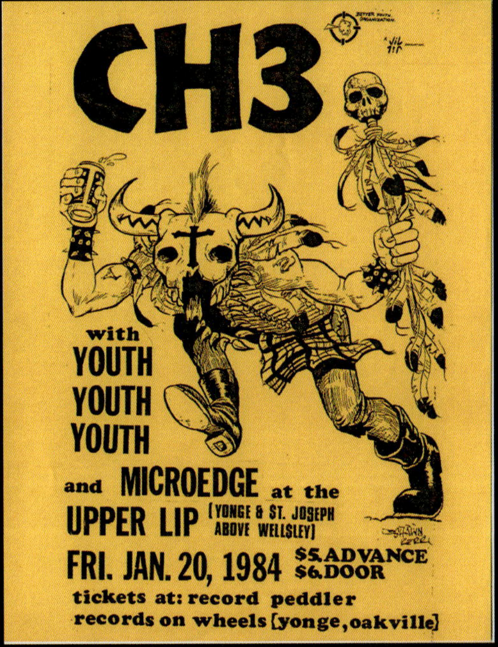

Shawn Kerri

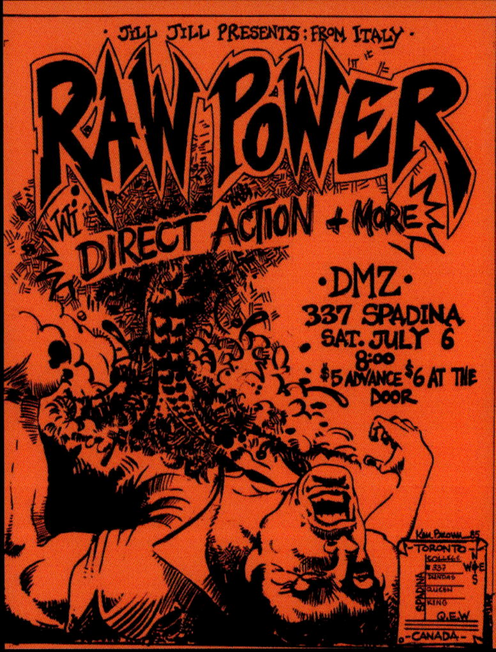

Ken Brown

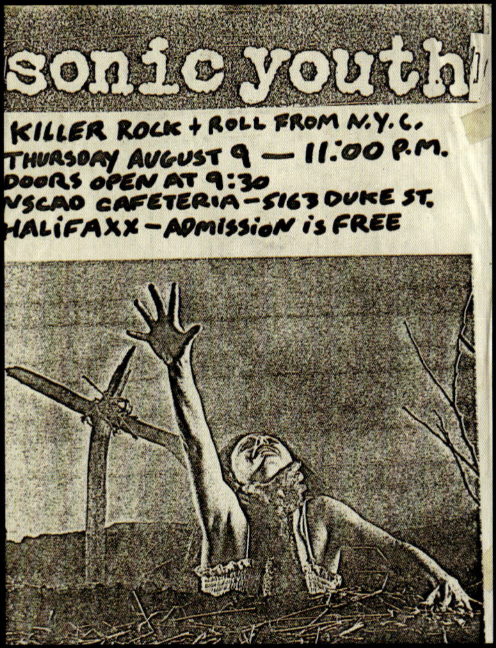

Thurston Moore

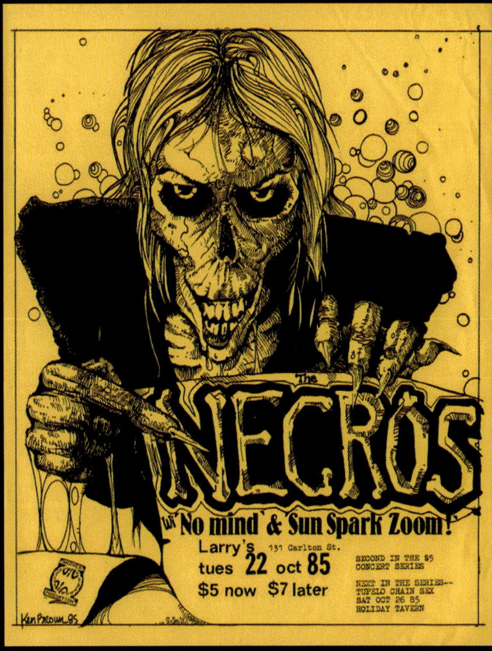

Ken Brown

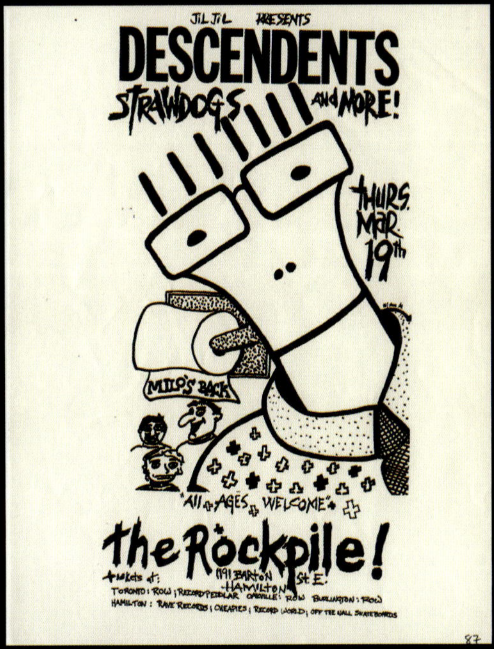

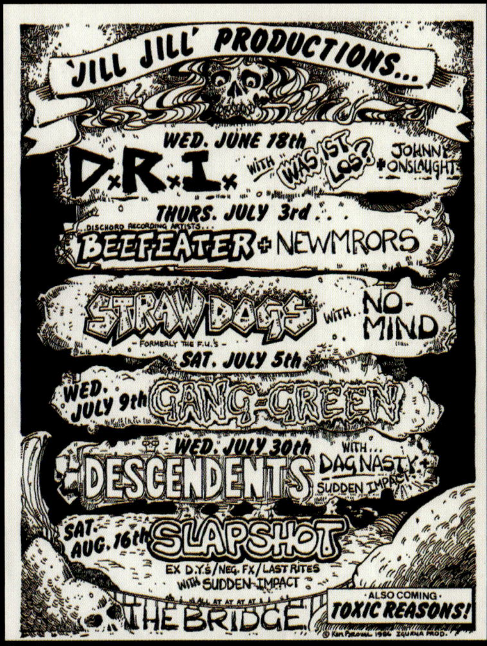

Ken Brown

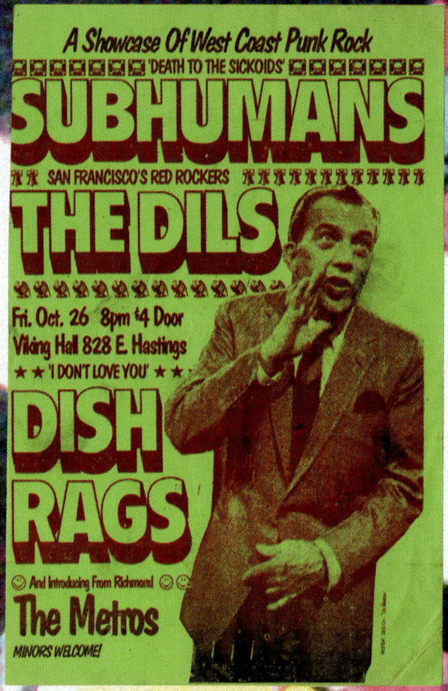

A Showcase Of West Coast Punk Rock
'DEATH TO THE SICKOIDS'
SUBHUMANS
SAN FRANCISCO'S RED ROCKERS
THE DILS
Fri. Oct. 26 8pm $4 Door
Viking Hall 828 E. Hastings
★ ★ 'I DON'T LOVE YOU' ★ ★
DISH RAGS
And Introducing From Richmond
The Metros
MINORS WELCOME!

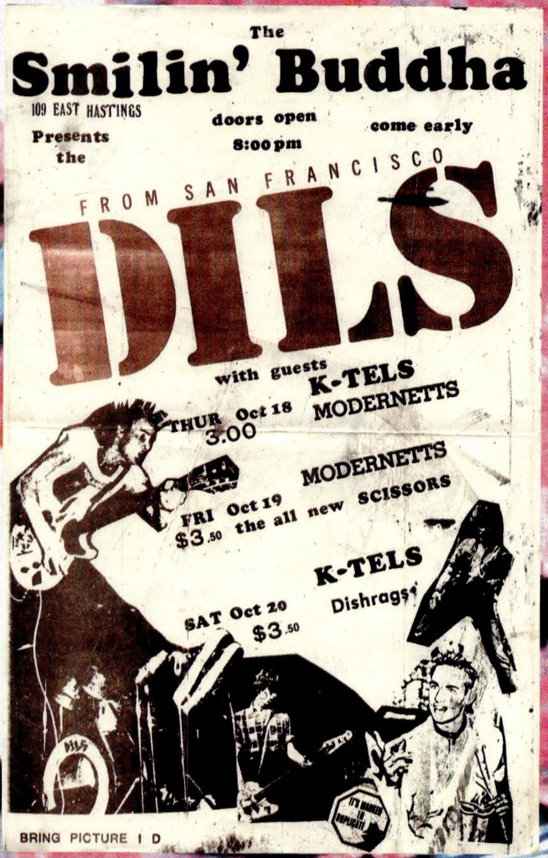

The
Smilin' Buddha
109 EAST HASTINGS
Presents
the
doors open
8:00 pm
come early
FROM SAN FRANCISCO
DILS
with guests
THUR Oct 18
3.00
K-TELS
MODERNETTS
FRI Oct 19
$3.50
MODERNETTS
the all new SCISSORS
SAT Oct 20
$3.50
K-TELS
Dishrags
BRING PICTURE I D

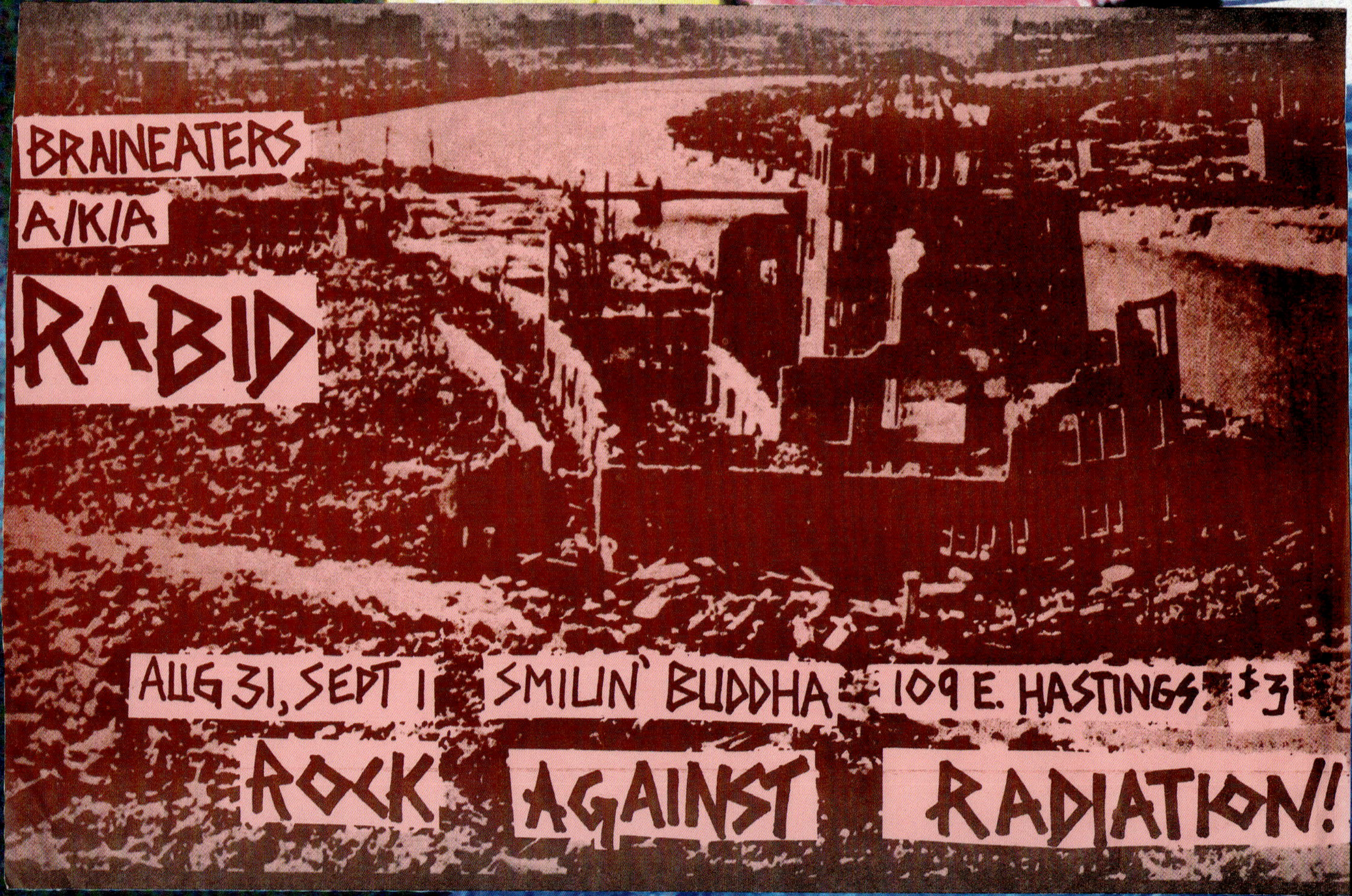

BRAINEATERS
A/K/A
RABID
AUG 31, SEPT 1
SMILIN' BUDDHA
109 E. HASTINGS
$3
ROCK AGAINST RADIATION!

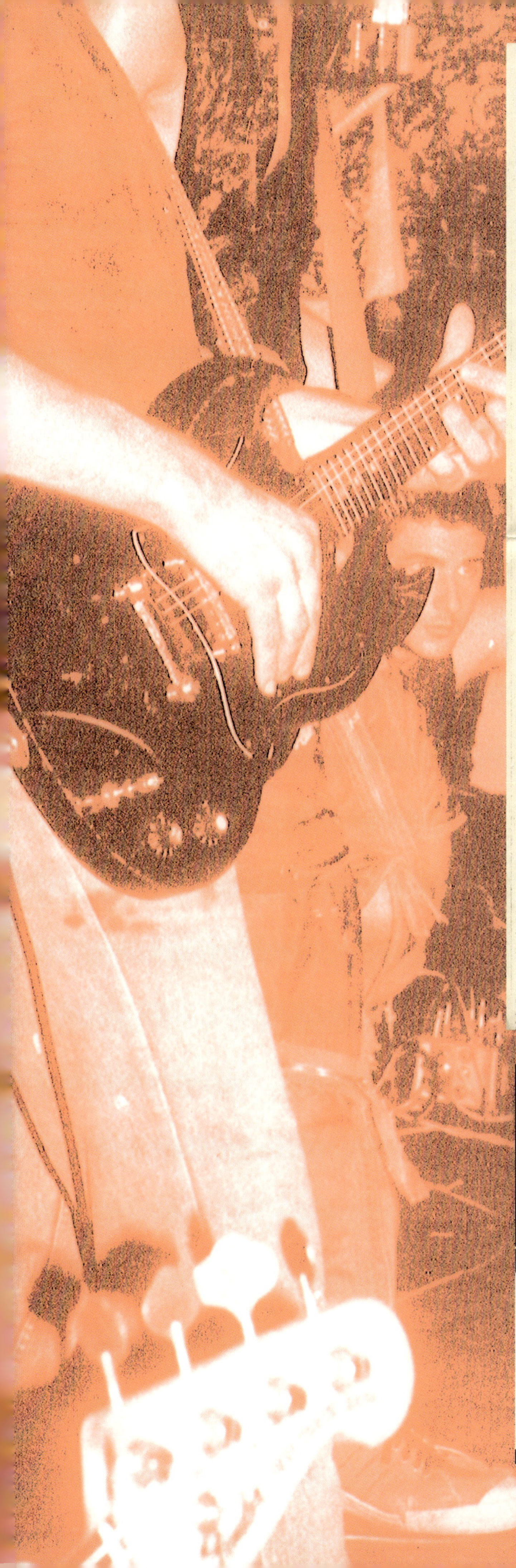

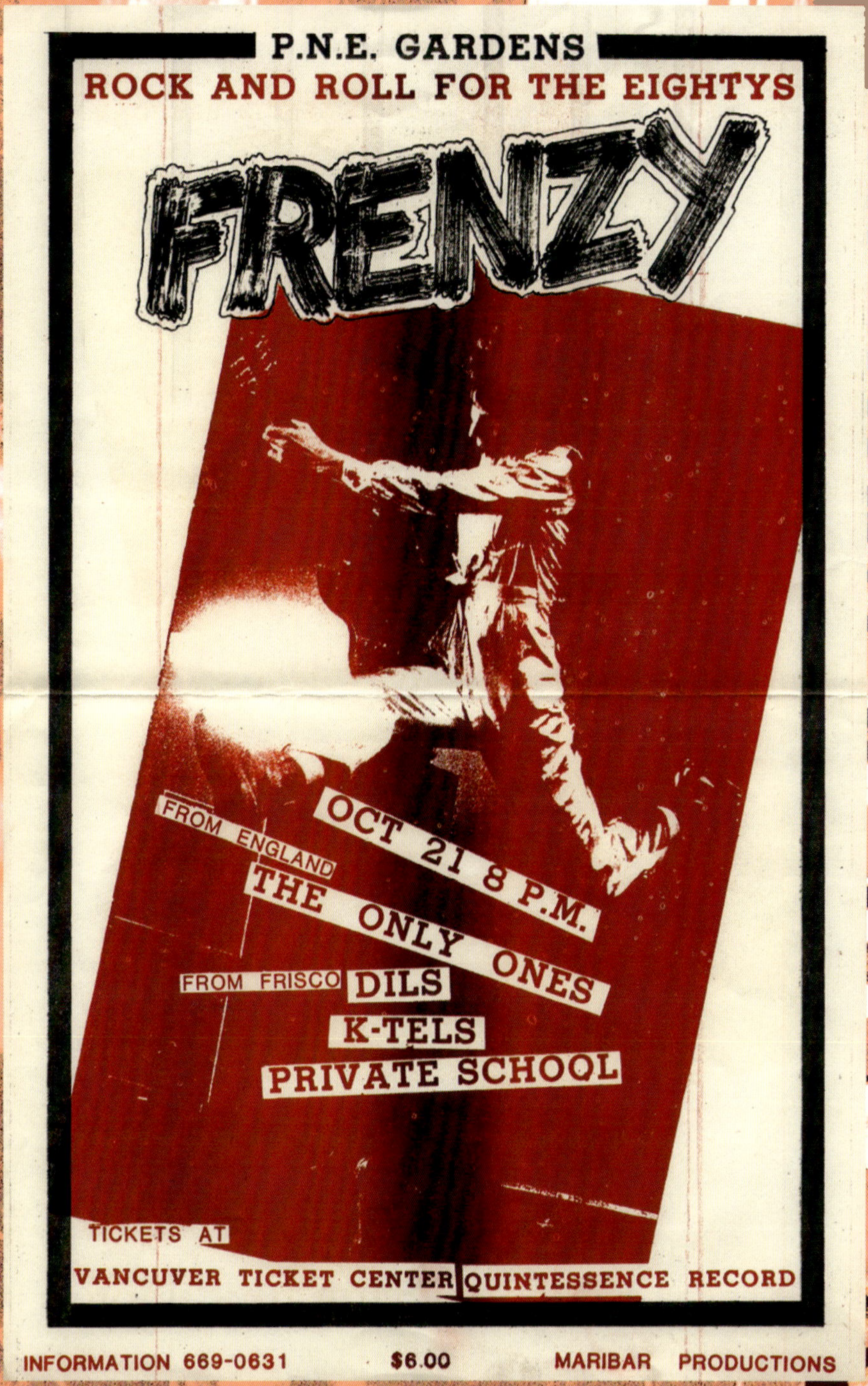
P.N.E. GARDENS
ROCK AND ROLL FOR THE EIGHTYS
FRENZY
OCT 21 8 P.M.
FROM ENGLAND
THE ONLY ONES
FROM FRISCO
DILS
K-TELS
PRIVATE SCHOOL
TICKETS AT
VANCUVER TICKET CENTER
QUINTESSENCE RECORD
INFORMATION 669-0631
$6.00
MARIBAR PRODUCTIONS

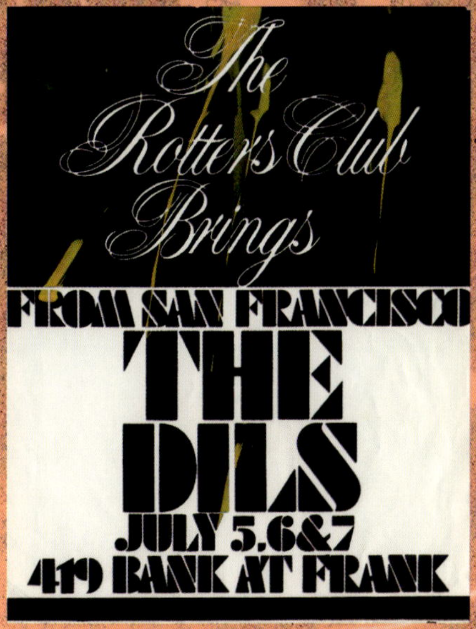
The Rotters Club Brings
FROM SAN FRANCISCO
THE DILS
JULY 5,6&7
419 BANK AT FRANK

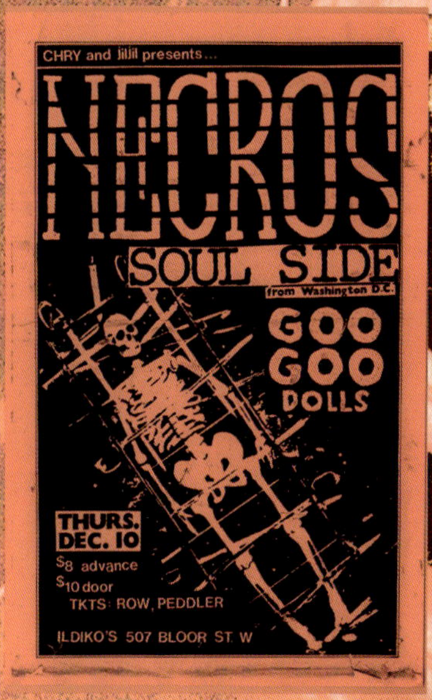
CHRY and presents...
NECROS
SOUL SIDE
from Washington D.C.
GOO GOO DOLLS
THURS. DEC. 10
$8 advance
$10 door
TKTS: ROW, PEDDLER
ILDIKO'S 507 BLOOR ST. W

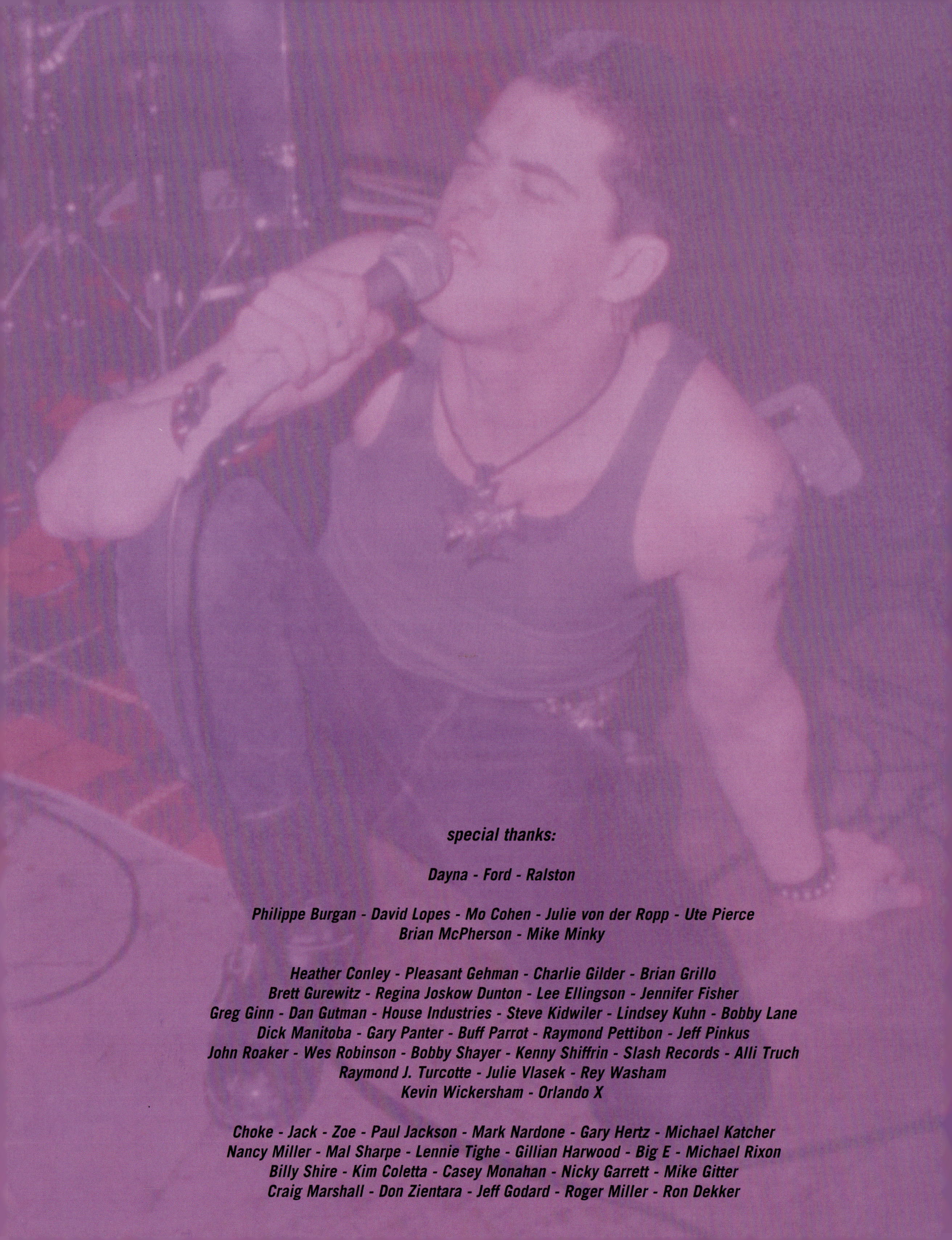

special thanks:

Dayna - Ford - Ralston

Philippe Burgan - David Lopes - Mo Cohen - Julie von der Ropp - Ute Pierce
Brian McPherson - Mike Minky

Heather Conley - Pleasant Gehman - Charlie Gilder - Brian Grillo
Brett Gurewitz - Regina Joskow Dunton - Lee Ellingson - Jennifer Fisher
Greg Ginn - Dan Gutman - House Industries - Steve Kidwiler - Lindsey Kuhn - Bobby Lane
Dick Manitoba - Gary Panter - Buff Parrot - Raymond Pettibon - Jeff Pinkus
John Roaker - Wes Robinson - Bobby Shayer - Kenny Shiffrin - Slash Records - Alli Truch
Raymond J. Turcotte - Julie Vlasek - Rey Washam
Kevin Wickersham - Orlando X

Choke - Jack - Zoe - Paul Jackson - Mark Nardone - Gary Hertz - Michael Katcher
Nancy Miller - Mal Sharpe - Lennie Tighe - Gillian Harwood - Big E - Michael Rixon
Billy Shire - Kim Coletta - Casey Monahan - Nicky Garrett - Mike Gitter
Craig Marshall - Don Zientara - Jeff Godard - Roger Miller - Ron Dekker

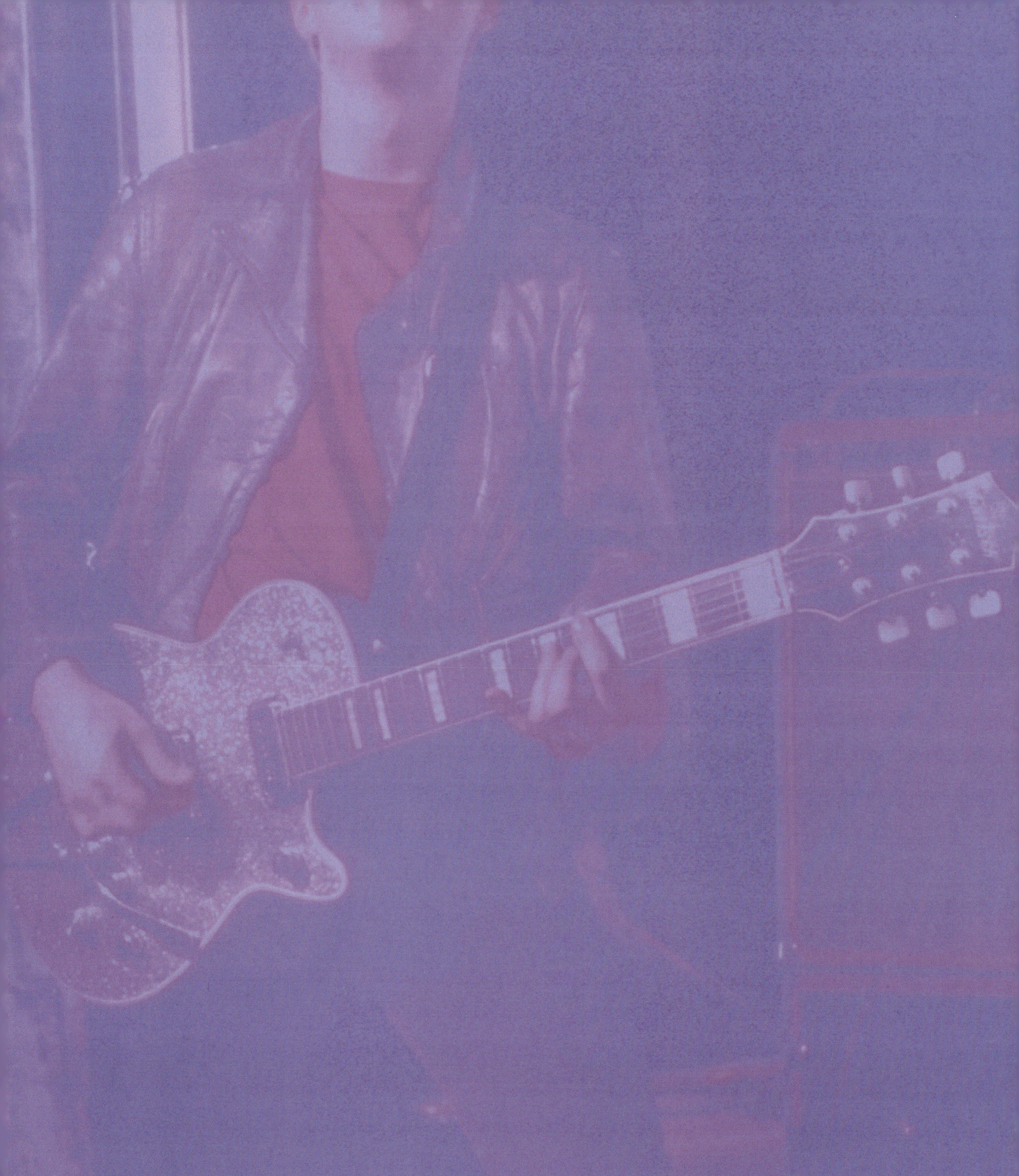

Darby & Billy Zoom photo from and by Jenny Lens - Mike Ness photo from and by Marla Watson
background photography by: Stacey Turcotte - John Susoeff - Kim Coletta - Dayna Turcotte - Beth Schneckenburger

Invaluable Production Assistants:
Jordan Edell - Nathan Ehrenfeld - Andrew Heilprin - Carl Swanberg - Chris Richardson

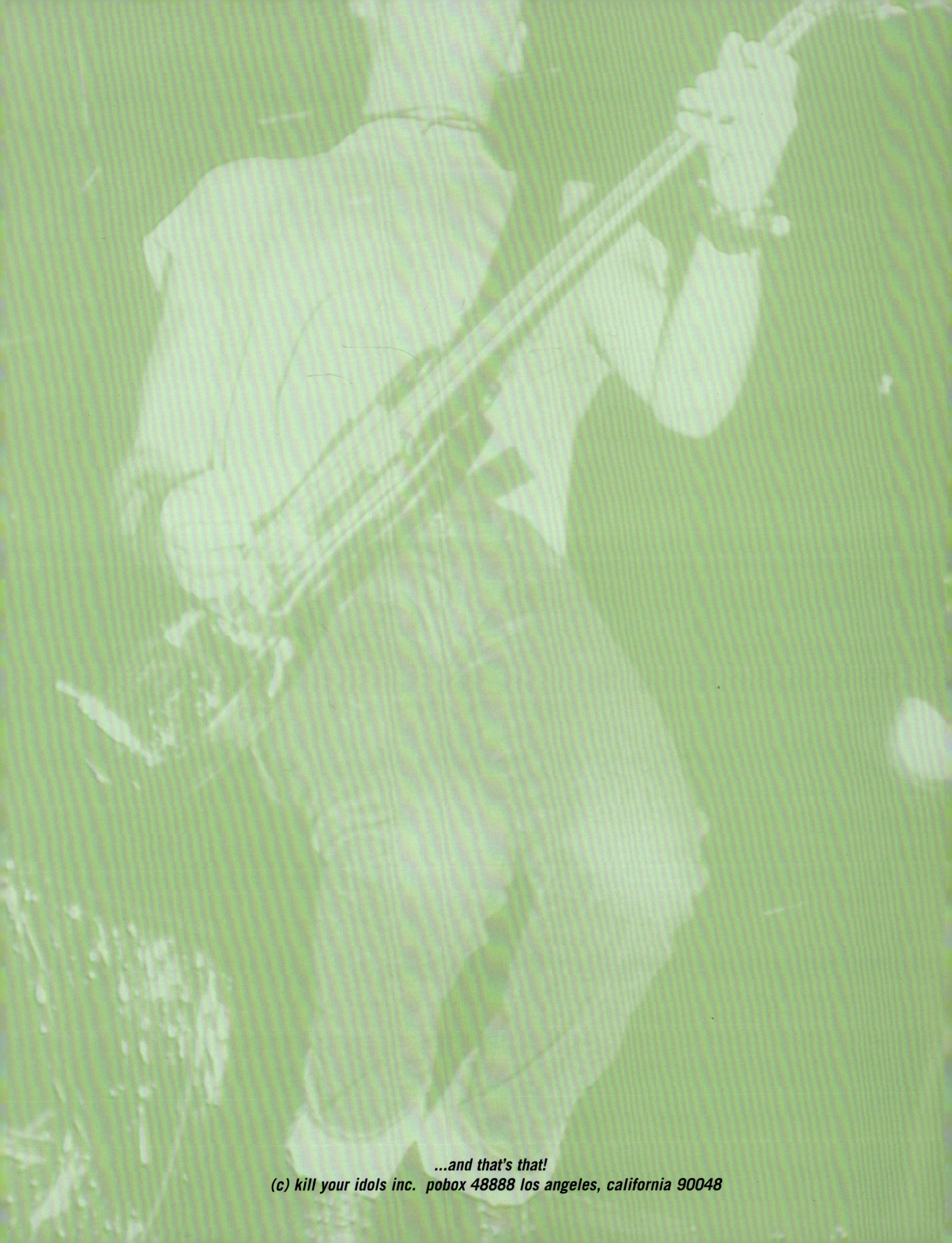

...and that's that!